CALCULATOR USERS GUIDE AND DICTIONARY

by
Charles J. Sippl

including:
An Index of Calculator Products and Manufacturers

FIRST EDITION
FIRST PRINTING 1976

Copyright © 1976, by
Matrix Publishers, Inc.

All rights reserved.

Library of Congress Catalog Card Number: 76-7886
ISBN: 0-916460-06-1
10 9 8 7 6 5 4 3 2 1

Published by Matrix Publishers, Inc., Champaign, Illinois 61820

Typeset by Graphic World, Inc.
Printed by Strathmore Company
In House Editor: Merl K. Miller

CALCULATOR USERS GUIDE AND DICTIONARY

BY
Charles J. Sippl

Author of Computer Dictionary and Handbook, Howard W. Sams and Co. Inc., Data Communications Dictionary, Van Nostrand-Reinhold, N.Y., Microcomputer Dictionary and Guide, Matrix Publishers, Inc. Programmable Calculators: How to Use Them, Matrix Publishers, Inc. and other computer and communications books; Computer Industry Lecturer and Consultant whose academic background includes teaching Computer, Operations Research and Business Administration Classes at: California State Universities at Los Angeles, Long Beach, and Northridge, and the University of California at Los Angeles (Extension). His BS degree is from the University of Wisconsin; MA from the University of Miami, with continued graduate work at University of California - Berkeley and UCLA, where his first "Computerman's Dictionary" was written in 1963.

FIRST EDITION, 1976
Copyright © Matrix Publishers, Inc., Champaign, Illinois 61820

ACKNOWLEDGEMENTS: Basic reference source for many of the terms and definitions in this dictionary is "Computer Dictionary and Handbook" published by Howard W. Sams & Co., Inc., 4300 West 62nd Street, Indianapolis, Indiana 46268. It is available through book stores, electronic parts distributors, or directly from the publisher. Approximately 15% of the more fundamental microcomputer definitions are excerpted from "Microcomputer Dictionary and Guide," Matrix Publishers, Inc., 1976. Many of the communications-oriented definitions can also be found, with significant elaboration, in the large volume, "Data Communications Dictionary," published in 1976 by Van Nostrand-Reinhold Company, New York.

How To Use This Book

The dictionary section of this book follows the standards accepted by most, but not all, modern lexicographers. All acronyms and terms of more than one word are treated as one word and abbreviations are also treated alphabetically. The letters "I/O" follow "Input-output" rather than appearing at the beginning of the I's.

For ease in quickly locating a specific term, the first and last entries on each page appear as reference words at the top of each page.

Extensive cross-referencing has been used as an aid in locating terms which you might look for in more than one place. For example, "ECL" may also be located as "emitter coupled logic." If you are not sure whether you want "memory" or "storage," check both; CMOS is filed as it would read as a word; commas and hyphens are disregarded. Again, think of each group of letters or words as a single word, including "ings" and "eds," then follow strict alphabetization to facilitate location efforts.

The author expresses his appreciation to all calculator manufacturers who forwarded photos, operation details, and other materials.

"This pocket calculator is far more than a revolution in technology... it is a revolution in individual management capability." "I believe the calculator will soon become as common as a pen. It will be difficult to locate many students, managers, scientists, business people, professionals... who do not carry one or do not have one very near by...". "It can be said that the microprocessor (the heart of advanced calculators) is the bridge between the impossible and the possible. Certainly it is the link between today's challenges and tomorrow's realities. Coupled with human imagination and concern, the microprocessor can undoubtedly propel us to a better world. We need only the inspiration and opportunity to explore the microprocessor's possibilities."..... These are random, anonymous quotes from Calculator Industry people.

Preface

Throughout history man has designed and built tools to extend his physical capabilities such as wheels to move his person and products faster and more conveniently, agricultural implements to increase his output and gathering of food and countless other extensions of his brawn but not his brain. Machines to count, measure, perform simple arithmetic and mathematics have remained few and relatively primitive for thousands of years. None of these are analytical, control or decision-making tools. The computer of the mid-twentieth century — our age — is the first tool that actually extends man's mental capabilities. The computer simulates sets of circumstances, uses data it has electronically gathered, and develops conclusions, problem answers and decisions based on programs that man or the computer itself has designed and predetermined. And due to the power of its programs, the computer can control countless other machines, processes and procedures and do so with speeds calibrated in minute fractions of seconds. Truly, the computer is one of man's greatest marvels and more than a tool, it is a masterful servant, and indeed, for many — also man's job-substituting competitor.

But today's computers still have many problems and inconveniences for most users. The complexity of most larger systems, the cost of the equipment, difficulties of computer programming techniques, etc. continue to preclude its use by the great majority of the world's citizenry. Where computers are installed the cost of computer time, the inconvenience of waiting for a turn and the problems of having to learn and remember special computer languages and rules almost prohibit their widest and best use by managers, teachers, researchers, and myriads of professional people who should be their most immediate and hardest users. But the ever-industrious and ingenious designers of calculating devices have evidently solved most of these problems, and this very sudden turn of events has taken place within the past three to four years.

The central processing unit (CPU) is the heart of all computers. It performs the arithmetic, procedural and processing control and communication to and from memory units within computer systems. Computer engineers have reduced the size of this powerful electronic unit to about the space occupied by one of the printed 'O's on this page. This is the microprocessor — a maze of electronic connections and switches on a 'chip' of silicon. Together with some input-output 'pins', a few thousand transistors and discrete semiconductor devices, all almost invisibly tiny, used as memory to store coded (1s and 0s) data, information and programs, a complete microcomputer can be built which in total can be held on the tip of one's finger. Perhaps the greatest miracle of all of this, however, is that microprocessor chip powerhouses are being mass-produced at rates of up to one million a month by large semiconductor and computer companies around the world. The cost for the majority of them is less than a hundred dollars — and the simplest ones, which still have the power and versatility of the huge vacuum tube computers of 30 years ago, sell for $10 and even less in quantities of 20,000 to 50,000.

These microprocessors, and their input-output plus memory attachments are now being used as the controllers of advanced calculators, replacing more than 70 million "older" calculators. Microprocessors are now appearing in countless electronic games, watches, appliances, computer terminals, communication devices, automobiles, medical and scientific instruments and devices — and the industry is only in its infancy. In this book we are concerned with how the microprocessors and microcomputers can function as mass-user calculators — from the simple $30 to $100 four-to-six function ($+$, $-$, $\times$, $\div$, $\%$, $\sqrt{}$) with memory and special function keys to the very masterful 'computing' calculators that have peripherals attached such as big-screen terminals, graphic plotters, voice-input and answerback, and scores of others. The latter are 'programmable' calculators that function almost exactly as computers but without the problems of complexity, big expense, special language programming headaches, waiting in line for service, etc. Programmable calculators are "personal" computers that are very easy to operate, simple to program by almost any user or to operate with insertable program strips, cards, cassettes, etc. They are available as hand-held, pocket-size calculators or small typewriter-size low cost number crunchers and processed information distributors on the desks of immediate users, such as, clerks, managers, students, grade-schoolers — anybody, really. How much are these 'programmable' calculators — in their simplest, most easy to use but very versatile form? The book opens with the analysis and explanation of the 'below $30' units.

Unfortunately, however, many current calculator users and potential purchasers are totally confused when they attempt to make the decisions concerning what type, model, brand, capacity, capability, etc. calculator to purchase. In the calculator marketplace there are hundreds of different models and makes with sales personnel making claims (and proving them) of rather fantastic utility for practically any type of customer . . . and at near unbelievable low prices for the many sundry and also really great services. The confusion (and often frustration) results, as with most new technologies, from a bewildering array of strange terminology. Almost without warning, terms such as: stacks, loops, registers, ROM (Read Only Memory), RAM (Random Access Memory), LED (Light Emitting Diode) and scores of other strange words and acronyms are thrown out to customers as though they were as common as "See Spot Run" of first-grade days.

This book has as its primary purpose to (1) help take most of the confusion out of the judgement of the types and capabilities of the calculators in the marketplace by analyzing the products available, (2) explain the criteria and procedures required to evaluate many of these machines for proper selection of the type of calculator unit or system best suited for individual application, and (3) to offer a rather complete dictionary section to assist the reader in unraveling the mysteries of the new and rapidly growing importance of modern calculating, processing, communicating terminology. The dictionary section is broad, comprehensive, tutorial. The design of the dictionary section (Part III) is multipurpose: for use as specific 'lookup' of a single word or phrase or as a reference for a conceptual search or for an analysis of a single concept, technique, product or procedure. Perhaps its greatest value for many is its 'browsing' characteristic. If the reader determines he or she desires to learn more about 'advanced calculators,' for example, *several pages* are available to offer the opportunity to study or explore the full range of capabilities, adaptations, developments, applications, etc. — all in one section. This type of topic grouping reflects the effort of the author to provide a concise encyclopedic aspect to assist the true enthusiast for a quick and convenient quest to gain succinct knowledge in larger distinctly pertinent 'subject areas' in contrast to brusk, curt non-explanatory tight phrasing of many dictionaries. In designing the dictionary section in this way, a few of the rules of strict modern lexicography have been 'bent' a bit. The reader is advised to carefully read the 'How to Use' section to facilitate his 'search and find' adventure into calculating and electronics. A companion text is available from Matrix Publishers, Inc. entitled, "Programmable Calculators:" How to Use them in Business, Science and Industry — At Home and On the Job". For those interested in the microcomputer per se, the publisher offers a 704-page "Microcomputer Dictionary and Guide" and several lively pragmatic applications and technical design professional and college level texts.

The programmable calculator is now a major 'consumer computer.' A few years ago calculators were basically for mathematicians, who compute complex formulas; statisticians, who evaluate models and project values and events; engineers, who need instant answers in design work; educators, who teach math, computer and other sciences, and research specialists, who reduce large amounts of statistical or control data and information. Now programmability provides 'custom design' for professionals, managers, and practically every type of worker to input and resolve problems of all ranges and nature. The machines have outstanding characteristics and permit immediate personal problem-solving "by the person with the problem when he or she has the problem." They are not 'remote' or difficult to use. Properly programmed, they practically *automatically* solve the problems *where* they happen, *when* they happen and provide analysis as to *why* they happen. The slight strain to learn to master especially the more advanced models of calculators is well worth the effort for any and every type of worker with a progressive, alert mind.

It must be remembered, however, that we all must make the assumption that whatever the manufacturers are offering in the calculator lines of today, something better will be available tomorrow. Neither the designers nor the manufacturers can specify for any set length of time what they intend to do . . . this year, or even this month. Using calculators for fun and profit is an adventure and a challenge that carries with it a very personally satisfying reward of continuous self-accomplishment and contentment.

Charles J. Sippl

DEDICATION

To Roger and Christine in partial reparation for all the hours I missed being with them while this project wound its way to completion . . .

Charles J. Sippl
May, 1976

TABLE OF CONTENTS

How To Use This Book			iv
Preface			v
Introduction—list of illustrations			x
Part I	Section 1	Hand-Held Calculators — How do They Work? What are the Differences?	7
	Section 2	The Concepts of Special Function Keys (SFKs), Preprogramming and Programmability	18
	Section 3	Selection Criteria for Evaluating Hand-Held Programmable Calculators	28
	Section 4	Advanced Hand-Held, Fully-Programmable Calculator Operating Characteristics	35
Part II	Section 1	Desk-Top Calculators and Computing Calculating Systems — What's Available and What are Proper Evaluating Techniques	43
	Section 2	Preprogrammed Desk-Top Calculators — Printers and Non-Printers, Some Examples	49
	Section 3	Programmable Desk-Top Calculators — 'Mind-Extenders' In Offices, Laboratories, and Executive Suites	53
	Section 4	Computing Calculators — Portable Computers With Attached, Simplified Keyboards, Immediate User Control	62
Part III	DICTIONARY SECTION		93
	EPILOGUE	The New Directions and Future of Programmable Calculators	421
	Appendix A	Desk Top Programmable Calculator Comparison Chart	423
	Appendix B	Manufacturer's Address List	426
		Index of Products	427

INTRODUCTION

Calculator industry specialists estimate that another 50 to 70 million calculators will be sold to North Americans from mid-1976 to mid-1978. The rate of sales jumped from a few million per year in the early 1970s to about 20 million in 1975. Exports of Japanese calculators to the U.S. in December, 1975 alone totalled 1,550,521, according to the Japanese Finance Ministry. The Japanese shipments to the U.S. for 1975 totalled 11,074,779 (of the 32 million Japan and the Far East produced). The U.S. produces and sells about 7 to 9 million, the majority of them being the more expensive or 'high-end' of the market. The retail prices of all units range from $5 to $10,000 — from shirt-pocket simple arithmetic units to very large calculator systems with practically all the power, peripherals, and versatility of medium-to-large computer-communications systems. Users range from 5-and 6-year-olds to atomic and space scientists — and practically everybody in-between.

Astronauts used them in outerspace; ocean bottom 'dwellers' use them as lifeline system controllers. Their real potential as sophisticated, customized personal processing and control instruments and expandable systems is now only being approached. As their range of cost-effective advantages becomes larger, their physical size and their costs become smaller. A scientific and commercial phenomenon unheard of in the annals of technological history. This remarkable achievement by the computer and calculator industry is causing both 'first-time' users and calculator veterans to 'trade-up' for ever-more capability — and the significant side-effect is a subtle reduction in the formerly almost all-pervasive 'fear of computers.' The problem of each user selecting the 'right calculator' for his specific range of tasks becomes more difficult as each new 'miracle' model emerges and the costs of 'unlimited — anybody can do it' programmability fall drastically. Excellent 'programmables' are available for under $30, and convenient and 'beautiful' hand-held machines that can accept 'pocketfuls' of 'miracle' programs for near-automatic operation are available for less than $400. The successful search and the purchase of just the right one that fits specific users job, hobby, or challenge can be a joy of personal fulfillment. The 'quick' buyer who fails to seriously evaluate and mentally digest the latest information of low cost available functions and capabilities will return to demonstrate his 'electronic brain' to his peers and associates only to become terribly dejected in frustration and depleted of funds that could have otherwise been well-spent. The information required and the 'understandability' knowledge desired relates to: 'preprogrammed' functions; internal and peripheral memories, alternate logic manipulation, and it goes on. The new terminology might be a little difficult at first, but it reflects the new nomenclature — new phrases and concepts that quickly become very standard, day-by-day conversational, common words of the computing, processing, communicating language of our new electronic world.

LIST OF ILLUSTRATIONS

Product	Page	Product	Page
Texas Instruments—TI-5050	5	Burroughs—C6451	50
Fondiller—Calcron	6	Burroughs—C6203	51
Litronix—2200	9	Casio—FX-3	51
Litronix—2290	9	Casio—162-F	52
Litronix—2290	11	Texas Instruments—SR-60	52
Sinclair—Scientific Programmable	15	Sharp—PC-1001	56
Novus—4510 and 4515	16	Compucorp—Alpha 327	58
Novus—6030 and 6035	17	Schematic drawing	58
National Semiconductor—4615	18	Rockwell—920	59
Rockwell—64 RD	23	Rockwell—930	59
Rockwell—44 RD	23	Rockwell—940	60
Monroe—360/65	26	Sharp—CS-364P	61
Sharp—EL-8300	26	Magnetic card	61
Sharp—EL-8200	26	Hewlett-Packard—HP-9815	64
Hewlett-Packard—HP-25	30	Hewlett-Packard—9815 and 9871	66
Texas Instruments—SR-56	30	Hewlett-Packard—9825A and 9866B	66
Texas Instruments—PC-100	31	Schematic drawing	68
Novus—4520-4525	32	Hewlett-Packard—HP-9800	68
Novus—6020-6025	32	Victor—480	70
Hewlett-Packard—HP-55	33	Canon—SX-100	71
Monroe—324	33	Canon—SX-310	71
Monroe—344	34	Sharp—CS-4500	72
Monroe—354	34	Monroe—1830	72
Hewlett-Packard—HP-65	36	Schematic drawing	73
Hewlett-Packard—HP-65	37	Monroe—1880	74
Hewlett-Packard—HP-65	38	Magnetic card	74
Monroe—Beta 326	40	Compucorp—402	77
Texas Instruments—SR-52	42	Compucorp—403	77
Texas Instruments—SR-52	43	Compucorp—450	78
Microelectronic circuit	45	Olivetti—P-652	78
Microelectronic circuit	45	Wang—600	81
Olympia—502	45	Wang—Basic 2200 S	85
Olympia—CPD575	47	Wang—2200 S	85
Olympia—CP181	47	Tektronix—4051	89
Burroughs	47	Tektronix—4051	89
Hewlett-Packard—HP-91	49	Tektronix—4924	90

CALCULATOR CLASSIFICATION SYSTEM

The maze of the calculator marketplace can be organized into a relatively basic structure of calculator types, their components and capabilities. On a rather primitive but functional basis the classifications fall into groups of threes — three general *classifications* of calculating instruments; three *types of operating units* in each classification; three primary characteristics of each type of unit, three types of memory; three types of logic; three types of software (programs) and 3 general classes of peripherals. This organization system hopefully will provide a pathway for the eager calculator purchaser — whether he or she is a high school student, a manager of a large bank or industry, or an ivory-towered superbrain about to solve man's toughest problems. Calculators are a blessing and a sound investment for each and all of them. They're fun — and they pay off in both the short and long run. How does one tell which are which? Let's try!

Practically all calculators are: Hand-Held (pocket); Desk-Top (display or printing, or both) or computing (control systems). These are the basic and broad classifications, and within *each class* the calculator will either be: (A) Basic — Four-to-Six Function; (B) Preprogrammed (Basic or Advanced) and (C) Programmable (Basic or Advanced).

CALCULATORS: CLASS AND FUNCTION STRUCTURE

CLASS

I. HAND-HELD
   A. Four-Six Function
   B. Preprogrammed
   C. Programmable

II. DESK-TOP
   A. Four-Six Function
   B. Preprogrammed
   C. Programmable

III. COMPUTING
   A. Prompting/Peripherals
   B. Exterior Memories/High Level Languages
   C. CRT Computing Systems

TYPE

A. FOUR-SIX FUNCTION
   1. Arithmetic
   2. Memory
   3. Special Function Keys (SFKs)

B. PREPROGRAMMED
   1. Slide-Rule/Scientific
   2. Business/Financial
   3. Professional/Specialist

C. PROGRAMMABLE
   1. Keyboard/Temporary
   2. Card, Tape, ROM (Permanent)
   3. Language/Interactive

MEMORY TYPES
1. Intermediate Storage
2. Addressable Storage (direct/indirect)
3. Automatic Input-Output Storage

LOGIC TYPES
1. Arithmetic
2. Algebraic
3. Reverse Polish Notation (RPN)

SOFTWARE (PROGRAMS)
1. Simple Formula
2. Decision-making
3. Interactive/microprogrammable

PERIPHERALS
1. Input-Output
2. Communication
3. Control (Remote)

The Hand-Held, Preprogrammed, and Programmable Classes all carry subgroups as either: Basic or Advanced.

Thus a Desk-Top (Class) Type B-2 would be a: Desk-Top Preprogrammed Business/Financial Calculator. Because its preprogrammed and not programmable, it would have no exterior software capability. But, it could have Memory Type 2, Indirect Addressable Storage, and Type 3 Logic, RPN, and Type 1 Peripherals, i.e., Input-Output (printer, or voice output).

It will be difficult to discover any calculator that does not fall within these three Broad Classes, Functional Types, or Memory, Logic, Software or Peripherals groups.

The Sections of Part I and Part II are organized within this Classification Structure — and the products and capabilities are related competitively, generally — as of late '76.

EVALUATION OF HAND-HELD CALCULATORS: THE BASIC TYPES AVAILABLE

The calculator selected should have individually desired capabilities and conveniences — the built-in functions, memories and other features required to solve many specific problems quickly, easily, accurately and without confusion. In most cases the simple unprogrammable or unpreprogrammed calculator will not suffice — even providing it can handle the required number of digits and may also include "%" and constant keys, i.e. special function keys or SFKs. Usually problems extend beyond basic arithmetic. The hard user needs a professional pocket calculator — designed and manufactured for day-in, day-out professional use.

Professional calculators are designed with the specific capabilities required to quickly and easily solve problems intrinsic to a specific discipline or application. The preprogrammed nomenclature on the keys give users a quick insight into the types of problems the calculator can help solve. Broadly speaking, there are four main types of professional pocket calculators: Those designed for the Scientific and Engineering disciplines, Statistics units, Business units for broad ranges and those units for more exacting Financial disciplines.

Scientific Preprogrammed and Key Programmable Pocket Calculators — Professional "scientific" calculators generally provide the standard log and trig functions, so users don't have to refer to tables or interpolate from those tables. They just press the keys to get their answer — an answer far more accurate than any slide-rule can give. These "full scientific" calculators also provide exponential, square root and reciprocal functions. But these are only SFKs.

For handling more advanced types of scientific, engineering, business, mathematical or statistical problems, users need an "advanced business, statistics, financial or scientific" calculator. These have all the built-in functions found in the preprogrammed machines, plus the SFKs for a variety of others, depending upon which models are selected. These may include: mean, standard deviation, linear regression (trend line), and U.S./metric conversions, and many others.

These advanced models also offer more memory power . . . more sophisticated trig functions, such as rectangular coordinate/polar coordinate conversion . . . selectable modes (degrees, radians and, possibly grads) . . . conversion between decimal angle and angle in degrees/minutes/seconds . . . and others.

This added fixed capability facilitates the handling of complex problems and can drastically reduce the time and effort necessary to solve them. For example, polar/rectangular coordinate conversions let users add or subtract vector components in seconds, simply by pressing one or a few keys. The fixed functions are programmed.

The more proficient type of low cost professional scientific pocket calculators are key programmable. When solving complex, repetitive or iterative problems, programming can be invaluable. Users enter their specific problem-solving sequence of keystrokes just once . . . then, with just one keystroke initiate the entire sequence — as often as they wish.

But whatever scientific calculator one chooses, the more functions and features it has, the more capability it has to solve more types of problems — even the most complex — faster and easier, reducing the work users have to do. And the less chance for errors. Users should compare functions and features carefully before they make their final selection. At $100 or less: 4-function with SFKs ("scientific"), preprogrammed or key programmable, are all true bargains.

Business Pocket Calculators — Pre- or Key Programmed — Although a scientific calculator may be used for solving the more basic types of business problems, Key Programmable calculators especially designed for business and/or financial problems can soon pay for themselves in terms of time and effort saved — because they are made to solve specific business problems — giving users the exact answer they need when and where they need them.

A business calculator should provide all of the fundamental financial functions to solve problems involving interest rates; rates of return and discounted cash flows; extended percent calculations; remaining balances, amortization and balloon payments. But in addition, a business calculator should help the modern business manager in planning, forecasting and decision analysis. For these problems, a business calculator should provide advanced statistical capability, mathematical functions, and extra memory power, i.e. be preprogrammed.

In addition to business pocket calculators, there are also "advanced business" or "financial" calculators. These usually have all of the functions found in business calculators, but will also have more specialized capabilities to solve problems involving depreciation, bond prices, yields, etc. And because the latter require a calendar, these types of calculators will have one "built-in," as part of the group of programs designed and fixed within the operating capability of the specialized machines — either hand-held, desk-top or computing calculating tools.

For the solution of many types of specialized business or financial problems, involving extended calculations or unique and complex formulas, a key programmable calculator can be a tremendous time-saver. Since users enter their problem-solving sequence of keystrokes just once — and then with one keystroke start an entire sequence — they reduce their error ratio and as a result, have confidence in their answers.

Another point to consider when selecting a business calculator, is the basic financial concepts a user works with daily as a decision maker handling business transactions. The calculator selected should help in making decisions, then users save far more than the calculator costs, the first week they use it. And this, applies to a basic business 4-function or pre- or key programmable type for a very nice return on investment.

Four Criteria (Features) for Determining Problem-Solving Capabilities — Before users make their final selection of a pocket calculator, they should take a close look at four features that can make their problem-solving easier and more reliable. These are programmable capabilities, memory power, the logic system, and peripherals.

Programmable Capabilities — To reduce the number of keystrokes, and keystroke errors, even low-cost hand-held calculators can be programmed

— directed to initiate the desired keystrokes automatically. A sequence of keystrokes is used to automatically solve a problem or series of problems. Once a calculator is programmed, all users have to do is key in the data — the numbers for the specific problems they are solving — and press one key to run the entire program. Other preprogrammed capabilities can be 'wired-in' also.

A pocket calculator may be either "key" programmable or "fully" or use exterior programmability. A key programmable machine can usually be key programmed up to 100 steps by pressing the keys. (Then the program is temporarily stored in the program memory, where it remains until removed or changed by the calculator operator or until the calculator is turned off.)

With a fully programmable pocket calculator, that same program can also be permanently stored on an external device (such as magnetic "strips" or cards) and re-entered in the program memory when needed. Programming can be an extremely useful feature, saving time and energy and helping to avoid keystroke errors. Depending on the model, a fully programmable calculator may have provision for editing a program (adding, deleting or changing steps) and such computer-like operations as branching — choosing between two alternate steps depending upon the outcome of a relational test. A fully programmable calculator can actually make logical decisions for users.

For occasional key programming, a "programmable" machine (i.e., one with temporary storage capability) should suffice. But if users frequently handle problems that can be permanently programmed, they should consider a "fully programmable" calculator, and record their programs on program cards, strips, cassettes, etc. Then their specific and general applications are already programmed for multiple users... amateur or professionals.

Memory Power. — Every pocket calculator should have at least one addressable memory — to store constants or other numbers used more than once in a calculation. The more memories a calculator has, the less writing down of numbers that users have to do. With certain calculators having addressable memories, users can do register arithmetic — they can directly add to, subtract from, divide into or multiply the contents of a register. This makes data manipulation exceptionally easy, even when working problems involving three simultaneous linear equations (or other 3 x 3 matrix inversions).

Besides addressable memories, certain pocket calculators have an automatic memory (also called an operational stack, a four-memory stack, etc.). Entries and intermediate answers are stored automatically, then re-entered into the calculation at the appropriate time. Obviously, this eliminates the need for users to write down and re-enter numbers, which could lead to errors, and it speeds the work.

Logic Systems. — A logic system is the "language" used to communicate with a calculator — the way in which users key in problems and the way the calculator is designed to handle the problems. One logic system may require users to restructure an equation to conform to the system; another may not.

The three most common types of logic systems used in professional pocket calculators are algebraic, arithmetic and RPN logic. Users may wish to check out these systems, and determine for themselves which is the easiest to use (especially important when solving complex problems)... which is the least confusing (so they can have confidence in their answers)... and which is the best to use for solving the kinds of problems they face regularly.

Peripherals Availability. — In addition to everything mentioned so far, users should also — before selecting a specific type calculator — consider peripherals of the physical units for fast input and output of calculator data and instructions ... cassettes, printers, readers, and the availability of accessories and wide-ranging applications books ... and, of course, one must remember, a good value in an adequate calculator that's capable of solving specific problems today ... may not help for tomorrow's problems. Programmables are best.

With all this in mind, users should study descriptions of each calculator type, compare the models, and select the one machine that comes closest to filling future needs. And those evaluating fully programmable calculators must carefully consider the types, quality and future programs (software) available or planned.

The Direction of Today's Calculator Buyers quests — A typical user today is a problem solver (and usually a multi-discipline problem solver). Users now expect more capability in the same package at a significantly lower cost. Pocket calculators have increased in number and complexity of functions and memory storage size. The gap between computer and calculator has gotten narrower and narrower. The alphanumeric input-output calculator, which has become a true computer by any definition, is now a reality in less than four years from the invention of the microprocessor. But these computers now remain in the form of a calculator. They sell better that way.

The user has grown in sophistication. Today's users have reached new skill levels and have mastered their present machines. They now want more capability, more memory, faster execution speeds, and more complex firmware (fixed programs). As long as there are more and more users experimenting with their machines, trying to solve their problems, there will be a need to share 'discoveries' and techniques. Through clubs, newsletters, and magazines, most calculator owners can become aware of applications information directly related to their job, hobby or specific calculator. Most want to acquire that information to stay ahead. Calculator user sophistication has become like various professional degrees. Alert and eager users continue to reach for levels of complexity and capability that represent new technical and mathematical vistas.

Today's pocket calculators are far from a complexity level that only a relatively few 'experts' can use them. Users are challenged, but they win. A few years ago the electronic slide rule that replaced volumes of mathematical tables was considered complex. Today every college campus has a large percentage of students using far more complex calculators like any other tool. Programmability rules today. Hundreds of thousands of 100+ step scratch-pad programmable machines that cost less than $100 are being sold. The straightforward four-function calculator has broken the $10

evaluation of hand-held calculators

price barrier. Successful users of scratch-pad programmable machines now want to move up to machines with editing and conditional branching capability. Many manufacturers are providing these machines and also provide "free" many applications programs to attract customers. Most new users will transcend the scratch-pad programmable storage and purchase fully programmable (looping and editing) machines without much hesitation. And the emphasis of this book attests to this. A majority of users now want units with program recording capability. And they also now or soon will want units which have larger 'mass' storage capability made possible by magnetic tape cassettes. The general trend will be toward plug-in ROM programs and programmable machines with more exotic firmware functions.

The user of today primarily applies his calculator to personal and business affairs. Data handling capability must be enough that the machine will take on such tasks as record keeping and measurement. Complex analysis of data is now possible because of the extensive firmware functions built into the machines. The capability of the machines will become so great that the challenge of calculating will consume considerable time. The longer run times of complex programs will upset the owners and a keyboard interrupt capability will be an expected feature; this will allow a short, quick keyboard, time or register inspection operation to be performed. And the previously executing program can wait and then continue with great user satisfaction. The complex, current high technology society is spawning whole new generations of users applying calculators not only to time and money problems, but to such problems as optimizing the route to take in going to work. Measurement and numbers will continually take on a greater meaning for people. The hardware and firmware are being made ready, only the dissemination of calculator progress information seems to be lagging.

Calculators for Elementary School Students — In education the calculator plays roles both subtle and obvious. Users can press keys in seconds. They can 'test' their answers faster than they can ask the question. When they make some rather dumb mistakes, there is no reprimand; no one to tell them how stupid they are, only a flashing display or other indication alerts them to improper operations. With instant, logically perfect responses from their machines, the users quickly refresh their basic math. Great numbers of teen-age and business users have reported that they were previously uninterested in mathematics, but now find themselves very involved because the mathematics gives them the answers they want — painlessly, precisely and fast.

Other educational uses for a programmable calculator are obvious. One popular program converts the HP-65 reverse polish into the algebraic logic of other machines — including second argument constant. This demonstrates and contrasts the two logic systems. The most spectacular and fun aspect of calculator education is games.

Recreation. — The kids and adults who 'play around' with numbers find this both recreational and educational. People who enjoy recreational math now spend hours experimenting with numbers. The fun and challenge pastime of devising words or expressions to be read from the display held upside down or to a mirror is well known; 'alphabets' and dictionaries have been published. Catalog houses and retailers have discovered that a surprising number of people buy pocket calculators for their amusement. Many popular types of programs are really games. The value of other games is becoming more and more recognized, as specifically designed by computer people as a means of teaching and, equally important, humanizing the computer. Games programmed for programmables cover a wide field.

Calculator to Develop Math Skills — One of the first calculators specifically made for developing individual mathematical computational skills has been introduced by Monroe, called Classmate 88. The machine uses an individualized instruction approach to generate unlimited drill and practice exercises for more than 70 computational skills. The calculator is used in conjunction with Operation Achievement, a skills program developed three years ago in Monroe's education center. The combination of the computer system and the skills program provide an innovative approach to developing a capability in addition, subtraction, multiplication, division, fractions, decimals and number concepts.

Classmate 88 comes with survey and diagnostic testing to determine exact competence levels for individual students. With a flick of the switch, the system generates random exercises in any of the 70 skill areas. When a skill area is selected and entered on the keyboard, the Classmate 88 prints a problem for that specific skill on a tape. The student works it manually on scratch paper, enters his solution into the machine and presses a "go" button.

The machine either accepts the answer as correct and automatically prints another problem or prints the student's answer and a red error indicator. The student then may do the problem again until he gets the correct answer or he may press a key to ask the machine for the right answer. Problems and student's answers are printed on the tape, providing the teacher with a record of the student's work.

SPECIAL COMBINATION CALCULATORS- WALLETS, WATCHES, VOICE ANSWERBACKS, BIORHYTHM

Texas Instruments Portable Electronic Hand-Held Printing Calculator, The TI-5050 — The TI-5050 performs chain calculations with all four functions. Users simply press a desired function key to use any result in the next problem. Repeated addition and subtraction is completed without reentering the number. Number entries are cleared with the CE key. A # key (non-add) prints reference numbers. The ↑ key feeds extra paper for easy tearoff. The unit sold for less than $130.00 in mid 1976.

Its dimensions: $8.7 \times 3.9 \times 2.7$ inches; weight 28 ounces. Includes carrying case, 2 inch thermal paper, adapter/charger, manual. High level buffering lets users make multiple entries while the calculator is still printing. Two-key rollover lets users press a second key even before their finger leaves the first. Familiar business machine entry sequence.

It's a decided improvement over Casio's printing ¼" tape machine . . . but, other competition is expected.

evaluation of hand-held calculators

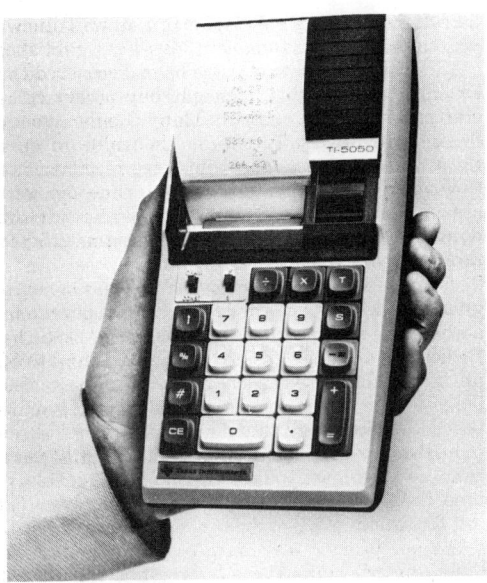

Texas Instruments TI-5050 Hand-Held Printing Calculator — The TI-5050 pictured above is a popular unit for those users who require only simple calculations. It has very little sophistication for engineers, businessmen, statisticians, or scientists, as do other Texas Instruments models. It is one of the best of the hand-held printers, however. Its competition, in 1976, was from the under $100 Casio, "Mini Calculator/Printer" using a narrow ¼" tape horizontally mounted within the case, and the Facit-Addo, Inc. unit model 1140 (1½ pounds), which uses a 2¼ inch tape (thermal) and has 8-digit capacity, floating decimal, automatic constant and percentage keys, permitting discount and markup calculations.

Shirt Pocket Calculator Users — For novelty and purpose there's a calculator that does fit in a users pocket. The Hanimex weighs only 3½ ounces. So users can keep it in their pocket comfortably all day long — at lunch, on the airplane and during all those times when they wish they had a calculator with them. The Hanimex is an eight-digit, 4-function, percentage calculator. There's an automatic constant on all four functions. The unit features algebraic logic (users perform functions exactly as they think), and the LED display has overflow indicators and a floating negative sign. The clear key doubles as a clear entry key, and the unit measures 11/16" × 2⅛" × 4⅜" — convenient for any pocket.

Calculators Vocalize Data Entries and Results — Master Specialties Co. (MSC's) ARC 9500 audio-response calculator talks to users with its solid-state natural-sounding synthesized voice. It announces each entry and the results of every calculation in a loud, clear voice, according to the manufacturer in Costa Mesa, CA. Talking calculators are used in the vocational education of the blind and in the reinforcement of basic math concepts for sighted students. In addition, sighted users find that it permits them to concentrate full visual attention on the input figures being entered without having to shift attention back and forth to look at the visual display. The ARC 9500 is an eight-function calculator and also has an eight-digit visual display.

A "Speech Plus," talking calculator was developed by Telesensory Systems, Inc. There are NO tapes in the calculator. Rather, the 24-word spoken vocabulary is electronically synthesized by a custom LSI microcontroller in conjunction with a single 16-k ROM. The firm specifically ruled out the use of tapes from reliability and cost considerations. The speech synthesizer is expandable to 64 words and is entirely contained on a single 4 in. × 6½ in. PCB, includes batteries, volume control, and loudspeaker.

Calculator/Wallet — Some manufacturers offer desk-top calendar-calculator combinations for business gift giving. Rockwell offers a combination wallet and built-in ultra-thin five function calculator, priced at $40. The unit includes a ballpoint pen, check or notebook pocket, and transparent credit card inserts. The calculator has a full four-key memory and functions include percent with automatic add-on and discount, square root and change sign. The 24K operates in algebraic logic and maintains trailing zeroes in add and subtract for monetary calculations. It positions the decimal point automatically and also performs chain calculations. Fairly impressive for a product that weighs less than half a pound and measures 5½ x 2¾ x ½-inches.

Calculates Biorhythms — The BIOLATOR is a dual function machine. It is an 8-digit, four-function calculator. Plus, it calculates a users biorhythm status for the day. They key in their birthdate, and the machine will automatically compute their physical, emotional, and intellectual condition for the day. A built-in 99-year calendar does it, can also be used for computing loans and interest. Made by Casio.

Mostek Calculator for Check Accounts — A semiconductor manufacturer, Mostek Inc. has introduced a purse-size, two-function calculator which is designed for computing checking account balances and is aimed at the female consumer market. Called the Checkmaster, the $39.95 unit, with a keyboard and six-digit LED display, automatically adds deposits and subtracts checks. The machine features a memory which retains the correct checking account balance even after the unit is turned off.

The battery-powered Checkmaster incorporates a single modified P-channel MOS chip and LSI circuitry. Also, the unit is designed in a case which opens and closes and holds a checkbook. The system automatically shuts off when the case is closed.

Initially, the unit was marketed by the JS&A National Sales Group, a Northbrook, Ill., mail-order distribution firm. In addition, the Checkmaster was marketed under the Corvus trade name by banks as a bank account premium and by retailers. Mostek, a Dallas-based firm, expected to sell about 250,000 units during the year 1976.

Here's how it works. — Users open their checkbook holder and turn on the built-in computer. Press the "Balance" key, and their bank balance is recalled on the display. The CheckMaster memory never forgets their balance — even months after they last recall it.

They enter the amount of their check, and press the "Check" key. The check amount is automatically deducted from their balance, and their new balance is displayed — and all with just one key stroke.

evaluation of hand-held calculators

Or they enter the amount of a deposit, and press the "Deposit" key. Their deposit is automatically added to their balance, and again, their new balance is displayed.

Watch/Calculator — A hit of the 1975 Christmas season, Time Computer Inc. introduced a solid gold Pulsar watch-calculator combination with a six-digit LED display. The calculator has five functions, plus memory, floating decimal, and display overflow. Originally priced at $3,950, it's designed around two C-MOS chips, one each for time and calculation. The watch uses four battery cells that should last for a year for 25 calculations and 25 time readouts a day.

The big drawback to the Pulsar calculator — in addition to its price — is that users have to use a special plastic stylus to key in information. Even though Time Computer supplies the retractable stylus mounted on the top of a ballpoint pen, the fact that the calculator can't be operated with an ordinary ballpoint tip means a user's $3,950 calculator isn't usable if the wearer forgets the stylus. But this problem probably will be overcome with later models, and certainly by competitors.

The Optel I Calculator/Watch — Multiplexed circuits connecting the display segments have helped cut the size of a calculator/watch combination so that it fits on the wrist. The all-electronic calculator/wristwatch was exhibited by Optel Corp., Princeton, N.J., in Switzerland at the Basel watch and jewelry fair in 1975. Prototypes were ready for sampling and small production quantities were scheduled. Called the Optel I, the calculator/watch is designed around complementary-MOS circuits and a field-effect liquid-crystal display. It uses multiplexing to wire the display segments, simplifying the design. The display has eight digits, six of which are used in the normal time-keeping mode to show hours, minutes, and seconds. All eight are operable when the device is switched by pushbutton to the four-function calculating mode.

Succeeding versions will have memory and calculator functions for scientific applications. Prices for the first two models were between $500 and $550 for the standard version and $975 for the fancier one. The Optel I packs three C-MOS chips into its case, measuring 3.3 by 4.57 by 0.953 centimeters. One chip contains the countdown circuitry for time-keeping, the second integrates the calculator circuitry, and the third the buffer and driver stages for the display. The 1-second time pulses are derived from a 32-kilohertz crystal oscillator whose frequency is counted down by a 15-step divider network. The power pack consists of four 1.5-volt silver-oxide batteries, each about 15 millimeters in diameter and 4 mm thick.

Wrist-Watch Size Calculators — Below is a handy calculator, it is a 17-key unit. Its tiny keys and readout use a layer of conductive rubber. The trend toward micro-miniaturization in electronics has been pushed ever further by the watch industry. Chomerics Inc. of Woburn, Mass. responded by introducing a keyboard measuring only ¾ x 1 inch with 17 keys of ⁵/₃₂-inch centers. The key array includes a moving decimal point, constant, clear, multiply, divide, add-equal, and subtract-equal keys that are as easy to read as a watch face. The full calculator would probably have either a four-digit liquid-crystal display or a six-digit light-emitting-diode (LED) readout.*

This pencil tip or stylus keyboard makes use of Chomerics' materials technology in conductive elastomers, paints, and inks, and its capability in full-size keyboards. The miniature keyboard uses the same materials as the large subassemblies, but they are put together differently. The keyboard consists of a tiny printed-circuit board, screened with a silver paint that provides a permanently conductive contact surface. Over this is laid a 0.005-inch-thick Mylar spacer with holes directly under the keys. A layer of conductive rubber, and a Mylar legend sheet has the keys on it. When the Mylar is deflected, an electrical impulse that is set up in the conductive rubber travels through the holes in the Mylar spacer to the printed-circuit board. The keyboard was developed as a result of inquiries from watch companies, and samples were supplied to at least 10 of them in mid-1974. In volume the manufacturer says the keyboards could sell for less than $2 each.

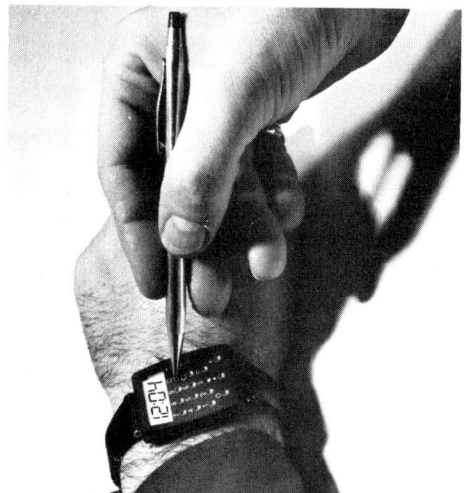

Calculator-Watch for Men Offered — Maybe! — A calculator-watch combination that can be worn on a man's wrist has been developed by Fondiller Corp. Called Calcron, the product is a scientific calculator and a man's digital wrist watch combined in a 1.5-inch-square case and less than 0.5-inch thick. The 40 functions of the keyboard — including trigonometric, logarithmic, exponential functions, square root, memory, chaining degrees and radian — use 20 buttons and operate by the use of a shift key like a typewriter's. Rechargeable nickel-cadmium batteries supply power for about 20,000 calculations. Retail price of the system is $500, including a battery charger. The calculator portion is priced at $300. The unit is said to have 40 functions in a 20-button keyboard through use of a shift key. Buttons on right give hours, minutes, seconds and data in the same 9-digit LED display used in calculators. The company also began working on a wrist watch for women to be called Femcron. It is not known if either unit is yet on the market.

*Slightly larger readout areas could accommodate several 'answer' lines, using an attached magnifier for improved clarity.

PART I — Section One

HAND-HELD CALCULATORS —
HOW DO THEY WORK?
WHAT ARE THE DIFFERENCES?

"My Calculator is Fine — But, I Want a better One." Now almost anyone can enjoy the speed, efficiency, accuracy, and computational power of personal programmability with a $30 Litronix, a $50 Sinclair, a $90 Corvus. Hewlett-Packard hand-held calculators and those from Texas Instruments, Monroe, Compucorp, others are a "tradeup" from these.

Programming is simply the ability of a calculator to learn, remember, and execute automatically a series of steps necessary to solve a particular problem. This is "real" calculating power, and it does not end. Once a user has taught the calculator the formula for any problem, all he must do is supply the known variables and start the program running.

But this is the "short" story. Programmable calculators give users much more. Their calculators can become a full computer . . . with:

- Full editing capability. Users can add or change steps at will . . . from a one-line to a 16-line display. (see: Advanced Desk-Top Computing Calculators, Part II, Section 4.)
- Direct branching. Users can solve problems requiring iterative routines. Can control machines and communicate around the world.
- Conditional testing. Users can program the calculator to make decisions or change conditions based on the data . . . decisions to jump to another program and another.
- Easy-to-understand keystrokes or programming languages . . . keyed in or entered by cards, tapes, cassetes, etc.

Before one buys a calculator, he or she must take a look at the programmable calculators from at least three to five sources.

One advanced scientific programmable pocket calculator offers eight addressable memories, full editing, and branching and conditional test capability . . . the stepup from the less than $100 models.

Another low-cost advanced scientific programmable calculator provides 20 addressable memories, editing, branching and conditional test capability, and also a 100-hour digital timer. These are KEYBOARD programmable units. The program must be keyed in when it is to be used. Others can be "automatically" programmed.

The best are fully programmable pocket calculators for scientists or business executives, etc., that let users prerecord their programs on magnetic cards for future use. The HP-65, for example, has nine addressable memories, full editing, and nine conditional tests. In addition, Application Pacs containing pre-recorded magnetic cards for many specific business and scientific disciplines are available which save users much time and effort. Attractively priced, the HP-65 and Texas Instruments SR-52 are only two of many bargains.

Programmable calculators take most of the repetition out of often used repetitive problems. If users want to save $ and frustration, they should take time to read about the specific advantages and price ranges on the following pages. Programmability is the "magic" word of calculators. The majority of the book is devoted to this capability — and the 'dictionary' section is designed to help the reader unravel the mysteries of "computing" calculators.

But to understand the calculator first . . . and programmable calculators next, it is necessary to start at the beginning — with the simple, straightforward four-to-six function machines often called "the adders". They add, then subtract by 'adding' algebraically — and multiply and divide by successive addition and subtraction — in split seconds.

HAND-HELD BASIC
4- TO 6-FUNCTION MACHINES

The Typical Pocket Size Four-to-Six Function Electronic Calculator with Memory Performance — The typical unit enables users to carry out calculations silently and accurately anywhere . . . in the home, office, plane or train . . . because it's battery operated. Its calculating capabilities include addition, subtraction, multiplication, division and arithmetic combinations. All keys of the unit are logically arranged according to their function, and conveniently located. Memory keys are color-coded. Most low-cost units have a standard 10 key keyboard with decimal point key. The nine function keys are self-explanatory and based on universal arithmetical language. A typical unit has a capacity of 8 digits, which is ideal for solving complex calculating problems. It includes full floating decimal point with automatic roundoff.

The operator can select the decimal placing of the result between 2 and 4 places.

Memory System, Constants and Clearing — The flexibility of the typical memory system allows the operator to work individual problems and store the results in memory until grand totals are required to complete calculations. When carrying out a series of multiplications and divisions the multiplier and divisor can be held constant. When switching on the calculator, the display is cleared automatically. Newly entered figures clear the display panel of any previous figures. The CLEAR (C) key clears the calculating register at the end of the calculation.

Standard Performance Highlights are:
Modern MOS-LSI technology.
8 digit capacity.
Addition, subtraction, multiplication and division.
Automatic percent calculation.
Constant in all four arithmetic functions.
Direct access independent memory.
Chain multiplication and division.
Choice of full floating or fixed 2-4 decimal system with underflow.
Leading zero suppression.
Mixed and chain calculations.
Automatic round-off.
Credit balance.

hand-held calculators

Automatic clear.
Operation: AC or rechargeable battery.
Result overflow indicator.
Battery low indicator.
Handy carrying case. (Litronix)

Units with capacities similar to the above usually sell for from $10 to $50, depending upon exterior quality, case, keyboard, brand name, etc. Texas Instruments TI-1250 with 4-key memory, percent key, automatic constants was from $15 to $20 in mid-1976 and its TI-2550II with square root, inverse, etc. was between $40 and $50. Other leaders were: Rockwell, Casio, Cannon, Norvus, Unitrex, Hewlett-Packard, Victor, Royal, Olympia, Lloyds, Melcor, Corvus, Sharp, etc. The products of most of these firms will be analyzed and evaluated in pages ahead.

The Basic Low-Cost Four-Function Calculator and its Competition with Under $50 Programmable Units — Almost without exception even the lowest cost calculators offer add, subtract, multiply and divide plus at least two other functions as single key operations. For example, the under $20 Litronix 1101P, designed for taxes, check-book, shopping budgets, performs all basic arithmetic functions plus chain and mixed calculations with complete ease. A powerful percent key makes quick work of add-on, discount, mark-up and yield calculations. Repetitive addition and subtraction calculations are equally simple. The constant switch permits multiplication or division by a number over and over without re-entering it. Repetitive addition and subtraction calculations are equally simple. A bright LED display provides ease of readability on these lower cost units. Thus, the percent function (or square root) plus the constant or chaining add to 6 functions. Three penlight size AA batteries, included with the 1101P, will provide up to eight hours of continuous use. Alkaline batteries will increase operation to up to sixteen hours. An AC adapter is available as an optional purchase. This unit eliminates the batteries and operates on normal house current. This, in essence, describes the "standard" 4-6 function calculator.

The Quick, Low-Cost Stepup — Add Memory and Special Function Keys (SFKs) — A typical unit adds the "unforgettable" Memory. In addition to all basic functions, it has a full accumulating memory (including exchange key), percent and square root keys and offers automatic constant for all four arithmetic functions. The under $40 Litronix 2200 series offers: on/off keys; an automatic system that remembers to turn itself off if users forget; and a flashing "Error" signal when improper sequential entries are attempted. The keyboard on the Litronix was patterned after the expensive Hewlett Packard unit and has a three button color-coded memory system. Instead of the conventional on/off switch the Litronix has on/off keys.

Three categories of "special purpose" extra function key machines are the (1) mathematician-engineering or "slide rule" units, (2) the research or statistical capability units, and (3) the business or financial function "special key units," as noted below.

An example of a typical slide rule calculator is the Litronix 2260. It has: automatic exponential notation override from eight digit floating decimal display; a memory[3] system — performs natural parenthetical entry of complete algebraic expressions, accumulating memory and store-recall-memory; advanced square/root system — does square and square root of sums, sums of squares and square roots without re-entering intermediate results; constant Pi (π); plus the on/off keys, automatic shut-off system and "Error" signal.

Three key memory. The memory system has three separate keys for data entry. Users can do calculations on the display, store the answers in a memory bank, and recall their total without erasing what was previously stored. The separate "on-key" replaces the standard "on-switch" thus eliminating this calculator's only moving part (a major cause of calculator problems).

The Litronix has an 'automatic constant' on all five functions and can do reciprocals, raise numbers to whole powers, compute square roots, and show overflow conditions. In addition, there's a floating negative sign, sign change feature, exchange key and a percentage system that gives intermediate percentage results with each calculation. Users can do invoice extensions, compound interest problems, or many other business and scientific calculations.

Many brands of calculators provide statistical data at user fingertips! They perform arithmetic mean, variance, standard deviation, sum and "x" and sum of "x^2" statistical calcualtions, plus a full accumulating memory and calculated square roots. Most are floating decimal calculators with an item counter, which provides a check on the number of data points entered. And statistical register protection prevents accidental destruction of data.

The "Preprogrammed" or Function-String Type Calculators — The third example of the stepup from four-six function machines is the first example of the important preprogrammed category. A more complete discussion is developed below, but the example of this very low cost unit explains a bit of the miracle of truly cost-effective calculators.

Ideal for the financial man or for those who need to balance a checkbook, compute sales commissions, perform invoice extensions, or determine the gross profit on the sale of a toaster, for example, many units like the Unitrex 80 F are well worth every penny of their $40.00 to $50.00 prices. And, they work very well for computing tax returns. If a user is into high finance, the many units including the 80 F will breeze through almost any problem. Mass-produced advanced technology permits advanced calculations at very low cost. The 80 F incorporates a sophisticated ROCKWELL integrated circuit that is preprogrammed to solve complex financial problems in seconds.

Some of the advanced and preprogrammed functions: Future trend forecasts, monthly payment of annuity, present and future value of annuity, payment amount for sinking fund, present and future value of compounded amount, depreciation calculations, bond value calculation, number of periods required to repay a loan, accumulated interest paid over a specific period, sell, cost and margin calculations, and more.

Also: logic selection switch, business (arithmetic), algebraic, summation and averaging, percent add-on and discount, constants, decimal selection, square root, four (4) memories, plus more.

The 80 F and competing similar units saves

hand-held calculators

users valuable time! For Example ... If someone invests $1500 at 7½% per year in an IRA or Keough retirement plan from age 35, and he wants to know the value of the plan at age 65, the Unitrex 80 F would tell the answer, $101,966.76 in less than 15 seconds. (It also computes the present value, $16,720.42) Only three (3) numbers had to be entered: 1500, 7½ and 25 (years). That is only one of the many problems programmed on the ROCKWELL or other manufacturer integrated circuits.

These units, or similar models are available at stores throughout the world or are highly advertised through special catalog distribution outlets such as Chafitz of Rockwell, Maryland, USA, JS&A National Sales Group, Northbrook, Illinois and many others. In sections ahead many highly specialized and "custom-designed preprogrammed units, such as the 'Bond-Trader' are evaluated and explained, most at significantly higher but still cost-effective prices.

A Unique "Any Cause" Full One Year Warranty and Unconditional Guarantee — Litronix, Inc. warrants its calculators in accordance with Federal minimum standards for Full Warranty for one year from the date of retail purchase by the original owner. In addition, Litronix unconditionally guarantees that the Litronix calculator will function properly for one year from the date of such retail purchase. Should the Litronix calculator cease functioning properly at any time within such one year period because of a defect, malfunction or any other cause, Litronix, without charge, will promptly repair the calculator or replace it with a new one. CONSEQUENTIAL DAMAGES FOR BREACH OF WARRANTY OR UNCONDITIONAL GUARANTY ARE EXCLUDED. No action for breach of warranty or unconditional guaranty may be commenced more than one year after the cause of action has accrued.

Designed for use in: Metric measurement — school and business, International business, Freight and shipping, Automotive and spare parts measurements

Full Accumulating Memory — stores and recalls subtotals of prior calculators.
Memory Exchange Key — permits data in display to be exchanged for data saved in memory at any time during calculations.
Metric Conversion Template — 16 preprogrammed conversion factors — converts English to Metric and Metric to English values.
Performs percent functions — including add-ons, discounts, markups and yields.
Automatic constant — performs repetitive addition, subtraction, multiplication and division.

Floating Decimal System — automatic decimal point positioning for full 8-digit accuracy.
Automatic Overflow Indicator — indicates when calculation exceeds the 8-digit capacity.
Algebraic Logic — lets users enter problems as they would state them.
Minus Sign — indicates when number in display is negative.
Flashing Error — indicates attempted division by zero.
Performs chain and mixed calculations.
Automatic Power Off — turns calculator off after 8 minutes of non-use.

$30 Programmable Consumer Calculator — "As common as the pen?..."

hand-held calculators

THE BIG SURPRISE: UNDER $30 PROGRAMMABLE CALCULATOR FOR CONSUMERS

Designed For Use In: Retailing, Accounting, Forecasting and Budgeting — The first programmable consumer calculator — it lists for $29.95 — can store and execute a sequence of 10 program steps. The 2290, developed by Litronix, Cupertino, CA, simplifies calculations wherever a repetitive sequence of steps is involved, such as in figuring markups or discounts on store inventory, or in calculating the prices and total of a string of purchases with the sales tax included. It is also suitable for solving math problems such as the sum of squares and the value of a string of parallel resistances. The calculator remembers a sequence of function-key operations up to a total of 10. This includes any sequence of plus-equals (+=); minus-equals (−=); multiply (×); divide (÷); percent (%); add to memory (M+); subtract from memory (M−); and recall memory (RM). Clear memory (CM) cannot be used in a program, but this function is programmed by depressing recall-memory twice.

The $29.95 calculator ($39.95 in the rechargeable version) does not have exotic programming and branching as the high-priced programmable scientific machines do. To insert a program in the 2290, the display and memory are first cleared. To instruct the machine to store the program, a "learn" (L) key is pressed. The sequence of data and function keys is then pressed in the proper order until the program sequence is finished, at which point a "stop" or S key is pushed. To execute a program, the numerical data are entered and an "execute" key (E) is operated in the proper sequence.

For example, the program to calculate the prices of a number of items, including a 6% sales tax on each, involves the following:

	Key Pressed	Display
Clear display	C/ON	0.
Clear memory	CM	0.
Enter tax (%)	6	6
Add to memory	M+	6.
Learn program	L	6.
Enter item price ($)	10	10
Multiply	×	10.
Recall tax from memory	RM	6.
Times percent	%	.6
Answer ($)	+=	10.6
Stop earning sequence	S	10.6

Now sales tax computations can be made by entering the price and depressing Enter. For example, the price of $11, $12 and $13 items, with tax, and calculated by:

	Key Depressed	Display
Enter price	11	11
Press enter	E	11.66
Enter price	12	12
Press enter	E	12.72
Enter price	13	13
Press enter	E	13.78

There is no need to press any of the program or function keys again.

From this point on sales tax computations are made simply by entering any article price and pressing the execute (E) key, which then displays the price-plus-sales-tax total.

While no square-root key appears, the internal "chip" has been designed to give that function in a nonorthodox manner. For example, to obtain a square root, the number is entered followed by depressing the divide-by and plus-equal keys.

The LED display on the 2290 is unusually bright because each digit draws 150 mA instead of the usual 100. Battery life with alkaline dry cells is 18 hours.

The 2290 also has standard four-function Litronix consumer-calculator features with a four-key accumulating memory, and the usual constant K. A significant battery-saving feature of the line is that the calculator automatically turns itself off after 12 minutes without an entry. (see the $50 programmable by Sinclair Radionics, Inc. and the low-cost units by National Semiconductor Corp, (Norvus), Hewlett-Packard and Texas Instruments.)

LITRONIX 2290 PROGRAMMABLE — The Electronic Calculator That Learns

Features:
- Dual Memory system:
  - Full Accumulating Memory — stores and recalls subtotals of prior calculations.
  - Program Memory — Can "learn" up to ten-step programs in special program memory.
- Stored Program steps can be "recalled" automatically for repeat calculations. User can just "enter" new data.
- Square root operation for additional calculating power.
- Floating Decimal System — automatic decimal point position for full 8-digit accuracy.
- Arithmetic Logic — allows entry sequence to follow adding machine format.
- Overflow Save — in case of overflow in display a single press of c/on clears the overflow condition and allows calculator to continue using the overflowed results divided by 10^8.
- Battery saving display flasher.
- Flashing Error Signal — indicates an improper sequence or out-of-range data.
- Learn Mode light indicates when learn mode is in use.
- Automatic power off after approximately 12 minutes of non-use.
- Comes with a durable carrying case.
- Operates on three penlight size AA batteries for up to 8 hours of continuous operation. Alkaline batteries will provide up to 16 hours of continuous operation.
- Deluxe, bright oversized LED Display.
- FREE AC Adapter included.
- ONE YEAR UNCONDITIONAL GUARANTEE.

OPTIONAL MODEL 2290R — RECHARGEABLE
The optional 2290R comes with an integral Ni-Cad battery pack and AC charger. When fully charged the calculator will provide up to 6 hours of normal use. The unit may be recharged in 12-14 hours.

DIMENSIONS AND WEIGHT
Width: 3¼ inches   Length: 6¼ inches
Depth: ⅞ inches   Weight: 7 ounces

OPERATING INSTRUCTIONS AND FUNCTIONS

The following is a summary of functions performed by individual keys. Users refer to these functions once they have learned how to use the

hand-held calculators

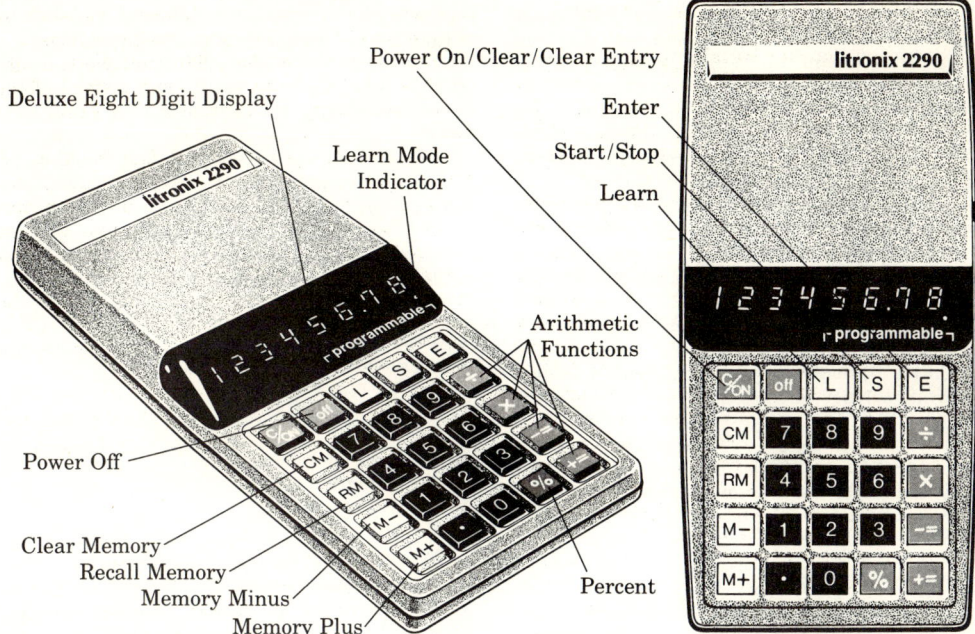

calculator. Various examples follow in order to show the simplicity of use of the calculator.

KEYS

C/ON Initial power on clears calculator, including memory. If last entry was a number, one press clears last entry. If display indicates overflow, one press clears overflow conditions. Two presses will clear claculator, but not program on data saved in memory.

OFF Turns calculator off. Once off, all data is erased from calculator, including that which was saved in memory and program.

CM Clear memory. Sets the value of memory to 0.

RM One press of key recalls data saved in memory to the display. Two presses of key clears data saved in memory.

M − Subtracts the display from data saved in memory. Repetitive subtractions of the display from data saved in memory can be done by pressing this key the specified number of times.

M+ Adds the display to data saved in memory. Repetitive addition of the display to data saved in memory can be done by pressing this key the specified number of times.

0 — 9 Number entry keys.

. Enters decimal point.

% Used in conjunction with ×, the % is used to find the percentage of a given number. Used in conjunction with + =, the % of a base number is added to that base in the display. Used with − =, the % of a base number is discounted from that base in the display.

When used in conjunction with ÷, the % function can be used for yield calculations.

+ = Directs calculator to add display to previous number when used in addition operation. If depressed twice or more in succession, the calculator remembers the original display and adds it to the current value of the display. If a previous multiplication or division has been entered, this key will complete the operation.

− = Directs calculator to subtract display from previous number when used in subtraction operation. If depressed twice or more in succession, the calculator remembers the original display and subtracts it from the current value of the display. If a previous multiplication or division has been entered, this key reverses the sign of the display, and then completes the operation.

× Directs calculator to multiply display by the following number. To multiply by a negative number, press ×, then the multiplier, then − = to complete the operation. If the preceding operation was a multiply or divide, it directs the calculator to complete that operation, display the results, and then multiply that display by the following number.

÷ Directs calculator to divide display by the following number. To divide by a negative number, press ÷, then the divisor then − = to complete the operation. If the preceding operation was a multiply or divide, it directs the calculator to complete that operation, display the results, and then divide that display by the following number.

SPECIAL COMBINATIONS

×, + = When these two keys are pressed consecutively, the calculator squares the number in the display.

÷, + = When these two keys are pressed consecutively, the calculator takes the square root of the number in the display.

PROGRAMMING KEYS

L Begins Learning Sequence and erases the previous program. Turns the learn light on and readies the calculator to accept program steps.

S Stops Learning Sequence and Starts Program Sequence. Turns off the learn light and readies the calculator to start accepting numbers at the beginning of the program.

E Enters the current value of display in the next data position in the program and continues running the program until the next data position.

hand-held calculators

DISPLAY

Error Signal — When an improper sequence of functions is entered into the calculator, the word "Error" will flash in the display. A single press of C/ON restores display.

Program Learn Indicator — A program learn indicator light appears at the left side of the display window when the L key is pressed and will go out once the S or E key is pressed.

Minus Sign — Appears immediately to left of the displayed number to indicate a negative number.

Decimal Point — Calculator automatically positions decimal point to maintain full eight digit accuracy.

Overflow Indication — A square around the decimal point will appear in the display when calculation has gone beyond capacity and refuses to permit further entries until C/ON has been pressed.

Battery Saving Display Flasher — After approximately 50 seconds of non-use, display will begin flashing on and off and continue to do this until approximately 12 minutes of non-use have passed at which time it will automatically turn itself completely off.

BATTERY HINTS

Battery Life — This calculator is designed to operate on 3 AA penlight batteries, which will provide up to 8 hours of continuous use. For the best cost power ratio for your unit, use leak-proof Alkaline Batteries, which will improve operating life up to 16 hours of continuous use. When the display becomes erratic, dim or refuses to turn on, the batteries should be replaced.

A.C. Adapter Operation — The A.C. Adapter/Battery Eliminator (Model #102 for 110 volt operation and Model #104 for 230 volt operation) will allow this unit to be used with normal A.C. Power. When the adapter is used, the internal batteries are automatically disconnected to conserve battery life.

Optional Model 2290R (Rechargeable) — This model comes with an internal battery pack that provides up to 6 hours of normal use. The batteries can be recharged in 12-14 hours with the enclosed A.C. Adapter/Charger (Model #102/103 for 110 volt operation, Model #104/105 for 230 volt operation.)

The battery pack should be recharged when the calculator display becomes erratic, dim or the calculator refuses to turn on. To obtain a maximum charge in a 12-14 hour time period, the calculator would be turned off during the charging, however, the calculator can be operated while the charger is connected. It is further recommended that if the machine has not been used for four or more weeks, it be recharged before using on battery power.

PROGRAMMING

What is a Program?

A calculator 'program' is simply a series of keyboard operations that must be done in a particular sequence to yield a correct answer — add, multiply, subtract, divide or other functions. Often this identical series of steps must be performed again and again — for example, to solve a recurring problem where only the 'numbers' change but not the way they must be manipulated. With its ability to be programmed, the 2290 'learns' these program sequences and can repeat them automatically, saving the user time and button pressing, and reducing the chance of error.

How to Write a Program

Users program their Litronix calculator by example. Press the L key, and the calculator clears any previous program it had remembered, and gets ready to learn a new program. The calculator will remember the sequence in which users enter numbers and save the function keys; each function key represents one program step. Learn mode lasts until users depress the S key, or until they have entered 10 program steps.

For example, consider computation of sales tax, to give total sales price. To teach their calculator to do sales tax calculations they do the following:

	Key Depressed	Displayed
Clear display	C/ON	0.
Clear memory	CM	0.
Begin learning	L	9.●
Enter price	10	10●
Press multiply	×	10.●
Enter sales tax rate	6	6●
Press per cent	%	0.6●
Press plus equals	+=	10.6●
Stop learning	S	10.6

The calculator has now learned how to compute add on tax. The price of a $10 object with 6% sales tax is $10.60. Now as an example, execute the program to calculate the total price of a $11 item with 6% sales tax.

How To Execute a Program

To execute a program, press the E key, after entering numbers, but not function keys, in the same sequence that you used when the L key was depressed. The calculator will sequentially substitute numbers you enter, one by one, into the learned program.

	Key Depressed	Display
Enter Price	11	11
Press Enter	E	11.
Enter sales tax rate	6	6
Press Enter	E	11.66

Note that the price was entered first, and sales tax rate second as in the learning sequence. See what happens if you enter sales tax rate first and price second.

Incorrect Use of Program

	Key Depressed	Display
Enter sales tax rate	6	6
Press Enter	E	6.
Enter Price	11	11
Press Enter	E	6.66

A completely meaningless answer results. Note that if the sales tax is constant, this program can be simplified so that only the price need be entered. The sales tax rate can be saved in the memory, and the RM key used in your program.

OPERATING EXAMPLES WITHOUT PROGRAMMING

	Key Depressed	Display
1. Entering Numbers		
Enter 25		
Clear display	C/ON	0.
Press 2	2	2
Press 5	5	25
2. Entering Numbers with Decimal Points		
Enter 3.141		
Clear display	C/ON	0.
Press 3	3	3
Press .	.	3.
Press 1	1	3.1

hand-held calculators

Press 4	4	3.14
Press 1	1	3.141

3. Entering Decimal Numbers Smaller than 1
Enter .651

Clear display	C/ON	0.
Press .	.	0.
Press 6	6	0.6
Press 5	5	0.65
Press 1	1	0.651

4. Entering Negative Value Numbers
Enter −1.2

Clear display	C/ON	0.
Press 1	1	1
Press .	.	1.
Press 2	2	1.2
Press minus equals	−=	−1.2

5. Clearing Entries

Enter 11.2	11.2	11.2
Press multiply	×	11.2
Enter 4	4	4
Press C/ON	C/ON	0.
Enter 17.5	17.5	17.5
Press C/ON	C/ON	0.
Enter 5	5	5
Press plus equals	+=	56.

6. 'Overflow'

Enter 888888.8	888888.8	888888.8
Press multiply	×	888888.8
Enter 999.9	999.9	999.9
Press plus equals	+=	8.8879991

The 'box' around the decimal point and the flashing display indicate the 'overflow' condition. Note that the calculated numbers are correct but the decimal point has been moved over 8 places to the left. The machine will not allow further entry until C/ON is pressed.

7. Addition of Whole Numbers
Add 40 and 47

Clear display	C/ON	0.
Enter first number	40	40
Press plus equals	+=	40.
Enter second number	47	47
Press plus equals	+=	87.

8. Addition of Number (Dollars) with Decimals (Cents)
Add $10.13, $6.00, $5.70

Clear display	C/ON	0.
Enter first number	10.13	10.13
Press plus equals	+=	10.13
Enter second number	6.00	6.00
Press plus equals	+=	16.13
Enter third number	5.70	5.70
Enter plus equals	+=	21.83

9. Subtracting Whole Numbers
Subtract 16 from 17

Enter number to be subtracted from	17	17
Press plus equals	+=	17.
Enter number to subtract	16	16
Press minus equals	−=	1.

10. Subtracting Numbers with Decimal
Subtract 4.2 and 6 from 3

Enter number to be subtracted from	3	3
Press plus equals	+=	3.
Enter first number to subtract	4.2	4.2
Press minus equals	−=	−1.2
Enter second number to subtract	6	6
Press minus equals	−=	−7.2

11. Chained Addition Subtraction and 'Repeat'
Add 5, 6.2, 6.2, then subtract 41.1, then add 12.8 and 12.8

Clear display	C/ON	0.
Enter first number	5	5
Press plus equals	+=	5.
Enter second number	6.2	6.2
Press plus equals	+=	11.2
Press plus equals	+=	17.4

Note that we do not have to enter the third number (6.2) since it is the same as the second, and Litronix calculator has a repeat operation function for addition and subtraction.

Enter fourth number	41.1	41.1
Press minus equals	−=	−23.7
Enter fifth number	12.8	12.8
Press plus equals	+=	−10.9
Press plus equals	+=	1.9

12. Multiplication of Whole Numbers
Multiply 21 by 15

Enter first number	21	21
Press multiply	×	21.
Enter second number	15	15
Press plus equals	+=	315.

13. Multiplication of Numbers with Decimals
Multiply 10.2 gallons by 57.9¢

Enter first number	10.2	10.2
Press multiply	×	10.2
Enter second number	.579	.579
Press plus equals	+=	5.9058

14. Chained Multiplication
Multiply 5 feet by 2 feet by 3½ feet

Enter first number	5	5
Press multiply	×	5.
Enter second number	2	2
Press multiply	×	10.
Enter third number	3.5	3.5
Press plus equals	+=	35.

15. Division, Including Decimal Values
Compute ⅝

Enter number to be divided	5	5
Press divide	÷	5.
Enter number to divide with	8	8
Press plus equals	+=	0.625

Calculating Per Cent (%)
The percent key has 3 uses.
(1) x is what % of y?
(2) What is x% of y?
(3) Compute what x% of y and then add or subtract that number to y.

(1) 3 is what % of 4?

Enter first number	3	3
Press divide	+÷	3.
Enter second number	4	4
Press per cent	%	75.

3 is 75% of 4

(2) What is 11.1% of 43?

Enter first number	43	43
Press multiply	×	43.
Enter second number	11.1	11.1

hand-held calculators

	Press per cent	%	4.773
	4.773 is 11.1% of 43		

(3) What is the new value of a $14 item if it is marked up 8%

	Key Depressed		Display
Enter first number	14		14
Press multiply	×		14.
Enter second number	8		8
Press per cent	%		1.12
Press plus equals	+ =		15.12

The price of the item is $15.12

Joice Black has a problem. She can buy 7 oz. of Brand X detergent for 59¢ or she can buy the economy size which is 16 oz. for $1.89. Which is the better value? To answer this question we compute the price per ounce. The smaller price per ounce is the better value.

7 oz. 59¢

	Keys Depressed	Display
Clear display	C/ON	0.
Enter price	.59	0.59
	÷	0.59
Enter quantity	7	7
	+ =	.08428571

16 oz. for $1.89

	Keys Depressed	Display
Clear display	C/ON	0.
Enter price	1.89	1.89
	÷	1.89
Enter quantity	16	16
	+ =	0.118125

At a little over 8¢ per ounce, the 7 oz. size is more economical than the 11¢ per ounce (16 oz.) container.

Mary Garcia wants to balance her budget. She will take her income and subtract her fixed expenses to arrive at the amount of money she is free to spend. Mary is paid $195 per week. She pays $140 a month for rent, $45 a week for food, $125 a month on her car, $10 a week for gas and oil, $40 monthly for her insurance bills, and $15 monthly for her utility bills. To calculate,

	Key Depressed	Display
Clear display	C//ON	0.
Clear memory	CM	0.
Enter weekly income	195	195
	×	195.
Enter number of weeks in month	4.3	4.3
	+ =	838.5
Store this value in memory	M+	838.5
Enter rent payments	140	140
Subtract from memory	M−	140.
Enter weekly food bill	45	45
	×	45.
Enter weeks in month	4.3	4.3
	+ =	193.5
Subtract from memory	M−	193.5
Enter monthly car payment	125	125
Subtract from memory	M−	125.
Enter weekly gas and oil bill	10	10
	×	10.
Enter weeks in month	4.3	4.3
	+ =	43.
Subtract from memory	M−	43.
Enter monthly insurance	40	40
Subtract from memory	M−	40.
Enter monthly utility bill	15	15
Subtract from memory	M−	15.

Mary now presses RM to recall memory and sees that she has $282 discretionary monthly income.

WITH PROGRAMMING

Jim Fournier, a small businessman, wants to discount his line of toasters. Before he finalizes this decision, however, he needs the new price of each toaster and the updated value of his inventory. To do this he teaches his Litronix calculator the following sequence.

	Key Depressed	Display
Clear display	C/ON	0.
Clear memory	CM	0.
Begin learning sequence	L	0.•
Enter price of toaster (top of line — the New Yorker)	49.95	49.95•
	×	49.95•
Enter discount rate	10	10•
Compute discount	%	4.995•
Discounted price	− =	44.955•
	×	44.995•

At this point, the display indicates what the cost of Jim's top of the line toaster would be with a 10% discount. Jim now enters the number of New Yorkers in stock.

	3	3•
	+ =	134.865•
Save updated value of inventory in memory.	M+	134.865•
Stop learning sequence	S	134.865

Memory now contains the new inventory value of Jim's 3 New Yorker toasters. Since Jim has 15 Angeleno toasters, he wishes to discount them 12% so that they will start moving. He does the following steps.

Enter price of toaster	39.95	39.95
	E	39.95
Enter discount rate	12	12
	E	35.156

The display now indicates what the new price of the Angelenos would be.

Enter number of toasters	15	15
	E	527.34

Using his program, Jim calculates the discount price for the rest of his toasters and generates this new table.

TOASTER	CURRENT PRICE	DISCOUNT RATE	NO. IN STOCK	NEW PRICE	NEW INVENTORY VALUE
New Yorker	49.95	10	3	44.955	134.865
Angeleno	39.95	12	15	35.156	527.34
Foridian	33.33	10	5	29.997	149.985
Franciscan	25.25	10	5	22.725	113.625
Bostonian	19.99	8	8	18.3908	147.1264
					1072.9414

Esther Edwards wishes to buy a new car. There are three dealers in town who offer the model she is interested in, the new California Motors compact, the Flash. The three dealers, Fred's Auto, Hiram's Motors, and Ron's Auto, are each offering a different 'deal.' Esther wants to determine which would be the best deal on a price basis, and what her monthly payments would be. These are the deals:

	Base Price	Yearly Add-On Interest Rate	Length Of Loan
Fred's	3500	7	3 Years
Hiram's	3750	6.5	3 Years
Ron's	4000	6	3 Years

hand-held calculators

Esther figures which is the best deal on her Litronix calculator. She teaches her calculator the following steps:

	Key Depressed	Display
Begin Learning sequence	L	0.
Enter price	3500	3500●
	×	3500. ●
Enter rate of interest	7	7●
	%	245. ●
	+=	3745. ●
	+=	3990. ●
	+=	4235. ●
	÷	4235. ●

The display now indicates the total price of the car. To find her monthly payments and to complete the learning sequence, Esther follows with:

Enter number of months	36	36●
Depress plus equals	+=	117.63888●
Stop learning sequence	S	

The price of Fred's car was $4235. The monthly payments will be $117.64.

To calculate Hiram's total price, Esther does the following:

Enter price of car	3750	3750
	E	3750.
Enter rate of interest	6.5	6.5
	E	4481.25
Enter number of months	36	36
	E	124.47916

Hiram's car will cost $4481.25 and will have monthly payments of $124.48.

The price of Ron's car will be calculated in the same manner.

Enter price of car	4000	4000
	E	4000.
Enter rate of interest	6	6
	E	4720.
Enter number of months	36	36
	E	131.11111

On the basis of price and monthly payments it is clear that Fred is offering Esther the best "deal."

The Sinclair Scientific Programmable for under $50...

Sinclair's Scientific Programmable is not an ordinary calculator. It has only 19 keys — and, for a programmable, a very low price — but its problem-solving capability exceeds that of any ordinary scientific calculator. The big plus is programmability — the ability to remember a calculation sequence of up to 24 steps entered directly from the keyboard. Once stored in the program memory, a calculation sequence can be recalled at the touch of a single key, and applied to new numbers to produce new results. For users who carry out repetitive calculations, the Scientific Programmable will save many key strokes and lots of time. It will also save users from errors, since the calculation sequence will be recalled exactly as originally entered, over and over again.

A distinct engineering achievement lies behind the capability and low price of this calculator. The Sinclair Scientific Programmable was one of the first among many programmable calculators to use a single integrated circuit. The entire logic, data storage and program storage of this calculator are contained in a single chip — a chip developed by Sinclair engineers. Others quickly followed, and one-chip machines are becoming standard.

Programmable characteristics

Entering a calculation sequence into the program memory is quite easy. Users press the BE key to tell the calculator to remember a sequence. They key in the calculation almost exactly as they normally would. They use VAR at the points where they'll want the program to stop, so that they can enter new numbers or display partial results. During entry the number of steps is displayed, so they won't exceed the program memory's capacity. When they've finished they press BE again to tell the calculator that the sequence is complete. The program is now available until they overwrite it with another program or until they switch the calculator off. To enter new numbers, they press EXEC, and get new results. The Scientific Programmable can be used as an ordinary scientific calculator. Even half-way through the execution of a program, users can stop, carry out a calculation from the keyboard, then press EXEC to continue execution of the program when they're ready. Once users have entered a program it is available at the touch of a key until they overwrite it with another program or switch off. But the program doesn't interfere with the calculator's normal operation in any way; it is stored in a separate program memory area and is available only when needed.

With the Sinclair Program Library users don't have to be programmers. For easier use of the Scientific Programmable's full problem-solving capability, each calculator comes with a fully documented library of hundreds of programs to solve standard problems, and complete instructions on how to use them. Typical programs and costs are shown below. As regards applications, the Scientific Programmable has many applications in areas of computation other than repetitive calculations. It can be used for the analysis of experimental data, the evaluation of integer functions, and with a variety of methods for the iterative solution of equations. They are dealt with in detail in the instruction book and Program Library. And, although the Scientific Programmable is no toy, it does play games — and wins! The display is a 5 digit mantissa with 2 digit exponent. Num-

hand-held calculators

ber entry is floating decimal point and/or scientific notation; results are in scientific notation. It uses Reverse Polish Notation logic. Its preprogrammed functions are sine, cosine arctangent (radians), log, alog (base 10), square root, reciprocal, change sign, clear/clear entry. It has memory to store, recall and exchange.

The Scientific Programmable is small enough to hold in one's hand and big enough to use on one's desk. It measures 6" x 2⅞" x 1¼", has non-slip rubber feet and a big green display. It uses a small, inexpensive 9v battery or the Sinclair AC adapter.

Sinclair Offers Free Custom Programming Service — If users have an application for the Sinclair Scientific Programmable which is not covered by the Program Library, Sinclair's software support team will devise a custom program to solve the problem. Users must write to Sinclair clearly explaining the problem and they will send a program that can be used with Scientific Programmable to solve it. There is no charge for this service.

AVAILABLE SINCLAIR PROGRAMS (mid-1976)   (Prices shown below are for complete sets)

GENERAL ARITHMETIC FORMULAE $2.00
Factorials
Polynominal Evaluation
Quadratic Equation
General Expressions
Series
Decimal to Binary Conversion
Complex Numbers
Determinants
Log Base Change

GEOMETRY $2.00
Triangles
Parallelograms
Circles
Right Parallelopiped
Cuboid
Cylinders
Cone
Sphere

STASTICS $1.50
Summations
Sample Variance
Probability
Quality Control
Error of Difference
Chi²
Simpson's Rule, Regression

FINANCIAL $1.50
Accumulation
Percentages
Compound Interest
Loan Repayment
Cash Flow

GENERAL APPLICATION $1.00
Fahrenheit to Centrigrade
Degrees minutes and seconds to Radians
Hours minutes and seconds to Decimal Hours
Tally Counter
Subtraction Game

ELECTRONICS $3.50
Ohms Law
Attenuators
Reactance-Frequency Chart
Frequency to wavelength
Amplitude of Harmonics of Waveforms
RCL Circuits
Decibel Conversion
Transistor Transconductance
M. O. S. Transistors
Power Amplifiers
H. F. Amplifiers
Negative Feedback
Thermal Noise
Power Supply Smoothing
Transmission Lines

RADIATION AND PROPAGATION $1.50
Aerials
Communication Theory
Radar Equation
Frequency, Angular Velocity
Characteristic Impedance
Skin Effect
Series Resonance

ELECTROSTATICS AND ELECTROMAGNETICS $2.00
Electrostatics
Capacitance
Inductance
Magnetostatics
Electric Flux Refraction
Electron Dynamics

ELECTRICAL MACHINES $1.00
DC Machines
Induction Motors
Transformers

MECHANICS $3.50
Parallelogram Law for Forces
Statistics in 3 Dimensions
Relativistic Effects
Frequency, Angular Velocity, Wavelength
Forces in Co-ordinate Systems
Tangenital and Normal Components
Energy in a Gravitational Field
Scalar Product
Motion due to various Force Fields
Moment of Inerta Theorems
Work Equation
Projectile Motion
Planetary Motion
Electron Dynamics
Escape Velocity
Doppler Effect
Mirrors and Lenses
Velocity of Sound

STRUCTURES $2.50
Beam Deflection Elastic Analysis
Beam Deflection
Struts
Elastic Bending
Elastic Strain Energy
Torsion of Tube
Complex Stresses
Cylinder Pressure Vessel
Strains due to Stress
Redundancy in Trusses

CENTERS OF GRAVITY & MOMENTS OF INERTIA $2.50
Laminae
Rods
Shells of Revolution
Solids of Revolution
Torroids

THERMODYNAMICS $1.50
Dryness Fraction
Polytropic Process
Heat Conduction
Heat Conduction (Shape Factors)
Radiation

FLUID MECHANICS $2.50
Hydrostatics
Pressure-Flow Measurement
Pipe Flow
Sudden Expansion
Free Surface Flows
Total Conditions
Compressible Flow
Perfect Gas Relations
Vortices
General

MATERIALS $1.50
Atomic Physics
Transport Properties
Ionic Bond
Elastic Properties
Stresses and Strains
X-ray Diffraction
Dislocations

Competing with the Sinclair Scientific Programmable is the Novus Programmable Mathematician above (right)

The Standard and Programmable Statisticians — Low cost units from Novus (National Semiconductor Corp). The Novus 6030 is a fully-featured pocket calculator priced within the means of all serious users, professionals and students alike. Especially dedicated to statistical problems, the Novus Statistician features pre-programmed, single-key calculations of most common statistical formulas. Countless hours can be saved in performing statistical calculations. And more important, the chances for calculating or entry errors are virtually eliminated. As an extremely accurate scientific tool, Novus 6030 is a valuable business machine that offers four-function performance (addition, subtraction, multiplication, division) as well as some important extras. Like automatic square roots, a live % key with automatic add-on or discount and net, a separate accumulating memory, standard deviation, coefficient of correlation, and regression line. Its handy business/commercial logic lets users perform addition and subtraction arithmetically (as on an adding machine) and multiplication and division algebraically.

Performance features are:
• Single-key summation of x, x^2 and n.

hand-held calculators

- Single-key calculation of a mean and standard deviation.
- Single-key summation of x and y values for linear correlation and regression.
- Single-key calculation of linear correlation coefficient and slope of curve.
- Single-key calculation of y-axis intercept or any point of y-axis.
- Separate keys to remove incorrect x and y values.
- Single key to enter frequency for standard deviation of grouped data.
- Mean and standard deviation calculated without destroying summations, enabling additions or deletions.
- Single key to clear all statistical summations.
- Square, square root and change sign functions.
- Automatic constant in multiplication and division.
- Automatic repeat addition and subtraction.
- Full accumulating memory with memory-plus and equals-plus.
- Floating entries and intermediate answers.
- "Live" % key with automatic add-on or discount and net.
- Indicator light for low battery condition.
- MOS/LSI solid-state circuitry for durability and dependability.
- Bright, eight-digit LED display.

Many important statistical formulas have been pre-programmed into the Novus 6030 to assure absolute accuracy. The possibility of entry errors is greatly reduced since most of the Statistician's special function keys require only single entries.

Call Clears all statistical summations.
r[reg] Linear correlation and regression.
y val y-intercept.
x[σ] Mean and standard deviation.
ΣY Summation of y values.
del Y Delete a y value.

The Novus 6035 adds Programmability Power
— Added keys on the Programmable Statician (6035) are:
del X Delete an x value.
ΣX Summation of x values.

Novus 6030 Statistician/6035 Programmable Statician

CHS Change sign.
M+ Adds displayed number to contents of memory.
$\sqrt{}$ Square root. Automatically determines square root of displayed number.
Freq Enters frequency of grouped data.
=+ Adds results of calculation to contents of memory.
[MR]/MC Memory recall displays contents of separate accumulating memory. Memory clear function erases contents of memory.
% Percent key.

The addition of learn-mode programming to the already powerful Novus Statistician creates a truly innovative combination of calculating power, convenience and affordability. The Statistician's programming capability means users can virtually eliminate the possibility of errors in performing repetitious calculations. Its unique programming features include:

- Simplified programming. Users simply engage a Learn Switch and perform a problem in normal manner. The Novus 6035 records the formula and lets users debug the program as it's written.
- The learn-mode capacity totals 100 separate steps.
- Several different programs can be contained at the same time.
- Constant factors can be entered as program steps.
- Delete feature lets users correct programs while they are writing them.
- Skip key permits skipping over entire programs to access additional programs within 100-step capacity.
- Programs remain intact until new programs are written over or until the Statistician is turned off.
- Users have total freedom to select keyboard entries as variables or constants.
- Automatic warning signal in display lets users know when they exceed programming capacity.
- The Novus Programmable Statistician is rechargeable and comes complete with nickel cadmium batteries, charger and attractive vinyl carrying case.

Which Low-Cost Calculator Is Best For Students and Engineers? — Prospective users who go about attempting to select the right calculator generally ask themselves two basic questions: 1. What types of problems will the calculator usually be used to solve? 2. What are the most difficult types of problems the calculator may be called upon to solve? If users can obtain a calculator with enough functions to satisfy both types of problem-solving situations at a satisfactory price, they should buy it. However many might make mistakes if they forego the more advanced capability — they will discover costs are so very low.

Most simple and compound arithmetical calculations can be done on four-function units. Engineers, however, would most likely want to add specialized functions such as reciprocal, squaring, and square-root calculation. In more advanced applications — such as in preparing mechanical drawings, doing geometric and navigation problems, trigonometric functions are needed. Rectangular-to-polar coordinate conversion keys are desirable because they minimize keystrokes and, therefore, shorten calculating time.

the concepts of special function keys (SFKs)

For many purposes and especially in the designing of electrical and electronic circuits the engineer uses logarithmic functions — common log, common antilog, natural log, natural antilog — and exponential functions, square roots, and nth roots. When working with statistics — such as those used in quality control and time analysis problems — the engineer should look for logarithmic, exponential, and factorial functions as well as mean and standard deviation capabilities.

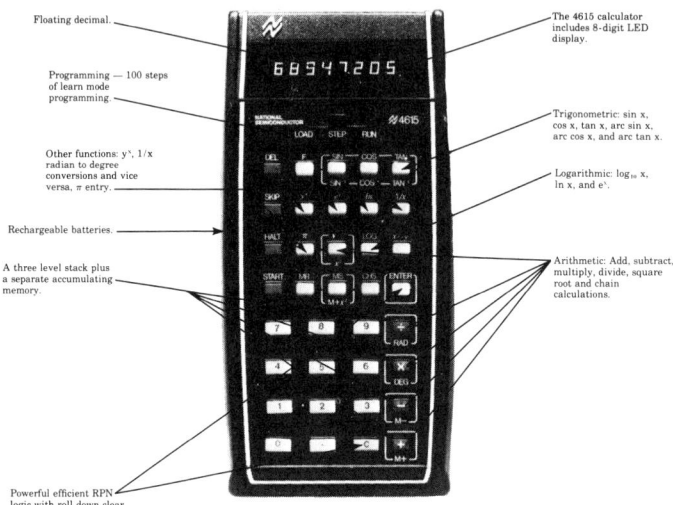

The National Semiconductor 4615 slide-rule calculator is a 100-step, keyboard programmable calculator with arithmetic, log and trig functions and features RPN (reverse Polish notation), three-level register stack and accumulating memory. The 4615 and 4640 professional calculators both carry the National Semiconductor name, while other consumer-oriented units bear the Novus label. The National Semiconductor 4640, 54-function scientific calculator features arithmetic, log and trig functions, commonly used statistical functions and a dozen conversion functions. It offers a 12-digit LED display which includes a 10-digit mantissa, two-digit exponent, and has 10-digit accuracy. A selectable display provides floating point, fixed point, and engineering notation and automatically overflows into scientific notation when necessary. Price was $89.95 in mid 1976.

PART 1—Section Two

THE CONCEPTS OF SPECIAL FUNCTION KEYS (SFKs), PREPROGRAMMING AND PROGRAMMABILITY

The modern pocket calculator has very quickly found use in practically all professions, many ranges of education, increasingly numerous types of recreation, and for the hobbyists, in challenging calculator modification. The first effective pocket calculator, the Hewlett-Packard HP-35 was introduced in January 1972. After two years and a few hundred thousand machines, practical applications information appeared in the literature. This related primarily to the organization of problem-solving equations and keystroke steps and sequences as related to simple and complex but pragmatic business and scientific problems. The goal of optimized key sequence simplicity was achieved while the simultaneous very rapid reduction in costs of products occurred. Within two years of acceptance of the introduction of the first pocket scientific calculator, the first "fully" programmable calculator, the HP-65 was introduced. This unit, and its numerous imitators, as noted on pages ahead, offers logical "compares", for branching to other program segments; editing, for correcting, changing, or adding, and most importantly, a magnetic card (strip) reader for accepting exterior programs. The applications for this type machine are so numerous, exciting and varied that sales zoomed, and the "pocket computer" concept was alive with excitement throughout all the already established calculator utilization areas and an uncountable number of new ones.

Programming meant that users now had a way

the concepts of special function keys (SFKs)

to get the machine to do exactly and quickly what they most wanted it to do and under their personal direction. It became very easy for the user to become quickly familiar with the calculator characteristics, while the exact opposite is true for users of computers. Most calculator owner's manuals offer very well developed explanations of machine utilization and capability. The new user's problems generally relate to input-output, memory space allocation, and specific routines. And a considerable amount of practice is required to follow the owner's manuals and to then proceed beyond with new profitable adventures. A surprising number of users develop their own special routines and programs.

The four-function hand-held or desk-top calculator was initially upgraded with memory, then two, three or more special function keys, as percentage, square root, constant, etc. Although these are often called 'preprogrammed' functions, they should not be confused with "preprogrammed machines". The preprogrammed calculators have all these capabilities, plus a lot more. They perform complete routines and often complex 'string' and branch calculations at the touch of a single key, calculations that would take several operations on four-function machines, with or without special function keys. They almost totally eliminate the tediousness of step-by-step pencil and paper notation and/or separate calculations. Preprogrammed machines effectively accomodate various disciplines, specific professions, etc. They are preprogrammed to solve problems unique to each of many types of engineers, (surveyors, hydraulics, etc.) businessmen, industrialists, scientists, and research workers — and many of these specialized units are compared in pages ahead. The scientist's or engineer's preprogrammed calculator, for example, does everything a complex slide-rule will do — but with greater speed, accuracy and computation range. These machines have from the usual several to a great many memory registers that store intermediate answers and constants, plus self-contained log, trig. statistics, and other tables — all called-up at the touch of a key. The businessman's preprogrammed calculator, for example, helps him solve time and money problems, because, like the 'scientific' and 'slide-rule' machines, not just a few SFKs, but complete specific programs and long specialized sequence strings are 'wired in' or preprogrammed. These are much more powerful than four-function "+" machines. They fill a gap, a wide gap, between electronic adding machines and big computers. It has been estimated that at least 40% and up to 70% of most business and scientific organization's computational needs fall within the capabilities of preprogrammed calculators. But, the nagging questions remain: How do potential users know which calculator best fits their need? What makes one machine a better cost-effective machine than another? Which is the best choice for ease of use — preprogrammed, programmable, pocket-size, desk-top etc.? By showing and evaluating alternatives, the pages ahead hopefully will assist users in making these decisions. The preprogrammed units next evaluated are a step-up from the very low-cost units analyzed.

Problem solvers in specific job classifications quite often solve very similar type problems, day in and day out. Auto dealers use calculators to instantly figure customers' deals. Government and municipal bond traders and financial managers use special preprogrammed calculators to instantly calculate sophisticated financial transactions. Accountants handle general business data problems from receivables to inventory reports, and the list goes on. Problem solvers are great potential machine buyers, and the thirst for 'how to use' information is far greater than the calculator industry realizes. The increasing size and popularity of 'User Groups', Calculator Clubs, Calculator newsletters and special magazines attest to this. Calculator manufacturers should provide greater support to these efforts to increase sales, reduce post-sales inquiries, publicize testimonials, disseminate applications information, provide education and training, encourage feedback among users, dealers, suppliers, and to keep customers happy. Happy customers generate other customers.

The preprogrammed units to be analyzed are often called "Answer Machines" because they are often not general purpose advanced calculators with basic computational keys and programming characteristics that require the user to have detailed mathematical knowledge or training. Instead they are dedicated specific purpose answer machines that pop out highly processed final accurate answers. They can, for example, compute the groundspeed of an airplane, given the direction of the wind and the speed and direction of the plane — without the user knowing the fundamentals of trigonometry, vector arithmetic, etc. Only the variables need be entered on appropriately designated keys after which the desired 'answer' key is pressed, in this case "Groundspeed." Thus, preprogrammed machines are dedicated calculators aimed specific users applications, or as is the case with 'combination calculators' (see pages ahead), they are general purpose units with some form of 'canned program' wired-in for unique applications. There are Navigation Answer Machines, Real Estate Answer Machines, as well as specialized preprogrammed units for carpenters, photographers, etc. From the manufacturer's standpoint, they can preprogram or reprogram various CPU or ROM (Read Only Memory) chips to achieve specific purposes — and great volume within these specifications reduces one-time unit costs very considerably—all to the benefit of users.

THE PREPROGRAMMED HAND-HELD CALCULATORS: AN EXAMPLE — THE ELECTRONIC SLIDE RULE HAD ITS DAY

Typical Available Functions of 'Slide Rule' Calculators:

Round-off — When a fixed decimal point is used, the operation automatically rounds off (either up or down) the last significant digit of an answer.

Truncate — Performed in lieu of rounding off, the answer is automatically cut down to the required number of fixed decimal places.

Memory — Used only to store intermediate results for future processing. Contents cannot be altered while in memory.

Addressable memory — Contains contents that can be processed independently.

Fixed decimal point — The position of the decimal remains fixed, limiting the number of digits that can appear to the right of the decimal point.

Floating decimal point — Automatically positions the decimal point in a given answer, making

the concepts of special function keys (SFKs)

for higher accuracy than can be achieved with the fixed decimal point technique.

Scientific notation — When answer overflows the number of available digits, it is automatically expressed in terms of powers of 10. Thus, a number range of 10^{-99} to 10^{+99} is obtained.

Repeat operations — Allows the addition and subtraction of a series of identical numbers by depressing the add or subtract function key repeatedly.

Constant operations — Operations can be performed on a series of numbers by a particular number without having to continually re-enter the constant.

Unit conversion — Automatically converts English units to metric and vice versa.

Percent — Automatically displays an answer in percentage terms when the percent key is used.

Constants — The display or entering of constants such as Pi or e at the push of a button.

Trig calculations — Used for analyzing and making calculations from the relations of sides and angles of triangles. Some calculators give the operator the option of obtaining the answer in degrees, radians, or grads.

Reciprocals (1/x) — Divides any number into one without having to enter the one and use the "divide" key.

Square (X^2) — Multiplies any number by itself without having to enter the number twice and using the "multiply" key.

Square root ($\sqrt{X}$) — Automatically calculates the quantity that, when multiplied by itself, will give the entered quantity. This capability (as with "square" and "reciprocals") is of great value where large and/or complicated numbers are involved.

Logarithms — Calculates common and natural logs by merely entering specific numbers and pushing the "log" or "ln" keys.

Statistical expression — To make statistical analysis easy, some technical calculators feature keys that provide a running total when adding numbers; compute the sum of the squares of all entries; calculate the arithmetic mean and standard deviation; and perform averaging and vector addition and subtraction.

The Quick Step-Up Alternative to Slide-Rule Calculators — The Low-Cost Key Programmable and the Fully Programmable Units — A typical programmable pocket calculator is the Hewlett-Packard HP-25. This under $200 unit has 8 logical compares, 4 comparing X to Y, and 4 comparing X to 0. Backstep, single step, and pause are other unique features to calculators in this price range. The inconvenience of having to key in the program each time is offset by the ability to review the program in the display. The ability to make logical comparisons gives the machine tremendous computing capability. With personal machines, speed is of secondary importance. If a problem takes 30 minutes to solve, the user simply sets the machine aside and does something else while the machine runs. The ability of the machine to go anywhere makes it the slave of the user, not the reverse.

The fully programmables offer programmed cards, tapes, ROMs, etc. First, the Cards . . . Purchased, preprogrammed cards are imprinted for specialized relabeling, and blank cards are also available for users who wish to write and store original programs. These magnetic cards have frosted white backing material for pencil notation and easy erasure. On several medium to low-priced units, one program containing up to 100 steps, or many programs totaling 100 steps, can be recorded on a single card. When a recorded program is no longer needed, the magnetic card can be erased on these units and reused to record another program. Accidental erasures can be prevented by clipping a corner of the cards. Sensors note the missing corner and deactivate the record function should it be called for. The manufacturers of programmable units maintain large libraries of both standard and user-contributed programs for the units. These are available to all owners for a small fee. The calculator itself no longer represents a significant investment for the individual, at from $300 to $800. This includes a 115/230-volt ac adapter-recharger, a soft carrying case with belt loop, a hard travel case, adhesive name tags, owner's manual, quick reference guide, and the standard Application Programs containing tape recorded programs, diagnostic program cards, magnetic head cleaning cards, and blank magnetic program cards. Buyers also receive subscriptions to newsletters, User Library Catalog, etc.

Several calculators run on rechargeable batteries or ac and include peripheral tape cassettes and drives through which the user can write or read over 100,000 program steps. This enables the storage and retrieval of an entire program library on a single cassette. Programmable from the keyboard, some "Computing" calculators can accept blocks of programs in 160 steps increments, with the added feature of one program segment being able to call another program automatically or store and recall data from tape. Some units use standard computer programming language (often a deterrent to unskilled users), but others utilize simple algebraic language. Equations are entered just as they are written, including parentheses and parentheses within parentheses. Editing, for example, has been greatly simplified. A user can move back and forth in memory one step at a time, inserting, deleting, or modifying any number of program steps.

Texas Instrument's Preprogrammed Advanced Math Calculators: SR-50-A, SR-51-A — Engineer . . . Scientist . . . Businessman . . . Geologist . . . Chemist . . . Statistician . . . Student . . . or for many other fields, if users are doing more than basic mathematics they might consider an SR-50A or SR-51A from Texas Instruments.

The SR-51A for example is designed for simple arithmetic to complex statistics. As regards math power, log and trig and hyperbolics and functions of x, the SR-51A has these and also statistical functions. Like mean, variance and standard deviation. Factorials, permutations, slope and intercept. Trend line analysis. And there's a random number generator. Plus 20 preprogrammed conversions and inverses. The list on page 21 is a closer look at the real math power users can get in both the SR-51A and the SR-50A:

Answers are calculated to 13 significant digits, rounded off and displayed to 10. And for maximum accuracy, all 13 are held inside for subsequent calculations. Scientific notation is automatic when users need it. For numbers as large as $\pm 9.999999999 \times 10^{99}$. Or as small as $\pm 1. \times 10^{-99}$.

the concepts of special function keys (SFKs)

FUNCTION	SR51A	SR-50A
Log, lnx	yes	yes
Trig (sin, cos, tan INV)	yes	yes
Hyperbolic (sinh, cosh, tanh, INV)	yes	yes
Degree-radian conversion	yes	yes
Deg/rad mode selection switch	yes	yes
Decimal degrees to deg. min. sec.	yes	no
Polar-rectangular conversion	yes	no
y^x	yes	yes
e^x	yes	yes
10^x	yes	no
x^2	yes	yes
$\sqrt{x}$	yes	yes
$\sqrt[x]{y}$	yes	yes
$1/x$	yes	yes
$x!$	yes	yes
Exchange x with y	yes	yes
Exchange x with memory	yes	no
% and Δ %	yes	no
Mean, variance and standard deviation	yes	no
Linear regression	yes	no
Trend line analysis	yes	no
Slope and intercept	yes	no
Store and sum to memory	yes	yes
Recall from memory	yes	yes
Product to memory	yes	no
Random number generator	yes	no
Automatic permutation	yes	no
Preprogrammed conversions	20	1
Digits accuracy	13	13
Algebraic notation (sum of products)	yes	yes
Memories	3	1
Fixed decimal option	yes	no
Keys	40	40
Second function key	yes	no
Constant mode operation	yes	no

SR-51A Preprogrammed Conversions

FROM	TO
mils	microns
inches	centimeters
feet	meters
yards	meters
miles	kilometers
miles	nautical miles
acres	square feet
fluid ounces	cubic centimeters
fluid ounces	liters
gallons	liters
ounces	grams
pounds	kilograms
short ton	metric ton
BTU	calories, gram
degrees	gradients
degrees	radians
°Fahrenheit	°Celsius
deg. min. sec.	decimal degrees
polar	rectangular
voltage ratio	decibels

The 3 Logic Forms — Academic Arguments — Three basic subdivisions of logic organization are used inside the present crop of personal calculators: arithmetic logic, algebraic logic, and reverse Polish notation. For the user, this means selecting among the several schemes that exist for entering data into the various brands of calculators. No one method provides serious learning problems, but some shoppers may find their choice of machine strongly influenced by past experiences with mechanical desk-top calculators or computers.

Calculators built with arithmetic logic are quickly spotted from two unique dual-function keys, plus-equals (+ =) and minus-equals (− =). These keys must be pressed after the last number to be added (or subtracted) as well as between each entry (thus, five-plus-three-equals-eight is 4 + = 3 + = 7; and five-minus-three-equals-two is 6 + = 3 − = 3). Multiplication and division keys are used just as when figuring with pencil and paper. This is the arrangement common to most mechanical calculators.

Separate plus, minus, and equals keys are found on machines with algebraic logic, and all calculations may be performed in the familiar handwritten sequence. This system has been adopted by many of the better grade portable calculators, including the scientific types. "Enter equations as you say them."

Most Texas Instruments' products, for example, allow a problem such as the sum of products — $(2 \times 3) + (4 \times 5)$ — to be solved by direct keyboard entry of all numbers and instructions in a left-to-right order. The sum of products capability puts calculator memory to a common but very useful purpose.

Reverse Polish notation, a part of all modern computer compilers for languages such as FORTRAN and ALGOL, is favored by most Hewlett-Packard, National Semiconductor and other calculators, and the field is becoming equally divided. Combined with a stack arrangement of memory registers, this system is said to be the most efficient way known for evaluating mathematical expressions and packing considerable calculating power into a small space. The stack memory is particularly useful for handling long, complex problems involving chain calculations.

Operation is based on the fact that arbitrary expressions can be specified unambiguously without parentheses by placing operations immediately before or after their operands. Thus, the expression $(a - b) \times (c - d)$ may be specified as $\times + ab - cd$ (Polish) or $ab + cd - \times$ (reverse Polish). With the help of a stack (last-in first-out) memory, the reverse Polish expression is evaluated as follows:

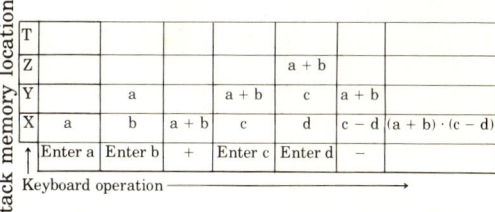

Though straightforward, note that the order of data entry is considerably different from a typical pencil and paper calculation.

Several brands of four-function, consumer and programmable calculators also use reverse Polish notation. In all cases, this logic system is immediately revealed by the keyboard, which lacks any type of equals function key.

RPN vx. algebraic — A manufacturer offers practical comparison using three representative calculators and "real-world" scientific problems.

Criteria for Evaluating a Scientific Pocket Calculator.

1. You are buying a scientific pocket calculator because you work with complex scientific problems. Therefore, the calculator itself shouldn't add complexity.
2. You should select the calculator that gives you the most confidence — confidence that you can trust the answers you get.
3. You should select a calculator that can solve

the concepts of special function keys (SFKs)

complex equations according to a consistent, easily remembered set of rules.
4. And, you should select a calculator that provides the features and functions you really need to solve your kinds of problems.

Comparison 1: simple arithmetic.
Let's start our comparisons with the very simple arithmetic problem.
Problem: $3 \times 4 = 12$

System	Solution	No. of Keystrokes
RPN:	3 ENTER↑ 4 ×	4
A:	3 × 4 =	4
B:	3 × 4 =	4

As can readily be seen, the RPN solution is based on a few simple rules. But, the fact that you can solve this problem on an algebraic machine just the way it's written offers a distinct advantage — one that explains why most pocket calculators use algebraic logic.

Chances are, though, that you wouldn't be looking at a scientific pocket calculator if you only needed to solve simple arithmetic problems. So, let's look at something a bit more complicated.

Comparison 2: sum-of-products.
This second problem is also one of the ones often used to explain the RPN method. But, let's see how calculators using the other two logic systems would solve it.
Problem: $(3 \times 4) + (5 \times 6) = 42$

System	Solution	No. of Keystrokes
RPN:	3 ENTER↑ 4 × 5 ENTER↑ 6 × +	9
A:	3 × 4 + 5 × 6 =	8
B:	3 × 4 = STO 5 × 6 + RCL =	11

The System A keystroke sequence is easy to remember since, as in the first problem, it follows the algebraic equation. Parentheses are not necessary because the operational hierarchy performs the second multiplication before the addition. It is worth noting, however, that the second intermediate answer is not displayed.

Because the System B calculator has only two internal working registers, it was not able to automatically store the first intermediate answer. Instead, the user must manually store and recall it (at the appropriate times) from the calculator's only addressable memory register. This, of course, means that you cannot use the register for storage of constants or other data.

Comparison 3: product-of-sums.
Problem: $(3 + 4) \times (5 + 6) = 77$

System	Solution	No. of Keystrokes
RPN:	3 ENTER↑ 4 + 5 ENTER↑ 6 + ×	9
A:	3 + 4 = STO 5 + 6 = × RCL =	12
B:	3 + 4 = STO 5 + 6 × RCL =	11

Although this problem is very similar to the previous one, it demonstrates some important points about the advantages of RPN over modified algebraic systems.
1. With RPN, both problems are solved in the same consistent way. The only difference is that the + and × operations are reversed — just as in algebraic equations.
   In both problems, the 4-register operational memory stack automatically saves and retrieves the intermediate answers. And, both intermediate answers are displayed as calculated so that you can check the progress of your calculation as you go.
2. With System A, there are significant differences between the solutions of these two very similar problems. This is because the effects of the operational hierarchy must be carefully considered before you key in your problem.
   If you forget that multiplication is performed before addition, you might key in the product-of-sums problem just as written: $3 + 4 \times 5 + 6 =$. And, you would get an incorrect answer because the operational hierarchy would interpret the problem as: $3 + (4 \times 5) + 6 = 29$.
   Another approach to this problem might be: $3 + 4$ STO $5 + 6 \times$ RCL $=$. This would also give you a wrong answer because the operational hierarchy would now interpret the problem as: $5 + [6 \times (3 + 4)] = 47$.
3. With System B, both problems are at least approached in the same, consistent manner. But, as can be seen in the other type comparisons, some calculators' limited storage capacity severely restricts their ability to solve complex problems unless the user writes down and re-enters intermediate answers.

As part of early efforts, HP and others carefully evaluated the strengths and weaknesses of the various languages which an operator might use to communicate with an electronic calculating device. Among those studied were:
- arithmetic or 'adding machine' language
- computer languages such as BASIC and FORTRAN (see ahead)
- various forms of algebraic notation, and
- RPN (Reverse Polish Notation), and parenthesis-free but unambiguous language derived from that developed by the Polish mathematician, Jan Lukasiewicz.

As might be expected, each of the languages described is found to excel in a particular application. For its biggest programmable desk-top calculators, HP selected BASIC. For its other powerful desk-top calculators, with less extensive storage capacity, HP chose algebraic notation... Which Texas Instruments prefers. But, given the design constraints of a pocket-sized scientific computer calculator, RPN was considered the simplest, efficient, consistent way to solve complex mathematical problems.

Several Major Manufacturers Claim RPN Offers 'Ease of Use' Advantages for Hand-Held Units — Compared to alternative logic systems, Hewlett-Packard and others believe that RPN — in combination with a 4-register operational memory stack — gives users these powerful advantages:
1. You can always enter your data the same way, i.e., from left to right — the same way you read an equation. Yet, there is no need for parenthesis key; nor for a complicated "operational hierarchy."
2. You can always proceed through your problem the same way. Once you've entered a number, you ask: "Can I perform an operation?" If yes, you do it. If no, you press ENTER↑ and key in the next number.
3. You always see all intermediate answers — as they are calculated — so that you can check the progress of your calculation as you go. Also important, you can review all numbers stored in

the concepts of special function keys (SFKs)

the calculator at any time by pressing a few keys. There is no "hidden" data.
4. You don't have to think your problem all the way through beforehand unless the problem is so complex that it may require simultaneous storage of three or more intermediate answers.
5. You can easily recover from errors since all operations are performed sequentially, immediately after pressing the appropriate key.
6. You don't have to write down and re-enter intermediate answers, a real time-saver when working with numbers of eight or nine digits each.
7. You can communicate with your calculator confidently, consistently because you can always proceed the same way.

- Reciprocal
- Register exchange
- Change sign
- Automatic constants
- Automatic repeat
- Scientific functions and arithmetic functions can be intermixed in chain calculations
- Dual clear entry/clear key

Display: Large, 12-digit, fluorescent display shows up to 8 significant digits in the mantissa plus 2 digits for exponent and 2 digits for sign of mantissa and exponent.
Keyboard: 37 key, deluxe, double injected, three color keyboard.

Rockwell Model 64RD/Electronic Advanced Slide Rule with Scientific Notation — With scientific notation, parentheses, an addressable memory and a big, bright green display for easy reading, the 64RD is designed for engineers and scientists. In addition to trigonometric, logarithmic and exponential functions, this model performs such complex calculations as polar/rectangular coordinate and degree/minute/second/decimal degree conversions.
Features:
- Extra-large, 12-digit, green display with scientific notation
- Algebraic logic
- Full floating and scientific notation entry capability
- Two levels of parentheses
- Addressable memory: store, recall, M+
- Trigonometric functions in either degrees, radians or grads
- Inverse trigonometric functions in either degrees, radians or grads
- Polar coordinates converted to or from rectangular coordinates in either degrees, radians or grads
- Degrees, minutes and seconds converted to or from decimal degrees
- Base e logarithm
- Base 10 logarithm
- Base e exponential
- Base 10 exponential
- Y^x for raising numbers to powers
- Constant π key
- Square root
- Square

The Rockwell Model 44RD/Electronic Slide Rule with Scientific Notation is — A portable calculator for engineering and higher math students that computes logarithmic, trigonometric and exponential functions. It also features a big, bright green display for easy reading, plus the following:
- Algebraic logic
- Full floating and scientific notation entry capability
- Parentheses — Two levels: one level available during trigonometric and logarithm calculations
- Store/recall memory
- Trigonometric functions in either degrees or radians
- Inverse trigonometric functions in either degrees or radians
- Base e logarithm
- Base 10 logarithm
- Base e exponential
- Base 10 exponential
- Y^x for raising numbers to powers
- Constant π key
- Square root
- square
- Reciprocal
- Change sign
- Automatic constants
- Automatic repeat
- Scientific functions and arithmetic functions can be intermixed in chain calculations.
- Dual clear entry/clear key

the concepts of special function keys (SFKs)

Display: Large, 9-digit, fluorescent display shows up to 8 significant digits in the mantissa for positive and negative results between 1 and $10^8 - 1$. Results outside this range are automatically displayed in scientific notations with a 5-digit mantissa and 2-digit exponent.
Keyboard: 36-key, double injected, three color keyboard

H-P-21 Offers 32 Built-in Functions ... An Addressable Memory ... The HP-21 is a low priced scientific pocket calculator. It is one of Hewlett-Packards' lowest priced scientific pocket calculators.

Its trigonometric capabilities are: Coordinate conversions — Converts polar coordinates to rectangular coordinates, or vice versa. This lets users do vector arithmetic quickly and easily. Angular mode selection — users flip a switch to perform trig operations in either of two angular modes: degrees or radians. They can also convert angles from one mode to the other push-button fast. Standard trig functions — The HP-21 gives all of the standard trig functions: Sin x, Arc sin x, Cos x, Arc cos x, Tan x and Arc tan x. The logarithmic capabilities include: Standard log functions — The HP-21 also gives all of the standard log functions: log x, ln x, e^x and 10^x. Register arithmetic — The HP-21 has an addressable memory for storing constants or other data, for use later on in a calculation. Any of the four arithmetic operations may be performed directly upon this stored data.

The HP-21 also includes a four memory stack, which makes possible the RPN logic system. Light-emitting diode display — Recessed for better contrast in harsh lighting. Displays up to 10 significant digits (eight plus two-digit exponent in scientific notation), and appropriate signs. Two selectable display modes: fixed point, with automatic overflow and underflow into scientific, and scientific with a dynamic range of 10^{99} to 10^{-99}. Automatic decimal point positioning. Selective round-off; range: 0-10 (in scientific, 0-8). "ERROR" appearing in display indicates improper operation. Lighted decimal points indicate low battery condition.
Keyboard commands: Trigonometric functions: 2 angular modes · Sin x · Arc sin x · Cos x · Arc cos x · Tan x · Arc tan x · Rectangular coordinates ↔ Polar coordinates
Logarithmic functions: Log x · Ln x · e^x · 10^x
Other functions: y^x · $\sqrt{x}$ · $1/x$ · π · Register arithmetic · Addition, subtraction, multiplication or division is serial, mixed serial, chain or mixed chain calculations
Data storage and positioning operations: Data entry · Stack roll down · x, y interchange · Data storage · Data recall · Change sign · Exponent entry
Memory: Four memory stack · Addressable memory

HP-35: 'Pioneer' Pocket Calculator Designed to Fit the Needs of Today's Engineering/Scientific World — Often called the "original electronic slide-rule," the HP-35 scientific pocket calculator offers features and functions not available on apparently similar models. Most important of these is the unique Hewlett-Packard four-register operational memory stack which automatically stores and retrieves intermediate answers during lengthy calculations and which virtually eliminates the need for scratch notes or the re-entry of data. Stack control keys permit roll-down of any entry to the display for review or further processing. The HP-35 also provides a separate, addressable storage register for selective storage or retrieval of constants or other data. Like all Hewlett-Packard pocket calculators, the HP-35 has a 200-decade range (10^{-99} to 10^{99}) and can display all numbers within this range with an accuracy of up to 10 significant digits while automatically positioning the decimal points.
Pre-programmed Functions
- Arithmetic: add, subtract, multiply, divide, square root.
- Trigonometric (decimal degrees): sine, arc sine, cosine, arc cosine, tangent, arc tangent.
- Logarithmic: common logarithm (base 10), natural logarithm (base e), natural antilogarithm (base e).
- Other: x^y, $1/x$, π, data storage and positioning functions.

HP45: An Advanced Scientific Pocket Calculator with Additional Pre-programmed Functions, Nine Addressable Memory Registers — The HP-45 scientific calculator is an advanced version of the popular HP-35 that offers many additional capabilities. In addition to the powerful operational stack, the HP-45 has nine addressable storage registers which can be used for register arithmetic as well as selective storage and retrieval of data. A 10th, "Last X" register automatically stores the last input argument permitting easy error correction or multiple operations on the same number.

The HP-45 performs all trig functions in any of three operating modes: decimal degrees, radians or grads. Answers in any of these modes can be converted to degrees/minutes/seconds and back again. A special key sets the display for either fixed-decimal or scientific notation, rounded to a specified number of decimal places (full accuracy is always maintained internally).
Pre-programmed Functions
- Arithmetic: add, subtract, multiply, divide, square root, square.
- Trigonometric (decimal degrees, radians or grads): sine, arc sine, cosine, arc cosine, tangent, arc tangent, rectangular/polar coordinate conversions, vector arithmetic, conversions between operating mode and degrees/minutes/seconds.
- Logarithmic: natural logarithm, natural antilogarithm, common logarithm, common antilogarithm.
- Statistical: mean, standard deviation, sum-of-the-squares, factorial.
- Other: y^x, $1/x$, π, %, Δ%, metric/U.S. unit conversion constants, register arithmetic, data storage and positioning functions.

HP-22 Offers a Combination of the Financial, Mathematical and Statistical Capabilities Needed in Modern Business — All the fundamental financial functions of the HP-22 are integrated with a comprehensive range of the statistical and mathematical functions needed in today's business world. With it, users can handle everything from simple arithmetic to complex time-value-of-money computations including interest rates; rates of return and discounted cash flows (net present value and internal rate of return) for investment analysis; extended percent calculations; accumulated interest/remaining balances, amortization and balloon payments. Users can

the concepts of special function keys (SFKs)

also handle planning, forecasting and decision analysis. The financial equations, statistical formulas and mathematical functions are built-in the HP-22. Users key in their data, press the appropriate keys, and see answers displayed — in seconds. The gold key relates to the gold legends on the keyboard, giving access to three additional financial functions and thirteen additional mathematical and statistical functions.

The financial capabilities.

12×	12÷	ACC	INT	BAL
n	i	PMT	PV	FV

The five keys in the top row of the HP-22 are the basic financial keys that replace equations and interest tables. To use any of the additional functions, users press the gold key first. When they enter three known values with the financial keys, they can solve for another unknown value. For example: enter amount of present value [PV]; they enter number of periods involved [n]; enter future value [FV]. Then, push [i] and get interest displayed automatically.

Expanded Percentages Capability — Percentage is the common standard of measurement in the business and financial world. For this reason, the HP-22 provides three separate percentage function keys. The [%] key is used to calculate a percentage. For example, to calculate 4% of a displayed number, users key in 4 and press the [%] key. There is no need to convert the 4% to its decimal equivalent of .04.

The [Δ%] key is used to compute the percentage difference (ratio of increase or decrease) between two numbers. The [%Σ] key is used to find what percentage one number is of another number or of a total sum. The HP-22 saves the base number for multiple percentage calculations of the same base number.

In addition to the financial capabilities, the HP-22 gives advanced statistical capabilities of planning, forecasting and analysis. Using the [Σ+] key, users can enter statistical data into five of the ten addressable memories, where it remains unaffected by most other calculations. What's more, using the [Σ−] key users can adjust or correct input data without having to repeat the entire calculation. For example, to project sales, users key in past performance data, then press the [LR] key. They key in the number of the forecast period and press the [ŷ] key to obtain sales at that future point in time. To obtain an average, they key in all data, then press the [x̄] key. To find standard deviation (a measure of statistical validity) they key in their data, then press the [s] key for the answer. The HP-22 gives virtually all the math capabilities needed in business, such as logs, antilogs, exponentiation and root extraction so users may work out their own solutions to unusual individual problems.

Expanded Memory Capacity — In addition to the 5 financial memories and the 4 operational stack memories, the HP-22 provides 10 addressable memories used to store data. Users press the [STO] storage key and one of the numerical keys. For example, to store a displayed value in the first addressable memory they press [STO] [0] and the value will be automatically stored in that memory. To recall the value, they press the [RCL] recall key and the [0] key and the value will again be displayed. For added convenience, register arithmetic can be performed with all 10 memories.

HP80: The Businessman's Pocket Calculator That's Preprogrammed to Solve Hundreds of Time-and-Money Problems — The HP-80 financial pocket calculator is a highly sophisticated computer-calculator which provides 36 separate financial capabilities, including bond yield and price, compound interest, mortgage payment and analysis, trend lines, rate of return analysis, accrued interest, discounted notes, true equivalent annual yield, annual percentage rate conversions, mean and standard deviation. And the HP-80 has a built-in 200-year calendar.

In short, the HP-80 can solve almost any business problem without resort to cumbersome tables or expensive computer time. The HP-80 features a 200-decade operating range, and provides answers with an accuracy of up to 10 significant digits. Or, users can round the display and number of decimal places from 0 to 6. Numbers too large or small for conventional, fixed-decimal notation are automatically displayed in scientific notation. The HP-80 also provides a four-register operational memory stack, and a separate addressable memory register for storage of constants or other data.

Besides offering the capabilities of the HP-22, the HP-80 provides the following: Amortized (direct reduction) loans (ordinary annuity). Users can solve for: the number of payments; the number of payments to reach a specified balance; payment amount; annual percentage rate, with or without fees; principal amount; amortization schedules; remaining balance (remaining principal, last payment, balloon payment) and accumulated interest; payment amount for loan with a balloon payment; annual percentage rate with balloon payment coincident with, or one period after, the last payment; price and yield of discounted mortgages (prepaid or fully amortized), and the mortgage factor for Canadian mortgages.

Loans with a constant amount paid toward the principal — With the HP-80 users can prepare a payment schedule showing the interest portion per payment and the remaining balance, when a constant amount is paid toward the principal.

Sinking funds (ordinary annuity) — The HP-80 can calculate: payment amount, interest rate, number of payments and debt retirement amount.

Consumer loans — Users press the keys to calculate the monthly payment amount, or to convert the add-on interest rate to the annual percentage rate of interest. And, using the Rule of 78's, they can use the HP-80 to calculate rebates.

Also, they can convert the annual percentage rate to the add-on rate.

Savings functions (annuity due) — Users can calculate the number of deposits, the rate of interest, the deposit amount and the future value.

Lease and rent functions (annuity due) — The HP-80 can be used to convert the add-on interest rate to the annual percentage rate, or vice versa.

Users can calculate: the number of payments; rate of interest; payment amount; payment amount with balloon payment or residual value, and present value.

Discounted cash flow analysis — Σ+ Σ−. Users can quickly and easily perform a discounted cash flow analysis, and calculate the net present value of even, uneven or deferred payment streams.

The HP-80 can also be used to calculate the dis-

the concepts of special function keys (SFKs)

counted or internal rate of return (iteration of above).

Equity investment analysis for income property — Users can use the calculator to solve for: equity yield rate; equity investment value and present value; and future value and overall appreciation/depreciation rate.

Bond functions —
YTM   INTR   BOND

The HP-80 has built-in function keys for bond calculations: "Yield-To-Maturity," "INTeRest" and "BOND". Users can calculate bond price, yield and after-tax yield, accrued interest (between coupons) and bond amortization. Users can also calculate a callable bond price and yield-to-call.

Commercial loans (short term notes) —
INTR

The HP-80's "INTeRest" key lets users calculate the accrued interest amount or the discount amount and annual yield for a discounted note (for either a 360- or 365-day year).

Calendar functions —
DATE
DAY

This key puts a 200-year calendar (1900 to 2099) at user fingertips. Users can find: the number of calendar days between two dates; the day of the week a date falls on; a future date, or a past date, given the number of days from a known date.

Depreciation functions —
COMPUTE
SOD

The HP-80 incorporates a unique key labeled "SOD" for calculating sum-of-the-years'-digits depreciation — amount of the remaining balance — on a full-year or partial year basis.

Users can also calculate the depreciation amount and remaining balance via the straight-line method, or via the declining-balance method (full year or partial year).

Statistical functions —
    Σ−   →Σ
TL Σ+   X̄

By using the "Trend Line" key, you can easily calculate: a trend line (time series linear regression) giving you the y-intercept (value at point 0); the number of time periods; the slope, and automatic projections.

The HP-80 can also calculate: the mean and the standard deviation, with the ability to change data points after a calculation and recalculate. The "Σ+" key provides running totals and computes the sum of the squares and the number of entries.

HP81: a Financial Desk-Top Calculator with all HP-80 Functions Plus Extended Calculations and Labeled Printout — The HP-81 financial desk-top calculator provides all HP-80 functions and prints complete, labeled schedules for 10 extended calculations including: interest per period, depreciation (three types), discounted rate of return, rule-of-78's prepayment, loan amortization and coupon equivalent yield. Users can also perform bond and note calculations in any of ten different modes. Available options include an LED display and a fully buffered keyboard. (more detail in the desk-top section)

Typical Specialist Calculator: the Monroe 360/65 Micro Bond Trader (More Than Just Portable) — It's a unique machine that handles all bonds: munis, corporates, governments, agencies, T-bills and notes (30/360s and Actual/365s). It also displays Yield-to-Call and Yield-to-Maturity at the same time. Or Price-to-Call and Price-to-Maturity at the same time. It can do production and extension. Calculate average life. accrued interest, after-tax yield. Even after-tax yield to dollar price. And yield means exact yield, not just an estimate. The display is big and bright. With the right number of decimal places (Six on governments; three on munis). Commas every three digits. And dates with dashes separating month, day and year.

Sharp's Low-Cost Metric-English Converter Calculator

Sharp's Low-Cost Financial and Banking, Two-Memory Calculator Offering: Mean, Standard Deviation, Linear Regression

the concepts of special function keys (SFKs)

THREE EXAMPLES OF OTHER LOW COST PREPROGRAMMED UNITS... MANY OTHERS ARE BEING MARKETED

Model F4146R Portable by Commodore — This is a 46 key, 14-digit rechargeable financial electronic calculator. Commodore's financial minicalculator is preprogrammed with many interest and financial tables. This reservoir of data combined with numerous keyboard features affords extensive operating capability across a wide range of business applications. Some of the many calculations users can solve with ease on the F4146R financial calculator are:

- Combined Compounded Amount and annuity problems
- Mortgage Calculations
- Effective yield calculations
- Add-on interest to effective yield conversion
- Amortization (depreciation, finance charges)
- All present value, future value and effective rate calculations
- All percent calculations
- All simple and compound interest assignments ... and more

In addition to being a financial unit, the F4146R is a powerful, two memory, exponential calculator with a bank of standard computing functions. Some features are:

14 Digit Display -1234.567891 -99 — The ten digit mantissa with its two digit exponent lets users tackle monetary computations considerably larger than the National Debt.

Logic — Algebraic logic permits easy, direct problem entry.

Financial Keys —
Features:
DIS The display key tells the calculator that a user wishes to recall on earlier entry. Pressing this key may be done just about any time during an example — to review an entry even several steps back.

Special Keys —
DP The Down Payment or Initial Deposit key saves time. With it users can compute annuity and savings calculations in which an initial deposit exists. (Without it, users would first have a lengthy preliminary example to solve.)

Δ% This is the Percentage Difference Key. It is employed when an example calls for instantly finding a profit margin. For instance, a firm's operating expense during December was $1.3 million. Sales for that month were $2.8 million. What was the firm's margin of profit for December?
Enter   Read
1.3 Δ% 2.8 =115.3846154
Answer: 115.38% Instantly, silently, easily.

% The "live" add-on/discount percent key, computes the percentage and sets it up to be either added to or subtracted from the display total.

Basic Financial Keys —
PV Present Value
FV Future Value
PMT Payment
I Interest (entered as a % per compounding period)
N Number of compounding or payment periods
CPT Compute Key. This key is pressed before the unknown fact is given: A $1000 Present Value, a 3-year savings period and a 7% annual interest rate, the user could determine the Future Value by simply entering the problem:

CLR	1000 PV	7 I	3 N	CPT	FV
Clear Machine	$ Present Value	Annual %	Number of Periods	Compute	Future Value

The display would read: 1225.043
Thus, the savings would be: $1225.04

Advanced Financial Keys —
PER The Period key eliminates extra key entries. It is used as a preface to enter a specific time base key.
For example:
8% compounded annually is entered: 8 I
8% compounded quarterly: 8 PER QTR I

Time Base Keys —
QTR SEMI YEAR DAY day WEEK MTH

INT Dollar Amount Interest Key. It is used with the Compute Key to perform discounted note and accrued interest calculations.

x↔y The Exchange Register Key takes a special meaning for those financial calculations which have two results. After one is displayed the second may be recovered by pressing the x↔y key: a) Discounted Note, b) Accrued Interest, c) Add on interest to annual % conversion.

Memory Keys —
STO 1 Storage or Memory Register 1
RCL 1 Memory 1 Recall
STO 2 Storage or Memory Register 2
RCL 2 Memory 2 Recall
Σ 1 Automatic Memory 1 Summation key

Scientific keys —
y^x "y" to the power of "x"
1/x Reciprocal or Inverse Key
+/− Change Sign Key

Melcor SC-655 Offers: 12 Memories, 50 Functions, 60 Keyboard commands — Combining its 12 accessible memories, 50 functions, straightforward algebraic logic and dual parenthesis levels, the Melcor SC-655 allows users to solve advanced problems with significant ease and flexibility for a hand-held calculator at such a low price. The Melcor Corporation, one with wide experience in the calculator field, took a look at the hundreds of electronic components that go into most calculators and figured out a way to simplify integrated circuitry design so that a full function scientific calculator — would have only 37 components.

The benefits are decreased cost — the fewer components, the less hand labor. And more reliability — the fewer components, the fewer the chances of failure. Made with TMC,™ Total Modular Construction, the SC-655 uses this advanced microcircuitry with only 30 components!

Some Basic Functions of the list: 50 functions and 66 keyboard commands. Includes: 10 digits plus scientific notation, Algebraic logic with two parenthesis levels, Sin, Cos, Tan (plus inverse), 1n, Log 10^x, e^x, pi, y^x, $\sqrt{x}$, x^2, 1/x, x↔y, and x→m exchange, sign change, n!, low battery indicator, automatic battery saving circuit (display blanking) and many other features. The Advanced Functions include: Combinatorial functions and binomial co-efficients, combinations, permutations, normal probability functions Pr(z), Gamma function, Γ(n), statistical functions: arithmetic mean, standard deviation σ, variance σ^2, sq. rt. of sum of squares $\|x\|$. Memory: 12 operator accessible memories with protected group memory which includes: Sum memory, sum of squares memory, index memory, plus much more.

Some preprogramed Sharp Electronics Corp. units are shown on these pages and a significant number of other units from Casio, Unitrex and other low-cost units are available throughout the world.

PART 1—Section Three

SELECTION CRITERIA FOR EVALUATING HAND-HELD PROGRAMMABLE CALCULATORS

Determining the selection of a four-to-six function calculator is a relatively simple matter (price, memory, SFKs, printers, etc.) when compared to the conflicts and comparisons of programmable units. The two basic types of hand-held programmable units are: keyboard programmables and card or exterior programmables. The differences are quite major and are related in detail below. However, the fundamental characteristics of calculators per se now become more significant, as programmables are judged. Quite often machines are grouped first according to the number of memories, then according to capacity. Some evaluators are concerned with the number of common problems which the machine can perform without re-entry of numbers, and the number of steps required for each problem, procedure or function. With the new and great popularity of preprogrammed and programmable units, these criteria have become relatively unimportant. What is important related to memories is that the units being evaluated have a significant number of them. What is even more important is the type of special functions the machine offers and/or its capability of accepting and executing a relatively large range of problems.

There are many features of machines that seriously detract from their utility. User's Groups and Clubs often warn of these: printers that use metal-treated, odd-size, tapes or inferior thermal paper; displays that are difficult to read from some angles; poorly designed keyboards and those with 'accident-prone' or unusually small or 'high' keys; noisy idling motors that keep 'gurgling' between computations; entries that require the determination of the power of 10 for that number prior to use; and the exorbitant prices of some units for the capability offered. Thus, the legibility of the display or printout, the ease of using the keyboard, the ease of performing calculations, the price and durability of the case, mechanical mechanisms, etc. all should be evaluated as well as the reputation of the manufacturer. Breakdowns are not infrequent, and a strong manufacturer will have a good service reputation for maintenance and repair procedures and reasonable costs.

If all of the above characteristics have been checked 'ok'; then, the evaluation becomes basically one of ranges of capability, utility, expandability, and ease of program use. To understand these criteria, more information on programmability is needed. Some evaluators suggest the best way to guage the power of a pocket calculator is to ask, "How much can it do easily?" Four-function, slide-rule and scientific types can do very limited amounts of computations easily. Preprogrammed units can do considerably more, in both ranges and complexity. Programmables have capabilities that are restricted only to the user's imagination and programming ability, for the great majority of practical purposes, at least. Programmability, at least for pocket calculators, is the ability to store instructions and to automatically execute them with a very few 'triggering' keystrokes. The ability to store (record) strings of keystrokes means that entire difficult formulas can be 'set inside' the unit and then produced by the touch of, in most cases, a single key. Most formulas then execute automatically, sequentially, precisely and very rapidly the steps keyed-in and output the results on display, on print, or both. Programmability assists most effectively the user-needed characteristics of visability, verifiability, and modifiability.

Keyboard programmables, or key programmable units are the lowest cost and simplest, and certainly the cheapest, as discovered in the first section of the book. Without the need to build in a magnetic card reader to accept program strips, etc., the programmability function is neither expensive nor difficult to design into a calculator. It is expected that most calculators of the future will contain this capability, providing more power, usability, and versatility. Such calculators provide the means of exploring, and for better understanding the mathematical concepts of the scientific world and the "scientific method" problem-solving procedures of the business and industrial world. Those young students using programmable calculators have been known to very quickly come to grips with math, and often with real enthusiasm and zeal, while without them, they remained confused, irritated, and uncomfortable with most aspects of it. Grade school teachers should be most anxious to introduce them early, to utilize the true value of calculators in the 'fun and learn' processes to stimulate the interest and progress made by these youngsters when they discover the drudgery is out of math — and the machine seeks and searches for the answers if they themselves can discover and understand the problem.

Because the difference between key programmables and card programmables is so distinct, little further discussion is needed here. The examples of product immediately ahead attest to the range of capability, but it might be best at this stage to introduce the concepts, now becoming very popular and wide-ranging, or dual and multi-color keys to expand the range of keyboard pre-programming and programmability. When using the Norvus 4515 Programmable for example, the key legend explains that this below $150 calculator uses three-stack RPN logic. Several of 36 keys do double duty by using a gold-colored shift key. When this is pressed, the function printed in gold beneath the key is brought into play instead of the one in silver above it. The programmable feature is controlled by four blue keys arranged vertically along the left side of the keyboard and labelled from top to bottom: DEL, SKIP, HALT, and START; plus a three-position slide switch at the top labelled: LOAD, STEP, RUN.

Learn-mode programming begins with the slide switch at LOAD. Users press START and then key in a sequence of steps to solve a problem. Users press HALT each time before they insert a variable. The calculator 'remembers' exactly, and

selection criteria for evaluating calculators

when users put the slide switch at RUN and press START, it will go through the same sequence of steps automatically, only stopping at any HALT for users to insert a new variable, and with the new answer displayed at the end of the sequence. This unit and others have 100 steps of programming available at one time so users can program these units with one large program or as many small programs as will fit into 100 steps. Pressing SKIP in the LOAD position terminates one program and marks the beginning of another. In the RUN position, the SKIP key is used as a kind of tab key to skip over unwanted programs to reach the one users want. The DEL key is used to erase, or delete, erroneous steps. With the switch in the STEP position, users can go through a program or programs a step at a time by repeatedly pressing the START KEY.

Programmable features really are time-savers and error-avoiders in situations requiring the repeated working of the same basic problem with different data used each time. The key-programmable units evaluated next are a step-up from the very low-cost units discussed in the first few pages of Part I.

PROGRAMMABLE HP-25 HAS BUILT-IN POWER TO SOLVE TECHNICAL PROBLEMS

Preprogrammed to solve 72 scientific, engineering and mathematical functions, the HP-25 saves users time solving difficult technical problems. In addition, it has 8 addressable memories, each capable of register arithmetic. The HP-25's programming power includes a 49-step memory. Each step in this memory can accommodate multi-keystroke functions, because the keycodes of all prefixed functions — including the register arithmetic functions — merge. Thus, users gain extra capacity. With the HP-25, users enter the keystrokes necessary to solve representative problems only once. Thereafter, they enter the variables and press the Run/Stop key for an almost instant answer. Users can add, change or skip steps and can program the HP-25 to perform direct branches of conditional tests. And the hand-held unit offers not only fixed and scientific but also engineering notation (i.e., exponent displayed as a multiple of $10^{\pm 3}$ as in giga and nano). The RPN logic system with 4-register stack allows users to evaluate any expression without copying parenthesis or worrying about hierarchies or restructuring before entering.

Preprogrammed functions of the HP-25 include log and trigonometric functions, the latter in degrees, radians or grads; rectangular/polar and decimal hours/hours-minutes-seconds conversions; mean and standard deviation; and summations. The main differences among the three calculators is HP's programmable line are that the HP-65 is fully programmable and available with preprogrammed cards and memory — not available in the HP-55 or HP-25. The HP-55 performs functions not available in the HP-25.

The calculator's 49 steps of program memory are coupled with merged keycodes that conserve steps to effectively expand memory capacity. An "Integer/Function" key permits storage of two numbers in a single memory and an "Absolute Value" key adds to the storage capacity and flexibility of the HP-25's programing. Users may perform full register arithmetic on the data in each of the eight addressable memories.

Keystroke programmability is the four-step answer to repetitive problem. Users:
1. Turn the HP-25 on and switch to PRGM;
2. Enter the keystrokes necessary to solve the problem and switch to RUN;
3. Key in a set of variables and press the R/S (Run/Stop) key;
4. Repeat step three for each iteration.

Users save time, gain precision and flexibility because they can verify formulas or test alternate approaches with near complete programmability. Users can add, check, or change program steps at will. They use the SST (Single-STep) or BST (Back-STep) key and Display to locate the steps they want to check or change, then enter their changes. The HP-25 displays all program steps, so they can always tell at a glance where they are in their routine. The HP-25 has a PAUSE key that lets users write one-second interrupts into their programs, in case they want to pick up intermediate results or verify the progress of a calculation. Thus the HP-25 is a complete keystroke programmable calculator.

With merged key codes each step in the HP-25's 49-Step memory can accommodate multi-keystroke functions, because the keycodes of all prefixed functions — including the register arithmetic functions — merge.

With branching and conditional test capability users can program the HP-25 to perform direct branches or conditional tests based on eight different logic comparisons. A program, in this case, is a sequence of keystrokes used to solve a problem. The HP-25 can retain and repeat a program up to 49 steps in length. So users don't have to press the same keys again and again when the same problem is worked with different data.

PRGM — RUN

Users set the HP-25 to PROGRAM mode by flipping a switch. They press the keys they'd normally press to solve the problem. (But don't enter the data). Their program is retained in the HP-25's program memory.

To solve the problem, they switch to RUN mode and enter the data. They then press the "Run/Stop" key to run their program. Seconds later, the answer appears on the HP-25 display. To solve other problems using the same program, they enter the new data and press the "Run/Stop" key again. Because their program does the calculation automatically — users just sit back and watch it — there's less chance for error than if they had to repeat the keystroke sequence themselves step by step. Also it takes but a fraction of the time.

The HP-25 can be programmed to make decisions because it can do conditional branching, using eight relational tests. Users can program it to test the relationship between two values, by means of these tests:

$x < y$ $x \geq y$ $x \neq y$ $x = y$ or
$x < 0$ $x \geq 0$ $x \neq 0$ $x = 0$

Depending on the outcome of the tests, the HP-25 will automatically skip a step of the program ... or it will continue through the program in sequence. Or, by the means of the "Go TO" key, users can program the HP-25 to branch directly to a specified step, and then continue executing the program.

selection criteria for evaluating calculators

Both types of branching — conditional and direct — are useful in solving a variety of programming problems.

Here are the other extras: engineering notation, RPN logic, an integer/fraction truncation key, absolute value key. The application manual supplied helps users to realize the full potential of their new scientific calculator. 54 programs are included from the varied areas of algebra, number theory, trig, analytical geometry, numerical methods, statistics, finance, surveying, navigation and even games.

HEWLETT-PACKARD'S LOW-COST HP-25 PROGRAMMABLE SCIENTIFIC POCKET CALCULATOR AIDS

HP-25 Applications Programs Book to Help Get the Most Out of the HP-25 — These HP-25 Applications Programs — 54 in 1976 — have been drawn from the varied areas of algebra and number theory, trigonometry and analytical geometry, numerical methods, statistics, finance, surveying, navigation, and games. Each program is furnished with a full explanation which includes a description of the problem, any pertinent equations, a list of keystrokes to be entered into program memory, a set of instructions for running the program, and an example or two, with solutions. To use these programs does not require any proficiency in programming. The first program in each chapter contains, in addition to the usual explanations, a more detailed description of the problem, a commented list of the program keystrokes with a step-by-step tracing of the contents of the stack registers, and a list of the keystrokes required to solve the example problem. Whenever an interesting programming technique is used in one of these programs, it is described in a short section headed "Programming Remarks."

SR-56 Hand-Held Key Programmable Calculator by Texas Instruments — In early 1976... expanding its hand-held programmable line, Texas Instruments Incorporated announced the key programmable SR-56, a 100 step, 10 memory calculator with an Algebraic Operating System featuring left to right entry and 9 levels of parentheses. Like TI's SR-52 hand-held card programmable, the SR-56 is compatible with thePC-100 print cradle, which allows complete tracing and printout of any calculator operation. Over 25 scientific and statistical operations are possible from the keyboard, and 2 looping capabilities and 4 levels of subroutines allow sophisticated programming approaches which are new to the general run available key programmable units.

The SR-56 is very suitable for students and professionals who frequently need to solve repetitive

This SR-56 is a 100-step, 10 memory Key programmable calculator with Algebraic Operating System and looping.

selection criteria for evaluating calculators

problems, or explore multiple options within single problems. Its ease-of-use, however, makes the SR-56 a desirable tool for businessmen or financiers who make forecasting and estimating decisions on the basis of extended calculations. The SR-56 uses the Algebraic Operating System (AOS) introduced by TI on its SR-52 and SR-60 models. With twenty-five (25) preprogrammed arithmetic and transcendental functions, the SR-56 is capable of handling quite difficult computational problems. Logs, trigs and coordinate-conversions are just a few of the transcendental functions. The SR-56's ten (10) user memories have full register arithmetic to facilitate their use and increase the calculator functionality.

A key programmable calculator, the SR-56 can "remember" up to 100 program steps. And with an extensive repertoire of conditional and unconditional branches, it is capable of solving problems previously solvable only on large-scale computers. There are three (3) unconditional branches and six (6) conditional branches which include four (4) levels of subroutines and two (2) loop control instructions. Two more features are unique to most hand-held programmables: (1) An independent test register permits comparison with the value in display at any point in a calculation without interfering with the processing in progress; (2) A dual function pause key allows the display to be viable during program execution for ½ second or provides for automatic single step program operation. Selected editing functions permit easy entry and correction of user programs. With single step and back step keys, the user can quickly sequence through its program memory to locate a program error. With the write-over capability of the calculator design, erroneous key pushes can be replaced with the proper key push while extra keypushes can be negated by using the NOP key. A 10 + 2 digit VLED display has full floating point with Scientific Notation format. Moreover, format is controllable via the fixed point option. The unit is fully rechargeable and comes complete with a standard charger. A 56-program applications booklet is included with the SR-56, with programs for Mathematics, Electrical Engineering, Statistics, Finance, Surveying and other disciplines.

Printers for TI Portables — The PC-100 print cradle permits TI's SR-52 and SR-56 hand-held programmable calculators to become desk-top printing calculators. When the calculator is locked into the cradle, the user is able to print anything shown in the display or print the step-by-step execution of a program. Print and paper advance controls permit the user to handle these functions on the PC-100 as well as on the calculator, and a "trace" key allows monitoring of all functions as they happen. The PC-100 has a thermal printer which prints 5 × 7 dot-matrix characters on a 2.5-in. tape. It prints 20 characters per line and sold for $295 in 1976.

Calculator Printer — Texas Instruments low-cost printer attaches to all of its hand-held programmable calculators. It's dubbed the PC-100, with the pc standing for "print cradle." The printer can be used for printing out program steps and problem solutions. The calculator is inserted into the cradle where it can be used for anything from printing out long amortization schedules for the business world, or listing every step in an iterative problem for scientists. The printer weighs approximately seven pounds and measures about 10 inches square and four inches high. Print and paper advance controls are built into the printer, which is fully controllable from the calculator keyboard or card program. The price seems reasonable at $295 — which means users can now have a complete stored program computer, including card input (cards about the size of gum sticks) and 20-column hardcopy for around $600.

selection criteria for evaluating calculators

Novus 4520 Scientist/4525 Programmable Scientist

Novus 6020 Financier/6025 Programmable Financier

The Novus Low-Cost Programmables — Novus, the National Semiconductor Co. line of programmables, represent currently three models, The Scientist, the Statistician, and the Financier. They are available as non-programmables also, at about $40 to $50 less cost.

The Novus 4525 Programmable Scientist offers all the features found on the basic Scientist. Its programming features include:
- Simplified programming. Users engage a Learn Switch and perform a problem in normal manner. The Novus 4525 records the formula and lets users debug the program as it's written.
- The learn-mode capacity totals 100 separate steps.
- Several different programs can be contained at the same time.
- Delete feature lets users correct programs while writing them.
- Skip key permits skipping over entire programs to access additional programs within 100-step capacity.
- Programs remain intact until new programs are written over or until the Scientist is turned off.
- Users have total freedom to select keyboard entries as variables or constants.

The Novus 6025 Financier is specifically dedicated to solving the kinds of problems that create the biggest problems for users. Time and money problems. The kind users work with every day in business and financial professions such as banking, real estate, insurance or accounting. The Financier has been pre-programmed to solve hundreds of these problems and more. Yet the Financier is as easy to operate as any basic adding machine. And it's priced, in many markets, somewhat lower than many comparable calculators on the market. The performance features of the Novus 6025 enable users to solve complicated problems such as present and future value, loan payments, depreciation, amortization, annuities, annual percentage rate conversions, sum-of-digits depreciation.

Professional engineers and scientists are offered the 4525 Novus Scientist priced within the means of most serious users, professionals and students alike. In addition to numerous pre-programmed arithmetic, trigonometric and logarithmic functions, the Novus Scientists feature a rollable 4-level stack, coupled with RPN (Reverse Polish Notation), for efficient evaluation of all mathematical expressions and are key-programmable.

Especially dedicated to statistical problems, the Novus 6035 Statistician features pre-programmed, single-key calculations of most common statistical formulas. What this means to most users is that countless hours can be saved in performing statistical calculations. Also, the chances for calculating or entry errors are virtually eliminated. The 6035 is a business machine that offers four-function performance (addition, subtraction, multiplication, division) as well as some important extras. Like automatic square roots, a live % key with automatic add-on or discount and net, and a separate accumulating memory and the unit is key programmable.

HPs Shirt-pocket Model 55 Machine Has Total of 86 Keyboard Functions and a 100-hour Digital Timer — Hewlett-Packard's HP-55 is a shirt-pocket calculator and unlike the earlier models, the machine is programmable. It has 49 steps of program memory, plus branching, testing, and editing capabilities. A built-in timer can also store and recall up to 10 elapsed-time readings.

Unlike the more-expensive HP-65, the model 55 has no provision for storing programs permanently on magnetic cards. When the calculator is shut off, the program is cleared from the memory, and must be reentered to be used again. However, the model 55 has more preprogramed functions than many pocket units, 86, compared with 51 for the -65 and 44 for the -45. And the model 55 has 20 addressable memories, 10 of which can be used to perform register arithmetic.

Perhaps the most unusual feature of the HP-55 is its inclusion of a digital timer — essentially a

selection criteria for evaluating calculators

high-quality digital stopwatch — which uses a crystal-controlled oscillator to measure intervals as long as 100 hours with a resolution of 0.01 second, and a maximum error of ±0.01%. While the timer is running, the user can acquire and store as many as 10 splits (elapsed-time readings within an event) simply by pushing digit keys 0 through 9. After the timer is stopped, the splits may be recalled and manipulated like any other data. Like other H-P pocket calculators, the HP-55 uses the RPN (reverse Polish notation) logic system with a four-memory operational stack of registers that holds intermediate answers and brings them back when they are needed in a calculation. It can work in three trigonometric modes: degrees, radians, and grads, and the user can convert from any one to any other. The machine will add and subtract degrees, minutes, and seconds (DMS), and can convert decimal degrees to DMS and vice versa. Single-keystroke polar-to-rectangular and rectangular-to-polar conversions are also included.

The HP-55's statistical functions, along with its 20 addressable memories, make possible the easy calculation of two-variable mean and standard deviations, as well as the performance of linear regression, linear estimate, and curve-plotting calculations. Further, the calculator can solve a set of four linear equations with four unknowns. Unlike the HP-45, which is preprogrammed with constants for use in English/metric conversions, the HP-55 actually performs the conversions with a single keystroke. The conversions include: inches and millimeters, feet and meters, U.S. gallons and liters, pounds mass and kilograms, pounds force and newtons, degrees farenheit and degrees celsius, and British thermal units and joules.

For ease of editing, debugging, and reviewing programs after they are written, the model 55 has a single-step key and a back-step key. While in the program mode, the calculator display shows a two-digit line number (from 00 to 49) and a two-digit keycode that tells what command or function was keyed in for that step. Thus, if the 24th step were the reciprocal function, the display would show "24 13," since the reciprocal key is the third key from the left in the first row of keys. Branching is accomplished by the HP-55 in one of three ways: by means of an unconditional "GO TO" command, or by means of two conditional tests, "X-Y" of "X less than or equal to Y" with the "GO TO" command implied. By comparison, the HP-65 has 100 steps of program memory and four conditional branching tests.

The 15-digit light-emitting-diode display can be formatted in a variety of ways at the user's discretion. It can show numbers in fixed-decimal-point or scientific notation, and can display from zero to nine places after the decimal point, in either mode, while the calculator maintains full accuracy internally. The unique, low cost HP-55 is equipped with a special "Last X" storage register that enables a user to correct an error in arithmetic or in number-entry without having to start over in the middle of a lengthy calculation. The "Last X" register can also be used to compute multiple operations of the same argument.

Calculator Counts Time, Too — Because the HP-55 programmable calculator contains built-in digital counter with 100-hour duration, It can store and recall up to 10 different finishes within one

event. Although it could be useful for sports buffs, the calculator is designed to fill the needs of the serious scientist, student or researcher. The calculator, as noted, is programmable to perform repetitive calculations

The Monroe 324 is a Hand-Held Programmable Scientific Unit — The Monroe 324 is a hand-held programmable with two 80-step program memories and was designed to meet the demand for a portable accurate powerful calculator in the engineering and scientific field. The 324 offers the scientist the convenience and capabilities of a computer in solving such problems as stress analysis, cut-and-fill calculations, circuit design, fluid mechanics, structural design and simultaneous equation solutions. Directly accessible from the Monroe 324 keyboard are 20 programmed operations for mathematics that in-

selection criteria for evaluating calculators

clude sine, cosine, tangent, arcsine, arccosine, arctangent, $\log_e$, e^x, $\log_{10}$, square root, reciprocal, degrees to radian, radians to degrees, degrees, minutes, seconds to decimals, degrees, entry, degrees or grad operation.

The Monroe 324 has ten independent storage registers with full arithmetic capability in all storage registers to store, recall and exchange control keys. Some of its other features include: a large, easy to read 10-digit display plus 2-digit exponent; automatic lighted commas for punctuation; zero suppression and separate error and overflow indication; arithmetic and function sequence including constants and data points are stored automatically when calculation is performed in load mode, and automatically executed when program switch is in "Run", program step numbers are displayed when program switch is in "Load" position. The unit is programmable and can loop and do conditional operations. Users do their special calculations the first time with the run/load switch in load. From there on, the unit does the calculations automatically until those program steps are overwritten or the power is removed.

Monroe Model 344 is a Hand-Held Statistical Programmable Unit — The Monroe 344 is a hand-held programmable with two 80-step program memories designed to meet the demand in the statistical field for a portable accurate, powerful compact unit. It offers the statistician the convenience and capability of a computer in solving complex formulas and problems algebraically. Preprogrammed into the Monroe 344 is a set of commonly used statistical functions that include: standard deviation (grouped or ungrouped), linear regression, Z-score, t- dependent and independent, logs and anti-logs, coefficient of correlation, expected y from regression coefficients, slope and intercept, square root, reciprocal, and integer-fraction separation.

The Monroe 344 has ten independent storage registers with full arithmetic capability in all storage registers to store, recall and exchange control keys. Arithmetic and function sequence including constants and data points are stored automatically when calculation is performed in load

mode and automatically executed when program switch is in "Run"; program step numbers are displayed when program switch is in "Load" position, and the unit is key programmable for special routine or programs developed by the user.

Monroe 354 Micro Surveyor is Hand-Held, Battery-Powered and Programmable — The Monroe 354 Micro Surveyor is a hand-held display programmable calculator designed for surveyor calculations in the field; as well as desk-top use for subdivision work in the office. The unit easily handles intersections, vertical angles, side shots, circular arcs as well as the standard direction/ length to latitude and departure conversions. As a surveyor works his way around a traverse, angles may be entered as bearings, field angles or azimuths from which the 354 accumulates the total area, including curved sections and perimeter length. There are 18 powerful special function keys for quickly and conveniently solving the most complicated surveying calculation.

The Monroe 354 is a dual program machine with two separate 80-step programs that can be stored in the memory at the same time. It can do complex calculations such as balancing area cut-offs, horizontal and vertical curves. In addition to the preprogrammed functions, there are a number of library programs that can be run on the Micro Surveyor. These include: Compass Rule Adjustment, Three Point Resection, Horizontal Curve Stacking, and over 30 more. The unit is also useful for tax assessors, land developers, real estate and land investment consultants. The Micro Surveyor adapts to AC current for office use. It's size: 5.5" x 9" x 2". It's weight is 3½ lbs.

PART 1—Section Four

Advanced Hand-Held, Fully-Programmable Calculator Operating Characteristics — For a great many professionals and hundreds of thousands of students — especially those in engineering, mathematics, statistics and management, the HP-65 fully programmable hand-held calculator was the most desired and valuable instrument available to them. In the section ahead, this unit is compared to the Monroe and Compucorp 326s, and the Texas Instrument SR-52, which was released in the first quarter of 1976. These are advanced units that utilize exterior or insertable magnetic cards (strips) and tapes, in the case of the Beta 326s. It can be predicted with a major degree of assurance that other units will soon be offered in direct competition with these and upgraded models from practically all will use cassettes (and plug-in Programmable ROMs — PROMs) as their counterpart desk units already do. Hewlett-Packard, for example, solved many design problems before they introduced the HP-65. One, for example, was how to get over 80 functions on a calculator with only 35 keys. As previously noted and detailed ahead, the face of multi-function keys offer one function; the lower portion of the key (in blue) offers another, and other function indicators are placed above keys (in gold). All three hand-held units to be analyzed are real challenges to users to make them more versatile and powerful, not only for evaluating formulas, but to their inventiveness in constructing their own complex programs, highly specialized, if desired, for bringing their hand-held units very close to the capabilities of full computers. A significant accomplishment for these units is the magnetic card read/write ability. After writing and debugging a program, the user has the ability to make a permanent record of his program on a magnetic card (tape, on the 326) and then at any time later to read the program back into the calculator. On the HP-65, for example, factory-supplied or user-developed programs can be read from or written into program memory by inserting a small magnetic card into the lower of two slots on the right side of the calculator. A two-track, self-clocking recording scheme is used to maximize the system tolerance to head skew and motor speed variations. When the W/PRGM RUN switch is in the RUN position, insertion of a card into the reader slot triggers the motor and read circuits.

Over the past few years, costs of manufacturing electronic calculators have been drastically reduced by technological improvements in design. Automated manufacture and testing has brought calculator prices within range of huge numbers of consumers, creating many mass markets. And calculator makers are still finding ways to lower manufacturing costs even further. Perhaps the greatest reductions in manufacturing costs have resulted from integration of the calculator functions on a single chip. This has led to a simple, low-cost assembly procedure: piercing together four major components — keyboard, integrated-circuit logic, power-supply unit, and display or printer. However, little value is added by a manufacturer that simply assembles these parts. The maximum value is added by making and integrating all the necessary components in the same factory. The ultimate in cost-cutting could be achieved by building the calculator from raw materials as a single part in a single assembly process.

In 1972, Hewlett-Packard introduced the HP-35 pocket scientific calculator, the first in a family of calculators that eventually grew to include many members, from the original HP-35 to the sophisticated fully programmable HP-65. The second generation of HP pocket calculators currently has four members, designated HP-21, HP-22, HP-25 and HP-27. The HP-21 is the basic scientific calculator that replaced the HP-35, the HP-22 is the business calculator, and the HP-25 is the programmable scientific calculator. State-of-the-art technology has been applied in the new family to achieve the major design goal of low cost with no sacrifice in reliability or quality.

The HP-27 is a six-ounce calculator that combines all of the most frequently used scientific and financial functions. Priced at $200, the unit provides compound interest and statistical capabilities as well as 28 exponential, log, trig and arithmetic functions, including time, angle, and coordinate conversion functions. It has 10 addressable memories for data storage, five financial memories, the last-x memory and four operational stack memories.

Most parts are common to all four calculators, the fundamental differences occurring in the read-only memory (ROM) that contains the preprogrammed functions. In each calculator is an integrated circuit that is a small, slow, but powerful microcomputer. It executes microprograms that are stored in the ROM. When the user presses a key, a microprogram is activated to perform the function corresponding to that key. The ROM comes in blocks of 1024 ten-bit words. Each block adds factory cost. But until all of the ROM has been allocated, features can be added, omitted, or modified and functions can be made more or less accurate without increasing factory cost at all. The firmware designer's challenge is to make these no-cost choices in some optimal way for each calculator.

Low power chips and displays will eventually cause replacement of expensive rechargeable batteries and chargers with disposable batteries. This will free the user from a wall adapter environment. In the calculator, the changes will be obvious as the component count diminishes and more of the discrete elements are included in the MOS chips, all accompanied by an increased functional capability. These advances will be due to improved architectural designs, greater chip component densities and larger chip sizes. Even with these future trends, case sizes are still expected to decrease slightly, though not as rapidly as in the past.

Preprogrammed selected custom features are offered in well chosen disciplines as noted. These dedicated calculators are basically professional machines whose special functions are dedicated to

advanced calculator operating characteristics

one specific application area. However, the programmable market share will increase and tend to serve these disciplines that are not served by dedicated calculators. This will be a result of several factors. Memory sizes will continue to increase with 100 to 200 registers being standard. The program memory will increase in size and free a user from the tedium of spending all day being "efficient" when he programs.

Programmables now have a software commitment for prepared, prepackaged, program libraries in both general and specific areas. This capability allows a programmable calculator to serve several different needs for an individual (i.e., a manager who performs statistical analysis, financial accounting, and personal financing in the course of a typical day). The library programs can provide a wider range of complicated functions with a high level of sophistication for a lower price than a comparable dedicated calculator. The programmable calculator will be enhanced with the advent of non-volitile memory and program areas which will allow the user to turn his calculator off and on and not lose its contents for a later session. The ability to read and write both memory and program areas of magnetic strips has become commonplace. In order to aid the owner in the use of more sophisticated calculators, hard copy units are now being offered. It has becom common to connect a professional pocket calculator to an inexpensive printing device to obtain an audit trail for both calculation and program executions. This also provides a listing of a stored program which will be a requirement as memory sizes increase. Enhanced operation has evolved due to the development of alphanumeric display capability on desk pocket calculators. This allows an interactive mode between the user and a program which he or she or someone else has written.

Although this book is not designed to evaluate microprocessors or instruct readers on the intracicies of microelectronics, certain facets can be briefly defined. Large Scale Integration (LSI) is a process that results in a layered structure of very tiny interconnected components with extremely complex and capable switching functions. Combined with Metal Oxide Semiconductor (MOS) devices, extremely low-cost memory and powerful control devices can now be contained, as previously noted, within wrist-watches. LSI became important in the early 1970s joining the advance of MOS technology. This packing and 'unitizing' severely reduced the number of components necessary to manufacture relatively sophisticated calculators. As component count and costs were reduced (mass-production), portable calculator power became one of the fastest growing professional and now, consumer products in the world. The heart of the low-end calculator, as noted above, is a single MOS/LSI circuit, usually supported by a bipolar drive circuit and an LED (Light Emitting Diode) display (no driver necessary with fluorescent displays). The principal non-semiconductor components are a keyboard, printed circuit board, case, battery, labeling overlays, packing box. Labor and marketing costs complete the total 'business' of calculators. For low-end calculators, 50% to 60% of the cost is represented by semiconductor content, if an LED is used. For high-end highly sophisticated units, the semiconductor content becomes even more dominant, with the other components shrinking rapidly in 'percent of the whole' costs. And fortunately, it is the cost of the conductor content that is being sharply reduced most rapidly by mass production and mass sales, most of the Research and Development already discounted to close to zero per unit or already totally recaptured. Some MOS/LSI single unit calculator chips are selling for less than 10% of their original selling price of just 18 months previous. All logic and input-output interfacing is on the single chip; LEDs are significantly more efficient and less costly, many being supplied as single components providing 14 seven segment digits for hand-held units; keyboards are very low cost single components; labor has become almost nonexistant as a cost. The time to assemble a whole calculator has been reduced to a matter of a very few minutes, even for on-shore U.S. labor — though slightly cheaper in some Asiatic countries. Only software costs are a bit high but might soon crash also.

Hewlett-Packards Advanced Fully Programmable HP-65 — Weighing only 11 ounces, the HP-65 battery-powered calculator enables users to write, edit, record and reenter the program steps used to solve frequently encountered mathematical problems. Each set of instructions tells the calculator tells it to perform certain calculations in sequence to provide an answer or a set of answers. Previously, programming was possible only with much larger and more expensive calculators and computers. With the HP-65, users can record programs on tiny magnetic cards for use as often as needed. When inserted into the calculator, the magnetic card instructs the machine to perform the calculations when the user presses the appropriate key. Up to 100 program steps can be recorded on a single card. HP-65 packs the equivalent of 75,000 transistors in its circuitry. It is designed for use in science, many types of engineering, medicine, surveying, statistics and mathematics. Because users can write their own programs easily, the HP-65 can also be used in areas such as business, education and navigation. No previous programming experience is necessary to use the calculator.

advanced calculator operating characteristics

The calculator is a wholly programmable instrument due to its features: a built-in magnetic card reader/writer, a 100-step program memory, 51 preprogrammed functions and operations, and 9 addressable memory registers. Users have it three ways: 1) As a user-programmed calculator, they program up to five functions callable from the keyboard or by other programmed functions, conditional skips based on logic comparisons, and branches. 2) With prerecorded program cards from Hewlett-Packard, many complex problems can be solved immediately. 3) As a keyboard-operated calculator, the HP-65 can perform all trig functions in three-angle modes, handle logarithms and permit register arithmetic. Other preprogrammed functions include: factorial, polar/rectangular coordinate conversions, square root, square, reciprocal, decimal/octal integer conversions, and the ability to add or subtract degrees/minutes/seconds.

Medical — The HP-65 is the first pocket-sized calculator to provide full programming capability for medical researchers, cardiologists and pulmonary specialists. In addition, medical users can get a total of 39 prerecorded programs which solve many frequently encountered medical calculations. Price of the HP-65 is $795.00 (U.S.), in 1976.

HP-65 Applications — An engineer or scientist in need of an on-the-spot answer in the laboratory, a pilot making an in-flight course correction, a surveyor running a traverse in the field, a businessman estimating returns-on-investment during a conference, a physician evaluating patient data — these illustrate the everyday examples of people whose professions require certain types of calculations over and over again. A programmable calculator is obviously of great assistance to such people. And now they can carry one of those around in their pockets. They offer the convenience and easy operation of a calculator, but the programmability makes them versatile enough to fit the needs of a wide variety of disciplines, including science, engineering, finance, statistics, mathematics, navigation, medicine, surveying, and many others.

In the interest of logical operation and simplicity, many different techniques were used in designing keyboard layouts. Keys of the same nature are grouped into clusters. Some nomenclature has been placed on the lower side of the keys to reduce busyness. Nomenclature for multiple-keystroke operations is color-coded to make the keystroke sequences associative. All functions are classified as immediate (+, −, ×, ÷), direct, inverse, or miscellaneous, and are grouped and color-coded accordingly. Key sizes, colors, value contrast, and nomenclature have all been chosen to guide the user.

HP-65 Programming — Perhaps, the first way to use the calculator is to write programs, incorporating the specific equations, constants and/or procedures users need for easy and rapid solution of all types of numeric problems. They simply make a list of the keystrokes needed to solve their problem using any of the arithmetic, log, trig and exponential functions on the keyboard. They set the HP-65 to WRITE PROGRAM and key in their program. Once their program is in the machine, they can record it on a magnetic card for future use anytime, anywhere. To run their program, they set the switch to RUN, key in their known

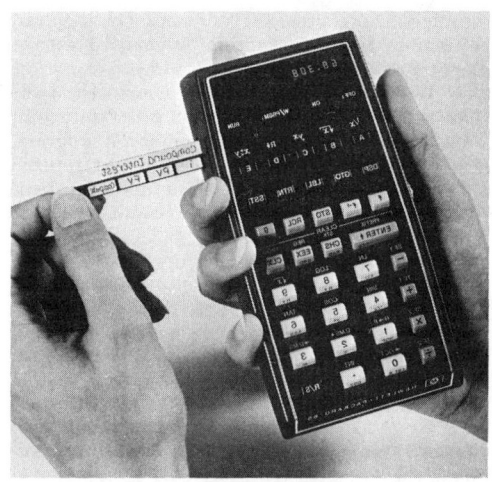

data and start the program running. The HP-65 will automatically execute entire calculations in seconds — as often as needed. Program memory is 100 steps long and there are logic tests, conditional branches — plus all the functions on the HP-65 keyboard. Users can easily chain programs for those unusually long or complex problems that cannot be solved in 100 steps. The second way to use the HP-65 is with the prerecorded magnetic program cards supplied in HP-65 Application Pacs. Each Pac contains as many as 40 programs dedicated to a specific discipline (e.g., electrical engineering, finance, statistics, marine navigation).

To use a pre-recorded program, users simply insert the appropriate card into the lower slot on the right side of the calculator. The instructions on the card will be automatically transferred to the HP-65's program memory in just 2 seconds. Next, users key in their known data and start the program running as described in the easy-to-follow instructions that come with each Application Pac.

These Keyboard Controls Give Full Programmability in a pocket calculator — These keys take the HP-65 out of the realm of the calculator and into the sophisticated world of computer technology. They permit users to write, record, save and read back their programs. They also set in motion the HP-65's other powerful programming functions.

To write or run a program . . .
W/PRGM   RUN
Set this switch to "WRITE PROGRAM" to enter or change any steps in the program memory and for recording programs, without altering any data stored in the four memory automatic stack or the addressable memories.

To structure a program . . .
LBL The "LABEL" key enables users to indicate and identify a series of steps within their program. Up to 15 labels are available by pressing this key and any digit (0-9) or letter (A-E) key.
GTO The "GO TO" key, in conjunction with a digit key, sets off a search in the program memory for the label with the same digit. It can be used from the keyboard when editing, or as part of a program.
A B C D E The User Definable keys are just what their name implies. They are letter labels for parts of a user program which can be

advanced calculator operating characteristics

executed directly from the keyboard. Or, they can be used to call a subroutine when used with a program.

RTN When the "RETURN" key is pressed, it enables to start at the beginning of program again. If this key is used as part of their stored program, it stops execution of their program and returns control to the keyboard for manual operation. When used as part of a letter subroutine, it returns control to the calling program.

R/S When this "RUN/STOP" key is included in users stored program, it will halt execution of the program and return control to the keyboard for manual operation. When used from the keyboard, it can stop a running program or start a stopped program at the next step.

To include conditional tests in a program...

SF 1 SF 2 Like a computer, the HP-65 can take alternate computational paths based on the condition of the two flags With the "SET FLAG 1" and "SET FLAG 2" keys, the flags can be set or cleared manually from the keyboard or automatically by an appropriate program step.

TF 1 TF 2 The condition of the flags can be tested automatically at any point in a user program by using the "TEST FLAG 1" and "TEST FLAG 2" keys to include an appropriate test flat instruction. A user program will either advance sequentially or skip over the next steps, depending on the condition of the tested flag.

$x \neq y$ $x \leq y$ $x = y$ $x > y$ These keys allow users to compare the values in the X and Y registers. If the test condition is not met, the program skips over the next two steps. If the test condition is met, the program continues with the next step. This allows the HP-65 to perform conditional branches based on the results of the test.

DSZ The "DECREMENT AND SKIP ON ZERO" key subtracts a "1" from the integer previously stored in addressable memory 8, then advances a user program depending on the value remaining in the memory. If the value in memory 8 is not equal to zero, the program advances to the next step. If it does equal zero, it skips the next two steps. "DSZ" allows users to loop through a portion of their program a pre-determined number of times.

NOP If this "NO OPERATION" key is included in a user stored program, it will advance the program to the following step. It is often used in conjunction with conditional-skip instructions.

To edit a program...

PRGM The "PROGRAM" key is used to clear the entire 100-step program memory, so users can begin keying in a new or revised program they have developed.

DEL This "DELETE" key erases a single program step and automatically moves the remaining steps up one place in the program memory to fill the resulting gap. To insert the corrected step, users key it in and the following steps will move down automatically.

SST When the HP-65 is in the "WRITE PROGRAM" mode, this "SINGLE STEP" key lets users step through each program instruction in the program memory, as the display shows a number for each step. This number represents the location (row and column) of the key corresponding to that particular instruction. For example, "34" refers to the key in row 3, column 4 — "RCL." (Exception: digit keys are represented by the numbers 00 to 09.)

If the "SST" key is used with the HP-65 in the "RUN" mode, you can execute a program one step at a time.

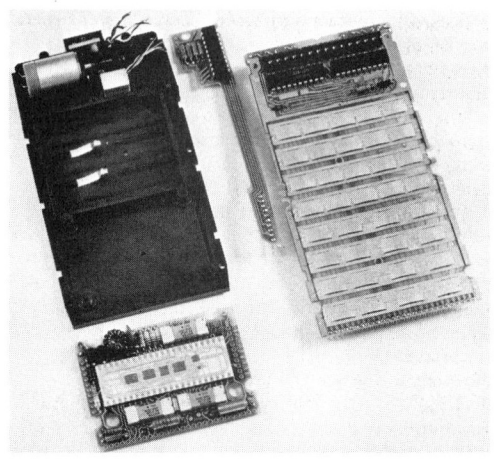

Inside the HP-65 — The HP-65 fully programmable calculator has four major subassemblies: (top left) a support plate with card reader head, motor and drive gears; (bottom left) a printed circuit logic board with 6-chip silicon hybrid which provides all control, timing, memory and arithmetic functions; (center) a card reader printed circuit board with amplification and control circuitry, and (right) a keyboard/display printed circuit board with cathode and anode LED drivers.

The HP-65 Advanced Scientific Pocket Calculator Functions and Features Built In — "Shift keys multiply the functions of many keys: f f^{-1} g To save space, many of the built-in functions are shown on the keyboard as alternate functions, and are indicated either above the key (in gold) or on the front side of a key (in blue). To activate them, users press the appropriate prefix "shift" key. Note that f^{-1} performs the inverse of the labeled gold functions.

Advanced trigonometric capability

$R \rightarrow P$ Coordinate conversions — Convert polar coordinates to rectangular coordinates, or vice versa. This lets users do vector arithmetic quickly and accurately.

DEG RAD GRD Angle modes — Users can calculate trig functions in any of three angular modes — degrees, radians or grads. Users can also convert from an angle in one mode to an angle in another mode with a few keystrokes.

D.MS Angle (time) conversions — In any of three angular modes, users can convert decimal angles (times) into angles (times) in degrees (hours)/minutes/seconds ... or vice versa.

$\rightarrow$ D.MS Angle (time) conversions — In any of three angular modes, users can convert decimal angles (times) into angles (times) in degrees (hours)/minutes/seconds ... or vice versa.

D.MS ± Angle (time) arithmetic — Users can add or subtract angles (times) in degrees (hours)/minutes/seconds.

Other specialized functions

INT Truncation — To truncate the displayed number to its integer value, press "f", then this key. To truncate it to a decimal fraction, first press "f^{-1}". In this way users can save memory storage space by retaining two numbers within a single memory. This is often used in programs.

advanced calculator operating characteristics

→OCT Octal conversion — Press the "f" key and this key to convert a decimal integer to octal. Press the "f⁻¹" key first to convert an octal integer to decimal.

Advanced memory power for faster, easier problem-solving

In addition to the 100 step-program memory, the HP-65 incorporates nine addressable memories.

These nine addressable memories make data manipulation easy. Users can store data in any memory... retrieve data from any memory... and even do register arithmetic.

The addressable memories are not only useful when operating the HP-65 as a scientific calculator — to accumulate sums, or to store constants or intermediate results — but are equally useful when working with a program. Data may be stored in any memory, then retrieved — either manually or automatically, as part of a program.

Plus other quality HP features...

The HP-65 also includes a four memory stack, which makes possible the famous RPN logic system, and a "Last X" memory.

Light-emitting diode display — Displays up to 10 significant digits, plus two-digit exponent and appropriate signs. Two selectable display modes: fixed point, with automatic overflow into scientific notation, and scientific with a dynamic range of 10^{99} to 10^{-99}. Automatic decimal point positioning. Selecting round-off; range: 0-9 decimal places.

Flashing display indicates improper operation; flashing decimal points indicate low battery.

The HP-65 outfit includes:
HP-65 Fully Programmable Pocket Calculator • Rechargeable battery pack • 115 or 230 Vac adapter/recharger • Soft carrying case • Safety travel case • Illustrated Owner's Handbook • Quick Reference Guide • pad of programming worksheets • Standard Pac of pre-recorded program cards • "Key Note" newsletter and Users' Library Catalog subscriptions.

To extend the usefulness of the HP-65 fully programmable scientific pocket calculator, Hewlett-Packard is offering many HP-65 application pacs of prerecorded programs in the fields of statistics, microwave circuit design and machine design, for example in mid 1976, each pac (above) sold for $45 and included 40 prerecorded magnetic cards, an operator's manual and a pad of blank programming pads. Examples of these three follow:

MACHINE DESIGN PAC I contains 35 programs that provide solutions for the machine designer in dynamics, vibration, linkages, cams, gears, springs, power transmission and machine geometrics.

STATISTICS PAC II contains 31 programs that provide solutions in the areas of general statistics, distribution functions, curve fitting, analysis of variance, test statistics, probability, quality control and queing theory. This is the second Stat Pac to be offered by HP for the HP-65.

EE PACK II contains 27 programs to assist the microwave circuit designer in making microwave measurements, designing transistor amplifiers, computing transmission line properties and certain system properties, and performing difficult related mathematical operations. HP offers many application pacs for use with the HP-65. They are in the fields of finance, mathematics, statistics, electrical engineering, chemical engineering (thermodynamics and transport processes), stress analysis, surveying, medicine, aviation and marine navigation.

Users start with the Standard Pac... a sampling of 17 pre-recorded program cards, plus three other cards to help insure the smooth operation of the HP-65. The pre-recorded cards are:
• Day of the week
• Mean, standard deviation, standard error
• Great circle navigation
• Integer base conversion
• Body surface area (Boyd)
• Pi network impedance matching
• EDM slope reduction — given elevation
• Temperature conversion
• Weight-mass conversion
• Volume conversions
• Compound interest
• Loan repayment
• Reconcile checking account
• Iterative solution of $f(x) = 0$
• Quadratic equation
• Areas and solutions of right triangle
• The game of NIMB (a game of logic users play against the HP-65)

Plus two diagnostic cards:
• User diagnostic program I
• User diagnostic program II

These two cards check the operating condition of the HP-65.

Also included is a special card to (occasionally) clean the program read/write head of the HP-65, and 20 blank program cards for do-it-yourself programming. Included, too, is a detailed manual on the Standard Pac, plus a set of 20 two-sided blank Pocket Instruction Cards (each having room for two program cards and their program instructions).

The HP-65 Users' Library* —Gives a subscription to the Catalog of Contributed Programs. The Users' Library contains thousands of programs — from a wide range of fields and application areas — contributed by HP-65 users, in addition to those developed and tested by Hewlett-Packard. All of the programs are listed and described in the Catalog of Contributed Programs, which is periodically updated. This sectionalized catalog makes it easy to select the particular program that will help quickly obtain the answer(s) to specific problem. The Catalog is indexed according to application area, key word and author. In addition, there is a section containing a short abstract of each program. The abstract provides information to help users determine whether a particular program will meet needs, or owners can use it to compare programs against each other when selecting between two or more alternatives. Any of the programs listed in the Catalog may be ordered from Hewlett-Packard, and owners may record them on blank program cards for repeated use.

The Monroe Beta 326 Programmable Hand-Held Calculator is also the Comucorp 326 — The Monroe or Compucorp Beta 326 is a powerful and easy to use hand-held programmable pocket calculator available with a tape cassette unit. Its features include:
• Built into the Beta 326 are over 100 preprogrammed operations for logarithms, trigonometry, statistics, metric conversions and the ability

*Available in continental U.S.A., Alaska and Hawaii only.

advanced calculator operating characteristics

to compute in degrees, grads, radians and degrees, minutes and seconds.
- Programs and data are stored on a tape cassette.
- By itself, the Beta 326 holds 160 program steps plus 12 data registers.
- All arithmetic operations are performed algebraically, just as they're written on paper. Plus parentheses, four levels deep.
- Using rechargeable batteries or AC current.

It includes a magnetic tape drive which allows users to read programs or data into the Beta 326. The tape drive can as easily receive programs or data from the Beta 326 and record them for future use. And an entire program library can be stored as a unit since a single 1½ ounce cassette holds over 100,000 program steps or 9,000 data values. Programmable from the keyboard, the Beta 326 also automatically accepts blocks of programs from tape in 160 step increments. Under program control, users can call another program and store or recall data from tape.

The Beta 326 does not use complicated computer language. It works algebraically. To add 2 and 2, users simply press 2 + 2 = and their answer appears. Users can nest parentheses to four levels to easily handle calculations such as $5 \times [4 - e \left(\frac{2}{[6 \times \ln(8/3)]} + .04 \right)]$. They key in the equation as it appears on paper. The display indicates the number of open parentheses. Users select the decimal setting, from 0 to 9 places, or scientific notation. All entries and results appear on a big, bright 12-digit display with automatic comma insertion on large numbers. Yet, at all times, users have the assurance that computations are accurate to 13 digits with a dynamic range of 10^{-98} to 10^{99}. If they want to perform the same arithmetic operations using the same constant repeatedly, they only need to enter their new variable and = . It's called constant arithmetic and it's very handy. If users make an illegal operation, such as attempting the log of -7, the display shows E-----. They simply press clear CLEAR and -7.0000 reappears. Twelve internal storage registers are used to store constants and intermediate results. And users can perform register arithmetic into and out of each register.

Over 100 Pre-programmed Operations Save Time and Memory — To save program memory and make calculations easier, over 100 pre-programmed operations for logarithms, trigonometry, statistics and even 24 metric conversions are hardwired into the unit. For example, users can perform trigonometric functions with a keystroke, determine the standard deviation of a sample of grouped or ungrouped data, and convert kilograms per square centimeter to pounds per square inch. For all trigonometric functions, the Beta 326 works in degrees, grads, radians, and degrees, minutes and seconds. All arithmetic operations can be performed using degrees, minutes and seconds (or hours, minutes and seconds) with the results formatted, 12 42 19 6000 . Programming is as easy as working from the keyboard.

Programming is a simple extension of the Beta 326's basic mathematical operation. Users enter their computation in load mode just as they would calculate it in run mode when solving the problem from the keyboard. They switch back to run and simply enter the variables.

Ease of use extends beyond elementary programming. Program editing has been made extremely easy. Users can move back and forth in memory, verifying, inserting, deleting or modifying any number of program steps. They can also step through a program to watch its execution one step at a time. Or they can automatically list the entire program. Jumping, branching, six levels of subroutines, labeled addressing and seven conditional statements for testing are all standard features.

In addition, Monroe and Compucorp offer program paks for a wide range of applications and other units. For example, the desk-top Alpha 325 model includes a printer in addition to 12-digit numeric readout and a tape cassette drive. Delivery began in 1975. The desk-top model now holds over 150,000 program steps on a single cassette and accepts blocks of programs in 416-step increments, compared with 160-step increments for the hand-held model. Both units can handle seven conditional tests, and nest subroutines six deep. CompuCorp and Monroe also supply software packs, including mathematics, beam design, circuit design, spring design, pathology and petroleum geology. Average price for software packs was $30.

The Monroe or CompuCorp Beta 326 can be interfaced to a standard teletype or CRT Display to perform input/output operations, thus giving printed output capability to a hand-held machine. It operates on rechargeable nickel-cadmium batteries or AC current and is priced with or without tape cassette. The Monroe/CompuCorp Beta 326 dimensions are 5" x 2" x 9", and it weighs 3½ lbs. Weight including the 392 cassette drive and carrying case is 10½ lbs.

Compucorp/Monroe Beta 326 with Tape Cassette Unit

Specifications: Monroe or Compucorp Beta 326 — Data Memory: All numbers are carried internally with 13 digit accuracy plus a two digit exponent. Twelve data storage registers which may be recorded on magnetic tape cassette.

Program Memory: 160 program steps which may be recorded on magnetic tape cassette.

Pre-programmed Operations: Reset, clear entry, set decimal point (0 to 9 digits to right of decimal point), exponent (scientific notation), enter and calculate with angles in degrees-minutes-seconds, enter and calculate with angles in decimal degrees or grads, decimal degrees to degrees-minutes-seconds, degrees-minutes-seconds to decimal degrees, square root, square, reciprocal, factorial, statisti-

advanced calculator operating characteristics

cal summation (number of data items, sum, sum of squares), delete data from summation, mean, standard deviation, sine, arc sine, cosine, arc cosine, tangent, arc tangent, to polar, to rectangular, degrees (or grads) to radians, radians to degrees (or grads), base e logarithm, base e antilogarithm, base 10 logarithm, base 10 antilogarithm, integer, fraction, absolute value, pi, e, round.

Arithmetic Functions: Add, subtract, multiply, divide, and a' (raise a number to a power), left and right parentheses (nesting to four levels).

English → Metric, Metric → English Conversions: Degrees Fahrenheit to degrees centigrade, inches to centimeters, inches/second to centimeters/second, inches/second^2 to centimeters/second,^{2} inches^3 to centimeters,^{3} feet to meters, miles to kilometers, miles per hour to kilometers per hour, U.S. gallons to liters, U.K. gallons to liters, pounds to kilograms, ounces to grams, pounds/inch^2 to kilograms/centimeter^2 pounds/feet^3 to grams/centimeter,^{3} degrees to grads.

Programming Operations: Addressing — Labeling (symbolic and relocatable addressing) with 13 different labels.

Jumping — 7 different conditional jumps to labeled addresses.

Jump > 0
Jump < 0
Jump ≥ 0
Jump ≤ 0
Jump ≠ 0
Jump = 0

Jump if keyboard entry has been made.

Subroutines — 7 conditional branches to labeled subroutines. Automatic return from subroutine to main program or another subroutine. Subroutines can be nested to 6 levels.

Additional operation: Identifiers to indicate points where variables are entered or the display of specific calculation results. Start or stop program execution. Pause in program execution.

Program Editing: Automatic display of memory location, code and symbol when entering programs from keyboard. Display shows present address and code plus codes at the previous and next program step. Trace feature while stepping through programs to observe operations as performed. Backspace and forward keys to permit corrections and changes in programs. Insert key to add steps in any part of the program at any time. Delete key to remove steps in any part of the program at any time.

Register Usage: Store and recall of all 12 registers. Exchange an entered number with the number in any of the 12 registers. Add, subtract, multiply, divide, and a^x into and out of data registers. Clear all registers, clear registers 1, 2, and 3 (group registers used in summation operation).

Other Features:
- Self testing — hardwired routine that automatically tests all the segments of the gas discharge display, and all the read only and random access memory chips.
- Tape cassette drive — manual controls for forward, rewind, record, stop, and eject tape cassette. Manual (or programmable) controls for writing reading data registers or programs onto or from tape cassette.

  Tape cassette drive plugs into and derives power through the Beta.
- Tape cassette medium — Programs and registers may be stored on either endless or straight line tape. Information is stored in blocks with 14 blocks on the endless tape and multiple files of 14 blocks each on the straight line tape. Each block can hold up to 12 data registers or 160 program steps as noted above.

Users can "talk" to the Compucorp Monroe Models 325 and 326 calculators through a Model 395 Teleprinter Interface if any device: 1) is 20 ma. current loop, EIA RS-323-C or CCITT V.24 compatible; 2) is ASCII at 110 baud, 10 cps alpha or program, 5 cps numerical data, half- or full-duplex; and 3) can terminate numerical entries or alpha strings with a Control A character. A Monroe Model 325 or 326 calculator with a Model 395 can: accept numerical data directly into the Entry register for calculating or storage in a data register; output a number from the Entry register through the Model 395; generate a Carriage Return and Line Feed for data formatting purposes; accept a string of alphanumeric characters (up to 72) and store it in data registers and output it to a Model 392 cassette drive or through the Model 395; and can output its program to a Teletype paper tape punch or read it back into program memory from the paper tape reader.

Texas Instruments Hand-Held Programmable SR-52 — This compact unit permits users to: Evaluate complicated functions. Calculate transcendental functions. Find the roots of: $F(x) = 0$. Find numerical solutions to ordinary differential equations. Invert and multiply matrices. Solve simultaneous equations. Integrate a function between arbitrary limits. Determine best-fit values for statistical samples. Users can set up calculations like these just once. Record them. Then use them for years. These units operate with three separate modes: Run mode. Calculate mode. Learn mode.

With a few keystrokes, the Run mode allows users to quickly solve complex problems with programs from prerecorded magnetic cards. The Calculate mode lets them solve problems manually. And with the learn mode, they can literally teach the SR-52 unique calculating methods. All modes can use nine levels of parentheses. 20 independent memory registers and 224 program locations with up to 72 labels. The procedure is:

1. Insert card. Send the A-side of the prerecorded magnetic card through first.
2. Remove card. And send the magnetic card through again. This time the B-side.
3. Slide the magnetic card into the window. A-side above keys A through E. The Read/Write keys let the SR-52 accept a magnetic card and run a program. Ten User-Defined Keys let users put in their known data, repeat a program as often as needed, change values of variables and solve for different unknowns. The stored program is not affected.

Using LEARN MODE, the SR-52 allows a personal approach to problem solving. It remembers up to 224 keystrokes. Users key-in their problem left-to-right as they would in calculate mode, using the following options for precise control:

- Preprogrammed "IF" Statements (8) make decisions based on the condition of the display.
- Decrement and Skip to Zero lets a segment of code be repeated a specified number of times.

advanced calculator operating characteristics

- User-defined Flags (5) determine the condition under which a program transfer is made.
- 3 Program Levels allows main program to call up to two levels of subroutines.
- Labels (72) name program segments.
- Indirect addressing (2 modes) extend the versatility of all memory-reference and branching instructions. Users trial-run their programs with editing and "debugging." They can move through problems a step at a time, forward or backward. Add more steps. Delete. Or write over steps. Then record.

SR-52 RUN MODE: Users load the contents of a magnetic card pre-recorded, or user-written. This puts the card's contents in memory. They start the card above the 5 user-defined keys representing 10 functions they can define. They enter numbers directly into the program. Or into one or more of the 20 addressable memory registers. They may do both. Execution is completely automatic. A program runs until it encounters a halt, which may be part of a program, or a keyed-in interruption. Users repeat a program as often as needed; change values of their variables, and solve for different unknowns. The stored program is unaffected.

With the SR-52 comes a Basic Library Program Manual and preprogrammed cards: Factors of an integer. Complex arithmetic. Reconcile checking account. Ordinary annuity 1 & 2. Permutations and combinations. Means and moments 1 & 2. Random number generator. Hi-pass active filter. Dead reckoning. Hyperbolic functions. Trend line analysis. Solution of quadratic equations. Conversions 1 & 2.

Additional Libraries may be purchased separately: Statistics. Math. Electrical Engineering. Finance. And more are on the way.

SR-52 CALCULATE MODE, operated manually, the SR-52 is an advanced professional calculator. All registers, internal and addressable, provide 12-digit numbers. Up to 10 digits show on the display, plus a scientific notation range from 10^{-99} to 10^{99}.

SR-52 with Inserted Program

SR-52 Operating Features — Program Transfer Statements or Branching. Program steps are usually processed as they're entered. But often clusters of steps need to be handled out of sequential order. This skipping around is called branching or transferring. There are two types:

A. Unconditional Transfer Keys

GTO Go To. A prefix key. Moves program counter to a new program location, defined either by a 3-digit program location or a label.

SBR Subroutine. A prefix key. Used with either a label or a 3-digit program location. Causes a transfer to a program segment to be used as a subroutine.

2nd IND GTO Indirect Go To. Transfers to the location in program memory specified by the contents of a memory register.

2nd IND SBR Indirect Subroutine. Transfers control to a program segment designated as a subroutine whose starting location is found in the specified memory register.

B. Conditional Transfers

These statements depend on tests. If test conditions are met, then transfer or branch takes place. Otherwise the regular sequence continues. Three types of tests are conducted: The display (positive, negative, zero, flashing, not flashing). Flags (set, not set). Contents of register 00 (zero or not zero).

C. Conditional Transfer Keys

2nd f pos If Positive. Tests display register for positive or zero. If it is, transfer occurs to a location or label. If the test fails, transfer does not occur.

2nd if zro — If Zero. Tests display register for zero. If it is, transfer occurs to a location or label. If not, no transfer.

2nd if err — If Error. Tests for an error condition (flashing display). If it is, transfer occurs to a location or label. If not, no transfer.

2nd dsz — Decrement and Skip on Zero. Decrements the contents of memory register 00, then tests these contents for zero. If it is not zero, transfer occurs to a location or label. If it is, no transfer.

D. Inverse Conditional Transfer Keys

Reverse all the above conditional transfers. For example, INV 2nd if pos tests the display and causes a transfer when the display is negative.

E. Flags

Flags are signals. The SR-52 has five. Each is set or reset by the user manually from the keyboard, or as part of a stored program. The flag's condition can be tested by the if flg transfer instruction.

F. Record Program Keys

2nd read Read/Write. Reads a program from a card into program memory.

INV 2nd Read Inverse Read/Write. Writes (records) a program on the magnetic card from program memory. After the card is labeled it is available at users fingertips for repetitive problem solving. They simply insert the card and operate the SR-52 in the Run mode. Users save time and effort, and have greatly reduced the chance of error since there are far fewer steps to perform. After they've completed their program they can store it and record it permanently, by running a magnetic card through the reader. Then it's in the SR-52 and on a card.

In early 1976, eighteen prerecorded programs come with an SR-52. And users can put them to work right away. No computer knowledge is necessary. There's no special entry system to learn. Three diagnostic cards are also supplied to reinforce program-building confidence. And users get a 96-page Basic Library Manual. Each program is supported by sample problems, user instructions and program listings.

TI's Printer Interfaces with Hand-Held Calculators — Model PC-100 is a peripheral printer which allows any TI hand-held programmable calculator to become a desk-top printer calculator. When the calculator is locked into the cradle, the user is able to print anything shown in the display or print the step-by-step execution of a program. The silent electronic printer has a 2.5 inch thermal tape allowing for 20 characters per line; each character is printed in a 5×7 dot matrix, and the printer is fully controllable from the calculator keyboard or card program. Priced at $295; it was available in early 1976.

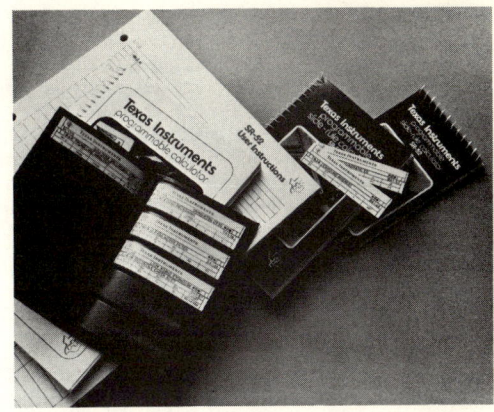

SR-52 Programs and Instruction Manuals

PART 2—Section One

Desk-Top Calculators and Computing Calculating Systems — What's Available and What Are Proper Evaluation Techniques — For managers in the sophisticated disciplines of business, science, and engineering, the eight-hour day has almost disappeared. The growing complexity of statistical and mathematical tools has made their work more precise. Simultaneously, this mountain of information has also placed a tremendous burden of data analysis and interpretation on their desks, a burden that often requires them to work evenings, weekends, and even holidays. For some, big computers help — but unless the problem is extremely complex or involves massive amounts of data, using the big computer can be more of a hassle than it's worth. The time spent writing programs or waiting turns on the computer has to detract from the time spent on truly productive work.

Now managers can put preprogrammed or programmable calculators on their desks and to greatly reduce their computational workloads. Replacing the big computer is not the purpose of calculators. But, they are designed to complement any computing tools presently in use — from adding machines to huge, general purpose computers. Various models allow users to fit the right machine to the right problem and greatly increase the utility and performance of both men and machines.

Just as craftsmen who work with their hands draw on a host of specialized tools to perform their tasks in the most efficient manner, managers in the new world of numbers, now have an entire range of special personal calculating tools to make their work most efficient, to make decisions when and where they arise or are needed. Programmable calculators can free users from the tedium and cost of data reduction.

Perhaps one of the most notable successes of mass market sales of calculators has been the current 'acceptance' of many computer concepts by the professionals and a sizable portion of the general public. The calculator concepts of memories, instructions, branching, programmability, interfaces, etc. are the same as those of computers. The fine line between 'keyboard microcomputers' that are becoming so popular with several hundred thousand computer 'hobbyests' and the advanced programmable 'computing' calculators is becoming near-invisible. Both are competing for applications including extensive communications capabilities. The 'basic fear of computers;' practically inherent in the beings of most businessmen, is being overcome — because of the much simpler decision-making capabilities of advanced calculators, which they do not fear. Indeed, some have become almost fanatic users; constantly seeking new challenges, new capabilities — which, are quite assuredly, capabilities of the microcomputer buried within each advanced calculator. The Tektronix 4051 BASIC Graphic Computing Calculator System analyzed on pages ahead combines convenient, compact storage, large-screen graphic display, and a general purpose interface bus by using the Motorola M6800 microcomputer chip. The first units of the Hewlett-Packard 9825 Computing Calculators used Intel's CPU microprocessor chip, and the competition has barely begun. The limits of programmable desk-top claculators are not presently foreseeable, neither are the numbers and types of the additional refinements and improvements being added practically monthly.

Many of the advanced units evaluated on the final pages of Part II have rapidly encroached upon the area previously dominated by various standard and minicomputers. MOS, RAM, and PROM circuitry were the major steps beyond the first integrated circuits (ICs) and hard-wired (fixed logic) systems of the immediate past. MOS-LSI for the calculators has provided greater speed, improved

desk-top calculators and systems

densities of memories, reduced costs, enhanced processing versatility, and announcements of these advances and new breakthroughs for calculators provide exciting reading and analysis for calculator enthusiasts. The number of users continues to multiply as the fertile minds of designers and power and press of marketing specialists take advantage of ever greater capability at ever reducing costs. The desk-top calculators decentralize and personalize the decision-enhancing powers of information processing systems — bringing to the individual what was previously only available to staff leaders or various top executives. Departmental managers, special research workers, project leaders, etc. can now cope with more data, explore with more insight, digest more facts, use more 'what if' techniques 'on the spot' and far more successfully than before with the recently offered preprogrammed or programmable desk-top calculators. Thus, better decisions are made — in the conference rooms, laboratories, in the field, ... wherever decisions must be made; better decisions with more accuracy and more options considered, from broader data bases, the information being instantly recallable. The advanced calculator is a powerful personal mathematical resource, without the user being required to possess programming experience or computing system expertise. The entry and recall systems are easy to use, flexible, and expandable at low cost and with little if any inconvenience. Personal problem-solving techniques and styles can be introduced and followed, professional capabilities are being magnified and made adaptable for faster, better procedures through the use of advanced calculators. Programmability has become a high-leverage investment as more important information processing tasks formerly controlled by computers are now available with true cost-effectiveness and accountable responsibility through the more satisfying use of advanced calculators. Increased capabilities through optimized models, advanced statistics by many users, etc. are a few examples.

We have noted that Casio and Canon, as well as Sharp, offered rather complete lines of below $30 hand-held calculators for housewives, golfers, engineers, businessmen, etc. with many varieties of special function keys. These lines carry over into the low-end desk-top four-function units, with or without standard size adding machine printers. The Ricoh 301P is offered by some catalog suppliers for less than $100 with four functions, chain/mixed calculations. 10 digits, two color print, credit balance, etc. One of the more popular units is the Lloyd's 12-digit high speed printer with a large display (not found on the Ricoh 301P) and live percent, overflow signal, memory signal, two-color printing, etc. Rockwell International's model 330 has 14-digit capacity, two independent memories, automatic square root, automatic constants, chain calculation, etc. Casio's line is nicknamed 'The Silencers' and is claimed to automatically eliminate idling noise between calculations. It has three read-out systems, print-with-display, display only, and print-answer-only. Monroe's model 1450 is part of a series of lightweight, desk-top calculators that offers 17 different keyboard options. They include choice of print and display, display only, two accumulators, percent change key, etc. The Adler Business Machine's electronic printing calculator model 1215P is a 12-digit unit with floating/fixed decimal system that has an override feature to accomodate additional decimals beyond the pre-selected decimal entry. Other features include underflow, add mode, percent key, complete memory bank, buffered keyboard for very rapid entry, indicator lights, etc. Facit-Addo, Inc. and Olivetti as well as Victor offer four-function desk-top models each with special functions and capabilities, and all are very competitive on a cost-effectiveness basis. However, as we will note below, these units are rapidly giving way to low cost preprogrammed and programmable units, and potential purchaser's should beware of overpaying for simple adders or adders with some few 'bells and whistles' when for the same or slightly increased costs they could own much better capability and quality performance. The standard four-function eight-digit LED, no memory units are admittedly already obsolete.

Quite basically Part I was concerned with the 'How to Use' and 'What to Evaluate' of Hand-Held Calculators. Part II is concerned with the same questions of desk-top units. Evaluation must begin with the simplest units, the four-to-six function units, most often simply called, 'adders.' Enumeration of the features is not meant to be considered recommendation of specific products. This is done to enlighten the reader to the enlarged range of alternative styles, capabilities, price drops, etc. Not all brands, models, or manufacturer lines can be included because of space limitations and changing developments. All calculator markets are volatile; all experience constant and great competitive pressures, a significant number of manufacturers or many of their models falling to the innovative advances of new technologies represented by continuous new entries and exits of companies and products. Two examples of typical advances are as follows: Mode Lamp — With those units having this feature, when a number is entered on the keyboard, the number will appear on the display; then when a function key is depressed ($+$, $-$, $\times$, or $\div$) a lamp will light on the display showing which function key has already been depressed. This feature is very useful to the operator in reducing errors as sometimes an operator will enter a number, and by being distracted, not remember if the function key has been depressed. The lamp will indicate this.

An innovative feature of some units is a mode of formatting the displayed result, called engineering notation. This is a selectable format that makes calculated answers easier to understand. Imagine a problem that deals in physical units of measure, such as seconds. Say the answer to the problem in scientific notation is 5.00 -05. Now this is a valid answer, but not as clear as it could be. Setting some units into engineering notation gives the answer as 50.0 -06 which is easy to read instantly as 50 microseconds. Engineering notation forces the power-of-ten exponent to be a multiple of three and adjusts the decimal point to give the correct answer. If the above answer is multiplied by 10, it gives 500. -06 or 500 microseconds. Multiplying again by ten gives 5.00 -03 or five milliseconds.

Also, the capability of any programmable calculator depends on software. Calculators that also have an abundance of programs available can save users much time. It is far easier to turn on a unit

desk-top calculators and systems

and start operating than it is to spend a day or so doing one's own programming — even then it's nice to have a machine that is easy to program. Evaluations ahead will emphasize this.

This microelectronic circuit, shown on the head of a match, contains as many components as 300 portable radios but produces no heat. The tiny circuits are manufactured by NCR Corporation in Dayton, Ohio, and others for use in computers and data terminals. See actual microprocessor "chip" held by tweezers below.

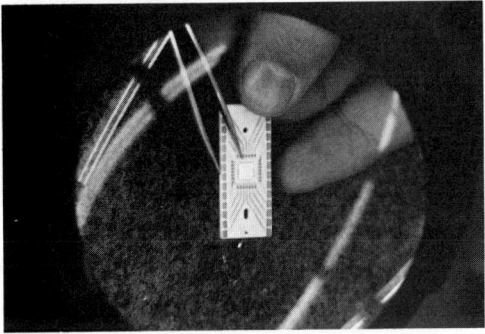

BASIC FOUR TO SIX FUNCTION NON-PRINTING DESK-TOP CALCULATORS — EXAMPLES OF EXTRA MEMORIES AND FUNCTIONS

The Olympia Line of Basic Desk-Tops — The Olympia CD 502 electronic display calculator, is representative of the range of Olympia calculators that technically incorporate the latest in electronic technology. The keyboard layout has 14-digit input/output capacity, two memories, complete decimal point and rounding technique, and facility for automatic square root, percentage and averaging calculations. Addition and subtraction are treated in the same way as on a standard adding machine, while for multiplication and division, flow arithmetic logic is used.

The Automatic percentage calculations include: Discount, bonus, sales (whether added or deducted, and with the results shown as gross or net amounts); all necessitate calculating with percentages. The CD 502 handles this easily. No more problems with the zeros when carrying out percentage calculations. Ideal for invoicing with "in-line" discounts without using the memory. The unit also includes automatic square root calculations.

With flexible memories accuracy can be achieved without any additional manual operations. Apart from the six-function calculating system, the CD 502 has two additional memory-registers: For immediate entry of results into the memory; For immediate direct entry of items (additions and subtractions) to the memory, the results of which can be recalled; For the transfer of a selected factor from a current series of calculations (FT function); For automatic processing of individual totals to make up the grand total (GT-function); For repeated feeding of additional constants into the arithmetical operation. Both memories have a 14-digit capacity, which also applies to the calculating register. The memories have individual decimal point placing as well as correct true-to-sign logic, and are protected against excess capacity results. For visual display, the clear, easy-to-read multi — digitron display panel has emerald green luminous figures and symbols. The display panel also includes the control signals for negative values, capacity overflow and memory registers in use.

The lower cost similar model CD 402 has automatic memory. The memory is important for commercial calculations, for direct entry of totals, for the automatic processing of products, quotients, totals or differentials. The CD 402 has good memory facilities with accumulating + and − keys, and additional result keys ∓ and ≡. The memory can also be used for recalling values (subtotals) or for the clearing of recalled totals. The contents of the memory are safeguarded against capacity overflow. It rejects an entry which may cause a capacity overflow, although it will cause an overflow in the arithmetical unit. On depressing the "C" key the CD 402 is once again ready for operation, while the original value in memory is retained in the register.

Reliability is achieved through simplified clearing technique. When switching the calculator on, all registers are automatically cleared. Newly entered figures clear the display panel of any previous figures. The arithmetic system and memory have their own clearing keys. Incorrectly keyed-in figures are cleared by simply depressing the "C" key. The CD 402 has a compact keyboard design to provide maximum operator efficiency. It has an attractive non-glare finish and overall elegant styling. It's neutral colors will fit the decor of any office.

Olympia 502 6-Function, 2-Memory Desk-Top Unit.

desk-top calculators and systems

Non-Printing Desk-Tops: the Casio 101-F and 121-F — Casio's unique technology in office machinery has developed this sophisticated calculator for people whose daily work involves complex figurework. It is a neat, compact unit, yet is sturdy enough for everyday heavy-duty use. It has a light-touch add bar, a spacious keyboard arrangement and other features specially designed to make sure that using it will never be tiring. The keys respond to the lightest touch and the green digitron tube, with a full 10-digit capacity, has large, read-at-a-glance figures.

The 101-F business machine has an independent memory . . . doubles the calculating range and raises efficiency by providing automatic accumulation, temporary storage and direct access to the memory. Other features are:
- Constants for $\times / \div$ . . . convenient capabilities for processing conversions and figurework involving repeat values.
- One-touch percentage facilitates mark-ups and discounts.
- One-touch square roots.
- Powers (x^2, x^3 . . .) and Reciprocals ($1/x$, $1/x^2$ . . .)
- Versatile decimal handling . . . fixed with round-off/cut-off or floating.
- True credit balance readings.
- Easy-to-read large green display.
- Memory lamp . . . indicates the memory storage is activated.
- Overflow indicator.

Although a compact unit, the 121-F is made for heavy duty operation. Special design features include a light-touch add bar and a sensible, spacious keyboard arrangement. All keys respond instantly, delivering to the bright green digitron tube (with a full 12-digit capacity) large, read-at-a-glance figures. Another advantage is that the 121-F automatically places comma markers between each group of three numerals for easier reading of large figures.

The Rockwell Low-Cost Non-Printing Desk-Tops — Other units in this class grouping are available from Rockwell, Texas Instruments and a score of other companies. Another example follows:

The Rockwell 310 offers a lot of calculating power and convenience at a modest price. It adds, subtracts, multiplies, divides, stores results in an accumulator memory, works percentage calculations automatically. The unit has add mode so users can add and subtract without worrying about a decimal.

The Rockwell International's model 330 calculator has 14-digit capacity, two independent memories, automatic square root, and a special function switch that performs various secondary calculations as an automatic by-product of the primary calculation. Features include percent key, repeat add/subtract, automatic constants, chain calculation capability, change sign key, and comma punctuation.

Victor's Scientific/Engineering Display Electronic Calculator Model 18/1721 The Scientific/Engineering model is 5" x 11¾" x 10" and weighs 6 lbs., 2 oz. And, it is capable of:

Trigonometric Functions. Automatically calculated sine, cosine, tangent, $\sin^{-1}$, $\cos^{-1}$, or $\tan^{-1}$, in degrees or radians.

Automatic Raising Key. Raises automatically "X" to the whole number or fractional "Y" power.

Logarithmic Functions. Automatically calculated the common or natural log of a value in the display.

Inverse Key. Conditions the calculator to calculate anti-logs or inverse trig functions.

Change Sign. The algebraic sign of a displayed value may be changed at the touch of a key.

Sequential Math. Only new entry need be keyed in problems like: $2 \times 3 \times 4$.

Automatic Square Root. The square root of any displayed number appears at the touch of a key.

Pi Key. Enters Pi (π) automatically as a displayed value.

Automatic Reciprocal Key to calculate the reciprocal of a value displayed.

Lloyd's Low-Cost Electronic Printing Calculator with 12 Digit High-Speed Printer (under $200) — Lloyd's advanced printing calculator is designed to perform complex business calculations in one-tenth the time it takes with conventional mechanical adding machines. More than a new device, it's a packaged system integrating advanced electronic business features including a high speed printer, live percent, automatic constant, a big, easy to read display, fully independent memory that permits automatic accumulation of the sums of products and quotients plus separate memory inputs. The Lloyd's system also offers a floating in/fixed out decimal switch. This switch automatically positions the decimal point at a choice of 2, 3, 4 or 6 decimal positions. Another important feature is the add mode for monetary calculations. With the add mode, there's no need to reenter the decimal — it's automatically positioned in the second place. These features will save time when doing invoice extensions, rate extensions, calculating commissions and the like! Additional features:
- 12 digit display
- printer/display operates independently
- buffered keyboard for fast operation
- Advanced Seiko auto start/stop printing head
- live percent • add mode • non add key
- automatic constant • item counter key (for averaging)
- overflow signal • memory signal
- fully independent memory with direct access from main register • two color printing
- full one year warranty
- floating or preset decimal with round off

OLYMPIA ELECTRONIC PRINTING/ DISPLAY CALCULATORS

Models CP162 and CPD575 — The Olympia CP 162 is ideally suitable for square root calculations, in addition to its computation and storage systems. Users enter the figures and press the square root key. The result is printed out immediately. Even if the square root calculations occur in the middle of a problem, they can be carried out there, and then the rest of the work can be continued in the usual way. Other features which make the CP 162 outstanding are: statistical spacing (groups of 3 digits) automatically permits easy reading of the paper roll. The decimal point technique offers a wide choice. All values and totals are printed out with the preselected decimal point, whether floating of fixed, within the range of 0 — 9 digits, with automatic underflow. The AM (adding machine fixed decimal point) technique. Ideal for those who do a great many additions, since it is not necessary to operate the decimal point key.

desk-top calculators and systems

The CP 162 has three selectable rounding-off facilities: a) no rounding off (truncating) b) according to the commercial 5/4 system c) rounding up (0/1). The Constants features are: Automatic constant first factor during multiplication. Automatic constant divisor during division. Repeat values of addition and subtraction.

The item counter records the number of additions and subtractions — a great advantage for calculating averages. The subtotal key permits the printout of sums for checking. The non-add key allows printing of dates and invoice numbers on paper rolls.

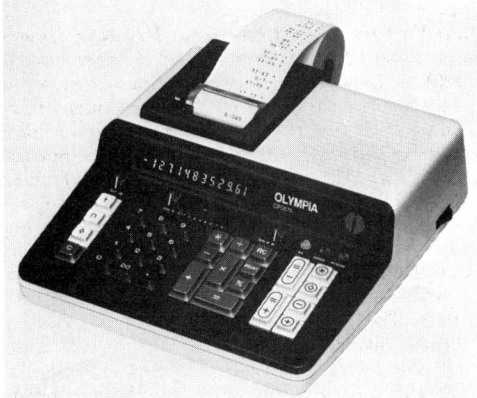

The Performance Highlights of the Olympia Model CPD575 — Modern MOS-LSI technology offers: High speed, silent epicyclic printing system: 2.5 lines per second. No moving parts when not performing calculations. Selectable: print only, display only, or print and display. Direct access independent memory with memory use light. Memory for grand total, multiplications and division. 12-digit capacity with 24-digit calculating capacity. Selectable print of an amount. Automatic percent calculation. 2 add mode positions: dollars and pennies, and pennies and mills. Large easy to read digitron display. Full-floating, floating-in, floating-out, fixed-out decimal system. 0-7 places. 2-color printout. Selective round-off. Constant in all four arithmetic functions. Mixed and chain calculations. Credit balance. Register change key. Non-add key. Sub-total key. Illuminated overflow indicator.

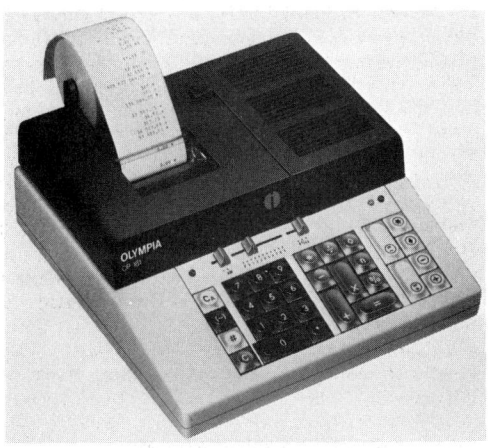

Microprocessor — Controlled Printer Unit — All over the world a calculator is judged on its capacity. The standard calculator employed in the international banks and clearing houses requires a capacity of 16 figures — and of course a memory. The Olympia 181 has these, as well as a host of other features. Professional features, like a computing memory suitable for storing values and results, and full algebraic sign logic and sign change are engineered into the CP 181. A simplified six-key layout insures maximum accuracy when carrying out memory computations through the use of a unique 2½ memory system. A three position selector provides the following round-off capabilities: a) Truncation (no rounding-off) b) Commercial 5/4 system c) Rounding-up (1/10).

Calculating percentages, among the most important type of computation for the businessman, is easily accomplished on the CP 181 with a percent key. Whether rebate, discount, bonus, sales tax, additions to and subtraction from percentages can be determined in seconds.

A full-floating, floating-in, fixed-out decimal system provides a decimal selection range of 0-9-F. The automatic value selector insures that decimal points are positioned accurately under each other during addition and subtraction. The model CP 181 is also equipped with Add Mode-the adding machine fixed decimal point system. All selected decimal point positions are automatically printed out and therefore, need not be keyed-in.

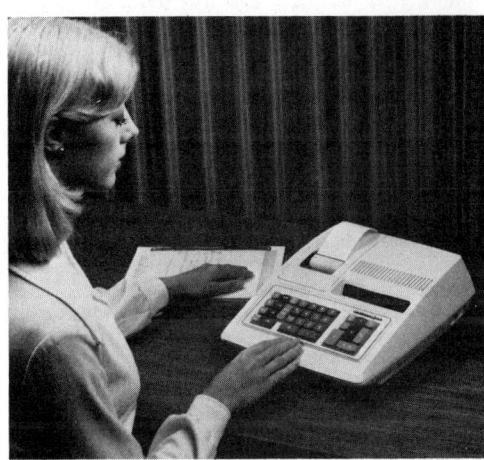

BURROUGHS CALCULATORS: FLEXIBILITY, SILENCE, COMPACT SIZE

In late 1975 Burroughs Corporation expanded its comprehensive range of electronic calculators with two series, the C 2400 and the C 2050. The C 2400 Series (above) includes two models, both featuring electronic display and printing capabilities. They can operate in either display-and-print mode or display-only mode. The display-only mode offers the advantages of silence, instant readability, and paper economy for random calculations and those applications not requiring a proof tape. The display-and-print mode is used when a printed record is needed. A large 12-digit Panaplex® display allows the user to verify indexed amounts before printing and provides easy reading of results. The two models in the C 2400 Series are the

desk-top calculators and systems

C 2436 and C 2456. The C 2456 has nine storage memories (eight more than the C 2436) and can operate in three application modes. Typical uses for these modes include:

- Accumulating indexed amounts in up to eight different categories.
- Automatically accumulating factors and results, or automatically accumulating debit and credit amounts with a count of each.
- Automatically increasing or reducing by a previously stored percentage.

Four to Six Function Printers: Casio R-200, an Example — Many low-cost units offer distinctive 2 color printing. The R-200 automatically and distinctively prints in two colors — green for entry, black for result — with the symbols showing operation performed. So now users can more easily trace and check those complicated calculations and records. Many units, Casio included, offer: "Silencers" that eliminate all idling noise because the printing drum is automatically stationary right after printing, there's no motor noise to distract. They offer a quiet office environment, no-power wastage. At least six similar models are being marketed.

A typical low-cost unit is the Casio, electronic printing and display calculator, the Model R-11. The unit features a double item counter system which shows on the print-out the number of separate items being added in each group and the number of group totals in the grand total. It also has a totalling system that produces total, grand total and accumulated total in a single series operation. The R-11 has a 12-digit working capacity, a memory for addition and subtraction, percent key, constant for multiplication or division, and printing in two colors.

Olivetti Corporation's Logos 68 electronic printing calculator has two independent direct access registers for addition, subtraction, accumulation and storage of constants and has an arithmetic unit comprised of three registers for multiplication, division, percentages, squaring, square root, and automatic recall of all results. It features floating-in/fixed-out decimal control, entry buffer, safety interlock.

The Underwood 481 is a versatile, general purpose, electronic printing calculator extremely quiet in operation — all idling noise between calculations has been eliminated. It has Accumulating memory, Automatic constant, Percentage key, Decimal places; Add Mode 2, 3, 4 and Floating, plus Recall of all entries and totals and a Buffered keyboard.

A line of 15 electronic calculators for business, professional, and home use has been introduced by Royal Typewriter Co., division of Litton Industries. The new products range from basic breast-pocket-size four-function/constant calculators to advanced scientific models. Two desk-top display models and three printers are included. All units that have display have the digitron type.

Ricoh of America, Inc., has offered the Esprint II, a calculator that measures, counts, and calculates. It uses plug-in accessories to count items or measure such things as length, square footage, volume, cubic yards, water volume, or irregular shapes right off the blueprints. It has a bright green, 12-digit, 4-symbol display and produces a two-color paper printout.

The 1176 is an electronic printing calculator from Facit-Addo, Inc., that has 12-digit capacity, automatic decimal underflow, full four-key memory, 0-7 or floating decimal selection, and add mode. Its two-key percentage system allows one-step percentage calculation. Wide tape; two-color printout with separation between hundreds, thousands, and millions; and automatic motor shutoff are features.

Adler Business Machines' electronic printing calculator model 1215P is a 12-digit unit with a floating/fixed decimal system that has an override feature to accomodate additional decimals beyond the pre-selected decimal entry. Other features include underflow, add mode, percent key, complete memory bank, buffered keyboard for rapid entry, easy-to-read printouts, indicator lights.

Another typical low-cost unit, the Rockwell 420P has an array of features to speed figurework and promote accuracy. Features are a keyboard designed for speedy touch operation, a powerful memory, 12-digit capacity, add mode, automatic item counter, percent key, exchange key (or optional square root), automatic constants, chaining etc. Plus a permanent record of all calculations on printed tape. Rockwell offers a rather full line including the thermal printer models 80R, 82R and the 415P.

Texas Instruments like a score of other firms continues to introduce new electronic printing calculators. The TI-500 desk-top model was the first printing calculator in the company's business line. The TI-500 has 12-digit capacity with comma punctuation, audit trail symbols and two-color printing on standard 2½-inch-wide paper tape. Credit balances are printed in red to insure easy readability. Among other features are add-mode, large plus key, add-on/discount per cent, repeat add and subtract, and selectable decimal and rounding positions. The unit weighs 7 pounds.

All Victor Series 1900 Matrix Printers offer 14 digit capacity. Automatic tape advance presents answers up front at the touch of a key. Automatic features include: constant multiplication and division, constant addition or subtraction as well as item count of all entries. Percentages are automatically pointed off. Sequential math ($2 \times 3 \times 4$) simplifies chain calculations and results of all calculations are automatically retained for use without re-entry. The Model 19/4462 with two Memories also has two memory registers. Amounts are stored in either register may be recalled for subsequent use. Addition and subtraction can be performed with either register. Lights show which registers contain amounts.

PART 2—Section Two

PREPROGRAMMED DESK-TOP CALCULATORS — PRINTERS AND NON-PRINTERS, SOME EXAMPLES

The above picture of the Hewlett-Packard HP-91 printing preprogrammed scientific calculator is a typical example of the display, printing, and expanded preprogrammed capability that has become available at very reasonable costs, $500 for this unit. As noted on pages ahead, it has a wide range of engineering capability, long battery life, large display, modern design, and other advantages. Undoubtedly, Hewlett-Packard intends to introduce more models in this series, quite likely business, financial, statistical, and other types of preprogrammed units. And, just as likely, imitators will bring out similar units and undercut the price — and often much of the capability. So, again the battle is on, and the reader will do well to evaluate carefully each of the several models before making a purchasing decision, being careful not to be confused about the primary characteristics of: Special Function Keys; Preprogrammed Features; Keyboard Programmability, and Full Programmability. The alert reader might again refer to the chart produced and explained on the first few pages of the book to note the broad classifications and type of unit categories.

Hewlett-Packard Preprogrammed HP-91 — In early 1976, Hewlett-Packard introduced the first in a new line of small, portable printing calculators. The HP-91 is a scientific calculator, and has all of the preprogrammed functions of the hand-held HP-45 plus 16 addressable memory registers, engineering notation, regression and linear, estimate capabilities, and three percentage functions. As it was introduced it was priced at $500. The HP-91 will print and display in fixed decimal, scientific notation and engineering notation and has four clearing operations and three printing modes.

The thermal printing system of the HP-91 employs a moving thin-film head to record and label calculations on heat sensitive paper. Because the HP-91 can print all calculations, users can print — with labels — statistical summations, contents of the operational stack, or the contents of all sixteen addressable memories. Users routine repetitive calculations can be performed by non-specialists and later checked for accuracy. Tape is available in 80-ft. rolls that accommodate 5,760 lines of printed data.

With switch set to ALL, the printer will show all entered data, functions, intermediate and final answers. With the switch set to NORMAL, the printer will record entered data and functions only. In this mode, intermediate and final answers may be printed by pressing the Print X key. With switch set to MANUAL, the printer will operate only when users press the Print X key or a list function. This mode is useful in conserving battery power or when the full printing capability of the HP-91 is not required.

The HP-91 will print and display in fixed decimal and scientific notation, common in many scientific calculators. It will also print and display in engineering notation, an important HP feature that displays values with exponents that are mul-

preprogrammed desk-top calculators

tiples of 3. This is useful in working with many units of measure, such as kilo (10^3), nano (10^{-9}), etc.

Its math capabilities include log and trig functions (the latter in degrees, radians or grads), rectangular/polar conversions and three separate percentage functions. Its statistical capabilities include summations, mean and standard deviation, linear regression, linear estimates (all for two variables) and factorial. All this, plus sixteen addressable registers, an automatic four-register stack, a Last-X register for easy error recovery and four clearing options.

Compared to algebraic logic, many users feel the RPN logic system is faster, more efficient and more versatile in solving the complex problems faced by today's professionals in science and finance. For calculations, it requires fewer keystrokes. Users don't need parenthesis keys and don't need to keep track of complicated hierarchies. Intermediate answers are displayed and stored automatically in an operational stack of four memories — no need to write them down and risk errors. The size and complexity of problems that can be handled with RPN logic are virtually unlimited.

The bright lighted display of the HP-91 shows up to ten significant digits, plus two digits exponent and appropriate signs. And the display is at a 45° angle that makes it easily read while seated at a desk or standing at a workbench or drafting board.

THE BURROUGHS PREPROGRAMMED SYSTEM

The Burroughs C 6451 is an example of a general-purpose calculator — plus a unique application calculator. Burroughs technologically sophisticated C 6451 is designed to handle time-consuming calculations involving units of measurement with a conversational simplicity never before offered in a desk-top calculator. The C 6451 features a Program Activator Panel. The user snaps the Program Activator Panel into place on the applicational keyboard of the C 6451.

The versatile Program Activator Panel . . .
- activates the measurement, liquid, or weight programs.
- combines the functions of the applicational keyboard with the computing and listing keys of the basic calculator.
- identifies the three common function keys (per, convert to and metric) and the nine unit entry keys which represent the units of measurement for the applications.
- permits computations and conversions for a broad range of liquid, weight or measurement applications.

Measurement, weight or liquid problems are entered on the keyboard in the same manner as they would be stated by the user. It's that simple. The C 6451 also provides protection for the future through its ability to handle conversions to and from the metric system of measurement.

The Burroughs C 7200 programmable printing calculator features 16 storage memories for storing factors and for automatic or manual accumulations. A buffered keyboard remembers which keys have been depressed and processes them sequentially. Programs are easily recorded onto magnetic cards, each card recording up to 408 program steps. All figures and instructions print clearly and quietly.

The C 6451 is an office quality display and print calculator that can add, calculate or convert in various units of measurement quickly and easily. (See Fig. B-1) This versatile calculator is designed to serve many types of business including the construction, transportation, textile, food processing and packaging industries, as well as educational institutions and governmental organizations. It can perform area calculations in yards, feet and inches; volume calculations, price-per-unit calculations, conversion to and from metric as well as to any equivalent units, and calculations involving fractions. Pounds and ounces, hours and minutes, gallons and pints can be added, multiplied or divided in exactly the same way as decimal amounts. The C 6451's simplicity is achieved by combining a standard calculator keyboard with unit entry keys for the different measure systems. Problems involving units of measurement are entered on the keyboard conversationally in the same manner as they would be stated by the user.

Advanced large-scale circuit technology gives the C 6451 the versatility to add, calculate or convert in several measurement systems. The systems are weight (avoirdupois, troy and metric); liquid (US, imperial and metric); measurement (linear, area and volume); time; quantities (gross, dozens and singles, fractions and decimals); and temperature (Fahrenheit and Celsius). The values and functions of the different systems are stored in micro-programmed read-only memories which are accessed by three interchangeable program activator panels. These program activator panels fit over the unit keys and can be changed easily. In a matter of seconds, for example, the user may change the labels and functions of the unit keys from tons, pounds and ounces to hours, minutes and seconds or one of the other measurement systems available. The C 6451 is designed to handle conventional business calculations as well as measurement applications and gives the user the advantages of both display and printing output. The display-only mode saves paper in random calculations where an audit tape is not required. The display-and-print mode provides both the legibility of the large Panaplex® display and a printed tape

preprogrammed desk-top calculators

which identifies each entry and calculation with symbols applicable to the measurement program in use. In 1976, purchase price of the basic C 6451 calculator with one program activator panel was $695. Prices range from $695 to $795 depending on the number of program activator panels provided.

Burroughs Introduces Pre-Programmed Electronic Calculator Designed for Financial Institutions — One of the Burroughs Corporation preprogrammed electronic printing calculator, the C 6203, is designed especially for commercial banks, savings and loan association, other financial institutions and financial management of large commercial organizations. The C 6203's versatile stored programs provide simple and rapid solutions to the complex computations which are part of the everyday work of departments handling installation loans, commercial loans, mortgages and savings accounts. The calculator's simplicity of data entry and rapid calculation eliminate the need for charts, rate books, tables and formulas. For example, computation of monthly payments of a conventional mortgage loan is performed by entering the principal amount, the annual interest rate, and the number of years of the loan. The automatic result shows the monthly payment, including principal and interest. Monthly payments on installment loans including credit life insurance and accident/health insurance can be computed quickly and can include "odd days" interest, frequently lost by an institution because of the number of references that must be made to rate books and charts.

Single or multiple payment commercial loans and amortization schedules can also be computed quickly and easily with the C 6203. The calculator also makes it easy for a savings department to determine how much a customer needs to deposit on a periodic basis to achieve a specific savings goal. General financial applications include such routines as equity calculation on a mortgage loan, equivalent interest rate on discounted notes, calculation of investment required to yield fixed periodic withdrawal, calculation of periodic withdrawal from a known investment, and others. The C 6203's eleven application programs, which are activated simply by depressing program selection keys, are stored permanently in read-only memory (ROM), consisting of large scale integrated circuit chips. Read-only memory contains all the program instructions required to permit fast, simple solution of the complex problems encountered by financial management and financial institutions. In addition, the calculator can be used for many general-purpose applications and as a standard four-function calculator with square-root capability.

The calculator has five storage memories used principally for storing of proof totals and/or accumulations, or both, resulting from executed programs. The "execute" key of the C 6203 is an important feature which contributes to simplicity of operations. After data is entered on the keyboard, depression of the "execute" key triggers completion of the selected program steps. The calculator's output tape provides printed results, and also provides a complete audit trail of data entry and computations. The new calculator, designed and manufactured by Burroughs, includes special internal diagnostic checkpoints and removable components, permitting fast, easy, maintenance in customer's offices. The calculator and the application programs were designed by a special task force which combined Burroughs technological advances and Burroughs lengthy experience with the requirements of financial institutions.

Casio FX-3 Scientific Calculator — The Casio FX-3 scientific calculator gives engineers, scientists and mathematicians fast, accurate solutions — from simple arithmetic to complex statistics . . . with pre-programmed switches, and keys for 25 essential scientific functions. Specifications of the capabilities: Normal functions — 4 basic functions, chain & mixed operation, constants in 4 functions, automatic accumulation in 4 functions, true credit balance and calculations involving decimal places. Scientific functions — trigonometrics either by degree, radian or grade, inverse trigonometrics, hyperbolics, inverse hyperbolics, common & natural logarithms, exponentiations (exponentials, squares & powers), factorials, square roots, reciprocals, sexagesimal/decimal conversion, register exchange, sign change, Pi entry and scientific notation mantissa display exchange. Preprogrammed or fixed program functions — polar ⇌ rectangular coordinates conversion, quadratic equation, statistics.

preprogrammed desk-top calculators

The Programmed Casio 162-F — The unit offers the calculating capacity needed for most office calculating work. It has an extensive 16-digit display to let users handle any large figures. As many as 7 memories (1 independent, 1 for constants and 5 for accumulating/data storage) plus an item counter facility, help to make working out tough problems easy, quick and convenient. A touch key deals in seconds with calculations that used to involve tedious references, such as percentages, square roots, powers, reciprocals and sign changes.

Casio's unique DATE key quickly traces days and dates and delivers answers to a multitude of financial calculations such as loans, deposits, interest, insurance, etc. The pre-programmed standard deviation functions are most helpful. The PROGRAM key computes the sum, arithmetical mean or standard deviation required in statistics by simply entering the data. Then users just depress the appropriate key to get their answer. In addition, users can swiftly process more complicated statistical calculations involving totalled data by using the seven memories.

Monroe's Desk-top Calculator Solves Statistical Problems — Preprogrammed into the Monroe Model 1930 is a set of commonly used statistical functions that include single variable (grouped or ungrouped) data summations; 2 variable data summations, standard deviation, mean and standard error of the mean; and linear regression with correlation coefficient slope and y-intercept. It calculates factorials, common and natural logarithms permutations and combinations, t-dependent, t-independent, and t-statistic; Chi-square, f, and t-distributions are available with the depression of a single key.

The Monroe 1930 has 10 independent storage registers with full arithmetic capability. Some of its other outstanding features include a buffered keyboard, automatic lighted commas for punctuation, zero suppression and separate error and overflow indication and 2-key rollover. Functions are accessible without double key depression or second function key. Results may be read through use of the display format switch in the units in which the statistician works.

Hewlett-Packard's HP-46 Gets the Best Features of The HP-45 — Plus a Printer — This desk-top counterpart to the HP-45 starts with the features users like best in the HP-45: 48 high-level functions and operation, plus addition, subtraction, multiplication and division. Mean and standard deviations. Conversions of length, weight and volume measurements to U.S. or metric standards. Conversion of vectors to either polar or rectangular coordinates. And up to 10-digit accuracy. But with the HP-45 users also get a printout of every step of every operation for fast and easy rechecking. The alphanumeric impact printer lets users list the contents of the operational stack and registers, gives them error indications, and prints symbols, numbers and letters in red or black, or both, on standard paper tape.

Hewlett-Packard's HP-81 is its Calculator for Business and Finance. It can evaluate complex time/money relationships as easily as doing sums on an adding machine. No matter what specialty, the computing power of the HP-81 gives an extra edge in making business decisions. The HP-81 contains 63 fundamental business and financial functions — instant solutions to thousands of business problems. And the HP-81 gives a fast, accurate, independent method of ensuring that users come up with accurate evaluations ... authoritative answers ... sound decisions. Available is an optional expedited entry keyboard that lets users enter a new problem while the HP-81 is solving the previous one.

The H-P 9000 line begins with the Model 9805, the more advanced models are discussed in the Computing Calculators Section. For the scientist working with statistics, the Model 9805 will solve many statistical problems encountered in day-to-day work. And once the data is entered, it will solve these problems with a single keystroke. Conveniently, with a single keystroke, it prints out sample size, mean, standard deviation, and correlation. Or calculates histogram cell statistics. Or predicts y from a known x. Or calculates linear or parabolic curve fit coefficients. Or evaluates t, including degrees of freedom. Users may add an HP X-Y plotter and see these solutions graphically presented, again at the press of a single key.

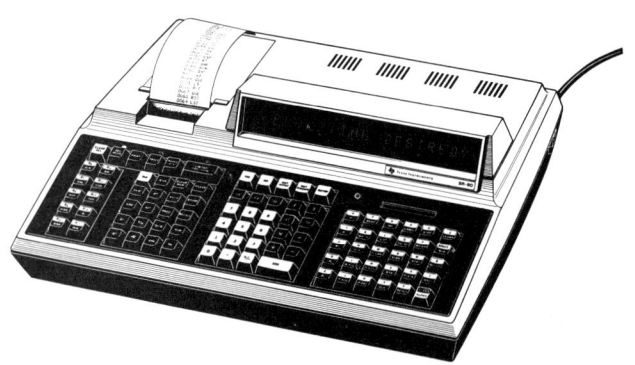

PART 3—Section Three

PROGRAMMABLE DESK CALCULATORS — 'MIND EXTENDERS' IN OFFICES, LABORATORIES, AND EXECUTIVE SUITES

A few years ago practically all offices, labs, statistics, engineering and research sections of business, educational institutions and industry were equipped with dozens to hundreds of 'adding' machines, some improved with a few special keys. Today, calculators are available to these users as powerful, flexible, immediately interactive 'systems' that rival small computers. Most of these are equally as easy to operate as the old fashioned types, and most are far less costly. They perform consistently, directly, and accurately hundreds of tasks that expensive computers perform at considerably more confusion, cost, and inconvenience. Many programmable calculators are available with peripherals, as noted on pages ahead, including: card readers, tape input-output units. X-Y plotters, output printers, digitizing devices, and scores of others. Keyboards are used not only for entering data for on-the-spot calculations but also for entering programs. And separate interchangeable keyboard sections are available for special functions on some units. Most of the program language appears on or is completed on the keyboard. Displays show calculated results, the input and the programs, and these range from a simple numerical presentation to a complete alphanumerical presentation including real-time (immediate response) output. Hard-copy output is becoming standard as are magnetic cards, ROMs, or cassette units for storage and read-in.

Low cost-calculator systems, analyzed on the pages ahead, can eliminate computer time-sharing and the usual 'waiting' for computer results. The calculator serves as a standard engineering, management and industrial monitoring tool when not being used in a total information system. They are significantly less expensive than complex computer systems. Wherever there are groups of engineers, departmental or general managers, or other professionals of various disciplines, there are places for calculators — especially when they are not trained in computer use. Advanced programmable calculators provide direct interaction because they are user-oriented machines with algebraic languages and alphanumeric printers.

Some calculators are used for electronic and electrical circuit design evaluation, for analysis of power lines and hardware designs, for statistical reduction and analysis, for management or operations research model building and problem solving, for metallurgical alloy evaluation, for scores of medical tests and analysis, and an almost unending array of other applications. The majority of these people really do not need a computer when advanced programmable calculators are available. Both take instructions, store information and perform rapid, complex mathematical operations. They compile, correlate and select. Both provide analysis capability and can work with the same peripherals thereby controlling components in a system. Users can quickly note by analysis of the models depicted on the following pages that today's programmable calculators are very comparable to minicomputers and small business computing systems. But there are some major beneficial differences.

Perhaps the most important advantages of the calculators are the accessibility and response immediacy. There are elements of participation with programmable calculators which users don't achieve with computers — large or small. The calculators are complete, approachable, self-contained without high support costs. The minicomputers with their assembly languages are often tedious things to program and control. Users often must lean on editor programs to assemble operating programs. Added memory to use higher level languages and the need for high priced peripherals push costs up and up. It is simple to compose, store, and adjust programs right on calculator keyboards, or copy them from handwritten notes. Most math functions are built into the machines, and users do not require algorithms or the necessity of converting them to and from binary languages. Calculators are now extremely versatile and flexible; they can be standalone units or used as dedicated or non-dedicated parts or controllers of systems, for data acquisition, monitoring, analysis. They are mathematical generators for graphic displays or plots, projectors of trends, and with magnetic tapes and cartridges, data is safe. Users can concentrate on ideas instead of on complex mechanics and equally complex computer methods. They are recorders, reporters, processors, manipulators, can be operated by stand-in clerks or managers themselves. Man-machine interaction is excellent with programmable calculators.

Examples of Programmable Calculator Applications — Advanced programmables offer fast, accurate solutions to mathematical, statistical and business problems. These systems can be programmed for very specific needs. Manufacturers now offer several series of complete calculating systems for specialized users:

For Auto Dealers — The desk-top programmable calculator is used by many auto dealers who have developed literally dozens of ways to reduce the cost, time and effort required to handle the mountain of paper work that is a part of every dealership. Not only do these calculators fill out all the forms required to complete the customer's sale, but at the end of every day they provide an up-to-the-minute analysis of sales and service revenues;

For Surveyors and Civil Engineers — A desk-top programmable calculator helps Surveyors and Civil Engineers solve complex problems quickly and easily. Surveyor programs are already prepared to handle traverse, inverse and slope/temperature corrections with keyboard entries. And, under full program control, the various systems drive very accurate flatbed plotters to automatically and quickly produce finished drawings from calculated data;

For Structural Engineers — Calculators are powerful tools for solving the tough analysis and

programmable desk calculators

design problems of steel and concrete structures with software developed to meet the needs of the most exacting Structural Engineering firms and Consultants. They can actually do the job of big computers or time-sharing services at a fraction of the cost;

For Teachers — Calculators are a learning assistant for the math teacher to aid in the explanation of math concepts for both gifted and slow learners;

For On-line Applications — Calculators form the data collection and mathematical manipulation end of a system interfaced with medical laboratory or other on-line devices that give users instantaneous solutions to complex equations, chemical analyses, and other mathematical oriented applications, and also give users a running hard copy result printed or plotted;

For Mathematicians — Calculators are a mathematician's aid in solving problems in general math or statistics that would require the use of a computer or many, many hours of calculations from tables or charts. Various series of calculators come with complete libraries of mathematical programs already for users to adapt to their individual problem.

For Scientists, Statisticians and Engineers — For the scientist, statistician, or engineer, calculators can be a complete answer book for problems from trigonometrics to hyperbolics, to multiple linear regression combined with the ability to print the results on a variety of output devices, including printers and plotters.

For Business and Industry — As a management tool for large and small companies alike. The calculator system gives users the problem solving efficiency of some large computers at the much lower cost of a programmable calculator or programmed accounting machine. Smaller companies are replacing accounting and bookkeeping machines and time-sharing services or service bureaus, by using programs developed for the various series programmable calculators. For example, they offer a solution to financial ratebook calculators for bankers, brokers and insurance or real estate salesman... from installment credit to investment analysis.

From the following pages users will see why these advanced calculators save time, money and frustration in processing difficult data handling problems. A typical application follows:

"We've had programmable calculators in operation for the last three months in our sales/service department where we use them to determine product selling prices and profitability of certain operations.

"The programmable permits us to get projections as to the selling price and profitability of products as new orders come in. To determine cost, it utilizes a cassette with prerecorded manufacturing formulas (size of box, cost to manufacturer, and suggested selling price.) Our financial statements have been reviewed and we know what our rate of profit has been over the past few years. Projected cost and selling price put out by the programmable include profit. It actually tells us what percentage of profit we can expect to recover for a particular item.

"We're not using the full capacity of each cassette. We maintain no more than two programs on any one cassette to protect outselves in case the information should be destroyed erroneously.

"Input of variable information is first prepared for the operator on a code chart by someone who knows the business. Then the operator need only refer to the chart. An automatic typewriter attachment enables us to type out readily usable forms. Other output (such as profitability analysis) is in code form, which is accessible only to management people who know the program.

"Before we installed the programmables, a salesman calling in for a quote had to wait for a reviewer to come up with all of the facts. If the reviewer was absent, the information did not go out. With the programmable, we can give the salesmen quotes at any time in about five minutes. Confidential information such as profitability considerations is coded for our protection."

Desk-Top Computing Calculator Systems, Two Examples of Many — Because of special features and high speed, the Hewlett-Packard 9825A can compute, handle peripherals, and control instruments, all effectively at the same time. By combining calculator and minicomputer features, HP's 9825A offers a "personal" computer oriented toward the solution of problems in the fields of engineering, research and statistics. A few features of this calculator: Multidimensional arrays allow users to organize data logically, thus saving program space and execution time. Memory load and record allows them to suspend processing, store the complete contents of memory on tape — including programs, data, and pointers — for continuation later on.

Direct memory access (DMA). This permits input speeds up to 400,000 16-bit words per second. Memory is expandable in 8K bytes to 32K bytes. Each bidirectional tape cartridge can store 250K bytes with an average access time of 6 seconds.

Accuracy to 12 digits with a dynamic range of 10^{-99} to 10^{99} and an internal calculation range of 10^{-511} to 10^{511} provides outstanding arithmetical capabilities.

Calculator/Controllers Offer Outstanding Interface Capability — Because of the 9825's vectored priority interrupt capability, available in the Extended I/O ROM, the calculator can act as a controller for several instruments or peripherals which require attention at unpredictable rates or times. Besides being used as a controller for instrumentation systems, it can also be used for pilot process control applications, remote data collection and production control.

As a controller, the 9825 can handle up to 45 measuring instruments simultaneously through its three I/O slots. Three optional interface cards are available: one for 16-bit parallel data, one for BCD devices, and a third — the HP-Interface Bus — for instruments that conform to IEEE Standard 488-1975.

Upper and lower case alphanumerics are available on both the 32-character LED display and the 16-character thermal printer. The 9825's high level programming language (HPL) offers power and efficiency of handling complex formulas and equations. HPL handles subroutine nesting and flags, and allows 26 simple and 26 array variables. With all this versatility and speed and weighing just 12 kg. (26 lbs), the 9825 can legitimately be considered a portable computer.

A Prompting, Programmable, Printing Calculator with an Alphanumeric Display that Communicates with the User — Strongly value-packed but at less than half the cost is Texas In-

programmable desk calculators

strument's SR-60. Its business capability ranges from solving intricate financial analyses and long-range forecasting, to simpler operations like payroll and amortization. For technology there are 46 scientific functions on the keyboard and 480 program steps for complex programming. This capacity can be expanded to 1,920 steps and 100 data memories with its optional module. Programming: The SR-60's unique 20-character display lets the user run alphanumeric programs which "ask" for information at successive stages of the problem. The SR-60 then waits for a user response before continuing. This dialogue allows even a novice to work with complicated problems immediately.

Programming is easy and straightforward yet flexible for the user with: 78 labels, 10 flags, 10 branches, 4 levels of subroutines, and 2 modes of indirect operation, and quite complete program editing capability. And, by using the printer users can list and trace the actual program execution. Programs are written and recorded on magnetic cards. With alphanumeric prompting, the cards can be used by assistants or secretaries. A person generally needs a minimum amount of instruction and a general concept of what's to be solved to have answers in seconds.

Ten prerecorded cards are included in the SR-60's Basic Library: Power transformer and filter design. Add-on rate installment loans and compound interest. Polynomial evaluation, cubic and quadratic equations. Basic statistics. Random number generator and diagnostics, etc. Well over 100 optional additional programs are available, including many on business. Printing: The SR-60's quiet printer provides a scaled replica of what appears on the alphanumeric display on 2½-inch thermal paper. Users can get a hard copy of any keyboard calculation that appears on the display, a complete program list of the contents of the data registers, whether entered from the keyboard or run from a program card.

A "Novice Helper" Feature: Desk-Top Programmable Calculator Prompts Users — The SR-60 programmable desk-top calculator features a display that communicates with the user. It includes a printer, magnetic card reader and additional function keys. With its "prompting" display, an SR-60 user can run alphanumeric programs which request information through the 20-character display at successive stages in a problem. The calculator then waits for a response before continuing with problem solving. The SR-60 is designed for both business and technical operations. For future development, the Key SR-60 is designed to accommodate I/O peripherals, which would expand its capability in data storage and variety of readout. The SR-60's silent printer gives a scaled replica of the display, with 20 characters per line on 2.5 inch wide thermal paper. Each printed character is also in a 5 x 7 dot matrix. Through the printer, the user can record results of keyboard calculations, any displayed item, complete program listings of data register contents, and a printed trace of the execution of any problem, whether entered from the keyboard or run with a program. Suggested retail price of the SR-60 was $1,695 and was available in early 1976.

The unit has 95 keys, including 40 for mathematical functions, 46 for scientific functions, and the rest mostly for instructions. It should be noted the 480 program memory locations and 40 data memories are expandable to 1,920 program locations and 100 data memories with a $700 optional module, making the total suggested price $2395. The unit can also be operated as a general purpose calculator. It has left-to-right algebraic entry and nine levels of parentheses to allow users to enter problems as they normally would say them. At the users' option, answers can be displayed, printed out on a dot-matrix thermal printer, or both. Some users suggest that the TI calculator is generally comparable in performance to Hewlett-Packard Co.'s 9815A ($2,900), Canon Inc.'s SX310 introduced in June '75 ($2,895), and Sharp Electronic Corp.'s recently introduced Model 2610 ($3,200).

TI originally shipped the SR-60 with 10 basic program cards. An additional 100 cards, designed for specific technical and business applications, were available priced from $95 each. TI was able to hold down the SR-60's manufacturing cost (and its price) by making almost everything in the unit, including the case.

Two diagnostic programs are also supplied to test the SR-60's internal operation. Users also get a Basic Library Manual which details each program, contains sample problems, user-instructions and program listings.

The SR-60 Basic Library offers a basic variety of mathematical programs. Programs that will add to user problem-solving capability: Six libraries containing well over 100 different programs are available. Finance, with 21 programs and Electrical Engineering with 16 programs were available first. The others: Math I, 20 programs. Math II, 18 programs. Statistics, 19 programs, and Surveying, 7 programs.

Here is a sampling of the kinds of problems the SR-60 can be programmed to handle:

Business — Profit and loss statements, Balance Sheets, Payroll, Trend lines, Economical ordering, Depreciation schedules, Crossover between straight line and declining balance, Loan amortization, Discounted cash flow, Simple and compound interest, Rule of 78's, Annuities, Days between dates, Date conversion, Bond yield.

Technology/Science — Evaluate complex functions, Evaluate polynomials with complex coefficients, Find real and complex roots of cubic and quadratic equations, Solve transcendental equations, Approximate integrals, Find approximate solutions of differential equations, Assist in power transformer design, Assists in filter design, Performance of many statistical calculations.

TISR-60 Prompting — The alphanumeric prompting feature used in conjunction with programming, displays letters, numbers and special symbols that let users make words and phrases that will later "ask" for entries or decisions to solve the problem. The SR-60's large (1¼ by 9¼-inch) 20-character light emitting diode display (5 by 7 dot matrix) "asks" users for their input, in terms they understand, at each stage of the problem — then waits for their keyed in response before it continues. So users really interact or "talk through" a problem — Users providing raw data, the SR-60 giving back complete answers. This rapid dialogue lets users solve a problem using different inputs, letting them explore multiple options. And, should the dialogue be interrupted, users leave the SR-60 on and its display will tell them where they are when they return.

The SR-60's prompting features helps users to know the problem by keeping track of steps and

programmable desk calculators

eliminating demands on their mental organization. As long as the user gives the appropriate input to each question, he doesn't need to know how to "solve" the problem — the SR-60 does it automatically.

Any program can be recorded on blank magnetic cards for continued use. Algebraic operating system (AOS) with 9 levels of parentheses solves problems with up to 10 pending operations. Entry is left-ro-right just as the problem is written. Results are displayed up to 10 digits, plus two more for power of 10 exponents. The SR-60's trace mode key automatically begins recording all calculations whether entered from the keyboard or run with a program. So users can see how the program is being executed. This is very useful for editing and debugging a program. It conveniently lets users verify that instructions are keyed in correctly and get a quick check on hastily constructed programs, or programs not carefully documented. Users verify that program results are based on correctly formulated problems.

SR-60 Keys and Programming Procedure — Programming is really no more than taking small problems and integrating them to solve bigger problems. On the SR-60 programming is merely listing the keystrokes necessary to carry the problem through to its solution. Some may still feel that programming is too complex for the untrained person to master. A view that probably is helped along by the vocabulary associated with programming. Words like direct and indirect addressing, conditional and unconditional branching, labels, and flags sound esoteric and abstract. Yet these words are just a shorthand use to describe manipulations almost anyone can grasp. In fact, they're not even mathematical.

Even though the SR-60 has many functions, no one can anticipate all their needs. Fifteen user-defined keys are provided to make them any function users may need. The Label key tells the SR-60 that the next key pressed will be a label. There are 77 keys, including the user-defined keys, that can be used as labels. If Positive, If Zero, and If Error are keys that test the contents of the display. Branching occurs if the conditions: positive, zero, or flashing display are true. Branching occurs if the conditions are not true when these keys are prefixed by the 2nd key.

Alternate calculating paths can be defined by the Set Flag key followed by a number from 0 through 9 then the Test Flag key tests the state of the flag — set or reset. The SR-60 branches if the specified flag is set, or continues sequentially if the flag is not set. 2nd, Test Flag reverses the sense of the test. The indirect addressing (IND) key is used with unconditional, conditional and data memory keys. An example: IND, TFLG, 2,05. means that SR-60 tests flag number 2, and looks at the contents of the data memory register 05 to find the program address to which to branch if flag 2 is set. The Que key halts the SR-60's operation and waits for a response from these keys: Yes, No, Not Known, Not Apply, Enter. Press Yes and the SR-60 branches to the first label which follows Que. Pressing No causes it to branch to the second label, and so on. These five label keys are equivalent to a five-way branch. The alphabetical letters and symbols on keys are activated by the Alpha key to enter prompting messages for display or print. The convenient Pause key permits a message or result to be displayed for about ½ second.

The SR-60's editing and debugging keys let users go through a program one step at a time. Or single-step backward through a program. The Insert key moves the current and all following instructions down one location so that a change can be made at any place within a program without rewriting it. Users remove the displayed instruction and move all following instructions up with the Delete key. The SR-60 can als print a trace, or a record, of all functions, numbers and calculations.

Two Prompting/Programming Examples That Show How Easy the SR-60 Operates

Compound Interest
(Solve for Present Value)

Step Prompting Message/ Printout	Your Response
1. Enter present value	Not known
2. Enter interest %	9
3. Enter no. periods	24
4. Enter future value	5000
5. Present value (Printed)	

Payroll Calculation*

Step Prompting Message/ Printout	Your Response
1. Enter employee card	Feed card into SR-60
2. Employee SSN (Printed)	
3. Company number (Printed)	
4. Regular hours	Enter straight time hours
5. Overtime rate 1	Enter time and one-half hours
6. Overtime rate 2	Enter double time hours.
7. Miscellaneous pay	Enter miscellaneous pay
8. Gross wages (Printed)	
9. Federal withholding tax (Printed)	
10. State withholding tax (Printed)	
11. Local withholding tax (Printed)	
12. FICA deduction (Printed)	
13. Voluntary deductions (Printed)	
13. Voluntary deductions (Printed)	
14. Total voluntary deduction (Printed)	
15. Net wages due (Printed)	
16. Year to date totals for each of above printed)	
17. Enter employee card for update	Feed card into SR-60 (records all year to date totals on employees card)

* Requires optional expansion module.

64-Step Programmable Calculator — The Sharp PC-1001 electronic calculator is actually a programmable unit, designed specifically for scientific and engineering use. It is capable of performing 15 different scientific functions including trigonometric, inverse trigonometric, hyperbolic, logarithmic, and exponential. It has 10 digits mantissa, two digits exponent, and eight memories. Programming of functions is already incorporated in the LSI, permitting instant computation of functions with the touch of a key. Both floating decimal point and exponential positioning systems are offered. In addition, 64 steps of programming or 8 registers are available for formula and equation evaluation.

BURROUGHS FINANCIAL BUSINESS MANAGEMENT SYSTEMS CALCULATOR

The Burroughs C 7200 Printing Programmable Calculator, combined with Burroughs Financial Program Products, can speed and simplify calculations for many financial computations. Below are just a few of the Program Products available in the comprehensive library:

Installment Loan
    Annual Percentage Rate
    (A.P.R.)
    Add-on Rate
    Discount Rate
Installment Loan
— Auto Dealer
Installment Loan
— Skip Payment
Installment Loan
— 90-Day Deferred Payment
Interest Scheduling
— Rule of 78's
Term Computation from
Monthly Payment, Principal, and Interest
Dealer Participation
Single-Payment Loan
— Simple Interest
Single-Payment Loan
— Simple Interest Discounted Single Payment Loan
— Simple Interest Discounted with Exact Proceeds and Fee
Savings Calculation
— Saving Deposit Compounded Daily, Monthly, Quarterly, Annually, Future Value — Present Value
Annuity Calculation
— Multiple Deposit Compounded Daily, Monthly, Quarterly, Semi-Annually, Annually
    Future Value —
    Present Value
Term Deposit Redemption
Mortgage Loan
— Monthly Payment
Amortization Schedule
Unpaid Principal and Equity Calculation
Continuous Compounding

The Wang 400 Series — This series offers users up to 320 program steps to help solve time-consuming everyday math problems rapidly because most Programmable Calculators of the standard programs needed like $\sqrt{x}$ and other basic functions are hard-wired. With 320 steps of Learn Mode Programming, the 400 series units permit users to write and design their own programs. The decision-making capabilities, such as "skip if+" or "skip if 0" can be written into user programs. Other functions permit automatic branching to any portion of the program as well as looping and stacking. The special function keys are molded, high rise permitting instant access to up to 32 hard-wired routines and up to 32 of the user's own programmed routines. Each register or program is clearly labeled with color-coded interchangeable routine strips. The 400 series can save up to 50 separate subtotals at once, and results can be recalled for use as needed. Two "scratch register", full number entry keys, and programming control and editing keys make the 400 series a strong desk-top competitor in its class.

The Wang 400 Series also offers several program libraries to aid users in special function calculating. The General Stat/Math library encompasses Regression Analysis, Binomial Coefficients, etc. The General Business library offers Investment Withdrawal, Average Growth Rates, etc. Also data or routines that are used routinely can be prepunched on standard 80 column cards with Wang's Punched Card Programmer precluding the need to reenter the data or program through the keyboard. Also, using the data or program steps that users mark with a pencil on special cards, the Marked Sense Card Programmer permits users to get information into the calculator automatically and quickly.

The "450 Scientist" model offers a Special Routine Strip indicating the hard-wired capabilities from r to $\log_{10} x$ for engineers to X! Mean, variance, standard deviation for statisticians plus 16 complete registers to perform direct and indirect storage routines in arithmetic. Each register offers complete single keystroke results, displayed instantly. To execute, users press one button — and the same keys can be used for other calculations. The model 452 Advanced Scientist adds hyperbolics and trigonometric functions to the capability of the model 450 with single commands. The model 462 Advanced Statistician offers fingertip control to make single keystroke statistical calculations. All 400 Series models can solve up to 6 simultaneous equations quickly and can complete matrix inversions up to 6×6 in less than 2 minutes.

Monroe 1400 Series Programmable Desk-Top Calculators — Another of the keyboard programmable series of printing calculators, the typical 1450 offers 17 different keyboard options. It also has a non-add/date key and a large display with choice of print and display or display only. Options include two accumulators, percent change key, percent plus key, and chain discount key. The provision for amendments in the series is the options specifically required for particular businesses or other users. In effect, users can build their own calculator by selecting from a total of 17 different options for the models 1440 and 1450. They cover independent accumulation, extra memories and constants, percent-change, mark-up, change sign, reverse key, item count, square root, sum of first factors, etc. Users can customize these functions to a single option key. A plug-in unit is sort of a black box. On it, users find the 16 function keys for these various options. This 'Customizer' is designed after individual consultation with the Monroe representative.

Computer Cassette Utility Built Into Calculator Line — The Compucorp line starts with the Alpha 325 a desk-top computer that has over 100 preprogrammed operations and can store both programs and data on a tape cassette. For greater portability users may choose the Beta 326, a hand-held unit with similar capabilities. The 325 does trig and algebra and handles calculations with up

programmable desk calculators

to four levels of paranthesis. Programs are accepted from tape in 416 step increments and the unit features 12 data registers, a two-color printer and 12 digit display. Computation is 13 digits with a range of 10^{-98} to 10^{99}. The 326 has no printer and holds 160 rather than 416 steps. Both units include 13-digit capability plus program commands for branch, six subroutine levels and seven conditional statements. Also edit operations such as verify, insert, delete or modify are easily done on the keyboard. As a bonus, the 325 will interface directly to a TTY. The 325 selling price is below $2000.

Programs and Data Are Stored on a Tape Cassette — All arithmetic operations are performed algebraically, just as they're written on paper. Plus parentheses four levels deep. It has both a printer and display, yet it takes up less room on desk than the average in-basket. A magnetic tape drive is included to allow users to read programs or data into the Alpha 325. The tape drive can as easily receive programs or data from the Alpha 325 and record them for future use. And a user's entire program library can be stored as a unit since a single 1½ ounce cassette holds over 150,000 program steps or 4,000 data values.

Programmable from the keyboard, the Alpha 325 also automatically accepts blocks of programs from tape in 416 step increments. Under program controls, users can call another program and store or recall data from tape. Besides providing a permanent record of computations, the printer is also extremely handy for listing program steps and data values, and for editing and verifying programs.

Over 100 Pre-Programmed Operations Save Time and Memory — To save program memory and make calculations easier, over 100 pre-programmed operations for logarithms, trigonometry, statistics and even 24 metric conversions are hardwired into the unit. For example, users can perform trigonometric functions with a keystroke, determine the standard deviation of a sample of grouped or ungrouped data, and convert kilograms per square centimeter to pounds per square inch. For all trigonometric functions, the Alpha 325 works in degrees, grads, radians and degrees, minutes and seconds. All arithmetic operations can be performed using degrees, minutes and seconds (or hours, minutes and seconds) with the results formatted, 11 28 33 6000 ; the printer formats 11 28 33 • 6

Programming Is as Easy as Working from the Keyboard — Programming is a simple extension of the Alpha 325's basic mathematical operation. Users enter computations in load mode just as they would calculate it in run mode when solving the problem from the keyboard. They switch back to run and simply enter the variables. Ease of use extends beyond elementary programming. Program editing has been made extremely easy. Users can move back and forth in memory, verifying, inserting, deleting or modifying any number of program steps. They can even step through a program to watch its execution one step at a time. Or they can automatically list the entire program. The printer provides a permanent record of all steps entered, with step number codes and mnemonics. Jumping, branching, six levels of subroutines, labeled addressing and seven conditional statements for testing are all standard features. In addition, Compucorp has written a program paks for a wide range of applications.

Compucorp Alpha 327 Offers An Optional I/O Peripheral Interface to Provide a Formatted and Typed Solution to Problems — Whether users are solving problems with keyboard calculations, using programmed solutions to problems in Engineering, Surveying, Science, Mathematics, and Statistics, estimating quantities for proposal preparation, or accumulating data on the tape memory for subsequent processing with typed results, the Alpha 327 provides a solution. A Tape Cassette Memory — gives users a massive storage of programs and data on inexpensive, widely available audio grade cassettes. Operates manually or under program control for automatic storage and retrieval of data and automatic sequencing of programs.

Programming Controls make it easy for users to Write, Track, and Edit programs. Programming is powerful yet simple. Users can be an expert in their field without becoming an expert in math. A Format key is used to control the significance of numbers displayed and printed. Regardless of the format setting, numbers are carried internally to 13-digit accuracy with 2 exponent digits.

Data storage register controls let users access 44 registers, directly or indirectly, and do math operations into and out of each register.

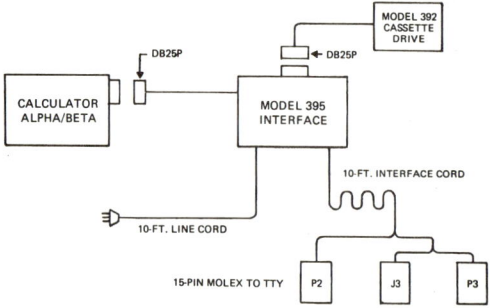

The Monroe 395 Teleprinter Interface — The Monroe 395 Teleprinter Interface was designed to enable Monroe Model 325, 326 and 1800 Series programmable calculators, as noted, to have the capability of direct on-line communication to line printers, teletypes®, laboratory/medical instruments, and phones with acoustic coupler or modem attachments. The Monroe Alpha 325 or Beta 326 Microprogrammable calculators when interfaced to the 395 teleprinter will: accept numerical data

programmable desk calculators

directly into the ENTRY register for calculation or storage in a data register; output a number from the ENTRY register through the 395 interface to the peripheral device; generate a Carriage Return and Line Feed on the peripheral for data formatting; accept a string of up to 72 alphanumeric characters, store them in data registers and then output to a Model 392 cassette or back through the 395 to the peripheral for additional use. The Models 325 or 326 calculator with 395 interface have the ability to output their programs to a teletype® paper-tape punch or read them back into program memory from a paper-tape reader. The 395 when used with the Model 325 or 326 calculators can be interfaced to devices having a 20mA current loop, EAI RS-232C or CCITT V.24 interface. The acceptable character coding is ASCII at 110 baud, 10 characters per second alpha or program, or 5 characters per second numerical data, either half or full duplex. The Model 395 Teleprinter Interface is priced at about $500.00.

Rockwell 900 Series of Desk-Top Programmable Calculators — The Rockwell 900 Series programmable calculators were designed for people who have never before used a programmable. It is a line of machines that will increase productivity in a full range of business calculations. In manufacturing and marketing companies. In banking. In insurance. In real estate, etc.

The Rockwell 900 series calculators are virtual desk-top computers that include a printer, a display, a magnetic card reader, and other auxiliary devices. The model 940 machines, for example will let users record programs for various business calculations on magnetic cards — once — then use those cards to automate the process thereafter.

The Magnetic card reader — To load a program, the operator depresses one key and inserts the card into the slot. The program loads instantly and the card pops up for removal. Each magnetic card can store 256 program instructions on each side, or a total of 512. Cards can be used for data storage as well as program storage. They are easy to handle and file, with the title of each program readily visible. Standard functions on the keyboard include reciprocals, powers, square roots, natural logs, and antilogs. The availability of these functions saves program steps in many business and scientific applications and greatly enhances the value of the 900 Series as problem solvers.

Programming power — The Rockwell 900 Series uses "keyboard" language, a straightforward calculator language. The calculators have full decision-making capability, with conditional or unconditional jumps. Direct addressing to permit jumps directly to a step number. Symbolic addressing to any label for simplified programming. The ability to list programs on the printed tape. Simple debugging and editing, with easy program expansion or contraction. Subroutine capability of nesting up to five levels deep. And memory indirect (INDIR), a powerful "pointer memory" that simplifies and shortens programs. All this means maximum flexibility and more computing throughout for users.

Rockwell Model 920 Specifications — Electronic 14-digit printing/display calculator, 10-key accumulator (+, −, S, T, Add Mode), calculator functions (×, ÷, %, =, constants), automatic item and accumulation counters, automatic 1st and 2nd

factor accumulations, 9 basic registers and optional expansion registers with direct register arithmetic, indirect register addressing, $1/x$, x^y, ln x, e^x, $\sqrt{}$, overflow and error detection, tape audit sumbols, 192 basic programming steps with optional expansion, program edit functions (replace, insert, delete, back-up, list, trace), subroutine nesting, conditional and unconditional program transfers (positive, negative, zero, no entry), absolute and label program addressing, magnetic card system with card validity test.

The Rockwell Model 930 — User Definable Electronic Printing/Display Programmable Calculator — The programming characteristics are: MODE CONTROLS: MANUAL, PROG, LIST, EDIT, RUN. PROGRAM CONTROLS: JUMP and GO SUB (conditional or unconditional), LABEL, INDIR, PRINT, SPACE, RETURN, STOP. MEMORY CAPACITY: Available with a basic 192 steps separate from data storage with optional expanded memory up to 960 steps, subroutine nesting to 5 levels, absolute, label, and indirect program addressing. EDITING CAPABILITIES: Replace, insert, delete, back-up, list, trace. Among the registers are: Basic memory registers 1 — 9 with M+, M−, = +, = −, ◊, *, EXCHANGE functions and accumulation counter, basic and expanded optional registers (up to 99) use ↑ M/IN, ← M/OUT with register arithmetic (+, −, EXCHANGE) and indirect addressing. The magnetic card system permits 32 data registers or 256 program instructions on each half card with card validity test.

programmable desk calculators

Fundamental specifications: Electronic 14-digit printing/display calculator, 10-key accumulator (+, −, S, T, Add Mode), calculator functions (×, ÷, %, =, constants), automatic item and accumulation counters, automatic 1st and 2nd factor accumulations, 11 user definable keys, 9 basic registers and optional expansion to 99 registers with direct register arithmetic, indirect register addressing, $1/x$, x^y, $\ln x$, e^x, $\sqrt{\ }$, overflow and error detection, tape audit symbols, 192 basic programming steps with optional expansion to 960 steps, program edit functions (replace, insert, delete, back-up, list, trace), subroutine nesting, conditional and unconditional program transfers (positive, negative, zero, no entry), absolute, label, and indirect program addressing, magnetic card system with card validity test.

The 930, in addition to its unique method of customized keys, also allows users to key in own programs through the simple-to-operate keyboard or they can select programs from a continually expanding program library. Program and data storage memories are expandable up to 960 steps and 99 memories. A versatile repertoire of programming instructions is available including: conditional and unconditional program transfers; absolute, label and indirect program addressing; replace, insert, delete, back-up, list, and trace functions; and a magnetic read/write card system with card validity test.

Rockwell Model 940 — Electronic Printing/Display Programmable Calculator with Financial Functions — The general specifications are: Electronic 14-digit printing/display calculator, 10-key accumulator (+, −, S, T, Add Mode), calculator functions (×, ÷, %, =, constants), automatic item and accumulation counters, automatic 1st and 2nd factor accumulations, 9 basic registers and optional expansion registers with direct register arithmetic, indirect register addressing, $1/x$, x^y, $\ln x$, e^x, $\sqrt{\ }$, period, interest, payment, present value, future value, APR/rate of return, depreciation, amortization, loan rebate/forecast, days, % change, overflow and error detection, tape audit symbols, 192 basic programming steps with optional expansion, program edit functions (replace, insert, delete, back-up, list, trace), subroutine nesting, conditional and unconditional program transfers (positive, negative, zero, no entry), absolute and label program addressing, magnetic card system with card validity test.

Rockwell 960 Scientific Unit — The Rockwell Model 960 Scientific Programmable Calculator brings together in one unit the ease of actual algebraic hierarchy language in pure equation form, the versatility of a print and display calculator, the immediate convenience of magnetic card data and program storage and a versatile set of scientific, conversion, statistical and user definable functions. Not a cure-all for the calculator market, but a finely honed tool for the scientist and his associates. This system allows users to write, edit, preserve and use programs to solve their equations and data handling problems with unprecedented cost efficiency.

Major Features:
- A complete natural algebraic language that recognizes hierarchy of mathematical functions, parenthetic implied multiplication and equation entry syntax.
- Logical, efficient programming with insert, delete, list, list and execute and automatic address update capability. Conditional program decisions based on size, sign, entry or flag. Numeric, label, indirect or computed program addressing. Numeric, indirect, incremental, and computed register addressing with register arithmetic into or out of any register. Multiple key stroke sequences are compiled to single or double word program steps saving valuable program area. Up to 1000 steps of very efficient programming are available.
- Formatted tape output with identifiers and red or black dotted line separators.
- Large, easy-to-read display for monitoring entry or output.
- 100+ scientific hand wired functions available from the keyboard or as program steps.
- Ten user definable keys to program for single key entry or operation.
- Output decimal formatting system which allows fixed 0-9 decimals, full floating, scientific notation or automatic Pico, Nano, Micro, Milli, Kilo, Mega, Giga, etc.

Rockwell 960 Decisions Capabilities —

	Conditional Statement	
Instruction Sequence	Jump	Subroutine Transfer
Transfer if the displayed value is positive	JUMP + ...	GO SUB + ...
Transfer if the displayed value is negative	JUMP − ...	GO SUB − ...
Transfer if the displayed value is zero	JUMP = ...	GO SUB = ...
Transfer if there is not a keyboard entry	JUMP ÷ ...	GO SUB ÷ ...
Transfer if the FLAG is set	JUMP × ...	GO SUB × ...

programmable desk calculators

Programming power relates to conditioned and unconditional program transfers of address, looping and subroutine nesting to six levels provide extremely efficient and powerful programming. Addressing of any step may be accomplished directly or indirectly. 100 labels are provided for symbolic addressing.

Editing aids include the ability to backstep and correct in program mode, list single step forward or reverse, list entire program, list single step with execution or list continuous with execution, single or multiple step delete and insert with automatic update of symbolic addresses, and error or overflow messages that call out the step number where the problem occurred. Step number is displayed and printed in program and edit mode along with a printed 6-column alphanumeric mnemonic for each instruction.

Rockwell User Definable Keys — The Rockwell 960 was designed with automatic permanent subroutines for most common scientific functions (i.e. SIN, COS, X^y, etc.). However, most realize that every professional scientist or engineer within his own discipline may have several valuable routines that are particularly important to his endeavors. To fill this need, Rockwell incorporated the ability of allowing the user to redefine the operation of ten keys. Therefore, by moving a switch to "CUSTOM", users can "customize" the keyboard operation of those ten keys to execute any desired preprogrammed routine.

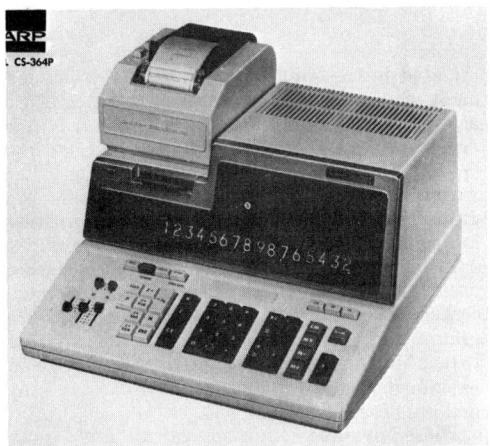

Sharp Offers the CS-364P-II Electric Calculator — It can program up to 144 main routine steps into nine groups and 144 subroutine steps with speed and convenience. The answer is printed too, if desired. (See above) Each program is stored on a magnetic card for future reference. Users insert the magnetic card into the slot conveniently located on the upper front below the printer, and the data is instantly printed out. The user's own specially programmed library of calculations is available anytime they need it.

LSI (Large-Scale-Integration) makes the difference. Thousands of parts are eliminated to provide maximum miniaturization. At the same time performance is significantly improved. The unit has 12 memory registers, 3 working registers and program storage. It can carry out the simplest to the most complex calculations up to 16 digits instantly. A special "DEBUG" mode enables logical thinking for mathematical calculations. And each program is easily and quickly checked by the "CHECK" mode operation. A special jump system also enables programs to be repeated, branched and jumped by simply pressing a button. Other extras include zero suppress system, electronic punctuation, rounding up/off/down device and automatic credit balance systems.

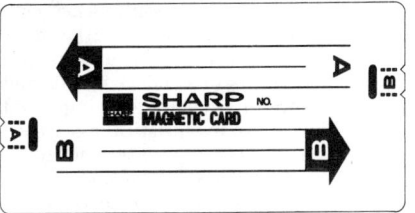

Magnetic Card Completely Independent Subroutines — Subroutines are completely independent of main routines and the subroutines alone may be recorded on the magnetic cards. They are also used for manual operation so users can get the answers to various kinds of functions with one-touch key operations. Users can develop external memorization of numerals. Operation DATA, RECORD gives the instruction to record the numbers stored in all the 12 memory registers on the magnetic card and DATA ENTER gives the instruction to transfer the numerals recorded on the magnetic card to memory registers.

Efficient Magnetic Card System — Once the programming is complete, programs are easily recorded on magnetic cards. Required programs are instantly written in program storage with a simple one-touch operation of the keys with the magnetic card inserted into the card reader. Convenient jumping system makes these units virtually a "mini-computer". Programs can be repeated, branched and jumped. The unit includes unconditional jump, negative jump and non-zero jump system and sub-routine jump for maximum versatile utility. The Programs are easily checked and corrected. The number of steps and instructions are displayed step by step when S key is depressed in "CHECK" mode. Programs can be optionally jumped by depressing numeral keys after touching → x < 0, x = 0, SUB keys. Programs can be corrected by depressing the CP key. The "DEBUG" function mode is for educational instruction. Effective for logical thinking in mathematics, intermediate results and next instruction of the operation process are displayed step by step when S key is depressed in "DEBUG" mode.

Personal Computing Power for Immediate Users — It has been concluded by many surveys, research reports and in-house analyses that many users have been spending too much money on computing. They generally need quicker answers for department heads even while they are planning the next step in a specific analysis. Advanced calculators can help very significantly. Many American and worldwide corporations are devoted to supplying information systems based on calculators to all types of operating and research sectors of modern industry. They serve government, educational institutions and professional disciplines including medicine, health care and the pure sciences, to mention only a sample of a vast range of users.

computing calculators

In particular, they provide software and systems using desk-top programmable computing calculators (under $6,000) that compete with mathematical and data reduction systems using time-shared terminals. They feel that personal, stand-alone units, having all the power and flexibility of time-shared use of computer mainframes, can be a superior alternative to getting mathematical and system computing done. Using a computer through a terminal often means that users are cramped with a small workspace, and saturation problems start troubling them when usage increases. Using calculator systems, they can check results and proceed without formal requests for computer time. Many firms specialize in statistical analysis, engineering, financial, etc. software and have put many millions of dollars in development of the fine pragmatic, documented and tested programs offered for individual types of computing. Leaders in many fields seem to agree with approaches of decentralized calculator-based computing.

Many major systems offer only a stereotyped analysis decided upon from the start by the accounting department and it does not always produce all the information the data can offer. And even the liberal printing-out of intermediate results at the end of a long calculation does not allow the user of information to involve himself in the analysis to the same degree as is possible if the calculations are broken down into smaller sections, the results of which are then inspected immediately. These considerations strongly favor the small advanced electronic calculators which are now becoming available at more reasonable costs.

Whether users presently have access to computers or they use older calculators, they should consult these pages to see what vast new ranges and kinds of problems small advanced calculator units sitting right on user desks can do. They might ask a calculator systems representative to arrange a demonstration. If information problems lie in applied statistics, management, engineering, finance or hundreds of other advanced concepts, calculators can really help resolve the problems and distribute answers quickly and directly.

PART 2 — Section Four

COMPUTING CALCULATORS: PORTABLE COMPUTERS WITH ATTACHED, SIMPLIFIED KEYBOARDS, IMMEDIATE USER CONTROL

It is perhaps only academic or even futile to attempt to establish a fine line between advanced programmable desk calculators and the expanding group of calculator systems which are being popularly called, 'Computing Calculators.' It is also certainly probable that various manufacturers would feel slighted if their top model, priced in the $4000 to $7000 range was not included in this 'supercalculator' group. Thus, it was decided to consider for inclusion in this classification (and price range) the 'top of the line' of most of the major large system calculator manufacturers and suggest that they all compete with each other — and with the bottom of the IBM line, its 5100 portable computer. Honeywell, Burroughs, and other major computer manufacturers are also stretching downward to meet in this 'simple keyboard, portable computer' battle.

Although the IBM 5100 sells for from $8,975 to $19,975, such leading advanced calculator manufacturers as Hewlett-Packard (the leader), Wang (22000 desk-top programmables have sold over the past ten years), Tektronix, Monroe, Victor, Sharp, Compucorp, and others use strong promotion lines stating their top units outperform the IBM 5100 and are available at far less cost. . . . "three to five times faster and as much as 40 percent less expensive." H-Ps 9825A was introduced at $5900 while its 9830 was selling for $6800. Potential users will find interesting performance comparisons.

These major advanced computing calculator systems have, in effect, combined calculator and mini-computer features to offer 'personal computers' oriented to the solution of problems in management, engineering, research and statistical areas as well as many other business, medical, scientific, and industrial control environments. Live keyboards let users examine and change program variables, call subroutines, record and list programs, etc. while other operations are in progress. Multidimensional arrays allow users to organize data logically. Memory load and record permits users to suspend processing, store the complete contents of memory on tape — including data, programs, and pointers — for continuation later on. Direct Memory Access, Vectored Priority, etc. are explained as the capabilities of particular units and are described on later pages.

These advanced computing calculators also use practically all types of regular computer peripherals, (with appropriate interfaces) high-level languages, such as BASIC, versions of IBM's PL-1, (or FORTRAN) such as Hewlett-Packard's HPL, and others. These units operate as time-sharing terminals of standard computer systems. (For example, the HP 9830), accepts plug-in ROMs, data communications packages (software) and protocols and uses standard modems. Keyboard overlays (templates), extensive plotting capabilities and the use of interface units for utilizing IBM Selectric Typewriters (the Tycom 9800 interface, for example) are all common attributes of top of the line calculators of several major suppliers. Tasks such as gathering and processing data, controlling numerical-input equipment, operating test equipment and providing terminal services are ideal for these calculators. Evaluations of capabilities relate to: peripheral capabilities; system speed; programming language; storage requirements; data input-output conveniences plus the other standards as: program documentation, vendor support, program security and facilities and environmental requirements, maintenance, and most importantly, total system cost. An operating system often forms the first part of supplied programs. Users can keep their programs on cassette tapes, in addition to the library of common test and diagnostic programs. Key advantages of advanced calculator systems are the systems control abilities to communicate with external devices, such as, instruments, graphic equipment, transducers, computers and computer components, relays, and other programmable equipment, especially that requiring feedback. The IEEE 488 interface is a major step toward direct calculator communication. Also on these major systems, checked out software, cards, tapes, etc., can be changed to firmware, often Programmable ROMs, providing tremendous flexibility. The use of the calculator's subroutine capability greatly simplifies user programming, and the separation of program and data-storage areas has become most efficient. Because those units that use BASIC are now given memory size in bytes, evaluators using registers, for program steps or data registers must make some conversions to properly judge merit. These major units now also offer CRT (Cathode Ray Tube) display and storage, Tektronix providing hard copy from the tube display.

THE BASIS OF ADVANCED CALCULATOR SYSTEM EVALUATION CRITERIA

The cost is always major in the selection of calculators, minis, and micros. The prime question is concerned with which will do the job adequately at the best price. Although the hardware price and the software development are primarily involved, users must be careful in pertinent evaluations to consider the total cost of getting the calculating equipment into a working distributed information system as very basic. The hidden costs of software development, interface design, service requirements, etc. are usually not significant with programmable calculators. High-speed and/or extra large memory formerly were not considerations, but the power and versatility of today's programmable calculators must often effectively fill the bill of particulars for high speed system integration. Many calculator-based software systems being sold today have been developed by system houses for custom applications, or have been designed by customer companies for their own in-house use. Customized calculator-based communication systems have also been developed and are currently operational in many manufacturing facilities. Many systems are selling fast because the relatively easily controlled and expandable speed, memory, and programming requirements all point to lower cost, simply operated programmable calculators as logical choices. At convenient points in time, fast decisions can be made to add the capability of testing other calculator control, processing or communication components for complete systems. Being added to many units are new levels of input-output versatility. These systems also have additional programming for more management-conceived applications and are opening the door for future programs and for applications not yet conceived. The speed, memory, and software requirements now satisfied by calculators are very similar to the original requirements of the medium to large standard computer systems of just a year or two ago. There is no doubt that the programmable calculator has the most economical and satisfactory solutions for the many thousands of systems in the accounting, engineering, educational, and general business fields. It's very easy to switch to divisional operators, and/or local manager control without retraining costs or divided responsibilities.

Significant addition of flexibility includes: data output that can be formated and listed with headings and other labels, allowing direct composition of reports and summaries and display of messages. Prompting permits notification of the operator for some action or interaction with the display, printer or audible device. Evaluators can expect that more units will be available with the BASIC language. The BASIC interpreter will be resident in ROM so users won't be bothered with the problem of loading interpreters. Complete computing calculator systems generally cost about $10,000 to $12,000, with all the 'bells and whistles,' but they are still more flexible, convenient, and cost-effective than practically all minicomputers and certainly more accomodating that small standard computers. Calculator system memories now routinely move up to 32,768 steps (or bytes). Tape cartridges can hold 250,000 bytes with 2750 byte/s transfer rates.

Direct User Decisions and Benefits — The calculator solution is usually under various specific managers' direct control. They have hands-on flexibility that will give them complete solutions in their own working environment. Selection of the proper tool in analyzing data and reaching conclusions generally depends upon the following:
1. The return of investment on labor and equipment,
2. Complexity of the problem,
3. Time available for a solution,
4. Degree of accuracy required,
5. Ease in learning to use the tool,
6. Proper size ratio of tool to problem.

The calculator solution to data analysis problems may well be the answer... and justified by any of the above considerations. The tools calculators can provide, are not only cost effective, but designed to solve the kind of problems which previously were either solved by hand or overwhelmed by an expensive computer. The calculator solution gives users flexibility, ease of operation, accurate documentation, and fast results. Results now can save considerable time and money.

The Mini Vs. Calculator Decision — The decision to use a programable calculator rather than a minicomputer will be most favorable when two or more of the following conditions are met:
- Input/output rates are less than 100 and preferably 10 or fewer per second.
- The equipment will be used for applications which require frequent program changes.
- Persons using or responsible for the installation are not adept at minicomputer programming in assembly language.
- Common sense is needed in deciding what needs to be controlled and what doesn't and to avoid both the oversimplified and the overcomplicated system.
- All computer purchases must be approved by people in the data processing department who

computing calculators

would consider only expensive exotic hardware.
- Total installed cost, including software and interconnection, is one of the most important considerations.
- The system will be used for hands-on experimental, demonstration, or training purposes or a simulator for distributed processing systems.

Within the above criteria, calculator-based systems have been successfully applied in areas such as:
- Automotive guaging and classification of power steering pump components.
- Automated quality control in the chemical and pharmaceutical industry.
- Data acquisition in agricultural yield analysis programs.
- Control of universal testing machines and electrohydraulic fatigue testers.
- Multipoint water quality analysis by government agencies.
- Control of cement composition as a function of elemental analysis and raw material cost.
- Determination of jet afterburner performance.
- Plant output and efficiency analysis in the manufacture of ceramic dinnerware.

With the advent of the new Basic language calculators oriented to data communication and remote control, a whole new range of applications is opened:
- Tank level gauging and inventory control in bulk storage terminals, including product accounting and billing.
- Monitor and control of smaller sewage treatment plants.
- Centralized logging of stack gas and effluent parameters in pollution control applications.
- Batching and weighing operations in animal feed production, ready-mix concrete plants, and similar activities.
- Control and water flow analysis of large-scale irrigation system.
- Pipeline condition monitoring systems.
- Supervisory data collection and overall plant control.
- Production and down-time monitoring of machine tools using remote counting techniques.

The H-P Model 9810 and the Recently Introduced Model 9815 — The Model 9810 is a programmable Calculator for Repetitive Problems. From keyboard to memory, peripherals to program packages users may configure their Model 9810 programmable calculator to satisfy many situations. Model 9810's do tasks from surveying problems to statistical analysis. Plug-in keyboard modules customize keyboards for the application at hand and sharply cut programming and computing time. An alphanumeric printer gives users clearly labeled output that can be read without decoding. And with 500 program steps and 51 data-storage registers of memory (both expandable) the Model 9810 has plenty of power for solving a system of 10 simultaneous equations or doing a complete regression analysis.

The H-P 9815 calculator combines keystroke calculating convenience, dedicated problem solving and an optional two-channel I/O to give users versatility and power in solving problems from the simple to the sophisticated. An AUTO-START capability and high-speed dual-track data cartrige capable of storing 96,384 bytes of data and programs are features that make the 9815A calculator a variable and easily customized choice for virtually any lab. Add optional interface capabilities and users can easily extend powerful 9815 desk-top computing capabilities.

The 13-opound (5.9 kg) calculator features the Hewlett-Packard stack-oriented logic system simplifying keystroke calculations and giving fast answers. The buffered keyboard contains 24 preprogrammed functions, 4 arithmetic keys plus keys for memory-stack manipulation and 15 special function keys. The thermal printer prints up to 16 characters per line at 2.8 lines per second. In addition, there is an easy-to-read numeric display. With the addition of the optional two-channel I/O structure, users can add 9815 Series peripheral devices, including the 9871 printer/plotter, (see ahead) The 9862 plotter, tape reader or tape punches, or a digitizer.

The 9815 also mates with BCD instruments and devices with 8-bit parallel interfaces. The 9815 accommodates the Hewlett-Packard Interface Bus, (HP-IB) allows users to control, gather, and process data from as many as 14 different HP-IB compatible test and measurement instruments. The 9815 contains computer language functions for programming power and performance. The standard 9815 has 472 steps of program memory and 10 data storage registers. An option is available to expand the calculator's internal memory to 2,008 program steps. Many standard problem solutions are available from the extensive library of pre-recorded programs in statistics, engineering, science and surveying.

Model 9815 Operating Characteristics — A series of keystrokes can be stored in the memory of the 9815 to solve the same problem many times. Then users recall the program any time they wish. They stroke the keys only once, the 9815 does it from then on. The 9815 provides them with a set of keys that lets them control their program. These keys are grouped on the left of the calculator keyboard. They provide appropriate instructions to organize and direct the execution of the program. The keystrokes reference easy-to-remember mnemonics like GO TO or STEP.

The programming language of the 9815 brings

computing calculators

together decision making ability and efficient execution. For example, the IF instruction acts as a qualifier for making decisions. Similarly, FOR NEXT loops automatically control repetition of program segments. GO TO, GO TO X, GO SUB X all identify branching instructions that tell the calculator where to execute the next step in computation. SUBROUTINES in 9815 logic can be nested up to seven deep. And FLAGS can be set to identify special program conditions. Users may want to modify or correct their program. The special editing features of the 9815 help them change program steps, update their program addressing, recall any program step, and step through any program sequence with ease and convenience. Simple and direct keystrokes establish a rapid and natural editing technique that is represented in three easy steps. First, users list their program. Program steps and instructions are labeled in language they understand. In most cases, error messages tell precisely what went wrong in concise phrases. Second, users identify the areas of the program they would like to change. They key in that particular address, and make that change. If this step requires that branching addresses in the program be changed, the 9815 takes care of it automatically. The third step in the editing process is simply to run the program to verify the changes.

H-P 9815 Cartridges, Overlays and Programs — A cartridge, key overlay, and AUTO START let users dedicate the 9815 to solve their problem. The cartridge carries the prerecorded program to the 9815. The overlay labels the 15 user-definable keys for single keystroke execution of program steps — that define a function special to various professions, unique operations, or commands required for peripherals. When users turn the power on, the AUTO START feature automatically loads File 0 and executes the program. Also Hewlett-Packard has an extensive library of programs for the 9815. This convenience establishes operation of various programs without extensive set-up procedures. Convenient prerecorded programs are available for complex problem solving in electrical engineering, statistics, medicine, and surveying — to name a few.

Changing applications is as easy as changing cartridges. The cartridge itself is small — smaller than the typical cassette, yet it can hold 96,384 bytes of data and programs. Or roughly 45 programs with 2,008 steps. So, anyone can have his own library of programs. Not only can the 9815 easily solve the problems of the engineer, it can also deal effectively with the problems of the statistician, the doctor, the analyst, and the businessman. Anyone who can insert a prerecorded cartridge and turn on the power can solve a problem on the calculator. Secretaries, clerks, and part-time help can operate the 9815 to get the solutions to problems.

Users Can Dedicate the 9815 as a Stand-Alone Calculator or as a Powerful System — Users can dedicate their units in seconds to solve their problems, not just as a stand-alone unit, but as a powerful system as well. Read-only memory built into each cable and into the calculator gives fast response to specific needs. Operation and language features that are built in establish the rapport that only a dedicated system can have. A cartridge. A template. Automatic operation. For example, the printer and the display interact to provide two kinds of immediately available information. The printer gives labeled copy that identifies both what was done and how it was done. The display tells where in the calculation procedure users are and the result of each intermediate calculation. The printer and display are the tools with which the 9815 closes the communication gap between man and machine.

Rapid calculations are standard because the 9815 combines buffered keyboard operations, the logic of an operational stack, and a rational key layout. The entire right half of the keyboard is designed especially for keystroke problem solving. The far right block of keys contain 24 preprogrammed scientific functions. The next group of keys lets users access the operational stack and perform four-function arithmetic. These keys are adjacent to the 10-key numeric pad. Thus, users can pull together the "adding machine" portion and the scientific functions for complex problem solving. The results are a matter of record because they can be printed for permanent reference. Complex scientific problems and four-function calculations can be handled in much the same way. Because many of the scientific functions users may need are preprogrammed, it takes no more keystrokes to find the log or sin of a number than it does to perform any of the math operations with the same number. Intermediate calculations are automatically stored in the four-register operational stack, or users can assign them to any of the 10 permanent storage registers or any of the data registers in calculator memory. This immediately accessible data is easy to manipulate, thus eliminating the need for pencil and paper notations. The 9815 always retains 12 significant digits of the result; and whatever scientific numeric format users choose, the answer is calculated to 12-digit accuracy.

The 9815 reacts to users special requirements — by allocating memory into either program steps and/or data registers. If users want 50 registers instead of the 10 permanent registers, they tell the calculator 5 0 SHIFT STORE. Thus, users can partition the basic memory of the 9815, which is 472 program steps, any way they choose. Optionally users can expand to 2,008 program steps, which increase the basic memory four times — all of which can be partitioned by them. The 9815 extends its memory with the data cartridge. Bidirectional search, coupled with interchangeable data and program storage, gives users power, flexibility, and speed. The tape drive can search at 1524mm per second (60 inches per second). It can read or write data and programs at 254mm per second (10 inches per second). This means that, in the time it takes a user to check his watch, the 9815 has loaded, checked, and is running a program 1,500 steps long.

Interfacing with the H-P 9815 Series — An optional I/O structure adds another dimension to the 9815. Users can choose whether or not they want the 9815 to be equipped with general interfacing capabilities. The 2-channel configuration in the back of the calculator gives users plug-to-plug compatibility with many HP 9800 Series peripherals. These peripherals allow them to extend the input and output capabilities of the 9815. Another advantage of choosing the I/O configuration is this calculator's easy connection to a wide range of digital voltmeters, counters, or other instruments.

computing calculators

Each peripheral for the 9815 is equipped with an individual interface. Users can plug one to another. Each dedicated peripheral cable contains read-only memory which, when the cable is connected, provides all the special language and unique programming instructions necessary. The HP 9871A Printer is a prime example. The 9871 extends the output capabilities of the 9815 by providing a full-character impact writer with a fixed carriage and a 96-character interchangeable disc. The 9871 fills forms, creates reports, and draws charts and graphs rapidly and easily under program control of the 9815.

The 9815 can control instruments, gather data, and process that data. For this purpose, three general types of interface cards are available: general 8-bit I/O, BCD input, and HP-IB. General 8-bit I/O provides compatability with tape punches, tape readers, instruments... The general 8-bit I/O has built-in I/O buffers, recognizes programmable logic levels, and is capable of handling input speeds up to 2,000 bytes per second. The BCD input card operates with digital voltmeters, electronic counters, and BCD measurement systems. It can handle both 9-digit input and 8-bit control output. The 9815 is plug-to-plug compatible with HP-IB instruments. Up to 14 HP-IB instruments can be interconnected to a single HP-IB interface card. With two I/O channels, the 9815 can have up to 15 different instruments distributed between its channels. And the 9815 is fully compatible with all Hewlett-Packard HP-IB instruments. This is a versatile calculator accepting 15 different instruments. The 9815 has some important features that simplify the task even further. Programmable data logic levels give the ability to tell the 9815 what to look for in + or − logic levels. The tape cartridge complements the system with 98,384 bytes of data storage. The cartridge and the AUTO START provide users with the capability for power-fail restart in remote locations when the 9815 is a part of an interfacing system. So no matter where users are, immediate data acquisition and instrumentation control become possible where they were uncomfortable before.

The HP 9871A printer extends the output characteristics of the 9800 series desk-top programmable calculators. This impact printer is a full-character, fixed carriage peripheral that can be used to fill out forms, create reports, draw charts and plot graphs using the bi-directional platen and carrier. It also features programmable horizontal and vertical tabulation. In addition to the standard 96-character, upper/lower case print wheel, optional interchangeable wheels are available for ASCII character sets and European character sets. The 9871 is a versatile printer, accommodating paper up to 15 inches (38 cm) wide and prints up to 132 columns at 10 characters per inch. Average printing speed is 30 cps. Six-part paper in single-sheet or continuous-feed form may also be used. The HP 9871A was priced at $3400 in 1976.

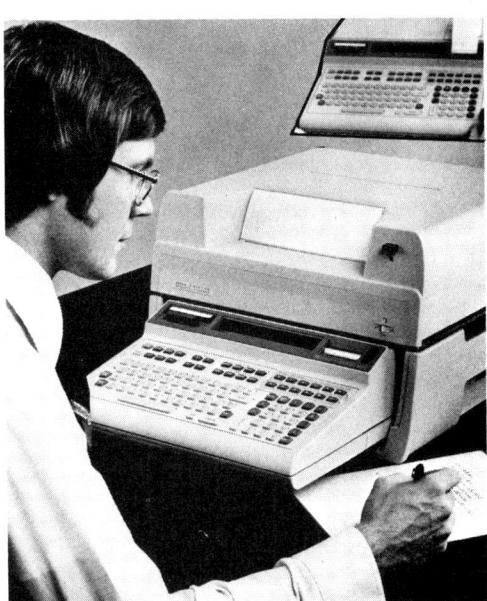

HP's 9825A Desk-Top Programmable Calculator with 9866B Printer — Hewlett-Packard introduced a new programming language. HPL designed for subroutine nesting and flags and which allows 26 variables and 26 multidimensional array variables. The 9825 also features 12 special function keys and shift functions that can allow 24 operations. The company said the live keyboard has never been featured on a desk-top calculator before and allows several additional functions.

The 9825 includes a 32-character LED display and a built-in 16-character thermal printer with upper and lower case alphanumeric readout.

The thermal line printer with upper and lower case and plotting capabilities is called the 9866B. The unit contains a 95-character ASCII set, upper and lower case alphabet and symbols reproduced by a 5 by 7 dot matrix and printer speed of 240 lines per minute, 80 characters per line. The 9866B in early 1976 cost $3,350 and is designed to be used with all H-P 9800 desk-top programmable calculators. Like the 9815, the 9825 calculator includes a dual-track cartridge with storage of 250,000 bytes, a 2,750 byte-per-second transfer rate, a search speed of 90 inches per second and a read/write speed of 22 inches per second.

HEWLETT-PACKARD'S 9815 DESK-TOP SCIENTIFIC CALCULATOR AND 9871 OUTPUT PRINTER

computing calculators

The 9825 comes with 8,000 bytes of internal read/write memory that can be expanded in 8K increments to 32K bytes. The unit also features four plug-in slots for optional ROMs.

HP Desk-Top Calculator Model 9825-A Capabilities — The powerful medium-priced desk-top programable calculator with many features previously found on minicomputers became available from Hewlett-Packard in early 1976. The 26-pound model 9825A, then priced at $5,900, is designed primarily for use in engineering, research and statistics. Its speed, interfacing abilities, and computer-like features make it particularly useful as the controller of an instrument system (see photo), for pilot process-control applications, remote data collection and production control. It also can be a powerful stand-alone computing tool.

A "live" keyboard allows users to change program variables, perform complex calculations, call subroutines and record and list programs while the calculator is performing other operations. This and various other significant features incorporated in the 9825A include: interrupt; input/output speeds up to 300,000 bytes per second; direct memory access; high-performance, bidirectional tape drive; multidimensional arrays; automatic memory record and load; extended internal calculation range ($\pm 10^{511}$ to $\pm 10^{-511}$), and optional plug-in read-only memory (ROMs). ROM add-ons include string operations, matrix manipulation, plotter control routines and I/O facilities. Three operational statistics software packages were available in early 1976 with more planned for release.

The 9825A uses a high-level programming language, called HPL, as noted, for controller applications as well as data processing. HPL handles subroutine nesting and flags and allows 26 simple variables and 26 multidimensional-array variables, limited only by the size of the calculator memory. Error locations are identified by a flashing cursor in the 32-character LED display. Fixed- and floating-point formats can be set by the user from the keyboard.

The 9825A's keyboard has 12 special function keys that, with a shift key, can handle 24 different operations. With the live keyboard, the user can perform simple calculations, examine and change program variables, and list programs while the calculator is performing other operations. Although the calculator appears to be doing these tasks simultaneously, the interrupt capability is actually apportioning operations on a priority basis. The speed of 9825A makes it seem as if everything is happening at once. The unit has a 32-character LED display and a thermal printer.

With search and rewind speeds of 90 inches per second and read/write speed of 22 in./s, the 9825A's built-in tape cartridge drive gives an average access time of 6 s. It provides automatic verification during recording.

The 9825A uses what HP calls second-generation n-channel MOS circuitry designed to provide high-speed internal calculation. The n-MOS chips consist of a binary processor chip, an input/output chip, and an extended math chip. There are four bipolar display chips. The 16-bit microprocessor employed in the 9825 has appeared also in H-P's 9871A printer/plotter. The chip, a custom 16-bit N/MOS microprocessor, was built at H-P's semiconductor facility. The 9815 calculator uses a Motorola eight-bit N/MOS microprocessor and was the first of the H-P desk-top calculators to use a microprocessor.

The HP 9825A functions as a systems controller. This means users can tackle sophisticated interfacing jobs without being a computer expert. The powerful and easy-to-use language HPL, high-speed data cartridge, live keyboard, interrupt, multidimensional arrays and high-speed input/output, are just a few of the versatile features that can make this possible. Also available: A choice of I/O methods and speeds: Formatted read/write up to 16K bytes/sec; Burst read/write up to 70K bytes/sec, Direct Memory Access (DMA) up to 400K transfers/sec. The power of 26 multidimensional arrays whose size is limited only by available memory and the flexibility of HPL's formula-oriented problem solving capability gives users easy-to-learn power.

Model 9825 System Performance — The 9825 Computing Calculator is a very versatile, very powerful device for high-speed problem-solving and for interfacing applications. It also offers these performance-oriented features:

- Vectored priority interrupt allows virtually simultaneous processing of multiple jobs. It's easily programmed to suspend processing, gather or send data and messages to instruments and peripherals, then automatically return to the original job.
- Live keyboard lets users interact with the system while a program is running to examine or change program variables — or even perform keyboard calculations.
- Up to 400k transfers per second direct memory access provides minicomputer speeds which allow real-time data acquisition and data transfer with high-speed devices.
- High-speed, 250k byte tape cartridge with 6-second average access time permits rapid processing of data and loading of programs.
- Multidimensional arrays allow users to organize data logically, thus saving program space and execution time. A 20 x 20 matrix can be inverted in 10 seconds.
- Buffered I/O increases throughput by providing a programmable software buffer between the program and an external device.
- Memory load and record allows users to suspend processing whenever they want and store the complete contents of memory on tape — including data and pointers — for continuation later on.
- High level language (HPL) offers users power and efficiency for handling equations, data manipulation, and input/output operations. Upper and lower case alphanumerics on both the display and printer.
- Interfacing to any of eight HP calculator peripherals through three I/O slots, and up to 45 different instruments via HP Interface Buses.
- Simultaneous processing of several diverse jobs. Operators using a 9825 to control an instrument test stand, and acquiring data from it at speeds in excess of 1000 bytes a second; then can print the results on the HP 9866B Thermal Line Printer. At the same time, the same 9825 can also be processing and plotting a statistical problem. And through the 9825's live keyboard, users can check the progress of either programs and can change parameters if they desire. It

computing calculators

seems the 9825 is doing all these operations simultaneously, thanks to its speed, buffered I/O, and interrupt capability.

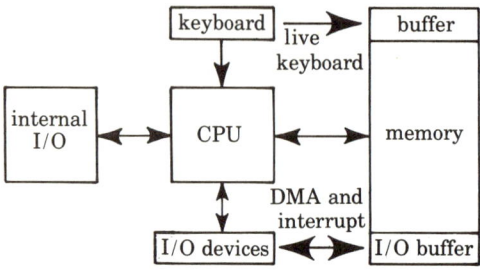

HEWLETT-PACKARD SERIES 9800, MODEL 30 CALCULATOR WITH PRINTER, PLOTTER AND CARD READER.

Hewlett Packard's 9830 is a 32-character-display, desk-top calculator providing a standard read/write memory of 4K bytes, expandable to 16K bytes. A built-in language compiler provides an additional 16K bytes of hard-wired memory. Further expansion is possible with read-only-memory (ROM) modules. Among features are: alphanumeric keyboard, built-in tape cassette, and BASIC language plus interface to a range of peripherals. (see below)

The HP 9830 Description — The HP 9830 is a general purpose, desk-top calculator with the power and peripherals necessary to solve complex engineering problems, provide reports for accounting services, generate medical diagnoses . . . in other words, compute answers for a wide range of applications.

The 9830 provides users with a standard read/write memory of 4K bytes, expandable to 16K bytes. And it has a built-in BASIC language compiler which provides an additional 16K bytes of hard-wired memory. Users can further expand the computational capacity and peripheral control functions with read-only-memory (ROM) modules. Using the ROM's and expanded memory features, the 9830 becomes a 48K-byte computing calculator.

Complementing the memory is a built-in cassette providing an additional 64K bytes of data or program storage. User programs or data can be entered into the 9830 by cassette or by the typewriter-like keyboard. During calculator programming or program execution, the 32-character LED display gives users crisp, alphanumeric messages or presents results.

The 9830 is designed to allow users to easily configure a system to meet their present needs and still allow for expansion to meet future needs. Users can choose from the tape readers, tape punches, typewriters, line and page printers, digitizers, plotters, data communications interfaces, cassette memories, a 4.8M byte mass memory subsystem, and a selection of general purpose interface cards, plus prerecorded software Pac's.

Features —
- Alphanumeric Keyboard
- 32-Character LED Display
- Built-in Tape Cassette
- Hard-wired BASIC Language
- Add-on ROM Memory
- Expandable Read/Write Memory
- 12 Significant Digits
- Full Trigonometric Capability
- Boolean Algebraic Capability
- Special Functions Keys
- Broad Range of Peripherals
- Instrumentation Control Capability
- Data Communications Interface

Mass Memory Subsystem Description — The HP 9880B Mass Memory Subsystem provides the HP 9830A Calculator with the large data storage capability required for applications such as payroll, account maintenance, inventory control, patient records, credit verification and large banks of data for structural design, statistical analysis and many other scientific, industrial and commercial fields.

The memory media of this peripheral is a permanently installed memory platter and an interchangeable cartridge (HP 12869A), each having a capacity of 2.4 million bytes; this is the equivalent of more than 600,000 total items of data of 12 digits each.

One of the main advantages of this system is data safety and security. Master data can be recorded on the removable cartridge, transferred into the calculator for manipulation, stored temporarily on the fixed memory platter for further use by the calculator's program and verification prior to modifying the master data on the removable cartridge. Also with this system, duplication of data files is easily accomplished. Year to date payroll data, inventory updating, account receivables and payables updating are just a few examples where this dual system offers great safety of the data base and affords the opportunity to verify the results prior to modification of master files. Should an error occur, it is easily corrected by repeating the operation, since the initial data still resides on the removable memory cartridge.

In addition to providing a large amount of data storage, the 9880B Mass Memory Subsystem is fast. A 10 x 10 array can be transferred to the cartridge in about 1 second and a typical 250 line program of 2000 words can be transferred in less than 2 seconds.

The HP 9880B Mass Memory Subsystem can be expanded in terms of increased data and program handling capacity. Up to two HP 9867B's can be connected to one HP 9830A Calculator through one HP 11305A Controller. The UNIT command enables the user to address any one of the desired memory platters.

Also, for increased versatility, up to four HP

computing calculators

9830A Calculators can be connected to the Mass Memory through the same Controller; however, only one calculator can be used to access the system at any one time. The HP 11305A Controller will sequentially service any of the four 9830A's requesting access to the mass memory.

Mass Memory Commands — As many as 10 data files can be used in one FILES statement at the same time.

Each file on the mass memory device is identified by a unique name of 1 to 6 characters in length.

Program and special function key files are accessed by using the SAVE, GET, and CHAIN commands.

Data files are created with the OPEN command; the user specifies the number of records to be reserved. The READ and PRINT statements permit both sequential and random data access.

Program and data files are erased from the mass memory by using the KILL command.

The IF END statement makes end of file processing routines easy to write.

The CATALOG command causes information about the files contained on the mass memory devices to be printed.

The UNIT command allows the user to access up to 4 mass memory platters from one calculator.

With the PROTECT command only authorized users, those who know the protection code, can access a data file. Also, protected files cannot be accidentally erased.

Special commands are also provided to allow the user to copy and to rename files and to create backup copies of files either on cassettes or on additional cartridges.

Many other commands and statements correspond to common time-share system commands and statements.

In conjunction with the String Variables ROM, strings can be stored as data, and they also can be used as variables for the access of files by name.

With the Matrix Operations ROM, two additional statements, MAT PRINT and MAT READ are available with the Mass Memory ROM.

Specifications —

Data Capacity Available to User
Bytes	4,866,048
Bytes per word	2
Words per record	256
Number of records	9,504 (4752/platter)
Maximum number of files	1,536 (768/platter)

Speed
Average access time	42.5 m sec.
Data transfer time	5.7 m sec.
	per 512 bytes
(Mass Memory to Calculator or vice versa)	

Specific Unit Descriptions — HP 9867B: Dual Platter (one removable, one fixed) Mass Memory Drive with interface cable (6 feet) and separate HP 13215A Power Supply.

HP 11305A; Controller. Provides the necessary interface to transfer data and programs bidirectionally between the HP 9830A Calculator and the HP 9867B Mass Memory.

HP 11273B: Read Only Memory, Calculator Interface Cable (10 feet) and Cassette for the HP 9830A Calculator. The ROM enables the HP 9830A Calculator to generate the necessary commands to write into and read from the Mass Memory. The cassette contains the program necessary to initialize a new memory cartridge and perform a system check out.

HP 12869A: Memory Cartridge has 2.4 million bytes capacity.

H-P 9000 Series Peripherals — Tape Punch users can add high-speed tape output to their HP system with a Model 2895B Tape Punch. The compact unit punches tape at 75 characters/second, permitting greatly improved throughput.

Card Readers — For big-batch processing capability, the high-speed Model 9869A Hopper Card Reader handles 80-column punched cards as well as mark-sense cards. It gives users speed and the versatility of formatted input. For smaller applications, the low-cost, hand-fed Model 9870A Card Reader optically reads mark-sense cards.

Paper Tape Readers — Data from analytical instruments, machine tools, and computer terminals goes directly into the Series 9800 calculator with paper tape readers. Model 9863A utilizes a pin-board programmer to make it easy to read a wide variety of formats at 20 characters/second. One Model 2748B Tape Reader is designed for high-speed, heavy-volume operations; it optically reads tapes at 300 characters/second.

Interfacing — With plug-in interface cards, the Series 9800 calculator takes on the ability to accept data from a large number of digital voltmeters, counters, and other instruments. By automating data entry users have a flexible lab processing center. The Model 9868A I/O Expander allows users to plug up to 13 peripherals or test instruments into the calculator.

X-Y Plotter — Histograms; pie charts; linear, log-log, and polar plots; circuit diagrams — these are just some of the things the Model 9862A X-Y Plotter can do. With a Peripheral Control Function Block, the plotter can automatically scale user data, generate words as well as numbers, and set up both axes complete with labels and tic marks — all in the designated units.

Line Printer — The HP 9881A LIne Printer is a low-cost, 5 x 7 dot-matrix printer which enhances the throughput of any 9800 Series calculator. Its unique print mechanism makes it quite enough for business environment and provides up to 6 consistent, clean copies. It prints at 200 lines per minute, regardless of the line length, and has full 132-column line width.

Digitizer — This is a specific machine that reads a curve, or any irregular shape, as a series of discrete points and then converts these to a series of digital X-Y coordinates. To make these entries, users trace the shape and the HP calculator prints out dimensions and area of the line or contained shape. With the Model 9864A Digitizer users can directly process graphical data such as X-rays, blueprints, strip-chart recordings, cut-and-fill profiles, to name a few.

CRT Display — Terminal Automatic formatting of repetitive data, business form filling and tax form preparation are some of the tasks which are for the HP 9882A CRT Subsystem. When users couple the advanced features of this CRT with those of the 9830 Calculator, their scrolling, cursor sensing, addressability, tabulation and positioning make even the big jobs seem smaller. The 5 in. by 10 in. display has an 1,920-character capacity in 24 lines of 80 characters per line.

computing calculators

Thermal Printer — For high-quality, hard-copy output the Model 9866A Thermal Printer operates at a fast, 250 lines/minute, equivalent to 3,600 words/minute. It's flexible, producing page-width, fully-formatted, alphanumeric text, tables, or simple plots. This option for the Model 9810, 9820 or 9830 carries a low price tag.

Typewriter — Tables, standard forms, letters, data listings — these are just a few of the data formats users can prepare with a Model 9861A Typewriter. And they can be produced with full alphanumeric capability, including upper/lowercase letters, punctuation marks, and symbols. The calculator, operating through a peripheral control block, automatically controls such things as tab setting and clearing, ribbon color, and vertical and horizontal spacing. But when the calculator is not running a typewriter program, the Model 9861A can be operated manually.

Tape Cassette — The high-speed Model 9865A Tape Cassette lets users store, update, and retrieve data and programs. A precision dual-motor drive protects irreplaceable data by eliminating the snarling and tape surge characteristic of capstan drive systems. And a fast bidirectional search feature lets users find any file on the tape... from any starting point... without rewinding. The 9865A has a minimum capacity of 6,000 registers; or 24,000 16-bit words for the Model 9820 and 9830; or 48,000 program steps for the Model 9810. Multiple cassette units can be used to speed data management and processing.

Victor Electronic Programable Printing Calculators — Some four models of Programable Electronic Printing Calculators head the Victor line of modern machines. They are all similar in basic design and function, but vary in numbers of registers and program steps (see chart). Programing data storage ranges from 128 to as many as 1,000 steps. This allows economical purchasing by fitting the specific calculator to the needs of the job.

All models share these functions and specifications: Operating simplicity, easy to use 10-key keyboard, 3 working registers, and 2 accumulating memories for standard electronic calculator functions. Totalling capacities to 14 digits on all four models. This also means accuracy to 13 decimal places. Prints sign (function) indication too. Mag Card Program Storage for convenience. Programs and/or data may be permanently stored on magnetic cards. Integral mag card reader/recorder permits programs to be written by and/or read into the calculator. Decision Making Commands. Users control a wide variety of conditional or unconditional symbolic jumping, looping and subroutine capabilities. Commands are keyboard-entered. Easily. Computer-like decision-making capabilities... with a 10 key calculator keyboard. Input Keyboard Logic in addition to programing and data control keys, the human engineered, color-coded keyboard includes these logical function keys: +, −, ×, ÷, S, T, √, %, EX (exchange), and N (count). Matrix Printer prints all entries and results for a permanent reference record. Uses a 5 x 7 matrix to form numbers and symbols. Large, legible and logical. High printing speed up to 110 characters per second (up to 5 lines).

Register and Program Steps Available

Model	Data Storage Registers	Program Steps (entirely separate from data storage)
4800	102	1000
4700	54	512
4600	6	128
4500	6	128

As noted above the 4800 offers a full 1,000 separate command steps. Three models provide a built-in reader/recorder for reading and preparation of magnetic cards that store program steps and data for general use. Subroutines conserve steps in applications that involve repeated calculations. Victor provides the applications programs either from their growing library or custom-tailored to specific user needs. With a few hours of instructions users can do their own programing.

Other characteristics are: a. Victor's matrix printer. Prints large, clear numbers, letters, symbols. b. Magnetic card reader/recorder. Program steps and data are recorded and read under machine control. Automatic verification. c. Mode selection. Simple lever device easily puts machine into programable, manual calculate or adding machine modes. d. Indicator lights. Provide quick indication of important operation steps. e. Programing control. Used only during creation of steps for new programs. (Other keys may also be used during program creation.) f. Arithmetic control and data entry. Standard keyboard arrangement for use during programmable and manual calculate modes. g. Memory/Data Storage. Provides direct access to accumulating memories and data storage registers during manual calculate mode. h. Program Storage — Integral magnetic card reader/recorder permits permanent storage of programs and/or data on magnetic cards that can be read into the calculator in seconds. i. Decision Making Commands — A wide variety of commands that provide conditional or unconditional symbolic jumping, looping, and subroutine capabilities are there at the touch of a few keys. Program Control — The utmost simplicity is provided by means of two program execute keys, j. User Definable Keys (Optional Feature) — Eight of the programing keys can be converted to user definable operation. In the CALC mode each key initiates a search for a specific tag in the program memory. The keys are labeled with the customer's description for the functions-eliminating operator errors. k. Function Keys — The hardwired key-

computing calculators

board functions for +, −, ×, ÷, S, T, √, %, EX, and N are there at a touch. 1. Color Coded Human Engineered Victor Keyboard — Convenient grouping of function keys respond instantly to the slightest touch. Smartly styled eye-appealing, the keys are color coded for immediate recognition and function control.

Features of the Canon SX 100, SX 310 and SX 320 — Built-in Magnetic Card Reader — The machines can make programs directly and store them on magnetic cards. The built-in magnetic card reader transfers programs or data from the machines to cards and vice versa.

Expanding Memory and Program Steps — The SX-100 has a working minimum of 20 data memories which can be expanded to a full 100. Its working mimimum of 200 program steps can also be easily increased to 1000. When using a data memory split into two sections, data storage capacity is doubled. This flexibility enables the SX-100 to perform an extremely wide range of complicated calculations.

Built-in Thermal Printer and Display — The SX Series' quiet, thermal printer prints out alphanumerics of input and output. Operations and results are easy to read on a display, too. Mode lamps indicate the calculator's mode, and an error if it has been made.

Alphabetical Capability — The SX Series can print a message in alphabetical form through manual operation of the keyboard or programmed instructions. Program calculations are easier to operate on messages proceeding from the calculator.

Making Tables — The SX Series prints solutions in any form or chart users desire. Users can get numbers, charts, graphs, pictures, labels, words — almost anything they desire — with paper 77mm or 140mm wide.

Algebraic Logic Sequence — Even the most complicated calculations can be performed by entering data in the same order as the algebraic expression of the calculation, including double parentheses. This logic entry system is much faster.

Special Function Keys — There are special function keys for trigonometric, inverse trigonometric, logarithmic (common and natural), exponential, reciprocal, n-th power, square, square root, factorial, absolute values, integers/fractions, decimals to degrees (and vice versa), constant pi (π) and e.

Other Special Features — It can perform:
- Conditional and unconditional branching
- Indirect memory addressing
- Memory splitting
- Symbolic addressing of subroutines
- Subroutine nesting up to two levels.

Calculating Capacity — Mathematical calculations are performed with full accuracy up to 14 digits and a 2-digit exponent. When special function keys are used, the same accuracy is maintained up to 12 digits and a 2-digit exponent. The SX-100 has a dynamic range of 10^{-99} to 10^{+99}.

Program Correction and Editing — Automatic printing of traced program steps. A stepback key for program correction. A key to insert additional steps and another to delete unnecessary ones in any part of a program.

Function Keys at User's Discretion — Users can customize each of the keys labeled A through E to perform specific functions at the touch of a single key.

Other SX-100, SX-310, SX-320 Capabilities —
Built-in Scientific Functions — Incorporates 15 easy-to-use micro-programmed functions.

Subroutine and Program Selection — For performing subroutine branching in program instructions and for program selection in manual operations.

Memory Control Keys — Memory can be used for both accumulation and storage.

Ten-Key Block — Exponent key makes it possible to input data in scientific or mixed notations.

Calculation Block — Equipped with fundamental functions $\sqrt{}$, $1/a$, a^2 and a^x.

Program Instruction Block — Employs 66 instructions, including branch commands and printer control instructions for obtaining exact desired output.

Program Control Block — Features complete editing facilities to decrease program checking time and simplify desired step settings. Completely furnished with mode and magnetic card reader control keys.

Expanding Memory and Program Steps of the SX310 and SX320. The SX-310 has a working minimum of 50 data memories which can be expanded to a full 500. Its working minimum of 500 program steps can also be easily increased to 4000. When using a data memory split into two sections, data storage capacity is doubled. The SX-320 has a working minimum of 100 program steps easily increased to 4000.

Peripherals: The SX-310 and SX-320 are sophisticated instruments fully capable of executing complex computations. However, in addition to the expandable memory capacity, a number of input and output peripherals can be interfaced to meet specific needs. 1) Typewriter 2) Tape puncher and reader 3) Others.

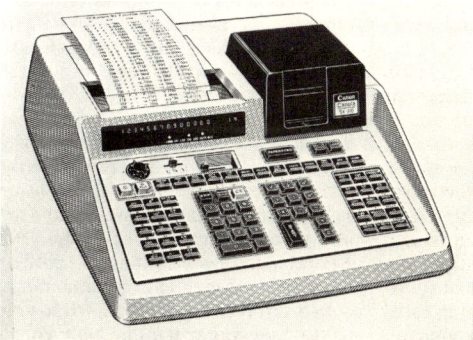

computing calculators

Canon's Programmable Calculators: The SX-100 and SX-310 — These conversational calculators have internal alphanumeric capability. They can be programmed to literally ask questions that elicit the proper responses. So users with virtually no training can process data and obtain meaningful results, fully labeled and formatted. Because these display-printing calculators produce hard copy on tape in 24- or 48-character widths, they give users complete freedom to format output as graphs, charts, etc. And since these calculators use algebraic logic they are easy to program, and are capable of conditional and unconditional branching, jumping and looping plus Indirect memory address and Subroutine nesting. Programs are stored on smooth-loading magnetic cards. Both come with a full complement of trigonometric function keys. But if users have no use for cosines and tangents, they can customize five of them as convenient program-select keys for their most recurrent problems.

Taken together, the SX calculators offer a wide and flexible range of capacities that can be arranged to suit users needs. The SX-100 comes with 50 memories and 500 steps that can be increased to 100 memories, 1000 steps. The SX-310's basic array of 50 memories, 500 steps can be incremented to a maximum of 500 memories, 4000 steps. The SX-310 is interfaceable with typewriters and other peripheral equipment.

Complete software packages are available. And Canon custom-tailors programs to users requirements.

Sharp CS-4500 Electronic Printing/Display Calculator with Interchangeable Cartridge Keyboards — The CS-4500 calculator offers interchangeable special applications. In addition to functioning as a 14-digit printing calculator, the CS-4500 features a keyboard of 8 special purpose keys that can be used for any number of special applications, merely by inserting a cartridge into the calculator. Cartridge and matching keyboard templates are available for a variety of business, financial, statistical and other applications. This means that a single CS-4500 can be utilized with a selection of cartridges to fill the needs of several departments within a business. If users want to do some invoicing they insert the Sharpvoicer cartridge, snap the Sharpvoicer template over the keyboard, and they're ready to do invoicing. After the invoicing is done and they want to figure some proration and distribution, they simply replace the invoicing cartridge and template with the Pro-Rater cartridge and template, and they can go. The Sharp users calculator library can have as many application keyboards on hand as they need to give them the benefits of several special purpose calculators without the cost of several calculators. Features of the CS-4501:

- Interchangeable cartridges for specialized applications. Provides calculating capabilities that approximate the level of programs of computers.
- 8 kinds of exclusive calculations with each cartridge.
- Once a calculation is chosen, other exclusive keys are electronically locked.

Monroe 1800 Series Tape Cassette Calculator Systems — The Monroe 1800 Series calculators are in effect, powerful and versatile microcomputer systems. The "brains" of this system is a user microprogrammable microprocessor, 7 kilobytes of ROM (Read Only Memory) operating system and hi-level instructions, and 1.5 kilobytes of working storage. This microprocessor subsystem is complemented by one of four keyboards for input, a 21 column printer for output and a magnetic card reader/writer for offline program and data storage.

All of these essentials are conveniently packaged in a rugged, desk-top unit with easy access I/O ports for additional system elements. Three of the models are offered with full program editing keyboards including the 1880 with mathematical and scientific ROM's, the 1860 with mathematical and statistical ROM's and the 1830 with 13 user-definable keys and mathematical and business ROM's. The Model 1810 offers additional user-definable keys in place of the programming keys of the 1830 with the same ROM functions.

In addition to the 100 plus instructions available in the keyboard code set, the 1800 Series offer user access to 256 microprogramming instructions for writing the user's own operating system and I/O control. The I/O capability of the 1800 Series ranges from a PIO (Peripheral Input-Output) bit-serial bus, up to 8-bit parallel input, byte or word transfer, Direct Memory Access (DMA) and interrupts. Main memory expansion in 512 byte increments are offered as options.

Monroe Model 1830 Electronic Programmable Printing Calculator — The Monroe Model 1830 is a desk-top unit that combines computer-like programmability with 13 user-definable keys that can be programmed to perform a wide range of special functions. The user also has access to internal read only memory (ROM) functions, not available as keys, such as raising a number to a power, square root, logarithm, antilogarithm, identifier routines, and simple and compound interest. The 1830 utilizes the straightforward arith-

computing calculators

metic operation of a standard manual calculator making it convenient to use for incidental calculations. Data storage consists of 64 main data registers with 10 seperate scratchpad registers, all of which function as complete four-rule (i.e.: add, subtract, multiply, divide) independent of 512 steps. Also a broad repertoire or computer-like program instructions is provided: unconditional or conditional branching, jumping, looping, and six-level nesting of subroutines. Simplified checking and debugging procedures speed up program verification and no special programming language is needed to write programs. Programs and/or data can be read directly into or out of the unit via the built-in magnetic card reader.

Monroe's Cassette System Characteristics — Monroe's low-cost tape cassette drive systems provide programming and storage expansion capabilities for 1800 series desk-top calculators. With the Monroe 392/1800 Cassette Drive System, 1800 calculator users are not limited in problem solving capacity by the number of program steps that can be stored in the machine at any one time. (See photo) Automatic program control allows users to write more sophisticated programs on preconditioned tapes. Large programs can be divided into a number of blocks, each holding 256 steps. A final command at the end of the block reads the next program into tape memory. This procedure can be repeated (up to 150 blocks) until the program has been completed. The 392/1800 system lets users access over 38,000 programming steps per side of tape. One convenient C30 Phillips type tape cassette is comparable to 150 individual magnetic cards, making reading and writing information more automatic, less time consuming.

The system's powerful interface assembly offers both READ ONLY and READ/WRITE ports, allowing the 1800 calculator user to selectively control the connected tape drive. Reading and writing operations can be done with single or dual tape cassette drives. However, dual drives make updating information easier, more convenient. The 392/1800 Tape Cassette Drive System can be used with any Monroe 1800 series calculator for storage of information, giving expanded capabilities many users require.

Manual or Programmed Tape Operations — Tape drives may be operated manually by touching the appropriate sequence of keys on the 1800 keyboard, or the 1800 may be programmed to operate drives automatically as part of the applications program. Preconditioned Tapes are an attractive extra. Preconditioning divides the tape into the number of blocks specified by the operator. Each block is assigned a number in sequence beginning with one.

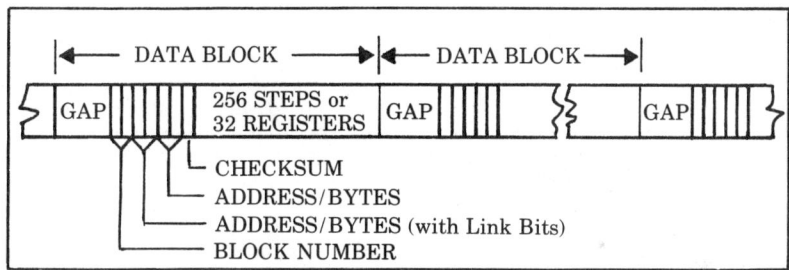

Automatic Error Checks — The 392/1800 system automatically checks for error conditions which affect operation or data information. Conditions such as: comparing sum of bits read with bits written; whether read/write head is past block requested; attempted read of block with no data; and preconditioning errors.

Add-on capabilities through peripherals expand the system. Peripherals such as the Monroe Model 300 I/O Writer or Model 395 Teleprinter Interface can be used with the 392-1800 system, allowing alphanumeric information to be written on or read from tape.

Basic 392/1800 Drive Functions — Functions which can be accessed manually or under program control. Users can:
- write a block of information on tape as part of multiple block file
- write a block of information on tape as single block file
- read a file of information from tape, using address recorded on tape to determine where in computer memory each block should be stored
- read a file of information from tape into specified address in computer memory (addresses recorded on tape are ignored)
- specify which drive information to be read from under manual or program control

Users can also duplicate tapes; update tapes with new or changed information; use pre-programmed tapes with up to 15 minutes of programmed material per side.

Monroe Model 1860 Scientific/Statistical Electronic Programmable Printing Calculator — The Monroe Model 1860 Electronic Programmable Printing Calculator combines the features of a scientific/statistical calculator, extensive problem-solving capability and hard-wired keyboard functions with versatile programming commands. The essentials are conveniently packaged in a rugged desk-top unit the size of a typewriter (with easy access I/O ports for additional system elements,) weighing only 22½ lbs. Thus it can be readily moved from one work station to another for maximum utility. The keyboard operation is simple and straightforward, following algebraic rules of equation solving and includes two-level nesting of arithmetic operations. By single keystroke operations, 28 mathematical and statistical functions can be provided. The 1860 offers optional user definable keys which allow the user to address up to three programs or subroutines by one key depression.

The Monroe 1860 provides 512 program steps with additional steps as an option in increments of 512 steps up to a total of 4096. It is designed to

computing calculators

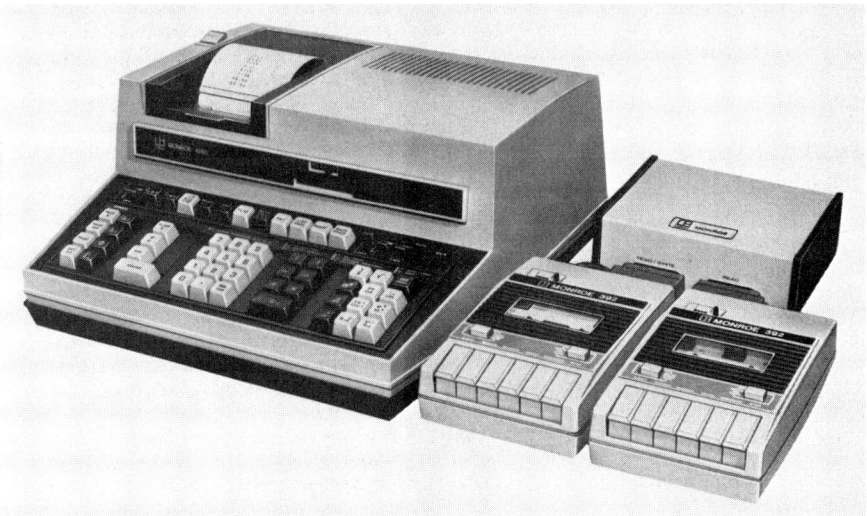

handle large quantities of data in its ten scratch pad registers and 64 main data registers which are expandable in increments of 64 registers to 512. The programming flexibility of the Model 1860 is further enhanced by symbolic addressing and indirect addressing techniques. A single key makes these two techniques immediately available to the user. There are 73 programs with 94 routines available in the Monroe statistical software library in addition to the 28 hardwired functions available on the keyboard to solve everything from single entry functions to complex problems requiring numerous data inputs such as regressions. The software program library also includes 50 programs for Chemistry, Science and Fluid Mechanics. Twenty-two Medical Laboratory Programs are available from Monroe including Electrophoresis and Radiommunoassay programs.

The automatic programmable tape drive control permits more sophisticated programs to be written as overlays on pre-conditioned tapes. Large programs may be divided into a number of blocks, each holding 256 steps. A command reads the next program or overlay of any number of blocks of memory at the appropriate locations. The 392/1800 system permits access of over 38,000 programming steps per side of tape. The system's powerful interface assembly offers both Read Only and Read/Write ports allowing the 1860 to selectively control the connected tape drives. The tape drives may be operated manually by touching the appropriate key sequence on the 1860. The 1860 may be programmed to operate drives automatically as part of the program. Reading and writing operations can be performed with single or dual tape cassette drives. Peripherals such as the Model 300 I/O Writer or the Model 395 Teleprinter interface can be used with the 392/1800 system, thus permitting alpha-numeric information to be written or read. Also using the Model 395 Teleprinter interface, the Model 1860 can be interfaced with an instrument acoustic coupler, line printer, Teletype or CRT terminal and can accept or output numerical data, alpha strings of variable lengths or programs.

Monroe Model 1860 Statistical Calculator —
The Monroe Model 1860 as an electronic programmable calculator designed for statistical applications combines algebraic and hard-wired keyboard functions with versatile programming commands. High-speed printed output is provided along with complete input/output peripheral capability which makes possible the use of a wide range of peripheral devices.

Keyboard operation follows algebraic rules of equation-solving, including two-level nesting of arithmetic operations. Single keystroke generation of 28 mathematical and statistical functions is also provided. Program and data storage memories are expandable at the user's option. A complete repertoire of computer-like programming instructions is provided: unconditional and conditional branching, jumping, looping, subroutines. Data may be stored and recalled under program control, and 6-level nesting of subroutines is possible. Simplified checking and debugging procedures speed up program verification. No special programming language is needed to write programs.

Model 1860 key features: Programmability — 512 steps in basic memory; expandable in increments of 512. Integral magnetic card reader. Symbolic addressing. Program editing flexibility. Data Storage — 10 scratch-pad registers. 64 main data storage registers; expandable in increments of 64. Full arithmetic capability in all registers. Direct and indirect register addressing. Keyboard Functions — Single keystroke generation of statistical functions. Input/Output Capability. Algebraic Operation. Simplicity — No need to learn computer language. Support — Access to large and growing library on programs provided by Monroe. Worldwide sales and service organization.

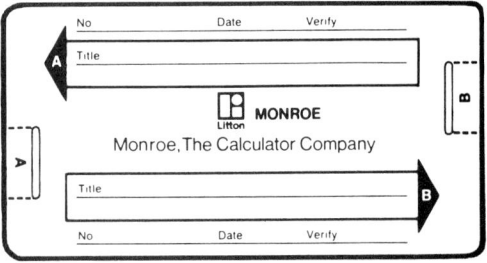

Magnetic Program Card — Capacity per side:

computing calculators

256 instructions or the contents of 32 data registers.

Monroe 1800 Peripherals — Complete I/O capability is built into the unit to allow interfacing with a wide range of peripheral devices.

General: Capacity — In all registers, 13-digit mantissa with 2-digit power-of-ten exponent within the range of ±99. Printout — High-speed, 2½ lines per second. Prints 10 significant digits of mantissa with sign and 2-digit exponent with sign. Red print for negative values. Commas to indicate thousands punctuation. Complete symbology for keyboard functions. Buffered Keyboard — Allows depression of a digit or a function key while calculator is still executing a previous instruction. Keyboard Interlocks — Preclude errors occurring from simultaneous depression of two or more digit keys. Decimal Format — User selects decimal position indicating number of digits to the right of the decimal point. Decimal shifts right automatically overriding selection if necessary. When input or results exceed a 10-digit mantissa, calculator automatically converts to exponential format. Dimensions — Length 15"; Width 14½"; Height 7". Weight — Approximately 22½ lbs. Power Requirements — Voltage* 90-110V; 105-125V; 180-220V; 195-235V; 210-250V. Frequency 48-70Hz. Operating Temperature Range — 32° F (0° C) to 104° F (40° C).

The Monroe 1860 as a "Laboratory Calculator" Monroe has dubbed its Model 1860, the "Laboratory Calculator." The programmable 1860 will handle many complex laboratory tests with the ease it takes to insert a small program card into the unit's self-contained magnetic card reader. Thirty-two Medical Lab programs were available early from Monroe to take the bothersome part of testing, the calculating portion, out of user hands. They depress the appropriate key and the specific test routine is ready to go, eliminating long hours. The Electrophoresis program, for example is put into the 1860 by a specific magnetic program card. First, a program identifier is printed. Then the date and the patient's number are entered. All users do is enter the data, depressing the RESUME key after each entry, and Monroe points out, . . . in less than 9 seconds, 13 results are printed out!

Users may wish to go a step further and have this calculated information in a plotted graph form. The Monroe 1860/310 lab system gives them the option of expanding this system to include a Model PL-2 XY Digital Plotter for a clear visual representation of the results. Or they may wish to have the results typed out alphanumerically. The Model 300 I/O Writer will automatically type out the results in whatever form they are accustomed to using. This convenient peripheral is ideally suited to the production of finished reports, completed documented problem solutions, and typing on pre-printed forms. For those using a counter (Liquid Scintillation, Gamma, etc.) with a printed tape output to perform their tests, many are undoubtedly wasting valuable hours calculating test results using data printed out on their lister. Instead they can team the counter up with a Model 310 Data Coupler interfaced with the 1860 and have a complete laboratory system. Custom-programmed for a nominal fee, this system will not only list the data but do all the calculations, showing the results on the tape printout.

Monroe Model 1880 Survey System — The 1880 is a compact, advanced system that will handle the everyday simple, as well as complex, mathematical problems of the surveyor. The Model 1880 Electronic Programmable Printing Calculator is specifically designed to perform surveying calculations; an optional Input/Output Writer accepts alphanumeric information from the calculator and prints it in standard format. An innovative development by Monroe, the two-unit Model 1880 Survey System is a simple push-button operation with programmed instructions which eliminate the tedious tasks of using tables, charts and non-programmable calculators to evaluate field book leg distances and angle measurements. For example, the loop traverse program simplifies the process of adjusting and balancing closure errors through automatic, accurate, high-speed electronic computation. It prints out in a matter of minutes, a complete display of all survey traverse output data in columnar format suitable for presentation to clients.

How it Works — First, the mathematical calculations required by land surveyors have all been previously stored in a series of credit-card sized magnetic program cards (20 in Monroe's library to date) containing 70 separate surveying routines. The program cards control the calculator's powerful computation capabilities, but users control the cards plus the calculator. Each card has a capacity of 512 instructions or steps, and multiple cards can be handled by the 1880 (a card is inserted into the slot above the keyboard and is automatically ejected in one second). Users then enter data direct from field notes. This not only triggers the solutions they need, but stores the data in the calculator memory for subsequent calculations. There is immediate access to as many as 126 stored points.

Monroe's 1880 Structural and Hydraulic Engineering Packages — A hydraulic engineering software package with a wide range of applications using the Monroe 1880 programmable calculator to perform its computations is a software package written in the language of the engineer. It offers a total of sixteen programs to provide the user with information to select the best design for the project. Previously most had been available only in packages designed for large main-frame computers. They now provide the user with more flexibility than many large scale computer programs offer. The programs provide valuable tools for the engineer in: backwater analysis for natural, trapezoidal or circular channels; the design of storm and sanitary sewer systems; culvert design for circular, box, or pipe-arch culverts; the Hardy Cross analysis of water distribution networks; Streeter-Phelps stream analysis; and gravity flow through elliptical, pipe-arch, circular, and trapezoidal channels.

The Monroe 1880 programmable calculator combines algebraic and hard-wired keyboard functions with powerful programming commands. As previously noted the keyboard operation of the 1880 is simple and straight forward. Single keystrokes can generate 27 mathematical functions. Programs and data-storage memories are expandable

---

*Voltage range dependent on local conditions; adjusted by Monroe service representative.

computing calculators

at the user's option. Data may be stored and recalled under program control.

Monroe's structural engineering software package is unique, powerful and yet flexible. With Monroe software, simple beam analysis can now be computed using one program. Frame analysis, which almost always required a computer, can now be done effectively on the calculator. This adaptable package has a wide range of applications which can be used in a variety of standard structural engineering computations. It is divided into 3 sections, encompassing Structural Engineering Programs, Steel Design Programs, and Concrete Design Programs.

Advanced Monroe Calculators Can Communicate with Peripherals, Laboratory and Medical Instrumentation and Over Phone Lines with Accoustic Couplers and Modems — When interfaced with the unique micro-programming of the Model 1800 Series calculators, the software-driven Monroe 395 Interface provides the user greater flexibility in full utilization of total system performance. Numerical data, alpha of variable length, and software program input or output are accepted. Data editing, validating, and output formatting can be readily incorporated into the software programs.

The 1800 Series Calculator with a Model 395 will interface to peripheral devices using 20 mA. current loop. EAI RS-232C or CCITT V. 24. The coding designated character acceptable is ASCII at 110, 150, 300, 600 or 1200 baud (or any two of these), either half or full duplex.

An 1800 Series calculator with a Model 395 Teleprinter Interface can accept or output numerical data, alpha strings of variable lengths or programs. Because the 1800 Series calculators are uniquely micro-programmable, the Interface is software driven. Users have flexibility in optimization of their total system performance. Data editing and validating as well as output formatting may be incorporated in the application software.

Compucorp 400 Series Computing Calculators — Compucorp has developed extended internal and external memory systems for the Monroe 1800 and Compucorp 400 series programmable calculators. Addition of the memories to existing calculators puts them in the small computer system category.

The internal memory development uses 4K random-access memories (RAM) to package 8K bytes of memory into the Monroe 1800/Compucorp 400 series. The external memory interfaces up to four floppy disk drives.

A Disk Operating System is said to be a complate file management system that allows the programmer to talk to the disk in terms of files and records and to access records based on numeric or alphanumeric keys. The operating system also contains standard utility routines such as sort and list.

The price of Model 491 dual disk memory was $6,000; the Model 88 8K internal memory $3,750 in early 1976. The 402 Computing calculating system is pictured above, and the 403 Data Collection System is shown on the next page.

The Compucorp 402 System —
- Completely programmed business computer requiring minimum operation intervention
- Powerful organization with a local data base using economical disk technology
- Specially designed for automatic invoicing, inventory control, accounts payable and receivable, payroll, management reports, etc.
- Local processing in batch or interactive mode
- Can be part of a distributed processing network through communications with a central computer
- Technology completely tested and reliable.

Description — The Compucorp 402 is designed mainly for commercial applications and is a free-standing, completely programmed disk based system. It consists of an 8K processor (Model 485), a double disk unit (Model 491-2), an operating system (DOS-K) and a 30 character per second printer (LA 36 DECwriter) or an RS232C compatible device. The system can be expanded to include up to two additional disks, another printer or video unit and one-half inch Mag Tape (Model 497) for those accounting and administrative applications requiring more capacity, and further processing on a larger computer.

System Components — Processor 485. This is a general-purpose digital processor with large memory capacity, powerful instruction repertoire, and extensive input/output facilities. Maximum memory size addressable by the processor is 16,384 8-bit bytes. Memory can be either RAM or ROM. Micro instructions are one or two bytes long and data are usually word oriented. Words are 8 bytes, or 16 BCD digits in length.

Memory: up to 8K bytes — Programmer functions: floating arithmetic, financial algebra, logarithms, peripheral control functions, etc. (with a total of 214 functions) User definable keys: these keys are named by the user to execute a particular application; example: keys can be labelled DATE, ACCOUNT NUMBER, INVOICE, SALES TAX, etc. The operator simply depresses the required user definable key and the operation is carried out. Printer: Tally roll printer which can be used for arithmetic operations and to print messages to guide the operator through a program. Magnetic card reader: it is used for program or data input and can be useful as a "magnetic key" to prevent access to confidential information by unauthorized personnel.

Unit 491 DISK — A flexible and interchangeable floppy disk opens a new dimension in the processing of commercial applications. The large capacity and random access facilities make the storage and retrieval of information easy and fast. For example, the operator inputs information from one source document, an order. From information stored on disk, the invoice is completed, customer account and inventory records updated, etc. When required, the operator can request an automatic print-out of reports — sales analysis, inventory, debtors trial balance, etc. Up to 315K bytes per disk and 1.2 M bytes per system can be organized in an integral data base that will include all the accounting information a company requires. Included in the disk unit is a communication interface (Model 495).

Operating system DOS-K — The principle function of DOS-K is handling the data files and changing programs. The information stored on disks constitutes a data base that can be accessed many different ways and following sequences that differ from the basic order. In this way long and costly data classifications (sorts) can be avoided because the data is already ordered in as many dif-

computing calculators

ferent ways as required by the application. For example, an inventory file can be accessed for the last movement date, for inactivity analysis or a supplier name or its physical position in the stock room to facilitate inventory checking, etc. All this is accomplished without moving the data on disks and using only the necessary time to read the records in the file sequence making it easier to produce management reports.

LA 36 Printer — Prints 30 characters per second using a dot matrix printer. It can handle variable size continuous stationery forms.

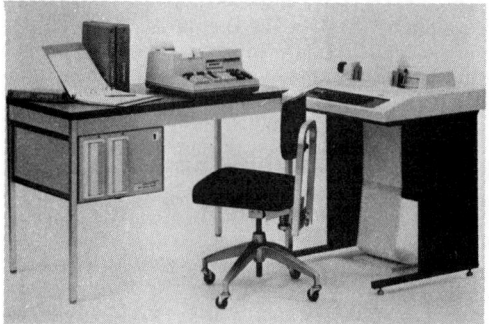

Compucorp 402 Options — Magnetic Tape Unit 497 (off-line data transmission). Allows the data transfer to and from large computers using ½" IBM compatible magnetic tape.

On-Line Data Transmission — Allows the communication between Compucorp systems or with other equipment through asynchronous channels of up to 4800 baud through telephone cables or other suitable media. Available routines allow the connection with a remote computer using 2740 protocol or similar. This includes transmission error detection and the automatic retransmission of messages.

Applications — The Compucorp 402 system allows it to be part of a distributed processing network in large organizations or to be a free-standing independent computer for medium-to-small size companies.

Free-Standing computer — The 402 system is an economic solution for the replacement of conventional accounting equipment (based on paper tape or ledger cards) by a disk based data system. The storage capacity and random access capabilities of the 402 system reduce the amount of operator intervention required. Sufficient information can be stored on disk which permits the simultaneous updating of all files in the accounting process. Ideal applications are invoicing, inventory control, accounts receivable, accounts payable and management reporting.

Other applications areas where high speed storage or retrieval of information is necessary are:
- stock market transactions
- property descriptions for real estate companies
- lists of names for direct mail campaigns
- itineraries for travel agencies
- customs classifications and documentation for freight forwarders
- patient medical record information for hospitals
- banking (general accounting, foreign exchange, etc.)
- project costs for construction companies
- quantity surveying

- engineering and estimating
- data entry applications.

Terminal network — The Compucorp 402 system can be used as controller of 485 processor network using terminals with access to a common data base for a system. Up to 15-20 terminals and response times of 3 to 10 seconds are typical features. Distribution is useful in:
- banking terminals or similar type applications
- cash register in supermarkets
- hotel accounting

The 402 system can also act as a terminal on line to a large computer.

Other Comucorp equipment — For more specific applications, the 485 processor can be replaced by the 425 for scientific calculations (hardwired trigonometrical functions available) or for the 445 for sophisticated statistical calculations (includes mean, standard deviation, student 't'-tests, multiple correlations, etc.).

Additional peripheral devices which can be connected are: 490 Mark Sense Reader, 492 Cassette Unit, 493XY Plotter, 495 IBM 735 Typewriter Interface.

Technical Data — Processor 485. Memory: RAM, up to 8K bytes in increments of 512 bytes with direct or indirect addressing; Machine cycle: 80 microseconds processing 8 or 64 bits per cycle; Operation system (firmware): ROMs, 7K bytes preprogrammed for the execution of 214 functions; Arithmetic unit: floating point, with 13 digit mantissa, two digit exponent and signs both binary or decimal; I/O Channels: two of 80 and 10 microseconds per character, serial, parallel and interrupt driven input/output is provided for. Printer: drum printer, numeric, 21 columns, 16 rows, 3 lines per second.

COMPUCORP 403 DATA COLLECTION SYSTEM

The Compucorp Model 403 Data Collection System is used to collect variable format data from local or remote data entry stations. The data can be assembled on IBM-compatible one-half inch magnetic tape, for processing on other computers, or on floppy disks for processing on Compucorp 400 Series systems. The system consists of a 400 Series CPU interfaced to the magnetic tape for data storage, a dual floppy disk for storage of data entry formats, and interfaces for up to four data entry terminals. The software operating system allows each of the terminals to act as a supervisory station, with the capability of calling any format

computing calculators

and edit routine stored on the disk. Formats can include protected fields and prompting messages displayed on the VDU terminal. Validation checks may be performed on incoming data; the cursor points to incorrect entries. Any validation routines may be programmed. Common routines are Mod 10 and Mod 11 check digit, range checking, all numeric fields, etc. Terminals can be located up to 1000 feet from the CPU. When remotely located, they can serve as a distributed data collection system. Since each terminal can call any entry format available on the disk, a single location can be used to enter many different kinds of data. The 403 System is a full 400 Series calculator system, and is program compatible with all other 400 System software. The Executive operates under DOS-K, Compucorp's extensive data base management system. The system is programmed in AL400 assembly languages.

Compucorp 450 Computing Calculator System — The Compucorp System 450 is a freestanding, fully programmable disk based computer system which can be configured to solve a wide variety of business and scientific applications.

The 450 is modular in design and can be expanded with Compucorp 400 series peripherals and a wide range of locally available printers, CRT display terminals, and communication equipment.

The basic 450 consists of a system cabinet containing a microprocessor CPU, 8K bytes of user memory, a dual floppy disk unit, magnetic card reader, and system printer. Next to the cabinet is a desk with a keyboard console containing four groups of keys for alphanumeric data entry, numeric data entry, programmable special functions, and program control. In addition to the compact console, the desk can contain a CRT and/or a printer.

Compucorp 450 Computing Calculator System Processor (CPU) — The CPU of the 450 is Compucorp's proprietary 3000 series microprocessor which is solving problems in over 100,000 installations throughout the world. It is a general purpose digital processor with large memory capacity, powerful instruction repertoire, and extensive input/output facilities. The CPU is supported by a 7K-byte ROM resident operating system and 8K bytes of user RAM memory. The ROM resident operating system provides the functions that solve user problems. It is a computer program consisting of over 7,000 instructions that serves users with I/O communications control, mathematical, and program execution, trace and editing functions. The Standard System 450 (see photo) is supplied with an operating system that also contains specialized functions for business and financial problems. Two optional operating systems are available, one with specialized functions for engineering and science and one with statistical functions. The user RAM memory provides 8,192 bytes of storage. The RAM memory is used to hold the program that is currently operating and the data the program requires. Each byte may contain a code for a program instruction, for a typed character, or for part of a number.

System 450/OPD CRT Display — The CRT display adds extremely rapid information displays and interactive data entry to System 450 performance. It provides transmission speeds up to 4800 Baud (480 characters per second) which fills its 1920 character screen in only 4 seconds. The screen is organized into 24 rows of 80 characters, both upper and lower case. The addressable cursor of the display offers the ability to guide the operator.

The Compucorp System 450 is Offered in 3 Configurations — The System 450 includes CPU, ROM operating system, 8K-byte RAM memory, dual floppy disk memory, dual telecommunication controllers, keyboard console, magnetic card reader, system printer, disk operating systems DDD and DOSK, AL400 Language Assembler, manuals and accessories. The System 450/OP includes all the items of System 450 plus a 30 character per second, 132 character width output printer. The System 450/OPD includes all the items of System 450/OP plus a 480 character per second, 1920 character CRT Display terminal. Any model of System 450 may be ordered with a scientific, statistical, or business operating system. Specifications are: Type 1 Scientific, Type 2 Statistical, Type 3 Business.

OLIVETTI P-652 ADVANCED PROGRAMMABLE CALCULATOR SYSTEM

The P 652 consists of:
- a central memory (RAM) of 4K semi-bytes
- standard keyboard functions with microprogrammed sequences for common mathematical routines and peripheral unit control
- an arithmetic-logic unit
- an operating keyboard with 10-key entry pad and function keys
- an integrated 30cps roll printer with 28 print positions
- an integrated unit for reading and recording magnetic cards
- an optional ROM for special mathematical and statistical functions

computing calculators

A serial I/O interface for connection of peripheral units is standard with the basic unit. An interface for the MLU 600 random access tape cartridge unit and DAS 600 Disc Unit is optional.

Central Memory (RAM) — This is a 2 μsec random access memory of MOS type integrated circuitry. Capacity is 4K semi-bytes of 4 bits each equivalent to 16,384 bits. It is possible to store 1800 alphanumeric characters (bytes) of 8 bits each; 1200 program instructions (Address and Operation) of 12 bits each. Registers may contain numeric data, alphanumeric data or instructions permitting 100% memory utilization. There are also: 2 operating registers (M and A), each of which may contain a number represented in floating point; 8 Base registers for indirect addressing each of which may contain a 4-digit integer without sign; 4 sense switches, each internally settable and having binary condition on or off; 60 extra bytes available through indirect addressing.

Olivetti P 652 Specific Features — There are 17 microprogrammed routines for the evaluation of:

sin x	e^x
cos x	b^x, to any base
tan x	Ln x
Rectangular to Polar	Log_{10} x
	$\sqrt{x}$
arcsin x	π
arccos x	
arctan x	Polar to Rectangular
arctan x	

For the trigonometric functions angles may be in either degrees or radians and the argument taken from either the M or A Operating register. Keys for these functions appear on the console for both manual operation and program compilations.

Optional ROM — This memory contains 20 microprogrammed routines for special mathematical and statistical functions with error correction procedures. These functions are accessed by the F key and the 10-key numeric keyboard.

Instruction Set — Over 70 generic instructions are available for arithmetic, transfer, logic, standard and optional ROM functions. 24 different conditions for branching to 110 different Labels. Both direct and indirect addressing available. Each 12 bit instruction consists of an address and operation. Peripheral commands use additional bytes for unit and mode identification.

Memory Origins — Dynamic partitioning of central memory is available through 110 different origin definitions, separate from the 110 Labels.

Subroutines — 110 Labels are available for subroutine definition with option of 4 different types of return jumps. Subroutines may be nested to 7 levels.

General Keyboard — Simplified numeric keyboard with 10 keys plus decimal point and algebraic negative sign which can be entered either before or after the number.

E key for entering numbers in scientific notation. Keyboard Clear key for clearing last figure or instruction entered. General Reset key for clearing central memory. Start/Stop key for data entry and program continue.

Operation Keys — Keys for addition, subtraction, multiplication, division, register accumulation, and register clearing. (See Standard Keyboard Functions for other basic mathematical functions.)

Data transfer keys featuring transfers among registers and both operating registers, M and A. Key for peripheral commands and format. Key for Reading a Magnetic Card (Variable Block Length). Key for Writing a Magnetic Card (Variable Block Length).

Special Keys — Key for routine selection. 100 routine labels may be referenced directly or indirectly. An additional 10 may be referenced indirectly. Key for subroutine selection. Key for indirect addressing. Key for addressing the Base Registers. Key for various condition setting and sensing. Key for various command modifications and to define memory partitions (origins).

Switches and Controls — Power supply on/off switch. Switch for Program printing. Single Step Switch for error location. A program may be either printed or executed in single step mode and instructions added or deleted without auxiliary cards. Decimal Wheel for setting 0-15 print decimals in fixed point, either rounded or truncated. Error light (red light) indicating operating error. Correct Operation light (intermittent green light). Read/Write light (yellow light). Program Switch for Setting program options or modes at the console. Switch for compiling programs keyed in through the keyboard.

Recording and Correction of Programs — The instructions are entered into memory through the machine's keyboard. Programs can be printed from memory either automatically, or step by step operator control. This allows accurate location of an error, which can then be corrected without complete re-entry of the program. Long programs may be recorded on a number of cards and executed sequentially.

Magnetic Card Read/Record Unit — This allows the program and data stored in the main memory to be recorded on magnetic cards, and conversely, the contents of a card to be loaded into the Main Memory. Positive Read/Write controls to prevent inadvertent erasure of card or internal memory.

Printing Unit — Serial printing using a revolving drum unit. The unit prints all keyboard entries and partial and final numeric results as required. Program listings may also be obtained. Error message for peripheral error conditions are automatically printed when they occur. General Reset, Read and Write commands all print, allowing an audit trail of operator actions. Capacity: 28 print positions for floating point or fixed point output, (rounded or truncated, with decimal point and sign) register identification and program symbols. Speed: 30 characters per second.

P 652 Systems — The MLU 600 magnetic tape cartridge unit may be connected to the basic unit through an optional interface. This provides a random access file in the form of replaceable magnetic tape cartridges, each equivalent to 22,400 instructions, 4,480 numeric data, or 33,600 alphanumeric characters. It is also possible to connect through the standard interface as many as 4 peripheral units simultaneously, such as: LN20 Paper tape reader, PN20 Paper tape punch, Editor 4/ST Input/output typewriter, XY Plotters. Many instructions such as: Gamma spectrometers, multichannel Analyzers, Liquid Scintillation counters, etc.

The DAS 600 Disc Unit specifications relate the characteristics of this random access memory for use with the P 652 programmable calculator. The P 652 is preset to operate with either the disc unit or tape unit depending upon the I/O ROM and in-

computing calculators

ternal interface cable it contains. The DAS is available in 40, 80, 120, or 160 kilobyte memory. The memory is composed of a non-interchangeable magnetic disc containing 32 concentric tracks. Reading and recording occurs through a series of fixed heads organized into groups of eight, with one head corresponding to one track exclusively. Thus, one group of 8 heads can read and/or record 8 tracks of information (40K bytes) and 4 groups of 8 heads can read the maximum of 32 tracks (160K bytes).

The P 652 Has Computer Type Architecture — Numeric Data — The P 652 can store up to 240 signed numeric data represented in floating point with 12 digit mantissa and exponent from −99 to +99. Numeric data may be entered in natural decimal or scientific notation. Printing is automatic for all input data and may be floating point, fixed-rounded or fixed-truncated for all output data. The contents of each machine register may be printed by a single instruction.

Alphanumeric Data — The P 652 can store up 1860 alphanumeric characters (bytes) using an ASCII character set. Input, processing, and output is available through many different media.

Program Instructions — The P 652 can store a resident program of up to 1200 program instructions. These are true single address computer instructions (address and operation) — not merely "steps". Long programs can be chained. Programs can be key-entered into the memory or by a magnetic card on which the program has been previously recorded. Registers may contain numeric data, alphanumeric data, or instructions, permitting 100% memory utilization.

Dynamic Memory Partitioning — 110 memory origins are available, permitting the creation of special "reserved" areas for system software. Memory origin definitions can be made either directly or indirectly.

Subroutines — 110 memory labels are available for subroutine definitions with the option of 4 different types of return jumps. Subroutines may be nested to 7 levels.

Indirect Addressing — 10 Base registers are available for indirect addressing of operands, labels, subroutines, and memory origins.

Easy Program Logic — Users don't have to be a computer professional to program the P 652. Its convenient keyboard language (all the convenience of a mnemonic assembly language) permits compilation of complex programs directly at the keyboard. No keypunching involved. There are 24 different conditions for branching to 110 different labels. Four sense-switches, which can be set internally or externally, and one console "program" switch permit greatly simplified operating procedures for even the most complex program.

Single Step Debugging — Users check and change programs instantly, step-by-step, through the single-stepping facility. Program code may be altered, inserted or deleted directly at the keyboard. Both program printing and execution may be inspected in this manner with complete access to intermediate results at any stage in execution.

Optional ROM — This memory contains 20 microprogrammed routines for special mathematical and statistical functions with error correction procedures. They give the operator or programmer facility for calling for matrix inversions, regressions, factorials, Gaussian frequency distribution, and complex number manipulation. These functions are accessed by the F key and the 10-key numeric keyboard.

Peripherals — It is possible to connect through the standard interface as many as 4 peripheral units simultaneously, such as: LN 20 Paper tape reader; PN 20 Paper tape punch; Editor 4/ST Input/Output typewriter; Instrument controllers for gamma spectrometers, multichannel Analyzers, Liquid Scintillation counters, etc.; XY Plotters. The standard interface permits a 3,000 character per second data transfer rate. The MLU 600 magnetic tape cartridge unit may be connected to the basic unit through an optional interface. This provides a random access file in the form of replaceable magnetic tape cartridges, each equivalent to 22,400 instructions, 4,480 numeric data, or 33,600 alphanumeric characters.

Both Basic and Applications Software — The Olivetti P 652 has one of the largest supporting software libraries in existence for this type of equipment. An extensive series in BASIC Software supplies the user with common (and some not so common) numerical routines and algorithms in the form of programs very much like a FORTRAN math or statistics library — although far more comprehensive. Utility routines for system configurations are also included. These programs stand on their own but the user can also incorporate the techniques into his own programs.

Olivetti BASIC Software consists of routines in: Frequency Distributions • Paired Data Analysis • Regression Analysis • Trend Analysis and Time Series • Statistical Significance • Analysis of Variance • Probability and Sampling Distributions • Stochastic Processes • Combinatorial Analysis • Generation of Functions • Solution of Equations • Linear Algebra • Curve Fitting • Optimization • Numerical Integration • Interpolation, and Differentiation • Differential and Integral Equations • Analytic Geometry • Elementary Functions • Higher Mathematical Functions • Non-Book Functions • Magnetic Card Utility Routines • Magnetic Tape Utility Routines. Highlights of the basic software library available for mathematical and statistical routines are: Multiple Linear Regression for 16 or Less, Independent Variables or polynominal fit to 13th degree, Eigenvalues of a Real Matrix of order 9 or less and new methods in general root finding, Revised-Simplex Linear Programming System, Exact probabilities for 2 x 2 and 2 x 3 Contingency Tables, Extensive Analysis of Variance software for Two Way, Three Way Layouts, Balanced and Unbalanced designs, Incomplete designs, factorial designs, hierarchical designs, etc.

Wang 600 Calculator Offers . . . the Power of a Small Computer — A selection of memory sizes, available in three models from 312, 824 to 1,848 program steps (bytes), make the 600 rival small computers for programming power. As users needs grow, the 600 grows up to a powerful 6K and more, if users add a Magnetic Tape Cassette Memory or Disk Storage unit. Any group of eight program steps can be converted to a storage register, up to a total of 231 storage registers. This allows optimum use of the combined program steps and storage registers to meet individual requirements. Direct and indirect addressing to all registers allows arithmetic operations to be completed quickly and easily. Various decision-making capa-

computing calculators

bilities include conditional and/or, unconditional looping and branching to 256 branch points as an aid for getting complicated problems solved by user's own programs. Nine different types of decisions give programming flexibility. For example, branching from a test with the computed "GOTO" command gets directly to any program step in memory. Subroutines can be nested 8-levels deep. Sixteen user-definable Special Function Keys can be assigned up to 32 specific subroutines, so users write their own programs, using single keystroke addressing for each application. For additional do-it-yourself programming, the 600 features a LEARN mode key. For easy debugging, the display shows the exact program step and code in the memory. From there users can DELETE, INSERT, BACKSPACE, of SEARCH FOR MARK AND STOP as needed. All programs can be recorded on cassette tapes for storage and future use. Every 600 contains sixteen high-rise finger-molded keys making available thirty-two subroutine identifiers for users own dedicated functions, giving users single keystroke operation for users own programs, calculations, or access to memory. Flexibility is built into this keyboard. Since the special functions are not hardwired, they are quickly and easily redefined to relate the day-to-day changes in the user organization's operation.

Visual Display — A standard feature on all 600's is the Panaplex® display. In RUN mode, the display offers a quick and accurate check on entered data. In LEARN mode users can almost see into the memory of the system. Displaying each program step and instruction lets them debug faster and more easily while stepping through a program. A PAUSE feature displays intermediate results in ½ second increments without printing out; saves both time and paper. Final results can be shown with a fixed or floating decimal point or in scientific notation.

Column Printer — The low-cost optional 20-Column Printer gives users hardcopy printout on input and output data at 160 lines per minute. Formatted output includes sixteen alpha characters for labeling. It prints results in fixed, floating decimal point or scientific notations. While running a program, a TRACE mode uses the printer to print interim results and program commands; the TRACE mode may be programmed to be turned on or off. In LIST mode a program can be sequentially printed out with numbered program codes to give a complete listing of an entire program or segments of program if users prefer.

Programming the Wang 600 — Because no special computer language is necessary, programming can be accomplished in the same way users would mathematically solve problems on a manual calculator. Each keystroke represents one program step. The LEARN mode switch allows a program to be keyed into calculator memory. The visual display shows the operator, the program step number and the program code of the next step. A program counter automatically increments each new program step. Another useful mode is LEARN AND PRINT. In this mode each program step learned into memory is automatically printed out on the optional printer. Once a program has been learned into memory, it can be executed by switching to the RUN mode. The program can also be recorded onto the magnetic tape cassette for future use, whereby the program can be automatically reloaded into memory from the tape cassette.

Corrections, changing program steps, or modifying program sections are easily accomplished by special features designed specifically for the do-it-yourself programmer. The TRACE mode which can be turned on or off (either manually or under program control) enables programs or portions of programs to be analyzed for possible errors. Single keystroke INSERT and DELETE commands change any program step. A STEP function advances the program one step at a time in either RUN or LEARN mode. The SET PC (Program Counter) key enables any specific program step to be directly accessed. Once accessed, the STEP and BACKSPACE functions provide single keystroke access to adjacent steps. The SEARCH FOR MARK AND STOP command allows direct unconditional branching to any designated mark in the program and then stops. All these features add up to easier programming and debugging in the shortest time possible.

Above — The Wang Model 600 Operating as the Input-Output and Control of Instrumentation — The Wang 600 is an advanced programmable calculating system with 16 high-rise, finger-molded special function keys that make available 32 subroutine identifiers for dedicated functions. Magnetic tape cassette records long, multi-program blocks; loads programs into memory, and is available for auxiliary storage. Visual display and optional plug-in ROM's (read only memory) are key features.

Magnetic Tape Cassette — Designed for both recording long multi-program blocks onto magnetic tape and loading programs into memory, the Cassette Tape option can also be used for auxiliary storage. A tape can hold up to 12 blocks of 1,848 program steps of 2,772 full storage registers per side. For automatic chaining of programs or data storage and retrieval, the 600 Tape Drive features programmable "READ" and "WRITE" commands . . . under complete program control. VERIFY insures that programs have been loaded and gives manual identification of individual blocks of programs. A parity check with a flashing ERROR INDICATOR LIGHT feature proves data has been entered correctly from the tape.

Plug-In ROM's — Optional plug-in ROM's (Read Only Memory) add up to 2,048 more program steps of single keystroke, hard-wired functions. Five low-cost special purpose ROM's are available for statistics, advanced statistics, formula programming (algebraic), extended alpha listing and

computing calculators

surveying. Custom ROM's are also available for specialized programs. Once a program has been reproduced on the custom ROM, it cannot be listed, looked at or printed. This feature gives complete privacy and assurance that unauthorized personnel cannot access a listing of programs. Yet with proper instruction, programs can be run with single keystroke operation.

The Wide Range of Wang 600 Peripherals Available —

1. Series 600 Programmable Calculator
2. Model 605-1A Micro Interface
   The Model 605-1A Micro-Interface allows direct input of data from external digital devices (digital voltmeters, panel meters, counters, digital clocks. etc.) into the Wang Model 600 Calculators. As an input only interface, it accepts numeric data of up to seven digits (28 bits) and sign in parallel. The ability to handle standard BCD 8, 4, 2, 1 code with TTL voltage levels makes this interface directly compatible to most digital meters for a variety of on-line applications. Combined with the Wang 600 Calculator, users have a low cost on-line system.
3. Model 622 Keyboard
   The Model 622 Keyboard inputs alphanumeric characters directly into the calculator's memory and is quite useful when information is frequently indexed and retrieved alphabetically of when output requires numerous alpha headings and messages. The keyboard is similar in layout to the Selectric® typewriter with a total of 88 alphanumeric characters (44 uppercase and 44 lowercase) plus calculator control functions. This layout makes operations easier for users familiar with typewriter keyboards.
4. Model 633 Paper Tape Editor
   A convenient method for transferring raw data into the Wang 600 Calculating System, the Model 633 reads numeric data from paper tape punched in the standard 8-level ASCII code. Combined with the calculator, this high-speed photo-electric reader is an efficient data reduction system for statistical analysis of raw test data.
5. Model 614 Mark Sense Card Reader
   Field statisticians, researchers and engineers can collect and record data on these cards at remote locations and then process the data on the calculator. The 614 reads standard size tab cards marked with soft lead pencil, and lets users enter programs and numerical data quickly, conveniently, (and economically) into the Wang 600 Calculator. Also, programs can be written off-line without using a calculator.
6. Model 629 Dual Magnetic Tape Cassette Reader/Recorder
   Large storage at low cost is one of the key features of the 629. Two independent tape drives can be individually addressed. Both have read/record features, rewind, search forward, and search in reverse direction. "Automatic verification" insures correct reading of data. Each holds a 150-foot tape cassette containing up to 115,200 program steps giving a combined total of 230,400 program steps or 28,800 full storage registers available between the two tapes. The 629 allows users to "read/write in place". This saves time and money in applications involving updating of data. Individual data blocks can be conveniently changed in place without disturbing other blocks on the tape.
7. Model 607 Teletype Interface And Control
   This interface is designed to be compatible with a Model 33 TEG Teletype or equivalent, and allows the user's Teletype to be tied on-line to the Wang 600 Calculating Systems. It gives users variety of input/output operations such as alphanumeric input from the Teletype, hard copy alphanumeric output to the Teletype and input/output of numeric data on punched paper tape.
8. Model 623 I/O Extender
   A choice of two models in this series, Model 623-3 and 623-6, extend the one I/O connector on the calculator to either three or six I/O connectors respectively for memory devices. Circuitry within the I/O extender isolates all memory peripherals from each other, eliminating electrical reflections and feedback from one device through the others.
9. Model 640 Dual Removable Flexible Disk Drive
   The Model 640 provides low-cost storage for the needs of smaller applications. The highly reliable flexible disk platters are the size of a 45 rpm record. Depending on the models chosen, each disk stores a maximum of 131,072 or 262,144 program steps (about two to three times the capacity of a tape cassette). The disks will not break and, because of their compact size and resistance to dirt, are easily stored. Access is quick (300 milliseconds per 256 bytes) and it uses a fixed contact head rather than a floating head. With software compatibility, users can easily upgrade from a Model 640 to a Model 630 as needs grow.
10. Model 630 Fixed/Removable Disk Drive
    The high end of the peripheral line fulfills the needs of those users who have extremely large storage requirements and work with great quantities of numbers. Three sizes are available; from 1,228,800 program steps to 4,915,200 program steps or 153,600 to 614,400 full storage registers. High speed, random access and large capacity are the main features of this Disk Drive. Five different types of Error checks are also incorporated into this reliable system.
11. Model 602 Plotting Output Writer
    Adds digital plotting, as well as fully-formatted alphanumeric output capability, to the Wang 600 Calculating Systems. High-speed stepping motors (about 400 steps/second) on both the X and Y axis plots points or alpha characters in increments as small as 1/100th of an inch. It can also be used as an Output Writer.
12. Model 612 Flatbed Plotter
    The Flatbed Plotter plots continuous line or point plotting of curves and data. It also gives full alphanumeric labeling of problems solved on the Wang 600 Calculating Systems. Besides plotting standard curves, the 612 also plots bar graphs, charts, pie graphs, and three-dimensional profiles. Alphanumeric characters can be programmed in a selection of fifteen different character sizes for labeling the 10 x 15 inches of plotting area.
13. Model 632A Digital Flatbed Plotter
    A versatile, large 31" x 48" Flatbed Plotter ex-

computing calculators

pands the plotting capability of the Wang 600 Calculating System to also include plots of subdivision plans, highway horizontal and vertical plans, electrical and mechanical drawings, and much more. It's flexible because users can use any type of paper including linen, vellum or mylar. Plus the option of using fiber tip, ball point, or drafting pens to draft finished plots titled, scaled, and labeled as needed.

14 **Model 621 High-Speed Printer**
Prints at speeds of 150 characters per second, up to 132 characters per line. Has full alphanumerics in two programmable character sizes. This highly reliable dot matrix impact printing technique generates four carbon copies in addition to the original. The 621 handles continuous pin feed paper from 4″ (10.2 cm) thru 14½″ (36 cm). A complete formatted page advance is controlled by prepunched paper tape.

15 **Model 641 Thermal Printer**
The Model 641's use of a special typing head, made up of 35 heating elements, and heat-sensitive paper eliminates the need for ribbons, ink, and the noise of impact line printers. The unit prints 56 alphanumeric characters, each composed of a 5 x 7 dot matrix, at a rate of 30 characters per second. Although the 80-column unit is small (weighing only 30 pounds), it is designed for high-volume printing applications.

16 **Model 601 Output Writer**
A modified Selectric Output Writer, has full format alphanumeric capability to give hard copy output of calculated results, final reports, forms, documents, etc. The 601 can also be used as an extra typewriter when needed.

17 **Model 611 Input/Output Writer**
The Model 611 combines the features of the Model 601 Output Writer and Model 622 input keyboard in one self-contained unit. It handles full alphanumerics for both input and output applications. The combined system can work in a convenient conversational mode under program control. Operating instructions in the user's language can be typed out and the operator can type in the required information — a two-wqy conversation between the calculator and user.

Software for the Wang 600 — Software in addition to hardware, Wang provides a very comprehensive programming library of application software/programming services available for calculators. Here are some of the applications that the Model 600 programmable calculators can perform:

Statistics	Bond Billing
Mathematics	Real Estate
Mechanical Engineering	Installment Loans
H.V.A.C.	Credit Unions
Sheetmetal	Auto Dealers
Electrical Engineering	Investment Analysis
Life Insurance	Banking
Bond Trading	Chemistry
Petro-chemical	Quality Control
Life Science	Time Study
On-Line Application	Surveying
Medical	Job-Cost Estimating
Medical-Pathology	Stock Market
Medical Histories	Accounting
Radiology	Structure

Wang Model 700 Calculator — Another of Wang's Advanced Programmable Calculators combines the easy keyboard operation of manual calculators with the sophistication and power of large programmable calculators, a valuable combination for the scientific and business user. The complete set of fully interfaced peripheral equipment, including an output writer, plotters, a paper tape reader, an on-line interface, a high-speed printer, a disk drive, a dual tape drive, plus various other input and output devices, can provide flexibility for designing the calculating system for every application.

The 700 Series Calculators feature sixteen user-definable special function keys. In a given program these keys are readily assigned specific functions or subroutines which can be executed by a single keystroke. This can allow the user to write specific single-keystroke programs in each application. A magnetic tape cassette drive, records programs for future reference. Programs can be chained together for automatic execution; specific programs can be loaded under program control.

Calculators are supported by a library of programs, which modify the machine for specific applications. Statistics, engineering, surveying, and medical programs can be entered into calculators with a single keystroke, enabling the evaluation of data entered either manually or automatically from various instruments. Available investment and financing programs compute, and actually type out legal contracts. The system can be further enhanced for automatic letter writing. Wang Laboratories provides software and field support enabling the system to be installed and operating on the day it is delivered.

Software — The library of programs available on the 700 includes volumes of Statistics, Surveying, Medical, Engineering, Insurance, Investment Analysis, Estimating, Bond Analysis and Data Acquisition as well as programs for Contract Preparation in financial and automobile dealer environments. In addition, Wang Laboratories maintains a staff of field analysts available to do custom programming, and to assist in modifying existing programs such that they meet specific requirements.

Education — Wang Laboratories offers periodic programming seminars on the 700, designed to develop and sharpen basic calculator skills. The courses concentrate on manual and programming techniques, with emphasis on the relationship of the calculator to various peripherals in a given calculating system.

In addition, the Wang customer organization, SWAP, provides the medium for interchange of programs and programming techniques among Wang users.

Specifications — An advanced programmable calculator with capacity of 960 program steps and 120 storage registers (or 1,984 steps and 248 registers). Users have sixteen user-definable special function keys for single keystroke calculation of exponential and logarithmic (to the base e and the base 10) functions with results displayed (in one of two visible registers) in floating or scientific notation (with dynamic range of 10^{+99} to 10^{-99}). All storage registers perform ADD, SUBTRACT, MULTIPLY, DIVIDE AND EXCHANGE operations either DIRECTLY or INDIRECTLY. The calculator is able to make decisions based on twelve

computing calculators

conditions. It is also able to store data and programs on a standard magnetic tape cassette for future access.

The 700 calculating system consists of a calculator and various input and output devices to communicate with the calculator. The 700 calculator is available in two different memory configurations:

700   960 program steps-120 total registers
720 1,948 program steps-248 total registers

If memory requirements expand, the 700 can be field-retrofitted to the larger storage capacity of the 720.

Magnetic Tape Cassette — The magnetic tape cassette drive provides for the storage of approximately 20,000 program steps per cassette, all 20,000 of which can be chained together for automatic execution under program control. A programmable SEARCH capability enables the calculator to automatically SEARCH, LOAD, and EXECUTE specific programs on tape.

Technical Functions — The set of single-keystroke technical functions includes the exponential and logarithmic (both to the base e and the base 10) functions. In addition, square, square-root, integer and reciprocal operations are performed as single keystrokes.

Programming — Programs are entered in either the LEARN mode by touching keys in the proper sequence or in the RUN mode by loading instructions from the magnetic tape cassette. In a program, 256 subroutine codes are available to define subroutines. Subroutines can be nested five levels deep. The 700 has full decision-making capability which enables the subsequent path of the program to be determined by the results of calculations. Iterations can thereby be set up which are performed until certain conditions are met. Debugging of programs is facilitated with a TRACE mode of operation. The STEP, INSERT, and DELETE available on the "C" versions of the 700 and 720 also are useful for program debugging.

Peripheral Equipment — The 701 Output Writer types alphabetic and numeric output from the calculator with full format control. In the 702 Plotter, complete digital plotting is combined with the alphanumeric capability of the 701. Plots are therefore easily titled and labeled. With the 703 Paper Tape Reader, raw data is automatically input into the Wang Calculating system providing for an efficient "data reduction" system. Programs and data can be prepared "off-line" and input automatically from the 704 Card Reader. Instrumentation and analytical equipment are interfaced directly to the calculator using the Model 705 Micro Interface. "On-line" data acquisition is therefore facilitated. With the 706 Teletype, input and output of alphanumeric data is readily accomplished in the Wang Calculating system. The 708 Extended Memory provides external storage in increments of 4,096 program steps.

Memory controller — This is an external core memory which is utilized to store from — or recall to — the main memory of the 700, program steps, data, or alphabetic information. The 708-1 can contain as many as eight 708-2 Core Modules and, as a result, has a peak capacity of 32,768 program steps.

Plotting Output Writer — A specially modified electric typewriter with the capability of producing formatted alphanumeric output. It not only plots a graph, but also labels points. (Also available as the 702-p, a portable unit with a separate electronics package.)

Micro Interface — The 705-1 is an interface which may be hooked directly on-line to most available digital voltmeters. It produces a low cost on-line data reduction system.

Teletype Terminal — For remote or local operation, the 707 constitutes a teletype terminal and control device. There are even acoustic coupler stations for remote operation of up to four terminals.

Large programs and sets of data can be stored easily and inexpensively on the 709 or 729 Dual Tape Cassette Drive. Each 150' tape cassette can store a maximum of 90,000 program steps or the contents of 11,250 storage registers. Over 262,000 program steps can be stored and accessed randomly on the 710 Disk. The Model 711 Input/Output Writer provides a convenient means for entering alphabetic information into the calculator as well as the printout capability of the 701 Output Writer.* With the 714 Marked Sense Card Reader, data and programs can be entered directly into the System. Since the cards are prepared "off-line" without tying up the calculator, the System is more efficient. The 718 Extended Memory provides additional storage capacity in increments of 1,024 program steps. Since the 700 Calculator can address multiple peripherals, more than one 718 can be incorporated into a single system. Hardcopy output is printed at 150 characters per second or up to 200 lines per minute on the 721 High Speed Printer. In the 700 Calculating System, the 722 Input Keyboard enables alphabetic, numeric and formatting instructions to be typed directly into the calculator. The 727 Communications Interface enables two calculators to communicate via voice grade telephone lines.

Digital Flatbed Plotter — The 732 provides continuous line or point plotting of data keyed in via the 700 keyboard. Circles, bar graphs, subdivision plans as well as highway horizontal and vertical alignment plans may be plotted on the 31" x 42" surface. Any type of paper as well as various types of pens may be used.

Dual Removable Flexible Disk — The 740 consists of two disk platters, both removable and easily stored. The storage capacity of each unit is divided between the two platters; 131,072 bytes or 262,144 bytes per platter depending on the model chosen. Data can be recorded on only one side of each platter and is transferred at a rate of 300 ms per 256 bytes.

Flatbed Plotter — The 712 provides alpha labelling of problems and draws plots automatically under either manual or program control. With the 712's range of 15 different sizes of alphanumeric labels, a user can draw finished plots that are labeled, titled and scaled anywhere on the 10" x 15" surface.

Alpha Input Keyboard (722) — A remote typewriter-like keyboard with full alpha. It may be used as an input-only keyboard with the 700.

I/O Buffer — The 723, which comes in a choice of two models, extends the one I/O connector on the calculator to either three or six I/O connectors for memory devices. Circuitry within the I/O extender isolates all memory peripherals from each

*The 701, 702, and 711 can be used as manual, electric typewriters when not being used with the Wang Calculating System.

computing calculators

other, eliminating electrical reflections and feedback from one device through the others.

Dual Magnetic Tape Cassette Reader/Recorder — The 729 contains two separately controllable magnetic tape cassette units for recording from — or reading data into — the main memory of the 700C or 720C Calculators only. Up to 115,200 program steps can be contained on the 729's cassettes.

Fixed/Removable Disk — The 730 adds considerable programming power to the Wang 700: up to 4,915,200 program steps or 614,400 storage registers. Under keyboard control, the 730 offers high-speed random access storage and retrieval of alphanumeric information.

Paper Tape Reader — With the 733, data is put in automatically, off-line. The 733 is an asset to any research situation when used in conjunction with analytical instruments that produce a punched paper tape. It is also an asset in the compilation of many data points, when great speed and accuracy are desired.

Thermal Printer — The 741 is an alphanumeric output-only unit featuring fast speed, quiet operation, and low cost. The 5x7 dot matrix print head contains 35 heating elements which generate a 56-character set. The desired character is produced prior to contact with the heat-sensitive paper rather than on impact. It prints a maximum 80-character line at a rate of 30 characters per second.

A Telecommunications Controller transforms the System 2200S into an intelligent terminal. It processes data efficiently and inexpensively, and then transmits the results to the main computer.

Various Input/Output Interfaces allow on-line data acquisition and reduction of the large amount of data from measuring instruments.

Printers provide ready printout in format for applications in banks, insurance companies, auto dealers and many other businesses.

Software — A variety of statistical, mathematical and utility programs. Specially designed for use in schools (many students use the 2200S). The Huntington 1 Package runs on the Wang System 2200S. The package is a compilation of computer programs, developed by teachers and students in conjunction with the Huntington Project under the direction of Ludwig Braun and Marian Visich, Jr., and supported by the National Science Foundation. Many software packages cover a wide variety of fields, including engineering, surveying, medical, insurance, banks and auto dealers. They can save users time and money every day.

Sales and Service — Wang Systems are sold and serviced from more than 100 offices across the United States and in 47 countries worldwide.

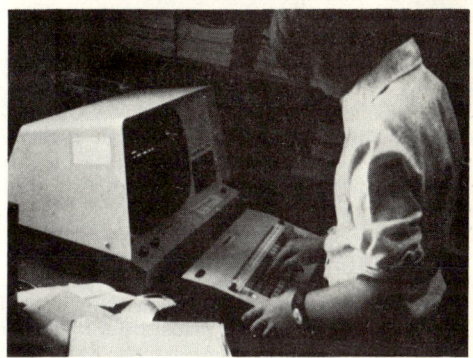

A Wang 2200S Computing System: Computer Power with Calculator Convenience — (see above) Computer power through a powerful, hard-wired BASIC language interpreter, 4K to 32K bytes of user memory, a 16-line CRT, and a most comprehensive line of peripherals describes the 2200S. Calculator convenience is through a typewriter-like keyboard which inputs complete BASIC verbs with a single keystroke each and accesses 32 subroutines in memory.

Instant-on powerful BASIC allows users to converse with the system through the touch of a key, or a glance at the silent screen. Users input program statements with a single keystroke each; renumber a program automatically in increments they determine; alter, insert, delete as they choose; the system will pinpoint and identify syntax errors for the ultimate in ease of programming. It handles a 16 x 16 matrix inversion with 4K bytes of memory, or a 61 x 61 matrix inversion with 32K bytes, and uses a MATRIX ROM to speed up the operations. It manipulates bits and bytes with assembler-like statements, such as AND, OR, XOR or ROTATE.

The unique line of peripherals includes small and large-format plotters, digitizers, medium and high-speed printers, paper-tape and batch card readers to adapt the system to user needs. Disk

The Wang BASIC Computer System 2200S — Wang offers "hands-on" computing in BASIC. The Wang System 2200S operates in "BASIC", a high-level, almost literal computer language. Users can converse through its TV-like screen, and it gives them the power they need to solve complex problems. By definition, the Wang System 2200S is a computer. The Wang System 2200S Central Processing Unit includes the powerful BASIC programming language (built-in for users convenience), and 4K to 16K bytes of working memory for programs and data. A built-in tape drive saves and loads users programs and data as they require. At users option, the system can handle one or more peripherals:

Card Readers for single card or batch processing: Particularly valuable for schools, program cards are an easy and inexpensive way for students to record their programs for later input into the Wang System 2200S.

A Digitizer enters graphic data "on-line" without time-consuming translation into numbers. It acts as a highly accurate and efficient input medium.

computing calculators

storage from 2 to 10 million bytes, and 9-track tapes give extra power. Users can add I/O interfaces for on-line data acquisition and reduction, or preprocess their data and transmit them to another Wang system or a foreign CPU.

Users can develop instant solutions through instant software: Wang's program library covers many aspects of Analysis of variance, Regression analysis, Sequential analysis, Nonparametric statistics. It contains a wide variety of mathematics and engineering programs and many utilities for plotting, sorting, disk and tape management.

Wang 2200S System Characteristics — The Display acts as conversation point with the Wang System 2200S: for program debugging, interrogation of results, display of graphs, program listings and so on. The Wang System 2200S automatically shifts in and out of floating point arithmetic when needed and provides 13-digit accuracy throughout its 10^{-99} to 10^{+99} range. Trigonometric arguments can be calculated in radians, degrees or gradians. The Dual-Purpose Keyboard allows users to type, as on a typewriter. Or program by entering the most commonly used BASIC instructions with a single keystroke. The sixteen keys across the top permit instant keyboard access to 32 subroutines or text entry strings. The Tape Drive permits "utility programs for loading and saving a program, users simply: LOAD "PROGRAMX" SAVE "PROGRAMX" The capacity of a tape cassette is 78K bytes. It can be protected against overwriting.

Several CPU Options Give System Flexibility — The standard version of the 2200S CPU includes the BASIC interpreter and 4K bytes of memory. One peripheral, for instance a printer, can be connected. To accommodate expanding needs users:

- Add memory in 4K-byte increments up to a maximum of 16K.
- Add three I/O slots and build the system that suits needs, for applications requiring additional tape cassette drives, card readers, interfacing or telecommunications.
- Add a Matrix ROM for faster, easier programming of complex mathematical problems.

For System compatibility — The Wang System 2200S is designed to be compatible with Wang's Series 2200 Computer System. It offers "hands-on" calculating and programming power. For example, in IMMEDIATE MODE, the Wang System 2200S will act like a calculator. Users enter multiple statements unnumbered in one line, and execute program immediately without entering it into memory. Example for "hands-on" computing and accuracy is: SELECT D EXECUTE (for input in degrees) :PRINT(ARCSIN(SIN(5 × 6)/LOG (EXP(3)))↑2 EXECUTE 100

To program the Wang System 2200S, users enter numbered single or multi-statement program lines, instruction by instruction. The Wang 2200S "BASIC" language includes such features as:

- 286 variable names each for numeric variables, numeric array variables, string variables and string array variables.
- One or two-dimensional numeric or alphanumeric string arrays.
- The passing of multi-argument lines to subroutines.

For program editing and debugging the Wang System 2200S:

- The whole program or sections thereof, including subroutines, can be automatically renumbered in increments users determine.
- A coded error pointer pinpoints and identifies syntax errors.
- For maximum ease in correcting errors, the EDIT feature allows users to alter, insert or delete alphanumerics in a program line, before or after entering it into memory.
- TRACE steps through the program and produces a printout or display whenever a variable receives a new value or a program transfer is made.
- HALT/STEP executes a program one step at a time.

Recently Wang introduced microprocessor-based peripherals and two software packages for multi-user distributed data processing. There are two new computers in the new line. One is the portable computer system (PCS), a 57-pound machine selling for $5,400. It will compete head-on with the IBM 5100. The PCS price includes a new processor in Wang's 2200 series, 8,000 bytes of semiconductor random-access memory, and 42,500 bytes of read-only memory. The PCS includes a 9-inch CRT display, full alphanumeric keyboard, a tape cassette for program loading and storage, and controllers for a new printer and plotter. The random-access memory is expandable to 32,000 bytes.

The second new processor is included in the 2200 series work station that might be laid out as a three-station multiprocessing system selling for $41,000. It includes the 2200 central processing unit with a five-megabyte disk, 16,000 bytes of memory, a 200-character-per-second printer, a removable floppy disk for program loading, disk multiplexer, and three hard-disk work stations.

The other hardware entries in the Wang line are a 120 character-per-second printer and a drum plotter based on an Intel 8080A microprocessor. Both are priced at $2,900, and both will eventually be sold to original-equipment manufacturers. There are also two new communications controllers, and two software packages — a management-planning system, and Wang/CASH accounting package.

Special Low-Cost Tektronix E-31 — With inherent capabilities identical to those of the 31, the E31 is exclusively a stand-alone processor. It is designed without add-on I/O capacity to offer significant savings to those not looking to expand their calculator into graphic, instrumentation or other systems. The E31 has a natural math keyboard and English-type programming. Its 35 built-in math functions and 24 user-definable keys permit short-cuts and shorthand calculations. The 512-step, 74-register memory is standard on the E31, expandable up to 16 times that capacity. In addition, there's magnetic tape storage to make programming power virtually unlimited.

There are many more convenience features that figure into the E31. Like complete alphanumerics; total editing ability; flashing display for illegal or overrange math operations; and an optional silent alphanumeric printer.

Silent Alphanumeric Thermal Printer Option —Some E31 Printer Features: The E31 Calculator Printer operates in alpha and numeric characters which makes it invaluable for two reasons. First, program listing. The printer, using English mnemonics, lists each program step in sequence. The second advantage, interactive programs.

When prompted by the program, the printer can ask the user for specific data input. Also, titled solutions are easily produced the same way. Thus, the printer not only provides for convenient execution but provides a printed copy of the program and each of its steps. Other E-31 Printer features include: a print display that results in the printing of the alpha information with whatever numerical data that is on the display. The printer can also be operated exclusively of any program. It has an automatic indication of overrange or illegal operations, and the thermal printing paper has a capacity of 18,000 lines per roll.

The standard E31 programmable calculator from Tektronix, Inc., has 512 program steps and 74 data registers. Memory expansion packs are available as options for expanding program steps and data registers. The unit has English-like programming keys and a simple keyboard that performs mathematical calculations the way users write them. It has more than 30 built-in math functions.

Tek-31 Programmable Calculator Computer Power, Calculator Ease — The Tek-31 is capable of dealing with complex problems, sophisticated programs and controlling systems. There are 35 math functions at user fingertips. Because the 31 follows natural math hierarchy to work problems users can enter data in a free format: ordinary floating, scientific floating or mixed decimal. Exponents, trig and hyperbolic functions are often solved on the keyboard. There is a full set of alpha characters. When users work this with the user-definable overlay, they get easy interaction between man and machine, for versatility. Many users customize with overlays. The overlays let them define 24 keys to specialize in many problem areas by changing the math function keys to a users own subroutines. They combine several functions they use often into one key and label it. When they need that complete operation, they press the customized key and get complex patterns resolved with one key stroke.

Alphanumeric Printer — The alphanumeric printer and keyboard work together to make operation quite easy. Besides giving hard copy printout of results, the printer aids programming. While users write a program, the printer copies it. This makes it easy to check for errors. Then it's simple to edit with the proper keys. The conversational ability of the 31 is especially useful for systems work. Users can set up a program and turn over the operation to practically anyone. The calculator will print instructions, telling the user when to input data on the keyboard or when to press a key to sample from a system component and when to turn on or off another instrument.

Tektronix 31/53 Calculator Instrumentation System — Tektronix' 31/53 system complete with plug ins, is ready for immediate data acquisition and analysis. Measures time, frequency, temperature, count, voltage, current, resistance and can compute displacement, volume or pressure. Processes, evaluates, documents and records.

Programming. An alphanumeric keyboard with user definable overlay or magnetic tape cartridge. Standard Software:
- Data Logging on alphanumeric printer with sampling rate and numbers; single or dual source.
- Data Reduction. Statistical summaries of variables and frequency distribution.
- Data Acquisition. Stores data internally and generates least squares curve fits for a line, expotential or power function.

Magnetic Tape Cartridge. Stores programs or data.

System Processor, 31 Programmable calculator. Natural math hiearchy. Alphanumerics with user-definable keys. Stores data, computes, outputs to printer, display terminal or X-Y plotter. Memory steps, 512 expandable to 8,192; Data registers, 74 expandable to 1,010.

Digital Display. 7 Segment Gas Discharge. 10 digit plus two exponents.

Data Acquisition. 153 Instrumentation Interface enables calculator to read instruments; supplies power to plug ins.

Optional Plug Ins. Users choose from four TM 500 modular test and measurement instruments. Up to 20 plug ins can be operated with additional interface units.

Direct Inputs. Any electrical signal — voltage, current, resistance, temperature, time, and frequency.

X-Y Plotter. Optional 4661 Digital Plotter gives fast, accurate graphic representations of data.

Graphic Terminal. Optional 4010 displays alphanumeric and graphic expression of calculator output. The 4010-1 is hard copy compatible.

PROM. A users own program up to 1,024 steps permanently resides in the calculator, without reducing MOS memory. Instant-on; more efficient operation.

Calculator System in Quality Control, An Example — A core memory manufacturer tests and matches magnetic characteristics of 50,000 cores from weekly production of eighty million. The former data acquisition system gave printouts of a 17-cell frequency distribution of each tested component. This meant manual processing of 30,000 printouts to produce closely-matched sets. The 31 calculator and 154 interface automated the system. Now, the calculator initiates tests, collects, processes and stores data. Then, compares data with acceptable test limits. Finally, it retrieves individual lot data, compares and matches similar components. The result is a saving of 34 manhours weekly and a production boost. Also, the calculator handles engineering and accounting work on the side.

30/10 Graphic Calculator Rapid and Interactive Graphics and Alphanumerics — Offers vivid descriptions of math concepts drawn on the 31/10 personal graphic calculator system. It's a good combination of mathematician and designer. The 31 programmable calculator has computational power and the 4010-1 Graphic Terminal is a big display system. With both machines sitting at users' desks, they have two keyboards to work with. The math keyboard of the calculator and the teletype keyboard of the terminal let users concentrate on ideas instead of mechanics, and their concepts take form on the bright screen because the system is fast. For example they tap the calculator's remote key to send these commands to the terminal: Erase screen. Accept X-Y coordinate data. Enable graphics. Start or start alpha. Print alpha. Make hard copies with optional hard copy unit. The big screen capacity — The 4010-1 terminal puts up 2590 characters. There are 35 lines of 74 upper case alpha and numeric characters per line.

computing calculators

As for graphics, it's fast with fineline draftsmanship. Drawing time is 2.6 ms. with 1024 by 1024 addressable points and 1024 on X by 780 on Y viewable points. Software lets users go to work immediately. They plug in a tape cartridge and get: automatic scaling, data plotting, X-Y coordinate value scaling, labelling and statistical operations. The 31/10 has capacity to meet many needs. Mathematical capacity via the 31 calculator with 35 math functions. Program and data storage memory — 74 data registers and 512 program steps. Both can grow with options. Users store the results on tape cartridge or print it on the 31 alphanumeric printer. The hard copy unit takes only 18 seconds to knock out the first copy and 10 seconds for extras.

User-Definable Overlays, An Example — There's a user-definable overlay which makes the calculator more approachable, yet still maintains the machine's basic math capability. Users custom label keys in their own language. For example, they might label a key standard deviation. Then, with a single keystroke, that function is executed. This feature allows even the inexperienced operator to use the machine, freeing the engineer from time spent entering data. The alphanumerics of the Tek 31 make interaction between users and the machine even easier. An example follows:

With its alpha capability, the calculator can communicate with user or his operator. It will ask for input instructions and label the results on the alphanumeric printer. An Example:

Use the definable overlay and 24 keys to deal with your special interests. Set up a subroutine for each of those 24 keys and then label your overlay. Your operator need only punch a key for the results you want. For example you could label keys magnitude, phase, real and imaginary to handle complex numbers.

Or for statistical work label them mean, variance, standard deviation and linear regression. A single keystroke does it.

There are other features which make programming simple: conditional and unconditional branching, editing, symbolic addressing and subroutine nesting.

Return addresses can be sequentially stored and recalled to permit nesting of subroutines, or can be used to compute a new starting point.

The growing trend of using programmable calculators as system processor-controllers makes good sense. They are flexible, easily programmed, adaptable, expandable — and extremely cost effective.

The calculator itself is a system — Users develop functional block diagrams. Data input via keyboard or magnetic tape. Data processing through tape input. Data manipulation and analysis by internal mathematical functions. Storage in machine memory, mag-tape, and disc. And data output through the alphanumeric printer.

Users, expand on that with interfaces and a wide range of instrumentation and they can see the calculator as the processor-manager of any system. Here is another specific example.

Interactive calculator replaces manual plotting — Radioimmunoassay techniques measure hormone and drug levels in the human body. Previously, it took half an hour of manual plotting to get test results after the radioactive complexes were counted.

Now, tape cartridge programs ask for information as the operator inputs data into the 31 keyboard. In five minutes, the calculator prints an alphanumeric plot of hormone concentrations.

Two peripherals make the system more useful and faster. Since the radioactive complex count comes from a TTY printer, a tape reader inputs data automatically into the calculator. And a 4661 digital plotter gives a graphic comparison to a standard curve.

Tek-31 Programming Procedure, an Example — In addition to conditional and unconditional branching, on the Tek 31 users have full editing capability, they can symbolically address and nest subroutines, and alphanumerics are as simple as typing one's name. With these features and the ease of programming, the computational power of a computer is available at user fingertips. And in a language they already understand.

Decision making within a user program is a simple matter with the "if" condition keys (conditional branching). The number in the display may be tested for less than zero, equal to zero, or greater than or equal to zero. In addition, users can test the condition of a programmable flag and test to see if the calculator has overranged or attempted an illegal math operation (indicated by a flashing display). If the conditions are not met, the sequentional program execution is interrupted and program control branches to the appropriate point in the program. In addition to these conditional branches, four types of unconditional branches are available.

If there is an error in programming, it's easy to examine the program, by → ← pressing step forward or step back to debug the program. The printer will list the program steps in English for users. Once users detect the error, they can insert, delete or overwrite a step. If necessary, the machine automatically renumbers the subsequent program steps. Symbolically labeling a subroutine allows users to call a subroutine by its name rather than by its location in memory. The calculator will remember the subroutine location. All users have to do is tell the calculator which subroutine they want. The calculator finds the subroutine, executes it and automatically returns.

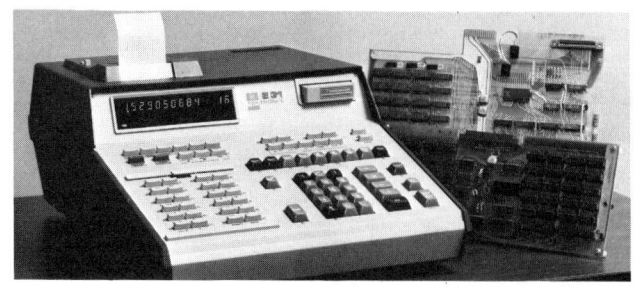

computing calculators

In order to return to the proper point in the program after branching to a subroutine, the calculator automatically remembers the return address. This return address may be sequentially stored and recalled to permit nesting of subroutines, or modified to alter the return address.

With the alpha capability in the Tek 31, the calculator actually communicates with the operator. Because the calculator can print instructions, ask for input and label results, an experienced operator is no longer a necessity. Any one who can press the start key can get the right answers.

Output — Reading the operations and results is easy in the large, bright display. Messages displayed tell users what mode they're in and if an error has been made. When users need hard copy, there's the silent alphanumeric thermal printer.

The wide variety of input and output peripherals users can interface to the Tek 31 can provide more power. These include the graphic computer terminal and x-y plotter.

Tektronix Intelligent Alternative . . . to Time-Sharing — Many computer users would like to reduce their time-sharing outlay, or even eliminate it. The 4051 offers them one fixed system charge, instead of the "fixed unknown" of time-share charges. In many cases, the 4051 can actually pay for itself in less than one year. The 4051 gives control of data and program libraries with increased reliability. Users get complete data security, low-cost local storage and fast, no-wait local input and output. Plus users acquire graphics software and capability that most commercial time-sharing services can't match. For users with in-house time-sharing, the 4051 promises reduced communications traffic, fewer system loading problems and greater accounting control. The individual user can keep personal projects local and uncomplicated. There are no sign-on protocols to interrupt the train of thought and no connect charges to worry about. This develops increased control, cost-effectiveness and creativity — and allows users interested in getting a graph to get one almost as easily as they get a number.

The 4051 uses an enhanced version of BASIC, a widely approved language for high-level language calculators. And it can operate like a desk-top calculator. Users are often surprised at the high quality of graphics they are able to generate at the first few sessions with the 4051: everything from bar charts, time plots and function plots to complex structures, and much more. The 4051's BASIC handles most application problems. For a user's most complex problems, the 4051's data communications option can put users on line to powerful graphic applications that few stand-alone calculators can offer. The 4051 offers interactivity with its Graphics flexible interface options software support; and compatibility with a whole line of Tektronix 4051 peripherals. The BASIC language built into the 4051 lets users interact with it quickly, easily and there's no daily tangle of paper tape loading. The 4051 is a well-designed, compact package. It's a desk-top system, not a whole-desk system. It's lower-cost and smaller than any ready-made mini-based system of equal ability. Plus, it includes a Tektronix terminal, which is necessary for users to add high-capability, low cost Graphics. It includes: Full 128 character set ASCII keyboard: upper/lower case; 96 printing characters; 32 control characters; upper case TTY mode. Color keyed multiple fonts: six built-in character sets: U.S.; Scandinavian; German; General European (Fr., Brit., It.); Spanish; plus special symbols.

The 4051 offers 10 user-definable keys to permit a call-up of 20 routines with shift control without typing or screen clutter. The screen is a 11" diagonal direct view storage CRT: upper case/lower case: 72 characters/line; 35 alphanumerical line/

The Tektronix 4051 BASIC Graphic Computing System — A compact data system that combines high-level BASIC-language interaction, built-in computing, and local tape memory — plus the unique graphic capabilities of the Tektronix display.

Many users are now looking for a compact computing system with local control, a convenient storage medium and enough computing power to handle their workload.

The manager . . . can interpret data, not just shuffle it. Forecasting comes alive, and costly errors are easy to spot.

The researcher . . . can spot check and analyze weeks of logged data, in seconds.

The engineer . . . can design, debug, and analyze without leaving desk-side.

The analyst . . . gains complete data security, with prompt access to unlimited taped programs.

The physician . . . can analyze patient data, obtain charts, input notes, with greater comprehension and speed.

Furthermore, with the data communications option, the 4051 distributes a user's computing by doing double-duty: as a graphic input/output terminal: and as an on-line tape storage facility.

computing calculators

page; 1024 x 780 addressable graphic points; keyboard or program control; no memory needed for display refreshing; no eye-fatiguing flicker. The tape unit is 3M cartridge with 300K capacity; the IEEE standard 488-1975-compatible interface is for plotters, instrumentation, etc.

The 4631 Hard Copy Unit — This offers a clear picture of user solutions. When a 4051 graphic display needs to be preserved, hard copies are the answer. They're convenient, permanent and easy to work with. The 4631 Hard Copy Unit is compatible with the 4010 family of display terminals and the 4006-1, as well as the 4051 BASIC Graphics System. The 4631 provides permanent, dry copies of any information displayed on the terminal screen. It can be multiplexed to make copies from up to four display terminals and/or display monitors. The 4631 is an easily installed, completely self-contained unit with attached stacking tray. It is small enough to fit on a table top, and light enough to be moved where needed. There are no messy chemicals to spill. It's clean and quiet enough to fit into the most sensitive system.

Copy time is 18 seconds for the first copy, 10 seconds for subsequent copies — efficient enough for computer time-conscious users. Its large paper roll (540 copies per roll) minimizes roll-loading downtimes. Interfacing to the 4051 is as simple as a plug-in. Operation is easy even for non-technical users. A harmonic connector on the 4631's timing board allows for format changes and copy time selection for greatest flexibility. Format A in position I, for example, gives copies of 11- or 19-inch displays in horizontal format. Format B, position II gives copies of 11-inch displays in vertical format. The unit offers flip-top maintenance. By lifting the cover, all electrical and mechanical components are readily accessible for easy repair. A special cover interlock automatically disables all hazardous voltages. Few mechanical or electrical or electronic adjustments are ever required, and all circuit boards can be quickly removed, or placed on an extender board for fast trouble-shooting. The image quality is high and dry. The 4631 uses 3M® Brand 777 Dry-Silver paper for the high image contrast needed for complex graphics and alphanumerics. It's as stable as wet-process printouts, but provides all the handling ease of dry, conventional paper; users can write on it or erase pencil marks from it without damage.

4924 Digital Cartridge Tape Unit — This inexpensive storage offers increased 4051 flexibility.

The 4051 BASIC Graphic Computing System contains its own built-in tape unit — but when pressed for time and pressing for optimum data handling capability, two tape drives are better than one. The 4924 Auxiliary Tape Unit not only enhances the built-in storage capacity of the 4051, it lets users perform tasks that no single tape drive can handle. Sort and merge operations are possible because input and output transactions can occur concurrently, with one tape unit for programs, the other for data copy tapes. Or users can double their on-line storage capacity with a highly reliable, cost-effective complement to the basic 4051 cartridge system. Each tape cartridge can hold about 300,000 bytes in high density storage. The 4924 is addressed by the same commands which control the onboard tape unit, including FIND, MARK, SAVE, OLD, PRINT, INPUT, READ, and WRITE.

The 4924 Includes Three Independent Modes of Operation — The first is on-line, in which the tape's logical organization precisely parallels the 4051's BASIC language tape command structure. The alternate, mode places the 4924 on-line to another controller which follows the IEEE (488-1975) standard protocol; and the off-line Talk-Only or Listen-Only mode, allows limited data logging capability. Talk Only mode allows independent transmission. The 4924 is immediately compatible with the 4051's IEEE standard interface. Up to 15 tape drives may be multiplexed to the 4051 at any time. Complete command summaries and operation instructions are provided with the user's manual which accompanies the 4924.

Tek 4921/4922 Calculator Flexible Disc — This mass memory device allows Tek calculators to perform jobs previously beyond the capacity of most calculators. It is available as the 4921 single disc and the 4922 dual disc units with option 4 calculator interface. It stores both program and data information in sector units. This means the calculator can engage in program library management, more sophisticated programs and handle large amounts of data. Operation is simple and straightforward. Keyboard commands from the calculator give access to the disc for read or write operations. Disc addresses and status are shown on the calculator display. The interface is optimized to make transfer of thousands of bytes of information as easy as transferring only a few.

Tek 4661 Digital Plotter — A clear picture gives a quickly-grasped idea of the calculator's mathematical data, but users need accurate detail also. The 4661 digital plotter can make quick and digitally accurate presentation pieces: statistical data, histograms, schematics, sales and production curves. Vectors are zipped out at 15 to 22 inches per second. While the pen is moving, the calculator is computing the next move. Precision drawing means no misinterpretation of data. Digital plotting keeps lines vector straight and insures absolute repeatability to within .005 inch. Scale controls give full scale plots within a 10 × 15 inch plotting area. Each axis can be separately reduced to half scale by front panel controls. Users can set their data zero point any place on the plot from the calculator or the plotter. Zero is set automatically for first quadrant operations on power up. Users can draw on any size paper they want — from sketch pad size to 11 x 17 inches easel-size. Electrostatic hold down keeps it in place.

Because users are replacing minicomputers with the Model 31 programmable calculator; using the 31/53 calculator instrumentation system; the 31/10 graphic calculator that uses the 4010 graphics terminal; the 4661 digital plotter and the 4922 flexible disk memory. Tektronix, Inc., moved quickly to bring out its 4051 BASIC Graphic Computing System.

The IBM 5100 Portable Computer — The competition to advanced programmable calculators, but at about twice the cost is the IBM 5100 compact, portable computer designed for personal use. Weighing less than 50 pounds, it can be carried in its own case and used in office or home — wherever there is a 115 A.C. grounded wall outlet.

It features an alphanumeric keyboard . . . a 15-key calculator pad . . . 14 interactive command keys . . . a video screen with a 1,024 character display . . . and a modular memory that can be increased from 16K to 64K positions.

Three Problem-Solver Libraries are available on tape cartridges. They contain the most often used analytical routines. These tested programs permit the user to concentrate on the solution of a problem rather than the operation of a computer.

The IBM 5100 Portable Computer is available with three language model options: APL, BASIC or both. All models are equipped with a tape cartridge specifically designed for high-speed data handling as well as high-capacity data storage. In addition, a TV monitor adapter is provided.

Options Available for the IBM 5100 Portable Computer — 5103 Printer — An 80 character per second, 132 print position printer.

5106 Auxiliary Tape Unit — Doubles the accessible storage capacity.

Communications Adapter — Permits access to remote data bases and program libraries.

Carrying Case — A case with a sturdy carrying strap is available.

The Mathematics Problem-Solver Library provides engineers and scientists with preprogrammed mathematical routines. The conversational nature of the programs enables the user to define a problem with a series of questions and answers. And to search for the solution with routines covering areas such as:
- Solutions to Simultaneous Linear Equations
- Matrix Eigenproblem
- Eigenvalues and Eigenvectors
- Integration
- Differentiation
- Interpolation, Approximation and Smoothing
- Zeroes and Extrema of Functions
- Ordinary Differential Equations
- Finite Fourier Transform
- Special Functions
- Linear Programming

The Business Analysis Problem-Solver Library consists of 30 interactive BASIC routines designed to provide business and financial analysts, product planners, economists and engineers with quantitative methods that might be impractical on a manual basis. Each routine can be used without the assistance of specialized data processing personnel.

The IBM 5100 enhances the problem-solving professional's capability to examine additional, alternative case studies . . . respond to requests for special financial studies . . . produce spread sheet, investment, break-even and time series analyses.

The Business Analysis Library provides the user with easy-to-operate procedures for:
- Leave vs. Purchase Analysis
- Cash Flow Analysis
- Forecasting
- Resource Projection
- Profitability Analysis
- Return-on-Investment Analysis
- Budgeting
- Financial Projection
- Spread Sheet Preparation

The Statistics Problem-Solver Library offers concise programs designed for the problem solver who uses statistical techniques. Each program guides users, at their own pace, through a set of procedural instructions. This interactive mode simplifies usage and enables the user to concentrate on problem solving.

The statistical analysis programs include:
- Regression and Correlation Analysis
- Multivariate Analysis
- Design Analysis
- Nonparametric Statistics
- Time Series Analysis
- Biostatistics

A

abbreviated addressing — A process of shortening the direct address mode by using only part of the full address and providing a faster means of processing data because of the specially modified code.

abscissa — The horizontal, or X axis on a graph or chart.

absolute address — 1. An actual location in storage of a particular unit of data; address that the control unit can interpret directly. 2. The label assigned by the engineer to a particular storage area in the computer. 3. A pattern of characters that identifies a unique storage location or device without further modification. (Synonymous with machine address.)

absolute coding — Machine language instructions, directly acceptable to a computer without further modification.

absolute value — Refers to the numerical value of a number or symbol, but without referring to its algebraic sign. Absolute value is signified by vertical lines on both sides of the number or symbol. Therefore, |7| is the absolute value of plus 7 or minus 7.

abstract quantity — A quantity which does not involve the idea of matter, but simply that of a mental conception: it is expressed by a letter, symbol, or figures. Thus, the number three represents an abstract idea, that is, one which has no connection with material things, while three feet presents to the mind an idea of a physical unit of measure called a foot. All numbers are abstract when the unit is abstract.

AC adapter — A typical Universal AC Adapter operates over 70 of the most popular calculator models from Alcor, APF, Commodore, Hanimex, Litronix, Melcor, Novus, Rockwell, Sharp, Texas Instruments, Unisonic, Unitrex . . . and others. A Voltage Selector Switch makes it useable on 3, 4½, 6, 7½ and 9 volt calculators. An exclusive quadplug with four interchangeable tips accommodates for differing polarities and a wide variety of calculator receptacles. It is also useable on radios, tape recorders, walkie-talkies and other non-rechargeable devices.

acceleration time — The time between the interpretation of instructions to read or write on tape, and the transfer of information to or from the tape onto storage, or from storage onto tape, as the case may be. (Synonymous with start time.)

access — Ability to store or retrieve information in a memory device.

access, direct — A memory device which allows the particular address to be accessed in a manner independent of the location of that address; thus, the items stored in the memory can be addressed or accessed in the same amount of time for each location. Thus, access by a program is not dependent upon the previously accessed position.

access, immediate — Pertaining to the ability to directly obtain data from, or place data in, a storage device or register without serial delay due to other units of data, and usually in a relatively short period of time.

accessory — An additional part or an added feature which is designed to increase the function or add to the value or capacity of equipment without redesigning or altering the basic function of the equipment.

access time — The interval between the insertion and completion of storage, or between the request for and delivery of data from a memory.

accidental stops, (calculators) — On most units pressing any key will stop a program. Users must be careful to avoid pressure on the keyboard during program operation or being clumsy when keyboarding.

accounting checks — Accuracy controls on input data that are based on such accounting principles as control totals, cross totals, or hash totals.

accumulator (AC) — The accumulator is a 4, 8, 12 or 16-bit register that functions as a holding register for arithmetic, logical, and input-output operations. Data words may be fetched from memory to the AC or from the AC into memory. Arithmetic and logical operations involve two operands, one held in the AC, the other fetched from memory. The result of an operation is retained in the AC. The AC may be cleared, complemented, tested, incremented or rotated under program control. The AC also serves as an input-output register. Programmed data transfers pass through the AC.

accuracy — The degree of freedom from error, or conformity to truth. Contrasts with precision; Example: an improperly computed 8-digit reading is more precise but less accurate than a properly computed 4-digit reading.

ac dump — The intentional, accidental, or conditional removal of all alternating current or power from a system or component. An a-c dump usually results in the removal of all power, since direct current is usually supplied through a rectifier or converter.

acquisition and analysis system calculator — One type calculator system masters a wide range of data acquisition and analysis operations. It can capture, translate, compare, analyze, record and store electrical measurement data. It's like a minicomputer system but without softwear or language problems. These systems replace manual logging; eliminate conversion tables and visual strip chart scaling. They are automatic and virtually free from human error. In effect, the calculator is the system processor-controller, working with a counter or multimeter — or two of a kind. The interface unit holds the plug-ins and translates messages between instruments and calculator. The calculator can control up to 20 plug-ins. This type desktop programmable system reads a vast signal range of time, frequency, voltage, current, resistance and counts events. Coupled with transducers, it gives readings in user terms, automatically: statistical parameters, averages, frequency distribution, group about the mean; it fits curve and logs data and times events; converts input and labels output on the alphanumeric printer.

acronym — A word formed from the first letter or

letters of the words in a name, term, or phrase; e.g., SAGE from Semi-Automatic Ground Environment, and ALGOL from ALGOrithmic Language.

action cycle — Refers to the complete operation performed on data. Includes basic steps of origination, input, manipulation, output, and storage.

actual decimal point — A decimal point used for "display" purposes; e.g., when a numeric value is listed on a printed report, the decimal point will often appear as an actual printed character. When specified for data to be used within a computer, it requires an actual space in storage.

adaptor, AC — A device which allows a battery-operated calculator to be run off standard current.

addend — The number or quantity to be added to another number or quantity (augend) to produce the result (sum).

adder — A device whose output is the sum of the quantities represented by the inputs.

addition, destructive — The sum appears in the location previously occupied by the augend which is thus lost. The addend remains in its original location.

addition, nondestructive — The first operand placed in the arithmetic register is the augend, the next operand is the addend, and the sum replaces the augend and thus becomes the augend for a subsequent addition.

add mode, floating point — Entries are automatically punctuated with the last two digits as decimals with no need to enter the decimal point. This feature is especially useful when working in dollar and cent calculations.

address — 1. A character or group of characters that identifies a register, a particular part of storage, or some other data source or destination. 2. To refer to a device or an item of data by its address.

addressable memory registers — Addressable memory registers make data manipulations much simpler. The user can store data in any register, retrieve data from any register, or even do register arithmetic, using or modifying data in any register.

addressable registers, hand-held programmables — On some units, registers $R_1, R_2, \ldots, R_9$ constitute the addressable registers. Their respective contents are referred to as $r_1, r_2, \ldots, r_9$. Operations refer to them by number. The registers are typically used to accumulate sums or to store constants or intermediate results. Users can store the value of the stack's X-register in any addressable register, or they can recall the value in any addressable register to the X-register. Additionally, they can store in any register an arithmetic sum, difference, product, or quotient of the contents of the given register and the X-register. For example, if R_5 contains 100 and if X contains 70, users can store the difference $(100 - 70 = 30)$ in R_5.

address, direct — An address that indicates the location where the referenced operand is to be found or stored with no reference to an index register or B-box. (Synonymous with first-level address.)

address, effective — 1. A modified address. 2. The address actually considered to be used in a particular execution of an instruction. 3. An address obtained by the combination of the contents of a specific index register with the address of an instruction. 4. The address used for the execution of an instruction. This may differ from that of the instruction in storage.

address, indirect — 1. An address that specifies a storage location whose content is either an indirect address or another indirect address. 2. A single instruction address that is at once the address of another address. The second address is the specific address of the data to be processed. This is classified as single-level indirect addressing. But, the second address could also be indirect, which is then second-level indirect addressing. This same process could develop third, fourth, fifth, and other levels of indirect addressing.

addressing level — 1. Zero level addressing, the address part of an instruction is the operand, for instance, the addresses of shift instructions, or where the address is the date (in interpretive or generating systems). 2. First level addressing, the address of an instruction is the location in memory where the operand may be found or is to be stored. 3. Second level of addressing (indirect addressing), the address part of an instruction is the location in memory where the address of the operand may be found or is to be stored.

address memory — Every word in memory has a unique address. A word may be defined as a set of bits comprising the largest addressable unit of information in a programmable memory. The address of a word is its location in memory.

addressing modes, microprocessor — Common addressing modes include direct, immediate and indirect. In the immediate mode, the instruction includes data, while in the indirect mode, an address preloaded into a register increases the address bits in an instruction. Variations and extensions of these modes are also used, so a basic instruction can be manipulated several times and ways.

addressing, symbolic — Refers to a fundamental procedure or method of addressing using an address (symbolic address) chosen for convenience in programming or of the programmer in which translation of the symbolic address into an absolute address is required before it can be used in the computer.

address, multiple — A type of instruction that specifies the addresses of two or more items which may be the addresses of locations of inputs or outputs of the calculating unit, or the addresses of locations of instructions for the control unit. The term multiaddress is also used in characterizing computers; e.g., two-, three-, or four-address machines. (Synonymous with multiaddress.)

address, register — 1. A permanent storage register or location within a machine, and the pattern of characters that identifies it. In some systems, channel addresses are identified by 3-digit reading. 2. An identifying name, label, or number for a source or storage location.

address, track — Binary codes on magnetic tape or disc to locate data stored in other tracks by actual code patterns as indicated by the address, or by completing a count, or by simply noting their positions.

address types — An address is a coded designation of the instruction or of the location of data or program segments in memory. The address may refer to storage in registers or the many types of memories. The address code itself may be stored so that a location may contain the address of data rather than the data itself. This form of addressing is quite common in microprocessors, but there is considerable variation due to the efforts to reduce execution time.

add-subtract time — Refers to the time required by a digital computer to perform addition or subtraction, not including the time required to obtain the quantities from storage and put the result back into storage.

add time, (in microseconds) — The time required to acquire from memory and execute one fixed-point add instruction using all features such as over-lapped memory banks, instruction look-ahead and parallel execution. The add is either from one full word in memory to a register, or from memory to memory; but not from register to register.

ADP (Automatic Data Processing) — 1. This acronym pertains to equipment such as EAM (Electronic Accounting Machines) and EDP (Electronic Data Processing) equipment units, or systems. 2. Data processing performed by a system of electronic or electrical machines so interconnected and interacting as to reduce to a minimum the need for human assistance or intervention.

ads (Address Data Strobe) — An output signal used to clock address information to the systems' memory or peripherals.

advanced calculator business applications examples — Inputs: New orders, packing slips, inventory receipts, vendor invoices, employee time cards, customer payments. Storage: Customer files, accounts receivable open items, open orders, inventory, employee files, accounts payable and vendor files. Outputs: Order acknowledgments, packing lists, invoices, invoice registers, customer statements, aged trial balance, paychecks, accounts payable, checks, check registers, stock status reports, inventory lists, operating statements, balance sheets.

advanced calculator business system — For small manufacturing concerns it might consist of the calculator with small memory, String Variable ROM, Peripheral Tape Cassette, Hopper Card Reader, and Typewriter. With this configuration, users could automate nearly every number-crunching task in a typical shop: payroll, billing, loan contracts, inventory control, etc. with efficient users getting vital management information to help them make sound decisions for cutting costs, bidding jobs, planning investments, and the like. As an added bonus, the advanced calculator could maintain a list of important customers, periodically mailing them "personal" letters describing important new products or services.

advanced calculator consulting engineering system — This could include cassettes, The RAM big memory, Matrix ROM, Page Printer and Plotter. Versatility is important. Not only will advanced units handle complex structural problems — steel and concrete column design, concrete beam design, pre-stress beam design, shear-and-moment plotting — but they'll handle most business problems as well.

advanced calculator communication capabilities — Several advanced calculators are now equipped for communications. The addition of Data Communications Interface (cable & control ROM) allows these units to connect with another terminal or with another calculator to act as a remote batch terminal to a larger computer for remote job entry, or to act as a timesharing terminal. Two BASIC statements defined by the control ROM are used to write messages in strings to, or read messages from, a remote terminal or computer asynchronously or synchronously at speeds from 110 to 9600 bits/sec on one specific unit. Another ROM adds IBM-type bisynch protocol, transmission error detection, ASCII-to-EDCDIC conversion, programmable error recovery for various BASIC language programs, and bisynch transparent text mode. A third ROM makes some units act and look like an interactive teleprinter to a time-sharing computer, allowing synchronous communication in BASIC and free text (which can include programs in other languages, such as FORTRAN). These units tend to keep semanticists busy with calculators that look like a remote terminal and act like a remote terminal *and* a minicomputer, and remote terminals that look like pocket calculators.

advanced calculator educational system — This would conceivably include an advanced calculator with small memory, String Variable ROM, Marked Card Reader, Page Printer, and Plotter. In this configuration, it's a strong, versatile educational tool which can be equally at home in the science, mathematics, business, or computer science class room. Calculators for both teacher and student, could help to raise scientific education out of the tedium of routine calculation and into the challenging arena of abstract concepts. A process that's enhanced by a complete package of educational programs and teaching materials. Some American educational software is considered the finest and most advanced. And it's available on all levels — from elementary through university.

advanced calculator research lab system — This would conceivably consist of an advanced unit with big memory, Matrix ROM, Page Printer, High-speed Tape Reader, and Plotter. At this level, a Fourier Analysis or a Two-Way Analysis of Variance would be finished instantly as would other problems. A 20×20 matrix inversion might take the better part of a minute.

advanced calculator terminal systems — As proven systems with many years of hard field use at many organizations, calculators have demonstrated abilities to disperse computing power to field offices for many tasks, sharply improving employee productivity while reducing operating costs. Many units are designed into fully programmable, multi-user systems using powerful processors and lines of peripherals to match user needs. Some units contain processors with 48K user memory. Users can simultaneously access the system and accomplish data entry, data processing, file management or report generation. Programming can be quickly accomplished in calculator BASIC language. Each user can run a separate program and access single or multiple public or restricted files. There's no spinning wheels trying to make a limited system fit specialized needs. Advanced calculators with inherent flexibility and powerful software lets the users at each remote site readily accomplish the task at hand.

advanced calculator vs minicomputer — The differences between minicomputers and calculators become less and less apparent. One might consider the capabilities of a medium-power advanced system. One specific device has 4K to 8K bytes of semi-conductor user memory, up to 16K bytes of preprogrammed read-only memory, a programming language, and even a 15KB "operating system." One of the features that marks it as a calculator is that its BASIC interpreter and many of its functions are hardwired. Another is that its keyboard, 32-character display, 80KB random-access tape cassette, and 80-column/250-lpm thermal printer are built into one unit. Also, its cpu takes 12 μsec to add two 16-bit words. Still, it offers its single user interactive debugging and keyboard functions like program scrolling, statement fetching, and program loading.

advanced programmable calculator system — A typical system combines the easy keyboard operation of manual calculators with the sophistication and power of large programmable calculators, a valuable combination for the scientific and business user. The complete set of fully interfaced peripheral equipment, including an output writer, plotters, a paper tape reader, an on-line interface, a high-speed printer, a disk drive, a dual tape drive, plus various other input and output devices, provides the flexibility for designing the calculating system for every application. Most calculator systems feature sixteen user-definable special function keys. In a given program these keys are readily assigned up to 64 specific functions or subroutines which can be executed by a single keystroke. This allows the user to write specific single-keystroke programs in each application and calculator cassette drive. A magnetic tape cassette drive can be provided when the user records programs for future reference. Programs can be chained together for automatic execution; specific programs can be loaded under program control. Most advanced calculators are supported by a library of programs, available on tape cassettes, which modify the machine for specific applications. Statistical, engineering, surveying, and medical programs can be entered into the calculator with a single keystroke, enabling the evaluation of data entered either manually or automatically from various instruments. Available investment and financing programs compute, and actually type out legal contracts. These systems can be further enhanced for automatic letter writing. Many major suppliers provide software and field support enabling their systems to be installed and operating on the day they are delivered.

advanced programmable desktop calculator, example — A typical example of an advanced desk-top programmable calculator is one well suited to a variety of scientific, engineering, research, and industrial applications. A specific unit contains a built-in thermal printer with alphanumeric, mathematic, and trigonometric functions and a high-speed bidirectional data cartridge. This almost standard model includes 472 program steps and 10 data registers. The memory can be expanded to 2,008 program steps. Input to the unit can be via the keyboard, which includes: 15 special function keys, 10-key numeric pad, program language and control keys, editing keys, and 28 scientific functions; or through the advanced series input peripherals. The units optional interface module provides the capability to interface to all of the supplier's peripherals and various instruments.

advanced programmable hand-held calculator — A typical advanced pocket calculator is a fully programmable instrument which features a built-in magnetic card reader/writer, a 100+-step program memory, 50+-pre-programmed functions and operations and up to 10 addressable data memory registers. These capabilities allow the units to be used in many ways: 1. With pre-recorded program cards from suppliers the units can be used by anyone to solve complex problems in such fields as electrical, chemical and mechanical engineering; statistics; mathematics; finance; medicine; navigation; aviation, and surveying. Users simply select the appropriate pre-recorded program card and pass it through the units built-in card reader. They key in known data and start the program running as described in the easy-to-follow instructions provided with each program. Various catalogs of Application Packages, each of which contains up to 40 pre-recorded programs, can be obtained from various pocket calculator dealers or via the mails. 2. As a user-programmed calculator, the units let users write programs of up to 100 or more steps and record them on blank magnetic cards (10 to 20 supplied) for future use anywhere, anytime. Depending on user's needs, a program can be simple or complex. It can incorporate any of the pre-programmed functions and operations on the machines or use conditional branches based on logic comparisons, loops and one-level subroutines. Various user-definable keys let them execute different segments of their program directly from the keyboard. Also important, some units offer full editing capability for fast, convenient program modification or correction.

alarm functions, calculator — Many units offer everything from a simple alarm indication in red on the printout, to a separate alarm relay on each channel, and functions in between. Alarms operate on a digital comparison basis. Digitized input data for a given channel is compared with digitized alarm setpoint values. Logic operates when limits are exceeded, placing that channel in alarm.

alarm, print function — A "print on alarm" feature adds to flexibility. On some calculators, the data system can be set to scan at its maximum rate over and over again without data output until a channel is detected in alarm. The calculator then prints out a complete data scan from memory, regardless of which channel is in alarm. A second mode is to set the system to scan (and print-on-alarm) all channels at the maximum rate, and automatically print out all channels at a desired interval even if there is no alarm. An alarm condition triggers a priority printout immediately, giving the system an effective alarm scan at one rate, print out at another.

alarm, print on change only feature — A "print-only-on-change-of-alarm status" option is similar to standard print-on-alarm feature, but causes printout of data frame whenever any channel changes alarm state. If any channel exceeds limits after previously falling within limits or vice versa, a scan printout occurs. This option is quite useful in production or QC testing of quantities of similar devices being cycled in ramp programs.

alarms, data acquisition system — This low-cost option presents the user with a great array of alarm flexibility as offered by many data acquisition systems. A part of the flexibility is built into the underlying architecture of the microprocessors, memories, and alarm programming by keys on a channel-by-channel basis. Often RAM locations are organized in a way that shares storage. Signal input channels and alarm setpoints are interchangeable, and thus result in a tradeoff of channels versus alarm setpoints. Various tables illustrate several possible interrelationships.

alarm totalizer — An alarm totalizer is a handy feature of the basic alarm packages. It displays the total number of channels in alarm on that scan and gives the viewer a quick understanding of the situation. This is standard on practically all alarm-equipped systems except those with certain custom options.

algebraic entry advantages — The case for algebraic is straight-forward: It lets users key the problem just as they would state it. Because it works the way they think, many people find it easier to master and more natural to use. That's why many manufacturers chose this method. For example, when users think in algebraic notation, they say, "Two times four equals eight". With RPN, they have to say, "Two and four multiplied". An oversimplification, but it points up the fundamental difference.

algebraic entry method (Texas Instruments Inc, others) — This technique lets users key the problem just as they would state it. A unique register system provides a sum-of-products capability directly at the keyboard. This ability to store the first product while the second is being calculated is in addition to the memory accessed by the memory keys. The efficiencies are suggested by this simple problem:

$(2 \times 3) + (4 \times 5) = 26$
TI's Algebraic Entry Method:
$2 \times 3 + 4 \times 5 = 26$
Reverse Polish Entry Method:
$2 \uparrow 3 \times 4 \uparrow 5 \times + 26$

algebraic entry vs Reverse Polish Notation — Most hand-held scientific calculators use either algebraic entry or Reverse Polish Notation (RPN). There are two basic schools of thought on which is best — each manufacturer advocating his own. And, to make it more confusing, a good case can be made for both by the careful selection of sample problems. In truth, there is no ultimate answer. Either system can be operated with ease by the experienced owner. And either can be a boon to the simple solution of the most complex problems. Many practiced users of RPN now swear by it. But owners of algebraic machines can find RPN awkward and confusing. It boils down to individual preference.

algebraic language — Many users prefer to key problems exactly as they would write them. Algebraic language used by many types of calculators permits the use of symbols, implied multiplication, nested parentheses, traditional formulas and other basic functions. The language helps to achieve programming and operating simplicity by providing branching and subroutining capabilities.

algebraic logic — The problem is entered as it would be written. To perform the problem (minus 5 plus 4 minus 3), the following sequence is followed: depress (minus), depress (5), depress (plus), depress (4), depress (minus). Depress (3). Algebraic logic is found on some minicalculators and the large programmable machines. Calculating machines used in offices before the introduction of electronic calculators (electromechanical machines), all use the adding machine logic. Office personnel accustomed to these machines might have difficulty in using a machine with algebraic logic and serious mistakes can be made. Machines with algebraic logic are more suited for the consumer market, or the programmer who has to enter very lengthy equations on the machine.

algebraic versus polish notation — Most calculator chips on the market today use one of two general approaches to data entry. One, algebraic notation, calls for data to be entered into the calculator in more or less the same way they are written on paper, so that the problem $(2 + 3 = 5)$ would be worked out by pressing keys 2, +, 3, =, in that order. (Sometimes a calculator has keys += and −=; these are also algebraic, with the convention that the sign of a number is entered after, rather than before, its numerical value, as in conventional handwritten notation.) Among the more widely known algebraic calculators are those manufactured by Texas Instruments.
The other general approach is called reverse Polish notation, devised by Polish mathematician Jan Lukasiewicz. It places the arithmetic operation after, rather than between, the two numbers on which it is executed. It makes parentheses unnecessary and simplifies the design of push-down stacks, which are required in calculators that can "remember" more than one number. Hewlett-Packard calculators use it, as shown by the "enter" key on their keyboards, which indicates the boundary between two successive numeric entries.

algorithm — A prescribed set of well-defined rules or processes for the solution of a problem in a finite number of steps, for example, a full statement of an arithmetic procedure for evaluating sin x to a stated precision. Contrast with heuristic.

allocate — Refers to assignment of storage in a computer to maintain routines and subroutines, thus fixing the absolute values of symbolic addresses.

alpha — The first letter of the Greek alphabet, and thus, a symbol representing first. 2. An abbreviation for Alphanumeric. 3. A feature of representation of data in alphabetical characters in contrast to numerical.

alphameric display operation, calculator — On some calculators light-emitting diodes (LEDs) provide a bright, 32-character display, which is easy to read over a wide range of angles and distances. Each of the 9/32 inch (.714 cm) high characters uses a 7 × 5 dot matrix to provide naturally-shaped numbers, letters, and symbols. When greater than 32 characters are being input, the characters will automatically shift to the left to allow room for the additional characters being keyed in. To view the beginning of the input, press →; this moves the character in the display to the right. Pressing ← performs the reverse operation. Although the display is 32 characters, an 80-character line can be keyed in with the automatic scrolling both for program lines and keyboard operations. (Some units)

alphanumerical — A coding system capable of representing alphabetical characters and other symbols as well as numbers.

alphanumeric keyboard, calculator — On some units the keyboard inputs alphanumeric characters directly into the calculator's memory and is quite useful when information is frequently indexed and retrieved aalphabetically or when output requires numerous alpha headings and messages. On these units the keyboard is similar in layout to the Selectric typewriter with a total of 88 alphanumeric characters (44 uppercase and 44 lowercase) plus calculator control functions. This layout makes operations easier for users familiar with typewriter keyboards.

alphanumeric string variables — Some versions of BASIC provide an additional variable form, the alphanumeric string variable. It is distinguished from numeric variables by the manner in which it is named, a letter or a letter and a digit followed by a $. String variables can be used in a program for the input, loading, storing, transferring, comparing, and printing of alphanumeric data.

alphanumeric typewriter keyboard — This enables upper and lower case alphabetic, numeric and system control instructions to be typed directly into the system, from a keyboard arranged like a typewriter.

alpha prompting capability — With the alpha capability in some units, the calculator actually communicates with the operator. Because the calculator can print instructions, ask for input and label results, an experienced operator is no longer a necessity. Any one who can press the start key can get the right answers.

ALU (Arithmetic-Logic Unit) — The ALU is the heart of and one of the essential components of a microprocessor. It is the operative base between the registers and the control block. The ALU performs various forms of addition, subtraction, and the extension of these to multiplication, division, exponentation, etc. The logic mode relates to the operations of gating, masking and other manipulations of the contents of registers.

ambient — Refers to atmospheric conditions and other disturbances surrounding a device.

ambiguity error — A gross error, usually transient, occurring in the reading of digits or numbers. An imprecise synchronism which causes changes in different digit positions, such as in analog-to-digital conversion. Guard signals can aid in avoiding such errors.

American Standards Code for Information Interchange (ASCII). — A universal code proposed by the American Standards Association, which now has as its collating sequence blanks, special characters, numbers, alphabet (with no gap between R and S in the alphabet).

analog — 1. The representation of quantities by means of continuous physical signals. 2. Generally the term refers to a physical system in which the performance of measurements yields information concerning a class of mathematical problems.

analog backup — Provision for control by analog instrumentation, in the event of a computer system failure.

analog computer — A computer which operates on the principle of creating a physical (usually electrical) analog of a mathematical problem to be solved. Variables such as temperature or flow are represented by the magnitude of a physical phenomenon such as voltage or current. These variables are manipulated by the computer in accordance with mathematical formulas "analoged" on it.

analog flatbed plotter — A typical unit provides continuous line or point plotting of curves and data, as well as full alphanumeric labeling of problems solved with some systems.

analog output — As opposed to digital output, the amplitude is continuously proportionate to the stimulus, the proportionality being limited by the resolution of the device.

analog-to-digital (A/D) conversion — Production of a digital output, indicating the value of an analog input quantity.

analog-to-digital conversion techniques — Much of the information required by a calculator for the various computations necessary in the processing system may be available as analog input signals instead of digitally formatted data. These analog signals may be from a pressure transducer, thermistor or other type of sensor. Therefore, for analog data an A/D (analog-to-digital) converter must be added to the system.

analysis of covariance program — Computes the statistics needed to perform an analysis of covariance on a single variable of classification with an associated variable in a randomized experiment.

analysis of variance program — The one-way analysis of variance tests the differences between the population means of k treatment groups. Group i (i = 1, 2, . . . , k) has n_i observations (treatment group may have equal or unequal number of observations).

analysis of variance, stat pack — An analysis of variance includes most commonly required analytical techniques for pre-analysis, analysis and post-analysis of commonly occurring statistical models. Each program allows graphic multiple comparisons; data transformations; plotting and listing of marginal means; analysis of marginal means with contrasts or orthogonal polynomials; automatic printout of significance levels; complete analysis of variance tables; and easy correction and manipulation of entered data. Among the programs included are: One-way analysis of variance, with balanced or unbalanced data, using a completely randomized design model. Two-way analysis of variance — either balanced via standard procedures with Tukeys test for zero interactions; or unbalanced, via least squares analysis or weighted squares of means. Three-way analysis of variance via least squares analysis, plus a generalization of Tukeys test for testing three factor interactions. Other programs include one-way analysis of covariance and latin square designs — with each analysis constructed to permit full plotting capability and graphic multiple comparisons.

analyst, systems — A person who designs information-handling procedures which incorporate computer processing. The systems analyst is usually highly skilled in defining problems and developing algorithms for their solution.

analytical statistics — The design and use of analytical statistics is to enable one to draw statistical inferences about the characteristics of the entire statistical "universe" of data from a small sample.

ancillary equipment — A term which is often interchangeable with peripheral equipment which relates to all types of input-output, communication and interface equipment.

AND — A Boolean logic operator having the property that all inputs must be true for the output to be true.

AND GATE — A component which implements the AND operator.

angular functions, calculator — Some scientific calculators provide users with 6 trigonometric functions. In addition, users have their choice of angular modes, various angle conversions, and angle addition and subtraction in degrees,

minutes, seconds, and hundredths of a second.
angular modes, calculator — Scientific units calculate trigonometric functions using angles expressed in degrees, radians, or grads (360 degrees = 2π radians = 400 grads). When some calculators are switched ON, they automatically are set in degree modes. In order to convert an angle from degrees to radians and back, Angular Mode Conversion procedures are provided.
ANSI (American National Standards Institute) — Formerly ASA and USASI, an organization that develops and publishes industry standards.
antilogarithm — The number from which a given logarithm is derived. For example, the logarithm of 4261 is 3.295. The antilogarithm of 3.295 would therefore be 4261.
APL language — A programming language developed by Iverson. An unusually extensive set of operators and data structures are used to implement what is considered by many to be the most flexible, powerful, and concise algorithmic/procedural language in existence. Primarily used from conversational terminals, its applicability to "production" job processing is limited but its value for educational and investigative work is great.
application package — A set of programs and/or subroutines used to solve problems in a particular application, i.e., business, scientific, financial, etc.
applications program — A program written to accomplish a specific user task (such as payroll) as opposed to supervisory, general purpose, or utility programs.
applications programs procedure — Preparation of applications programs can be broken down into the following steps:
1. Write the source program. The cost of this step will be proportional to the length of the program, and therefore will be a function of the memory required by the CPU. A good operating system will further reduce the size of source programs by providing commonly used subroutines such as mathematical functions, input/output drivers, and program execution scheduling.
2. Generate an object program. Costs will be insignificant for this step if the user is programming in a higher level language. If the source program is in assembly language, a relocatable assembler and linking loader will provide a significant saving over an absolute assembler and loader.
3. Debug the object program. The cost of this step will be determined by the debug system software provided.
applications software, calculator — Various software packages are: Finance, Structural Engineering, Statistics, Electronic Engineering, Mathematics, Education, and many more. Depending on specific needs, users can buy one program to solve one particular problem. Or they can get an entire library that will take care of most of the problems in their business.
applications support — Applications support packages assist users in: (1) evaluating the operation of the microcomputer family of parts in an actual application, (2) reducing the engineering time and development costs required in developing and constructing prototype systems using the microcomputer family of parts, (3) comparing user's system software and firmware programs, (4) reducing the time required to evaluate and debug system hardware, software and firmware, (5) providing a working model of the user's system.
application study — The detailed process of determining a system or set of procedures for using a calculator for definite functions or operations, and establishing specifications to be used as a base for the selection of equipment suitable to the specific needs.
APT (Automatically Programmed Tools) — A language for programming numerically controlled machine tools. ANSI standard is close to approval. There are many other similar languages with different names.
area by double meridian distance program — This program computes the area of a straight-sided closed figure from the bearings and lengths of its sides. It is generally more accurate than methods which calculate area from the coordinates of the figure.

$$\text{Area} = \frac{1}{2} \sum_i \text{DMD}_i \times \text{Latitude}_i$$

$$\text{DMD}_i = \text{DMD}_{i-1} + \text{Departure}_{i-1} + \text{Departure}_i$$
where
$$\text{Departure}_i = \text{Dist}_i \sin \text{Az}_i$$
$$\text{Latitude}_i = \text{Dist}_i \cos \text{Az}_i$$

Note: Angles are input as bearing and quadrant code. The quadrant code is 1 for NE, 2 for SE, 3 for SW, and 4 for NW.
area of a polygon program — If the x-y coordinates of the vertices of a polygon are known, the area can be found by the following formula: Area = ½ [$(x_1 + x_2)(y_1 - y_2) + (x_2 + x_3)(y - y_3) + \ldots + (x_n + x_1)(y_n - y_1)$] Traverse the coordinates clockwise for a positive area.
area of a triangle a, b, c program — Given three sides of a triangle this program computes the area by the following formula:

$$\text{Area} = \sqrt{s(s - a)(s - b)(s - c)}$$

where $s = \frac{1}{2}(a + b + c)$

area of a triangle a, b, C program — Given two sides and an included angle of a triangle this program computes the area by the following formula:

$$\text{Area} = \frac{1}{2} ab \sin C$$

The angle C can be in any angular mode but if in degrees it is assumed to be in decimal degrees.
area of a triangle a, B, C program — Given two angles and an included side of a triangle this program computes the area by the following formula:

$$\text{Area} = \frac{a^2 \sin B \sin C}{2 \sin(B + C)}$$

Angles B and C can be in any angular mode. If in degrees all angles are assumed to be decimal degrees.
area of a triangle [$(x_1, y_1), (x_2, y_2), (x_3, y_3)$] program — Given the coordinates of the vertices of a triangle, the area is found by the following formulas:

$$\text{Area} = \tfrac{1}{2} \text{ Determinant of D where}$$

$$D = \begin{bmatrix} x_1 & y_1 & 1 \\ x_2 & y_2 & 1 \\ x_3 & y_3 & 1 \end{bmatrix}$$

Therefore,
Area = ½[$x_1(y_2 - y_3) + x_2(y_3 - y_1) + x_3(y_1 - y_2)$]

argument — An independent variable, for example, in looking up a quantity in a table, the number, or any of the numbers, that identifies the location of the desired value.

arithmetic and harmonic progressions program — Provides options to: (1) display the terms of an arithmetic progression; (2) find a particular term of an arithmetic progression; (3) find the sum of an arithmetic progression; (4) display the terms of a harmonic progression.

arithmetic and logical (ALU) operations, microprocessor — In most systems all arithmetic and logical operations utilize the accumulator, with the second operand coming either from the general registers or the main memory. Several different addressing methods may be used for accessing the main memory including: immediate, absolute, indexed and auto-increment modes. Instructions to manipulate the index registers make other addressing modes, such as stack addressing, easy to implement. A large complement of move instructions allows data transfers between the accumulator, the general registers and the memory in many combinations.

arithmetic and logic chip (ALU) — That CPU chip logic which actually executes the operations requested by an input command is called the Arithmetic and Logic Unit (ALU), since in every case some combination of arithmetic and/or logical operations is required. A part of CPU chip logic, the Control Unit, decodes the instruction (stored in the instruction register) in order to enable the required ALU logic, and thus implement the arithmetic and/or logical operations required by the instruction.

arithmetic, control, and timing circuit (ACT) — Refers to a circuit that combines the functions of the first generation's arithmetic and register circuit, a control and timing circuit, and the clock driver circuit in a programmable calculator.

arithmetic expression — An expression containing any combination of data-names, numeric literals, and named constants, joined by one or more arithmetic operators in such a way that the expression as a whole can be reduced to a single numeric value.

arithmetic, fixed-point — 1. A method of calculation in which operators take place in an invariant manner, and in which the computer does not consider the location of the radix point. This is illustrated by desk calculators or slide rules, with which the operator must keep track of the decimal point. Similarly with many automatic computers, in which the location of the radix point is the programmer's responsibility. (Contrasted with floating-point arithmetic.) 2. A type of arithmetic in which the operands and results of all arithmetic operations must be properly scaled so as to have a magnitude between certain fixed values.

arithmetic, floating-decimal — A method of calculation which automatically accounts for the location of the radix point. This is usually accomplished by handling the number as a signed mantissa times the radix raised to an integral exponent; e.g., the decimal number + 88.3 might be written as $+.883 \times 10^2$; the binary number $-.0011$ as $-.11 \times 2^{-2}$. (Contrasted with fixed-point arithmetic, definition 1.)

arithmetic logic (calculator) — Many calculators use this mode of operation (since the circuitry is simpler). This logic cannot directly multiply two negative numbers and give a positive answer. Also, addition and subtraction operations are not done in the same sequence as written in the original equation.

arithmetic mean — 1. It is the most generally used measure of central tendency. 2. Its value is affected by the value of every item in the series. 3. A type of average, obtained by adding quantities together, then dividing by the number of quantities. Also refers to a figure midway between two extremes, usually found by adding the extremes and dividing by two. More accurately found by adding all values in a list and dividing the total by the number of values in the list. 4. It may be used in further algebraic calculations. The algebraic sum of the deviation of the values from their arithmetic mean is zero. 5. The sum of the squares of these deviations is less than the sum measured from any other value in the series. Often the arithmetic mean gives a misleading impression as an average because of the influence of extremes in its values. In other cases, it does not give the correct answer to a problem of averaging; e.g., determining the average of a group of ratios or the average of rates of change. For these the geometric and harmonic means are utilized.

arithmetic operation — In a calculator, the operations in which numerical quantities make up the elements of the calculation, including the fundamental arithmetic operations such as addition, subtraction, multiplication, comparison, division.

arithmetic products — A result developed as two numbers are multiplied as in decimal notation, $6 \times 10 = 60$. In data processing, the product is the result of performing the logic AND operation.

arithmetic registers, microprocessors — Arithmetic (or ALU) registers are those on which arithmetic and logic functions can be performed; the register can be a source or destination of operands for the operation. Registers that can supply but not receive operands for the ALU are not considered arithmetic registers by many evaluators.

arithmetic shift — 1. A shift that does not affect the sign position. 2. A shift that is equivalent to the multiplication of a number by a positive or negative integral power of the radix.

arithmetic unit — A computer subsystem in which arithmetic and logical operations are performed.

armed interrupt — Interrupts may be armed or disarmed. An armed interrupt accepts and holds the interruption signal. A disarmed interrupt ignores the signal. An armed interrupt may be enabled or disabled. An interrupt signal for an enabled condition causes certain hardware processing to occur. A disabled interrupt is held waiting for enablement.

armed state — The state of an interrupt level wherein it can accept and remember an interrupt input signal.

artificial intelligence — Research and study in methods for the development of a machine that can improve its own operations. The development or capability of a machine that can proceed or perform functions that are normally concerned with human intelligence as learning, adapting, reasoning, self-correction, automatic improvement. In a more restricted sense, the study of techniques for more effective use of digital computers by improved programming techniques.

ARU (audio-response unit) — A device that can connect a computer system to a telephone to provide response to inquiries made.

ASCII — American National Standard Code for Information Interchange, X3.4—1968. The standard 8 level code, a character set consisting of 7-bit coded characters plus a parity bit, is used for information interchange among data processing systems, communications systems, and peripheral equipment. The ASCII set consists of control characters and graphic characters. Synonymous with USASCII.

ASCII Code — American Standard Code for Information Interchange; a code which relates 96 displayed characters (64 without lower case) and 32 non-displayed control characters to a sequence of 7 "on" or "off" choices.

assemble — 1. In digital computer programming, to put together subprograms which finally make up a complete program. To perform some or all of the following functions: 2. Translation of symbolic operation codes into machine codes. 3. Allocation of storage, to the extent at least of assigning storage locations to successive instructions. 4. Computation of absolute or relocatable addresses from symbolic addresses. 5. Insertion of library routines. 6. Generation of sequences of symbolic instructions by the insertion of specific parameters into macro instructions.

assembler — The essential capability of an assembler is to translate symbolically represented instructions into their binary equivalents. A well designed computer is reflected in a versatile, efficient assembly language instruction set. It is a computer program which operates on symbolic input data to produce from such data machine instructions by carrying out such functions as, translation of symbolic operation codes into computer operating instructions, assigning locations in storage for successive instructions, or computation of absolute addresses from symbolic notation.

assembler error messages — The ability of assemblers to detect and point to a variety of errors in source statements is a valuable feature on many systems. These errors are often syntactic — they deal with misuse of the actual language. Assemblers normally cannot catch logic errors in the program, errors of intent or other subtle problems. A statement that contains an error is often printed in the list file with a code letter — a flag — beside it. Or the entire error message may be printed. Some common errors that can be detected include duplicate address labels, undefined label and unrecognized instruction mnemonic (due perhaps to the misspelling of an operation code). Other detectable errors include undefined operand field names, wrong number of operands and an invalid number in the number system chosen. In addition an assembler could be made to detect the error of an address referred to the same ROM page, as in a short jump when a long jump is required. Not all errors of syntax are flagged in current microprocessor assemblers. For example, when the labeled address for a jump or call instruction is not the start of an executable instruction, the error is not generally detected.

assembler language — A source language that includes symbolic machine language statements in which there is a one-to-one correspondence with the instruction formats and data formats of the computer.

assembly — Refers to a process in which instructions written in symbolic form by the programmer are changed to machine language by a computer.

assembly, conditional — Conditional assembly permits the assembler to include or delete sections of code, which may vary from system to system, such as the code required to handle optional external devices.

assembly language — Most microprocessor programs are written as a series of source statements using mnemonic symbols that assist in the definition of the instruction and are then translated into machine understandable object code, e.g. binary 0s and 1s.

assembly language components — The characteristics of symbolic assembly language programs and the mechanisms by which such programs are translated into executable machine programs include the assembler, the assembly language character set, statements, expressions, machine instructions, error processing and the assembly listing.

assembly language processor — A language processor that accepts words, statements and phrases to produce machine instructions. It is more than an assembly program because it has compiler powers. A macro-assembler permits segmentation of a large program so that positions may be tested separately. It also provides extensive program analysis to aid in debugging.

assembly program — Refers to a computer program flexible enough to incorporate subroutines into the main program. It is a program to translate a program written in pseudo-language (symbolic language) to a corresponding program in machine language. Principally designed to relieve the programmer of the problem of assigning actual storage locations to instructions and data when coding a program and to permit use of mnemonic operation codes rather than numeric operation codes. The address scheme used may be either numeric or mnemonic. The numerical systems utilize small blocks of code written in a numbering system allowing easy insertions, deletions and amendments to the program. The mnemonic system uses alphanumeric names in referring to locations in storage. In both cases, the pseudo-addresses are converted to machine-coded addresses by the assembly program before the program is finalized for computer use.

assembly system — 1. An automatic system (softwear) that includes a language and machine-language programs. Such supplementary programs perform such programming functions as checkout, updating, and others. 2. An assembly system comprises two elements, a symbolic language and an assembly program, that translate source programs written in the symbolic language into machine language.

associative storage registers — Concerns various registers which are not identified by their name or position but which are known and addressed by their content; used to locate indexed items. (Clarified by mapping, memory.)

assumed decimal point — The point within a numeric item at which the decimal point is assumed to be located. When a numeric item is to be used within a computer, the location of the as-

asynchronous data set interface — Typical units provide two-way communications with Bell 103 or 202 Data Sets or equivalent. Operates from 26 to 3110 baud in simplex, half-duplex or echoplex mode. Programmable character size is from 1 to 8 bits plus an optional parity bit.

asynchronous device — A unit which has an operating speed not related to any particular frequency of the system to which it is connected.

asynchronous multiplexer — A typical unit provides interfacing for up to 16 communications devices at programmable rates from 57 to 2400 baud, with automatic speed detection at seven standard rates including that of the IBM 2741. Operates in full duplex, half duplex or echoplex modes with automatic answering and automatic break detection. Programmable functions include parity generation and checking, split speed operation, and character length selection from 5 to 12 bits.

asynchronous transmission — The transmission process such that between any two significant instants in the same group (block or character), there is always an integral number of unit intervals. Between two significant instants located in different groups, there is not always an integral number of unit intervals.

audio-cassette record interface — A device that allows virtually unlimited memory storage for data or software. Operates by modulating audio frequencies in the record mode. Demodulates recorded data in playback mode.

audio response — A form of output which uses verbal replies to inquiries. The calculator can be programmed to seek answers to inquiries made on a time-shared on-line system and then to utilize a special audio response unit which elicits the appropriate pre-recorded response to the inquiry. Inquiries must be of the nature which the audio response has been prepared.

audio response calculator — An audio response calculator announces each entry and the results of every calculation using a solid-state synthesized voice stored on ROMs after digitizing. The CMOS circuits pronounce the ten numerals and the four algebraic functions of the calculator. They include: inverse, square root, square, and percent plus memory. The calculator's use was for vocational education of the blind and in the early development, an audio reinforcement of basic math concepts for sighted students.

audio response calculator modes — Learning Mode — This mode is used until operator becomes familiar with keyboard. Each entry produces an audio output associated with that entry. It has a keyboard lockout feature which guarantees audio output before new entry. This will prevent loss or clipping of words. Fast Mode — Standard calculator mode except function entry and answers are audibly announced. Calculator Mode — Performs as a standard calculator and only provides audio output upon demand by depressing repeat (R) key.

audio response calculator operation — Talking Calculator with solid-state voice. An Audio Response Calculator originally used in vocational education for the blind, and it continues to be used in this important field. Recent technological advances have permitted both cost and size reductions to extend its use into other applications. The unit is an 8-function calculator that provides both an 8 digit visual display and voice readout for the basic four functions plus all numeral entries and results. Each spoken word is digitized and stored permanently in its own individual Read-Only Memory (ROM) for a clear, natural-sounding voice readout. The solid-state operation of the system provides years of maintenance-free operation and audio output. In addition to the numeric-words zero to nine, the voice system in the calculator includes the words "plus", "minus", "times", "divice", "equals", and "point" for decimal point. The operator inputs the data through a standard keyboard with easily-learned key positions with touch sensitivity. In the learning mode, as each key is depressed, the number or word associated with that key is announced through a speaker in a natural-sounding male voice. When the "equals" key is depressed, the voice announces "equals" and then voices the number of the total that has been calculated by the arithmetic section of the calculator. A "point" is included in the numeric callout for the decimal point when required.

audio system — Relates to various types of special equipment which have capabilities of storing and processing data obtained from voice sources, either recorded or transmitted. Voice answer back (VAB) systems are a type of audio output system as a contrast.

auditing — Source data, methodology, and report conclusions and sums are checked for accuracy and validity as well as credibility in the auditing process through the use of studied techniques and information sources.

audit trail — 1. The trail or path left by a transaction when it is processed. The trail begins with the original documents, transactions entries, posting of records and is complete with the report. Validity tests of records are achieved by this method. 2. An audit trail must be incorporated into every procedure; provision for it should be made early so that it becomes an integral part. In creating an audit trail it is necessary to provide: (A) Transaction documentation which is detailed enough to permit the association of any one record with its original source document. (B) A system of accounting controls which provides that all transactions have been processed and that accounting records are in balance. (C) Documentation from which any transaction can be recreated and its processing continued, should that transaction be misplaced or destroyed at some point in the procedure.

auto state, data acquisition calculator — Places system in "powered-down" conservation mode by shutting off motors, displays, circuits, and peripherals during lulls between data scan outputs. System goes into AUTO as main power is turned on.

auto-indexing — The use of specified memory locations for address incrementing operations; when referenced, contents of auto-indexed locations are incremented and used as addresses.

auto loader — A program that allows program loading to be initiated automatically, remotely, or from a front panel switch. The signal operation provides loading from Teletype, paper tape, cassette, magnetic tape, and/or disk.

automata theory — Relates to the development of

theory which relates the study of principles of operations and applications of automatic devices to various behaviorist concepts and theories.

automated production management — Management using the assistance or under the control of data processing equipment which relates to production planning, scheduling, design or change, and control (reporting) of output.

automatic accumulating register — The results of calculations are automatically added to, or subtracted from, the register contents. There are $(+, =)$ and $(-, =)$ and other keys which complete the function and automatically add or subtract the result from the total in the register. On most calculators, there is an accumulator or sigma (Σ) key which, when engaged, causes all results to accumulate in the register.

automatic calling units — In order to use the automatic dialing feature of calculator batch terminal programs, an Automatic Calling Unit must be provided. The 25-pin connector on the 11284A Interface labeled ACU is designed to meet the EIA RS 366 specification for interfacing to Automatic Calling Units. In the United States and Canada, this is the Bell System Data Auxiliary Set 801 or an equivalent unit provided by an independent supplier. The Bell 801A is designed for systems where manual dialing is used, and the Bell 801C is designed for systems where TOUCH TONE® is available. In other countries, consult the Postal Telephone and Telegraph authorities.

automatic checking — Processors are constructed and designed for verification of information transmitted, computed, or stored. The procedure is complete when all processes in the machine are automatically checked, or else the check is considered a partial verification. Partial checking concerns either the number or proportion of the processes that are checked, or the number and proportion of the machine units that are assigned to checking.

automatic coding — 1. A technique by which a machine translates a routine written in a synthetic language into coded machine instructions, e.g., assembling is automatic coding. 2. Various techniques and methodology by which a computer is utilized to translate programs from formats which are quick and easy for programmers to produce, into formats which are convenient and efficient for the computer to execute.

automatic controller — A mechanism which measures the value of a variable, and limits deviations from a desired reference.

automatic display switching — Many calculators switch the display from fixed point notation to full scientific notation whenever the number is too large or too small to be seen with a fixed decimal point. This feature keeps users from missing unexpectedly large or small answers.

automatic error-correction — A technique, usually requiring the use of special codes and/or automatic retransmission, that detects and corrects errors occurring in transmission. The degree of correction depends upon coding and equipment configuration.

automatic error detection — The program itself, or the program embedded in a more complicated system, is usually designed to detect its own errors, print them out with the cause and, if so signed, take steps to correct them.

automatic interrupt — 1. Interruption caused by program instruction as contained in some executive routine; interruption not caused by programmer but due to engineering of devices. 2. An automatic program-controlled interrupt system that causes a hardware jump to a predetermined location. There are at least five types of interrupts. (1) input/output, (2) programmer error, (3) machine error, (4) supervisor call, and (5) external (for example, timer turned to negative value, alert button on console, external lines from another processor). There is further subdivision under the five types. Unwanted interrupts, such as an anticipated overflow, can be masked out.

automatic loader — This is a loader program implemented in a special ROM (Read-Only Memory) that allows loading of binary paper tapes or the first record or sector of a mass storage device. The program is equivalent to a bootstrap loader plus a binary loader. When an automatic loader is installed, it is seldom necessary to key in a bootstrap program to load the binary loader.

automatic loader diagnostic — This program aid reads out and verifies the contents of the automatic ROM (Read-Only Memory). It verifies proper sequencing when the automatic loader switch is depressed.

automatic or manual constant — Refers to a calculator feature that simplifies reciprocal and squaring computations. Usually, a switch controls the constant, which is locked in the logic store and used as required.

automatic reset — Refers to a stepping relay that returns to its home position either when a pulsing circuit fails to energize its driving coil within a given time or by an overload relay that restores the circuit as soon as the cause of the overload is corrected.

automatic routine — A routine that is executed independently of manual operations, but only if certain conditions occur within a program or record, or during some other process.

automatic RUN mode, small calculators — Some units can be used to automatically execute a list of operations with the PRGM-RUN switch set to RUN if they have previously been recorded in program memory. Instead of users having to press each key manually, the recorded operations are executed sequentially in automatic RUN mode when users press R/S (run/stop). They press only one key and the entire list of recorded operations is executed very quickly.

automatic sequencing — Refers to the ability of a computer to perform successive operations without the necessity of additional instructions.

automatic test systems — Various systems are supplied with Unit Under Test (UUT) adapter modules that provide a general purpose cabling interface between the system stimulus, measurement, and switching modules and the UUT. Many Automatic Test Systems are general-purpose systems based on modular building-block techniques, that provide a wide latitude in testing capabilities, with easy expansion to handle future testing needs. The Systems cover stimulus-response testing over the frequency range of dc to 18 GHz. Some systems are, at the same time, fully standardized and fully flexible in configuration and operation. The broad testing capabilities of these type systems lie in the fact that they are supplied with a standard paper-tape or disc-based controller while all stimulus, measurement, switching, and interface hardware are available as options. Some automatic test systems incorporate Extended BASIC as the primary test language. Additionally, the disc-based systems incorporate a software control executive.

automation — 1. The implementation of processes by automatic means. 2. The theory, art, or technique of making a process more automatic. 3. The investigation, design, development, and application of methods of rendering processes automatic, self-moving, or self-controlling. 4. The conversion of a procedure, a process, or equipment to automatic operation.

auto programming — A ROM provides automatic custom programming and turn-on of a calculator to same initially pre-programmed system and channel settings each time, on various data acquisition systems.

auto response calculator characteristics —
- Portable — Small package that is easily picked up with one hand and carried from one place to another.
- 8-Digit Visual Display — Large characters for good visibility by partially sighted and sighted operators.
- Keyboard — Human engineered for multiple finger data entry and ease of operation.
- Audio Repeat Key (R) — Used to announce information on display at any time.
- Audio Reset Key (AR) — Used to silence the audio output. This is particularly effective when users desire a two or three place floating decimal point; any numbers beyond this are meaningless.
- Jack for external speaker or head-set for private listening.
- Tone for overflow condition.
- On-off switch and Volume Control.
- 115 or 230 V operation.
- Operating instructions with each unit.
- Rechargeable battery operation. (See talking calculator features)

auto start switch, calculator — The AUTO START Switch begins some calculator operations when the power is turned on, thus eliminating complicated set-up keystrokes and giving users power-fail recovery for interfacing applications.

auxiliary processor — A specialized processor such as an array processor, fast fourier transform (FFT) processor, or input/output processor (IOP) generally used to increase processing speed through concurrent operation.

auxiliary PROM module — Generally, the auxiliary PROM chips are the same physically as the control PROMs (256×8 bits). However, the auxiliary PROM module often is inerfaced as an I/O module which means that data stored on these PROMs can be accessed only as data. The PROMs therefore cannot contain control programs to run many types of microcomputers or calculators.

auxiliary routine — A routine designed to assist in the operation of the calculator and in debugging other routines.

auxiliary storage — A storage device in addition to the main storage of a calculator, e.g., magnetic tape, disk or magnetic cards. Auxiliary storage usually holds much larger amounts of information than the main storage, and the information is accessible less rapidly.

average and range chart program — Computes the averages and ranges of sample data as well as the control limits and other summary statistics. Provides the option to base the control limits on the computed values of average and/or range or the standard values of average and/or sigma. An additional option permits correction of erroneous data and/or the computation of revised control limits upon the removal of unwanted data.

average and sigma chart program — Except for the computation of sigma and its associated limits, program is similar to average and range in computations and options. An additional option to suppress the printing of the individual subgroup data is provided, since average and sigma charts are often applied to larger subgroups.

aviation program pack — Various programs devoted to pre-flight planning, flight management and in-flight navigation.

axes key — Establishes plotting scale for x and y axes; also establishes "tic mark" interval for drawing axes. (some units)

B

background program — A program that is not time-dependent. This program is of a lower priority than the foreground or main program and is at halt or standby while the main program runs.

backspace key (shift key) — Allows entry of numbers while the calculator is executing previous calculations.

Back Step and Single Step keys — The "Back STep" and "Single STep" keys let one review the entire memory one step at a time, in either direction. If one wants to change the program, he or she simply stops it at the appropriate step and keys in a new entry, which will overwrite the previous one. To test a program a step at a time, users switch to RUN and press "SST" repeatedly. One may see the numeric code when he or she presses the key and see the intermediate solution when the key is released. (some units)

back step key — On some systems the Back Step Single steps backward through a program in the learn mode. The Delete key removes displayed instructions and automatically shifts following instructions up when in the learn mode.

back-up system — 1. Systems that combine several sophisticated error detection and correction techniques which spot and correct equipment and transmission errors. 2. Systems that take over when the primary system is down for various reasons.

backward-forward counter — A counter having both an add and subtract input, and capable of counting in either an increasing or a decreasing direction.

B address — The higher order position of the instruction code indicating the location of data to be processed.

balanced line — A transmission line consisting of two conductors, in the presence of ground, capable of being operated in such a way that the voltages of the two conductors at all transverse planes are equal in magnitude and opposite in polarity with respect to ground; the currents in the two conductors are equal in magnitude and opposite in direction.

balancing error — A specific error which in effect balances or offsets another error, i.e., two offsetting errors of equal values or same numbers of opposite signs could exist and would be most difficult to detect or correct because the various check totals would agree or compare favorably.

band — 1. A group of tracks on a magnetic disc or on a magnetic drum. 2. In communications, the frequency spectrum between two defined limits.

base — The radix, or quantity of characters employed in a numbering system; e.g. 2-binary; 8-octal; 10-decimal; 16-hexadecimal.

base number — Specifically, the radix of a number system. For example, 10 is the radix, or base number for the decimal system. 2 is the radix for the binary system (base 2).

base time — A designed and precisely controlled function of time by which some particular process or exercise is controlled or measured.

BASIC — Beginner's All-purpose Instruction Code. A common high-level time-sharing computer programming language. It is easily learned and used for direct communication between teletype units and remote calculators or computers. The language is similar to Fortran II and was developed by Dartmouth College for a General Electric 225 computer system.

BASIC conversational language features — BASIC is a conversational programming language developed at Dartmouth College that employs simple English-type statements and familiar mathematical notations to perform an operation. It is one of the simplest computer languages to learn. And once it is learned, BASIC offers the facility of advanced techniques to perform intricate manipulations or express a problem efficiently. With BASIC, even the novice programmer can solve complex data acquisition and processing problems with a minimum amount of effort. Some calculators use extended BASIC which is implemented as an incremental compiler which combines the interactive capabilities of an interpreter with the speed of a compiler. Features of extended BASIC include:
- String capability; users can have Dartmouth-compatible string support complete with string arrays and functions.
- A "CALL" statement that allows easy interfacing of assembly language functions; the function can be called by name and passed several parameters.
- Interrupt-driven support for standard devices.
- Sequential and virtual memory file support for unit mass storage devices.
- CHAIN and OVERLAY statements to accommodate programs many times larger than available memory.

BASIC CRT calculators — An increasing number of more-powerful calculators have been introduced in which a high-level language, BASIC, is used. With alphanumeric displays, the calculator using BASIC can be operated in a conversational mode or its CRT display is used as an alarm or annunciator panel. As the BASIC language is oriented to time-sharing telecommunication applications, these devices have serial input-output capabilities which allow data communication or process control via simple twisted pair wires or, using a modem, the telephone system. Since the Basic compiler is hardwired in read-only memory, program execution by calculator often is faster than that by minicomputer when a similar high-level language is used.

BASIC, data management capabilities — In addition to the computation facilities normally found in BASIC, various versions of extended BASIC provide extensive character string manipulation and powerful data file management abilities. Disk files may be both sequential and direct access. Files may be created and purged under program control. New statements and functions make it easy to develop file-oriented applications accessed by multiple terminals concurrently. Each program may access up to 16 data files at the same time, and each file can be opened and closed dynamically, on some systems.

BASIC, extended (graphics) — Extended BASIC includes: All the standard BASIC COMMANDS. System operating commands, featuring: APPEND (retrieves and attaches a stored BASIC program to one already in the workspace, to effectively overlay larger programs); CALL (passes control to an optional ROM pack firmware routine; SET (sets to RAD/DEG/GRAD units); TRACE (line-at-a-time) or NORMAL execution, KEY or NOKEY (to enable user function keys).
- A full range of built-in math functions.
- Powerful MATRIX COMMANDS, featuring, at no extra cost: DIM; MAT INPUT; MAT PRINT; MAT READ; and MATRIX arithmetic functions.
- Totally unique GRAPHICS COMMANDS, the Tektronix 4051 BASIC: AXIS; DRAW/RDRAW/ MOVE/RMOVE (draws or invisibly moves to new absolute or relative position); GIN (returns x and y locations of graphic cursor); MAT DRAW/MAT RDRAW/MAT MOVE/MAT RMOVE (instant lines from any data matrix); ROTATE; and more.
- Output formatting commands, rare in BASIC.
- Unique INTERRUPT control for the peripherals.

BASIC, graphic extensions — BASIC graphic extensions offer important BASIC extensions, including: special graphic primitives, file system data access; matrices for powerful graphic manipulation; exceptional string functions for text handling; and high level interrupts to access the processor whenever users need it.

BASIC, hard-wired — Some Central Processor Units (CPUs), with hardwired BASIC interpreters offer programming power capable of executing sophisticated programs, the CPUs include: an additional 3 I/O slots for a Matrix ROM a Programming ROM and a General I/O ROM. A number of peripherals also are available on various systems.

BASIC keyword keyboard — This contains single keys for most BASIC language verbs and commands. The keyboard also contains all alphabetic characters as well as all control keys needed to program some systems.

BASIC language — The highest level of digital problem-oriented programming language available for programming electronic calculators at present. It is generally compatible with BASIC used on various minicomputers, thus making a

BASIC language calculator — Most units offer powerful capabilities: typewriter-style keyboard, magnetic tape cassette programming and data recording; large memory option, etc.

BASIC language calculator components — An increasing number of general purpose, programmable calculators designed for a wide range of applications use the universally accepted language called BASIC. This easy-to-use language couples simplicity with power and appeals to the new calculator owner as well as the experienced programmer. The users automatically inherit a comprehensive range of proven software packages, including finance, mathematics, statistics, and education. For one specific series a minimum unit provides 3520 8-bit bytes (1760 words) of user read/write memory. This can be expanded to 15,808 bytes (7904 words). In addition, the user can select from a wide range of read-only-memory (ROM) plug-in blocks for increased computational capability or peripheral control, or both. The unit allows up to 16K bytes of add-on ROM for a total of eight plug-in blocks. A broad range of peripherals is available with this type calculator series to allow the user maximum flexibility in putting together that specific system required to solve his problem.

BASIC language calculator, mass memory — Some advanced programmable calculators in many respects perform like a powerful computer—complete with BASIC language and up to 16K bytes of read/write memory. Many can be dramatically extended with a Mass Memory that provides another 4.8 million bytes of rapid-access storage. They not only accommodate a complete range of input/output peripherals, some convert to a remote batch or timeshare terminal. And others also provide easy interfacing for instrument control, data acquisition, and processing. Users find it convenient and cost-effective to combine all this power and convenience with calculator operating simplicity. Users can take it out of the box, set it on their desk, and it's ready to go. The BASIC language is already hardwired into the CPU, so it doesn't use any read/write memory. New users can start solving problems the moment they turn it on. In fact, a lot of the input, output, and storage need is also built in: the alphanumeric keyboard and display, the thermal printer, and the magnetic tape cassette (for both input and storage). These units then become powerful computation systems that are simple to operate, immediately accessible and reasonably priced.

BASIC language, extended — Simple enough for the novice to use, some versions of extended BASIC include an English-oriented conversational BASIC language processor, which permits the development and execution of BASIC programs from all user terminals simultaneously. A few simple statements formed with meaningful words provide the basic capabilities for manipulating data, performing calculations, and controlling program flow. Yet these versions of extended BASIC are versatile and powerful enough for more advanced users to efficiently implement sophisticated applications involving data base management and remote job entry to central IBM and CDC and many other computer systems.

BASIC, multi-user — This is an interpretive system that provides interactive entry and execution of programs written in the popular BASIC language developed by Dartmouth College. Multi-user BASIC supports up to nine concurrent users in some systems and provides many language extensions and features not usually included in the BASIC language. A 'desk calculator' mode of operation allows immediate execution of statements without the need to write a complete program. This feature is useful for program debugging as well as for performing calculations. In addition to all the elementary and advanced features normally included in the BASIC language, some versions include extensions for string operations, matrix operations, trigonometric functions, random numbers, etc.

BASIC non-programmable commands — BASIC commands provide the user with a means of effectively controlling the system. Commands are used primarily to instruct the system to perform actions on BASIC programs (i.e., listing, loading, renumbering).
BASIC commands are entered one line at a time. They differ from BASIC statements because they are not preceded by line numbers, and only one command can be entered on each line. All the BASIC commands are executed immediately.

basic operating system (BOS) — One of many fundamental operating systems; (See operating system)

basic stat key — Calculates and prints number of entries, mean, and standard deviation. May be pressed during any analysis in order to review data. (some units)

basic telecommunications access method — An access method that permits read/write communications with remote devices. Abbreviated BTAM.

BASIC-using communications calculators — The new breeds of BASIC-using calculators are ideally suited to serial data transmission systems as the language of their compilers was developed expressly for remote time-sharing use. In addition, they provide serial ASCII outputs to other RS232-C voltage or 20/60 mA current loop standards, making connection to serial systems a matter of attaching both ends of a twisted pair. This it is practical for the industrial user to install rather complex systems himself using inhouse electricians. Some parameters must be sacrificed for both the programming convenience of a high level language and the noise insensitivity and installation ease of serial data transmission. Often the parameter sacrificed turns out to be speed.

batch processing — 1. In computer terminology, batch processing refers to a specific method of processing in which a number of similar input items are grouped for processing during the same machine run. 2. Batch processing computer systems generally do not require immediate updating of files. In batch processing, data is gathered up to a cutoff time and then processed.

batch system flexibility, calculator — Some of the standard features of the calculator batch terminal which can be easily changed to suit particular needs are:
- Data transmission: 2000 bits-per-second (Optionally, 1200, 1800, 2400, 3600, or 4800 bits-per-second).
- Mode: half duplex (Optionally, full duplex).

batch terminal applications, calculator

- Terminal position: primary or secondary binary synchronous terminal.
- Output page width: 80 columns (132 columns on some systems).

Simple, step-by-step instructions on how to change a batch terminal environment are given for most of the common options so that the unit batch terminal can fit exact needs.

batch terminal applications, calculator — The calculator as a batch terminal can be used at many points throughout a typical organization wherever stand-alone processing is required and large amounts of data must be transmitted at high speed with accuracy between two points. To name only a few:

- Remote job entry (RJE).
- Preparing numerical control tapes.
- Payroll.
- Inventory control.
- Structural design.

Unit batch terminal brings all of the applications available at the central computer to the remote location.

batch terminal calculator — The following equipment is required for operation of an advanced calculator as a batch terminal:

- An advanced Calculator with 3808 or more words of memory.
- String Variables ROM.
- Thermal Printer or equivalent.
- Data Communications Interface.
- Binary Synchronous ROM.
- Modem.

Optional additions to the batch terminal environment may include one or more of the following groups of equipment:

- Mass Memory Subsystem.
- External Cassette.
- Calculator Card Reader with Extended I/O ROM.
- Tape Reader with Option—Extended I/O ROM.
- Line Printer Subsystem (132-column output).

A larger calculator memory (7808 words) and a wide variety of other peripherals can also be included in the calculator batch terminal environment. A user's particular application will determine which of the many series peripherals best suits user needs.

batch terminal characteristics, calculator — With the calculator batch terminal, the calculator will emulate the operation of an IBM 2780 remote batch terminal. Card image input can be via the calculator card reader or from paper tape, tape cassette, or mass memory. Output can be to an 80-column thermal printer, a 132-column impact printer, or to a magnetic storage media; such as, tape cassette or mass memory.

batch terminal editing system, calculator — Included with the calculator batch terminal programs are two very powerful editing systems: one for the cassette-oriented batch terminal and one for the mass memory-oriented batch terminal. Each of these systems allows users to add, delete, and insert 80-column, card-image data into an existing data base, on the cassette or the mass memory. This provides a fast, convenient medium for data storage before the information is transmitted over the data communications link. Now users can eliminate punched cards or paper tape as their data storage medium if this is desired. To use the cassette-based editing system, it is necessary to have an External Cassette in the calculator batch terminal configuration. For the mass memory-based editing system, the calculator Mass Memory Subsystem is required.

batch ticket — A document used for control of groups of source documents.

batch total — 1. The sum of certain quantities, pertaining to batches of unit records, used to verify accuracy of operations on a particular batch of records; e.g., in a payroll calculation, the batches might be departments, and batch totals could be number of employees in the department, total hours worked in the department, total pay for the department. Batches, however, may be arbitrary, such as orders received from 9 A.M. to 11 A.M. on a certain day. 2. Each or any of a number of sums that can be calculated from a series of records which are intended to serve as aids to check the accuracy of computer operations.

battery control — Various indicators alert users when the batteries are low. Some are battery-saver circuits that cut off the display after about 15 seconds to prevent excessive battery drain (the display is restored when any key is pushed).

battery life indicator — Refers to a meter or warning light that indicates the status of the battery life within an electronic calculator.

battery, low power operation — Operating some calculators for more than 2 to 5 minutes after a low power indication first occurs may result in wrong answers. The battery pack must be replaced or recharged by connecting the calculator to the battery charger. Users must be sure to turn off the calculator before connecting the recharger to the calculator. They also must be sure to start with at least partially charged batteries before using the card reader/writer on some systems.

battery pack — These units generally provide backup power to support components, as RAM etc. Time of support is dependent upon the amount of RAM for example, to be kept under power; 4K bytes can be supported for 8 hours. 20K bytes can be supported for 1 hour in some systems.

baud — 1. A unit of signalling speed equal to the number of discrete conditions or signal events per second. For example, one baud equals one-half dot cycle per second in Morse Code, one bit per second in a train of binary signals, and one 3-bit value per second in a train of signals each of which can assume one of eight different states. 2. In asynchronous transmission, the unit of modulation rate corresponding to one unit interval per second, i.e., if the duration of the units interval is 20 milleseconds, the modulation rate is 50 baud.

baud rate — A type of measurement of data flow in which the number of signal elements per second is based on the duration of the shortest element. When each element carries one bit, the Baud rate is numerically equal to bits per second (bps).

Bayes' formula program — Suppose $E_1, E_2, ..., E_n$ are n mutually exclusive and exhaustive events, and A is an event for which the conditional probabilities, $P[A/E_i]$ of A given E_i, are known. If $P[E_i]$ are given, then the conditional probability $P[E_k/A]$ of any one event E_k given A is

$$P[E_k/A] = \frac{P[E_k]\, P[A/E_k]}{\sum_{i=1}^{n} P[E_i]\, P[A|E_i]}$$

where k can be 1, 2, ..., or n.

Bayesian statistics — Refers to a branch of statistics that is concerned with estimates of (prior) probability distributions, as subsequently revised (posterior distribution) in order to incorporate new data by means of Bayes' equation. Often used in medical diagnostic programs as an alternative to analytical, sequential, or programmed diagnostic procedures.

B box — A register that contains a quantity which may be used to modify addresses. (Synonymous with B-register.)

BCD, binary coded decimal — A type of positional value code in which each decimal digit is binary coded into 4-bit 'words'. The decimal number 12, for example, would become 0001 0010 in BCD; as based on and sometimes called the 8421 code.

It derives its name from the value assigned to each of 4 bit positions, with each set of 4 bits equal to 1 decimal.

Decimal Digit	8421 Binary
0	0000
1	0001
2	0010
3	0011
4	0100
5	0101
6	0110
7	0111
8	1000
9	1001

BCD interface, calculator-controlled systems — A BCD interface that provides calculator control over storage readers, meters, counters and multichannel analyzers provides the means to configure a complete system for data-acquisition, control, stimulus of programable instruments, data-logging, or process control. The unit is designed for advanced programable calculators and provides direct parallel access to the display register and to the internal memory. The peripherals present the data to the interface in bit-parallel, digital-parallel format. The unit then transfers the data to the calculator in bit-parallel, digit-serial format. When the calculator is in the direct-memory-access mode, data can be transferred at 15,000 samples per second on some systems.

BCD interface, general purpose calculator — One type Binary Coded Decimal unit is a full bit parallel input-output interface. It gives calculators access to A/D and D/A converters, scanners, programmable power supplies, and realtime clocks. It also works with many straight binary and binary octal code instruments. On one type, 64 bit parallel inputs lay a big pipeline for user data to flow through—up to 15,000 samples per second using the keyboard or DMA (Direct Memory Access). With the 56 programmable outputs and the calculator's six triggers users can make up a system that can do a lot in the area of high speed signal analysis or multipoint data acquisition. (some systems)

benchmark — In relation to microprocessors the benchmark is a test point measuring the performance characteristics of products offered. A benchmark program is a routine or program selected to define or compare different brands of microprocessors. A flow chart in assembly language is often written out for each microprocessor, and the execution of the benchmark time, accuracy, etc. is evaluated.

benchmark evaluation problem — 1. A problem used to evaluate the performance of hardware or software or both. 2. A problem used to evaluate the performance of several computers relative to each other, or a single computer relative to system specifications.

benchmark problem routine — A routine used to determine the speed or specific performance of a computer or calculator. One method is to use one-tenth of the time required to perform nine additions and one complete multiplication. A complete addition or a complete multiplication time includes the time required to procure two operands from storage, perform the operation and store the result, and the time required to select and execute the required number of instructions to do this.

beta probability program — Refers to a Beta Distribution. Given the parameters Alpha and Beta, and a random variable x, this program will determine the Beta Distribution, $f(x)$.

bidirectional — Generally refers to interface ports or bus lines that can be used to transfer data in either direction, e.g., to or from the calculator.

bidirectional lines — With bidirectional and asynchronous communications on a bus, devices can send, receive, and exchange data at their own rates. The bidirectional nature of a bus allows utilization of common bus interfaces for different devices, and simplifies the interface design.

bidirectional operation — An operation in which reading, writing, and searching may be conducted in either direction, thus saving time and providing easy access to stored information.

bifurcation — A condition where two, and only two outcomes can occur—such as on or off, 0 or 1.

bili — A specific prefix which designates the quantity one billion (10^9 power); i.e., synonymous with kilomega. Billibits mean one billion bits; billicycle, one billion cycles per second.

binary — A characteristic, property, or condition in which there are but two possible alternatives, e.g., the binary number system using 2 as its base and using only the digits zero (0) and one (1).

binary-coded character — Can refer to an alphabetic letter, a decimal digit, a punctuation mark, etc., as represented by a fixed number of consecutive binary digits.

binary-coded decimal (BCD) representation — A system of representing decimal numbers. Each decimal digit is represented by a combination of four binary digits (bits), as follows:

Binary	Decimal	Binary	Decimal
0000	0	0101	5
0001	1	0110	6
0010	2	0111	7
0011	3	1000	8
0100	4	1001	9

binary coded decimal (place value) — The 8421 system represents each digit by 4 binary digits with each place value equal to 8^2, 4^2, 2^2, and 1^2, reading from left to right. A conversion of the decimal number 3571 to 8421 BCD equivalent under the place value concept would be as follows:

Digit:	3	5	7	1
Binary value:	0011	0101	0111	0001
Place value:	8421	8421	8421	8421

binary counter — Flip-flop or toggle circuit which gives an output pulse for two input pulses, thus dividing by two.

binary digit (bit) — 1. A numeral in the binary scale of notation. This digit may be zero (0), or one (1). It may be equivalent to an on or off condition, a yes, or a no. Often abbreviated to (bit). 2. The kind of number that computers use internally. There are only two binary digits, 1 and 0, otherwise known as "on" and "off".

binary dump program — A program that provides a means for printing, displaying or punching a binary paper tape copy of any portion of memory. The output may be selected as either absolute or binary relocatable.

binary loader — This is used to load a binary format, such as those produced by the Binary Dump program, the Link Editor, or an assembler into memory.

binary loader, tape — In some systems a binary loader is used to load binary object tapes obtained from the assembler or debugging utility. Each tape is made up of a number of lead records which contain address data, object data, and checksum data. The loader reads the object tape via the teletype reader and processes each record sequentially by placing the object data into the memory locations specified by the address data.

binary, ordinary — Expression of binary numerals in a system of positional notation in which each successive digit position is weighted by a factor of two times the weight of the prior position. An example: 1011 binary represents: $1 \times 2^3 + 0 \neq 1 \times 1^1 + 1 \times 1^0 = 11$, i.e., eleven.

binary point — The point mid-way between integral powers of two in a particular binary number.

binary row — 1. Pertaining to the binary representation of data or punched cards in which adjacent positions in a row correspond to adjacent bits of the data; for example, each row in an 80-column card may be used to represent 80 consecutive bits or two 40-bit words. 2. A method of representing binary numbers on a card where successive bits are represented by the presence or absence of punches in a successive position in a row as opposed to a series of columns.

binary synchronous (bisync) — A specific mode of synchronous transmission, faster than STR (Synchronous Transmit Receive) and largely replacing it in newer terminal devices (e.g., IBM 2780 series) and computes communication adapters (e.g., for IBM System 3 and System 7).

binary-to-decimal conversion — The actual process of converting a binary number to its equivalent in conventional decimal notation.

binomial distribution — 1. Refers to a statistical distribution applicable to processes involving a number of individual observations with each, of which a specific event may or may not be associated. A special case of multinomial distribution where several events may be associated with each observation. 2. The binomial distribution is concerned with two mutually exclusive categories, occurrence and non-occurrence of a particular event. (Success or failure, heads or tails, hit or miss, etc.)

binomial program — Refers to a Binomial Probability Distribution. Computes individual and cumulative terms of the binomial probability distribution for given values of R, N, and P.

Biolator calculator — A "Biolator" calculator designed to help a person determine his ability to cope with everyday problems at any given time measures an individual's biorhythm and is intended to replace the tables and charts normally used to compute biorhythms. Casio calls its new machine a Biolator. To operate the Biolator, the user enters the year, month and day (in that order) and pushes the special "date" key between each computation and the minus key after the last entry. Then the same is done for a person's date of birth. Next, he presses the special "bio" key after the last entry and the person's biorhythm will appear on the large display area in three sets of digits (example: -05.02.12-). The first set of digits represents the physical condition, the second, the sensitivity (emotional) and the third, the intellectual. The biorhythm is then interpreted by using the permanent chart on the reverse side of the calculator.

Biolator calculator features — The Biolator features a 99-year calendar function which allows the user to calculate the day of the week for the years 1901 to 1999, and automatically computes the number of settlement days of account payments, bank interest or promissory notes. It allows a person to calculate the number of days since his birth. The day of the week is expressed in digits from zero to six with a table labeled on the calculator to convert the numbers into the day of the week. Also, the biorhythm graph is provided above the numerical display. (Casio)

biometrics — The science of statistics when applied specifically to biological observations.

bipolar — Refers to conventional circuitry now widely used. Bipolar is an older technology than MOS. It is used for most transistors found in radios and for most small-scale and medium-scale integrated circuits. It is faster than MOS technology, but the circuits use more current, hence they heat up more. This imposes limits on the number of transistors that can be put on a single chip.

biquinary — A two-part representation of a decimal digit consisting of a binary portion with values of 0 or 5, and a quinary portion with values of 0 through 4; e.g., the number 7 is coded as 12 which implies 5 and 2.

bit — 1. Bit is an abbreviation for binary digit. Most commonly a unit of information equalling one binary decision, or the designation of one of two possible and equally likely values or states, usually conveyed as 1 or 0 of anything used to store or convey information. (such as 1 or 0, which may also mean "yes" or "no".) 2. A single character in a binary number. 3. A single pulse in a group of pulses. 4. A unit of information capacity of a storage device. The capacity in bits is the logarithm to the base two of the number of possible states of the device.

bit density — A specific number of bits of information contained within a given area, such as the number of bits written along an inch of magnetic tape.

bit memory organization — Each element of a memory is a binary digit (BIT), capable of representing 1 or 0. At any instant during the execution of a program, memory is a grid of binary ones and zeroes.

bit, parity — A check bit that indicates whether the total number of binary "1" digits in a character or word (excluding the parity bit) is odd or even. If a "1" parity bit indicates an odd number of "1" digits, then a "0" bit indicates an even number of them. If the total number of "1" bits, including the parity bit, is always even, the system is called an even-parity system. In an odd-parity system, the total number of "1" bits, including the parity bit, is always odd.

bit rate — 1. The speed at which bits are transmitted. 2. The rate at which binary digits, or pulses representing them, pass a given point on a communications line or channel. (Clarified by baud and channel capacity.)

bit/slice — Refers to microcomputer chip that is a quarter or an eighth of an entire processor. When a cpu is too complex or would dissipate too much heat to be put on a single chip, it is sliced into two- or four-bit chunks which are then wired together on circuit cards.

bit stream — Referring to a binary signal without regard to groupings by character, word, or other unit. A line signal.

bit string — A one-dimensional array of bits ordered by reference to the relations between adjacent numbers.

bivariate normal probability program — Refers to a Bivariate Normal Distribution. This program calculates f(x, y) for the general form of the two dimensional normal frequency function.

black box — A generic term which can describe any unspecified device performing a special function where the inputs produce specific outputs.

blank card programming procedure — On a piece of paper, or a program form (supplied), make a step-by-step list of the keystrokes needed to solve a problem. On one system users then, with the unit set in the "WRITE PROGRAM" mode, press the keys (except those for entering data) in the proper sequence. The resulting program is stored in the program memory until the unit is turned off, but can also be permanently recorded on a blank card. Users then label the program card and insert it in the slot directly above the User Definable Keys to identify how they are to be used. With the unit set in the "RUN PROGRAM" mode users key in the known data for the problem they want to solve, and run the program. On these units they can change any part of the program by deleting keystrokes and adding new ones. Or clip a corner of the card to prevent erasure or modification.

blast — The release of various specified areas or blocks of either main or auxiliary storage no longer needed by an operational program. This type program will execute a blast macroinstruction which causes the control program to return the address of the area blasted to its list of storage available for use by future operational programs.

blinking display, hand-held programmable — The display blinks when any of several improper operations are attempted. Depressing any key stops the blinking without otherwise performing the key function. CLX is the recommended blink stopper. Various manuals list these improper operations.

block diagram — 1. A chart setting forth the particular sequence of operations to be performed for handling a particular application. Used as a tool in programming. 2. A sequential, graphic representation of operations of the various computer machines through the use of symbols which represent functional steps rather than the physical structural details. The block diagram is usually the gross or macro diagram for the entire integrated system or large application areas. Flow charts then provide the specific detail of various operations.

block length — A measure of the size of a block, usually specified in units such as records, words, computer words, or characters.

blocks — Records are transferred to and from tapes in the form of blocks (sometimes called physical records). A block (physical record) may contain one or more records (logical). Records may be reduced to blocks on tape to reduce the acceleration and deceleration time.

blue-ribbon program — Handwritten and independently designed by a programmer and so checked that no mistakes or bugs are therein contained; i.e., the blue-ribbon or star program should thus run correctly the first time, excepting machine malfunctions. Same as program, star.

board — An electrical panel which can be altered with the addition or deletion of external wiring. Also known as a plugboard, panel, or wire board.

Boolean algebra — A mathematical system of logic named after George Boole, the famous English mathematician and logician. It deals with classes, propositions, on-off circuit elements, etc. Associated by operators as AND, OR, NOT, EXCEPT, IF... THEN... which permit computations and demonstrations as in any other mathematical system.

Boolean calculus — Basically Boolean algebra modified to include the element of time.

Boolean operator — An operator (gate) used in Boolean algebra as applied to logic units of computer architecture, i.e., the result of any operation is restricted to one of two values, generally represented as 1 or 0.

Boolean variable — The use of two-valued Boolean algebra to assume either one of the only two values possible. Examples: true or false; on or off; open or closed. Basically, all digital computers use the two-state or two-variable Boolean algebra in construction and operation.

bootstrap — 1. A technique or device designed to bring itself into a desired state by means of its own action, e.g., a machine routine whose first few instructions are sufficient to bring the rest of itself into the computer from an input device. 2. To use a bootstrap. 3. That part of a computer program used to establish another version of the computer program.

bootstrap input program — Very popular programs which have simple preset computer operations to facilitate information or program input reading and which also contain instructions to be read until the program is assembled or executed, i.e., one instruction pulls other preset instructions.

bootstrap loader — A bootstrap loader is input when there is no loader in main memory. The bootstrap loader will sequentially read into memory any series of bytes generally making no checks for error. The bootstrap loader may be keyed into the computer via the console, or more frequently, it will be implemented in Read Only Memory, where it can never be erased. The principal criterion for the bootstrap loader is that it contain as few instructions as possible, in case it has to be keyed in via the computer console. The bootstrap loader can be used to load an absolute loader into main memory.

BPS — Bits per second. In serial transmission, the instantaneous bit speed with which a device or channel transmits a character.

braille calculator — A braille calculator is a standard portable five-function calculator with a floating decimal point equipped with a single braille cell. Within the cell is a two-by-three array of six solenoids underlying a similar array of small pins. Energizing the solenoids forces the pins above the cell surface in various patterns that represent the decimal point and the numerals 0 to 9 in braille. To activate the cell, the blind person simply presses a read button on the front of the calculator. This action starts transferring the contents of the visual readout, one decimal place at a time, to the braille cell. If a number is repeated on the visual display, the set of pins representing it momentarily submerges, before reappearing as the next number in the sequence.

branch — 1. Concerns the capability and procedure of a microprocessor program instruction designed to modify the function or program sequence. The actual modification is an immediate change in direction, meaning or substance of intent of the programmer. 2. To depart from the normal sequence of executing instructions in a computer. Synonymous with jump. 3. A sequence of instructions that is executed as a result of a decision instruction.

branching — When applied to computer technology, branching is a method of selecting, on the basis of the computer results, the next operation to execute while a program is in progress.

branching; hand-held calculators — Branching is accomplished by many units in one of three ways: by means of an unconditional "GO TO" command, or by means of two conditional tests, "X-Y" or "X is less than or equal to Y" with the "GO TO" command implied. Some popular units offer 100 steps of program memory and four conditional branching tests.

branching, pointer (small calculators) — In some cases, the program pointer is rerouted or "branched" to a new line number. The "branch" can be made unconditionally or dependent on the outcome of a comparison of data values in the X- and Y-registers.

branching, simple (small calculators) — In a program, GTO [line number] branches program execution to the line specified. Program execution continues at the new line with the exception of line 00; at line 00 program execution always halts. The line number must be a valid two digit entry from 00 thru 49. (some units)

branch instructions — An instruction logic which when executed may cause the arithmetic logic unit (ALU) to obtain the next instruction from some location other than the next sequential location. A branch is one of two types: conditional, unconditional.

branch-on indicator — Branching takes place when appropriate indicators (switches, keys, buttons, etc.), or conditions, have been set to point to a particular group of registers, i.e., a branch may occur dependent upon whether the magnetic tape units are ready to receive a new block of data.

branch-on switch setting — Refers to branching that is often designed for the use of certain memory locations or index registers to set the value of the switches. The presetting of a switch may cause the program to branch to the appropriate one of N points, where N is the number.

branch operation — Refers to an operation that replaces the updated instruction address portion of the program status word with a new instruction address, either unconditionally or only if specified criteria are satisfied.

breadboard — Usually refers to an experimental or rough construction model of a process, device, or construction.

breadboard output card — A card that allows user to design and build a custom analog or digital output card. Card includes basic address, storage and control signal buffer circuits.

breakpoint — 1. Relates to a specific point in a program usually indicated by a breakpoint flag that requests interruption of the program to permit the user an opportunity to check, correct or modify the program before continuing its execution. 2. A place in a routine specified by an instruction, instruction digit, or other condition, where the routine may be interrupted by external intervention or by a monitor routine.

b-register — 1. A computer register that has the capability of storing a word which can change an instruction before it is carried out by the calculator.

BTAM basic telecommunications access method — An IBM designation that refers to the use of macro instructions to achieve data communications with specific terminals.

bucket — Refers to a slang expression used to indicate some portion of storage specifically reserved for accumulating data, or totals, e.g., "throw it in bucket 1," is a possible expression. Commonly used in initial planning.

buffer — A 'machine' designed to be inserted between other 'machines' or program elements to match impedances, peripheral equipment speeds, to prevent mixed interactions, to supply additional drive or relay capability or simply to delay the rate of information flow. Buffer types are classified as inverting or non-inverting.

buffered asynchronous communications interface — Typical units provide two-way communications with Bell 103 or 202 Data Sets or equivalent units at speeds up to 9600 baud. Unique features are a 128-character first-in/first-out buffer, and a special recognition/interrupt feature with a 256 special character memory. They operate in simple, half-duplex, or echoplex mode, often with hardware break detect capability.

buffered keyboard — This function allows depression of a digit or function key while calculator is still executing a previous instruction.

buffered keyboard for rapid entry — Some units impose no limitations on the speed of the operator's entries. The buffered keyboard permits continuous entries while the unit is still working on a complicated problem. Information is stored and then processed when the unit is able to compute it.

buffering, simple — A technique for obtaining simultaneous performance of input/output operations and computing. This method involves associating a buffer with only one input or output file (or data set) for the entire duration of the activity on that file (or data set).

buffering, terminal — The communications adapter can provide additional buffering capacity so that the data can be received faster than the terminal can be acted upon without slowing down the communications system.

buffer storage — 1. A synchronizing element between two different forms of storage, usually between internal and external. 2. An input device in which information is assembled from external or secondary storage and stored ready for transfer to internal.

buffer storage device — 1. A storage device in which data are assembled temporarily during data

buffer storage locations transfers. It is used to compensate for a difference in the rate of flow of information or the time occurrence of events when transferring information from one device to another. 2. A portion of main storage used for an input or output area.

buffer storage locations — A set of locations used to compensate for a difference in rate of flow of data, or time of occurrence of events, when transmitting data from one device to another, and importantly also to retain temporarily a copy of the data as a safeguard against faults and unintentional erasures.

buffer storage, numerical control — In an NC system, storage positions for data, usually a complete block(s) of data. This storage is to prevent delays in the transfer of data due to tape reader speed. The data in buffer storage does not actively control the machine.

bug — 1. A program defect or error. Also refers to any circuit fault due to improper design or construction. 2. A mistake or malfunction. 3. An integrated circuit.

bug patches — As bugs are uncovered in a program, patches can be inserted and documented in order to fix the mistakes. When a number of patches have been made, they should be incorporated into the source program and the program should be reassembled. This insures a well documented program.

building block principle — Relates to a system designed to permit the addition of other equipment units to form a larger system. Also called modularity.

built-in programmability calculator — Some units are designed with programmability built-in. Users can write their own sophisticated program applications of up to a full 320 steps. Or, users can combine pre-programmed steps or hard-wired routines and save hundreds of their own steps. Supplier developed complete libraries aid users in getting the job accomplished as quickly and easily as possible.

bulk memory — A high-capacity auxiliary data storage device such as a disc, cassette or cartridge.

burst — 1. Refers to separation of continuous-form paper into discrete sheets. 2. In data transmission, a sequence of signals counted as one unit in accordance with some specific criterion or measure.

burst mode — A mode of communications between the processor and I/O devices. When a signal from an I/O device operating through the multiplexor channel indicates burst mode, the receiving unit continues to fetch bits until the unit is finished.

bus — 1. As applied to computer technology, one or more conductors used as a path over which information is transmitted. 2. A circuit over which data or power is transmitted. Often one which acts as a common connection among a number of locations. (Synonymous with trunk.) 3. A path over which information is transferred, from any of several sources to any of several destinations.

bus-calculator systems — The development of powerful but easily programmed desk calculators and smart instruments that are able to talk to each other over a standardized data bus has made application of the systems approach to laboratory instruments economically feasible. Many owners now use non-dedicated data acquisition and analysis systems using programmable bench instruments under calculator control. Many documents are available that describe the systems concept in terms of several interesting applications where data were gathered and manipulated by the calculator in such a way as to make the final results easy to interpret. The availability of built-in computing capability has effected a significant change in the design of data acquisition signal processing, instrumentation, and measuring systems. Some of the most productive systems can be found in the areas of signal processing systems, geophysical data acquisition systems, navigational systems, and many others.

bus cycles — The typical bus cycles (with respect to the processor) are: Data word transfer in: Equivalent to read operation; Data word transfer in, followed by word transfer out: Equivalent to Read/Modify Write; data word transfer in, followed by byte transfer out: equivalent to Read/Modify Write; data word transfer out: equivalent to Write operation; data byte transfer out: equivalent to Write operation.

bus available (BA) signal — The bus available signal will normally be in the low state; when activated, it will go to the high state indicating that the microprocessor has stopped and that the address bus is available. This will occur if the halt-line is in the low state or the processor is in the WAIT state as a result of the execution of the WAIT instruction. In some systems at such time, all three-state output drivers will go to their off state and other outputs to their normally inactive level.

business application — Close groupings of related activities for treatment as specific units; e.g., inventory-control processes, order and sales entires, customer-credit reports and accounting, automated purchasing models, and others may be treated as units for conversion to electronic data processing and operating systems.

business management calculator — These units are efficient management tools that enable managers to forecast the future, faster, more easily and with greater certainty, using the same data they use now. The calculator's financial, statistical and mathematical capabilities help managers not only perform most time-value-of-money calculations; they perform the statistical and mathematical calculations users need to forecast scientifically; e.g., linear regressions, curve fits. Most types also assist in extended percent calculations. They offer separate percent keys that let users make all sorts of percent calculations with a minimum number of keystrokes. One unit contains an expanded memory of 19 registers. In addition to the five financial registers, and four operational stack registers, this unit offers 10 that are addressable in which users can store and retrieve data.

business management calculators, hand-held — Several types of business management pocket calculators put an ideal combination of financial, mathematical and statistical functions at users fingertips. With them they can handle everything from simple arithmetic to complex time-value-of-money computations. They can even handle planning, forecasting and decision analysis. And, users can approach business problems in a variety of ways to arrive at intelligent decisions and recommendations based on facts. Many of these special units automatically calculate discounted cash flows; percentages; ratios; proportions; compound interest; remaining balance; annuities; depreciation; mean and standard deviation; rate of return; amortization and more.

business system, programmable calculator-based — A business system for small manufacturing concerns might consist of a programmable calculator with small memory, a string variable ROM, a peripheral tape cassette, a hopper card reader, and a typewriter. With this configuration, a user could automate many number-crunching tasks in his shop: payroll, billing, loan contracts, inventory control. The system can enable the businessman to get vital information to help make decisions for cutting costs, bidding jobs, planning investments, and the like. The system could also maintain a list of important customers, periodically mailing them "personal" letters describing new products and services.

bus priority structure — Since many busses are used by processors and I/O devices, there is a priority structure to determine which device gets control of the bus. Often every device on the bus which is capable of becoming bus master is assigned a priority according to its position along the bus. When two devices which are capable of becoming a bus master request use of the bus simultaneously, the device with the higher priority position will receive control.

bus system — Refers to a system or network of paths within the calculator designed to speed data flow. Several important types of busses in microprocessor systems are labeled: data bus, address bus, control bus, etc.

bus system, multiple — The microprocessor size and type dictates the bus structure which is an important factor affecting performance. The common bus approach is defined as the case where a single bus is used alternately for data, addresses, and control signals. A multiple-bus system uses at least one separate, dedicated bus for data and another for addresses. Control signals may or may not have a dedicated bus. By using a multiple-bus system, data and addresses can be the same cycle without waiting for a serial usage of a common bus.

bust — The bad performance of a programmer or a machine operator.

byte — An IBM developed term used to indicate a specific number of consecutive bits treated as a single entity. A byte is most often considered as a single entity. A byte is most often considered to consist of eight bits which as a unit can represent one character or two numerals.

byte addresses — Some computer words are divided into a high byte and a low byte. In some systems word addresses are always even-numbered. Byte addresses can be either even-or odd-numbered. Low bytes are stored at even-numbered memory locations and high bytes are odd-numbered memory locations.

byte storage — A byte is composed of eight bits plus a parity bit, and represents one alphabetic or special character, two decimal digits, or eight binary bits of information. The availability of expandable bytes provides even the smallest user with the ability to integrate communications network control and real-time data processing in the same processor, and, as a byproduct, run conventional programs during those time periods when real-time transactions are not being proposed.

C

cable — Assembly of one or more conductors within an enveloping protection sheath so constructed as to permit the use of conductors separately or in groups.

cache memory — A limited-capacity, very fast semiconductor memory which can be used in combination with lower cost, but slower large-capacity memory, giving effect to a larger and faster memory. Look-ahead procedures are required in the progress of the programs to affect locating and depositing the right information into the fast memory when it is required.

CAD (Calculator Aided Design) AC analysis program — This program is patterned after the well known ECAP circuit analysis program written by IBM. Features of the program are:
- Up to 9 nodes and 48 components can be analyzed concurrently,
- Components allowed are resistors, capacitors, inductors, and voltage-controlled current sources,
- The precision and dynamic range of the Calculator make it possible to transform other active elements, such as, op-amps, into the required form,
- Data input is simplified: users need only specify the element values and node interconnections,
- Circuit topologies can be stored on tape cassette for future recall,
- Analysis is available in the swept frequency mode with either log or linear sweep; components and circuits can be modeled and analyzed.

CAD — engineer tutorial systems — If an engineering design problem is too troublesome for manual analysis but does not warrant the time and expense of a computer, many try the Calculator-Aided Design solution. It can save time and money and give hands-on accessibility and accurate answers in a few minutes. Suppliers can help users take the drudgery out of their work and give them more design time. For more information on CAD programs — the time savers — EEs should call nearest supplier Calculator Field Engineers.

calculate mode — The calculate, or manual mode is the foundation for many developments of programming efficiency. Many amateurs use this mode to begin building their own programs. As they work with a programmable unit, most will quickly discover new dimensions of its flexibility and power — perhaps far more than they initially expected.

calculating, card-programmed — Card-programmed calculating uses many connected or separate routines. That is, a calculator CPU reads from electronic cards the various factors for calculating, and the codes instruct the machines about calculations to be made, thus, involving multiple steps of data processing.

calculating manually — Users control every step of the calculation by pressing keys in the actual order of execution: users enter data, perform functions, store results, control display, etc., by pressing keys.

calculating operation, average — An indication of the calculating speed of the computer determined by taking the mean time for nine additions and one multiplication.

calculating oscilloscope advantages — The unit gives users the precision of a digital oscilloscope for data acquisition and display *plus* the built-in capability of a microprocessor for data reduction. Users can make exact calculations of rise times, integrals, differentials, peak areas, RMS values, peak-to-peak measurements, n-point averaging, and an almost unlimited range of other operations. It increases productivity by letting users measure, display, digitize, store, and process data faster and more accurately than ever before. The unit will analyze data and, through conditional branching, function as a decision making instrument. It is easily programmable — without computer instructions — so repetitive operations can be completely automated. Its mainframe, through modular design, has provisions for a wide range of plug-in modules to let users expand their system to meet individual requirements. It can be interfaced to control other equipment. (some units)

calculating oscilloscope, programmable — To many this is the ultimate instrument for the acquisition, processing and manipulation of electrical data. It substantially eliminates the need to compromise many requirements with a jumbled array of separate instruments. The programmable calculating oscilloscope is a unit that combines the capabilities of a digital oscilloscope and a microprocessor in a single mainframe. It brings users flexibility, convenience, accuracy and reliability.

calculation, double or reverse — Double or reverse calculation is the calculation, recalculation, and then comparison of the two results to prove accuracy. It is commonly used in payroll and other calculations for which no predetermined control total can be developed. In the recalculation, factors are reversed; the original multiplier becomes the multiplicand and the original multiplicand becomes the multiplier.

calculator accounting — Some accounting calculators offer full electronic accounting capabilities for departments or small offices. The office-sized calculator comes pre-programmed to do receivables, invoicing, sales journals, inventory, general ledger, and payroll. They handle both cut and continuous forms, and ledger cards with or without magnetic recording.

calculator acquisition and analysis system — One type advanced calculator system masters a wide range of data acquisition and analysis operations. It can capture, translate, compare, analyze, record and store electrical measurement data. It's like a minicomputer system. But in an easy-handling form with a lower price. And, software or language problems are easily solved. It replaces manual logging. Eliminates conversion tables and visual strip chart scaling. It's automatic and free from human error. The calculator is the system processor-controller, working with a counter or multimeter—or two of a kind. The interface unit holds the plug-ins and translates messages between instruments and calculator. The calculator can control up to 20 plug-ins. (some systems)

calculator add-on capabilities (peripherals) — Peripherals such as Input Writer, Output Writer or Teleprinter Interface can be used with some systems, allowing alphanumeric information to be written on or read from tape.

calculator adaptability — One of the primary advantages of a programmable calculator is adaptability. It can be used for quick keystroke calculations, dedicated problem solving, programmable problem solving, and interfacing. Compact and lightweight, the unit sits anywhere on a desk to calculate problems from simple addition to complex math encountered in such fields as statistics, science, and engineering.

calculator-aided design (CAD) — Programmable calculators can slash days, even weeks, from an electronic design schedule. A user has complete interactive control of the design process. It is no longer necessary to interface with a time-sharing system, or wait for a data processing center to run a job. The user enters component values and an X-Y plotter, can draw a Bode diagram that shows the effect of those changes. This entire process is done automatically—on the plotter or built-in printer, completely documented—before a design is committed to time-consuming breadboarding. There are CAD programs available for network analysis, filter design—all giving improved efficiency from concept to hardware.

calculator-aided design applications — Larger calculators equal the computer in data handling and calculating power. This is made possible by such features as increased key functions, printing capability, peripheral devices and computer-like compatibility with interfacing. Among the peripherals are X-Y plotters, card readers, tape readers and punches, typewriters, line printers, digitizing devices, magnetic-tape cassettes and disc memories. In perspective, a programmable calculator is an engineering tool designed for scientific usage with hands-on accessibility. Unlike computers, calculators are molded to fit typical engineering work spaces and provide on-the-spot solutions. Computational speed (a bench-mark factor used in assessing computer performance) is definitely a factor in large "number-crunching" programs. However, for most engineering design problems, the total engineering solution time overshadows the computational speed. A calculator also provides a capacity for dialogue, for iterations of solutions, and for direct hands-on interaction by the design engineer. As an extra advantage for calculator-aided design applications, some calculators are directly compatible with peripheral tape or disc memory and other capacity-building equipment. Graphic displays that effect the quickest interpretation of solutions are conveniently interfaced to calculators.

calculator aided design systems — Network analysis, control systems, logic simulation, magnetics, microwave and other engineering problems can be solved with the calculator-aided design procedures. This software system can slash days—perhaps weeks—from user design schedules. It concerns fully-proven combinations of computing calculators and engineering software that can give users fast, accurate solutions to their most complex problems.

calculator "answering machines" — A method of reducing software support costs and maintaining a high semiconductor ratio is to effectively design machines with more of the software converted to silicon chips, instead of developing general purpose advanced calculators with basic computational keys and programming capability, which requires the user to understand both the programming characteristics of the calculator and the detailed mathematical concepts of his or her application. Many dedicated special purpose "answer machines" are now being marketed for specific applications. The keys of many of the answer machines are hardware programmed to give final results of a problem. For example, it is possible to compute the ground speed of an airplane given the direction of the wind and speed and direction of the plane on an advanced calculator if one knows the fundamentals of trigonometry and vector arithmetic. Many pilots and all navigators do. These problems can be solved on an "answer machine" type calculator by entering the variables using appropriately designated input keys and simply pressing the desired answer key, in this case one probably marked "groundspeed". A minimum of sustaining software is required and all those civilian pilots who didn't do well in math are potential customers.

calculator applications (four function units) — The majority of users buy calculators for balancing checkbooks, keeping track of grocery totals, doing their income tax and occasionally computing how many miles per gallon their car is getting. Low-end calculators easily provide enough function capability for most non-professional uses—usually too much. Accumulating memories, percentage keys with convenient methods of computing add-on or discount values, automatic constants and even square root keys are now standard functions for calculators that are considered low-end or four-function products.

calculator as a budget-priced business computers — Many calculators function as stand-alone computers, as remote job entry stations, or as satellite terminals. They may be used by small companies as a first computer, or by larger firms as part of a distributed computing network. Based on sophisticated microprocessors, some systems have 16K+ of memory, CRT consoles, dual floppy-disk drives, plus line printers. They can be expanded to larger configurations and have full ranges of systems software, including business-oriented languages.

calculator, audible — An audible calculator, called Speech Plus, has a 24-word vocabulary built into a speech-generating read-only memory custom IC that announces every entry and result. It has six basic functions, including square root and per cent, accumulating memory, automatic constant, a change of sign key, a floating decimal point, and an eight-digit visual display. The speech key can be pressed repeatedly to announce what is on display.

calculator-based data acquisition system — Various specific data acquisition and process control subsystems and programmable desk calculators combine to create a highly versatile data acquisition, data logging and small-scale process control system at surprisingly low installed cost. Programming expense is reduced one or two orders of magnitude because no knowledge of special programming languages is required — a series of keystrokes control the operation of the entire system. Programs and data are stored in memory or on magnetic tape with the calculator's built-in digital cassette recorder. Full alpha-numeric printout of data is achieved by an IBM "Selectric" typewriter, properly interfaced.

calculator-based HP-IB multiprogrammers — Unless users automatic systems require the high-speed execution of a computer, there's a good chance they can take advantage of the economy, flexibility, and ease-of-programming offered by a calculator-based HP-IB — Multiprogrammer. The heart of the HP-IB — Multiprogrammer approach to real-time system design is the HP Programmable Calculator. Any of several calculators can be used: Model 9830A, 9820A, 9821A, 9815A and 9825A.

calculator-based multiprogrammer system — Process engineers can now plug together and program their own automatic test and process control system quickly and economically. It's all made possible with a calculator-based Interface Bus. One Multiprogrammer System is designed for ease in communicating bi-directionally with a user's process instrumentation. A basic system includes the controller, a desk-top programmable calculator connected via the bus to a multiprogrammer interface unit, a multiprogrammer, and from 1 to 15 randomly-addressable I/O cards that plug into the mainframe. Up to 15 extender mainframes, each holding 15 plug-in cards, can be combined permitting system expansion up to 240 I/O channels controlled by a single calculator.

calculator-based variables monitoring system — Monitoring the pH and precisely controlling the amount of caustic that should be used to neutralize the acid in order to prevent damage to the bacteria in a municipal sewage plant is a complex process. A calculator helps control the effluents from some manufacturing plants. One specific Data Acquisition System is coupled with a programmable calculator providing a system that replaced multiple recorders previously required throughout the facility. The system is programmed for precise pH levels. It continuously monitors pH and indicates an alarm condition when the limits are not in specification. Measuring multipoint physical parameters to monitor or analyze phenomena and control devices will provide many varied applications of the system. Transmission of the data may be possible over thousands of miles using a Common Carrier Interface and an optional modem.

calculator-based system approaches — Firmly established as a valuable tool for the engineer, the calculator has recently found its way into systems. Programmable desk calculators, for example, offer a useful alternative to minicomputers in the design of small-scale data acquisition and process control systems. Many documents refer to Calculator Based Data Acquisition and Process Control Systems. They point out the advantages of the "intelligent" programmable approach as compared to hardwired systems and will assess the relative merits of the scientific desk calculator vs conventional minicomputers for those applications. In addition to detailing keyboard-oriented programming techniques and operator-interactive systems using programmable calculators, they also provide a checklist to aid in selection of the appropriate type of calculator, memory capacity, and peripheral equipment. Potential users will gain from evaluations of data acquisition, processing and display—calculator-based systems. They should also examine hardware versatility and the ability to acquire information from a variety of sources; processing—particularly capabilities, software requirements, and speed-cost tradeoffs; and diverse utilization of processed information.

calculator batch terminal components — The following equipment is required for operation of a calculator as a batch terminal: A calculator with up to 4K words of memory, string variables ROM, a thermal printer or equivalent, a data communications interface, binary synchronous ROM, and modem. Optional additions to the batch terminal environment may include one or more of the following groups of equipment: mass memory subsystem, external cassette, calculator card reader with extended I/O ROM, tape reader with extended I/O ROM, line printer subsystem. A large calculator memory and a wide variety of other peripherals can also be included in a batch terminal environment.

calculator-batch terminal operations — Refers to the various flows of information through the advanced calculator during various batch operations. Also concerns the use of intermediate data storage on cassette or mass memory. Before data is transmitted or stored on the intermediate storage for future transmission, it is blocked in a 400-character buffer, in some systems. Before data is printed, often such data in 400-character buffer is unblocked.

Other functions performed by the batch calculator include data checking on received data and retransmission of improperly transmitted data. If line errors make data communication impossible or the connection is not maintained for some other reason, an error message is displayed at the calculator. Also, the number of message blocks transmitted or received is printed at the end of each transmission.

calculator business system — Complete business system calculator configurations can be delivered with all of the programs to handle the acccounting and administrative needs for a particular business. For example, the package for wholesaler/distributor handles the order writing and invoicing, inventory accounting and control, accounts payable, aged accounts receivable, and sales analysis. Each of the functions generates all necessary reports and documents for both management analysis and day-to-day running of the business. (some systems)

calculator capability range — Four function calculators perform arithmetic operations. Scientific calculators perform a broad range of math functions and evaluate most math formulas quickly. Programmability adds to the already impressive power of the scientific calculator. In simple terms, programmability for pocket calculators is the ability to store and then automatically execute keystrokes. Evaluating formulas typically involves fixed keystroke procedures. The ability to record keystrokes means that entire formulas can be recorded and then be produced by the touch of a key. Entire formulas can be made as easy to use as the addition operation of a four function calculator.

calculator capacity, non-programmable — The capacity of a calculator is the maximum number of digits that can be entered or obtained in a result. In most machines, the capacity is equivalent to the number of digits in the display. In a few machines, it is larger than the number of digits in the display and a flip-flop key is used to show the full result. Where this is the case, it is noted in a table supplied with the unit.

calculator card reader — Users can input data on punched or marked cards to their calculators. Various programmable calculators can use a companion card reader that reads 128-character Hollerith code and converts it to 7-bit ASCII for the calculator. Some type card readers operate at 300 cards/minute. Owners can use either 40- or 80-column format. They can design owners cards, thanks to a special command that transmits all the marks on the card without regard to coding. Data is stored in intermediate buffers for optimum transmission, which means users operate on blocks of data rather than stacks of cards. With the card reader, users can program various series calculators at their desks or at home. Applications include payroll, quality control, inventory control, education, medical records, and consumer surveys.

calculator cartridge memory — Users can extend some memories with data cartridges. Bidirectional searchs, coupled with interchangeable data and program storage, provides power, flexibility, and speed. Some tape drives can search at 1524mm per second (60 inches per second). Users can read or write data and programs at 254mm per second (10 inches per second). This means that in the time it takes to check the time on a watch, for example, the calculator has loaded, checked, and is running a program 1,500 steps long.

calculator character-impact printer — Various manufacturers offer page-width printers for use with Advanced Series programmable calculators. The platen accommodates, on some units, paper up to 15 inches wide and prints up to 132 columns at 10 characters per inch. The 96-character interchangeable print disc provides full character impact on the fixed carriage, yet it is quiet enough to allow operation in office environments, at least for some models. Bidirectional motions of the platen and print mechanism provide plotting capabilities for charts and graphs. Programmable tabulation, both horizontal and vertical, simplifies plotting and form filling on this printer. Special enhancements include programmable top of form, form length, and form feed. Some units are fully self-contained and can be easily interfaced to Advanced Series programmable calculators. The optional form feed mechanism available on some models offers clear multiple copies, as well as continuous Z-fold paper handling capabilities. These units can be used in scientific, industrial, and commercial applications.

calculator, children's "Mickey Math" — A low-cost electronic calculator designed specifically for the children's market was announced mid-1975 and designed to appeal to children as well as adults with a sense of humor, Mickey Math™ features a colorful picture of cartoon favorite Mickey Mouse[c] arrayed in a sorcerer's costume. Furnished with an illustrated instruction booklet written for the younger set, the instrument is a full four-function, algebraic logic calculator with a floating decimal and six-digit readout.

calculator chip — A typical calculator chip might have the following characteristics:

- Five function ($+, -, \times, \div, \%$) eight digit display;

calculator 'chips', advances

- Percent discount and percent add-on;
- Memory with automatic accumulation;
- Algebraic keyboard with full chaining;
- Automatic constant factor on five functions;
- Floating decimal mode; decimal wraparound on overflow.
- Automatic power-on clear; leading zero suppression;
- For use with LED (direct drive) fluorescent, or gas discharge displays;
- Square root; entry; percentage mark-up; percentage difference;
- Register exchange; change sign; fixed decimal point with 5/4 rounding;
- Conversion of liters/gallons, kilograms/pounds, and centimeters/inches; and
- Constant conversion modes.

calculator 'chips', advances — Low power chips and displays will eventually cause replacement of expensive rechargeable batteries and chargers with disposable batteries. This will free the user from a wall adapter environment. In the calculator, the changes will be obvious as the component count diminishes and more of the discrete elements are included in the MOS chips, all accompanied by an increased functional capability. These advances will be due to improved architectural designs, greater chip component densities and larger chip sizes. Even with these future trends, case sizes are still expected to decrease slightly, though not as rapidly as in the past. Memory sizes will continue to increase with 10 to 20 registers being standard. The program memory will increase in size and free a user from the tedium of spending all day being "efficient" when he programs. (See microcomputer section for 'chip' discussion of components and capabilities.)

calculator circuit, all-in-one — One type of all-in-one calculator chip incorporates support functions, allowing a powerful scientific calculator to be constructed by the addition of LED display, segments driver, and digits driver.

calculator circuit system kits — A typical 'kit', a programmable calculator data system, accepts BCD inputs from any source. It performs arithmetic calculations $(+, -, \times, \div)$ and provides outputs for printers, machine control functions, LED displays, d/a converters, etc. It supplies eight latched BCD decades and a multiplexed seven-segment output. The system is TTL-compatible and operates from a +5-V supply. The module is externally programmable—it accepts function commands from external keyboards, ROMs, switches, or any other BCD device. Other models come with thumbwheel programming switches, an eight-digit LED display, and are housed in small instrument cases.

calculator circuit, test instrument — A typical unit is designed to test all types of calculator chips and chip sets. It will reject devices on the basis of failures in substrate continuity, logic functions, input or output tests, power drain, and bounce delay. All data for test voltages, limits, categorization, input stimuli, and output results are stored in a random-access memory. To minimize job setup time, performance boards (plug-in units containing the device adapter, pin assignment, level shifting, other chips in the set, and any special circuitry required for a particular device) are used for each device type. New programs are generated and edited by means of a separate keyboard unit

calculator control (major microprocessor)

that plugs into the mainframe. Once a program is in memory and has been verified, it can be stored quickly on a magnetic card for future use.

calculator code — The code by which data are represented within a calculator, for example a Binary Coded Decimal. Also referred to as machine language.

calculator code types — There are two general means of solving problems on professional calculators. One method involves the algebraic form with anything from no operational precedence to full algebraic hierarchy. The other method involves the computer-like stack commonly referred to as reverse Polish notation (RPN). Large segments of users find the algebraic form more natural than the RPN as a consequence of the familiar forms from high school or college math courses, however, once users are familiar with RPN, they often prefer this form.

calculator communications — As calculator control expanded and different or more complex situations were met, calculator manufacturers developed the hardware-interrupt capability. Calculator manufacturers rely generally on asynchronous mode, data is only transmitted when the readiness of both devices has been established, usually by some form of handshake procedure. Bytes can be offered to external devices in two basic ways. All the bits may be transferred at once on different lines (parallel), or they may be transmitted one at a time on a single line (serial). The former method is commonly used between local system components, while the latter is useful for long-distance communications.

calculator communications, example — From the calculator, data is sent to the teletypewriter with supplementary housekeeping characters. A carriage return and line feed are inserted after each four channels of data so that page copy is produced. Various types of printout can be formatted for easy interpretation of the data. Channel number is clearly identified, decimal point printed, and engineering units shown on many systems. The standard interface includes a 10-foot interconnect cable with spade lugs at the teletypewriter end for direct attachment to its input terminal strip.

calculator-controlled plotter — One type calculator plotter provides permanent graphic solutions to problems solved by advanced programmable calculators. The plotter graphs the point specified by the X and Y coordinates stored in two of the calculator data registers when the plot command is given. The relationship between the variables is usually programmed in the calculator which then controls the plotter. The calculator can also be used in the manual mode to transfer data coordinates directly to the plotter. Maximum plotting capability is obtained with the plotter which provides complete alphanumeric plotter output, axis generation, automatic function scaling, and special symbol point plotting. This allows the user to produce finished plots that are titled, scaled, and labeled as he desires.

calculator control (major microprocessor) — For the Motorola M6800 microprocessor which the semiconductor firm disclosed in early 1974 the Hewlett-Packard model 9815A programmable desktop calculator was the first major commercial application (late 1975). The Motorola part was selected for the calculator because of its fairly fast operation, compatible chip set, and minimal requirement for external circuitry. It's in complete control of the machine, including operation of a built-in tape transport, display, and thermal printer. The microprocessor also controls the timing and handshaking routines for optional input/output interfaces, which includes the IEEE standard interface, binary-coded decimal, and general interface options along with circuitry designed to talk to specific HP instruments.

The calculator itself can store up to 472 program steps and has 10 data registers. Memory is expandable to 2,008 program steps and can be allocated to any combination of program steps and data registers. The tape transport uses a cartridge designed by HP in conjunction with 3M Co., Saint Paul, Minn. Each cartridge can store 96,384 bytes of data on a 140-foot-long tape. The microprocessor allowed a reduction in size for the calculator's control circuitry from four boards to one. This, added to the lower-cost thermal printer and tape transport, resulted in a calculator priced at less than half the cost of a similarly equipped model 9810 programmable unit.

calculator conversions — One single-chip calculator array can perform 360 different pre-programmed conversions or up to three user-programmable conversions. The array also includes such basic features as algebraic entry, two parentheses levels, scientific notation and natural logarithms. Three full-feature accumulating memories are accessible to a user. Each is separately addressable from a keyboard with Store, Recall and M⁺ keys. The calculator array operates with a 40-key board and a 12-digit display.

calculator customization — Whatever a users's discipline, from physicist to financier, engineer to biochemist, there is some available programmable calculator that is the right system. The modular structure of the many units allows users to help design the calculator that best suits them. From special keyboards to memory, peripherals to program packages, users can configure their system to satisfy practically any situation—including a tight budget. Interfaces are also available which allow many series calculators to accept data from a large number of digital voltmeters, counters, and other instruments.

calculator data acquisitions system components — The systems have a calculator and an instrumentation interface with built-in power supply which holds two plug-ins, standard software overlays, and cables. Software tapes provide automatic data acquisition and processing. Counters provide accurate time base, measure direct frequency and totalize events to 9,999,999. The seven digit LED display positions decimals and blanks leading zeroes; measures frequency to 110 MHz, etc. Other operations include:
- Data logging on alphanumeric printer with sampling rate and numbers, single or dual source.
- Data reduction. Statistical summaries of variables and frequency distribution.
- Data acquisition. Stores data internally and generates least squares curve fits for a line, exponential or power function.

Standard accessories include:
- A verification program
- power cord
- magnetic tape cartridge (6000 step capacity)
- two user-definable overlays.

Interface features are:
- Can transmit to calculator all data on digital display
- Programmable interface pulse outlets. Trig out, front and back panels 12 μs width
- Logic levels are TTL compatible $\geq$ 2.4V high $\leq$ .8V low
- Calculator display flashed by interface with a $\geq$ 2 μs momentary short or pulldown to ground

calculator/data tablet combination — A desktop graphic data-processing system designated the Calcutizer combines a data tablet with a programmable calculator to form a "smart" data-tablet system. Developed by Talos Systems Inc., the Calcutizer consists of an integrated hardware and software package. Data tablets and digitizers measuring from 11 by 11 inches to 44 by 60 in. of active area are available. A programmable calculator with a printer or—as an option—one of the more powerful series calculators is interfaced to the digitizer. Standard packages of statistical and graphic software are available.

The engineer or scientist can use the Calcutizer to perform calculations in seconds or minutes, in his office. Many previous data-reduction systems involved delays for batch-mode processing or connection to costly time-share systems. The input for the system is the Talos data tablet. Both tablets and digitizers developed by the company are based on closed-loop, all-electronic servo circuitry instead of the technique of pen-displacement detection used in other systems. In addition to the standard hardware of the Calcutizer system, an optional plotter for hard-copy graphics is available. The company also makes the Telenote system, which transmits handwriting over telephone lines.

calculator decision-making capabilities — Decision-making capabilities are an essential requirement of all but the simplest kind of program. A programmable calculator must therefore handle programs that are constructed with decision (or branch) points. Different sequences of commands are performed depending on the value, or almost any other aspect of a number, or a logic condition at a specific branch point in a program. Many simple condition decisions are: negative numbers, zero, switch settings, greater than, less than, etc. Most can be combined to create highly complex multi-branched programs, but overall simplicity is still retained. The programmer can spell out singly, each condition to be tested in a multiple-branch despite increasing complexity. A capacity of 4,000 program steps can solve highly complex branching problems and is available on many models.

calculator decision-making IF key — Users press the IF key for decision making or conditional branching. They test a displayed number for less than, equal to or greater than zero or test the condition of a programmable flag. Some test for over-ranges or illegal math operations. If the conditions aren't met, the program branches to the appropriate point. There are also four types of unconditional branching in some units.

calculator design constraints — Procedures for making hand-held programmable calculators, require the solution to the following problems: (1) determination of current drain of the chip set; (2) suitable small display that is legible and requires low drain; (3) physical limit of keyboard, based on human engineering aspects. The first problem is resolved using the MOS chips. The second item is met by using optoelectronic light emitting diodes (LED) and rechargable batteries. The space requirements of the keyboard can be met using the KLIXON® type design. This led to the generation of portable calculators that were approximately 6×3×1 inches for a volume of less than 20 cubic inches. This reflects current sizes today although there are some simple calculators that are approximately 5 cubic inches in volume. All logic and input/output interfacing is included on a single MOS/LSI chip. Most calculators can operate directly off a single nine volt battery. LED displays have been made more efficient, which reduces the amount of current needed and allows the MOS logic chip to drive the display directly without bipolar drives. Both LED and fluorescent type displays are being fabricated as single components that provide as many as 14 seven segment digits for hand-held scientific calculators. Keyboards are also single components and new techniques have cut their cost substantially.

calculator display organization — A typical basic calculator organization is a mechanization that provides 704 words of microprogramming and 76 words of memory storage for working registers, display and memory registers. In one unit the I/O circuit provides 12 outputs and 12 inputs, for strobing and encoding keyboards, driving segmented displays and sensing discrete switch settings. The CPU has 8 discrete inputs and 4 discrete outputs which interface directly with the accumulator, bringing the total number of interface pins to 20 inputs and 16 outputs. The unique characteristics of this organization allow the user to emulate a ROM program before committing the microprogram to a MOS ROM, thereby guaranteeing product operation and performance prior to a volume procurement. In addition, the ability to readily add ROM, RAM and I/O circuits provides upward compatibility from the smallest product configuration to one requiring a large amount of memory and interface. All internal signal levels between circuits in the system are MOS compatible impedance and voltages while all external data lines on the I/O are TTL compatible. A single crystal and +5v, −12v power supplies are all that is required to have a complete operating system. The microprogram, for this type of product, is typically written such that the keyboard is periodically scanned in a predetermined sequence. The closure of a keyboard switch is a signal to the processor to carry out some operation or subroutine sequence as a function of the key which is depressed. This sequence of instructions is completely determined by the microprogram stored in the ROM.

calculator dual magnetic tape cassette reader/recorder example — Large storage at low cost is one of the key features of some units. Two independent tape drives can be individually addressed. Both have READ/RECORD features, REWIND, SEARCH FORWARD, and SEARCH in reverse direction. "Automatic verification" insures correct reading of data. Each holds a 150-foot tape cassette containing up to 115,200 program steps giving a combined total of 230,400 program steps or 28,800 full storage registers available between the two tapes. The unit allows users to "read/write in place". This saves time and money in applications involving updating of data. Individual data blocks can conveniently changed in place without disturbing other blocks on the tape.

calculator editing system — Included with some calculator batch terminal programs are editing systems. Some for the cassette-oriented batch terminal and some for the mass memory-oriented batch terminals. Each of these systems allows users to add, delete, and insert 80-column, card-image data base, on the cassette or the mass memory. This provides a fast, convenient medium for data storage before the information is transmitted over the data communications link. Users can eliminate punched cards or paper tape as a data storage medium if this is desired. To use the cassette-based editing in some systems, it is necessary to have an External Cassette in the batch terminal configuration. For the mass memory-based editing system, a mass memory subsystem is required.

calculator extended memory — On some systems provides additional storage capacity in increments of 1,024 program steps. Since many calculators can address multiple peripherals, more than one memory module can be incorporated into a single system.

calculator family plotters — Several firms have introduced high speed, high resolution digital plotters, plug-compatible with their calculators families. Uses of these Digital X-Y Plotters include bar charts, graphs, point plots, diagrams and other graphics. The digital design provides excellent linearity and the simplified circuitry eliminates downtime. When the specific plotter is given a set of coordinates to move to, it calculates the distance on each axis and internally computes the ratio of speeds in x and y directions to make the move smoothly. The plotter knows how far the pen has to travel and governs its acceleration accordingly, eliminating the slew, waviness, or overshoot associated with most analog plotters. On some units vectors of any length may be plotted. Front panel selection of full or half scale may be selected independently for each of the x and y axes.

calculator, first generation — 1. A data processor especially suitable for performing arithmetical operations that requires frequent intervention by a human operator. 2. Generally and historically, a device for carrying out logic and arithmetic digital operations of any kind.

calculator, flat bed plotter — The Flat Bed Plotter plots continuous line or point plotting of curves and data. It also gives users full alphanumeric labeling of problems solved or programmed on calculating systems. Besides plotting standard curves, these units also plot bar graphs, charts, pie graphs, and three-dimensional profiles. Alphanumeric characters can be programmed in a selection of fifteen different character sizes for labeling the 10 × 15 inches of plotting area on some units.

calculator flexible disc — One mass memory device allows the calculator to perform jobs previously beyond the capacity of calculators. It is available as a single disc and as dual disc units with optional calculator interface. It stores both program and data information in sector units. This means the calculator can engage in program library management with more sophisticated programs and handle large amounts of data.

Operation is simple and straight forward. Keyboard commands from the calculator give access to the disc for READ or WRITE operations. Disc addresses and status are shown on the calculator

display. The interface is optimized to make transfer of thousands of bytes of information as easy as transferring only a few. Some typical specifications are:
- 64 data tracks per disc
- 32 sectors/track
- 128 steps/sector; 16 registers/sector
- Read after write error checking
- 128 character buffer
- 160 ms rotational latency
- 15 ms track-to-track access plus 5 ms head setting time
- 1 in 10^{11} bit error rate
- 10^7 pass/track disc life
- 5 year head life

calculator, four-function 'scientific' — The simple four-function calculator offers the engineer and other users almost as much versatility as much more expensive scientific units. By altering the order in which some computations are performed, and by adding some extra steps, users can develop the basic calculator to do operations like squaring, square-rooting, summing of products, summing of quotients, trig ratios, and exponents. But usually before users can do this, they must simplify the complex engineering formulas. The reduction simply eliminates some factors in the equation that would not affect the result by more than a few percent. Once the formulas are reduced there are many areas where the four-function calculator can be used to predict design trend quickly without lengthy analysis. Areas where this applies include power-supply filter design, signal filter design and RMS signal calculations.

calculator-host system, example — Some calculators can be used in both small and large control systems. Often they can be used in a large distributed-processing system. For example, a pipeline company that already has a master control center might want to expand the control network by buying several remotely controllable systems from a supplier and linking them by telephone lines to the master control. Or, they might use a similar host-satellite organization with other serial data channels for master and local control in a large multiphase process plant. In one example, the OEM computer subsystem must communicate with the master control, calculate process-control parameters, transfer data to and from local controllers via d-a and a-d converters, accept information from a keyboard, and display system status. These requirements can all be met by variations of I/O configurations. So a single subsystem calculator board in each satellite system can implement all the required functions.

calculator input/output writer — One unit combines the features of the Output Writer and the calculator Input keyboard in one self-contained unit. It handles full alphanumeric for both input and output applications. The combined system can work in a convenient conversational mode under program control. Operating instructions in the user's language can be typed out and the operator can type in the required information—a two-way conversation between the calculator and user.

calculator instrument and peripheral control — Calculator systems can control instruments, gather data, and process that data. For this purpose, three general types of interface cards are available: general 8-bit I/O, BCD input for some systems. For example, general 8-bit I/O provides compatability with tape punches, tape readers, instruments . . . The general 8-bit I/O has built-in I/O buffers, recognizes programmable logic levels, and is capable of handling input speeds up to 2,000 bytes per second. In one system, the BCD input card operates with digital voltmeters, electronic counters, and BCD measurement systems. It can handle both 9-digit input and 8-bit control output. The Hewlett-Packard Systems are plug-to-plug compatible with HP-IB instruments. Up to 14 HP-IB instruments can be interconnected to a single HP-IB interface card. With two I/O channels, the 9815H-P calculator can have up to 15 different instruments distributed between its channels. And, of course, the H-P9815 is fully compatible with all Hewlett-Packard HP-IB instruments.

calculator-instrumentation systems, black boxes — Some users, by connecting one end to an instrument or black box and the other end to their computing calculator, have an automatic instrumentation system. Then the calculator controls all those things that take up so much valuable time —adjusting controls, making measurements, and extracting meaningful answers from masses of data. The systems can free users from serving as the interface. They put a connector on the end of the cable and, for all practical purposes, they have a computer-controlled system that can be easily tailored to the job at hand. Most users don't have to replace their present instruments or redesign their black boxes if they have any of the common interfaces. Binary, BCD, ASCII data codes (parallel or serial) suppliers have interface cards that handle just about any problem that may arise.

calculator instrumentation system capabilities — Users may have a powerful, yet inexpensive calculator combined with a power supply and system software and add the instrumentation modules they need and it's still portable. With the calculator, users can read input from DMM's and counters, can log data selectively, calculate results and output data or trigger signals. Programming is little more than natural math, and many users write their own. Also standard software gives users data logging (on the optional printer) and data capture on the calculator at operator selected intervals. For numerical monitoring or analysis, there are other units with plug-ins.

calculator interface couplers — A series of interface systems now act as couplers between the input/output bus of programmable calculators and laboratory or process instruments. The systems consist of a mainframe and PC cards for the specific calculator models to be used together with card-rack assembly that accommodates 8, 10, or 16 plug-in function cards. Standard function cards include a/d converters, multiplexers, six-digit parallel BCD data input, six-digit high-speed counters, and ten channel, four-digit counters. A special card provides simulated interrupt capability for the calculator. Many other interfaces are possible.

calculator interface, instruments — Calculator interfaces have been designed to get digital outputs (BCD or binary) from all types of measuring instruments (DMV, counters, transient recorders, correlation analyzers, temperature ph, etc.) into any of the popular programmable calculators. One device accepts the parallel data from the instruments, serializes it, formats it, decodes it, and sends the data to the calculator. A 26 step program provides the ability to present any character at any time to the calculator, thereby allowing existing software for the calculator to be used without modification. (Many other examples.)

calculator interfaces, "smart" terminals — With special interfaces many calculators (Wang 600 or 700 for example) can communicate between themselves, with any serial asychronous ASCII terminal, and with other computers at speeds from 110 to 9,600 bits per second. The interface handles all the necessary translation, formatting, buffering, and serializing, so that simple input/output procedures with the Wang are retained. Usually, existing software operates with attached terminals such as CRTs or printing terminals without modification. A terminal's keyboard can be used in place of the calculator keyboard for data input simply by using a Group 1 command instead of a "STOP" code on some units. With these units the Wang Calculator, as an example, may be programmed to perform either as a remote computer or as a "smart terminal". Communication can occur through standard modems or by directly plugging into the computer port or terminal connector. The WU-X is supplied with both male and female RS-232-C connectors, and contains a switch that allows reversing the transmit and receive lines so that the Wang system can be connected to virtually any terminal or computer.

calculator internal operation — A typical calculator module is operated in a sequential manner, one program step at a time. On initialization, input data is strobed through a multiplexer into a PROM. The calculator then accepts each BCD digit as fast as its own internal clock will allow. The MUX automatically stops after it has strobed the five channels. On the next externally applied programming pulse, another number, representing one of the four functions ($+ - \times \div$) is transmitted into the calculator. Other data may then be entered in similar fashion, including longer equations that are formed by using the remaining program capacity available in the front panel switches or the PROM programmer. Upon conclusion of the equation, a number representing the equals ($=$) sign is entered. The calculator then provides the output, which is available as a 7-segment display signal or as 8 latched outputs. In some systems, the minus sign from the calculator is decoded in the module and is made available as an output, for applications where an equation may go through zero and a decision must be made accordingly.

calculator languages — Potential calculator buyers first evaluate the various languages that an operator might use to communicate with an electronic calculating device. Among those available are:
- computer languages such as BASIC and FORTRAN,
- various forms of algebraic notation, and
- RPN (Reverse Polish Notation), a parenthesis-free but unambiguous language derived from that developed by the Polish mathematician, Jan Lukasiewicz.

Each of these languages has been found to excel in a particular application. For its biggest programmable desk-top calculators, most manufacturers select BASIC. For other powerful desk-top calculators, with less extensive storage capacity, many chose algebraic notation. But, given the design constraints of a pocket-sized scientific computer calculator, RPN might be the simplest, most efficient, most consistent way to solve complex mathematical problems, according to Hewlett Packard and several other makers. Most suppliers use versions of both RPN and algebraic — others use plain English.

calculator/laser controlled measuring machine — An example of a complete electronics package for a laser transducer system is a laser-controlled measuring machine. The three-axis measuring machine is used for checking the dimensions of parts. The system uses a Hewlett-Packard (HP) 9820A Calculator as a controller and data handler. It also uses three 10783A Numeric Displays to display displacement information along the X-axis, the Y-axis, and the Z-axis and one 10745A HP-IB I/O card to get instructions into the system from the controller and to get displacement data and error information back out to the controller for distribution to the displays. A system similar to this has been built in the laboratory. The 9820A program includes preset capability and complete error sensing and identification routines with printout of errors. The update rate is quite adequate for measuring machine applications.

calculator LEARN capability — With LEARN capability, some calculators can communicate with the engineer and his operator. It will ask for input instructions and label the results on the alphanumeric printer. Operators can use the definable overlay and 24 keys to deal with special interests. Users set up a subroutine for each of those 24 keys and then label the overlay. An operator need only punch a key for the results he wants. For example, users could label keys magnitude, phase, real and imaginary to handle complex numbers. Or for statistical work they could label them mean, variance, standard deviation and linear regression. A single keystroke does it.

calculator, marked sense cards — With a special Marked Sense Card Reader, data and programs can be entered directly into the system. Since the cards are prepared "off-line" without tying up the calculator, the system is more efficient.

calculator mass memory system — Inventory control, payroll, order processing, and other large-data-base applications are within the capability of the more powerful desktop calculators that include BASIC language. Their BASIC-language programming capability along with alphanumeric string and matrix manipulation, give them tremendous data handling versatility. As a result, many users have developed applications that require storage capacity much larger than standard tape cassettes can provide. Typically, these applications also call for random data access, and therefore are not conveniently run on any magnetic tape system. One obvious answer is a disc drive and they are now available as peripherals to the units. Such applications include inventory control, payroll processing, order processing, account maintenance and others. The various disc drives have been slightly modified with removable disc cartridges, and others have one fixed disc and one removable cartridge. Each fixed disc or cartridge can typically store 2.4 million 8-bit bytes of data. Data access is rapid and, most important, the drives have proven high data-handling reliability.

calculator "micro" interface — One company offers a "Micro" Interface that allows direct input of data from external digital devices (digital voltmeters, panel meters, counters, digital clocks, etc.) into their calculators. As an input only interface, it accepts numeric data of up to seven digits (28 bits) and sign in parallel. The ability to handle standard BCD 8, 4, 2, 1 code with TTL voltage levels makes this interface directly compatible to most digital meters for a variety of on-line applications. Combined with the calculator, users have the lowest cost on-line system available.

calculator-oriented microprocessors — Its applications range from small business machines to minicomputers. It reduces the requirements for circuit boards and connectors and shortens design time.

calculator output, visual/hardcopy — On advanced systems the printer and the display interact to provide two kinds of immediately available information. The printer gives users labeled copy that identifies both what was done and how it was done. The display tells users where in the calculation procedure they are and the result of each intermediate calculation. The printer and display are the tools with which these units close the communication gap between man and machine.

calculator peripheral system capabilities — Many calculator manufacturers provide a variety of peripherals and peripheral interfaces for use with their systems. At minimum, a workable programmable calculator requires some form of input/output device (large keyboard or switches and display, CRT terminal, or paper-tape reader/punch). Many applications also require peripheral data storage, either in the guise of floppy disks or magnetic tape. Also, a special group of packaged software items provided in ROM or on paper tape or mag tape. This varies widely among calculator manufacturers. Many units, especially those slated for industrial control, come with special-purpose assembly languages. Assembler programs facilitate the translation of such low-level languages into machine code on a line-for-line basis. Some general-purpose calculators have compilers that allow the translation of high-level languages, like FORTRAN and BASIC, into machine language. Other frequently provided software includes editors, used for making changes in programming, conversion routines, debug monitors and PROM programmers, and operating systems to monitor the partition of time between the various peripherals in the calculator system.

calculator plug-in ROM's — Optional plug-in ROM (Read Only Memory) for some units adds up to 2,048 more program steps of single keystroke, hard-wired functions. Five low-cost special purpose ROM's are typically available for statistics, advanced statistics, formula programming (algebraic), extended alpha listing and surveying. Custom ROM's are also available for user's own specialized programs. Once a program has been reproduced on the custom ROM, it cannot be listed, looked at or printed. This feature gives users complete privacy and assurance that unauthorized personnel cannot access a listing of programs. Yet with proper instruction, user's programs can be run with single keystroke operation.

calculator pointer — The pointer is an internal part of the calculator. It determines which memory location is executed or displayed.

calculator printer characteristics — A recently introduced printer extends the output characteristics of advanced series desk-top programmable calculators. This impact printer is a full-character, fixed carriage peripheral that can be used to fill out forms, create reports, draw charts and plot graphs using the bi-directional platen and carrier. It also features programmable horizontal and vertical tabulation. In addition to the standard 96-character, upper/lower case print wheel, optional interchangeable wheels are available for ASCII character sets and European character sets. The calculator is a versatile printer, accommodating paper up to 15 inches (38 cm) wide and prints up to 132 columns at 10 characters per inch. Average printing speed is 30 cps. Six-part paper in single-sheet or continuous-feed form may also be used.

calculator, professionally dedicated — Various dedicated calculators are aimed at specific user applications or as a general purpose calculator that uses some form of "canned programs" for unique applications. This approach usually uses magnetic cards, or some equivalent, to input the programs. The additional components necessary to read the programs tend to also reduce the ratio of semiconductor content. The dedicated stand alone concept becomes even more attractive if the same semiconductor components used for, say a navigation dedicated machine are also used in a real estate or photographers or carpenters dedicated machine. As long as the change from one application to another is simply the reprogramming of a standard chip, this is essentially true. Even though each of the applications is not huge by itself, together they represent enough volume to reduce semiconductor costs over time. Software costs are imposed during development phases and very little sustaining expense is necessary, thereby its effect on unit cost also decreases as volume accumulates.

calculator program analysis — Corrections, changing program steps, or modifying program sections are easily accomplished by special features designed specifically for the do-it-yourself programmer. In some units, the TRACE mode which can be turned on or off (either manually or under program control) enables programs or portions of programs to be analyzed for possible errors. Single keystroke INSERT and DELETE commands change any program step. A STEP function advances the program one step at a time in either RUN or LEARN mode. The SET PC (Program Counter) key enables any specific program step to be directly accessed. Once accessed, the STEP and BACKSPACE functions provide single keystroke access to adjacent steps. The SEARCH FOR MARK AND STOP command allows direct unconditional branching to any designated mark in the program and then stops. All these features add up to easier programming and debugging on some advanced units.

calculator programmability — One valuable and interesting addition to the growing list of available calculator functions is the programming feature. This is the ability of the calculator to remember (or save) a key sequence in a program area. This sequence can be executed at the user's discretion. This programmability in effect allows the user to define his own "function" keys or to execute the same key sequence repeatedly. A major inconvenience has been the loss of this program when the calculator is turned off. One solution has been to record the program on magnetic strips, cards, or tape cassettes for subsequent re-entry. There will be other future solutions to this problem.

calculator programming, hand-held — Programming is simply the ability of a calculator to learn, remember, and execute automatically a stored series of steps necessary to solve a particular problem. Once taught the calculator has the formula for the problem, all users do is supply the known variables and start the program running. But many hand-held programmable calculators give more, such as:
- Full editing capability to add or change steps at will;
- Direct branching to solve problems requiring iterative routines;
- Conditional testing to program the calculator to make decisions based on the data, all completed with various...
- easy-to-understand keystroke programming languages.

calculator programming operations, hand-held — To key a program into some machines, users press the successive keys with the switch in W/PRGM position. Then, by passing an unprotected magnetic card through the right lower slot of the calculator, users can save the program (contents of the 100-step program memory) for future use. (Some units) Four major headings of programming are: • Looking at a program. • The Control Operations needed in programs to start, to repeat, and to stop. • The Editing Operations that allow users to correct and change programs in memory. • Test Operations that allow user programs to make decisions.

calculator programming procedures — To create a program, users need to:
1. Define the problem.
2. Work out the keystroke sequence that solves the problem.
3. Add control operations for automatic execution.
4. Key the keystroke sequence, including control operations, into program memory.
5. Edit, verify, and record the sequence for later use.
6. Run the sequence, automatically, with user data.

calculator, remote — Some desk calculators allow simultaneous on-line computing service for many engineers, scientists, and mathematicians from their home or office. In a time-sharing system, the terminal can be a remote calculator that provides direct, remote access to the computer. Remote connections can be made anywhere, via standard telephone channels. Through the common-user dial network, users query the computer from a keyboard containing conventional functions and symbols of mathematics. Answers are immediately shown on the remote calculator display panel. All features of the powerful digital computers can be made instantly available at low cost.

calculator RS-232-C interface — Takes advantage of the calculator's programming and processing ability. Provides a two-way bit serial communication path for a host of RS-232-C devices. Also works with 20 mA current loop devices. It uses ASCII code so a user's calculator can converse with teleprinter terminals, CRT terminals, paper tape/punch readers and digital tape cassettes. This specific interface is compatible with Decwriter LA30, GTE Typewriter Terminal model 5741, NCR typewriter terminal model 260-6 ASR, Teletype model ASR33, Texas Instruments models 733KSR and 733ASR, Tektronix Computer Display Terminals 4010, 4012, 4013, 4014, 4015, 4023.

calculator RUN mode — In RUN mode SST executes the program step denoted by the program pointer. In the case of single stepping a call to a user defined function, (A, . . . E) the entire function executes (as one step) before returning control to the keyboard. (Some units)

calculators as medical test components — A calculator can replace some traditional medical test devices. And, it gives faster, more complete analyses in many cases. For example, the calculator with programs on magnetic tape cartridges analyzes half a dozen lung tests gathered by instrumentation. Programs can be changed or altered easily on the magnetic tape cartridges. This flexibility was not available on various old system's built-in programs. The calculator's alphanumeric printer gives the technicians a better understanding of results than the old numeric printer it replaced.

calculators, satellite processors — Various advanced calculators can be a remote batch terminal, timeshare terminal, and satellite processor, all in one unit. As a satellite processor, these powerful, often BASIC language calculators give fast solutions to most of their computational problems. And by keeping these small- or intermediate-size jobs out of the data processing stream, these units help make better use of all their computing resources. Data can be gathered from many sources because the calculators accommodate instrumentation and a complete line of input/output peripherals, including plotters, digitizers, and line printers.
To convert these units to a computing data terminal, users simply add Data Communications Interfaces and ROMs. Then they can communicate with another terminal or another calculator, function as a binary synchronous remote batch terminal to a large computer, or serve as a timeshare terminal. Users find that they then become an economical alternative for connecting to remote batch or time-sharing services — especially since calculators have so many of the features they need to improve data processing capabilities.

calculators, scientific programmable — Many of these units produce fast, accurate answers to complex everyday scientific and engineering problems. They are ideal as a desk-top scratch pad for scientific programmable calculations. Typically they feature a 10-digit display that automatically operates in scientific notation. Results of the functions can be computed in degrees or radians at the touch of a switch. Difficult programming of functions are "inside" incorporated. Users in some systems compute instantly with just a one-touch key operation. A total of 15 or more scientific functions are hardwired in, including trigonometrical, inverse trigonometrical hyperbolic, exponential, and logarithmic. Some units offering 64 or more steps of programming on 8 or more registers are available for formula and equation evaluation. Users choose several decimal point positioning systems including the floating decimal point and the exponential system with scientific notation capacity from $10^{-99''}$ to $10''$ -1 and 0.

calculator software, hand-held — A major factor in user acceptance of any programmable calculator is software. Program development can be time consuming and the user who must develop his own programs from scratch is severely limited in the extent to which he can take advantage of a machine's problem solving power. Most manufacturers have attacked the problem on two fronts. Sizable program libraries covering applications in such diverse fields as medicine, surveying, mathematics, statistics and electronic engineering are already available at extra cost. A sampling of these application packages is included with the calculator as are programs for personal use and many blank strips. For one type the EE software package alone comprises 35 programs and 114 more were quickly available in the areas of mathematics and statistics. And since the user can record his own programs, routines that have been developed for other machines can, in some cases, be adapted to many types of units.

calculator special communication interface — These units add a new dimension to the various calculator product lines. This special communication interfaces allows one calculator to "talk" to any number of remote calculators over telephone lines. Since these units are directly compatible with many telephone company modems they allow remote units in field locations to communicate with central installations. One manufacturer features three modes of information transfer: 1) calculator memory to another calculator memory, 2) calculator memory to Writer, 3) Writer to another I/O Writer.

calculator structure — New directions in computing occurred with the emergence of calculator chips. The present calculator can be defined as a small highly specialized computer. The memory structure consists of both a fixed and variable memory. The fixed portion, a read-only memory (ROM), provides a system of control program called firmware — meaning unchangeable instructions. This contrasts with general-purpose computers programmed by software, and random-logic systems that use hard-wired circuitry.

calculator subsystem components — For programmables two components are very basic — a high-density nonvolatile program memory and a flexible input/output interface that preserves the general-purpose nature of the calculator as a programmable component. The I/O interface should provide a large number of parallel I/O lines in configurations flexible enough to handle a variety of peripheral devices as well as a versatile serial I/O port for use in data communications.

calculator system monitor-controller — Some calculator systems monitor, log, process and analyze changes in a heating-airconditioning system. It computes BTU consumption as adjustments are made. The program tells a scanner where to take readings from electrical and temperature probes and transducers in the water, air and power lines. Digital voltmeters relay their readings to the calculator where data is processed. It's a precise and low cost way to experiment with variables that can add up to savings in energy costs.

calculator system peripherals Users can print, process and store more. They get full page reports from teleprinters and enlarge the calculator's data handling capability to many thousands of data points through the use of paper tape readers or tape cassettes. They feed data from cards, tape or disc into the calculator and gather information from analytical instruments and data acquisition systems for storage, processing and printout. One system's Standard Accessories are:
- calculator cable
- termination pack
- connector guide
- instruction manual

calculator tape cassette — Designed for both recording long multi-program blocks onto magnetic tape and loading programs into memory, the Cassette Tape option on some units can also be used for auxiliary storage. A tape can hold up to 12 blocks of 1,848 program steps or 2,772 full storage registers per side. For automatic chaining of programs or data storage and retrieval, one type Tape Drive features programmable "READ" and "WRITE" commands . . . under complete program control. VERIFY insurer that programs have been loaded and gives manual identification of individual blocks of programs. A parity check with a flashing ERROR INDICATOR LIGHT feature proves data has been entered in correctly from the tape.

calculator tape cassettes and cartridges — Several calculators have built-in cassettes for program data, or special key storage. In addition to the internal cassette some advanced calculators can operate with 9 or more peripheral cassettes. Files may be recalled from the cassette, modified, and restored in the same location, thus eliminating the need for a second tape unit. All files are numbered sequentially and a high-speed bi-directional search is used to locate a specified file from any point on the tape; program execution times are significantly reduced by eliminating the need for tape rewind in order to begin searching for a file.

calculator tape cassette storage characteristics — Cassette storage may be optimized by selecting different file sizes which correspond to the program length and/or data storage of the program. Several Cassette Memories may be used in a system and each can be selectively addressed. The cassette system has an interrupt mode for simultaneous calculator operation and cassette file search. A single tape cassette can hold up to 80,000 bytes (40,000 words) depending on the file structure set up by the user. The following tape cassette commands are programmable: MARK, STORE, LOAD MERGE, LINK, REWIND, FIND, STOREKEY, LOADKEY, STOREDATA, LOADDATA, and TLIST. These commands are also available in keyboard mode.

calculator teletype system example — Users have two keyboards to work with. The math keyboard of the calculator and the teletype keyboard of the terminal let users concentrate on ideas instead of mechanics. They see concepts take form on the bright screen, and they work easier because the system is fast. For example, they tap the calculator's remote key to send these commands to the terminal: Erase screen. Accept X-Y coordinate data. Enable graphics. Start or start alpha. Print alpha. Make hard copies with optional hard copy unit. The system has big screen capacity. One peripheral terminal is very big. Users can see 2590 characters without squinting. There are 35 lines of 74 upper case alpha and numeric characters per line.

calculator terminal — Some programmable calculators are not intelligent terminals but rather communicating calculators. Some provide the communications capability of a time-sharing or remote batch terminal, while retaining all the computing capability of powerful, programmable, BASIC language calculators. Some units calculate and can perform most daily computations right at the user's desk. They then collect data that can be transmitted to a large batch computer for further processing and central data base storage. In addition, the computer can send unformatted information directly to some calculators with the final report format determined by a calculator program.

calculator terminal applications, batch — Some batch terminals can be used at many points throughout a typical organization wherever stand-alone processing is required and large amounts of data must be transmitted at high speed with accuracy between two points. To name a few:
• Remote job entry (RJE).
• Preparing numerical control tapes.
• Payroll.
• Inventory control.
• Structural design.
Interactive batch terminals bring all of the applications available at the central computer to the remote location.

calculator terminal system flexibility — Some of the standard features of a calculator batch terminal which can be easily changed to suit particular needs are: (1) data transmission — 2000 bits-per-second (optionally, 1200, 1800, 2400, 3600, 4800 or 9600 bits-per-second). (2) mode — half duplex (optionally, full duplex). (3) terminal position — primary or secondary binary synchronous terminal. (4) output page width — 80 columns or 32 columns. Step-by-step instructions on how to change batch terminal environments are given for most of the common options so that the batch terminal can fit exact needs.

calculator timer — With the mode switch set to TIMER, some units can be used as a timer with a range from 0 to 100 hours. The basic operation is relatively easy. Users press to clear the timer and (run/stop) to start and stop it. When running, the X-register increments every .01 seconds with .01% accuracy (about ± 1.5 seconds in 8 hours). But there are other operations involving the timer. The timer can be started anywhere within the 0 to 100 hour range. Starting times, however, are keyed into the X-register in RUN mode. The times must be keyed in using a specific format. The H-P 55 is one with this timer capability. (See manual for specific operating instructions)

calculator/typewriter system — A specific interface unit designed with the cooperation of Hewlett-Packard engineers, is a specially designed system to allow the use of an IBM Selectric Typewriter as an output writer for the Hewlett-Packard 9800 series calculators. The interface and the baseplate which attaches to the IBM Selectric typewriter not only provide an electro-mechanical interconnection between the calculator and the typewriter, it also converts the ASCII code from the calculator to the particular code of the typewriter, thereby making them compatible. This is unique to the Tycom system and is bone of the interface systems available which can make this conversion. The baseplate used on the Interface Unit is called a "Buffered Applique". The buffer is, in fact, the logic and the ROM which converts the ASCII to typewriter code. Also mounted on the Applique are the electro-mechanical components which cause the typewriter to type when certain codes are sent to it. Between the baseplate on the typewriter and the Hewlett-Packard calculator is the Interface and power supply. This box is 8" x 9" x 6" and contains the power supply for the entire system plus self testing circuitry which allows the operator to test the system for faulty operation independent of the calculator.

calculators vs minicomputers — Advanced programmable calculators are used often when there's a need for the performance of a minicomputer without their costs and complexity. In education, business, industry, medicine, scientific research. advanced calculators are replacing minis for three major reasons: A programmable calculator is a powerful computational tool with natural math and/or alpha languages to make them easy to use and at low cost. An advanced calculator also makes possible automatic systems which were not possible with the dedicated mini for the same reasons. High cost, lack of acceptance by operating personnel, and programming difficulty. For example, an advanced calculator is used as the intelligence unit in machine tool measurement systems. Its computational power and man-machine interaction make it a natural for easy system control. The user-definable overlays allow a computing system which is extremely simple to operate. Key labelling and sequencing are logical. With this and the alphanumeric printer, instructions guide the operator. This simplicity takes only a few hours to train operating personnel.

calculator/watch — Multiplexed circuits connecting the display segments have helped cut the size of a calculator/watch combination so that it fits on the wrist. The all-electronic unit is designed around complementary MOS circuits and a field-effect liquid-crystal display. It uses multiplexing to wire the display segments, simplifying the design. "Throwaway" batteries are warranted to last a year, even with an average of 100 calculations per day. The display has eight digits, six of which are used in the normal time-keeping mode to show hours, minutes, and seconds. All eight are operable when the device is switched by pushbutton to the four-function calculating mode.

calculator/watch components — One unit packs three C-MOS chips into its case, measuring 3.3 by 4.57 by 0.954 centimeters. One chip contains the countdown circuitry for time-keeping, the second integrates the calculator circuitry, and the third the buffer and driver stages for the display. The 1-second time pulses are derived from a 32-kilohertz crystal oscillator whose frequency is counted down by a 15-step divider network. The power pack consists of four 1.5-volt silver-oxide batteries each about 15 millimeters in diameter and 4 mm thick.

calculators, wrist types — Similar to various hand-held calculators are new popular types users can wear on their wrists. One (of many) company has developed a 40-function, nine-digit readout electronic calculator and digital watch — all contained in a package 1½ inches square and less than ½ inch thick. The calculator is operated by 20 buttons. Twice that number of functions is attainable by employing a shift key, "like a typewriter." And when its not calculating, the nine-digit LED display on the device will tell time in several different ways.

calculus, Boolean — An extension of Boolean algebra which includes other variables, such as time, step functions, changes of state, delay.

calculus of variations — A specific calculus which relates to the maxima/minima theory of definite integrals. The integrands are functions of dependent variables, independent variables, and their derivatives.

calibrated instrumentation — A procedure to ascertain, usually by comparison with a standard, the locations at which scale/chart graduations should be placed to correspond to a series of values of the quantity which the instrument is to measure, receive, or transmit.

calibration accuracy — Calibration accuracy is the limit of error in the finite degree to which a device can be calibrated. (Influenced by sensitivity, resolution, and repeatability of the device itself and the calibrating equipment.) Usually it is expressed in per cent of full scale.

calibration check option, data acquisition systems — Equipped with this option, the user has a readily available self-contained reference voltage source. It eliminates the need for expensive and bulky equipment for field checks of the analog circuit integrity of some units. The option mounts on the power supply printed circuit card in the rear of some units. The output is an accurate, regulated DC source of 20 millivolts, 200 millivolts, and 2 volts, fed to three separate sockets. These can be connected by test lead to any input terminal. A pushbutton switch selects positive or negative polarity for the calibration signals.

call — The branching or transfer of control to a specified closed subroutine.

call instructions — A call is an operation which brings into action a specific subroutine generally consisting of specific entry conditions which jump to the entry point of the subroutine. The operation begins with the execution of just one instruction referred to as a call instruction.

CAM devices (content addressable memory) — Refers to R/W RAMs with an access mechanism that retrieves the addresses of data which match an attribute presented to the inputs. Most are programmed by writing into the array via a separate addressing and control path.

cancel character — A specific control character designed to indicate that the data with which it is associated are erroneous or are to be disregarded.

CANCL status word — This status word indicates that the remote computing system has deleted some information.

capacity — 1. The limits, both upper and lower, of the items or numbers which may be processed in a calculator register — in the accumulator. When quantities exceed the capacity, an interrupt develops and requires special handling. 2. The total quantity of data that a part of a calculator can hold or handle, usually expressed as words per unit of time. 3. The capability of a specific system to store data, accept transactions, process data, and generate reports.

capacity, storage — The number of elementary pieces of data that can be contained in a storage device. Frequently defined in terms of characters in a particular code or words of a fixed size that can be so contained.

card — 1. A machine-processable information storage medium of special quality paper stock, generally 7⅜ × 3¼ inches, but other standards exist for other types. 2. An internal pluggable unit for printed-circuits wiring and components.

card address backplane — The key to one system's flexibility is its unique "card address" backplane. This printed circuit backplane, which serves as the bus, assigns an address to each card or module. Users plug into it. The result is that users can assemble nearly any combination of memory and interfacing modules and plug them into the standard backplane — and still have a system that requires no hard wiring. The program in the CPU refers to the address of each card in the package.

card annotating, magnetic — Users can write on the non-magnetic side of their card using any writing implement that does not emboss the card. It is customary to write a program name on the top and to write symbols identifying the functions of the top row keys in the spaces below. Annotating magnetic cards with a typewriter may impair the read/write properties of the cards.

card care and maintenance (magnetic) — Users should try to keep their cards as clean and free of oil, grease, and dirt as possible. Dirty cards can only degrade the performance of the card reader. Cards may be cleaned with alcohol and/or with a soft damp cloth.

card chassis — A typical Memory Card Chassis is designed to accommodate up to 33 memory and control cards for mounting in a 19" relay rack. The chassis features the use of full PC back plane for power and ground and can be wired for a number of memory sizes and configurations. It can also be used in multiple for larger memory configurations. One unit is 10.5" high, 12" deep, and can be used with an in-CAB memory cabinet.

card column — 1. A line of punch positions parallel to the Y datum line of a punch card. 2. A single line of punch positions parallel to the short edge of a 3¼ by 7⅜ inch punched card.

card design features — The most valuable electrical and packaging features are: Ease of assembly, convenience in check-out, access and identification for handling and troubleshooting, and choice of connector termination.

card, event sensing — Typical card compares digital input with reference data stored on card. A service request is generated when data sets do not match. Another type generates a service request on positive and/or negative transitions of any of 12 input lines and stores the event.

card field — The fixed columns on a punch card in which the same type of information is routinely entered.

card image — A representation in storage of the holes punched in a card, in such a manner that each card hole is represented by one binary digit and the unpunched spaces are each represented by the other binary digit.

card, magnetic head (cleaning) — Users minimize the exposure of a calculator to dusty, dirty environments by storing it in the soft carrying case when not in use. Each card pack contains one head cleaning card. The magnetic recording head is similar to magnetic recording equipment. As such, any collection of dirt or other foreign matter on the head can prevent contact between the head and card, with consequent failure to read or write. The head cleaning card consists of an abrasive underlayer designed to remove such foreign matter. However, use of the card without the presence of a foreign substance will remove a minute amount of the head itself. Thus, extensive use of the cleaning card can reduce the life of the card reader. If users suspect that the head is dirty, or if they have trouble reading or writing programs, they should use the cleaning card; that's what it is for. However, if one to five passes of the cleaning card does not clear up the situation, they should send the calculator in for servicing.

card-programmed calculating — Card-programmed calculating uses many connected or separate machines. That is, an accounting machine reads from punched cards the various factors for calculating, and the codes instruct the machines about calculations to be made, thus, involving multiple steps of data processing.

card punch — A machine which punches cards in designated locations to store data which can be conveyed to other machines or devices by reading or sensing the holes.

card reader, calculator — A low-cost card reader for use by many calculators is a compact, hand-fed card reader that is designed specifically for such data or program input. It reads standard 96-character Hollerith code on either pencil-marked or punched cards. Cards may also be custom-designed to suit various applications. The unit weighs just 18 oz. (0.5 kg). It's small and quiet enough for desk-top use in any business environment. The power required for operation is supplied from the calculator. Cards may be used to input patient histories, shipping and receiving orders, field research data, and any statistical analysis.

card reader diagnostic — Refers to tests for both the controller and the printer by printing known test patterns.

card reader, magnetic (calculators) — Various built-in card readers allow users to make and reuse permanent recordings of programs and data. Recording programs is a simple task and they are easily protected against accidental re-recording by removing a perforated tape at the end of the card, for some units.

card reader operation, intelligent terminal — Punched or pencil marked data on mark sense cards can be optically read into some systems, either by hand-feed with the Mark Sense Card Reader, or up to 300 cards per minute with a Hopper-Feed Mark Sense/Punched Card Reader. Standard 80-column cards, punched in Hollerith code with any standard key-punch, or punched in binary code, can be read at up to 300 cards per minute into the system with the same Hopper-Feed Punched Card Readers.

card reader punch subsystem — A typical card punch and reader provides fully buffered on-line 80 column punching, reading and printing on standard cards. One typical single peripheral device punches and prints at rates of 45 to 75 cards per minute and reads at 200 cards per minute.

card readers, advanced calculators — A typical high-speed unit is a Hopper Card Reader that handles 80-column punched cards as well as mark-sense cards. For smaller applications, the low-cost, hand-fed Card Reader optically reads mark-sense cards.

cards, interfacing — Examples are five interface cards: One is a Page-Width Printer Interface Card; another is an interface card for a specific Plotter. One type of BCD I/O requires 8-digit BCD input with high speed mode and 8-bit parallel output. A device for general I/O is a bidirectional 8-bit parallel interface which enables users to connect to various types of calculator peripherals. The general interface for I/O will accept up to 14 interconnected instruments. Once users have set up their system, the units can be used to control the data flow to and from their instruments while gathering and processing that data.

cards, micrologic — Typical micrologic card offerings are:
- Standard Gate/Flip-Flop Cards
- Arithmetic Logic, Counters, Converters
- Timing and Delay Circuits
- Analog Components for A to D and D to A conversion
- Line, Relay, Lamp Drivers
- Stepping Motor Controls
- Pulse and Signal Shapers
- High Level DC and AC Opto-isolated Input/Output

card, stepping motor control — Typical card used to drive stepper motor and pulse-update type controls. Can be programmed to generate from 1 to 2047 pulse outputs to either of two terminals.

caret — A symbol (an inverted v) used to indicate the location of an insertion.

carrier — 1. A particular wave which has constant amplitude and frequency, and a phase which can be modulated by changing amplitude, frequency, or phase. Also, an entity which has the ability to carry an electric charge through a solid. For example, holes and conduction electrons in semiconductors. 2. A continuous frequency capable of being modulated or impressed with a second (informative carrying) signal.

carrier system — A means of obtaining a number of channels over a single circuit, or path, by modulating each channel upon a different carrier frequency and demodulating at the receiving point to restore the signals to their original form.

carry — A type of signal produced in an electronic computer by an arithmetic operation on a one-digit place of two or more numbers expressed in positional notation and transferred to the next higher place for processing. Also, a signal or expression which may arise when the sum of two digits in the same digit place equals or exceeds the base of the number system being used.

carry, cascaded — In parallel addition, a carry process in which the addition of two numerals results in a partial sum numeral and a carry numeral which are in turn added together, this process being repeated until no new carries are generated.

carry time — 1. The time required for transferring a carry digit to the higher column and there adding it. 2. The time required for transferring all the carry digits to higher columns and adding them for all digits in the number.

carry types — 1. If a carry into a digit place will result in a carry out of the same digit place, and if the normal adding circuit is bypassed when generating this new carry, it is called a high speed carry, or standing on nines carry. If the normal adding circuit is used in such a case, the carry is called a cascaded carry. If a carry resulting from the addition of carries is not allowed to propagate, e.g., when forming the partial product in one step of a multiplication process, it is called a partial carry. If it is allowed to propagate, the process is called a complete carry. If a carry generated in the most significant digit place is sent directly to the least significant place, e.g., when adding two negative numbers using nine complements, that carry is called an end around carry. Synonymous with cascaded carry, complete carry, end around carry, high-speed carry, and partial carry. 2. A signal or expression in direct subtraction, as defined in 1 above which arises when the difference between the digits is less than zero. Such a carry is frequently called a borrow. Related to borrow. 3. The action of forwarding a carry. 4. The command directing a carry to be forwarded.

cartridge and cassette classifications — Cassette and cartridge drives are usually classified under one of two broad headings: 3M and Philips types. Measuring $4'' \times 6'' \times 0.665''$, the 3M cartridge holds 300 ft. of ¼" tape and incorporates all required tape guidance and tensioning equipment within its case. Standard Philips-type cassettes hold 300 ft. of 0.15" tape in a $4'' \times 2½'' \times ½''$ package, although such variations as a 150-ft.-long, ¼"-wide version are available. For applications not suiting either type of drive, users can also choose among several custom-built drives.

cartridge, calculator — One Advanced Data Cartridge provides 96,384 bytes of program and data storage. Bidirectional search speeds of 1524mm per second and read/write speeds of 254mm give quick access to data and programs.

cartridge disc subsystem — A typical system provides 15 megabytes of storage using a cartridge disc drive and 10 megabytes of removable storage on a front loading cartridge. The storage control unit will address up to eight drives and can provide multiaccess for up to eight CPU's. This provides capacity of 15 to 118 megabytes of storage at 25 ms access time.

cartridge, dual track (calculator) — A dual-track cartridge stores 96,000 bytes of data with a search speed of 60 inches per second and a read/write speed of 20 inches per second. It is priced under $3000 and is widely available.

cartridge-printer advanced calculator — One type is a desk-top programmable calculator that features a built-in high speed data cartridge, a 16-character alphanumeric thermal printer, an autostart switch, programming keys that double as special function keys, and two optional I/O channels. These capabilities allow the unit to be used in basic ways: It provides for quick keystroke calculations by having 28 built-in scientific functions along with the powerful Reverse Polish Notion Logic System used by many pocket calculators, a buffered keyboard, large display, and readable permanent printout, provide users with advanced problem solving at their fingertips.

cartridge program versatility (calculator) — Changing applications on advanced units means changing cartridges. New cartridges are small — smaller than the typical cassette, yet they can hold 96,384 bytes of data and programs, or roughly 45 programs with 2,008 steps. Practically anyone can have his own library of programs. Not only can these systems easily solve the problems of the engineer, they can also deal effectively with the problems of the statistician, the doctor, the analyst, and the businessman. Anyone who can insert a prerecorded cartridge and turn on the power can solve a problem on these calculators. Secretaries, clerks, and part-time help can operate them to get the solutions to their problems, leaving more free time to pursue the creative side of their profession.

cartridge recorder characteristics — Many digital cartridge recorders use the quarter-inch 3M cartridge. Tape format and cartridge referencing on top of the baseplate complies with the proposed ANSI/ECMA/ISO standards. Special features in cartridge convenience and reliability are offered as follows:
- Easy cardridge insertion, yet very positive locking in position with high forces (and electrical ejection).
- Rugged capstan motor with optical encoder for servo feedback, write clock generation and formatting by means of distance measurements, thus making the data handling completely insensitive to speed variations.
- Optional formatter can handle up to 4 drives on a bus.
- Tape speed of 10-30 ips in read/write and 90 ips in search result in 48 k bits/s data rate and low search times.
- Packing density is 1600 bpi phase-encoded and cartridge capacity is over 2.5M bytes when using all four tracks.

The modular construction enables users to configure a system of their special needs:
Built-in, single and double table top, single and double rack mount models are available.

cardridge system, midget — Some systems are small. One complete Read System (hand-held) is only $3'' \times 5½'' \times 2''$. Write is even smaller: $3'' \times 5½'' \times 1½''$. Read-Write and Read-After-Write are $3'' \times 5¾'' \times 3''$. The various tape cartridges are midget. Roughly $1½'' \times 2½'' \times 0.2''$. Small enough, and thin enough, to pop into an envelope and drop in the mailbox without protective packaging. But the capacity is surprisingly big: 42,000 bytes (336,000 bits) in the maximum tape length. More than big enough for lots of jobs. Current drain is milli. 160 milliamps for either Read or Write, and 170 mA for Read-Write or Read-After-Write.

cartridge tape system capabilities — Many cartridge tape systems offer minis up to 23+ megabytes of storage with a minimum use of panel space. One type handles up to 8 tape drives (four in each 8½" panel), and that means almost 18 kilobytes per square inch. Another system comes with one or two tape drives in just 5¼". Others take no panel space at all — they're suitcase portable. Many types are completely modular thus permitting field expansion to the maximum capacity of drives in just minutes; like five per drive.

cascade connection — Refers to two or more similar component devices arranged in tandem, the output of one connected to the input of the following device.

cassette — A self-contained package of reel-to-reel blank or recorded film, videotape, or electronically embossable vinyl tape for recording of sound or computer input signals, which is continuous and self-rewinding. Similar to a cartridge, but of slightly different design.

cassette data transfer rate — This is directly proportional to read/write speed: it is the product of that quantity and the drive's recording density.

cassette diagnostic — Refers to a test for all functions of the cassette controller and up to four cassette drives, in some systems.

cassette drive, dual tape — This consists of two tape drives housed in a single unit. The tape drives are identical in operation and performance. One controller board operates both tape drives, but both tape drives operate independently, with separate device addresses.

cassette drive, single tape — This is fast and easy to operate. The magnetic tape cassette provides a low cost bulk storage system for both programs and data. A 150-foot tape has a capacity of 78,000 (8-bit) bytes, with a transfer rate of 326 bytes per second.

cassette encoding methods — These fall into two broad categories: clocked and self-clocked. Clocked recording systems employ an extra recording track, which lies next to the data track and contains synchronizing pulses, either prerecorded or recorded concurrently with the data. Self-clocking techniques, on the other hand, employ a data encoding pattern that regularly changes states and thereby provides synchronization. Self-clocking techniques usually employ some form of phase encoding, which, in addition to requiring only one track, conforms to ANSI's standards.

cassette memory, built-in — Allows users to store and retrieve programs and data quickly and conveniently. The built-in cassette memory permits users to store programs and data on removable cassettes. When users need information again, they drop in a cassette, press the control keys, and are ready to go.

cassette (Phillips-type) calculator systems — For systems where cassettes are desired for data storage. The calculating units can use standard Phillips-type cassettes for both program and data storage on reliable, time proven, dual cassette drives. The inexpensive cassettes are easily handled and stored by office personnel unfamiliar with data processing equipment. Each cassette will store approximately 250,000 characters (using both sides). The amount of data stored will depend on the record length. These cassette-based units will also find application where equipment space is at a premium. No other support devices are necessary other than the communications adaptor, if used, and the system may be easily operated in a desk-top location. Memory for the Cassette can be 4 or 8K of solid-state memory. Automatic program re-loading will occur if a power outage occurs, on some systems.

cassette read/write speeds — These usually vary with the type of drive mechanism employed. For drives incorporating a capstan/pinch roller mechanism, tape transport speeds usually range from 0.001 to 20 ips. Cassette units with direct-reel drives operate at up to 40 ips.

cassette recorder — Off-line data recording is the specialty of many types of write-only cassette systems. These units accept data in most popular forms — either 8 parallel TTL or CMOS levels and serial RS232C or teletype current loop data. Input rate can be up to 1200 baud. These units then format and buffer the data before recording it on a certified digital cassette in blocks of up to 256 8-bit bytes. Block size is switch selectable by the operator and max storage/cassette is 1.2M bits. Generally, each stand-alone system includes carrying case, power supplies, front-panel controls and I/O connectors. Recorded tapes are directly readable on many calculators and computers.

cassette ROM — A built-in cassette ROM lets users perform control functions such as load, rewind, and store with two or three keystrokes.

cassette start/stop time — This is the period required to bring the tape to 95% of a preset speed or to drop it to 5% of that speed. Excessive start/stop time can produce inefficient data storage for block or incremental operation. A drive's start/stop speed should be fast enough to start and stop the tape in about 75% of the length of the inter-record gap separating the successive blocks of data. Thus, for a standard gap of 0.7″, the transport should be able to start and stop in 0.52″. To maintain gap-length compatibility, start/stop time must decrease.

cassette tape drives — The heart of most cartridge tape systems is the tape drive. With the 3M data cartridge, it's packed to 2.5 + megabytes at 1600bpi with 30 ips read/write, has 6 kilobytes/second transfer, plus 90ips search and rewind. The ANSI-compatible units are packed with trouble-saving features for the volume user.

cassette vs cartridge costs — Though standardized for most computer applications, both cassette and cartridge drives differ enough in electronic and mechanical designs to make choosing the proper unit difficult. Generally, a 3M-type cartridge drive is mechanically simpler than a cassette unit, at the cost of incorporating a more complex mechanism within the cartridge.

cassettes vs cartridges — Cassette recorders have grown rapidly in popularity and applicability until today they occupy a significant and continually expanding position in the digital data-recording market. Compact, economical and easy to use, they have proven particularly useful in low-volume, serial data storage applications. More recently, drives utilizing 3M-types ¼″ tape cartridges, and other cartridge types, have also begun to find use in applications requiring intermediate amounts of storage, where neither cassette or reel-to-reel recorders have proven practical. Although they rival the recording densities of ½″ open-reel tape, such cartridges also offer the convenience of snap-in Philips-type cassettes.

catastrophic failure — A failure which is total or nearly so, such as: breakdown of the power supply, making all circuits inoperative. Any type of failure which renders the useful performance of the calculator to zero.

cathode-ray tube (CRT) — 1. A tube which has an electron beam which can be focused to a small cross section on a luminescent screen and can be varied in position and intensity to produce a visible pattern. Abbreviated CRT. 2. An electronic vacuum tube containing a screen on which information may be stored by means of a multigrid modulated beam of electrons from the thermionic emitter storage effected by means of charged or uncharged spots. 3. A storage tube. 4. An oscilloscope tube. 5. A picture tube.

cell — The storage for one unit of information, usually one character or one word. 2. A location specified by whole or part of the address and possessed of the faculty of store. Specific terms such as column, field, location, and block, are preferable when appropriate.

central processing unit (CPU) — 1. A unit of a computer that includes the circuits controlling the interpretation and execution of instructions. Synonymous with mainframe. Abbreviated CPU. 2. The central processor of a computer system contains main storage, arithmetic unit, control registers, and scratchpad memory.

central processing unit operation, 4-bit system — A 4-bit central processing unit consists of a central processing unit (CPU) and a memory that has a stored sequence of instructions for the CPU. The CPU is operated by a clock circuit to alternately fetch and execute the memory instructions. The CPU fetches an instruction by sending an address from a program address counting register to the program memory. The program memory decodes the address and instruction in an instruction register where it is decoded and executed. The CPU performs control and data transfer functions and communicates with program memory, RAM registers and I/O ports by connecting appropriate elements of the system to the 4-bit CPU bus. In addition to an instruction register and program address counter, the CPU contains a program address counter stack, an arithmetic logic unit (ALU) with a four-bit accumulator register, and 16 or more four-bit registers for intermediate data storage.

central processor organization — The computer can be divided into three main sections: arithmetic and control, input/output, and memory. The arithmetic and control section carries out the directives of the program. The calculations, routing of information, and control of the other sections occur in this part of the processor. All information going in and coming out of the central processor is handled by the input/output section. It also controls the operation of all peripheral equipment. The memory section is the heart of the central processor; it provides temporary storage for data and instructions. Because of its importance, the total cycle time of the memory is the main determining factor in the overall speed of the processor.

central processor unit (CPU), microprocessor — The central processor performs control, input-output, arithmetic, and logical operations by executing instructions obtained from the memory sources. Most instructions use a 4, 8, 12 or 16-bit machine word. Depending on the number of separate memory accesses required, the processor may require one, two, or three memory cycles to complete execution of an instruction. The typical processor logic includes a parallel arithmetic unit (ALU) that performs two's complement arithmetic operations, and a parallel shifter unit (s) that performs logical and shift operations, etc.

central terminal unit (CTU) — This unit supervises communication between the teller consoles and the processing center. It receives incoming messages at random intervals, stores them until the central processor is ready to process them, and returns the processed replies to the teller consoles which originated the transactions.

chad — The tiny piece of paper removed when a hole is punched into a card or paper tape.

chain — 1. Any set of records or items linked together either physically or logically in a specified sequence. 2. Pertaining to a routine in specified segments which are run through the computer in tandem, only one being within the computer mainframe at any one time and each having access to the output from previously executed segments. The order in which the segments are executed may be data dependent.

chain arithmetic, calculator — Users quickly learned how to key numbers into calculator stacks and perform calculations with them. In each case they first needed to position the numbers in the stack manually using the ENTER key. However, the stack also performs many movements automatically. These automatic movements add to its computing efficiency and ease of use, and it is these movements that automatically store intermediate results. The stack automatically "lifts" every calculated number in the stack when a new number is keyed in because it knows that after it completes a calculation, any new digits users key in are a part of a new number. Also, the stack automatically "drops" when users perform a two-number operation. After any calculation or number manipulation, the stack automatically lifts when a new number is keyed in. Because operations are performed when the operations are pressed, the length of such chain problems is unlimited unless a number in one of the stack registers exceeds the range of the calculator (up to $9.999999999 \times 10^{99}$). In addition to the automatic stack lift after a calculation, the stack automatically drops during calculations. (some units)

chain calculations — Refers to the operating features of some calculators that include performance of chaining calculations with basic functions by simply pressing the desired function key to use any result in the next problem. Repeated addition and subtraction occurs without re-entering the number. Number entries are cleared with the CE key. A # key (non-add) prints reference numbers on some units.

chain/constant switch — The Chain/Const switch permits normal chain calculations or multiplication and division by a constant without re-entering numbers on various units.

chain discount key — Refers to the capability to compute chain or serial discounts without re-entry, as well as complementary percentages or meaningful intermediate results. Users enter the exact amount of each discount and the chain discount key computes and prints the percentage. At completion of the problem an (=) key provides the final net . . . on some units.

chained files — Chained files are ideal for the user desiring open-ended sequential data handling. These data files consist of a series of data blocks chained together with forward and backward pointers.

chained list — A list of items, each of which contains an identifier for the next item in a particular order, but such order does not have any particular relation to the order in which they are stored.

chained record — Physical records, located randomly in main or auxiliary memory modules, that are linked or chained by means of a control field in each record which contains the address of the next record in the series or chains. Long waiting lists or files can be connected or chained in this way.

chaining — A system of storing records in which each record belongs to a list or group of records and has a linking field for tracing the chain.

chaining, tape cassette unit — Some calculators

can be ordered with the magnetic tape cassette drive. Programs and data can therefore be recorded for future reference. Since the instruction to LOAD information from tape is programmable, programs can be chained together for automatic execution to a maximum of approximately 22,000 program steps. A selective SEARCH capability enables the calculator to find a specific block of information and load it into memory. Data can also be stored on tape under program control for future reference.

change sample key — Calculates t for both paired and unpaired data. CHANGE SAMPLE key used to change from one data array to the next. (some units)

CHAN INTVL (channel interval) data acquisition calculator — Key displays the time interval in seconds between measurements of individual channels. Channel interval is settable between 0 and 99 seconds.

chain, Markov — An often used statistical model for determining the sequence of events in which the probability of a given event is dependent only on the preceding event.

change sign key — Reverses negative entries or results to their positive equivalents or the reverse without re-entry or manipulation with a single key depression.

channel — 1. That portion of a computer's storage medium which is also accessible to a given reading station. 2. That part of a communication system that connects the message source with the message sink. In information theory in the sense of shannon the channel can be characterized by the set of conditional probabilities of occurrence of all the messages possible received at the message sink when a given message emanates from the message source. 3. A path along which signals can be sent, e.g., a data channel, output channel. 4. The portion of a storage medium that is accessible to a given reading or writing station, e.g., track, band. 5. In communication, a means of transmission. Several channels may share common equipment. For example, in frequency multiplexing carrier systems, each channel uses a particular frequency band that is reserved for it.

channel adapter — A device which permits the connection between data channels of differing equipment. The device allows data transfer at the rate of the slower channel.

channel, analog — Usually refers to a channel that will pass alternating current, but not direct current. A switched voice channel is an analog channel, while most teletypewriter circuits are digital (d-c) channels. If an analog channel is said to carry digital data, it is actually carrying analog representations of the digital data in the form of various frequencies.

channel block, channel pair, and individual channel programming — It is possible to set all channels in some systems simultaneously to a common set of variables. Blocks of channels may be programmed, such as all MV channels. Pairs of channels are programmed as standard for four functions: I-O, correction function, range, units, but an option is available to permit these parameters to be programmed on a channel-by-channel basis. (some calculator systems)

channel capacity — 1. The maximum number of binary digits or elementary digits to other bases which can be handled in a particular channel per unit time. 2. The maximum possible information transmission rate through a channel at a specified error rate. The channel capacity may be measured in bits per second or bauds.

channel, data — The bidirectional data path between the I/O devices and the main memory in a digital calculator that permits one or more I/O operations to take place concurrently with computation.

channel, dedicated — A specific channel that has been reserved or committed or set aside for a very specific use or application.

channel, duplex — A channel providing simultaneous transmission in both directions.

channel, half-duplex — A channel capable of transmitting and receiving signals, but in only one direction at a time.

channel, information — The transmission and intervening equipment involved in the transfer of information in a given direction between two terminals. An information channel includes the modulator and demodulator and any error-control equipment irrespective of its location, as well as the backward channel, when provided.

channel, input/output — A specific channel which permits simultaneous communications, and independently so, between various storage units or any of the various input or output units. Such a channel is the control channel for most peripheral devices and quite often performs various checks on data transfers such as validity checks, etc.

channel number — A three digit number that identifies a channel, in some units.

channel pair — Two consecutive channels (six wires), consisting of one even number and one odd number channel. Example: Channel 2 and 3. Many functions in calculators are programmed by channel pairs rather than individually to save time.

channel, simplex — A channel which permits transmission in one direction only.

channel, tape — In perforated tape, channels are longitudinal rows where intelligence holes may be punched along the length of the tape. Also known as levels or tracks.

channel-to-channel connection — A device for rapid data transfer between two computers. A channel adapter is available that permits the connection between any two channels on any two systems. Data is transferred at the rate of the slower channel.

character — One of a set of elements which may be arranged in ordered groups to express information. Each character has two forms: 1. a man-intelligible form, the graphic, including the decimal digits 0-9, and letters A-Z, punctuation marks, and other formatting and control symbols; and 2. its computer-intelligible form, the code, consisting of a group of binary bits.

character, blank — A specific character designed and used to separate groups of characters. In some calculators an actual symbol such as * is used to signify a blank and thus assurance is positive that a blank space did not develop from machine malfunction or keypunch operator error.

character element — 1. A basic information element as transmitted, printed, displayed, etc. or used to control communications, when used as a code. 2. Groups of bits, pulses, etc. occurring in a time period normally representing that for a character or symbolic representation.

character, erase — A character which most often

character, error — represents a character to be ignored or signifies that the preceding or following item is to be ignored as prescribed by some fixed convention of the machine or as programmed. It may signify that some particular action is to be prevented, or it may signify an erase or destroy action on a tape or disk.

character, error — One of the control characters used to indicate that an error in data preparation or transmission has occurred. It also usually signifies that a certain predetermined amount of coming or recently transmitted data should be ignored.

character, escape — 1. The control character with a time-sequence characteristic which serves to assign, either temporarily or permanently, various new or different meanings to specific coded representations. Examples are: locking-shift characters, nonlocking shift characters, shift-out or shift-in characters, font-change characters, etc. Thus, escape characters permit a limited code to represent a wide range of characters since it assigns more than one meaning to each character representation. 2. A character used to specify that the succeeding one or more characters are expressed in a code different from the code regularly or currently in use.

character fill /to) — To replace all data in a storage location or group of locations with the repeated representation of a specific character, usually zeros of Xs.

character, illegal — A character or combination of bits which is not accepted as a valid representation by the machine design or by a specific routine. Illegal characters are commonly detected and used as an indication of machine malfunction.

characteristic — The integral part of a logarithm; the exponent of a normalized number.

characteristic overflow — A situation developed in floating-point arithmetic if an attempt is made to develop a characteristic greater than a specified number.

characteristic underflow — A situation developed in floating-point arithmetic if an attempt is made to develop a characteristic less than a specified number.

character, least significant — The character in the rightmost position in a number or word.

character, most significant — The character in leftmost position in a number or word.

character reader — A specialized device which can convert data represented in one of the type fonts or scripts read by human beings directly into the machine language. Such a reader may operate optically, or if the characters are printed in magnetic ink, the device may operate magnetically or optically.

character recognition — 1. The computer process of reading, identifying, and encoding a printed character. 2. The technology of using a machine to sense and encode into a machine language characters which are written or printed to be read by human beings.

character, redundant — A character specifically added to a group of characters to insure conformity with certain rules which can be used to detect computer malfunction.

character set — An agreed set of representations, called characters, from which selections are made to denote and distinguish data. Each character differs from all others, and the total number of characters in a given set is fixed; e.g., a set may include the numerals 0 to 9, the letters A to Z, punctuation marks, and a blank or space. (Clarified by alphabet.)

character shift-in (SI) — 1. A code extension character used to terminate a sequence that has been introduced by the shift-out character, that makes effective the graphic characters of the standard character set. 2. A code extension character that can be used by itself to cause a return to the character set in effect prior to the departure caused by a shift-out character.

characters, machine readible — The symbols (printed, typed or written) that can be interpreted by both people and optical character recognition equipment.

character string — 1. A group of characters in a one dimensional array in an order due to the reference of relations between adjacent numbers. 2. A sequence or group of connected characters, connected by codes, key words, or other programming or associative techniques.

character strings (BASIC) — Character strings are any sequence of letters, numbers, and symbols enclosed in quotation marks. Character strings are some times called string constants, literal strings, literals, or just plain "strings." Normally, a character string represents a message to be printed on the GS display or a piece of written text. Digits entered as part of a character string cannot be used in math computations; they are treated just like any other symbol. The length of a character string is limited only by the size of the random access memory.

charge — 1. Quantity of unbalanced electricity in a body; i.e., excess or deficiency of electrons, giving the body negative or positive electrification respectively.

check — 1. A verification of the correctness of equipment operation, partially or in full. Also the verification of progress of the existence of certain prescribed conditions and/or the correctness of results. 2. A process of partial or complete testing of the correctness of machine operations, the existence of certain prescribed conditions within the computer, or the correctness of the results produced by a program. A check of any of these conditions may be made automatically by the equipment or may be programed.

check, arithmetic — An operation performed by the calculator to reveal any failure in an arithmetic operation. Can also be used to ascertain whether the capacity of a register has been exceeded after an operation.

check, automatic — Refers to various provisions constructed in hardware for verifying the accuracy of information transmitted, manipulated, or stored by any unit or device in a calculator. Synonymous with built in check, built in automatic check, hardware check.

check bit — A binary check digit, for example, a parity bit.

checkbook calculator operation — Users may open their checkbook holder and turn on the built-in computer. They press the "Balance" key, and their bank balance is recalled on the display. The CheckMaster memory never forgets their balance — even months after users last recall it. Users enter the amount of their check, and press the "Check" key. The check amount is automatically deducted from their balance, and their new balance is displayed with just one key stroke. Or users can enter the amount of a deposit, and press the "Deposit" key. Their deposit is automatically added to their balance, and again, their new balance is displayed.

check, built-in — A provision constructed in hardware for verifying the accuracy of information transmitted, manipulated, or stored by any unit or device in a computer.

check character — One or more characters carried in such a fashion that if a single error occurs (excluding compensating errors) a check will fail, and the error will be reported.

check digit — 1. An alarm signal which consists of a digit carried along with a machine word. It can report information about the other digits in the word. If a single error occurs, the check fails and an alarm signal is initiated. 2. Relates to one or several digits generated and carried in calculator processes for ascertaining error and accuracy control of data in batch processing, in real-time, or in subsequent operations; i.e., often periodically regenerated and compared with the original data.

check, even parity — 1. One or more redundant digits in the word as a self-checking or error-detecting code to detect malfunctions of equipment in data-transfer operations. (Related to forbidden-combination check and parity check.) 2. An extra or redundant digit related to the group of digits to be checked by a specific rule for double check.

check indicator — A device that displays or indicates a check result and announces an error has been made; or a checking operation has determined that a failure has occurred.

check-indicator instruction — A specific instruction designed to direct a signal device to be turned on to call an operator's attention to the fact that there is some discrepancy in the instruction then in use.

checking, automatic — Refers to the numerous internal checks that continually monitor the accuracy of the system and guard against incipient malfunction. Typical are the parity and inadmissible-character check, automatic readback of magnetic tape and magnetic cards as the information is being recorded. The electronic tests which precede each use of magnetic tape or magnetic cards to ensure that the operator has not inadvertently set switches improperly. These internal automatic tests are supplemented by the instructions which may be programmed to ensure proper setup of certain units prior to their use. Console switches are designed to protect against inadvertent or improper use, and interlocks are provided on peripheral units to guard against operator error.

checking, pre-edit programs — A pre-edit checking of the application or operational program before the test run — a pre-edit run can remove such things as disobedience to established supervisory care, program segmentation rules, etc.

checking, redundant — The specific use of added or extra digits or bits in order to diagnose, detect, or cause errors which can arise as a result of unwarranted dropping or gaining of digits or bits.

check, limit — A type of check on the input for the purpose of ensuring that only valid codes or transaction types are permitted. If, for instance, there are only four transaction types, the limit check will reveal an error situation if a transaction other than the four is encountered. A limit check will detect transposition errors as in the case where an 83 was mistakenly input as a 38. In such a case the 38 would show up as an error.

check number — A number composed of one or more digits and used to detect equipment malfunctions in data-transfer operations. If a check number consists of only one digit, it is synonymous with check digit. (Related to check digit.)

checkout — The application of diagnostic or testing procedures to a routine or to equipment. Same as debug.

checkpoint — 1. A point in a computer routine at which it is possible to store sufficient information to permit restarting the computation from that point. 2. A point at which information about the status of a job and the system can be recorded so that the job step can be later restarted. 3. To record such information.

checkpoint and restart, basic procedures — Checkpoint and restart procedures are techniques associated with calculators to make it possible, in the event of an error or interruption, to continue processing from the last checkpoint rather than from the beginning of the run. These techniques are included in applications which require many hours of processing time, since heavy machine scheduling and deadlines generally do not permit a complete rerun. To establish checkpoints, processing intervals are determined, each being based upon a certain number of items, transactions, or records processed. At each interval or checkpoint, the stored program identifies input and output records and then records them along with the contents of important storage areas such as counters and registers; at the same time, accuracy of processing up to that point is established. Restart procedures are the means by which processing is continued after an error or interruption.

check problem — 1. A test problem which can indicate an error in programming or operation of a calculator. When it is solved incorrectly, an error in programming or operation is indicated. 2. A problem chosen to determine whether the calculator or a program is operating correctly.

check proof total — One of a number of check totals which can be correlated in some manner for consistency or reconciliation in a range, set or distinct calculation.

proof total check — One of a number of check totals which can be correlated in some manner for consistency or reconciliation in a range, set or distinct calculation.

check register — 1. A feature in some calculators which temporarily stores information for comparison with a second transfer of the same information to verify that the transferred information agrees precisely. 2. A register used to store information temporarily where it may be checked with the result of a succeeding transfer of this information.

check reset key — A pushbutton that when pushed acknowledges an error and resets the error detection mechanism indicated by the check light. This is required to restart a program after an error has been discovered in batch mode.

checkout routine — Refers to various routines to aid programmers in the debugging of their routines. Some typical routines are; storage, printout, and device print-out.

checksum — A summation of digits or bits in a computer according to an arbitrary set of rules. Usually used for checking purposes.

check, summation — A redundant check in which groups of digits are summed, usually without regard for overflow, and that sum checked against a previously computed sum to verify accuracy.

check, validity — A check based upon known limits or upon given information or calculated results; e.g., a calendar month will not be numbered greater than 12, and a week does not have more than 168 hours.

chemical engineering program pack — Various programs to help in thermal and transport science calculations such as: equations of state, compressible flow, incompressible flow, heat exchange analysis, natural convection, black body thermal radiation, curve fitting and unit conversions.

chip — Refers to the tiny piece of silicon on which an integrated circuit is built. The circuits are mass-produced on circular sheets of silicon called wafers which are then cut into dozens of individual chips. Chips are square or rectangular in shape and range in size from under a tenth of an inch on a side to over a quarter an inch.

chip calculator — An example is a minimum PPS (parallel processing system) configuration. It is a 2-circuit implementation consisting of one CPU and a ROM/RAM. (The clock chip is a low cost oscillator-driver circuit and is assumed with any given configuration.) This minimum organization is useful as a special purpose dedicated calculator or processor. One such system can receive 4-bit BCD data through four of the 8 discrete inputs and transmit 4-bit BCD data out through the four discrete outputs. The user can configure any combination of ROM, RAM and I/O circuits as may be required for a particular equipment implementation and can therefore trade off memory circuits to achieve the most cost-effective approach.

chip, circuit — In a calculator, a single device composed of transistors, diodes, and other components as interconnected by various chemical processes. It usually has been cut from a larger water, usually of silicon.

chip microprocessors — Chip microprocessors have brought complete computers on a single chip of silicon. No larger than a 1/4 inch square, they contain all the essential elements of a central processor, including the control logic, instruction decoding, and arithmetic processing circuitry. To be useful, the microprocessor chip or chips are combined with memory and I/O integrated circuit chips to form a "microcomputer", a machine almost as powerful as a minicomputer. They usually fill no more than a single printed circuit board and sell for less than $100.

chip, MOS — The internal electronic circuitry of most electronic calculators is designed with MOS/LSI (Metal-oxide semiconductor) fabrication to achieve Large Scale Integration. (LSI) A chip process provides electronic calculators with the miniaturized circuitry necessary to make them perform accurately and rapidly. A mounted and wired chip is approximately the size of a dime, and contains the equivalent of thousands of transistors and other electronic components to become, in effect, a dedicated microcomputer.

chips, CPU and I/O advanced calculators — An example: the Hewlett-Packard 9815A, is a desk-top programmable calculator with alphanumeric keyboard and matrix printer, plus numeric display. It was designed to use the minimum of I/O chips and reduce size and weight drastically from previous models. It was designed to use Motorola's M6800 microprocessor family to develop the HP-9815A with only one-third the volume and weight of the HP9810. The HP9815A uses the MC6800 as its CPU. A single MC6820 PIA (Peripheral Interface Adapter) handles all internal and external I/O.

chips, I/O — To complete their microcomputer product line, each manufacturer tries to offer a complete set of I/O interface chips. I/O chips are implemented in MOS or bipolar technologies depending on the requirements. Those designed to fit a particular device to a microprocessor save the designer-programmer time in development and reduce the overall number of chips in the microcomputer. The next step is to make these interface chips parameter selectable so that several models of one kind of peripheral can be handled by one chip.

chips, memory — The memory section of a microcomputer usually accounts for a major portion of the chips. All three kinds of memory are used. Random access memory (RAM) chips are used primarily for variable data and scratch pad. Read-only (ROM) chips are used to store instruction sequences. Programmable Read-Only Memory (PROM) chips are used for quickly tailoring the general purpose calculators for specific applications. RAMs are expensive compared to ROMs, but the data in the ROMs must be stored at the time they are created, so there is a production delay associated with them as well as a "programming" cost. PROM chips, some of which can be erased by ultraviolet light and reprogrammed, are used in place of ROMs when small quantities are involved, they are not cost justified in large runs.

chip system — Refers to a multiplicity of chips, together with addressing logic, interfacing circuits, sometimes power supply, other packages on a circuit board (or boards), in convenient form for use as a subunit of a calculator system.

chip technology, LSI — The large-scale integration (LSI) technology used to build calculator chips primarily centers around metal oxide semiconductor (MOS) devices. Chip densities of MOS devices range from 500 to 10,000 transistors per chip. The chip's size typically ranges from 0.15 inch square to 0.25 inch square. The chips are mounted into dual in-line packages (DIPS) which typically have 18,24, or 40 pins for mounting on a printed circuit card. The p-channel MOS (PMOS) had been the predominate technology for the calculator chips and most of the 4-bit and 8-bit processors. The PMOS 8-bit microprocessors with especially good design are still sometimes competitive with the newer NMOS 8-bit chips. PMOS processors typically are offered with a family of interface chips tailored to reduce the demands on the programs to support external devices. NMOS, however, has become the preferred approach by many of the IC manufacturers.

circuit — 1. A communications link between two or more points. See channel. 2. The conductor or system of conductors through which an electric current is intended to flow.

circuit analyzer — A device consisting of several instruments or instrument-circuits combined in a single enclosure used to measure two or more electrical quantities in a circuit. Also called a multimeter.

circuit, integrated (IC) — Refers to one of several logic circuits, gates, flip-flops which are etched on single crystals, ceramics or other semiconductor materials and designed to use geometric etching and conductive ink or chemical deposition techniques all within a hermetically sealed chip. Some chips with many resistors and transistors are extremely tiny, others are in effect "sandwiches" of individual chips.

circuit, linear — A circuit whose output is an amplified version of its input or whose output is a predetermined variation of its input.

circuit load — Usually a percentage of maximum circuit capability to reflect actual use during a period of time; i.e., peak hour line load.

circuit, printed — Refers to resistors, capacitors, diodes, transistors and other circuit elements which are mounted on cards and interconnected by conductor deposits. These special cards are treated with light sensitive emulsion and exposed. The light thus fixes the areas to be retained and an acid bath eats away those portions which are designed to be destroyed. The base is usually a copper clad card.

circuits, control — The circuits which cause the calculator to carry out the instructions in proper sequence, and which can control by permitting only the coded conditions to continue or function.

circulating storage — A device or unit which stores information in a train or pattern of pulses, where the pattern of pulses issuing at the final end are sensed, amplified, reshaped and re-inserted into the device at the beginning end.

clear — An activity to place one or more storage locations into a prescribed state, usually zero or the space character. Contrast with set.

cleared condition — Usually concerns destructive reading in which a flux configuration is permanently changed to some predetermined state and is also called the cleared condition. Also called a zero condition. (different in various calculators)

clear entry data acquisition calculator — Key cancels numeric key input data in case of keying mistake. Works like CLEAR ENTRY on a calculator.

clear entry key — The Clear Entry key generally clears last entry made with 0 through 9 keys. Also stops flashing display without affecting displayed number. The Clear Key clears display and calculation in progress; does not affect contents of memory registers, flags, counters, program memory, or fixed decimal, on most systems. The Clear Memories Key clears all memory registers.

clear key — A function key to delete an entry, or an entire series of entries from a calculator. The key may be titled (C-), (C), (CE), (CA) or (AC). Some electronic calculators have only a (C) key which may, at first depression, clear the last keyboard entry, and, at second depression, clear everything. It generally has no entry capability.

clear x key, small calculator — CLX prepares the displayed X-register for a new number by replacing any number in the display with zero. Any new number then writes over the zero in X. For example, to press CLX to change the stack.

click-thrust keyboard, calculators — Some units have taken the full-thrust keyboard feel and added a click to provide a "click-thrust" keyboard. Not only do users get a very positive data entry feel, but the chance of false entry is greatly minimized by the unique widely-spaced keys.

clock — A device which generates periodic synchronization signals.

clock, 1000 days — This allows time readout of 999 days, 23 hr., 59 min., 59 sec. on all output devices. Display indicates only hr., min. and sec. This option precludes I.D. number and dual rate features such as integrator reset.

closed loop — 1. A circuit in which the output is continuously fed back to its source for constant comparison. Also a group of indefinitely repeated calculator instructions. 2. The complete signal path in a control system represented as a group of units connected in such a manner that a signal started at any point follows a closed path and can be traced back to that point.

closed-loop system — Refers to a feedback control system involving one or more feedback control loops, which combine functions of controlled signals and of commands, in order to keep relationships between the two stable.

closed routine — A computer routine that is entered by basic linkage from a main routine rather than being inserted as a block of instructions within a main routine.

CMOS Refers to Complimentary Metal-Oxide Semiconductor. This uses the least power of the several MOS technologies. It is the type of MOS used in digital watches to conserve battery life. It is more difficult to fabricate than either p- or n-channel MOS but is expected to dominate MOS circuitry in the future.

CMOS advantages — Complementary MOS is a new technology that uses both p- and n-channel devices on the same silicon substrate. Basic CMOS construction uses n- and p-channel devices connected in series. Only one device is turned on at one time, keeping power dissipation low. Switching of devices through the active region and charging and discharging of capacitance are main causes of dissipation. Major advantages are 1. low power dissipation, 2. good noise immunity (45% of drain voltage), 3. high fanout to other CMOS, 4. allowance for very wide power supply variations, 5. shorter propagation delay than with p-MOS (approximately 60 ns), and 6. full temperature range capabilities. Chip size, however, is larger than p-MOS. CMOS is used in battery-operated systems, aerospace logic systems, and portable digital communications equipment. It is also used for components in digital instruments which operate in noisy environments.

coaxial cable — Refers to a specific cable consisting of one conductor, usually a small copper tube or wire, within and insulated from another conductor of larger diameter, usually copper tubing or copper braid.

COBOL — Common Business Oriented Language. 1. A data processing language that makes use of English language statements. 2. Pertaining to a computer program which translates a COBOL language program into a machine language program.

CODASYL — Conference on DAta SYstems Languages. The conference which developed COBOL.

code — 1. A system of characters and rules for representing information. 2. Relates to transformations or representations of information in different forms according to a preassigned convention. 3. Digital codes may represent numbers, letters of the alphabet, control signals, and the like, as a group of discrete bits rather than as a continuous signal.

code, error-detecting — A code in which errors produce forbidden combinations. A single error-detecting code produces a forbidden combination if a digit gains or loses a single bit. A double error-detecting code produces a forbidden combination if a digit gains or loses either one or two bits and so forth. (Synonymous with self-checking code, and related to self-checking number.)

code machine — The absolute numbers, names or symbols assigned by the machine designer to any part of the machine.

code, micro- — 1. An instruction written by a programmer or systems analyst in a source program to specify and execute a routine to be extracted from the computer library to give the processor program information and instructions required to regularize the routine to fit into the specific object program. 2. A system of coding making use of suboperations not ordinarily accessible in programming; e.g., coding that makes use of parts of multiplication or division operations. 3. A list of small program steps. Combinations of these steps, performed automatically in a prescribed sequence to form a macro operation like multiply, divide, and square root.

code, minimum-access — A system of coding which minimizes the effect of delays for transfer of data or instructions between storage and other machine components. (Related to optimum code, minimum-latency code, and minimum-access coding.)

code, mnemonic — An instruction code using conventional abbreviations instead of numeric codes in order to facilitate easy recognition. Examples: MLT for multiply, SUB for subtract, instead of "12."

code, numeric — A system of numerical abbreviations used in the preparation of information for input into a machine; i.e., all information is reduced to numerical quantities.

code, operation — 1. The symbols that designate a basic calculator operation to be performed. 2. A combination of bits specifying an absolute machine-language operator, or the symbolic representation of the machine-language operator. 3. That part of an instruction that designates the operation of arithmetic, logic, or transfer to be performed.

code, pseudo- — 1. A code which expresses programs in source language; i.e., by referring to storage locations and machine operations by symbolic names and addresses which are independent of their hardware-determined names and addresses. (Contrasted with machine-language code.) 2. An arbitrary code, independent of the hardware and designed for convenience in programming, that must be translated into computer code if it is to direct the computer.

code, symbolic — A code that expresses programs in source language; i.e., by referring to storage locations and machine operations by symbolic names and addresses which are independent of their hardware-determined names and addresses.

code (to) — Refers to an action to originate, structure or devise a program. To code most often concerns the analysis of the problem, preparation of the flow chart, designing and testing a set of developing subroutines, and the specification of the input and output commands and formats.

coding — The ordered list of computer instructions required to solve a problem.

coding tools — IC manufacturers are giving more attention to the phase of calculator design, generally called coding, with improved tools and techniques to simplify the designer's task.
The basic tools available are these:
- Assemblers.
- Editors.
- Loaders.
- Compilers.
- Microprogramming.

In addition hardware or software simulators are available for program testing and error locating.

coefficient matrix — The matrix of left-hand side coefficients in a system of linear equations. It is to be distinguished from the matrix obtained by appending the right-hand side, which is called the "augmented matrix" of the system. It may be thought of as including a full set of logical vectors to convert inequality constraints to equations. In the case of the modified simplex array it also contains the objective function coefficients.

coefficient of correlation — The coefficient of correlation is widely used as a measure for the spread of a set of points about the line of regression. In turn, this will determine whether or not a linear relationship exists between two variables. If the points cluster about the line of regression, they indicate a linear relationship. If they are, however, widely scattered, the linear relationship is in doubt.

coefficient of determination, calculator use — To establish how well the data fits the linear regression, users may want to calculate the coefficient of determination (r^2). The coefficient of determination is a value between 0 and 1. At $r = 0$, there is no fit. At $r^2 = 1$, users have a perfect fit. The traditional equation for r^2 is:

$$r^2 = \frac{[\Sigma(x - \bar{x})(y - \bar{y})]^2}{[\Sigma(x - x^2)][\Sigma(y - y)^2]}$$

On some units, however, the most efficient way to calculate r^2 is to use this equivalent equation:

$$r^2 = \frac{n\Sigma xy - \Sigma x \Sigma y}{n(n - 1) s_x s_y}$$

COGO (COordinate GeOmetry) — A language useful for solving coordinate geometry problems in civil engineering. Can be used as geometrically oriented urban data-management systems under ICES.

column printer — Some manufacturers are offering low-cost optional column printers which give calculator users hardcopy printout on input and output data. One unit prints out 20 columns at speeds of up to 160 lines per minute. Formatted output can include sixteen alpha characters for labelling. It prints results in fixed and floating decimal point or scientific notation. While running a program, a trace mode may use the printer to print interim results and program commands; the trace mode may be programmed to be turned on or off. In list mode, a routine can be sequentially printed out with numbered codes to give a complete listing of an entire program or segments of the program, as necessary.

column printer commands (calculator) — The optional column printer (some units) prints input and output data at a rate of 160 lines per minute. The format of the output is programmable such that fixed or floating point or scientific notation can be designated. Sixteen letters are available for labeling appropriate lines. A programmable TRACE mode uses the printer to print interim answers while a program is being run. In addition a program LISTING can be executed on the printer, whereby the four-digit program codes are sequentially printed out and numbered.

column vector — One column of a matrix consisting of a single column. The elements of the column are interpreted as the components of the vector.

combination program — A combination is a selection of one or more of a set of distinct objects without regard to order. The number of possible combinations, each containing n objects, that can be formed from a collection of m distinct objects is given by

$$_mC_n = \frac{m!}{(m-n)!\,n!} = \frac{m(m-1)\ldots(m-n+1)}{1\cdot 2\cdot\ldots\cdot n}$$

where m, n are integers and $0 \leq n \leq m$.
This program computes $_mC_n$ using the following algorithm:
1. If $n \leq m - n$

$$_mC_n = \frac{m-n+1}{1}\cdot\frac{m-n+2}{2}\cdot\ldots\cdot\frac{m}{n}.$$

2. If $n > m - n$, program computes $_mC_{m-n}$.

Notes:
1. $_mC_n$, which is also called the binomial coefficient, can be denoted by C_m^n, $C(m,n)$, or $\binom{m}{n}$.
2. $_mC_n = {_mC_{m-n}}$
3. $_mC_0 = {_mC_m} = 1$
4. $_mC_1 = {_mC_{m-n}} = m$

combined arithmetic operations calculator — When a new number is entered after a calculation, most units automatically save the result of that calculation. This permits serial calculations $(4 + 6 + 8 + 10)$ as well as chain $(12 \times 5) + (11 \times 4) + (10 \times 3)$ and mixed chain calculations $(5/2 + 5/3 + 5/4) \div (3 \times 213.8)$.

COM (computer output microfilm) — Refers to outputting computer information onto microfilm through a COM printer.

comma indicator — A means of separating numbers into 3-digit units for easy reading, with a decimal point at the base.

command — 1. For calculators, an electronic pulse, signal or set of signals to start, stop or continue some operation. It is incorrect to use command as a synonym for instruction. 2. The portion of an instruction word which specifies the operation to be performed.

comment — Concerns various types of expressions which serve to identify or explain one or more steps in routines but which have no effects on the execution of such routines or programs.

common business oriented language (COBOL) — A specific language by which business data processing procedures may be precisely described in a standard form. The language is intended not only as a means for directly presenting any business program to any suitable computer, for which a compiler exists, but also as a means of communicating such procedures among individuals.

common carrier — Organizations licensed and regulated by the U.S. Federal Communications Commission and/or various public utility commissions and required to supply communications services to all users at published prices.

common hardware — Refers to items that are usually expendable such as, plugs, sockets, bolts, etc. and are items commonly used to construct or repair machines or components.

common language — 1. A technique which reduces all information to a form that is intelligible to the units of a data-processing system. This enables units to talk with one another. 2. A language or macro code which can be read or written by many different machines or by various groups of users. 3. A single code used by devices — typewriters, calculators, transmitters, and others — manufactured by different companies.

common mistakes, small calculators — The mistakes users of some systems are most likely to make are listed here for convenience:
1. Forgetting that prefix keys are not combined with conditional branch instructions when writing your program.
2. Omitting a prefix key or using the wrong prefix key for a calculation.
3. Losing the T-register contents because the stack has lifted a terminated number.
4. Performing a trigonometric function in wrong angular mode.
5. Trying to perform a calculation involving both X- and Y-registers with the numbers in the opposite registers because x:y was not pressed.
6. Failing to key in both digits following a branch instruction.
7. Positioning the program pointer at the wrong line in memory before an editing operation.

common programs — Programs or routines which usually have common and multiple applications for many systems; i.e., report generators, sort routines, conversion programs which can be used for several routines in language common to many computers.

communicating calculator — The advanced Programmable Calculator is not an intelligent terminal but, rather, a communicating calculator. Nevertheless, it provides the communications capability of a time-sharing or remote batch terminal, while retaining all the computing capability of a powerful, programmable, BASIC language calculator. (some units)

These units can perform most of the user's daily computations right at his desk. Then, data collected at the time can be transmitted to a large batch computer for further processing and central data base storage. In addition, the computer can send unformatted information directly to the advanced calculator with the final report format determined by a user program. Or, one calculator batch terminal may send messages or data to another calculator batch terminal using the calculator batch terminal programs.

communicating calculator advantages — The special features of many communicating calculators are things like both high-speed and low-speed transmission, asynchronously or synchronously. Or the editing, programming, and memory features that help reduce lengthy and costly on-line editing and programming; and various other specific uses.

communication calculator line problems — Calculator-based systems share a common problem with minicomputer devices — noise on data transmission lines. Glitches, spikes, and line-frequency AC signals plague even the best-engineered data acquisition systems. Although output control signals do not suffer these problems to the same extent because of their low impedance nature and the low frequency response properties of control elements, noise factors must be considered at both ends of the system.

communication control character — Refers to a specific character which designates the operation to be performed by some peripheral device. As with other characters it is represented by a pattern of printed binary digits or holes in tapes or cards. Its execution usually causes control changes on printers. For example, back space, skip line or rewind on tapes. Other types of characters relate to EOM, such as end-of-message, etc.

communication link — 1. The means of connecting one location to another for the purpose of transmitting and receiving information. 2. A channel or circuit intended to connect other channels or circuits.

communications calculators, terminals — Several companies have added a data communications capability to their various desk-top calculators, which allows them to operate as programmable terminals accessed through BASIC instructions. By adding interface cables and plug-in read-only memory (ROM) modules, the units can communicate with another terminal or units can operate like a binary synchronous remote batch terminal using 2780 emulation mode on-line to an IBM 360/370 mainframe, or operate as a time-sharing terminal. By adding an on-line programmable BASIC capability, the calculator becomes a terminal input device for business and/or scientific applications. When attaching the interface and the interface control ROM, one type calculator/terminal can interface with RS 232 modems, automatic dialers and other communications devices. Asynchronous or synchronous data rates from 110- to 9,600 bit/sec can be supported, and the terminals can have error detection and ASCII to Ebcdic conversion features depending on the ROM modems that are installed. Dual capabilities can be included so the device can operate as both a binary synchronous batch terminal and an interactive time-sharing device depending on the application. This specific calculator includes a thermal printer as a built-in capability. In addition, an 80-column card reader, 200 line/min printer and disk memory with up to 10M bits of memory can be installed on the system.

communications control — Generally, once the mode instructions (and sync characters if the synchronous mode is used) are loaded, the interface is ready for use. A command instruction controls the operation of the selected format. Functions such as enable, transmit/receive, error-reset, and modem controls are provided by the command instruction. Also, the CPU can read the status of a communications device at any time during operation. In data communications, a processor must often read device status to ascertain if errors have occurred or if other conditions require the processor's attention.

communications control device — The data devices that can be attached directly to the system channel via a control unit designed to perform character assembly and transmission control. The control unit may be either the data-adapter unit or the transmission control.

communications modems — An important element of any communications system are the modems (MODulator/DEModulator) which connect the communications multiplexor from the remote outlet to the interface device in the computer center. On the transmission end, the modulator converts the signals or pulses to the right codes and readies them for transmission over a communication line in altering current. On the receiving end a demodulator reconverts the signals to direct current for communication to the computer via the computer interface device. The computer operates on direct current.

communication theory — A branch of mathematics that is concerned with the properties of transmitted messages. The messages are subject to certain probabilities of transmission failure, distortion, and noise.

commutative operation — Concerns a specific type of set theory or dyadic operation in which the order of the operands is immaterial, i.e., the dyadic operator X is commutative if and only if $X(A, B) = X(B,A)$.

commutator — See multiplexer.

compare — 1. To determine whether a particular quantity is higher, equal to, or lower than another quantity, or to determine whether one piece of data is exactly like another. 2. To examine the representation of a quantity to discover its relationship to zero, or to examine two quantities usually for the purposes of discovering identity or relative magnitude.

comparing unit — 1. An electrochemical device used to compare two groups of timed pulses and signals, either identity or nonidentity. 2. Comparing is the automatic checking of cards on a match or nonmatch basis. With this machine, feeding, punching, and segregating are controlled by comparing cards from two separate files for a match or nonmatch condition. Comparison of both alphabetical and numerical data may be made on selected columns or fields, or on entire cards.

compatibility, firmware — Compatibility among data processing systems facilitates execution or conversion of existing programs, data interchange, and the implementation of compilers having equivalent execution-time semantics. Compatibility can be achieved via the basic hardware design or by (software or firmware) interpretation. Firmware, or microprogramming, has attracted attention in this context as promising hardware-like compatibility with software like implementation techniques.

compatibility, software — Compatibility among data processing systems facilitates execution or conversion of existing programs, data interchange, and the implementation of compilers having equivalent execution-time semantics. Compatibility can be achieved via the basic hardware design or by (software or firmware) interpretation.

compatibility test — Specific tests run to check acceptability of both software and hardware as a system, i.e., to test component workability.

compilation time — The time during which a source language is compiled (translated) as opposed to the time during which the program is actually being run (execution time).

compile, machine language — To prepare a machine language program from a computer program written in another programming language by making use of the overall logic structure of the program, or generating more than one machine instruction for each symbolic statement, or both, as

compiler

well as performing the function of an assembler.

compiler — A program which translates from high-level problem-oriented computer languages to machine-oriented instructions.

compiler advantages — Many microcomputer manufacturers offer compilers that allow programs to be written in a high-level language. Some benefits are: A short readable compiler statement corresponds to many symbolic assembly-language statements. Compilers eliminate the need to write detailed codes to control loops, to access complex data structures or to program formulas and functions. With programming details lessened, errors are reduced. High-level language programs are compact, easy to read and much easier to write. The net result could be excessive storage space and slower execution, when compared with an assembly-language program. Generally a choice between the two approaches depends on the degree of optimization required and the design time allowable.

compiler, BASIC microcomputer — One of the first resident code-emitting, high-level BASIC microprocessor language compilers became available in a stand-alone program development system in 1975. The language is tailored to meet the needs of the logic designer as well as providing a useful tool to the professional programmer. One of the unique features of these systems is that they allow the programmer to combine assembly language with BASIC in instances where memory utilization and execution time are critical.

compiling routine — A computer program more powerful than an assembler. In addition to its translating function which is generally the same process as that used in an assembler, it is able to replace certain items of input with series of instructions, usually called subroutines. Thus, where an assembler translates item for item, and produces as output the same number of instructions or constants which were put into it, a compiler will do more than this. The program which results from compiling is a translated and expanded version of the original. (Related to assembler.)

complement — A number which is derived from the finite positional notation of another by one of the following rules: True complement — Subtract each digit from 1 less than the base; then add 1 to the least significant digit and execute all required carries.

Base minus 1's complement — Subtract each digit from 1 less than the base (e.g., 9's a complement) in the base 10, "1's complement in the base 2, etc.

complement, twos — Two binary numbers, a value divided by subtracting an original number from the base number (or a power of the base number). For decimal numbers the equivalent of the twos complement would be the tens complement.

complete clearance key — One key clears all constants, storage, sums and the contents of every register and memory, on some units.

complete operation — Refers to those operations which inlude 1. obtaining all operands from storage, 2. performing the operation, 3. returning resulting operands to storage, and 4. obtaining the next instruction.

complex number — The combination of real number and an imaginary number in the form of (a + bi) is called a complex number as (5 + 2i) which is the same as $(5 + 3\sqrt{-1})$. The number on the left part of the pair is the "real part"

computer, asynchronous

of the complex number, while the right part is the pure imaginary part of the complex number.

component — One of the essential functional parts of a subsystem or equipment, possibly a self-contained element or a combination of parts, assemblies, attachments, or accessories.

component, solid-state — A component whose operation depends on the control of electric or magnetic phenomena in solids, e.g., a transistor, crystal diode, or ferrite.

component stress — The particular factors of usage or test, such as voltage, power, temperature, frequency, etc., which tend to affect the failure rate of component parts.

composition errors — Errors that are detected as soon as the user enters the offending statement. He may immediately substitute a correct statement.

compound amount program — This program applies to an amount of principal that has been placed into an account and compounded periodically, with no further deposits. The important variables in this case are the number of compounding periods n, the periodic interest rate i, the principal or present value PV, the future value of the account FV, and the amount of interest accrued I. Any of these may be calculated from the others by these formulas:

$$n = \frac{\ln (FV/PV)}{\ln (1 + i)} \qquad i = \left(\frac{FV}{PV}\right)^{1/n} - 1$$

$$PV = FV(1 + i)^{-n}$$

$$FV = PV(1 + i)^n \qquad I = PV[(1 + i)^n - 1]$$

compound interest — The calculator solves any of four variables (PV, FV, I, N) in classical compound interest equation.

compute bound — Generally refers to the limiting output rate because operations are delayed awaiting completion of a computation operation. Synonymous with compute limited; contrast with print bound.

compute limited — A situation in which the calculator time is the delaying factor in receiving output.

computer — A device with a stored program capable of accepting information in the form of signals or symbols, performing prescribed operations on the information, providing results as outputs, retaining programs for other conversions and operations and capable of switching and control performance over peripheral units of processing and communications.

computer aided design (CAD) — Refers to the capability of a computer to be used for automated industrial, statistical, biological etc. design through visual devices.

computer-aided instruction (CAI) — An educational concept which places the student in a conversational mode with a computer which has a pre-programmed study plan. The programmed course selects the next topic or phase of study according to previous responses from the student, allowing each student to progress at a pace directly related to his learning capability.

computer, asynchronous — Refers to those types of computers in which the performance of each operation starts as a result of a signal either that the previous operation has been completed, or that the parts of the computer required for the next operation are now available. Contrasted with computer, synchronous.

computer circuits — Circuits used in the construction of digital computers are the following: storage circuits, triggering circuits, gating circuits, inverting circuits and timing circuits. In addition, there may be other circuits used in smaller quantities such as power amplifiers for driving heavier loads, indicators, output devices, and amplifiers for receiving signals from external devices, as well as oscillators for obtaining the clock frequency.

computer, digital — A computer which processes information represented by combinations of discrete or discontinuous data, as compared with an analog computer for continuous data. More specifically, it is a device for performing sequences of arithmetic and logical operations, not only on data, but also on its own program. Still more specifically, it is a stored-program digital computer capable of performing sequences of internally stored instructions, as opposed to calculators, such as card programmed calculators, on which the sequence is impressed manually. (Related to data-processing machine.)

computer language — A programming procedure or language in which instructions are computer instructions only. A machine language as contrasted to a problem-oriented language must be compiled to a computer language before a machine can use it directly.

computer learning — That process by which computers modify programs according to their own memory or experience, i.e., changes of logic paths, parameter values. An example is a chess-playing computer. 2. In process-control, an analog computer can alter its parameters by a continuous process according to temperatures, or other reports it receives.

computer network — Basically, two or more interconnected computers with the advantage of permitting geographical distribution, and thus economy, of computer operations. Such a network also permits parallel processing, time-sharing combinations of send-receive communications, multi-point remote entry and output, and locally controlled and maintained data banks and switching centers.

computer operation — 1. The electronic action resulting from an instruction. In general, it is a computer manipulation required to secure results. 2. One of many designed or predetermined operations which are built-in or performed directly, i.e., jump, subtract.

computer-oriented language — A related term for a programming language requiring a low degree of translation. Such programs usually run very efficiently on a related computer but require very extensive translation or compiling on another variety of computer.

computer science — The entire spectrum of theoretical and applied disciplines connected with the development and application of computers. Contributions have come mostly from such fields as mathematics, logic, language analysis, programming, computer design, systems engineering, and information systems.

computer service organization — 1. Various companies which offer and contract maintenance and operation of computers not owned or leased by them for charges and fees commensurate with the size and complexity of the system. 2. Organizations which provide either personnel or total systems planning, operation, and other related support for customers. The national organization is ADAPSO (Association of Data Processing Service Organizations).

computer word — Relates to that sequence of bits or characters treated as a unit and capable of being stored in one computer location. Synonymous with machine word.

computing solution with calculators — Calculators are available for routine, basic arithmetic and statistics, or the most subtle mathematical and complex analysis. Calculators help derive the essential truths from data. And they do it at a price most can afford, both in terms of capital outlay and operating overhead. There are many variations of calculators — hand-held, programmed, programmable — coupled with a wide range of options and peripherals. Users can choose the precise combination of functions, memory, input, output, and storage features that fit specific problem and budgets. Typical calculators do sums, means, and variance at a single keystroke. Some can handle variable, multiple-linear regression with transformations in a matter of minutes. Hundreds of programs, ranging from quality assurance to modeling, from non-parametric statistics to high-level analysis are also available. Insertable programs are fully documented and precisely designed for calculator operation and are some special features that match solutions to varying problems. The capability of these programs is endless.

concentrator — The polling of local lines or resolution of contending terminals, the checking and formatting of messages, the correction of errors, guidance to operators and similar tasks, are typical of those conveniently performed by a concentrator with a reasonable degree of processing power.

concordance — Refers to various alphabetic lists of words and phrases appearing in a document, with an indication of the place those words and phrases appear.

concurrent — Refers to the occurrence of two or more events or activities within the same specified interval of time. Contrast with consecutive, sequential, simultaneous.

concurrent control system — Relates to an environment which allows the system to react immediately to the inquiries, requests and demands of many different users at local and remote stations; it allows for the stringent demands of real-time applications; it is able to store, file, retrieve, and protect large blocks of data, and it makes optimum use of available hardware facilities, while minimizing turn-around. Only through central control of all activities can this environment of the combined hardware and software be fully established and maintained to satisfy the requirements of all applications; this responsibility for efficient, centralized control is borne by the executive. This system controls and coordinates the functions of the complex internal environment, and by presenting a relatively simple interface to the programmer, relieves him of concern for the internal interaction between his program and other coexistent programs.

concurrent processing — 1. The ability to work on more than one program at the same time. This

conditional branching decisions   **conductor**

is a valuable feature of some computer systems. The result is a better utilization of time by taking full advantage of the high speed of the central processor. 2. Concerns the processing of more than one independent task simultaneously by a single computing system involving interlaced time-sharing of at least one section of hardware, which is generally the control unit and memory-address register or the multiplexing unit, for selecting individual control units and memory-address registers for each task. 3. The operation of a computer which has some or all of the program for more than one run stored simultaneously in its memory, and which executes these programs concurrently by time-shared control. See multiprogramming.

conditional branching decisions — Often during calculations users need to look at an intermediate answer in order to determine what calculation to perform next. This decision-making capability can also be programmed on the unit. The calculator can test for two separate conditions and then branch program execution accordingly. (Some units)

conditional branching, "if" condition keys — On some units decision making with a program is a simple matter with the "if" condition keys (conditional branching). The number in the display may be tested for less than zero, equal to zero, or greater than or equal to zero. In addition, users can test the condition of a programmable flag and test to see if the calculator has overranged or attempted an illegal math operation (indicated by a flashing display). If the conditions are not met, the sequential program execution is interrupted and program control branches to the appropriate point in the program. In addition to these conditional branches, four types of unconditional branches are available on some units.

conditional branching, small calculators — On some units, the eight different program instructions give the ability to make decisions within a program depending on the outcome of a comparison of data values. These "conditionals" transfer program execution based on the outcome of the test. If the answer is YES, program execution continues sequentially downward. If the answer is NO, the calculator branches. To key in the program set the mode users switch to PRGM and press PRGM to clear program memory and display step 00. (some systems)

conditional jump — A specific instruction which will basically depend upon the result of some arithmetical or logical operation or the state of some switch or indicator as to whether or not that instruction will cause a jump or skip to another preset instruction.

conditional key — Each value is tested in X-register against that in Y-register or 0 as indicated. If true, calculator executes instruction in next program memory step. If false, calculator skips next step.

conditional operators, calculator — Typical conditional operators include: $x = y$, $x < y$, $x \geq y$ (comparison). $x = 0$, x positive, x negative (test x registers). If flag set, if flag clear (test flags).

conditional skip functions — Among the most powerful features on some calculators are the conditional-skip functions which enable the calculator to choose which calculations to do next. For example, one unit provides two flags which can be set or cleared either from the keyboard or by an appropriate program step. The condition of these flags can be tested at any point in the program by including an appropriate test-flag instruction. The program will then either advance sequentially or skip over the next two steps depending on the condition of the tested flag.

conditional stop instruction — An instruction that can cause a program to be halted if some given condition is discovered; i.e., the program may be required to stop if it finds that a keyboard switch has been set by the operator.

conditional transfer — An instruction which, if a specified condition or set of conditions is satisfied, is interpreted as an unconditional transfer. If the condition is not satisfied, the instruction causes the calculator to proceed in its normal sequence of control. A conditional transfer also includes the testing of the condition. Synonymous with conditional jump and conditional branch.

conditional transfer key examples —(1) If Positive. Tests display register for positive or zero. If it is, transfer occurs to a location or label. If the test fails, transfer does not occur. (2) If Zero. Tests display register for zero. If it is, transfer occurs to a location or label. If not, no transfer. (3) If Error. Tests for an error condition (flashing display). If it is, transfer occurs to a location or label. If not, no transfer. (4) Decrement and Skip on Zero. Decrements the contents of memory register 00, then tests these contents for zero. If it is not zero, transfer occurs to a location or label. If it is, no transfer.

conditional transfers — These statements depend on tests. If test conditions are met, then transfer or branch takes place. Otherwise the regular sequence continues. Three types of tests are conducted: The display (positive, negative, zero, flashing, not flashing). Flags (set, not set). Contents of register 00 (zero or not zero), on some systems.

conductive elastomers — Conductive elastomeric materials are formed from a rubber made conductive by incorporating a metalized filler or carbon. Originally used for gasketing against electromagnetic and radio-frequency interference, recent large-scale production of digital calculators has opened up a large new market for conductive elastomers as connectors for the liquid crystal readouts. As opposed to metals, the elastomers filled a need for a high-contact density, shockproof, springy, reliable connectors.

conductive elastomers, applications — An example: Some keyboards make use of new materials technology in conductive elastomers, paints, and inks and their capabilities in full-size keyboards. The miniature keyboard on some 'Wrist Calculators', for example, use the same materials as the large subassemblies, but they are put together differently. The keyboards consist of a tiny printed circuit board, screened with a silver paint that provides a permanently conductive contact surface. Over this is laid a 0.005-inch-thick Mylar spacer with holes directly under the keys. A layer of conductive rubber, and a Mylar legend sheet that have the keys on it follow. When the Mylar is deflected, an electrical impulse that is set up in the conductive rubber travels through the holes in the Mylar spacer to the printed-circuit board.

conductor — 1. A body of conductive material constructed so that it will carry an electric current. 2. That part of an electrical circuit which carries the current, as opposed to the dielectric.

conduit — A tubular raceway for holding wires or cables designed specifically for this purpose.

confidence interval — A range of values with a preassigned degree of confidence which includes the true characteristic of the lot.

confidence level — A measure of confidence concerning a statistical calculation might be stated as follows: "We are 95% confident that, from a universe believed to be stable, the true mean will fall between x_1 and x_2."

connector, variable — 1. A flowchart symbol representing a sequence connection which is not fixed, but which can be varied by the flowchart procedure itself. 2. The device which inserts instructions in a program corresponding to selection of paths appearing in a flowchart. 3. The computer instructions which cause a logical chain to take one of several alternative paths. (Synonymous with N-way switch and programmed switch.)

consoles, CRT (Cathode-ray tube) — Cathode ray tube (CRT) display consoles have received much interest and attention, a CRT terminal overcomes most of the disadvantages of a typewriter console. Its display rate is very fast — thousands of characters per second. It is quiet. Its output is flexible, easily modified and rearranged. The more sophisticated forms of CRT consoles have pictorial capabilities allowing line segments to be displayed. Pointing facilities, such as light pens, allow users to easily designate symbols or vectors of interest.

constant — A fixed value or an item of datum that does not vary.

constant, calculator — Allows repetitive calculations using the same number without having to reenter that number for each calculation.

constant-factor storage key — Automatically stores a constant for use in percentage computations, factor equivalent conversions, fractional equivalent conversions or mark up. One key does it all.

constant(s) — 1. Refers to those quantities or messages which will be present in the machine and available as data for the program, and which usually are not subject to change with time. 2. A character or group of characters usually representing a value key or standard, used by the calculator to identify, locate, measure, or test in order to make a decision.

constant storage — A part of storage designated to store the invariable quantities required for processing.

constant words — Descriptive data that is fixed and does not generally appear as an element of input.

constraint — An equation or inequality relating the variables is an optimization problem. A feasible (primal) solution must satisfy all the constraints including column-type restrictions (bounds, non-negativity, etc.)

constraint matrix — In linear programming, the augmented matrix of the constraint equations; it is the matrix formed by the coefficient columns, or left-hand sides, and the column of constants.

consulting engineering system, programmable calculator-based — Some dedicated consulting engineer systems include a programmable calculator with large memory, a matrix ROM, a page printer, and plotter. This type of system generally has the necessary versatility to handle complex structural problems — steel and concrete column design, concrete beam design, pre-stress beam design, shear-and-moment plotting. This same system can also handle a firm's business problems such as payroll, billing, business communications, etc.

contact — A current-carrying part of a relay, switch, or connector designed to open or close associated electrical circuits.

contact alignment — Refers to electrical contacts and the sidewise movement or play in mating contact pins or other devices for plug or other contact insertions or surfaces.

contingency interrupt — Refers to events in which a program is interrupted if any of the following events occur at the operator's console: the operator requests use of the keyboard to type in information: a character has been typed in or out; a type-in has been completed; or the operator requests a program stop. Contingency interrupt also occurs if an arithmetic operation resulted in an overflow, an invalid operation code was specified, or the clock was addressed after clock power was removed.

continuous simulation — Refers to a type of simulation which may be represented by continuous variables. The system is therefore suitable for representation by a set of differential equations. These may be further classified as linear or non-linear. Examples are: missile flights, medical devices, etc.

continuous variable — In contrast to discrete variables, a variable is continuous if it can assume all values of a continuous scale. Such quantities as length, time, and temperature are measured on continuous scales and their measurements may be referred to as continuous variables.

cycle operation variable — See operation, variable cycle.

control — 1. Those parts of a calculator which carry out instructions in proper sequence, interpret instructions, and apply proper signals. 2. Frequently, it is one or more of the components in any mechanism responsible for interpreting and carrying out manually-initiated directions. Sometimes it is called manual control. 3. In some business applications, a mathematical check. 4. In programming, instructions which determine conditional jumps are often referred to as control instructions, and the time sequence of execution of instructions is called the flow of control.

control action — The operations performed by or for a control system in processing, testing, or manufacturing.

control algorithm — A mathematical representation of a control law, indicating action to be performed.

control block — Refers to the circuitry that is designed to perform the control functions of the calculator CPU. It is designed to handle the decoding of microprogrammed instructions; to generate the internal control signals that perform the requested operations, and to carry out other basic operating functions.

control card — A card containing input data or parameters for a specific computer program application of a general routine.

control, cascade — Refers to an automatic control system in which various control units are linked in sequence, each control unit regulating the operation of the next control unit in line.

control character — 1. A character whose occurrence in a particular context initiates, modifies, or stops a control function. A control character may be recorded for use in a subsequent action. A control character is not a graphic character, but may have a graphic representation in some circumstances. 2. A character whose occurrence starts, changes, or stops a process. 3. A character used to cause nonprinting functions such as line feed and carriage return, to occur. 4. A character which controls an operation, such as recording, interpreting, transferring, transmitting, etc.

control 'chip' — Refers to a 'chip' that provides the microinstruction address sequence for the memory and control for a calculator data access port. This often contains the following features: programmable translation array (PTA)-provides a decoding mechanism for generating microinstruction addresses from macroinstructions; location counter (LC)-stores the address in the read only memory (ROM) from which accesses are being made; return register (RR)-used to hold a microsubroutine address; data transfer control logic-provides control and timing signals for data/address port; interrupt logic-provides control over three internal flags for the processor and four external flags for the system. (Some units.)

control circuits — The digital computer circuits which carry out instructions in proper sequence. They also interpret instructions and apply the proper commands to the arithmetic element and other circuits in accordance with interpretation.

control counter — A device which records the storage location of the instruction word which is to be operated upon following the instruction word in current use. The control counter may select storage location.

control data — One or more items of data which control the identification, selection, execution, or modification of another routine, record file, operation, data, value, etc.

control field — A constant location where control information is placed, usually in a sequence of similar items in a calculator.

control function — Refers to various actions that affect the recording, processing, transmission or interpretation of data, e.g., starting or stopping a process; carriage return; font change; rewind; end of transmission. Synonymous with control operation.

control, input/output — Directs the interaction between the processing unit and input/output devices.

control instructions — The instructions in this category are used to manipulate data within the main memory and the control memory, to prepare main-memory storage areas for the processing of data fields, and to control the sequential selection and interpretation of instructions in the stored program.

controlled variable — A quantity, condition, or part of a system which is subject to manipulation, regulation, or control by computer.

controller — A module or specific device which operates automatically to regulate a controlled variable or system.

controlling system — Generally refers to a feedback control system; i.e., that portion which compares functions of a directly controlled variable and a set point, and adjusts a manipulated variable as a function of the difference. It includes the reference input elements: summing point, forward and final controlling elements, as well as feedback elements (including sensing element).

control logic, on-chip — The on-chip control logic decodes instructions and coordinates instruction execution with memory and I/O operations, which are often managed by the system controller. In some units the CPU selects memory locations and I/O devices by means of a three-state, 16-line address bus. The system controller operates a three-state, eight-line, bidirectional data bus and the control bus.

control memory block — The control memory block is a separate section of most systems, as selected by the designer. Any microprogram storage included on LSI circuits results in design constraints. Microprogram storage can vary up to several thousand words, depending on system complexity, and often is optimally built with individual ECL PROMs and ECL RAMs. (See microcomputer section for discussion of ECL.)

control mode — A specific type of control action to be calculated or processed.

control operation communication — Refers to various actions and interpretation of data, e.g., starting or stopping a process, carriage return, font change, rewind and end of transmission.

control operations — Operations control of installation administration and workflow includes instructions from and to the computer operator, administrative records, logs of system operation, and the control over library programs.

control program (microprocessor) — A specific designed sequence of instructions that guides the CPU through the various operations otherwise programmed. Most often this program is permanently stored in ROM memory where it can be accessed but not erased by the CPU during operations.

control programs — Control programs contain many routines that would otherwise have to be put into each individual program. Such routines include those for handling error conditions, interruptions from the console, or interruptions from a communications terminal. There are also routines for handling input and output equipment. Because these routines are prewritten, the programmer is saved a good deal of effort and the likelihood of programming-errors is reduced.

control register — Also called instruction register, the control register stores the current instruction governing the operation of the calculator for a cycle.

control register function — Virtually all modern programmable calculators use a microprogrammed instruction set. Microprogramming permits emulation or modifying of systems to meet specific customer requirements, and designing the software to take advantage of existing hardware. The control register function has the necessary logic to accomplish such microprogram control. Often, important features of this circuit include: 4-bit width and expandable to larger words; storage and logic to address the control memory circuits and handle status, branching, and interrupt operations; and inputs/outputs necessary to interface with other sections of the system.

control routine — 1. Refers to primary routines which control loading and relocation of routines and in some cases makes use of instructions which are known to the general programmer. Effectively, control routines are part of the machine itself

control routine interrupt

(synonymous with monitor routine, supervisory routine, and supervisory program). 2. A set of coded instructions designed to process and control other sets of coded instructions. 3. A set of coded instructions used in realizing automatic coding.

control routine interrupt — A routine entered when an interrupt occurs that provides for such details as the storage of the working details of the interrupted program, an analysis of the interrupt to decide on the necessary action, and the run of control to the interrupted program.

control section — Refers to the primary sequence of instructions or data within a program that can be transferred from outside the program segment in which it is contained. The control section can be deleted or replaced with a control section from other program segments. Microprocessors are changing the structure and procedure of many such devices and systems.

control sequence — Refers to the normal order of selection of instructions for execution. In some calculators one of the addresses in each instruction specifies the control sequence. In most other calculators, the sequence is consecutive except where a transfer occurs.

control statements — 1. Generally these are statements which are used to direct the flow of the program, either causing specific transfers or making transfers dependent upon meeting certain specified conditions. 2. Instructions which convey control information to the processor, but do not develop machine-language instructions, i.e., symbolic statements.

control system — A system which is manipulated to achieve a prescribed value of a variable or response to an action.

control system design, calculator applications — Engineers assigned to develop control systems for STOL aircraft have overcome a host of highly complex aerodynamic problems. The control system designers often have turned to an advanced calculator. As they start they enter results from wind tunnel tests into the calculator, along with data on the aircraft's mass and inertia. The unit quickly computes the static and dynamic derivatives for various trim conditions required to set up a dynamic model of the aircraft for each flight condition. (There are approximately 120 different flight conditions.) The calculator also computes transfer functions and the roots of the characteristic polynomial. And then, using a root-locus plotting program, it designs single-loop control systems. These calculations that once took days are now done in about ten minutes.

control total — 1. The summation of some field from each record in an arbitrary grouping of records; the number is often used for checking machine and program data reliability. 2. A sum of numbers in a specified record field of a batch of records determined repetitiously during the processing operation, so that any discrepancy from the control indicates an error. A control total often has some significance in itself, but may not, as for example, when a control total is determined as the sum of identification numbers of records. (Related to hash total.)

control unit — The portion of a computer that directs the sequence of operations, interprets the coded instructions, and initiates the proper instructions to the computer circuits.

control word — 1. A word, usually the first or last of a record, or first or last word of a block, that carries indicative information for the following words, records, or blocks. 2. A word which is used to transmit processing information from the control program to the operational programs, or between operational programs. Most systems normally contain the several significant fields within the record.

conventions — Concerns various standard and accepted procedures in programs and systems analysis and the abbreviations, symbols, and their meanings as developed for particular systems and programs.

conversational calculator systems — The conversational ability of calculator terminals is especially useful for systems work. Users can set up a program and turn over the operation to anyone. The calculator will print instructions, telling a "stand-in" when to input data on the keyboard or when to press a key to sample from a system component. When to turn on or off another instrument.

conversational language — Refers to various languages that utilize a near-English character set which facilitates communication between the computer and the user. For example, BASIC is one of the more commonly used conversational languages.

conversational processing — The user is said to be communicating with the system in a conversational manner when each statement he enters through the terminal is processed (translated, verified, and, if desired, executed) immediately. The system then sends a reply to the terminal. The information contained in the reply varies. For example, it might be a message indicating that the previous statement contained an error. Operations in the conversational manner must be in either of two possible modes — the program mode, or the command mode (some computers).

conversion equipment — Refers to the equipment that is capable of transposing or transcribing the information from one type of data processing medium to render it acceptable as input to another type of processing medium.

conversion key — Converts amounts to the proper decimal value on a per factor basis (per C, per M, per dozen, etc.) also performs metric conversions.

conversions, calculator — Most scientific calculators allow users to convert from polar coordinates to rectangular coordinates and vice versa. They also enable users to convert to or from several English and metric units.

conversions functions — These include: Degrees to Radians. Assumes angle displayed is in degrees and converts it to radians (Independent of the Angular Mode switch). Radians to Degrees. Assumes angle displayed is in radians and converts it to degrees (Independent of the Angular Mode switch). Degrees/Minutes/Seconds to Decimal Degrees. Converts the number displayed from degrees/minutes/seconds to decimal degrees. Decimal Degrees to Degrees/Minutes/Seconds. Converts the number displayed from decimal degrees to degrees/minutes/seconds. Examples are:
Polar to Rectangular. Converts as follows: r STO 00, Θ 2nd P/R → y, RCL 00 → x.
Rectangular to Polar. Converts as follows: x STO 00, y INV 2nd P/R → Θ, RCL 00 → r.

conversions, single-stroke — Most units are preprogrammed with constants for use in English/

metric conversions. Most popular units actually perform the conversions with a single keystroke. The conversions include: inches and millimeters, feet and meters, U.S. gallons and liters, pounds mass and kilograms, pounds force and newtons, degrees farenheit and degrees celsius, and British thermal units and joules.

converter system, a/d — An a/d Converter samples analog data at specified rates and allows the program to store the equivalent digital value for subsequent processing. Sample and hold circuitry ensures accurate conversions, even on rapidly changing signals, by holding the input voltage constant until the process is completed. On some systems the maximum throughput rate for a single channel is approximately 35 KHz. A 16-channel single-ended multiplexer can be included. The input voltage range can be program selectable for unipolar (OV to +5V), or bipolar (−2.5 to +2.5V) operation.

coordinate conversions — Users convert polar coordinates to rectangular coordinates, or vice versa. This lets them do vector arithmetic quickly and accurately using two modes: Angle mode — users can calculate trig functions in any of three angular modes — degrees, radians or grads, and can also convert from an angle in one mode to an angle in another mode with a few keystrokes. Angle (time) conversion — In any of three angular modes, users can convert decimal angles (times) into angles (times) in degrees (hours)/minutes/seconds... or vice versa.

coordinates — Coordinates are elements of reference by means of which the relative positions of points in a plane may be determined with respect to the ordinate axis and the abscissa axis. These elements, the objects to which reference is made, and the method of making the reference, constitute a system of coordinates.

coordinates, rectangular — A set of three lines, called axes, that intersect at a common point in space in a way that each line, or axis, is perpendicular to the plane containing the other two.

core — Refers to tiny 'doughnuts' of magnetizable metal that can be in either an on or off state and can represent either a binary 1 (on) or binary 0 (off). Commonly called magnetic core and used as the basic type of main memory for many computers.

core memory vs semiconductor memory — Possibly the biggest boost to semiconductor memory development in the past year stems from the profusion of microcomputers and calculators finding their way into distributed data processing systems and remote industrial controls. And as microcomputerized controllers head toward environmentally hostile areas like factory workstations, oil fields and cargo docks, the need for reliable and nonvolatile memory increases. Power-interruption-proof memories may thus take on added importance in this highly competitive market, and the stage is set for core memory to make a comeback. New core memories, like many recently introduced, will offer high densities and TTL compatibility, as well as meeting semiconductors' speed capabilities with the added advantage of nonvolatility.

correction program — A particular routine which is designed to be used in or after a calculator failure, malfunction or program or operator error and which thereby reconstructs the routine being executed before the error or malfunction and from the most recent or closest rerun point.

correlation measurements — Three basic important measures of correlation are: 1. The line of regression that is fitted to the points on the scatter diagram in such a way that the sum of the squared deviations from the line is at a minimum. The line of regression gives the average change in y resulting from any given change in x. 2. The standard error of estimate (S_y) equals $\sqrt{\Sigma d^2/N}$, where d represents the deviation from the line of regression. S_y indicates, in absolute terms, the error that may be expected from any group of estimates made from the line of regression. 3. The coefficient of correlation (r) is a relative measure of the degree of relationship between two variables. It indicates the degree of improvement in the ability to estimate y from x over estimates of y made from the mean of the y variable alone.

CORR FUNCT correction function data acquisition — Key displays channel pair correction function code in memory such as thermocouple correction or alarm. Users key in new numeric code and enter.

cosine integral program — The cosine integral is denoted by Ci (x) and is defined as follows:

$$\text{Ci}(x) = \gamma + \ln x + \int_0^x \frac{\cos t - 1}{t} dt$$

where $x > 0$, and $\gamma = 0.5772156649$ is Euler's constant.

Also, a Taylor series expansions yields

$$\text{Ci}(x) = \gamma + \ln x + \sum_{n=1}^{\infty} \frac{(-1)^n x^{2n}}{2n(2n)!}$$

This program computes successive partial sums of the series. When two consecutive partial sums are equal, the value is used as the sum of the series.

cost/effectiveness — Constructed or designated measure of performance for distinct evaluations of systems, products, or endeavors. It is most often expressed as a ratio of some reference measure of cost and/or performance.

counter — A device or memory location whose value or contents can be incremented or decremented in response to an input signal.

counter, B-line — A specification or name for the index register, which is a special counter which can be set to any desired number from storage, changed by a certain number, and tested to see if the new number is equal to another number in storage. Index registers are useful for address modification and in problems involving repetitive calculations.

counter, cycle index — Utilized to count the number of times a given cycle of a program instruction has been done. It can be examined at any selected time to determine the number of repetitions still required in a loop.

counter, program — A register that holds the identification of the instruction word to be executed next in the time sequence, following the current operation. The register is often a counter which is incremented to the address of the next sequential storage location, unless a transfer or other special instruction is specified by the program.

counters, advanced calculators — Provide accurate time base, measure direct frequency and totalize events to 9,999,999. The seven digit LEDs display positions, decimal and blanks for leading zeroes. Some units measure frequency to 110MHz. Others count to 550 MHz with 10X prescale, with 50 ohm input. Others have capabilities for period and ratio averaging including six functions: period, ratio, frequency, time A-B, time manual and totalizing. Other units perform direct measure to 225 MHz and have pulse width and events A during B capabilities.

counting and timing — The most common functions performed by men and/or machines today are counting and/or timing. Because of this, many firms have introduced very comprehensive lines of integrated circuits to perform these functions. Electronic timing, unit counting, frequency measurement, frequency/time base generation, clocking, and so much more can now be accomplished simply, with a minimum of cost. For maximum user convenience suppliers group the products into four categories; eternally settable counter/timer; frequency and/or unit counter; complete timer/counter/stop-watch; and low power crystal frequency generators.

(A) Externally settable counter/timer circuits are a family of devices which can generate accurate, externally settable time delays from microseconds to five days.

(B) Frequency and/or unit counter is a 7-digit fully integrated circuit. To count units, users add an LED display, two resistors, a capacitor and control switches. For use as a timer or frequency counter, in addition to the above users also add an oscillator/controller circuit.

(C) A counter/timer/stopwatch comes complete in a single IC package. It works beautifully from a stack of three NiCad batteries. To make a system, users need to add only a quartz crystal, trimming capacitor, four switches and an 8-digit LED display.

(D) Low power crystal frequency generators provide low power operation plus the outstanding accuracy and stability of high frequency crystal circuits.

coupling — The association of two or more circuits so that power may be transferred from one to the other.

covariance and correlation coefficient program — For a set of given data points $\{(x_i, y_i), i = 1, 2, ..., n\}$, the covariance and the correlation coefficients are defined as:

$$\text{covariance } s_{xy} = \frac{1}{n-1}\left(\Sigma x_i y_i - \frac{1}{n}\Sigma x_i \Sigma y_i\right)$$

$$\text{or } s_{xy}' = \frac{1}{n}\left(\Sigma x_i y_i - \frac{1}{n}\Sigma x_i \Sigma y_i\right)$$

$$\text{correlation coefficient } r = \frac{s_{xy}}{s_x s_y}$$

where s_x and s_y are standard deviations

$$s_x = \sqrt{\frac{\Sigma x_i^2 - (\Sigma x_i)^2/n}{n-1}}$$

$$s_y = \sqrt{\frac{\Sigma y_i^2 - (\Sigma y_i)^2/n}{n-1}}$$

Note:
$-1 \leq r \leq 1$

CPU (central processing unit) — The CPU is the primary functioning unit of any computer system. Its basic architecture consists of storage elements called registers, computational circuits designed as the Arithmetic-Logic Unit (ALU), the Control Block, and Input-Output ports. A microprocessor built with LSI technology often contains a CPU on a single chip. Because such a chip has limited storage space, memory implementation is added in modular fashion on associated chips. Most microprocessors consist of several CPU chips and others for memory and I/O.

CPU chip — A CPU chip may be visualized as one universal chip which performs the functions of numerous individual chips. The CPU chip requires two sets of input signals to generate one set of output signals. The input and output signals correspond to the chip inputs and outputs. The instruction signals tell the CPU chips which individual logic chip to emulate. In order for a CPU chip's versatility to be useful, it must emulate logic equivalents to more than one chip.

CPU chip circuit — Contained on some CPUs are an arithmetic logic unit, (ALU) an accumulator, a scratch-pad memory, a status register, several bidirectional I/O ports, clock circuits to control all chips in the system, an interrupt control circuit, and a power-on detect circuit that disables the interrupt system and assures that processing starts from a unique address when power is first applied.

CPU computer card — The CPU chip requires certain input signals, and generates output signals which must be interpreted in a very specific way. These requirements will hold (with variations) for the simple CPU chip or the more complex CPU chips. For some applications the CPU chip is all the computer that is needed. An electronic calculator or a simple signal sensor/controller could be built using a CPU chip, plus limited and specialized external logic that satisfies the needs of the CPU chips but falls short of supplying capabilities commonly associated with a computer.

Computer designs have evolved to fill a need in the marketplace, and thus for many applications the most economical way of including computer capability in a product is via the standard expansion of a CPU chip into a computer card. For example, every microcomputer CPU chip must operate in conjunction with a memory module, and must have CPU-to-memory interface logic; if the CPU communicates with standard peripheral devices (e.g., a teletype, disk unit, or line printer), the computer card will supply the necessary interface between the CPU chip and peripheral device controller. Following is the extra logic needed to convert a CPU chip into a computer card:

COMMUNICATIONS — the ability to transmit data between the CPU chip pins and external devices.

TIMING — a clock that generates timing signals used by the CPU chip.

CONTROL LOGIC — The means for knowing where data is to be read, and where data must be sent.

CPU editor, calculator — Full editing capacity can be achieved as the CPU devices read the PROM contents and store them in RAM. The data can be edited, changed, and then written to PROM from RAM. Generally entire PROM chips are programmed serially from address 00 to FF for some. The Editor includes the keyboard programmer.

CPU section — Three primary sections of microprocessors are ROM, RAM, I/O, and they are fairly well standardized. The CPU section is characterized by wide variations among available units. It contains the following functions: microinstruction decode and control, registers, arithmetic unit, timing and control. The partitioning and complexity of these chips give microprocessors varying characteristics and capabilities, such as instruction set, word length, speed, memory capacity, etc. Some microprocessors are on a single chip while others are distributed on more than one chip. Single chip units are generally less expensive but also less flexible. Multiple chip designs make use of more silicon area and can generally offer more functions.

CPU, single-chip, second-generation — First-generation microcomputers are mostly p-channel MOS single-chip, nonmicroprogrammed devices. Using n-channel MOS many second-generation CPUs rely on greater chip density to provide more computer-like performance. Direct memory addressing (as in minicomputers) is available; but indirect and indexed addressing is not. Word size is 8 bits; typically there are seven 8-bit accumulators and a stack. The following features have been added to the first generation CPU chip to produce a second-generation chip: 1) separate address pins transmit memory addresses, independent of the 8-bit data bus, 2) A special signal indicates whether data is being input or output on the data bus. 3) The interrupt enable feature has been added. This allows a program to disable or enable the interrupt line. 4) a special signal indicates whether a read from memory or a write to memory is occurring. This signal greatly simplifies the logic external to the CPU chip.

CPU slices — CPU slices are generally 2 or 4 bit parts of a CPU. Users must define an instruction set and the architecture which executes that instruction set, then develop the interface between that architecture and the memory containing the control program and the I/O system which connects into devices, and then provide a system package. The CPU slice approach was initially represented by the Intel 3001, 2 bit CPU slice followed by several other 4 bit CPU slice offerings.

criterion — Refers to a value used for testing, comparing, or judging; e.g., in determining whether a condition is plus or minus, true or false; also, a rule or test for making a decision in a computer or by humans.

critical path method (CPM) — The longest time path in a project which has to be done as quickly as possible. Because the overall time required to complete the project cannot be less than that required along the critical path, it requires the most careful monitoring. Any delay along this path causes whole project to be delayed, while minor delays along noncritical paths do not. See PERT network, Project Evaluation and Review Technique.

crossfooting — Crossfooting is the addition and/or subtraction of factors in a horizontal spread to prove processing accuracy. It can be used on a payroll register to prove that the final totals of net pay and deductions equal the final total earnings; this provides control on report preparation as well as calculating and card-punching operations. In posting transactions to records that are stored in a calculator (i.e., accounts receivable), crossfooting is used to prove the accuracy of posting either as each transaction is posted, or collectively at the end of the run or both.

cross validation — The verification of results by replicating an experiment under independent conditions.

CRT audio signal — A CRT Audio Signal is a programmable alarm to notify the operator of various conditions requiring attendance, such as errors, incoming messages, or program completion.

CRT (Cathode Ray Tube) — A type of display which looks like a television tube. It is capable of multi-line displays, and can show the contents of several registers simultaneously.

CRT character/block mode with full editing
- Teleprinter compatible operation in character mode; local data preparation in block mode.
- Efficient data correction with character insert and delete; line insert and delete.
- Off-screen storage allows use of forms over 24 lines in length.
- Programmable, protected fields for forms entry.

CRT computing calculators — Operating much like a computer and receiving "instructions" in widely used BASIC Computer Language, many desk-top units are capable of very sophisticated data processing operations and can store and retrieve literally millions of "bytes" of information, yet their cost compared to computers is relatively, very low. Some use a CRT Display (TV tube-like screen) and give users a unique ability to review information or results instantly. Some systems have CRT units with up to 20 peripheral devices available to help users get the information the way it is most useful to them for specific businesses and professions.

CRT control, calculator — Although some engineers choose to use standalone calculators, programmed in algebraic language through a numeric and function keyboards, others choose those which are programmed in BASIC. These more capable units are used to permit operator interaction through a typewriter-like keyboard and alphanumeric display.

CRT Display size — Usually refers to the diagonal measurement of a terminal's CRT screen. Display configuration refers to the way in which data can be presented on that screen. Most of the alphanumeric units in various surveys can display 1920 characters, in formats of 74 to 80 characters/line. Other configurations are also available, however. The capabilities of the graphic terminals are measured by the number of addressable points on their screens.

CRT edit functions — The edit functions of a CRT terminal include the ability to insert or delete characters or entire lines, the ability to position the unit's cursor and the ability to define certain protected data fields on the terminal's screen. Generally, the more numerous its editing capabilities, the more "intelligent" users can consider a CRT terminal to be.

CRT modular microprocessor architecture
- One chip microprocessors control memory allocation, data communications, keyboard scanning, and Mini Cartridges.
- Plug-in modules minimize down time.
- Single button Self-Test for instant verification of terminal operation. (some units)

CRT raster-scan terminals — Raster-scan CRT terminals, as opposed to storage-tube types, require memory to refresh the characters displayed on their screens. Additionally, those terminals with more than rudimentary "intelligence" also incorporate memory to store the programs that control their special functions, such as editing capabilities. Many of the more intelligent terminals, especially those used for distributed data processing, also have some form of peripheral storage — hard- or floppy-disk, or tape.

CRT storage — 1. Often this relates to the electrostatic storage characteristics of cathode-ray tubes in which the electron beam is used to sense the data. 2. The storage of data on a dielectric surface, such as the screen of a cathode-ray tube, in the form of the presence or absence of spots bearing electrostatic charges; these spots can persist for a short time after the removal of the electrostatic charging force. 3. A storage device used as in the foregoing description.

CRT substitutes — There will be more use of visual-display screens — like mid-size television screens — that will rid the viewer of the fatiguing flicker of cathode ray tube screens. The new screens use neon gas, sandwiched between the front and back of the display. The screens are referred to as gas plasma, gas panel or gasp, are about half-inch thick and are flat. Also, look for chip screens. These use electrically sensitive particals that make up characters or numerals when lit. Chip screens, too, are flat and flicker-free, many are used in word processing (WP) systems. They are inexpensive systems relative to the cost of many older intelligent terminal-WP configurations. Equipment costs have gone down because of microcomputer circuitry. Also, this new technology treats laser beams as if they were electronic circuits. This reduces the size and cost of the power input. The moves from electronic to laser circuitry are analogous to the moves from tube to transistor technology.

CRT subsystem, programmable calculator — One specific CRT subsystem is a special configuration of the HP 2640A intelligent terminal. It has been designed to interface with the HP 9830 BASIC language calculator to provide a high speed entry system for users who work with business forms. It can be operated in either a block or character mode for sophisticated data entry applications. The easy-to-read, 5×10 inch, inverse video (black on white) display is available with standard 128-character Roman font. The terminal generates characters with a high-resolution (7×9) dot matrix in a 9×15 dot character cell. The microprocessor-controlled operating characteristics of the terminal, combined with its RAM semi-conductor memory, provide a smart (dynamically allocated) memory that can store more than 200 lines of data that are viewable 24 lines at a time. The 9882A comes with 3K bytes of memory, which can be expanded in a 2K byte step-up to 5 bytes. (H-P stands for Hewlett-Packard Co.)

CRT terminals classifications — With a growth rate that could be termed explosive, distributed processing applications in turn stimulate the proliferation of offerings in the CRT-terminal marketplace. Users can expect the spectrum of terminal types to continue to widen, spanning simple, "non-intelligent" Teletype replacements and increasingly versatile and powerful "intelligent" units. The difficulty that pervades the CRT-terminal marketplace is the current lack of agreement among manufacturers as to exactly what constitutes "intelligence." Most makers cite one or more characteristics, such as editing capability, cursor addressability by a host computer, software checks of alphanumeric characteristics, and protected data fields, as characteristics of such intelligence. Rather than classify the terminals by their degree of intelligence, much of the industry has chosen a more clearcut classification scheme. The entries basically are either alphanumeric (able to display numerals, letters and certain other specialized symbols) or graphic (able to display diagrams). A third entry under the type subheading — "alphanumeric and graphic" — encompasses those units that are primarily alphanumeric but also have a graphic capability, albeit limited.

CRT terminal ('smart') — Various types operate character-by-character as a completely interactive terminal or can act on one block at a time. Text can be composed and edited locally, so users can verify and correct data before it's transmitted to the computer. Various other 'standard' features include: inverse video, 50 to 400 lines of off-screen storage with scrolling and page select capability, many special function keys for user-defined routines, and extensive editing features often up to four 128-character sets can reside concurrently and be intermixed on the screen. A standard 5×10 inch screen provides a 1,920 character capacity of 24 lines of 80 characters.

CRT transmission mode — The data transmission mode of a CRT terminal is usually either full or half duplex, although other modes are possible. The first mode allows the terminal to simultaneously and independently send and receive information, while the second allows such independent communication to proceed only in one direction at a time. The terminal's data transfer mode, on the other hand, is defined to refer to the method by which the unit sends and receives information. Generally, the terminal can either transfer data as it is generated — character-by-character — or in blocks.

cued stops, calculators — If memory space permits, it is sometimes helpful to put a familiar number into the X register before stopping for data. Thus when the program stops, the displayed number identifies the desired input. For example if a user's program requires 8 stops for input, it is very helpful to have the numbers 1, ..., 8 appear so he knows which input is needed. If a cue number is created as a program step immediately preceding the R/S, it is not lifted into the stack and the number is overwritten by the data users key in. (Cue numbers generated by other means will be lifted.) (Some systems)

curve conformity — Relates to curves, the closeness to which they approximate a specified functional curve (i.e. logarithmic, parabolic, cubit, etc.) and usually expressed in terms of nonconformity; i.e., the maximum deviation between an average curve and a specified functional curve. The average curve is determined after making two or more full range traverses in opposite directions. The value of non-conformity is referred to the output unless otherwise stated. See linearity.

curve fitting — The process of obtaining a specific representation of a curve by a mathematical expression or equation.

curve fitting-linear regression program — When investigating the relationship between two variables in the real world, it is a reasonable first step to make experimental observations of the system to gather paired values of the variables, (x, y). The investigator might then ask the question: What mathematical formula best describes the relationship between the variables x and y? His first guess will often be that the relationship is linear, i.e., that the form of the equation is $y = a_1 x + a_0$, where a_1 and a_0 are constants. The purpose of this program is to find the constants a_1 and a_0, which give the closest agreement between the experimental data and the equation $y = a_1 x + a_0$. The technique used in linear regression by the method of least squares.

The user must input the paired values of data he has gathered, (x_i, y_i), i = 1, ..., n. When all data pairs have been input, the regression constants a_1 and a_0 may be calculated. A third value may also be found, the coefficient of determination, r^2. The value of r^2 will lie between 0 and 1 and will indicate how closely the equation fits the experimental data: the closer r^2 is to 1, the better the fit. (See appropriate manuals for formulas)

curve, Gaussian (random-error concept) — A "random error of sampling" is a variation due to chance alone. If the sample is truly random, small errors will be more numerous than large errors and positive errors will be as likely as negative errors, thus giving rise to symmetrical, bell-shaped "normal curve of error." The concept was first investigated by the German mathematician, Karl F. Gauss, and the curve is often called the Gaussian curve.

customizer, calculator — One firm has a little plug-in that is a type of "black-box" that has a total of 16 different option keys. Each one performs a different function or sequence of functions. The supplier representative demonstrates when he brings the Customizer to customers to show exactly how each option operates. The users tell him which ones they want and which ones they don't. Proper key overlays are installed on the Customized units.

custom program initialization option — Where some systems are to be applied primarily to a single task, a special ROM can be supplied that contains all control, system, and channel setting initialization. Some keyboards permit making local variations to the special program, or complete override of the entire special program as with the many advanced calculators.

custom ROMs (PROM) — With custom-programmed ROMs, the manufacturer places the binary information (links or no links) into the memory as specified by the user. Custom programming of ROMs is expensive when only small quantities are ordered. To reduce the high cost of small quantities of ROMs, manufacturers offer the field-programmable ROM or PROM. The PROM is an ordinary ROM that has all of its on-chip fuses intact. A 256-bit PROM would have 256 of these fuses, one for each bit of memory. The user can program information into the PROM quite simply by blowing selected on-chip fuses. The fuses are blown open by passing a specific amount of current through them.

Cybernetics — 1. The science of systems of control and communication. 2. The diverse field encompasses (a) integration of communication, control, and systems theories; (b) development of systems engineering technology; and (c) practical applications at both the hardware and software levels. Recent and projected developments in Cybernetics are taking place in at least five important areas: technological forecasting and assessment, complex systems modeling, policy analysis, pattern recognition, and artificial intelligence. Applications have moved far beyond the feedback control systems described in Norbert Wiener's book "Cybernetics" first published 25 years ago.

cycle — An interval of space or time in which one set of events or phenomena is completed. In alternating current, the time for a change of state from a value through a positive and negative maximum, back to the same value.

cycle, action — Specifically refers to the complete operation performed on data. Includes basic steps of: origination, input, manipulation, output and storage.

cycle availability — That specific time period during which stored information can be read.

cycle check — A method of error detection which checks every nth bit, n + 1 bit, n + 2 bit, etc. It is more powerful and efficient than horizontal checks, vertical checks, or combinations of both.

cycle code — Refers to any binary code which changes by only one bit when going from one number to the number immediately following.

cycle counter — A mechanism or device which measures the number of times a specified cycle is repeated.

cycle, index — 1. The number of times a cycle has been executed, or the difference between the number of times a cycle is desired and the number of times it has been repeated. 2. The number of cycle iterations in digital computer programming. A cycle index register may be used to set the number of cycles desired. Then with each cycle iteration, the register count is reduced by one until the register reaches zero and the series of cycles is complete.

cycle interrupt — The change (by sequence or specific operation cycle) of control to the next or a specific function in a predetermined manner or order.

cycle shift — Refers to the removal of digits of a number or characters from a word from one end of the number or word and their insertion, in the same sequence, at the other end.

cycle time — 1. The period required for a complete action. In particular, the interval required for a read and a write operation in working memory, usually taken as a measure of calculator speed. 2. Length of time for the calculator to make a complete scan of data measurements at the programmed rate, plus the time to output the scan to one or more output displays or devices.

cycle (verb) — 1. Refers to performance of a non-arithmetic shift in which the digits dropped off at one end of a word are returned at the other end in circular fashion, cycle right and cycle left. 2. To repeat a set of operations a prescribed number of times including, when required, supplying necessary address changes by arithmetic processes or by means of a hardware device such as a b-box or cycle-counter.

cycling — Refers to the periodic change imposed on controlled variable or a function by a controller.

D

daisy chain bus — A daisy-chain bus is very similar to the party-line, except that the connections are made in serial fashion. Each unit can modify the signal before passing it on to the next device. This approach is used mainly for signals related to interrupts or polling circuits. Whenever a device requires service, it blocks the signal. A priority is thus established, since the devices that are closest to the microprocessor usually have the first chance to request service.

data — 1. A representation with characters or analog quantities to which meaning is assigned that expresses facts, concepts, or instructions in a formalized manner suitable for communication, interpretation, or processing by automatic or human means. 2. Information which can be produced or processed, by a calculator, computer or control system.

data access systems — Various data access systems offer users multi-terminal, on-line data processing capability with unique, concurrent multi-terminal remote job entry (RJE) available at each terminal. These systems offer combinations of capabilities made possible by the use of state-of-the-art processors with high speed semiconductor memories. A system processor is dedicated to disk storage management (up to 8 disk drives), program interpretation and computing. Additionally, communications processors assure fast response to users at terminals and efficient use of peripheral devices. These processors manage local peripherals, asynchronous terminal communications at speeds up to 2400 baud, and synchronous communications to various type computers at speeds up to 4800 baud.

data acquisition calculator architecture — Basic system architecture is always a three-way tradeoff of versatility (how many functions?), capacity (how many channels?), and practicality (how costly?). Some specific advanced calculators provide the optimum combination of characteristics for 8 out of 10 applications in standard configurations; the others can be met optimally with special plug-in ROMs.

data acquisition calculator capabilities — Advanced rugged calculators provide a great shortcut to large-scale data gathering. Functionally, they are standardized data acquisition systems, under the control of a tiny microprocessor. These solid state integrated circuit "computers on a single chip," combined with RAMs (random access memory devices), ROMs (read-only memory devices), and PROMs (programmable ROMs), are keyboard programmed with one finger. Most are designed for the toughest industrial conditions where noisy signals are the rule, not the exception. Guarding and isolation are standard features to assure accurate measurement. The circuitry is generally reliable, readily serviced, and backed by a nationwide service organization. When users need a dependable data gatherer — in the laboratory, in the field, in the plant — wherever data originates, they consider the calculator to save from 20 to 80% of the alternative cost of any comparable hard wired system.

data acquisition calculator inputs — Some systems will handle up to eight types of functional ranges at one time. The basic system can take up to 248 analog channels, up to 16 digital inputs. Virtually any type of transducer at any signal level is acceptable, including nonlinear thermocouples. Functional ranges are set up for individual channels, pairs of channels, blocks of channels, or for the entire system by keyboard. Automatic channel circuit checking, as for thermocouple burnout, is a basic benefit. (some systems)

data acquisition calculator output — On some systems, data in digits may be displayed channel-by-channel on a LED panel readout. Further, the basic calculator can send data to two peripheral transmission or recording devices such as the internally mounted printer, modems, Teletype, paper or mag tape recorders. Up to four peripheral outputs can be handled on an optional basis on some systems. A valuable feature is the ease of printing out data in engineering units such as °F, °C, MV, R/M, and many other standard symbols. Alarm outputs consist of relay closures and red printouts, together with an appropriate symbol to indicate high or low alarm. Using the keyboard, alarms may be set on individual channels, and if desired, some systems will print only on alarm.

data acquisition calculator system, example — One specialized system includes:
- Self-contained up to 64 channels, expandable to 248 analog channels.
- Low level sensing to 1 microvolt resolution, 0 to 40 MV or higher input ranges. Measurement immune to noise, uses dual slope integration with one cycle of line frequency sample period. Isolation relay three-wire switching, 200 VDC common mode. Guard shield envelope surrounds all analog elements. Auto signal source check.
- Handles mixed multiple thermocouples, millivolts, volts, non-linear functions, process signals, digit BCD inputs.
- Crystal controlled clock, memory save option, battery-saver electronics, calibration check, make it ideal for field use.
- Versatile output combination of on-board printer, paper and mag tape, Teletype, modem. High/low alarms optional each channel.
- Microprocessor allows optional special ROM programs such as ratios, rates of change, accumulation, math functions, dedicated initialization ROM with keyboard override.

data acquisition, calculator system output — System outputs are another flexible part of calculator data systems. The benefit is the ability to feed data to two output devices in a pre-determined sequence with a standard system. Any two of the following may be key-selected on some systems:
On-board digital printer, 21 columns,
Paper tape perforator,
Magnetic tape recorders,
ASR33 Teletype and compatible devices,
Data telemetry interface, RS-232-C compatible.

data acquisition, calculator system sequence — Sequentially, output flows as follows: a complete data scan is made without interruption. All analog data is scanned first, then all digital inputs. Conversion of linearization, as for thermocouple channels, is performed as received. The entire scan is stored in memory. Control then passes to the key-programmed output instruction. Output device No. 1 receives the frame header line, specified analog channels, digital channels, and a record separator (printer line feed or interrecord gap). Sequence is repeated for output device No. 2. Cycle time for the above sequence is the scan time plus cumulative device output times. Interchangeability of an output device involves only change of an output PC board, a ROM and a plug-in cable.

data acquisition system CPU organization — The central processing unit of some systems is a powerful, thoroughly proven 4-bit microprocessor coupled to up to 16 read-only memories (ROMs), and 32 random access memories (RAMs) busconnected. Memories contain instructions for linearizing thermocouple signals, for scaling, for applying coefficients, for data handling, for reading out measurements directly in engineering units, for alarm setpoints, for temporary memory, and data formatting. While such power sounds expensive, it results in a lower cost data system than most comparable predecessors. The secret is that the microprocessor performs the signal processing, interfacing, and formatting tasks that formerly required hundreds of TTL logic packages and dozens of mechanical switches. Users get higher value, simplicity, and reliability.

data acquisition system, programmable calculator-based — A data acquisition can make pressure, temperature, fuel flow and engine speed calculations, and provide personnel with a complete printout of this data. Data from the sensors, converted to digital form by a group of individual instruments can be placed in the memory of a calculator. Conversion to engineering units combined with standardization of data to compensate for variables such as air temperature, air density, and fuel density is accomplished and all of the corrected data can be printed out, completely formatted with alphanumeric headings and engineering unit indications by various automatic typewriters. Hardcopy output can become a permanent report of performance of a particular engine combination.

data acquisition systems — Data acquisition systems are used in three basic areas: research and development laboratories, process industries, and factory production. In laboratories they monitor electrical and physical parameters of experimental systems. In process industries they monitor process parameters, calculate and predict trends, and occasionally control the process itself on the basis of these calculations. Finally, in factory production, they permit more complete testing of the factory's product in less time — for example, testing printed circuit boards for faulty, incorrect, or missing components. Data acquisition is not necessarily complex. It can be as simple as a digital voltmeter and a printer, logging voltage measurements that represent other variables, such as pH or temperature. On the other extreme, it can involve data from multipoint transducers, periodically scanned under the control of a computer. The latter reduces data online and makes appropriate calculations to correlate data, test limits, and predict trends.

data-adapter unit (communications) — The data-adapter unit greatly expands the input/output capabilities of the system. It provides direct connection of a variety of remote and local external devices to a system. These devices include the data-collection system, the data-communication system, process-communication system, telephone terminals, telemetry terminals, and control and data-acquisition equipment.

data base — The set of data or information on which operations and conclusions can be based. This is the set of data that is internally accessable to the computer and on which the computer performs.

data base management — A systematic approach to storing, updating, and retrieval of information stored as data items, usually in the form of records in a file, where many users, or even many remote installations, will use common data banks.

data bus — Most calculators communicate externally through the use of a data bus. Most are bidirectional, e.g., capable of transferring data to and from the CPU, storage and peripheral devices.

data bus components — A typical System Data Bus is composed of three signal buses. An example is a data bus that consists of 16 bidirectional data lines. The timing bus provides the basic system clocks as well as address and data strobes which indicate when data is valid on the bus. The control bus provides a priority system for bus access, signals to indicate whether the current transaction is a read or write from memory or a peripheral, an extended cycle signal, and a response line to indicate that a peripheral device has accepted an order sent over the system bus.

data capture — A method employed by point-of-sales terminals whereby customer account numbers, the amount of the purchase, and other information are automatically recorded, and sent to the computer to be processed.

data cartridge — A typical high-speed data cartridge provides up to 96,384 bytes of program and data storage. Dual-track, 140 foot magnetic tape can be searched bi-directionally at 60 inches a second.

data chaining — Refers to the gathering (or scattering) of information within one physical record, from (or to) more than one region of memory, by means of successive I/O commands.

data channel — Refers to a bidirectional data path between the I/O devices and the main memory in a digital calculator that permits one or more I/O operations to happen concurrently with computation.

data chip — A data chip generally incorporates the paths, registers, and logic to execute microinstructions. It can offer the following features: 1. Register File — provides multiple registers for storage of frequently required data. 2. Arithmetic and Logic Unit (ALU) performs the arithmetic and logic operations necessary for instruction execution. 3. Condition Flags Logic — monitors the status of the result from the ALU section. 4. Data/Address Port — provides access to the data address lines.

data-collection system — This system gathers manufacturing information from electronic in-plant reporting stations and transmits it directly to the computer. The information is processed as it is received. Reports can be produced which indicate, for example, job cost or machine utilization.

Information can enter the processor in several ways, including punched card, plastic badge, keyboard or data cartridge. The latter logs production data on a pocket-sized recording device that the employee maintains at his work station.

data communication interface RS-232-C — Designed for compatibility with modems and other conventional data couplers. Serial data transfer, USACII code.

data communications — Generally relates to the movement of computer-encoded information by means of electrical transmission systems.

data communications control unit — The unit that scans the central terminal unit buffers for messages, and transfers them to the central processor.

data communications interface firmware module — The Data Communications Interface Option increases terminal scope from desk-top graphic computing system to intelligent graphic terminals, by enabling several data communications modes. On some systems the backpack includes two plug-in spaces to hold firmware ROMs for specialized applications. ROM options will be coming steadily from many firms. User-designed ROMs will also fit its versatile design.

data communications interface output — Practical remote use of most calculators is enhanced by the capability of the RS-232-C interface. It permits use of the system with a variety of receivers and transmitters through land lines, at radio frequencies, literally any telemetering medium. The interface is a recognized standard of the Electronic Industries Association (EIA) and is the basis of all U.S. data communications. Further, the interface meets the code of the International Committee CCITT (Consultative Committee on International Telegraphy and Telephony). Advantages are that two-way interaction is possible in several modes, and transmission rates can equal that of high-speed teleprinters. Data transmission may be initiated from either the calculator end or the other end of the line.

data communications interfaces — Typical data communication interface cards permit various calculator and computer series users to transmit data through a wide variety of privately-owned and common-carrier communication facilities. All communication interfaces conform to EIA specification RS-232, provide programmable character size, programmable parity checking, and a variety of programmable or jumper selectable data rates. All interfaces can be operated under program or DMA control.

data-communication terminal — A data station is an all-purpose remote communication terminal which can be used for a broad range of applications involving direct, on-line data transmission to and from the company. Branch offices, warehouses, remote reporting locations throughout a plant, or any other company outpost can communicate directly with a centrally located computer via the data station. When not being used for actual on-line transmission (remote mode), the data station can be used off-line (local mode) for activities such as data preparation and editing.

data, continuous — 1. Continuous measures are those which may conceivably be found at any point along a continuous scale. Examples are thermometers, speedometers, and analog computing devices. 2. Sometimes used in a broad sense to indicate all quantitative data, including that of a quantal nature.

data design — A particular layout or format of calculator storage or machine storage allocation, i.e., for input and output and most often related to flow charts and diagrams to define procedures and practices for problem solution.

data design layout — 1. A predetermined arrangement of characters, fields, lines, punctuation, page numbers, etc. 2. A defined arrangement of words, totals, characters, stubs, headings, etc. for a desired clear presentation of data or print-output, such as a financial record.

data element — A specific item of information appearing in a set of data, i.e., in various sets of data, each item is a data element, the quantity of a supply item issued, a unit rate, an amount, and the balance of stock items on hand, etc.

data element dictionary (DED) — An organized listing of data elements (and their associated information) in a given system.

data entry — The writing, reading, or posting to a coding form or to a terminal or processing medium, of information or instructions. A datum or item which is usually entered on one line, a single entity of processing.

data entry, calculator keys — Digit Keys are used to enter numbers 0 through 9 to a limit of 10-digit mantissa and a 2-digit exponent, on various hand-held systems.

data entry, free format (calculator) — Users can enter data in a free format: ordinary floating, scientific floating or mixed decimal. Exponents, trig and hyperbolic functions are relatively easy to solve on many keyboards. There are more than numbers on most keyboards. There are full sets of alpha characters. When users work these with the user-definable overlays, users get easy interaction between man and machine. And that means increased versatility for advanced calculators.

data entry terminal calculators — Compact portable calculator terminals are designed for simple, serial interactive communication with a computer. A data entry terminal generally consists of a 16-character keyboard, a communications interface module, status indicators, a power supply and a numeric display.

A typical 16-character keyboard contains the numeric characters 0 through 9, and the alphabetic characters A through F. The units transmit the key codes and receive at typical rates of 110 and 300 baud standard. Most are prewired to accept a numeric display option which enables them to display numeric data, 0 through 9, and a decimal point. The decimal point can be program-controlled; its particular location depends on the data or character codes received. Optional numerical display clusters of 4, 8, and 12 characters are available. A plus-or-minus sign can be substituted for a numeric character.

Communicating with a computer using the terminal is similar to using a teletypewriter. In some units, the 16-pad keyboard is not just limited to a 16-character repertoire. There can be virtually countless numbers of functions as determined by the user. By using simple programming techniques, the 16 characters can be software-interpreted as commands, or instructions.

data entry terminal, microprocessor — Microcalculator terminals and data collection devices allow low cost entry functions to be put back onto

data format

the immediate user. Later, data can be transmitted directly to service bureaus, or data collected and converted onto floppy disks or tape cassettes which can be mailed in to the service center. A big advantage is that the data finally entering the host computer is cleaner, and reruns are reduced. Specific kinds of collection devices can be custom-designed for payroll, accounts receivable, and other applications, or designed and programmed for specific customers.

data format — Rules and procedures describe the way data is held in a file or record, whether in character form, as binary numbers, etc.

data-formatting statements — Refers to various statements that instruct the assembly program to set up constants and reserve memory areas and to punctuate memory to indicate field boundaries.

data handling — Scanning, monitoring, analog-to-digital conversion, print-out, and similar devices designed to simplify the use and interpretation of data.

data-handling system — 1. A system of automatic and semi-automatic devices used in the collection, transmission, reception, and storage of information in digital form. 2. A system in which data is sorted, decoded or stored in a particular form; related to data reduction.

data hierarchy — Structuring data into the subsets within a set, such as bit, byte, character, word, block, record, file, and bank.

data input bus (DIB) — Some calculators feature a single bus structure; the processor, memory, and input-output channels all sharing a common Data Input Bus (DIB). The Data Input Bus is the mechanism whereby address information and data are transferred between the switch register (SR) and the processor, between the processor and the memory, between the memory and the input-output interface, and between the processor and the input-output interface.

data input cards — A data input card is designed to transfer up to a maximum of six binary-coded-decimal (BCD) digits of data from devices such as counters, digital voltmeters, digital multimeters and similar devices which provide a "print command" pulse indicating the availability of valid data. Data must be valid for a minimum of five milliseconds after the print command transition. Either positive-going or negative-going print command transitions can be selected by a link on the card. Provision is also made for either a normal or inverted polarity indication which issues a "change sign" command to the calculator.

data item — 1. Sometimes called a datum. A single unit of information of a specific kind pertaining to a single thing. 2. A specific member of a data set denoted by a data element; for instance Monday, the name of a specific member of the set of the days of a week. The week is the data element. Monday the data item, and 05 could be the data code.

data manipulation — The performance of data-processing chores common to most users, such as sorting, input/output operations, and report generation.

data manipulation, calculator — Four accumulators provide temporary on-chip storage for intermediate and arithmetic results, thus reducing program length, instructions during program operation and the number of memory operations. Ten addressing modes provide easy access to system memory. That means short, simple and efficient programs for users. (some units)

data medium — The selected medium used to transport or carry (communicate) data or information. Punched cards, magnetic tapes, and punched paper tapes — and lately portable disks, are examples, most often easily transported independently of the devices used in reading or interpreting such data or information.

data organization — Also known as data-set organization. Pertains to any one of the data management conventions for the spatial or physical arrangements of the records of a data set. The five data management organizing methods are sometimes defined as: 1. sequential 2. partitioned 3. indexed sequential 4. direct 5. telecommunications.

data origination — 1. The translation of information from its original form into a machine-sensible form. 2. The act of creating a record in a machine-sensible form, directly or as a by-product of a human-readable document.

data path — The data path is a transfer bus for input/output and data handling operations. Data path width is suggested by applications where random logic suggests individual bit manipulation. Numeric operations such as calculators suggest a 4-bit width for BCD representation. Alphanumeric data handling suggests an 8-bit representation and scientific processing suggests larger byte sizes. Regardless of what byte size the applications suggest, data path width is actually only limited by the speed desired in performing the operation. A one bit microprocessor can handle a sixteen bit operation and, in the same sense, a sixteen bit microprocessor can do individual bit manipulation. The real tradeoff is between speed and cost.

data paths and I/O capability — Some systems provide an extremely fast elementary input/output capability. The data paths and control functions are often simple elements that are sequenced from the control memory with flexible disciplines. The fact that the control memory is very fast means that microprograms (firmware) in the control memory can implement facilities with a high degree of versatility in timing, data paths and I/O capabilities such as priority interrupts, fully buffered data channels, macroprogrammable transfers, and special purpose communication multiplexer channels. This basic I/O element is always the I/O bus and varies for cell systems.

Data-Phone — A product trademark of the A.T. & T. Company to identify the data sets manufactured and supplied by the Bell System for transmitting data over the telephone network. It is also a Bell System service mark to identify the transmission of data over the telephone network (Data-Phone Service).

data plotting package — Including routines which draw and label axes, this package also allows user input of data minimums, maximums and increments. The program allows for easy data entry and subsequent screen plotting. For convenience, all routines can be called from user's own programs.

data plotting packages — Some data plotting packages include routines which draw and label axes, allowing the user to input data minimums, maximums and increments. Some programs allow for easy data entry and subsequent screen plotting. For convenience, all routines can be called from user's own programs. One manufacturer offers an optional data plotting package. It consists of a program which includes an automatic graphing system with a memory option; it also allows for use of an overlay for user selection of the desired interaction level. Besides providing for automatic scaling and tic labels, this plot allows arbitrary graph location on the screen. The result is the plotting capability for multiple graphs and/or multiple lines per graph. Any and all programs, whole or part, may be used as subroutines in any user-written program. This and other plotting packages present the user with versatility in graphing capability.

data processing — 1. Any procedure for receiving information and producing a specific result. 2. Rearrangement and refinement of raw data into a form suitable for further use. 3. The preparation of source media which contain data or basic elements of information, and the handling of such data according to precise rules of procedure to accomplish such operations as classifying, sorting, calculating, summarizing, and recording. 4. The production of records and reports. (Synonymous with data handling.)

data processing calculator system — When owners connect advanced programmable calculators to their computers they put full computing capability right on the user's desk – where it often belongs. They put an end to the data processing run-around because the calculator can be a remote batch terminal, timeshare terminal, and satellite processor, all in one unit. As a satellite processor, one type powerful, BASIC language calculator gives fast solutions to most of the user's computational problems. And by keeping these small- or intermediate-size jobs out of the data processing stream, the calculator helps users make better use of all users computing resources. Data can be gathered from many sources because the calculator accommodates instrumentation and a complete line of input/output peripherals, including plotter, digitizer, and line printer. To convert the calculator to a computing data terminal, users simply add a Data Communications Interface and ROMs. Then it can communicate with another terminal or another calculator to function as a binary synchronous remote batch terminal to a large computer, or serve as a timeshare terminal. Users find that the calculator then becomes an economical alternative for connecting to remote batch or time-sharing services – especially since it has so many of the features users need to improve their data processing capabilities.

data processing, centralized — The processing of all data involved with a given activity at a given location and usually in one building housing the equipment configuration.

data processing, decentralized — The housing of data by individual subdivisions of an organization or at each geographical location of the parts of an organization.

data processing, graphic — A letter or other drawn, diagrammed (or an omission of such) character or figure which can be reproduced or transmitted in some way through an electronic data system, usually by an ordered set of pulses.

data processor — 1. A device capable of performing operations on data, such as a digital computer, analog computer, or a desk calculator. 2. A person processing data. 3. A standardized term representing any and all devices which have the capability of performing the reduction, summarizing, processing, or input and output of data or information, and including calculators, punched card equipment, computers, and subsidiary systems.

data purification — The reduction of the number of errors as much as possible prior to using data in an automatic data processing system.

data record — A collection of facts, numbers, letters, symbols, etc., that a program can process or produce.

data reduction — 1. The art or process of transforming masses of raw test or experimentally obtained data, usually gathered by instrumentation, into useful, ordered, or simplified intelligence. 2. The process of transforming raw data into useful form by smoothing, adjusting, scaling and ordering experimental readings.

data reliability — A ratio used to measure a degree to which data is error free.

data saving and loading, terminal systems — DATALOAD and DATASAVE commands read or write lists of variables and arrays from or onto a tape cassette or other selected storage device on some systems. Also, the COM Clear statement clears some or all previously defined common variables for a more efficient use of memory space in program overlaying (chaining).

data set — 1. Usually refers to unique combinations or aggregations of data elements. Examples are the sales order, accounts-receivable ledger card, sales summary report, payroll register, etc. It should be noted that a data set is a potential combination of data elements. Not all data elements need be present at one time. For example, a payroll-register entry for a given employee may contain only one or two of several possible deductions. 2. An electronic device that provides an interface for the transmission of data to remote stations. 3. The terms modem and data set are often used interchangeably.

data sink — A communications term referring to a device capable of accepting data signals from a transmission device. It may also check these signals and originate error control signals. Contrast with data source.

data source — A communications term referring to a device capable of originating data signals for a transmission device. It may also accept error control signals. Contrast with data sink.

data source interface — A typical unit provides 32 input lines for sensing external voltages relative to an externally provided reference level.

data station — A multipurpose remote-terminal calculator can be used for a broad range of communications applications, as well as for off-line jobs. This device gives branch offices, warehouses, remote reporting locations throughout a plant, or any other company outposts, the power to prepare source data locally and communicate directly with a centrally located computer. The data station features a wide choice of input/output devices, including paper tape and punched-card equipment, a keyboard, page printers, and an optical bar-code reader that introduces new applications possibilities.

data stream — Generally all data transmitted through a channel in a single read or write operation.

data summarization and histogram program

data terminal — Refers to a Data Summarization and Histogram Plot. This program calculates Mean, Variance, Standard Deviation, Skewness, Kurtosis, and the range for either Grouped or Ungrouped Data which is drawn either from a finite or infinite population. Also computes cell midpoints and frequencies of observations within each cell for summarizing data into a simple histogram of eight cells. The cell interval is constant.

data terminal — 1. A device which modulates and/or demodulates data between one input/output device and a data-transmission link. 2. Various typewriter, audio, or visual devices for inputting or receiving output of computers.

data terminal ready — Refers to an EIA RS-232-C designation applied to a control circuit used by a terminal or computer to tell its modem that the terminal or computer is ready for operation. In some applications this circuit is used to enable the modem to answer or terminate calls.

data terminal, video — In many systems video-data terminal and interrogator units include a processor which combines data entry and display. Each video data terminal operates over a single communications line and contains its own storage and character generator, capable of providing a selected character subset for display of up to 480 characters on various sized screens.

data, transaction — A set of data in a data-processing area, a record of occurrence of a new event or transaction, in which the incidence of the data is essentially random and unpredictable. Hours worked, quantities shipped, and amounts invoiced are examples from, respectively, the areas of payroll, accounts receivable, and accounts payable.

data transfer — There are generally three types of data transfer: programmed data transfers, program interrupt transfers, and direct memory access transfers. Programmed data transfer is the easiest and most direct method of handling data I/O. Program interrupt transfers provide an extension of programmed I/O capabilities by allowing the peripheral device to initiate a data transfer. The data break system uses direct memory access for applications involving the fastest data transfer rates.

data transfer, calculator — Data transfer between a calculator CPU and communications channels or terminals requires a serial I/O interface. In a conventional system, an extra board is needed to provide the control logic, serialization logic, and communications clocks. However, some programable communications-interface devices provide a universal synchronous/asynchronous receiver/transmitter (USART) on a single LSI chip. Often the USART is programmed by system software to operate in synchronous or asynchronous mode with user-defined data formats and "handshaking" sequences. The inclusion of the USART jumper-selectable RS-232-C and teletypewriter interfaces, together with a variable baud-rate generator often eliminates the need for an additional board.

data transmission systems — A series of circuits, modems, or other devices which transfer or translate information from one site or location to another.

data validity — Refers to various measures of verifiability of data, i.e., the results of specific tests performed on the data such as the forbidden code check. Such tests and checks verify the reliability of the data and thus its validity or degree of acceptability.

data word — 1. A word which may be primarily regarded as part of the information manipulated by a given program. A data word may be used to modify a program instruction, or to be arithmetically combined with other data words. 2. A data word often consists of 36 bits (or six 6-bit characters). Data is transferred on a word basis, 36 bits in parallel (some computers).

dating routine — A routine that computes and/or stores, where needed, a date such as current date, expiration date of a tape, etc.

datum — The quantities, characters, or symbols on which operations are performed by computers and other automatic equipment, and which may be stored or transmitted in the form of electrical signals, records on magnetic tape or punched cards, etc.

db — Abbreviation for "decibel." A unit expressing the ratio of two voltages, currents, or powers. It is equal to 20 times the common logarithm of the ratio of two voltages across or two currents through equal loads, or 10 times the common logarithm of the two powers. One db is approximately the smallest change in audible power that can be recognized by the human ear.

dc — An abbreviation for: direct current, direct coupled, digital computer, direction cycle, direct cycle, display console, decimal classification, data conversion, design change and detail condition.

dc analysis program, calculator — Networks that are strictly resistive can be quickly and easily analyzed by this program. Additionally, active devices, provided they can be modeled by only resistive elements and voltage-controlled sources, can be analyzed.
Features of the program include:
- Networks with up to 7 nodes and 15 branches can be analyzed,
- Input requirements consist of element values and node connections,
- Networks may be stored on tape cassette for future recall,
- Networks may be edited easily to show the effect of different elements, values, or connections,
- Tabular output includes node voltages, element currents and power dissipation.

Users can easily determine nodal voltages, power dissipation, etc., for complex resistive networks and perform bias-point analyses right at their desks. They also have the calculator printout to document their circuit configuration and analysis results.

dc couple — Refers to a modem or device which transmits a steady state of pulses rather than oscillating or alternating.

dc dump — A withdrawal of direct-current from a calculator which may result in loss of stored information.

de — Abbreviation for: display element, digital element, decision element, display equipment, division entry.

dead front — Concerns the act of joining of a connector that is designed in such a way that the contacts are recessed below the surface of the connector's body, in order to prevent accidental short-circuits, and to prevent the contacts from contacting other objects.

dead time — Any definite delay deliberately

debug — placed between two related actions in order to avoid overlap that might cause confusion or to permit a particular different event such as a control decision.

debug — 1. An instruction, program, or action designed in calculator software to search for, correct, and/or eliminate sources of errors in programming routines. There are many types of 'bugs' or 'glitches' that can be located by single step testers, specifically designed programs, or operational procedures. 2. To locate and correct any errors in a computer program. 3. To detect and correct malfunctions in the computer itself.

debug aids, program — DEBUG routines are relocatable object programs that provide aids for the efficient development of user's programs. The programs are designed to be used with many keyboards to allow the operator to perform the following debugging functions: printing the contents of registers or selected areas of memory; modifying the contents of registers or memory locations; providing instruction breakpoint halts or "snapshots" during the execution of a user's program; allowing the initiating of execution at a special point in a program; and searching memory.

debugged program — Refers to various programs that will perform actions in the logical sequence expected and produce accurate answers to one or more test problems which have been specifically designed to execute all foreseeable paths through the program.

debuggers — Debuggers are a class of system software that is designed to help the programmer discover the causes of problems found during the runtime testing in the checkout phases of his software development. Their features include the ability to stop the executing program and inquire as to the state of the machine. The machine state includes the content of all memory locations and registers. The features of the debuggers are a function of the machine architecture and special hardware facilities. Another type of debugger is called a "simulator." The simulator is a software program that takes as input the machine code for the "target" machine and simulates the target machine's changes of state on a "host" machine while offering various debugging facilities. However, the simulator cannot duplicate the actions of the input and output, particularly when the peripheral device timing is part of the run-time and check-out.

debugging programs, small calculators — Even the most experienced programmer finds "bugs" in his programs. These bugs range from mistakes in the original equations to mistakes in keying in the program. Wherever they occur, they need to be corrected and many units are designed to make this error-checking process as easy as possible. One method is to use program stops. Many times a "bug" in a program will stop program execution. To help identify why the calculator stopped in the middle of a program, users examine program stops. On some units the execution of a R/S in a program halts program execution at the R/S. Users can also execute line 00. Whenever line 00 is executed in a program, program execution halts at line 00, in some units. Another way is to press any key. Pressing any key (even accidentally) halts program execution. If a program has been stopped by pressing a key, be careful not to restart program execution in the middle of a digit entry key sequence within the program or between a prefix key and the corresponding operation. Use BST or SST to reposition the program pointer in either of these cases. (some units).

decay time — The time in which a voltage or current pulse will decrease to one-tenth of its maximum value. Decay time is proportional to the time constant of the circuit.

decentralized data processing — The housing and handling of data by individual subdivisions of an organization or at each geographical location of the parts of an organization.

decibel — 1. A standard unit expressing a loss or gain in transmission power levels. Abbreviated db. The term "dbm" is also used, when a power of one milliwatt is the reference level. Db indicates the ratio of power output to power input:

$$db = 10 \log \frac{P_1}{10 P_2}$$

decimal — 1. Pertaining to a characteristic or property involving a selection, choice, or condition in which there are ten possibilities. 2. Pertaining to the number representation system with a radix of ten.

decimal, binary coded (BCD) — Describing a decimal notation in which the individual decimal digits are represented by a pattern of ones and zeros, e.g., in the 8-4-2-1 coded decimal notation, the number twelve is represented as 00010010 for 1 and 2, respectively, whereas in pure or straight binary notation it is represented as 1100. Related to binary.

decimal, fixed — Restricts the number of decimals to that preselected.

decimal, floating — Refers to the absence of restrictions on the position of the decimal point.

decimal format, calculator — In some units the user selects the decimal position indicating number of digits to the right of the decimal point. Decimal shifts right automatically overriding selection if necessary. When input or results exceed a 10-digit mantissa, calculator automatically converts to exponential format.

decimal point display, multiple — For some calculators, the battery provides approximately 3 hours of continuous operation. By turning off the power when the calculator is not in immmediate use, the battery power will be conserved. To conserve power without losing program or results, users leave the calculator on, key in a • , and leave it there until ready to resume calculation. On these units, all decimal points light in the display when 2 to 5 minutes of operation time remain in the battery pack. Even when all decimal points are turned on, the true decimal position is known because an entire digit position is allocated to the true decimal position.

decision — 1. Most often concerns a comparison to determine a verification concerning the existence or non existence of a given condition as a result of developing an alternative action. 2. The computer operation of determining if a certain relationship exists between words in storage or registers, and taking alternative courses of action. This is effected by conditional jumps or equivalent techniques. Use of this term has given rise to the misnomer "magic brain"; actually, the process consists of making comparisons, by use of arithmetic, to determine the relationship of two terms, e.g.

decision box — equal, greater than, or less than. 3. Usually by comparison, a determination is completed concerning the existence or nonexistence of a given condition as a result of developing an alternative action.

decision box — A rectangle or other symbol on a flow chart used to mark a choice or branching in a sequence of programming.

decision branching — Like a computer, some units can be programmed to make decisions, because they can do conditional branching. Users can program them to test the relationship between two values, by means of these tests:

$$x < y \quad x \geq y \quad x \neq y \quad x = y$$

Depending on the outcome of the tests, the units will automatically skip a step of the program . . . or they will continue through the program in sequence. Or, by means of the "GO TO" key, they can program the unit to branch directly to a specified step, and then continue executing the program.

decision, logical — The choice or ability to choose between alternatives. Basically, this amounts to an ability to answer yes or no with respect to certain fundamental questions involving equality and relative magnitude; e.g., in an inventory application, it is necessary to determine whether or not there has been an issue of a given stock item.

decision making capabilities, calculator — . . . Some Series Calculators give users decision making capabilities like those of larger programmable calculators or even computers . . . Decisions like "skip if +" or "skip if $\emptyset$" . . . can easily be written into programs. Users can automatically "branch" to any portion of their program as well as loop, giving them extreme application flexibility.

decision making commands, calculator — These include a wide variety of commands that provide conditional and unconditional symbolic jumping, looping, and subroutine capabilities. They are available with the touch of a single key or a small combination of them.

decision making loops, calculator — In some units nine different decisions can be made in which the subsequent path of the program is determined by the results of calculations. Loops or iterations can thereby be set up which are performed until certain conditions are satisfied. Unconditional branchings to a specified location of the program are done with a simple SEARCH statement.

decision plan — A system or procedure used for making managerial decisions; i.e. rules either prepared in advance of specific events or developed at the time or on the scene and applied by men, machines, or combinations of these. Such plans include the exception principle, internal decision-making procedures, manual interrupt and intervention, variable or stochastic processing, and various adaptive and heuristic plans.

decision rules — The programmed criteria which an on-line, real-time system uses to make operating decisions. It is important to periodically review the decision rules which are being used by a system, because the nature of the problems to be solved changes over time and because new situations may have arisen which were not at first anticipated.

decision table — A table of all contigencies that are to be considered in the description of a problem, together with the actions to be taken. Decision tables are sometimes used in place of flowcharts for problem description and documentation.

decision table components — Decision tables are convenient where action or consequences can be set as results of a preceding set of "AND" conditions. A table is usually set up as a set of columns, the upper part of each column contains a list of conditions which may or may not be satisfied. The lower part of the column lists a set of actions to be taken of the set of conditions if satisfied. The rows of the table may indicate the type of conditions or the type of action.

deck — A collection of cards, commonly a complete set of cards which have been punched for a definite service or purpose.

deck, instruction — A deck of punched cards containing the data that defines the operations to be performed by a data processing system. The instructions comprising a program may be in machine language code or in the form of a compiler.

declaration — A declaration is represented by one or more instructions which specify the type, characteristics, or amount of data asssociated with identifiers.

declarative macro instruction — Utilized as a portion of an assembly language to instruct the compiler or assembly program to perform some action or take note of some condition. When used it does not result in any subsequent action by the object program.

decode — 1. To apply a code so as to reverse some previous encoding. 2. To determine the meaning of individual characters or groups of characters in a message. 3. To determine the meaning of an instruction from the set of pulses which describes the instruction, command, or operation to be performed. 4. To translate coded characters to a more understandable form.

decoder-drivers, calculator — The most common are the combined decoder-drivers intended primarily to drive LED displays. To be found in DIP packages, they are the standard products of such firms as Fairchild Semiconductor, Motorola, National, RCA and Texas Instruments. Monsanto markets its own drivers to drive its LED devices. Both bipolar (TTL) and MOS (including CMOS) technologies are employed.

decoders, seven-segment — Most common seven-segment decoders are in 16-pin DIP packs. Four pins are assigned to the input code; seven are assigned to output. In addition, one pin is assigned as lamp test LT. When it is set at logic "0", all segments will be illuminated to determine if there are any faults. Two other pins relate to the blanking function, that is, they can be used to switch off unnecessary zeros in a multidigit display to eliminate confusion in reading.

decoding — 1. Performing the internal operations by which a calculator determines the meaning of the operation code of an instruction, also sometimes applied to addresses. In interpretive routines and some subroutines, an operation by which a computer determines the meaning of parameters in the routine. 2. Translating a secretive language into the clear.

decoding functions, display — The task of decoding decimal input signals into switching drive signals for all displays, including the higher voltage gas-discharge devices, can now be handled by the main logic chip. Newer calculator and watch chips already include these functions. But many circuits still require drivers and their importance is expected to continue.

decrement — 1. A programming device or instruction designed to decrease the contents of a storage location. 2. The quantity by which a variable is decreased. 3. In some computers, a specific part of an instruction word. 4. To decrease the value of a number.

dedicated — Generally refers to machines, programs, or procedures that are designed or set apart for special or continued use. For example, a dedicated microprocessor can be one that has been designed or specifically programmed for a single or special group of applications, such as computerized games, appliances, traffic lights, calculators, etc. ROMs, as control devices, are usually the means of developing dedicated microprocessors. 2. Synonymous with leased or private lines or machines usually referring to communications equipment. 3. Reserved or committed to a specific use or application.

dedicated, leased line, private — A service offered by the common carriers in which a customer may lease, for his exclusive use, a circuit between two or more geographic points.

dedicated problem solving — One typical unit offers several software packages which include a prerecorded cartridge, special function key overlay, and easy-to-follow instructions for each program. All users do is set the switch to auto-start, slip in the cartridge, put the overlay in place, and turn on the unit. The first file will be automatically loaded and the program executed. The tedious set-up work is done for users.

dedicated problem solving (calculator) — On some advanced programmable calculators, a cartridge, key overlay, and AUTO START let users dedicate the calculator to solve specific problems. The cartridge carries the prerecorded program to the unit. The overlay labels up to 15 user-definable keys for single keystroke execution of program steps — that define a function special to a specific profession, unique operation, or a command required for peripherals. When users turn the power on, the AUTO START feature automatically loads File 0 and executes the program, on some systems.

dedicated, specific task calculator components —
(1) Dedicated, specific task applications
(2) Fixed program by special ROM
(3) Easy modification of program by keyboard
(4) Alarm system option
(5) Input guarding and measurement method
(6) Memory save optional feature
(7) Special system options

dedicated, specific task calculator systems — Many users need a thoroughly reliable data acquisition system devoted to monitoring a process, a specific set of plant operating equipment, or repetitive quality assurance testing on large batches of products. These systems can be furnished as a custom engineered data system expressly and economically designed to get specific data at lowest operating cost. These systems offer the possibility of revising the data input, format, processing, alarms, and outputs now or in the future. The calculator keyboard permits individual channel changes or sweeping system-wide changes with fingertip control. If the data system environment is industrial, with noise and off-ground signals on channels, calculators provide the proven trouble-free combination of channel isolation plus common mode rejection gained through experience with hundreds of systems. Memory save option guards the system against power outage amnesia.

definable keys and tape cartridges — Many advanced programmable calculators combine sophistication and simplicity. Sophistication for the power users need; simplicity for the ease of operation they want. Most users are not required to be able to program to use the calculator's potential. Many simply approach the calculator with a key overlay and a program cartridge. To operate they can place the overlay over the user definable keys, slip in the cartridge, and turn on the power. The calculator automatically loads and executes File 0 on some prerecorded cartridges they have chosen from available supplier-provided software. Problem solving begins at once.

define — To establish a value for a variable or symbol or to establish what the variable represents.

definition — 1. The resolution and sharpness of an image, or the extent to which an image is brought into sharp relief. 2. The degree with which a communication system reproduces sound images or messages.

degradation — A special condition when the system operates at reduced levels of service. Circumstances such as this are usually caused by unavailability of various equipment units or subsystems.

DEG/RAD keys — Refers to Angular mode selection—users flip a switch to perform trig operations in either of two angular modes: degrees or radians. Users can also convert angles from one mode to the other push-button fast.

DEL — The delete character.

delay, circuit — The time between phases is the circuit delay—the time it takes to change state after receiving an input signal.

delayed access — Access which is delayed because of procedures relating to batch processing or the inherent slow speed of input/output of storage devices.

delay element — Refers to that circuitry or electronic mechanism which accepts data temporarily, and emits the same data after a specific interval.

delete key — The Delete key removes displayed instruction and automatically shifts following instructions up when in the learn mode.

delta — The Greek letter delta (Δ) represents any quantity which is much smaller than any other quantity of the same unit appearing in the same problem. Also refers to a magnetic cell, the difference between the partial-select outputs of the same cell in a one state and in a zero state.

demand processing — The processing of data as quickly as it becomes available or ready. This is real-time and thus avoids the need for storage of any appreciable amount of unprocessed data.

demodulation — 1. Also called detection, usually refers to the operation on a previously modulated wave so that it will have substantially the same characteristics as the original modulating wave. 2. The process of retrieving an original signal from a modulated carrier wave. This technique is used in data sets to make communication signals compatible with business machine signals.

demodulator—modulator (modem) — Refers to the common device which can perform both modulation and demodulation for signals transmitted through communications facilities.

demultiplexer — A device used to recover individual signals, which have been combined for transmission over a single channel.

density, bit — The number of binary digits that are stored in a given linear area or volume.

dependent variable — A variable whose value is determined by some function of another quantity or representation, i.e., the standard expression is $y = f(x)$, where y is considered the dependent variable because its value is determined by the value of x and the nature of the function to be performed.

depreciation schedules straight line program —

Let PV = original value of asset (less salvage value)
n = lifetime number of periods of asset
B_k = book value at time period K
D = each year's depreciation
k = number of time period, i.e., 1, 2, 3, ..., or n

Then, B_k and D can be calculated by the following formulas:

1. $D = PV/n$
2. $B_k = PV - kD$

depreciation schedules sum-of-the-year's digits program —

Let n = life time number of periods of asset
S = salvage value
D_k = depreciation over time period k
B_k = book value at time period k
PV = original value of asset (less salvage value)
k = number of time period, i.e., 1, 2, 3, ..., or n

Then, D_k and B_k can be calculated by the following formulas:

1. $D_k = \dfrac{2(n - k + 1)}{n(n + 1)} PV$
2. $B_k = S + \dfrac{(n - k) D_k}{2}$

depreciation schedules variable rate declining balance program —

Let PV = original value of asset (less salvage value)
n = lifetime periods of asset
R = depreciation rate (given by user)
D_k = depreciation at time period k
B_k = book value at time period k
k = number of time period, i.e., 1, 2, 3, ..., or n

Then, D_k and B_k can be calculated by the following formulas:

1. $D_k = PV \dfrac{R}{n} \left(1 - \dfrac{R}{n}\right)^{k-1}$
2. $B_k = PV \left(1 - \dfrac{R}{n}\right)^{k}$

If R = 2 the program gives the double declining balance method. If R = 1.5 the program gives the 150% declining balance method.

descriptive statistics — Descriptive statistics involves methods that, essentially do not go beyond the arithmetic data. Inductive statistics involves generalization, predictions, estimations, and decisions. Descriptive statistics are also called arithmetic statistics and include such parameters as mean, median, mode, and standard deviation.

design simulations — Prediction and evaluation of component, network, or system characteristics; for example, filter synthesis or dynamic analysis of control systems.

design verification — Proving that the finished design meets the operating specifications for the finished product or system; for example, checking heat loss and gain vs. capacity for a finished heating, ventilating, and air conditioning system.

desk check — A procedure of analyzing or inspecting a written program or specific instructions for errors in logic or syntax without the requirement or use of computing or peripheral equipment.

desk-top calculators — Some desk-top calculators enable users to log, compare, and analyze data the moment it arrives, and to eliminate all manual entries. These systems can store data and match many of the capabilities of minicomputers. Calculator systems combine the stand-alone data recorder with the data analysis computer. New systems are especially useful in quality control testing and monitoring; design engineering testing and documentation; production testing, monitoring and control; and in various scientific and medical laboratories. Systems include the calculator, a mainframe power source, and interface plug-in, standard software for data acquisition, and standard accessories and options. Actual data acquisition is accomplished by other instruments which are plugged into the calculator mainframe in any desired configuration.

desk-top lock-in printer (for hand-held units) — Some hand-held users are able to plug their units into a printing unit and get a tape copy of their calculations fast. Some units provide lock-on security as well as power. Generally they also print instructions or results without halting program execution, and can trace step by step. With printers, users are able to verify that keyed-in instructions match those on their Coding Form. Users can have quick program documentation for ready reference and have the means to verify that a program was based on correct formulation.

destructive read — The sensing of data using a process which inherently destroys (erases) the record of the data which has been read. In some core storage, reading is destructive, but such data is usually regenerated after each readout. In tapes, drums, disks, etc., reading is usually accomplished without destruction.

destructive test — A test of equipment capability in which results prove to be a cause of permanent degradation due to the type of performance exacted from the equipment tested; for example, the application of excess power, voltages, heat, etc., to cause eventually the circuits or elements to burn, shatter, burst, or otherwise be destroyed.

detail chart — A flowchart in minute detail of a sequence of operations. The symbols of the detail chart usually denote an individual step or computer operation. A detail chart is more detailed than a logic chart, usually reflects the particular computer characteristics and instructions, and facilitates the actual coding of the program in the manner intended by the programmer preparing the chart.

detail record — The specific listing of data which is a unit part of a major classification of larger segments or a total classification of data.

determinant and inverse of a 2×2 matrix program —

Let $A = \begin{bmatrix} a_{11} & a_{12} \\ a_{21} & a_{22} \end{bmatrix}$ be a 2×2 matrix.

The determinant of A denoted by Det A or |A| is evaluated by the following formula:

$$\text{Det } A = a_{22} a_{11} - a_{12} a_{21}$$

Also, the program evaluates the multiplicative inverse A^{-1} of A. The following formula is used:

$$A^{-1} = \begin{bmatrix} a_{22}/\text{Det } A & -a_{12}/\text{Det } A \\ -a_{21}/\text{Det } A & a_{11}/\text{Det } A \end{bmatrix}$$

determinant of a 3×3 matrix program —

Let $A = \begin{bmatrix} a_{11} & a_{12} & a_{13} \\ a_{21} & a_{22} & a_{23} \\ a_{31} & a_{32} & a_{33} \end{bmatrix}$ be a 3×3 matrix.

The determinant of A denoted by |A| or Det A, is calculated by expanding A by minors about the first column. The formula is:

$$\text{Det } A = a_{11} \begin{vmatrix} a_{22} & a_{23} \\ a_{32} & a_{33} \end{vmatrix} - a_{21} \begin{vmatrix} a_{12} & a_{13} \\ a_{32} & a_{33} \end{vmatrix} + a_{31} \begin{vmatrix} a_{12} & a_{13} \\ a_{22} & a_{23} \end{vmatrix}$$
$$= a_{11} [a_{22} a_{33} - a_{23} a_{32}] - a_{21} [a_{33} a_{12} - a_{32} a_{13}] + a_{31} [a_{23} a_{12} - a_{13} a_{22}]$$

deterministic simulation — A simulation in which a fixed relationship exists between input parameters and output results for each action, value, event, etc. such that given input parameters will always result in the same output. (Contrast with simulation, stochastic.)

device character control — A control character which is used to control various devices associated with computing or telecommunications systems, i.e., particularly the switching to on or off of the devices.

device independence — Refers to the ability to request I/O operations without regard for the characteristics of specific types of input/output devices.

device selection, terminal system — On some units, the SELECT statement is used both in the Immediate Mode and under program control to select a device for particular I/O operations (PRINT, INPUT, TAPE, DISK). Device selections are maintained independently for input and output operations, allowing programs to be modified easily to work with any I/O device.

DFT — Diagnostic function test.

DFT table — An area of main storage that serves as a logical connector between the user's problem program and a file. The DFT table can also be used to provide control information for any transfer of data.

diagnostic — Refers to the detection, discovery, and further isolation of a malfunction and/or mistake.

diagnostic compiler — The compiler diagnostics are of four categories:
precautionary — Print warning message and continue compilation.
correctable — Try to correct the error, print explanatory message, and continue compilation.
uncorrectable — If intent of programmer cannot be determined, print a diagnostic message, reject the clause or statement, and continue compilation.
catastrophic — When so many errors have occurred that no more useful diagnostic information can be produced, terminate the compilation.
Other outputs from the compiler include extensive diagnostic messages, source-language listings, machine-language listings, and special cross-reference listings of name definitions and their references.

diagnostic function test (DFT) — A program to test overall system reliability.

diagnostic routine — 1. A routine designed to locate a malfunction in the calculator or a mistake in coding, or both, 2. Routines for diagnosing programming mistakes are most often service routines, whereas routines for diagnosing mistakes in data are usually specific to a particular application.

diagnostics, microprogrammed — Diagnostics and service aids may be easily implemented in the control portion of the system with ROMs. Some very small systems store their diagnostics in ROM control. Many models of large systems also do this and this trend will spread. Microprogrammed implementations are oriented toward servicing and diagnostics. For example, large portions of the control network can be checked by putting parity on the output of the control store. Furthermore, the microprocessor can both set and test internal control states not available to the machine language programmer.

diagnostics, system — A program resembling the operational program rather than a systematic logical-pattern program which will detect overall system malfunctions rather than isolate or locate faulty components.

diagnostic terminal — Some communications adapters will turn off a terminal when there is a terminal malfunction and send a message to the host computer stating whether the line, communications adapter or terminal is malfunctioning.

diagnostic test — The running of a machine program or routine for the purpose of discovering a failure or a potential failure of a machine element, and to determine its location or its potential location.

diagnostic trace routine — A particular type of diagnostic program designed to perform checks on other programs or to demonstrate such operations. The output of a trace program may include instructions of the program which is being checked and intermediate results of those instructions arranged in the order in which the instructions are executed.

dichotomy — A division into subordinate classes; e.g., all white and all nonwhite, or all zero and all nonzero.

dictionary — A book or list of code names or keys used in a program, routine, or system with the description or identification of their designed or intended meaning in that program, routine, or system.

dictionary, automatic — The component of a language-translating machine which will provide a word for word substitution from one language to another. In automatic-searching systems, the automatic dictionary is the component which substitutes codes for words or phrases during the encoding operation. (Related to machine translation.)

dictionary, data element (DED) — An organized

dictionary, reverse code

listing of data elements (and their associated information) in a given system.

dictionary, reverse code — An alphabetic or numeric alphabetic arrangement of codes, associated with their corresponding English words or terms. Related to code, dictionary.

difference of two proportions program — Confidence Interval on the Difference of Proportions. This program computes confidence intervals on the difference between two proportions using a normal approximation.

differential equation — An equation which contains derivatives of differentials of an unknown function, i.e., the solution satisfies the equation identically throughout some interval of x. The general solution represents the set of functions that satisfy the equation. Related to physical problems, the arbitrary constants are determined from additional conditions which must be satisfied. Most differential equations result from mathematical relations and descriptions of motion and change.

differential equation, partial — Refers to differential equation which contains more than one independent variable and/or derivatives or differentials of more than one independent variable.

differentiate — 1. To find the derivative of a function, 2. to deliver an output that is the derivative with respect to time of the input, or, 3. to distinguish objects or ideas from others.

differentiation — A process of the calculus for determining rates of change and especially for finding maximum and minimum as well as points of inflection.

digital — Pertaining to the utilization of discrete integral numbers in a given base to represent all the quantities that occur in a problem or a calculation. It is possible to express in digital form all information stored, transferred, or processed by a dual-state condition; e.g., on-off, open-closed, and true-false.

digital/analog converter (DAC) — Converts digital signals into a continuous electrical signal suitable for input to an analog computer.

digital (BCD) input — An important system option of data acquisition units is the digital input port. It permits taking data directly from such sources as digital counters, digital voltmeters, digital output transducers such as encoders, and similar devices. This capability makes data acquisition systems available at reasonable prices. On some systems a total of 16 different digital input devices, each with up to 8 digits of BCD (binary coded decimal) data, may be used. Digital channels are scanned after all specified analog channels, and the combined scan is outputted as programmed. Digital input circuit cards are housed in a special card cage at the rear of some units. One card handles each digital channel, and eight cards fit in one cage. If only digital channels are used, all 16 cards may be housed internally. Any additional analog channel inputs would require a separate enclosure. (some systems)

digital computer — A computer which processes information represented by combinations of discrete or discontinuous data as compared with an analog computer for continuous data. More specifically, it is a device for performing sequences of arithmetic and logical operations, not only on data but its own program. Still more specifically it is a stored program digital computer capable of performing sequences of internally stored instructions, as opposed to calculators, such as card programmed calculators, on which the sequence is impressed manually. Related to machine, data processing.

digital flatbed plotter — Typically this provides continuous line or point plotting of curves and data. The plotting surface is 31 inches by 48 inches. The plotter uses any type of paper including vellum, linen and Mylar. Fiber tip, ballpoint, or drafting pens can be used. (Some units)

digital input — On some units digital input cards accept 12 bits of data from digital measuring instruments, push-buttons, switches, relays and other digital devices in the form of logic levels or contact closures. Digital data sources with more than 12 bits of data use several digital input cards.

digital interface — A digital interface is designed as a general purpose input/output system for some electronic programmable calculators. It allows these versatile highly-sophisticated systems to be used in a wide variety of data acquisition, process control, and data collection, system control, and similar applications by putting the calculator "on-line" to the outside world. The system provides calculators the input/output versatility of conventional minicomputer systems while retaining the low-cost, ease of programming, and computational ability characteristic of programmable calculators as a group.

Most laboratory instruments, process signal conditioning systems, voltmeters and other instruments, manufactured in the last five years are equipped with binary-coded-decimal or binary digital outputs. A digital interface provides the means for connecting these devices to the calculator. Transfer of data from instruments and control systems is by means of individual plug-in cards designed for a specific application. There are, for instance, cards for digital voltmeters, clocks, timers, etc. Other cards are used for output functions such as relay contact closures, data output from the calculator for external displays, counter preset systems, and similar applications, as well as analog inputs by means of an analog-to-digital converter card in conjunction with both reed-relay and MOS multiplexer cards.

digital — logic types — The most 'regular' types of digital logic families of elements are the transistor-transistor-logic (TTL), emitter-coupled logic (ECL), and the complementary metal-oxide semiconductor logic (CMOS). Each of these families has its own set of parameters and applications, and each is encountered in many modern microprocessor applications. The TTL family has been the most widely used of the three families.

digital plotter, calculator — Generally pictures give a quickly-grasped idea of a calculator's mathematical data. But users need accurate detail also. A typical digital plotter can make quick and digitally accurate presentation pieces: statistical data, histograms, schematics, sales and production curves. On some units Vectors are printed out at 15 to 22 inches per second. There's no lag. While the pen is moving the calculator is computing the next move.

digital system, man-machine — An organization of people, digital computers and equipment to regulate, and control events and achieve system objectives.

digital timer, calculator — A unique, useful feature of some calculators is a 100-hour digital

digital-to-analog (D-A) conversion — Production of an analog signal, whose instantaneous magnitude is proportional to the value of a digital input.

timer. It's accurate to ±0.01% and measures time in hours, minutes, seconds, and even hundredths of a second. And users can store up to 10 different points in time while it is running.

digital-to-analog (D-A) conversion — Production of an analog signal, whose instantaneous magnitude is proportional to the value of a digital input.

digital to analog converter (DAC) — A typical unit provides two analog output channels ranging from 0 to +10 volts with 8 bits per channel resolution. Also provides two logic level outputs for external device control.

digital X-Y plotter — One manufacturer has introduced a high speed, high resolution digital plotter, plug-compatible with other calculators. Uses of the digital x-y plotter include bar charts, graphs, point plots, diagrams and other graphs. The digital design provides excellent linearity and the simplified circuitry eliminates downtime. When the plotter is given a set of coordinates to move to, it calculates the distance on each axis and internally computes the ratio of speeds in x and y directions to make the move smoothly. The plotter knows how far the pen has to travel and governs its acceleration accordingly.

digitize — A process which is used to convert an analog measurement of a specific physical variable into a number expressed in digits in a system of notation.

digitizer — A digitizer is a device that reads a curve, or any irregular shape, as a series of discrete points, and then converts these to a series of digital X-Y coordinates. To make these entries, the digitizer is used to trace the shape and the calculator prints out the dimensions and area of the line or contained shape. Some digitizers allow the user to directly process graphical data such as X-rays, blueprints, strip-chart recordings, cut-and-fill profiles, to name a few.

digitizer accuracy — The sum total of all factors which tend to cause deviations in coordinate outputs and actual point locations. The accuracy specification should assume that all factors are at their adverse limits. For the Graf/Pen accuracy is within 0.1% of full scale.

digitizer, advanced calculator — A typical digitizer reads a curve or any irregular shape as a series of discrete points into the calculator then prints out the dimensions of the line and the area of the contained shape.

digitizer, calculator — This is a unique machine that reads a curve, or any irregular shape, as a series of discrete points, and then converts these to a series of digital X-Y coordinates. To make these entries, users trace the shape and their calculator prints out dimensions and area of the line or contained shape. With the Digitizer users can directly process graphical data such as X-rays, blueprints, strip-chart recordings, cut-and-fill profiles, to name a few.

digitizer repeatability — The deviation obtained when a single point is digitized an infinite number of times. For the Graf/Pen it is ± 1 count. Thus, for a point with a coordinate reading of 085.6 millimeters, no matter how many times the point is digitized the reading will always be 085.5, 085.6 or 085.7 millimeters.

digitizer tablets — Most digitizers have sensing devices imbedded in a special "tablet" on which material to be digitized must be placed. To sense the location of the stylus used to draw or trace lines, the stylus must exert pressure on or be within capacitive distance of the tablet.

digit(s), equivalent binary — The number of binary digits required to express a number in another base with the same precision, e.g., approximately 3-1/3 binary digits are required to express in binary form each digit of a decimal number. For the case of coded decimal notation, the number of binary digits required is usually 4 times the number of decimal digits.

diode — 1. A device having two terminals which conducts electricity more easily in one direction than in the other. 2. A device utilized to permit current flow in one direction in a circuit, and to inhibit current flow in the other direction. In computers, these diodes are primarily germanium or silicon crystals. 3. A vacuum tube with two active electrodes.

diode-transistor-logic, (DTL) — Logic employing diodes with transistors used only as inverting amplifiers.

DIP devices — More and more devices are becoming available in DIP form. Quite complex systems can be built. Some typical applications include:
- Multiword input and/or output devices.
- Programmable instrument interfaces.
- Interprocessor buffers.
- Custom peripheral controllers.

Interfacing of:
- Microprocessors
- A/D converters
- Multiplexers
- Counters
- Shift Registers
- ROM and RAM memories
- Arithmetic logic units
- Programmable logic arrays (PLA)

DIP — Dual In-Line Package — 1. The most popular IC packaging in the mid-1970s in the plastic dual-in-line case, using plastic for economic reasons and the dual-in-line package (DIP) configuration for manufacturing efficiency. 2. Chips are enclosed in Dual In-Line Packages which take their names from the double, parallel rows of leads which connect them to the circuit board. DIPs are sometimes also called "bugs."

direct-access — A type of storage medium which allows information to be accessed by positioning the medium or accessing mechanism directly to the information required, thus permitting direct addressing of data locations.

direct data capture — A technique employed in cash registers, or on sales slips whereby customer account numbers, the amount of the purchase, and other information are automatically recorded, read by an optical reading device, and sent to the computer to be processed. Its use permits the generation of more timely and accurate transaction data.

direct digital control (DDC) — Control action in which control is obtained by a digital device which establishes the signal to the final control element.

direct-insert routine — 1. A separately coded sequence of instructions that is inserted in another instruction sequence directly in low order of the line. 2. A directly inserted subroutine to the main line program specifically where it is required. 3. A subroutine that must be located and inserted into the main routine at each place it is used.

directly proportional — A term used in contradistinction to the term inversely proportional. Two quantities are directly proportional when they both increase or decrease together, and in such a manner that their ratio shall be constant.

direct memory register addressing keys — The Store Key stores a displayed number into one of many addressable memory registers. The Recall Key displays data stored in a selected register. The Exchange Key exchanges contents of a selected register with the displayed number.

direct numerical control (DNC) — A system connecting a set of numerically controlled machines to a common memory for part program or machine program storage, with provision for on-demand distribution of data to the machines. Direct numerical control systems typically have additional provisions for collection, display or editing of part programs, operator instructions, or data related to the numerical control process.

directory — A group of records containing information used in locating and retrieving elements of the disk-resident system. There are six directories in the basic operating system, system directory, transient directory, core image directory, macro directory, relocatable directory, and phase directory.

direct reference address — A virtual address that is not modified by indirect addressing, but may be modified by indexing.

disabled — 1. Refers to a state of the central processing unit that prevents the occurrence of certain types of interruptions. Synonymous with masked. 2. In communications, pertaining to a state in which a transmission control unit cannot accept incoming calls on a line.

disc drives — Typical disc drives are highly reliable, random access, moving-head memory devices, compactly designed for use as peripheral units in large, small and now, microcomputer systems. Typically a photoelectric positioning system, working in conjunction with a velocity transducer and voice coil driven actuator, provides fast and accurate head positioning over a wide temperature range. Cartridge interchangeability between drives is becoming standard. A typical dual platter disc drive utilizes one permanent disc and one removable cartridge to provide 4.9 million bytes of storage. Some reliable drives have an average access time of less than 30 milliseconds, and a data transfer rate of 2.5 million bits per second.

discontinuous — Broken off, interrupted, gaping. Discontinuous function is one which does not vary continuously as the variable increases uniformly. The function

$$\frac{b}{a}\sqrt{x^2 - a^2}$$

is a discontinuous function.

discrete — Pertains to separate and distinct parts of data such as holes in a card, or graphic characters.

discrete data — A representation for a variable which may assume any of several distinct states; i.e., sex, race. Usually coded. Conventional usage in computing excludes measures of a quantal nature (i.e., number of children in a family). (Contrast with continuous data.)

discrete programming — A class of optimization problems in which the values of all the variables are restricted to integers. Normally, the optimization problem without this integer restriction is linear programming, additional adjectives indicate variations; for example, integer quadratic programming, etc.

discrete proportion — Discrete proportion is one in which the ratio of the first term to the second is equal to that of the third to the fourth; thus, $3:6::8:16$. The proportion $3:::12:24$ is not a discrete but a continued proportion, or a geometrical progression. A discrete quantity is one which is discontinuous in its parts.

discrete series — A discrete series is one in which the differences between successive observations are always finite in character, that is, there are no values falling between the observed values. For example, shoes are made in sizes 5, 5½, 6, 6½, etc. Since no shoes are made in intermediate sizes — e.g., between 5 and 5½ — the differences between sizes are always finite.

discrete simulation — The major components of the system are individually identifiable (discrete). Example: queuing networks.

discrete units — Distinct units of a digital nature as opposed to a continuous information flow, which is analog.

discrete variable — A variable is said to be discrete if it assumes only a finite number of values or as many values as there are whole numbers. The number of heads which we obtain in, say, 10 flips of a coin is a discrete variable because it cannot assume values other than 0, 1, 2, 3, ... and 10.

discrimination — Refers to the skipping of various instructions as developed by a predetermined set of conditions as programmed. If a conditional jump is not used, the next instructions would follow in the normal proper sequence.

disc storage — A computer memory device capable of storing information magnetically on a disc similar in appearance to a phonograph record.

disjunction — The logical operation which makes use of the OR operator or the logical sum. The disjunction of two variables, or expressions, may be written as A + B, A, OR B, A union B. These may also be described as a union when using Venn diagrams.

disk — A flat circular magnetic plate, on which data can be stored by selective magnetization.

disk accessing — Refers to the process of or methods used in transferring data to and from a disk file. Disk units and access routines vary widely in their sophistication: access can be accomplished either by using physical addresses (actual disk locations) or various levels of symbolic or keyed-record addressing procedures. Some disk drives can locate a desired record using addressing logic contained within the unit itself to find a keyed record, thus leaving more productive time available to the central processing unit while the record is being sought.

disk average access time — Included in access time is latency which typically ranges from 12.5 to 20 milliseconds.

disk cartridge bit density — Although bit densities are almost always 2200 bits per inch, the new generation of disks has increased density to over 4000 bpi, with resulting increases in transfer rates and capacities.

disk cartridge drive capacity — Most manufacturers list unformatted capacity in megabytes to achieve a common spec. However, OEM manufacturers usually speak of unformatted capacity in terms of bits, and end-user manufacturers specify formatted capacity in terms of words. In the fixed-removable systems, the drive capacity is equal to that of the fixed plus removable disk. Drive capacities generally range from 2.5 to 10 MB. (megabits — 1 million bits

disk cartridge software — Diagnostics and drivers are usually supplied with the disk system. In some cases, independents also offer an operating system, and in other cases the systems are software compatible with certain mini disk operating systems.

disk cartridge speed — Disk rotational speed is usually 1500 or 2400 rpm. Transfer rates and access times improve with higher disk rotational speed. If both speeds are available, 1500 rpm is used to determine the specs.

disk cartridge track density — Track densities are typically 100 or 200 tracks per inch.

disk cartridge transfer rate — Rates are usually 200 or 312 kilobytes per second. However, recent innovations have increased the rate to over 500 KB per second. Most new high transfer rates are due to intelligent controllers.

disk cartridge types — Exceptions to the norm can result by increasing bit densities, providing intelligent controllers, or increasing rotational speed. Disk cartridges come in two versions: the top loading IBM-standard 5440 cartridge type and the front loading IBM-standard 2315 cartridge type. There's a one-drive cabinet with either one fixed, one removable, or one fixed combined with one removable disk. Fixed disk drives are not generally used with calculators.

disk cartridge vs floppy disk — The single-platter disk cartridge is just as removable as a disk pack with specifications on the same order of magnitude, but a lot smaller and less expensive. Drive costs are about three times that of a floppy, but performance characteristics are an order of magnitude better. Whereas the floppy has an access time averaging 300 milliseconds, the disk cartridge averages 55 milliseconds. The floppy stores 250 kilobytes per drive, the cartridge drive stores up to 10 megabytes up to 53 MB. Some floppies have approached the cartridge's transfer rate of 187 kilobytes per second, but most are an order of magnitude lower.

disk drive system — A typical unit consists of a floppy disk drive, power supply (110-125 v AC, 60 Hz), cooling fan, disk buffer and address select electronics. It is capable of storing up to 300,000 words on a flexible disk. Up to 16 disk drives can be controlled by one disk controller.

disk editing — A TEXT EDITOR can be loaded into a microcomputer from a floppy disk in less than two seconds. The user can edit a named disk file, merge files, combine files, and reassign the input and output devices at any time during the editing process using the logical I/O assignment feature of microcomputer monitors.

diskette operating systems — Diskette operating systems substantially reduce the time required to assemble, edit and execute programs. On many systems a diskette operating system is available to speed the microcompute development cycle. One diskette operating system includes an intelligent disk controller, a diskette drive and a powerful software system called IDOS. Users save a great deal of time and effort with IDOS, because they can assemble, edit and execute programs in seconds. Equally important, IDOS includes comprehensive file management capabilities which enable users to symbolically represent program and data files. This makes development work easier. For example, when users begin an assembly operation, they can load the macro assembler into the MDS in seconds. They name source and destination files, and IDOS automatically takes care of the assembly operation without any further action. Symbolic disk files can be created, edited and executed quite easily.

diskette sectoring — There are two methods of sectoring: hard-sectoring and soft-sectoring. Hard-sectoring identifies each sector by holes punched in the diskette (one hole per sector). Soft-sectoring identifies the sectors by magnetic codes written on the diskette. Both methods, however, have a hole, called the index hole, in the diskette to identify the beginning of the tracks, which start on the same radius. When the diskette spins, a beam of light is detected by a photoelectric cell that signals the controller that the track has begun.

disk file — 1. Refers to various disk units consisting of a drive, channel, and the fixed or removable disks. 2. An associated set of records of the same format, identified by a unique label.

disk file management — Basically a microcomputer Disk Operating System (MDOS) provides total file management capability. Named disk files of varying lengths can be created and deleted quickly and easily. Any logical input or output device can be assigned to any named disk file on any one of up to eight floppy disk drives. Named disk files can be copied, merged, assembled, joined and otherwise manipulated as the user desires. Upon command, the directory of a diskette on any floppy disk drive can be listed on the console output device.

disk file subsystem — A typical unit provides 23.4 million bytes of storage using a standard 11 high removable pack. The controller handles up to 2 drives for a maximum capacity of 46 million bytes. Average access time is 32 milliseconds for some units.

disk memory — A non-programmable bulk-storage random access memory consisting of a magnetizable coating on one or both sides of a rotating thin circular plate. Memory latency time is of the order of hundreds of milliseconds.

disk operating system (DOS) — Many such programs are data communications oriented disk based operating systems. They feature both multi-terminal and multitasking capabilities and allow full control of both hardware and software operations through the system console, or any batch input device.

disk operating system (DOS)/support components — In many systems, DOS supports the following languages: assemblers and utilities; BASIC and FORTRAN IV languages; complete macro assemblers; text editors, as flexible symbolic and character oriented editors for generating and easy maintenance of source files; link editors, that link together user and library programs into a single load file — the resulting file can be output to specified devices; object loaders which are specific relocating and linking loaders that load both object and binary programs into memory from practically any specified device, and other I/O devices.

disk operating system, ROM — Many users suggest any program can be enabled in a ROM. Here are some common examples: 1. A computer system that uses a disk may have a ROM program to load the first disk sector into the beginning of memory. By storing initial operating system programs on the first sector of disk, users can instantly address the computer system. 2. If data collection is accompanied by fast Fourier transform, the Fourier transform programs (and coefficient tables) may be enabled in a ROM. 3. Any frequently exercised mathematical routines could be enabled in ROM's. Such routines may include: numerical integration, statistical tests, mathematical functions such as x^n, $x^{1/n}$, Sin s, Cos x, etc. Although it is less frequently used on a day-to-day basis than other computer capabilities, Read Only Memory is valuable for very specific applications in a computer system.

disk operation — Refers to a system that can address numerous disk drive units with varying capacities from 0.25 to 10 megabytes.
Each disk operates in two modes: automatic file cataloging and absolute sector addressing. With catalogue operations, programs and data files can be saved and accessed automatically by name, without keeping track of sector addresses on the disk. The absolute disk operations permit the user to specify disk sector addresses when saving and loading programs and data. An extensive set of support operations is provided, including the ability to copy backup disk platters and list the catalogue index in a single statement.

disk pack — Refers to various removable direct access storage devices containing magnetic disks on which data is stored. Disk packs are mounted on a disk storage drive, such as the IBM 2311 Disk Storage Drive.

disks, multiple fixed — Multiple fixed disks provide an avenue for capacity expansion while still preserving the utility of the removable cartridge. Each additional fixed disk allows an increase in storage from a minimum of 5 MB up to 10-20 MB. This feature allows electronic track switching up and down the cylinders and sharply reduces time delays due to moving head seeks. The addition of fixed heads on one or more fixed disks strongly enhances program and file swapping performance. Improvements of this kind put cartridge disks into respectable competition with the currently available "5 high" and "10 high" disk pack systems in capacity, performance and economics. Moreover, the multiple fixed disks plus removable cartridge combination provides a backup capability not available in removable disk pack systems that have no fixed disk storage.

dispatching system — One of the basic applications of real-time, communication-based systems, dispatching systems respond to demand by assigning resources to meet it, then reporting accordingly. For example, a system that assigns inventory to fill orders. In this case a dispatching system must reduce the recorded balances, prepare the appropriate documents for the warehouses where the items are stocked, and issue reorder documents when inventory levels become too low. The dispatching system also performs such functions as financial accounting, payroll, and management reports on daily operations.

display — 1. Lights, annunciators, numerical indicators, or other operator output devices at consoles or remote stations. 2. An electronic means for output display of numeric entries and answers. The five basic technologies are: LED (light emitting diode), LCD (liquid crystal display), gas discharge, fluorescent tube display, and cathode ray tube display (CRT).

display and readout brightness — One major problem concerning the brightness of displays and readouts stems from the industry's use of two units of measurement. LEDs, for example, are most commonly specified in millicandelas (mcd), a measure of luminous flux per unit solid angle. On the other hand, incandescent displays are usually specified in ft-lamberts, often referred to as luminance or intensity per unit area. For conversion purposes, ft.-lamberts = $1/\pi$ (cd/ft^2), where ft^2 refers to the area of the display surface.

display and readout characteristics — When deciding on a display to incorporate into a design, users should consider three important selection factors: power budget, ambient lighting condition and message format. When one of these factors forms a paramount constraint in a specific design, the choice becomes easy. For example, when only microwatts are available to power a specific display, liquid crystal technology becomes the choice. Or, if a user display must operate in intense sunlight, high-brightness and (high-power-consuming) incandescent technology takes precedence. When long messages must be displayed, high-voltage gas-discharge panels, which can read-out up to eight lines of 32 characters each, become the technology of choice.
Rarely, however, are design choices so clear. In most cases users must trade-off power, brightness, size, packaging and display message flexibility. For these situations, light emitting diode displays appear to offer the most versatility. Users can get them in character heights ranging from 0.09" to 1", in at least four colors, with medium-level power consumption, with built-in decoding and latch circuitry, and with a variety of character formats and packaging configurations, some with built-in magnifying lenses.

display and readout packages — Displays come in a variety of packages, ranging from standard-size DIPs to nonstandard modules and panels. Besides the display itself, the packages often contain additional circuitry. Such circuitry may include decoders, drivers and latches, as well as special circuitry for display multiplexing, storage registers and provisions for shifting decimal points and accessing signs.

display and readout types — To economize on the number of active display elements within each readout, purely numeric characters are most commonly formed with an array of seven illuminated segments. Said to be invented by Dialight, the seven-segment format can be implemented with LEDs, LCDs and incandescent units, using monolithic elements on discrete illuminators. For more complex character shapes, like alphanumerics and special symbols, most displays use dot matrices, most commonly 5×7 or 7×9.

display, blurring (small calculators) — During execution of a stored program, the display continuously changes and is purposely illegible to indicate that the program is running. When the program stops, the display is steady.

display control — A typical display control unit displays data in the form of a 1024 by 1024 dot array. Under program control, a bright dot may be produced at any point in this array. A series of these dots may be programmed to produce graphical output. Some display controls offer four program-controlled modes in which the scope can intensify a point and then have two D/A converters with either a ±5V or a ±0.5V full scale output and all the necessary circuitry for scope control.

display, data acquisition calculator — On some systems an eight-digit light emitting diode (LED) display reads out time or data as directed by the keyboard. Direct 8 digit display gives time in days, hours, minutes, seconds (to 99 days, 23 hours, 59 minutes, 59 seconds). Decimal point and minus sign are displayed on data. Overrange data values are flagged by a letter L. As an option on slow scan systems, channel number and data reading may be displayed. (some systems)

display, fixed (programmable calculators) — Fixed notation is specified by pressing DSP · followed by the appropriate number key to specify the number of decimal places (0-9) to which the display is to be rounded, in some units, fixed notation allows all answers to be displayed with the same precision. The display is left-justified and includes trailing zeroes within the setting selected.

display functions — These develop power-on and numerical information. They also provide indications of a negative number, decimal point, overflow, underflow and error and displays 10-digit mantissas and 2-digit exponents, on most units.

display hand-held calculator — The 15-digit light-emitting-diode display on many units can be formatted in a variety of ways at the user's discretion. It can show numbers in fixed-decimal-point or scientific notation, and can display from zero to nine places after the decimal point, in either mode, while the calculator maintains full accuracy internally, on some units.

display, hand-held programmable — On some units, the display is used to show results, operational errors, low battery conditions, programs in execution, and program steps. Additionally, in some units, W/PRGM mode, the display allows users to "see" each step of a program in memory.

display, highliting — Data can be distinguished or emphasized on a CRT display by reversing the field, blinking, underlining, changing color, changing light intensity or some combination of the above. A keyboard terminal should have at least three different methods of emphasizing or highliting information on the display.

display interface circuits, calculator — There are three kinds of seven-segment numeric display interface circuits. The simplest is the integrated circuit driver which consists of four or more transistors in one package. The second type, the decoder-driver, performs a conversion function in addition to the driving function and may, in addition include a latch function. The third type is the counter-decoder-driver which includes the counting function.

display module — An optical device which stores computer output and translates this output into literal, numerical or graphic signals which are distributed to a program-determined group of lights, annunciators, and numerical indicators for use in operator consoles and remote stations.

display multiple decimal point (small calculators) — On some units all decimal points light to warn that users have 2 to 5 minutes of operating time left on battery power. They must either:
1. Operate from ac power
2. Charge the battery pack
3. Insert a fully charged battery pack

display operations — Refers to power-on and numerical information. Provides indication of a negative number, decimal point, overflow, underflow and error. Displays 10-digit mantissa and 2-digit exponent on some systems.

display register — The display register consists of up to twelve (or more) indicators that display the contents of the register selected by the display switch.

display, scientific (programmable calculator) — This is useful when users are working with large or very small numbers and allows answers to be displayed with the same number of significant digits. It is specified by pressing DSP followed by the appropriate number key to specify the number of decimal places to which the mantissa is rounded. On some units the display is left-justified and includes trailing zeros within the selected setting.

display setting, small programmable units — Some units display up to 15 characters: mantissa sign, 10-digit mantissa, decimal point, exponent sign, and 2-digit exponent. In RUN mode, the display shows a rounded version of the number in the X register. Two display modes (fixed and scientific notation) with a variety of rounding options may be selected from the keyboard. (Rounding options affect the display only; most units always maintains full accuracy internally.)

displays, gas-discharge (neon) — Gas-discharged (neon) displays are generally eye pleasing with their pleasant orange color and they can be produced in reasonable size. However, this display is the most difficult to interface with digital logic as most gas-discharge displays require at least 180 V to guarantee proper operation. Even if this high voltage is available in the system, it is generally beyond the normal limitations of common IC technology, thereby requiring use of discrete transistors or expensive dielectrically-isolated IC's to provide the required interface.

displays, light emitting diodes (LEDs) — Light-emitting diodes (LEDs) are often compatible with common TTL levels. Generally they can be operated from the logic power supply and driven by either open-collector gates, IC drivers or discrete transistors. The high operating speed of LEDs permits the use of multiplexing circuitry to reduce driver count. The biggest disadvantages of LEDs are their small size and limited color selection.

displays, liquid-crystal — 1. Recently developed liquid-crystal panels display alphanumeric characters. The displays may be 20 or more characters long. However, the best length is closer to 10 characters because of the many interconnections required for a longer display. Each character is defined by a five-by-seven matrix and as many as three complete displays can be multiplexed at the same time. The units operate in a reflective dynamic-scattering mode, which tends to offer a longer life than the field-effect mode popular for watches, although threshold voltage is higher, and contrast lower. 2. While liquid crystal displays have the lowest power requirements and in many instances can be driven directly from the MOS logic, they produce no light but merely scatter ambient light. Despite their large character size, liquid crystals are often criticized for their poor compatibility with the human eye.

display station — Used to display alphameric information in a visual input/output system. It provides rapid man-machine communication by direct cable connection to the computer via a display control, or by remote transmission over telephone lines.

display terminal — Soft displays combine a method of generating characters and a viewing surface for displaying these characters. Under today's technology, the soft display for the system is likely to be a standard TV tube with 525 scan lines to the inch. Some of the key features of the display are: capacity, quality, highlighting.

display terminal interface — A typical unit provides local two-way communication with a keyboard/display terminal. Data rates from 110 to 9600 baud are automatically determined by the terminal external clock signal.

display types — Cathode Ray Tube, plasma and liquid crystal displays, light emitting diodes (LEDs), incandescent and fluorescent displays and "Nixie" tubes are becoming solidly established in circuit design as the trend to digital readout continues. The design engineer faces an unusually formidable task in determining the type of display most suitable and practical for his product.

display unit — Generic term used to describe any of the scores of output devices which provide visual representation of data.

distributed computer systems — The arrangement of computers within an organization, in which the organization's computer complex has many separate computing facilities all working in a cooperative manner, rather than the conventional single computer at a single location. Versatility of a computer system is often increased if small computers in geographically dispersed branches are used for simple tasks and a central computer is available for larger tasks. Frequently an organization's central files are stored at the central computing facility, with the geographically dispersed smaller computers calling on the central files when they need them. Such an arrangement lessens the load on the central computer and reduces both the volume and cost of data transmission.

distributed computing, calculator — Sales and service from hundreds of locations around the nation bring users close to reality with solutions to their problems. The advanced programmable calculators provide them with the convenience of desk-top calculation and the adaptability to change from one problem to the next quickly and easily, plus the power to quickly solve these problems. These capabilities — quick keystroke calculations, dedicated problem solving, programmable problem solving, and interfacing — now give users a new perspective on distributed computation.

distributed-intelligence system — Each processor in a distributed-intelligence microcomputer system (DIMS) performs some combination of these four basic activity functions: 1. Local input/output or hardware controller activity. 2. Information concentration and temporary storage. 3. Information processing. 4. Remote input/output and communication. Items below list typical combinations found in a variety of applications. The first activity, local functions, can be divided over several microcomputers or combined into one processor. The local interface may deal with a broad variety of contrasting I/O characteristics that includes: high-speed/low-speed; electromechanical/electronic; decimal/binary; analog/digital; interrupt/polled DMA; unformatted/formatted; human/machine; simple/complex, and single-cycle/multicycle.

distributed-intelligence system applications — Some applications examples are: 1. Modular instruments. 2. Terminal (POS, data collection) system controller. 3. Network of remote sensors, interpretation and communication to larger host computer. 4. Modular data collection device with display. 5. Scientific computer network or minicomputer emulation. 6. General-purpose controller/processor applications. 7. Multiprocessing system or dedicated support system.

distributed-intelligence system capabilities — Distributed-intelligence systems differ from multiprocessing systems in the way that tasks are handled. Although both systems are multiple processors, the tasks assigned to a distributed system remain fixed. By contrast, in a multiprocessing environment, a continuous stream of assignments is fed to a single node and allowed to unburden the processors. And the allocation of tasks is performed by complex algorithms present in the software operating system. Each processor in a distributed-intelligence microcomputer system (DIMS) performs some combinaton of these four basic activity functions: 1. Local input/output or hardware controller activity. 2. Information concentration and temporary storage. 3. Information processing. 4. Remote input/output and communication.

distributed processing, I/O — Distributed processing techniques applied to I/O transfer functions include two aspects: Intelligent serial and parallel I/O ports and Direct Memory Access (DMA) control. The combination of these two techniques provides a powerful method of I/O control and frees the CPU of all details of block transfer activities.

distributed processing, peripheral control — The peripheral controller function of microcomputers is similar to that used in levels of calculator systems. A controller is designed and built to control various peripheral devices such as magnetic tape drive, a printer, a magnetic disk system, a modem interface, or a keyboard/display function. The only difference is that the controller functions can now be reduced to one or two MOS/LSI chips by using the same techniques as have been so successfully applied to microcomputer CPU designs. In pursuing this philosophy, the following are typical peripheral control functions: 1. Keyboard/display. 2. Keyboard/printer. 3. Display. 4. Printers. 5. Magnetic card reader. 6. Modem. 7. Floppy disk controller.

distributed systems — Refers to various arrangements of computers within an organization in which the organization's computer complex has many separate computing facilities all working in a cooperative manner, rather than the conventional single computer at a single location. Versatility of a computer system is often increased if small computers in geographically dispersed branches are used for simple tasks and a powerful central computer is available for larger tasks. Frequently an organization's central files are stored at the central computing facility, with the geographically dispersed smaller computers calling on the central files when they need them. Such an arrangement lessens the load on the central computer and reduces both the volume and cost of data transmission.

distributed systems test capability — Particularly useful and advantageous in multiple test station applications (remote test sites) are various Distributed Systems Test capabilities. A distributed system consists of a central computer or calculator system and a number of satellite systems (usually one at each remote site). Satellites commonly concentrate the measured data prior to transmission to central. Satellites and central share the use of peripherals (disc, line printer, card reader, plotter, etc.), thus minimizing total system cost. The concept and applications of distributed systems tests are often complex.

divergent series — A divergent series is an infinite series in which the sum of the terms is greater than any definite quantity, if enough terms are taken.

DMA (direct memory access) — A procedure or method designed to gain direct access to main storage to thereby achieve data transfer without involving the CPU. This means that the CPU must be periodically disabled while DMA is in progress. The manner and modes of achieving this differ considerably in the many microprocessor models that have DMA capability.

DMA channel — The direct memory access (DMA) channel capability permits faster data transfer speeds. The basic approach is to bypass the registers and provide direct access to the memory bus. Another significant feature included in some of these is a vectored interrupt capability. The number of separate interrupt lines accommodated typically is four or more. These newer designs have been referred to as the second-generation in microprocessors. Second generation features include: separate address and data bus lines; multiple address modes (e.g., direct, indirect, relative, and indexed), more instructions, more versatile register stack operation, vectored interrupts, direct memory access, standard RAM and ROM. The result of these improvements is 10 times faster operation for typical instruction times, over first generation micros.

DMA channel multiplexer — Typically, various multiplexer channels are packaged on three standard circuit board types which plug directly into any of the major calculator slots. One board contains all the common circuitry and eight asynchronous channels. A second board contains up to 24 additional asynchronous channels, and a third contains up to 8 synchronous channels. Thus the complete I/O system to handle 128 asynchronous lines or a combination of 104 asynchronous lines and 8 synchronous lines is packaged on six boards. (some types)

DMA control — Various types of controls depend on the speed of the processor. Higher throughput results can be obtained from the use of a direct-memory-access (DMA) bus. In this arrangement, a peripheral device communicates directly with memory without disturbing the CPU. Interfacing is more complex because request and acknowledge signals must be exchanged between the device and an autonomous bus controller. When a single bus is used, data and addresses must be time-multiplexed, and latches must be provided to hold the address stable while memory or a peripheral are accessed.

DMA data transfers — In order to effect DMA data transfers, a device controller has buffers to hold the current memory address (to or from which data are to be transferred) and the word count. After transferring the data address to the inbus data lines, the device controller logic must increment the memory address and decrement the word count.

document (noun) — Any representation of information which is readable by human beings, usually used in connection with information of interest to the originator of a data processing activity, rather than to the operators of the computer, more commonly applied to input information than output.

documentation — Refers to the orderly presentation, organization and communication of recorded specialized knowledge, in order to maintain a complete record of reasons for changes in variables. Documentation is necessary not so much to give maximum utility as to give an unquestionable historial reference record.

documentation book — All the material needed to document a computer application, including problem statement, flow charts, coding, and operating instructions.

documentation components — Such documents usually contain: 1. The name of the responsible individual who ordered or is directing the program. 2. A brief outline of the system, with some notes relating from the benefits to be obtained. 3. A type of "handbook" is developed for use by those who will use the system and programs, explaining such things as: paper flow, coding required, and output file instructions. Other items explained are equipment utilization change-over procedure, systems test data, program descriptions, etc.

documentation, program — This is a vital part of programming. Documentation is required so that programs can be modified, so that people can be trained, and so that machine operators know how to run programs and diagnose the problems if they occur.

document, original — A specific document originally designed to be used by data processing system and which supplies the basic data to be input to the data processing system. Many resulting errors are attributed to errors in the source document.

domain — The set associated with the variable is the domain. A set could be all real numbers, for example. The set on which the function is defined is the domain of the function.

DOS (disk operating system) — Relates to the tape operating system TOS, this is a versatile operating system for IBM System 360 installations having direct-access storage devices. This simple operating system supports almost every peripheral device available for System 360.

DO statement, range — All FORTRAN statements included in the repetitive execution of a DO loop operation.

dot matrix impact printer — A typical dot-matrix impact printer utilizes a serially-driven printing element consisting of 7 print solenoids and print wires. The print wires are arranged vertically with respect to the printed media. The printing element is driven across the print area from right-to-left at a constant speed. External electronics "clock" the print pulses to the solenoids to form characters of almost any desired density and font configuration. Because the printing element travels at a constant speed, there is no need for a complex "feed-back" system from the printer to the electronics to determine the proper timing of print pulses. The printing element is positively driven via a spirally-grooved plastic drum which in turn is driven by a synchronous motor. A second (and identical) motor accomplishes document feed. Standard document feed is performed at the rate of 10 lines per second. The unit incorporates a wide metal "plate" to facilitate document insertion and removal. When the document is properly inserted, an optional switch closure is effected to act as a signal to the external electronics. (some units)

dot matrix printer — A typical 31-column dot matrix printer, designed for numeric-only applications, requires no strobe of incoming data. Its input may be decimal or BCD character serial, and it interfaces with TTL and CMOS. An internal buffer collects data asynchronously and prints on command at 110 cps. Additional features include a printer-busy signal, paper wind-up motor and provision to keep printed data under keylock but observable by the user. Some printers come with or without an internal power supply, and packaging may be customized for special OEM requirements.

double length — Pertaining to twice the normal length of a unit of data or a storage device in a given computing system; e.g., a double-length register would have the capacity to store twice as much data as a single-length or normal register; a double-length word would have twice the number of characters or digits as a normal or single-length word.

double or reverse calculation — Double or reverse calculation is the calculation, recalculation, and then comparison of the two results to prove accuracy. It is commonly used in payroll and other calculations for which no predetermined control total can be developed. In the recalculation, factors are reversed–the original multiplier becomes the multiplicand and the original multiplicand becomes the multiplier. When processing with unit record equipment, if the recalculation is performed in a separate run, then proofing of the result can also be verified.

double precision — Pertaining to a quantity having twice as many digits as are normally carried; e.g., a double-precision number requires two machine words in a fixed-word machine.

DPMA certificate — A certificate given by the Data Processing Management Association which indicates that a person has a certain level of competence in the field of data processing. The certificate is obtained by passing an examination that is offered yearly throughout the United States and Canada.

driver — A program or routine that controls external peripheral devices or executes other programs.

driver, bus — In some systems outputs of both the Word Counter and BA Counter are connected to a set of BUS drivers so that the counter contents can be gated to the DATA BUS when the appropriate enable signals (BA TO BUS L and WC TO D BUS L) are asserted. In addition, the BA register has a set of drivers with independent outputs to allow it to drive the address bus when the BA TO BUS L input is asserted.

driver-decoder calculator application — A typical application for a driver is as interface between a calculator chip and the display where the decoding has been performed by the chip. Thus the outputs are in seven-segment form. The driver's function is to provide current or voltage gain between the chip and the display. Hand-held calculators usually use monolithic LEDs. The anode segments are formed by chemical etching on a common-cathode substrate. For driving in the multiplex mode they require anode segment drivers (current sources) and cathode digit drivers (current sinks).

drivers and decoders, calculator — The increasing popularity of pocket calculators, digital instruments and digital watches and clocks has led to the development of classes of integrated circuits called display drivers and binary coded decimal (BCD) to seven-segment decoders. A need for separate drive circuits for numeric displays — at this time predominantly light-emitting diode and neon gas-discharge types — arose because conventional bipolar TTL logic could not supply sufficient voltage, current or both to drive the segments of the displays. This need is already changing: MOS (including CMOS) is now capable of driving some displays directly, as the input power requirements are decreasing for some of the newer LED and liquid crystal numerics.

drop dead halt — Concerns a type of halt which may be deliberately programmed or may be the result of a logical error in programming, but from which there is no recovery.

dual in-line package (DIP) — The most popular IC packaging in use in the mid 1970s is the plastic, dual-in-line case, using plastic for economic reasons and the dual-in-line package (DIP) configuration for manufacturing efficiency.

dual magnetic tape cassette reader/recorder — Large storage at low cost is one of the key features of the dual magnetic tape cassette reader/recorder. Two independent tape drives can be individually addressed. Both have read/record features, rewind, search forward, and search in reverse direction. On some models, "Automatic Verification" insures correct reading of data. Many also allow the user to "read/write in place." This saves time and money in applications involving the updating of data. Individual data blocks can be conveniently changed in place without disturbing other blocks on the tape.

dual magnetic tape cassette reader/recorder, calculator — One type contains two separately controllable magnetic tape cassette units for recording from – or reading data into – the main memory of some types of calculators only. Up to 115,200 program steps can be contained on the various cassettes.

dual-purpose keyboard — Users type, as on a typewriter or program by entering the most commonly used BASIC instructions with a single keystroke. The sixteen keys across the top permit instant keyboard access to 32 subroutines or text

dual removable flexible disk, calculator — One type consists of two disk platters, both removable and easily stored. The storage capacity of each unit is divided between the two platters; 131,072 bytes or 262,144 bytes per platter depending on the model chosen. Data can be recorded on only one side of each platter and is transferred at a rate of 300 ms per 256 bytes.

dual removable flexible disk drive — Dual removable flexible disk drives provide low-cost storage for the needs of smaller applications. The highly reliable flexible disk platters are the same size as a 45 rpm record. The disks will not break and, because of their compact size and resistance to dirt, are easily stored. Access is quick (300 milliseconds per 256 bytes) and uses a fixed contact head rather than a floating head. With software compatibility, a user can easily upgrade as storage requirements change.

dual systems — Special configurations which use two calculators to receive identical inputs and execute the same routines, with the results of such parallel processing subject to comparison. Exceptionally high reliability requirements are usually involved.

dummy — Generally refers to an artificial address, instruction, or record of information inserted solely to fulfill prescribed conditions, such as to achieve a fixed word length or block length, but without itself affecting machine operations except to permit the machine to perform desired operations.

dummy argument — A prototype card field in a macro-definition that is variable and is to be replaced with a parameter (quantity or symbol) when the macro-operation is used. It is also called a dummy definition.

dummy instruction — Refers to an artificial instruction or address inserted in a list of instructions, solely to fulfill prescribed conditions (such as word or block length) without affecting the operation.

dummy load — 1. Refers to devices such as a resistor, in which the output power can be absorbed. A dummy load is used for simulating conditions of operation for test purposes. 2. To effect the finding, and transfer to storage of a program or set of programs without execution to determine that all relevant specifications and components exist in the proper forms in the library.

dump — 1. Frequently referred to as power dump, meaning to withdraw all power from a computer, either accidentally or intentionally. Also, to transfer all or part of the contents of one section of computer memory to another section. 2. A small program that outputs the contents of memory onto hard copy which may be listings, tape or punched cards.

dump, A.C. — Refers to the removal of all alternating current power intentionally, accidentally or conditionally from a system or component. An A.C. dump usually results in the removal of all power, since direct current is usually supplied through a rectifier or converter.

dump and restart — Concerns specific software routines for taking program dumps at specified times, and for restarting programs at one of these points in the event of program failure.

dump, binary — Refers to a dump or printout of the contents of a memory unit in binary form onto some external medium such as paper tape or printout forms.

dump, change — Concerns a print-out or output recording of the contents of all storage locations in which a change has been made since the previous change dump.

dump check — A check which usually consists of adding all the digits during dumping, and verifying the sum when retransferring.

dumping — Many techniques are designed to provide a periodic "write out" of a complete program and its data; i.e., the contents of the working storage area, to a backup storage or memory unit. A dumping program usually incorporates restart procedures to thereby enable the program to be resumed at the last dump point in the event of interruption due, for example, to a machine failure, or some other job interruption. A periodic dump, therefore, avoids having to start from the original beginning if some unforeseen event causes erasure.

dump point — Refers to a designed point in a program at which it is desirable to write the program and its data to a backing storage, as a protection against machine failure. Dump points may be selected to effect dumping at specific time intervals or at predetermined events in the running of the program.

dump, post-mortem — A listing of the contents of a storage device taken after a routine has been run in order that the final condition of sections of storage may be recorded for debugging purposes.

dump, program — As a last resort users can request a Dump program to list in hexadecimal format the contents of memory at any point in program execution that they choose.

dump, RAM — To copy the contents of all or a part of a storage, usually from an internal storage such as a RAM, into an external storage such as a printout. The process of copying, and also the data resulting. The dump does not eliminate the data stored. A snapshot dump is the copying of the contents stored in memory at one address into a calculator display.

duodecimal — 1. Pertaining to a characteristic or property involving a selection, choice, or condition in which there are twelve possibilities. 2. Pertaining to the numeration system with a radix of twelve.

duplex — In communications, this is a simultaneous twoway and independent transmission in both directions (sometimes referred to as "full duplex"). Contrast with half-duplex.

duplex channel — A communication system — in which each terminal can simultaneously receive and transmit data.

duplication check — A check which requires that the results of two independent performances, either concurrently on duplicate equipment or at different times on the same equipment, of the same operation, be identical.

dynamic — Pertaining to a quantity that is affected by time, energy or power, and therefore indicates a relatively transient or unstable condition.

dynamic check types — A self-checking code or error-detecting code uses code expressions such that one or more errors in a code expression produces a forbidden combination. A parity check makes use of a self-checking code employing bi-

dynamic dump

nary digits in which the total number of 1's or 0's in each permissible code expression is always even or always odd. A check may be made either for even parity or odd parity. A redundancy check employs a self-checking code that makes use of redundant digits called check digits. Some of the various names that have been applied to this type of check are forbidden-pulse combination, unused command, improper instruction, unallowable digits, improper command, false code forbidden digit, non-existent code, and unused code.

dynamic dump — A dump that is performed periodically during the execution of a program.

dynamic error debugging — Where possible simple checkout routines should first be run in a single step mode. After they are working at low speed, the routines should be run as closely as possible to full system speed to locate dynamic errors.

dynamic gain ratio — The specific magnitude ratio of the steady state amplitude of the output signal from an element or system to the amplitude of the input signal to that element or system, for a sinusoidal signal, i.e., it is often expressed as a ratio, or in decibels as 20 times the log of that ratio for a specified frequency.

dynamic mapping system — Some systems provide the capability to address memory configurations up to 1 million words from four independent memory spaces with no degradation in performance. They allow page by page read and write memory protection and allow programs and data to be accessed from non-contiguous pages of memory. Some systems accomplish this by the addition of many new memory management instructions.

dynamic memories — Usually refers to delay lines or their semiconductor equivalents, where stored information is inserted and propogates through the storage medium, and is only available for reading when it emerges at the other end; it must then be re-inserted, or it will be lost.

dynamic memory card — A typical dynamic memory card contains 4,096 words of memory. Maximum access time is 420 nanoseconds. An automatic refresh cycle is performed every 32 clock pulses at sync time. If the card is addressed at the same time that refresh occurs, the calculator is given one or two wait states during refresh. Otherwise, the processor is unaware that refresh is occurring. Has write protect capability. Variable address circuitry allows user to provide a starting address in memory at any one of 16 locations — 4K, 8K, 12K, 16 K, etc. (some units)

dynamic programming — The essence of dynamic programming is that an optimum decision must be made at every stage of a multistage problem. When considering only a single stage, there may appear to be a number of different decisions of equal merit. Only when the effect of each decision at every stage on the overall goal is determined can the final choice be made. This integration of the cumulative effect of a path of decisions through each stage of the network is the real essence of dynamic programming.

dynamic RAM — Data is stored capacitively, and must be recharged (refreshed) periodically (every 2 ms. or so) or it will be lost.

dynamic relocation program — The moving of a partially executed program to a different location in main memory without detrimentally affecting its ability to finish its normal processing.

dynamic response — The specific behavior of the output of a device as a function of the input, both with respect to time.

dynamic stop — A specific stop in a loop which consists of a single jump instruction which effects a jump to itself.

dynamic storage — 1. Refers to stored computer data which remain in motion on a sensing device. For example, an acoustic delay line, magnetic drum, as opposed to static storage. 2. The storage of data on a device or in a manner that permits the data to move or vary with time, and thus the data is not always available.

E

EAROM (electrically alterable ROM) — Electrically alterable read-only memories are commercially available as MNOS EAROMs. These non-volatile memory devices, with operating power down to $3\mu2$/bit, are programmed much like ordinary RAMs. They have no fusible links and do not require UV irradiation. Read cycle time is reportedly 10-20 μ s; write time is on the order of 1 ms. (See: electrically alterable ROM definitions)

EAROM disadvantages — EAROMs have several inherent disadvantages. First the price, when compared to masked MOS ROMs is very high. Reprogrammability does help to reduce true cost of EAROMs but isn't sufficient in large volume applications to warrant EAROM use. The second problem with EAROMs is testing. As it takes a very long time to write a single data pattern into an EAROM, testing multiple data patterns can take up to 20 or 30 minutes while similar tests on R/W RAMs would take a matter of 30 seconds to 1 minute to complete the same test patterns. Another problem with EAROMs is their comparatively slow speeds. A 340NS access time prevents EAROMs from addressing the high speed applications currently served by bipolar PROMs.

earth stations — Ground terminals that use antennas and associated electronic equipment to transmit, receive and process communications via satellite. Future cable systems may be able to interconnect to domestic communications satellites, creating regional and national cable networks.

EBCDIC code — An acronym for Extended Binary Coded Decimal Interchange Code. A standard code consisting of a character set consisting of 8-bit coded characters; used for information representation and interchange among data processing systems, communications systems, and associated equipment. Used especially by IBM.

ECL — Refers to Emitter-Coupled Logic. This is the fastest technology in the bipolar family. ECL has been fabricated into large-scale integrated circuits only recently. The Amdahl system uses LSI ECL and other commercial systems also do.

ECL (emitter-coupled logic) advantages —

Some designers predict computer logic will eventually be designed completely around ECL (emitter-coupled logic). The ECL approach often is preferred since the devices are inherently very uniform and very stable, and are excellent for driving lines. ECL is very fast, so users must design with the higher speed in mind and follow certain layout rules. The approach also can necessitate use of multi-layer printed circuit boards. That's advantageous in terms of packaging density. ECL is also advantageous because it requires only a one volt swing in 3 to 4 nanoseconds, while a typical Schottky T²L requires a 5 volt swing in the same time frame. ECL also inherently generates less noise, which is a benefit.

edit — To modify a calculator program, or alter stored data prior to output.

edit and debug functions, hand-held units — These functions allow trial-run programs to move through a program a step at a time, forward or backward, to add more steps, delete, or write over steps, then record.

editing, calculator programs — Refers to automatic printing of memory location, code and mnemonic symbols when entering programs from the keyboard. Display shows present address and code plus codes at the previous and next program step. A trace feature is used while stepping through programs to observe operations as performed. Backspace and forward keys permit corrections and changes in programs at any time. A delete key removes steps in any part of the program at any time. Such are the editing capabilities of some mid-size desk-top calculators.

editing capability, built-in — One of the outstanding features on some calculators is built-in editing capability. Under program control data in a program can be inserted, deleted or changed on existing programs. The user can back step or forward step and review the last and the current instruction step at the same time on display.

editing, hand-held calculators — For ease of editing, debugging, and reviewing programs after they are written, some models have a single-step key and a back-step key. While in the program mode, the calculator displays show a two-digit line number (from 00 to 49) and a two-digit keycode that tells what command or function was keyed in for that step. Thus, if the 24th step were the reciprocal function, the display would show "24 13," since the reciprocal key is the third key from the left in the first row of keys.

editing operations, programmable calculator — Users edit with the mode switch set to W/PRGM on some systems. The edit operations make it easier to key in programs because, in case of mistakes, users can correct a wrong step by (1) stepping through your program using SST until the wrong step is in the display, (2) pressing "g" (delete program step) and by reentering the step correctly. To insert an operation following the one on display, users key it in. Now they will be able to step through their program and insert a step between any two steps.

editing, program — Program editing consists of automatic listing of memory locations, code and symbols while entering programs from a keyboard with a trace feature, while stepping through programs to observe operations as performed. Backspacing a key permits correction of program entry errors in some systems. The insert key permits adding steps in any part of the program at any time. Hardwired keyboard routines for some units are included for common trigonometric, logarithmic and statistical functions.

editing terminal — Concerns a system for providing the following editing capabilities: 1. replacement of characters; 2. insertion, deletion and movement of characters, words, sentences, paragraphs and blocks; 3. field checks which include the number of, sequences of and types of digits; 4. zero fill, left or right; 5. batch balance; 6. check digit verification.

editor — An editor is a general-purpose text editing program used to prepare source program tapes. Original text entered via the teletypewriter and held in memory may be changed and corrected. The user can insert, delete or change lines of text, insert, delete and change characters within a line without retyping the line, locate lines containing key words and list or punch any portion of the text. Text may be punched using either the teletypewriter or the high-speed punch. If further correction is necessary, the tape may be read into memory via the teletypewriter or a high-speed reader, corrected, and a new tape punched. Some editors require a minimum of 4K of RAM memory and are supplied on a binary tape with a User's Manual.

edit ROM — Character Edit ROM gives additional flexibility and ease in recalling and editing program lines and numeric or alpha numeric data input lines.

educational system, programmable calculator-based — An educational system would conceivably include a programmable calculator with small memory, a string variable ROM, marked card reader, page printer, and plotter. In this configuration, it is most versatile—equally at home or in the science, mathematic, business, or computer science classroom. For both teacher and student, the programmable calculator can raise scientific education out of the tedium of routine calculation and into the challenging arena of abstract concepts, a process that is enhanced by offerings of complete packages of educational programs and teaching materials. Some current lines of educational software are available for many educational levels. Since budgeting is always an important educational systems consideration, most of the equipment and software can be leased annually, often for less than the price of a teaching assistant's monthly salary.

EE pack I — Programs selected from the following electrical engineering application areas: impedance matching, filter design, transmission line calculations, parameter conversion, power supply design, transistor biasing, control system and waveform analysis.

EE pack II — Programs assist the microwave circuit designer in making microwave measurements, designing transistor amplifiers, computing transmission line properties and certain system properties, and performing difficult related mathematical operations.

EEROM programmer — A device that provides a means of programming a single EEROM or an EEROM module from paper tape or from an integral hex keyboard and display. EEROMs are electrically eraseable and, therefore, need not be removed from the module or socket to be erased and reprogrammed. Included is a RAM buffer which permits editing of any EEROM. Some equipment may also be used as a ROM emulator.

effective address — 1. A modified address. 2. The address actually considered to be used in a particular execution of a computer instruction. 3. An address obtained by the combination of the contents of a specific index register with the address of an instruction. 4. The address used for the execution of an instruction. This may differ from that of the instruction in storage.

effective speed — Speed (less than rated) which can be sustained over a significant period of time and which reflects the slowing effects of control codes, timing codes, error detection, retransmission, tabbing, hand keying, etc.

EFTS — Electronic Funds Transfer Systems (EFTS) describes various electronic communications systems which transfer financial information from one point to another. Although EFTS encompasses many diverse electronic automation projects, it is most frequently used to describe three types of systems: Automated Clearing Houses, Automated Tellers, and Point-of-Sale Systems.

EIA — Abbreviation for Electronic Industries Association.

EIA interface — Refers to a set of signal characteristics (time duration, voltage and current). For connection of terminals to modem units, and specific physical coupler dimensions specified by the Electronic Industries Association.

EIA standard code — A code or coding system conforming to any one of the standards established by the Electronic Industries Association.

electrical contacts — Concerns various paths, joints or touchings of the two halves of a connector or those at points joined in electrical connections.

electrical engineering I tape package — A single large program which performs microwave and general active and passive circuit analysis, with Smith chart, rectangular or polar plotting. Includes binder, manual, overlays and one tape cartridge. Prerequisite: 24K bytes memory.
Tape Cartridge or Manual only

electrically alterable ROMS (EAROMs) — EAROMs are available with 450 nanosecond to 3 μsec access times and in sizes from 2K bits to 8K bits. Prices range from .5¢ to .6¢ per bit and have been decreasing quite rapidly over the past 3 years. The speed of EAROMs make them ideal for replacing MOS ROMs in low volume applications or in bread-boarding systems which later convert to pin compatible masked MOS ROMs. EAROM speeds are an excellent match to available microcomputer memory speed requirements making them ideal programmable logic elements for machine controllers which demand program nonvolatility. The nonvolatile nature of EAROMs also make them suitable as memory replacements for portions of main memory in minicomputer semiconductor memories. Portions of programs which must remain intact through power failures and battery depletions can be written into EAROMs which then are placed in the memory space of the minicomputer, microcomputer or calculator.

electrically programmable ROM-(EPROM) — A typical unit is a 512×8 electrically programmable ROM suited for high performance microcomputer systems where fast turnaround is important for system program development and for small volumes of identical programs in production systems. It has an access time of 100 nanoseconds. It is fully decoded. Chip select lines are available which permit easy system memory expansion. This unit is a Schottky Bipolar device.

electrochromeric displays (ECDs) — Electrochromic displays are low-voltage, low-current devices that chemically transform themselves from a transparent to an opaque state when tickled by an external electric field. Even after this field is turned off, the devices maintain their opacity; only when subjected to a field with the opposite polarity do they return to their initial state. Thus electrochromism can find uses both in displays and in information storage devices. The devices can operate in either a transmissive or a reflective mode, against any color background. They do not require polarizers, and are claimed to have distinctly superior appearance, contrast and legibility in dimly lit ambients. In addition, they are legible over wide viewing angles and compatible with IC technology.

electron — One of the natural elementary constituents of matter which carries a negative electric charge of one electric unit and has approximately 1/1840th the mass of a hydrogen atom or 9.107×10^{-28} gram.

electronic — Any system or device in which electrons flow through a vacuum, gas, or semiconductor. Also pertains to devices, circuits, or systems using the principle of electron flow through a conductor such as an electronic control, equipment, instrument, or circuit.

electronic control — General description of a control of machinery, traction, lifts, etc., which includes essential electronic switching and timing of operations, with or without tape triggering.

electronic data-processing (EDP) — 1. Any machine or group of machines which has the capability to automatically enter, receive, classify, sort, compute and/or record alphabetical or numerical accounting or statistical data (or all three) without the intermediate use of tabulating cards. 2. Data processing by way of electronic equipment, such as an internally stored program, electronic digital computer, or an automatic data processing machine.

electronic funds transfer system (EFTS) — 1. A type of national banking or money settlement and clearing function. 2. Various pre-authorized or scheduled transfers of funds, predominantly local in nature. 3. Various transfers and financial services triggered or provided at points of sale, predominantly retail.

electronic industries association (EIA) — A trade association of the electronics industry which formulates technical standards, disseminates marketing data, and maintains contact with government agencies in matters relating to the electronics industry.

electronics — 1. Branch of science that deals with the study and application of electron devices, e.g., electron tubes, transistors, magnetic amplifiers, etc. 2. The field of science and engineering concerned with the behavior of electrons in devices and the utilization of such devices.

electronic slide rule — Most electronic slide rules no longer omit the transcendental functions. The new units not only include the trig and log functions but add hyperbolic functions as well. All major types can calculate x! and operate in either a degree or radian mode. Most units provide the

electrostatic storage user with a key to convert between degrees and radians.

electrostatic storage — 1. The storage of data on a dielectric surface such as the screen of a cathode ray tube, in the form of the presence or absence of spots bearing electrostatic charges, that can persist for a short time after the electrostatic charging force is removed. 2. A storage device so used.

elevation angle — A measurement of an angle in the vertical plane from some stated reference, most often the horizontal plane.

emitter coupled circuits (ECL) — These circuits do not saturate, obviating either Schottky clamps or gold doping. However, to realize ECL's speed potential, one or two extra diffusions are needed in manufacturing. The net result: ECL memories are faster than TTL but more expensive. Certainly, for applications requiring small memories to be mixed with ECL logic, there will always be a requirement for ECL memories. Also, since ECL memories are faster than CMOS and N-channel, they will be used in applications that need extra speed. Since this is not true with TTL, ECL should eventually become a more important memory form than TTL.

empirical — Pertaining to a statement or formula based on experience or experimental evidence.

emulate — A procedure designed to imitate one system with another such that the imitating system accepts the same data, executes the same programs, and achieves the same results as the imitated system. Contrast with simulate.

emulation — Refers to various techniques using software or microprogramming in which one computer is made to behave exactly like another computer; i.e., the emulating system executes programs in the native machine language code of the emulated system. Emulation is generally used to minimize the impact of conversion from one computer system to another, and is used to continue the use of production programs — as opposed to "simulation" which is used to study the operational characteristics of another (possibly theoretical) system.

emulation, control store RAM — It is highly desirable to be able to load any one of a number of library programs into a control store. The machine can then use a small amount of control storage to perform a number of different emulations or operations in sequence. For example, a computer running in a time-sharing, batch and remote batch environment might want to emulate the performance of a specific computer for a batch problem. It could do so and then change its control store and operate as a completely new computer.

emulator — 1. Refers to various devices or computer programs that emulate. 2. The combination of programming techniques and special machine features that permits a given computing system to execute programs written for another system.

emulator system — A device or computer program that imitates one system with another so that the imitating system accepts the same data, executes the same programs, and achieves the same results as the imitated system.

enabled — 1. Refers to a state of the central processing unit that allows the occurrence of certain types of interruptions. Synonymous with interruptable. 2. In communications, pertaining to the state in which a transmission control unit can accept incoming calls on a line.

encoder — An electromechanical transducer which produces a serial or parallel digital indication of mechanical angle or displacement.

end of data marker — Refers to a character or code that designates that the end of all data held on a specific storage unit has been reached. Not to be confused with end of file marker.

end of file (EOF) — Refers to the termination or point of completion of a quantity of data. End of file marks are used to indicate this point.

end of message (EOM) — Refers to a specific character or sequence of characters which indicates the termination of a message or record.

end of run routine — A specific routine provided by the programmer to deal with various housekeeping operations before a run is ended; i.e., rewinding tapes, printing control totals, etc.

end of transmission (EOT) — Refers to a unique character or group of characters used to denote the end of a data transmission to or from a remote terminal.

energy monitoring calculator — Quality control testing, laboratory and production instrumentation, and other applications. Calculators enhance system's potential. Users add the mainframes and modules they need to have a graphic calculator system for many polution monitoring systems.

engineering calculator, hand-held — A standard unit performs logarithms, trigonometrics, hyperbolics, powers, roots, reciprocals, factorials, linear regression, mean, variance and standard deviation. Many memories, scientific notation, preprogrammed engineering conversions, rechargeable batteries, AC Adapter/Charger and case are usually included.

engineering, calculator systems — An example is a system that reads a vast signal range of time, frequency, voltage, current, resistance and counts events. Coupled with transducers, it gives readings in digits automatically. It gives statistical parameters, averages, frequency distribution, group about the mean, fits curves. It logs data and times events. It converts input and labels output on the alphanumeric printer. (some units)

engineering-graphics and alphanumerics — Engineers often need vivid descriptions of their math problems. Their concepts can be drawn on their personal graphic calculator system. The system becomes a combination of mathematician and designer. The programmable calculator has the computational power, and the Graphic Terminal has the artistic skill. With both machines sitting at an engineer's desk, he has two keyboards to work with. The math keyboard of the calculator and the teletype keyboard of the terminal lets him draw the shape of his thoughts as he builds them. This lets him concentrate on ideas instead of mechanics. He can see his concepts take form on the bright screen. This permits him to work easier because the system is fast. For example, he can tap the calculator's remote key to send these commands to the terminal: Erase screen. Accept X-Y coordinate data. Enable graphics. Start or start alpha. Print alpha. Make hard copies with optional hard copy unit. (some systems)

engineering logic diagram — A specific logic diagram that has been referenced or addended with detailed information relating to circuitry, chassis layout, terminal identification, etc. showing gates, circuits, etc. used in the logic as well as types and rating of the circuit elements.

engineering notation — Special to some pocket calculators is engineering notation, which allows all numbers to be shown in a modified scientific notation with exponents of 10 that are multiples of three (e.g., 10^3, 10^6, 10^{12}). Whichever notation is selected, the user always maintains the complete 10-digit number internally. Also, the unit switches the display automatically from fixed point notation to full scientific notation whenever a number is too large or too small to be seen in fixed point notation.

engineering notation display — Engineering notation allows all numbers to be shown with exponents of ten that are multiples of three (e.g., 10^3, 10^{-6}, 10^9). This is particularly useful in scientific and engineering calculations, where units of measure are often specified in multiples of three. See the prefix chart below.

Multiplier	Prefix	Symbol
10^{12}	tera	T
10^9	giga	G
10^6	mega	M
10^3	kilo	k
10^{-3}	milli	m
10^{-6}	micro	μ
10^{-9}	nano	n
10^{-12}	pico	p
10^{-15}	femto	f
10^{-18}	atto	a

engineering, system — A method of engineering which takes into consideration all of the elements in the control system, down to the smallest valve, and the process itself. It is believed to have the most promise as an intelligent approach leading toward fuller industrial automation.

English-metric conversions — This program allows conversion between the most commonly used metric and English units of length, weight, and temperature. The metric units used are centimeters, kilograms, and degrees centigrade. The English units to which these can be converted and vice versa are inches, pounds (avdp.) and degrees Fahrenheit.

entering programs, advanced calculators — For example, to enter a program into the program memory, on some units, users tell the calculator the starting point of the program by pressing GO TO followed by the desired memory address. Then to tell the calculator to remember the keystrokes of the program, users press LEARN and enter the program. To print any results they press PRINT DISPLAY. To end the program and reset the calculator they press RESET. They exit the learn mode by pressing LEARN.

enter transfers, small calculators — Enter also prepares the X-register for a new number by terminating the old number and copying it into the Y-register. A new number then writes over the number in the X-register without lifting the stack. (some units)

entry — 1. A statement in a programming system. In general each entry is written on one line of a coding form and punched on one card, although some systems permit a single entry to overflow several cards. 2. A member of a list.

entry block — A block of main-memory storage assigned on receipt of each entry into a system and associated with that entry throughout its life in the system.

entry name — A name within a control section that defines an entry point and can be referred to by any control section.

entry point — 1. Refers to various specific locations in a program segment which other segments can reference. 2. The point or points at which a program can be activated by an operator or an operating system.

entry, remote job — The inputting of the job information to the main computing system from a remote device. Frequently abbreviated RJE.

environment — The elements and/or factors influencing or affecting the design and operation of a device or system.

EPROM erasure — Electrically programmable Read Only Memory (EPROM) is ideally suited for uses where fast turn-around and pattern experimentation are important. Some types are packaged in a 24-pin dual in-line (DIP) package with a transparent lid. The transparent quartz lid allows the user to expose the chip to untraviolet light to erase the bit pattern. Therefore, unlike a metal mask Read Only Memory where a pattern cannot be changed, a new pattern can be written in to the EPROM devices. As supplied or erased, all data bits in EPROM are initially interpreted as zeroes (output high), with programming operation forcing zeroes to ones or leaving zeroes unchanged. Ultraviolet erasure of the EPROM restores the data to all zeroes.

CAUTION: When using an ultraviolet source of this type, care should be taken not to expose the eyes or skin to the ultraviolet rays, as damage to vision or burns may occur. Also, these shortwave rays may generate considerable amounts of ozone which is potentially hazardous.

equate — To establish a variable, segment, or file name which is to be replaced at each appearance by a second named identity; this may be utilized for testing, measuring, etc. or whenever a substitute identity or quantity is desired. (Contrast with equivalence, which establishes identicality of identities.)

equation statements — In high level languages (e.g., BASIC, FORTRAN, PL/1, etc.), equation statements are effectively instructions to replace the variable named to the left of an equals sign ($=$) with the value or evaluated expression to the right. This may appear as a mathematical or algebraic equation (e.g., $I = J/3 + K$) but does not necessarily require algebraic validity. E.g., $I = I + 3$ is invalid as an algebraic equation but is valid as a computer language stagement and actually rather common; it may be paraphrased "Add three to the current value of 'I' to form a new value for 'I.'"

equivalent binary digits — The number of binary digits required to express in binary notation a number expressed in another number representation system. For example, approximately $3\tfrac{1}{3}$ times the number of decimal digits is required to express a decimal numeral as a binary numeral.

equivalent equations — Two equations or equation systems in the same unknowns which have the same set of solutions.

erasable programmable ROM (EPROM) — Once programmed, erasable programmable read only memories (EPROMs) allow the programmed contacts to be restored to their initial state, such that they can be re-programmed as often as desired.

erasable storage — 1. A storage device whose

data can be altered during the course of a computation. 2. An area of storage used for temporary storage. 3. A storage medium which can be erased and reused repeatedly, e.g., magnetic drum storage, magnetic tape storage, magnetic disk storage, etc.

erase — 1. Much like clearing; to destroy data stored on a magnetic drum, tape, or any other storage device so new data may be recorded. 2. To replace all the binary digits in a magnetic storage device by binary zeros. 3. To replace all the binary digits in a paper tape by punched holes; more correctly called rubout or letter out.

error — 1. Refers to any incorrect step, process, or result in a computer or data-processing system. The term also refers to machine malfunctions or "machine errors," and to human mistakes or "human errors." 2. Any discrepancy between a computed, observed, recorded, or measured quantity and the true, specified, or theoretically correct value or condition. Contrast with mistake.

error, balanced — 1. A set of error values with maximum and minimum equal in magnitude but opposite in sign. 2. Range of error values that average a zero value.

error burst — A sudden outbreak of errors in a short amount of time compared to the period of errors immediately before and after the occurrence.

error condition — Concerns the state that results from an attempt to execute instructions in a calculator program that are invalid or that operate on invalid data.

error, conscious — An error that was instantly recognized as such by an operator, but was such that his reflex actions were unable to prevent.

error control — Refers to various provisions or arrangements to detect the presence of errors. In some systems, refinements are added to correct the detected errors, either by operations on the received data or by retransmission from the source.

error control, step forward — step back — On some units when there is an error in programming, it's easy to examine the program, by pressing step forward or step back to debug the program. The printer will list the program steps in English. Once users detect the error, they can insert, delete or overwrite a step. If necessary, the machine automatically renumbers the subsequent program steps.

error correction, automatic — Refers to various techniques, usually requiring the use of special codes and/or automatic retransmission, which detect and correct errors occurring in transmission. The degree of correction depends upon coding and equipment configuration.

error correction code — A digit or digits, carried along with a moved computer word or record, which may be used to partially reconstruct the moved record in case of partial loss.

error detecting code — 1. Refers to a system of coding characters in a computer such that any single error produces a forbidden or impossible code combination. 2. A code in which each expression conforms to specific rules of construction, so that if certain errors occur in an expression the resulting expression will not conform to the rules of construction and, thus, the presence of the errors is detected. Synonymous with self-checking code.

error detection routine — A routine used to detect whether or not an error has occurred, usually without special provision to find or indicate its location.

error, generated — Refers to the total error determined by combining the effect of using inexact or imprecise argument with the inexact formula. These errors are compounded by rounding off.

error, inherent — The error in the initial values, especially the error inherited from the previous steps in the step-by-step integration. This error could also be the error introduced by the inability to make exact measurements of physical quantities.

error interrupts — Special interrupts are provided in response to certain error conditions within the main calculator. These may come as a result of a programming fault (e.g., illegal instruction, arithmetic overflow), a store fault (parity error) or an executive system violation (attempt to leave the locked-in area or violation of guard mode). These faults have special interrupt locations in central store and are used by the executive system to take remedial or terminating action when they are encountered.

error notation, calculators — On some units logical errors and improper calculations beyond range of machine (division by zero) are automatically noted — with a reference to an explanation in operating manual!

error, parity — Indicates that during a course of the previous block transfer of data a parity error was detected, or one or more bits have never been picked up or dropped out from either the timing track or the mark track.

error, propagated — An error occurring in a previous operation that spreads through and influences later operations and results.

error quantization — A specific gauge or measure of the uncertainty, particularly that of the irretrievable information loss, which occurs as a result of the quantization of a function in an interval where it is continuous.

error, quiet — These are errors that occur in manual-mechanical systems and are corrected by competent people close to the system before they spread throughout the process or system.

error range — 1. The range of all possible values of the error of a particular quantity. 2. The difference between the highest and the lowest of these values. 3. The binary program with its associated subroutines will not fit into the available main memory. The names of any missing subroutines are listed following this message.

error rate — The total amount of information in error, due to the transmission media, divided by the total amount of information received.

error recovery procedures — Procedures designed to help isolate and, where possible, to recover from errors in equipment. The procedures are often used in conjunction with programs that record the statistics of machine malfunctions. Abbreviated ERP.

error report — Relates to a list of error conditions generated during the execution of a specific program. Errors caused by incorrect or unmatched data.

error, rounding — The error resulting from rounding off a quantity by deleting the less significant digits and applying some rule of correction to the part retained. For instance, 0.2751 can be rounded to 0.275 with a rounding error of .0001.

(Synonymous with round-off error, and contrasted with truncation error.)

error routine — An error routine provides a means of automatically initiating corrective action when errors occur, such as tape read and write, or disk seek, read, and write. It is executed after the programmed check establishes an error. The error routine should cause the operation to be performed at least one more time (in some cases several). If the error persists, processing is interrupted and the condition is signaled on the display. The operator's instruction manual should include procedures for correction and resumption of processing.

errors, completeness — Errors of completeness are discovered when the user signifies that his program is complete by entering the END statement. Some errors (e.g., invalid subscript value, reference to an undefined variable, arithmetic spills, etc.) can be detected only during execution. In this case, after a display of the error condition and its location, execution is interrupted and the calculator reverts to READY status. The user then either immediately corrects his error or proceeds with the rest of his program.

errors, composition — Errors that are detected as soon as the user enters the offending statement. He may immediately substitute a correct statement.

errors, entry (calculator) — Algebraic calculators perform complex chain calculations in the order in which they are entered, rather than according to the standard mathematical hierarchy (in which exponentiation is done first, then multiplication and division, then addition and subtraction). For example, most users are aware that AB & CD must be entered as

$$A \times B + (C \times D) =.$$

Entering it as

$$A \times B + C \times D =$$

gives the erroneous answer (AB + C)D.

error signal — 1. A signal whose magnitude and sign are used to correct the alignment between the controlling and the controlled elements of an automatic control device. 2. Relating to closed loops, that specific signal resulting from subtracting a particular return signal from its corresponding input signal.

errors, instrumentation — Where input into a system is directly from instruments such as pressure gauges, limit checks are imposed to prevent instrumentation errors. If these limits are violated, control may be assumed by a violation subroutine for immediate corrective action.

errors, sampling — 1. The error is a statistic due to a finite number of samples. 2. Errors arising from improperly selected samples, or samples improperly collected so that the samples are not representative.

error, semantic — Those that are concerned with the meaning or intent of the programmer and are definitely his responsibility. Consequently, he is provided with an extensive set of debugging aids for manipulating and referencing a program when in search of errors in the logic and analysis.

errors, solid — An error that always occurs when a particular piece of equipment is used.

error, standard — The standard deviation when it is considered as a measurement of error.

errors, static — An error that is independent of the time variable, as contrasted with dynamic error, which depends on frequency.

errors, syntactic — Syntactic errors are considered the responsibility of the system and are further categorized as follows:
Composition — Typographical errors, violations of specified form, of statements and misuse of variable names (e.g., incorrect punctuation, mixed-mode expressions, undeclared arrays, etc.).
Consistency — Statements that are correctly composed but conflict with other statements (e.g., conflicting declaratives, illegal statement ending a DO range, failure to follow each transfer statement with a numbered statement, etc.).
Completeness — Programs that are incomplete (e.g., transfers to nonexistent statement numbers, improper DO nesting, illegal transfer into the range of a DO loop, etc.).

error, timing — The program was not able to keep pace with the tape transfer rate or a new motion or a selected command was issued before the previous command was completely executed.

errors, uncorrectable — If intent of programmer cannot be determined, the CPU prints a diagnostic message, rejects the clause or statement and continues compilation.

error, unbalanced — Those errors or sets of error values in which the maximum and minimum are not opposite in sign and equal in magnitude, as contrasted to balanced errors, i.e., the average of all the error values is not zero.

ESC, escape character — 1. A control character to signal a change in the meaning of one or more of the characters that follow it. 2. A data communications term representing the use of a control character which, when combined with one or more succeeding characters, forms an escape sequence and the development of additional data communications control operations.

etched circuit — Relates to integrated circuits and the particular construction is a geometric design or pathing arrangement to form active elements by an etching process on a single piece of miconducting material.

even parity check — The method of detecting when bits are dropped by adding one bit to all odd numbers of bit patterns to signify a character; thus, all characters would be represented by an even number of bits. A failure to have such representation would be called a parity error.

event chain — The series of actions that result from an initial event. An example is order processing, inventory adjustment, shipping document preparation, etc., resulting from a sale.

event counter card — An event counter card consists of six individual binary-coded-decimal counter circuits which may be connected into three 2-digit, two 3-digit, or one 6-digit counter units simply by changing a set of jumpers. Individual, programmable "start," "stop," and "reset" controls are provided for each counter subgroup.

event sensing — It is often necessary for a system to respond quickly to alarm conditions, operator intervention or other requests for immediate service. This service request is made via a program interrupt generated by either an event sense or a process interrupt card.

exception-principle system — An information system or data-processing system that reports on situations only when actual results differ from planned results. When results occur within a normal range they are not reported.

exception reporting — A record of departures from the expected or norm. Oftentimes, maximum or minimum limits are the set parameters and the normal range lies within these end numbers or expectations. Reports that have results which exceed these parameters become the basis for an exception reporting output.

exception scheduling routine — When messages or situations occur that require exceptional action, the exception scheduling routine separates them from the normal scheduling loops or routine. The exception action is performed and the system returns to its normal routine.

excess-3 BCD (XS-3) — A variation of 8421 BCD code in which the natural binary sequence of values from 3 through 12 respectively represent the decimal numbers 0 through 9. Used for convenience in forming nine's complements.

exchange key — The exchange key tells the calculator to exchange the x and y quantities in y^x or $\sqrt[x]{y}$ before the function is processed. It changes operands in (x) and (÷) and enters dual arguments for polar-rectangular conversions, decibel conversions, and permutations. (some units)

exclusive OR — 1. A logical operator having the property that if P is a statement and Q is a statement, then the OR of P.Q. is true if and only if at least one is true; false if all are false. P or Q is often represented by P + Q, PUQ. See inclusive OR and exclusive OR.

exclusive segments — Segments in the same region of an overlay program, neither of which is in the path of the other. They cannot be in main storage simultaneously.

EXEC — 1. An abbreviation for Executive Statement. 2. An abbreviation for the Executive system.

execute phase — Refers to a specific part of the cycle of the calculator's operation wherein a command in the program register is performed upon the address indicated. The act of performing a command. See also fetch phase.

execute statement — A basic job control command which identifies a load module to be accessed and executed, plus the specification of job steps.

execution cycle — Refers to a portion of a machine cycle during which the actual execution of the instruction takes place. Some operations (e.g., divide, multiply) may need a large number of these operation cycles to complete the operation, and the normal instruction/operation alternation will be held up during this time. Also called operation.

execution time — 1. Relates to the specific time required to carry out an instruction or procedure or cycle. The time is often expressed in clock cycles. Because the clock frequency is known, the actual time can be calculated accurately, although clock frequencies can be varied. 2. The portion of an instruction cycle during which the actual work is performed or operation executed, i.e., the time required to decode and perform an instruction. Synonymous with time, instruction.

executive — Software which controls the execution of programs in the computer or calculator based on established priorities and real-time or demand requirements.

executive cycle — Refers to a specific period of time during which a machine instruction is interpreted and the indicated operation is performed on the specified operand.

expected values — Generally, the summation of the products of all possible outcomes after each is multiplied by the probability that it will occur, and tables constructed to indicate these values.

explicit address — Refers to an address reference that is specified as two absolute expressions. One expression supplies the value of a displacement. Both values are assembled into the object code of a machine instruction.

exponent — A number placed at the right and above a symbol in typography to indicate the number of times that symbol is a factor, e.g., 10 to the 4 equals $10 \times 10 \times 10 \times 10$, or 10,000.

exponential — Of or pertaining to exponents or to an expression having exponents or a quantity that varies in an exponential manner instead of linearly.

exponential curve regression program — Least Squares Fit, Exponential Curve. This program uses the least squares fit method to fit N pairs of (X, Y) data points to the exponential function $Y = AE^{bx}$. Y must be greater than zero.

exponential equation — A name given to an equation in which the unknown quantity enters an exponent; thus $A^x = b$ is an exponential equation. Every exponential equation of the simple form $a^x = b$, may be solved.

exponential probability program — Refers to an Exponential Distribution. This program calculates the probability distribution of a random variable with exponential distribution function.

exponential quantity — A single quantity which increases or decreases at the same rate as the quantity itself.

extended addressing — Concerns a specific type of addressing mode designed as an operation that can reach practically any place in memory.

extended arithmetic element EAE — Refers to a fundamental central processor logic circuit element which provides hardware-implemented multiply, divide, and normalize function.

extended binary coded decimal interchange code — A set of 256 characters, each represented by eight bits. Abbreviated EBCDIC. See also binary coded decimal character code.

extend (extended data transfer) — An input signal that allows the processor to accommodate a slow memory or peripheral.

extension register — A computer register used as an "extension" of the accumulator register or the quotient register.

external delays — This is lost time which occurs beyond the control of engineers, operators, or maintenance men. Examples are power failure, ambient conditions outside the prescribed range, or transmission difficulties or faults.

external device code (ED) — 1. An address code of an external device that specifies what operation is to be performed. 2. In some systems all external devices are connected to the processor by a common cable that carries an external device address code and a code which specifies what operation is to be performed. Only that device whose address is on the lines will respond to an instruction on the common cable. No instruction will be initiated unless it is accompanied by a start signal. When a device recognizes its address and receives a start signal, it will start the essential information from the operation code in flip-flops and initiate the specified operation.

external device status — External devices re-

external interrupts

spond with both their busy status and their interrupt-request status whenever they recognize their own address. They do not clear out an interrupt request until the interrupt succeeds. The processor notifies an external device that its interrupt has been recognized by sending out an interrupt reset signal.

external interrupts — External interrupts are caused by either an external device requiring attention (such as a signal from a communications device), keyboard switching, or by the timer going to zero.

external memory — 1. The storage of data on a device that is not an integral part of a calculator, but in a form prescribed for use by the calculator. 2. A facility or device, not an integral part of a calculator, on which data usable by a calculator is stored, such as off-line magnetic-tape units or punch-card devices. (Contrasted with internal storage.)

external registers — Refers to those registers, which can be referenced by the program and are located in control store as specific addresses. These are the location (registers) which the programmer references when he desires that some sort of computational function be carried out.

extra accumulator keys — Extra accumulators function as completely separate accumulating memories with complete transfer capability.

extract — To replace the contents of specific columns of a quantity (as indicated by some other quantity called an extractor) by the contents of the corresponding column of a third quantity. To remove from a set of items of information all those items that meet some arbitrary criterion.

extract instruction — A specific instruction that requests the formation of a new expression from selected parts of given expressions.

extrapolate — 1. To estimate the value of a function for variables lying outside the range of the known values. 2. As regards curve characteristics, to extend a curve beyond the limits of known points by continuing the trend established over known points.

extrapolation — The process of deducing a value greater or less than all given values of a function or graph assuming that a projection of the function or graph would continue to satisfy the same relationships as the portion whose values are known.

F

facsimile — 1. Refers to a process by which pictures are scanned and the information converted into signal waves which produce a likeness of the subject copy at another remote point. 2. A system for the transmission of images. The image is scanned at the transmitter, reconstructed at the receiving station, and duplicated on some form of paper. Abbreviated FAX.

fact correlation — A process which is an integral part of linguistic analysis and adaptive learning which uses methods of manipulating and recognizing data elements, items, or codes to examine and determine explicit and implicit relations of data in files, i.e., for fact retrieval rather than document retrieval.

factorial — Let n be a positive integer. The notation n! is read as "n factorial," and represents the product of all positive integers from 1 to n, that is n! = 1, 2, 3, ... n. Thus 4 factorial or $4! = 4 \times 3 \times 2 \times 1 = 24$. Factorial notation is used most importantly in combination, permutation, and other counting techniques.

factorial function key — Factorial function allows rapid calculations of combinations and permutations... to reduce problem-solving time to seconds. Calculators can quickly find the factorial of positive integers.

factorial operator — An operator which applies to a number in a specific way, i.e., if n is the number being considered, then n factorial (written n!) is equal to $n \times (n-1) \times (n-2) \ldots 1$, it being understood by convention that $0! = 1$.

factor, scale (multiplier) — A particular number used as a multiplier, specifically chosen so that it will cause a lot of quantities to fall within a given range of values.

fail-safe control — A system of remote control for preventing improper operation of the controlled function in the event of a circuit failure.

fail-safe system — A system which continues to process data despite the failure of parts in the system. Usually accompanied by some deterioration in performance.

fail-soft system — A calculator system which will continue to run (with deteriorated performance) despite failure in parts of the system.

failure logging — In some systems an automatic procedure whereby the maintenance section of the monitor, acting on machine-check interrupts (immediately following error detection), records the system state. This log is an aid to the customer engineer in diagnosing intermittent errors.

failure, mean-time-to — The average time the system or a component of the system works without faulting. (MTTF)

failure prediction — Refers to various techniques which attempt to determine the failure schedule of specific parts or equipments so that they may be discarded and replaced before failure occurs.

fallback — Refers to a specific condition in processing when special calculator or manual functions must be employed as either complete or partial substitutes for malfunctioning systems. Such procedures could be used anywhere between complete system availability and total system failure.

fallback, recovery from — The restoration of a system to full operation from a fallback mode of operation after the cause of the fallback has been removed.

false add — To form a partial sum, that is, to add without carries.

family — In mathematics, a set of functions, curves, etc., which can be generated by varying one or more of the parameters of a general form.

fan-in — The number of inputs available to a specific logic stage or function.

fan-out — The number of circuits which can be supplied with input signals from an output terminal of a circuit or unit. The changes of digital circuits depend basically on the number of devices that can drive or be driven by one circuit of a specific type, and the number of elements that one output can drive is related to the power available from the output and the amount of power required for each input.

fast response — This is dependent on the situation; on a desk calculator, a fast response would be a 30-second answer: in computer-assisted instruction, it would be a response time of up to 10 seconds; in inputting information, it would be an instantaneous response (less than 1 second) to the teletype terminal from the computer, BSW.

F/A switch — This switch permits users to choose full floating decimal (F) or add-mode (A) operation. In add mode, the decimal is automatically positioned at two places for easy entry of dollars and cents without using • key on some models.

fault — Refers to various physical conditions that cause a device, a component, or an element to fail to perform in a required manner, for example, a short circuit, a broken wire, an intermittent connection.

fault, intermittent — A fault that occurs seemingly in no predictable or regular pattern.

fault-location program — Concerns various programs for identification or information regarding faulty equipment. It is designed and used to identify the location or type of fault and is often part of a diagnostic routine.

fault, permanent — Faults are failures in performance in the manner required or specified. Sporadic faults are intermittent while permanent faults are repetitious, but these may either escape attention when they do not result in failure to perform some particular tasks, or are known and easily correctable.

fault time — The period during which a calculator is malfunctioning or not operating correctly due to mechanical or electronic failure, as opposed to available, idle time, or stand-by time, during which the computer is functional.

fax — Transmission of pictures, maps, diagrams, etc. by radio waves. The image is scanned at the transmitter and reconstructed at the receiving station. (Synonymous with facsimile.)

feasibility study — 1. Usually the initial procedures and criteria for determination of suitability, capability, and compatability of calculator systems to various firms or organizations. A preliminary systems analysis of potential costs savings and new higher level of operations, decision making, and problem-solving capacity as a result of computer procurement. 2. A study in which a projection of how a proposed system might operate in a particular organization is made to provide the basis for a decision to change the existing system.

feedback — When applied to a transmission, feedback is the return of a fraction of the output to the input. In a closed-loop system, it is the part of the system which brings back information about the condition under control.

feedback control — Action in which a measured variable is compared to its desired value, with a function of the resulting error signal used as a corrective command.

feedback control action — That designed control action in which a measured variable is compared to its desired value to produce an actuating error signal which is acted upon in such a way to develop a reduction in the magnitude of the error.

feedback loop — A closed signal path, in which outputs are compared with desired values to obtain corrective commands.

feedforward control action — That control action designed so that information concerning one or more conditions that can disturb the controlled variable is converted into corrective action. This minimizes the deviations of the controlled variable, i.e., feedforward control can be combined with other types of control to anticipate and minimize deviations of the controlled variable.

fetch — 1. The particular portion of a calculator cycle during which the location of the next instruction is determined. The instruction is taken from memory and modified if necessary. It is then entered into the register. 2. To bring a program phase into main storage from the memory image library for immediate execution. 3. The routine that retrieves.

fetching, demand — A memory multiplexing design in which segments are kept on a backing storage and only placed in an internal storage when computations refer to them.

fetch instruction — Refers to a basic instruction or procedure to locate and return instructions that are entered in the instruction register. Generally the next, or some later step in the program, will cause the microprocessor to execute that segment of the program related to the fetched instructions.

fiber optic communications — One optical system consists of three basic components: a pulsed-light source (laser or light-emitting diode), a 2000-foot connecting cable containing over 100 thin glass fibers (approximately 0.004 in. diameter) and a silicon-optical detector as the receiver. The experimental system, still in its development stage, is designed to carry high-speed multiplexed telephone information for relatively short distances, such as the few miles between telephone switching offices in any one city. Currently, such interoffice links use twisted-pair copper conductors, a transmission process that requires the placement of an electric repeater approximately every mile. Since signal attenuation is lower in fiber-optic cable this system won't require field repeaters. Additional benefits include greater message-handling capability due to the very wide bandwidth, a potentially lower cost than conventional systems, and conservation of natural resources (primarily copper).

Two signal data rates will be used. The higher rate (44.7 Mbits/sec) is transmitted by a miniature laser that uses a chip of aluminum gallium arsenide no larger than a grain of table salt. The lower rate (1.544 Mbits/sec) uses a light-emitting diode. Both types of light source, as well as the silicon-optical detector, are packaged so that a field technician can easily connect them to an individual strand of the fiber-optic coupling cable. Joining the two hair-thin fibers end-to-end by means of a simple connector, was an important engineering achievement.

fibonacci search — A search based on dichotomy and developed in such a way that in each step, the original set or the remaining subset, is subdivided in accordance with successive smaller numbers in the specific Fibonacci series. When the number of items in such a set is not equal to a Fibonacci number, the number of items in the set is assumed to equal the next higher Fibonacci number.

field alterable ROMs — Generally these work with many popular advanced calculators. They are often packaged on a single PC board. Some field-alterable ROMs can be programmed at the single-bit level. With capacitive type units, the alteration is almost as simple as a pencil erasure. Any discrete bit in storage can be reprogrammed repeatedly, even while the system is operating.

field calibration check, data acquisition systems — Particularly useful for setting up the calculator . . . the field is a 3-level accurately regulated voltage source, with a polarity switch. Its connections can be jumped to channel terminals to check internal circuit calibration and simulate transducer outputs.

field data gathering system, calculator — When users need to gather data in the field, away from power lines, they look for basic power and clocking systems that are designed for mobile or remote applications. The standard AUTO mode powers-down some units between scans to reduce battery drain. Users need a pre-set program, a customized ROM program they can tailor their system to specific requirements, reducing on-site hassle and time. An optional memory save feature lets the system "keep its wits" during a temporary engine generator outage. Self-calibration simplifies field checkout. If lightning or static electricity threaten the field setup, the calculator is ruggedized up front for extra protection. A carry case is usually available.

field data gathering system calculator components — Some characteristics are:
(1) Clock timing
(2) AUTO mode power conservation
(3) Custom initialization feature
(4) Memory save option
(5) Self-calibration option
(6) Noise rejection and common mode protection
(7) Field cases

field monitoring, calculator — Installed in a pollution monitoring trailer, in a proving ground vehicle, out on the edge of a corn field, one type calculator brings back the data in the form users want it—as a digital printout, telemetered to a computer, even integrated to show such parameters as solar radiation, or smoke density per 15 minute period. Calculators are designed to be rugged and versatile.

FIFO advantages — The first in/first out memory has both advantages and disadvantages when compared to the conventional random access memory (RAM). The RAM allows a system to address any memory location, to write in new data, or to read existing stored data. Data is not lost to memory during a read operation and can be used as often as necessary. The random access memory gives a system maximum flexibility for reading stored data, but requires keeping knowledge of where in memory information is stored and addressing that location. For applications where it is desirable to read out information in the same order that it was written, a FIFO greatly simplifies system operation. (some types)

figures shift — A function performed by a teletypewriter machine that causes the machine to shift to upper case for numbers, symbols, etc., when initiated by the figures-shift character.

file addressing — Some data records have a particular key or code which identifies the data. When the program is given this key it can locate and use the data at the particular file address.

file, chained — To conserve searching time and space, some computer files are in chains. Each data item or key in a record in the chain has the address of another record with the same data or key. To retrieve all data which contain the given key, only the first address need be found, since the next address is adjacent to it, and that one is adjacent to the next, etc.

file conversion — The transformation of parts of records, customer account records, employee records, and the like from their original documents into magnetic files by the computer.

file, data — Aggregations of data sets for definite usage. The file may contain one or more different data sets. A permanent data file is one in which the data is perpetually subject to being updated; e.g., a name and address file. A working data file is a temporary accumulation of data sets which is destroyed after the data has been transferred to another form.

file maintenance — Modification of a file to incorporate changes that do not involve arithmetical operations; for example, insertions, deletions, transfers, and corrections.

file mark — An identification mark for the last record in a file. One of the several labels to indicate end-of-file; i.e., file marks may be followed by trailer label, file mark, and reel mark.

file, master — The overall file or grouping of records having similar characteristics, but which contain the data which is considered permanent by nature of its contents, such as employee pay data, exemptions claimed, department wage rates, etc.

file organization — The procedure of organizing various information files; these files are often random-access files to develop maximized use of storage and swift retrieval for processing.

file preparation — The ordering, sorting, and handling of parts records, customer account records, employee records, and the like from their original or copied documents into a form suitable for transformation via the computer onto magnetic files for storage.

file protection — A device or method which prevents accidental erasure of operative data on magnetic tape reels.

finance pack — Programs address the frequently encountered problems in investment analysis, loans, savings annuities, leases, depreciation, business statistics, and other business applications.

financial "answer machine" calculator — Some manufacturers have produced "answer machines," not "equation-solvers." This means that the power of the basic unit's hardware has to be harnessed in such a way that the real complexity of solving many problems must be invisible to the user. In the final design of some specialist calculators the user need only enter the parameters of the problem into the unit and press a key for his answer. One specific financial unit has over 30 hard-wired programs implemented in the design. These programs essentially replace all of the commonly used financial tables, such as compound interest, annuities, bonds, and so on. Also, other difficult problems, such as time-series, linear regression analysis and standard deviation, are made extremely simple.

financial calculator applications example — One accountant reports that he does cash flow reports, studies sales trends, works out alternative sales terms and financing arrangements, and makes better lease or buy decisions. The calculator also helps control and price inventory, helps the firm produce more timely and meaningful financial statements. The calculator also estimates the weight of any number of steel bars — whatever their size, shape, or length — without the use of tables.

financial pocket calculator — Several types of financial pocket calculators offer wide ranges of financial problem-solving power. One specific unit has 36 separate financial functions allowing users to automatically compute bond yield and price; conversions from add-on interest to APR; sum-of-the-digits depreciation schedules and Rule of 78's interest rebates and more — plus all the financial functions of standard business calculators. In addition, other capabilities give users a built-in 200-year calendar so that they can quickly figure the exact number of days in a bond or loan transaction; mean and standard deviation; and trend-line analysis using linear regression.

finite — A quantity that has a limit or boundary, in contrast to infinite, that has no limit.

finite difference interpolation program — Interpolates for data points in the region of tabulated data for uniformly spaced abscissas, with a specified spacing. The equation used is the backward interpolation formula of Gauss, which uses pairs of data points and sets up the cubic equation for interpolation.

firmware — 1. A term usually related to microprogramming and those specific software instructions that have been more or less permanently burned into a ROM control block. 2. An extension to a computer's basic command (instruction) repertoire to create microprograms for a user-oriented instruction set. This extension to the basic instruction set is done in read-only memory and not in software. The read-only memory converts the extended instructions to the basic instructions of the computer.

firmware, calculator — Many manufacturers sell read-only memories (ROMs) for special routines, generally called "firmware." Several manufacturers sell basic firmware in the form of separately marketed, preprogrammed ROMs (PROMs), which the user selects to fit his unique requirements and plugs into special slots in the mainframe. The ROMs provide various mathematical and statistical functions as well as special input/output routines for mass-storage devices and other peripherals.

firmware, compatibility — Compatibility among data processing systems facilitates execution or conversion of existing programs, data interchange, and the implementation of compilers having equivalent execution time semantics. Compatibility can be achieved via the basic hardware design or by (software or firmware) interpretation. Firmware, or microprogramming, has attracted attention in this context as promising hardware-like compatibility with software-like implementation techniques.

firmware limitations — Firmware generally is limited to moving data through the data paths and functional units already present; able to process effectively only the instruction formats, data types and arithmetic modes that are defined for the hardware. Attempting to use firmware for new formats, types and modes is inherently awkward and might result in poor performance, and that unless special compatibility hardware is added, not normally practical for users, the advantages of microprogramming for this purpose are limited.

first in/first out memory — The first in/first out memory (FIFO) is an important building block for modern digital systems. In calculator systems, the FIFO is used for stack registers where register outputs are sequentially read in the same order that data was entered. A FIFO also simplifies many information handling operations such as high speed compiling and code conversions. Equally important to internal use in a system is the performance of a FIFO as an interface element between two subsystems. It is possible the two subsystems will not share a common clock and the FIFO must operate asynchronously. In this case, data input is controlled by the device supplying information and the read function is controlled by the system using the information. Also, the two systems can be operating at different data rates where several words are stored prior to being read. For example, a lower speed peripheral system may load data at a slow rate to be read by a CPU in a high speed burst.

fixed-cycle operation — 1. A type of operation where a fixed amount of time is allowed for a specific operation. 2. A synchronous or clock-type arrangement in which events occur as a function of measured time.

fixed-in point — Decimal point position is set by a switch. Entries must be made with decimal keying. Any entries that exceed the fixed number of positions will be truncated (dropped).

fixed length record — A record whose number of characters is fixed. The restriction may be deliberate to simplify and speed processing or may be caused by the characteristics of the equipment used.

fixed-out point — Decimal point position is preset to the desired number of positions for the answer. Any excess decimal positions in answer are used to round off, or are truncated depending on the option selected.

fixed point — A notation or system of arithmetic in which all numeric quantities are expressed by a predetermined number of digits with the point implicitly located at some predetermined position; contrasted with floating point.

fixed point arithmetic — 1. A method of calculation in which operations take place in an invariant mannner, and in which the computer does not consider the location of the radix point. This is illustrated by desk calculators or slide rules, with which the operator must keep track of the decimal point. Similarly with many automatic computers, in which the location of the radix point is the programmer's responsibility. Contrasted with arithmetic, floating point. 2. A type of arithmetic in which the operands and results of all arithmetic operations must be properly scaled so as to have a magnitude between certain fixed values.

fixed point arithmetic library — A typical fixed point arithmetic library is a group of subroutines that perform most common single, double and triple precision arithmetic functions. Some of these subroutines are: Single Precision Signed Multiply, Half-signed Multiply; Signed Multiply and Add; Half-signed Multiply and Add; Uncorrected Fractional Divide. Some double precision subroutines are: Double Precision Negate; Add, Subtract, Unsigned Multiply, Half-Signed Multiply, Divide, etc.

fixed point display formats — When one first turns on the power the display is rounded to two decimal (usually) places. By pressing "f" "FIX" and a number key (0 to 9), one can specify the number of decimal places. Or one can select scientific notation, by pressing "f" "SCI" and a number key to specify the number of decimal places (up to seven digits after the decimal point. (Some units).

fixed point operation — A calculation of numbers in which the arithmetic point, binary or decimal, is assumed to be or is held at a specific relative position for each number.

fixed-point system — Refers to a notation system whereby a number is represented by a single set of digits and the position if the radix point is not expressed numerically.

fixed/removable disk, calculator — One type adds considerable programming power to the calculator up to 4,915,200 program steps or 614,400 storage registers. Under keyboard control, the unit offers high-speed random access storage and retrieval of alphanumeric information.

fixed/removable disk drive, calculator — The high end of one peripheral line fulfills the needs of those users who have extremely large storage requirements and work with great quantities of numbers. Three sizes are available; from 1,228,800 program steps to 4,915,200 program steps or 153,600 to 614,400 full storage registers. High speed, random access, and large capacity are the main features of Disk Drive. Five different types of Error check are also incorporated into this reliable system. (some models)

fixed sequential format — Means of identifying a word by its location in the block. Words must be presented in a specific order and all possible words preceding the last desired word must be present in the block.

fixed variable — 1. A variable in the problem (logical, structural, primal, or dual) fixed at zero level for feasibility. 2. A variable to be bounded away from zero is sometimes "fixed" at its bound in a bounded variable algorithm so that the transformed variable associated with it is then feasible at zero level, thus permitting arbitrary upper and lower bounds.

fixed word length — Having the property that a machine word always contains the same number of characters or digits.

flag — Refers to a bit (or bits) used to store one bit of information. A flag has two stable states and is the software analogy of a flip-flop.

flag bit — Refers to a specific information bit that indicates a type or form of demarcation that has been reached. This may be carry, overflow, etc. Generally the flag bit refers to special conditions, such as various types of interrupts.

flag operations, calculator — Flag are signals. Some units have five. Each is set or reset by user. Manually from the keyboard, or as part of a stored program. The flag's condition can be tested by the IF FG transfer instruction. Users can manually control program options directly from the keyboard before execution with flags.

flags for programmed decisions, calculators — Some calculators have two flags (called flag 1 and flag 2) available for use. A flag is an invisible piece of information with just two possible conditions: on or off. The flag operations are very basic to many calculators. Users can set a flag on or off by using the Set Flag operations. These operations can be executed from the keyboard or from a program. The reason for setting a flag is so that a program can later make a decision based on the condition of the flag (using the test flag operations).

flag signals — Flag signals, flags set, cleared, tested etc. include data entry, error detection, and error override. Change flag without stopping program execution is an added feature on some systems.

flashing display, small calculators — On some units the display flashes when any of several improper operations are attempted. Pressing any key stops the flashing without performing the key function.

flashing display stops (small calculators) — Errors that cause a flashing display, if executed in a program, also stop the program. Users stop the flashing by pressing any key. Some users can identify the reason for the stop by switching momentarily to PRGM mode to see the keycode of the improper operation. A list of these operations can be found in most specific unit's handbooks.

flip-flop — A device capable of assuming one of two stable states, in which interconnected symbols are used to represent operations, data, flow, and equipment.

flip-flop circuit — 1. A type of circuit having two stable states and usually two input terminals (or signals) corresponding to each of the two states. The circuit remains in either state until the corresponding signal is applied. Also, a similar bistable device with an input which allows it to act as a single-stage binary counter. 2. A bistable device; a device capable of assuming two stable states; a bistable device which may assume a given stable state depending upon the pulse history of one or more input points and having one or more output points. The device is capable of storing a bit of information; controlling gates, etc.; a toggle.

floating decimal point — Relates to a system in which each entry may contain the decimal point in any position. The number and decimal point will be properly positioned automatically when displayed.

floating-in, decimal — Decimal point position is not preset. It is entered with number of proper insertion point. Each entry can have a different number of decimal positions.

floating out decimal — Decimal is automatically aligned in the answer by the calculator.

floating point — A form of number representation in which quantities are represented by a bounded number (mantissa) and a scale factor (Characteristic or Exponent) consisting of a power of the number base, e.g., $127.6 = 0.1276 \times 10^3$ where the bounds are 0 and 1.

floating point arithmetic — Arithmetic used in a calculator where the calculator keeps track of the decimal point (contrasted with fixed point arithmetic).

floating point shift — A shift in 4-bit increments, performed on a short-format or long-format floating-point number.

floating-point system — A numbering system in which an added set of digits is used to denote the location of the radix point.

floppy disc specifications — Typical characteristics are: Data Capacity: Tracks per Surface, 77; Sectors per Track, 26; Bytes per Sector, 128; Bytes per Surface, 256.2K; Transfer Rate (bits per second), 250 K. Access Time: Rotation (RPM), 360; Rotational Latency, 167; Positioning Time: Track to Track, 10 milliseconds; Head Stabilization, 20 milliseconds; Head Load, 40 milliseconds.

floppy disc system, diskette — A floppy disc system provides calculator users a low-cost, random access, mass storage disc with storage capacity typically from 242K bytes to a total of 968K bytes. The diskette is an economical, flexible, oxide-coated, Mylar disc enclosed in a plastic protective jacket. Many floppy systems meet IBM format, recording, and medium specifications which enhances the diskette usage as a transportable medium. Technically the floppy disc is a combination of magnetic tape and disc technologies. The diskette recording medium has the appearance of a 45 RPM record; the circular diskette is packaged in an 8-inch square plastic case. The disc drive's head moves radially across the diskette as do large disc. Data may be read from or written to the diskette by specifying a track and sector address. The read/write head moves radially across the surface to the specified track and waits until the specified sector is brought to the read/write head through disc rotation.

floppy disc system configuration — The following are some standard floppy disc kit options available

- Master kit. This kit includes one floppy drive, 7" × 19" × 15" chassis which can house two drives, power supply for two drives, floppy CRU controller, and a 12-foot cable assembly.
- Secondary kit. This kit includes disc drive, mounting hardware, and cable assembly. This unit mounts either in the master kit chassis or the floppy disc expansion kit.
- Floppy disc expansion kit. This kit includes a floppy disc expansion chassis and power supply for two drives. The expansion kit allows the user to expand a master kit to a total of four drives.

floppy disc system features — The following are primary features of floppy disc available for calculator users:
Recording medium is removable diskette (oxide-coated, Mylar disc) enclosed in plastic case; IBM-compatible; Rack-mountable; Four disc drives per controller with overlapped seek capability; Power supply capable of handling two disc drives; Additional individual disc drives available for expansion; Head loading and unloading feature; Internal on-board diagnostics; Cyclic redundancy error checking of sectors; Basic write protect feature; Mechanical door interlock to ensure that diskette is completely inserted in drive; Power failure detection to prevent data alteration during ac power loss.

floppy disk automatic error recovery — When a sector read, or read ID fails, controller automatically retries, and if required wipes the diskette and retries. If failure persists, host is notified.

floppy disk automatic seek verify — After seek completion a read ID is effected to ensure desired track was reached (not done for write unformatted commands).

floppy disk characteristic — With the recent introduction of dual density drives, inner-track bit density for floppies has doubled from 3200 bpi, the standard concentration for conventional drives. Accordingly, unformatted capacity per disk has risen from 3.2 Mbits for conventional systems to 6.4 Mbits for dual density machines.

floppy disk diagnostics —
SELF DIAGNOSTIC: At power up an initializing sequence self-tests the controller, the floppy disk drive and the diskette.
HOST DIAGNOSTIC COMMANDS: Allow isolation of faults within the subsystem.
- DIAGNOSTIC READ
  Transfers the internal registers of some type units to the host for diagnostic purposes. (NOTE: Register zero contains a sense byte detailing the nature of a failure.)
- LOOPBACK
  A diagnostic oriented command reflecting output data back to the input.

floppy disk drive, low cost — One unit combines the best of both worlds with this type floppy-disc drive; both worlds being IBM-formatted soft sectoring and 32-hold hard sectoring. For even greater versatility users add an optional sector generator and create their own hard sectored format using IBM diskettes. Typical specs for this drive include 3.2M-bits storage capacity, 6 msec track-to-track access, 176-msec random access seek, and head-positioning lead screw reliability of 3.2×10^9 steps. To eliminate ground loops and decoupling problems, an internal dc/dc converter provides a negative power supply voltage. A single interface cable can connect up to 4 drives, since each drive has its own unit-select decoding circuitry. In addition, a status connector on the unit provides continuous monitoring of the index, sector and ready signals. This allows simultaneous track seeking independent of the CPU with an interrupt signal returned when the seek is complete. Features include a mechanical write-enable switch, automechanical interlock, clock/data separator, error flag signal and low current stand-by operation.

floppy disk host commands, examples —
WRITE FORMATED
The normal write command executed by: (1) reading a sector to verify correct track ID, and (2) writing the sector buffer data.
WRITE UNFORMATED
Similar to the write formated except the read before write is omitted; used for diskette initialization.
READ
Seek the desired track and sector and subsequently loads sector data into the sector buffer.
COPY WRITE
Host software driver performs fast sector data moves either disk to disk, or with sectors of the same disk (without passing the data through the host computer or calculator).

floppy disk IBM compatibility — This actually encompasses two types of compatibility: media compatibility and plug-to-plug compatibility. A floppy disk is media compatible if data written on it by an IBM disk system can be read by another manufacturer's machine. An IBM-compatible disk has the same physical parameters, composition and format as IBM's product. The IBM floppy-disk format, incidentally, specifies a number of characteristics, including 77 tracks per surface, 26 sectors per track and a data record of 128 bytes per sector. In addition, the format is characterized by preambles, address marks, sync bytes and error codes arranged in a specified order and in specified locations within each sector. Plug-to-plug compatibility refers not to the floppy disk, but the disk drive itself. A plug-to-plug compatible floppy system is functionally equivalent in every respect to an IBM system, which it can replace if necessary without disrupting the host processor's operations.

floppy disk illegal command checking — Ensures the controller does not inadvertently destroy data with an erroneous host originated command eg., write track 78, etc.

floppy disk interface — A host-controller interface bus represents the minimum lines required to support an asynchronous byte communication protocol between host computer and controller. An 8 bit input bus can be used for status and data transfers, an 8 bit output bus can be used for commands and data transfers and five control lines are used for I/O bus information definition and byte handshaking. Input/output bus can also be tied together to further reduce interface lines (12 lines total), giving a bidirectional byte bus.

floppy disk printer interface — Due to the I/O space limitation of many microcomputers and calculators, a subchannel address capability is provided along with the internal microcode for controlling a printer (a standard feature of the controller). The hardware interface is simply an edgeboard connector.

floppy disk sectoring — Sectoring divides the diskette into equal-sized pie slices. Each track cuts across each sector to form a matrix of track and sector units that are the "mailbox" addresses of the user's data. In the IBM format, 77 tracks and 26 sectors form 2,002 mailboxes that each store 128 bytes. Three of the tracks, however, are reserved by IBM for a table of contents, maintenance and as extra tracks, should up to two regular ones go bad. Thus the 74 used tracks store 242K bytes of the user's data.

floppy disk systems — A typical floppy disk provides random access program/data storage. Hard-sector formatted, each disk holds over 300,000 data bytes. Because many floppy controllers have all of their intelligence in microcode, some microcontrollers offer features not practical in designs implemented with hard-wired logic. The host-calculator driver need only issue a small sequence of commands to write or read data from the disk.

floppy disk systems (for microcomputers and calculators) — Cheaper but slower than their rigid counterparts, floppy disks currently compete with low-cost tape cassettes and cartridges as program loaders and testers, and as peripheral memories for dedicated systems. As the proliferation of LSI technology steadily drives down the cost of IBM-compatible and other drives, however, floppies may gradually supplant their tape and cassette rivals in these dedicated applications. Moreover, they will find growing applications as main memories in microcomputer and advanced calculator based systems. With microcomputers and LSI circuitry, the floppy disk will form a principal building block in future small systems and will play a major role in the gradual decentralization of many larger computer systems. New systems concepts provide CRTs and calculators as terminals.

floppy disk track-to-track access time — This is given as 10 ms by most manufacturers, refers to the period a floppy's head requires to move from one data track to the adjacent track on the disk. Users should distinguish track-to-track access time, however, from average head positioning time, which, with average latency and settling time, constitutes one of the three components that make up average access time. The difference arises because the typical addressing command requires the moving head to cross many data tracks, not just one. Users can, however, use track-to-track access time to calculate average positioning time by multiplying it by one-third the total number of tracks and adding head settling time (typically 10 ms) and head loading time (typically 50 ms) to this product. For a floppy disk with 77 tracks and a track-to-track access time of 10 ms, average positioning time equals 310 ms.

flow chart — 1. Usually a programmers tool for determining a sequence of operations as charted using sets of symbols, directional marks, and other representations to indicate stepped procedures of computer operation. Flowcharts also enable the designer to conceptualize the procedure necessary and to visualize each step and item on a program. A completed flowchart is often a necessity to the achievement of accurate final code. 2. A graphical representation for the definition, analysis, or solution of a problem, in which symbols are used to represent operations, data, flow, equipment, etc. Contrast with block diagram. 3. A flowchart represents the path of data through a problem solution. It defines the major phases of the processing as well as the various data media used.

flow tracing — A type of diagnostics and debugging in which the programmer specifies the start and end of those program segments where he wishes to examine the contents of various registers and accumulators. The program will run at machine speed until it encounters the desired segments, and the printing commences and is terminated when the end of the program segment is encountered. It is also possible to then include "snap-shot" traces which indicate the contents not only of the various accumulators and registers, but also of specified memory locations.

forecasting — Refers to various types of plans and determinations concerning potential future situations. Many forecasts are unhappily based on projection and analysis of past results instead of being viewed in the light of very current experience. Statistical procedures and probabilities, as well as new operations research techniques for modern forecasting, make use of such factors and techniques as seasonal variation, trends, random variables, queuing, econometrics, etc.

foreground — 1. In multiprogramming, refers to the environment in which high-priority programs are executed. 2. Under time sharing option (TSO) the environment in which programs are swapped in and out of main storage to allow CPU time to be shared among terminal users. All command processor programs execute in the foreground. Contrast with background.

foreground/background technique — Automatic execution of programs on a priority basis, allowing the lower-priority programs to execute when higher-priority programs are not utilizing the system.

foreground job — 1. A high-priority job, usually a real-time job. 2. A teleprocessing or graphic dis-

formal logic

play job that has an indefinite running time during which communication is established with one or more users at local or remote terminals. 3. Under TSO, any job executing in a swapped region of main storage, such as a command processor or a terminal user's program. Contrast with background job.

formal logic — The study of the structure and form of valid argument without regard to the meaning of the terms in the argument.

format — The arrangement of data according to a fixed plan or design.

format, packed — A binary-coded decimal format in which two decimal digits are represented within a single byte of storage, accomplished by eliminating the zone bits.

formula language — The second level of programming language available for user-programmable electronic calculators. It uses formula statements, mathematical in nature, and is constructed in the same way as it would look if written on paper to be solved by hand.

formula programming, calculator — In some units the Formula ROM provides an additional set of twenty-five instructions to the calculator's such that problems can be solved algebraically, in exactly the same sequence as they are written on paper. In addition one- or two-dimensional subscripting simplifies the manipulation of the elements of the matrix. The ROM does not interfere with the regular calculator keyboard operations or with its ability to use peripheral devices.

FORTRAN Assembler — An assembler written in ANSI FORTRAN is available for some systems. This allows maximum transferability to a wide variety of large computer systems and the advantage of file management and text editing capabilities of large general-purpose computer systems. The assembler can contain the following features: relocatable- or absolute - load - module generation; conditional assembly features; global symbols for communication between independent assemblies; wide variety of assembly-time operators (+,-,*,/, AND, OR, NOT); local symbols, error messages, including error position in the source line, etc.

FORTRAN — (Formula Translation): A problem-oriented computer programming language initially designed for use by scientific and engineering personnel for the solution of problems which can be expressed in algebraic notation.

FORTRAN IV — FORTRAN IV is an optimizing compiler implementing ANSI Fortran X3.9-1966 plus many extensions. It permits the user to write his program in a higher level language to save programming time. The compiler operates in an Operating System (OS) in most cases, and produces object code optimized for minimum memory utilization.

Fourier analysis — The determination of the harmonic components of a complex waveform either mathematically or by a waveanalyzer device.

Fourier principle — Principle which shows that all repeating waveforms can be resolved into sine wave components, consisting of a fundamental and a series of harmonics at multiples of this frequency. It can be extended to prove that nonrepeating waveforms occupy a continuous frequency spectrum.

Fourier series — A mathematical analysis permitting any complex wave form to be resolved into a fundamental, plus a finite number of terms involving its harmonics.

Fourier transform — A mathematical relation between the energy in a transient and that in a continuous energy spectrum of adjacent component frequencies.

four-register operational stacks — Four-register operational stacks can hold intermediate solutions. They can retain as many as four intermediate solutions in sequence, and automatically position them for use on a last in, first out basis. The stack design also permits X and Y register exchange and roll-up or roll-down of any entry to the display for review or operation.

fourth generation — Computer systems designed with the extensive usage of integrated circuits.

fox message — A standard message used for testing telegraph circuits and machines because it includes all the alphamerics as well as most of the function characters. The message is: THE QUICK BROWN FOX JUMPED OVER A LAZY DOG'S BACK 1234567890 (STATION NAME) SENDING.

FPLA characteristics — Some enhanced FPLA families of devices have field programmability, I/O organization, 50 ns speed, and also chip enable features. These offer distinct usage benefits in both tristate and open collector devices.

FPLA device (field programmable logic array) — A PLA where the internal connections of the AND and OR gates can be programmed by passing high current through fusible links.

FPLA editing — A critical feature of FPLAs, absent in bipolar PROMs, is their editing capability. A number of modifications can be incorporated in a program already stored in the FPLA. Specifically in some FPLAs, product terms can be added or deleted from any output function, and input variables can be deleted from any output function, and input variables can be deleted from any product terms. Also, outputs programmed active-high can be reprogrammed to active-low. This offers a good degree of flexibility, comparable to the versatility afforded by erasable MOS PROMs.

FPLA vs PROM — The structure and use of Field Programmable Logic Arrays can be understood if one compares them more to memory than to logic. An FPLA is basically a PROM with one very important difference — its versatility makes it a great deal more useful. To grasp the similarities, one must examine PROMs. Industry jargon refers to PROMs as 1K, 2K, 4K, etc. These usually imply standard organizations such as 256×4, 256×8, 512×8, respectively. The larger in each pair of numbers refers to the number of words in a PROM, and the second represents the number of bits in each word. The product of both numbers (approximately 1K, 2K, 4K) gives the total number of storage bits contained in the PROM. This aspect of PROMs carries over to FPLAs, meaning that FPLAs will be described as 48×8, for a total working storage density of 384 bits. Since the key word here is "working," although an FPLA appears to be a relatively small PROM, its usefulness is vastly magnified because of the difference in input structure.

fractional conversion key — Enters any fraction as any part of any operation exactly as it is written and automatically converts it to its decimal equivalent without interrupting computations.

frame — Generally refers to a record consisting

of a printout of the programmed channel number, measurement data, units, and alarm condition of each channel together with a frame identification number and time of scan.

f ratio of two variances program — Given data from two samples, of Sizes N1 and N2, this program will calculate the variances of the two samples and the F-Ratio.

free field — A property of information-processing recording media which permits recording of information without regard to a preassigned or fixed field; e.g., in information-retrieval devices, information may be dispersed in the record in any sequence or location.

frequency — 1. Refers to the number of recurrences of a periodic phenomenon in a unit of time. Electrical frequency is specified as so many cycles per second. Frequency is symbolized by f. 2. The number of times an electromagnetic signal repeats an identical cycle in a unit of time, usually one second. One Hertz (Hz) is one cycle per second. A KHz (Kilohertz) is one thousand cycles per second; a MHz (Megahertz) is one million cycles per second; a GHz (Gigahertz) is one billion cycles per second. 3. The rate of recurrence of some cyclic or repetitive event, such as the rate of repetition of a sinewave electrical current, usually expressed in cycles per second, or Hertz.

frequency and/or unit counter for display — A typical unit is a 7-digit frequency or unit counter for use with a LED display. As a unit counter, users need only add display, two resistors, a capacitor, and control switches. As a frequency counter in addition to the above, users can add an oscillator controller. These units are useful for: unit counters, frequency counters, period counters and offer low operating power dissipation, internal store capability, internal inhibit to counter input, to test speed-up points and to protect terminals against static discharge.

frequency counter — A typical unit has been designed to provide the oscillator and gating functions to convert the unit into a 6 or 7 decade frequency counter. Using a 6.5536MHz quartz crystal oscillator this frequency counter has two count windows, either 0.01 sec or 0.1 sec. The maximum input frequency can be as high as 2MHz. The total current consumption with the display off is less than 1mA and with all digits lit is typically 120mA from a 5 volt supply, thus making this system ideal for portable battery operated systems as well as for low cost line operated instrumentation equipment.

frequency distribution — Usually concerns table showing the number of occurrences of each value displayed in an ordered array or pattern.

frequency-division multiplexing — A technique for sharing a communication channel, by using each signal to modulate the frequency of a subcarrier.

frequency measurements — A pulse counter card accumulates counts over a precise time interval when a programmable timer card is connected to the enable line of the counter. The program divides the count by the time interval to measure frequencies from 200 kHz to 0.001 Hz.

frequency reference card — Typical card provides six separate square wave outputs derived from a 1MHz crystal. Often used with 69435A counter cards for time interval measurements.

f test of sample variances program — Computes the F Ratio from Sample Variances and the associated upper tail area of the cumulative F-Distribution function to enable hypothesis testing of Sample Variances.

full adder (parallel) — A parallel full adder can be developed from as many three-input adders as there are digits in the input words. The carry output of each operation is connected to one input of the three-digit adder corresponding to the next significant digit position. (Some systems)

full-duplex — Refers to a duplex operation that is simultaneous communication between two points in both directions.

full shift capability — Some systems provide a full complement of shift instructions which can be: single or multiple place; left or right; logical or circular. Compare this with the basic single place shift found in most minicomputers.

function — 1. One quantity (A) is said to be a function of another quantity (B) when no change can be made in B without producing a corresponding change in A and vice versa. Thus, in the equation $y^2 = R^2 - X^2$, Y is a function of X, and Y is also a function. 2. A specific purpose of an entity or its characteristic action. 3. In communications, a machine action such as a carriage return or line feed. 4. A quantity whose value depends on the value of one or more other quantities.

function, continuous — A function in which the difference between any two consecutive states is less than any assignable quantity. In such a function, if we suppose the independent variable to pass through every possible state from one given value to another, the function will pass, by imperceptible degrees, through every state from the first to the last. A function that follows this law is said to be subject to the law of continuity.

function, control — 1. A nonprinting bit configuration that causes a machine action such as line feed, carriage return, etc., but has no affect on data. 2. The machine operation caused by 1.

functional design — The specification of the working relations between the parts of a system in terms of their characteristic actions.

functional diagram — 1. A specific type of block diagram which represents the functional design and special symbols called functional symbols. Functional design relates to the specification between all parts of a system, including the logic design and equipment used. A graphic representation showing the operational aspects of a system.

functional key — A terminal key, such as the attention key, that causes the transmission of a signal not associated with a printable character. Detection of the signal usually causes the system to perform some predefined function for the user.

functional requirement — A document most often prepared by systems analysts or operations-research staff people explicitly detailing one of the functions to be performed by the system. Specifications concerning the manner in which the function will be completed often accompany the message. Functional requirements provide a basis for: guiding and assisting people who prepare programs; preparing instruction manuals; obtaining management acceptance of management procedure or policy changes to further integrate a computer "total system."

function evaluation program — Calculation of Arbitrary Functions at a Point or Over a Given Interval. For any function (programmed by the user) this program will calculate the value of the function at any given point or at a specified sequence of increments over any chosen interval.

function-evaluation routines — A set of commonly used mathematical routines. The initial set of routines will include sine, cosine, tangent, arcsine, arccosine, arctangent, square root, natural logarithm, and exponential. These routines will be written in fixed and floating point.

function, explicit — A function whose value is expressed directly in terms of the variable; thus, in the equation $Y = AX^2 + BX^{1/2} + C$, Y is an explicit function of $X(Y = fX)$. The term stands opposed to implicit function, in which the relation between the function and variable is not directly expressed.

function, exponential — A function in the mathematical form of: $f(x) = kb^x$, k and b are constants.

function generator — A computing element designed with an output of a specified nonlinear function of its input or inputs. Normal usage excludes multipliers and resolvers.

function hole — A specific hole punched into a card which indicates the type or nature of data or information coming or which of various functions a particular peripheral unit is to perform or which instructions are to be followed. Also called: control punch, function hole or designation punch or hole.

function, implicit — An expression in which the form of the function is not directly expressed, but which requires some operation to be performed, to render it evident. Thus, in the equation $ay^3 + bxy + cx^2 + dy + ex + f = 0$, y is an implicit function of x.

function key — 1. A specific key on a keyboard (for example, CR, LF, LTRS, FIGS, etc.) which, when operated, causes a receiving device to perform a certain mechanical function so that a message will be received in proper form. 2. A special key or set of keys which allows functions to be specified characteristic of given applications environment. 3. Keys on keyboards of input/output or specialized terminals which are used to query the system or have it perform certain operations. For example, on a remote-inquiry terminal used in a stock quotation system, a three letter combination identifies any stock, and earnings, sales, dividends, volume, etc. can be displayed, by punching the right function key.

function keys, cathode-ray tube (CRT) — Fixed and variable function keys have been added to various CRT consoles. A function key when depressed transmits a signal to the computer which can be equated to a prestored typewriter message of many strokes. Function keys by thus saving user actions provide convenience and ease of operation and increased response rate of the user. Special consoles of various types have been developed for a particular user. Examples are: airline agent's sets, badge readers, stock broker's inquiry consoles and many others.

function, objective — An objective function of the independent variable function whose maximum or minimum value is sought as an optimization problem.

function punch — A specific hole punched into a card which indicates the type or nature of data or information coming or which of various functions a particular peripheral unit is to perform or which instructions are to be followed. Also called: control punch, function hole or designation punch, or hole.

functions — If two variables x and y are so related that, whenever a value is assigned to x, one or more corresponding values of y are determined, then y is called a function of x. If just one value of y corresponds to each value of x, y is a single-valued function of x. If y is a function of x it is referred to as the independent variable, y the dependent variable. Independent variables are usually plotted on the horizontal axis.

functions accuracy, calculator — The accuracy of many operations (trigonometric, logarithmic, and exponential) depends upon the argument. The answer that is displayed will be the correct answer for an input argument having a value that is within $\pm N$ counts in the 10th (least significant) digit of the actual input argument. For example, 1.609437912 is given as the natural log of 5 when calculated on some units. However, this is an approximation because the result displayed (1.609 437912) is actually the natural log of a number between 4.999999998 and 5.000000002, which is ± 2 counts (N = 2 for logarithms) in the 10th (least significant) digit of the actual input argument.

functions library (elementary) — A typical offering of many manufacturers is a set of subroutines to perform the most common mathematical functions using floating point number format. Some are: Square Root; Exponentiation; Hyperbolic Tangent; Arctangent; Sine; Cosine; Natural Logarithm; Common Logarithm; Base 2 Logarithm, etc.

functions of x and y program — Can be used to find: (1) y raised to the x power for any real y and x (if y is negative, x must be an integer); (2) logarithms of y to base x; (3) y (mod x) = y − x (integer part of [y/x]); (4) permutations of y things taken x at a time; (5) combinations of y things taken x at a time.

functions, process — Specific collective functions performed in and by the equipment in which a variable or number of variables is or are to be controlled, but not concerned with any automatic control equipment, as stated.

functions, trigonometric — Specific mathematical functions of an angle or an arc. The most common are: sine, cosine, tangent, cotangent, secant and cosecant. If θ is the angle formed by r and the x axis, and P is a point on r having "a" as its abscissa and "b" as its ordinate, then: sine $\theta = b/r$; cosine $\theta = a/r$; tangent $\theta = b/a$; cosecant $\theta = r/b$; secant $\theta = r/a$ and contangent $\theta = a/b$.

function table — 1. Refers to two or more sets of data so arranged that an entry in one set selects one or more entries in the remaining sets, for example, a tabulation of the values of a function for a set of values of the variable, a dictionary. 2. A device constructed of hardware, or a subroutine, which can either decode multiple inputs into a single output or encode a single input into multiple outputs.

function, transfer — 1. A mathematical expression frequently used by control engineers which expresses the relationship between the outgoing and the incoming signals of a process, or control element. The transfer function is useful in studies of control problems. 2. A mathematical expression or expressions which describe(s) the relationship between physical conditions at two different points in time or space in a given system, and perhaps, also describe(s) the role played by the intervening time or space.

function words — The function word contains

the operating instructions for the peripheral units, its format depending upon the particular subsystem.

fuse — A protective device, usually a short piece of wire or chemical compound, constructed to melt and break a circuit when the current exceeds its rated capacity.

G

games calculators play — When some clever person figured out that 71077345 viewed upside down on a calculator spelled "SHELLOIL," a new game was popularized: calculator word games. Unfortunately, the vocabulary is limited to I, E, H, S, L, B and O, with G and D possible depending upon the calculator and the viewer's imagination. While some unkind people might wish a T possible to combine with IDIOS. A book has been published (28-pages) entitled "Games Calculators Play." Included are more than 250 words and 57 games.

game theory — A mathematical process of selecting an optimum strategy in the face of an opponent who has a strategy of his own.

game theory, decision-making — Game theory is a mathematical theory dealing with decision-making in a competitive situation in which both parties are active and have an effect on the final outcome. The object is to arrive at an optimal course of action through consideration of all possible moves and chance happenings.

game theory models — The theory of games is a branch of mathematics that aims to analyze various problems of conflict by abstracting common strategic features for study in theoretical "models," — termed "games" because they are patterned on actual games such as bridge and poker. By stressing strategic aspects, that is, aspects controlled by the participants, it goes beyond the classical theory of probability, in which the treatment of games is limited to aspects of pure chance. Zero-sum, two-person games can be solved by linear programming methods.

gamma function program — This program approximates the value of gamma function $\Gamma(x)$ for $1 \leq x \leq 70$.

$$\Gamma(x) = \int_0^\infty t^{x-1} e^{-t} dt$$

1. $\Gamma(x) = (x - 1)\Gamma(x - 1)$
2. For $1 \leq x \leq 2$, polynomial approximation can be used.

$\Gamma(x) \cong 1 + b_1(x - 1) + b_2(x - 1)^2 + \ldots + b_8(x - 1)^8$

where $b_1 = -0.577191652$, $b_2 = 0.988205891$
$b_3 = -0.897056937$, $b_4 = 0.918206857$
$b_5 = -0.756704078$, $b_6 = 0.482199394$
$b_7 = -0.193527818$, $b_8 = 0.035868343$.

Note: This program can be used to find the generalized factorial x! for $0 \leq x \leq 69$.

$$x! = \Gamma(x + 1)$$

gamma probability program — Refers to a Gamma Probability Distribution. Calculates the Gamma Probability Distribution for a given argument. Another program computes the probability of a random variable which has a Gamma probability distribution. It also computes the Mean and Variance of the specified Gamma Distribution. This distribution requires two parameters, Alpha and Beta, as input, both of which must be greater than zero.

gantt chart — A chart of activity against time; such charts have historically been used to schedule or reserve resources for specific activities. Critical path method (CPM) and project evaluation and review techniques (PERT) are devices which have offered substantial improvement in scheduling and allocations; a Gantt chart can be used to express the resource allocation schedule decided upon using PERT/CPM.

gap — 1. An interval of space or time used as an automatic sentinel to indicate the end of a word, record, or file of data on a tape, e.g., a word gap at the end of a word, a record or item gap at the end of a group of words, and a file gap at the end of a group of records or items. 2. The absence of information for a specified length of time or space on a recording medium, as contrasted with marks and sentinels which are the presence of specific information to achieve a similar purpose. Marks are used primarily internally in variable word length machines. Sentinels achieve similar purposes either internally or externally. However, sentinels are programmed rather than inherent in the hardware. Related to file and symbol, terminating. 3. The space between the reading or recording head and the recording medium, such as tape, drum, or disk.

gap digits — Digits are sometimes included in a machine word for various technical reasons.

gap, interrecord — An interval of space or time deliberately left between recording portions of data or records. Such spacing is used to prevent errors through loss of data or over-writing and permits tape stop-start operations.

gap length — The dimension of the gap of a reading and recording head measured from one pole face to the other. In longitudinal recording, the gap length can be defined as the dimension of the gap in the direction of tape travel.

garbage — A slang computer term for unwanted and meaningless information carried in memory or storage. Also referred to as hash.

gas discharge displays — Gas discharge displays are devices that use the glow produced by ionized neon gas to form alphanumeric characters. For calculator applications these characters are usually in the form of a 5-by-7 or 7-by-9 dot matrix. There are two kinds of gas discharge, or plasma displays, dc and ac. Dc displays are the most widely available. In dc plasma panels, a glass plate with an array of holes is sandwiched between top-wire anodes above the glass, cathode strips and bottom-wire anodes below it. The holes from cells for the neon gas become visible when the proper voltages are applied.
Burroughs' Self-Scan II uses this principle. The Self-Scan II is a basic 20 character display that uses a 5-by-7 dot matrix to produce 0.7-inch high characters.

gas-discharge tube decoder-drivers — Gas-discharge tubes require decoder-drivers and segment-digit drivers with significantly higher breakdown voltages than are needed with LEDs. New techniques such as dielectric isolation permit circuitry to withstand higher voltages. However, for driving anodes and cathodes, the device need not withstand the full 180 to 200 V drop and ratings of 50 V can be satisfactory.

gate — 1. A circuit having one output and several inputs, the output remaining unenergized until certain input conditions have been met. When used in conjunction with computers, a gate is also called an AND circuit. A gate can also be a signal to trigger the passage of other signals through a circuit. 2. An electrode in a field-effect transistor. 3. A device having one output channel and one or more input channels, such that the output channel state is completely determined by the input channel states, except during switching transients. 4. A combinational logic element having at least one input channel.

gating circuits — The digital calculator carries out its tasks by performing "logical operations" on information expressed in binary form, that is, information represented by strings of "1's" and "0's." When the information is expressed in this form, operations of any complexity can be performed by building up arrays of circuitry using only a few basic operations. These are Boolean functions and inversions. These functions can be achieved in a variety of ways using electronic circuits.

Gaussian curve (random-error concept) — A random error of sampling is a variation due to chance alone. If the sample is truly random, small errors will be more numerous than large errors and positive errors will be like negative errors, thus giving rise to symmetrical, bell-shaped "normal curve of error." This concept was first investigated by the German mathematician Karl F. Gauss, and the curve is often called the Gaussian curve.

Gaussian distribution — Widely encountered spread of values about a nominal mean in systems where statistically large numbers of readings are obtained. Characterized by equal probabilities of values with equal positive and negative deviations from the mean. Also normal distribution.

GDO — Grid-dip oscillator.

GE — Greater than or equal to. See relational operator.

generalized routine — A computer routine designed to solve a class of problem. The routine can be specialized to solve a specific problem when appropriate values are supplied.

general NC language processor: A computer program developed to serve as a translating system for a parts programmer to develop a mathematical representation of a geometric form with the use of symbolic notation.

general purpose interfaces — General purpose interfaces are contained on individual plug-in I/O cards. In addition to the appropriate data registers, each interface generally has independent flag and control logic, allowing two-way communication between series computers and calculators, and one or more external devices. All interfaces operate under either program or direct memory access control. A wide choice of interfaces allows external connection via floating contact closures, DTL/TTL, transistor, or differential logic.

general purpose program — Designed to perform some standard operations. The particular requirements of any run of the programs are provided by means of parameters which describe the needs of the run. It is similar to a generator, but differs in that it usually requires parameters each time it is run; whereas a generator produces a specific program which can later be used without parameters.

general register — A register used for operations such as binary addition, subtraction, multiplication, and division. General registers are used primarily to compute and modify addresses in a program. They have also found increasing utilization as replacements for special registers, such as accumulators, particularly in microprogrammable processors.

general register unit — In some systems, the general register unit (GRU) serves as a scratch pad memory for the microprogram. It is used for storage of program counters, accumulators, general registers, memory address registers and status information. An address multiplexer is provided to allow addressing from the instruction control unit (ICU) or the status register. The GRU also contains a skeletal interrupt system which facilitates microprogram emulation of an n-level priority interrupt structure.

generate — 1. An activity designed to produce a program by selection of subsets from a set of skeletal coding under the control of parameters. 2. To produce assembler language statements from the model statements of a macro definition when the definition is called by a macro instruction.

generated address — A number or symbol which is generated by instructions in a program and is thus used as an address part, i.e., a generated address.

generator program — A large detailed program which permits a computer to write other programs automatically. Generators are usually of two types. 1. The character controlled generator, which operates like a compiler in that it takes entries from a library tape, but unlike a simple compiler in that it examines control characters associated with each entry, and alters instructions found in the library according to the directions contained in the control characters. 2. The pure generator is a program that writes another program. When associated with an assembler a pure generator is usually a section of program which is called into storage by the assembler from a library and then writes one or more entries in another program. Most assemblers are also compilers and generators. In this case the entire system is usually referred to as an assembly system. (Related to problem-oriented language.)

generator, random-number — A special machine routine or hardware designed to produce a random number or series of random numbers according to specified limitations.

generator, report — A technique for producing complete data processing reports giving only a description of the desired content and format of the output reports, and certain information concerning the input file.

generator, RPG — Most report program generators provide a convenient programming method for producing a wide variety of reports. These may range from a listing of a card deck or tape reel to a precisely arranged, calculated, and edited tabulation of data from several input sources.

generic — 1. Of, applied to, or referring to a kind, class or group. 2. Inclusive or general-opposed to specific and special.

geometric mean — This is the nth root of a product of n numbers. G.M. = $\sqrt[n]{X_1 \cdot X_2 \cdot \ldots X_n}$. Where a large number of values are involved, it is more convenient to find the logarithms of the numbers, divide the sum of the logarithms by the number of items, and look up the antilogarithms of the quotient.

geometric mean program — For a set of n positive numbers $\{a_1, a_2, \ldots, a_n\}$, the geometric mean is defined by

$$G = (a_1 \, a_2 \ldots a_n)^{\frac{1}{n}}.$$

geometric progression program — Can be used to: (1) display the terms of a geometric progression; (2) find the value of a particular term of a geometric progression; (3) find the sum of the first n terms of a geometric progression; (4) find the infinite sum of a geometric progression if the ratio of two successive terms has an absolute value less than one.

get — 1. Refers to an activity to develop or make a record from an input file available for use by a routine in control of the machine. 2. To obtain or extract a coded or transformed value from a field (as to GET a numerical value from a series of decimal digit characters). 3. To locate and transfer a record or item from storage. (Contrast with put).

gibberish — Usually a total accumulated for control purposes when handling records by the addition of specific fields of each record, although the total itself has no particular sense or meaning; i.e., an accumulation or indicative data such as customer's account number, etc.

giga — a Prefix signifying one billion, or 10^9.

gigacycle — One kilomegacycle, or one billion cycles.

gigahertz — A term for 10^9 cycles per second, used to replace the more cumbersome term kilomegacycle.

GIGO (Garbage in-Garbage Out) — A specially coined term used to describe the data into and out of a computer system — that is, if the input data is bad (garbage in) then the output data will also be bad (garbage out).

global — Pertaining to that part of an assembler program that includes the body of any macro definition called from a source module and the open code portion of the source module. Contrast with local.

global variable — Refers to a variable whose name is accessable by a main program and all its subroutines.

goal-setting — Use of the computer or calculator in economic and financial planning and control. Modern computer communication networks provide corporate and governmental planners with the data base, mathematical tools, and simulation capabilities necessary for effective planning. Using modern simulation techniques, decision makers are able to try out, on-line, the effects of different changes before any final decisions are made.

GOMPERTZ curve regression program — This program fits observed data to a Gompertz curve given by the following growth or strategic function: LOG Y = LOG A + C^X LOG B. The program calculates LOG A, C, LOG B and Y for each X.

GO TO (FORTRAN statement) — An instruction in a general purpose programming language that directs the computer to leave the current sequence of instructions and begin operating instructions at another (specified) point in the program.

GO TO key, small calculators — Followed by a two-digit number, causes calculator to execute the instruction at the specified step number next, and continue program execution sequentially from there.

Graf/pen data entry — This technique enters both graphic and alphanumeric data automatically by requesting the user to simply trace a curve, circle a printed character or make a checkmark with a pen or cursor. If not restricted to a "tablet", the Graf/Pen can be mounted on a drawing table, a blackboard, a projection screen, a CRT display or any other flat surface. The system permits human judgement and cuts graphic data entry time. Users have experienced reduction of 90% compared with manual scaling and keyboard entry. It has become widely applicable and is currently used for such diverse purposes as planning radiographic treatment in medicine and as entering part numbers in order processing and inventory control. The technique is systems oriented and interfaces are available to almost every kind of minicomputer, programmable calculator of RS-232 device. Complete off-line systems use punched paper or magnetic media.

graphic calculator system — A calculator graphics system consists of two basic components: the advanced programmable calculator and the display terminal. Linked by an interface, the terminal provides the calculator with the capability of presenting data in alphanumeric and graphic form. Straightforward Plots are possible. Two preprogrammed plot program tapes are supplied as part of some systems. The programs take the mystery out of creating graphics while providing efficiency of system operations. Also offered are various Function Plots.

Designed to enable the user to plot any user-defined single variable function, automatic scaling routines assure good representation of data and optimum screen area usage. Interactive operation will, however, allow the user to specify minimum and maximum values for X and Y coordinates, the coordinate of axis intersection and the independent variable increment. Some systems offer Optional Function Plots. Used with memory options, one package provides not only the above but also automatic scaling with axis labeling.

graphic display — A communications terminal (linked to a computer) which displays data on a (television-like) screen, usually a CRT — cathode ray tube.

graphic plotter, example — Using a highly efficient data transfer format, one type high speed X-Y plotter can plot up to seven vectors per second in any direction. Each data coordinate is expressed with a binary number and represented by the bit pattern of two successive ASCII characters. Thus, only 4 characters are required to define any move. ASCII characters are accepted at 10 or 30 cps through a standard RS232C compatible interface. Operating in parallel with data communications terminals, graphs can be plotted on any size paper up to 27.9 × 43.2 cm (11 × 17 in). Paper is held by an electrostatic paper holdown. Front panel controls allow adjustment of graph limits to fit a plot to any preprinted grid. Four colors of ink are avail-

graphic plotters — able in disposable pens. Pens are changed quickly and easily so that plots may be superimposed in color for comparison. With the proper interface, advanced calculator owners can add a fast digital X-Y plotter to thereby display the data in easy-to-understand charts and graphs.

graphic plotters — Most series of graphic plotters are designed to provide high quality graphics with absolute address coordinates that assure high accuracy over the entire plotter area. Front panel scaling controls allow users to choose any plot size or position up to 11×17 inches on some systems. Electrostatic paper hold down and disposable ink cartridges are available in four colors to provide operator convenience on various systems.

graphic solution — A solution obtained with graphs or other pictorial devices, as contrasted with solutions obtained by the manipulation of numbers.

graph, stacked — A graph with two or three x scales and the same number of y scales plotted in such a way that there are discrete plotting grids placed one above the other.

graph, standard — A graph plotted with one x scale and one or two associated y scales forming a single plotting grid.

gray code — A positional binary number notation in which any two numbers whose difference is one are represented by expressions that are the same except in one place or column and differ by only one unit in that column or place.

ground — Relating to an electric circuit, a point considered to be at nominal zero potential and to which all other potentials in the circuit are referred, often, but not always, connected to the actual surface of the earth; as a verb, to connect to a ground.

grouped records — Refers to the result of the combining of two or more records into one block of information on tape to decrease the wasted time due to tape acceleration and deceleration and to conserve tape space. This is also called blocking of records.

group indication — A device on some calculators which permits the first item of a series of same or similar data or information to be printed and also inhibits some of the printing of the rest of the set or series. Same as group indication.

group mark — A mark that identifies the beginning or end of a set of data, which could include words, blocks, or other items.

group theory — A study, in the mathematical sense of the rules, for combining groups, sets, and elements; i.e., the theory of combining groups.

guard bit — 1. Refers to a special bit contained in each word or specific groups of words of memory designed to indicate to computer hardware units or software programs whether or not the content of that memory location may or may not be altered by a program. 2. A bit designed to indicate whether a core or disk memory word or group of words is to be filed or protected.

gulp — Generally, a small group of bytes, similar to a word or instruction.

H

half-adder — Refers to a circuit with two input and two output channels for binary signals (0, 1).

half-duplex — Permits one-direction, electrical communications between stations. Technical arrangements may permit operation in either direction but not simultaneously. Therefore, this term is qualified by one of the following suffixes: S/O for send only; R/O for receive only; S/R for send or receive.

half-duplex channel — A communication system which permits transmission only one way at a time.

halfword — Refers to a contiguous sequence of bits or characters which comprises half a computer word and is capable of being addressed as a unit.

halt — A condition which occurs when the sequence of operations in a program stops. This can be done to a halt instruction being met or due to some unexpected halt or interrupt. The program can normally continue after a halt unless it is a drop dead halt.

halt, data acquisition calculator — Stops output and blocks next scan by canceling NEXT SCAN time setting. After HALT, system will return to operation when new NEXT SCAN time is entered.

halt, drop dead — Refers to a machine halt from which there is no recovery. Such a halt may be deliberately programmed. A drop dead halt may occur through a logical error in programming. Examples in which a drop dead halt could occur are division by zero and transfer to a non-existent instruction word. Synonymous with dead halt.

halt indicator — The halt indicator is illuminated whenever the processor is in the HALT mode.

halt, nonprogrammed — Refers to an inadvertant machine stoppage, not due to the results of a programmed instruction, such as an automatic interrupt, manual intervention, machine malfunction, power failure, or other cause.

hand-held calculator print cradle — A typical print cradle permits some types of hand-held programmable calculators to become desk-top printing calculators. When the calculator is locked into the cradle, the user is able to print anything shown in the display or print the step-by-step execution of a program. Print and paper advance control permit the user to handle these functions on the print unit as well as on the calculator, and a "trace" key allows monitoring of all functions as they happen. The print unit has a thermal printer which prints 5×7 dot-matrix characters on a 2.5-in. tape. It prints 20 characters per line.

hand-held calculators, dual programming memories — Some models of Scientist and Statistician calculators feature two scratchpad program memories, with 80 steps each. These units enable the user to have two separate programs in memory at the same time. The user performs his calculations once and it is available for automatic execution. In addition, the user may verify his program while entering it. Specific programming simplifies calculations for scientific and statistical users. The statistical model, for example, can be programmed to perform such analyses as non-linear regression, chi square, and analysis of variance. Most models are battery operated, have multiple storage registers, and calculate with 13-digit or higher accuracy. Some units feature mathematical and trigonometric special function keys; others offer single-key special statistical operations.

hands-on — Refers to a person having experience of operating computer equipment.

hands-on background — The prior work experience developed by actually operating the hardware and often used as a criteria of programmer capability and knowledge.

handshake I/O control — Provision for handshake I/O control allows convenient interfacing with peripherals of varying response time. Control flags and jump condition inputs are useful to reduce hardware decoding and software overhead. If multiple devices are to be connected over the same I/O lines, three-state or open-collector TTL logic is often required to drive the bus. The microprocessor I/O circuitry should directly interface with these signals for most systems.

handshaking — 1. A descriptive term often used interchangeably with buffering or interfacing, implying a direct connection or matching of specific units or programs. Some computer terminal programs are called 'handshaking' if they greet and assist the new terminal operator to interface with or use the procedures or programs of the system. Other handshaking relates to direct package-to-package connections as regards circuits, programs, or procedures. 2. Exchange of predetermined signals when a connection is established between two data set devices.

hang-up — 1. A condition in which the central processor of a calculator is attempting to perform an illegal or forbidden operation or in which it is continually repeating the same routine. 2. An unplanned calculator stop or delay in problem solution, e.g., caused by the inability to escape from a loop. 3. A nonprogrammed stop in a routine. It is usually an unforeseen or unwanted halt in a machine pass. It is most often caused by improper coding of a machine instruction or by the attempted use of a non-existent or improper operation code.

hang-up prevention — The calculator logic must be designed or modified so that no sequence of valid or invalid instructions can cause the calculator to come to a halt or to go into a nonterminating uninterruptible state. Examples of this latter case are infinitely nested executions or non-terminating indirect addressing.

hard copy — Typewritten or printed characters on paper produced by a calculator at the same time the information is copied or converted into machine language that is not easily read by a human.

hardware — Refers to the metalic or 'hard' components of a calculator system in contrast to the 'soft' or programming components. The components of circuits may be active, passive, or both.

hardware assembler (microprocessor) — Often consists of PROMs that plug into simulation boards, enabling the prototype to assemble its own programs.

hardware interrupt facility — A hardware interrupt facility permits input-output operations to be scheduled under interrupt control. The interrupt facility may be selectively enabled or disabled under program control. When the interrupt facility is enabled, a device generates a processor interrupt each time it is ready to receive or transmit data. Use of the interrupt facility enables input-output operations to be performed simultaneously with computing.

hard-wired numerical control — A numerical control system wherein the response to data input, data handling sequence, and control functions is determined by the fixed and committed circuit interconnections of discrete decision elements and storage devices. Changes in the response, sequence, or functions can be made by changing the interconnections.

hard-wired serial interface — A typical unit provides high-speed, asynchronous, long distance, point-to-point data transfer between two calculators or computers.

hard-wire logic — Refers to logic designs for control or problem solutions that require interconnection of numerous integrated circuits formed or wired for specific purposes and relatively unalterable. A hard-wired diode matrix is hard-wired logic whereas a RAM, ROM, or CPU can be reprogrammed with little difficulty to change the purpose of operation. Hard-wired interconnections are usually completed by soldering or by printed circuits and are thus hard-wired in contrast to software solutions achieved by programmed microcomputer components.

harmonic mean program — For a set of n positive numbers $\{a_1, a_2, ..., a_n\}$, the harmonic mean is defined by

$$H = \frac{n}{\frac{1}{a_1} + \frac{1}{a_2} \ldots + \frac{1}{a_n}}.$$

hash — 1. Considered to be computer or program garbage specifically recorded on tapes to fill or comply with restrictions on conventions of starting procedures, block sizes, and others. 2. Same as garbage.

hash total — A summation for checking purposes of one or more corresponding fields of a file that would ordinarily not be summed.

HASP — 1. An extension to the System/360 Operating System that provides supplementary job management, data management, and task management functions such as control of job flow, ordering of tasks, and spooling. 2. Acronymn for Houston Automatic Spooling Operation. An IBM computer configuration for its 360 and 370 computer series. Several companies have provided their own remote job-entry system to fit the IBM equipment.

header — The initial portion of a message containing any information, control codes, and so on that are not part of the text (e.g., routing, destination addressee, and time of origination.)

header label — Refers to a designed block of data at the start of a magnetic tape file which contains descriptive information to identify the file; e.g., file name, reel number, file generation number, retention period, and the data when the data was written to tape.

header table — Refers to specific records which contain the description of information designated in a classification or group of records, which follows this initial document.

head gap — 1. The space between the reading or recording head and the recording medium, such as tape, drum or disk. 2. The space or gap intentionally inserted into the magnetic circuit of the head in order to force or direct the recording flux into the recording medium.

heading — In ASCII and communications, a sequence of characters preceded by the start of a heading character used as machine sensible address or outing information. Contrast with text.

heirarchy, program operations — Many flowcharts show the general programming sequence, starting with a power-off cold data system. Most of the operations are linear, simplifying the programming. Most users realize that while a given program may involve many steps, most are repetitive and simple.

help program — HELP is a program and a system of files that provide assistance to the engineer or programmer in the use of software and the hardware. Also provides up-to-date information on improvements and new developments to a specific microcomputer family of components and software.

hertz — 1. A unit of frequency equal to one cycle per second (now also used in the United States). 2. A hertzian wave is the wave used in radio communication; it is produced by an alternating current at the sending station and received by the aerial of the receiving set. Named after Heinrich Hertz (1867-94), a German physicist. A generalized expression referring to all radio waves or oscillations of electricity in conductor producing electromagnetic radiation.

hesitation — A temporary halt or temporary suspension of operations in a sequence of operations of a calculator in order to perform all or part of the operations from another sequence.

heuristic — Solutions are considered with the objective as being satisfactory relative to the constraints of time, funds, personnel available and the stated "confined use" of the solution as advice of a "better" though not especially the best alternative to present usage; heuristic solutions serve to "find out"; a solution which could contribute to the reduction of time and funds necessary for an algoristic solution (i.e., as closed linear-programming models) which require highly structured models, exhaustive computation if complex. Heuristic models provide executive-accepted "better for now and for the purpose" resolutions of problems which are more flexible to model, permit faster testing and evaluation, and fit any type of problem which contains elements which can be measured and associated.

heuristic — Pertaining to exploratory methods of problem solving in which solutions are discovered by evaluation of the progress made toward the final result. Contrast with algorithm.

heuristic routine — A routine by which the computer attacks a problem not by a direct algorithmic procedure, but by a trial and error approach frequently involving the act of learning.

Hewlett-Packard interface bus controller — Allows any H-P processors to interface with instruments that are programmable via the HP Interface Bus. The HPIB is Hewlett-Packard's implementation of IEEE Standard 488-1975, "Digital Interface for Programmable Instrumentation."

hexadecimal — Refers to whole numbers in positional notation with 16 as the base. Hexadecimal uses 0 through 16, with the first ten represented by 0 through 9 and the last six digits represented by A,B,C,D,E, and F.

hexadecimal calculator/converter — The unit operates as follows: users enter any number in base 8, 10, or 16. Then at the touch of a key, that number is converted to either of the other two bases. And users can add, subtract, multiply or divide again in all three number bases. For mode conversions in the automatic mode, pressing the desired base key converts both the calculator display number and operation to the selected base. In the manual mode, users enter numbers in one base and then press one of the other two base keys. The calculator converts the entered number to the selected base and is ready for the next entry.

hexadecimal-decimal-octal calculator — Users can store, recall and sum numbers with the calculator memory. Memory keys operate on the memory and display only, without affecting previous instructions. And all internal operations and data are converted to the selected number base upon recall. For example, when users enter a base 16 number and later recall it in base 10, the number is converted to display in base 10.

hexadecimal-decimal-octal calculator manual operation — The unit lets users operate in either automatic or manual mode conversions. In the automatic mode, pressing the desired base key converts both the calculator display number and operation to the selected base. In the manual mode, users simply enter numbers in one base and then press one of the other two keys. The calculator converts the entered number to the selected base and is ready for the next entry.

hexadecimal function (HEX) (BASIC) — The HEX function is a form of literal string that enables use of any 8-bit codes in BASIC programs. Each character is indicated by two Hexadecimal digits (0-9, A-F). The HEX function can be used wherever literal strings enclosed in double quotes can be used.

HEX/octal/decimal calculator — Only in the last two years have we seen advances in circuit design technology that permitted powerful calculators to be designed into pocket-size packages. This type calculator is probably most useful to systems analysts in IBM shops, as it is basically a hexadecimal organized calculator that can be used to calculate addresses in HEX, octal, and decimal equivalents. The unit is also a standard four-function calculator for performing those operations in any of the three number bases. MOS/LSI circuitry performs the computations and drives the display.

hierarchical — An arrangement of programming procedures from highest and most powerful to lowest and least powerful. With many calculator systems control commands preceed individual channel control commands.

hierarchical file system — The utilization of a three level hierarchical file system using symbolic file, record, and item names eliminates the requirement for a separate and complicated data base definition language. Simple, English-type commands like "up-date," "write," "get," "put," "add," "delete," "copy," "lock," and "unlock," are used to set up and access the system. (available on some intelligent disk systems).

hierarchy, memory — Refers to a set of memories with differing sizes and speeds and usually having different cost-performance ratios (i.e., expensive/fast to less expensive/slower). Faster access sections contain a main computer memory hierarchy, might consist of a very high-speed, small semicon-

high level language

ductor memory, a medium-speed core memory and a large, slow-speed core.

high level language — A problem oriented language for communication with the computer using simple rules (syntax). The statements of a high level language are broken down into a number of machine instructions. The translation is accomplished with a compiler or translator allowing a greater degree of independence between computer systems. For example FORTRAN, APT, COBOL.

high level language comparisons — 1. Such languages are usually problem-oriented or procedure-oriented programming languages as distinguished from machine-oriented and/or mnemonic languages. Machine languages are the final target languages, after compiling, while high level languages are source languages for many programmers and users. Examples of high level languages are: COBOL, BASIC, FORTRAN, ALGOL, etc. 2. A language in which each instruction or statement corresponds to several machine code instructions. High level languages allow users to write in a notation with which they are familiar rather than a language oriented to the machine code of a computer. Contrasted with low-level language.

high level software — Like other programming tools, the compiler approach automates the production of programs to counteract the rapidly increasing cost of software production at a time when hardware costs are decreasing. And, in addition to rapid production turnaround, the programs can be fully checked out early in the design process. What's more, the self-documentation of compiler/interpreter programs enables one programmer to readily understand the work of another, which dramatically reduces program-maintenance costs and provides transportability of software between programmers and to other processors as they are introduced. Additional cost reductions also result from standardization of parts and modules, and alterability of the final program often outweighs benefits of random-logic-designs or custom-chip fabrication.

high-order — Pertaining to the weight or significance assigned to the digits of a number; i.e., in the number 123456, the highest order digit is one; the lowest order digit is six. One may refer to the three high-order bits of a binary word as another example.

high-order digit — A digit that occupies a more significant or highly weighted position in a numerical or positional notation system.

high-speed bus — A set of wires or "path" which is used to transfer numbers (electrical pulses) which represent data and instructions to various registers and counters. However, on-off and similar transfer lines or control signals are not considered as digit transfer buses.

high-speed tape reader subsystem, advanced calculator — A typical unit combines the Photo Reader and Optional Interface Card. The unit optically reads tapes at 300 characters/second.

histogram — 1. An experimental frequency distribution which shows the number of quantities of particular magnitudes. 2. Represents the measurements or observations constituting a set of data on a horizontal scale and the class frequencies on a vertical scale. The graph of the distribution is then constructed by drawing rectangles, the bases of which are determined by the corresponding class frequencies.

histogram key — Calculates complete histogram on data set. Resulting printout includes cell number, lower bound of cell, number of occurrences in cell, relative percent frequency of cell. (some units)

histogram plot — In some calculators, a histogram package allows users to specify the minimum and maximum values and establish cell width. Some programs use consecutively entered values to establish mean, standard deviations, and percentage of occurrences per cell. Upon key command, accumulated cells are plotted on the axis. At any point, the user may return to input mode and add new data. In addition, a memory option offered by some manufacturers includes automatic scaling and labeling. Additionally, it allows cell plotting three ways: occurrences per cell, percentages per cell and pie charts.

hit — 1. Refers to momentary electrical disturbance on a circuit. 2. A successful comparison of two items of data. Contrast with match.

hold instruction — A computer instruction which caused data called from storage to be also retained in storage after it is called out and transferred to its new location.

hole — 1. As related to punched cards, the removal of paper to affect a contact and detecting a binary digit. As related to transistor theory, a vacancy in a crystal lattice caused by the absence of an electron in an order structure of covalent bonds, thermal agitation will break the bond, causing the electron to move away from its atom, leaving the hole behind. The electron may fill another hole left by another electron, and the hold may be considered to have a positive charge equal to that of an electron. The movement of holes and electrons constitutes current flow, and upon the application of an electric field, the flow becomes ordered, rather than random as it is under thermal agitation. 2. A freely moving positive charge in a doped semiconductor crystal.

Hollerith code — An alphanumeric punched card code invented by Dr. Herman Hollerith in 1889, in which the top three positions in a column are called "zone" punches (12, 11, and 0, or Y, X and O, from the top downward), and are combined with the remaining punches, or digit punches (1 through 9) to represent alphabetic, numeric, and special characters. For example, A is a combination of a Y (12) and a 1 punch; an L is a combination of an X (11) and a 3 punch, etc.

Hollerith system — A widely used system of encoding alpha-numeric information onto cards. The mainstay Hollerith card is synonymous with punch card. Such cards were first used in 1890 for the U.S. census, and are named after the inventor, Herman Hollerith.

horizontal parity check — The comparison of the number of bits tallied and totalled along channels as related to a previously determined quantity.

host computer — 1. The primary or controlling computer in a multiple computer operation. 2. A computer used to prepare programs for use on another computer or on another data processing system; for example, a computer used to compile, link edit, or test programs to be used on another system.

housekeeping — Pertaining to a computer routine, those operations, such as setting up constants and variables for use in the program, that contribute directly to the proper operation of the computer but not to the solution of the problem.

housekeeping character — A letter, digit, or other symbol that controls the operation of a peripheral device in addition to formatting and data characters. Example: Characters such as carriage return, line feed, and record separation are generated and put out by the Teletype interface, other peripherals.

housekeeping operation — A general term for the operation that must be performed for a machine run usually before actual processing begins. Examples of housekeeping operations are: establishing controlling marks, setting up auxiliary storage units, reading in the first record for processing, initializing, set-up verification operations, and file identification.

HP-IB calculator interface — The 59405A connects the HP 9820A, 9821A and 9830A calculators to the HP Interface Bus. It provides both control and data capability for up to 14 additional HP-IB controlled devices, and uses only one I/O slot on the calculator. Included with the interface are the I/O card, an appropriate ROM for I/O control, a 4 m (13.2 ft) HP-IB cable, and a User's Guide. The User's Guide describes how the calculator can be used to communicate with and control instruments and accessories.

HP interface bus operation — All active interface circuitry is contained within the various HP-IB devices, and the interconnecting cable (containing 16 signal lines) is entirely passive. The cable's role is limited to that of interconnecting all devices together in parallel, whereby any one device may transfer data to one or more other participating devices. Every participating device (instrument, controller, accessory module) must be able to perform at least one of the roles of TALKER, LISTENER or CONTROLLER. A TALKER can transmit data to other devices via the bus, and a LISTENER can receive data from other devices via the bus. Some devices can perform both roles (e.g. a programmable instrument can LISTEN to receive its control instructions and TALK to send its measurement). A CONTROLLER manages the operation of the bus system primarily by designating which devices are to send and receive data, and it may also command specific actions within other devices. A minimum HP-IB system configuration consists of one TALKER and one LISTENER, but without a CONTROLLER. In this configuration, data transfer is limited to direct transfer between one device manually set to "talk only" and one or more devices manually set to "listen only" (e.g. a measuring instrument talking to a printer, for semi-automatic data logging). The full flexibility and power of the HP-IB become more apparent, however, when one device which can serve as CONTROLLER/TALKER/LISTENER (e.g. calculator or computer) is interconnected with other devices which may be either TALKERS or LISTENERS, or both (e.g. frequency synthesizers, counters, power meters, relay actuators, displays, printers, etc.), depending on the application.

human control, indirect — As contrasted with direct control when one unit of computers is controlled by the other unit without human intervention, and the first unit is said to be on-line to the second, if human intervention is necessary, the first unit is said to be off-line to the second and is under indirect control of the second while an operator is acting as a human link in the specific control chain.

human engineering — The science and art of developing machines for human use, giving consideration to the abilities, limitations, habits and preferences of the human operator.

human factors — Refers to the designated application of phychology and related social sciences to systems involving humans and human behavior.

hunting — A continuous attempt on the part of an automatically controlled system to seek a desired equilibrium condition. The system usually contains a standard, a method of determining deviation from this standard, and a method of influencing the system such that the difference between the standard and the state of the system is brought to zero. (Clarified by servomechanism.)

hybrid computer — A computer designed with both digital and analog characteristics, combining the advantages of analog and digital computer when working as a system. Hybrid computers are being used extensively in simulation process control systems where it is necessary to have a close representation with the physical world. The hybrid system provides good precision than can be attained with analog computers and greater control than is possible with digital computers, plus the ability to accept input data in either form.

hydraulics program package — These programs include:
- Gravity Flow Programs: Round Pipes, Pipe-Arches, Elliptical Pipes, Trapezoidal Channels
- Water Surface Profile, (Backwater Curve Analysis) Direct Step Method, Standard Step Method
- Design of a Water Distribution Network, using the Hardy Cross Method
- Design of a Non-Looping Water Distribution Network
- Circular Culvert Design
- Box Culvert Design
- Pipe-Arch Culvert Design
- The Streeter-Phelps Equation
- Storm Sewer System Design
- Sanitary Sewer System Design
- Equivalent Pipe Calculations

hyperbolic functions — The calculator returns values for sinh, cosh, tanh, arc sinh, arc cosh, arc tanh.

hyperbolic functions program — This program evaluates the six hyperbolic functions by the following formulas:

1. $\sinh x = \dfrac{e^x - e^{-x}}{2}$
2. $\cosh x = \dfrac{e^x + e^{-x}}{2}$
3. $\tanh x = \dfrac{e^x - e^{-x}}{e^x + e^{-x}}$
4. $\operatorname{csch} x = \dfrac{1}{\sinh x} \ (x \neq 0)$
5. $\operatorname{sech} x = \dfrac{1}{\cosh x}$
6. $\coth x = \dfrac{1}{\tanh x} \ (x \neq 0)$

hypercube, multi-microcomputer systems — Called the Hypercube, one system uses an array of 32, 162 or 512 microprocessors to provide claimed computational power up to that of some of the largest computers of today. The continued growth of data communications as an integral part of data processing introduces many control tasks in linking together remote locations with a central facility. If one includes the capability of introducing processing facilities at the various points in a network where data comes together, the opportunities for using low-cost processing elements–i.e., microprocessors–are manifold. Applications include multiplexing, network control, front-ending, traffic monitoring and routing, etc. Multi-microprocessors have a strong future both as stand-alone processing elements and as logic components in large computers using new architecture.

hypergeometric program — Refers to a Hypergeometric Probability Function. Computes the individual and the cumulative hypergeometric distributions. The Mean, Variance, and Standard Deviation of the Distribution are also computed.

hypertape unit — Magnetic tape units which use cartridges, house the supply and take up reels, and perform automatic loading.

hysteresis — The difference between the response of a system to increasing and decreasing signals.

I

IBM desk-top computer model 5100 — The system is a single card 16-bit μP, 16k words of 354-nsec RAM and up to 158k bytes of ROM. This is the heart of the IBM 5100 portable computer. It has a full keyboard with function keys and calculator cluster, 16×64-char. CRT display, and built-in tape cartridge drive for a complete unit. The ROM stores interpreters for APL and/or BASIC high-level languages. RAM storage can be increased to 64k words. Using modified 3M ¼-in. tape cartridges, the 5100 can store 204k chars. and access them at 40 ips (2850 cps). Display versatility includes standard white-on-black formatting, reverse video, and expansion of left or right 32 characters. IBM has done the programming for over 100 interactive routines prerecorded on tape cartridges. Users need a few more cartridges for computer-aided instruction in programming. Also available are diagnostics that tell users why the program doesn't work and a separate set lets them know if the hardware is at fault. An optional printer and extra tape unit are offered.

IBM-type diskette — One Advanced Electronics Diskette is the type used with the IBM 3740 and 3600 data systems; however, the data is stored at twice (double) the density of the IBM data. By doubling the density, over twice the storage capacity per diskette is achieved compared to the IBM 3740 and 3600. Diskettes are protected in accordance with ANSI recommendations. Programs and data may be stored on both sides of the diskette, thereby more than quadrupling the storage capacity compared to the IBM formatted diskettes. Each Diskette is certified to be free from defects.

IBM-type floppy disk — Many Floppy Disks read and write double-density data on IBM type diskette media on one unit. Closing the spring-loaded front door panel engages the Floppy Disk and the drive mechanism which rotates the media at a constant 360 rpm. The DC drive motor is completely independent of line frequency, a highly desirable feature for varying power conditions. A DC stepper motor drives a precision lead screw which positions the read-write head at 11 milliseconds per track. MFM recorded data is transferred between the head and the media in bit serial form at 500,000 data bits per second. For additional long life, the drive has a ferrite ceramic READ/WRITE head. Up to 4 completely independent floppy disk drives fit in a single cabinet. Up to 2 drives fit in each cabinet.

ID codes-data acquisition caculator — Users press ID to read frame identification and other special function codes. Key initiates procedures to change frame identification and special function codes.

identifier — 1. A symbol whose purpose is to identify, as to indicate or name a body of data. 2. A key.

identify — Refers to an equation or quite simply a statement that two expressions are equal. When an equality is true at all times and for all values of the symbol for which the numbers are defined, it is an identity. The symbol $\equiv$ means, "is identically equal to" and is generally used to emphasize this trait of relationship.

identifying error stops, calculators (blinking display stops) — Errors that cause a blinking zero display, if executed in a program, also stop the program. Users can identify the stop by switching momentarily to W/PRGM to see the code of the offending operation. (some systems)

idle light — On some calculators an idle light flashes to indicate an illegal operation has been performed. For example; dividing by zero, square root of a negative number, log of zero or negative number, entry or result of more than the capacity of the display, raising a number to zero or negative power, depressing two keys simultaneously, depressing keys too quickly in sequence.

IDP, Integrated Data Processing — 1. A system that treats as a whole all data-processing requirements to accomplish a sequence of data-processing steps or a number of related data-processing sequences, and that strives to reduce or eliminate duplicating data entry or processing steps. 2. The processing of data by such a system in which all procedures are in some way tied to the computer.

IDS (Input Data Strobe) — An output signal that enables external devices that are sending data to CPU.

IEEE — Institute of Electrical and Electronics Engineers.

ier register — The register that contains the multiplier during a multiplication operation.

If Flag Key — The If Flag Key tests to see if a specified flag is set. If it is, then transfer occurs to the location or label. If flag is reset, no transfer occurs. For example, 2nd if flg 3 0 1 1 means if flag is set, transfer to program location 011. Or, 2nd if flg 3 A means if flag 3 is set, transfer to that segment of the program labeled A.

ignore — 1. A typewriter character indicating

that no action whatsoever be taken, i.e., in teletype or flexowriter code, a character code consisting of holes punched in every hole position is an ignore character, this convention makes possible erasing any previously punched character. 2. An instruction requiring nonperformance of what normally might be executed, i.e., not to be executed. This instruction should not be confused with a no op or do nothing instruction, since these generally refer to an instruction outside themselves.

I²L advantages — I²L (Integrated Injection Logic) circuit techniques offer capabilities that make next generation high performance, low cost, systems possible. Since it is manufactured with todays TTL bipolar technology, it does not require major new technology research; the process is in production now. Because I²L is made from a standard bipolar process, I²L circuit designs can be made to interface with many other circuits.

These characteristics make I²L a universal logic form for medium performance, minimum cost applications. Internal logic can be totally separated from the interface resulting in optimum density, correct logic interface; thus ease of use for the system logic designs.

illegal — The status of a program which has attempted to perform a non-existent instruction, or to violate the program area reservation check.

illegal-command check — A specific check, usually programmed or automatic, to test for the use of occurrence of codes which have no real assigned meaning or validity, i.e., illegal characters. Checks can be designed to have a flip-flop signal occur when the presence of illegal digits occur, i.e. to record or indicate the event.

illegal Display, hand-held programmable — During execution of a stored program, the display continuously changes and is purposely illegible to indicate that the program is running. When the program stops, the display is steady.

illegal operation — The process which results when a calculator either cannot perform the instruction part or will perform with invalid and undesired results. The limitation is often due to built-in constraints.

image sensors — Sensors known as charge-coupled devices (CCD), and nickel-size silicon chips containing over 120,000 electronic elements. When an image is focused on the CCD, the sensor's electronic elements transform the picture into individual electrical charge packets. These packets are then read out very rapidly by charge transfer techniques. The resulting information then can be processed and displayed as a TV picture. In the CCD, half the electronic elements form the imaging array and the other half are for storage and readout. The CCD is being developed as part of broadly-based efforts aimed at developing all solid-state TV systems and applying CCD technology to a wide range of other applications such as space exploration, closed-circuit television, military programs, surveillance systems, telephone systems transmitting TV pictures, by consumers with home video records, and in broad Lange camera applications.

imaginary number — 1. Relating to mathematics, a number whose square is negative. 2. If the number has the property that when multiplied by itself has yields of negative number, it is an imaginary number, i.e., the square root of −4 does not exist in the number system, it is neither +2 or −2.

immediate access — Pertaining to the ability to obtain data from or place data in a storage device or register directly, without serial delay-due to other units of data, and usually in a relatively short time period.

immediate addressing — 1. A specific mode of addressing in which the operand contains the value to be operated on, and no address reference is required. 2. A particular system of specifying the locations of operands and instructions in the same storage location, i.e., at the same address. An address part contains the value of an operand rather than its address.

immediate instructions — Some systems provide a full complement of immediate instructions. The address portion of the instruction can contain the 8-bit operand itself, rather than an address. Only half as much memory is needed since both instruction and operand are contained in a single word. Immediates include: Add, Subtract, Load and Compare.

imperative statement — 1. Action statements of a symbolic program that are converted into actual machine language. 2. A statement consisting of a verb and its operand(s), also a series of such statements. A statement expresses a complete unit of procedure.

implicit function — An expression in which the form of the function is not directly expressed but which requires some operation to be performed, to render it evident. Thus, in the equation $ay^2 + bxy + cx^2 + dy + ex + f = 0$ y is an implicit function of x.

in-circuit symbolic de-bugging — The hardware and software aspects of the Intellec MDS (Intel. Corp.) ICE-80 offer prototyping and production test of user systems. ICE-80 is a unique development system that provides full emulation and debug features while operating inside the user system. The user can get extensive information on the interplay of his software and hardware without introducing extraneous hardware or special debug software into his working system.

incomplete gamma function program —

$$\gamma(a, x) = \int_0^x e^{-t} t^{a-1} dt$$

$$= x^a e^{-x} \sum_{n=0}^{x} \frac{x^n}{a(a+1)\ldots(a+n)}$$

where $a > 0$, $x > 0$. This program computes successive partial sums of the above series. The program stops when two consecutive partial sums are equal and displays the last partial sum as the answer. Note: When x is too large, computing a new term of the series might cause an overflow. In that case, display shows all 9's and the program stops.

incomplete routine — A routine in a library of a programming system that requires parameters to be supplied by a macrostatement or main routine.

increment — An added part or portion as differentiated from decrement representing a decreasing portion. Mathematically an increment is the average rate of change of a variable, y, with respect to a variable, x, within a given interval or $\Delta y/\Delta x$ where delta (Δ) represents a small change.

incremental data — Often refers to specific data which represents only the change from that data which just preceded it; hence, in incremental positioning each move is referenced to the prior one.

incremental representation — A method of representing a variable in which changes in the values of the variable are represented, rather than the values themselves.

increment operation — A software operation most often associated with stacks and stack pointers. Bytes of information are stored in the stack register at the addresses contained in the stack pointer. The stack pointer is decremented after each byte of information is entered into the stack; it is incremented after each byte is removed from the stack. Increment also refers to various addressable registers.

independent — One quantity is said to be independent of another with which it is connected, when it does not depend on it for its value. In this case, the term is nearly synonymous with arbitrary, but not quite. In an equation containing more than one variable, as does the equation of any magnitude all the variables, except one, are independent; that is, any value may be assigned to them at pleasure, and the corresponding value of the other will be found for the solution of the equation. Thus, in the equation of the straight line,

$$Y = AX + b,$$

we may take X as the independent variable in which case, whatever be the value assigned to it, the corresponding value of Y may be found.

independent conformity, curve — A calculated value of nonconformity determined after any translation and/or rotation of the actual curve is made to minimize the maximum deviation.

independent equations — A set of equations none of which can be expressed as a linear combination of the others. With linear equations, the condition for independence is that the matrix (coefficient columns) shall be nonsingular or, equivalently, have rank equal to the number of equations.

independent events — Two events are said to be independent if the occurrence of either in no way affects the occurrence of the other.

independent linearity, curve — A calculated value of non-linearity determined after any translation and/or rotation of the actual curve is made to minimize the maximum deviation from a straight line.

independent operation — Operations which do not inhibit the operation of any unit which is not directly connected or involved in the operation concerned.

independent routine — A routine that is executed independently of manual operations, but only if certain conditions occur within a program or record, or during some other process.

independent variable — A variable whose value is not a direct function of some other variable and does not depend on another variable. The independent variable is usually plotted as the abscissa (horizontal line) on an axis.

index — An integer used to specify the location of information within a table or program.

index, citation — An index or reference list of documents that are mentioned in a specific document or document set. The references are mentioned or quoted in the text. The citation index lists these references.

index, cycle — The number of cycle iterations in digital computer programming. A cycle index register may be used to set the number of cycles desired. Then with each cycle iteration, the register count is reduced by one until the register reaches zero and the series of cycles is complete.

indexed files — The indexed structure is ideal for applications involving a heavy volume of random access. This structure consists of a series of pointers to data blocks scattered throughout the disc. It has the open-ended characteristics of chained files with the access speed of contiguous files.

indexing — A calculator technique of addressing modification that is often implemented by means of index registers, external commands or events.

indexing, coordinate — An indexing scheme by which descriptors may be correlated or combined to show any interrelationships desired for purposes of more precise information retrieval.

index, KWIC — A permuted title index based upon use of keywords or phrases extrinsically or automatically identified. (Key-Word-In-Context.)

index number — To measure the changes in the large number of constantly varying items in the data, it is necessary to resort to some relative averaging device that will serve as a yardstick of comparative measurement. The index number is such a device. The index number measures fluctuations during intervals of time, group differences of geographical position or degree, etc.

index number, array — A number used to identify the position of a specific quantity in an array or string of quantities. That is, in array A, the elements are represented by the variables $A(1)$, $A(2) \ldots A(50)$: The indexes are $1, 2, \ldots 50$.

index, permuted — A form of document indexing developed by producing an entry in the index for each word of specific interest and by including the context in which it occurs, most often restricted to title words.

index register — 1. A register that contains a quantity to be used under direction of the control section of the computer hardware; e.g., for address modification and counting. 2. A device that permits automatic modification or an instruction address without permanently altering the instruction in memory. 3. A register to which an arbitrary integer, usually one, is added (or subtracted) upon the execution of each machine instruction. The register may be reset to zero or to an arbitrary number. Also called cycle counter and B-box.

index registers, 4-bit (calculator) system — The index registers in some 4-bit systems consist of sixteen 4-bit registers which can be directly operated on by various instructions, either individually or in pairs. The registers are organized as the even numbered and the odd numbered registers, or as seven pairs, each pair consisting of one even and one odd numbered register. When the registers are being used with the 4-bit accumulator by various instructions they are used individually. When data is loaded directly from program memory or if the registers are used for address control, they are used in pairs because of the 8-bit requirement for these functions.

index value — Pre-set value of a controlled quantity at which an automatic control is required to aim; also desired value.

index word register — A register which contains a quantity which may be used to modify addresses under direction of the control section of the computer. (Sometimes known as b-box)

indicator, branch-on — Branching takes place when appropriate indicators (switches, keys, buttons, etc.), or conditions, have been set to point to a particular group of registers, i.e., a branch may occur dependent upon whether the magnetic tape units are ready to receive a new block of data.

indicator chart — Refers to a table or schematic used by a programmer during the logical design and coding of a program to record items about the use of indicators in the program. A portion of program documentation.

indicator, check — A device which displays or announces that an error has been made or that a checking operation has determined that a failure has occurred.

indicator, machine check — A protective device which will be turned on when certain conditions arise within the machine. The machine can be programmed to stop or to run a separate correction routine or to ignore the condition.

indicator, overflow — A signaling device that indicates the occurrence of an overflow; for instance, a number too large to be contained in a given register.

indicator, overflow check — A device which is turned on by incorrect, or unplanned for, operations in the execution of an arithmetic instruction, particularly when an arithmetic operation produces a number too large for the system to handle.

indicator, read-write check — A device incorporated in certain calculators to indicate upon interrogation whether or not an error was made in reading or writing. The machine can be made to stop, re-try the operation or follow a special subroutine depending upon the result of the interrogation.

indicators — Refers to various devices which register conditions, such as high or equal conditions resulting from a comparison of plus or minus conditions resulting from a computation. A sequence of operations within a procedure may be varied according to the position of an indicator.

indirect address — An address specifying a storage location, which in turn contains either a direct or another indirect address.

indirect addressing — 1. Refers to the procedure of addressing a memory location that contains the address of data rather than the data itself. 2. A form of computer cross-referencing, in which one memory location indicates where the correct address of the main fact can be found. 3. Any level of addressing other than the first level of direct addressing. Translation of symbolic instructions into machine-language instructions.

indirect and direct memory register addressing — On some units the direct register addressing instruction: 5 STO 10, means to store 5 directly in register 10, as shown in some sketches. Indirect addressing, on the other hand, increases the versatility of all memory registers and allows users to store the address of another memory register for future use.

indirectly controlled system — A specific portion of the controlled system in which the indirectly controlled variable is changed in response to changes in the controlled variable.

indirect memory address keys (algebraic logic) — Indirect Store. Indirect Recall. Indirect Exchange. Indirect Add. Indirect Subtract. Indirect Multiply. Indirect Divide. Example: the indirect address instruction: 5 IND STO 10 means to store 5, not in register 10, but in the register whose address is found in register 10. Thus, if 15 were previously stored in register 10, then 5 IND STO 10 would mean store 5 in PROD register 15. Register 15 has been indirectly addressed by the given instruction. (some units)

indirect register addressing — Many calculators provide certain keys dedicated to special registers whose contents are then used to address other registers. This feature is called indirect addressing. The data contents of these special registers can be automatically changed as directed by the program. Indirect addressing is particularly useful in loop portions of a program. An instruction in the loop may designate such a special register each time the loop makes its sequence. The contents of the special register can be changed before the start of a succeeding loop sequence. This provides considerable flexibility in programming complex sequences as other registers, indirectly addressed by each circuit of the loop, call up new data, of programming routines.

industrial CRT alarm calculator systems — The vast majority of industrial processes have such inertia that speed seldom is an overriding factor, especially for supervisory control applications. The use of standard serial ASCII as the communications code allows installation of conventional CRT terminals as input/output devices but even more usefully as status or alarm indicators. Input to the calculator via terminal keyboards is limited to "line" or "page" mode as the calculator, lacking an interrupt structure, must maintain control over the I/O process at all times. Conventional time-sharing is no longer impractical with calculator-based systems. CRT alarm systems can be created for industrial processes which are fairly sophisticated and much less costly than their hard-wired counterparts.

industrial process control — Industrial processing applications are as wide and varied as the degrees of control that individual processes may require. Some general process-control application areas are: precious metals production, cement production, environmental control, pilot plants, chemical processes, petroleum refining and many others. The data acquisition and control system provides maximum flexibility in the types of process data that it can accept, and the variety of output signals and data format that a calculator may exercise.

inequalities, linear programming — The mathematical problem of minimizing or maximizing a linear function of n variables, subject to n independent restrictions, such as requirements that each variable be non-negative, and also subject to a finite number of other linear constraints. The latter are either equalities or weak inequalities ($\leq$ or $\geq$); strict inequalities of the form $<$ or $>$ are not admissible. An exact solution or other termination to this problem is furnished by the simplex method or one of its variants.

inequality — A proposition (or relation) which relates the magnitudes of two mathematical expressions or functions A and B. Inequalities are four types; A is greater than B ($A > B$); A is less than B ($A < B$); A is greater than or equal to B ($A \geq B$); A is less than or equal to B ($A \leq B$). The first two types are called strict, and the last two are relaxed or weak. The process of identifying a functional argument or range of arguments which makes the proposition true is called solving the inequality, or obtaining a feasible solution to the inequality.

infeasible or unbounded solutions, linear programming — A technique for finding the best solution from among all solutions of a system of linear inequalities. The variables are usually processing or scheduling variables in some physical situation; the inequalities are obtained from the physical constraints on these variables; and the criterion for "best solution" is the value of some given linear function of all the variables. When a solution fails to exist, the system is said to be infeasible or to have no feasible solution. When the best solution is infinite in one or more variables, the system is said to be unbounded.

infinity — A term employed in mathematics to express a quantity greater than any assignable quantity of the same kind. Mathematically considered, infinity is always a limit of a variable quantity, resulting from a particular supposition made upon the varying element which enters it.

inflection point — The point where a curve changes direction.

information — The meaning that a human assigns to data by means of the known conventions used in their representation.

information bits — The fundamental unit of measurement for information is the "bit." One bit of information is one answer to one question, expressed in binary (yes or no) form. Basic information theory, derived from logical principles, provides that all information, no matter how complex, can be represented by some collection of bits. Physicists generally agree that bits can travel as fast as the speed of light, and that the minimum mass or energy required of a bit can be made indefinitely small if the space and time required to contain it be made indefinitely large. The limiting product of the energy and time requirements of a bit is closely related to the very small Plank's constant of the quantum theory, 6.626×10^{-27} erg-seconds. Despite rapid advances in electronics technology in recent years, the theoretical limits have not been even remotely approached.

information-feedback system — An error-control system using message feedback when an erroneous group is received from the sending station.

information heading — Messages are composed of data and control. The control information is contained in that portion of the message called the heading. Some typical heading information is the following: identification of the originating station; identification of the sending and receiving device or process; the priority of the message; the security class of the message; routing information concerning the distribution of the message once it has reached its destination; message processing information concerning its status as data or control.

information processing — A less restrictive term than data processing, encompassing the totality of scientific and business operations performed by a computer.

information processing calculator system — The programming versatility of electronic calculators makes them ideal for processing information from automated chemical analysis equipment. A brand called "AutoAnalyzers" represents widely-used equipment of this type. A Pharmaceuticals company in California, has applied a 16-channel high-speed analog-to-digital conversion system and a system time clock, in conjunction with an advanced programmable calculator and disk memory, to provide a complete information processing and data storage system. Data from research and production gas chromatographs is handled in a similar fashion to that of the AutoAnalyzer except that peak area is determined rather than peak height. Chromatographic data reduction, including retention times and percent concentration of the individual components, can be provided by the system. Data is accepted either directly from the chromatographic detector or through one or more digital integrators.

information retrieval system — A system for locating selecting on demand certain documents, or other graphic records relevant to a given information requirement, from a file of such material. Examples of information retrieval systems are classification, indexing, and machine searching systems.

information theory — The mathematical theory concerned with information rate, channels, channel width, noise and other factors affecting information transmission. Initially developed for electrical communications, it is now applied to business systems and other phenomena which deal with information units and flow of information in networks. 2. Mathematical analysis of efficiency with which communication channels are employed — the aim being to find the most efficient system of coding for any channel.

information-transfer paths, calculator — On some systems, using the information-transfer paths in the system, all data transfers between the calculator and the mass memory go through the cache memory. All addresses, commands, and status information are processed through the input/output structure. The basic difference is that cache-memory transfers go directly to the calculator read/write memory and are much faster than transfers through the calculator I/O structure.

inherited error — A calculator or computer error which has incorrect initial values, especially that error accumulated from prior steps in a step-by-step integration.

in-house — Pertains to system development or operation performed by an organization's own staff, as opposed to contracting the work to an outside organization.

initialization — 1. Concerns specific preliminary steps required before execution of iterative cycles to establish or determine efficient start procedures. Usually a single, nonrepetitive operation after a cycle has begun and/or until a full cycle is again begun. 2. Supplying a previously programmed set of instructions from a special ROM at the time a calculator is powered on.

initialization step, calculator — Generally, the initialization step, clears the registers, asks for the minimum and maximum value of x's with the width of the cells, and also accepts input value and adds 1 to the counter representing the particular cell in which that value falls. Its next sequence is to count that input. It is now ready to accept another data value. This step in the program will continue as long as users enter values and press "continue". When users want to discontinue input and calculate the results, they press the keys to begin the output part of the

initialize

program. Each cell is read in separately and the % of total is calculated and printed. (some systems)

initialize — 1. Refers to a program or hardware circuit which will return a program, a system or a hardware device to an original state. 2. To set an instruction, counter, switch, or address to a specified starting condition at a specified time in a program.

initial program loader — 1. The initialization procedure (program) that causes an operating system to commence operation. Abbreviated IPL. 2. The method that allows a program to be loaded so that the program can proceed to run under its own control.

in-line processing — Refers to various systems whereby transactions are processed in the line, or in the sequence in which they arrive, without the need for sorting.

input — 1. An adjective referring to a device or collective set of devices used for bringing data into another device. 2. A channel for impressing a state on a device or logic element. 3. Pertaining to a device, process, or channel involved in an input process or to the data or states involved in an input process. In the English language, the adjective "input" may be used in place of "input data," "input signal," "input terminal," etc., when such usage is clear in a given context. 4. Pertaining to a device, process, or channel involved in the insertion of data or states, or to the data or states involved. 5. One, or a sequence of input states.

input area — The internal storage area in a calculator or computer into which data from external storage is transferred.

input block — A section of a calculator's internal storage reserved for receiving and processing input data.

input buffer register — A device that receives data from input devices (tape, disk) and then transfers it to internal computer storage.

input bus control — The input bus control manipulates the source of data to the input bus port. The input bus can receive data from either the shift network or the accumulator. In addition, this control circuit can inhibit data from being routed to the input bus. This allows the input bus to enter data into the accumulator, or to be used for other system functions.

input key, data acquisition calculator — Overrides AUTO control to place system in full power-on readiness with components active. INPUT mode alerts system to receive keyed instructions. (some units)

input device — The mechanical unit designed to bring data to be processed into a computer, e.g., a card reader, a tape reader, or a keyboard.

input editing — Refers to various types of input that may be edited to convert to a more convenient format for processing and storage than that used for entry into the system; and to check the data for proper format, completeness, or accuracy. Often, input must be formatted as most convenient for preparation by humans, and then must be reformatted.

input interface controller (BCD 10-digit-parallel) — This is an input only interface. It is directly compatible to most digital meters for on-line applications. It automatically converts each BCD digit to an ASCII equivalent code. It also can receive up to 40 bits of parallel binary data. (some units)

input/output control system (IOCS)

input/output — 1. Commonly called I/O. A general term for equipment used to communicate with a computer. 2. The data involved in such communication. 3. The media carrying the data for input/output. 4. The process of transmitting information from an external source to the computer or from the computer to an external source.

input-output bus — Input-output bus provides scores of parallel lines for data, command, device address, status, and control information. This eliminates the timing problems created when data and address lines are time-shared. It makes interfacing easier, faster, and less expensive. Memory and input-output interfaces connect directly to the main bus. Each operates at its own pace. Under Direct Memory Access (DMA), this means that transfers can be made directly between external devices and memory without affecting the central processor, if desired.

input/output channel — Refers to a specific channel which allows independent communication between the memory exchange and the input/output exchange. It controls any peripheral device and performs all validity checking on information transfers.

input-output channel bus — Central processor communication paths, consist of a high speed data bus, a high-speed input/output bus for calculator peripheral equipment, and a low speed bus buffer channel for slower process equipment.

input-output code, calculator ROM — In some units for input and output operations all information exchange between the calculator and a peripheral device consists of data being transferred character by character in an 8-bit parallel fashion on some units. Alternatively, a 12-bit parallel character series can be output, if required. The calculator generally sends and receives one 8-bit character at a time; if another character is to be sent or received, the calculator will wait until the device is ready. On some units there is no provision for system-interrupt operation when using the I/O ROM, i.e., the peripheral device cannot initiate or call for input or output operation. The calculator must be in complete control of each peripheral device while the device is involved in I/O operations.

input/output concepts — The I/O concepts of a particular calculator will determine the control signals required in the system and interface hardware, the extent to which the processor itself acts as the I/O controller, and the software options available for dealing with data at the ports. One system approach has centered on the microbus structure in which both memory and I/O interfaces exist in the same address space. The interfaces are individually programmable to provide I/O management. They generate and receive all I/O control signals in the system. They are programmed by control words passed over the system bus. The result of this is minimization of hardware controls required on the system bus together with simplicity and generality of I/O programming.

input/output control — Input/output control, includes physical and logical control over I/O records, files, and units; buffer control: teleprocessing terminal and message handling; random access I/O control; labeling of files, and error-recovery procedures.

input/output control system (IOCS) — A group of macro-instruction routines for handling the transfer of data between main storage and external storage devices. IOCS consists of two parts: physical IOCS and logical IOCS.

input-output, customized — Many sophisticated calculators must be capable of interacting with an enormous variety of external devices, including switches, motor drives, bistable sensors, analog-to-digital and digital-to-analog converters, lamps, displays, keyboards, printers, teletypewriters, communications modems, cassettes, and other computers. The CPU must have access to these devices to obtain system information and to respond with control, status, and numerical information. Because the possible combinations of devices, modes, and techniques are virtually unlimited, the programmable-LSI interface components are designed to implement most combinations that might want.

Programable configurations can accommodate the various operating modes and protocols for data transfer. Their applications are primarily limited only by the room available on a board for the devices, interconnection traces, line drivers, and terminators. The programable LSI devices enable the user to customize the I/O interface with control words contained in the system program. The appropriate words are placed in the initialization section of the program, and the CPU transfers the words to registers in the peripheral-interface devices. The only additional customization required is to plug suitable line drivers and terminators into the sockets associated with the parallel I/O ports.

input-output device controllers — Input-output controllers consist of the necessary logic circuitry required to interconnect one or more peripheral devices with the input-output interface. Each input-output or direct memory access (DMA) controller depending upon which channel is interfaced. An input-output controller is normally identified with a single device; however, certain types of controllers may accommodate multiple devices of the same physical type.

input/output drivers — The list is long; some are: Teletype driver, to assist the programmer in writing efficient teletype input/output routines; Paper Tape Driver documentation to assist the programmer in writing efficient reader/punch subroutines; Card Reader Driver, provides for input from an 80 column punched card reader and code conversion from Hollerith to ASCII; Line Printer Driver, documentation to assist the programmer in writing efficient line printer output subroutines; Cassette I/O Driver, for convenient operation of digital cassettes. Supports high speed search as well as normal input/output functions; Magnetic Tape Driver, provides for all read, write, rewind and skipping functions for 9-track magnetic tapes; Moving Head Disk Driver, sets up and controls all disk positioning functions and data transfers via Direct Memory Access (DMA) . . . supports overlapped seeks on up to four drives; CRT Driver, documentation to assist the programmer in writing efficient CRT input/output subroutines, and others.

input-output interface — A typical input-output interface might incorporate two input-output channels, a processor input-output /PIO) channel, and a direct memory access (DMA) channel. The PIO channel interfaces with the processor via the data input bus and provides simplex character-oriented data transfer capability. The DMA channel interfaces directly with the memory, via the data input bus, and provides high-speed, record-oriented data transfer capability at rates of up to 500,000 or more words per second. The typical input-output interface incorporates two or more input-output channels, a processor input-output channel, and a direct memory access input-output channel.

input/output interface module, CRT — Some calculators have I/O modules that contain the CRT or other display and keyboard interfaces. The keyboard interface can provide not only for the input of characters, but also support of the mini-operator console located on the keyboard. Typically the console functions include two switches: system reset and, initial program load (from cassette tape), and two status displays: run/halt, and interrupt enable. All other front panel functions and debugging aids can be provided by an interactive debugger through the CRT display.

input-output limited — Refers to a system or condition which the time for input and output operation exceeds other operations.

input-output models — Such classes of models as these are derived from assumptions about economic variables and behavior which take account of the general equilibrium phenomena and are concerned with the empiricial analysis of production, i.e., especially intermediate uses and final output. The problem is to investigate what can be produced and the quantity of each intermediate product which itself must be used up in the production process. Various data are obtained initially which attest to available resources and current state of the technology.

input/output operation — In some units the input/output section acts as an autonomous processor which runs independently of the instruction-execution cycle, scanning the input channels for the presence of input or output word transfer requests and transferring data between the channels and central storage, controlled by the input/output access-control location associated with the channels.

input/output port — A typical input/output port consists of an 8-bit latch with tri-state output buffers along with control and device selection logic. Also included is a service request flip-flop for the generation and control of interrupts to the microprocessor. The device is multimode in nature. It can be used to implement latches, gated buffers or multiplexers. Thus, all of the principal peripheral and input/output functions of a microcomputer system can be implemented with this device. Some units require only .25 μA input current, permitting direct connection to MOS data and address lines of the CPU's.

input/output processor (IOP) — A secondary processor dedicated to transfer operations to and from main memory. (Clarified by processor, peripheral.)

input/output request words — Control words for input/output requests that are stored in the Message Reference Block until the I/O is completed.

input/output, simultaneous — Generally refers to calculators or computers which can handle other operations concurrently with input and output operations, most often using buffers which hold input/output data and information as it arrives and on a temporary basis, while other operations are executed by the CPU. Thus, the computer need not wait for data from the very slow I/O units and may instead take it from the faster part of the buffer in massive quantities instead of as it arrives from slower units or terminals.

input/output system bus — Many input/output systems have provisions for up to 240 devices, organized along a common bus. Communication along these busses is on a byte-by-byte basis under program control. However, high speed devices can communicate directly with memory through the use of a multi-port memory module. Many devices can be attached to one multi-port memory module. It is also possible to connect two or more systems to the same multiport module to allow interprocessor communications. Generally the parts of these systems are modular to allow configurations to meet any users needs as precisely as possible. Interfaces are available for a wide variety of applications including synchronous and asynchronous serial communications, control of AC devices D/A and A/D converters, and peripherals ranging from teletypes to flexible disk drives.

input/output table — A plotting device used to generate or to record one variable as a function of another variable.

input/output unit — Those devices, modems, terminals or various pieces of equipment whose designated purpose relates to manual, mechanical, electronic, visual or audio entry to and output from the computer mainframe or calculator unit.

input/output writer, calculator — Provides a convenient means for entering alphabetic information into the calculator as well as the printout capability of the various Output Writers.

input/output writer capability — Some examples:
- Permits alpha string (messages) and formatted numeric input and output
- Serves as an on-line keyboard for directly entering alphanumeric codes into various model calculators
- Headings, titles, messages easily inserted into programs requiring formatted or columnar output
- Ideally suited to production of finished reports, completely documented problem solutions, typing on preprinted forms

input process — The transmission of data and its reception from peripheral hardware or as an exchange of external storage to internal storage.

input program — A routine which directs or controls the reading of programs and data into a calculator system. Such a routine may be internally stored, wired, or part of a "bootstrap" operation and may perform housekeeping or system control operations according to rules.

input register — A specific register which receives data from input devices to hold only long enough to complete transfer to internal storage, i.e., to an arithmetic register, etc., as directed by the program.

input storage — 1. Refers to a device that holds each bundle of facts while it awaits its turn to be processed. This allows successive bundles to be compared to make sure they're in the right order or for other control purposes. 2. Any information that enters a computer for the purpose of being processed or to aid in processing. It is then held until signaled for use by the control program.

input translator — Refers to a section of some programs that convert the incoming programmer's instructions into operators and operands understood by the calculator. This scan or search also checks the input items for desired properties and, in many cases, outputs appropriate error messages if the desired properties of the input do not conform to the proper syntax.

input work queue — A list or line of jobs ready or submitted for processing but not yet begun or in process. Usually, these tasks are input on a first-come, first-served basis such as: an input queue consists of programs, data, and control cards settled and waiting in the input job stream. Schedulers and special operating systems handle and control such queues differently.

inquiry — Refers to a technique whereby the interrogation of the contents of storage may be inititated at a local or remote point by use of a keyboard, touchtone pad, or other device.

inquiry and transaction processing — Refers to various types of teleprocessing applications in which inquiries and records of transactions received from a number of terminals are used to interrogate or update one or more master files maintained by the central system.

inquiry, keyboard — Interrogation of program progress, storage contents, or other information by keyboard maneuvering.

inquiry station — The remote terminal device from which an inquiry into computing or data processing equipment is made.

inquiry terminal — On some units information is placed into the calculator through the alphanumeric keyboard and is simultaneously displayed on the screen. The unit then displays a reply to the inquiry on the screen. Information is displayed many times faster than that produced by an operator by means of a typeout. To reuse the display after the inquiry has been answered requires only a press of the erase button.

insert key — The insert key moves the current and all following instructions down one location when in the learn mode, in some units.

instability — The measure of the fluctuations or irregularities in the performance of a device, system or parameter.

installation and cabling, interface — Various series universal digital interface systems are plug-compatible with series calculators. Generally, specific modification of the calculator or special wiring is required for their use and, when the calculator is not being used on-line, it may be devoted to conventional manual data entry problems without the necessity of disconnecting the interface. Input/output connections to the individual series data and control cards are made through printed circuit connectors located at the rear of the mainframe assembly.

instantaneous access — Refers to directly obtaining data from, or placing data into a storage device or register without serial delay due to other units of data, and usually in a relatively short period of time.

instantaneous power — For a circuit or component, the product of the instantaneous voltage and the instantaneous current. This may not be zero even for a non-dissipative (wattless) system on account of stored energy, although in some cases its time integral must be zero.

instruction — 1. A statement that specifies an operation and the value or locations of its operands. 2. Information which, when properly coded and introduced as a unit into a digital machine, causes the calculator to perform one or more of its operations. An instruction commonly includes one or more addresses.

instruction accumulator — Instructions are the means for the accumulator to perform data manipulations and arithmetic operations. Memory is passive; users can write into it, and can read back what they wrote, and that is all. Therefore a calculator will need a more flexible storage area in which data manipulation will take place; most will call this storage area an Accumulator or Working Register and it is built from flip-flops, or logic that allows each bit to be set to 0 or 1 based on the status of other accumulator bits or based on the results of any other logical sequence. The electronic logic that determines whether a bit is to be set to 1 or 0 is collected into a part of the calculator called the Central Processing Unit.

instruction address bus, calculator — On some units, when the calculator is in use, every keystroke places a corresponding keycode on the I_A (instruction address) bus. This code is stored in the buffer of the program storage circuit. If the calculator is in W/PRGM mode, the code is then inserted into the program memory. If the calculator is in RUN mode, the keystroke is executed.

instruction address register (IAR) — The register which contains the address of the instruction to be executed next, but subject to branching, interrupts, etc.

instruction, arithmetical — Specifies an arithmetic operation upon data, e.g., addition or multiplication. Arithmetical instructions form a subset of the machine instruction set to be considered separately from logical instructions.

instruction, calculator — A bit pattern that is interpreted by the executing control hardware in a wired control machine or by a microprogram in a microprogrammed machine.

instruction check, unallowable digit — A character or combination of bits which is not accepted as a valid representation by the machine design or by a specific routine and suggests malfunctions.

instruction, clear — That specific instruction which replaces data or information in storage or in registers, accumulators, etc. with zeros or blanks, i.e., to place various binary devices into zero states.

instruction code — Concerns various symbols, names and definitions of all the instructions which are directly intelligible to a given calculator or a given executive routine.

instruction, control — The instructions in this category are used to manipulate data within the main memory and the control memory, to prepare main-memory storage areas for the processing of data fields, and to control the sequential selection and interpretation of instructions in the stored program.

instruction control unit — Many systems operations are controlled by the instruction control unit (ICU) which contains a read-only memory (ROM) in which the micro-instructions are stored, and address control logic to allow microprogram branching.

instruction diagnostic — A device that completely tests all CPU instructions in all modes including operation under interrupt.

instruction examples, calculator — The programming language of some units brings together decision making ability and efficient execution. For example, the IF instruction acts as a qualifier for making decisions. Similarly, FOR NEXT loops automatically control repetition of program segments. GO TO, GO TO X, GO SUB X all identify branching instructions that tell the calculator where to execute the next step in computation. Subroutines of some logic types can be nested up to seven deep. And flags can be set to identify special program conditions.

instruction execution logic — In some units the instruction-execution logic causes each instruction to be retrieved-or fetched- from memory, decoded and then executed. The instruction logic performs these functions in the following three ways:
1. The contents of the Program Counter (PC) are sent to the Memory Address Register (MAR) to define the location of the next instruction.
2. The contents of the memory at the address are loaded into the (IR) instruction Register.
3. The execution of the instruction in the IR may then involve many steps and many transfers between memory and the General Purpose Register (GPR) file.

instruction groups, microprocessor — Most CPUs have many instructions which are extremely useful and extend their ranges of applicability. The instruction groups are as follows:
- Data register and memory transfers;
- Conditional or unconditional branches and subroutine calls;
- I/O operations;
- Direct Load/Store Accumulator;
- Save, Restore Data Registers, Accumulator and Flags;
- Double Length Operation in Data Registers include: Increment/Decrement/Addition,
    Direct Load/Store (H and L),
    Load Immediate,
    Index Register Modification;
- Indirect Jump;
- Stack Pointer Modification;
- Logical Operations;
- Binary Arithmetic;
- Decimal Arithmetic;
- Set and reset interrupt enable flip-flop;
- Increment/Decrement Memory or data registers.

instruction, hold — A calculator instruction which caused data called from storage to be also retained in storage after it is called out and transferred to its new location.

instruction, macro — 1. An instruction consisting of a sequence of microinstructions that are inserted into the object routine for performing a specific operation. 2. The more powerful instructions that combine several operations in one instruction.

instruction, microprogrammable — Generally all instructions which do not reference main memory (do not contain a memory address) can be microprogrammed, allowing the programmer to specify several shift, skip, or input/output transfer commands to be performed within one instruction.

instruction modification — Refers to an alteration in the operation code portion of an instruction or command such that if the routine containing the instruction or command is repeated, the calculator will perform a different operation.

instruction, multiple address — An instruction consisting of an operation code and two or more

instruction, no address — An instruction specifying an operation which the computer can perform without having to refer to its storage unit.

instruction, nonperformance — An instruction requiring nonperformance of what normally might be executed, i.e., not to be executed. This instruction should not be confused with a NO-OP or Do-Nothing instruction.

instruction, no-op — 1. An instruction that specifically instructs the calculator to do nothing but process the next instruction in sequence. 2. A blank instruction. 3. A skip instruction.

instruction, n-plus-one address — Refers to a multiple address instruction in which one address specifies the location of the next instruction of the normal sequence to be executed.

instruction, null — One which performs no action during the operation of a program. Occasionally used to provide for future changes to the program, but more often used to complete a set of instructions where the machine code system requires instructions to be written in complete groups.

instruction, operational-stop — An instruction that can stop the calculator either before or after the stop instruction is obeyed, depending on the governing criterion.

instruction path, microprocessor — The instruction path is a transfer bus for retrieving instructions from the program memory. Instruction word width is determined by the size of the instruction set which affects processing power.

instruction, privileged — Protection against one problem subprogram misusing another problem subprogram's I/O devices is provided by restricting all I/O commands to the supervisor state. A subprogram requests I/O action by issuing a supervisor call instruction. The supervisory subprogram can then analyze this request and take the appropriate action.

instruction, programmed — Special subroutines called programmed instructions, may be used as if they were single commands by employing one of the programmed instructions of the repertoire. This capability allows the programmer to define his own special command, through the use of subroutines, which may be changed by the operating routine if desired.

instruction, pseudo — 1. A symbolic representation in a compiler or interpreter. 2. A group of characters having the same general form as a computer instruction, but never executed by the computer as an actual instruction. Synonymous with quasi instruction.

instruction register, current — The control section register which contains the instruction currently being executed after it is brought to the control section from memory.

instruction register (IR) — The instruction register is a 4, 8, 12 or 16-bit register that is used to hold the instruction currently being executed by the processor.

instruction register, sequence control — A hardware register which is used by the calculator to remember the location of the next instruction to be processed in the normal sequence, but subject to branching, execute instructions and interrupts. Synonymous with instruction address register (IAR).

instruction repertoire — The set of operations that can be represented in a given operation code.

instruction set — 1. The set of instructions that a calculating, computing or data-processing system is capable of performing. 2. The set of instructions that an automatic coding system assembles. 3. Instruction sets consist of an operator part, one or more address parts, and some special indicators, usually, and serve to define the operations and operands. It is the total structured group of characters to be transferred to the calculator as operations are executed.

instruction set components — One typical large instruction set has 128 instructions including:
- the floating point group
- the memory reference group
- the register reference group
- the I/O group
- the extended arithmetic group
- the indexed group
- the data communications group

instruction set expandability — A typical medium-scale MPU has a set of 72 basic instructions usually listed in alphabetical order. These include binary and decimal arithmetic functions, as well as logical, shift, rotate, load, store, branch, interrupt and stack manipulation functions. Most of the instructions have several variations and most can be used with several memory addressing modes. Thus, the total complex of instructions available to the programmer actually is 197, for one MPU model. MPU means micro processor unit, the 'heart' of advanced calculators.

instruction sets, microprocessor — From a programmer's point of view, microprocessor instructions break down conveniently into the following:
- Data movement.
- Data manipulation.
- Decision and control.
- Input/output.

Data can be moved about between a variety of internal sources and destinations. The most complex locations are those in memory — usually a RAM or RAM bank — since a variety of addressing modes can be used to specify location. The effective address of a memory location to be read or written can be given immediately by bits in the instruction being executed. In current microprocessors the immediate data may be 4, 8, 12 or even 16 bits long. Immediate data may be interpreted as a location (or displacement) in a previously selected page (or location) or memory.

instruction, shift — Specific instructions which will shift the number either to the left or to the right within an arithmetic register. A shift operation is principally equivalent to multiplying or dividing by the radix of the number base in use, depending upon the direction of the shift. In a decimal computer, a shift of one place to the right is equivalent to dividing by 10, a shift one place to the left is equivalent to multiplying by 10.

instruction, skip — An instruction having no effect other than directing the processor to proceed to another instruction designated in the storage portion. (Synonymous with skip, and no-op instruction.)

instruction, supervisory — This instruction is designed and used to control the operation or execution of other routines or programs.

instruction time — The portion of an instruction cycle during which the control unit is analyzing the instruction and setting up to perform the indicated operation. Same as time, execution.

instruction, trapped — A special instruction

instruction variable-length — which is executed by software routine in cases where the necessary hardware is absent and in cases where the CPU is not in the state required or an instruction whose execution was stopped or cancelled.

instruction variable-length — A feature which increases main memory efficiency by using only the amount necessary for the application and increases speed because the machine interprets only the fields relevant to the application. Half-word (2 byte), two-halfword (4 bytes), or three-halfword (6 bytes) instructions are used on some systems.

instruction words, location — Some calculators manipulate memory data according to a list of instruction words stored in the same memory. The Program Counter (PC) defines the location of the next instruction to be executed. The Instruction Register (IR) holds the instruction word for the current instruction being executed.

instrumentation — The application of devices for the measuring, recording and/or controlling of physical properties and movements.

instrumentation, calculator — Calculators generally cost much less than minicomputers. The programmable calculators open up whole new areas of measurement and control for automation techniques. They can also be used to streamline automation instrumentation systems, many of which use inflexible hard-wired logic or relatively inflexible paper tape. The use of calculators in measurement instruments and automated control systems is expanding rapidly. Special-purpose calculators began to appear in 1974. They were not simple desk-top instruments, but extended their capabilities over large areas. Different versions were rack-mountable and ruggedized to adapt to different environments. Calculators benefited greatly from computer technology. They adopted interrupt and special processing, and calculator I/O structures to permit simpler and more efficient routing of information within the system, as well as to peripherals. Users and designers of these systems expanded their planning horizons, and upward compatibility within calculator product lines grew quickly and significantly.

instrumentation calculator interface — Instrumentation and analytical equipment are interfaced directly to many calculators using special design interfaces. "On-line" data acquisition is therefore facilitated.

instrumentation calibration — A procedure to ascertain, usually by comparison with a standard, the locations at which scale/chart graduations should be placed to correspond to a series of values of the quantity which the instrument is to measure, receive, or transmit.

instrumentation control calculator — Some advanced system calculators accept 15 different instruments. These units have some important features that simplify the task even further. Programmable data logic levels give them the ability to tell calculators what to look for in + or − logic levels. Various tape cartridges complement some systems with 96,384 bytes of data storage. The cartridge and the AUTO START provide some systems the capability for power-fail restart in remote locations when the calculator is a part of an interfacing system. With advanced interface systems, immediate data acquisition and instrumentation control become possible where they were uncomfortable or impossible before.

instrumentation correction — Refers to the calculated difference between the true value and the indication of the measured quantity; i.e., a positive correction denotes that the indication of the instrument is less than the true value.

instrumentation error — Where input into a system is directly from instruments such as pressure gauges, limit checks are imposed to prevent instrumentation errors. If these limits are violated, control may be assumed by a violation subroutine for immediate corrective action.

instrumentation programming, calculator — Flowchart and program statements illustrate the ease of generating programs to control instruments. One type program scans selected channels, programs the digital voltmeter to range and function, measures thermocouple voltage on each channel, converts this voltage to degrees Celsius, and prints results on the calculator's printer.

instrumentation system, calculator — Refers to a powerful, yet inexpensive calculator combined with a power supply and system software. Users add the instrumentation modules they need. With the calculator, users can read input from DMM's and counters and can log data selectively, calculate results and output data or trigger signals.

instrument calculator control components — The system components generally include the advanced system calculator with any of the presently available options; a modified interface plug-in; and software for data acquisition and analysis. On some systems among the basic features: up to two numerical inputs can be acquired from two digital multimeters or two digital counters; two output signal lines can be activated for controlling external equipment; and a standard software package is provided that can be used for data logging (on printer) and data capture (in advanced calculator registers) with selectable sampling rates.

Capabilities vary depending on which version of some series calculator is used and the options that it incorporates. One type system with a printer can perform the following tasks: data logging on the printer at a preset sampling interval or under operator control; data monitoring and programmed decision making; mathematical operations on input data such as integration, differentiation, transformation, statistical reduction; and output stimulation and regulation of external equipment.

Another system with a printer can accomplish all of the above operations plus: direct data capture (3-4 samples per second) in registers, stored for later printout; graphic analysis or computation; extensive statistical reduction and regression analysis of input data; operator prompting and output labeling of interactive operator controlled measurements, such as in calculator based testing and evaluation; and long-term data monitoring and storage of data on mag tape. The software, recorded on magnetic media, allows the operator to select the number of samples to be taken, the sampling rate, and data limits to allow data collection to be terminated.

instrument calibration system — A typical Instrument Calibration System brings to the calibration laboratory a cost-effective solution to calibrating the myriad complex instruments in use today. The system incorporates a wide variety of calibration-quality instruments, easily recognized by those involved in cal lab work as required for calibration purposes. The system calibrates a wide variety of passive meters, multimeters, electronic meters (voltage, current, VSWR, power, etc.), differential voltmeters, digital voltmeters, frequency counters, and oscilloscopes along with their plug-ins and amplifiers. In addition, the system can optionally calibrate signal sources and generators, oscillators, pulse generators, and function generators.

instrument control, calculator — Instruments having a BCD output can be read by the calculator under program control. The calculators may also control external equipment. With these capabilities, the advanced units can automatically acquire and store data, perform statistical analyses of these data, and list the data on the optional calculator printer. These systems also have provisions for powering many of the standard plug-ins. Typical of the applications to which these systems may be applied are automatic data collection from laboratory experiments, automatic counting and sizing of produced goods, monitoring of heating and air conditioning efficiency, stimulation and measurement of equipment or component performance, calibration of medical radiotherapy equipment and monitoring of pollutant levels (with limit alarm provisions).

instrument digital interface units — Various digital interface units are designed for use in general purpose input/output systems for some electronic programmable desk calculators to allow these versatile highly-sophisticated systems to be used in a wide variety of data acquisition, process control, and data collection, system control, and similar applications by putting the calculator "on-line" to the outside world. These units provide advanced calculators with the input/output versatility of conventional minicomputer systems while retaining the low cost, ease of programming, and computational ability characteristic of programmable calculators as a group.

instrument programmability — The programmability of microprocessors allows inclusion within the instrument of diagnostic aids for troubleshooting and self-checking. More generally, programmability simplifies tailoring for the user of instrument function and interface characteristics. Prior to microprocessors, manufacturers had very limited ability to make custom changes unless a quantity order was involved. Microprogrammed instruments, because of adaptability through software, promise to resist obsolescence longer than conventionally designed instruments. Control programs may be changed in the field to update and improve the performance of microprogrammed instruments.

INT — The INTeger/FRACtion truncation function allows one to keep only the integer or fractional portion of a number. This is especially useful in base conversion, random number generation, or for storing two numbers in one memory.

INTCP — Intercept.

integer — A whole number as distinguished from a fraction; this is, a number that contains the unit (one) an exact number of times.

integer programming — 1. A class of optimization problems in which the values of all the variables are restricted to be integers. Normally, the optimization problem without this integer restriction is a linear program; additional adjectives indicate variations — for example, integer quadratic programming. 2. In operations research, a class of procedures for locating the maximum or minimum of a function subject to constraints, where some or all variables must have integer values. Contrast with convex programming, dynamic programming, linear programming, mathematical programming, nonlinear programming, quadratic programming. 3. Loosely, discrete programming.

integral — 1. The result of integration either of a function or of an equation; an expression whose derivative is the integrand. 2. An expression which after being differentiated will produce a given differential. 3. In numeric notation, the integral or integer is contained in the places to the left of the assumed point. The decimal 2345.67 has four integral places.

integrand — 1. When a unit has two input variables (x and y) and one output variable (z) which is proportional to the integral of (y) — the y is the integrand. 2. A calculus expression, i.e., the math expression or function which is operated upon in the process of integration.

integrated circuit (IC) — 1. A combination of interconnected passive and active circuit elements incorporated on a continuous substrate. 2. Also called a functional device. An interconnect array of conventional components fabricated on and in a single crystal of semiconductor material by etching, doping, diffusion, etc. and capable of performing a complete circuit function.

integrated circuit advanced technologies — Basically new IC fabrication techniques include: advances in photolithographic techniques, electron beam microfabrication, ion implantation, heterojunction device processing, vapor phase epitaxy and silicon-on-sapphire devices, others.

integrated circuit chip board — The Random Access Memory is an example of an Integrated circuit chip to store data for future access by the control ROM or PROM. A typical RAM module consists of 8 RAM chips (2.56k total storage) on a RAM printed circuit board. A RAM module performs two functions. As a Random Access Memory it stores N bits per chip (N chips per module) arranged as N registers of twenty N-bit characters each. As a vehicle of communication with display devices each chip is provided with N output lines and associated control logic. Since there are 8 RAM chips on the board, in small systems, 32 output lines (8 RAM × 4 output lines/RAM) are available. These output lines are often connected to lights on the console.

integrated circuit packaging — An integrated circuit package is expected to satisfy a large number of partly conflicting requirements: low cost, mechanical strength, high packing density, hermeticity, low parasitic reactances, low thermal resistance, and ease of handling and testing. No single circuit package exists which ideally fulfills these characteristics. For a majority of monolithic analog circuits, the package choice is narrowed down to three most commonly used package types. These are the TO-5, the Flatpack, and the Dual-In-Line (DIP) packages.

integrated data processing — 1. Refers to an information processing system which is organized, directed and carried out according to a systems approach. 2. Complete machine control of a sphere of

interest. 3. A system that treats as a whole, all data processing requirements to accomplish a sequence of data processing steps, or a number of related data processing sequences, and which strives to reduce or eliminate duplicating data entry or processing steps. 4. The processing of data by such a system. Synonymous with IDP.

integrated injection logic (I^2L) — I^2L is characterized by some observers as the bipolar LSI of the future. Its primary advantages are increased density, good speed-power product, versatility, and low cost. The technology is capable of squeezing 1,000 to 3,000 gates, or more than 10,000 bits of memory, on a single chip. It has speed-power product as low as 1 picojoule, compared to 100 pj with TTL logic. It can handle digital and analog functions on a single chip and is made with a five mask process without the need for current-source and load resistors.

integrated monolithic circuit — Several logic circuits, gates, flip flops are etched on single crystals, ceramics or other semiconductor materials and designed to use geometric etching and conductive ink deposition techniques all within a hermetically sealed chip. Some chips with many resistors and transistors are extremely tiny, others are in effect "sandwiches" of individual chips.

integrated system — The combination of processes which results in the introduction of data which need not be repeated as further allied or related data is also entered. For example: Shipment data may also be the basis for inventory inquiries, invoicing, marketing reports, etc.

integrator — A device which integrates an input signal, usually with respect to time.

integrator package — The optional integrator package functions by allowing the user to measure and record data values representing the total area under the curve or average values over a preselected period of time. Ten channels can be handled by one package. Average values are highly desirable in monitoring where the signal intensity may vary widely, as in solar radiation studies, air pollution investigations, and meteorological parameters. By using the option, large savings in data reduction time result.

integrity — Preservation of data or programs for their intended purpose.

intelligence — The developed capability of a device to perform functions that are normally associated with human intelligence, such as reasoning, learning, and self-improvement. (Related to machine learning.)

intelligence, artificial — The study of computer and related techniques to supplement the intellectual capabilities of man. As man has invented and used tools to increase his physical powers, he now is beginning to use artificial intelligence to increase his mental powers. In a more restricted sense, the study of techniques for more effective use of digital computers by improved programming techniques.

intelligent cable — General-purpose intelligent Cables are standard, low-cost parallel interfaces for many computers in LSI families employing distributed I/O systems. This system frees the OEM system designer from many complex problems and costly development time usually associated with peripherals interfacing. Many low to medium-speed peripherals and special-purpose intelligent cables completely eliminating the need for higher-cost special-purpose interfaces.

intelligent cable calculator-systems — Users dedicate their units as stand-alone calculators or as a powerful system. They have taken command of a powerful stand-alone or system problem solver. As a problem solver any user can dedicate his unit in seconds to solve accounting problems, but not just as a stand-alone unit, but as a distributed system as well. Read-only memory built into each cable and into the calculator gives fast response to remote station needs. Operation and language features are built in to establish the rapport that only a dedicated system can have. A cartridge can act as a template for one problem or be the base of many automatic operations.

intelligent cable features — These include:
- TTL-compatible negative-true logic
- Low-power Schottky design
- High noise immunity
- Hand-shaking or Strobed I/O discipline
- Controls multiple devices
- Half-duplex or Simplex
- Microprogrammed interface control
- Automatic Error Detection
- Two Standard I/O programming modes
- Standard Ribbon cabling
- Simplified mounting

intelligent keyboard systems — Refers to various intelligent keyboard systems that perform the combination of alphanumerics and numerics for all the applications specially designed to provide the following functions: keying, displaying, editing, calculating, storing, compressing, communicating, printing.

intelligent terminal — A terminal with some level of programmable "intelligence" for performing pre-processing or post-processing operations.

intelligent terminal development — In the past decade, large numbers of computer terminals have been developed and installed to link subscribers in remote locations to a central processor or a central data base. These terminals served only as input/output devices. As the amount of data communications traffic increased, however, computers and transmission lines became overloaded. Users began to explore the possibility of not only collecting data at the terminal but also of sorting and organizing it to minimize computer time required. From this exploration, came the development of "intelligent terminals" which allowed processing to be distributed between the computers and the terminals in a network.

intelligent terminals, remote — In more sophisticated remote-batch terminals a small computer is included to store programs, to control the I/O equipment, and to do some preprocessing functions (e.g., code conversion and editing) and output processing functions (e.g., formatting). In such terminals the use of a microcomputer reduces the amounts of data transmitted to and from the larger central computer, provides flexible control.

interactive calculator plotting example — Radioimmunoassay techniques measure hormone and drug levels in the human body. Previously, it took half an hour of manual plotting to get test results after the radioactive complexes were counted. Now, tape cartridge programs ask for information as the operator inputs data into the calculator keyboard. In a few minutes, the calculator prints an alphanumeric plot of hormone concentrations. On some units two peripherals make the system more useful and faster. Since the radioactive complex count comes from a TTY printer, a tape reader inputs data automatically into the calculator. And a digital plotter gives a graphic comparison to a standard curve.

interactive calculators — Thanks to various, semi-natural and algebraic languages and their conversational, alphanumeric displays and alphanumeric printer, users key in many intricate mathematical problems in the same form they'd write them on paper. This allows them to easily solve complex interactive problems; such as, modeling electronic circuits, including schematics, parts specifications, and cost figures.

interactive ROM, calculator terminal — With the Interactive ROM installed received characters go directly to the calculator's display. When a carriage return character is received, the line is transferred to the printer and the display is cleared. Characters to be sent are typed into the display and sent by pressing the special function key labeled TRANSMIT. A special function key template for the Interactive ROM is necessary.

interactive terminals — Interactive terminals are generally equipped with a display, a keyboard and an incremental printer. Optionally they also include a tape subsystem. Such terminals support interactive, conversational, demand, inquiry, and transaction oriented applications.

interactive processing — A development made possible by the advent of time-sharing, interactive processing involves the constant interplay of creative and routine activities with the routine jobs being relegated to the computer so that man is left free to exercise his imagination and judgment.

interactive system calculator — A system in which bilateral communication is established between a calculator or operating program and a user.

interchange, exchange equals key — If multiplication or division has been conditioned, the exchange key will interchange the first and second factors and execute the conditioned operation as for equals. The printer will print EX to the right of the second factor to denote the operation. For addition or subtraction this key will interchange the input register and the accumulator if the printer is off. If the printer is on, this key will be ignored. (some systems)

interconnection line — Also called tie line. A transmission line connecting two electric systems or networks and permitting energy to be transferred in either direction. Larger interconnections are often called interties, giant ties or regional interconnections.

interface — 1. Refers to instruments, devices or a concept of a common boundary or matching of adjacent components, circuits, equipment, or system elements. An interface enables devices to yield and/or acquire information from one device or program to another. Although the terms adapter, handshake, buffer have similar meaning, interface is more distinctly a connection to complete an operation. 2. A common boundary — for example, physical connection between two systems or two devices. 3. Specifications of the interconnection between two systems or units.

interface bus applications — Thanks to the various interface busses, users can couple the speed and computational power of advanced calculators with the measurement capability of electronic counters and other state-of-the-art accessories. Many new application notes describe how these versatile low-cost combinations solve difficult measurement problems. One typical application note provides an example of a simple data acquisition system using low-cost counter modules, an interface, and some specific model calculators. A multimeter/counter measures frequency, ac volts, dc volts, or resistance and outputs these measurements to the calculator. The calculator computes the mean, standard deviation, and peak-to-peak deviation of the data and even plots a histogram.

interface bus, calculator — One type Hewlett-Packard (HP) Interface Bus can be used with HP 8620 sweepers to achieve calculator control of frequencies from 3 MHz to 18 GHz. The 8620A Opt E45 sweeper with appropriate RF plug-in becomes a source with 1000 points per band programmability. The HP 86290A, to 18 GHz plug-in, is ideal for HP-IB systems because of its flexibility, frequency accuracy and linearity. The bus-controlled 8620A/86290A can quickly step through as many as 3000 frequencies — typically with ± 5 MHz accuracy. For higher accuracy, add the HP 5340A counter plus D/A converter to automatically correct frequency to within 100 kHz. Even greater precision (to 25 Hz) can be obtained by phase-locking the sweeper to the HP 8660 synthesized signal generator and programming both the sweeper and 8660 via the HP-IB. Precision power level control of the sweeper is also possible using the 436A digital power meter.

interface bus, data gathering system — One type automatic data gathering and reduction is a compact low-cost system that scans up to 520 channels under calculator control; measures dc, ac and ohms at up to 4 readings/second; then calculates results either on-line or off-line. The interface bus teams a multimeter and a scanner with a programmable calculator. The system measures:

- dc in 5 ranges from 100 mV to 200 V with 1 μV resolution
- ac in 4 ranges from 1V to 200 V with 10 μV resolution over a frequency range of 20 Hz to 100 kHz
- resistance from 100Ω to 10 MΩ with 1 mΩ resolution

With the appropriate transducer, can also measure pressure, torque, velocity, acceleration, and weight.

interface bus, instruments — An interface standard for products means users can conveniently interconnect a wide range of instruments, calculators, and other devices having stimulus, response, display, control or computational capabilities. Also, users can now assemble relatively low-cost systems with minimum engineering effort. Various Interface devices accommodate high and low-speed devices in the same system. Some can interconnect as many as 15 devices — voltmeter, printer, signal source, calculator, digital clock, etc. — over a total distance of up to 20 meters. Devices are linked via a passive cable network having 16 signal lines. These signal lines carry all information (addresses, commands, program data and status data) at data rates up to 1 megabyte/sec on some units. Simple interface bus configurations do not require the use of a controller such as a calculator or computer. In most cases, programmable calculators are the ideal controllers for customer-assembled systems whenever some degree of data manipulation is required.

interface, calculator terminals — Several makers of programable calculators now offer communications interfaces. Originally, these interfaces were designed simply to make the calculator operate as a remote printer for other calculators, but because many users indicated a desire to apply calculators as terminals, other terminal functions have been added. These features include alphanumeric character manipulation, an input-output structure that is compatible with other terminals and computers, at least 2,000 to 4,000 bytes of expandable buffer memory, and a page-width printer or similar output device. Mass storage such as disk or tape is also helpful for batch applications. For timesharing applications, a typewriter-like keyboard is the most efficient keyboard format.

interface cards, data communications — Data communication interface cards permit calculator users to transmit data using a wide variety of privately-owned and common-carrier communication facilities. Most communications interfaces conform to EIA specification RS-232C and CCITT specification V.24.

interface cards, optional — On one unit, three optional interface cards can be accommodated simultaneously in I/O slots. These are a 16-bit parallel cards that may be used for general-purpose interfacing, a BCD card for use with BCD devices, and an HP-IB card for instruments that conform to IEEE Standard 488-1975. (some units)

interface channel peripheral — That interface form (matching) previously designed or agreed upon so that two or more units, systems, programs, etc., may be easily joined or associated.

interface circuits, gas-discharge displays — Interface circuits are used for mating gas-discharge displays to logic, overcoming the problem of driving a high-voltage display from a low-level output. Typical anode supply voltages exceed 108 V, where the capabilities of both MOS and conventional TTL would be exceeded.

interface command, three operational modes — In TERMINAL mode, data is directed from a terminal keyboard to the host computer, or from the host to terminal screen. The interface emulates a graphic terminal. In COMMUNICATIONS mode, data is sent and received via the terminal system internal tape unit, at speeds many times faster than keyboard or paper tape transmission permits. In the PROGRAMMED I/O mode, the terminal systems BASIC can access the RS232 interface as device number 40. In this mode, BASIC can communicate through the interface without operator intervention. (Some systems)

interface, common carrier, HB-IB (Hewlett-Packard Corp). — This offers separate system components up to 3000 feet using dedicated line. An Optional modem provides systems communication over direct or dial-up telephone lines. The HP-IB/Common Carrier Interface is designed to overcome the older HP-IB length restriction of 50 feet. Up to 3000 feet of additional length can be obtained with just two CCI modules, while with the optional modem, length is limited only to the distance covered by available telephone networks. The CCI module converts all HP-IB data and control lines to a serial bit stream of digital information. This information can be sent in this form to another CCI up to 3000 feet away, or it can be fed into a modem for conversion to a data format that can be used over voice-grade telephone lines. The same CCI/Modem combination must be used at each end of the phone line.

interface, communications — The transfer of data between the processor and the standard communication subsystem takes place through input data leads, connected to the processor input channel, and output data leads, connected to the processor output channel. In addition to the data leads, there are several control leads which are used to control the flow of data.

interface controller (RS-232-C) I/O — This allows direct asynchronous input and output of data between a Teletype or other 8-level ASCII device and the host terminal. The controller is excellent for linking the host terminal to a local unit or for monitoring instruments. Laboratory or medical instrumentation which is RS-232-C and 8-level ASCII-compatible can be supported, as well as Teletype 33, 35's equipped with EIA, RS-232-C adapters. Operation is selectable at 110, 150, 300, 600 or 1,200 baud. The controller can be used with the host terminal CPU alone; the CRT is not required. (on some systems)

interface design — For unique user applications such as on-line installations which require specialized input/output equipment, engineering staffs will design the necessary interface units as part of services to their customers. Then, they will fabricate these units for particular systems under close supervision by the same engineers that designed them. These engineers, who are naturally quite familiar with the logic and requirements, are best qualified to do this important work.

interface, EIA — Refers to a standard set of signal characteristics (time duration, voltage and current) specified by the Electronic Industries Association for use in communications terminals. Also includes a standard plug/socket connector arrangement.

interface functions — A calculator must have an efficient way of interfacing with peripheral input/output (I/O) equipment. Peripheral Interface Adapter (PIA), provides a flexible method of connecting byte-oriented peripherals to the MPU. Data flows between the MPU and the PIA on the system data bus.

interface, general purpose — General purpose interfaces are contained on individual plug-in I/O cards. In addition to the appropriate data registers, many interfaces have independent flag and control logic allowing two-way communication between the computer, and one or more external devices. Most interfaces operate under either program or direct memory access control. A wide choice of interfaces allows external connection via floating contact closures, DTL/TTL, transistor or differential logic.

interface, hand calculators — The hand calculator is an attractive input device since it is built with storage and display room for at least eight digits. It is designed for minimum size, cost and power consumption. And it has a calculating capability frequently useful prior to storage. In addition, a simple eight-digit interface turns hand calculators into input devices for many accessories such as digital recorders, etc.

interface, IEEE standard 488-1975 — The IEEE Standards Board has approved IEEE Standard

488-1975 "Digital Interface for Programmable Instrumentation", as published in April 1975.[1] The IEEE standard is based on work initiated by the IEC, and follows the general concepts of the draft Standard document now under consideration by IEC member nations. The HP Interface Bus is Hewlett-Packard's implementation of IEEE Standard 488-1975.

interface link, computational power-standalone — One type BASIC graphic computing system is a uniquely capable desk-top processor, with up to 32K of personal problem-solving power. But when users plug in the versatile data communications interface they may enter a single command, and the interface serves up all the capabilities of a full range graphics Computer Display Terminal.

interface option, calculator — One type permits eight process control monitors to be combined with an easily programmable data manipulator. The package includes an interface board for the monitor, cable, and sample program listing, and is compatible with calculators and related peripherals. With it, the process monitor is put under calculator control for acquiring time and data from low level analog sensors. No computer is needed to process analog data, since the calculator is programmable by math keystrokes.

interface options — One option now lets users explore all kinds of options: on-line and batch processing; taped data storage; programmed input and output; interactive communication in any language. It allows users to communicate to terminals, terminal-like equipment, or host computers via a bit serial interface that conforms to RS232 A, B and C standards.

interface output, calculator — The standard output of type interface is for 20 milliampere, 2 wire current loop operation, with simplex (one way) operation — the basic input for ASR33 devices. Standard output data rate is 110 Baud (10 characters/sec.). For higher speed devices, calculators can output at appropriately higher rates as an option. A standard capability of the interface shuts down the teletypewriter motor between data scans when the calculator is in auto mode. Operating life of the teletypewriter is thus extended dramatically.

interface, paper tape — Usually the paper tape perforator interface is furnished with an interconnect cable if the calculator recorder is furnished by the same manufacturer. If no recorder is specified, only the mating plug to the interface output connector is furnished.

interface, power expansion (calculators) — The memory limits of advanced programmable calculators can be expanded to over 500 times standard capacity with the use of interfaces which link the calculator to flexible disks. The calculator flexible disk interface allows the disks to provide mass memory, dedicated either to data storage or programs or both. Single disk expands the memory capacity to 256 times the standard capacity and the dual disk doubles that capacity. Two different types of write protect can be utilized for securing the information on flexible disk. One, a tab which is inserted manually on the disk envelope, protects the entire disk; the other protects tracks 0 through 9 from erasure while allowing the remainder to be available for normal read-write operation.

interface, processor — The transfer of data between the processor and the standard communication subsystem takes place through input data leads, connected to the processor input channel and output data leads, connected to the processor input channel, and output data leads, connected to the processor output channel. In addition to the data leads, there are several control leads that are used to control the flow of data.

interface ROM — A special ROM enables the calculator to interface with any modem that conforms to EIA specification RS-232-C and with automatic dialers that meet EIA spec RS-366. Two Basic statements are defined by the control ROM to allow the user to write or read messages in strings from a remote terminal or a computer via telephone lines. Other features include programable parity, automatic answering, programable end-of-transmission character, and either half- or full-duplex modes. Still other features can be added with two additional ROMs. One ROM allows the terminal to operate with a binary-synchronous protocol. It also adds error detection and ASCII-to-EBCDIC conversion so that the user can connect the calculator as a remote-batch terminal without modifying software drivers at the computer. One other significant feature is programable error recovery. In a data-communications mode, errors (incorrect commands or codes, for example) can often be automatically remedied. The special ROM, therefore, includes the ability to take different actions for different types of errors.

The main storage in the interface is programed with the actions to be taken, and the ROM includes the commands to jump to this area of storage after identifying the type of error. The ROM also allows use of transparent text in the binary synchronous protocol, so that special characters can be used, with appropriate coding that warns the receiving end of their presence. (some systems)

interface ROM, communications — A special ROM, (communications) allows some calculators, when operating in an asynchronous mode, to function as interactive teleprinters to a time-shared computer. The calculator can transmit and receive BASIC programs or free text, which can include programs written in other languages, such as FORTRAN. Two of the calculator's 10 special-function keys are defined to correspond to teleprinter SHIFT and CTRL keys. Two other keys are defined to send a line from a display, and to receive program lines into the calculator memory.

interface satellite — One type data communications Interface option draws out the full potential of a intelligent desk-top graphics terminal. It combines the potential of central computer communications with the promise of keeping line and time charges to a minimum. Users switch at will between complex programs in the host and subordinate BASIC programs locally. They extract detailed solutions from the mainframe, then formulate graphic conclusions with the interface's self-sufficient processing power.

interface signal characteristics, example — The RS-232-C transmits data in serial binary form, 10 bit USASCII code. Standard output data rate: 1200 Baud. Other rates available are 110, 300, 2400 Baud. Built-in nine-second default time, if no response to request-to-send signal is received. Voltage levels supplied for bi-polar signaling are +12 VDC and −10 VDC. Power supply protection and current limiting are provided. The RS-232-C is type D, half duplex operation. In addition

interface, standard

to the conventional data communications telemetry applications, the RS-232-C interface affords access to a host of data terminal devices. A customized RS-232-C interface is offered for most terminals. Other specific variations may be tailored to virtually any device in the RS-232-C family. Calculator output may be configured either at the data set or the data terminal end of the RS-232-C circuit. This choice is normally predicated by the receiving device. Affected items are control signals, data signal locations and the connectors.

interface, standard — That specific form of interface (matching) previously designed or agreed upon so that two or several units, systems, programs, etc. may be easily joined or associated.

interface, standard memory — A typical unit enables the CPU devices to utilize standard memory components — PROMs, ROMs, RAMs, in a memory array to facilitate system program development. Most units contain an I/O bus enabling expansion of the ROM I/O ports; typical commands such as, READ PROGRAM MEMORY (RPM) and WRITE PROGRAM MEMORY (WPM) allow the user to store data and modify program memory. Basic units directly address 4K of program memory. Programs generated using the interface may be committed to ROM with no software changes.

interface terminal device — The interface between the terminal device and the communications network is usually a multiplexer or concentrator. A multiplexer is a non-programmable device with predetermined speed selections and a concentrator is a programmable computer. Concentrators offer a number of advantages over multiplexers. Multiplexers employ fixed time slots on the high speed link to transmit data from the terminal and/or other devices being multiplexed and cannot take advantage of under utilization of some devices to accommodate increased utilization on others. Concentrators, on the other hand, with their buffering capability and programmed logic can use the high speed link to the optimal advantage of all devices.

interface types — Various interfaces can be categorized into three distinct types for some systems. 1. Slave — This interface usually has no provision in its control logic to become Master. It will only transfer data onto and off the BUS by command of a Master device. 2. Interrupt — This interface generally has the ability to gain Mastership of the bus in order to give the Central Processor the address of a subroutine which the processor will use to service the peripheral. 3. DMA — This interface has the ability to gain Mastership of the Bus in order to transfer data between itself and some other peripheral. A single interface may employ all three of the above types.

interface types, calculator — There are two main approaches to the dedicated interface and the general-purpose coupler. The dedicated interface connects a single peripheral device directly to the calculator's internal bus. Many times four or more interface cards are used. The calculator has full control over the bus, directing and routing data between itself and the peripheral, on most systems. The general-purpose coupler, however, provides its own external bus system, and couplers with as many as eight and more interface channels are available. Thus up to eight different devices can be simultaneously connected to a standard calculator operation.

interfacing, advanced calculator example

By using a general-purpose coupler, with an ASCII input-output card, and a programmable power supply, one can make an automatic stimulus source for testing. Combine this with a DVM and a data scanner (often part of the DVM), and have an automatic test system for circuit boards. The different functions of DVMs — such as ac or dc, volts or milliamperes, or ohms — and their ranges are also controlled by the calculator.

interface, user — Some user interface logic consists of logic added to a specific module by the user to suit his specific interface requirements. In one type module, of the 40 IC device positions in the user's portion of the board, 16 are dedicated for 14-pin devices and have prewired power and ground connections. The remaining positions accommodate either 14 or 16-pin devices, or a number of 22, 24, or 40-pin devices (with a corresponding reduction in the total device capacity). Two sections of the board, if free of IC devices, are useful for installing discrete components in plated-through holes. Various modules may include (optional) ribbon cable connectors for interconnection between the interface and external devices or other modules.

interfaced bus architecture, calculator — Programmable calculators with a bus architecture are easy to interface with digital devices that use standard codes. Digital volt-meters, counters, X-Y plotters and tape-cassette units are only a few of the peripherals that may be used. In fact, a variety of standard packages are available for interfacing calculators with peripherals that use BCD and ASCII codes. A calculator, an interface card set and a DVM make an inexpensive measuring, data-processing and logging system. The voltages measured automatically by the DVM are fed into the calculator, and they can be converted to other units of measurement, if desired. A complete statistical analysis can be done. And a printer, usually part of the calculator, makes the system a data logger.

Further, while serving in such dedicated systems, the calculator can still be used for its basic purpose — calculating. Built into its language is the ability to disconnect from the interface; there is no need to physically reconfigure the system in any way. (some systems)

interfacing, advanced calculator — One supplier offers many interface cards designed for those customers who desire to build custom, calculator-controlled instrumentation systems. These cards are:

- I/O Interface — an 8-bit parallel input/output card with TTL compatible drivers and receivers.
- BCD Input Card — 9 digits of 8421-coded BCD data, plus other functions (input from instrument to calculator only).
- Serial I/O Interface — bit serial input/output card conforming to RS-232-C recommended specification.
- Data Communications Interface — allows a calculator to communicate with other calculators and computers via telephone lines and modems which meet EIA Specification RS-232-C.
- Binary Synchronous ROM — when used with a bus allows a unit to act as a remote batch terminal emulating IBM 2780.
- Interactive ROM — when used with a bus allows a unit to act as time-sharing terminal emulating ASCII Teleprinter.

interfacing, advanced calculator example — A

interfacing, bus

specific interfacing capability is provided calculators through an optional two-channel I/O module. It allows a choice of seven different peripherals to work with advanced calculator units including page printers. Users just plug them in, and they're ready to go. Specific interface cards and cables allow users to control, gather and process data from a variety of instruments. And by adding Interface Busses of various types, up to 14 instruments can be monitored simultaneously.

interfacing, bus — Physically a bus is an etched board with rows of module connectors soldered to the board. The pin assignment can be the same on all connectors. One of the most popular busses consists of 96 signals which feed to 96 pins on the connectors. The user is generally only concerned with those signals that control data transfers, address memory, or contain the data to be transferred. However, additional signals, such as timing, are readily available on the bus to accommodate various tailor-made requirements in the event that the user should design and build his own interface module. A typical bus structure employs bidirectional data and control lines plus a few unidirectional control signals. Each bus line is a matched and terminated transmission line that must be received and driven with devices designed for that specific application. A module may have an unused bus driver for bus receiver circuits that can be used with TTL devices, provided the loading rules are observed.

interfacing, calculator — Advanced units provide the capability of controlling the data flow to and from test instruments, gathering that data, and processing that data, For example, the optional interface bus is becoming standard for a majority of advanced units. I/O can accept up to 14 interconnected devices. Many units have available general purpose I/O cards to help make connections to calculators quickly and easily. Once users have set up their systems, they can develop exceptionally capable instrumentation controllers and processors.

interfacing peripherals, calculator — For many programmable calculators reading and writing operations can be performed with single or dual tape cassette drives. Peripherals such as Input-Output writers or teleprinter interfaces can be used with these systems, thus permitting alphanumeric information to be written or read. Also, using the proper interface, the units can be interfaced with an instrument acoustic coupler, line printer, teletype or CRT terminal and can accept or output numerical data, alpha strings of variable lengths or programs. Other calculator systems can use plotters, voice response units, etc.

interfacing, plug-in cards — With plug-in interface cards, some series calculators take on the ability to accept data from a large number of digital voltmeters, counters, and other instruments. By automating data entry users have a flexible lab processing center, as well as a powerful number cruncher. One Model I/O Expander allows users to plug up to 13 peripherals or test instruments into a calculator.

interference — Electrical or electromagnetic disturbance that causes undesirable responses in electronic equipment not designed to radiate electromagnetic energy.

interim reports — Single-record inquiries, or interim reports, may be produced in seconds or minutes on a demand basis. Exception reports may be prepared automatically to signal activity requiring management attention.

interlace — To assign successive storage location numbers to physically separated storage locations in order to reduce access time.

interlocks, keyboard — Keyboard interlocks preclude errors from simultaneous depression of two or more digit keys.

intermediate cycle — An unconditional branch instruction that may address itself, i.e., a branch command is called, executed, and a cycle is set up, which may be used for stopping a machine.

intermittent control — Control system in which a controlled variable is monitored periodically, an intermittent correcting signal thus being supplied to the controller.

intermittent error — The sporadic or intermittent equipment error which is difficult to detect as the fault may not occur when the diagnostics are run.

internal calculator functions Refers to wide ranges of hard-wired functions, such as, raising a number to a power, square root, logs, antilogs, interest, hundreds more.

international electrical units — (ohm, watt, amp, volt). Values of the practical units adopted internationally until 1947, since then MKSA units have been employed. The international watt differed by 16 parts in 10^5 from the absolute watt (1 J/sec). MKSA — meter, kilowatt, second, ampere.

interpolation — 1. The process of finding a value between two known values on a chart or graph 2. General procedure for determining values of a function between known or observed values, i.e., entries in a table of logarithms. There are various procedures, depending on the assumption of a curve (line or parabola) which fit localized values, imitated electrically in some controls for machine tools.

interpreter — There are occasions when neither assembly language nor a compiler language is adequate. It will take too long to write and debug short programs whenever users want to run another trial-and-error calculation. An interpretive language fills this need. An interpreter is a program which operates directly on a source program in memory. The interpreter translates the instructions of the source program one by one and executes them immediately. It is not common practice to use interpreters to translate and execute source programs, since they are slow, but they have several advantages on specific problems.

interpreter, BASIC — A BASIC interpreter refers to the set of microprocessor instructions which give the system the ability to understand and execute BASIC statements. The BASIC interpreter resides in the Read Only Memory and is part of the operating system.

interpreter (interpretive routine) — An executive routine which, as the computation progresses, translates a stored program expressed in some machine-like pseudo-code into machine code and performs the indicated operations, by means of subroutines as they are translated. An interpretive routine is essentially a closed subroutine which operates successively on an indefinitely long sequence of program parameters (the pseudo-instructions and operands). It may usually be entered as a closed subroutine and executed by a pseudo-code exit instruction.

interpreter routine — An executive routine

which translates a stored machinelike pseudocode into a machine code and performs the operations indicated by subroutines during computation.

interpretive interaction calculators — Applications involving network synthesis, analysis, electronic circuit modelling, transfer-function evaluation, and trial and error iteration are all engineering problem areas comfortably handled with advanced calculators. While computation alone seldom gives the complete solution, meaningful engineering answers can be derived from interpretive interaction with the calculator output in terms of graphics, printed tables, and calculator-synthesized circuit configurations.

interpretive program — A calculator program in which coded instructions are translated into machine operation codes, in a stepwise fashion, as computation progresses.

interpret program — 1. A calculator program that translates and executes each source language statement before translating and executing the next one. 2. A device that prints on a punched card the data already punched in the card. 3. To translate non-machine language into machine language. 4. To decode.

interrecord gap — 1. Also referred to as interblock space. The space between records on magnetic tape caused by starting and stopping the tape motion. This gap is used to signal that the end of a record has been reached. 2. An interval of space or time, deliberately left between recording portions of data or records. Such spacing is used to prevent errors through loss of data or overwriting, and permits tape stop-start operations.

interrupt — 1. A break in the execution of a sequential program or routine, to permit processing of high-priority data. 2. Various interrupts relate to the suspension of normal operations or programming routines of microprocessors and are most often designed to handle sudden requests for service or change As peripheral devices interface with CPUs, various interrupts occur on frequent bases. Multiple interrupt requests require the processor to delay or prevent further interrupts; to break into a procedure; to modify operations, etc. and after completion of the interrupt task. to resume the operation from the point of interrupt.

interrupt capabilities — Many applications require asynchronous or unpredictable events control and an interrupt capability. Throughput increases, since the processor can perform useful work concurrent with I/O (input/output) operations. The major characteristics of this capability include interrupt latency (time to recognize the interrupt and branch to the service routine), response (time to identify the interrupted device and begin execution of the device service code) and software overhead (to get to the service routine and return to the main program). Single line, multilevel and vectored interrupts offer various speed-hardware tradeoffs. Cascaded interrupt capability (interrupting an interrupt) is essential if slow and fast devices are to be mixed in a system. Interrupt enable flags are used to mask or unmask individual levels.

interrupt card — Interrupt cards are often eight and ten channel devices which are utilized by the calculator to sense the occurrence of an external event. Electronic programmable calculators do not ordinarily possess the hierarcical interrupt structure associated with minicomputers and thus it must be simulated. Some interrupt cards provide two outputs, the first indicating if any of the 8 or 10 interrupts have been set by the external device and the second providing an appropriate output data signal when the program reaches a set flag as the interrupts are scanned under program control.

interrupt, contingency — In some systems the program is interrupted if any of the following events occur at the operator's console: the operator requests use of the keyboard to type in information; a character has been typed in or out; a type-in has been completed; or the operator requests a program stop. Contingency interrupt also occurs if an arithmetic operation resulted in an overflow, an invalid operation code was specified, or the clock was addressed after clock power was removed.

interrupt, controller — Interrupts can be generated by the controller for various conditions, including the detection of an error condition or the sensing of a special character that requires immediate action. Typical conditions that may generate interrupts are receipt of end-of-message or end-of-block (EOT or EOB characters), either on receiving or transmitting. The availability of an interrupt feature relieves the computer of the need for time-consuming scanning to sense these special conditions. Some controllers send interrupts to the processor after the receipt of each character from the line; others — the message-oriented controllers — only send interrupts at the end of the message or end of transmission.

interrupt control routine — A routine entered when an interrupt occurs that provides for such details as the storage of the working details of the interrupted program, an analysis of the interrupt to decide on the necessary action, and the return of control to the interrupted program.

interrupt, cycled — The change (by sequence or specific operation cycle) of control to the next or a specific function in a predetermined manner or order.

interrupt device — External interrupts are caused by an external device requiring attention (such as a signal from a communications device), console switching, by the timer going to zero, and by other procedures.

interrupt, error — Special interrupts are provided in response to certain error conditions within the calculator. These may come as a result of a programming fault (e.g., illegal instruction, arithmetic overflow), a store fault (parity error) or an executive system violation (attempt to leave the locked-in area of violation of guard mode). These faults have special interrupt locations in central store and are used by the executive system to take remedial or terminating action when they are encountered.

interrupt function, priority — Priority interrupt functions usually include distinguishing the highest priority interrupt active, remembering lower priority interrupts which are active, selectively enabling or disabling priority interrupts, executing a jump instruction to a specific memory location, and storing the program counter register in a specific location.

interrupt identification — Various I/O interrupts are caused by an I/O unit ending an operation or otherwise needing attention. Identifications of the device and channel causing the interruption are often stored in the old Program Status Word (PSW). In addition, the status of the device and channel is stored in a fixed location.

interrupt, internal — A feature of peripheral equipment using an external device which causes equipment to stop in the normal course of the program and perform some designated subroutine.

interrupt, live keyboard — A live keyboard, claimed to be a "first" for desk-top calculators, permits a user to perform simple calculations, examine and change program variables, and list programs while the calculator is performing other operations. Actually, an interrupt capability apportions operations on a priority basis, but the process is so fast that everything appears to happen at once. The live keyboard can be turned on or off under program control. Available in an extended I/O ROM (input/output read-only memory), this interrupt capability allows the calculator to control instruments or peripherals, print, plot, and run programs at the same time on an operator-determined priority schedule. On the calculator this is accomplished by simple keyboard commands; on a minicomputer the operator would have to write a program in assembly language.

interruption, machine — Machine-check interruptions are caused by the machine-checking circuits detecting a machine error. The system is automatically switched to a diagnostic procedure.

interruption, program check — An interruption caused by unusual conditions encountered in a program, such as incorrect operands. Abbreviated PCI.

interrupt mask bit — A specific bit designed to prevent the CPU from responding to further interrupt requests until cleared by execution of programmed instructions. It may also be manipulated by specific mask bit instructions.

interrupt, not-busy — When an external device recognizes its address and is not busy, it sends a response on the not-busy line to the calculator. If no such response is received, the processor will assume that the addressed device is busy. The processor will send a start signal only if a not-busy response is received. If a device is disconnected, it will appear as busy.

interrupt priority system — Using various priority interrupt systems, each class of interrupts is assigned a priority, where interrupts of a given class inhibit all interrupts of lower priorities until the higher priority interrupt is completely processed. However, an interrupt of higher priority can interrupt an interrupt of lower priority before it is completely processed.

interrupt priority table — A table that lists the priority sequence of handling and testing interrupts used when a computer doesn't have fully automatic interrupt handling capability.

interrupt, processor — In many systems, processor interrupts are automatic procedures designed to alert the system to conditions arising that may affect the sequence of instructions being executed.

interrupt, processor-dependent — 1. An example of a processor-dependent interrupt condition is the "presence bit condition" caused by a program being executed on a processor that is executing an operand call which addresses a descriptor with a presence bit of zero. 2. Another example of a processor-independent interrupt condition is an I/O finished condition caused by the I/O hardware when an I/O operation has been completed.

interrupt schemes, time sharing — An interruption is the cessation of normal sequencing and branching under program control when an internal fault (such as, arithmetic overflow) or an event external to the running program occurs. Interrupts may be categorized in five classes: (1) input/output or channel, (2) external, (3) machine malfunction, (4) program fault, (5) supervisory call (on master/slave mode computers).

interrupt signal feedback — Refers to a steady signal indicating that an interrupt signal has advanced its associated interrupt level to the waiting or active state; the signal is dropped when the interrupt level is reset to the disarmed or the armed state.

interrupt, software priority — The developed programmed implementation of specific priority interrupt functions.

interrupt types — Several types of calculator can accommodate single-line multilevel and vectored interrupts, and they save essential registers automatically. A complete saving must be programmed. In one single-line interrupt system, device-interrupt requests are ORed together to form one request line. The program identifies the device and resolves priority. A multilevel scheme employs several single-level sense lines to handle additional interrupts. For very fast response, the vectored interrupt directly branches to a memory location that corresponds to a specific interrupt.

interrupt vectoring — Handling interrupts in some systems is a problem of software polling. A polling sequence usually has a corresponding program. Such a polling approach is usually the lowest cost alternative for identifying interrupts, but may in some instances be too slow. For many applications, hardware may be added to the system to achieve priority encoding of the various interrupt requests. The encoded value of the interrupt request can then be used as a system address to transfer control to the appropriate response routine. This is referred to as "interrupt vectoring."

interrupt, voluntary — An interrupt to the processor or operating system caused by an object program's deliberate use of a function known to cause an interrupt, and hence under program control.

interval — If a variable, x, can take as its values all real numbers lying between two given numbers, a and b, then its range is called the interval a, b. This is commonly written $a < x < b$ or $a \leq x \leq b$ according to whether the values a and b are excluded or included. The expressions "near to" or "neighborhood of" can be more precisely stated by using the concept of an interval.

interval, confidence — It is now claimed with a possibility of 0.95 that the interval from $x \pm (1.96\sigma/\sqrt{n})$ contains μ, the interval given is called a 95% confidence interval. We are 95% sure (we can assert with a possibility of 0.95) that this interval contains the mean of the population.

interword gap — The time period and space permitted between words on a tape, disk, drum, etc. Usually, such space allows for controlling specific or individual words, for switching.

inventory control — The practice to hold stocks to meet demands. Even though stocks are held, temporary shortages are sometimes experienced, probably due to a sudden rise in demand or delay in production.

inventory control system, automated — A systems approach to inventory control, involving attempts to maintain stocks at the minimal level necessary to meet expected demand with an adequate margin of safety. As a stand-alone application, it has value for critical supplies having limited "shelf-life" (e.g., short-lived radio isotopes, blood banking) and has broader application when it exists as a phase of an integrated supply/requisition/order system.

inventory master file — Relates to permanent stored regularly updated inventory information retained for future use.

inventory, real-time processing — A system that can be depended on to provide the information necessary to base this minute's or this hour's decisions on information up to date as of the minute or the hour.

inventory records — A complete listing of file contents by records series together with sufficient supporting information to enable a proper evaluation of file functions and activities.

inventory stock report — A specific report showing the current amount of inventory on hand for each item carried in inventory.

inverse conditional transfer keys — In general they reverse most or all of the conditional transfers. For example, INV 2nd if pos tests the display and causes a transfer when the display is negative.

invert — Refers to various steps to place in a contrary order. To invert the terms of a fraction is to put the numerator in place of the denominator, and vice versa.

inverter — 1. A circuit which takes in a positive signal and puts out a negative one, or vice versa. 2. A device that changes AC to DC or vice versa. It frequently is used to change 6 volt or 12 volt direct current to 110 volt alternating current. 3. Arrangement of modulators and filters for inverting speech or music for privacy.

investment, business calculators — Although a scientific calculator may be used for solving the more basic types of business problems, calculators especially designed for business and/or financial problems can soon pay for themselves in terms of time and effort saved — because they are made to solve business problems — giving the exact answers when and where they are needed.

involuntary interrupt — Refers to an interrupt which is not caused by an object program but which affects the running of such a program. For example, the termination of a peripheral transfer will cause the operating system to stop the object program momentarily while the interrupt is serviced. Such an interrupt is involuntary.

I/O (input-output) — Refers to devices, programs, or procedures for accepting or outputting information. As regards microprocessors specifically, package pins are tied directly to the internal bus network to enable I/O to interface the microprocessor with the associated equipment or programs.

I/O architecture, microcomputer — A microcomputer's I/O architecture generally breaks down into these areas:
- transfer techniques,
- instruction formats,
- busses,
- bus structures,
- interrupt schemes,
- memory-access techniques.

Most microprocessors allowed for three types of I/O transfer techniques — programmed transfer, interrupt-program control and hardware control. In the first two cases, found in most simple applications, the microprocessor controls the transfer. In the third case, system hardware controls transfer.

I/O buffer — Permits data-word transfer to and from memory to proceed without main program attention. May be programmed so that when I/O transfer is complete, the calculator generates an internal interrupt.

I/O bus lines — Parallel lines and control logic are referred to collectively as the I/O bus. They transfer information between microprocessor and I/O devices. The bus contains three types of lines: data, device address and command. Data lines consist either of one bidirectional set or two unidirectional sets. In the latter case, one set is used exclusively for inputting of data to the CPU and the other for out-putting of data. In most cases the width of the bus — number of lines — equals the word length of the microprocessor.

Device-address lines are used to identify I/O devices. The theoretical maximum number of available address lines changes significantly from one microprocessor to another. Command lines allow a peripheral to indicate to the CPU that it has finished its previous operation and is ready for another transfer end.

I/O bus structures — I/O bus structures employ several schemes. A radial system is one of the simplest, but it limits the number of I/O units. A party-line system reduces the number of lines needed for a distributed system. The latter system also comes in a daisy-chain version, which connects devices serially.

I/O channels, optional (calculator) — I/O channels provide users with the capability to configure input and output peripherals into a computing system. Plus, users can interface to instrumentation to acquire, process or control data.

IOCS — An abbreviation for input/output control system. Specialized program generally related to large scale operations.

I-O, data acquisition calculator — This key displays the input-output code in memory for a particular channel pair previously selected. To change, users key in new numeric code and enter.

I/O expander advanced calculator — A typical I/O Expander allows users to plug up to 13 peripherals or test instruments into their calculator.

I/O extender, calculator — One manufacturer offers a choice of two models in series, these two models extend the one I/O connector on the calculator to either three or six I/O connectors respectively for memory devices. Circuitry within the I/O extender isolates all memory peripherals from each other, eliminating electrical reflections and feedback from one device through the others.

I/O interface controller (8-bit-parallel) — This allows interface of external equipment enabling parallel 8-bit data to be transmitted from or received by the system.

I/O interface controller (RS-232-C) — This allows attachment of a Model 33 Teletype as a terminal for a system, generating hardcopy and inputting programs and data stored on Teletype punched paper tape. It also supports the interface of other Teletype compatibile instrumentation or terminals at 110, 150, 300, 600 or 1,200 baud.

I/O interfacing, advanced calculators — An optional I/O structure for many advanced programmable calculators permits users to choose whether or not they want their units to be equipped with general interfacing capabilities. One model 2-channel configuration in the back of the calculator gives it a plug-to-plug compatibility with many of its special series peripherals. These peripherals offer users capability to extend their input and output versatilities. There are various other advantages for choosing these I/O configurations. The calculator's easy connection to a wide range of digital voltmeters, counters, or other instruments can be achieved with "good" interfaces.

I/O memory addresses — It is almost always possible to use memory addresses for I/O devices. I/O ports are considered as if they were RAM locations; an input is performed by reading memory and an output by writing into it. Though a program may look somewhat more obscure (I/O operations become more difficult to spot if the program isn't documented), operations performed on input data can be those associated with RAM data. For example, add, compare and test bits. This technique also allows for a number of I/O devices, limited only by the size of the memory that can be addressed by the microprocessor.

ion implantation (I^2) — Refers to a process that can be used with all variations. It allows accurate control of dopants or impurities introduced into the silicon — in essence, a costlier, more controllable alternative to thermal diffusion. The process can selectively change the threshold voltage of MOS transistors to produce devices with no overlap capacitance. Although it has not yet demonstrated significant advantage in memories, I^2 is a potentially valuable processing tool, and may eventually be used to varying degrees in all complex integrated circuits.

I/O ROM general — On some system a general I/O ROM provides additional input and output statements which can vary signal sequence parameters to interface more easily non-standard peripherals and provide additional character and data conversion capability.

I/O subsystems, hard-wired — In previous calculators parallel I/O subsystems have often been accommodated simply by providing optional hardwired — and thus predefined — input and output interfaces. Although many requirements for I/O configurations can be met in this way, often the available configurations in I/O subsystems are inefficient because they do not directly match the desired application. For example, a standard parallel I/O-board option might provide, say, 16 inputs and 16 outputs, but the user requires four inputs and 18 outputs. Hence, two I/O boards would be needed, even though only one third of their capacity could be used. Newer units avoid such inefficiencies; software-configurable I/O interfaces increase the designer's freedom. If one changes types of peripherals and data-transfer techniques during system development or in different models of the system, one often accommodates these changes simply by modifying system software.

IOT instructions — A class of instructions dealing with IOT, input/output and transfer.

I/O writer, input mode operation — Messages in this mode, all alphanumeric keystrokes of I/O Writer, as well as SPACE, BACK-SPACE, CR/LF, INDEX, SET TAB, TAB and CLEAR TAB may be programmed into memory of a calculator. This is actuated by a READ-ALPHA command from a calculator. To terminate input to the calculator, the MARGIN RELEASE is depressed during last input keystroke to take a calculator out of alphanumeric input mode.

Data in this mode, all numeric keys (0 — 9) on the I/O Writer as well as change sign (—), exponent (E) and decimal point (·) can be transferred to keyboard register of a calculator for use as input to a program being executed. The MARGIN RELEASE is depressed with the last numeral entered in order to terminate numeral entry. (some units)

IPL (initial program loader) — An initial program load or a program that reads the supervisor into main storage and then transfers control to the supervisor.

ipot — Abbreviation or slang for inductive potentiometer, a precision type of toroidally-wound automatic transformer provided with one or more adjustable sliders.

IPS — Inches per second.

irreversible process — That mechanism with a flux change within a magnetic material in which the flux does not return to its initial state when the disturbing magnetic field is removed.

ISO (International Standards Organization) code — Codes authorized by the ISO to represent alphabetic, numeric, and special characters.

item — 1. A set of one or more fields containing related information. 2. A unit of correlated information relating to a single person or object. 3. The contents of a single message.

item advance technique — A programming technique which groups records in specific arrangements disregarding location aspects of the data.

item counter — Counts the number of calculations preceeding the final result.

item size — 1. The magnitude of an item, usually expressed in numbers of fields, words, characters or blocks. 2. The number of BCD or alphanumeric characters in an item.

iterate — To repeatedly execute a loop or series of steps, e.g., a loop in a routine.

iterative — Refers to a procedure or process which repeatedly executes a series of operations until some condition is satisfied. An iterative procedure can be implemented by a loop in a routine.

iterative operation — The standard, usual, or automatic repetition of the solution. For example, a set of equations with successive or changed combinations of initial conditions. or simply the use of different parameters and the use of the same computing program.

iterative process — A process for calculating a desired result by means of a repeating cycle of operations, which comes closer and closer to the desired results, i.e., the arithmetical square root of n may be approximated by an iterative process using additions, subtractions, and divisions only.

ITS — Invitation To Send. A specific Western Union term used for a character sequence sent to an outlying teletypewriter terminal which polls its tape transmitter.

J

jack — 1. A socket to which the wires of a circuit are connected at one end, and into which a plug is inserted at the other end. 2. A connecting device to which a wire or wires of a circuit may be attached and which is arranged for the insertion of a plug.

jacks, pocket calculators — The introduction of pocket calculators featuring internal access connectors or jacks has been recent. Considering the overall capabilities of pocket calculators, the addition of I/O (input/output) connectors has greatly increased their versatility. Such jacks permit their use as counters, for example, or permit data to be recorded on accessory equipment. In addition, an output jack permits a pocket calculator to be used as a portable control unit for various types of electronic instruments or as an input device for computers and microprocessors.

jargon — A vocabulary used by a specific group of people but not generally nor universally accepted in fields other than the one in which it originated.

JCL (job control language) — Refers to specifications (on tapes or punched cards, usually) that declare the environment in which a job (series of computer programs) is to be run.

JFET — Junction field effect transistor.

job — Usually refers to an externally specified unit of work for the computing system from the standpoint of installation accounting and/or operating system control. A job consists of one or more job steps.

job batch — A succession of job definitions that are placed one behind another to form a batch. Each job batch is placed on an input device and processed with a minimum of delay between one job or job step and another.

job control — A program that is called into storage to prepare each job or job step to be run. Some of its functions are to assign I/O devices to certain symbolic names, set switches for program use, log (or print) job control statements, and fetch the first program phase of each job step.

job control language-JCL — 1. The JCL for modern operating systems may be quite complex and there are probably nearly as many user-prepared jobs which fail to execute due to JCL errors as failures due to compiler language errors. 2. A programming language specifically used to code job control statements.

job control processor — The processing program that reads and interprets job control statements and sets up the system to execute a specific program using specific resources.

job control statement — Any one of the control statements in the input stream that identifies a job or job step or defines its requirements and options.

job entry, remote (RJE) — A situation in which a central computer accepts and processes jobs from a remote location.

job flow control — Job flow control includes: I/O transition between jobs and job segments, unit assignments, initial loading and initialization when the computer is first turned on; control between jobs; and control over the type of operation mode, ranging from simple stacked jobs through teleprocessing systems performing concurrent operations.

job input stream — The input usually consisting of tapes or punched cards which is often the first part of an operating system. The stream contains the beginning of job indicators, directions, programs, etc.

job library — A concatenation of user-identified partitioned data sets used as the primary source of load modules for a given job.

job management — Relates to specific functions which are performed by special programs such as: job schedulers or master schedulers in tandem or combination.

jobname — The name assigned to a JOB statement; it identifies the job to the system.

job-oriented terminal — 1. A terminal designed for a particular application. 2. A terminal specially designed to receive source data in an environment associated with the job to be performed, and capable of transmission to and from the system of which it is a part.

job output device — A device assigned by the operator for common use in recording output data for a series of jobs.

job processing — The reading of job control statements and data from an input stream, the initiating of job steps defined in the statements, and the writing of system output messages.

job processing control — Job-processing control program is generally part of the control section which starts job operations, assigns input/output units, and performs functions needed to proceed from one job to another.

job-request selection — The use of information contained in the job-request schedule to select the next job to be initiated. Selection is based on the priority and precedence assigned to the job, the sequence relationship of this job to other jobs with the same priority and precedence, and the availability of facilities required by the job.

job scheduler — The control program function that controls input job streams and system output, obtains input/output resources for jobs and job steps, attaches tasks corresponding to job steps, and otherwise regulates the use of the computing system by jobs.

job statement — A special control statement usually related to input job stream which marks the beginning of a series of job control statements for a specific job. Previous history (i.e., termination circumstances) of the last job have no impact on subsequent steps if separated from them by a job statement, whereas steps not separated by job statements may abort succeeding ones if errors occur.

job step — A job step consists of the external specifications for work that is to be done as a task or set of tasks. It is also used to denote the set of all tasks which have their origin in a job step specification. A job stream consists of a set of computer jobs or job steps in an input queue awaiting initiation and processing.

job step initiation — The process of selecting a job step for execution and allocating input/output devices for them.

joint probability — The possibility that both A

JOVIAL (Jules own version of IAL) and B will occur. If A and B are independent, neither influencing the other, joint probability is the product of their separate probabilities.

JOVIAL (Jules own version of IAL) — A language containing facilities for numerical computations and some data processing. Most widely used for command and control applications. A new version of JOVIAL called JOVIAL/J73 has been developed; it will probably become the new standard language for command and control applications.

joystick, plotter control — One type Joystick lets users move the cross-hair cursor in x-only and/or y-only directions because of mechanical detents which guide the level along axis lines unless more pressure is applied for freer movement. This gives the unit a combination of free-form and guided direction needed for interactive graphics. Some Joysticks have several exclusive features which are designed to increase flexibility and ease of use. By entering the basic command, POINTER, one type will put the pointer on-screen, allow movement, and return coordinates on any alphanumeric keystroke. An exclusive X-Y zero button on the Joystick control panel immediately returns the cursor to center screen when desired.

jump — The Jump instruction or operation, like the Branch instruction, is designed to control the transfer of operations from one point to another point in a control or applications program. Jumps differ from Branches by avoiding the use of the Relative Addressing mode, in most microprocessors.

jump operation — The calculator or computer departs from the regular sequence of instruction executions and jumps to another routine or program, or even some preceding or forward instructions to alter control, repeat a process or loop, etc.

jump routine — A routine designed to have the calculator depart from the regular sequence of instruction executions and jump to another routine or program, or even some preceding or forward instructions to alter control, repeat a process or loop, etc.

junk — A slang expression that refers to garbled or otherwise unintelligible sequence of signals or other data, especially as received from a communications channel, i.e., hash or garbage.

K

K — 1. Commonly used to describe the amount of addressable storage units of computer systems. K in computer terminology equals 1,024. For example, 64K signifies 65,536 storage units. 2. Symbol for cathode or dielectric. 3. Abbreviation for Kelvin or kilo.

Karnaugh map — A tabular arrangement which facilitates combination and elimination of duplicate logical functions by listing similar logical expressions.

KB — Kilobytes per second.

kc (kilocycle) — 1000 cycles per second. Now called kiloherz (kHz).

KDS — Key display system.

Kendall's coefficient of concordance program — Suppose n individuals are ranked from 1 to n according to some specified characteristic by k observers; the coefficient of concordance W measures the agreement between observers (or concordance between rankings).

$$W = \frac{12 \sum_{i=1}^{n} \left(\sum_{j=1}^{k} R_{ij} \right)^2}{k^2 n(n^2 - 1)} - \frac{3(n + 1)}{n - 1}$$

where R_{ij} is the rank assigned to the ith individual by the jth observer. W varies from 0 (no community of preference) to 1 (perfect agreement). The null hypothesis that the observers have no community of preference may be tested using special tables or, if n > 7, by computing

$$\chi^2 = k (n - 1) W$$

which has approximately the chi-square distribution with n − 1 degrees of freedom.

key — 1. A group of characters usually forming a field, utilized in the identification or location of an item. A marked lever manually operated for copying a character; e.g. typewriter paper-tape perforater, card punch manual keyboard, digitizer or manual word generator. 2. That part of a word, record, file, etc., by which it is identified or controlled. 3. The field by which a file of records is sorted into order; e.g. the key for a file of employee records by a number, department, or letter.

keyboard — 1. A device for the encoding of data by key depression which causes the generation of the selected code element. 2. The portion of the supervisory printer via which the operator can communicate with the system. 3. Keyboards fall into three basic types — alphanumeric, numeric variety and mixed. Alphanumeric keyboards are used for word processing, text processing, data processing and teleprocessing. Numeric only keyboards are used on touch-tone telephones, accounting machines and calculators. The touch-tone telephone has come into significant use as a calculator and data input and voice output device.

keyboard, advanced calculator, special function keys — In addition to a typewriter-like section, a calculator-key section, and command keys, one keyboard contains 12 special function keys. Using a shift function, 24 different operations can be handled. These keys also aid in program writing and in peripheral and instrument control, and can be used as immediate execute keys, as call keys for subroutines, and as typing aids.

keyboard, calculator (BASIC language) — Calculator keyboards have been designed for maximum user flexibility. The major portion of some BASIC keyboards duplicates that of a typewriter or teletype. The numeric keys are repeated in normal desk-top calculator sequence. Other groups of keys include the arithmetic operators, the special function keys, the edit keys, display control keys, and a group of program keys.

keyboard commands: examples (hand-held programmable units) — Trigonometric func-

tions: angular modes (degrees, radians, grads) · Sin x · Arc sin x · Cos x · Arc cos x · Tan x · Arc tan x · Rectangular coordinates ↔ Polar coordinates · Decimal angle (time) ↔ Angle in degrees (hours)/minutes/seconds
Logarithmic functions: Log x · Ln x · e^x · 10^x
Statistical functions: Mean and standard deviation · Positive and negative summation giving n, Σx, Σx^2, Σy, Σxy
Other functions: Integer (gives only integer portion of number) · Fraction (gives only fractional portion of number) · Absolute (gives absolute value of x) · y^x · $\sqrt{x}$ · $1/x$ · π · x^2 · % · Register arithmetic in all addressable memories · Addition, subtraction, multiplication or division in serial, mixed serial, chain or mixed chain calculations
Data storage and positioning operations: Data entry · Stack roll down · x,y interchange · Data storage · Data recall · Change sign · Enter exponent
Warning indicators: "Error" appearing in display indicates improper operation. All decimal points lighted indicates low battery.
keyboard, companion — An auxiliary keyboard device which is usually located remotely from the main unit.
keyboard control keys — On most CRT terminals control keys move and control the cursor, switch the terminal from one application to another, switch the communication disciplines, and cause the performance of other functions.
keyboard data acquisition system — For most calculator systems control and data entry functions are keyed directly from a human-engineered keyboard. The big benefit of keyboard control is maximum versatility in establishing operational sequences, channel-by-channel functional programming, setting precise timing intervals, setting alarm points, calling in math functions and other algorithms, and other manipulations. Keys are rated for 2 million operations. As a special option the keyboard may be remotely located up to 30 feet away. (some systems)
keyboard, design — Regardless of the professional discipline, astronomy, securities analysis, neurosurgery, plasma physics, users can literally design their own programmable calculator keyboard to execute their particular functions. Some keyboards can be customized by specifying the functions for individual banks of keys, or a group of banks. This may be accomplished by inserting a plug-in block, then placing the associated key identification template on the keybank. The system is ready to solve problems. Many programmable calculator manufacturers offer several plug-ins, such as a mathematics block, a user-definable block, and a peripheral block. In some calculators, all three may be used at one time.
keyboard design, calculator — A typical modular calculator keyboard system is designed to provide the design flexibility desk-top calculator manufacturers need for quick and inexpensive model changes. Various type keyboards consist of a series of keyswitch clusters that can be arranged on a PC board in any desired keyboard layout. Most are supplied fully assembled, pretested, and ready for the calculator. High-volume price of highest quality keyboard systems is in the low $.20 range per key position with price including cost of final assembly, labor for insertion of keyswitches, soldering, cleaning, and testing. Some competitive keyboard prices are said not to include these costs. The competition is rough. Some save as much as $.05 to $.10 per key position installed by mass overseas purchases. Also, some design concepts also enable calculator manufacturers to change models with only a PC board revision. Some suppliers have an established library of available cluster models. Most keyboards are compatible with MOS circuits. Insulation resistance is 1000 megohms at 50 V dc. Dielectric strength is 250 V minimum on some units.
keyboard design, user — Whatever discipline, from astronomy to securities analysis; neurosurgery to plasma physics, users can literally design the keyboard that works best to execute the functions they use most in the course of their work, at the touch of a single key. On one specific unit they can customize the three left-hand key banks by specifying the functions for individual keys, an entire bank of keys, or a group of banks. To accomplish this users insert a Plug-In block, then place the associated key identification template on the key bank and they're ready to start solving problems. On some units users have a choice of several Plug-Ins: a Mathematics block, a User Definable block, Peripheral block, are examples. They may be used at one time in a system or a user may use one User Definable block to control one, two, or three key banks. More Plug-Ins are planned for the near future by many manufacturers.
keyboard, display console — 1. Some keyboard consoles make possible interpretive operations. Often a particular job is assigned by the computer program and the keys for that job are identified by removable illuminated overlays. 2. An operator control panel for those processors where the display is used in place of the typewriter control console.
keyboard displays, calculator — The more conspicuous developments in the calculator field have been made in the methods of display. The buyer will find a wide array of displays including light-emitting diode (LED), liquid-crystal, and gas-filled glass-tube displays. The legibility of a display has much to do with individual preference, because displays come in all sizes and in red, green and silver colors.
While many of the more sophisticated minicalculators now use either LEDs or liquid crystals, most manufacturers believe that liquid crystals will be the displays of the future. They consume less power than the other types and require hardly any maintenance. The problems to be overcome are poor visibility at low light levels, slow response time, and failure in extreme temperature environments. A large display costs more than a small one. The more digits in display, the more expensive the machine will be. The prospective buyer must decide how important visibility is to him, and determine the accuracy his particular uses require.
keyboard display station — The keyboard display station is a valuable tool for on-line program debugging. Programs are displayed on the keyboard/display station with mnemonic and location in a format identical to the programmer's coding sheet, a "page" of coding at a time. The editing features of the keyboard/display station are used to make corrections to the program. The program-

mer may "thumb through the pages" of his program stored in memory just as he can thumb through his coding sheets. In a data-acquisition system, the keyboard/display station may also be used for "quick-look" display of test data or results, as the test progresses. The ability to address locations on the keyboard/display station screen by the computer permits the output of only the changing information by the computer at very rapid per character rate, rather than requiring a complete "page" of information for each change. This light demand on computer time permits a continuous presentation of important test parameters as they change.

keyboard, edit keys — The edit keys should make it possible to easily replace, insert, delete, and move characters, words, sentences, paragraphs and blocks.

keyboard electronic eraser — When users make a mistake, some units not only let users know there's an error, but precisely what and where the error is.

Suppose, for example, a user keyed in the expression, 20: If $XI > (X2 + 3.41/XI$ Then 45, as part of a program. He would hear a soft "beep" and the display would immediately light up with: ERROR 16 LINE 20.

Checking the list of error notes, a user would find he forgot the right parenthesis after XI in line 20. On some units to correct an error, or to modify a program, the special editing keys at the top of the keyboard let users make their changes without disturbing the remainder of the program. They just recall the text they wish to change – then delete, replace, or insert the appropriate information.

keyboard encoder — One type of 99-key four-mode encoder simplifies the customer-encoding of keyboards. The IC identifies each key and mode with a simple binary number. With that binary input, a PROM may be programmed within a few hours. The IC features a 10-bit code output, an on-chip clock generator, built-in keybounce suppression, complete N-key rollover, electronic shift lock, error detection for simultaneous key depressions, complete compatibility with TTL logic signals and operation with standard $+5$ and -12 V supplies.

keyboard entry — 1. An element of information inserted manually, usually via a set of switches or marked punch levers, called keys, into an automatic data-processing system. 2. A medium for achieving access to, or entrance into, an automatic data-processing system.

keyboard, entry and inquiry — The use by an operator of a keyboard to provide a computer with information and to establish what is stored in any specific location.

keyboard features — Keyboards are the part of the calculator that interfaces with the operator, they should be designed in a manner that makes the operator as comfortable and efficient as possible. The most important design features are: layout, N-key rollover, edit keys, function keys, numeric pad, and control keys.

keyboard function keys — Many suppliers offer terminal function keys that make it possible to strike one or two keys to call out strings of characters and formats, send a unique distinct code to the computer which may represent any amount of data, and to conveniently activate the calculator peripherals.

keyboard, human engineered — On some units the keyboard is human engineered, with finger-tip-fitting, color-coded, functionally-grouped keys. Often-used keys are made oversized for convenience. Half-size keys in the three left-hand key-blocks allow room for overlays to label their special functions assigned by the plug-in ROM's. Powerful individual keys are usually included, such as the ERASE key, which clears the entire memory and all flags. (some units)

keyboarding — A procedure for operating at typewriter-like keyboards to produce copy and machine readable data.

keyboard inquiry — A technique whereby the interrogation of the contents of a calculator's storage may be initiated at a keyboard.

keyboard interface, microcomputer — One unique board has the numerals 0-9, and six special-function keys that are electronically interpreted in hexadecimal. They make up the microcomputer input/output port. Two more control keys interface as additional bits in input. The remaining two keys are related to the system interrupt function. The display interface has six LED digits driven by microcomputer output ports. Decoders display the numerals 0 through 9, and the hexadecimal numbers from A through F thus: A, B, C, D, E, F.

keyboard interlocks — This function precludes errors occurring from simultaneous depression of two or more digit keys.

keyboard-language, calculators — Programmable calculators are ready to use right out of the shipping carton. On keyboard-language calculators a complete operation — such as add, subtract or multiply — is normally defined by a single key. When the key is pressed in the operate mode the operation takes place immediately. Many functions that need several operations — such as storage, search, printing and many user-defined specials — can often be done with at most two key strokes. Programming a keyboard-language calculator is done by switching it to its learn-program mode and pressing the keys in the same sequence that users would to make calculations directly. Thereafter the calculator can repeat a complex sequence automatically, stopping only to wait for new data at selected points or to take prestored data from the memory or registers.

Keyboard-language calculators are easy to master. With almost no experience in programming, users can operate a unit with fair efficiency almost immediately and program effectively in days. The keyboard calculator is powerful. The simpler unit can execute sequentially about 500 programmed steps, and more advanced machines can handle several thousand.

keyboard, live — On some units this lets users interact with the system while a program is running to examine or change program variables — or even perform keyboard calculations.

keyboard lockout — An interlock feature which prevents sending from the keyboard while the tape transmitter or another station is sending on the same circuit, to avoid breaking up the transmission by simultaneous sending.

keyboard mode, BASIC language calculator — Some models of calculators are very powerful programmable BASIC language terminals. But they also are very easy to use in simple keyboard operation. Some features which make this so: The EXECUTE key, when pressed will cause the calculator to execute what is currently shown in the display. If the display line contains an arithmetic expression the calculator will perform the indicated operations and display the results. Pressing CLEAR RESULT EXECUTE displays the numerical value of the last arithmetic statement that was executed. The result key can also function as an "accumulator" for "adding machine" calculations.

Pressing RECALL will result in bringing the last line that was executed to the display. This allows the user to alter or edit the line without rekeying the entire expression.

keyboard N-key rollover (at least 3-key rollover) — The rollover feature makes it possible to strike a series of keys simultaneously and the characters displayed in the order that the keys are released. N-key rollover is necessary for a typist to type at full speed without locking the keyboard or dropping characters.

keyboard, numeric pad — The numeric pad makes it possible to efficiently enter numeric and accounting data.

keyboard output code — Output code is a set of unique electrical signals which identify and differentiate each character on a keyboard. The American Standard Code for Information Interchange (ASCII), used primarily in data communications applications, employs a variety of bit-set sizes to encode characters (seven-bit and 12-bit coded sets are among the popular types). EBCDIC primarily suits data processing applications involving keypunch, key-to-magnetic tape, key-to-disk and key-to-cassette devices. BCD forms a third popular output code category, and other types are also in use.

keyboard personalization, calculator — For expediency in keyboard personalization, users select an appropriate User Definable Function keyblock and they can customize each of the nine (or more) keys labeled f_1 through f_9 to perform their functions at the touch of a single key. For example, if users are financial businessmen, key f_1 could become an amortization key. Users load a program for amortization, defined as f_1, into memory, and they have single key calculating for amortization. From then on, all they need to do is enter the data, press f_1 (amortization) and their answer is displayed. These single key functions are fully protected by the calculator's automatic "bookkeeping" system — until users want to change them, that is. If users find at any time that a function is getting less use than they anticipated and would like another in its place, it's a simple matter to delete this function and add a new one, without disturbing any other functions or programs. (advanced units)

keyboard printer — The keyboard printer permits keyboard insertion of transaction data and printed page output of calculator responses at speeds related to the common-carrier service available. Either telegraphic or voice grade lines can be utilized. The keyboard and printer can be used separately or in combination. The keyboard contains a full four-bank set of keys, 10 numeric, 26 alphabetic, 10 special character keys, and a space bar. The printing unit prepares a copy of all transaction data as it is typed on the keyboard. Calculator responses are also printed by the printing unit. (some units)

keyboard printers, buffered — There are two main types of keyboard-printers in use, those that include some type of buffering from the line and those that transmit directly to the line when a key is depressed. The buffering allows several transactions or messages to be batched and editing and corrections to be performed off-line, therefore ensuring accuracy. In addition, buffering makes better use of the transmitting facility because of a higher transmission speed; that is, more terminals can share a dedicated (private) line for a given response time than if nonbuffered terminals are multipointed on a line. Less time is also required for a dial-up connection where charges are based on time and distance. Buffering also allows fixed or repetitive information to be added to a transaction without the need for manual entry during each occurrence.

keyboard/printer time-sharing — This unit can be arranged for split operation for each user station. Printer should be independent of keyboard and operated on a full-duplex circuit. Proper provision must be made for typing into the calculator's communication system, either locally or remotely through private lines or the switched network.

keyboard rollover — Rollover is a mechanical capability that prevents keyboard operators from depressing more than one key at the same time. Two-key rollover limits this protection to the simultaneous action of two keys. N-key rollover prevents the simultaneous action of n keys, where n can be any number up to the maximum number of keys on the board.

keyboard send/receive (KSR) — A combination teletypewriter transmitter and receiver with transmission capability from keyboard only.

keyboard, special key/modules — On some systems, users can design their own keyboards, with special plug-in modules that give them single keystroke solutions for statistics, mathematics, or special functions for a host of disciplines.

keyboards, personal customization — For the ultimate in keyboard personalization, some choose the User Definable Function Plug-In, and they can customize individual keys with the operations uniquely important to them. These will typically be the commonly used formulas that are the foundation of their discipline. The electrical engineer, for instance, will probably want his voltage, impedance, capacitance, and true RMS functions; the physicist, his mass, velocity, and acceleration functions; the chemical engineer, his fluid-flow and heat transfer functions. With one User Definable Plug-In users can customize 5, 15, or 25 keys on some models.

keyboards, scientific/numeric — Rapid calculations are fast for advanced systems that combine buffered keyboard operation, the logic of an operational stack, and a rational key layout. The entire right half of some keyboards is designed especially for keystroke problem solving. The far right block of one unit's keys contain 24 preprogrammed scientific functions. The next group of keys lets users access the operational stack and perform four-function arithmetic. These keys are adjacent to the 10-key numeric pad. Thus, users can pull together the "adding machine" portion and the scientific functions for complex problem solving. Their results are a matter of record because they can be printed for permanent reference.

keyboards, touch sensitive membrane — Available in both custom and standard designs, the monopanel keyboards offer many options previously unavailable in the keyboard industry. Utilizing touch-sensitive membrane technology, the boards are designed for long trouble-free life. Lack of any mechanical linkage wearout problems further enhances keyboard reliability. The layer construction of the boards incorporates a tough membrane with a conductive rear surface. Contact closure is effected when the membrane is moved approx. 0.005 in. A 2- to 4-oz. touch sensitivity is required for switch operation.

keyboard, supervisory — The supervisory console includes the operator's control panel, a keyboard and typeprinter, and a control unit for the keyboard and typeprinter. Optionally, a paper-tape reader and punch may be connected to the calculator through the same control unit. Information transfer between the calculator and any single device is performed and an output channel is assigned to the keyboard auxiliaries. Two switches mounted on the control unit permit selection of the paper-tape reader or the keyboard, and the paper-tape punch or the type printer (some calculators).

keyboard switching — Keyboard switching methods vary widely. Reed switches, for example, incorporate two plated reeds cantilevered from each end of a sealed glass tube, which can be either evacuated or filled with inert gas. Reed switches handle up to 100V. Mercury-filled flexible-tube mechanisms employ a plunger that opens circuits by pinching a plastic tube and separating the mercury column within it. When the tube assumes its original shape and the mercury flows together again, the circuit closes. Non-coding mechanical contact, in which keyboard operation depends on contact between the upper and lower layers of a printed circuit board, typically lasts for more than 100 million operations and exhibits little contact bounce. Mechanical switches, however, often suffer from oxidation and build-up on their contact mating surfaces. In magnetic resistor switching, the presence or absence of a magnetic field alters the switch's resistance and produces a regular on-and-off motion in a transistor. As with other contactless devices such as the proximity transducer, which generates up to eight parallel outputs and provides self-coding switches, magnetic resistor switches eliminate the need for delay circuits. Other switching types include capacitor couplings, ferrite cores, Hall-effect semiconductors, and elastomeric conductors.

keyboard time-out, (remote calculating system) — Many keyboards are equipped with a time-out feature, that causes the keyboard to lock if more than 15 seconds elapse between the sending of characters. If a time-out occurs after the partial typing of a line, any information typed on that line up to that point will be discarded. To avoid this loss of information, the user may press and release "Shift" before the 15-second limit has been reached; this action may be repeated as necessary to prevent a time-out. By pressing "Shift," the user can prevent a time-out without affecting the input information.

keyboard versatility — Keyboards offer designers of equipment for the rapidly growing data-handling-machine market a variety of equipment types, sizes and options. This flexibility means users can effectively specify a custom keyboard, with all its associated engineering features, almost at the price of an off-the-shelf model. If users keep abreast of the various keyboard models and options currently available on the market, they can reduce their purchase price even more. The most popular keyboard models and their specifications offer varying encoding methods, character sets and switching techniques — information users will require to pick the device best suited to their system.

key (button), activate — Same as initiate button. A primary switch on various keyboard panels which when pressed or initiated will cause the first part or step of a program cycle or a procedure to begin. Same as start key, button or switch.

key, check reset — A pushbutton that when pushed acknowledges an error and resets the error detection mechanism indicated by the check light. This is required to restart a program after an error has been discovered in batch mode.

key, constant — This latching key allows the use of the first factor in multiplication or the second factor in division as a constant for future operations.

key-driven — Any device for translating information into machine-sensible form, which requires an operator to depress a key for each character, is said to be key-driven.

key, function — 1. A specific key on a keyboard (for example, CR, LF, LTRS, FIGS, etc.) which, when operated, causes a receiving device to perform a certain mechanical function so that a message will be received in proper form. 2. A special key or set of keys which allow functions to be specified characteristic of given applications environment.

keying — The forming of signals, such as those employed in telegraph transmission, by the interruption of a direct current or modulation of a carrier between discrete values of some characteristics.

keying order, RPN system — Some systems can save a number in each of the four registers. Most problems can be solved by keying in the numbers in the same order as they appear in the original expression, that is, from left-to-right. To work a problem, users key in the first number. If there is an operation they can perform at this point, they do it. If there is not, they press ENTER↑. Now they key in the next number. They perform any operation that can be done ($+,-,\times,\div$, etc.). If there is no operation they can perform, they ENTER↑ this number and repeat the procedure, keying in the next number.

keying programs — On some systems, to key in a program, users switch to PRGM mode. They should see 00 in the display. They then key in the listed keys. They are not executed but instead stored in program memory for later execution. The first key is ENTER↑. When users key it in, the display changes to : 01.41 The number 01 designates the first line of the program. The number 41 designates the key stored in that line. Users can tell what key it is by simply counting down four rows to find the first key. They should arrive at the ENTER↑ key. The codes are simply the number of rows down and the number of keys across. The digit keys are the exception. Their codes are 00 thru 09 depending on the key. The second key is 3 and the display changes to: 02.03. If there had been a previous program in memory, it would not make any difference. Each key overwrites one line in memory. Users never have to clear program memory before keying in a new program. (some units)

key, load — A control key, or similar manual

key phrase codes, Hewlett-Packard (HP-25) — device, which is used to input data or instructions into a calculator or control system. The instructions are usually made up of computer routines.

key phrase codes, Hewlett-Packard (HP-25) — The HP-25 (among others) merges keystrokes into key phrases using a microcoded finite state machine. The machine carefully checks for undefined key sequences. When a valid key phrase is completed, an eight-bit code is fabricated. If the calculator is in run mode, the code is immediately decoded and executed. In program mode, the code is copied into the program memory and then decoded to generate the row-column display. The data registers used for program storage are 56 bits long. Each register can contain seven key phrase codes. Seven such registers comprise the program memory, so all together there are 49 key phrase locations. The HP-25 contains a data storage integrated circuit with sixteen registers of 56 bits each (14 BCD digits). Seven registers are for user programming, eight are for user data, and one is used for the LAST × function.

key phrase programming, calculator — The real power of some calculators is easy programming. One type programming is based on key phrases rather than keystrokes. A key phrase is simply a sequence of keystrokes that together perform one function or operation. For example, both f SIN and STO + 5 are key phrases, but they contain two and three keystrokes, respectively. The program memory contains numbered locations for 49 key phrases. When the user writes a program, one type calculator merges keystrokes into key phrases and stores the instructions in program memory.

key, protection — An indicator designed to allow the program access to sections of memory which the program may use, and a denial of access to all other parts of memory, i.e., a memory-protection device with a key which is numbered by the calculator. Usually such keys are for most locations in memory, and when a storage key differs from the program protection key, the program can be interrupted and taken over by a supervisory program to handle the problem which arises.

keypunch — 1. Refers to a special machine to record information in cards or tape by punching holes in the cards or tape to represent letters, digits, and special characters. 2. To operate a device for punching holes in cards or tape.

key, start — Refers to a specific push button located on the control panel designed to initiate or resume the operations of the equipment after an automatic or programmed stop.

key, stop — A push button on the control panel which causes a halt in the processing, but often only after the completion of an instruction being executed at a given moment.

key, storage — A special set of bits designed to be associated with every word or character in some block of storage, which allows tasks having a matching set of protection key bits to use that block of storage.

keystroke program control — In advanced calculators a series of keystrokes can be stored in the memory of these units to solve the same problem many times. Then users can recall the program any time they wish. They stroke the keys only once, the unit does it from then on. Many calculator systems have capabilities to provide users with sets of keys that let them control many programs. These keys are grouped on the left of the same calculator keyboards. They provide appropriate instructions to organize and direct the execution of the program. The keystrokes usually reference easy-to-remember mnemonics like GO TO or STEP.

key-tape program memories, calculator — On some advanced units there is one continuous memory, which holds 512 program steps, and users can branch to any step. The versatility of these units allows users to develop an overlay to label 24 user-definable keys for specific problems. For example, if a user is an electrical engineer dealing with complex variables, he may label keys magnitude, phase, real and imaginary. A single keystroke would give him any of these parameters. If he is dealing with statistics, he might choose to label some of the keys mean, variance, standard deviation, linear regression. While he's using the overlay in his own language, he may still maintain the full mathematical capability of the calculator. A magnetic tape can also be used to store or load programs or data. And it can also be used to expand the number of steps or data registers available.

keyswitch calculator on a substrate — A soda-glass substrate carries keyswitch contacts and the front half of a liquid-crystal-display package on one side. The other side contains the rear half of the display and the interconnecting calculator circuitry.

key tape load — A specific control push button which causes the first tape unit to read and transfer data into internal storage until the inter-record gap is sensed, at which time the internal storage is read for the first instruction.

key, tape skip — A particular operator control key which, when depressed, advances the tape until a tape skip restore character is sensed.

key typeout, respond — A particular push button on a console inquiry keyboard which locks the typewriter keyboard and permits the automatic processing to continue.

key-verify — To use the punch card machine known as a verifier, which has a keyboard, to make sure that the information supposed to be punched in a punch card has actually been properly punched. The machine signals when the punched hole and the depressed key disagree.

keyword — Refers to various significant or informative words in a title, abstract, body, or part of the text that generally are utilized to describe a document. A keyword or set of keywords may describe the contents of a document, label the document, and/or assist in identifying and retrieving the document.

keyword-in-context (KWIC) — 1. An index which lists available computer programs in alphabetical order with entries for each keyword in the title. 2. There is an index entry for each significant keyword in the title. Certain words are not accepted as indexing words but will be printed as part of the title. A KWIC index is prepared by highlighting each keyword of the title in the context of words on either side of it and aligning the keywords of all titles alphabetically in a vertical column.

kickstand, calculator — A kickstand elevates the calculator at an angle to make the display easier to read. On some models it doubles as a carrying handle. Some can be fastened to a desk and the calculator locked in place to prevent theft.

kilo — A prefix meaning one thousand. Its abbreviation is K; e.g. 1K = 1024 and 8K means 8192 in computer use refers to the power of two closest to a number; e.g., 4K word memory is actually 4096 words.

kilobauds — Refers to high capacity data channels. For special applications, some data channels capable of 20 kilobauds have been placed in service.

kilocycle — Abbreviated kc. One thousand cycles per second.

kilomega — A prefix meaning one billion; i.e. a kilomegacycle means one billion cycles (same as billicycle and gigacycle), and a kilomegabit means one billion bits (same as billibit).

kit, floating-decimal calculator (integrated circuit) IC — Developed using a metal gate, a p-channel MOS process with low end-product cost as the primary objective, one IC allows a complete 4-function, 6-digit calculator to be built using only a keyboard, a LED display stick, a digit driver, and a 9-V battery. Leading- and trailing-zero suppression allows easy reading of the right-justified display and conserves battery power. Battery life is from 10 to 20 hr, depending on battery type. Other features include algebraic key entry notation, floating point I/O, and chain operations. Keyboard decoding and key debounce circuitry, clock and timing generation, and output 7-segment display decoding are all included on the chip and require no external discrete components.

kits, calculator — Along with other suppliers, the National Semiconductor Corporation made it possible for equipment manufacturers and hobbyists to design moderately priced programmable calculators when it introduced a series of four special-function single-chip calculator IC's together with a compatible programmer chip capable of converting any of the four chips into a fully programmable "learn mode" calculator. Using these new devices, a programmable calculator can be assembled with only three IC's, a LED display, an appropriate keyboard, a dc power source, and a few small components.

National's five IC's include the slide-rule circuit, the business and financial calculator, the statistical calculator, the international conversion calculator, and the calculator programmer. All four calculator chips provide standard arithmetical functions. In addition, these units offer a complete set of log and trig functions while some provide a single-key computation of present and future value of compound interest, deposit or sinking fund amounts, payment or loan installments, and sum-of-the-digits calculations. The slide rule includes linear correlation and regression, y-intercept, mean and standard deviation, summation of X or Y values, and related statistical functions. The international is designed to provide automatic conversions of length, volume, area, or temperature between two different measuring systems, such as British and metric. Finally, the programmer circuit, used in conjunction with any of the calculator chips, can provide computational programs of up to 102 steps. All of the circuits in the new series feature automatic display cutoff to conserve battery power, trailing zero suppression, power-on clear, and a low battery signal display (when used with a suitable digit driver).

kludge — A computer mimic or humorous term indicating the black box or computer. A kludge is slang for, or representation of, an endearment of the pet computer; i.e., "our kludge".

KWIC — A permuted title index based upon use of keywords or phrases extrinsically or automatically identified (See Key-Word-in-Context.)

L

label — 1. Various labels are concerned with or correspond to numerical values or to memory locations in tapes, discs, etc. The specific absolute address is not necessary in most cases because the intent of the label is a general destination. Labels are a requisite for jump and branch instructions as regards software. 2. A set of symbols used to identify or describe an item, record, message, or file. Occasionally it may be the same as the address in storage. 3. A code name that classifies or identifies a name, term, phrase or document.

labeling, calculators — On some units any part of a program may be labeled by using LABEL and another key for the symbol. This part of the program is then executed by pressing EXECUTE and the appropriate symbol. Labeling provides branch points for "if" conditions or can be used to denote the beginning of separate, independent programs. Users may also use labeling to create subroutines. Usually a subroutine is called from a main program. Upon completion of the subroutine the calculator returns to the main program at the proper location. To accomplish this on some units the RETURN ADDRESS, GO TO DISPLAY sequence is programmed at the end of the subroutine.

label key — The Label key saves the code of the next pressed key as a non-executable label, thus naming a program segment. Up to 72 are available by using first and second level keys including the 2nd key with 0 through 9, on some systems.

labels, future — Future labels are labels which are referenced by the programmer in the operand field of a statement and have not been defined previously. Since an address cannot be assigned to this reference the label is put into a symbol table as an unassigned label, accompanied by the address of the command which referenced it.

laboratory calculator-to-calculator communication — Calculator-to-calculator communication can be employed simply to move data from one machine to another. In a typical system, a calculator interfaced to a blood analyzer in one clinical laboratory collects data on blood samples and stores this information on disc files. Another clinical laboratory 40 miles away performs the same data collection onto tape cassettes. This data is also forwarded via 300 bit/second acoustic couplers to the disc files at the first calculator. Thus, the calculator disc is used as a local data base for the two laboratories.

laboratory data acquisition calculator — Some users need a versatile data acquisition system that can be set up for one use, easily modified, and completely reprogrammed for another use — all by keyboard control. An advanced calculator general purpose data system can be easily adapted for specific experiments and tests.

If users need to handle a variety of input signals, measure at different rates — fast or slow scan, obtain direct outputs or use computerized reduction, a calculator is a most versatile input/output data formatting system. For program documentation, a program printout option automatically records the full keyboard setup for the various experiments.

laboratory data acquisition calculator capabilities — Some examples are:
(1) Lab applications, custom-designed
(2) Easy setup, modification by keyboard
(3) Digital inputs from specialized lab instruments, counters
(4) Input flexibility, programming, versatility
(5) Measurement method flexibility
(6) Many different outputs
(7) Special functions options simplify reduction
(8) Program printout options.

laboratory data collection, logging and reduction — Programmable calculator users can eliminate most errors and drudgery associated with manually copying data generated by laboratory test equipment. Using available interfaces and data acquisition sub-systems with programmable calculators, chromatographs, Auto-analyzers, spectrophotometers, universal testing machines and similar systems can be placed "on-line". Savings in labor costs often pay for the entire system in less than one year. No knowledge of computer programming languages or techniques is required. A system can be operating the same day it is received.

laboratory experiments and tests — Calculator users can make the general purpose calculator into a data acquisition system tailored to their project just by pressing the keyboard. For example, one day the system may be set up to handle 10 thermocouple channels, 10 MV channels, and 10 BCD channels, with alarms on 12 channels. The following day it could be keyed to handle 45 analog channels with low and high level alarms, outputting nonalarm readings into a tape recorder and printing out only when one or more channels go into alarm. Instant versatility benefits every lab. This is accomplished by programming and ROM customizing.

language — A set of symbols, rules, and conventions utilized for representing and communicating information or data between people, or between people and machines.

language, APL — A programming language developed by Iverson. An unusually extensive set of operators and data structures are used to implement what is considered by many to be the most flexible, powerful, and concise algorithmic/procedural language in existence. Primarily used from conversational terminals, its applicability to "production" job processing is limited but its value for educational and investigative work is great.

language, APL capabilities — Some users feel APL is the most powerful language in small computers today. It uses concise symbols to solve complex problems, including matrix commands that use a single symbol to solve multiple equations. APL routines are as close to the original mathematics as possible and take up just a fraction of the space required for the same routines written in other high level languages.

language, artificial — A language specifically designed for ease of communication in a particular area of endeavor, but one that is not yet natural to that area. This is contrasted with a natural language which has evolved through long usage.

language, assembly — Instructions include machine operation codes and symbolic addressing. The output may be absolute or relocatable. The assembly language can feature page-free programming.

language, assembly-output — A symbolic assembly-language listing of the binary object program output of the compiler is optional at compile time. The listing contains the symbolic instructions equivalent to the binary code output from the compiler. This assembly-language output listing is useful as a debugging aid. By including certain pseudo-operations codes in in-line assembly language; the assembly-language output can be assembled by the assembler. This will allow modification of programs at the assembly-language level.

language, command — 1. The language which is recognized by the executive and utilized to issue control commands to the system. 2. A source language which is usually structured with procedural instructions. Such a language has capabilities of causing the execution of many functions, most of which are basic or used repetitively.

language, common business oriented — A specific language by which business data processing procedures may be precisely described in a standard form. The language is intended not only as a means for directly presenting any business program to any suitable computer, for which a compiler exists, but also as a means of communicating such procedures among individuals. The acronym for it is COBOL.

language, conversational — A language utilizing a near-English character set which facilitates communication between the computer and the user. For example, BASIC is one of the more commonly used conversational languages.

language, high-level APL — This high-level language for problem solving lets users enter a concise expression of complex mathematical statements. APL contains mathematical operators that allow users to perform array processing functions, trigonometric and hyperbolic functions, as well as common arithmetic, logical, and relational operations. Some features are:
- Treats scalars, vectors, and arrays with equal ease
- Lets users store data or the results of computations using a variable name. As users refer to variable names, APL automatically supplies their current value
- Permits previously defined programs to be used as a function
- Performs operations on arrays of up to 63 dimensions (some systems)

language, machine-code — A system of combinations of binary digits used by a given calculator. Synonymous with machine code, and contrasted with symbolic code.

language, native — A communication language or coding between machine units or modules which is peculiar to or usable for a particular class or brand of equipment.

language, MPL — Motorola's microcomputer

language based on PL/I (Programming Language 1).

language, PL/M — PL/M is a high level language concept developed by Intel Corp. to meet the special needs of microcomputer systems programming. Programmers can utilize a high level language to efficiently program microcomputers. PL/M is an assembly language replacement that can fully commmand the 8080 CPU and future processors to produce efficient run-time object code. PL/M was designed to provide additional developmental software support for the MCS-80 microcomputer system, permitting the programmer to concentrate more on his problem and less on the actual task of programming than is possible with assembly language. Programming time and costs are reduced, and training, documentation and program maintenance are simplified. User application programs and standard systems programs may be transferred to future computer systems that support PL/M with little or no reprogramming. These are advantages of high-level language programming that have been proven in the large computer field and are also available to the microcomputer user.

language, problem- or procedure-oriented — Languages used by the programmer to state the definition of a problem are procedure-oriented. ALGOL, COBOL, and FORTRAN are examples of problem languages. Problem languages are closely related to the type of problem being stated, i.e., algebraic statements from mathematical problems (ALGOL, FORTRAN) and narrative English statements for commercial problems (COBOL). Procedure or problem languages should not be confused with machine language. A source program is written in a problem-language by the programmer. This source program is then translated into the object program (machine language) by a compiler program.

language processor — A general term for any assembler, compiler, or other routine that accepts statements in one language and produces equivalent statements in another language.

language, programming types — The major kinds of programming languages are as follows: 1. Assembly, or symbolic machine languages — one-to-one equivalence with computer instructions, but with symbols and mnemonics as an aid to programming. 2. Macroassembly languages, which are the same as assembly or symbolic machine languages, but which permit macroinstructions (which see) for coding convenience. 3. Procedure-oriented languages for expressing methods in the same way as expressed by algorithmic languages (which see). 4. Problem-oriented languages for expressing problems (which see). Procedure-oriented languages (which see) may be further divided into: (a) Algebraic languages (numerical computation), (b) String-manipulating languages (text manipulation), (c) Simulation languages (such as GPSS, DYNAMO) and (d) Multipurpose languages (such as PL/I).

language, report program generator (RPG) — A popular, problem-oriented language for commercial programming, especially in smaller installations. Like COBOL, RPG has powerful and relatively simple input/output file manipulation including table look-up, and reporting capabilities, but is relatively limited in algorithmic capabilities.

language rules — Most language rules are basically designed to: 1. Prevent the programmer from making nonsensical or disallowed statements of computer operations. 2. Allow a "shorthand" for commonly made code sequences. Additionally, translators themselves have control options that invoke or specify various services that contribute to the programmer's efforts like object listings and data maps.

language, source — The original form in which a program is prepared prior to processing by the machine.

languages, programmable calculator — General mathematical languages are often used on many programmable calculators. The task of software development is thus quite arbitrary. Many programmable calculators feature hard-wired functions such as the trigonometric functions, logarithmic and exponential functions. Because they are decimal machines, there is no need to convert to or from binary or to incorporate algorithms to perform floating point operations. Programming mathematical functions into the calculator becomes almost as easy as copying equations from paper onto the keyboard. A great many entries into the calculator market feature the high-level easy-to-learn BASIC. Each programmable calculator also has its own programming language. Most of these languages follow the rules and symbols of mathematics. Only a few of these calculators do not observe math hierarchy strictly. The majority still treat the various math operators on a first-come, first-served basis. Many consider the calculator languages as high-level languages and as such they carry the same ease-of-use as other standard high-level languages. The calculator fortunately doesn't need additional memory to support the math languages. The high-level languages on most calculators do generally result in slower speed and a lack of bit-manipulation capability. A few calculators do offer hidden instructions which allow bit manipulation. The decimal nature of the calculator also means slower speed than is obtainable on the binary machines. Execution of single keyboard-strokes on calculators is usually in the millisecond range.

language statement — A statement that is coded by a programmer, operator, or other user of a computing system, to convey information to a processing program such as a language translator or service program, or to the control program. A language statement may request that an operation be performed or may contain data that is to be passed to the processing program.

language, synthetic — A pseudocode or symbolic language. A fabricated language.

language, target — The language into which some other language is to be properly translated.

laser memory — Experiments over the past four or five years have indicated the feasibility of using extremely fine laser beams to produce and to read optical patterns (films or holes) so small that an entire telephone directory would be contained on an area the size of a postage stamp. While not yet commercially available, such devices could solve problems which currently are not approachable due to unavailable cheap and large memory capacity.

LAST X, calculator — In addition to the four stack registers that automatically store intermediate results, some units also contain a separate automatic register, the LAST X register. This register preserves the value that was in the displayed X-register before the performance of a function. To place the contents of the LAST X register into the display again, users press f LAST X.

latching — Arrangement whereby a circuit is held in position, e.g., in read-out equipment, until previous operating circuits are ready to change this circuit; also called locking.

LCDs-liquid crystal displays — Refers to displays that are sandwiches of two glass plates, spaced typically about .0005" apart with a nematic liquid crystal solution between them and hermetically sealed at the perimeters.

LC (library of congress) — A prefix or suffix which indicates a Library of Congress subject or document number.

LE — Less than or equal to. See relational operator.

leader — 1. A record that precedes a group of detail records, giving information about the group not present in the detail records, e.g., beginning of batch 17. 2. An unused or blank length of tape at the beginning of a reel of tape preceding the start of the recorded data.

leading zeros — Zeros preceding the first non-zero integer of a number. Leading zeros may be employed in the numeric fields of numerical control input blocks to indicate the assumed position of the decimal point within the field.

leapfrog test — Refers to a unique program designed to discover computer malfunction, characterized by the property that it performs a series of arithmetical or logical operations on one group of storage locations, transfers itself to another group of storage locations, checks the correctness of the transfer, then begins the series of operations again. Eventually, all storage positions will have been occupied and the test will be repeated.

learning — That feature of various unique programs which are designed to improve the efficiency of computers by altering programs using the computer's own experience as the basis. Instructions for program modification are written which analyze programming and processing results and then take corrective action based on predesigned branches or alterations due to a specific computer's characteristics and happenings.

learn and print mode — In some units the LEARN mode switch allows a program to be keyed into calculator memory. The visual display shows the operator the program step number, and the program code of the next step. A program counter automatically increments each new program step. Another useful mode is LEARN AND PRINT. In this mode each program step learned into memory is automatically printed out on the optional printer. Once a program has been learned into memory, it can be executed by switching to the RUN mode. The program can also be recorded onto the magnetic tape cassette for future use, whereby the program can be automatically reloaded into memory from the tape cassette. (some units)[21]

learning, computer — That process by which computers modify programs according to their own memory or experience, i.e., changes of logic paths, parameter values. An example is the now famous chess-playing computer. 2. In process-control, an analog computer can alter its parameters by a continuous process according to temperatures or other guage reports it receives. Examples are adaptive autopilots for aircraft, which explore different alternatives.

learning, machine — The capability of a device to improve its performance based on its past performance.

learning, programmed — An instructional methodology based upon alternating expository material with questions coupled to branching logic for remedial purposes. May be implemented in book form ("Programmed Text") or in computers (Tutorial computer-assisted-instruction, CAI).

learn mode, calculator — Some units have a "learn" approach to problem solving. Users simply key-in their problem left-to-right as they would in calculate mode, using the following options for precise control:

- Preprogrammed "if" Statements (8). Makes a decision based on the condition of the display.
- Decrement and Skip on Zero. Lets a segment of code be repeated a specified number of times.
- User-defined Flags (5). Determines the condition under which a program transfer is made.
- Program Levels (3). A main program can call up to two levels of subroutines.
- Labels (72). Name program segments.
- Indirect Addressing (2 modes). Extends versatility of all memory-reference and branching instructions.

Users may trial-run their program. Editing and "debugging" are easy. Users move through problems a step at a time, forward or backward. They may add more steps. Delete. Or write over steps. Then record.

LEARN mode operation, calculator — Operators should use the Coding Form (it comes with the unit) and make a list of the keystrokes needed to solve a problem. They begin by setting the unit in the learn mode using the Coding Form as a ready reference to key in the steps leading to the solution of a problem. Users key-in their problem left-to-right as they would in the calculate mode. They can construct a program of up to 224 steps (000 to 223) and store it in the program memory, in some units.

least significant character — The character in the rightmost position in a number or a word.

LED alphanumeric display — On some units Light-Emitting Diodes (LEDs) provide a bright, 16-character display, which is easy to read over a wide range of angles and distances. Each of the 9/32 inch (.714 cm) high characters uses a 7×5 dot matrix to provide naturally-shaped numbers, letters, and symbols on these various advanced units.

LED light emitting diode display calculator — LED displays as used in calculators have eight to nine digits and are commonly monolithic devices with common cathodes. With character heights of about 0.1 inch, the current requirement for red is about 5 mA per segment but this may rise to 80 mA under short-pulse time sharing conditions. For green this may run to 10 mA under dc conditions or as high as 1 amp for short-pulse strobing. Some of the newer LED 1/3-inch numerics are based on conventional GaAsP and GaP chips and consequently have the same electrical characteristics as discrete lamps; these call for currents of 10 to 20 mA but may be operated under strobed conditions to 150 mA.

LED (Light-emitting diode display readout — Often recessed for better contrast in harsh lighting, displays show up to 10 or more significant digits (eight plus two-digit exponent in scientific notation), and appropriate signs. Two selectable display modes: fixed point, with automatic overflow and underflow into scientific, and scientific with a dynamic range of 10^{99} to 10^{-99}. Other features: automatic decimal point positioning. Selective round-off; range: 0-10 (in scientific, 0-8). "ERROR" appearing in display indicates improper operation. Lighted decimal points indicate low battery condition. (some hand-held units)

left shift — Relates to a shift operation where the digits of a word are displaced to the left. This has the effect of multiplication in an arithmetic shift.

leg — A course or path taken in a routine from one branch point to the next.

legend — A table of symbols or other data placed on a map, chart, or diagram to assist the reader in interpreting it.

level of addressing — 1. Zero level addressing, the address part of an instruction is the operand, for instance, the addresses of shift instructions, or where the address is the date (in interpretive or generating systems). 2. First level addressing, the address of an instruction is the location in memory where the operand may be found or is to be stored. 3. Second level of addressing (indirect addressing), the address part of an instruction is the location in memory where the address of the operand may be found or is to be stored.

levels of confidence — To indicate in quantitative terms what degree of confidence may be placed in certain inferences drawn from the facts obtained from a random sample.

lexeme — The written word, particle, or stem that denotes the meaning.

lexicon — A vocabulary, not necessarily in alphabetic order, with definitions or explanations for all terms.

librarian — A program that creates, maintains, and makes available the collection of programs, routines and data that make up an operating system. Librarian functions may include system generation and system editing.

library — Refers to a collection of standard and proven routines and subroutines by which problems and part of problems may be solved, usually stored in relative or symbolic coding. (A library may be subdivided into various volumes, such as floating decimal, double-precision, or complex, according to the type of arithmetic employed by the subroutines).

library, basic software — A comprehensive library of utility software is available for many calculators. A typical library includes: loading and debugging program, text editor, resident assembler, floating point package, cross assembler, PROM programming software, tape conversion program, multiply/divide package.

library, electronic — A general purpose library system whereby the user sits at a computer terminal and can call for viewing on his CRT any author, title or subject in the card catalogue, or any page of any book in the library. At the press of a button any lines or pages can be printed for him to take home. The tremendous potential of the electronic library can be appreciated if one realizes the materials of several libraries may become available to millions of users through the usage of computer utilities.

library, subroutine — A set of standard and proven subroutines which is kept on file for use at any time.

library, user — A basic library of general-purpose software is furnished by manufacturers to perform common jobs; to this the user can add his own often-used programs and routines. Programs in the library can be conveniently assembled into an object program by the use of macroinstructions.

LIFO — 1. Refers to Push Down Stack procedures and means: Last-In-First-Out, a buffer procedure. 2. A queue discipline wherein the newest entry in a queue or file is the first to be removed.

light emitting diodes (LEDs) — Discrete light-emitting diodes, available in several colors can be bought in ultraminiature form with a body size only slightly larger than the head of a pin. These devices can develop a brightness of around 1,000 foot-lamberts at drive levels of 10 ma or so. A component application that could impact display technology in the years ahead is the use of LEDs in analog-type indicators that have no moving parts. The indicator, could be used as a car radio dial or as a temperature or liquid level indicator. From a linear array of LEDs, an IC selects diode and turns it on and off, depending on the analog value to be represented.

light pen — An important tool for terminal operators, this optional device can, when used in conjunction with the incremental display, greatly extend its usefulness. It is a high speed, photosensitive device that can cause the computer to change or modify the display on the cathode-ray tube. As the pertinent display information is selected by the operator, the pen signals the computer by generating a pulse. Acting upon this signal, the computer can then instruct other points to be plotted across the tube face in accordance with the pen movements, or exercise specific options previously programmed without the need for separate input devices.

light, thermal — A display signal which is visible to machine operators when internal equipment temperature is higher than a designed level.

limit — A value toward which a varying quantity may approach to within less than any assignable quantity, but which it cannot pass. Thus, the quantity $a^2 + 2ax^2$ varies with x, or it is a function of x, and approximates towards a^2 in value as x is diminished, and may, by giving a suitable value to x, be made to differ from a^2 by less than any assignable quantity. Thus, a^2 is, properly speaking, a limit of the expression, which in this case may be found by making x = 0.

limited — A word attached to another word or term to indicate the particular machine activity which needs the most time, i.e., tape-limited, input-limited, etc.

limited checks — A check made on input data to insure that it does not exceed a maximum figure.

limited, compute — A situation in which the computation time is the delaying factor in receiving output.

limited, input — The time that the central processing unit waits for delivery of input items. This restricts the speed of the operation.

limited, input/output — On buffered computers, a section of a routine in which the time required for computation is exceeded by the time required for input/output operations.

limited, output — The speed restriction on a process or on equipment which causes other operations to await the completion of an output operation. This causes other equipment to have idle time.

limiter — A device that reduces the power of an electrical signal when it exceeds a specified value. The amount of reduction or compression increases with an increase of the input power.

limits, operative — A calculated range of operating conditions to which a device may be subjected without permanent impairment of operating characteristics. Most often such performance characteristics will not be stated in the region between the limits of normal operating conditions and operative limits.

linear — 1. Relating to order in an algebraic equation in which all of the variables are present in the first degree only, i.e., an equation in which none of the variables are raised to powers other than unity or multiplied together. 2. Having an output that varies in direct proportion to the input.

linear equations — Linear equations are those graphed as a straight line. Since a straight line is determined by two points, to plot the graph of a linear equation plot two points and draw a straight line through them.

linear, exponential and power equations regression program — Analysis of Ungrouped Data Using Various Regression Techniques. This program uses the least square fit method to fit N pairs of X, Y (X not equal to 0) data points to one of these three curves: (1) Linear Regression, (2) Exponential Curve, (3) Power Curve.

linear interpolation program — If $(x_1, f(x_1))$ and $(x_2, f(x_2))$ are two points of a function $f(x)$, then the function at x_0 can be approximated by the following formula:

$$f(x_0) \cong \frac{(x_2 - x_0) f(x_1) + (x_0 - x_1) f(x_2)}{(x_2 - x_1)}$$

This is called the linear interpolation formula. Of course, x_2 cannot equal x_1.

linearity — The relationship between two quantities when a change in a second quantity is directly proportionate to a change in the first quantity.

linearity, deviation from — Deviation from linearity is the maximum deviation of output from the most favorable straight line that can be drawing through the input-output curve. The method of determining the most favorable line must be stated. This may be expressed in percent of output full scale.

linearity error — An error due to or caused by the departure from linearity of a nominally linear unit. To rated load divided by the no load voltage.

linearization — A mathematical procedure which is incorporated in a post-processor to subdivide simultaneous linear and rotary machine slide motions into smaller segments so the tool motion resulting from the consecutive subdivisions will result in a straight line on the surface of the part within a part programmer's specified tolerance.

linearization, calculator control — Many transducers are nonlinear. Although they may sometimes be assumed linear over a restricted range, nonlinearities must usually be taken into account over an extended range—for example, with tables or calibration curves, which may either be imprecise or use large memory spaces. In data acquisition systems, the calculator provides a powerful tool for linearization, correcting the measurement with a power-series polynomial that describes the thermocouple table. For example, a polynomial of degree 5 can describe a particular thermocouple to an accuracy of 1° C over its entire operating range. Execution time is saved by using the polynomial in its nested form.

linear key — Completes linear curve fit calculation using least squares technique. Prints out A, B, and correlation coefficient r^2 for straight line $y = A + Bx$. (some units)

linear optimization — Refers to procedures for locating maximum or minimum values of a linear function of variables which are subject to specific linear constraints which may or may not be inequalities.

linear program — Refers to an algorithmic program used to develop a class of problems satisfied by a set of solutions, the requirements being to select the least costly (or the most profitable) solution belonging to the set.

linear programming — Refers to a mathematical method of sharing a group of limited resources among a number of competing demands. All decisions are interlocking because they must be made under a common set of fixed limitations.

linear-programming-control language — The language used to prescribe the course of a linear-programming run on a computer. The language consists mainly of verbs (agendum names), which call in a body of code (program or subroutine) embodying the desired algorithm for execution.

linear-programming inequalities — The mathematical problem of minimizing or maximizing a linear function of n variables, subject to n independent restrictions, such as requirements that each variable by non-negative, and also subject to a finite number of other linear constraints. The latter are either equalities or weak inequalities ($\leq$ or $\geq$); strict inequalities of the form $<$ or $>$ are not advisable. An exact solution or other termination to this problem is furnished by the simplex method or one of its variants.

linear programming, resource allocation — Linear programming (LP) is a mathematical technique in which the best allocation of limited resources may be determined by manipulation of a series of linear equations. Each factor in the problem is evaluated against all other factors in relation to the long-range goals, yielding optimum paths of action for management consideration.

linear regression programs —

(1) Linear Regression (Grouped Data). This program calculates the Standard Deviation, Mean and Standard Error of Group Data X and Y and also calculates the correlation coefficient, slope and intercept of the linear regression. The maximum and average deviation and the bias are also calculated.

(2) Hypergeometric Probability Function. Computes the individual and the cumulative hypergeometric distributions. The Mean, Variance, and Standard Deviation of the distribution are also computed.

(3) Linear Regression with Correlation Coefficient and Standard Error of Estimate. This program fits the equation Y equals A plus the quantity B times X to variable data by the

method of least squares and checks the validity of the fit by means of the linear correlation coefficient and the standard error of estimate.

(4) Linear Regression and Pearson Correlation Coefficient for Ungrouped Data. This program computes the slope and the Y-Intercept of the line most closely approximating a set of N Data points.

(5) Linear Regression and Correlation Coefficient, Ungrouped Data. (Plotter Option.)

linear unit — A device which follows the rules of mathematical linearity, i.e., in which the change in output due to a change in input is proportional to the magnitude of that change and does not depend on the values of the other inputs, i.e., adders, scalars, and integrating amplifiers, whereas multipliers and function generators are often designed as nonlinear.

line control unit — A special purpose processor used to control input and output from communications lines that are not directly connected to the main computer.

line printer, calculator — A calculator Line Printer Subsystem consists of a specific Line Printer which is a reliable, low-cost, 5 × 7 dot-matrix printer. One unique print mechanism makes it quiet enough for any business environment and provides up to 6 consistent, clean copies. It prints at 200 lines/minute regardless of the line length and has full 132-column line width. The unit includes the specific Line Printer Interface Card.

line printing — Printing one line of characters across a page; i.e., 100 or more characters simultaneously, as continuous paper advances line by line in one direction past type bars or a type cylinder that contains all characters in all positions.

line speed — 1. The maximum rate at which signals may be transmitted over a given channel. 2. The normal operating speed of a communications system. Refers to the automatic machine speed, as opposed to the slower speed of any associated manual operations.

line status — The status of a communication line such as receive, transmit, or control.

link — 1. That part of a subprogram that connects it with the main program. 2. A process to gather or unite two or more separately written, assembled, or compiled programs or routines into various single operational entities, i.e., to complete linkage. Some computer systems have special programs called linkage editors to correct address components into symbols or to perform relocation to avoid overlapping.

linkage — 1. Specific instructions that are related to the entry and re-entry of closed subroutines. 2. The interconnections between a main routine and a closed routine; i.e., entry and exit for a closed routine form the main routine. 3. In programming, coding that connects two separately coded routines.

linkage editor — A standard service routine to convert outputs of assemblers or compilers to forms which can be loaded and executed by combining separately developed object modules, or incorporating all or parts of previously processed load modules into a new load module. The linkage editor also replaces or inserts control sections, creates overlay facilities, or resolves symbolic cross references between various input modules. Usually linkage editors are run before programs are ready for load in OS, DOS, or TOS operations, i.e., disk and tape operating systems.

link, communication — The physical means of connecting one location to another for the purpose of transmitting information.

linking — Linking means that an analysis may be continued in a second program based on the results stored in the memory registers by the first program. For example, the programs in one section, that calculate a certain type of statistic, can be linked to the same type of programs in another section. The information does not have to be re-entered.

linking loader — The bootstrap loader can be used to load a linking loader into main memory. The linking loader is a relocatable loader — it completes memory address calculations that were partially processed by the relocatable assembler, allowing users to load and execute a program anywhere in memory.

liquid crystal displays (LCDs) — Although LEDs continue to dominate the readout market, liquid-crystal displays have made some notable technical gains. No longer, for example, are they strictly edge-mounted devices. At least one manufacturer has developed a dual-in-line configuration facilitating wider conductive patterns and therefore less susceptibility to opening. Recently this company has equipped its dual-in-line devices with special substrate clips that permit the displays to be plugged directly into pc boards in order to mount them.

liquid crystal displays, calculator — Liquid crystals have unusual properties that enable them to be employed in numeric display panels. They belong to a class of chemicals which flow like liquids yet have molecules that form chains like crystals. Normally transparent, they turn opaque when subjected to an ac or dc electric field. Liquid crystals are sandwiched between glass plates, masked to form numeric segments. When a voltage is applied to electrodes across the transparent material, the material composition changes so that it no longer transmits light.

liquid crystal display operations — Liquid crystal displays now compete with gas discharge displays for computer terminal applications. These systems are capable of displaying more than 600 alphanumeric symbols and are a major step toward the use of large-area liquid crystal display systems in computer terminals.

In operation, the liquid crystal — an organic compound — undergoes a change in transparency when voltage is applied to it. This change can be clearly seen in high ambient light. An important plus of liquid crystal displays is that they need only a few microwatts of power to induce this change.

LISP (list processing) — This is an interpretive language, developed for manipulation of symbolic strings of recursive data, i.e., used to develop higher-level languages.

list — 1. A string of items written in a meaningful format that designates quantities to be transmitted for input/output.

list, chained — A set of items each of which contains an identifier for the next item in a particular order, but such order does not have any particular relation to the order in which they are stored.

list key — On some units this latching key automatically inserts the decimal point in a figure entry at positions 0-11 according to the decimal switch setting. If a decimal point is entered manually in a figure entry it will be entered and displayed as usual, but when printed will be aligned and printed according to the decimal switch position with excess decimal digits truncated. The list mode will be applied to all factors in addition and subtraction and to the first factor on multiplication and division.

list processing — Refers to a method of processing data in the form of lists. Usually, chained lists are used so that the logical order of items can be changed without altering their physical locations.

list processing languages — Specific languages developed for symbol manipulation and used primarily as research tools rather than for production programming (i.e., LISP). Most have proved valuable in construction of compilers and in simulation of human problem solving. Other uses have been generalization and verification of mathematical proofs, pattern recognition, information retrieval, algebraic manipulation, heuristic programming and exploration of new programming languages.

list, punch-down — A list of items where the last item entered is the first item of the list, and the relative position of the other items is pushed back one. (LIFO)

list, push-up — A list of items where each item is entered at the end of the list, and the other items maintain their same relative position in the list.

list structure — A specific set of data items combined because each element contains the address of the successor item or element, i.e., a predecessor item or element. Such lists grow in size according to the limits of fixed storage capacity, and it is relatively simple to insert or delete data items anywhere in a list structure.

literal — 1. A word, number, or symbol which names, describes, or defines itself and not something else that it might represent. 2. An item of data with its value as stated or listed. Example would be 490, a literal; thus, 490 is its value. 3. An item in a source language whose representation in characters remains unaltered during the operation of the appropriate program, i.e., in the instruction, If X = 10 print—STOP, the word STOP is the literal.

live keyboard, advanced calculators — Besides possessing capabilities of minicomputers such as being able to call subroutines, record and list programs while the calculators are performing other operations, these advanced units include two-level priority interrupt, direct memory access (DMA) with input speeds of up to 400K 16-bit word/sec., bi-directional tape drive, multi-dimensional arrays, automatic memory record and load, extended internal calculation range and optional plug-in ROM. Some of the units use a programming language called HPL-for Hewlett-Packard Language, that handles subroutine nesting and flags.

live keyboard calculator applications — Useful in engineering, research and statistics applications and also for text string manipulation, sorting, and editing functions, the Hewlett-Packard (H-P) 9825A offers one of the first desk-top calculators to feature a live keyboard, allowing the user to perform simple calculations, examine and change program variables, and list programs while the calculator is performing other operations. The 9825A can be asked to do a great many things simultaneously (update files, plot print, monitor an oven temperature range, and more) with very little degradation in performance. The interrupt structure of the 9825A is unique and versatile. The 16-bit machine uses a 12K system ROM (organized in bytes), and adds from 8-32K of RAM, plus the optional plug-in memories. For interfacing, the 9825A accommodates three optional interface cards simultaneously.

live keyboard calculator control capabilities — Various advanced programmable desk-top calculators use up to 12 function keys to aid in program writing using a new calculator language, called HPL. Several of these advanced systems are very efficient in peripheral and instrument control. Their interrupt capabilities allow the calculators to act as controllers for several instruments or peripherals which require attention at unpredictable rates or times. One unit has a 32-character LED display and a built-in 16-character thermal printer which provides upper- and lower case alphanumeric readout. The tape cartridge, three optional interface cards, impact printer/plotter, paper tape punches and paper tape readers all add to its system capabilities. Internal read/write memory is expandable to 32K bytes.

load — 1. The power consumed by a machine or circuit in performing its function. 2. A resistor or other impedance which can replace some circuit element. 3. To fill the inner storage of a computer with information obtained from auxiliary or external storage. 4. The process of reading the beginning of a program into virtual storage and making necessary adjustments and/or modifications to the program so that it may have control transferred to it for the purpose of execution. 5. To take information from auxiliary or external storage and place it into main storage.

load and go — A computer operation and compiling technique in which pseudo language is converted directly to machine language and the program is then run without the creation of an output machine language.

loader — A program that operates as or on input devices to transfer information from off-line memory to on-line memory.

loader, bootstrap — Enables users to enter data or a program into the RAMs from a teletypewriter, paper tape, or keyboard, and execute the program from the RAMs. Often consists of a PROM that plugs into the phototyping board.

loader capabilities — There are a number of capabilities that a loader must have in order to be effective and useful:
1. It must load a string of bytes into memory, storing words into designated memory addresses.
2. It must check that each byte was correctly transmitted by the input device. (Usually it makes a parity check.)
3. It must insure that each word is a valid instruction, part of an instruction, or data; this is done by checking special format codes that were imbedded into the byte string when it was recorded.
4. It must check that the right number of bytes were read, usually this number is recorded

form operations such as: LOAD — Load the contents of a memory byte and store it in the 8-bit accumulator. Memory is read, bit by bit and as each bit of the memory byte is read, the next sequential accumulator bit will be set or reset to reproduce the status of the memory bit just read. STORE — Store the contents of the 8-bit accumulator in a memory byte. This will be the reverse of the load process. A calculator will perform a variety of other operations.

loading routine — A routine which, once it is itself in storage, is able to bring other information into storage from cards or tape.

loader types — A number of loaders are available to complete various coding processes. Many types can be stored in ROMs. Assembled programs are often loaded into read-only memory. They can also be loaded into RAMs, in which case a bootstrap type is often used. A relocating loader automatically adjusts program addresses and loads the resulting instructions. Some loaders have linking capability that lets users employ routines with undefined labels. These types supply the missing cross-references between separate routines.

loading (bootstrap) — 1. Refers to a particular routine placed in storage for the purpose of reading into storage another program, routine, or various data. 2. A single subprogram that loads a complete object program.

loading, block — A technique for program loading in which the control or other sections of the program or program segment are loaded into adjacent positions in the main memory.

loading error — The error found in the output of the calculator which came about as a result of a change in value of the load which was supplied.

loading-location misuse errors — 1. A loading location specification was made but no load or execute was specified. 2. The loading location specified was not within the available range of memory. 3. The loading location is assigned as the first available location.

local control — That carried out directly and not from a remote control console.

local (load-on-call) — A program overlay procedure for loading one of several subprograms into main memory for execution only when required by the currently executing program.

local variable — A variable whose name is known only to the subprogram to which it belongs.

location counter — 1. The control section register which contains the address of the instruction currently being executed. Variously called the instruction counter, program address counter, etc. 2. A counter that is incremented by one for each word the assembly program generates in the object program.

locations, protected — Locations reserved for special purposes, and in which data cannot be stored without undergoing a screening procedure to establish suitability for storage therein.

lock-in printer — Calculator capabilities of one unit are:
- Print out an entire program.
- Print calculate mode results.
- Print instructions or results without halting program execution.
- Trace program execution step by step for error detection.

lockout, keyboard — An interlock feature that prevents sending from the keyboard while the tape transmitter or another station is sending on the same circuit.

lock-up table — A method of controlling the location to which a jump or transfer is made. It is used especially when there are a large number of alternatives, as in function evaluation in scientific computations.

log — 1. Refers to the process of recording everything pertinent to machine run including, identification of the machine run, record of alternation switch settings, identification of input and output tapes, copy of manual key-ins, identification of all stops, and a record of action taken on all stops. 2. A collection of messages that provides a history of message traffic.

logarithm — The logarithm of a number is the exponent indicating the power to which it is necessary to raise a given number, called the base, to produce the original number.

logarithm, applications — Logarithms are particularly useful to the scientist and engineer. For example, sound level is measured on a logarithmic scale (in decibels). Another example is the Richter scale, used by seismologists to measure the magnitude of earthquakes, which operates on a logarithmic basis so there is a 10-fold increase in magnitude from one unit to the next. And there are many other relationships that are logarithmic.

logarithm characteristic — The non-negative decimal part of a logarithm is called the mantissa, and the integral part is called the characteristic of a logarithm. For example, in the log $1830 = 0.2625 + 3$. 0.2625 is the mantissa and 3 is the characteristic, or 1 less than the number of integers. See any math text for use and rules of logarithms.

logarithmic curve — A particular type of curve on which one coordinate of any point varies in accordance with the logarithm of the other coordinate of the point.

logarithmic functions — Many units compute both natural and common logarithms as well as their inverse functions (antilogarithms).

logarithmic scale — A scale on which the various points are plotted according to the logarithm of the number with which the point is labeled.

logic — Mathematics dealing with the relationships among conditions or events.

logic — 1. As regards microprocessors, logic is a mathematical treatment of formal logic using a set of symbols to represent quantities and relationships that can be translated into switching circuits or gates. Such gates are logical functions such as, AND, OR, NOT, and hundreds of others. Each such gate is a switching circuit that has two states, open or closed. They make possible the application of binary numbers for solving problems. The basic logic functions electronically performed from gate circuits is the foundation of the often complex computing capability. 2. The science dealing with the criteria or formal principles of reasoning and thought. 3. The systematic scheme which defines the interactions of signals in the design of an automatic data processing system. 4. The basic principles and application of truth tables and interconnection between logical elements required for arithmetic computation in an automatic data processing system. Related to logic, symbolic.

logical add — An operation performed in Boolean

algebra on two binary digits at a time in such a way that the result is a one if either one or both digits are a one, or zero if both digits are zero. The logic operator is the OR operator.

logical circuit — 1. A group or set of logic elements interconnected or integrated to carry out the design of the processing task as part of the total computer logic design. 2. One of many types of switching circuits such as AND, OR, NAND, etc., gates which can perform various logic operations or represent logic functions.

logical comparison — The consideration of two things, with regard to some characteristics, to obtain a yes if they are the same, or a no if they are different.

logical difference — Refers to set theory in which all members of one set which are not members of another, given the elements of each specific set; i.e., if set A includes 1, 3, 5, 7, 9 and 11 and set B includes 2, 3, 4, 5, 6 and 7, the difference is 3, 5, and 7.

logical element — The smallest building block in a computer or data processing system, which operators can still represent in an appropriate system of symbolic logic. Typical logic elements are the AND gate and the "flip-flop." A logical expression using the logical operators AND, OR, and NOT. The numeric expression is arranged in such a way that the numeric result is a logical 1 or a logical $\emptyset$. A logical expression may be part of a larger numeric expression involving relational operators and/or arithmetic operators.

logical expression — In assembler programming a conditional assembly expression that is a combination of logical terms, logical operators, and paired parentheses.

logical flow-chart — A detailed solution of the work order in terms of the logic, or built-in operations and characteristics, of a specific machine. Concise symbolic notation is used to represent the information and describe the input, output, arithmetic, and logical operation involved. The chart indicates types of operations by use of a standard set of block symbols. A coding process normally follows the logical flowchart.

logic, algebraic (calculator) — Separate plus, minus, and equals keys are found on machines with algebraic logic, and all calculations may be performed in the familiar hand-written sequence. This system has been adopted by many of the better grade portable calculators, including the scientific types. A typical unit, for example, allows a problem such as the sum of products — $(2 \times 3) + (4 \times 5)$ — to be solved by direct keyboard entry of all numbers and instructions in a left-to-right order. The sum of products capability puts calculator memory to a common but very useful purpose.

logic, arithmetic (calculator) — Calculators built with arithmetic logic are quickly spotted from two unique dual-function keys, plus-equals ($+=$) and minus-equals ($-=$). These keys must be pressed after the last number to be added (or subtracted) as well as between each entry (thus, five-plus-three-equals-eight is $5 += 3 += 8$; and five-minus-three-equals-two is $5 += 3 -= 2$). Multiplication and division keys are used just as when figuring with pencil and paper. This is the arrangement common to most mechanical calculators.

logical operation — 1. A logical or Boolean operation on n-state variables which yields a single n-state variable. Operations such as AND, OR, and NOT on two-state variables which occur in the algebra of logic, i.e., Boolean algebra. 2. The operations of logical shifting, masking, and other nonarithmetic operations of a computer. (Contrasted with arithmetic operation.)

logical relation — Relates to assembler programming. A logical term in which two expressions are separated by a relational operator. The relational operators are EQ, GE, GT, LE, LT, and NE. See also arithmetic relation.

logical shift — A shift in which the sign is treated as another data position.

logical sum — A result, similar to an arithmetic sum, obtained in the process of ordinary addition, except that the rules are such that a result of one is obtained when either one or both input variables is a one, and an output of zero is obtained when the input variables are both zero. The logical sum is the name given the result produced by the inclusive OR operator.

logic analysis — The delineation or determination of the specific steps required to produce the desired output or intelligence information from the given or ascertained input data. The logic studies are completed for many computer processes, programs, or runs.

logic analyzers — Practically all analyzers share a number of features that have become synonymous with the word "analyzer." Included are multiple input lines, or channels, internal storage, the ability to recognize and trigger on a preset digital word, and the ability to look forward or backward in time — that is, to look along a sequence of data events that occur either before or after a reference event. It is this last feature that makes the analyzer so useful and perhaps the most exciting piece of test gear to come along in recent years.

Some vendors list glitch detectors, special outputs or triggers, plus other capabilities as essential to an analyzer. Others don't. Still others see multichannel units as cumbersome and limited to laboratory use. The latter, of course, offer compact units, with limited features aimed at field-service requirements. Because the analyzer is still growing up, and will likely continue to change over the next few years, there's no single satisfactory definition of what an analyzer should be. In fact, the word "analyzer" is a misnomer. The products that now use the name are actually data grabbers, manipulators or displayers, and it's the user who does the analyzing, not the instrument.

logic analyzers, display — Logic analyzers provide a fast, simple, easy and accurate way to look at digital signal streams. Highs and lows are displayed by "on" and "off" states of LED's when working with truth-tables or timing diagrams. It is possible to look backwards as well as forwards in time from a triggered event. Waveform storage lets the user conveniently capture single-shot or transient bit streams. Logic analyzers offer an ease of operation and display interpretation not offered by other methods of monitoring digital bit streams.

logic, Boolean — A mathematical analysis of logic. Applications of Boolean logic include information retrieval and circuit-switching designs.

logic card — Refers to a group of electrical components and wiring circuitry mounted on a board which allows easy withdrawal and replacement from a socket in the equipment. Each such card is related to a basic machine function and on discovery of a bug in that function the card can be replaced.

logic chart — A flowchart of a program or portions of a program showing the major logical steps intended to solve a problem. The symbols of the logic chart usually denote routines and subroutines and should represent the computer run in terms of highlights and control points. The level of detail in a particular logic chart may vary from one run to another and from one program to another, depending on the requirements of the program, and at the prerogative of the person preparing the chart.

logic, computer — The logical operations of the computer, consisting entirely of five operations — add, subtract, multiply, divide and compare. This simple processing logic is enough to allow the computer to accomplish its entire potential of tasks when properly programmed.

logic control — Generally this relates to the sequence of steps or events necessary to perform a particular function. Each step or event is defined to be either a single arithmetic or a single Boolean expression.

logic design simulation, calculator — With some units the state variable approach lets users analyze control systems up to the 10th order — within minutes. Given a forcing function, users must determine if the system be stable, if it will oscillate, or if it will go completely unstable, building up in oscillation until it tears itself apart or begins to smoke. With an advanced calculator and a state variable program, users have their answer in minutes — with no tedious transforms to manipulate, no breadboard or prototype to build, no turnaround problems with batch or time-share systems. The control system doesn't have to be an electronic circuit. It can be mechanical, hydraulic, optical, or hybrid. The calculator will predict the dynamic time response of any type of system that can be described with linear differential equations or transfer functions.

logic, diode-transistor (DTL) — The earliest form of integrated circuits combining a diode and a transistor in monolithic structure.

logic, emitter-coupled (ECL) — A logic circuit in which the circuit generates its own clock pulse, independently of the clock pulse for logically preceding or following circuits. This allows different circuits to work at their own speeds and not be dependent on a clock pulse which must run at the speed of the slowest circuit.

logic, formal — An objective study of the structure, form, and design of valid arguments, and disregarding for this purpose the meaning and importance of the terms of the argument itself.

logic, graphic system — In a specific graphic system, the principle of truth tables, also, the interconnection of on-off, true-false elements, etc., for computational purposes.

logic level — The voltage magnitude associated with signal pulses representing ones and zeros in binary computation.

logic notation systems — There are three basic subdivisions of system organization used inside the present crop of personal calculators: arithmetic logic, algebraic logic, and reverse Polish notation. For the user, this means several schemes exist for entering data into the various brands of electronic wizards. No one method provides serious learning problems, but some shoppers may find their choice of machine strongly influenced by past experiences with mechanical desk-top calculators or computers.

logic product — The result developed from the AND operation as contrasted with arithmetic product.

logic, programmed — The internal logic design which is alterable in accordance with a precompleted program which controls the various electronic interconnections of the gating elements, i.e., the instruction repertory can be electronically changed, or the machine capability can be matched to the problem requirement.

logic, RPN (calculator) — Reverse Polish notation, (RPN) a part of all modern computer compilers for languages such as FORTRAN and ALGOL, is favored by Hewlett-Packard for personal calculators (HP-35, -45, -65, and -80 others). Combined with a stack arrangement of memory registers, this system is said to be the most efficient way known for evaluating mathematical expressions and packing considerable calculating power into a small space. The stack memory is particularly useful for handling long, complex problems involving chain calculations.

Operation is based on the fact that arbitrary expressions can be specified unambiguously without parentheses by placing operators immediately before or after their operands. Thus, the expression $(a - b) \times (c - d)$ may be specified as $\times + ab - cd$ (Polish) or $ab + cd - \times$ (reverse Polish). With the help of a stack (last-in–first-out) memory, the reverse Polish expression is evaluated as follows:

Stack memory location							
T							
Z					a + b		
Y		a		a + b	c	a + b	
X		a	b	a + b	c	d	c − d	(a + b)·(c − d)
↑	Enter a	Enter b	+	Enter c	Enter d	−	
	Keyboard operation →						

Though straightforward, note that the order of data entry is considerably different from a typical pencil and paper calculation.

Several brands of four-function consumer calculators also use reverse Polish notation. In all cases, this logic system is immediately revealed by the keyboard, which lacks any type of equals function.

logic shift — 1. A type of shift in which all bits or characters are treated the same, i.e., no special consideration is made for the sign position as in an arithmetic shift. 2. A shift that affects all positions.

logic, solid-state — Microelectronic circuits are a product of solid logic technology (SLT) and make up many systems basic circuitry. These microminiaturized computer circuits are called logic circuits because they carry and control the electrical impulses that represent information within a calculator. These tiny devices operate at speeds ranging from 300 down to 6 billionths-of-a-second. Transistors and diodes mounted on the circuits are only 28 thousandths of an inch thick (some systems).

logic, symbolic — 1. The study of formal logic and mathematics by means of a special written language which seeks to avoid the ambiguity and inadequacy of ordinary language. 2. The mathematical concepts, techniques, and languages as used in definition (1), whatever their particular application or context. (Synonymous with mathematical logic, and related to logic.) 3. Exact reasoning about relations, using symbols that are efficient in calculation. A branch of this subject known as Boolean algebra has been foundational.

logic systems — A logic system is the "language" used to communicate with a calculator — the way in which users key in problems and the way the calculator is designed to handle the problems. One logic system may require users to restructure an equation to conform to the system; another may not. The two most common types of logic systems used in professional pocket calculators are algebraic and RPN logic. Users may wish to check out both systems, and determine which is the easiest to use (especially important when solving complex problems) . . . which is the least confusing (so they can have confidence in answers) . . . and which is the best to use for solving the kinds of problems they face regularly.

logic technology, solid (SLT) — Refers to microelectric circuits used as basic components of the system; transistors and diodes mounted on the circuits as small as 28 thousandths of an inch square.

logic, transistor-transistor (TTL) — An integrated circuit in which two transistors are combined in one monolithic structure. These circuits are generally faster, easier to construct, and hence cheaper than DTL circuits.

longitudinal parity check — The data line terminal at the transmitting end generates a longitudinal parity character during the transmission of the data characters. This is essentially a count for even parity of all of the bits in each one of the bit levels for all data characters in the message including the start-of-message code but not the end-of-message code. This same count is also being generated for the bits of the data characters entering the data-line terminal of the receiving end.

look-up, table (TLU) — A process or procedure for searching identifying labels in a table so as to find the location of a desired associated item. By extension, a digital computer instruction which directs that the above operation be performed. The technique is used primarily to: 1. obtain a derived value for one variable given another where the relationship cannot be easily stated in a formula or algorithm; 2. to convert a discontinuous variable from one form to another (e.g., convert from one code to another), or 3. to provide conditional (logical) control functions (e.g., converting from disk keys from symbolic to actual addresses or determining which of several discrete processes should be applied for a given state).

loop — 1. Basically a self-contained series of instructions in which the last instruction can modify and repeat itself until a terminal condition is reached. The productive instructions in the loop generally manipulate the operands, while bookkeeping instructions modify the productive instructions, and keep count of the number of repetitions. A loop may contain any number of conditions for termination. The equivalent of a loop can be achieved by the technique of straight line coding, whereby the repetition of productive and bookkeeping operations is accomplished by explicitly writing the instructions for each repetition. Synonymous with cycle 1. 2. A communications circuit between two private subscribers or between a subscriber and the local switching center.

loop checking — A method of checking the accuracy of transmission of data in which the received data are returned to the sending end for comparison with the original data, which are stored there for this purpose.

loop, closed — Concerns a signal path in a control system represented as a group of units connected in such a manner that a signal started at any point follows a closed path and can be traced back to that point.

loop computing — Those instructions of a loop which actually perform the primary function of the loop, as distinguished from loop initialization, modification and testing, which are housekeeping operations.

loop, dynamic — A specific loop stop consisting of a single jump instruction which causes a jump to itself. A loop stop is usually designed for operating convenience such as to indicate an error.

loop, feedback — Refers to basic systems which use feedback and have loops which connect the input and output, or internal processing loops which rely on various signals or evaluations of conditions or results.

looping N times, programmable calculator — The loop operation is useful in repeating a labelled segment of a program a given number of times. The repeated segment is called a loop. Rule: To execute a labeled program segment n times, preset n in R_8 and end the segment with a loop to determine whether or not to repeat the segment. (some systems)

loop, nesting — Nesting loops usually contain a loop of instructions which then also contains inner loops, nesting subroutines, outer loops, and rules and procedures relating to in and out procedures for each type.

loop, open — 1. Pertaining to a control system in which there is no self correcting action for misses of the desired operational condition, as there is in a closed loop system. 2. A family of automatic control units, one of which may be a computer, linked together manually by operator action.

loop operation — Refers to a loop which has an associated set of instructions which restore modified instructions or data to their original or initial values at each entry to the loop, or a sequence of instructions which may be obeyed repetitively.

loop, program — A series of computer program instructions that are repeated a number of times.

loop, outside — Outside loops are most often considered for nested loops when loops within it are entirely contained. The outside loop executes the control parameters that are being held constant while the current loop is being carried through possible values.

loop testing — That particular procedure developed to determine whether or not further loop operations are required.

loop testing process — A specific process used to determine the need for loop operations; the process of repeating program instructions which are portions of programs which repeat themselves a number of times until a program result is achieved.

loop update — The process of supplying of cur-

low order — That which pertains to the weight or significance assigned to the digits farthest to the right within a number; e.g., in the number 123456, the low order digit is six. One may refer to the three low-order bits of a binary word as another example.

LP (linear-programming) — Linear programming (LP) is a mathematical technique whereby the best allocation of limited resources may be determined by manipulation of a series of linear equations. Each factor in the problem is evaluated against all other factors in relation to the long-range goals, thus yielding optimum parts of action for management consideration.

LPL (list programming language) — An interactive language based on LISP 1.5 but with a notation more like FORTRAN and ALGOL. Implemented on: IBM System/360.

LPM — Lines per minute.

LSD — Least significant digit.

LSI — Large-scale integration refers to a component density of more than 500 per chip.

LSI microprocessor — An LSI microprocessor is essentially a complete system on one chip, or at most a few chips. Sometimes called a microcomputer, the system normally consists of a CPU, a RAM, an I/O, and a ROM. The ROM is predesigned and can be customized by programing. In examining the semantics of microprocessing, it should be pointed out that the CPU was introduced first. Most people call the combination of CPU with a ROM and a RAM a microprocessor. Some LSI microprocessor systems are complete sets with no interfacing circuitry needed, and they contain a variety of LSI I/O circuits. Therefore, some industry people now call a completed system a microcomputer — a set of system-designed LSI circuits which have been programmed in the ROM to perform unique functions. All microcomputers contain a small memory which is satisfactory for any manual input, such as a keyboard.

LSI vs electromechanical devices — Large-Scale Integration (LSI), the judicious packing of thousands of transistors and associated components on a single integrated circuit, has produced many "dedicated" LSI devices. They have given a lower price/performance ratio to a host of consumer and industrial products — such as calculators, wristwatches, cardiac pacemakers, digital voltmeters, microprocessors — and the list continues to grow. LSI pervades an increasing number of products that once relied on either electromechanical devices or numerous discrete components arrayed over several circuit boards.

LT — Less than. See relational operator.

LUF — Lowest usable frequency.

M

machine code — 1. The absolute numbers, names, or symbols assigned by the machine designer to any part of the machine. 2. Same as operation code.

machine cognition — Refers to optical machine reading and pattern recognition. Certain machines have capability to optically sense a displayed character and to select from a given repertorie of characters, the specific character which is nearest in shape to the character which is displayed. The various shapes of characters are based on statistical norms, and if different shapes arise new characters join the repertorie. This suggests a type of artificial learning, i.e., perception and interpretation are based on experience. Optical character recognition must be part of the scheme. Machine learning is based on artificial perception or machine cognition.

machine cycle — The shortest complete process or action that is repeated in order. The minimum length of time in which the foregoing can be performed.

machine design program pack, calculator — Various programs aid the machine designer in dynamics, vibrations, linkages, cams, gears, springs, power transmission, and machine geometrics.

machine error — A deviation from correctness in data resulting from an equipment failure.

machine-independent — An adjective used to indicate that a procedure or a program is conceived, organized, or oriented without specific reference to the operating characteristics of any one data-processing system. Use of this adjective usually implies that the procedure or program is oriented or organized in terms of the logical nature of the problem, rather than in terms of the characteristics of the machine used in solving it.

machine instruction — 1. A code element, which upon machine recognition, causes a predefined sequence of operations. 2. An instruction that the particular machine can recognize and execute.

machine language — The final language all computers must use is binary. All other programming languages must be compiled or translated ultimately into binary code before entering the processor. Binary language is machine language.

machine language coding — Coding in the form in which instructions are executed by the calculator. Contrasted to relative, symbolic, and other nonmachine language coding.

machine learning — The ability of a device to improve its performance based on its past performance. Related to artificial intelligence.

machine logic — 1. Built-in methods of problem approach and function execution; the way a system is designed to do its operations; what those operations are, and the type and form of data it can use internally. 2. The capability of an automatic data-processing machine to make decisions based upon the results of tests performed.

machine operation — A predetermined operation set which a calculator is designed, built and operated to perform directly, i.e., a jump, etc.

machine processible media — The physical character of the mode of input or output such as punch cards, magnetic tape, disk packs, etc., in optical scanning unit, such media is most often hard copy.

machine readable — Relates to the capability of being able to be sensed or read by a specific device;

i.e., tapes, cards, drums, disks, etc. are capable of being machine readable.

machine run — The execution of one or several machine routines which are linked to form one operating unit.

machine translation — The automatic transmission from one representation to another representation. The translation may involve codes, languages, or other systems of representation. (Related to automatic dictionary.)

machine word — 1. A unit of information consisting of a standard number of characters which a computer regularly handles in a register. 2. A unit of information of a standard number of characters which a machine regularly handles in each transfer, i.e., a machine may regularly handle numbers or instruction in units of 4, 8, 12, 16, 32 binary digits, each is then the machine word.

macroassembler — A macroassembler simplifies coding when similar sections of code are used repeatedly, but variations preclude the use of conventional subroutine techniques. With a macroassembler, a single instruction yields the necessary expansion without undue complexity.

macroassembler, resident — The resident macroassembler enables users to efficiently translate assembly language programs into the appropriate machine language instructions. The full macro capability eliminates the need to rewrite similar sections of code repeatedly and simplifies user's program documentation. And the conditional assembly feature of the macroassembler permits users to include or delete optional code segments which may vary from system to system.

macro command — Refers to those programs that are formed by strings of standard, but related, commands. Such strings are usually brought into operation by means of a single macro command or instruction. Any group of frequently used commands or routines can be combined into a single macro command — and the many individual instructions thus become one.

macrogeneration — The many-for-one concept or process of generating several machine-language instructions from one macrostatement in source programs.

macroinstruction, debug — One of several types of macroinstructions which generate a debugging program testing capability within a particular program.

macroinstruction limitations — Various macroinstructions control the translation procedure and do not necessarily develop usable machine-language programs. A predefined macroinstruction whose expansion provides some system service or linkage to a system service routine, e.g., GET, PUT, CALL AND SAVE.

macroinstruction linkage — A macroinstruction that provides logical linkage between programs and subroutines and that will save data needed by another program.

macroprogramming — The process of writing machine procedure statements in terms of macro instructions.

macros, programmer-defined — Segments of coding, which are used frequently throughout a program, can be defined at the beginning and used and referenced by a mnemonic code with parameters. This increases coding efficiency and readability of the program.

macrosystem — A programming system with symbolic capabilities of an assembly system and the added capability of many-for-one or macroinstruction development.

macrotrace — An error detection aid such as memory and file dumps, loggings, and simulators. A macrotrace records pertinent information when macroinstructions are being executed; the macrotrace can print out the record of macros or it can record them; and also dump working storage and the needed registers.

magnetic card reader, built-in — One type magnetic card reader built into a basic model allows users to make and reuse permanent recordings of programs and data. Two sizes of cards, 6 inches (15,2 cm) long and 10½ inches (26,7 cm) long, are available on these units. Recorded programs are easily protected against accidental rerecording by removing a perforated tab at the end of some cards.

magnetic-card reader/writer-H-P (Hewlett-Packard) — The HP-65's built-in magnetic card reader/recorder uses mylar-based ferrite-oxide-coated cards 0.95 cm wide and 7.1 cm long. Each card can store 100 program steps or 600 bits of information. A two-track self-clocking recording scheme is used to maximize the system's tolerance to head skew and motor speed variations. When the right-hand switch just below the display is in the RUN position, insertion of a card into the reader slot in the right side of the calculator triggers the motor and read circuits. All 100 program steps on the card are read into the calculator's memory.

When the same switch is in the W/PRGM position, insertion of a card triggers the motor and writing circuits, and the contents of the calculator's memory are written on the card. A card that has the file-protect tab (upper left corner) clipped off will not trigger the writing circuits; the program on the card is thereby protected against accidental erasure.

magnetic disk — Refers to a storage device or system consisting of magnetically coated disks, on the surface of which information is stored in the form of magnetic spots arranged in a manner to represent binary data. These data are arranged in circular tracks around the disks and are accessible to reading and writing heads on an arm which can be moved mechanically to the desired disk and then to the desired track with data written sequentially as the disk rotates. Related to storage, disk.

magnetic disk, calculator — The magnetic-disk memory available for some units can outperform multiple cassettes in a single unit and with greater data-access speed and greater freedom in data manipulation. Blocks of data can be read or recorded in random order, thus overcoming the sequential constraints imposed by a tape unit. This imposes less of a need for careful planning in program preparation. Many units have replaceable disks. Such units can thus store as much data as tape units can.

magnetic tape — Flexible plastic tape, e.g., 0.5 in. wide, on one side of which is a uniform coating of dispersed magnetic material, in which signals are registered for subsequent reproduction. Used for registering television images or sound or computer data.

magnetic tape cassette — Designed for both recording long multi-program blocks onto magnetic tape and loading programs into memory, a cassette tape option can also be used for auxiliary storage. A tape can hold up to 12 blocks of 1,848 program steps or 2,772 full storage registers per side. For automatic chaining of programs or data storage and retrieval, some tape drives feature programmable "READ" and "WRITE" commands... under complete program control. VERIFY insures that programs have been loaded and gives manual identification of individual blocks of programs.

magnetic tape drive — Relates to the mechanism that moves magnetic or paper tape past sensing and recording heads. This mechanism is usually associated with data processing equipment.

magnetic tape, end of (EMT) — The point on a reel of magnetic tape that indicates the end of usable tape for recording purposes.

magnetic tape recorders, calculator use — On some units for recording large quantities of data from the calculator the reel-to-reel magnetic tape recorder is recommended in 7-track (EBCDIC) or 9-track (EBCDIC) configurations. Choice of 7- or 9-track is dictated by the machine input chosen for data reduction. The primary advantage of magnetic tape recording is recording speed coupled with high density storage. The disadvantages are vulnerability to dirty environmental conditions, particularly dust, which can cause errors and data loss. Temperature and humidity changes can cause tape drive problems, and finally, operators cannot verify visually whether data is being recorded.

magnitude, relative — The relationship or comparison of the magnitude of one quantity to another, most often related to base magnitude and expressed as a difference from a percentage of the base or reference.

mail box — A 'Mail Box' is often referred to as a set of locations in a common RAM storage area, an area reserved for data addressed to specific peripheral devices as well as other microprocessors in the immediate environment. Such an arrangement enables the co-ordinator CPU and the supplementary microprocessors to transfer data among themselves in an orderly fashion with minimal hardware.

mainframe — Refers to the basic or main part of the computer, i.e., the arithmetic or logic unit. The central processing unit.

main memory — Usually the fastest storage device of a calculator and the one from which instructions are executed. (Contrasted to auxiliary storage.)

main storage — 1. Usually the fastest storage device of a computer and the one from which instructions are executed. 2. Program addressable storage from which instructions and data can be loaded directly into registers from which the instructions can be executed or the data can be operated upon.

major total — The result when a summation is terminated by the most significant change of group.

management information system (MIS) — 1. Refers to various management activities performed with the aid of automatic data processing. 2. An information system designed to aid in the performance of management functions.

management programs, calculator — Some typical examples are:
   Spread Sheet Analysis
   Investment Analysis
   Break Even Analysis
   Depreciation Analysis
   Time Series Analysis
   Graphic Presentation

management reports — 1. Those reports, formal or informal, prepared on a recurring basis and distributed at specific intervals, passing from one level of company management to another and/or one organization to another. They contrain statistical and/or operating information reflecting utilization of resources, status of operations or provide other administrative information useful in judging progress, forming decisions, or directing operations. 2. The management function which assures that administrative reports are kept to a minimum and that those required are well presented, accurate, and timely.

management science — The field of management science is extending the computer far beyond the automation of routine accounting operation and into the complex decision-making process of management. Through revolutionary-computer programming techniques such as simulation, the objective, scientific approach of management science is providing increased management capability and control. In addition to the physical or operational processes like inventory management, product planning and control, resource allocation or market forecasting, this also includes the fiscal processes such as bond management, capital investment, risk analysis, profit planning and product pricing. Manufacturer's broad resources are preparing to meet management's growing demand for this expanded capability and to extend the tradition of total systems capability into new revolutionary data-processing techniques and applications.

management science (operations research) — A relatively new area of computation processes and techniques designed to be mathematical tools directed toward the solution of sets of problems concerned with optimizing the management function and math models of business (conflicting interest) situations. Its task is to analytically resolve control variables to optimal decisions. Some complex models are expressed and solved with the simplex method, matrix algebra and the computer. Among the OR computational techniques are: linear programming, game theory, econometrics, input-output, queue analysis (waiting lines), simulation, critical-path method (CPM), Project Evaluation and Review Techniques (PERT) and others.

Manchester code, tapes — Manchester code is extremely easy to generate, decode, and synchronize, and is the basis for the CUTS (Computer Users Tape System) recording method proposed as an outgrowth of a 1975 meeting of microcomputer hobbyists in Kansas City, Missouri.

manipulated directly controlled variable — That specific quantity or condition which is varied as a function of the actuating signal so as to change the value of the directly controlled variable. Most practical control systems have several manipulated variables. It is thus necessary to state which manipulated variable is meant. In process control activity, the one immediately preceding the directly controlled system is usually intended.

manipulated variable — In a process that is desired to regulate some condition, a quantity or a condition that is altered by the calculator in

man-machine dialogue

order to initiate a change in the value of the regulated condition.

man-machine dialogue — A specialized form of interactive processing between man and machine in which the human operator carries on a dialogue with the machine through a console or some other I/O device. (related to conversational or interactive computing).

man-machine simulation — The scope of simulation clearly includes models of systems in which human beings participate (operational or behavioral models). However, the possibility also exists of incorporating people within the model. In other words, the model is no longer completely computer-based but requires the active participation of a man.

MAN REC (manual receive) data acquisition — Manually starts an immediate scan and output of one data frame. Overrides scan interval setting temporarily. Will initiate program printout or alarm settings printout if pressed after minus key or alarm keys are actuated on systems with these optional features. (some calculators)

mantissa — The fractional part of a logarithm; e.g., in the logarithm 2.5, 2 is the characteristic and 5 is the mantissa.

mantissa, scientific notation — In scientific notation, the term mantissa refers to that part of the number which precedes the exponent. For example, the mantissa in the number $1.234E+200$ is 1.234.

manual backup — An often used alternate method of information handling or process control by which manual activities or adjustments of final control elements take place in the event of a failure in the computer system.

manual flag operation — On some units users can have the program automatically set the flag based on data. And the program tests the flag's condition to automatically guide the program to the correct conclusion.

manual or programmed tape operations — Calculator tape drives may be operated manually by touching the appropriate sequence of keys on the keyboard, or the unit may be programmed to operate drives automatically as part of the applications program.

manufacturing testing applications examples — Some typical test systems are:
- multipoint circuit board testing
- high volume component and transducer testing and calibration
- manufacturing process monitoring and control
- others.

map — 1. Refers to activities to transform information from one form to another. 2. A listing provided by a compiler to enable a programmer to relate his data names to the main addresses within the program.

mapping, main memory — On some units main memory is mapped for protection and relocation in four separate maps: system data, system code, user data, and user code. Up to 128 kilobytes are addressable through each map. Memory mapping automatically reallocates user code or noncritical operating system code to alternate physical memory pages upon detection of a parity or uncorrectable memory error.

marginal — The economists' term for the derivatives or rate of change of a function with respect to quantity. "Incremental" and "variable" are often used in an exactly synonymous sense.

mark up key

Thus, the composite terms: "marginal cost" (of production), "marginal revenue" (from sales), "marginal value" (of a capacity, of sales, of supplies, etc.). The coefficients of a linear programming model are themselves all marginal figures, for example: The cost coefficient of an activity is the marginal cost of performing the activity; the coefficient in a material-balance row is the marginal consumption or production of the material.

marginal test — A preventive-maintenance procedure in which certain operating conditions are varied about their normal values in order to detect and locate incipient defective units, e.g., supply voltage or frequency may be varied. (Synonymous with high-low bias test, and related to check.)

mark detection — A type of character recognition system which detects from marks placed in areas on paper or cards, called site areas, boxes, or windows, certain intelligence or information. Mark reading results from optical character recognition or mark-sensing systems which seek out the presence or absence of pencil marks or graphite particles, such as on college or school exams, census returns, etc.

Markov chain — A model often used for determining the sequence of events in which the probability of a given event is dependent only on the preceding event.

mark scan — To mark scan is to read a document for a specific mark in a particular location. The mark may be made by a pen or pencil, since the operation is usually based on optical scanning and light reflectance. Mark scanning differs from mark sensing because mark sensing requires an electrographic pencil with conductive ink.

mark sense card programmer, calculator — Some units allow users to enter programs with all their series calculators by marked sense cards. Instructions coded are simply marked on the special cards and transferred electronically into the memory for instant program operation.

mark sense card reader — Field statisticians, researchers and engineers can collect and record data on these cards at remote locations and then process the data on the calculator. The reader reads standard size tab cards marked with soft lead pencil, and lets the user enter programs and numerical data quickly, conveniently (and economically) into the calculator. Also, programs can be written off-line without the calculator.

mark sense card reader, calculator — With the Mark Sense Card Reader, data and programs can be entered directly into system. With this low cost reader the cards are prepared "off-line" without typing up the keyboard (making the system more efficient) and are manually fed into some systems.

mark sense cards, calculator — Using the data or program steps that users mark with a pencil on special cards, the Marked Sense Card Programmer lets users get information into the calculator automatically and fast . . . when they don't have time to wait for keypunching operations. Either way, the "system" approach helps them with your time-consuming repetitive calculations, just like a small computer.

mark sensing — 1. The electrical sensing of manually recorded conductive marks on a non-conductive surface. 2. The automatic sensing of manually recorded marks on a data medium.

mark up key — Computes mark up on the selling

price automatically printing both the amount of the mark up and selling price. Can also be used with constant mark up percentages to eliminate re-entry.

"M" ARY — More than two states or conditions as compared with binary, meaning two states.

mask — 1. Usually a device made of a thin sheet of metal which contains an open pattern used to shield selected portions of a base during a deposition process. 2. A machine word that specifies which parts of another machine word are to be operated on.

masking — A technique for sensing specific binary conditions and ignoring others. Typically accomplished by placing zeros in bit positions of no interest, and ones in bit positions to be sensed.

mask register — The mask register functions as a filter in determining which portions of words in masked operations or logical comparisons are to be tested. In repeated masked-search operations, both the mask register and the repeat counter must be loaded prior to executing the actual search command (some systems).

mass-memory — An auxiliary bulk memory providing rapid-access storage capacity.

mass memory advantages — One of the main advantages of such systems is data safety and security. Master data can be recorded on the removable cartridge, transferred into the calculator for manipulation, stored temporarily on the fixed memory platter for further use by the calculator's program and verification prior to modifying the master data on the removable cartridge. Also, with such systems, duplication of data files is easily accomplished. Year-to-date payroll data, inventory updating, account receivables and payables updating are just a few examples where this dual system offers great safety of the data base and affords the opportunity to verify the results prior to modification of master files. Should an error occur, it is easily corrected by repeating the operation since the initial data still resides on the removable memory cartridge.

In addition to providing a large amount of data storage, such Mass Memory Subsystems are fast. A 10 × 10 array can be transferred to the cartridge in about one second, and a typical 250-line program of 2000 words can be transferred in less than two seconds.

mass memory calculators — Several types of powerful desk-top calculators offer BASIC-language programming, along with alphanumeric string and matrix manipulation to give them tremendous data handling capability. As a result, many users have developed applications that require storage capacity much larger than standard tape cassette can provide. Typically, these applications also call for random data access, and therefore are not conveniently run on any magnetic tape system. Such applications include inventory control, payroll processing, order processing, account maintenance and others.

The most obvious answer is a disk drive, and many are now available as peripherals to advanced units. Some have been slightly modified and given new model numbers. Some have one removable disk cartridge while others have one fixed disk and one removable cartridge. Each fixed disk or cartridge can store 2.4 million 8-bit bytes of data. Data access is rapid and, most important, the drives have proven high data-handling reliability. (some models)

mass memory calculator software organization — In one system control firmware and speed-sensitive mass memory commands are stored in the read-only memory (ROM). A prerecorded support cassette is used to record bootstraps (routines to execute other mass memory commands) on the platter when the system is turned on.

mass memory controller — Provides the necessary interface to transfer data and programs bi-directionally between the Calculator and the Mass Memory units.

mass memory expansion — Mass Memory Subsystems can be expanded in terms of increased data and program handling capability. Up to four units can be connected to one Calculator through one Controller. The UNIT command enables the user to address the desired memory cartridge in some systems. Also, for increased versatility, up to four Calculators can be connected to the Mass Memory through the same Controller; however, only one calculator can be used to access the system at any one time. Various Controllers will sequentially service any of the four calculators requesting access to the mass memory.

mass memory handshake operation, calculator — Generally the calculator and the controller operate asynchronously. To guarantee that they do not get out of step and misinterpret data, all address and command signals from the calculator are flagged and receipt acknowledged by the controller. Each time the controller acknowledges receipt of an address byte, the calculator checks the status lines to determine whether an error occurred. The controller does not always immediately acknowledge receipt; tests may be made on the information or some other operation performed first, but all transmissions are eventually acknowledged. On some specific systems if an address error is detected during the transmission or reading of addresses, three attempts are made before the operation is terminated by the calculator. If a checkword error is detected in trying to read the data, ten attempts are made before the calculator gives up and displays an error message to the user. This technique makes momentary errors recoverable so the system is not affected by them.

mass memory modes, calculator — Data can be stored in mass memory files in serial or random modes. In the serial case, the complete file is considered a serial access storage device. In the random case, a file can be used as a random access storage device in which logical records (256-word subfiles) can be modified independently on some units. The data files that will be accessed by a given program must be declared by name in a FILES statement before data storage or retrieval is attempted. A maximum number of ten files can units.

mass memory multi-disk controller — On one system the controller can handle up to four platters and four calculators. Operation is not time-shared: only one calculator at a time can access a mass memory. At least two platters are recommended so backup copies of data can be made easily.

mass memory 1-K ROM — Although it would be impractical to provide all types of software as firmware because this would consume most of the add-on ROM capability of the calculator, the memory problem is often solved by adapting a software organization design with ROM.

The single 1K Mass Memory ROM provides the controlling firmware and all the speed-sensitive mass memory commands. Additional mass memory commands that are to be executed from the keyboard or infrequently in a program are stored on each mass memory platter during initial turn-on. When these commands are encountered in a program or executed from the keyboard, the mass memory ROM fetches the corresponding bootstrap — i.e., software needed to accomplish the particular function — from the mass memory, transfers it to the calculator read/write memory (RWM), and executes it. A bootstrap fetch operation is accomplished within 50 milliseconds in some systems.

mass memory ROM control, calculator — In some systems controller instructions and functions are stored in a 256-state bipolar ROM. One bit of the current ROM address determines whether the transition to the next address is qualified or unconditional.

mass memory subsystem — A mass memory Subsystem provides user calculators with large data storage capability required for applications such as payroll, account maintenance, inventory control, patient records, credit verification and large banks of data for structural design, statistical analysis and many other scientific, industrial and commercial fields.

The memory media of this peripheral can be a single interchangeable cartridge with a capacity of 2.4 million bytes; this is the equivalent of more than 300,000 items of data of 12 digits each. In addition to providing a large amount of data storage, the Mass Memory Subsystem is fast. A 10 × 10 array can be transferred to the cartridge in about 1 second and a typical 250 line program of 2000 words can be transferred in less than 2 seconds.

mass memory system, advanced calculator — Besides the disk drive, some new mass memory systems include plug-in read-only memory (ROM) blocks as installed in one of eight ROM slots to expand the calculator's instruction repertoire. An interface cable assembly containing interface circuitry and a small cache memory connects the calculator to the disc drive controller. Another cable assembly connects the controller and the disk drive on some units.

master clock — 1. The primary source of timing signals used to control the timing of pulses. 2. The electronic or electric source of standard timing signals, often called "clock pulses," required for sequencing computer operation. This source usually consists of a timing-pulse generator, a cycling unit, and sets of special pulses that occur at given intervals of time. In synchronous computers the basic time frequency employed is usually the frequency of the clock pulses.

master control — 1. An application-oriented routine usually applied to the highest level of a subroutine hierarchy. 2. A computer program to control operation of the system, designed to reduce the amount of intervention required of the operator. Master control schedules programs to be processed, initiates segments of programs, controls input/output traffic, informs operator and verifies his actions, and performs corrective action on program errors or system malfunction.

master control program — Refers to calculator program designed to control the operation of the system. It is designed to reduce the amount of intervention required of the human operator. The master control program provides the following functions: schedules programs to be processed, initiates segments of programs, controls all input/output operations to insure efficient utilization of each system component, allocates memory dynamically, issues instructions to the human operator and verifies that his actions were correct, performs corrective action on errors in a program or system malfunction.

master control program procedures — The master control program:

1. Controls all phases of a job set-up; directs program compiling, and debugging, allocates memory, assigns input-output activity, schedules and interweaves multiple programs for simultaneous processing.
2. Directs all equipment functions and the flow of all data; provides for comprehensive automatic error detection and correction.
3. Directs the operator with printed instructions.
4. Adjusts system operation to changes in system environment.

master record — The basic updated record used in the next file-processing run. A master record is most often a magnetic tape item. Visual copies for possible analysis and alteration are usually developed.

master scheduler — Refers to the control scheduler that permits the function of a control program that allows an operator to initiate special actions or to cause requested information to be delivered which can override the normal control functions of the system.

master/slave accumulator — The master/slave accumulator provides for fast, iterative computer operations needed in high-performing systems. These may include repeated add with accumulated sum, multiply, divide, and multiple-shift operations. A multiplexer circuit feeds the accumulator from one of three possible sources — the results of the shift network, the input bus, or the output bus. A fourth condition inhibits the accumulator clock so that stored data is retained. The accumulator is the only section of some 4-bit slices that requires clock operation. This is done to eliminate possible race conditions when the circuit is connected within a system.

mathematical analysis — Includes arithmetic and algebra; deals with numbers, the relationships between numbers, and the operations performed on these relationships.

mathematical control mode — A specific type of control action such as proportional, integral or derivative.

mathematical logic — Frequently referred to as symbolic logic. Exact reasoning concerning non-numerical relations by using symbols that are efficient in calculation.

mathematical model — 1. A series or organization of equations that are a mathematical representation of a "real world" problem or process in a skeletonized form, but with precise measurements of the relationships of the variables, parameters, and constants. Each model has some objective function (goal or target) and decision rules (values to be determined) which will solve the problem to develop the answer or range of alternatives. 2. A mathematical representation of a process, device, or concept. 3. A mathematical representation that simulates the behavior of a process, device, or concept.

mathematical operator — A symbol that indicates briefly a mathematical process, which describes the relations and restrictions which exist between the input variables and the output variables of a system.

mathematical programming — A mathematical theory for optimizing a set of variables controlling a process for a given set of parameters.

mathematical simulation — The use of a model of mathematical equations in which computing elements are used to represent all of the subsystems.

mathematics — Involves the definition of symbols of various kinds and describes the operations to be performed, in definite and consistent ways, upon the symbols; a symbolized and extended form of logic to form the patterns of scientific phenomena, the laws obeyed, and the uniformities displayed. Although mathematics does not provide these, it expresses and interprets them and helps to deduce their consequences, or to forecast what will happen if they hold. Mathematics points and advises where to look for verification or contradiction of hypotheses.

mathematics function keyblock — If a user chooses the Mathematics Function Keyblock for his advanced calculator he will have single key control of powerful mathematics statements and additional capability for subroutine control and peripheral control. In addition to the functions shown on the keyboard, in one system, pressing the key labeled TABLE N followed by keys 1, 2, 3, ... 9, or FMT gives him access to 10 more functions. On one unit functions 1-9 are: SET DEGREES; SET RADIANS; SET GRADS; $\log_{10}X$; 10^x; degrees/minutes/seconds to decimal degrees conversion; decimal degrees to degrees/minutes/seconds conversion; X!; and Round. TABLE N, FMT is an automatic scaling control for use with the X-Y Plotter; it saves users from manual data scaling routines. For added flexibility, users can program the key labeled DEFINABLE f( ), to perform any function they wish. Once the key has been programmed, users need only press it to execute their function.
No programming is required for any of the functions in this keyblock (with the exception of DEFINABLE f( )). Users merely enter the data, press the appropriate key, and their answer is displayed, instantly. These functions have a separate (ROM) memory block dedicated to them so they do not draw upon the main calculator memory — leaving it fully available for further problem solving needs.

mathematics I, tape pack — Twenty two programs of commonly used numerical analysis techniques such as, conversions, function analysis and plots, integration, differential equations, and systems of linear equations. Includes binder, manual, overlays and one tape cartridge. Prerequisite: 8K bytes of memory. Tape Cartridge. (some units)

math-pack — Mathematical and statistical programs for simplifying such scientific and engineering applications as solution of simultaneous linear equations, matrix algebra, multiple linear regression, roots of a polynomial, and least squares polynomial fit. (some firm offerings)

matrix — A two-dimensional rectangular representation of quantities, manipulated in accordance with the rules of matrix algebra. Also, a network of input and output leads, with logic elements connected at intersections.

matrix algebra tableau — The current matrix, with auxiliary rows and/or columns, as it appears at an iterative stage in the standard simplex method computing form of solution.

matrix, computer — Relating to computers, a logic network in the form of an array of input leads and computer logic.

matrix, coefficient — The matrix of left-side coefficients in a system of linear operations. It is to be distinguished from the matrix obtained by appending the right side, which is called the augmented matrix of the system. It may be thought of as including a full set of logical vectors to convert inequality constraints to equations, and in the case of the modified simplex array it also contains the objective function coefficients.

matrix inversion program — Inverts an N BY N Matrix. The maximum value of N which can be handled is defined by the following relationship N Squared less than or equal to R where R is the number of main data registers available.

matrix math — Matrix Math — is of great value to scientists and engineers because it simplifies the manipulation of complex algorithms. One particularly nice feature of a Matrix Math ROM is that it lets users find Determinants directly — with a single command on some calculators.

matrix operations — Matrix operations are extremely valuable to the engineer and scientist for solving a set of simultaneous equations or performing a regression analysis. Structural and electronics engineers find the determinant operation (not available in standard BASIC) particularly useful in their design problems.

matrix printing — The printing of alphanumerical characters by means of the appropriate selection of pins contained in a rectangular array on the printing head.

matrix, semantic — A graphical device for plotting in a standard conventional form whatever precise elements of meaning have been ascertained from the semantic analysis of a concept.

matrix storage — Storage, the elements of which are arranged such that access to any location requires the use of two or more coordinates, for example, cathode ray storage, magnetic core storage.

matrix switch — An array of circuit elements interconnected specifically to perform a particular function as interconnected, i.e., the elements are usually transistors, diodes, and relay gates completing logic functions for encoding, transliteration of characters, decoding number system transformation, word translation, etc., and most often input is taken along one dimension while output is taken along another.

matrix table — A specific set of quantities in a rectangular array according to exacting mathematical rules and designs.

mean — The mean of two quantities is the quantity lying between them and with them by some mathematical law. There are several types of means, the main ones being the arithmetical mean and the geometrical mean. The arithmetic mean, or average of several quantities of the same type, is their sum divided by their numbers. For example, the arithmetical mean of 10, 12, 17, and 25 is $\frac{64}{4}$ or 16. The arithmetical mean is understood when the word mean is used alone. The geometrical mean of two quantities is the square root of their product; the geometrical mean of 2 and 8 is $\sqrt{16} = 4$. The greater of the given quantities is as many times greater than the mean, as the mean is greater than the least quantity. Such is the idea of the geometrical mean. In a geometrical progression, each term is a geometrical mean between the preceding and succeeding terms; in an arithmetical progression each term is an arithmetical mean between the preceding and succeeding terms.

mean, geometric — This is the nth root of a product of n numbers. $G.M. = \sqrt[n]{X_1 \cdot X_2 \cdots X_n}$. Where a large number of values are involved, it is more convenient to find the logarithms of the numbers, divide the sum of the logarithms by the number of items, and look up the antilogarithms of the quotient.

mean, standard deviation, standard error for grouped data program —
Given a set of data points

$$x_1, x_2, ..., x_n$$

with respective frequencies

$$f_1, f_2, ..., f_n$$

the program computes the following statistics:

$$\text{mean } \bar{x} = \frac{\Sigma f_i x_i}{\Sigma f_i}$$

$$\text{standard deviation } s = \sqrt{\frac{\Sigma f_i x_i^2 - (\Sigma f_i)\bar{x}^2}{\Sigma f_i - 1}}$$

$$\text{standard error } s_{\bar{x}} = \frac{s_x}{\sqrt{\Sigma f_i}}.$$

measured signal — A designed electrical, pneumatic, mechanical, or other variable which is applied to the input of a device. It is the analog of the measured variable produced by a transducer, if such is used.

measured variable, physical — A specific physical quantity, condition, or property which is to be measured, often referred to as the measurand. Such common measured variables are: pressure, temperature, rate of flow, thickness, speed, etc.

measurement/control systems, industrial — Measurement control systems made possible with the use of programmable calculators can greatly improve productivity. Their applications include material handling, process control, information networks, and quality control. Industrial measurement and control systems can ensure material is on hand, when needed, in the right quantity. They can control the manufacturing process; and when the job is done, they can check the quality of the finished products automatically. The system can also be integrated into a plantwide information network for management reports and data processing.

measurement error — The total anticipated error due to 1. sampling inadequacy or variability; 2. sample preparation variability; 3. instability or lack of precision in read-out or transducer systems.

median — The value of the middle item when the items are arranged according to size. If there is an even number of items, the midpoint is taken as the arithmetic mean of the two central items. The median is an average of position while the arithmetic mean is a calculated average. The median is computed as follows: 1. Arrange the items according to magnitude (this is called an array), 2. Record the size of the middle value. If there is an even number of items in the array there will be two central values; thus, the arithmetic mean of these two values is taken as the median.

median and range chart program — This program computes the sample statistics and the control limits for median and range control charts.

medical instrumentation calculator — One calculator system with programs on magnetic tape cartridges analyzes half a dozen lung tests gathered by instrumentation. Programs can be changed or altered easily on the magnetic tape cartridges. This flexibility was not available on most old system units. The calculator's alphanumeric printer gives the technicians a better understanding of results than the older numeric printers now replaced.

medical pack — Programs applicable to these types of medical calculations and conversions: ventilator set-up and calibration; analysis of cardiopulmonary function, acid-base balance, blood gases and respiratory status.

medium, empty — Usually printed forms or blank paper tapes, invoices, etc., which are bases or media on which data has been recorded only to develop a frame of reference to determine the feasibility of such instruments to be used later as data carriers.

medium, input/output — The vehicle or material designed and used to carry recorded data, i.e., a punched card, magnetic tape, microfilm, etc. The medium is the carrier of data and instructions to and from a computer. A specific register that contains modifiers of instructions before execution, or a register that controls actions under the direction of the computer or program.

medium, nonerasable — Paper tapes are examples of nonerasable media used to drive various production machines. It is quite uncommon to use paper tape as an intermediate memory because it is nonerasable.

mega — Prefix denoting 10^6 (one million) Abbreviated M.

membrane keyboards, touch-sensitive — Standard custom monopanel keyboards have no mechanical linkages. Layer construction incorporates a tough membrane with conductive rear surface which effects contact closure when moved approximately 0.005". Required touch sensitivity is 2 to 4 oz. typ. A standard series includes 12- and 16-position spst, black on white nomenclature, and black or white plastic bezel, with or without mounting flange.

memories, calculator types — Most conventional CPU boards contain read/write memory, but nonvolatile program storage has often required an additional memory module or a separate solid-state read-only-memory board. In most systems, programs are stored in nonvolatile memory to eliminate the need to reload read/write memory every time the system is turned on.
However, some systems provide all three types of necessary memory right on the board: EPROM for program development, small-volume system production, and applications where programs are subject to change after the system is manufactured; masked ROM for moderate-volume production of system with unchanging program requirements; and RAM to store data, variable parameters, and subroutines that are subject to dynamic change. The recent development of the 8,192-bit EPROM, which stores 1,024 bytes, has made practical the packaging of all three types of memory on one board. Typically, four 8708s,

which are two to four times as dense as previous designs, can be plugged into the board, and they are interchangeable with 8,192-bit masked ROMs. Some system's EPROM/ROM sockets allow the user to plug in program memories in 1-kilobyte increments by simply inserting as many as four of the 8,192-bit devices. The EPROMs are normally used for program development because they can be erased and reprogramed through all the development cycles of the OEM's system prototype. Also, many manufacturers prefer to ship new products with EPROMs to accommodate special customer requirements. Calculator manufacturers with unchanging programs and large production volume can reduce costs by plugging in masked ROMs after the programs have been developed. A typical 1-kilobyte read/write memory contains eight 1,024-bit (256 × 4) static RAMs.

memory — 1. One of the three basic CPU components, main memory stores information for future use. Storage and memory are interchangeable expressions. Memories accept and hold binary numbers or images. 2. In order to be effective, a computer must be capable of storing the data it is to operate on as well as the program that dictates which operations are to be performed. Not only must the memory unit of a computer store large amounts of information, the memory must be designed to allow rapid access to any particular portion of that information. Speed, size and cost are the critical criteria in any storage unit. Various types are: disc, drum, semi-conductor, magnetic core, charge-coupled devices, bubble domain, etc.

memory address keys, indirect — These include: Indirect Store. Indirect Recall. Indirect Exchange. Indirect Add. Indirect Subtract. Indirect Multiply. Indirect Divide. Example: the indirect address instruction: 5 IND STO 10 means to store 5, not in register 10, but in the register whose address is found in register 10. Thus, if 15 were previously stored in register 10, then 5 IND STO 10 would mean store 5 in PROD register 15. Register 15 has been indirectly addressed by the given instruction.

memory address register (MAR) — 1. While accessing memory, the MAR register in some systems contains the address of the memory location that is currently selected for reading or writing. The MAR is also used as an internal register for microprogram control during data transfers to and from memory and peripherals. 2. The memory address register is a 4, 8, 12 or 16-bit register that is used to hold the address of a data word to be read from, or written into, memory. 3. The location in main memory that is selected for data storage or retrieval is determined by the memory address. Some registers can directly address all words of the standard main memory or of any preselected field extended main memory.

memory address, virtual — Often interpreted as addressing (1) a particular character relative to the beginning of a page, (2) a particular page relative to the initial point of that segment, and (3) a particular large memory segment or book. Thus programs can be addressed into noncontiguous areas of memory in relatively small blocks.

memory allocation, calculator — Advanced calculators react to many special requirements. Users can allocate memory into either program steps and/or data registers. If they want 50 registers instead of the 10 permanent registers, they simply tell some calculators 5 0 SHIFT STORE. Thus, they can partition the basic memory of these units which is 400+ program steps, and any way they choose. Optionally they can expand some units to 2,008 program steps, which increases the basic memory four times — all of which can be partitioned by plan or design.

memory, advanced calculator — One standard advanced calculator includes 8 kilobytes of internal read/write memory, which is expandable in 8-kilobyte increments to 32 kilobytes. Optional ROMs can be added in four plug-in slots in the front of the calculator: STRINGS, which provides string arrays; 32,767 characters; functions like length, position, value, and capitalization; and concatenation; ADVANCED PROGRAMMING: MATRIX ROM provides standard operators like invert (40 x 40 in 70 s), transpose and multiplication, multidimensional array operators, and scalar multiply; PLOTTER; GENERAL I/O and EXTENDED I/O and other ROMs are available.

memory, backing — Considered to be the same as auxiliary storage, i.e., those units whose capacity is relatively larger than working (scratchpad or internal) storage but of longer access time, and which transfer capability is usually in blocks between storage units.

memory, BASIC — This generally refers to the Read/Write Random Access Memory that contains BASIC programs and data, as opposed to the Read Only Memory which contains the BASIC interpreter.

memory board — A typical semiconductor memory board can be configured in 4K word increments up to 32K words. It provides addressing for up to 32K words, refresh and standby logic, the bus interface, and the first 4K words of memory. The system is driven by the microprocessor and contains up to 16K words per board.

memory bus — The CPU communicates with memory and I/O devices over a memory bus. In different calculators this bus has various names, including I/O bus, data bus or one of a host of proprietary names.

memory, cache — Refers to units with limited capacity but very fast semiconductor memory which can be used in combination with lower cost, but slower large-capacity memory, giving effect to a larger and faster memory. Look-ahead procedures are required in the progress of the programs to affect locating and depositing the right information into the fast memory when it is required.

memory, cache (calculator) — One type cache memory is a 256-word (512-byte) MOS read/write memory. It allows data transfer from the calculator at one rate and to the mass memory at a different rate. This avoids any synchronization or timing problems between the two components. The full 256-word contents of the cache memory are transferred during any read/write operation with the mass memory. The cache memory appears to the calculator as an extension of its own memory, but is not accessible by the user.

memory, calculator (simple) — A 'constant' or a 'memory' facility is used when a problem requires the repeated use of a single constant. Users key this in only once and then multiply, divide, add, or subtract with this constant by simply pressing the constant key. A 'memory' allows users to park a displayed number in invisible storage with a

memory capacity, calculator — stroke of a key for as long as they like; then the touch of another key magically brings it back, over and over again, for use in a problem. This saves having to write down sub-totals and partial answers to problems before proceeding.

memory capacity, calculator — The amount of memory provided by calculator manufacturers varies widely and depends in part on the units' intended applications. Generally, the minimum read/write memory provided is about 512 bytes. Additionally, 1K of read-only memory is also usually available. Users can usually expand RAM and ROM to a combined total capacity of up to about 64K, or more with very large systems.

memory, cartridge capacity example — Each cartridge on some units provides 2.4M bytes of storage. In addition, 7K of system software resides on each platter after it is formatted for system use.

memory cassette, calculator example — Some advanced calculators feature a built-in cassette for program, data, or special function key storage. In addition to the internal cassette these calculators can operate with up to nine peripheral cassettes. Tape and data manipulations not usually available on large computer magnetic tape systems are easily performed on calculators. Files may be recalled from the cassette, modified, and restored in the same location, thus eliminating the need for a second tape unit. All files are numbered sequentially and a high-speed bi-directional search is used to locate a specified file from any point on the tape; program execution times are significantly reduced by eliminating the need for tape rewind in order to begin searching for a file.

memory, cassette characteristics (calculator) — Cassette storage may be optimized by selecting different file sizes which correspond to the program length and/or data storage of the program. Several Cassette Memories may be used in a system and each can be selectively addressed. One cassette system has an interrupt mode for simultaneous calculator operation and cassette file search. A single tape cassette can hold up to 80,000 bytes (40,000 words) depending on the file structure set up by the user. The following tape cassette commands are programmable: MARK, STORE, LOAD MERGE, LINK, REWIND, FIND, STOREKEY, LOADKEY, STOREDATA, LOADDATA, and TLIST. These commands are also available in keyboard mode. (some systems)

memory chips, high density — As regards development of higher density memory chips, considerable work is in progress in this area, with several firms reporting positive results. Utilizing a combination of ion implantation and electron-beam lithography techniques, IBM's Research Division, for example, has already achieved a tenfold increase in the packing density of LSI memory chips on an experimental basis. The IBM process permits the fabrication of memory chips with a storage density of five million bits per square inch.

memory, circulating shift register (calculator) — On one popular unit the memory itself contains no absolute addresses. Instead, it is a circulating shift register organized into six-bit words. One word is a marker that denotes the boundary between the beginning and the end of the memory. Another word is a pointer which denotes the last step executed in run mode, and the last step filled in program mode. As a program runs, this pointer is moved down through memory. Branching is accomplished by moving the pointer to the location of the destination label. User-defined function calls are implemented by leaving the main pointer at the call and activating a second pointer at the function location. When the return to the calling location occurs, the second pointer is deactivated and the first pointer reactivated. Neither the marker nor the pointers subtract from the 100 user steps.

memory, content-addressed — A memory in which the storage locations are identified by their contents rather than their addresses. Enables faster interrogation to retrieve a particular data element.

memory-device access times — Typical access times have been reported as follows:

TTL RAM	60 ns
MOS RAM	300 ns
Core	500 ns
Bubbles (Fast Auxiliary Config.)	0.5-1 ms
Head/Track Disk/Drum	8 ms
Moving Head Disk	50 ms
Floppy Disk	100 ms
Bubbles (Endless Loop Config.)	1 s
Cassettes	10 s
Tapes	10 s

memory diagnostic — Refers to a routine that checks all memory locations for proper functioning using a set of worst-case pattern tests. By relocating quality control diagnostics into various positions in memory, the memory diagnostic is able to test all of memory.

memory (direct) register addressing keys, calculator — Store. Stores displayed number into one of many addressable memory registers. Recall. Displays data stored in a selected register. Exchange. Exchanges contents of a selected register with the displayed number. Sum. Algebraically sums displayed number to contents of a selected register and retains result. Subtract. Subtracts displayed number from contents of a selected register. Product. Multiplies contents of a selected register by the displayed number and retains result in that register. Divide. Divides contents of a selected register by the displayed number and retains result in that register.

memory dump — Generally refers to a listing of the contents of a storage device, or selected parts of it. (1) Dynamic — A dump of certain sections of memory under program control as a main routine is being executed. (2) Differential — A dump of only those words or characters of memory which have been changed during the execution of a routine, determined by a diagnostic routine which re-reads the original contents from auxiliary storage and compares them with the present contents.

memory, dynamic — Refers to a characteristic of the storage of data on a device or in a manner that permits the data to move or vary with time, and thus the data is not always available instantly for recovery; i.e., acoustic delay line, magnetic drum, or circulating or recirculating of information in a medium.

memory efficiency, calculators — Many units are offering efficient usage of all memory. Memory structure, language, addressing . . . all these things were designed to ensure efficient use of internal memory. The idea is to provide users with the most memory power possible no matter which size they order. Consider the following capabili-

ties available on most advanced units:
- No artificial partitioning — programs and data share the same storage.
- No waste — after program entry, all unused memory is available for data.
- Editing leaves no gaps — the units automatically repack memory.
- Automatic allocation — programs are converted to machine code and efficiently fitted into storage.
- A choice of addressing — any combination of direct, indirect, relative, and symbolic addressing to decrease program length and the amount of storage required can be used.

memory equals + key — On some units this key operates in the same manner as the equals key when multiplication or division has been conditioned and adds the answer to the memory contents. If multiplication or division has not been conditioned, this key will add to memory the contents of the input register.

memory expansion, calculator — To facilitate customizing, programmables are divided into two classes: those whose memories can be expanded both externally and internally, and those whose memories can only be expanded internally. For those users who will not require the super memory capacity available with add-on devices, small, low-cost units are fine. Some typical units have 120 storage registers or 960 program steps. The more powerful advanced units have even more storage registers for up to 1984 program steps. And tapes, cassettes, ROMs and RAMs extend this even further.

memory expansion, capability — By expanding the memory capability of the programmable calculator with peripherals such as highspeed magnetic tape cassette systems, external semiconductor or core memory, and disc drives, calculator manufacturers have made it practical to "close the loop," using the calculator for supervisory control in conjunction with conventional electronic process controllers and sensing instrumentation. Although programing often is complicated by external memory transfer instructions, the simplified "program step/data register" orientation of the calculator language is preserved and thus, too, is its low programing cost.

memory extender — A typical memory extender provides fully powered channels for up to 8 additional memory modules. Some units have 16K word memory modules, and the memory extender can have a capacity of 131,072 words of semiconductor memory. Using 8K word modules, the extender can hold 65,536 words of memory. The power supply for the memory extender is comparable to the M/30 power supply to assure maximum reliability in a micro or minicomputer system. A Power Fail Recovery system is often available that will support a memory system for a minimum of hours in the event of a total power failure.

memory, FIFO — FIFO memories offer the system designer many advantages. They operate with a minimum of addressing logic. Their separate write and read address inputs eliminate critical timing. Users can use a multiport register to get new levels of speed, flexibility and performance in a FIFO design for computer, calculator or communication systems.

memory fill — Refers to the placing of patterns of characters in the memory registers not in use in a particular problem to stop the calculator if the program, through error, seeks instructions taken from forbidden registers.

memory, floppy disk format — A typical low-cost floppy disk-format allows storage of over 300,000 bytes. Since the disk is hard sectored (32 sectors for each track), users write 137 bytes on each sector, 9 of which are used internally (track#, checksum) leaving 128 data bytes per sector, 4096 per track. One floppy diskette is supplied with each drive; extra floppies are available for purchase. On some systems, software driver for the floppy disk is available at no charge and is supplied with the disk as a source listing. The disk operating system — which has a complete file structure and utilities for copying, deleting and sorting files — costs extra. Extended BASIC, which uses random and sequential file access for the floppy disk, is also available.

memory, floppy disk system — Various Disk systems offer the advantage of nonvolatile memory, plus relatively fast access to data. A low cost Disk Controller consists of two PC boards (over 60 I.C.s) that fit in the chassis. They inter-connect to each other with 20 wires and connect to the disk through a 37-pin connector mounted on the back of the unit. Data is transferred to and from the disk serially at 250K bits/sec. The disk controller converts the serial data to and from 8-bit parallel words (one word every 32 μ sec). The CPU transfers the data, word by word to and from memory, depending on whether the disk is reading or writing. The disk controller also controls all mechanical functions of the disk as well as presenting disk status to the computer. All timing functions are done by hardware to free the computer chip for other tasks. Since some floppy diskettes are divided into 32 sectors, a hardware interrupt system can be enabled to notify the CPU at the beginning of each sector. Power consumption is approximately 1.1 amperes from the +8v (VCC) line for the two boards.

memory high-speed — 1. A high-speed random access data storage device utilizes arrays of ROMs, RAMs and PROMs, usually employed as a working memory. 2. A data storage system, particularly for use with calculating elements and machines.

memory, "LAST x" — Some units have nine or more addressable memories and a special "LAST x" memory that automatically stores the last number users key in for easy error correction and multiple operations on the same number.

memory light — A light which indicates there is a number in the memory.

memory load and record operation — Allows users to suspend processing whenever they want and store the complete contents of memory on tape — including data and pointers — for continuation later on.

memory, main — Usually the CPU or fastest storage device of a calculator and the one from which instructions are executed. Contrasted with auxiliary storage.

memory map list — In some systems a memory map is provided at compile time on an optional basis. The memory map is a listing of all variable names, array names, and constants used by the program, with their relative address assignments. The listing will include all subroutines called and last location when called.

memory, microcomputer — The typical micro-

memory, off-line

computer main memory has a capacity of 4096 or more 4, 8, 12 or 16-bit words with a read/write cycle time of 1.5 microseconds (or faster). The memory is often non-volatile; if power is removed, data stored in memory is not lost. The processor and input-output interface communicate with the memory by way of the data input bus. Various hardware registers are used to hold memory address information and data received via the bus: the memory address register and the memory data register.

memory, off-line — Any memory medium capable of being stored remotely from the calculator, which can be read by the calculator when placed into a suitable reading device.

memory options, advanced calculators — Generally, a wide range of memory options lets users expand the capability of some machines as their needs expand. For example, in these units by simply plugging in IC's and changing a few jumpers users can have up to 8192 program steps and 256 registers or 2048 steps and 1000 registers.

memory (+0) or (−) keys — These keys provide access to the memory. They can alter the contents by adding to the existing total or subtracting from it.

memory power — Even pocket calculators should have at least one addressable memory — to store constants or other numbers used more than once in a calculation. The more memories a calculator has, the less writing down of numbers that users have to do. With certain calculators having addressable memories, users can do register arithmetic directly add to, subtract from, divide into or multiply the contents of a register. This makes data manipulation exceptionally easy, even when working problems involving three simultaneous linear equations (or other 3 x 3 matrix inversions). Besides addressable memories, certain pocket calculators have an automatic memory (also called an operational stack, a four-memory stack, etc.). Entries and intermediate answers are stored automatically, then re-entered into the calculation at the appropriate time. Obviously, this eliminates the need to write down and re-enter numbers, which could lead to errors, and it speeds the work.

memory protect — Memory protect is available for use in many processors. It protects the integrity of operating systems against accidental modifications. Memory protect sets up a fence which divides memory space into two segments, separating the operating system from user programs. If any part of a user program seeks to modify system space, the system interrupts and takes control. This is a necessity for many real time environments and other highly interactive systems.

memory, random access (RAM) — A memory whose information media are organized into discrete locations, sectors, etc., each uniquely identified by an address. Data may be obtained from such a memory by specifying the data address(es) to the memory.

memory ranges, calculator — Most advanced units have a good memory to start with and can grow more. One type has 512 program steps and 74 data registers in the standard machine. Users can add memory in blocks of 512 program steps and 64 data registers up to 2,048 steps and 256 registers. Then, in various combinations it can go to 8,192 program steps or 1,010 registers. Program and data are always stored separately. The magnetic

memory, secondary

tape cartridges can hold programs or data, adding even more memory without detracting from the machine's internal memory. For instant "on use" programs, user plug in PROMs hold 1,024 program steps. If they need still more, the optional flexible disc with built-in interface puts a vast memory bank at user disposal.

memory, read-only (ROM) — Refers to memory that cannot be altered in normal use of the calculator. Usually a relatively small memory that contains often-used instructions such as microprograms or system software as firmware.

memory recall — A key which allows the current contents of the memory to be displayed.

memory register — A register in which the contents can be added to or subtracted from. The contents are available until the register is cleared.

memory registers, addressable — These can be used for storage and retrieval of data, or to perform register arithmetic. A 10th ("Last X") register lets users recall last input argument for error correction or for multiple functions of same argument. (some units) (see registers)

memory, ROM advantages — Data processing requires large segments of read-write memory to solve the data manipulation type of problem. Often this memory is used for loadable program storage and bulk data storage. The fixed nature of dedicated control designs needs only ROM program storage, which deserves as much credit for the hard-wired logic replacement revolution as the microprocessor. Dedicated control systems previously hard-wired to perform the logic functions can be designed with the same permanence and yet enjoy the standardization and flexibility of storing logic sequences in ROM.

memory save — Provides battery-powered carry-over through power outages up to 10 minutes to prevent loss of program storage. This is powered-down non-operational mode. (some units)

memory save option, data acquisition system — In a power outage on some systems RAM memories that contain the program and the last data scan lose their stored information. In systems equipped with a custom initialization ROM, restoration of power automatically restores the full program to the RAMs, starts the clock and initiates data scanning in the AUTO mode. But for some applications a pre-programmed ROM is not desired for each different setup. To avoid program data loss, and timing loss, the memory save option powers the RAMs for ten or more minutes from an internal bank of batteries. These cells are kept fully charged during normal operation, and are automatically cut in if a transient or outage occurs. If more than 10 minutes of protection are desired, additional batteries or a UPS can be provided. The memory save option returns the system to scanning in the AUTO mode when line power is restored.

memory, scratchpad — Refers to the central, high-priority, small, immediate access memory area of the CPU, with a significantly faster access time than the larger main store. This is normally used by the hardware and/or operating system for storing microcodes, most frequently used operands, groups of object program instructions or registers.

memory, secondary — A particular storage which is usually of large capacity, but also with longer access time, and which most often permits the transferring of blocks of data between it and the main storage.

memory, semiconductor (LSI) — 1. Semiconductor flip-flop circuits could provide large scale storage units. Although the semiconductors are very fast, most require the continuous application of power to retain the data stored in them. They were originally used primarily for microcomputer storage registers and computational logic units (such as the arithmetic logic unit). 2. A memory whose storage medium is a semiconductor circuit most often used for high-speed buffer memories and for read-only memories, but now becoming primary storage devices for most computers. Large-scale integration (LSI) semiconductor memories now have potential to supersede core memories for most purposes. Charged-coupled devices (CCD's) and magnetic bubbles that represent bits as regions of charge or as magnetism that can be moved electrically on a fixed substrate are an important recent contribution to memory technology.

memory, serial — Refers to a type of memory whose information media is continuous. Data is identified in its content or form. Data may be obtained only by performing a serial search through the contents of the memory.

memory-sharing, calculator — Because a programmable calculator system is generally dedicated to a single, specific task at any given time, the sharing of peripherals by more than one calculator is not usually a system requirement. However it is sometimes desirable to share a large data base that is stored on discs or tapes. Two calculators can share a tape or disc unit by using a special Tee coupling system. If calculator A addresses the memory unit, the circuitry in the Tee sends a busy signal to calculator B, and vice versa. This system of sharing is particularly satisfactory for problems that call for infrequent reference to the memory unit. (some models)

memory sharing, disk (calculator) — It should be emphasized that most calculator systems are not time-shared systems in the usual sense. Only one calculator can access a disk platter at any given time. The remaining calculators in the system can access their respective cache memories during this time. The cache memory remains dedicated to the calculator, not to the controller on these specific systems. It is true, however, that two or more users can be working on different applications and sharing one or more mass memories, and in most such situations, neither user would notice that someone else was using the system. An order processing system, for example, might have someone entering new orders, another preparing shipping papers and updating inventory records, and still another preparing order acknowledgments and billing customers. The new order entries could be transferred from a holding file to the main data base at the beginning of each day.

memory stack, calculator — On some units data areas for programs are organized in main memory as stacks. A stack is a storage allocation method where the last item added is the first item removed. The CPU has registers that automatically keep track of the last area allocated in a stack. The use of the stack means that data areas for a procedure's private variables are allocated dynamically (when the procedure is called into execution), keeping the amount of memory space required by a program to a dynamic minimum. The stack also provides the mechanism for passing parameters to procedures and saving and restoring the calling environment (this applies to calling both an application's own procedures and operating system procedures).

memory stack, microcomputer — One memory stack provides last-in, first-out storage and is located in main memory. Advanced programming techniques, such as re-entrant, recursive and Polish mode programming, are conveniently implemented using the stack. Its exact location is under control of the user. Thus, for a user with a main program of 8K words, over 56K of RAM is available for the stack! One of the eight registers is generally assigned as a stack pointer, which contains the address of the next available memory location in the stack.

memory, static — A memory device containing no mechanical moving parts or one that contains fixed information.

memory subtotal key — On some units it recalls the memory and prints and displays the memory contents aligned to the decimal switch.

memory, virtual — A technique that permits the user to treat secondary (disk) storage as an extension of main memory, thus giving the virtual appearance of a larger main memory. A type of memory with the capability of using a type of algorithm of the paging or segmenting type. In this manner a larger memory is simulated than actually exists.

memory, virtual (pointer) — Virtual memory systems are designed for storage efficiency. Some computers are structured so that parts of programs and data may be scattered through main memory and auxiliary storage. Various pointers or sets of pointers automatically keep track of the location of these program portions. The user of computers so designed may be unaware of this scattering procedure and most often operates computing procedures as though he were using normal memory.

mesh — To combine in an arrangement according to some rule, two or more sequences previously arranged according to the same rule, to obtain a single sequence of items without any change in the number or type of items.

message blocks — Some terminals can support a number of high-speed devices, such as line printers and card readers, which may be capable of simultaneous operations. In order to reduce the transmission overhead, messages exchanged between such devices and the application programs may be blocked and unblocked at various points in the system. The blocking operation consists in the concatenation of several messages into a single transmission or physical record. This is done to reduce the frequency of the delays due to changing the transmission direction of the communication link.

message, fox — A standard message which is used for testing teletype circuits and machines because it includes all the alphanumerics on a teletypewriter as well as most of the function characters such as space, figures shift, letters shift, etc. The message is: The quick brown fox jumped over a lazy dog's back 1234567890 - - - sending." The sending station's identification is inserted in the three blank spaces which precede the word sending.

message, start of (SOM) — Character or group of characters transmitted by the polled terminal and indicating to other stations on the line that what follows are addresses of stations to receive the answering message.

message switching — Refers to the telecommunications application in which a message is received at a central location, stored on a direct-access device until the proper outgoing line is available, and then transmitted to the appropriate destination.

metal oxide semiconductor (MOS) — 1. In MOS technology, amplification or switching is accomplished by applying a signal voltage to a gate electrode. The resulting electrostatic field creates a conduction channel between the two diffused regions in the silicon crystal structure, called the 'source' and the 'drain'. 2. MOS is part of the acronym MOSFET, the FET meaning Field Effect Transistor. Thus MOS-LSI are types of transistors for Large Scale Integrated (LSI) metal-oxide semiconductor components for calculator memory units.

method study — Relates to the utilization of certain methods for recording and examining existing and proposed techniques of working in order to improve them.

MICR — Refers to Magnetic Ink Character Recognition. Machine recognition of characters printed with magnetic ink. Contrast with OCR.

microcircuits — 1. Miniaturized circuitry components common to the so-called third generation of computer equipment. Microcircuits frequently reduce cost, increase reliability, and operate faster than tubes and many transistors. 2. A specialized electronic circuit composed of elements which are fabricated and interconnected to make them inseparable and miniaturized.

microcode — 1. A system of coding making use of suboperations not ordinarily accessible in programming; e.g., coding that makes use of parts of multiplication or division operations. 2. A list of small program steps. Combinations of these steps, performed automatically in a prescribed sequence, form a macrooperation like multiply, divide, and square root.

microcoding — Alterable machine structure is often called firmware. The trend toward standardization of LSI products on just memory and processor is being accompanied by a trend toward microcoding, especially for the sake of simplicity and flexible uniformity. Lower cost and ease of debugging processor hardware are the driving forces that favor microcoding. The variability in machine characteristics desired by the user is taken care of by providing different microcode memories. Many microprocessors consist of two Dual-In-line Packages (DIPS). One is the processor itself, the other is microcode memory. In the past this memory most frequently was Read-Only-Memory (ROM), but more often than not it is now Read-write random access (RAM) and can be loaded by the user to emulate his favorite machine. Such user-loadable microcode allows tailoring the machine to suit a particular language, and this in turn makes it competitive with much larger and more expensive machines that cannot allow any modification of their basic structure because system security would be compromised. This at last allows machine structure, the hardware, to reflect softwear needs, e.g., "firmware."

microcoding algorithms — Although production of efficient microcode is an iterative process, the first step is the choice or design of an algorithm. This may involve such constraints as accuracy, execution speed, microinstructions required, or even available design time. Next, a functional flow chart is drawn to outline the sequence of various operations and any conditional operations. This flow chart is then expanded to sufficient detail that it can be translated to microinstructions and implemented on a calculator simulator. More often than not there are implementation errors to correct; sometimes the entire algorithm is faulty, requiring a new design. When the design is complete, integrated-circuit read-only memories are produced.

microcomputer — A general term referring to a complete tiny computing system, consisting of hardware and software, that usually sells for less than $500 and whose main processing blocks are made of semiconductor integrated circuits. In function and structure it is somewhat similar to a minicomputer, with the main difference being price, size, speed of execution, and computing power. The hardware of a microcomputer consists of the microprocessing unit (MPU) which is usually assembled on a PC board with memory and auxiliary circuits. Power supplies, control console, and cabinet are separate.

microcomputer advantages — Engineers are becoming more aware of the ways in which microcomputers can be applied to solve their problems. There are five basic reasons why many engineers have begun to use microcomputers: 1 Manufacturing costs of products can be significantly reduced. 2. Products can get to the market faster providing a company with the opportunity to increase product sales and market share. 3. Product capability is enhanced allowing manufacturers to provide customers with better products which can frequently command a higher price. 4. Development costs and time are reduced. 5. Product reliability is increased which leads to a corresponding reduction in both service and warranty costs.

microcomputer applications — The advantages of small size, low weight and power and high reliability also gain the ability to easily modify and enhance microcomputer system functions through software changes. In addition, the reduction in parts count has cut inspection costs for incoming parts and has resulted in reduced material costs for chassis, interconnects, and power supplies. Microprocessors fill the needs of low cost applications, such as, electronic games, small-intersection traffic-control signals, simple industrial systems, appliances, vending machines, and for more complex control functions as editing typewriters, measurement systems, accounting machines, etc.

microcomputer cards versus a CPU chip — Often the addition of a little logic has converted a hard-to-use CPU chip into an easy-to-use computer card. The process of converting a CPU chip into a computer card illustrates some key factors which a user must evaluate before deciding which to buy. The vital ingredient is to provide an interface between CPU chip pins and data busses that connect to external memory and peripheral devices. If the CPU chip is to be used in a computerlike application, that is all the logic the computer card requires, since standard memory control logic and I/O device control logic will complete the interface.

microcomputer communications — Four data input/output (I/O) paths typically will be required: a) CPU to memory, b) memory to CPU, c) CPU to peripheral devices, d) Peripheral devices to CPU. It is logical to differentiate between memory and peripheral devices during I/O operations. Memory I/O is very fast, and occurs during the instruction fetch phase of every instruction's execution; also memory is addressable to a very elementary (byte or word) level. Peripheral device I/O is too slow to constitute an integral part of instruction execution, and must be treated as an accessory to CPU operations.

microcomputer CPU — In general aspects, the CPU consists of the following: program counter (PC), instruction register (IR), instruction execution logic, a memory-address register (MAR), a general-purpose register (GPR) file, and an arithmetic and logic unit (ALU).

microcomputer development system — A typical Microcomputer Development System is a complete system for software development and PROM programming and is equipped with the following major items: Basic Processor, Console Card, Teletypewriter Interface, 4352 bytes of RAM, sockets for 768 bytes of PROM, PROM Programmer, CLD-528-8 enclosure (with logic and PROM Programmer power supplies, fully wired and assembled), ODT on PROMs, and Assembler, Editor and PROM Programmer Control Program binary tapes and User's Manuals.

microcomputer disadvantages — Microcomputers have several disadvantages. Despite adequate speed for many applications, microcomputers cannot address high speed data acquisition, high speed data communications, and high speed large screen CRT refreshing. As microcomputer speeds increase due to technology and design improvements microcomputers will move into some of these applications. Microcomputer testing, due to the high level of integration, is extremely difficult. Truly effective diagnostics haven't been developed for most new microprocessors, placing the burden on the user to find effective diagnostic methods.

microcomputer disk development system (MDOS) — Features a self diagnostic capability and a comprehensive repertoire of hardware error checks for error-free data. Software development on this system has several advantages.
- During the assembly process, the entire program listing need not be printed to find assembly errors. Instead, MDOS prints out only those statements which contain assembly errors.
- Because the editor program is stored on the disk, modification of the program procedes quickly and efficiently.
- The high-speed printer allows the maintenance of current, error free listings.
- The need to handle paper tape is virtually eliminated (except in writing ROMs).

microcomputer execution cycle — The steps required for a microcomputer to execute an instruction are: 1) The instruction, in a binary code, is fetched from its memory storage location, and held in the microcomputer's instruction register. 2) The microcomputer decodes the instruction code. 3) The microcomputer executes the operations requested by the decoded instruction.

microcomputer functional organization — Bus and control signals of the microcomputer are in four functional categories: data, addressing, control, and supervisory. Data moves in and out of the MPU usually on 8-bit, bi-directional data bus. A 16-bit address bus enables the MPU to directly address up to 65,536 memory locations on some systems. The control bus handles the signals required to regulate and control system operation. These include Read/Write and Memory Address signals from the MPU, an Interrupt Request signal from the peripherals and Reset and timing signals that are common to the supervisory signals. On these basic systems supervisory signals are used for timing and control of the MPU itself. They consist of complementary clock inputs, Halt and Three-state Control lines, a Non-maskable Interrupt input, a Reset, a Data Bus Enable signal, and a Bus Available line from the MPU. While not used in every application, all the signals required for Direct Memory Access (DMA) and multiple processor operation are usually provided. Programmable registers within some microcomputers include two 8-bit accumulators and a 6-bit condition code register. A program counter, a stack pointer, and an index register, each 16 bits long, are provided for controlling program flow. In addition to an MPU, microprocessor based systems must have some read/write memory for temporary storage of data and variables and some read-only memory for storage of constants and the control program.

microcomputer kit — Modular interfacing kits permit customer interfacing of user peripherals, production-control units and laboratory instruments. For example, such kits feature prewired backplane units that accommodate typically from 6 to 18 logic modules. The user selects the necessary modules and wires the proper mating connector to the standard 40-conductor cable.

microcomputer (μ) C-based calculator interface — A μC-controlled interface unit, can join any of the estimated 25,000 existing Wang 600 and 700 programmable calculators that can now communicate with a wide variety of devices, between themselves, and with other computers and calculators at rates from 110 to 9600 bits per second. The interface unit's μC is programmed to perform such functions as translation, formatting, buffering and serializing. Simple I/O procedures — one of the major features of programmable controllers — are still retained. When using communication-oriented peripherals — units not previously available for these calculators — the μC makes it possible to use existing software. Also the unit can handle data from instruments and special-purpose apparatus. The interface unit can transmit or receive all 128 ASCII codes. The calculator can then be dedicated to the manipulation of the pertinent data just as if it had been keyboard entered.

microcomputer memory types — Many microcomputer systems currently have two memory types, semiconductor RAM and ultraviolet erasable ROM. Others provide a mixed memory board composed of RAM and fusible link ROM. Some kits have all the common memory types currently available — semiconductor RAM, erasable ROM, fusible link ROM and core.

microcomputer program library — A typical library includes: text editor, assembler, and loader, subroutine for driving, RAM test program, program to control the tape motion of tape drives, logic subroutines AND, XOR, IOR, LOGIC, decimal addition routine, exerciser programs, teletype keyboard input routines, PROM programming software package, A-D converter using DAC,

PRQM duplication and verification program, BCD to binary conversion routine, and others.

microcomputer prototype system — Prototyping tools are developed for the microprocessor user to devise hardware and software systems around their microprocessors. They include a chassis, programmers control panel, power supplies, and generally one or more 8K-byte RAMs (Random Access Memory), in addition to the microprocessor cards themselves. With a Teletype, the system provides all equipment and software necessary for the immediate evaluation and use of microprocessor cards and LSI devices. The prototype system is especially useful for the development of application software and equipment interfaces.

microcontroller — Another all-purpose word, this can mean a microprogrammed machine, a microprocessor or a microcomputer used in a control operation — that is, to direct or make changes in a process or operation. But there's a narrower definition, more in keeping with the prefix, in which microcontroller refers to any device or instrument that controls a process with high resolution, usually over a narrow region.

microcontroller applications — There are generally three classes of control applications: Device Control: A single machine tool or computer peripheral is sequenced through its different operations; Data Control: data from one or more sources must be moved to one or more destinations or multiple low speed data paths are concentrated into a higher speed data path. Examples include multiple channel analog acquisition systems, data communication message switches, or data communication line controllers. Process Control: Discrete inputs from measured process variables are used in a closed loop enrivonment. Examples of assembly line control are automobile or appliance manufacture of continuous steel/aluminum smelting operations.

microcycle, calculator — The cycle of control which performs the fetch and execution of a microinstruction.

microelectronics — The entire body of electronic art together with, or applied to, the realization of electronic systems by using extremely small electronic parts.

microfilm, computerized — Microfilm which is produced from magnetic tapes. Special equipment is used for this conversion activity.

microfilm, computer output (COM) — Normal printed output of a computer reduced to one of several available microforms by a special output device that takes the place of the line-printer. The COM device allows high-quality output at speeds of 5000 or more lines per minute.

microfilm image — The legend contained in a microfilm frame; the reproduction on microfilm of the words, numbers, and other information on a document.

microfilm reader — 1. A device for viewing a microimage, consisting of a projector and a screen. 2. A unit of peripheral equipment which projects film to permit reading by clients or customers of that stored on the film, such as microfilm or microfiche, or a device which converts patterns of opaque and transparent spots on a photofilm to electrical pulses which correspond to the patterns.

microfilm reader-printer — A machine which combines the ability to read clearly the film on the screen and obtain a copy of the document being viewed by pushing a button on the machine.

microinstruction — A bit pattern that is stored in a microprogram memory word and specifies the operation of the individual LSI computing elements and related subunits, such as main memory and input/output interfaces.

microinstruction, calculator — A bit pattern normally stored in control memory which controls, at a primitive level, the processor hardware.

microinstruction sequence — The series of microinstructions that the microprogram control unit (MCU) selects from the microprogram to execute a single macroinstruction or control command. Microinstruction sequences can be shared by several macroinstructions.

microinstructions/microprograms — In a general sense, any sequential logic device can be viewed as transferring information from one set of storage elements to another through a logic network. In the case of a computer, the execution of an instruction involves a sequence of information transfers from one register in the processor to another, some of which takes place directly and some through an adder or other logical network. A machine or computer instruction is made up of a number of these transfers which can be likened to a program and hence, the term for individual steps is microinstruction and the sequence of steps a microprogram.

microinstruction storage — In most applications the microprocessor based system will be built with microprograms residing in ROMS or PROMS. Therefore, it is important that a form of ROM simulation which offers facilities to easily load, examine and modify storage be available during microprogram development. Easily alterable microcode is essential during development so that trial and error techniques may be used for debugging. A large number of short sequences of one or more instructions will be executed in order to become familiar with the microprocessor chip set and to exercise all of the combinations that the microinstruction set offers. Most of the familiarization programming must be done before the final version of the microprogram can be started. During microprogram development hundreds of changes will be made to the program to locate errors quickly and to experiment with different routines to develop a more efficient program. Without the ability to quickly alter program content, debugging becomes tedious and time consuming.

micro interface — Refers to a calculator interface which may be hooked directly on-line to most available digital voltmeters. It produces the lowest-cost on-line data reduction system on the market.

microminiaturization — 1. Production and use of circuit components of very small dimensions, involving vacuum-deposited films, e.g., Nichrome on ceramic rods for resistors, oxide layers for capacitor dielectrics. 2. The process of reducing the size of parts, photographs, or printed materials for more economical, convenient storage or packing. Microminiaturized circuits are usually etched, evaporated, or electronically deposited metals, inks or other materials to form extremely tiny monolithic chips, blocks or other integrations. See large scale integration (LSI).

micron — A unit or length equal to one-thousandth of a millimeter, i.e., one-millionth of a meter or 39-millionths of an inch.

microoperation, calculator — A primitive hardware operation — e.g., addition, shift, transfer into a register, etc.

microperipheral printer — The low cost of microcomputers has created a need for comparably priced peripherals (so the peripherals won't cost more than their bosses!) One unit is a 160 cps printer with EIA and asynchronous bit parallel ASCII interface for use with microcomputers. An electric discharge printer is used for printing 20 columns across 2¼-inch paper. Prices in 1976 were as low as $395 in quantities of 100. The unit has been designed to facilitate custom interfaces and these can be obtained from the manufacturer.

microprocessing unit (MPU) — The main constituent of the hardware of the microcomputer. It consists of the microprocessor, the main memory (composed of read/write and read-only memory), the input/output interface devices and the clock circuit, in addition to buffer, driver circuits and passive circuit elements. The MPU does not contain power supplies, cabinet and control console and is normally understood to be an assembled printed-circuit board. The level of sophistication of the MPU is that of the named microcomputer.

microprocessor — The semiconductor central processing unit (CPU) and one of the principal components of the microcomputer. The elements of the microprocessor are frequently contained on a single chip or within the same package but sometimes distributed over several separate chips. In a microcomputer with a fixed instruction set, it consists of the arithmetic logic unit and the control logic unit. In a microcomputer with a microprogrammed instruction set, it contains an additional control memory unit.

microprocessor adaptability — Microprocessor adaptability ranges from devices which already incorporate some degree of automation, such as numerically controlled machine tools or laboratory blood analyzers, to products, such as appliances for which digital control hasn't been considered because of cost of complexity. Used with data terminals, MPUs can provide higher levels of interactivity among operators while reducing the traffic burden on communication channels. Machines in industrial, commercial, and consumer use can be given capabilities for adapting to loads or demands, operating in a variety of modes, and performing monitoring and control functions automatically.

microprocessor architecture — Architectural features include: general-purpose registers, stacks, interrupts, interface structure, choice of memories, etc. General-purpose registers are used for addressing, indexing, status and as multiple accumulators. They simplify programming and conserve main memory by eliminating memory buffering of data. Multiple accumulators are especially important for ROM programs that have no writeable memory.

microprocessor cache memory — A typical cache memory consists of a cluster of bipolar units arranged in four blocks of four words each. Each memory board contains one cache. When addressing memory, the CPU checks cache and main memory. If the work is in cache, the data are transferred. An error check doesn't require extra CPU time. Error-detection/correction memories use 5 bits more than noncorrecting units. The extra bits are for a computation made by both memory and CPU when they exchange data.

microprocessor calculator — Usually a large scale integrated (LSI) logic circuit that supervises and controls the interconnection, sequencing, timing, measurement, input and output, and other functions of a calculator.

microprocessor cards — Typical microprocessor cards are often flexible, low-cost, self-contained 8-bit parallel processors and controllers. They are designed for computer-oriented equipment such as data terminals, test systems, communications equipment, machine tool controllers, process control systems, and calculator or device controllers. With them the system designer can have a proven, totally debugged processor that he may customize to his immediate application by programming rather than by hardwiring. This technique can save considerable cost, both in terms of money and developmental time — in contrast to costly in-house-developed processors or controllers that use hard-wired or permanent logic.

microprocessor central processing unit — A microprocessor Central Processing Unit (CPU) typically contains all of the functions of an ordinary central processor. Some models add some time and money saving features uniquely their own. For instance, dedicated CPUs can eliminate the need for external RAM circuits in many applications. Clock and power-on-reset circuitry, normally requiring additional integrated circuit packages can be included on-chip. CPUs can also contain 16 bits of fully bidirectional input and output lines internally latched (for strong output data) and capable of driving a standard TTL load. Other items can also be added as specific applications require.

microprocessor chess game — The set is a hand-held calculator in which a chess algorithm is stored and into which a player feeds his moves. The calculator, after analyzing the position of the pieces, responds with countermoves indicated on an 8-digit diode display. Basic to one set is an F-8 microprocessor developed by Fairchild Camera & Instrument Corp.

microprocessor chip — Standing alone, a microprocessor chip can do nothing. It functions only in the context of a microcomputer system, in which appropriate integrated circuit chips are incorporated to complement the basic function of the microprocessor (μP): to serve as a central Processing Unit (CPU) in which logic and arithmetic operations and data transfers between registers, memory, and the outside world are performed. One specific microcomputer system with 4K of solid-state memory and a control panel is built around the Intel 8080 microprocessor chip. Except for a power supply, it is completely operational. The system is bus structured and has all important inputs and outputs connected to a solderless breadboarding socket, permitting interfacing with scores of devices.

microprocessor chip, an example — The typical microprocessor chip itself is a 40 pin eight bit parallel processor with sixteen memory/peripheral address lines and an eight bit bi-directional data bus. On one unit is a full compliment of 72 basic instructions with five possible addressing modes (direct, relative, immediate, indexed and extended). There are six internal registers (program counter, stack pointer, index register, accumulator A, accumulator B and condition code register). Since the pushdown stack is located within user memory, it is easily accessable and space limited only by the programmer and the amount of RAM memory available. The processor has both maskable and non-maskable interrupts which are executed as jumps to specific memory locations. Restart is also executed as a jump, but in this system the restart jump transfers system control over to terminal control via the mini-operating system ROM.

microprocessor chip, ROM — A typical microprocessor ROM gives the user the ability to:
1. load user programs or data into memory from either the keyboard or tape (where applicable)
2. execute user programs
3. list user programs or data within specified memory locations on the terminal or tape (where applicable)
4. print the data contents within the internal CPU registers
5. change the data in specified memory locations or the CPU registers

microprocessor compiler — The microprocessor compiler, which is a basic program, translates the source program into machine language. These compilers, which can be run on a medium- or large-scale computers, are available from several nationwide time-sharing services.

microprocessor components — The microprocessor is the Central Processing Unit of a microcomputer and is usually fabricated on one or two chips. Their fundamental components are: ALU, Arithmetic-Logic Unit, Control Block, and Register Array. When joined with various memory chips and input-output capability, they become microcomputers. Each microprocessor is supplied with an instruction set and each make or model has a varying capability.

microprocessor-controlled terminals applications — Microprocessors tend to control all functions in terminals that they can, for example, the CRT is hardware generated; the terminal can have RAM display memory; the processor can directly control the cursor; the processor can directly control the I/O. Debugging routines, register and memory dumps, memory data modification, and breakpoint insertion capabilities are a few of the other microprocessor control characteristics of 'intelligent' terminals.

microprocessor control terminals — Much of the power and versatility of terminals is obtained through a sophisticated microprocessor. This device manages memory allocation, data communication functions, keyboard scanning operations, and display functions.

microprocessor debugging program — A debugging program usually resides in the microprocessor memory and is used during application program development to assist in debugging. It permits debugging via the keyboard. The program is usually a formatted tape cassette tape or a paper tape that is punched in binary code, directly transferable into the memory of the MPS.

microprocessor design criteria — The ultimate goal, from design concept through development and production, is to produce the most versatile, efficient, cost-effective microprocessor system possible. To accomplish this, five stringent parameters can be set forth as guidelines:
—Minimum Parts Count
—Cost Effectiveness
—Simple Peripheral Interfaces
—Easy Expansion through Modular Architecture
—Simplified Programming and Debugging

For solving complex problems, the microprocessor devices should be able to be connected as subsystems into a synergistic system of independent microprocessors.

microprocessor internal components — A basic microcomputer generally is composed of five sections: MPU and clock, memory, control and instructions, I/O port, and power supply. The MPU and clock are usually on one chip. The LSI chip basic internal arrangement centers on the operating elements as instruction decode and control, instruction register, data and address registers and buffers, 8 or 16-bit index registers, or 16-bit program counter, 8 or 16-bit stack pointer, 8-bit accumulators, condition code register, and ALU (Arithmetic Logic Unit).

microprocessor interrupt system — From time to time, a microprocessor must examine the state of its interrupt system to determine whether an interrupt is pending. If one is, the processor must suspend its normal execution sequence and enter an interrupt sequence in the microprogram.

microprocessor microinstructions, calculator — In one calculator microprocessor, the microinstruction address was only eight bits long. Each 256-word ROM would turn itself on or off as ROM-select instructions dictated. There was only one level of subroutine and the return address had only eight bits. Another calculator microprocessor uses a twelve-bit address. A given ROM responds only when it sees an address it contains. Subroutines can be located on different ROMs and easily returned to the correct next instruction. The new processor can save two twelve-bit subroutine return addresses. Two levels make it possible for one subroutine to call another.

microprocessor purchase criteria — The importance of individual microprocessor characteristics depends basically on specific application needs. A checklist of key features to consider before making a selection follows:
- Word length;
- Architecture;
- Speed;
- Programming flexibility;
- Completeness. (How many additional circuits are needed to make it work?);
- Available design aids (both hardware and software).

microprocessor semantics — Originally the word microprocessor was used to define MOS-LSI circuit sets organized like a computer — CPU, RAM, ROM, and I/O circuits. "Micro-" was applied for various reasons: the MOS-LSI systems were smaller, slower and less powerful than a "mini"; they were programmed through microinstructions. Early practices in applying microprocessors found semiconductor firms selling sets of CPUs, ROMs, and RAMs, with equipment manufacturers supplying the TTL circuitry. Microprocessor means to many the subsystem of combined CPU, ROMs, and RAMs. The microprocessor system phrase is beginning to be used to indicate a programmed microprocessor (CPU-ROM-RAM) with integrated MOS-LSI I/O circuits. A "microprocessor unit" is an alternate term for microprocessor system. Some firms have begun to use microcomputer as another equivalent term for either microprocessor or microprocessor system — i.e., CPU, RAMs,

I/Os, and microprogrammed ROMs. It is best to reserve the term, microcomputer, for a full microprocessor system: CPU, RAMs, I/Os, and microprogrammed ROMs.

microprocessor (16-bit) controlled calculator — The Hewlett-Packard 9825 desk-top programmable calculator is controlled by a 16-bit N-MOS microprocessor built by the firm. It features 500 instructions, high speed parallel arithmetic operations and is available with memory ranging from 8K bytes to 32K bytes. It uses a LED display, interrupt capabilities including eight levels of software interrupt, and two levels of hardware interrupt and statistics hardware. It is an algebraic calculator, and does not use BASIC software. The unit employs plug-in read-only memory (ROM), and extra ROMs and memory can be increased as optional features. The unit also includes a built-in 16-character thermal printer with a 2.8 lines per second speed and a bidirectional cartridge, a four-memory input stack, 472 steps of program memory and 10 data storage registers.

microprocessor "slices" — An important variation to the fixed-word length 4-bit, 8-bit microprocessor designs is the building block design with either 2-bit or 4-bit "slices" which can be used to build up 8-, 12-, 16-, 24- and 32-bit wide architectures. The longer word length for both addressing and instructions provides higher throughput and easier programming while the shorter 4-bit word length uses less hardware and smaller memories. There are many examples of this modular approach where 4-bit slices can be used to build up the registers, arithmetic logic unit (ALU) and I/O data lines to 32-bit widths. Software support and I/O interfaces for these models are not practical.

microprocessor stack operation — One unit has 65k bytes of memory, and it is fabricated with NMOS technology so that it has only a 2 microsecond instruction cycle. A portion of the external memory can be used as a last-in, first-out stack, addressed by the stack pointer upon the execution of a CALL, RETURN or RESTART instruction. Moreover, not only the program counter but also the data registers, the accumulator and the flags can be saved in an external pushdown stack. As a result, multiple interrupts can be easily handled — similar to the way a mini does it.

microprocessor support — These items generally range from papertape readers and punches through floppy disks and large moving head disks. Complete lines of peripheral systems, peripheral controllers, diagnostics and software can be available to assist in developing microcomputer-based products and also for use within these products. Support permits the user to concentrate on designing his product, not spending time designing special interfaces. A complete line of general purpose interfaces is also a vital support necessity. Some systems are also supported by many chassis types, power supplies and types of consoles.

microprocessor support ICs — Support ICs, include: prototyping systems, design kits, development tools and other aids for the microprocessor user.

microprocessor terminal — The microprocessor can be either hardwired with PROMs and ROMs or with a user programmable random access memory (RAM), to provide alterable intelligence capabilities to terminals.

microprocessor unlimited peripheral and memory expansion — Using a bus system where all input/output connections merge into a common line, an external card can be plugged into any slot and it will function properly. The only qualification is that each card have an address decoder to allow the specific card to take what data it needs from the common bus and put data on the bus as required. Some processor buffers are designed to drive 300 external cards, which should be adequate for most applications.

microprocessor variations — Every microprocessor is different. Variations occur in architecture, chip layout, the random logic of the CPU, the fabrication processes and the instruction languages. There are also variations in I/O capabilities and pin count (18 to 48), the various bit sizes (4, 8, 12 and 16 bits) and the different bus organizations and there is no way to test all units. And, in fact, no one — neither the manufacturer nor the user — knows how to test a microprocessor fully.

microprocessors vs dedicated control — Microprocessors with ROM memory satisfy a wide range of random logic product applications. They offer cost advantages and ease of use for fast market response to high volume products, plus flexibility and a standard approach to one-of-a-kind products. In addition, microprocessors satisfy random logic design needs, such as low power, small size, and reliability.

microprogram — 1. Microprogramming became popular with the introduction of minicomputers a decade or more ago. It generally refers to computer instructions which do not reference the main memory. It is a technique to design subroutines by programming the very minute computer operations. As regards microprocessors, microprograms can implement a higher language program by storing microinstructions in ROM. 2. A program of analytic instructions which the programmer intends to construct from the basic subcommands of a digital computer. 3. A sequence of pseudo commands which will be translated by hardware into machine subcommands. 4. A means of building various analytic instructions as needed from the subcommand structure of a computer. 5. A plan for obtaining maximum utilization of the abilities of most calculators by efficient use of the subcommands of the machine. 6. A type of program that directly controls the operation of each functional element in a microprocessor. 7. A program of microcode; using basic subcommands.

microprogram, calculator — A sequence of microinstructions. The machine-level instruction is normally interpreted by a microprogram.

microprogram, calculator chip — A typical calculator chip is merely a microprocessor that has a built-in microprogram to solve arithmetic functions. So, for simple numerical calculations, many designers do not seek trouble with more versatile microprocessors. They take advantage of a calculator's powerful arithmetic internal instruction set. The software is already written.

microprogram control — A ROM and counter form the basis for execution control logic. To select and generate a timing sequence, users set the counter to the start value and increment it for each step. The ROM decodes each counter value to activate appropriate ROM-output lines. This technique is called microprogram control, since the contents of the ROM control the sequence of operations.

microprogram debugging — After the user has checked out as much of the system as possible with diagnostic programs, he is ready to begin debugging his microcode. The diagnostic checkout will tend to increase user confidence that the problems he encounters are in fact errors in the microprogramming and not hardware system problems. Microprograms are definitely easier to debug if they have been written in assembly language. For this purpose, the user can either write his own assembler or make use of the assembly program which permits him to generate an assembler to fill his need.

microprogrammability, user — User microprogrammability can be an extremely valuable feature. It allows the user to customize the calculator, dramatically increasing performance, increasing software security, or adding features that are important to a particular application but are not offered in the base instruction set. Input/output is another area that can benefit from special microprogramming. Since I/O is under direct microcode control, the application of microcoding for higher throughput in I/O-intensive applications should be very effective.

microprogrammable calculator I/O capabilities — I/O facilities include:
A) Serial and parallel 8-bit ports for slow to medium speed devices such as keyboards, card readers, and typing devices, etc.
B) Externally accessible STATUS lines into and FLAG lines out of the CPU to provide the handshaking capability necessary for the control of communications with peripherals.
C) A DMA port for high speed (up to 50K bits/sec) data transfer formatted 4-bit parallel, nibble serial.
D) Externally accessible STATIC SWITCH lines that can be individually tested by the CPU's unusually large (more than 230) and powerful instruction set.
E) Two vectored interrupts with software disable and enable commands. The vector addresses may be specified by software.
F) For input/output alone, a repetoire of 19 single-byte, machine-level and over 20 hi-level language instructions is provided to implement data and control transfers via the various ports of some systems.

microprogrammable calculator memory — On some units seven kilobytes of ROM and 512 bytes of RAM are used to implement the operating system and a repertory of hi-level instructions and mathematical functions. This microprocessor subsystem is complemented by 1K of RAM (optionally expandable) for program and data storage, one of four keyboards, one of two 21 column printers and a magnetic card reader/writer. Three of the keyboards have full program editing capability including those which have mathematical and scientific ROM's. Other units have mathematical and scientific ROM's and another series has mathematical and financial ROM's and 13 keys whose function is defined by the application program. These units offer additional program definable keys in place of the programming keys.

microprogrammable calculators — Microprogrammable series calculators are powerful and versatile self-contained Microcomputer systems which can be microprogrammed by users to customize the system to their unique requirements. An important measure of a microprocessor's power is its ability to communicate. To fulfill the demanding requirements of today's advanced instruments and peripherals, several modes of data transfer and control are necessary. One specific series of microprocessor systems uniquely satisfies this need with 7 input and 4 output ports with several data rates and formats.

microprogrammable instruction — All instructions which do not reference main memory (do not contain a memory address) can be microprogrammed, allowing the programmer to specify several shift, skip, or input/output transfer commands to be performed within one instruction.

microprogrammable processors — Microprocessors are CPUs implemented in microelectronics. A microprogrammable processor is one in which the instruction set is not firmly fixed; in which the instruction set is defined in a memory, the contents of which are fetched and used to control the internal data paths of the computer. Because the interpretation of the instruction is in a memory and the contents of memory can be changed, the meaning and effect of the instruction can be changed. This is called microprogramming.

microprogrammed microprocessor — In a microprogrammed processor, operations on the fundamental register-transfer level can be programmed. These basic operations are the elements of conventional machine instructions. With minicomputers or largescale computers, microprogramming employs a single high-speed memory whose outputs control the data paths in the systems either directly or through decoding logic. This memory is then programmed — in a manner analogous to conventional machine or assembly-language coding — to provide the functions needed for the processor's instruction set.

microprogramming techniques — There are very few techniques that have been widely publicized for writing efficient microprograms or developing efficient microcode. A few of the more frequently used techniques discussed often which are finding application in microprogramming are: 1. Indexing, 2. Subroutines, 3. Paramaterization. Many arithmetic operations are made up of a sequence of repetitive operations. For example, a multiply is made up of a sequence of adds and shifts. This sequence will be executed over and over again until the operation is completed. Index registers have been used in computers to count the number of times one goes through a sequence of instructions. The same technique is applicable to microprogramming.

microprogramming vs fixed instruction — Some microprocessors come with fixed instruction sets, around which software must be developed for an application. Other units offer options for microprogramming. This is the ability to alter or totally change the original instruction set. In essence, users program the microprocessor's internal microinstructions to obtain a macroinstruction set that is tailored to the application. The advantages of microprogramming include increased speed, since microinstructions are executed considerably faster than macroinstructions are. Also, the technique allows a more detailed level of control that can be used to reduce hardware; the program controls more functions.

microwave transmission — Transmission of voice, television, or data signals by means of highly directional, high-frequency radio waves that are received and transmitted from one line-of-sight station to another, until a terminal is reached. The microwave signals are electromagnetic wave in the SHF (superhigh frequency) portion of the ratio frequency spectrum (above 890 MHz). Their wavelengths are sufficiently short to exhibit some of the properties of light. Microwaves are usually used in point-to-point communications because they are easily concentrated into a beam. In addition to the microwave transmission used by the communications common carrier, many privately owned microwave systems are in service.

miniaturization — Refers to specific reduction of size for the purpose of increasing packing density of magnetic, electromechanical parts, or components of circuits, single or integrated. Miniaturization or microminiaturization reduces power requirements, delay of signal propagation and the distance signals must travel as well as space necessary for packing.

mini cartridge — The minicartridge looks like a cassette, but works like a 6″ by 4″ cartridge. The unit is smaller in length than a cassette (3″ to 4″), and also not as wide (2½″ to 2¼″). The maximum storage capacity is also smaller by 54%: 140′ of .15″ tape is used on the cartridge, while some cassettes have 300′ of .15″ tape. Actual storage, however, is dependent upon the encoding density and number of tracks, which means that the potential of the cartridge will depend upon the drives developed for it. The H-P (Hewlett Packard) minicartridge drive records on only one track at 800 bpi for storage of 115K bytes. H-P estimates their (and 3M's) minicartridge will last six to seven times longer than the cassette.

minicartridge control, calculator — On some units, memory load and record operations are performed via a minicartridge. The 2-track tape holds up to 250 kilobytes of data and has a 2.7 kilobyte/s transfer rate. If power should fail, an autostart feature permits information to be reloaded into calculator memory from the cartridge after power has been restored. Tape cartridge commands permit the user to load and record data, programs, or the entire memory. After tape files are recorded, they are automatically verified against the calculator memory.

minicartridge drives — On some cartridge drives, bidirectional search and rewind speeds are 90 in./s (2286 mm/s) and read/write speed is 22 in./s (559 mm/s). Average access time is, therefore, 6 s. Transfer rate is 2750 bytes/s, typical access rate is 14,300 bytes/s, typ rewind time is 19 s end-to-end, and typ erase time is 40 s for one entire track. Since the calculator always knows the location of the tape, it is able to search in either direction for the next bit of information, thereby saving time. Also, an operator can interrupt a long program, load the data onto the cartridge, run a short program, and then restart the first program.

mini cartridge, example — One type contains two tape transports which utilize the unique Mini Cartridge. Shirtpocket size, each cartridge contains precision tape guiding mechanics to assure interchangeability. Control of tension by an isoelastic band allows constant speed drive by a single motor. Full width recording increases data reliability and reduces dropout sensitivity. It stores up to 220 kilobytes formatted data (ASCII or binary). Variable length records (1 to 256 bytes) store data in ASCII or binary format. Up to 255 files may be addressed directly. Recording of 800 bits per inch allows many hours of typing to be stored on a single cartridge. Reading and writing of data are performed at 10 inches per second. Fast access of files is provided by high speed search of 60 inches per second for average access time of 10 seconds.

mini cartridge mass store characteristics — On some units 220 Kilobytes of Mass Storage is available. Other features are: 10 seconds average access time with high speed search.

- Each Mini Cartridge stores up to 110 kilobytes (formatted) in ASCII or binary data formats.
- Miniature in size (2″ × 3″ × ½″); contains precision tape guiding mechanics to assure interchangeability.
- Single motor drive means simple, high reliability mechanism.
- Single track, full width recording increases data reliability and reduces dropout sensitivity.
- Data integrity is assured with write protect lock, beginning and end of tape markers, and covered tape path.
- Unique isoelastic band controls tape tension to minimize tape wear.

minicomputer — 1. Generally a minicomputer is a mainframe that sells for less than $25,000. Usually it is a parallel binary system with 8, 12, 16, 18, 24 or 35-bit word length incorporating semiconductor or magnetic core memory offering from 4K words to 64K words of storage and a cycle time of 0.2 to 8 microseconds or less. A bare minicomputer (one without cabinet, console and power supplies) consisting of a single PC card can sell for less than $1,000 in OEM quantities. 2. These units are characterized by higher performance than microcomputers or programmable calculators, richer instruction sets, higher price and a proliferation of high level languages, operating systems, and networking methodologies. Examples HP 21MX Series, DEC PDP 11 Series, Data General Nova Series, General Automation Inc., Computer Automation Inc. products and those from scores of other innovative companies.

minicomputer communication processors — Minicomputers are being applied as efficient, low-cost front-end processors where they connect between a central computing facility and a communications network, performing communications control functions for the central computer.

minicomputer software — Minicomputer software has made great strides during the last 5 years. Many minicomputers support FORTRAN II and IV, BASIC and/or Assembly Languages. In addition, some minicomputers support ALGOL, RPGII, SNOBOL, COBOL, ATLAS, and Systems Programming Languages. Minicomputer operating systems have also made great strides in recent years. High performance Real Time, Multiprogramming, Multitasking, Time-sharing, Networked and Batched Systems have all been successfully implemented on minicomputers. The net result of the combination of high level, interactive languages and sophisticated operating systems on minicomputers has been extremely low cost, easy to use programmable logic for solving significant problems. High level languages provide powerful and flexible man-machine interfaces while operating systems manage significant system resources. These resources are placed at the disposal of the application system designer in such a manner that he orchestrates their use with dramatically reduced effort. Over time, this designer-machine in-

minimax — In game theory and other payoff tabular decisions, one of the methods of evaluating acts under uncertainty is to follow the principle of looking only at the worst possible consequence of each act and then to choose the act for which the worst consequence is the least desirable of the worst. This process thus minimizes the maximum loss or damage. This is contrasted to the maximin, a process in which one conservatively chooses the strategy to minimize or select the largest of the minimum gains. The saddle point is thus the maximum of the row minima (maximin) and the minimum of the column (minimax) when both occur at the same point in the payoff table.

minimum latency routine — Programming in such a way that minimum waiting time is required to obtain information from storage. Contrasted with random-access programming.

mini-printer calculator — A calculator's printing head is the electromechanical device that prints the paper tape. On a standard 8-digit printing calculator with vertical tape, a printing head has eight rows of ten digits or a total of 80 separate digits. When calculations are performed, all eight rows must respond. By using a single horizontal printing disc, the Mini-Printer requires only ten digits in one row.
Shown actual size:

$2 \times 3 = 6 \ldots 3 \times 6 = 18 \ldots T24 \ldots$
MEMORY TOTAL AND RECALL
$5 \div 3 = 1 \cdot 6666666$
FLOATING DECIMAL
$\ldots 144 \sqrt{12} \ldots$
SQUARE ROOT
$2 - 3 \div 5 \times 6 + 3 = 1 \cdot 8$
CHAIN CALCULATIONS
$56 - 567 = -511$
NEGATIVE BALANCE

The Mini-Printer uses standard paper — readily available $5/16''$ ticker tape. The tape costs only 30 cents a spool and gives over 10,000 impressions. (In a standard printer, that's equivalent to 1,250 rows of eight digits each row.) The ink cartridge will last over 100,000 impressions or almost a year and costs $2.50 to replace. (some units)

mini thermal printer, calculator — Refers to an alphanumeric output-only unit featuring fast speed, quiet operation, and low cost. One 5×7 dot matrix print head contains 35 heating elements which generate a 56-character set. The desired character is produced prior to contact with the heat-sensitive paper rather than on impact. It prints a maximum 80-character line at a rate of 30 characters per second.

minor control change — When control changes of different levels of significance are used, they can be given distinguishing titles — minor control change, then intermediate, or next major — to establish a hierarchy related to the importance of the data.

minor control data — The items of data, one or more of which are used to select, execute, identify, or modify another routine, record, file, operation, or data value.

minuend — The quantity from which another quantity is subtracted or is to be subtracted.

minus, data acquisition calculator — Allows entry of negative numeric values. Also special functions that permit arranging the system for continuous print. Also provides for setting of channel constants by blocks of channels. Key sets up a display of the channel constants code settings.

minus indicator (negative indicator) — A visual indicator, generally a minus sign ($-$) light to indicate a negative entry or answer. In many electronic calculators, the ($-$) occupies one of the display positions, reducing a negative number to a maximum of seven digits (for eight digit electronic calculators).

minus zone — The bit positions in a computer code that represent the algebraic minus sign.

misfeed — When cards, tapes, or other data or storage media fail to pass into or through a device properly. Causes may be damaged, misprogrammed, or missensed input.

(MIS) management-information system — A communications process in which data are recorded and processed for operational purposes. The problems are isolated for higher-level decision-making, and information is fed back to top management to reflect the progress or lack of progress made in achieving major objectives. An MIS gives the executive the capability of controlling the operation of a firm on a real-time basis.

mistake — A human failing; e.g., faulty arithmetic, use of incorrect formula, or incorrect instructions. Mistakes are sometimes called gross errors to distinguish from rounding and truncation errors. Thus, computers malfunction and humans make mistakes. Computers do not make mistakes and humans do not malfunction, in the strict sense of the word. (Contrasted with error.)

mixed calculations — The ability of an electronic calculator to perform multiple kinds of calculations within the same problem without continuously having to depress the ($=$) key.

MKS system — With recommendations accepted by the IEEE and many other engineering groups and organizations, the MKS (meter-kilogram-second) system is used in preference to the CGS (centimeter-gram-second) version of the metric system. The metric system uses a series of multipliers, all powers of ten, which, together with Greek and Latin terminology, indicate the actual size of its units. A kilogram, for example, is 10^3 or 1000 grams.

mnemonic — Assisting or intended to assist, memory; of or pertaining to memory; mnemonics is the art of improving the efficiency of the memory (in computer storage). See also label.

mnemonic code — Often referred to as 'memory codes' these are designed to assist programmers to remember instructions corresponding to a given operation. MPY for multiply, for example. Source statements can be written in this symbolic language and then translated into machine language.

mode, burst — The movement of a continuous bit stream between devices until an interruption of completion of the stream occurs. Compare with mode, byte.

mode, byte — The movement of one byte at a time between devices, separated by an interrupt and release of channel control. Used in multiplexing, the byte mode permits the handling of data from several low-speed devices simultaneously.

mode, compute — Also known as the operate mode, the input signals are connected to the computing units (analog computer), including integrators for the generation of the solution.

mode, control — The mode of operation in which characters on a line are interpreted for communications control.

mode, conversation — A condition of real-time communication between one or more remote terminals and a time-sharing computer, in which each entry from a terminal elicits an immediate response from the computer. The remote terminal thus can control, interrogate, or modify a task within the computer. Contrasts with mode, reactive.

model building — A problem is encountered in a "real world" setting, i.e., an environment. It must be translated in quantitative terms it must be abstracted from its environment, simplified, stripped of its complexities. It must be expressed in relationships — variables, constants, parameters, symbolically, as $Y = mx + b$. Verbal vagueness and ambiguity are replaced with specific and precise definition of the situation. Next forms of several functional relationships are adopted which link the variables and parameters. Finally, established is a criterion by which a decision may be judged, that is explicit and a unique objective function or range. Users solve the model by selected technique to find the value of the decision variables which optimize the objective. Evaluations and tests follow.

model, iconographic — A pictorial representation of a system and the functional relationships within.

modeling, conceptual — A method of making a model to fit the results of a biological experiment, then conducting another experiment to find out whether the model is right or wrong. The models are created continuously, and are tested and changed in a cyclic manner. The physical sciences have developed through the years in this way, but there has been little use of the approach in biology, mainly because the kind of mathematics that developed is not well suited to biology. But now calculators can get around this problem, and the important technique of conceptual modeling is beginning to be used in biology, business, psychology, sociology, etc.

model, mathematical — The general characterization of a process, object, or concept, in terms of mathematics, which enables the relatively simple manipulation of variables to be accomplished in order to determine how the process, object, or concept would behave in different situations.

models, input-output — Such classes of models as these are derived from assumptions about economic variables and behavior which take account of the general equilibrium phenomena and are concerned with the empirical analysis of production, i.e., especially intermediate uses and final output. The problem is to investigate what can be produced and the quantity of each intermediate product which itself must be used up in the production process. Various data are obtained initially which attest to available resources and current state of the technology.

models, organizing and communicating — Models have been used for centuries by designers, inventors, and engineers to put ideas into physical form. The model serves two necessary and useful purposes — comprehension and communication. Details of a new design often become too numerous and elaborate for visualization, and a model is required to put the ideas into tangible form such that each part can be tried and fitted to the others until a workable system has been achieved. Thus a model assists comprehension because it is in precise mathematics or symbols. A model often provides a superior means for communicating ideas. When a model is used, attention can be focused on a particular feature without isolating it from the rest of the system, the basic ideas under discussion can hardly be mistaken, and the discussion can be held to the point in question. Thus, a model is useful for organizing and communicating ideas.

model statement — A statement in the body of a macro definition or in open code from which an assembler language statement can be generated at pre-assembly time. Values can be substituted at one or more points in a model statement; one or more identical or different statements can be generated from the same model statement under the control of a conditional assembly loop.

models, utility — After the installation has been completed, the utility model of the system continues to be useful. It provides a basis for restudy to improve the system. It provides a basis for system changes necessitated by changing business conditions and new demands by management. The model provides a starting point for studies to extend electronic processes to new areas of application.

model symbols — The symbols such as squares, circles, etc., convey no information and must be labeled. They localize a point of interest, but convey only the most general notion of intent. The finished model must include adequate description with each symbol to explain what the operation does. Liberal use of foot-notes is recommended to explain the "why" of operations which are not straightforward.

modem — Refers to a MODulation/DEModulation chip or device that enables computers and calculators to communicate over telephone circuits.

modem, asynchronous — In asynchronous mode one character is sent at a time, preceded by a "start" signal and terminated by a "stop" signal. FSK modulation is usually employed; there the BPS and baud are equal. Since the transmission rate is determined by the digital signal, it may vary up to the maximum supported. The existing conventional rates are 110, 134, 150, and 300 BPS. Provision may exist in the character code (i.e., ASCII) for error detection in the form of character parity.

modem chip — Users can build a microprocessor chip into stand-alone MODEM systems or data storage, remote data communication terminals, or I/O interfaces for minicomputers. Users can develop it in full or half duplex, simplex, automatic answering or disconnect, answer only or answer/originate configurations. They can add output buffer, input filter, and threshold detector for a modem with supervisory controls for handshaking routines between remote modems and local control signals to the data handling system. Some are compatible with 100 Series data sets, 1001 A/B data couplers and include interfaces to telephone lines. Various units are TTL compatible and operate from a +5V power supply.

modem functions — The modem performs a transformation between the digital signal acceptable to the terminal, and network ports and the host computer and the analog signal employed for transmission. In the modem, the square-edged pulse train from the computer or terminal is transformed to fit in the telephone channel frequencies between 300 and 3330 Hz.

modem market changes — The current very rapid use of LSI circuitry for modem technology has been remarkable in recent years, primarily concerning telephone line standards and the adoption of baseband standards promulgated by the Electronic Industries Association. From a marketing standpoint, prophets suggest that a trend to LSI modems, mounted within terminal cabinets, will put an end to an industry dominated by manufacturers of stand-alone units. Others have said that all-digital communication networks, which eliminate the need for modems, will account for the industry's collapse. But despite these predictions, the industry, now characterized by almost 50 suppliers producing $50 to $60 million in modems each year, keeps on growing. Projections indicate that the number of modem installations will rise to about 5 million in 1980, from 1975 figure of 1.5 million. Currently, nearly two-thirds of all installed modems operate at speeds below 2400 bps, 42% can send and receive simultaneously and 31% can automatically answer an electronic request to send data. (1976)

modem operations — Because most data communication applications require the use of telephone lines as channels, modems operating at low transmission rates, up to 9600 bps, must take full advantage of limited bandwidths. At low speeds, frequency-shift modulation — using alternating tones to represent ones and zeros — suffices, but at high rates modems employ 4-, 8- or 16-phase-shift keying.

modem standards — Because of standards development by the EIA, most modems accept data in RS-232C format, which specifies signal levels and pin connections. The European data input standard is termed CCITT V.24. Conformance to these digital interface standards by peripheral and computer manufacturers has simplified the process of modem selection.

modem, synchronous — In the synchronous mode, characters are sent in a continuous stream, thus requiring three levels of synchronization: bit, character and message. Transmission is synchronized by a clock internal to the modem. This fixed rate transmission does not require start and stop bits.

modes, communication — Each channel is capable of operating in three different communication modes: input, output, or function. The input and output modes are employed when transferring data to or from the central computer. The function mode is the means by which the central computer establishes the initial communication path with a peripheral subsystem. During this mode of transmission, the central computer sends one or more function words to a peripheral subsystem. These function words direct the units to perform the desired operation (some computers).

mode, single step (hand-held programmables) — The Single Step operation in W/PRGM mode, SST advances the program pointer to the next memory location, displaying the code. Repeated use of the key enables users to review a program and to position the pointer for editing.

modes, learn, run, calculate — With a few keystrokes, the run mode allows users to quickly solve complex problems with programs from prerecorded magnetic cards. The calculate mode lets them use a hand-held unit as a powerful calculator to solve problems manually. And with the learn mode, users can literally teach the hand-held unit unique calculating methods. In some units all modes can use nine levels of parentheses. 20 independent memory registers and 224 program locations. When users combine this capability with pre-recorded programs, or programs they originate themselves, they have an extremely valuable computational resource at their fingertips.

mode, time sharing (Ready) — A user task in "ready" status can be executed or resumed. Usually a separate queue of ready tasks is maintained by the executive. Whenever a processor is available, the executive activates the task at the head of the ready queue changing its status to "running."

modular — A degree of standardization of computer-system components to allow for combinations and large variety of compatible units.

modular calculator — Various modular claculators on the market that can grow or change to meet new needs offer upgrading without costly modifications. If users buy a basic model and later find that they need more memory, a printer, alphanumeric capability, a different keyboard configuration, or an input or output peripheral; often some of them can be plugged into the existing model of some lines. Not only can users keep up with the growing complexity of their needs for computation — but their investment is protected from obsolescence ... if their systems are modular.

modularity — 1. A condition in the determination of the design of the equipment and programming systems such that the hardware and software components can be readily identified, altered, or augmented without replacements of particular units or sections. 2. Operating system programs conform to specific standards, so that control programs will have an identical interface with all processing programs. These standards are well documented so that user-written programs can follow the same conventions. The user is free to supplement supplied programs to meet special situations. By following the rules indicated in the standards, portions of control or processing programs can be changed or replaced in modular fashion.

modularity design — The processor, memory, device interfaces, backplane, and interconnecting hardware can be modular in design. Module selection, such as the type and size of memory, and device interfaces, enable custom tailoring to meet specific application requirements.

modulation — The variation of a signal or energy waveform in accord with some characteristic of another waveform.

modulation, amplitude (AM) — Refers to the basic form of modulation in which the amplitude of the carrier is varied in accordance with the instantaneous value of the modulating signal.

module — 1. A program unit that is discrete and identifiable with respect to compiling, combining with other units, and loading, e.g., the input to, or output from, an assembler, compiler, linkage editor, or executive routine. 2. A packaged functional hardware unit designed for use with other components.

module, communications — In some computer configurations, a high-speed data link connecting the input processor and supervisory computer.

Using this link, selected data is passed from the input computer to the supervisory computer for optimizing and feedforward calculations and the results cascaded to the input computer for adjustments to program limits and set points.

module, input — The device or collective set of devices used to bring data into another device, or a channel, or process device for transferring data from an external storage to an internal storage.

modulo-n check — 1. A check that makes use of a check number that is equal to the remainder of the desired number when divided by n, e.g., in a modulo check, the check number will be 0, 1, 2, or 3 and remainder of A when divided by 4 must equal the reported check number B, otherwise an equipment malfunction has occurred. 2. A method of verification by congruences, e.g., casting out nines. Related to number, self checking.

monadic — Refers to an operator that has only one operand.

monitor — 1. Unit in large computers which prepares the machine instructions from the source program, using built-in compilers(s) for one or more program languages; and feeds these into the processing and output units in sequence, once compiling is completed. It also controls time-sharing procedures. 2. A device that observes and verifies the operations of a data processing system and indicates any significant departure from the norm. 3. Software or hardware that observes, supervises, controls, or verifies the operations of a system.

monitor-controller, calculator — One type calculator system monitors, logs, processes and analyzes changes in a heating-air conditioning system. It computes BTU consumption as adjustments are made. The program tells a scanner where to take readings from electrical and temperature probes and transducers in the water, air and power lines. Digital voltmeters relay their readings to the calculator where the data is processed. It's a precise and low cost way to experiment with variables that can add up to big savings in energy costs today.

monitoring and measuring calculators — Some calculators control data logging and, at the same time, perform other required calculations, such as transducer linearization or statistical analysis. A data acquisition system can measure multiple physical parameters and monitor devices. It's also suited for research work, as well as production testing. Users can test 100% of their pc boards or other electronic devices, at a fraction of the cost of a computerized system. If users need to obtain or send data elsewhere from their test site some firms offer an optional common carrier interface, and Data Access Arrangements (DAAs) can be rented from the phone company or others for remote transmission.

monitoring system, microprocessor — Monitoring chores, simple control functions are being provided for automatic light control and real-time clock generated interrupt signals at fixed, preset, intervals on some systems. The processor recognizes the time of each interrupt, and it can dim the lights or turn them off to conserve electricity. Light-control commands employ flag bits provided by the CPU chip. Another function is temperature control of the buildings through the regulation of heater and air conditioners.

monitor, microcomputer — A typical basic monitor system includes a CPU Board, with a console board, a keyboard with fully-decoded digits; a Breadboard, for assembling custom circuitry; and a PROM/RAM board, with a minimum 256 bytes of RAM, and a PROM containing a versatile monitor program. Fully assembled and tested, these systems are available as a monitor system.

monitor, microprocessor — Some systems reside in PROMs in the mainframe. They provide an operating system enabling program development to be carried out with a wide range of peripherals. Debugging is fast because users can do real-time break pointing, and can examine and modify all memory and CPU status information. Linkage points are available which permit user access to monitor routines. (some units)

monitor, operating system — Generally, most monitors exercise primary control of the routines that compose the operating system. It is the operating system which turns the calculator into a flexible tool allowing the user to achieve maximum use of the hardware's advanced design features.

monitor, real-time — The executive system is an operating and programming system designed to monitor the construction and execution of programs, to optimize the utilization of available hardware, and to minimize programmer effort and operator intervention. The executive system, as a monitor, provides for concurrent processing and real-time operation in a classical monitor environment. The executive system is of modular construction, tailored to each user's equipment configuration and applications requirements. Extensions to the system for peripheral devices and application programs may be added, altered, or deleted as required, on some systems.

monolithic — Refers to the single silicon substrate in which an integrated circuit is constructed. See: integrated circuit.

monomial — Refers to an algebraic expression consisting of but one term. For example, xy, 3ab, and 2y are monomials.

monte carlo method — A trial and error method of repeated calculations to discover the best solution of a problem. Often used when a great number of variables are present, with inter-relationships so extremely complex as to forestall straightforward analytical handling.

morpheme — An element of language which relates and connects images or ideas in sentences; i.e., the relation between a noun and a verb.

morphology — The branch of linguistic study that deals with the history and functions of derivational forms and inflections.

MOS — Metal Oxide Semiconductor — 1. Refers to the layers of material, and indirectly to a fundamental process for fabricating ICs. MOS circuits achieve high component densities. 2. The basic technology is a circuit structure called MOSFET, the FET representing Field Effect Transistor or Transfer. It concerns metal on or over silicon oxide or silicon. The metal electrode is the gate; the silicon oxide is the insulator, and the carrier-doped regions in the silicon substrate become the drain and source. The result is a sandwich very much like a capacitor, the sandwich effect causing MOS to be somewhat slower in speed than bipolar. MOS advantages are: process simplicity, functional density, ease of interconnection on chips. MOS broke the LSI barrier — and bipolar has done the same.

MOS calculator chip set — One type calculator

set of two MOS chips reportedly contains the complete electronics for 12-digit, 4-function calculators, including the drive circuitry for gas discharge displays. The two chips, contained in one 40-lead and one 28-lead silicone-molded DIP, include the clock oscillator, power-on clear circuitry, floating decimal point for input, selectable fixed decimal point in the display, selectable rounding (up, down or 5/4), exchange key, constant factor, percent add-on and discount, full memory, automatic underflow and overflow protecting the 12 most significant digits.

MOS circuits — Refers to Metal-Oxide Semiconductors. These are semiconductors using a technology which offers very low power dissipation and hence can be made into circuits which jam transistors close together before a critical heat problem arises. Most monolithic memories, calculators and electronic watches use this technology.

MOS multiplexer — One typical high speed MOS multiplexer is capable of selecting up to 16 input channels. Four basic versions of the multiplexer card assembly are available having 4, 8, 12 and 16 input channels. "A" suffix models are capable of operation from -5 to $+5$ volts, while the "B" suffix version operates from -10 to $+10$ volts.

mother board line buffering — Some types of mother boards provide the line buffering and address decoding for up to eight interface boards. Although one of the eight must be the control interface (serial), the other seven may be any combination of serial and parallel interfaces the user may choose to have. For those demanding even more interfaces often a 50 line processor buss may be paralleled onto another Mother Board with power supply expanding the interfacing to one control interface (serial), plus any combination of up to fifteen serial and parallel interfaces, on some systems.

movable heads — Reading and writing transducers on bulk memory devices which can be positioned over the data locations.

moving average — The moving average is the average of the last N data items input; data may be input continuously. However, only the last N items are retained. The output is the average of these last N items. N must not exceed the number of main data registers in the user's machine.

MPL compiler — MPL is a high-level, user-oriented programming language for the Motorola M6800 Microprocessor. The language is a subset of PL/I with features chosen for applicability to the microprocessor environment. MPL was designed to simplify the translation from functional requirements for a microprocessor application to operating M6800 programs. The MPL language and its associated compiler provide a powerful software tool which can significantly reduce the time and costs associated with microprocessor software development and maintenance.

MPS — 1. Microprocessor system or series. 2. Meters per second.

MPS interface modules — In developing an interface structure for an MPS system, the user can take two approaches: (1) design the interface using a wire wrap board, or (2) use available series modules. In either case, a wide variety of MPS-compatible modules and accessories are available off-the-shelf. Typically a device selector may be used to decode the device address from the processor. Other modules serve as efficient input and output interfaces. For custom interface circuitry, wire wrappable modules provide a foundation upon which to build integrated circuit interfaces.

MPU — Microprocessor unit.

MQ — An abbreviation for Multiplier-Quotient register.

MSD — Most significant digit. See digit, significant.

MSG — Most significant character (left-most).

MSI — Medium-scale integration is a measure of the number of circuit components, like transistors, formed on a single chip.

MTBF — An abbreviation for Mean Time Between Failures.

mu — Greek letter used as symbol for amplification factor; micro-; micron; permeability.

multi-access — Multi-access systems permit several people or groups to transact with the computer through the operator's console or many on-line terminals. Access points are generally connected to the central processor by data transmission lines from remote terminals which can be typewriters, visual display units, CRTs (Cathode-Ray Tubes), or satellite processors. Multi-access multiprogramming systems have been installed by many universities, laboratories, businesses, and research groups. Most operate in a conversational mode with fast response time and are controlled by operating systems.

multidimensional arrays — Allows users to organize data logically, thus saving program space and execution time. A 20×20 matrix can be inverted in 10 seconds on some units.

multi-function keys — On some units many keys now perform three commands. Some commands are labeled in gold above a key, or labeled in blue on the underside of a key, and activated by first pressing the appropriate gold or blue prefix key(s).

multi-function scanner, calculator-based data acquisition systems — In the usual data acquisition system, a scanner switches several inputs one by one to a single instrument for measurement and recording. It can serve as a programmable switch for actuating external processors or for distributing power and/or signals. It can also connect more than one channel at a time so it is able to make the multiple connections needed for four-wire resistance or floating bridge measurements. Where there may be more than one measuring and/or stimulus channel to be connected to a multiport device, a scanner can also be configured to make the multiple switch closures needed for matrix switching. A scanner is designed to work an interface bus in calculator-controlled systems. It is addressable and once addressed. It accepts and stores channel addresses until it receives the EXECUTE command, which then causes the indicated channels to open or close.

multijob operation — The simultaneous, concurrent, or interleaved execution of job parts, steps, or segments from more than one job. A type of multiprogramming, when each job or part waits for some external event to occur before it can continue processing: or each job, job part, or step has its own instruction and data areas and may be shared.

multi-length arithmetic — Arithmetic accomplished using two or more machine words to store each operand, most often to attain greater precision in the result. Arithmetic involving the generation of a result which requires to be stored in two or more words.

multi-level interrupt structure — The communication interfaces and modem controllers should be capable of generating interrupts requesting service from the program, and to notify the program of changes in the condition of some of the communication control lines such as data carrier, data set ready, clear-to-send, etc. For a dynamic communication system, in which conditions are changing rapidly, the program should have the capability of suppressing interrupts, and/or selectively modifying the conditions which can cause interrupts.

multilevel priority interrupts — In many large systems interrupt provisions have been made to facilitate the priority requirements of various subroutines. Specifically, the interrupt requests of these subroutines are handled by the central processor in the sequence of the highest priority. If a priority subroutine requests an interrupt, it will have priority over all subroutines of lower priority, even though they have previously requested an interrupt.

multimeter, data acquisition system — A typical digital unit offers:
- low level measurements with 5 digit resolution.
- added flexibility of dc or ac volts and resistance measurement capability.
- four readings/second.
- cost saving, built-in self-test.
- easy system expandability with an interface bus.

multiple bus architecture — The multiple bus architecture greatly minimizes the number of components required to build high-performance systems. A complete functional system can be implemented without external multiplexers or ancillary logic. The use of bipolar computing elements means that byte swapping, and other special functions, may be implemented directly with no external logic required.

multiple calculators and platters, calculator mass memory — Some mass memory systems have extremely large storage capacities. Each disk, or platter, as it is frequently called, can store 2.4 million bytes. Therefore, one mass memory is usually enough for an individual user. For applications that require still more storage, some Controllers can handle up to four platters in the same system, giving a total storage capacity of 9.6 million bytes. This offers many important system advantages.

multiple-length arithmetic — Arithmetic accomplished using two or more machine words to store each operand, most often to attain greater precision in the result. Arithmetic involving the generation of a result which requires to be stored in two or more words.

multiple precision — The use of two or more computer words to represent a single numeric quantity or numeral, i.e., with twice as many or more digits as are normally carried in a fixed-length word.

multiple precision arithmetic — A feature of the computer system which allows more than one word to be used to accomodate a quality expressed in more than one word length; this avoids the cutoff of a lesser significant digit.

multiple programming — The programming of a computer by allowing two or more arithmetical or logical operations to be executed simultaneously parallel. (Contrasted with serial programming.)

multiple regression program — (1) This program calculates the coefficients of the normal equations which are required for determining the regression equation. The program is done in two parts, Part 1 is for the data entries and the summations for the normal equations; Part 2, a modified version of solution of N-Simultaneous equations, determines the coefficients of the regression equation. (2) Multiple Linear Regression Analysis. Given a set of user-defined transformation function, sets of observed values for several independent variables X, and the corresponding values for the dependent variable Y, this program uses a least square fit method to perform a linear regression on the transformed independent variable, finding the coefficients A_j in the equation. As many as 15 independent variables can be accommodated in a -44 memory configuration; as many as 9 different transformation functions can be applied to each of the independent variables. (3) Multiple Regression, Three Variables. Makes the necessary computations for a multiple regression study between two independent and one dependent variable. Program computes the coefficients of the model, $Y = AX_1 + BX_2 + C$, along with the multiple and partial coefficients of correlation to enable significance testing via t tests or Anova.

multiple storage controller, calculator — For applications that require more storage, some Controllers can handle up to four platters in the same system, giving a total storage capacity of 9.6 million bytes. This offers some important advantages to the user. For example, he can access separate data bases stored on different cartridges and process the data on another platter. It also makes duplication of important data bases very simple. To match this storage and accessing capacity, the controller can also handle up to four calculators in the same system. Any of the four calculators can access any of the four platters connected to the system. Each platter contains the full system software and is not dependent on any of the others for its operation. (some systems)

multiplex channel — Some synchronous multiplex channels can each receive and transmit synchronous data at any rate selected by the modem up to 50,000 baud. The synchronous mux generates the flag sequence to provide the synchronizing character, converts the outgoing message from parallel to serial form, inserts a zero bit following five one bits to distinguish between a flag sequence and data, and generates the 16-bit Cyclic Redundancy Check (CRC) codes.

For incoming data, the process is simply reversed. The mux sense the flag sequence, checks for and extracts the zero bit, converts data from serial to parallel form, examines the CRC word, and packs the 8-bit characters in memory.

multiplex data terminal — A device that modulates and/or demodulates data between two or more input/output devices and a data transmission link.

multiplexer channel — 1. The communications multiplexer channel is a data processing and communications "coordinator." Systems equipped with communications multiplexer channels can manage the myriad data-transfer problems inherent in complex configurations. 2. A channel designed to operate with a number of I/O devices simultaneously. Several I/O devices can transfer records at the same time by interleaving items of data.

multiplexing — Refers to a process of transmitting more than one signal at a time over a single link, route, or channel in a communica-

multiplex (MUX)

tions system. There are many types of multiplexing, and microprocessors are playing a significant part in the development of low-cost multi-switching control that multiplexers require.

multiplex (MUX) — To interleave sequentially and transmit two or more messages on a single data channel. In some calculators the MUX cards feed each channel in turn into the measuring circuit and microprocessor under control of the program.

multiplex (mux) port — Some asynchronous mux ports have two data lines (incoming and outgoing) and two control lines (the outgoing Device Control line and the incoming Device Status line). The mux transmitter receives the data from the computer, converts it from parallel to serial form, inserts a start and stop bit, inserts a parity bit (if enabled), and transmits the data at the rate selected for the port.

The receiver portion reverses the process. Circuitry on the mux checks each port once per 100 microseconds for an input request. When such a request is found, the mux reads the control word for that port and carries out the indicated operations — including access of the automatic buffer or interrupt of the computer, depending upon the conditions.

multiplicand — The quantity which is multiplied by each digit of the multiplier to form the product in the operation of multiplication.

multiplication — Actions or processes which result in multiplying, i.e., determination of the product by repeatedly adding the same quantity (multiplicand) a discrete number of times (multiplier) which involves the shifting of the radix point (or decimal point in decimal computers or values) to the right.

multiplication function example, calculator — On some units this offers a product up to 12 digits. If answer causes overflow or underflow, 12 most significant digits are displayed and printed.
If overflow occurs, printer prints error symbol in red. "K" key for constant factor operation (first factor in multiplication) allows simple power calculations. Signed results on display. Results printed in red (negative) or black (positive) Algebraic logic. Solution time is 250ms max at 100kHz with display only.

multiplication key — On some units this key conditions the calculator for multiplication and will also execute a previously conditioned multiply or divide operation. The answer will be displayed but not printed. Multiple depressions of the "X" key are ignored. (some units)

multiplication shift — A shift which results in multiplication of the number by a positive or negative integral power of the radix, with special treatment to the sign digit. With floating-point numbers, only the fixed-point part is treated.

multiplication table — A specific area of storage that holds the groups of numbers to be used during the tabular scanning of the multiplication operation.

multiplier — The operand which controls the repetitive addition of the multiplicand in the operation of a multiplication.

multiplier, coefficient constant — A device, such as a linear amplifier, that develops an output equal to an input multiplied by a constant.

multiplier, constant — A computing element that multiplies a variable by a constant factor.

multiprogrammer controller

multiplier, electronic — An all-electronic device capable of forming the product of two variables. Examples are a time-division multiplier, a square-law multiplier, an AM-FM multiplier, and a triangular-wave multiplier.

multiplier factor — In multiplication, when the method of performance makes a distinction between two factors, they are called the multiplier factor and the multiplicand.

multiplier, functional — A device which will take in the changing values of two functions and put out the changing value of their product.

multiplier-quotient register — Refers to a specific register in which the multiplier for multiplication is placed and in which the quotient for division is developed.

multiplier unit — A unit which is capable of generating a product from the representations of two numbers, often formed by repeated additions of the multiplicand or multiples of it. See adders, subtracters, etc.

multiprocessing — 1. Refers to various computer configurations consisting of more than one independently initiable processor, each having access to a common, jointly-addressable memory. 2. Processing several programs or program segments concurrently on a time-share basis. Each processor is only active on one program at any one time while operations such as input/output may be performed in parallel on several programs. The processor is directed to switch back and forth among programs under the control of the master control program.

multiprocessing efficiency — Two or more processors are put in the system configuration. One processor is assigned to control the system, with the others subordinate to it. All processors have direct access to all memory; each can perform computations and request input/output on individual programs stored in system core memory. Multiprocessing is more economical. Throughput and reliability are retained without resorting to interconnection of multiple computers with redundant unused circuits.

multiprogrammer, bidirectional system interface — The Multiprogrammer mainframes and plug-ins function together as an integrated unit possessing many built-in systems features. Among these features are:
(1) Digital data storage on plug-in output cards to reduce controller processing overhead. (2) The ability to program most output cards to a safe state (in case of system failure or alarm). (3) The ability to program specific output cards individually or in selected groups. (4) The generation of a service request when digital lines being sensed change state. (5) The program selection of data transfer rates between the controller and the Multiprogrammer to proceed either at the maximum possible rate or at a rate governed by a particular device being controlled by a plug-in card. (6) A front-panel switch register on the mainframe which permits manual control of the system.

multiprogrammer control — On some systems each Extender mainframe accommodates up to fifteen programmable plug-in cards. Up to fifteen extenders can be chain-cabled together to obtain up to 240 individually addressable I/O channels. Extenders may be separated from one another by up to 30 meters.

multiprogrammer controller — One unit con-

multiprogrammer functions

trols the bidirectional transfer of data between the Multiprogrammer Interface and the plug-in cards installed in the Multiprogrammer and Extender Mainframes. The unit has a basic 15-channel (plug-in card) I/O capacity.

multiprogrammer functions — Stimulus, measurement, control, acquisition. Combinations of these four functions are essential to every automatic system. Various company manuals illustrate these capabilities in a simplified form and list the plug-in cards used in implementing each function. Complete specifications on the Multiprogrammer mainframes and plug-in cards are provided in a Multiprogrammer Brochure. (Hewlett-Packard Co.)

multiprogrammer I/O cards — Several different types of multiprogrammer input and output cards are available to interface with process instruments. Input card functions include current monitoring, voltage monitoring, digital input, counting, and event sensing. Output functions cover stimulus and control including voltage, current, resistance, relay contacts, digital bit patterns, stepping motor control, time and frequency references. Cards may be added or changed as the functions of a real-time test and control system change.

multiprogrammer kit, HP-IB — This is designed for do-it-yourself system solutions. Multiprogrammer building-block components include an interface unit, two types of mainframes, and a family of programmable plug-in cards.

For small systems, users can start with a calculator, interface unit and a Mainframe with from one to 15 plug-in cards. The cards are randomly addressable by the program allowing them to be mixed in any order within the mainframe; users can add cards to the system as their needs change. The calculator program "writes" data on output cards or "reads" data from input cards. An output or "write" operation is carried out by simply setting up the proper modes, addressing the desired card and depositing data bits in the card's storage registers. Conversion circuits then develop the output function (contact closures, D/A conversion, stepping motor drive, etc.) unique to that type of output card. To "read" data, the calculator sends out the desired input card's address and reads in digital data from the external device.

multiprogrammer mainframes — Multiprogrammer mainframes and plug-ins function together as an integrated unit possessing many built-in systems features. Among these features are:
- Digital data storage on plug-in output cards to reduce controller processing overhead.
- The ability to program most output cards to a safe state (in case of system failure or alarm).
- The ability to program specific output cards individually or in selected groups.
- The generation of a service request when digital lines being sensed change state.
- The program selection of data transfer rates between the calculator and the Multiprogrammer to proceed either at the maximum possible rate or at a rate governed by a particular device being controlled by a plug-in card.
- A front-panel switch register on the mainframe which permits manual control of the system and thus enhances serviceability.

multiprogramming — A technique whereby two or more routines or programs may be executed concurrently by a computer through an interweaving process using the same arithmetic and logic units.

multiprogramming interrupts — Some computers are equipped with a set of control signals which are referred to as interrupts. Whenever certain conditions exist, a control signal will direct the central computer to execute the word (instruction) at a specified address in central store. Each interrupt is activated by unique conditions and directs the computer to a correspondingly unique address in central store. The occurrence of an interrupt terminates guard mode, program lockin, and central-store address assignments.

multiprogramming, time-share — Refers to procedures for handling numerous routines or programs seemingly simultaneously by overlapping or interleaving their execution, that is, by permitting more than one program to time-share machine components.

multiprogramming, master-slave — Refers to a system designed to guarantee that one program cannot damage or access another program sharing memory. The unique operating technique in changing from slave to master mode makes multiprogramming not only practical, but foolproof.

multiprogramming memory protect — This hardware function provides positive protection to the system executive routine and all other programs. It not only protects against processor execution, but also against I/O data area destruction. Because it is a hardware function rather than software, it reduces multiprogramming complexities.

multireading feature — With the utilization of storage, cards are read only once and data from each field is read out of the storage on the following cycles, thus separate cycle reading for each line of print is unnecessary.

multireel sorting — The automatic sequencing of a file having more than one input tape, without operator intervention.

multisequencing — The simultaneous execution of several parts of a program by separate central processing units.

multistation — Any network of stations capable of communicating with each other, whether on one circuit or through a switching center.

multitasking — Refers to procedures in which several separate but inter-related tasks operate under a single program identity; differs from multiprogramming in that common routines and data space as well as disk files may be used. May or may not involve multiprocessing.

multithread — Used on a program which can have more than one logical path through it being executed simultaneously.

multivariate analysis programs — Examples are: Discriminant Analysis, Canonical Correlation, Factor Analysis, others.

mylar — A Dupont trademark for polyester film often used as a base for magnetically coated or perforated information media.

N

nano — Prefix for 10^{-9} (a billionth) times a specified unit.

natural function generator — Relates to either an analog device or a specific program based on some physical law, such as one used with a digital computer to solve a particular differential equation.

navigation program pack — Various programs to assist the marine navigator in piloting and dead reckoning, celestial navigation and relative motion problems.

NC — Abbreviation for numerical control.

n-channel MOS (NMOS) — With N-channel, higher substrate doping levels are practical, which means that transistors can be placed closer together, further increasing the packing density. However, in the N-channel manufacturing process the silicon surface becomes very lightly doped, resulting in increased leakage currents. Unless processing is carefully controlled, a wide variation in leakage occurs both initially and with time. This fact relates to memory circuit selection — dynamic circuits are much more sensitive to leakage current and its changes than static circuits. This is a major reason why many choose a static design for their N-channel memory components.

n-channel, p-channel — Refers to two kinds of transistors that can be fabricated using MOS technology. They are named for the type of charge carrier used for the channel through which controlled flows of current pass. N-channel is generally faster but harder to fabricate. Users may be familiar with PNP and NPN transistors which are the corresponding types of bipolar circuitry.

N/C (numerical-control) machines — A punched paper or plastic tape with magnetic spots is used to feed digital instructions to a numerical-control machine, i.e., an automated cutting or forming machine thus guided. Tolerances as fine as 1/10,000 of an inch are achieved on unattended units. Tapes are developed from digital computer programs.

N count key — Automatically counts the number of factors entered in addition or subtraction, or the number of problems completed in accumulative multiplication or division.

N/C system (numeric control) — Refers to a system which uses prerecorded intelligence prepared from numerical data to control a machine or process. The N/C system consists of all elements of the control system and of the machine being controlled that are, in fact, a part of the servomechanism.

negative — 1. Less than zero. 2. The opposite of positive. 3. A terminal or electrode having an excess of electrons. The electrons flow out of the negative terminal of a voltage source, toward a positive source. Abbreviated neg. 4. Relating to gating, the same as NOT, i.e., negative AND is the same as NOT AND or NAND, negative OR is the same as NOT OR or NOR, etc.

negative binomial — Refers to a Negative Binomial Probability Function. Computes individual and cumulative terms of the negative binomial function.

neon gas discharge tubes — Neon gas-discharge tubes and panels call for their own decoding and driving schemes. Some circuits have been developed for multiplexing them which reduces the number of active components in driving the display. Capacitors are used in level shifting from MOS output levels to the high voltage on either the anode or cathode side of the display.

nest — 1. Refers to an activity to embed a subroutine or block of data into a larger routine or block of data. 2. To evaluate an nth degree polynomial by a particular algorithm which uses (n-1) multiply operations and (n-1) add operations in succession.

nested two factor analysis program — This program determines the Analysis of Variance for a two-factor experiment where the second factor is nested within the first. This experiment is also called a Hierachal Design.

nesting loop — Refers to nesting loops that usually contain a loop of instructions which then also contain inner loops, nesting subroutines, outer loops, and rules and procedures relating to in and out procedures for each type.

nesting storage types — As data is transferred into storage, each word in turn enters the top register and is then "pushed down" the column from register to register to make room for the subsequent words as they are assigned. When a word is transferred out of the storage, again only from the top register, other data in the storage moves back up the column from register to register to fill the space left empty. This is accomplished either through programs or the equipment itself.

nesting subroutines, calculator — This refers to the technique of having one subroutine call another. On most units, each time subroutines are linked, the return address register is updated. This process of updating the return address register destroys any previous address. That means to "nest" subroutines successfully, users want to preserve the return address in some other register prior to calling the next subroutine. This is accomplished by storing the return address in a different register. When they want to return to the main program, they "recall" that register, instead of the "return address" register, to return to the main program. By using unique "save" registers, subroutines can be nested to as many levels as users think they'll need. (some units)

nesting, two-level calculator — Some programmable calculators which follow the algebraic rules of equation solving for keyboard entry permit two-level nesting. By a single keystroke 28 or more mathematical and statistical functions can be provided. These units offer optional user-definable keys which allow the user to address up to three programs or subroutines by one key depression. Some units provide 512 program steps with additional steps as an option in increments of 512 steps up to a total of 4096. Also, symbolic addressing and indirect addressing techniques make two routines immediately available to users on each designed key.

network — 1. A combination of elements. 2. An interconnected system of transmission lines that provides multiple transmissions between loads and sources of generation. 3. A series of points connected by communications channels. 4. The switched telephone network is the network of telephone lines normally used for dialed telephone calls. 5. A private network is a network of communications channels confined to the use of one customer.

network analysis program, circuit (CNAP) — Users can model a complex, active circuit design and have complete solutions automatically documented within a few minutes. They simply enter component values and node interconnections and define the plotter interval and bounds. The calculator takes it from there and quickly solves the problem using an HP (Hewlett-Packard) software routine patterned after the well-known ECAP circuit analysis program. User response data is printed in tabular form by the calculator while the plotter produces a Bode plot showing predicted amplitude and phase response. If circuit performance doesn't meet user specifications, it's a simple matter to modify component values and rerun the program until the user gets optimum results.

network, ARPA — The Advanced Research Projects Agency network enables computers to share their computing and storage capacities with each other and thus make their combined data processing power available to a large number of users. Utilizing 50-kilobit phone lines and packet switching, it has become the largest inter-computer network by linking over 40 computers of many different kinds. The network has achieved high reliability, coast-to-coast transit times under ½ second per message, and its incremental communication costs are about 30 cents per megabit. Further advances, including satellite extensions, megabaud data rates, communications security, and remote job entry devices, are under development.

network calculator — Combination of resistors, inductors, capacitors, and generators used to simulate electrical characteristics of a power generation system, so that the effects of varying different operating conditions can be studied in computers.

network intelligence, microcomputer — Distributed-intelligence systems can be more efficiently built with the new generation of microcomputers. The computational and control capabilities allow each micro in the network to perform a dedicated task. The over-all network can provide hardware and software redundancy at an attractive price — compared with a single large processor. Common-memory, software and hardware techniques provide one of the newest ways to handle the necessary intercommunication between subsystems. Microcomputer sets that include CPU, memory and I/O adapters can be purchased for less than $50. In a distributed-intelligence system, each of these units or processors has a dedicated function, typically I/O oriented. Since the system is oriented towards maximum I/O throughput, processor cross-communication is held to a minimum.

network node A network node performs a number of network internal functions and can be the network interface to the outside world. A node controls outgoing traffic on some or all of the channels connected to it through a channel allocation mechanism. If the node is simply a multiplexer, this function is performed by hardware that multiplexes the outgoing channels in either the frequency or time domain.

network processor — A network processor that incorporates 16K RAM chips, is designed for use at intermediate network locations. One type allows up to 64 local displays to access a central data base of up to 270M bytes through direct channel connection of two display processors. The system includes multiple DMA channels, software and hardware error recovery facilities, firmware diagnostics, a memory relocation and protection system, and communications control for up to six highspeed lines.

network processors, microcomputer — More complicated algorithms and the declining cost of programmable processors have made it attractive to replace hardwired multiplexes with microcomputers. They improve the efficiency of the network by permitting more sophisticated line control procedures, which may also facilitate recover from failure situations. Some of the functions previously performed by the main computer, or the front-end processor, may be delegated to the concentrator giving a more immediate response to the terminal.

network services — Refers to services which attract users to networks which are: access to computer power, programs, and data bases. They are primarily functions of the host systems on the network. These networks ought to be completely transparent with respect to the delivery of these services.

new input queue — A group or a queue of new messages that are in the system and are waiting for processing. The main scheduling routine will scan them along with other queues and order them into processing.

next chan (channel), data acquisition calculator — Key selects current channel plus one for monitoring and/or programming. A programming shortcut!

next scan, data acquisition calculator — The time set for the next scan is displayed when this key is pressed. Key initiates procedures to change or establish a new next scan time.

NiCd — NiCd (nickel Cadmium) batteries are the power supply for most electronic calculators with rechargeable batteries.

nickel-cadmium batteries — Nickel-cadmium batteries are becoming ever more popular in cordless consumer products and electronics building. Although initial cost may seem to be high, nickel-cadmium cells can be recharged so often that their per-unit-of-use performance actually makes them less expensive than almost any other type of battery in the long run. Aside from rechargeability and reasonable cost, these batteries can often directly replace ordinary disposable carbon-zinc cells.

Just as there are differences between bipolar and field-effect transistors (although they are both transistors), there are basic differences between nickel-cadmium cells and other types. Indeed, there are different types of nickel-cadmium batteries, too.

nickel-cadmium battery advantages — Sealed nickel-cadmium cells have a number of outstanding characteristics that make them good first choices for everyday use. They are reusable, permitting up to 1000 charge/discharge cycles. Their terminal voltage during discharge holds relatively constant. And they require no special care. There are some minor disadvantages. High initial cost is one, although it is counterbalanced by the fact that the cells are reusable. Another is that the typical nickel-cadmium cell, when compared with the same-size carbon-zinc cell, has a lower capacity and a lower terminal voltage (1.2 V as opposed to 1.5 V for the carbon-zinc cell). The balance, however, is in the nickel-cadmium cell's favor when it comes to long life, convenience of use, and reliability.

nickel-cadmium battery characteristics — General details are: The energy that a nickel-cadmium battery supplies is stored in the chemical compounds formed in the cell. The active material in the cell is nickel hydroxide in the positive plate and metallic cadmium in the negative plate. During discharge, the cadmium metal supplies electrons to the external circuit and becomes oxidized to cadmium hydroxide, while the nickel hydroxide accepts electrons from the circuit and goes to a lower valence state. The reverse process occurs during the recharging.

nine edge — The lower or bottom edge of a Hollerith card. This edge is most commonly used for entering the equipment first because of equipment requirements.

nine's complement — Incorporated in some ALUs is a 9's complement circuit to generate the necessary BCD complement functions. The 9's complementer is used with the following BCD instructions: A minus 0, 0 minus A, 9's comp A. and 9's comp 0. The 9's complement circuit is automatically enabled when the above functions are selected by the ALU select lines, and requires no special attention.

NIXIE display indicators — Some display capabilities concern NIXIE indicator tubes. The tubes are all-electronic, gas filled, cold-cathode indicators that display numerals, letters, or special symbols. These devices are one of the industry's widely used electronic readouts and are ideal for converting electromechanical or electronic signals directly to readable characters. NIXIE tube assemblies and display systems fall into two distinct categories, numeric and alphanumeric. The numeric types are generally used in digital voltmeters, frequency counters, and other devices where digital information of a decimal nature must be displayed. The alphanumeric types are used in schedule boards, arrival-departure displays, computer readout panels, stock-quotation systems, and in other applications where a minimum of 36 characters (ten numbers and 26 letters) are required. (Burroughs)

noise — An unwanted component of a signal or variable which obscures its information content.

nominative testing — Standards of performance that are established for the testing of both quantitative and qualitative system performance.

non-add key — A key which allows numbers, symbols, etc. to be printed by the electronic calculator but not entered into the calculations.

non-add print key — On some units this key prints the figure entered on the keyboard along with the (#) symbol, discards the figure, and clears the input register.

noncalculator calculator chip applications — Calculator chips can be used: to assemble computers; for specialized types of watches and clocks; laboratory, industrial and service test equipment; medical instruments; process monitors; communications equipment; surveillance and security systems; and automotive, appliance and industrial controls. Under development and scheduled for early release are varieties of wrist game units following the successes of miniature combination calculator wristwatches.

non-data operation — Any use of an input/output device that does not involve the transfer of data.

nondestructive read — A reading of the information in a register without changing that information.

non-equivalence operation — A logical operation applied to two operands producing a result depending on the bit patterns of the operands and according to rules for each bit position, e.g., p = 110110, q = 011010, then r = 101100.

non-erasable storage — Storage media which cannot be erased and reused, such as punched paper tapes and punched cards.

nonlinear control — On-line process control by an analog computer is essentially an extension of conventional control techniques to the next stage of complexity. More input variables can be accommodated and more complex compensation, often nonlinear in nature, can be used to stabilize process operation for a wide variety of disturbances.

nonlinearity — Refers to a relationship between the output and input which is not representable by a straight line. The output signal does not vary directly as the input signal but is also related to other operating parameters such as hysteresis or friction.

nonlinear programming — An inclusive term covering all types of constrained optimization problems except those where the objective function and the constraints are all linear. Special types of nonlinear programming for which some theory has been developed are convex programming, concave programming, and quadratic programming.

nonlinear system — Refers to a model or any system whose operation cannot be represented by a first order mathematical equation.

non-parametric statistics programs — Some types are: Kendall Rank Correlation; Kendall Coefficient of Concordance; Sign Test; Wilcoxon Matched Pairs Signed Rank Test; Mann-Whitney U-Test; Friedman Two-way Analysis of Variance; Cochran Q-Test; Biserial Correlation; Point Biserial Correlation; Tetrachoric Correlation; Phi Coefficient.

non-return to zero (NRZ) — A mode of recording in which each state of the medium corresponds to one binary state. In the mode, the state of the recording medium changes when the information changes from 1 to 0 or from 0 to 1. Note: NRZ modified is also often called NRZ1.

non-return-to-zero "change" recording — A special method of recording developed to use 0s and 1s as represented by two specified but different conditions of magnetization.

non-volatile memory — 1. A memory type which holds data even if power has been disconnected. A magnetic memory is non-volatile, an ultrasonic one is volatile (it does not comply with the above criterion). 2. One example of a non-volatile, electrically alterable, read-only memories (EAROM) are the tiny memory devices that perform as follows: 1. They can store data for years without power. 2. They're non-destructive and immune to external power interruptions. 3. They let users erase stored information in just one second, without ultraviolet irradiation. 4. They let users alter the memory as often as needed — up to a million times. 5. They're particularly useful for communications, computer peripherals, and very low power applications. 6. They are standard products and offer custom capability.

non-volatile PROM — The PROM is a member of the standard ROM family of memories. Once it is programmed, its memory is nonvolatile, which means that if power is removed from and then re-applied to the PROM, the stored information remains intact. By contrast, a RAM (random-access memory) has a volatile memory; if power is interrupted, when it is again applied, whatever information was stored in the memory will be erased.

nonvolatile storage — Storage media which retain information in the absence of power and which will make the information available when power is restored.

NO OP — Refers to an instruction commanding the calculator to do nothing, except to proceed to the next instruction in sequence.

"NO OPERATION" key — If a "NO OPERATION" key is included in a stored program, it will advance the program to the following step. It is often used in conjunction with conditional-skip instructions.

NOR — A combination of the logic functions NOT and OR.

NOR GATE — A component which implements the NOR function.

normal probability distribution program — Refers to a Normal Probability Distribution, Subroutine. Calculates the cumulative normal probability distribution for a given argument. Refers also to the Area Under Normal Curve. Computes normal curve probabilities for normal distributions with any Mean and Standard Deviation, by conversion to the standard normal with Mean, 0.0 and Standard Deviation, 1.0.

normalize — 1. In programming, to adjust the exponent and fraction of a floating-point quantity so that the fraction lies in the prescribed normal, standard range. 2. In mathematical operations, to reduce a set of symbols or numbers to a normal or standard form. (Synonymous with standardize.) 3. To alter or position into a regular or standard format as to right- or left-justify.

normalization routine — Concerns a floating-point arithmetic operation which is related to normalization of numerals in which digits other than zero are developed in the low order; i.e., less significant positions during the left shift.

normalized form — Concerns a special form taken by a floating-point number which has been adjusted in such a way that its mantissa lies in a specified range.

normal state — Refers to the condition of operation wherein the instructions are concerned with the conventional aspects of computation (adding, subtracting. information transfer, etc.). The detection of an exceptional condition (interrupt) that occurs while in this state suspends operation in this state and processing continues in control state.

normative testing — Standards of performance that are established for the testing of both quantitative and qualitative system performance.

NOT — A logic operator implying the converse of an input.

notation — 1. A manner of representing numbers. Some of the more important notation scales are:

Base	Name
2	binary
3	ternary
4	quaternary, tetral
5	quinary
10	decimal
12	duodecimal
16	hexadecimal, sexidecimal
32	duotricenary
2, 5	biquinary

2. The act, process, or method of representing facts or quantities by a system or set of marks, signs, figures, or characters.

notation, engineering — An innovative feature of some units is a mode of formatting the displayed result, called engineering notation. This is a selectable format that makes calculated answers easier to understand. Imagine a problem that deals in physical units of measure, such as seconds. Say the answer to the problem in scientific notation is $5.00-05$. Now this is a valid answer, but not as clear as it could be. Setting some units into engineering notation gives the answer as $50.0-06$ which is easy to read instantly as 50 microseconds. Engineering notation forces the power-of-ten exponent to be a multiple of three and adjusts the decimal point to give the correct answer. If the above answer is multiplied by 10, it gives $500.-06$ or 500 microseconds. Multiplying again by ten gives $5.00-03$ or five milliseconds.

notation, fixed decimal point — Refers to the position of the decimal that remains fixed, limiting the number of digits that can appear to the right of the decimal point.

notation, floating decimal point — Automatically positions the decimal point in a given answer, making for higher accuracy than can be achieved with the fixed decimal point technique.

notation, positional — A method of representing numbers in which the digits are arranged sequentially, each succeeding digit understood as being interpreted as the coefficient of successive powers of an integer referred to as the base of the number system. For example, in the decimal number system, each succeeding digit is interpreted as successive powers of the base 10.

notation, radix — 1. An annotation consisting of a decimal number, in parentheses, written as a subscript suffix to a number, its decimal value indicating the radix of the number; e.g., $11_{(2)}$ indicates the number 11 is in the radix of two, $11_{(8)}$ indicates the number 11 is in the radix of eight. 2. A number written without its radix notation is assumed to be in the radix of ten. (Synonymous with base notation.)

notation, scientific — Quantities are expressed as a fractional part (mantissa) and a power of ten (characteristic).

notational system — The methods for notation systems used to represent numbers which indicate quantities. Most numeration systems use methods for representing quantities by a sequence of digits after coefficients multiply successive powers of certain radixes. Various types of number systems are unary, binary, ternary, up to sexagenary, representing 60 where as binary is two, octal is 8, etc.

notched tab cards, calculator — On some units programs can be stored on magnetic cards for later use. Cards can be recorded and rerecorded as many times as desired. To protect a recorded program on a card, further recording can be prevented by clipping the notched tab on the upper left corner of the card. Users may write on the card and place it in a slot above the keys A through E, thereby labeling any specially defined keys. (some units)

NOT operation — A Boolean operation on one operand in which the result has the alternative value of the operand, i.e., if the two possible states of the operand are represented by a zero or a one, the corresponding results are one or a zero. Same as negation, Boolean complementation, or inversion.

NOW, Negotiable Order of Withdrawal — These certificates concern third party transfer powers for savings banks and savings and loan associations such that check-like documents called NOWs can be used with savings accounts, this permits transfers and cash withdrawals from interest-bearing accounts.

NRZI — Non-return to zero one.

NSEC — Nanosecond, one billionth of a second.

null — 1. A balanced condition which results in zero output from a device or system. 2. To oppose an output which differs from zero so that it is returned to zero.

null character — Refers to a special control character that serves to accomplish media fill or time fill, for example, in ASCII the all zeros character (not numeric zero). Null characters may be inserted into or removed from, a sequence of characters without affecting the meaning of the sequence, but control of equipment or the format may be affected. Abbreviated NUL. Contrast with space character.

null cycle — The time necessary to cycle through a program without introducing data. This establishes the lower bound for program processing time.

null string — The notion of a string depleted of its entities, or the notion of a string prior to establishing its entities.

number, base — The quantity of characters for use in each of the digital positions of a numbering system. In the more common numbering systems the characters are some or all of the Arabic numerals as follows:

System Name	Characters	Radix
BINARY	(0,1)	2
OCTAL	(0,1,2,3,4,5,6,7)	8
DECIMAL	(0,1,2,3,4,5,6,7,8,9)	10

Unless otherwise indicated, the radix of any number is assumed to be 10. For positive identification of a radix 10 number, the radix is written in parentheses as a subscript to the expressed number, i.e., $126_{(10)}$. The radix of any nondecimal number is expressed in similar fashion, e.g., $11_{(2)}$ and $5_{(8)}$.

number, call — 1. A group of characters identifying a subroutine and containing: (a) information concerning parameters to be inserted in the subroutine, (b) information to be used in generating the subroutine, or (c) information related to the operands. 2. A call word if the quantity of characters in the call number is equal to the length of a computer word.

numerator — In a fraction, the number which is understood to be divided by the other.

numeric — Composed of numerals; the value of a number as opposed or contrasted to character representation.

numerical analysis — 1. The study of methods of obtaining useful quantitative solutions to mathematical problems, whether or not an analytic solution exists, and the study of the errors and bounds on errors in obtaining such solutions. 2. The use of numerical methods to solve mathematical equations of a form which involves more complex processes or relationships, e.g., integration, by means of trial and error.

numerical control — 1. A manufacturing technique controlled automatically by orders (called commands). These are introduced in the form of numbers — which may be entered by a decade switch, or by a dial switch like the one on a telephone. 2. Refers to the control of machine tools, drafting machines, and the like, by punched paper or magnetic tapes suitably encoded with directive information. As most numerically controlled devices have very limited logical or arithmetic capability (to keep costs low), they rely on their input tapes for detailed and explicit guidance. This may mean 8 bits for every 0.001 of motion, or a great amount of data on the tape. It is common for a computer to prepare the control tapes, using information presented in a more manageable and concise form.

numerical control (APT) — An example of the APT (automatically programmed tools) system, developed by aerospace industry combine and currently supported by IITRIIS: Using APT, the designer describes his tool and the desired part in a high-level, geometrically oriented language. A preprocessor program accepts the high-level language and digests it into a simpler, formalized internal representation. The central program (tool independent) converts the material, tool, and geometrical information into tool motion commands. A postprocessor program prepares the tool motion information in a format suitable for the particular control mechanism being used. If desired, a simultaneous output for a numerical control drafting machine permits preparation of detail blueprints while the robot tool is making the part.

numerical control, direct (DNC) — A system connecting a set of numerically controlled machines to a common memory for a part program or machine program storage, with provision for on-demand distribution of data for the machines. Direct numerical control systems typically have additional provisions for collection, display or editing of part programs, operator instructions, or data related to the numerical control process.

numerical data — 1. Numerical operations are usually programmed using octal (8) or hexadecimal (16) numbers. Thus a hexadecimal, 8-bit computer would subdivide each 8-bit word into two hexadecimal digits. 2. Data in which information is expressed by a set of numbers or symbols that can only assume discrete values or configurations.

numerical-control machines — A punched paper or plastic tape with magnetic spots is used to feed digital instructions to a numerical control machine, e.g., an automated cutting or forming machine thus guided. Tolerances as fine as 1/10,000 of an inch are achieved on unattended units. Tapes are developed with digital computer programs.

numerical format, calculator — A numerical

format to be displayed and printed, on some units can be specified as either fixed point or floating point, with the desired number of digits. The commands are given either in a program or from the keyboard. For example, 1356.4255 may appear in the following formats:

FIXED	(3)	1356.426
FLOAT	(9)	1.356425500E 03
FLOAT	(3)	1.356E 03

Dynamic range: $-9.99999999999 \times 10^{99}$ to -10^{-99}, 0, and $+10^{-99}$ to $+9.99999999999 \times 10^{99}$ with 12 significant digits, 10 of which are displayed.

numerical tape — A punched paper or plastic tape used to feed digital instructions to a numerical control (N/C) machine.

numeric code — A system of numerical abbreviations used in the preparation of information for input into a machine, i.e., all information is reduced to numerical quantities.

numeric constant — Any real number that is entered as numeric data; also the contents of a numeric variable.

numeric expression — Any combination of numeric constants, numeric variables, array variables, subscripted array variables, numeric functions, or string relational comparisons inclosed in parentheses, joined together by one or more arithmetic, logical, or relational operators in such a way that the expression, as a whole, can be reduced to a single numeric constant when evaluated.

object code — The basic program; the output from a compiler or assembler which is itself executable machine code or is suitable for processing to produce executable machine code.

object deck — A stack of punched cards forming a computer program in machine language. Usually prepared from an equivalent source deck by the compiler for the machine.

objective, design — The planned performance goal based on or chosen prior to the developed operations. The technical estimates of performance requirements, but awaiting confirmation, i.e., standards designed to be met.

objective function — An objective function of the independent variable function whose maximum or minimum value is sought as an optimization problem.

objective functions (LP) — Linear program problems, for example, must have a mathematical statement of goals, usually the maximization of profits, efficiency, resources or the minimization of costs, etc. The model seeks for its solution the decision rule which, when implemented will achieve the goal thus expressed as the objective function.

object language — Refers to the language which is the output of an automatic coding routine. Usually object language and machine language are the same, however, a series of steps in an automatic coding system may involve the object language of one step serving as a source language for the next step and so forth.

object program — 1. A source program that has been automatically translated into machine language. 2. The final or 'target' program is referred to as the object program. The source program is developed first, and this is translated into the machine program for internal computer operation. 3. A set of machine language instructions for the solution of a problem, obtained as the end result of a compilation process. It is generated from the source program. 4. The absolute coding output by a processor program. See source program.

object program development — Users write programs in many programming languages. On some systems, translator modules of the operating system will translate the applications program into executable machine code; other modules of the operating system will add utility routines (e.g., to read from and write to I/O devices), thus generating executable object programs.

object-program preparation — Conversion of programs from one of several easy-to-use source languages, or from certain competitive system languages, to a specific machine code.

object time — The time at which an object program is executed, as opposed to the time at which a source program is translated into machine language to create an object program.

observational relationship, synthetic — A relation existing between a concept that pertains to an empirical observation. Such relationships are not involved in defining concepts or terms, but in reporting the results of observations and experiments.

OCR, Optical Character Recognition — Refers to recognition by machines of printed or written characters based on inputs from photoelectric transducers. Contrast with MICR.

octal number complements — Octal notation is used in source language and program testing diagnostic printouts. The octal or base 8 number system expresses values as multiples of powers of 8. Octal notation is a fixed-length system of binary notation. The binary number is interpreted octally by grouping the bits into bytes of three, starting from the right, and interpreting each byte into its octal equivalent. Within each byte the bit positions are weighted with the value of 4, 2, and 1, or 2^2, 2^1, and 2^0. If, after grouping the bits in the fashion described, the most significant byte contains less than three bits, as many binary zeros are implied to the left as are required to bring the numbers of bits in that group to three. For example, the binary number 10011101101 is interpreted octally as follows:

| (0)10 | 011 | 101 | 101 |
| 2 | 3 | 5 | 5 |

odd-even check — Refers to an automatic computer check in which an extra digit is carried along with each word, to determine whether the total number of 1's in the word is odd or even, thus providing a check for proper operation.

odd-parity check — Refers to a popular check by summation in which the binary digits, in a character or word, are added, and the sum checked

ODS (output data strobe) — An output signal that enables external devices that will receive data from CPU.

OEM — Original Equipment Manufacturers — The OEM has a well-defined problem. He needs a computer powerful enough to answer his product's requirements, with enough performance margin to accommodate the growth he expects in the future. Initial cost is important to him, since any savings are translated directly into profit. And because maintenance costs come right out of the same profit, he demands unfailing reliability. Besides these requirements, the OEM has other needs — unique to him — which further separate him from the end user. He needs to get his product to the marketplace fast, to establish his position before the competition can react. This means he wants to shorten his development cycle. He needs working hardware and software so he can get going on his prototype.

off-line — Refers to equipment or devices not under direct control of the central processing unit. Also concerns a description of terminal equipment not connected to a transmission line.

off-line operation — 1. Refers to an operation which is independent of the time base of the actual inputs. 2. In a computer system, this refers to the operation of peripheral equipment independent from the central processor, e.g., the transcribing of card information to magnetic tape to printed form.

off-line storage, calculators — Some units offer unlimited off-line storage. The built-in cassette memory offers users greater convenience and capacity. And some standard units include control ROMs that take care of bothersome tasks like program linkage so users can easily handle any size program. One cassette gives a bulk storage capacity for roughly 40 times as much data and programs as the basic internal memory of many advanced calculators.

offset deviation — A deviation from steady-state of the controlled variable when the set point is fixed. Such an offset resulting from a no-load to a full-load change (or other specified limits) is often called "droop" or "load regulation."

off-the-shelf — 1. Relates to production items which are available from current stock and need not be either newly purchased or immediately manufactured. 2. Also relates to computer software or equipment that can be used by customers with little or no adaptation, thereby saving them from the time and expense of developing their own software or equipment.

ohm — The unit of resistance, usually defined as the resistance, at $0°C.$, pg a uniform column of mercury 106.300 cm long and weighing 14.4521 grams. One ohm is the value of resistance through which a potential difference of one volt will maintain a current of one ampere. MKSA unit of resistance, such that 1 ampere through it produces a potential difference of 1 volt.

OLRT — Acronym for On-Line Real-Time operation.

omni constant — Refers to the calculator cabability for adding consecutively in any steps of any predetermined size, raise the power of any number in consecutive steps.

on-board digital printer, data acquisition systems — On some calculator systems direct printout with an on-board printer that prints out digital data on Z-fold paper is a standard feature. The printer is of the flying drum type, proven dependable in hundreds of data systems. Where readable data is desired, some printing units are very reliable because there are no mysterious conversions to perform or cryptic symbols to decipher. Users get all the data in engineering units.

on-demand system — A system from which information or service is available at time of request.

one-address instruction — An instruction consisting of an operation and exactly one address. The instruction code of a single-address computer may include both zero and multi-address instructions as special cases.

one factor analysis program — Analysis of Variance, One-Way-Classification. Computes the statistics needed to perform an Anova Test on a single variable of classification with replication.

one-for-one — Relates to a phrase often associated with an assembly routine where one source language instruction is converted to one machine language instruction.

one-port, two-port RAM — Refers to Random Access Memory that can be designed to fetch more than one piece of data at a time. The number of simultaneous paths to and from memory equals the number of ports. Multiport memory using many small-scale chips is not new, but today there is a move toward LSI multiport chips which can double system performance.

one's complement — The binary bit which, when added to 1 or 0, equals 1. Synonymous with the inverse binary state of any given bit.

one-step operation — A method of operating an automatic computer manually, in which a single instruction or part of an instruction is performed in response to a single operation of a manual control. This method is generally used for detecting mistakes.

one-to-one — A relation between individual members of one set and individual members of another set, i.e., each member of one set has a specific relation to one member of the other set.

on-line — Relates to equipment, devices, or systems in direct interactive communication with the central processing unit. May also be used to describe terminal equipment connected to a transmission line.

on-line calculators — Many users couple a programmable calculator directly to instruments to process and record data while an operation or experiment is in process. Such on-line use is made possible by the calculator's I/O architecture. However, special interface circuits for the instruments are usually necessary. They may often be obtained from the calculator manufacturer, or in some cases the user can design and build his own. Also custom-designed and prepackaged interface systems are available for some classes of instrumentation. No matter what the source, the interface circuit must perform the following general functions:
- Match the voltage levels to and from the I/O bus of the calculator.
- Translate codes acceptable to both the calculator and the instruments.

- Provide a GO signal to return control to the calculator after data have been transferred. Also, by multiplexing techniques, the interface can greatly increase the number of available input ports for data-scanning applications.

on-line data processing — Data processing in which all changes to relevant records and accounts are made at the time that each transaction or event occurs. The process usually requires random access storage. See on-line processing.

on-line debugging — Relates to the act of debugging a program while time sharing its execution with an on-line process program. On-line debugging is accomplished in such a way that any attempt by the "slave" program undergoing debugging to interfere with the operation of the process program will be detected and inhibited.

on-line diagnostics — Relates to the running of diagnostics on a system while it is on-line but off-peak to save time and to take corrective action without closing down the system.

on-line direct control — When one unit of peripheral equipment is under the control of another unit without human intervention, the controlling unit is then on-line to the second unit which is direct control of the first. If human intervention is necessary the controlling unit is said to be off-line to the second, but the controlling unit has indirect control over the second unit while an operator acts as the link in the control sequence.

on-line plotter — A local or remote digital incremental plotter — in either on-line or off-line operation with a digital computer — provides a high speed plotting system of versatility and reliability. For on-line operation with medium-size computers, a small adapter unit converts the computer output signals to a form suitable for driving a plotter. No modification to the basic computer circuitry is required. Adapters are available for all standard medium-scale digital computers. The plotter can be used for off-line operation with virtually any medium or large-scale calculator also.

on-line, real-time operation (OLRT) — A special system plan and operation in which the input data to the system are given directly from the measuring devices, and the computer results are thereby obtained during the progress of the event. For instance, the data that are received from measurements during a run, with real-time computation of dependent variables during the run, enables the computer to make changes in its output.

on-line storage — Storage devices, and especially the storage media which they contain, under the direct control of a computing system, not the off-line or shelf-storage of these media.

on-line system — 1. A system which eliminates the need for human intervention between source recording and the ultimate processing by a computer. 2. A system in which the input enters a computer from the point of origin and the output goes directly to where it is used.

on-line teller system (bank) — If the volume of savings account and mortgage loan activity warrants, these transactions may be handled in real time by the on-line teller system. Teller consoles at each window at each office may be linked to the computer and the on-line central file.

on-line testing — In a telecommunications or teleprocessing system, any testing of a remote terminal or station that is performed concurrently with execution of the user's programs — that is, while the terminal is still connected to the central.

on-off keying — That in which the output from a source is alternately transmitted and suppressed to form signals.

open collector output card — Typically provides 12 open-collector driver outputs. IC buffers on the card act as switches for voltage up to 30 volts dc and currents up to 40 mA.

open-ended — 1. The quality by which the addition of new terms, subject headings, or classifications does not disturb the preexisting system. 2. Having the capability of being extended or expanded.

open loop — Refers to a control system in which there is no self correcting action for misses of the desired operational condition, as there is in a closed loop system. 2. A family of automatic control units, one of which may be a computer or calculator linked together manually by operator action.

open routine — Concerns that type routine which can be inserted directly into a larger routine without a linkage or calling sequence.

open shop — Describing the operating of a computing facility where most productive problem programming is performed by the problem originator rather than a group of programming specialists. The use of the computer itself may also be described as open shop when the user also serves as the operator, rather than a specially trained computer operator.

open subroutine — Relates to various subroutines inserted directly into the linear operational sequence, not entered by a jump. Such a subroutine must be recopied at each point that it is needed in a routine.

operand — The fundamental quantity on which a mathematical operation is performed. Usually a statement consists of an operator and an operand. The operator may indicate an 'add' instruction; the operand thus will indicate what is to be added.

operand call syllable — A syllable which specifies that an operand be brought to the stack, either directly from the program reference table or indirectly by means of a descriptor.

operand example — Any one of the quantities involved in an operation. Operands may be numeric expressions or constants. In the numeric expression $A = B + 5*C$, the numeric variables B and C, and the numeric constant 5 are operands.

operand field — The portion of an immediate-addressing instruction word that contains the immediate operand value, with negative values represented as twos complements.

operating conditions — Those various conditions, such as, ambient temperature, ambient pressure, vibration, etc. to which many devices are subjected, but not including the variable measured by the device.

operating modes, calculator — Operating Modes include: RUN — manual operation and program execution. PGRM — writing and editing programs. AUTO START — automatic tape rewind, load file 0, execute program when power is switched on, etc.

operating programs, general-purpose — Plans or instructions for controlling input-output operations, remote data transmission, and multiple users which can be used and re-used to control these operations. Since these control programs are generally applicable to all users, they are usually prepared by calculator manufacturers.

operating ratio — The ratio of the number of

operating system — hours of correct machine operation to the total hours of scheduled operation, e.g., on a 168-hour week scheduled operation, if 12 hours of preventive maintenance are required and 4.8 hours of unscheduled down time occurs, then the operating ratio is (168 16.8)/168, which is equivalent to a 90 percent operating ratio. Synonymous with computer efficiency.

operating system — 1. A basic group of programs with operation under control of a data processing monitor program. 2. An integrated collection of service routines for supervising the sequencing and processing of programs by a calculator. Operating systems may perform debugging, input-output, machine accounting, compilation and storage assignment tasks.

operating system, disk (DOS) — A more powerful twin of TOS, this is a versatile operating system usually for IBM System installations having direct-access storage devices. These simple operating systems support almost every peripheral device available for System 360 or 370.

operating system, floppy disc — Several firms have developed floppy disk operating systems for microprocessor and calculator systems that obviate any need for paper tape or cards. Source programs written and edited at the system keyboard and stored on the floppy may then be assembled immediately with macroassembler units under operating system control. Assembled programs may be stored on disk in binary form, then loaded into the processor through a DOS Linking Loader, along with other object modules and the DEBUG programs. DOS packages include dual-drive floppy disk, interface, cable, software and documentation.

operating systems, executive — The executive program generally brings together selected components of a computer's system software to make an Operating System. Designing an operating system has many of the same problems as designing a programming language; there is very much an operating system can usefully do, and too often all will not fit in the available main memory. As a result, most computers provide a number of different operating systems. Three types are:
— A free standing operating system
— A disk operating system
— A real time operating system

operating system, time-sharing — The operating system is a collection of programs remaining permanently in memory to provide overall coordination and control of the total operating system. It performs several functions. First, it permits several users' programs from interfering with other users' programs. Each program is run for a certain length of time, then the monitor switches control to another program in a rotating sequence. Switching is frequent enough so that all programs appear to run simultaneously. Another function of the time-sharing monitor is to process input/output commands.

operation — 1. Generally refers to the action specified by a single calculator instruction or pseudo-instruction. 2. An arithmetical, logical, or transferal unit of a problem, usually executed under the direction of a subroutine.

operational stack — In some units a four-register stack lets users store and retrieve intermediate solutions at the appropriate time. The stack design permits roll-down of any entry to the display for review or other operation. The operational stack, coupled with reverse Polish notation, provides an efficient means for evaluating mathematical expressions on some calculators.

operational stack, 4-register (calculator) — The basic capability is for automatic storage and retrieval of intermediate solutions. The stack design permits review of stored data at any time. ((see: stack)

operation, average calculating — A representative operation which might serve as a base or indication of calculating speeds of various machines, i.e., a number representing, for example, two additions and one multiplication and the time to calculate this, or more commonly accepted, nine additions and one multiplication.

operation, bookkeeping — A calculator operation which does not directly contribute to the result, i.e., arithmetical, logical, and transfer operations used in modifying the address section of other instructions, in counting cycles and in rearranging data. Synonymous with red tape operation.

operation cycle — That portion of a machine cycle during which the actual execution of the instruction takes place. Some operations (e.g., divide, multiply) may need a large number of these operation cycles to complete the operation, and the normal instruction/operation alternation will be held up during this time. Also called execution cycle.

operation (OP) code — That part of an instruction designating the operation to be performed.

operation RUN STOP — If R/S is keyed in and a stored program is not executing, the stored program starts executing at the step denoted by the program pointer. If executed in a stored program, R/S stops the program, displaying the X-register and allowing keystrokes from the operator. If a R/S in a program is immediately preceded by a numerical entry from the program, the automatic lift is disabled upon return to the keyboard. This allows a program to display prompting information that will not be lifted in the stack if users enter a number from the keyboard. Except for this case, R/S does not affect the stack lift. In a program, R/S must have an ENTER separating the R/S from succeeding digit keys. (some units)

operation, add — An "add" instruction in which the result is the sum, and the result is usually apparent in the storage location previously occupied by one of the operands.

operations analysis — Refers to the scientific approach to solving operational problems (some methods used are linear programming, PERT, statistical theory, etc.

operations, constant — Operations can be performed on a series of numbers by a particular number without having to continually re-enter the constant.

operation, single step — A method of operating an automatic computer manually in which a single instruction or part of an instruction is performed in response to a single operation of a manual control. This method is generally used for detecting mistakes.

operations manual — The manual which contains instructions and specifications for a given application. Typically includes components of operators manual, programmer reference manual, and sometimes also includes a log section.

operations research — Using analytical methods adopted from mathematics for solving operational problems, the objective is to provide man-

operations research, management science

agement with a more logical basis for making sound predictions and decisions. Among the common scientific techniques used in operations research are the following: linear programming, probability theory, information theory, game theory, monte-carlo method, and queuing theory.

operations research, management science — The vast area of computation devices and techniques which concerns itself with mathematical tools directed toward the solution of sets of problems concerned with optimizing the management function and math models of business (conflicting interest) situations. Its task is to analytically resolve control variables to optimal decisions. Some complex models are expressed and solved with the simplex method, matrix algebra and the computer. Among the OR computational techniques are: linear programming, game theory, econometrics, input-output, queue analysis (waiting lines), simulation, criticalpath method (CPM), Project Evaluation and Review Techniques (PERT) and others.

operator — A symbol which represents an operation be performed on one or more operands.

operator console — In some systems, that particular device or part of the mainframe which enables the operator to communicate with the computer, i.e., it is used to enter data or information, to request and display stored data, to actuate various preprogrammed command routines, etc.

operator, logical — Operators which return logical 1's and Ø's, specifically, the AND, OR, and NOT operators. "True" operations return "1", "false" operations return "Ø".

operator, postfix — A notation system where the operator appears after the operand, for example, AB + = A + B. It is used in Polish notation.

operator symbol — A symbol indicating the operation to be performed on two operands. That is, in the express X + Y, the plus sign (+) is the operator.

optical character recognition (OCR) — Refers to a process of using photosensitive devices to identify graphic characters, often of special type-font origin.

optical scanner — A special optics device which scans patterns of incident light and generates analog/digital signals which are functions of the incident light synchronized with the scan, the primary purpose being to generate or "read" digital representations of printed or written data.

optical scanner, bar-code — An optical-scanning unit that can read documents encoded in a special bar code, at a hundreds character-per-second speed, in an element in the data station. The scanner opens up various systems concepts for such tasks as billing, couponing, retail-item control, and other forms of returnable media. The scanner can read either lithographed or computer-printed bar codes. As it scans, it transfers the encoded data to a buffer for direct transmission or to displays, paper tape and printers for pretransmission editing (some systems).

optimization, linear — Quite specifically this refers to procedures for locating maximum or minimum values of a linear function of variables which are subject to specific linear constraints which may or may not be inequalities.

optimization, nonlinear — A mathematical technique or procedure for the determination of a maximum, minimum, or an attempted optimum value of variables which are subject in the model to predetermined nonlinear constraints, as expressed by sets of inequalities or equations. This is contrasted to linear optimization in which constraints are linear, i.e., in a certain sense, proportional.

optimize — To arrange the instructions or data in storage so that a minimum amount of machine time is spent for access when instructions or data are called out.

optimizing control action — Various control actions which automatically seek and maintain the most advantageous value of a specified variable, instead of maintaining it at one set value.

OR — A logic operator having the property that if P and Q are logic quantities then the quantity "P OR Q" assumes values as defined by the following table:

P	Q	P OR Q
0	0	0
0	1	1
1	0	1
1	1	1

The OR operator is represented in both electrical and FORTRAN terminology by a "+," i.e., P + Q.

organizing and communicating models — Models have been used for centuries by designers, inventors, and engineers to put ideas into physical form. The model serves two necessary and useful purposes — comprehension and communication. Details of a new design often become too numerous and elaborate for visualization, and a model is required to put the ideas into tangible form such that each part can be tried and fitted to the others until a workable system has been achieved. Thus a model assists comprehension because it is in precise mathematics or symbols.

order — 1. A defined successive arrangement of elements or events. This term is losing favor as a synonym for instructions, due to ambiguity. 2. To sequence or arrange in a series. 3. The weight or significance assigned to a digit position in a number.

ordering bias — The degree to which a set of data departs from random distribution. An ordering bias will increase or decrease the effort necessary to order a set of data from the effort anticipated for random distribution.

ordinate — Vertical or Y distance on a graph.

origin — 1. The absolute storage address of the beginning of a program or block. 2. In relative coding, the absolute storage address to which addresses in a region are referenced.

original document — The document initially used by a data processing system and which supplies the basic data to be input to the data processing system. Many resulting errors are attributed to errors in the source document.

origination, data — The act of creating a record in a machine-sensible form directly, or as a by-product of a human readable document.

O. R. (operations research) — The use of analytic methods adopted from mathematics for solving operational problems. The object is to provide management with a more logical basis for making sound predictions and decisions. Among the common scientific techniques used in operations research are the following: linear programming, probability theory, information theory, game theory, monte-carlo method, and queuing theory.

OS/VS — Operating System/Virtual Storage.

output — 1. Processing results, such as answers to mathematical problems, statistical, analytical or accounting figures, production schedules, etc. 2. Information transferred from the internal storage of a computer to secondary or external storage; information transferred to any device exterior to the computer. 3. Information transferred from internal storage to external storage or to an on-line output device. 4. The state of a sequence of states occurring on a specified output channel. 5. The device or collective set of devices used for taking data out of a device. 6. A channel for expressing a state on a device or logic element.

output block — Refers to a segment of the internal storage reserved for output data. Also called output area, or output working storage.

output channel — The result or output from a specific device and through a channel for the planned conveyance of data from that source.

output device — The part of a machine which translates the electrical impulses representing data processed by the machine into permanent results such as printed forms, punched cards, or magnetic writing on tape.

output formats — Programmable calculator users may spend minutes or seconds finding the solution to a problem, then spend hours putting the results in final form. In many applications, all users need the answer, with a hard copy for reference. If so, then some very basic equipment will do the job. A built-in alphanumeric display and printer can show the formula being used, and data as it is being entered (with labels, if desired) and the labelled solution. For more formal data presentations, the I/O structure can be altered and refined to allow the user to plug-in the peripheral appropriate to the need, such as an analog X-Y plotter, a typewriter, paper tape punch, etc.

output process — A procedure designed to deliver data through various devices, systems, subsystems, or programming commands.

output record — 1. Refers to a specific record written to an output device. 2. The current record stored in the output area prior to being output.

output register — The basic register which holds data until it can be output to an external device.

outputs, data acquisition calculator — On some systems besides display, any two output devices can be handled at one time. The other outputs include interfaces driving:
- ASR33 Teletype and compatible devices with a 20 milliamp current loop.
- IBM-compatible 7-track magnetic tape recorder.
- IBM-compatible 9-track magnetic tape recorder.
- Paper tape perforator, 8-track, ASCII code.
- Modem data telemetry, RS-232-C compatible.

output state — The determination of the condition of that specified set of output channels, i.e., positive or negative, one or zero, etc.

output stream — Refers to diagnostic messages and other output data issued by an operating system or a processing program on output devices especially activated for this purpose by the operator. Synonymous with job output stream, output job stream.

output table — 1. Refers to a peripheral output device that plots the curves of variables as functions of other variables. 2. A hard copy output device which presents the results of a plotter system, which is designed to develop curves, graphs, chart, and other graphic output.

output unit — The unit which delivers information in acceptable language to a point outside the calculator.

output work queue — Various data which are output are often not immediately printed or punched into final form, but are stored on some type of auxiliary storage device and become part of a queue which is programmed with control information for disposition of this information. Often the calculator system is printer-bound or can operate only as fast as the printer can perform.

output writer — A service program which moves data from the output work queue to a particular output device, i.e., a printer, card punch, or terminal. The output writer thus transfers the actual output, often from an output work queue to an output device.

output writer, calculator — On one system, a modified Selectric® Output Writer has full format alphanumeric capability to give hard copy output of calculated results, final reports, forms, documents, etc. The unit can also be used as an extra typewriter when users need it.

over-capacity — The information contained in an item of information which is in excess of a given amount.

overflow — A condition that exists when an entry or an answer is too large for the capacity of the machine. The working register has been exceeded and the excess digits "overflow". The rightmost digits, the least significant ones, are not displayed.

overflow and underflow examples, small calculators — In many systems, program execution halts when any register overflows (numbers with a magnitude greater than $9.999999999 \times 10^{-99}$). If the overflow appears in the X-register, it is easy to determine the operation that caused the overflow by switching to PRGM mode and identifying the code in the display. Occasionally, however, the overflow will occur in one of the data storage registers and occasionally in the Y-register. If a program seems to have stopped arbitrarily and users are sure that they did not press any keys, they should check these other registers.

overflow, arithmetic — 1. Concerns an arithmetic operation, the generation of a quantity beyond the capacity of the register or location which is to receive the result; over capacity; the information contained in an item of information which is in excess of a given amount. 2. The portion of data that exceeds the capacity of the allocated unit of storage. 3. Overflow develops when attempts are made to write longer fields into a field location of a specific length; a 12-digit product will overflow a 10-digit accumulator.

overflow check indicator — A device that is turned on by incorrect or unplanned for operations in the execution of an arithmetic instruction, particularly when an arithmetic operation produces a number too large for the system to handle.

overflow indication — When more than nine consecutive digits are entered, one type calculator prints ENT OVF to indicate entry overflow. The CE or T key will clear this overflow condition. If a multiplication or division result contains more than nine digits to the left of the decimal, RES OVF is printed and the overflow condition is automatically cleared. The calculator is automatically cleared when ADD OVF is printed, indicating addition overflow.

overflow indicator — 1. A signaling device that

indicates the occurrence of an overflow; for instance, a number too large to be contained in a given register. 2. When the calculator's computing capacity is exceeded, the display will usually produce the answer with some special symbol and only the most significant digits displayed. (This assumes that the calculator can display only N digits.) 3. A bi-stable trigger which changes state when overflow occurs in the register with which it is associated. It may be interrogated and/or restored to the original state.

overflow, link (L) — This one-bit register serves as an extension of the accumulator. The content of this register can be program sampled and program modified. Overflow into the link from the accumulator can be checked by the program to greatly simplify and speed up single- and multiple-precision arithmetic routines.

overflow records — Those which cannot be accommodated in assigned areas of a direct access file and which must be stored in another area where they can be retrieved by means of a reference stored in place of the records in their original assigned area.

overlap — To perform central processor functions simultaneously on several instructions, for example by obeying an instruction in, say, three states. These may be decode, access operands, and perform function. The central processor can then have three separate instructions passing through these stages together.

overlap processing — Processor operations performed at the same time by using different parts of the circuitry, for example, read-process-write, or any two of these. (spooling)

overlay program — Concerns a program in which certain control sections can use the same storage locations at different times during execution.

overlay region — Relates to a continuous area of main storage in which segments can be loaded independently of paths in other regions. Only one path within a region can be in main storage at any one time.

overlays, customized calculators — Some overlays let users define 24 keys to specialize in specific problem areas by changing the math function keys to their own subroutines. They combine several functions they use often into one key and label it. When users need that complete operation they press their customized keys to get complex patterns resolved with one key stroke.

overlay segments — Relating to an overlay program structure that is not resident in main memory simultaneously with other parts. Very large programs are often segmented into overlays, and such segments are called into memory from auxiliary storage and thus main memory capacity is not overstrained. Overlay segments are ordered as "first-level," "second-level" etc.

overlays, memory — 1. In many types of systems, the monitor remains resident in lower memory at all times. Object programs are loaded into memory, starting at the end of the monitor. The program loader resides in upper memory. Object programs cannot be loaded into the loader area. This area can be overlayed by common storage. Part of the loader can also be overlayed by library subroutines. 2. In addition, programmers can specify that sections of their own program may overlay each other when needed.

overlays, segmentation — A segment of a program is defined as that portion of memory which is committed by a single reference to the loader. Usually a segment overlays some other segment and may have within itself other portions which in turn overlay one another, i.e., subsegments. That part of a segment which is actually brought into memory when the loader is referenced is called the fixed part of a segment. Segments are built up from separate relocatable elements, common blocks, or other segments.

overlay supervisor — A control routine that initiates and controls fetching of overlay segments on the basis of information recorded in the overlay module by linkage editor.

overload — An analog computer overload relates to a condition existing within or at the output of a computing element that causes a substantial computing error because of the saturation of one or more of the parts of the computing element.

overload level — The operating limit of a system, component, etc.; that point at which operation ceases to be satisfactory as a result of signal distortion, overheating, damage, etc.

override decimal system — One type override feature accommodates additional decimals beyond the pre-selected decimal entry. This means the operator can make subsequent decimal adjustments during entry. There is also separate decimal selection for entry and results to assure correct decimal point placement automatically for 0-2-3-4-6-8 decimal places.

override interrupt — An optional group of power on/off interrupts which have the highest priority and which cannot be disabled or disarmed.

overrun — Overrun can usually occur when data are transferred to or from a non-buffered control unit operating with a synchronous medium, and the total activity initiated by the program exceeds the capability of the channel.

overwrite — Refers to the activity of placing information in a location and destroying the information previously contained there.

P

pack — 1. The combination or consolidation of several short fields into one larger field. 2. To combine two or more units of information into a single physical unit to conserve storage. For example, the fields of an employee's pay number, weekly pay rate, and tax exemptions may be stored in one word, each of these fields being assigned a different location within the word.

package, plastic — A typical plastic dual-in-line package (DIP) is the equivalent of the widely accepted industry standard, refined by manufacturers for MOS/LSI applications. Many packages consist of a silicon body, transfer-molded directly onto the assembled lead frame and die. The lead frame is often Kovar or Alloy 42, with external pins tin plated. Internally, some use 50 μ in. gold spot on each die attach pad and on bonding fingertips. Gold bonding wire is attached with thermocompression gold ball bonding technique. Materials of the lead frame, the package body, and the die attach are all closely matched in thermal expansion coefficients, to provide optimum response to various thermal conditions. During manufacture every step of the process should be rigorously monitored to assure maximum quality of the plastic package. Generally they are available in 14, 16, 18, 22, 24, and 40 pin configurations.

package, software — A computer program or set of programs used in a particular application such as a payroll/personnel package, scientific subroutines.

packaging, microprocessors — Package size is important to many system designers, particularly those with cramped layouts for product design. In general package sizes with small numbers of pins are easier to physically install into a system, while microprocessors in packages with large numbers of pins are easier for interfacing.

packet transmission — Refers to use of short standardized packets. A packet-switching network is able to store and forward messages very rapidly, typically within a fraction of a second. This is made possible by the use of very high-speed switching computers in which messages (packets) are stored in fast-access core memory exclusively, rather than on the slow-access storage devices (electromechanical disk drives) employed in conventional message switching systems.

packing factor — 1. The number of pulses or bits of information that can be written on a given length of magnetic surface. 2. Refers to the number of units (words, bits, characters, etc.) that can fit in something of defined size (per inch, per record, etc.)

pack (to) — Refers to process of compressing data in a storage medium by taking advantage of known characteristics of the data, in such a way that the original data can be recovered.

pad, pushbutton dialing — A twelve-key device to originate tone keying signals. It usually is attached to rotary dial telephones for use in originating data signals.

page — The concept of dividing computer memory into sections, the sizes of which are dependent on the direct addressing capability of the computer programming instruction set.

page address — The 8-high order bits of a virtual address or an actual address, which represents a page of memory (some computers).

page addressing — A procedure of memory addressing utilized with some specific computers. The addressing capability is limited to less than the total memory capacity available. But, using page addressing, memory is divided into segments (pages) each of which can be addressed by the available addressing capability.

page characteristics — 1. Typically it is a set of 4096 consecutive bytes. Applied to main storage, a set of 4096 consecutive bytes, the first byte of which is located at a storage address that is a multiple of 4096 (an address whose 12 low-order bits are 0). 2. The subdivision of a program which can be moved into main memory by an operating system or hardware whenever the instructions of that subdivision need to be performed. A program will be divided into pages in order to minimize the total amount of main memory storage allocated to the program at any one time. The pages will normally be stored on a fast direct access store.

page, entry — The point, in flowchart symbols, where the flowline continues from a previous page due to space limitations on the original or previous page.

page-turning — 1. A technique of providing large single level memory, usually with dynamic memory relocation. 2. A procedure for moving complete pages of information between main memory and auxiliary storage units, to permit several simultaneous programs in execution to share main memory, or to permit cyclic scheduling for time allotments.

page-width printer, calculator — A typical unit is a page-width impact printer for use with the various programmable calculators. It features a bidirectional carrier and platen which holds paper up to 15 inches wide and can handle up to 6 part forms. The unit prints at 30 characters per second and will print up to 132 columns at 10 characters per inch. It includes a 160 character buffer which automatically fills if characters are received faster than the print rate.

paging — Refers to a procedure for transmitting pages of information between main storage and auxiliary storage, especially when done for the purpose of assisting the allocation of a limited amount of main storage among a number of concurrently executing programs.

panel, graphic — A master control panel which, pictorially and usually colorfully, traces the relationship of control equipment and the process operation. It permits an operator at a glance, to check on the operation of a far flung control system by noting dials, valves, scales, and lights.

panel, removable — Some systems are designed with a removable front panel. Removing the front panel exposes the LSI modules and cables. This enables replacement or installation of a module from the front. The power supply is often located on the right-hand side when viewed from the front. The power supply contains three or more front panel switches and indicators which are accessible through a cutout in the front panel. Therefore, when the front panel is removed, the lights and switches are still attached and functional.

paper feed key — This key advances the printer tape as long as it is held down.

paper tape — Refers to strips of paper capable of storing or recording information. Storage may be in the form of punched holes, partially punched holes, carbonization or chemical change of impregnated material, or by imprinting. Some paper tapes, such as punched paper tapes, are capable of being read by the input device of a computer or a transmitting device by sensing the pattern of holes which represent coded information.

paper (tape) advance key — A key which electronically advances the paper tape on printing calculators.

paper tape automatic development system — Typically this is a stand-alone system for the paper tape oriented small memory user. It consists of the most commonly used loaders and utilities supplied on a single paper tape with a small executive that causes the utilities to be loaded at the highest possible memory address (regardless of memory size) to leave maximum room for the

paper tape coil

users program. Such a system includes programs such as, Debug, Binary Load, Binary Dump, Binary Verify, and Object Loader.

paper tape coil — The roll of paper tape as coiled and ready for use at the punch station, but one which may be blank or punched in preparation for working.

paper tape editor, calculator — A convenient method for transferring raw data into the Calculating System, these units read numeric data from paper tape punched in the standard 8-level ASCII code. Combined with the calculator, this high-speed photo-electric reader is an efficient data reduction system for statistical analysis of raw test data, on some systems.

paper-tape processing — A processing device in which the message is typed in hard-copy form on a machine that simultaneously punches a paper tape. Then the tape is placed in a teletype transmitting machine for transmission over the wire at maximum transmitting speed.

paper tape reader, advanced calculators — Data from analytical instruments, machine tools, and computer terminals goes directly into a calculator. A typical unit reads a wide variety of formats at 20 characters/second.

paper tape reader and monitor — A typical high speed paper tape reader provides calculator systems with a high speed paper tape input. This translates into a significantly faster development cycle due to a marked reduction in the time required for repetitive program loading, assembly, and editing operations. Typical monitor software provides key capabilities which significantly enhance the systems performance of the various units, enable all systems software to utilize the high speed reader features and is callable by user written application programs. The monitor also provides dynamic I/O reconfiguration permitting instantaneous reassignment of physical devices to logical devices.

paper-tape systems — Systems having paper-tape equipment with no mass storage device have an operating system contained on binary paper-tape reels. The binary reels are of two types–format binary and absolute binary. Format binary programs are loaded by the system loader. Absolute binary programs may be loaded by the monitor or by a "PRESET" operation.

parabola key — Completes parabolic curve fit calculation using least squares technique. Prints A, B, C and correlation coefficient r^2 for parabola $y = A + Bx + Cx^2$. (some units)

parabolic regression program — This program uses the method of least squares to approximate the parabolic curve which best fits a set of data points (X, Y). The program will also plot the curve that best fits the set of data points.

paragraph — A pertinent or allied group of sentences, or those which are related logically and which are smaller or subgroups of pages as described in some computer systems.

parallel — The simultaneous transfer and processing of all bits in a unit of information.

parallel access — 1. Simultaneous access to all bits in a storage location comprising a character or word. Equal access time for any bit, character, or word in a storage device. 2. The process of obtaining information from or placing information into storage where the time required for such access is dependent on the simultaneous transfer of all elements of a word from a given storage lo-

parameters, sorting

cation. (Synonymous with simultaneous access.)

parallel action — Binary addition in which all digits are added simultaneously.

parallel I/O interface — The programable peripheral-interface chip, Intel type 8255, has 24 parallel I/O lines organized into three 8-bit ports, one of which (port C) can be separated into two 4-bit sections. The read/write control logic interprets commands from the system program and sets up the configurations of the ports. The chip is n-channel MOS in a 40-pin package.

parallel running — 1. The checking or testing of newly developed systems by running comparatively in conjunction with previously existing systems. 2. The running of a newly developed system in a data processing area in conjunction with the continued operation of the current system. 3. The final step in the debugging of a system; this step follows a system test.

parallel storage — 1. Computer storage where all bits, words, or characters are equally available. 2. Refers to storage in which all bits, characters, or (especially) words are essentially equally available in space, without time being one of the coordinates. Parallel storage contrasts with serial storage. When words are in parallel, the storage is said to be parallel by words. When characters within words (or binary digits within words or characters) are dealt with simultaneously, not one after the other, the storage is parallel by characters (or parallel by bit respectively).

parallel transmission — A system for sending all bits of a particular character simultaneously.

parameter — 1. Variable which, for a particular purpose, combines other variables in computers. 2. Arbitrary constant, which has a particular value in specified circumstances in physics. 3. Variable which can take the place of one or more other variables in mathematics. 4. In a subroutine a quantity which may be given different values when the subroutine is used in different main routines or in different parts of one main routine, but which usually remains unchanged throughout any one such use; in a generator, a quantity used to specify input/output devices, to designate subroutines to be included, or otherwise to describe the desired routine to be generated.

parameter, macro — Refers to specific symbolic or literal elements in the operand part of a macro statement and which will be substituted into specific instructions in the incomplete routine to develop a complete open subroutine.

parameter, program — A parameter incorporated into a subroutine during computation. A program parameter frequently comprises a word stored relative to either the subroutine or the entry point and dealt with by the subroutine during each reference. It may be altered by the routine and/or may vary from one point of entry to another.

parameters, report generation — Manufacturers furnish a program for automatic creation of reports according to user specifications. To use the report generator, the programmer merely prepares a set of parameters defining control fields and report lines. These parameters are used as input to the report generator that produces a symbolic program. The assembled version of this program accepts raw data as input, edits it, and generates the desired reports.

parameters, sorting — The response to the requirement for specifications for a sort/merge

parameter testing

generator. Parameters are used to fix input and output formats, computing configuration, location of keys, and so on.

parameter testing — Tests of individual sections or subroutines of a program to assure that specified inputs produce the desired outputs.

parameter word — A word in a subroutine which contains one or more parameters which specify the action of the subroutine, or words which contain the address of such parameters.

parametric programming — A method for investigating the effect on an optimal linear-programming solution of a sequence of proportionate changes in the elements of a single row or column of the matrix. Most commonly, the method is applied to either the objective-function row or the right-side column.

parametric subroutine — A subroutine which involves parameters, such as a decimal-point coded subroutine. The computer itself is expected to adjust or generate the subroutine according to the parametric values chosen.

parentheses, algebraic hierarchy — Using left-to-right entry. One enters calculations exactly as he writes them. A user combines a 3-level algebraic hierarchy with 9 levels of parentheses. This lets user enter problems containing up to 10 pending operations. This means users don't have to presolve the problem or search for the most appropriate, efficient order of execution. The unit does this automatically. (some units)

parentheses keys — Parentheses keys generally alter order of processing according to standard algebraic rules. Nine levels possible on many units.

parity bit — 1. The parity bit is used to check that data has been transmitted accurately; a receiving device counts the 'on' bits of every arriving byte; if odd parity is specified, an error condition will be flagged any time an even number 'on' bits are detected, since at least one bit must have been lost or gained in transmission for an even number of 'on' bits to remain. 2. A binary digit appended to an array of bits to make the sum of all the bits always odd or always even.

parity check, even — A parity check counting the number of binary ones which is always maintained as an even number. If the ones in the data part of the word or character are even, the parity bit is a zero, if odd, the parity bit is a one.

parity check, odd — A check by summation in which the binary digits, in a character or word, are added, and the sum checked against a single, previously computed parity digit; i.e., a check tests whether the number of ones in a word is odd or even (synonymous with odd-even check, and related to redundant check and forbidden-combination check).

parity or mark-track error — Indicates that during the course of the previous block transfer, a data parity error was detected or one or more bits have been picked up or dropped out from either the timing track or the mark track.

parity, tape — That particular application of parity checking codes or devices when transferring data to or from magnetic or paper tape.

part, address — 1. A part of an instruction word that specifies the address of the operand. 2. The part of an instruction word that defines the address of a register or location.

partial correlation program — Given the simple correlation coefficients of three variables, X,

path, critical

Y and Z, this program computes the partial correlation coefficients for each combination of two variables.

partial product — A particular result developed by multiplying the multiplicand by one of the digits of the multiplier, i.e., there are as many partial products in a multiplication operation as there are significant digits in a multiplier, as partial sums are shifted and added to obtain the final product.

partial sum — A particular result obtained from the addition of two or more numbers without considering carries, i.e., in binary numeration systems, the partial sum is the same result as is obtained from the exclusive OR operation.

partitioning — Subdividing one large block into smaller subunits that can be handled more conveniently, e.g., partitioning a matrix.

pass — 1. The travel of magnetic tape past a read head, or travel of cards through a card feed; that portion of a program that can be accomplished during the foregoing. 2. A single execution of an instruction group that constitutes a loop. 3. A complete cycle of reading, processing and writing, i.e., a machine run.

passive network synthesis, calculator — On some calculators transfer function analysis software takes the drudgery out of designing passive networks. Users give the calculator center frequency, terminal impedance, 3dB bandwidth, pass band ripple, and the low-pass prototype order (number of poles). The calculator immediately computes the element values for a band pass filter with Butterworth, Tchebycheff, or user-defined responses. It then prints a schematic of the synthesized circuit. From this output, users can proceed directly to a breadboard verification with all network values neatly documented.

pass, single and multiple — 1. A single pass program generates the desired end result in one computer run. 2. A multiple pass program generates intermediate outputs which require additional processing to obtain the end result.

patch — Section of coding inserted into a routine to correct a mistake or alter the routine; explicitly transferring control from a routine to a section of coding and back again.

patchboard — A removable board containing hundreds of terminals into which patch cords (short wires) are connected, which determine the different programs for the machine. To change the program, the wiring pattern on the patchboard or the patchboard itself must be changed.

patch cord — A handy flexible connector conductor with receptacles or connectors at each end and which is used to interconnect sockets of plugboards.

patching — Correcting or changing the coding by overlaying it with another instruction or group of instructions.

patch routine — 1. Enables octal changes (or corrections) to be made to specified programs at object program execution time. Changes occur in main memory only and do not affect the object program stored on the run tape. 2. A specific correcting routine written of a sequence on the program chart and referring to a correct sequence.

path — A series of segments which, as represented in an overlay tree, form the shortest distance in a region between a given segment and the root segment.

path, critical — The longest time path in a proj-

pattern recognition

ect which has to be done as quickly as possible. Because the overall time required to complete the project can not be less than that required along the critical path, it requires the most careful monitoring. Any delay along this path causes the project to be delayed, while minor delays along noncritical paths does not. See PERT.

pattern recognition — Cybernetic principles are now in widespread use for both character recognition and picture recognition. Applications for the former include scanning equipment used by post offices and banks to sort mail or read credit cards. Even the U.S. Government has gotten into the act with automated hardware which scans and then speeds the processing of social security claims and income tax forms. Picture recognition is somewhat behind character recognition in widespread commercial use. Active research and development of picture recognition is concentrated on software for automatic image interpretation of data gathered by the remote sensing of chromosome structure, cell images, fingerprint patterns, and very simple 3-dimensional objects.

pattern sensitive fault — A fault that appears in response to some particular pattern of data. Contrast with program sensitive fault.

pause feature — A valuable feature on some units is the "PAUSE" key. One can use it to momentarily interrupt (about one second per Pause command) the program execution and display the contents of the X register. This gives the opportunity to review or write down intermediate results.

pause and compare, calculator — On some pocket units eight comparisons allow the program to react depending on the data in the calculation stack. Together with the GTO (GO TO step number) operation, programs can branch and loop based on numeric results. A function that is new to pocket calculators is PAUSE. When encountered in a program, the calculator stops for a second, displays the most recent result, and then continues the program. This is useful when programming iterative functions because one can watch the function converge or diverge.

payments mechanism — A payments mechanism is any device, instrument or system which accomplishes the transfer of money. Existing payments mechanisms are: cash; checks; credit cards; and miscellaneous devices such as traveler's checks. EFTS devices or systems are also payments mechanisms, such as automated check clearing, point-of-sale systems, automated tellers, bill payment systems, etc. Within specific contents, "payments mechanism" might refer to any of the above or even to associated systems such as existing credit authorization systems.

PBX (private branch exchange) — A manual or dial exchange, connected to the public telephone network, located on a customer's premises and operated by his employees.

pc board types — Circuit boards can be classified in many ways. Simple, complex, combinational logic, sequential logic — these are types of boards typically tested. All of these can be tested because all the logic components are readily understood and accessible. Recent LSI boards and devices have caused some changes in testing procedures. These changes make some boards very difficult to impossible to test. The main problems are due to unavailable information about the logic within an LSI device and inability to access control and test points within the device.

peripheral

pen, light — An optional device, used in conjunction with the incremental display, that can greatly extend its usefulness. It is a high speed, photosensitive device that can cause the computer to change or modify the display on the cathode-ray tube. As the pertinent display information is selected by the operator, the pen signals the computer by generating a pulse. Acting upon this signal, the computer can then instruct other points to be plotted across the tube face in accordance with the pen movements, or exercise specific options previously programmed without the need for separate input devices.

pen (light) control — A light pen for communication between operator and processor. When this pen-like device is pointed at information displayed on the screen, it detects light from the cathode-ray tube when a beam passes within its field of view. The pen's response is transmitted to the computer, which relates the computer's action to the section of the image being displayed. In this way, the operator can delete or add text, maintain tighter control over the program, and choose alternative courses of action.

percent change key — Automatically compares any two factors, printing the actual numeric difference between them and the percentage of difference as well.

percent function example, calculator — This function presents answers to multiplication and division in percent form and offers signed results on display. Results are printed in red (negative) or black (positive) and some units offer the discount feature. After execution of a multiplication problem by the percent key, the answer can be added or subtracted from the first factor by pressing the + or − key. Solution time is 290 ms max at 100kHz with display only on some units.

percent key — On some units this key allows entry of factors in percent form. If multiplication or division has been conditioned, this key will execute the problem as for equals with the displayed and printed answer as a percentage. Conditions the machine for the discount (add-on) sequence.

percent minus key — Reduces any number by any percentage or simple discount, printing both the amount of discount and net. ALL in one operation.

percent operation — Calculations requiring percentage add-ons or discounts are solved with the % key . . . audit symbols "A" or "D" are printed beside the respective result. Some models will also print the ratio of two numbers as a percentage when the numbers are entered as a division problem and completed with the % key.

percent plus key — Adds a tax or percentage increase to any value. Computes and prints both the amount of increase and gross with a single key.

performance evaluation — The analysis in terms of initial objectives and estimates, and usually made on-site, of a data processing system's productivity and capabilities, to provide information on operating experience and to identify corrective actions required if any.

peripheral — Usually input/output equipment used to make hard copies or to read in data from

peripheral and memory expandability

hard copies (typer, punch, tape reader, line printer, etc.). Paper tape is considered hard copy for this definition.

peripheral and memory expandability, calculators — One basic calculator has 167 registers. Options for obtaining an initial configuration of 423, 935, or 1447 total registers are also available. Additional memory may be added later by service personnel in increments of 512 registers (to a maximum of 1447 registers). As an example of calculator power, the basic memory is sufficient to solve 16 simultaneous linear equations with 16 unknowns (70 with the fully-expanded memory). Other systems are equally or more powerful (see text).

peripheral control block — Provides in some systems enhanced general interface capabilities. Special features include tape translation, general instrument control (via an ASCII bus), formatted read/write, and calling special internal code programs. Other peripheral control blocks provide simple direct control over the various peripherals. Some peripheral control blocks have three groups of functions: plotter, typewriter, and systems. The latter facilitates program and data transfers between the various elements of a system such as calculator to peripheral.

peripheral control, input/output — Some peripheral control lines can be programmed to act as an interrupt input or as a peripheral control output. As an output, these lines are often compatible with standard TTL; as an input the internal pull-up resistor on one line represents one standard TTL load. The functions of these signal lines are programmed with the control register.

peripheral control switching unit — A unit which permits any two processors to share the same peripheral devices.

peripheral control transfers — Peripheral controls regulate the transfer of data between the central processor and peripheral devices. Specifically, they reconcile the mechanical speeds of the peripheral devices with the electronic speed of the central processor, and minimize the interruption of central-processor activity due to peripheral data transfers.

peripheral device control, PLA — For a Central Processor Unit to communicate with a peripheral device, the CPU must select the device and the mode of communication. During an Input-Output instruction, the CPU transmits the device address and control information to select a unique device in a specified mode. A PLA (Programmed Logic Array) can be used to monitor the device address and control field bus to issue appropriate control signals to the devices.

peripheral equipment — 1. Units which work in conjunction with a calculator but are not a part of it (e.g., tape reader, analog-to-digital converter, typewriter, etc.). 2. In a data processing system, any equipment, distinct from the central processing unit, that may provide the system with outside communication or additional facilities. 3. The auxiliary machines which may be placed under the control of the central calculator. Examples of this are card readers, card punches, magnetic tape units and high-speed printers. Peripheral equipment may be used on-line or off-line depending upon computer design, job, requirements and economics.

peripheral processor

peripheral interface adapter (PIA) — Some microprocessors have incorporated LSI devices exclusively dedicated to enhance their I/O capabilities and thus simplify the interfacing task of the design engineer. For example, several firms provide microprocessors with special peripheral interface adapters (PIA) that act like a universal I/O interface. The typical PIA offers two 8-bit, 3-state buses to interface with peripherals, along with the ability to service four independent interrupt lines. The unit also provides handshake control logic signals for synchronizing I/O devices to the microprocessor.

peripheral interface cards — A number of optional interface cards are available for many large systems, for a selected set of standard peripherals. The interfaces are implemented as printed circuit cards that plug into the chassis assembly.

peripheral interface channel — That interface form (matching) previously designed or agreed upon so that two or more units, systems, programs, etc., may be easily joined or associated.

peripheral power, advanced calculators — Large advanced calculators equal the computer in data handling and calculating power. This is made possible by such features as increased key functions, printing capability, peripheral devices and computer-like compatibility with interfacing. Among the peripherals are X-Y plotters, card readers, tape readers and punches, typewriters, line printers, digitizing devices, magnetic-tape cassettes and disc memories. In perspective, a programmable calculator is an engineering tool designed for scientific usage with hands-on accessibility. Unlike computers, calculators are molded to fit typical engineering work spaces and provide on-the-spot solutions. Computational speed (a bench-mark factor used in assessing computer performance) is definitely a factor in large "number-crunching" programs. However, for most engineering design problems, the total engineering solution time overshadows the computational speed. A calculator also provides a capacity for dialogue, for iterations of solutions, and for direct hands-on interaction by the design engineer. As an extra advantage for calculator-aided design applications, some calculators are directly compatible with peripheral tape or disc memory and other capacity-building equipment. Graphic displays that effect the quickest interpretations of solutions are conveniently interfaced to calculators.

peripheral processing, concurrent — Service functions can be performed on a peripheral system that serves as an auxiliary to a larger system, or they can be performed on one system concurrently with other types of processing, such as stacked job processing, in a way that ensures that the data-processing facilities of the system are efficiently employed. When peripheral and stacked job processing are performed concurrently, it is possible to incorporate in the operating system optional features that are designed to enable the operator to mount files for one job while other jobs are being processed.

peripheral processor — For some environments, input and output are best processed by two interconnected computers wherein one computer handles the input/output for the other. The control programs of the operating system provide the

peripherals, advanced calculators   **permuted index**

capability to handle this mode of operation for a configuration of equipment in which a very high-speed, high-storage capacity central processing unit performs calculations upon data supplied by a smaller computer that schedules, buffers, and controls the flow of input data, intermediate results, and output data to and from the larger unit. Usually in this configuration the larger unit is termed the host and the smaller one is called peripheral, but either one may actually be in control of the other's operations and schedule.

peripherals, advanced calculators — Typical peripherals available for advanced calculators are input/output devices such as: High Speed Tape Readers, Tape Punches, Card Readers, Tape Cassettes, Tape Cartridges, Paper Tape Readers and Punches, I/O expanders, Digitizers, Plotters, Visual Display Terminals, and many more.

peripherals, advantages — Peripherals can overcome many limitations of the manual stand-alone calculator. They can reduce dependence on manually keyed inputs. They can overcome the limitations in electronic-display calculators of a single-number output, if many numbers are needed for data evaluation. And they can extend memory size. Manual input in a stand-alone calculator can cause operator fatigue, with resulting data-entry errors in lengthy calculations. And it consumes lots of time. The operator is forced to watch the display to determine when he must enter more data. Even under program direction, the calculator stops every time data are needed and transfers control to the keyboard. The operator must enter the data and transfer control back to the program by inserting the GO key. Large amounts of data make the chances of error high. Finding an erroneous or missing entry can be difficult, and correcting it can be burdensome. Single-number visual output, another limitation, often forces an operator to write down a number, return control to the calculator, write down another number — and continue this slow process. But a wide variety of peripherals are available to cope with both input and output limitations and with the small memories that are soon overloaded as auxiliary devices are added.

peripheral equipment, custom-tailored (calculator) — Users can add peripheral equipment to tailor the input, output, and control to their special situation on many units. Fully compatible I/O structures let users interface their calculator to a broad selection of versatile and capable peripherals.

peripherals availability — Some types include:
Cartridge Disc Drives
Disk Pack Drives
Phase Encoded Magnetic Tape Drives
NRZI Magnetic Tape Drives
Plotters
Card Readers
Optical Mark Readers
Paper Tape Readers and Punches
Printing Terminals
CRT Terminals
Line Printers
Card Reader/Punch
Most of these devices are interfaced with standard hardware, software drivers, diagnostics and are available without need for significant modification.

peripherals, calculator — Various models accept up to four peripherals at one time (up to five if a unitized printer is included). This can be expanded to 13 peripherals with the use of the same types of I/O expanders. This virtually limitless I/O capability coupled with the broad range of other series peripherals allows the user to configure the exact system necessary for his application. The peripherals now available for use with many calculators are:
Marked Card Reader
Output Typewriter
X-Y Plotter
Paper Tape Reader
Digitizer
Tape Cassette
Page Width Printer
I/O Expander
Hopper Card Reader
Teletype
Paper Tape Punch
Paper Tape Reader

peripheral subsystem — Quite generally a subsystem is designed to be a group of one or more peripheral units of the same type connected to an available input/output channel. Each subsystem is controlled by a channel synchronizer/control unit that interprets the control signals and instructions issued by the central processor, affects the transfer of data to or from the selected unit and the central processor indicates to the central processor the status of the available peripheral units, and informs the central processor when errors or faults that affect the operation of the subsystem occurs.

permanent error — An error which is not eliminated by reprocessing the information a limited number of times.

permanent fault — Faults are failures in performance in the manner required or specified. Sporadic faults are intermittent while permanent faults are repetitious, but these may either escape attention when they do not result in failure to perform some particular tasks, or are known and easily correctable.

permutation — The number of possible sequences of n items taken c at a time:

$$p \binom{n}{c} = \frac{n!}{(n-c)!}$$

permutation program — A permutation is an ordered subset of a set of distinct objects. The number of possible permutations, each containing n objects, that can be formed from a collection of m distinct objects is given by

$$_mP_n = \frac{m!}{(m-n)!} = m(m-1)\ldots(m-n+1)$$

where m, n are integers and $0 \leq n \leq m$.
Notes:
1. $_mP_n$ can also be denoted by P_n^m, $P(m,n)$ or $(m)_n$.
2. $_mP_0 = 1$, $_mP_1 = m$, $_mP_m = m!$

permuted cyclic code — Refers to a specific code in which characters are represented by words of a fixed number of bits but which are arranged in a sequence so that the signal distance between consecutive words is 1 or unity.

permuted index — A form of document indexing developed by producing an entry in the index for each word of specific interest and by including

personal (calculator) computing systems — Like a computer, some units operate with lightning speed. Like a computer, many advanced calculators can execute highly sophisticated programs involving looping, branching, and five-level or higher subroutines.
Unlike a computer, advanced calculators offer instantaneous turnaround, ease of operation, and low initial cost which can be rapidly amortized. They will fit on top of a desk and can be operated without special programming experience. For many smaller operations, they can be a smart and economical alternative to a computer. If buyers are already computer users or owners, calculators still make a lot of sense: users can slash their terminal time and streamline their work flow by turning over many of the computer's chores to the instantly accessible programmable calculators.

personality modules, PROM programmers — Personality modules are used to accommodate the specialized interfacing and programming instructions for current and future varieties of PROMs. Options for teletype, paper tape reader, and general-purpose interface (minicomputer) are offered to make various PROM programmers more powerful and versatile.

PERT — Program evaluation and review technique. Critical path analysis using computer techniques.

PERT/COST — A PERT program for providing management with cost control for all phases of a project.

PERT/COST system — A generalized program designed to facilitate planning, scheduling, control, and monitoring of both large- and small-scale research and development projects.

PERT, early start dates — Used in an optimistic time estimate in which each job is started as early as possible to estimate the duration of the entire task.

PERT, free float — Certain stops used to halt particular tasks where no action would have resulted in an overall delay in the project.

PERT, latest start dates — Used in estimating the completion date of a particular task. Each job is arranged to start as late as possible so that the entire task is completed on the required date.

PERT (program evaluation and review technique) network — Use of PERT requires an extensive analysis of an overall project in order to list all the individual activities, or jobs which must be performed in order to meet the total objective. These activities are then arranged in a network that displays the sequential relationship among them. This analysis must be extremely thorough and detailed if it is to be realistic. PERT provides a means of reporting and analysis for project administrators. Information required can be developed and areas which impose the greatest time restrictions on the completion of a product can be high-lighted. Areas with an excess of time for completion, called slack areas, are also high-lighted.

PERT/TIME — A PERT program which allows management to plan, schedule, and direct programs and projects, as well as evaluate progress during project execution.

phoneme — A primitive unit of auditory speech in a given language.

phonetic system — The specific equipment which has features for starting and acting upon data from the voice source or having a voice-form output.

physical processing — The processing of data by an object program at the physical record level with the function of packing and unpacking logical records left to the user program. Contrast with logical processing.

physical simulation — The use of a model of a physical system in which computing elements are used to represent some but not all of the subsystems.

PIA bus interface — The PIA (Peripheral Interface Adapter) in many systems is used to provide 8 or 16 bits of external interface and four control lines at addressable locations in standard system memory. The I/O bits can be accessed in two words of 8 bits each, but each I/O bit is individually programmable to act as either an input or an output.

P.I. codes — Program indicator codes. When two or more programs are used in the same program tape, the use of PI codes permits automatic selection of programs and permits switching from one program to the other.

piece work programming — The programming technique of using an outside service organization to prepare programs for which payment is arranged by accomplishment, other than on a time-cost basis. Software companies are usually consulted for the above.

Pi key — The Pi key enters pi to 12 digits. Generally, the display indicates value rounded off to 10 digits.

pilot system — Relates to a specific collection of file records and supplementary data obtained from the actual operations of a business over an extended period and used to effect a realistic system for testing by closely simulating the real world environment.

pi-network impedance matching program — A pi-network impedance matching program illustrates the power of some pocket computers. Such a network is often used to match between two resistances R_1 and R_2. Given the values of R_1 and R_2, the frequency, and the circuit Q, the calculator determines network inductance and capacitance values in 20 keystrokes.

pipelining — Concerns the beginning of one instruction sequence before another has been completed. Once a technique used on supercomputers, pipelining is now used to speed execution on machines of all sizes.

place value — The representation of quantities by a positional value system.

plant — The usage in programming is to put or place an instruction which has been formed during the execution of a routine in a storage location, in such a way that it will be obeyed at some later stage in the execution. Thus, plants give the computer the ability to control and execute its own programs by using the ability of the computer to prepare or select instructions or subroutines on the basis of results obtained.

PLA (programmed logic arrays) — 1. A PLA is an orderly arrangement of logical AND and logical OR functions. In application they behave very much like a glorified ROM, but PLA is devoted primarily with a combination device. 2. A Programmable Logic Array is an alternative to ROM which uses a standard logic network programmed to perform a specific function. PLAs are implemented in either MOS or bipolar circuits.

plasma display — Some plasma display graphics terminals incorporate microprocessor technology in combination with the natural graphics medium of the plasma panel. Complete selective write and erase of each dot makes possible displays which can be altered. Many include communications interfaces such as standard RS-232C with ASCII format. Baud rates are selectable and special control codes may be specified to satisfy a user's interface requirements. Some options include APL character set, extended ASCII characters, space overwrite latch, variable writing modes, variable character size and addressable cursor. Supporting software for some models is written in FORTRAN.

platter organization, disk example — Each platter, removable or fixed, represents a separate mass memory system. As such, each platter is independent and must have its own directory area, bootstraps, and so on. The platter organization is as follows for one system:
Any location on the platter is defined by three variables: head, cylinder, and sector.[6] CYLINDER defines the radial position. There are 203 cylinders, 0 through 202, numbered from the outside of the platter towards the center. SECTOR defines the angular position around the platter. There are 24 sectors, numbered 0 through 23. A thin metal skirt on the hub of the platter has 24 slots cut into it to define precisely the start of each sector. An index slot provides a reference for sector 0. HEAD 0 and HEAD 1 specify the upper and lower platter surfaces, respectively. Each platter is divided into two areas, the system area and the user area. The system area is used by the mass memory system.

PL/M compiler language — PL/M is a high level language concept developed by Intel Corp. to meet the special needs of microcomputer systems programming. Programmers can utilize a high level language to efficiently program microcomputers. PL/M is an assembly language replacement that can fully command the 8080 CPU and future processors to produce efficient run-time object code. PL/M was designed to provide additional developmental software support for the MCS-80 microcomputer system, permitting the programmer to concentrate more on his problem and less on the actual task of programming than is possible with assembly language. Programming time and costs are reduced, and training, documentation and program maintenance are simplified. User application programs and standard systems programs may be transferred to future computer systems that support PL/M with little or no reprogramming. These are advantages of high-level language programming that have been proven in the large computer field and are also available to the microcomputer user.
PL/M is derived from IBM's PL/I, a very extensive and sophisticated language which could become a widely known and used language in the near future. PL/M is a subset of PL/I with emphasis on these features that accurately reflect the nature of systems programming requirements.

PL/1 (programming language) — Compilers are provided for use in compiling object programs from source programs written in this programming language. This language has some features that are characteristic of FORTRAN and incorporates some of the best features of other languages, such as string manipulation, data structures, and extensive editing capabilities. Further, it has features not currently available in any language. The language is designed to take advantage of recent developments in computer technology and to provide the programmer with a flexible problem-oriented language for programming problems that can best be solved using a combination of scientific and commercial computing techniques. It is designed to be particularly useful for the increasing number of semicommercial, semiscientific applications such as information retrieval and command and control applications.

plot, histogram — This special package allows users to specify the minimum and maximum values and establish cell width. The program will use consecutively entered values to establish mean, standard deviations and percentage of occurences per cell. Upon key command, accumulated cells are plotted on the axis. At any point, the user may return to input mode and add new data. (some units)

plot key — Plots last curve fit or histogram completed using scale factors established using AXES key. (some units)

plotter — Refers to a visual display or board in which a dependent variable is graphed by an automatically controlled pen or pencil as a function of one or more variables.

plotter, advanced calculator — One unit has a 96-character interchangeable printing disc which is externally programmable along with such functions as space, backspace, carrier return, horizontal and vertical tabs, line feed and reverse line feed, top of form, and form length. These programmable functions along with the bidirectional motions of the platen provide plotting capabilities for charts and graphs and simplifies form filling.

plotter, calculator time-sharing terminal — An accounting department provides an example of a calculator used as a time-sharing terminal in control of a plotter. As a terminal, the machine can access programs and data relating to corporate accounting from a central computer at corporate headquarters. Among this data is a file containing monthly inventory data for each division, set up during a recent drive to reduce inventory. This information is organized as X-Y coordinates and can drive a remote on-line plotter. Without a plotter, some designs can turn the calculator into a front end for an off-line plotter. Some calculators can be driven by a BASIC program that also adds titles to, and labels the axes of, the completed plot.

plotter control ROM — The Plotter Control ROM provides some calculators with the additional commands that are necessary for the control of plotters. The specific ROM expands the language of some models to include all the commands illustrated in various tables without sacrificing any of these model's Special Function Keys or read/write memory.

plotter, digitizing — Some digitizing plotters (terminals) have built-in joystick control. Users the context in which it occurs, most often restricted to title words.

personal (calculator) computing systems — Like a computer, some units operate with lightning speed. Like a computer, many advanced calculators can execute highly sophisticated programs involving looping, branching, and five-level or higher subroutines.

Unlike a computer, advanced calculators offer instantaneous turnaround, ease of operation, and low initial cost which can be rapidly amortized. They will fit on top of a desk and can be operated without special programming experience. For many smaller operations, they can be a smart and economical alternative to a computer. If buyers are already computer users or owners, calculators still make a lot of sense: users can slash their terminal time and streamline their work flow by turning over many of the computer's chores to the instantly accessible programmable calculators.

personality modules, PROM programmers — Personality modules are used to accommodate the specialized interfacing and programming instructions for current and future varieties of PROMs. Options for teletype, paper tape reader, and general-purpose interface (minicomputer) are offered to make various PROM programmers more powerful and versatile.

PERT — Program evaluation and review technique. Critical path analysis using computer techniques.

PERT/COST — A PERT program for providing management with cost control for all phases of a project.

PERT/COST system — A generalized program designed to facilitate planning, scheduling, control, and monitoring of both large- and small-scale research and development projects.

PERT, early start dates — Used in an optimistic time estimate in which each job is started as early as possible to estimate the duration of the entire task.

PERT, free float — Certain stops used to halt particular tasks where no action would have resulted in an overall delay in the project.

PERT, latest start dates — Used in estimating the completion date of a particular task. Each job is arranged to start as late as possible so that the entire task is completed on the required date.

PERT (program evaluation and review technique) network — Use of PERT requires an extensive analysis of an overall project in order to list all the individual activities, or jobs which must be performed in order to meet the total objective. These activities are then arranged in a network that displays the sequential relationship among them. This analysis must be extremely thorough and detailed if it is to be realistic. PERT provides a means of reporting and analysis for project administrators. Information required can be developed and areas which impose the greatest time restrictions on the completion of a product can be high-lighted. Areas with an excess of time for completion, called slack areas, are also high-lighted.

PERT/TIME — A PERT program which allows management to plan, schedule, and direct programs and projects, as well as evaluate progress during project execution.

phoneme — A primitive unit of auditory speech in a given language.

phonetic system — The specific equipment which has features for starting and acting upon data from the voice source or having a voice-form output.

physical processing — The processing of data by an object program at the physical record level with the function of packing and unpacking logical records left to the user program. Contrast with logical processing.

physical simulation — The use of a model of a physical system in which computing elements are used to represent some but not all of the subsystems.

PIA bus interface — The PIA (Peripheral Interface Adapter) in many systems is used to provide 8 or 16 bits of external interface and four control lines at addressable locations in standard system memory. The I/O bits can be accessed in two words of 8 bits each, but each I/O bit is individually programmable to act as either an input or an output.

P.I. codes — Program indicator codes. When two or more programs are used in the same program tape, the use of PI codes permits automatic selection of programs and permits switching from one program to the other.

piece work programming — The programming technique of using an outside service organization to prepare programs for which payment is arranged by accomplishment, other than on a time-cost basis. Software companies are usually consulted for the above.

Pi key — The Pi key enters pi to 12 digits. Generally, the display indicates value rounded off to 10 digits.

pilot system — Relates to a specific collection of file records and supplementary data obtained from the actual operations of a business over an extended period and used to effect a realistic system for testing by closely simulating the real world environment.

pi-network impedance matching program — A pi-network impedance matching program illustrates the power of some pocket computers. Such a network is often used to match between two resistances R_1 and R_2. Given the values of R_1 and R_2, the frequency, and the circuit Q, the calculator determines network inductance and capacitance values in 20 keystrokes.

pipelining — Concerns the beginning of one instruction sequence before another has been completed. Once a technique used on supercomputers, pipelining is now used to speed execution on machines of all sizes.

place value — The representation of quantities by a positional value system.

plant — The usage in programming is to put or place an instruction which has been formed during the execution of a routine in a storage location, in such a way that it will be obeyed at some later stage in the execution. Thus, plants give the computer the ability to control and execute its own programs by using the ability of the computer to prepare or select instructions or subroutines on the basis of results obtained.

PLA (programmed logic arrays) — 1. A PLA is an orderly arrangement of logical AND and logical OR functions. In application they behave very much like a glorified ROM, but PLA is devoted primarily with a combination device. 2. A Programmable Logic Array is an alternative to ROM which uses a standard logic network programmed to perform a specific function. PLAs are implemented in either MOS or bipolar circuits.

plasma display — Some plasma display graphics terminals incorporate microprocessor technology in combination with the natural graphics medium of the plasma panel. Complete selective write and erase of each dot makes possible displays which can be altered. Many include communications interfaces such as standard RS-232C with ASCII format. Baud rates are selectable and special control codes may be specified to satisfy a user's interface requirements. Some options include APL character set, extended ASCII characters, space overwrite latch, variable writing modes, variable character size and addressable cursor. Supporting software for some models is written in FORTRAN.

platter organization, disk example — Each platter, removable or fixed, represents a separate mass memory system. As such, each platter is independent and must have its own directory area, bootstraps, and so on. The platter organization is as follows for one system:
Any location on the platter is defined by three variables: head, cylinder, and sector.[6] CYLINDER defines the radial position. There are 203 cylinders, 0 through 202, numbered from the outside of the platter towards the center. SECTOR defines the angular position around the platter. There are 24 sectors, numbered 0 through 23. A thin metal skirt on the hub of the platter has 24 slots cut into it to define precisely the start of each sector. An index slot provides a reference for sector 0. HEAD 0 and HEAD 1 specify the upper and lower platter surfaces, respectively. Each platter is divided into two areas, the system area and the user area. The system area is used by the mass memory system.

PL/M compiler language — PL/M is a high level language concept developed by Intel Corp. to meet the special needs of microcomputer systems programming. Programmers can utilize a high level language to efficiently program microcomputers. PL/M is an assembly language replacement that can fully command the 8080 CPU and future processors to produce efficient run-time object code. PL/M was designed to provide additional developmental software support for the MCS-80 microcomputer system, permitting the programmer to concentrate more on his problem and less on the actual task of programming than is possible with assembly language. Programming time and costs are reduced, and training, documentation and program maintenance are simplified. User application programs and standard systems programs may be transferred to future computer systems that support PL/M with little or no reprogramming. These are advantages of high-level language programming that have been proven in the large computer field and are also available to the microcomputer user.
PL/M is derived from IBM's PL/I, a very extensive and sophisticated language which could become a widely known and used language in the near future. PL/M is a subset of PL/I with emphasis on these features that accurately reflect the nature of systems programming requirements.

PL/1 (programming language) — Compilers are provided for use in compiling object programs from source programs written in this programming language. This language has some features that are characteristic of FORTRAN and incorporates some of the best features of other languages, such as string manipulation, data structures, and extensive editing capabilities. Further, it has features not currently available in any language. The language is designed to take advantage of recent developments in computer technology and to provide the programmer with a flexible problem-oriented language for programming problems that can best be solved using a combination of scientific and commercial computing techniques. It is designed to be particularly useful for the increasing number of semicommercial, semiscientific applications such as information retrieval and command and control applications.

plot, histogram — This special package allows users to specify the minimum and maximum values and establish cell width. The program will use consecutively entered values to establish mean, standard deviations and percentage of occurences per cell. Upon key command, accumulated cells are plotted on the axis. At any point, the user may return to input mode and add new data. (some units)

plot key — Plots last curve fit or histogram completed using scale factors established using AXES key. (some units)

plotter — Refers to a visual display or board in which a dependent variable is graphed by an automatically controlled pen or pencil as a function of one or more variables.

plotter, advanced calculator — One unit has a 96-character interchangeable printing disc which is externally programmable along with such functions as space, backspace, carrier return, horizontal and vertical tabs, line feed and reverse line feed, top of form, and form length. These programmable functions along with the bidirectional motions of the platen provide plotting capabilities for charts and graphs and simplifies form filling.

plotter, calculator time-sharing terminal — An accounting department provides an example of a calculator used as a time-sharing terminal in control of a plotter. As a terminal, the machine can access programs and data relating to corporate accounting from a central computer at corporate headquarters. Among this data is a file containing monthly inventory data for each division, set up during a recent drive to reduce inventory. This information is organized as X-Y coordinates and can drive a remote on-line plotter. Without a plotter, some designs can turn the calculator into a front end for an off-line plotter. Some calculators can be driven by a BASIC program that also adds titles to, and labels the axes of, the completed plot.

plotter control ROM — The Plotter Control ROM provides some calculators with the additional commands that are necessary for the control of plotters. The specific ROM expands the language of some models to include all the commands illustrated in various tables without sacrificing any of these model's Special Function Keys or read/write memory.

plotter, digitizing — Some digitizing plotters (terminals) have built-in joystick control. Users move the pen to the desired position on the plot and press the CALL key, and the unit calls out the x-y data points. It's the equivalent of a built-in graphic tablet. A GIN command causes the plotter to send the current XYZ pen co-ordinates. If the pen is outside the page boundaries, boundary values are sent and a bell on the plotter signals the operator. (some units)

plotter, 4-color (calculator) — Users can plot up to 7 vectors per second in any direction with one type high-speed digital plotter. The x-y plotter works with a time-share system and operates in parallel with user terminals so they get both graphs and printouts. The plotter accepts bit-serial ASCII data at the rate of 10 or 30 characters per second. It can plot graphs on any size paper up to 11 by 17 in. (28 by 43 cm). Unlike the "staircase" drawings from incremental plotters, the unit draws a clean, smooth, continuous line. If there is an error in data transmission, that point is omitted and the next correct point is plotted. Four colors of ink are available, and the pens are disposable for convenience. Users simply snap out an empty pen, and snap in a new one. A picture may well be worth a thousand numbers.

plotter, interactive digitizing operation — One unit automatically adjusts for a 10″ × 15″ plot. There's no need to worry how the last plot was set up. When users wish to set a different plotting area or adjust to a new paper size, they use the set control buttons on the front panel to define the new area. Once it starts moving, the digital stepping motors and internal vector generator work at high speed, with microprocessor-controlled acceleration and deceleration. Repeatability is good. There is no servo hysteresis, no drift as in potentiometric feedback systems. And no slidewires to clean, no moving electrical contacts, no servo adjustments to be made. There are many new types of plotters.

plotter, joystick control — The Joystick is accurate to .1% for exacting input. Its sensitive control of the cursor, activated on some units by the POINTER command makes it easy to be accurate. One supplier claims it has none of the overshoot or backlash problems which often plague input devices, and which require the user to slowly "rock" a cursor into place. Joystick, users position the cursor the first time, quickly, precisely. Users move the center lever in the direction they want to move the cursor; speed is controlled by the angle or distance of the lever from the center position. When users want to stop the cursor, they release the lever to its natural vertical position. Users aren't required to keep adjusting the unit. It has less than one addressable point drift. And if ever the need arises, two drift trim tabs let users individually adjust the x and y axes.

plotter-printer, calculator — A printer that extends the output characteristics of advanced series desk-top programmable calculators is on impact printer with a full-character, fixed carriage that can be used to fill out forms, create reports, draw charts and plot graphs using the bi-directional platen and carrier. It also features programmable horizontal and vertical tabulation. In addition to the standard 96-character, upper/lower case print wheel, optional interchangeable wheels are available for ASCII character sets and European character sets. The printer, accommodates paper up to 15 inches (38 cm) wide and prints up to 132 columns at 10 characters per inch. Average printing speed is 30 cps. Six-part paper in single-sheet or continuous-feed form may also be used.

plotter systems, calculator — Adding a graphic plotter to a calculator system provides hard copy graphic solutions to problems solved by many of the advanced programmable calculators. Whether user applications require the production of graphs under total program control or by manually entering data coordinates through the calculator, the plotters provides fast, accurate transformation of tabulated data into meaningful graphics. Features of some plotters include the use of disposable ink pens facilitating the rapid changing of ink colors plus the ability to plot on any paper up to 10 × 15 inches. Maximum plotting versatility is obtained with a plotter ROM which provides complete alphanumeric capability, X-Y axis generator, automatic function scaling and special symbol plotting. The end result is a finished plot that is completely titled, scaled and labelled.

plotting, automatic — In many diverse areas of industry and science, a clear graphical representation of results is essential for rapid interpretation and evaluation of data. From weather mapping to business and stock market reports, from engineering design investigations to insurance actuarial graphs, in research laboratories and in computer laboratories, graphs of X vs Y plots are required for summarizing and presenting information in concise form. This need has been further accentuated by modern high-speed calculators. The rapid production of vast quantities of data by these machines requires especially fast and accurate plotting equipment.

plotting board — Refers to an output unit which plots the curves of one or more variables as a function of one or more other variables.

plotting board, hard copy — A hard copy output device which presents the results of a plotter system, which is designed to develop curves, graphs, chart, and other graphic output.

plotting output writer — Refers to a specially modified typewriter with the capability of producing formatted alphanumeric output. It not only plots a graph, but also labels points. (Also available as a portable unit with a separate electronics package.)

plotting output writer, calculator — Adds digital plotting, as well as fully-formatted alphanumeric output capability, to some types of Calculating Systems. High-speed stepping motors (approx. 400 steps/second) on both the X and Y axis plots points or alpha characters in increments as small as 1/100th of an inch. Users can also use it as an Output Writer.

plotting packages — Included are routines which draw and label axes, allowing a user input of data minimums, maximums and increments. Some programs allow for easy data entry and subsequent screen plotting. For convenience, all routines can be called from user's own programs on some calculators.

plug-in blocks, keyboard — Many mathematics users need an interactive, problem-solving system — a system that can play back their ideas in mathematical or alpha terms, instantly. Several models offer them the opportunity to select from special keyboard plug-in blocks, so they can personalize their problems solving capabilities to their specific discipline. These function blocks are completely interchangeable and require absolutely no modification to the calculator or any special tools or skills to install. To install the math functions for example, merely insert the math memory block in the slot at the top of the calculator, place the key identification template over the left-hand block of keys, and users are ready to start solving complex mathematical problems with the touch of a single key. This special feature on several systems vastly extends user calculating power, simplifies programming, and reduces computing time.

plug-in cards, calculator systems — Most laboratory instruments, process signal conditioning systems, voltmeters and other instruments, manufactured in the past five years are equipped with binary-coded-decimal or binary digital outputs. A typical digital interface provides the means for connecting these devices to the calculator. Transfer of data from instruments and control systems is by means of individual plug-in cards designed for a specific application. There are, for instance, cards for digital voltmeters, clocks, timers, etc. Other cards are used for output functions such as relay contact closures, data output from the calculator for external displays, counter preset systems, and similar applications, as well as analog inputs by means of an analog-to-digital converter card in conjunction with both reed-relay and MOS multiplexer cards.

plug-in data input card — A typical data input card is designed to transfer up to a maximum of six BCD digits of data from devices such as counters, digital voltmeters, digital multimeters and similar devices which provide a "print command" pulse indicating the availability of valid data. On some units, data must be valid for a minimum of 5 milliseconds after the print commmand transition. Either positive-going or negative-going print command transitions can be selected by a link on the card. Provision is also made for either a normal or inverted polarity indication which issues a "change sign" command to the calculator.

plug-in event counter card — A typical card consists of six individual binary-coded-decimal counter circuits which may be connected into three 2-digit, two 3-digit, or one 6-digit counter units simply by changing a set of jumpers. Individual, programmable "start," "stop" and "reset" controls are provided for some counter subgroups.

plug-in ROM block, calculator — A 1K ROM plug-in block contains software to allow the calculator to read and write on the mass memory. Prerecorded cassette contains system software. Interface cable assembly contains calculator interface card and 256-word cache memory. (some systems)

plug-in ROM calculators — Peripheral and memory expandability is available using Read Only Memory (ROM) plug-in ROM's after added internal memory, and control of external peripherals, providing capabilities to match any type of application. One basic calculator has 173 registers. A 429- or 1453-register memory can be supplied plus more ROM, either with the original shipment or installed later by users or service personnel. Tape cassettes, cartridges and disks add to this. An example of 9 desk-top unit's power: the basic memory is sufficient to solve 17 simultaneous linear equations with 17 unknowns. With the 429- or 1453-register memory, the number of equations that can be solved are 34 and 71, respectively.

plug-in unit — 1. An assembly of electronic components of a standard type, wired together, which can be plugged in or pulled out easily. 2. A self-contained circuit assembly.

plug-in, user-definable — As a primary advance in keyboard personalization and specialization, some manufacturers offer a user-definable function plug-in, allowing them to customize individual keys with the operations uniquely important to them. These are typically the commonly used formulas that are the foundation for a particular business or discipline. An electrical engineer uses voltage, impedance, capacitance, and true RMS function programs. A physicist uses mass, velocity, and acceleration functions. A chemical engineer uses fluid-flow and heat transfer functions. One user-definable plug-in can allow the customization from five to twenty-five keys.

plug, program-patching — A relatively small auxiliary plugboard patched with a specific variation of a portion of a program and designed to be plugged into a relatively larger plugboard patched with the main program.

PM (phase modulation) — 1. A method of angle modulation in which the amplitude of the carrier wave remains constant while varying in phase with the amplitude of the modulating signal. 2. One of three ways of modifying a sinewave signal to make it "carry" information. The sinewave or carrier has its phase changed in accordance with the information to be transmitted.

PMOS — P-channel MOS refers to the oldest type of MOS circuit where the electrical current is a flow of positive charges.

p-n-p type junction — The contact interface surface or immediate area between n-type and p-type semiconducting material. Transistor action takes place at the junction of these differently doped materials. Junction transistors may be p-n-p type or n-p-n type for the emitter, base and collect or electrode materials, respectively.

pocket calculators, business — Some of these feature many preprogrammed operations especially designed to solve business problems. While having deceptively fewer keys, they can solve specialized problems in compound interest, discounts, markups, remaining principle on a mortgage, future value of an annuity, depreciation, statistics, bond prices and yields, etc., far quicker than can scientific calculators.

pocket calculators, complex problem-solving — Most calculator users are solving complex mathematical questions with previously unrealized degrees of accuracy by using a hand-held calculator pre-programmed with extensive financial problem-solving routines. Generally the math calculator is capable of performing the four basic arithmetic functions and is programmed for financial routines such as linear regression (trend line) analysis, sum-of-the-year's digits and declining balance depreciation, discounted cash flow analysis, and yield-to-maturity bond calculations. The programs are activated by depressing one of several function keys. Each key executes a specific program. For example, once historical data is entered for trend line analysis, the operator specifies a future month and depresses the trend line key to display projected trends.

pocket calculators, programmable — Some advanced units are close to being a personal, portable computer. Like a computer, they accept and

point (base) — remember programs (fed in via the keyboard or tiny, magnetic program cards), execute them at the touch of a button. Some use RPN logic to solve extremely complex problems in seconds. Once the unit is programmed to solve a problem, it can run the program any number of times with different data. And, since users can feed in a new program card in a few seconds, they can rapidly customize the calculator to meet their specific needs of the moment. Most users don't have to know much about computers to operate their machines.

point (base) — The dot that marks the separation between the integral and fractional parts of a quantity, i.e., between the coefficients of the zero and the minus one powers of the number base. It is usually called, for a number system using base two, a binary point. For base ten, a decimal point, etc. See also notation.

point coefficient, floating — That specific part of a floating point number or representation that expresses the number of times that the number base with exponent is to be multiplied, i.e., the number 5.06 in the number 5.06×10^{18}, is the floating-point coefficient. This means it will be expanded by 10^{18}.

point, graphic — The tip of the writing tool on a graphic device (i.e. the tip of the pen on an X-Y plotter, or the writing beam on a graphic system display.

pointer — 1. A word giving the address of another main memory storage location. 2. Pointers automatically step through memory locations. Automatically stepping forward through consecutive locations is known as autoincrement addressing; automatically stepping backwards is known as autodecrement addressing. These modes are particularly useful for processing tabular or array data.

pointer movement, programmable calculator — On some units the program memory circulates continuously, its beginning and end denoted by a marker. The main pointer moves as programs are entered or executed. A second pointer is activated when a user-defined function is called.

pointer, program — On some units, when a stored program is executed, the pointer points to the next executable memory word and the buffer contains a copy of that word. The buffer contents are decoded and placed on the I_s bus as a microinstruction that causes the calculator to enter a subroutine in the ROM to service the key that was pressed.

pointer, register — The portion of the program status double-word that points to a set of 16 general registers to be used as the current register block. (some units)

pointer setting, program (small calculators) — On some units programs do not need starting statements. However, the program pointer must be positioned at the line at which users want the program to begin. Most programs will start at line 00. Users can set the program pointer to line 00 by pressing GTO 0 0 (read "go to zero zero") in RUN mode. Similarly, users can set the program pointer to any line in a program in RUN mode by pressing GTO and then keying in the desired line number. Also, on some systems, invalid addresses are numbers outside the range 00 thru 49. When an invalid address is used in RUN mode, the program pointer does not move and the display is also invalid. In PRGM mode, the GTO is omitted and the subsequent key is stored in program memory. Another way to set the program pointer to line 00 is to press the same key that clears prefix keys: BST. This is for the user's convenience so that they can perform this particular pointer operation in RUN mode by pressing one key instead of three.

Note: On some systems, users must always use two digits for designating line numbers following the GTO key. For example, to set the program pointer to line 6 users must press GTO 06.

pointer, stack — In nested storage types (pushdown), the address of the location at the top of the column is often called the stack pointer and is held in a preassigned register.

pointer, virtual memory — As an aid for storage efficiency some computers are designed so that parts of programs and data may be scattered through main memory and auxiliary storage. Various pointers or lists of pointers automatically keep track of the location of these program portions. The user of calculators so designed may be unaware of this scattering procedure and most often operates calculating procedures as though he were using normal memory.

point of no return — A first instance in a program in which a rerun is no longer possible, since data may no longer be available.

point-of-sale — Point-of-Sale (POS) systems are systems for automating various aspects of retail operations. Such systems are electronic and many directly involve EFTS. The general types of functions performed by POS systems are: 1. Inventory control and other functions internal to the retail establishment. Data entered on an electronic cash register becomes input to a store-wide or chain-wide file of such data. 2. Credit authorization. A purchaser's credit card is read by a terminal and a central computer verifies that the card is valid and that the purchaser's credit is sufficient to cover a sale. Such systems provide the means for establishing a zero floor limit for all credit transactions. 3. Credit verification. A merchant obtains verification from a bank's central computer that a purchaser's demand account balance is sufficient to cover a sale. 4. Electronic funds transfer. Some EFTS projects include POS terminals which are card-activated and which debit a customer's account and credit a merchant's account in order to effect payment for a sale. All POS functions could be integrated in a single EFT system. In such an integrated system, communications between banks and retail terminals would be handled by special switching and processing centers. Compatibility and standardization of POS/EFTS are important. Some standardization of cards and terminals may be necessary, since merchants may be unwilling to handle several different types. On the other hand, sharing of terminals may pose antitrust problems.

point of sale central controller — A typical central controller polls up to 120 of the data entry stations and records the data on nine-track magnetic tape. The central controller can also operate directly on-line with the computer as well as recording on magnetic tape.

point of sale terminal — Transaction or point-of-sale terminals for source data collection are used in applications such as department store sales, supermarket check-out, and factory data collection. These terminals provide a very easy interface for an unskilled operator, have built-in means of controlling or improving the user's accuracy, and in many cases provide a means of automatically reading some form of coded label or tag on the merchandise. Frequently, these terminals can be hard wired to a computer in the same physical facility, but in other cases a communications line tie-in to a remotely located computer is required.

point of sale terminal, programmable — These terminals are programmable and perform arithmetic operations. They contain both a read-only microprogram memory and magnetic-core memory. The terminals can operate either on-line over a communication link with a central computer or can store transaction data on a magnetic tape which can then be polled by the computer automatically.

point of sale terminals, stand alone — Most of these are designed primarily for off-line operation in multiterminal installations. A central unit is used to record data from multiple point-of-sale units connected by direct wiring on a nine-track magnetic tape. The central unit includes: 1. a magnetic tape unit, 2. a control unit, 3. a communications interface, 4. a scanner or multiplex unit, 5. a buffer. Arithmetic operations are performed in the terminal, which is programmable to a limited extent.

point of sale terminal users — There are many kinds of applications where general-purpose keyboard/printer or CRT terminals are not adequate for the users' requirements. In these cases, special terminals are required. The point-of-sale terminal is an example of this which has matured to the point that it is becoming a major market. Cash point and transaction terminals lead the list. Other examples are found in accounting firms, large libraries, hospitals, doctors' offices, lawyers' offices, civil engineers, architects, schools, banks.

point, radix — The dot that delineates the integer digits from the fractional digits of a number; specifically, the dot that delineates the digital position involving the zero exponent of the radix from the digital position involving the minus-one exponent of the radix. The radix point is often identified by the name of the system, e.g., binary point, octal point, or decimal point. In the writing of any number in any system, if no dot is included the radix point is assumed to follow the rightmost digit. (Synonymous with point.)

point-to-point circuits — Private communication lines for the exclusive use of the purchaser, and which join together one or more points.

point-to-point control system — A control system which is concerned only in going from one point to another without regulating the path it takes to arrive at the second point.

poisson parameter interval program — Confidence Interval on Poisson Parameter. This program determines a confidence interval on the parameter Theta of the Poisson distribution.

poisson program — This program calculates the probabilities for a poisson distribution given mean value (m) and value of the integer (C).

polar coordinate conversion key — Converts x, y rectangular coordinates placed in S- and Y-registers to polar magnitude and angle.

polar coordinates — A mathematical system of coordinates for locating a point in a plane by the length of its radius vector and the angle this vector makes with a fixed line.

polarity — 1. A condition by which the direction of the flow of current can be determined in an electrical circuit (usually batteries and other direct-voltage sources). 2. Having two opposite charges, one positive and the other negative. 3. Having two opposite magnetic poles, one north and the other south. 4. Distinction between positive and negative electric charges (Franklin). 5. Distinction between positive (north) and negative (south) magnetic poles of electro or permanent magnet; these poles do not exist, but describe locations where magnetic flux leaves or enters magnetic material. 6. General terms for difference between two points in a system which differ in one respect; e.g., potentials of terminals of a cell or electrolytic capacitor, windings of a transformer, video signal, legs of a balanced circuit, phase of an alternating current.

Polish, Cambridge — Used in the LISP language, the Polish operators = and × are allowed to have more than two operands.

Polish notation — 1. A distinct technique or device credited to the Polish logician J. Lukasiewicz for treating algebraic statements as manipulatory strings of symbols followed by manipulatory strings of operations. 2. A specific form of prefix notation.

poll — Refers to a systematic method, centrally controlled, for permitting stations on a multipoint circuit to transmit without contending for the line.

polling — 1. Refers to an important multiprocessing method used to identify the source of interrupt requests. When several interrupts occur simultaneously, the control program makes the decision as to the one that will be serviced first. 2. Refers to a technique by which each of the terminals sharing a communications line is periodically interrogated to determine whether it requires servicing. The multiplexor or control station sends a poll which, in effect asks the terminal selected, "do you have anything to transmit". 3. A flexible, systematic, centrally-controlled method of permitting terminals on a multi-terminal line to transmit without contending for the line. The computer contacts terminals according to the order specified by the user, and each terminal contacted is invited to send messages.

polling characters — Refers to a set of characters designed to be peculiar to a terminal and the polling operation. Response to these characters indicates to the computer whether or not the terminal has a message to send.

polling interval — Refers to a time interval set between polling operations if no data is being transmitted from the polled station.

polling list — Concerns a specified list containing control information and names of entries in the terminal table. The order in which the names are specified determines the order in which the terminals are polled.

pollution control terminal — A low-cost real-time terminal collects data from air-pollution control instruments and interfaces with the telephone line to permit later polling by a central computer. Another manufacturer has developed a real-time terminal which interfaces a mass spectrometer with a time-sharing system over a telephone line. This terminal converts outputs of the mass spectrometer to ASCII code, automatically dials up the time-sharing system, provides the necessary handshaking signals (i.e., log-on and log-off messages), and transmits mass-spectrometer data to the time-sharing system for analysis and storage. The results of the analysis from the time-sharing system are transmitted back to the terminal, where they are printed on a Teletype-like printer. This provides an alternative to other mass-spectrometer systems which include a minicomputer (or in some cases a larger computer) as part of the system.

polynomial regression statistics package — Permits degree of fit operations via graphical and objective techniques. In using graphic techniques, the operator simply need select a degree of fit, plot the curve against the data — then continue to select degrees by the press of a key until a satisfactory graph is obtained. Calculations by objective techniques will display the residual error, orthogonal polynomial sum of squares, F test of significance and R-square. Regression coefficients with t-tests, residuals, plots, the Durbin-Watson test and others may all be printed for any degree selected, without re-entering data.

polyvalent notation — A method for describing salient characteristics, in condensed form, using two or more characters, where each character or group of characters represents one of the characteristics.

polyvalent number — A number, consisting of several figures, used for description, wherein each figure represents one of the characteristics being described. (Similar to polyvalent notation.)

portable data medium — The selected medium used to transport or carry (communicate) data or information. Punched cards, magnetic tapes, and punched paper tapes — and lately portable disks, are examples, most often easily transported independently of the devices used in reading or interpreting such data or information.

portable disk pack components — A typical pack is comprised of a clear plastic cover, five double-surface disks, and a bottom cover assembly. The disks are composed of a base material of aluminum, coated with a layer of ferro-magnetic material dispersed in an organic binder. Data is stored on the disk in 8 bit bytes as saturated depositions forming magnetic dipoles. Each surface is burnished to a smoothness of 2.0 μ inches. Data is stored on five surfaces. The sixth surface is used for servo positioning data. The remaining four surfaces are reserved for protection of the previous six surfaces when the pack is mounted in the drive. The pack is returned to the canister for external storage.

port operation, advanced units — On some systems the six keyboard data-input lines and two control lines are brought in through port 1, the six display-output lines are sent out through port 2, and the remaining I/O functions are provided by port 3. The LSI device generates both keyboard and display-interrupt requests and sends them to the CPU via two lines of port 3. Interrupt requests can be initiated whenever the keyboard has a data input to be sent to the CPU or whenever the display is ready to receive data from the CPU; that is, when an input buffer on the chip is full or an output buffer is empty. Also, the CPU can query the programable peripheral interface to obtain data defining either peripheral's status. Four other lines of port 3 are used for handshaking with the two peripherals. In that way, 20 parallel I/O lines are needed to complete the interface, and some units have 28 lines available for other interface applications in the OEM system.

ports, input-output — Each processor can have a number of I/O ports. Some are associated with external system activity; others, for information exchange with other system processors. In practice, ports are part of the I/O section of a processor. Low-cost microcomputers are particularly adaptable to communications via their I/O ports. Because of the rapid real-time response possible, some multiprocessor systems can be designed for functions such as these:
- Control of a common interprocessor bus.
- Interrogation and preprocessing of remote sensors.
- Packing and unpacking of control information to and from remote locations.
- Minimization of intersystem cabling by concentration of information.
- Performing automatic calibration at remote location.
- Support of multipartition systems.
- Pipelining of arithmetic or algarithmic calculations in systems like FFT analyzers.
- Performing diagnostic monitoring.
- Control of security systems.

POS — See point-of-sale.

positional notation — 1. The procedure used in conventional number systems wherein the value assigned to a particular digit is determined by the symbol used (for example, 3) and by the position of the symbol relative to the radix point (for example, 300.0). 2. A number representation by means of an ordered set of digits, such that the value contributed by each digit depends on its position as well as on the digit value. 3. A method of representing numbers in which the digits are arranged sequentially, each succeeding digit is interpreted as the coefficient of successive powers of an integer referred to as the base of the number system. For example, in the decimal number system each succeeding digit is interpreted as successive coefficient powers of the interger or base 10.

positional operand — In assembler programming, an operand in a macro instruction that assigns a value to the corresponding positional parameter declared in the prototype statement of the called macro definition.

positional parameter — A parameter that must appear in a specified location, relative to other parameters. See also keyword parameter.

position control system — Discrete position control system as opposed to contour control system. A positioning system in which the controlled motion is required only to reach a given end point, with no path control during the transition from one end point to the next.

position decimal point key — On some units this positions the decimal point in the number entry. As digits are indexed after the decimal point key is operated, the decimal point on the display moves to the left one position for each digit indexed. Repeated pressing of the decimal point key is ignored.

positive feedback — The process by which the amplification is increased by having part of the power in the output circuit returned to the input circuit in order to reinforce the input power.

post — 1. To enter a unit of information on a record. 2. To record in a system control block the occurrence of an event for later interrogation by a procedure whose action is dependent upon the status of the event.

post editing — An editing procedure or process on

the output of a prior operation, especially those related to accounting, or programs which might have syntax or construction errors.

posterior probability — The revised estimate of probability incorporating additional information, usually developed using the Bayes equation.

post-processing calculator, example — One example of post-processing with the calculator used as a batch terminal is numerical control (NC) tape preparation by a midwest-based manufacturer. Programs written in the APT (Automatic Programming of Tools) language and JCL (Job Control Language) are stored as card images on a tape cassette. This is done directly from the calculator keyboard under control of a BASIC-language program. The BASIC program not only allows generation of the card images but also editing, including deleting or inserting cards. When the tape cassette is ready, the calculator signs on to the company's IBM computer to send the card images. Output from the APT processor is a listing with job statistics and EIA data for an NC control tape. The job statistics are routed to the printer; but the EIA data is put on tape cassette and later used off-line to generate the final punched tape on the calculator's peripheral tape punch. Further post-processing includes reading the tape via a peripheral tape reader and verifying the NC program by plotting the NC machine movements on the calculator's X-Y plotter.

post mortem — 1. A diagnostic routine for locating a malfunction in a computer or an error in a coding problem. Should a tape problem come to a standstill, the computer will print out — either automatically or when called for — any information concerning the contents of all or part of the registers in the computer. 2. A routine which, either automatically or on demand, prints information concerning the contents of the registers and storage locations at the time the routine stopped, in order to assist in the location of a mistake in coding. See routine. 3. Refers to listing of the contents of a storage device taken after a routine has been run in order that the final condition of sections of storage may be recorded for debugging purposes.

post mortem routine — Concerns service routine useful in analyzing the cause of a failure, such as a routine that dumps out the content of a store after a failure. Related to post mortem.

postmultiply — To multiply a matrix "A" by some conforming matrix "B," that is, by a matrix "B" that has as many rows as the given matrix "A" has columns ($A \times B$).

postprocessor — Refers to a set of computer instructions which transform tool centerline data into machine motion commands using the proper tape code and format required by a specific machine control system. Instructions such as feed rate calculations, spindle speed calculations, and auxiliary function commands may be included.

postulate — To assume without specific proof; to accept a proposition without immediate empirical evidence; to accept as evident from general life experience or general acceptance. For example, to postulate by an analogy, projection, or extrapolation; to petition that such knowledge has already been developed.

power equation regression program — Least Squares Fit for Power Curve. This program uses the least squares fit method to fit N pairs of (X, Y) data points to the power curve Y equals A times the quantity X raised to the B power.

power-fail/auto restart — Whenever DC power sequencing signals indicate an impending AC power loss, a microcoded power-fail sequence can be initiated. When power is restored, the processor can automatically return to the run state. Four options are available for power up sequencing on some systems.

power fail recovery system (PFR) — A Power Fail Recovery System is available for situations where total line failure might be experienced. This system, with charging and automatic switching circuitry, provides for automatic computer restart without operator intervention after a power failure. It maintains solid state memory data integrity for up to two hours.

power-on clear circuit — One type power-on clear circuitry is entirely self-contained on the data chip with the exception of an external capacitor and an optional diode. The circuit contains 2 threshold detectors guaranteeing a minimum turn-on hysteresis of one volt. Two flip-flops are used to ensure that the trailing (synchronizing) edge of the synchronous clear signal is sharp and stable. The power-on clear delay time must be a minimum of 64 clock times (640μsec @ 100kHz) after both V_{DD} and V_{GG} supplies have reached 90% of full voltage. In most systems, a 10μfd or less capacitor is sufficient to produce the required delay.

power source — There are three sources of power for electronic calculators: AC (alternating current), throwaway batteries, and rechargeable batteries. Some electronic calculators have the ability to work on several of these sources.

power supply — One specific unit uses a semi-regulated ferroresonant device, reliable low-cost power supply. Regulation begins at the power supply, and precise regulation is accomplished by individual solid-state 3-terminal voltage regulators built into each of the hardware modules plugged into the backplane.

power supply circuit — 1. A unit that supplies electrical power to another unit. It changes AC to DC and maintains a constant voltage output within limits. 2. An electronic circuit which converts an input ac voltage into an output dc voltage.

power switches — Rear panel switches permit user selection to match power sources of 100, 120, 220, or 240 V (+5%, −10%), at 48 to 66 Hz. Power consumption is 1.7, 1.5, 0.8, or 0.75 A, respectively on some advanced units for these voltages.

PPS, parallel processing — Processor is a general term used to determine the arithmetic and control section of a general purpose computer. Micro means small. In microprocessors, this is a small set of circuits which can be used to build equipment requiring digital data processing. This includes calculators, cash registers, credit terminals, electronic scales, billing machines, process controllers and general purpose data processors. Several firms describe the MOS/LSI circuit sets: "Parallel Processing Systems (PPS)."

PPS circuits — Various calculator circuits include: CPU, RAM, ROM, ROM/RAM, I/O Clock. In one PPS, or parallel Processing System, this compatible group has been configured to maximize circuit density, processing speed, and low power consumption. The CPU with its 12-bit parallel address bus directly outputs instruction words to the CPU in the form of 8-bit parallel information. The RAM can transmit and receive 4 bits of data in parallel during one cycle time. It is this parallel organization, along with a sophisticated time sharing technique, which results in unusually high data rate from a seemingly slow clock system.

pragmatics — A particular study of the range or extent to which practical use may be used in constructions of a problem, i.e., opposite from theoretical or ideal.

precision — 1. The quality of being sharply or exactly defined — i.e., the number of distinguishable alternatives from which a representation was selected. This is sometimes indicated by the number of significant digits the representation contains. 2. The degree of discrimination with which a quantity is stated, e.g., a three-digit numeral discriminates among 1000 possibilities. Precision is contrasted with accuracy, i.e., a quantity expressed with 10 decimal digits of precision may only have one digit of accuracy.

precision, double length — Pertaining to twice the normal length of a unit of data or a storage device in a given computing system; e.g., a double-length register would have the capacity to store twice as much data as a single-length or normal register; a double-length word would have twice the number of characters or digits as a normal or single-length word.

precision, single and double — All numbers in a computer are binary numbers (no decimals). In single precision the largest number that can be represented is dependent on the size (number of bits) in a single word. As an example, a 32 bit word has one of the highest.

precision, triple — The retention of three times as many digits of a quantity as the computer normally handles.

precomplier program — A unique program which is designed to detect errors and provide source program correction before the computation of the object, deck, or program.

preconditioned tape automatic error checks, (calculator) — Some calculator tape systems automatically check for error conditions which affect operation or data information. Conditions such as: comparing sum of bits read with bits written; whether read/write head is past block requested; attempted read of block with no data; and preconditioning errors.

preconditioned tape drive functions calculator) —
Functions which can be accessed manually or under program control are:
- write a block of information on tape as part of multiple block file
- write a block of information on tape as single block file
- read a file of information from tape, using address recorded on tape to determine where in calculator memory each block should be stored
- read a file of information from tape into specified address in computer memory (addresses recorded on tape are ignored)
- specify which drive information to be read from under manual or program control

Users can also duplicate tapes; update tapes with new or changed information; use pre-programmed tapes with up to 15 minutes of programmed material per side. (some systems)

preconditioned tapes, calculator — Automatic program control allows users to write more sophisticated programs on preconditioned tapes. On some systems large programs can be divided into a number of blocks, each holding 256 steps. A final command at the end of the block reads the next program into tape memory. This procedure can be repeated (up to 150 blocks) until the program has been completed.

predefined process — A process that is identified only by name and that is defined elsewhere.

pre-edit programs — A checking of the application or operational program before the test run. A pre-edit run can remove such things as disobedience to established supervisory, main memory program segmentation rules, etc.

prefix keys, unconditional transfer — Typical are: GO TO. A prefix key. Moves program counter to a new program location, defined either by a 3-digit program location or a label.
Subroutine. A prefix key. Used with either a label or a 3-digit program location. Causes a transfer to a program segment to be used as a subroutine. Indirect GO TO. Transfers to the location in program memory specified by the contents of a memory register. Indirect Subroutine. Transfers control to a program segment designated as a subroutine whose starting location is found in the specified memory register.

prefix multipliers — Prefixes which designate a greater or smaller unit than the original, by the factor indicated. These prefixes are:

Prefix	Symbol	Factor
tera	T	10^{12}
giga	G	10^{9}
mega	M	10^{6}
kilo	k	10^{3}
hecto	h	10^{2}
deka	da	10
deci	d	10^{1}
centi	c	10^{-2}
milli	m	10^{-3}
micro	u	10^{-6}
nano	n	10^{-9}
pico	p	10^{-12}
femto	f	10^{-15}
atto	a	10^{-18}

prefix notation — Refers to a technique of forming one-dimensional expressions without need for brackets by preceding, with a string or vector of operators, an operand string or vector which may itself contain operators upon operands.

preliminary review — Refers to an examination or evaluation of matters related to processing procedures of an organization in an attempt to offer guidance in the preparation of plans, proposals, or goal-designs previous to installation of calculator system equipment.

premultiply — To multiply a matrix "B" by some conforming matrix "A" — that is, by a matrix "A" that has as many columns as the given matrix "B" has rows (A × B).

prenormalize — To normalize the operands of an arithmetic operation before the operation is performed.

preprocessing calculator application — One BASIC-language emulation program can be revised to include preprocessing and postprocessing at the calculator. Preprocessing might include collecting and organizing information into a format required by an applications program at the calculator. As a postprocessor, the calculator might generate locally formatted reports based on raw data received and stored.

preprocessor — 1. A computer program that will take a specific set of instructions (describing the parts program) and translate them into the format required to be run on the processor program. 2. Refers to emulation, a program that converts data from the format of an emulated system to the format accepted by an emulator.

pre-programmable hand-held calculator — Typical programming features are: up to 50-step program memory; conditional branching based on any of eight relational tests ($x < y$, $x \geq y$, $x \neq y$, $x = y$, $x < 0$, $x \geq 0$, $x \neq 0$, $x = 0$); direct branching; ability to review or execute programs step-by-step; ability to add or modify program steps; PAUSE and NO-OPERATION program instructions.

pre-programmable hand-held calculator memory, display — Typical memory: eight addressable registers; four-register operational stack; "last x" register; typical display: up to 10 significant digits in fixed-decimal notation; up to 8 significant digits plus 2-digit exponent in scientific or engineering notation (in engineering notation all exponents are displayed as multiples of ± 3); full display formatting in any mode with selective roundoff; indicators for improper operations; low battery; line-number/key matrix program display.

pre-programmed calculators — A typical pre-programmed scientific unit offers 72 preprogrammed functions and operations plus eight addressable memories. Users can do register arithmetic on all of them. Because the unit is programmable, the user enters the keystrokes necessary to solve repetitive problems only once. Thereafter, they enter the variables and press the RUN/STOP key for an almost instant answer. Users can add, change, or skip steps and can program the units to perform direct branches or conditional tests. They can display answers in fixed decimal, scientific or engineering notation.

pre-programmed calculators, financial institutions — Some programmed electronic printing calculators, designed especially for commercial banks, savings and loan associations, and other financial institutions, use stored programs to provide simple and rapid solutions to the complex computations which are part of the everyday work of departments handling installment loans, commercial loans, mortgages, and savings accounts. The calculator's simplicity of data entry and rapid calculation eliminate the need for charts, rate books, tables and formulas. For example, computation of monthly payments of a conventional mortgage loan is performed by entering the principal amount, the annual interest rate, and the number of years of the loan. The automatic result shows the monthly payment, including principal and interest. Monthly payments on installment loans including credit life insurance and accident/health insurance can be computed quickly and can include "odd days" interest, frequently lost by an institution because of the number of references that must be made to rate books or charts. General financial applications include such routines as equity calculation on a mortgage loan, equivalent interest rate on discounted notes, calculation of periodic withdrawal from a known investment, and others.

pre-programmed control ROM — The programming of integrated circuit microprocessors is not microprogramming; it is programming of the plain ordinary kind. However, there are microprocessors available on the market that are both programmable and microprogrammable, for example, the National GPC/P. In that computer, the definition of the instructions (the microinstructions) are stored in a read-only memory (ROM) which is part of the control chip which makes up part of the CPU. That one chip (CROM: Control Read-Only Memory) can be bought from National in a pre-programmed form, or the customer can define the contents. (Since the microprogram is placed into the CROM by mask programming, the user must have a high volume to warrant the expenses involved in defining his own contents.)

pre-programmed conversions, calculators —

FROM	TO
mils	microns
inches	centimeters
feet	meters
yards	meters
miles	kilometers
miles	nautical miles
acres	square feet
fluid ounces	cubic centimeters
fluid ounces	liters
gallons	liters
ounces	grams
pounds	kilograms
short ton	metric ton
BTU	calories, gram
degrees	gradients
degrees	radians
°Fahrenheit	°Celsius
deg. min. sec.	decimal degrees
polar	rectangular
voltage ratio	decibels

pre-programmed functions, calculator — Many units are pre-programmed to perform all these functions Angle ($\angle$) Conv. Degrees/Minutes/Seconds, $+$, $-$, $\times$, $\div$, $1/x$, y^x, x^2, $\sqrt{x}$, LN, LOG, e^x, 10^x, %, Δ%, SINE, ASN, COS, ACS, TAN, ATN, N!, MEAN, STANDARD DEVIATION, TO POLAR/RECTANGULAR, RECTANGULAR/TO POLAR . . . and many more.

pre-programmed functions, hand-held programmables — Typical trigonometric (all in decimal degrees, radians, or grads) are: Sin x; Arc Sin x; Cos x; Arc Cos x; Tan x; Arc Tan x; logarithmic: Log x; Ln x; e^x; 10; others are: y^x; $\sqrt{x}$; $1/x$; π; x^2; n!; conversions between decimal angle (degrees, radians, or grads) and degrees/minutes/seconds; rectangular/polar coordinate conversion; decimal/octal integer conversion; degrees (hours)/minutes/seconds arithmetic; integer/fraction truncation; absolute value; full register arithmetic.

pre-programmed operations — To save program memory and make calculations easier, some mid-size desk calculators permit the storage of over 100 pre-programmed operations for logarithms, trigonometry, statistics and 24 metric conversions as hard-wired capability. For example, users can perform trigonometric functions with a keystroke, determine the standard deviation of a sample of grouped or ungrouped data, and convert kilograms per square centimeter to pounds per square inch.

pre-programmed vs programmable calculators — Programming calculators possess a learning capacity that results in increased flexibility of use. In contrast with preprogrammed calculators, programmable machines are characterized by operator-generated software, sometimes consisting of many variables, looping statements and testing functions.

Interacting with the calculator, the design engineer typically generates his program via the keyboard, or he loads a canned software program (from magnetic cards, mag tape, cassette, or even by calling up a program from a peripheral high-speed disc memory). The designer can interact with a calculator by observing peripheral outputs of plotters or by modifying circuit parameters upon displayed program requests. Should he be confronted with a real number-crunching problem, calculators are now available with memory capacities of up to 32k bytes of read/write memory (R/W) and 32k or more bytes of read-only memory (ROM).

pre-recorded program application cards — Like a computer, many calculators can be programmed so that they go through a step-by-step routine at just the touch of a few keys — to solve even extremely complex, lengthy or repetitive problems quickly, easily and accurately. But instead of bulky reels of tape or stacks of keypunch cards, the owners use tiny, magnetic program cards. One type is less than 1.3 by 7.6 cm in size. Each card contains a program directing the unit to perform a predetermined routine, to solve a specific problem or series of problems.

A particular program can be a relatively simple or intricate sequence of steps. Some cards store a program of up to 100 steps. If a program greater than 100 steps is required, it may be stored on two or more program cards.

Because the program card has all of the steps pre-recorded, users only have to feed in the known data — the calculator will do the work. Hundreds of pre-recorded program cards, packaged in Application Packs are available from stores, manufacturers and clubs. Packs contain up to 40 programs, plus a manual with step-by-step instructions for running each program. Other programs are longer, Individual Application Pack programs, and programs contributed by owners are available through various supplier-sponsored Users' Libraries.

pre-recorded program calculating, small units — By using pre-recorded magnetic cards (like those supplied in the packages shipped with many calculators) users can do highly complex calculations with minimal effort or study of the calculator itself. Users load a card into the calculator and let the stored program handle the busy part of the calculation. Typically, they just key in the data and start the program running. The program stops when it needs more data or when it displays a result.

preserve — The function or procedure designed to retain information in one storage device after transferring it to another device, in contrast to clear.

preset — 1. Refers to an activity to set the contents of a storage location to an initial value. 2. To establish the initial control value for a loop.

preset parameter — A parameter incorporated into a subroutine during input.

presettable I/O conditions — 1. Presettable I/O conditions allow the programmer to verify microinstructions that perform I/O data transfers before actual peripherals are connected to the system. 2. A single set of switches can be used to present the I/O bus input. It might also be helpful to provide a register that can be used to trap and display data transferred out during an I/O microinstruction.

pressure sensitive (elastic) keyboard — A recent development in keyboards. The keys do not move, but pressure makes contacts to provide conduction. Mass produced, this type of keyboard may bring about a significant reduction in costs.

preventive maintenance — Precautionary measures taken on a system to forestall failures rather than to eliminate them after they have occurred.

prewired external circuitry — Refers to connectors that are prewired to extend some I.O. systems. Because some units use the wire wrap technique, it is not difficult for the user to arrange the connectors in any way that is convenient.

PRGM mode, small calculator — The PRGM (program) mode for some small calculators provides for the recording in a part of the calculator called program memory, for later execution. All operations on the keyboard except three can be recorded for later execution with the PRGM-RUN switch set to PRGM. The three operations that cannot be recorded on some systems are SST, BST, and f PRGM. These three operations work in the PRGM mode to help users write and record their programs.

PRGM-RUN switch — Function keys are recorded in program memory. Display, on some systems, shows program memory step number and the keycode (keyboard row and location in row) of the function key. Function keys may be executed as part of a recorded program or individually by pressing from the keyboard. Input numbers and answers are displayed, except where indicated.

prices, implicit — Same as marginal values, shadow prices, dual-variable levels, etc. — that is, numbers giving the incremental worth of a relaxation of one unit in the right-hand side of a constraint.

primary store — 1. The main store built into a calculator, not necessarily the fast access store. 2. Relatively small immediate or very rapid access store incorporated in some calculators for which the main memory is a slower secondary store.

primitive — The most basic or fundamental unit of data, i.e., a single letter digit, element, or machine code as primitive when related to the ultrasophisticated codes or languages now available. Also refers to first or second generation computer equipment.

print cradle, calculator — The print cradle permits the hand-held programmable calculator to become a desk-top printing calculator. When the calculator is locked into the cradle, the user is able to print anything shown in the display or print the step-by-step execution of a program. Print and paper advance controls permits the user to handle these functions on the printer as well as on the calculator, and a "trace" key allows monitoring of all functions as they happen on some units. One unit has a thermal printer which prints

5 × 7 dot-matrix characters on a 2.5-in. tape. It prints 20 characters per line.

printed circuit — 1. A circuit in which interconnecting wires have been replaced by conductive strips printed, etched, etc., onto an insulating board. It may also include similarly formed components on the baseboard. 2. Refers to resistors, capacitors, diodes, transistors and other circuit elements which are mounted on cards and interconnected by conductor deposits. These special cards are treated with light sensitive emulsion and exposed. The light thus fixes the areas to be retained and an acid bath eats away those portions which are designed to be destroyed. The base is usually a copper clad card.

printed-circuit assembly — A printed-circuit board to which separable components have been attached. 2. An assembly of one or more printed-circuit boards, which may include several components.

printed-circuit board — 1. Also called a card, chassis, or plate. An insulating board onto which a circuit has been printed. 2. The printed-circuit or PC board should more accurately be termed a printed-wiring or PW board to reflect its true function. Basically it is an insulating board complete with metallic wiring paths for point-to-point connections, but may also include metalized connecting surfaces and heat sinks or heat radiators. They may be single-sided, double-sided or multilayer — actually sandwiches of boards where high density interconnections are required.

printed circuit boards, calculator — Easy access to interior of some calculators is provided by hinged printed circuit boards. One complete unit weighs only 26 lb and is about half the size of earlier calculators.

printed circuit card — A card, usually of laminate or resinous material of the insulating type, used for the mounting of an electrical circuit. Together, the base and circuit make up the card.

printed component — A type of printed circuit intended primarily for electrical and/or magnetic functions other than point-to-point connections or shielding (e.g., printed inductor, resistor, capacitor, transmission line, etc.).

printed element — An element, such as a resistor, capacitor, or transmission line, that is formed on a circuit board by deposition, etching, etc.

printed wiring — A conductive pattern formed on the surface of an insulating baseboard by plating or etching.

printer, advanced calculator — Some models of Page-Width Printers are designed specifically for various models of calculators. One type printer is a quiet thermal printer capable of printing 80 characters per line. It can print the same numbers, symbols, and letters that can be displayed by the calculator. The characters are generated from a 5 × 7 dot matrix.

printer, advanced calculators — For greater printing speed, a line printer may be added to some systems. Printing speeds to 1000 lines/min and higher at 80 or 132 char/line are then possible. Line printers are cousins to the column printer, but with proper buffering and programming, the format flexibility of a typewriter can be attained. Often the buffering and control circuitry are built into the printer.

printer, alphanumeric (calculator) — A quiet thermal printer is built into some basic type calculators. One unit can print the same numbers, symbols, and letters that are displayed, as well as user instructions, alpha labels for program results, and other alphanumeric messages. On this unit the maximum printer line length is 16 spaces. This does not limit the program line length, which can be up to 68 keystrokes.

printer, calculator chip control — Typical single-chip calculator circuits provide almost all the circuitry required for a 12-digit printing calculator. They replace earlier 3- to 5-chip sets. The circuits are organized as a single-chip computer with on-chip CPU, RAM, ROM, buffers and key scan, printer control, clock and voltage regulator. In some systems they drive the popular Seiko 104 EA7261 or 310 EA7251 OEM printers; however, the ROM can be changed to drive other printers. A single additional chip can drive a fluorescent display and requires no external components.

printer, desk-top — One type desk-top line printer produces 80 columns of 5 × 7 dot matrix characters at 100 characters per second × 70 lines per minute. The impact head prints bidirectionally on a 8½" roll paper using a conventional teletype ribbon. The line printer will print up to four copies of any item. Reliability is provided by a mechanism which contains no brakes, clutches, dampers or stepper motors. All control electronics including one-line buffer and self-test circuitry are contained on a single 5" × 15" printed circuit card. The specific model was expressly designed for the simplicity, reliability and extremely low cost required by current small-scale data handling systems and terminals. Vibration and wear are minimized because the print head moves uniformly in both directions and pauses only at the end of each line. Opto-electronic sensing is used to accurately position each dot and permit characters to be printed on the fly. The line printer comes with complete control electronics including a printer control card (some units).

printer, electrostatic — A device for printing an optical image on paper in which dark and light areas of the original are represented by electrostatically charged and uncharged areas on the paper. The paper is dusted with particles of finely powdered dry ink and the particles adhere only to the electrically charged areas. The paper with ink particles is then heated, causing the ink to melt and become permanently fixed to the paper.

printer, high-speed — A printer which operates at a speed more compatible with the speed of computation and data processing so that it may operate on-line. At the present time a printer operating at a speed of 250 lines per minute, 100 characters per line is considered high-speed. Synonymous with HSP.

printer-limited — Often, the timing restrictions on a process due to the slowness or inadequacy of the printing equipment, whereby other operations must await the completion of the printing unit.

printer, line — A printer in which all characters across an entire line of type of printed in one print cycle. Contrasts with printer, page.

printer, microprocessor control — A microprocessor helped cut the cost of Hewlett-Packard's (HP) model 9871A page-width printer. But in this case, HP decided to make the microprocessor itself. A major objective in the printer's design was that it be self-contained, with no external power supplies or control electronics, but without a microprocessor, they would have had to build some sort of discrete processor or go to some other drive system. The HP division decided to build its own because none of the processors commercially available at the time could do the job.

The microprocessor, a parallel 16-bit n-channel, metal-oxide-semiconductor device, has a typical execution time of 1 microsecond for a 16-bit instruction. In the printer, it receives and accepts 7-bit codes from a calculator or other controller, then determines whether the code must be stored or if the printer is ready. Next it locates the printer's character wheel and carrier, calculates the movements necessary to position the paper, controls the positioning stepper motors, and commands the hammer to fire.

printer, page — A printer that prints characters one at a time in page format. Contrasts with printer, line.

printer/plotter peripheral, calculator — Some advanced calculators use a Page-width Printer/Plotter. One unique bi-directional platen and 96-character printing disk lets users run program-formulated charts and graphs; tables and text. It works with specific series of computing calculators.

printer, serial — A device capable of printing characters, one at a time across a page. Many variations in serial printers exist, i.e., typewriter, stylus or matrix serial printer, and high-speed, multiple-line stylus or matrix serial printer.

printer, xerographic — A device for printing an optical image on paper in which dark and light areas of the original are represented by electrostatically charged and uncharged areas on the paper. The paper is dusted with particles of finely powdered dry ink and the particles adhere only to the electrically charged areas. The paper with ink particles is then heated, causing the ink to melt and become permanently fixed to the paper.

print functions example, calculator — On a typical unit one print line contains 12 digits plus decimal point, commas, and 2 symbols. It provides leading zero suppression. Negative answers and error/overflow indication are printed in red and printer motor shut-off 10 seconds after last key entry.

printing, detail — A card to hard-copy operation. A data processing function for preparing documents from series of punched cards. Automatic addition, or cross-subtraction may be combined in the same operation.

print-on-alarm — A data system condition in which continuous scanning of data channels takes place, but output of data is initiated only when an alarm condition is encountered.

printout — Sometimes an instruction to cause the printing of data in storage or from other external storage media into hard copy.

print-out, dynamic — A sequential operation of printing as part of a calculator run and during the run instead of at the end of the run.

print-out, large bold — Some units contain silent, electronic printers. The printer provides up to nine digits on two-inch thermal printing paper. In addition to normal audit-trail symbols, it prints 0.T or 0.00T each time the power switch is turned on. The letter K is printed each time the Chain/Const switch is moved to Const, and NK is printed when moved to Chain.

print-out, memory — A listing of the contents of a storage device, or selected parts of it. (Synonymous with memory dump and core dump.)

print positions — The maximum number of characters which can be printed on single line.

print wheel — A single element providing the character set at one printing position of a wheel printer.

priority — Degree of precedence or urgency. Message switching systems usually have the ability to recognize and handle several grades of priority.

priority indicators — Code signals which form a queue of data awaiting processing so that this is handled in order of importance.

priority interrupt function — Priority interrupt functions usually include distinguishing the highest priority interrupt active, remembering lower priority interrupts which are active, selectively enabling or disabling priority interrupts, executing a jump instruction to a specific memory location, and storing the program counter register in a specific location.

priority interrupts, multilevel — Interrupt provisions have been made to facilitate the priority requirements of various subroutines. The interrupt requests of these subroutines are handled by the central processor in the sequence of the highest priority. If a priority subroutine requests an interrupt, it will have priority over all subroutines of lower priority, even though they have previously requested an interrupt.

priority interrupts, multiple vectored — Multiple peripheral control is made easier by hardware-vectored, priority interrupt control lines. These lines allow processors to rapidly identify and service interrupting devices. The benefits are faster interrupt response and lower memory cost.

priority interrupt system — 1. A priority interrupt system allows high speed interrupt processing without the customary wasted time for saving registers and status. This is facilitated by providing a separate register set for each interrupt level, so an interrupt routine can use a full register set without affecting the registers of the interrupted routine. Each interrupt level can be individually enabled or disabled. 2. The priority interrupt system provides for internal processor interrupts, I/O peripheral device interrupts, and groups of individual external interrupts, each with its own unique interrupt memory address and priority assignment.

priority processing — A type of time-sharing or facility-sharing in which the programs to be run are selected by priority rules or criteria.

priority scheduling system — A unique type of job scheduler, in larger systems, so designed that a resultant improved system performance is achieved by means of input/output queues.

priority structure — The organization of a system for processing. The priority structure of the system depends not upon the number of instructions but upon the complexity of the programs. The structure can range from systems with no priority to multicomplex organizations with multilayers of interrupts and multilevels of priority.

priority switch table — A specific table in computer storage that contains the status of devices operating in interrupt mode.

private automatic branch exchange (PABX) — A private automatic exchange that provides for the transmission of calls to and from the public telephone network.

private (dedicated) line characteristics —

1. Data set may be telephone company type or other vendor. 2. Service terminal is charged for on a monthly rental basis plus a one-time installation charge. 3. The transmission speed may require additional monthly line conditioning charges for each termination or drop point on the line including the computer location. 4. Mileage is charged for on a monthly rental basis with no installation charge.

private line or private wire — Refers to channel or circuit furnished a subscriber for his exclusive use. Also called leased line.

privileged instructions — Protection against one problem subprogram misusing another problem subprogram's I/O devices is provided by restricting all I/O commands to the supervisor state. A subprogram requests I/O action by issuing a supervisor call instruction. The supervisory subprogram can then analyze this request and take the appropriate action.

probable error — The amount of error which, according to the laws of probability, is most likely to occur during a measurement.

probability distribution — A mathematical model showing a representation of the probabilities for all possibilities for all possible values of a given random variable.

probability distribution tables — These are tables that show the relative frequencies of each subset into which the total population is divided or segmented. Such tables can be read to show the probability of occurrence of each value so listed.

probability of proportions program — This program calculates the probability of a given proportion (y) of an event occurring in N trials.

probability theory — A particular branch of theory which pertains to measured likelihood of occurrence of chance or random events, and used to predict, analyze, or anticipate behaviors of groups, samples, and events.

problem — A set of circumstances, situations, or states which develop when some unknown information is to be discovered, i.e., a solution is sought from some known information and a procedure is understood to acquire the unknown.

problem, benchmark — A routine used to determine the speed performance of a computer. One method is to use one-tenth of the time required to perform nine complete additions and one complete multiplication. A complete addition or a complete multiplication time includes the time required to procure two operands from storage, perform the operation and store the result, and the time required to select and execute the required number of instructions to do this.

problem, check — A problem chosen to determine whether the calculator or a program is operating correctly.

problem definition — Refers to the act of compiling logic in the form of general flow charts and logic diagrams which clearly explain and present the problem to the programmer in such a way that all requirements involved in the run are presented.

problem description — A statement of the problem. The statement may also include a description of the method of solution, the solution itself, the transformations of data and the relationship of procedures, data, constraints, and environment.

problem identification — Compiling logic in the form of general flow charts and logic diagrams which clearly explain and present the problem to the programmer in such a way that all requirements involved in the run are presented.

problem language — The language a calculator programmer uses in stating the definition of a problem.

problem-oriented language — 1. A programming language that is especially suitable for a given class of problems. Procedure-oriented languages such as FORTRAN, ALGOL; simulation languages such as GPSS, SIMSCRIPT; list processing languages such as LISP, IPL-V; information retrieval languages. 2. A programming language designed for the convenient expression of a given class of problems.

procedure-oriented language — A programming language designed for the convenient expression of procedures used in the solution of a wide class of problems.

problem program — Any of the class of routines that perform processing of the type for which a computing system is intended, and including routines that solve problems, monitor and control industrial processes, sort and merge records, perform computations, process transactions against stored records, etc.

problem-solver libraries, financial (calculator) — To assist users in performing financial analyses, some problem solver libraries provide routines for:
- Return on investment
- Discounted cash flow
- Multiple loan analysis
- Single loan analysis
- Lease vs. purchase
- Make vs. buy
- Break-even under certainty
- Break-even under uncertainty
- Depreciation
- Growth rate
- Moving average
- Seasonal analysis
- Cyclical analysis
- Auto covariance/autocorrelation
- Crosscovariance/crosscorrelation
- Exponential smoothing
- Simple regression
- Histogram

problem-solving conversational approach — In practice, users set up a dialogue with the calculator and talk to it, through the keyboard, and it talks to them through its display. Here's how the concept works for a Capital Investment Analysis program. As users proceed, the calculator gives them operating instructions. For instance, it tells when to enter data. WHAT IS THE INITIAL INVESTMENT? HOW MANY CASH FLOWS? It shows data for verification. PERIOD (3), CASH FLOW = $1250
If users have a question, they can recall the program, line-by-line, to check the operations. 560 LET TI = B9/((A4 + 1) − X)
And, it will display labeled solutions THE RATE OF RETURN IS 19 PERCENT (some units)

problem-solving, heuristic — A series of rules that systematically vary models through formal mutations and regenerative recording.

problem, test — A problem chosen to determine whether the computer or a program is operating correctly.

problem, trouble-location — A test problem

procedure — whose incorrect solution supplies information on the location of faulty equipment. It is used after a check problem has shown that a fault exists.

procedure — The step-by-step process for the solution of a problem, especially the machine instructions embodying the solution.

procedure-oriented language — 1. Refers to various machine-independent languages which describe how the process of solving the problem is to be carried out. Usually oriented toward a specific class of procedures, i.e., FORTRAN is oriented toward algebraic procedures. COBOL is oriented toward commercial procedures. 2. A problem-oriented language that facilitates the expression of a procedure as an explicit algorithm. For example: FORTRAN, ALGOL, COBOL, PL/I.

procedures and parameters, calculators — Programs are functionally separated into blocks of machine instructions called procedures. A procedure, like a program, has its own private data area (actually in the program's data area). The real power of procedures is that they can be called into execution from any point in a program (including other procedures and themselves); the hardware automatically saves the calling environment when a procedure starts executing and restores the calling environment when the procedure finishes. A programmer can write procedures that receive parameter information (arguments), perform computations using the parameters, then return results to the caller.

process — 1. A course of events occurring according to an intended purpose or effect. 2. A systematic sequence of operations to produce a specified result. 3. To perform operations on data.

process control — 1. Automatic control of industrial processes in which continuous material or energy is produced. 2. Pertaining to systems whose purpose is to provide automation of continuous operations. This is contrasted with numerical control, which provides automation of discrete operations.

process control, industrial — Industrial processing applications are as wide and varied as the degrees of control that individual processes may require. Some general process-control application areas are: precious metals production, cement production, environmental control, pilot plants, chemical processes, petroleum refining and many others. The data acquisition and control system provides maximum flexibility in the types of process data that it can accept, and the variety of output signals and data format that a calculator may exercise.

process control loop — A system of feedback devices linked together to control one phase of a process.

process-control-oriented programmable calculator — More powerful and versatile than a programmable controller or a microcomputer, various advanced programmable calculators include many features usually found only on minicomputers. One type desk-top unit is easier to use than a minicomputer and can be operated as a calculator at the same time that control programs are running. Although intended as a controller for an instrument system or a pilot process application, for remote data collection, or for production control, the calculator can also be used as a stand-alone computer.

One firm has designed a medium-priced unit primarily for use in engineering, research, and statistics. Some of its features are interrupt capability, input speeds of up to 400,000 words/s and output speeds of up to 200,000 words/s (16-bit words), live keyboard, direct memory access, bidirectional tape drive using mini-cartridges, multidimensional arrays, automatic memory record and load, internal calculation range of $\pm 10^{511}$ to $\pm 10^{-511}$, and optional plug-in read-only memories.

process-control system — A system whose primary purpose is to provide automation of continuous operations.

processing, automatic data — Data processing performed by a system of electronic or electrical machines so interconnected and interacting as to reduce to a minimum the need for human assistance or intervention. (Related to automatic data-processing system.)

processing, background — Work which has a low-priority and is handled by the calculator when higher priority or real-time entries are not occurring. Batch processing such as inventory control, payroll, housekeeping, etc., are often treated as background processing but can be interrupted on orders from terminals or inquiries from other units.

processing capacity — Often the maximum limitation of places of a number which can be processed at any one time. An example is 12 place number.

processing ratio — The end result in calculating the time equipment is being used properly, including lost time because of human error and the total available time.

process, iterative — A process for calculating a desired result by means of a repeating cycle of operations, which comes closer and closer to the desired result, i.e., the arithmetical square root of n may be approximated by an iterative processing using additions, subtractions, and divisions only.

process-limited — Refers to the restriction of the speed of the processing unit controls, i.e., the processing time as contrasted with input/output limited.

process optimization — An extensive process-controller program, based on the model of the process, directs the DAC (data acquisition and control) system. Process data is continuously collected and analyzed for computation of optimum operating instructions. These instructions are given to the process operator via an on-line typewriter.

processor — A central control unit or set of compiler programs which provide translating assembling, and related software functions for a given programming language. 2. In hardware; a data processor. 3. In software, a computer program that performs functions such as a compiling, assembling, and translating for a specific programming language.

processor, basic instructions — Processor Modules execute basic instructions which can be functionally grouped into five categories: Register operations; Accumulator operations; Program counter and stack control operations; Input/Output operations; Machine operations.

processor-controller calculators — The growing trend of using programmable calculators as system processor-controllers makes good sense. They are flexible, easily programmed, adaptable, expandable — and extremely cost effective. The calculator itself is a system — Data is input via keyboard or magnetic tape. Data processing is through tape input. Data manipulation and analysis is by internal mathematical functions. Storage is in machine memory, mag-tape, and disc. And data output is through the alphanumeric printer. Many expand on this with interfaces and a wide range of instrumentation and users can see the calculator as the processor-manager of practically any system.

processor, front-end — A typical technique being used to handle many asynchronous lines is the small computer that serves as a line controller for the large processor. The small computer not only can serve as a line scanner and controller, but can handle a number of "supervisory" tasks that would normally be done by the large processor, such as error detection, character echoing (on a full duplex line), user validity checking, etc. There are two basic design approaches to the communication front end of a small processor: single bit buffers and line scanning.

processor, input/output (IOP) — A secondary processor dedicated to transfer operations to and from main memory. (Clarified by processor, peripheral.)

processor interface — The transfer of data between the processor and the standard communication subsystem takes place through input data leads, connected to the processor input channel, and output data leads, connected to the processor output channel. In addition to the data leads, there are several control leads that are used to control the flow of data.

processor interrupt — In most unique systems, processor interrupts are automatic procedures designed to alert the system to conditions arising that may affect the sequence of instructions being executed.

processor-limited — A system having the overall processing time dictated by the speed of the central processor instead of the speed of the peripheral equipment.

processor storage — General purpose storage that is part of a central processing unit. Synonymous with real storage.

processor storage relocation — The processor must have the ability to relocate programs in storage during normal processing, since many different types of transactions may necessitate bringing a program from file storage into a location in main storage for which the program was not assembled.

process, predefined — A type of identified process which is defined and delineated in another location in greater detail than the subject one.

process queue, DASD — A queue in which the queue control block resides in main storage, and the message-segment chain resides in a Direct-Access Storage Device. These queues contain message segments that are sent to a message processing program.

product area — Some calculators have an area in main storage to store results of multiplication operations specifically.

production application, calculator — A typical gaging system is used to measure the thickness of power steering hydraulic pump components, classify these components into groups for fit and reject those which fall outside acceptable production tolerances. All of the measurements, computations and decisions regarding group number, flatness and effective height, are made by the calculator and are output through its printer. (some units)

production automation applications — Some of the areas in which these versatile systems are providing solutions to control problems are: Machine Tool Control: Automatic Surface Grinder Control; Automatic Brake And Shear Control; Automatic Turret Lathe Control. Remote Monitoring And Control: Environmental Monitoring For A Nuclear Power Station; Programmable Remotes for Supervisory Control; Programmable Analog And Digital Alarm Systems; River Water Temperature Monitoring For A Public Utility; Data Monitoring Systems. Material Handling Control: Automatic Stacker Crane Control In A Frozen Foods Warehouse; Automatic Batch Weighing And Mixing Of Animal Feed, Liquid Laundry Detergent And Other Products; Automatic Weighing Of Railroad Freight Cars; Conveyor Sortation Systems; Automatic Cart Loader For Product Containers. Industrial Computer Control: Automatic Testing And Automatic Testing And Data Logging; On-line Parts Check Inspection Systems; Automatic Motor Armature Winding Machine Control; Automatic Assembly And Test Of Thermostats, Tape Cassettes, And Heart Pacemakers; Submerged Arc Welder Control. Traffic Control: Intersection Control Systems; Freeway Ramp monitoring And Control Systems.

production calculator/controller — If user has been working with BASIC language programming, some calculators are optimum controller. They combine the high level BASIC language with many unique programming and editing features to shorten usual programming time. The major portion of the keyboard duplicates that of a typewriter or teletype. On one unit, twenty special function keys can be defined by functions or subprograms to simplify system programming. Program, data, and special function key storage is easily and quickly done on the built-in cassette memory with up to 40,000 word capacity (16 bit words). Operator system interaction is greatly simplified with the 32 character alphanumeric display and the 80 character thermal printer. Of several types of controllers, one typical unit has a large memory option with 7.9K (16 bit words) of user read-write memory.

production data analysis — Characteristics usually pertain to:
- output in engineering units
- transducer linearization and compensation
- average values and standard deviations
- trend analysis
- design computations
- real time process profile
- efficiency and fast time information
- go/no-go limit testing
- comparison with historical test data

production data analysis calculator system — In the field of data acquisition, two general measurement solutions have been available. The simplest alternative is the basic data logger (voltmeter/scanner combination with printer or punched tape output) which has no on-site computational capability for analyzing data. When simltaneous data analysis or closed loop control based on measurement results are required, an on-line computerized voltmeter/scanner system is used. One major system enables users to move up to on-

line data analysis for reliable real-time results without committing the money and support required for a highly capable and complex computer data acquisition system. In a typical application the system will:
(1) Control the system instruments,
(2) Acquire and convert analog data from physical sensors to digital form,
(3) Correct the data for nonlinearity and offset and convert it to meaningful scientific units,
(4) Determine test results,
(5) Control processes or set alarms,
(6) perform high level statistical and historical analysis, and
(7) Log or display results.

The most significant effect is an increase in accuracy and dependability, while at the same time releasing skilled people from the costly routine of meter reading and performing other test procedures.

production routine — That routine which produces the results of the problem or program as it was designed, as contrasted with the routines which are designed for support, housekeeping, or to compile, assemble, translate, etc.

production run — A run that fulfills the program objective. It occurs after the projected program has been successfully checked out.

production system calculator — One type calculator system's computational power and interactivity has practically eliminated human error and double production of precision electronic components. It eliminates hours of test equipment stabilization time, hand logging and visual comparison of tables. The operator presses a key as each part is tested for voltage drop. The calculator's program applies a formula to compute the voltage reading and oven temperature relationship. Then it accepts or rejects the part. The alphanumeric printer labels results and groups acceptable parts into three grades.

product mix, linear programming — Linear programming will indicate how raw materials should be combined to produce the highest possible profits for the company, given a set of raw materials with given characteristics and a given set of market prices for finished products. Blending of gasoline is an example of this type of application.

professional calculator (preprogramming) — The professional calculator is pre-programmed so that one or two key strokes will do what might require a half dozen operations on a simpler calculator. An advanced scientific calculator can convert polar coordinates to rectangular coordinates and vice versa. It can calculate trig functions in any of three angular modes — degrees, radians, or grads — and can convert decimal angles into degrees, minutes, and seconds. It performs metric/U.S. conversions, calculates the factorial of positive integers, and simultaneously calculates the mean and standard deviation of an x value. Typically they have several addressable memories instead of only one, and users can perform register arithmetic.

program — 1. A set of instructions arranged in a proper sequence for directing advanced calculators in performing a desired operation or operations (e.g., the solution of a mathematical problem or the collation of a set of data). 2. To prepare a program (as contrasted with "to code"). 3. A sequence of audio signals transmitted for entertainment or information. 4. The basic computer preparation procedure. The computer is practically useless without accurate worthwhile programming. Programs are designed and written to solve problems, control processes and procedures and are referred to generally as software. 5. A plan for the solution of a problem. A complete program includes plans for the transcription of data, coding for the computer and plans for the absorption of the results into the system. The list of coded instructions is called a routine; to plan a computation or process from the asking of a question to the delivery of the results, including the integration of the operation into an existing system. Thus programming consists of planning and coding, including numerical analysis, systems analysis, specification of printing formats, and any other functions necessary to the integration of a calculator in a system.

program, calculator — 1. A series of detailed statements for calculations necessary to solve a problem. The programmable electronic calculators store this sequence of instructions in memory and require that the operator enter the variables. All programmable electronic calculators have the ability to "learn" the steps of a program as they are keyed, but many also offer the ability to store programs on cards ROMs, RAMs for tapes for reuse. 2. A sequence of detailed instructions designed for the operations necessary to solve a problem. After the first sequence of entries only the variable numbers used need to be entered on the keyboard and then the manual activation of the control keys.

program advantages, low cost calculators — Programs are written to save time on repetitive calculations. Once users have written the keystroke procedure for solving a particular problem and recorded it in the calculator, they need no longer devote attention to the individual keystrokes that make up the procedure. They can let the calculator solve each problem for them. And because users can easily check the procedure in their program, they have more confidence in the final answer since they don't have to worry each time about whether or not they have pressed an incorrect key. The calculator performs the drudgery, leaving user's minds free for more creative work.

program, applications — A program written to accomplish a specific user task (such as payroll) as opposed to a supervisory, general purpose, or utility program.

program, assembly — Also called a translator. A process which translates a symbolic program into a machine-language program before the working program is executed. It can also integrate several sections or different programs.

program attention key — On a display device keyboard, a key that produces an interruption to solicit program action that does not require the reading of data from the display buffer. Abbreviated PA key.

program, automatic recovery — A program enabling a system to remain functioning when a piece of equipment has failed. The automatic recovery program often activates duplex circuitry, a standby machine, or switches to a mode of degraded operation.

program, background — This program is of lower priority than the foreground or main program and is at halt or standby while the main program runs.

program, blue-ribbon — Handwritten and independently designed by a programmer and so checked that no mistakes or bugs are therein contained; i.e., the "BR" program should thus run correctly the first time, excepting machine malfunctions. Same as program, star.

program, calculator (low cost) — For small units a program is nothing more than a sequence of manual keystrokes that is remembered by the calculator. Users can then execute the program as often as they like with less chance of error. The answer displayed at the end of execution is the same one users would have obtained by pressing the keys one at a time manually. No prior programming experience is necessary for most small calculator programming.

program chaining — Situations may arise where programs are too long for computer memory. A convenient technique to use if this problem arises is to break the programs into segments and store these segments on tape cassettes. The segments are then loaded into the memory one segment at a time and executed. This procedure is termed "PROGRAM CHAINING".

program, check — 1. A system of determining the correct program and machine functioning either by running a sample problem with similar programming and a known answer, or by using mathematical or logic checks such as comparing A times B with B times A. 2. A check system built into the program or calculators that do not have automatic checking. This check system is normally concerned with programs run on machines which are not self-checking internally. Synonymous with routine check and related to check, automatic.

program checkout — A standard runthrough of a program on a calculator to determine if all designs and results of a program are as anticipated.

program, coded — A program which has been expressed in the code or language of a specific machine or programming system.

program, compatible — Relates to those features of equipment or programs which are acceptable or workable to various types of calculator or those peripheral machines or programs which can be substituted for use in various brands or types of machines.

program, compiling — A unique but basic translating program designed to transform, to assemble, or to structure programs expressed in other languages into same or equivalent programs expressed in terms of the particular machine language for which that particular machine was designed. Compiling programs or compilers most often include assemblers (or programs) as well as diagnostic and generating programs within them.

program, control — 1. A control system which automatically holds or changes its target value on the basis of time, to follow a prescribed program for the process. 2. A sequence of instructions which prescribe the series of steps to be taken by a system, a computer or any other device.

program control calculator applications — Output cards having programmable reed-relay contact closures are available for operating alarms, lamps, opening and closing valves, bins or providing stimuli to external systems. Thus the calculator, under program control, can analyze incoming data, print out a summary of the information received, make decisions and control processes all under program supervision.

program control transfer — The transfer of operational control among two or more independent programs being operated concurrently. This function makes possible the operation of compute-limited programs concurrently with I/O (input/output)-limited programs. Operational control is transferred to a compute-limited program whenever the I/O-limited programs must wait, pending completion of requested I/O functions. This function of the executive program allows an installation to make maximum use of its total system facility.

program, correction — Most users can rest assured that the first time they assemble or compile a program, it will contain errors in logic and instruction syntax. If a user's program is written in a compiler language, the source and object programs will be too unlike for them to follow and understand object program execution steps; nearly all program corrections must be made by generating results, then checking through logic to determine why the results are wrong.

program counter — 1. The program counter contains the address of the next instruction byte to be fetched from memory and is automatically incremented after each fetch cycle. 2. One of the registers in the CPU that holds addresses necessary to step the machine through the various programs. During interrupts, the program counter saves the address of the instruction. Branching also requires loading of the return address in the program counter.

program counter (PC) example — The typical program counter is a 4, 8, 12 or 16-bit register that holds the memory address of the next instruction to be processed. The execution of each instruction causes the program counter to be loaded with the address of the next instruction to be executed.

program creation, recording and execution, user — No prior programming experience is necessary to program on many calculating units. Users easily define the five top row keys to calculate functions of their own creation for use alone or with other programs. They plan their problem in terms of the keystrokes needed for calculation and the additional keystrokes needed to control their program. Users set the mode switch to W/PRGM position and key the keystroke sequence into memory. They may then record their program for future re-entry by merely passing a magnetic card through the calculator. Upon switching back to RUN mode, they can execute their stored program. (some systems)

program, cross-assembler — Microcomputers generally do not have enough memory or are not equipped with the necessary peripheral devices to support many utility programs. In such a situation, another computer is used to perform the assembly or compilation, and the programs used are called cross-assemblers or cross-compilers. For example, a microcomputer program might be cross-assembled on a time-sharing system. Punched tape output from the time-sharing terminal would then be loaded into the microcomputer for testing.

program debugging, TRACE, INSERT and DELETE — The TRACE mode can be turned on and off, in some units either manually or under program control enabling programs or portions of programs to be analyzed for possible errors. The

STEP function causes one step of the program to be executed each time the key is depressed.

Insert and Delete: INSERT AND DELETE commands permit the insertion or deletion of a program step with a single keystroke. The SET P.C. (Program Counter) command enables any specific program step to be accessed. Once a step is accessed the STEP and BACKSTEP functions provide single keystroke access to adjacent steps.

program development system — For program development, some suppliers provide a microprogramming development package, whereby users can make, simulate, and debug programs on a system that has a CRT display, keyboard, dual or single floppy disk drives and optional hard copy printer.

program, diagnostic trace — Refers to a particular type of diagnostic program for the performance of checks on the other programs or for demonstrating such operations. The output of a trace program may include instructions of the program which is being checked and intermediate results of those instructions arranged in the order in which the instructions are executed.

program documentation (microprocessor) — Refers to documentation for programs included in most microprocessor manuals; includes the program name and function, required hardware and software, details of the user-program interface, and a listing of the program.

program editing — Ease of use on some calculator systems extends beyond elementary programming. Program editing has been made relatively easy as users can move back and forth in memory, verifying, inserting, and deleting or modifying any number of program steps. Users can also step through a program to watch its execution one step at a time. Or they can automatically list the entire program. The printer provides a permanent record of all steps entered, with step number codes and mnemonics. Jumping, branching, six or more levels of subroutines, labeled addressing and seven or more conditional statements for testing are some standard features — plus varieties of program packs for wide ranges of applications are available on some mid-size desk units.

program editing, calculating — On some units editing a program is particularly easy. In program mode, the display shows the step number and the key phrase stored there. The key phrase is displayed as the row-column coordinates of the keystrokes that make it up. The digit keys are represented by a zero followed by the digit, and the other keys are described by a row digit followed by a column digit. (some units)

program editing, terminal systems — On some systems the RENUMBER command assigns an entire program, or a specified segment of a program, with user-selectable, equally incremented statement numbers. Errors are corrected in a statement by backspacing in an unexecuted line to the point where the error was made and properly re-entering the remainder of the line; deleting the entire line by reentering the line number, followed by a CR/LF command; or replacing the line completely by reentering the line number followed by the correct program statement. The Character EDIT ROM (Optional or standard on some models) provides cursor positioning and single character editing. Additional statements can be inserted into a program by entering a line numbered between two existing line numbers. The new line automatically is inserted between the two original line numbers.

program edit keys — Program edit keys allow the user to edit user-written programs. He can single-step through a program and add or delete individual steps at will, making it much easier to "de-bug" or modify a program.

program, editor — These are often string editing programs that instruct the CPU to search out and alter certain blocks of data (strings) in the program being developed. The editor is very useful when users desire to change an instruction they've repeated throughout a program.

program error — A mistake made in the program code by the programmer, keypuncher, or a machine-language compiler or assembler.

program error dump — The dumping onto tape, etc. by a priority program of information and main storage so that the cause of an equipment or program error interrupt may be assessed by the analysts.

program evaluation and review technique (PERT) — Use of PERT requires an extensive analysis of an overall project, in order to list all the individual activities or jobs which must be performed in order to meet the total objective. These activities are then arranged in a network that displays the sequential relationships among them. This analysis must be extremely thorough and detailed if it is to be realistic, and it will require application of all the talents and experience available to the organization. PERT provides a means of reporting an analysis for project administrators. Information required can be developed and areas that impose the greatest time restrictions on the completion of a product can be highlighted. Areas with an excess of time for completion, called slack areas, are also highlighted.

program, executive — Refers to various programs that control loading and relocation of routines and in some cases make use of instructions which are unknown to the general programmer. Effectively, an executive routine is part of the machine itself (synonymous with monitor routine, supervisory routine, and supervisory program). 2. A set of coded instructions designed to process and control other sets of coded instructions. 3. A set of coded instructions used in realizing automatic coding. 4. A master set of coded instructions.

program, externally stored — A program which is stored in one of many input devices or media and which must be read from the medium or device by connection and interrogation or interpretation, i.e., programs on tapes, cards, disks, etc., rather than wired or internally stored types.

program generator — Generally a large detailed program which permits a computer to write other programs automatically. Generators are usually of two types. 1. The character controlled generator, which operates like a compiler in that it takes entries from a library tape, but unlike a simple compiler in that it examines control characters associated with each entry, and alters instructions found in the library according to the directions contained in the control characters. 2. The pure generator is a program that writes another program. When associated with an assembler a pure generator is usually a section of program which is called into storage by the assembler from a library and then writes one or more entries in another program. Most assemblers are also compilers and generators. In this case the entire system is usually referred to an assembly system. (Related to problem-oriented language.)

program instruction — Refers to designed sets of characters, together with one or more address (or no address), that define an operation and which, as a unit, causes the computer to operate accordingly on the indicated quantities; a machine instruction to specific functions. Types: actual, arithmetic, blank, branch, control, direct, effective, execution, executive, extract, halt, hold, jump, machine, macro, programmed, and psuedo.

program, internally stored — Refers to a set or sequence of instructions; i.e., program or routine that is stored within the calculator (internal memory) as contrasted to those programs which might be stored externally on cards, paper, or magnetic tapes, etc.

program interrupts, addressing — Various events can lead to a program interrupt. Each interrupt is to a unique fixed memory address that is associated with the event that caused it. Addresses are reserved for these interrupts. Each external device has an interrupt address that is equal to its external device address. An external device may have more than one interrupt event and each event may have its own interrupt address. Interrupts may occur only at the end of program instructions. It is important to the programmer that each type of interrupt results in transfer of control to a different memory address. This makes it unnecessary for the program to scan interrupt events to see what has happened. A subroutine for each interrupt event may be in the memory. (Some systems.)

program interrupt (trapped) — Six events can cause the program of the calculator to be interrupted: (1) busy, (2) add overflow, (3) divide overflow, (4) operator, (5) external device, and (6) index overflow. An interrupt trap associated with each event may be set under program control to either respond when the event occurs or to ignore it. Many addresses in memory are reserved for external device interrupt. Each interrupt occurs at its own address so it can lead to its own unique subroutine. Upon completion of the subroutine, control can be returned to the original program at the point of interruption (some calculators).

program language types — Basically, the major kinds of programming languages are as follows: 1. Assembly, or symbolic machine languages — one-to-one equivalence with computer instructions, but with symbols and mnemonics as an aid to programming. 2. Macroassembly languages, which are the same as assembly or symbolic machine languages, but permit macroinstructions for coding convenience. 3. Procedure-oriented languages for expressing methods in the same way as expressed by algorithmic languages. 4. Problem-oriented languages for expressing problems Procedure-oriented languages may be further divided into: (a) Algebraic languages (numerical computation), (b) String-manipulating languages (text manipulation), (c) Simulation languages (such as GPSS, DYNAMO) and (d) Multipurpose languages (such as PL/I).

program, learning — The unique program designed to alter itself by making changes based on the experience of the program and results unknown until portions of the program have been run. For example, a program designed to increase efficiency and provide instructions for program modification or a predestined basis, concerning various analysis techniques built into the program itself resulting in corrective action or alternations of program instruction based on various criteron established within the program.

program libraries, supplier — Most suppliers maintain an extensive library of programs for customers. This emphasizes convenience and allows users to establish operations of various programs without extensive set-up procedures. Convenient prerecorded programs are available for complex problem solving in electrical engineering, statistics, medicine, and surveying — to name a few.

programmable — Capable of being set to operate in a specified manner, or of accepting remote setpoints or other commands.

programmable calculator — Programmable calculators are available at prices ranging from $29 to $11,000 and with simple instruction execution times ranging from about $10\,\mu$sec to $300\,\mu$sec. A high level man-machine interface is one of the most attractive features of these popular forms of programmable logic. In the simplest form, programmable calculator programming is accomplished by keystrokes stored to form a sequence of operations. This sequence can then be repeated on demand by the user. Higher level programmable calculators include simple storage devices to allow easy program change and storage. As one approaches the very high end of the programmable calculator spectrum, they begin to look like minicomputers. Programmable calculators in this class are elements in data communications nets, perform remote job entry (RJE), function as instrumentation system controllers, and have disc, cartridge and line printer peripherals. BASIC is run interpretively on several calculators in this class with programming facilitated by special keys and alphanumeric keyboards. Even these high level calculators maintain their dual nature so that simple problems can be quickly solved by several keystrokes while more difficult problems demand a programming effort.

programmable calculator advantages — Programmables offer a software commitment for prepared, prepackaged, program libraries in both general and specific areas. This capability allows a programmable calculator to serve several different needs for an individual (i.e., a manager who performs statistical analysis, financial accounting, and personal financing in the course of a typical day). The library programs can provide a wider range of complicated functions with a high level of sophistication for a lower price than a comparable dedicated calculator. The programmable calculator is now enhanced with the non-volatile memory and program areas which allow the user to turn his calculator off and on and not lose its contents for a later session. The ability to read and write both memory and program areas on magnetic strips has become commonplace. In order to aid the owner in the use of more sophisticated calculators, a hard copy capability is offered. It is relatively simple to connect a professional pocket calculator to an inexpensive printing device to obtain an audit trail for both calculation and program executions. This also provides a listing of a stored program which will be a requirement as memory sizes increase. Enhanced operation is available with the development of alphanumeric display capability on pocket calculators. This allows an interactive mode between the user and a program which he or someone else has written.

programmable calculator, algebraic — Many scientific and engineering-oriented, programmable calculators use algebraic language and observe the hierarchy of mathematics. These instruments feature programmable-ROM memories, expandable program memory, in external magnetic storage capacity, and are available with printer, plotter, and display. Problems are entered just as users would write their equations. Numbers can be entered from the keyboard in scientific notation, floating point, or in mixed format, and will be displayed in the same form. Although data entry is limited to a 10-digit mantissa in some units, all calculations are performed on a 12-digit mantissa, which is maintained in the working registers and rounded off for display as a 10-digit mantissa plus 2-digit mantissa plus 2-digit exponent, ensuring accuracy and reducing round-off errors. In addition to those keys normally found on a standard calculator, the keyboard contains mode selection, memory addressing, and control keys as well as 24 mathematical function keys, which, when depressed, perform common mathematical operations (eg., $\sqrt{X}$, $1/x, x^2$). (some units)

programmable calculator, BASIC language — Some advanced programmable calculators developed present the user with various choices in the system's primary elements. To enter programs and data into these units, a standard keyboard is offered and has the ability to enter BASIC language keywords with a single keystroke in addition to the alpha characters. They are often designed with a full teletype keyboard in addition to the 10-key numeric section for applications requiring the entry of large quantities of alphanumeric data. Some units have keyboards that offer 32 special function keys that may be used for manually-operated programs and text entry or for user-defined functions under program control. There is a choice of using a CRT display and magnetic tape cassette singularly or in combination. The Central Processing Units contain the extended BASIC in a read-only MOS memory and a random-access MOS memory of 4K expandable to 32K. For ease in programming, these calculators handle both numeric and alphanumeric string variables and two-dimensional arrays.

programmable calculator — BASIC (example) — A typical BASIC Language Calculator has the power and memory of a minicomputer without the limitations and expense usually encountered. Generally, these Programmable Calculators use a handwired BASIC language compiler which allows the user to communicate with and program the read/write (R/W) memory (in English) without disturbing or diminishing the R/W memory itself. Also these units employ plug-in, read-only memories (ROM's) which perform additional user (or peripheral) functions with the main R/W memory ... again, without reducing memory size or disturbing the user.

The R/W user memory, therefore, is always reserved and ready for programs and data. There is no loading of compilers or use of valuable memory for functions other than program or data. User frustrations are eliminated. A maximum of 8,000 16-bit words of user R/W memory is available on some units (in increments of 2,000 and 4,000 words). One specific model comes already equipped with a 7,500-word hardwired BASIC language compiler. Additionally, a total of 8 plug-in ROM's provide up to 8,000 words of read-only-memory over and above the R/W and compiler memories. The result: one 8,000-word unit in reality can be a 23,500-word computational system with 8,000 words of true, usable R/W memory available at all times. Some units can also be interfaced to Mass Memory Subsystems which provide up to 1.2 million words (2.4 million bytes) of extra, accessible memory. The entire system is completely accessible and not subject to time-share, batch-processing, or other delays. In conjunction with a companion Thermal Page Width Printer, neat, formal analysis can be silently printed at 250 lines per minute, 80 characters per line. Other peripherals, such as card readers and graphic plotters, can be added as required to many systems.

programmable calculator batch terminal — Although designed as stand-alone machines, advanced calculators have several capabilities that allow them to be conveniently converted to terminals. These include alphanumeric character manipulation (strings), a general input/output structure, 4,000 to 16,000 bytes of expandable buffer memory, and page-width, high-speed printers. For timesharing applications, their typewriter-like keyboards are easier to use than those which have the letters and numbers arranged in another format. For remote batch, the calculator mass memory allows efficient use of the communication link and provides ample storage for input and output data. The Hewlett-Packard 9830A's and some others use the program language BASIC, which is well known to users of timesharing systems.

programmable calculator bus control — The microcomputer within the calculator connected to a common bus controls the time allocation of the bus for peripherals and performs arithmetic and logic operations and instruction decoding. It often contains multiple high-speed general-purpose registers which can be used as accumulators, address pointers, index registers, and other specialized functions. The processor can do both single and double operand addressing and handle both 16-bit word and 8-bit byte data. The bus permits data transfer directly between I/O devices and memory without disturbing the processor registers. Some microcomputer processors are implemented with several LSI 40-pin chips. The chips are the control chip, the data chip, and two microm (microcode read-only memory) chips in a small system.

programmable calculator capabilities — Programmable calculators must remember keystrokes and be versatile and powerful in evaluating formulas. Formulas typically are defined with functions and variables. A programmable calculator must have: (1) a broad range of math functions; (2) formula solving and chain calculation abilities; (3) data storage registers. If any of the above is not present then the ability to remember keystrokes has limited value. One popular model has: (1) over 80 pre-programmed functions; (2) the significant power and simplicity of RPN and the stack for chain calculations; (3) nine addressable storage registers which, in programming, take on the role of variables in equations. To make programs simple to execute, the example unit has five user definable keys: A B C D E. Each of the five keys can be used to execute one program, allowing the user to easily access up to five different programs in the calculator at any given time. The unit features a unique "keyboard programming language" which makes writing programs very similar to using the calculator manually. Programs are lists of keystrokes stored and then executed automatically.

programmable calculator colored key example — As the key legends depict, various advanced slide-rule calculators have three-stack RPN logic. Several of the 36 keys are made to do double duty by use of a gold-colored shift key, on one unit, when this is touched before pressing a key, the function printed in gold beneath the key is brought into play instead of the one in silver above it. The programmable feature is controlled by these four blue keys arranged vertically along the left side of the keyboard and labelled from top to bottom: DEL, SKIP, HALT, and START; plus a three-position slide switch at the top labelled: LOAD, STEP, RUN.

programmable calculator components, basic — Many basic programmable calculators can be subdivided into five functional sections. These are the MPU and clock, the memory, an I/O port, control and indication, and the power supply. The first three of these sections, along with the power supply regulation components, are often located on the main printed circuit board.

programmable calculator computer capability — By most definitions, a computer is a device or system capable of solving problems by accepting and retaining data, performing prescribed operations on that data, and supplying and/or storing the results of those operations. If the capability of accepting and retaining a planned program of operations is added to a calculator chip, then, in effect, the calculator/programmer combination becomes a basic computer.

Not too long ago, a programmable calculator required several LSI chips to provide the necessary calculation, memory and programming functions, keyboard debounce circuits to prevent false entries, separate segment and digit drivers for the display, a multidigit display, power supply regulation circuits and, of course, a suitable keyboard. However, commercial programmable calculators cost as little as thirty or forty dollars now.

programmable calculator communications ROM (Read Only Memory) — Advanced calculators were originally intended to fill a gap between programmable calculators and computers. They were designed as a stand-alone computing systems that are compact, inexpensive, and easy to use. Options are provided by plug-in read-only memory (ROM) blocks. A terminal ROM, one of the first ROMs introduced, gave the calculator its original capability to act as a timesharing terminal. With the terminal ROM the calculator acted like a teleprinter. Programs could be prepared off-line and edited in the calculator memory, and programs could be received into memory from a time-sharing system.

However, users were not satisfied simply to emulate a teleprinter. Requests were received for a mode that would allow blocks of data to be sent to a computer automatically. Also, the calculator was growing as a small computing system. The addition of a disc with a maximum capacity of 4.8 million bytes, a hopper-fed card reader, and a medium-speed line printer meant that more and more data could be handled. The need arose to move locally collected information to a larger computer, or to input data from a larger data base to a local data base at the calculator.

programmable calculator concepts — To reduce the number of keystrokes, and keystroke errors, many pocket calculators can be programmed and directed to initiate the desired keystrokes automatically. A program is a sequence of keystrokes, used to solve a problem or series of problems. Once a calculator is programmed, users key in the data — the numbers for the specific problems being solved — and press one key to run the entire program. Some programmables can usually be programmed only by pressing the keys. (Then the program is temporarily stored in the program memory, where it remains until removed or changed by the calculator operator or until the calculator is turned off.) With a fully programmable pocket calculator, that same program can also be permanently stored on an external device (such as magnetic cards) and re-entered in the program memory when needed. Depending on the model, a programmable calculator may have provision for editing a program (adding, deleting or changing steps) and such computer-like operations as branching — choosing between two alternate steps depending upon the outcome of a relational test. A programmable calculator can also make logical decisions.

programmable calculator, data acquisition system — One typical system offers:
- powerful, yet easy-to-use, programmable calculator steps,
- high level data analysis and instrument control.
- easily learned programming language.
- conversational interaction with operator requiring less operator skill.
- easy system expandability with H-P interface bus and calculator I/O and memory options.

programmable calculator data communications terminal — By adding an interface cable and plugging in a pair of special read-only memories, the user of an HP 9830A BASIC-Language Programmable Calculator and quite likely other calculators as well can convert his machine to a versatile data communications terminal. The calculator can be a time-sharing terminal with the ability to exchange programs and data with a timesharing computer, can act as a binary synchronous remote batch terminal to a remote computer, and can communicate with another calculator or terminal. (H-P means Hewlett-Packard)

programmable calculator decisions — Decision-making capabilities are an essential requirement of all but the simplest kind of program. A programmable calculator must therefore handle programs that are constructed with decision (or branch) points. Different sequences of commands are performed depending on the value, or almost any other aspect of a number, or a logic condition at a specific branch point in a program. Many single condition decisions — negative numbers, zero, switch settings, greater than, less than, etc. — can be combined to create highly complex multi-branched programs, but over-all simplicity is still retained. The programmer spells out singly, each condition to be tested in a multiple-branch program no matter what the complexity is. A capacity

programmable calculator, hand-held

of 4000 program steps can solve highly complex branching problems, on some units.

programmable calculator, hand-held — Some hand-held programmables are three machines in one. The first way to use these calculators is to write specific programs, incorporating the exact equations, constants and/or procedures one needs for easy and rapid solution of all types of numeric problems. Often users make a list of the keystrokes needed to solve the problem using any of the arithmetic, log, trig and exponential functions on the keyboard. They next set the keyboard to WRITE PROGRAM and key in the program. Once the program is in the machine, users can record it on a magnetic card for future use anytime, anywhere, after they verify that solution.

To run the program, users set the switch to RUN, key in their known data and start the program running. The machine will automatically execute the entire calculation in seconds — as often as they need it. Some calculators (hand-held) have program memories 100 steps long, and they offer logic tests, conditional branches — plus all the functions on the complex keyboards. Users can also chain programs for unusually long or complex problems that cannot be solved in 100 steps. Another way to use the calculator is with the pre-recorded magnetic program cards supplied in special cards of application packs. Each pack contains as many as 40 programs dedicated to a specific discipline (e.g., electrical engineering, finance, statistics, marine navigation).

programmable calculator input-output — On some units for less highly engineered units, input is usually by a 10-key keyboard. More complex models accept keyboard, paper tape, punch tape, hopper type, mag card, mag tape, and optical paper tape editor input. Output encompasses typewriters, printers, plotters, paper tape, mag tape, CRT's and even includes telecommunication capabilities.

programmable calculator interface — A calculator interface allows direct input of data from external digital devices (digital voltmeters, panel meters, counters, digital clocks. etc.) into some programmable calculators. As an output only interface, it accepts numeric data.

programmable calculators — intelligent terminals — A question frequently asked is, are calculators intelligent terminals? Probably the best answer is, "No, they're intelligent calculators that have data communications capability." Most intelligent terminals might be better described as preprogrammed terminals for specific applications. Typically, the intelligent terminal may be used to enter data from keyboard to storage based on a form, or to emulate the functions of popular hardwired terminals, the most prominent being IBM 2780. Although the several calculators can emulate the IBM 2780 and can be used to enter data based on a form, this is not their primary function. They perform best as a stand-alone processors that have data communications capability.

programmable calculator interfacing — There are two main approaches to calculator interfacing: the dedicated interface and the general-purpose coupler. The dedicated interface connects a single peripheral device directly to the calculator's internal bus. As many as four interface cards are used. The calculator has full control over the bus,

programmable calculator microprocessor

directing and routing data between itself and the peripheral. The general purpose coupler, however, provides its own external bus system, and couplers with as many as eight interface channels are available. Thus, up to eight different devices can be simultaneously connected to some calculators.

programmable calculator limitations — Programmable calculators do have several shortcomings. Compared to minicomputers, even the highest level programmable calculator is quite slow but not for its price. Programming keystroke tabulations on even higher level versions, can be very time-consuming and quite frustrating. Calculator I/O operations are often slow and difficult to program which decreases programmable calculator effectiveness in I/O intensive applications. Where complex programming time, performance or broad I/O capability is of the essence, minicomputers or microcomputers are a better buy than programmable calculators. When straight calculations represent the vast majority of all calculations and ease of use for these problems is important, a programmable calculator is a much better fit.

programmable calculator limits — There is a limit to the size of a problem that many algebraic calculators can handle. Available memory capacity is the main limiting factor. Although peripherals like cassettes can substantially expand the memory, use of a calculator beyond a certain point is inefficient. A computer may better handle problems reaching this scale. Unfortunately there is little agreement among calculator manufacturers and users on how to measure this capability. Some users say the number of registers is the determinant factor. Others say the number of program steps that can be handled is a better indicator of a calculator's limitations. But different calculators may use different percentages of their memory for a particular step, and not all registers are the same size or can do the same functions. Comparison is difficult, but not impossible.

programmable calculator magnetic cards — A significant achievement in the design of programmable calculators, for example, was the magnetic card read/write ability. After writing and debugging a program, the user has the ability to make a permanent record of his program on a magnetic card and then at any later time read the program back into the calculator.

The programming power of these units allows extremely complicated programming procedures. For versatile problem solving the designers of these units wanted the users to have the ability to make a permanent record of programs and then rerecord them into the calculator whenever they wished. These units have a built-in magnetic card read/write ability. Programs can be read from or written into program memory by inserting a small magnetic card into the lower of two slots on the right hand side of some calculators.

programmable calculator microprocessor module — A typical processor module is built around a set of four N-channel metal oxide semi-conductor (MOS) chips, which include control and data elements as well as several microcoded read-only memories (microms). The latter are programmed to emulate the various mini-computer instruction sets along with routines for on-line debugging techniques (ODT), operator interfacing, and boot-strap loader capability. A processor also might contain a 16-bit buffered parallel input/output (I/O) bus, a 4096-word MOS random-access memory (RAM), a real-time clock input, priority interrupt control logic, power-fail/auto restart, and other features to provide stand-alone operation. The entire processor, plus all of the above-mentioned features can be contained on one 8.5 by-10-inch printed circuit board.

programmable calculator, natural math hierarchy — Features on some advanced units are:
1. The unit is an instrument that follows natural math hierarchy, with a keyboard that thinks of calculations the way users do;
2. With 24 user-definable keys, programming can be tailored to any particular discipline;
3. Data entry: fixed point, floating point or scientific floating point;
4. By pressing the alpha mode, each key functions is a different alphabetical character;
5. Two memory systems are built in: the data portion, consisting of 74 registers, allows storage of any 12 digit numbers.

One unit's program memory consists of 512 steps:
6. Any program, subroutine or data can be permanently stored on magnetic tape cartridges;
7. The optional thermal printer is for listing and writing interactive programs;
8. User-definable PROM capability;
9. 30 built-in math functions;
10. Electronic display consisting of 10 digit mantissa plus 2 digit exponent.

programmable calculator "package", hand-held — Typical "packages" come equipped with customized software and documentations, operating guides for quick reference to keystrokes and basic operations. Owner's Manuals give comprehensive, detailed information with numerous examples. Basic Library Program Manuals show owners how to use their prerecorded programs, also prerecorded program cards which users can put to work immediately. Various diagnostic cards let users check for programming accuracy. Head cleaners remove oxides and foreign particles from the magnetic read/write head. Blank magnetic cards let users develop their own programs. Other items are a carrying case for preprogrammed and prerecorded cards. A 100-sheet tablet of User Instructions and Coding Forms to make the user's own special programs easy to build. An AC adapter/charger is used while operating or for fast battery recharge from 115 V/60 Hz wall outlet. A sturdy vinyl, cushioned carrying case with pockets for the Operating Guide and program card case is usually also available for new owners.

programmable calculator power — Two of the most important considerations when evaluating a programmable calculator's power are its memory and its processor. To those doing relatively simple problems but working with massive quantities of data (inventory control for example), power is mass storage capability. To those doing complicated problems with relatively small amounts of data (such as finding the roots of polynomials), power is a big processor. For those doing vector analysis in multiple coordinate systems, both are essential. For this reason, manufacturers are offering several types of memory offering maximum flexibility. Users now have the opportunity to select both the size and the type of memory that suits their problems and applications. If problems or procedures change, a modular structure can allow the user to change the system as his problems and requirements change. Many calculators use the most advanced MOS/LSI technology for their internal memory. Users can obtain true computer power at a calculator price.

programmable calculator program (cards) — The HP-65 programmable calculator has built-in magnetic card reader/recorder that uses mylar-based ferrite-oxide-casted cards that are .95 cm wide and 7.1 cm long. Each card stores 100 program steps in 600 bits of information. A two-track self clocking recording scheme is used to maximize the system's tolerance to head screw and motor speed variations. When the W/PRGM RUN switch is in the RUN position, insertion of a card into the reader slot triggers the motor and the read circuits. All 100 program steps are read into the calculator's memory. In the W/PRGM, insertion of a card triggers the motor and writing circuits, and the entire contents of program memory (600 bits) are written on the card.

programmable calculator program modifications — A key design consideration of calculators is to optimize the user's ability to modify his programs. Ideally, instructions can be inserted into or deleted from any part of program memory. This is accomplished in some models through the use of a 600 bit shift register (each program memory position is six bits). When an instruction is keyed into memory, all instructions below it shift down one position. Similarly an instruction can be pulled out of a memory and all instructions below it shifted up one position. To give the programmer flexibility this unit was equipped with a complete set of program control instructions including: (1) A — E keys, (2) a subroutine capability. (3) numeric conditionals. (4) flags. (5) branching. (6) program interrupts. (7) an automatic counter for looping. These instructions extend the programming power to applications which require looping or iteration and also allow efficient utilization of program memory when areas of programs are duplicated.

programmable calculator, self-clocking two-track recording technique — When some models record a program on one of the small magnetic cards, they place two side-by-side tracks of varying magnetic flux on the card. One track represents the logical 1's in the binary data stream coming from the program memory, and the other track represents the logical 0's. The 1 track contains a flux reversal for each 1 in the data sequence and no flux change for each 0. The 0 track contains a flux reversal for each 0 and no flux change for each 1. The technique is self clocking because there is a flux transition for each bit. Thus no separate clock track is needed. The scheme also maximizes the system's tolerance to head skew and motor speed variations. The data can be recovered correctly even with a transition in the other. By contrast, other two-track schemes usually have one clock track and one data track, and may misread data when there is only minor misalignment of clock and data transitions.

programmable calculator systems capability — A calculator with enhanced versatility and with terminal functions fits into the small-computer category, since its instruction set can be customized on ROMs and it can store programs and data in its mass magnetic-tape or disk memory. But it is often more generally useful than a computer in that its programs are easier to access and its customizable keyboard makes it easier to operate.

programmable calculator terminal — When an operation has to handle sophisticated mathematical computations and also needs to access a remote computer, a programable calculator with plug-in communications options will reduce use of the central computer for calculations and also provide interactive or batch terminal capabilities. A typical calculator of this sort has added ROM, RAM for versatility above sophisticated minicomputer-based intelligent terminals.

programmable calculators vs minicomputers — For the past several years programmable calculators have been approaching those capabilities once solely in the minicomputer's domain. Today's calculators have sufficient memory capacity and language to displace minicomputers in most instrumentation systems. Technology has accelerated their capability to the point where they can do the same job as minicomputers — yet more people find them easy to understand, and use them because they need not wait for a computer programmer or for keypunch service. When applying a programmable calculator in an instrumentation system memory very fast minicomputer cycle time is seldom a limiting factor. Instead, speed restrictions are almost always imposed by digitizing of analog signals. Many physical parameters do not change fast enough to justify data rates exceeding easy calculator speeds of 10,000 measurements per second, and most, such as temperature, require only a few readings per second.

programmable calculators vs minicomputer "overkill" — The range of applications for programmable calculators is no longer limited in comparison to full-service minicomputers. The simplicity of operation and the many programming conveniences as well as the reduced installation costs, make them very attractive, despite their slower speed. A large majority of industrial processes do not require the great versatility that minicomputers offer, nor is speed always an overriding factor. The decision to use programmable calculators rather than minicomputers is most favorable when some of these conditions are present: (1) when input-output rates do not require speeds over 100 characters per second, (2) when the people using the instrument are not particularly adept at minicomputer assembly language programming, (3) when plug-in convenience is paramount because of the lack of electronic wiring and fabrication needed for other computers, and (4) when the equipment will be used for specific applications which do not require frequent program changes.

programmable calculators vs preprogrammables — Programmable calculators actually "learn" everyday business, scientific or other operations in order to handle them with very little operator intervention. The operator merely keys in the variables. Actually, the preprogrammables are hard-wired for specific programs in advance. On the other hand, programmables are more flexible, allowing the user to create or alter programs. Less complex programmables may not have internal memory but they could have from 2 to 64 storage registers in addition to the one the operator uses for calculations. The majority of machines, however, have two types of memory: one for stored data and the other for program instructions.

programmable clock — A programmable clock offers several methods for accurately measuring and counting time intervals or events. It can be used to synchronize the central processor to external events, count external events, measure intervals of time between events, or provide interrupts at programmable intervals. It can be used to start the A/D converter at predetermined intervals or from an external logic input. In some systems the clock operates in one of two program modes: single interval or repeated interval, and have seven programmable frequencies: 1MH$_z$ to 100 H$_z$, an external input, and an auxiliary input (on the backplane wiring). A counter can be preset for a number of time pulses or events to occur before an interrupt (or A/D counter start) is initiated. This counter can be read from the processor at any time to determine timing status.

programmable communications controller — Most units are complete ready-to-use firmware programmable systems incorporating enclosure — front panel — power supply — indicators and displays and card rack for additional memory and communications interfaces. EIA RS-232, CCITT V.24 — Telegraph TTY — Auto Answer and Originate. Synchronous or asynchronous, etc. Most are fully developed products. All are printed circuit construction. Interface modules, cables and all hardware needed for any communications application, often are available off the shelf. Various flexible units are not application dependent. Programmable Read Only Memorys control unit functions. Firmware is also available for many applications — special firmware can be provided by suppliers, or users can develop their own with an inexpensive development system.

programmable communications controller capabilities — Programmable Communications Controllers have been applied to many situations in the field of communications — here are a few: PROTOCOL CONVERTER — Supports terminals or other devices operating over communication lines with various protocols. COMMUNICATIONS CONCENTRATOR — Multiple terminals are multiplexed onto one line with error correction and contention. POLLING CONTROLLER — Several terminals can be polled and communicate with a CPU port that does not support polling. TERMINAL CONTROLLER — Speed and code translation — contention between multiple terminals for one port — protocol conversion so port can be used with normally unsupported devices.

programmable controller (PC) — Quite often now PCs replace solid-state logic modules. They are used for industrial controls as direct replacements for electromechanical control relays. PCs are designed to provide the user with the benefit of solid-state reliability while avoiding its pitfalls. PCs are provided with shielding or noise immune logic — i.e. designed-in isolation from high voltage inputs and outputs. In addition, the control logic — rather than being point-to-point wired as with solid-state modules — is programmable. PCs can be programmed in a familiar manner — often directly from a ladder diagram. Therefore, minimal training is required to implement a PC. More effort can be spent on designing the control logic rather than designing a control panel.

programmable controller capability — Solid state controllers are designed to replace relay-logic control and to automate systems. Low-cost and compact, many provide a programmable automatic control system that exceeds the performance of any conventional hardwired relay control panel in controlling, monitoring and protecting industrial machines, processes and production lines. The controller permits revision and reprogramming of the system without disturbing equipment, control devices or cables; without rewiring the control panel, and without losing the program security inherent in hardwired systems. The simple modular construction of the many controllers permits the system designer to choose both the size and characteristics needed for his control system. By using standard modules, he can tailor the controller to handle as few as 16 inputs and 8 outputs, and as many as 512 inputs and 256 outputs... with or without timing and counting. He can also perform arithmetic and shift register functions.

programmable DC voltage and current — On some units the output voltage (up to 100V) and current (up to 1000A) of thirty different power supplies can be programmed to provide bias in automatic test systems or control of electromechanical process equipment.

programmable graphic terminal calculator — The graphic terminal opens the skills of graphics with alphanumerics and provides added dimensions to calculator users. Fast x-y plots are as easy as specifying x, y coordinates. And alphanumerics is as simple as typing one's name. Users can program alphanumerics into the calculator from either the terminal or calculator keyboards. The terminal will format and print alphanumerics and data output under full program control. Rapid presentation of data or calculated results as well as graphical presentation of information for analysis or decision making is well within the capability of this device. The various brands of graphic terminal combinations provide a powerful and versatile team for data analysis and presentation in the computational office or laboratory.

programmable hand-held calculator, full capability — In these units programs are stored on tiny magnetic program cards. One of the cards can be slipped into the calculator and in two seconds the program is duplicated in the calculator's memory and the card exits for use another time. Users can buy these prerecorded magnetic cards with programs for solving problems in any math-connected discipline, or they can custom-record your own programs on blank magnetic cards for repeated use.

programmable instrument accessory examples — A timing generator and a digital clock are good examples of ASCII-programmable instrument accessories. The two modules are compatible with various interface busses and, as such, can be linked to counters, digital voltmeters, and other instruments.
One model timing generator provides precision time intervals from 1 μs to greater than a day. These time intervals are defined by start/end pulses and the interface bus start/end "flags." This flexible way of defining time intervals permits use in a wide variety of hardware and software applications. For example, the unit can be used to provide delayed gating pulses to counters or digital voltmeters to obtain frequency or voltage vs. time information. It can also be used to schedule subroutine execution in computer/calculator programs or to measure the time between events with μs resolution. The digital clock displays calendar and time data (month, day, hour, minute, second) and can be used for time logging to printers and calculators.

programmable I/O interfaces — The single-board computer — a standard plug-in "super component" — has become a reality with the introduction of 8,192-bit erasable programmable read-only memories (EPROMs) and programmable ISLI/O-interface components. The programmable interfaces allow the OEM to use software to customize the parallel I/O ports and communications interfaces, eliminating the previous need for inefficient hard-wired ports or I/O boards specially designed and manufactured for a custom application.

programmable logic — Programmable logic can be used to solve problems ranging from extremely simple combinations of elementary logic to controlling the financial system and production flow of an entire corporation. The tools to support development of these systems range from simple Karnaugh maps to extremely complex operating systems and high level languages. In surveying this spectrum of devices and tools, one encounters a myriad of tradeoffs which confuse the path to the best price performance solution to the problem at hand. This is further compounded by the speed with which new devices and tools are developed and the dynamic nature of the roles and characteristics of existing devices.

programmable logic array (PLA) — PLAs provide the sum of partial product outputs for a given set of inputs. This is accomplished by mask programming the interconnections in the input array of AND gates and the connections of the outputs of these AND gates to the inputs of output array of OR gates.

programmable logic spectrum — The programmable logic spectrum breaks down into two distinct categories — programmable logic devices and programmable logic systems. Each of these categories can be further broken down and ordered by the flexibility and capability of their individual elements. Programmable logic devices can be defined as relatively simple entities which, of themselves, do not compromise an entire computing system. Included in this category are random logic, FPLAs, PLAs, ROMs, EAROMs, RAMs, CAMs, and microprocessors. Programmable logic systems, on the other hand, are self-contained ASMs including all of the elements of a computer-control, arithmetic and logic functions, memory, I/O and the required software to make them implement the desired functions. Included in this category are microcomputers, programmable calculators, minicomputers, and large scale computers. Obviously this spectrum is wide, overlapping and replete with jargon that blurs distinctions between devices, systems, and categories.

programmable logic types — Logic has two significant forms — combinatorial logic and sequential logic. Combinatorial logic circuits produce outputs dependent only on input states and delays encountered in the logic path. Sequential logic, on the other hand, produces output dependent on input states, delays, the presence of a discrete timing interval (Tn), and the previous state of the logic array.

programmable LSI — Programmable LSI has drastically simplified the phases of the design cycle that generally have defied automation because of the amount of manual engineering work traditionally required. Detailed development and laborous, time-consuming debugging generally ruled in the past. Even these phases can now be largely automated by a software design approach — an approach, moreover, that can be implemented with a microcomputer as the development tool. Thus the smallest companies can share in the benefits of design automation. By the same token, automation for many companies will become mandatory, at least to the extent that the profitability of new designs depends on keeping development costs down and on penetrating new markets as soon as possible. More engineers are becoming involved in programming because the time has arrived when programmable LSI is high in performance for most digital systems. Compared to the earliest MOS microprocessors, the new microcomputer systems have 100 to 1,000 times more capabilities.

programmable memory — Refers to a type of memory whose locations are addressable by the calculator's program counter, i.e., a program within this memory may directly control the operation of the arithmetic and control unit.

programmable peripheral circuits — Many new peripheral circuits for microprocessors, offer a new dimension for LSI support chips in that they are all programmable. This allows the system designer maximum flexibility which results in lowered system cost. The five circuits provide functions for serial I/O timing, byte-oriented I/O, direct memory access and interrupt control.

programmable problem solving — One advanced calculator includes 472 program steps and 10 data registers and can be expanded to 2008 steps. The memory can be allocated by users into any combination of program steps and data registers they wish. The programming language includes such sophisticated features as FOR-NEXT loops; symbolic, absolute or calculated addresses; automatic address updating during editing; descriptive error messages; and subroutines nested to 7 deep. The unit has the programming power and memory flexibility to handle many of the most complex computational problems.

programmable read only memory (PROM) — PROMs are user programmable ROMs with commercially available speeds from 20NS to 1.5 sec and bit densities between 256 and 4096 bits. PROM prices range lower than 3c per bit in volume and have been dropping dramatically during the past few years. PROMs have found application in every area where ROMs have been used and created applications of their own. The lack of mask charges makes it feasible to use ROMs in low volume applications. Wide availability of PROM writers and PROM writing services has made it possible to get overnight service on PROM patterns. This significantly reduced design time for micro-coded systems. Quick turnarounds on PROM patterns combined with pin and speed compatibility with existing ROMs makes it possible to replace ROMs with PROMs. This avoids production line shutdowns when ROM errors are discovered. This aspect of PROMs solves two of the major problems encountered with ROMs. The other major problem associated with ROMs — that of high cost to repair errors in existing units is compounded by the fact that PROM prices above 1K bits are higher than equivalent ROMs. Thus users have either a high cost, quick fix for field systems or a delay to wait for ROM masks and parts.

programmable read only memory, PROM example — The Intel 1302 is a fully decoded 256 word by 8-bit metal mask ROM. It is ideal for large volume production runs of systems initially using the 1702A erasable and electrically programmable ROM. The 1302 is entirely static — no clocks are required. Inputs and outputs of the 1302 are DTL and TTL compatible. The output is three-state for OR-tie capability. A separate chip select input allows easy memory expansion. The 1302 is packaged in a 24 pin dual-in-line hermetically sealed ceramic package. It is fabricated with p-channel silicon gate technology. This low threshold allows the design and production of higher performance MOS circuits and provides a higher functional density on a monolithic chip than conventional MOS technologies.

programmable timer card — It can be programmed to generate crystal controlled, one-shot timing pulses. Time increment is variable from 1 μs to 40 days.

programmable timer/counter applications — Applications for these versatile devices include appliance timers, darkroom timers and process timers. They can also be used in programmable calculators. The internal clock can be disabled and the unit will count external pulses for programmable summing, loading or inventory applications. The internal clock can also be synchronized with the (m)th harmonic of an external sync and with the selectable counter, can provide a large number of nonharmonic frequencies from a single reference. Finally, they can be used as logic controlled switches in ramp type D-to-A and A-to-D converters.

programmable timing card — A programmable timing card is designed to provide a controlled interval signal to the calculator to allow synchronization of timing of measurements, output control signals, or the preparation of printouts.

programmable timing card, calculator — A typical programmable timing card is designed to provide a controlled interval signal to the calculator to allow synchronization or timing of measurements, output control signals, or the preparation of printouts. Various cards are available, which are designed for use in conjunction with time-of-day clocks. A typical card receives a 1 Hz input signal from the time base of the clock and provides 1, 2, 5, 10, and 30 seconds, 1, 2, 5, 10, and 30 minutes, and 1 hour timing signals. They often incorporate a crystal time base having an accuracy of one part to the 10^5 and provides additional timing intervals of 0.01, 0.02, 0.1, 0.2 and 0.5 second intervals. Intervals are generated by addressing the timing card. The calculator will then be disabled until a "go" command is triggered by expiration of the selected interval.

programmability and definable keys, user programming — Highly sophisticated calculations can be achieved by sequences of keystrokes. Since many calculators are truly programmable, including both branching and testing capabilities, it is quite possible to set a program to iterate all night. Typical programs can consist of up to 100 memory locations and more. Key functions can be defined to a particular use by loading an appropriately prerecorded magnetic card. Users first plan the function, key it into memory and then test it.

If it tests satisfactorily, they will record it on a magnetic card for future use.

program, macroassembly — A language processor that accepts words, statements and phrases to produce machine instructions. It is more than an assembly program because it has compiler powers. The macroassembler permits segmentation of a large program so that portions may be tested separately. It also provides extensive programming analysis to aid debugging.

program maintenance — A specific computer program most often consisting of various diagnostic routines, checking or test routines, and other types designed to complete the removal or reduction of malfunctions, mistakes, and errors and to thus repair or maintain programs and routines.

program maintenance procedures — Concerns various, quite specific diagnostic checking and test routines which are designed by manufacturers or software companies for purposes of removing, or at least reducing, machine malfunctions, human errors, or programmer mistakes. Other procedures help to maintain programs and routines in proper working order and in a ready status with current information, such as dates, etc.

program, master control — The master control program:
1. Controls all phases of a job set-up; directs program compiling and debugging, allocates memory, assigns input-output activity, schedules and interweaves multiple programs for simultaneous processing.
2. Directs all equipment functions and the flow of all data; provides for comprehensive automatic error detection and correction.
3. Directs the operator with printed instructions.
4. Adjusts system operation to changes in system environment.

program master-file update — Programs from the old master file are deleted, corrected, or left unchanged and new programs are added from the transaction tpae. Updating can include changing of program job assignments. A new program master file is produced.

program, mathematical — Considered by many to be the same as linear programming but not committed to be so defined because of sophisticated uses of research-type operations used as decision tools by modern management science enthusiasts.

programmed check — 1. A means of checking for the correctness of a calculator program and machine functioning, either by running a similarly programmed sample problem with a known answer (including mathematical or logical checks) or by building a checking system into the actual program being run. 2. A check of machine functions performed by the machine in response to an instruction included in a program.

programmed input-output — For greater flexibility, programmed I/O provides transfers between the external interface and some specific registers. It is especially effective in applications where data must be examined immediately upon input (such as message handling, keyboard response, etc.) or where data is the result of a computation which must be output immediately.

programmed input/output channel — Program control of information transfer between the central processor and an external device provides the fastest method of operating on data received from peripheral equipment. The programmed input/output channel allows input directly to the accumulator where the data can be acted on immediately, eliminating the need for a memory reference by either the channel or the program. Likewise, output data may be sent directly from the accumulator to an external device.

programmed learning — Refers to an instructional methodology based upon alternating expository material with questions coupled to branching logic for remedial purposes. May be implemented in book form ("Programmed Text") or in computers (Tutorial computer-assisted-instruction, CAI).

programmed magnetic card calculator — One type magnetic-card programmable hand-held calculator executes programs prerecorded on $2\frac{7}{8} \times \frac{5}{8}$-in. magnetic cards and can learn original programs written by the user. True algebraic entry allows problems to be entered exactly the way they are normally written. This is accomplished with a three-level hierachy and nine levels of parentheses. The unit can store up to 224 program steps and numbers on a single magnetic card. Twenty independent addressable memory registers permit addition, subtraction, multiplication and division of any displayed quantity with any memory register without affecting the keyboard calculation in progress. And trig and logs, powers and roots, factorials, reciprocals, three conversions and pi can be directly executed from the keyboard. Ten decision instructions and five user-set flags allow the user to program repetitive decision and branch-program segments automatically.

programmed selective dump — A library subroutine that is called to be used when other computer programs are running and a dump is desired. See selective dump.

programmed timer/counter — The current interest in microprocessors, ROM's, PROM's, etc., requires timers which can be programmed electronically. Generally there are two ways of using readily available TTL/MSI logic to accomplish this. Although one is available as a timer and the other as a counter, the choice of an external or internal clock would allow either circuit to perform either function.
One circuit typically uses a standard series TTL four bit magnitude comparator to compare the digitally programmed input with the various counter outputs. The Greater, Less Than and Equal waveforms provide several outputs to choose from. An external start pulse triggers the timer and the $A < B$ output is used as a reset.

program memory, calculator — One type program memory is designed to act like a carousel. The memory is implemented in a dynamic shift register. Program words, a pointer, and a beginning-of-memory marker circulate continuously in this register, a complete circulation taking a approximately $3\frac{1}{2}$ milliseconds. The pointer always points to the next program word and can move freely within the memory. Thus program steps can be inserted into the program or deleted from it at any point, without re-keying the other steps. Addressing is symbolic rather than absolute, and label-searching hardware is built into the program storage circuit.

program shortcuts, calculator — Indirect addressing of data registers shortens the number of program steps needed for successive operations. Saves time and memory. Conditional and uncon-

program tests, calculator — Some programs may contain three types of tests to allow conditional execution of all operations. These are x-y comparisons ($x \neq y$, $x \leq y$, $x = y$, $x > y$), four flag tests, e.g. there are two flags, each of which may be set or cleared and then tested for set or clear; and decrement and skip zero.

program memory control keys, calculator — Return. Ends a program segment which defines a subroutine and returns control to the point of the call. Reset. Resets the program counter to location 000 and resets all flags. Halt. Stops program execution and returns control to keyboard.

program memory, numeric code — One low-cost unit's program memory consists of 49 steps, numbered 01 through 49. A program remains stored for as long as one leaves the unit turned on, or until one erases or changes program. The program memory uses a simple numeric code, based on the position of each key on the keyboard. For example, "31" means "3 rows down, 1st key" —the "ENTER" key. To conserve steps, each prefixed function (e.g., "f""$\bar{x}$") takes only one program memory step.

programmer — 1. One who prepares programs for a machine. 2. A person who prepares instruction sequences without necessarily converting them into the detailed codes. 3. A person who prepares problem solving procedures and flow charts and who may also write and debug routines.

programmer, EEROM — A unit that provides a means of programming a single electrically erasable ROM (EEROM) or an EEROM module from paper tape or from an integral hex keyboard and display. EEROMs are electrically erasable and, therefore, need not be removed from the module or socket to be erased and reprogrammed. Included is a RAM buffer which permits editing of any EEROM. The equipment may also be used as a ROM emulator. Optional expansion capability sufficient to interface with modem and cassette devices is also available.

programmer, systems — This individual is primarily concerned with writing either operating systems (computer internal control programs) or languages for computers. System programmers produce these control programs and/or monitors that operate central processing and peripheral equipment. They write test programs that detect errors and malfunctions. They design utility programs to control formats of output and do sorting and merging of files. It is they who are primarily responsible for the efficiency of many computer systems.

program, micro — 1. Refers to a program of analytic instructions which the programmer intends to construct from the basic subcommands of a digital computer. 2. A sequence of pseudocommands which will be translated by hardware into machine subcommands. 3. A means of building various analytic instructions as needed from the subcommand structure of a computer. 4. A plan for obtaining maximum utilization of the abilities of a digital computer by efficient use of the subcommands of the machine.

programming — 1. Definition of a computer problem resulting in a flow diagram. 2. Preparing a list of instructions for the computer to use in the solution of a problem. 3. Selecting various circuit patterns by interconnecting or "jumping" the appropriate contacts on one side of a connector plug.

programming, advanced calculators — Following are some features which make programming simple: conditional and unconditional branching, editing, symbolic addressing and subroutine nesting on some units. The procedure follows: Press the GO TO key and the address of the program starting point. Press LEARN and enter the program. (Up to 512 steps on the standard machine.) Press PRINT DISPLAY to get results printed. PAPER FEED gives a blank line between results printed. Stop the program by pressing RESET and exit the learn mode by pressing LEARN.

programming and storage registers (calculator) — In one system programs are entered in either the LEARN mode by touching keys in the proper sequence, or in the RUN mode by loading instructions from the magnetic tape cassette. The Storage Registers characteristics are: All storage registers of the unit are accessible either by DIRECT ADDRESSING or by INDIRECT ADDRESSING. Each of the basic 16 hardwired registers can perform ADD, SUBTRACT, MULTIPLY, DIVIDE, EXCHANGE and TOTAL operation. In addition, the remaining software registers can perform these six operations when addressed INDIRECTLY. Subroutines characteristics are: 256 separate subroutine codes are available to define subroutines. Subroutines can be nested eight levels deep.

programming, applications — Applications programs range from sorting, payroll processing, and billing, to linear programming, matrix manipulation, and simulation. Whenever applications programs can be sufficiently generalized, the computing system provides and maintains them. Among the standard applications programs available are: (1) linear programming; (2) APT III; (3) PERT/COST; (4) mathematical subroutines. etc.

programming, background — Refers to a type of programming of no specific urgency as regards time but which may be preempted by a program of greater urgency and priority. Contrast with foreground programming.

programming, BASIC — Many units are programmed in BASIC, a formal, interactive language similar to FORTRAN. Depending on user needs, they may choose to do all their own programming. If they've already been working with BASIC, they can, with minor modifications, use existing programs. Since BASIC is a standard computer language, users will find there are many programs already written and available at nominal cost.

programming, calculator — The calculator is programmed either by use of the keyboard or by magnetic cards. The program mode allows entry of program instructions, via the keyboard, into program memory. Programming consists of pressing keys in the proper sequence. Users can store programs or large amounts of data on tapes, ROMs, handy magnetic cards, etc. for instant entry into their units.

programming, calculator (low cost) — Low cost calculator programming is as simple as pressing the keys one would manually press to solve various problem. But even though small calculator programming is simple to understand and use, it is very powerful, featuring:

- An obvious programming language.
- 49 usable steps of program memory.
- The ability to combine several keystrokes into each step.
- Decision-making capability for sophisticated routines.
- Several editing operations to facilitate corrections.

Together these features provide users with the tools necessary to tackle complex problems with significant confidence.

programming, conversational — A technique used in instructing the computer to perform its operations, whereby common vocabulary can be utilized by the user to describe his procedures most accurately. If a statement cannot be understood by the computer, it asks the user for a clarified instruction. This conversational procedure continues until the user has selected the series of statements in the proper sequence which will solve his problem. Conversational programming saves the user the inconvenience of having to study other programming languages extensively before he can solve his problem.

programming, convex — An operations research term for the development of nonlinear programming procedures in which the function to be optimized and the constraints are convex or concave functions of the independent variables, i.e., not related to programming in a computer sense.

programming, digit-entry routine (calculator) — A specific algorithm that demonstrates appreciable complexity is the digit-entry routine. Designing this seemingly trivial function so as to seem trivial to the user required considerable patience and careful thought. Usually, any entry will produce an undesirable result unless the designer specifically accounts for it. Values must be displayed as keyed in, yet they must be normalized to some internal form.

programming, dynamic (cost problem) — A method for optimizing a set of decisions that must be made sequentially. Characteristically, each decision must be made in the light of the information embodied in a small number of observables called state variables. The incurred cost for each period is a mathematical function of the current state and decision variables, while future states are functions of these variables. The aim of the decision policy is to minimize the total incurred cost, or equivalently the average cost per period. The mathematical treatment of such problems involves the theory of functional equations, and usually requires a calculator or computer for implementation.

programming EAROMS — Programs may be manually written into Electrically-Alterable ROMs (EAROMS). The EAROM to be programmed is inserted in the COPY socket, and the starting address is selected by setting up the eight ADDRESS toggle switches on the panel. After the LOAD button is depressed, data to be written is programmed on the front panel DATA switches. Using one specific programmer, with the COPY/1 step switch in the 1 STEP position, the programmed data will be written into the selected address when the START switch is depressed. The unit will then automatically advance to the next address, and the data programming step is repeated.

programming features, advanced calculators
— Typical are:
- Conditional branching
- Unconditional branching
- Single key register arithmetic
- Indirect addressing
- Complete editing: insert, delete, step forward, step back
- Symbolic addressing of subroutines
- Subroutine nesting
- Programmable flag

programming features, hand-held programmables — Typical are: 100-step program memory; built-in magnetic card reader/writer; five user definable keys; automatic counter; conditional branching based on any of four relational tests ($x = y$, $x \neq y$, $x \leq y$, $x > y$); direct branching; two flags; ability to review or execute program step-by-step; ability to add, delete or modify program steps; single-level subroutining.

programming features (hand-held runs) — Program writing capability • Single step execution or inspection of a program • Pause (to display intermediate result) • Program editing capability • relational tests: $x < y$, $x \geq y$, $x \neq y$, $x = y$, $x < 0$, $x \geq 0$, $x \neq 0$, $x = 0$ • Conditional branching • Direct branching, etc.

programming flexibility — Many systems offer a degree of programming flexibility that can be determined from an examination of the instruction set. Multiple addressing modes conserve main memory, simplify programming and increase speed through single-word memory-reference instructions. For programs stored in ROM or PROM, indexing or pointer addressing are often the only means to access data tables in program loops. Other useful capabilities include bit and byte manipulation, multiply and divide, double-precision arithmetic, normalize and I/O control instructions.

programming keys, calculator — The Programming Keys allow users to write and edit programs, plus they double as special function keys which can be defined to execute a program or a part of a program at the touch of a single key, as components of advanced programmable calculators.

programming logical simplicity — Most calculators have been designed for simplified programming in order to give four important user benefits: 1. Rapid learning — most people can program most of the functions with only one or two hours of familiarization with a calculator language. 2. Quick pickup — after weeks or months away from some specialized gear, controls have to be relearned from scratch. Not so with calculator languages because the heirarchical programming procedures flow logically downward from establishing overall system variables . . . and millions have used these systems. Yet, programming may be performed in any order. 3. Quick debug — order of operations is flexible, permitting changes in individual program variables or the system as a whole at any time. 4. Fail safety and diagnostic dumps — systems won't be damaged by invalid commands or data. As an option, any settings in memory can be printed out for fast checking with Program Printout on many advanced systems.

programming, mathematical — Techniques of finding an optimum value of a function of many variables when these variables are subject to restrictions in the form of equations or inequalities. The term is usually restricted to problems so complex that they require a digital computer for their solution. Special types of programming are linear programming, quadratic programming, and nonlinear programming.

programming, micro — The programmer technique of using a certain special set of instructions for an automatic computer that consists only of basic elemental operations, and combining them into higher-level instructions. He may then program using only the higher level instructions; e.g., if a computer has only basic instructions for adding, subtracting, and multiplying, the instruction for dividing would be defined by microprogramming.

programming modes, calculator — On some units programs are entered in either the LEARN mode by touching keys in the proper sequence or in the RUN mode by loading instructions from the magnetic tape cassette. For example, in a program, 256 subroutine codes are available to define subroutines. Subroutines can be nested five levels deep. A typical unit has full decision-making capability which enables the subsequent path of the program to be determined by the results of calculations. Iterations can thereby be set up which are performed until certain conditions are met. Debugging of programs is facilitated with a TRACE mode of operation. The STEP, INSERT, and DELETE available on some versions are also useful for program debugging.

programming technology, calculator — Programming technology continues to evolve. Keyboard programming was introduced first. Algebraic or formula programming came next. Here, availability of keys for percentages, parenthesis, and mathematical problems allows for programming mathematical instructions. A few more highly engineering programmables feature BASIC language commands. An English language, BASIC communicates with the user through typewriter or display in a conversational mode.

program modification — It may be necessary to modify a calculator program after it has been written. Incidental debugging or changes in technical specifications may call for altering values. Or in using a calculator for a problem with many unknowns, an engineer can interact directly with the machine and continually change the program. To modify a program for any purpose — debugging, revision or interaction — a user can take advantages of built-in features of some calculators such as: step-mode operation — any program can be stepped through — one instruction at a time — by the use of calculator switches, keys and combinations of both. Another procedure is the back-up function. Typical calculators have a back-up key to step the program back one step with each depression of the key. This may be the quickest way to the desired program point. Another technique is the program insert. An insert key is available on a number of calculators. This puts the machine into a mode that permits the insertion of new program steps. The inserted material becomes a standard part of the original program. A few other alternatives are: program delete when program steps can be deleted on many calculators by a key-operated delete, and program listing when a complete printout of the program can be called at any time. Virtually all programmable calculators have this last feature.

program modification, calculator — For users who want to modify or correct their programs, the special editing features of advanced units help to change program steps, update program addressing, recall any program step, and step through any program sequence with relative ease and convenience. Simple and direct keystrokes establish a rapid and natural editing technique that is represented in a few easy steps. First, users list their program. Program steps and instructions are labeled in languages users understand. In most cases, error messages tell users precisely what went wrong in concise phrases. Second, users can identify the areas of the program they would like to change. They can key in that particular address, and make the change. If this step requires that branching addresses in the program be changed, the calculator takes care of it automatically. The third step in the editing process is simply running the program to verify the changes.

program modification characteristics — It may be necessary to revise or modify a calculator program after it has been written. Initial debugging or changes in technical specifications may call for altering values. Or in using a calculator for a problem with many unknowns, an engineer can interact directly with the machine and continually change the program. To modify a program for any purpose — debugging, revision or interaction — a user can take advantage of built-in features like:

• Step-mode operation — Any program can be stepped through — one instruction at a time — by the use of calculator switches, keys and combinations of both.

• Back-up function — Typical calculators have a back-up key to step the program back one step with each depression of the key. This may be the quickest way to the desired program point.

• Program insert — An insert key is available on a number of calculators. This puts the machine into a mode that permits the insertion of new program steps. The inserted material becomes a standard part of the original program.

• Program delete — Program steps can be deleted on many calculators by a key-operated delete.

• Program listing — A complete printout of the program can be called for at any time. Virtually all programmable calculators have this feature.

program, monitor — A specific program developed to indicate the progress and other characteristics of work in various computer systems.

program, overlays — Programs or runs too large for memory can be divided into logical segments or overlays. (One program overlays another or several segments may be in memory at the same time.) Overlays are also used when various operations occur infrequently such as deduction for Community Chest, union dues, etc. The overlays are called in only when the functions they perform are required. An overlay subroutine is provided to call in these overlays. These subroutines function in a manner similar to the system supervisor.

program parameter — A parameter incorporated into a subroutine during computation. A program parameter frequently comprises a word stored relative to either the subroutine or the entry point and dealt with by the subroutine during each reference. It may be altered by the routine and/or may vary.

program, partial — A specific program incomplete by itself and generally a specification of a process to be performed on data. It may be used at more than one point in any particular program, or it might be made available for inclusion in other programs, i.e., a subroutine, and which is often called subprogram, incomplete program, etc.

program printout option — An inexpensive option, this feature permits the user to obtain a printout, or dump, of the overall system and channel-by-channel program, including all alarm setpoints. Initial programming can be verified more conveniently than with the display, and the hard copy of the program may be saved along with data. From this handy reference an old program may be keyed in at any time. Printout includes the following for some programs.

Present time
Interval between channels
Reference channel number
Identification of channels with alarms
Data identification number
All channel pair constants (gain, I-O, correction functions, units)

When the alarm option is present, actual alarm high and low setpoints may be printed, also.

program reference table (PRT) — Refers to an area in memory for the storage of operands, references to arrays, references to segments of a program, and references to files. Permits programs to be independent of the actual memory locations occupied by data and parts of the program.

program register — 1. Register in the control unit that stores the current instruction of the program and controls calculator operation during the execution of the program. 2. A temporary storage device or area which retains the instruction code of the instruction being executed.

program relocation — The execution of a program or location which is different than the location from which the program was originally assembled.

program restriction — A limitation in the performance of a tape transport falling within the specified normal range of operation of the unit and requiring modification of the command sequences to obtain normal accuracy in recording and reproduction of information.

program rewriting, calculator — Programming some types of calculators is completed by writing out the problem in ordinary math language, and then transferring that formula direct to the program memory. For example: $A + B \times C = D$ translates to $K0 + K1 \times K2 = K3$ (in the Tekronics model 21 desk-top).

To program this into memory, there are a few simple things users must tell the calculator. They must tell it where they want to start. So they press GO TO followed by the memory block they want to go to, f2 for example. Next, they tell it they want it to remember. They press LEARN. The calculator is in the learn mode and ready to accept the information they want it to remember. They press the keystrokes they want it to learn: $K\,0 + K1 \times K2 = K3$. If they want a printed copy of the result, they press PRINT DISPLAY.

To tell the calculator that they have finished, they program press END. They tell the machine to stop remembering by pressing LEARN. This takes the calculator out of the learn mode. To execute the program they press f2. Somewhere in the program they might want to direct the calculator to another point in memory. To unconditionally branch to that point, they press the key (f0 through f7) which identifies it. The calculator will go to that point and start execution there.

program run — Refers to the actual processing of or by a calculator program.

program running, calculator — On some systems, when a program is run, the calculator executes each line sequentially downward by means of a program "pointer." The calculator executes the instruction at which the program pointer is pointing. The pointer then increments one step downward* and points to a new instruction. After executing line 49, for example, the pointer automatically returns to line 00 and program execution stops. (some units)

program runs — A run is the same as a program except that a program refers to the writing or coding of the job, whereas the run refers to the acutal running of the program. Consequently, programs and runs are synonymous except to denote the time and action being performed.

program saving, calculator — To save the program, users pass a blank card through the calculator, switched to W/PRGM. They write the new definitions of keys A, ..., E on the magnetic card together with the program title. They then fill out the User Instruction Form to remind how to run the program at a later time. They can write their instructions on the Pocket Instruction Card and carry the magnetic program card with them. There are many possible ways to write programs which give users the required answers. Doubtless many can think of other ways. Some may wish to build variable entry capability into the program instead of storing them manually. Others may wish to have programs calculate differently, etc.

program saving, loading and chaining, terminal systems — Programs, or specified portions of programs, can be saved (recorded) on tape cassettes (or other selectable storage device) for future use. When needed, the programs are loaded into system memory to replace or append an existing program. Loading can be executed from the keyboard, or under program control, to facilitate chained program operation. The command SAVE P protects a program from being copied on another tape or listed. On some systems loaded protected programs cannot be accidentally modified. Any attempt to modify a loaded protected program results in an error message being displayed.

Saved programs can be identified by an alphanumeric name and then loaded by searching for the specified program name with the LOAD command, on some units.

program scheduler — A facility that allocates use of the central processing unit among programs in storage, based on priority.

program, segmented — Refers to one written in separate segments or parts. Only one, or some, of the segments may fit into memory at any one time, and the main portion of the program, remaining in memory, will call for other segments from backing storage when needed, each new segment being utilized to overlay the preceding segments.

program-sensitive error — An error arising from the unforeseen behavior of some circuits when a comparatively unusual combination of program steps occur during a run.

programs, packaged — These are various programs or routines which have been written by various individuals or organizations that are available from computer manufacturers of software companies.

program specification — The precise and ordered definitions of logic and scope of processing functions that are performed by particular programs or program segments.

program statements — The user's program is made up of program statements. When entered from a terminal, these statements are always retained in storage as part of the active program. If the user has a statement in his program that refers to an executable program statement within the program, he should assign a statement number to the statement referred to.

program status word (PSW) — A computer word containing information used in interrupt processing and for other purposes.

programs status word (PSW) storage — The PSW is stored at a fixed location, the address of which depends on the type of interruption. The system then automatically fetches a new PSW from a different fixed location, the address of which is also dependent on the type of interruption. Each class of interruption has two fixed locations in main storage — one to receive the old PSW when the interruption occurs, and the other to supply the new PSW that governs the servicing of that class of interruption. After the interruption has been serviced, a single instruction uses the stored PSW to reset the processing unit to the status it had before the interruption (some computers).

program step — Refers to a phase of one instruction of command in a sequence of instructions. Thus, a single operation.

program stop — A stop instruction built into the program that will automatically stop the machine under certain conditions, or upon reaching the end of the processing, or completing the solution of a problem.

program storage — Refers to a portion of the internal storage reserved for the storage of programs, routines, and subroutines. In many systems protection devices are used to prevent inadvertent alteration of the contents of the program storage.

program tape — Refers to a specific tape which contains the sequence of instructions required for solving a problem and which is read into a calculator prior to running a program.

program test — Refers to a system of checking before running any problem in which a sample problem of the same type with a known answer is run.

program tester — A program tester is available that enables a program or part of a program to be loaded and dynamically and selectively tested in accordance with simple and concise specifications expressed in terms of symbols and definitions used in the original source program. A variety of testing and monitoring facilities are provided by the program tester including file and storage display facilities designed to simplify the analysis of programming errors.

program, TRACE — This type program instructs the CPU to display the contents of any combination of registers or memory throughout the execution of the program being developed. Unlike many debug routines which instruct the computer to halt at certain selected breakpoints, trace programs allow users to command the computer to print the contents of any selection of registers in memory and then resume program execution, all automatically.

program transfer statements (branching) — Program steps are usually processed as they're entered. But often clusters of steps need to be handled out of sequential order. This skipping around is called branching or transfering. There are two types: conditional and unconditional.

programs, user — A group of specific programs, subprograms or subroutines that have been written by the user as contrasted to manufacturer supplied programs.

progression — 1. A discrete series in which the terms increase or decrease according to a uniform law. 2. A discrete series that has a first but no last element and the intermediate elements are related by a uniform law to the other elements.

PROM — 1. Programmable Read-Only Memory is generally any type which is not recorded during its fabrication but which requires a physical operation to program it. Some PROMs can be erased and reprogrammed through special physical processes. 2. A semiconductor diode array which is programmed by fusing or burning out diode junctions.

PROM and EROM — Information stored in the ROM can be altered electrically or through a combination of ultra-violet light erasing and electrical writing, but not at normal operational speeds and voltages.

PROM calculator chip advantages — A calculator chip, when controlled by a PROM and with the help of several mux/demux circuits, can handle arithmetic computation more efficiently than a microprocessor, and the calculator needs no software.

PROM contents — The PROM is a read-only memory — its contents cannot be altered accidentally by loss of power, by programming error, or by malfunctions in other system logic. However, the memory is endlessly erasable and reprogrammable. It is erased by exposure to a dosage of 6 Watt-sec/cm^2 of 254 nm ultra-violet light through a small quartz window on the circuit package. The required dosage is such that the memory may be exposed to direct sunlight or artificial lighting for prolonged periods. After the PROM is erased, the user's program is written into the memory using programming equipment that is available from suppliers. This accessory employs either punched tape or typed instructions to program and check PROMs. PROM memory cards and PROM chips are sold separately, so that users can set them up as desired. The user may program PROMs and place them on various memory cards as needed for his application.

PROM copying — "Clean" PROMS may be programmed from previously-written PROMS. Using one specific programmer the "written" PROM is placed in the MASTER socket and the "clean" PROM in the COPY socket. The RESET button is

PROM, plug-in option (calculator) — depressed; then the START button, the programmer automatically copies data, advances address, and repeats the operation until the maximum address is reached. The START light goes out the the programmer stops.

PROM, plug-in option (calculator) — Plug-in PROM's are available on many advanced units so users can have their favorite programs kept inviolate and ready for use at a moment's notice without tying up the flexible magnetic storage portion of the calculator.

PROM programmer — A typical PROM programmer peripheral can program Programmable Read Only Memories by plugging personality cards into the appropriate PROM programmer card socket. One PROM programmer includes provisions for two personality cards and corresponding zero-insertion force PROM programming sockets (one 16-pin and one 24-pin). When users plug the appropriate personality card into the PROM programmer mainframe, they can program and verify PROMs. Using a system console, they can select the input device containing the PROM image. The input data is then read into the RAM memory system and the PROM is automatically programmed and verified when the user issues a simple command from the console.

PROM programmer capabilities — Various separate PROM programmers in desk-top enclosures can program or copy one PROM at a time in less than 1 minute via a control program run on a development computer. The control program detects error or non-zero PROM at the start and verifies after each programming cycle. Several PROM programmers offer several features: PROM chips in both sockets (the original PROM and the duplicate) may be examined directly; the programmer can automatically check each byte of a PROM to be burned; if any byte has already been burned, no burning takes place and the computer prints the address and present contents of the first PROM byte in error; all errors can be accompanied by an explanatory error message.

PROM programmer card — A typical card allows blocks of memory to be automatically programmed into programmable read only memories. The PROMs often used are bipolar Schottky PROMs with 70 nanosecond access time. Each PROM can be organized as a 256×4 memory. Thus, two PROMs are required to achieve a 256×8 memory. Many cards include external test sockets for programming.

PROM programmer equipment — PROM programming equipment and software is available for use with various microcomputer systems. In addition, PROM programmers are available for use at the offices of various representatives and distributors throughout the United States.

PROM programmer keyboard — One type features hexadecimal keyboard entry of data and address and offers the following:
- Auto-copy between selectable min and max addresses.
- Program or List addresses sequentially or randomly.
- Verify master to copy while reading or writing.
- Stop on error detect.
- Display Data and Address.

PROM programming — To store microprograms, the PROM has to be programmed and machine language programming is the basic method of programming. The machine language user is expected to have sound understanding of the microcomputer organization and the significance of the instruction set.

PROM programming methods — Three available methods of programming PROMs are: simple keyboard entry devices, keyboard entry with some internal buffering and possibly external teletype interface, and highspeed paper tape input type PROM programming machines. One high-speed system developed is called a portable editor, because it is a buffered unit in a portable case with a 120 CPS paper tape reader on the front.

PROM programming steps — There are generally five necessary steps to a program PROMs so that the microcomputer can control various systems.
1. The designer lists the sequence of mechanical operations needed.
2. From this sequence of operations a program sheet is written.
3. The program sheet is used as a guide to enter the information on the keyboard of the compiler.
4. The information from the compiler is now entered into a blank PROM that is plugged into the program unit.
5. Now the programmed PROM is plugged into a memory card. On small systems as many as 8 PROMs can be plugged into one memory card. The microcomputer is turned on and the computer turns the solenoid valves on and off in the proper sequence. Feedback signals are sent to the computer from the limit switches to control the functioning of this machine.

prompting calculator — A desk-top programmable calculator that can prompt contains a 20-character alphanumeric LED display, a thermal printer and a magnetic-card reader. The card reader takes $2 \times 10\text{-}\frac{1}{2}$-in. cards. Up to 480 program steps can be stored in the machine. There are 40 data memories. These can be expanded to 1920 program steps and 100 data memories with an optional module. Prompting is a conversational function where the user asks questions using its display. Using algebraic notation and nine levels of parentheses, the calculator has 46 scientific functions and can be programmed using 78 labels, 10 pending operations, 10 flags, 10 branches, four levels of subroutines and two modes of indirect addressing. Editing of the program is simplified with insert, delete, step, backstep and go-to keys. The calculator can accommodate a variety of peripherals as well.

prompting display — Prompting displays on some calculators allow amateurs and novices to work complicated business and scientific problems very quickly. The prompting display assists the user to run alphanumeric programs and receive operating instructions on a LED display at successive stages in a problem. The calculator waits for a response before continuing with the problem.

PROM reading — In the READ or LIST mode, on some units, data in a PROM may be read out via the data displays. Users select the address to be read via the keyboard and observe the displays. Each operation of START button increments the address so that only the starting address needs to be entered to read a sequential portion of PROM. The address and data are displayed each time.

PROM/RAM board — A PROM/RAM board is a

basic memory component for many computer systems. With room for up to 2K bytes or more of programmable read only memory (PROM) and 1K bytes or more of random access memory (RAM), the board supports a system monitor program, and provides space for storage of users' programs. The memory address of each block of PROM and RAM is user-selectable. An optional WAIT circuit on the board allows the user to accommodate slow memory chips to a fast CPU on some systems.

PROM verifying — Using a specific programmer, data may be verified while writing a copy or reading a copy. With the VERIFY switch on, data in the master is compared to data in the copy. Any difference in the data will light the ERROR indicator, stop the programmer, and display the address in error (if a write operation) or the data in error (if a read operation).

PROM vs EAROM (Electrically Erasable ROM) — Both the EAROMs and the PROM are non-volatile, i.e. they retain their ones and zeros even when the power is turned off, and they both are field reprogrammable. The EAROM, however, has three key advantages:
(1) It costs less per bit.
(2) Data can be erased and changed in the memory using only electrical signals. An ultraviolet light source is not needed.
(3) EAROM data can be changed directly in the host system. It does not have to be physically removed to be programmed.

proof check total — One of a number of check totals which can be correlated in some manner for consistency or reconciliation in a range, set, or distinct calculation.

proof listing — Refers to a designed report prepared by a processor which shows the coding as originally written, any comments that may have been written, and the machine language instructions produced.

propagation loss — The transmission loss for radiated energy traversing a given path. Equal to the sum of the spreading loss (due to increase of the area of the wavefront) and the attenuation loss (due to absorption and scattering).

proportional, directly — A term used in contradistinction to the term inversely proportional. Two quantities are directly proportional when they both increase or decrease together, and in such a manner that their ratio shall be constant.

proportionally — Refers to a specific constant ratio of incremental cause and effect. Proportionality is a special case of linearity in which the straight line passes through the origin. Zero-error reference of a linear transducer is a selected straight-line function of the input from which output errors are measured. Zero-based linearity is transducer linearity defined.

proportion interval program — Confidence Interval on a Proportion. Given a sample of size N in which each element is random and independent, and D of the elements satisfy a criterion, this program determines a confidence interval on the estimate of the proportion P, the probability of an element satisfying the criterion, where $P = D/N$.

proprietary program — When the development of a program is controlled by an owner through the legal right of possession and title, it is a proprietary program. Commonly, the title remains with the owner and its use is allowed with the stipulation that no disclosure of the program can be made to any other party without prior agreement between the owner and user.

proposal — A statement by a contracting or consulting firm describing how it would carry out a project described by the sponsoring agency or customer, usually in the form of a Request for Proposal (RFP). Proposals normally include information describing the qualifications of the people who would work on the project, a project management plan, and a budget or price for the project.

proration problems — These are rapidly solved with most units. The percent key not only can be used simultaneously with the constant, but also with the automatic memory accumulation key to achieve instant solution of a percentage distribution computation.

protected locations — 1. Refers to locations reserved for special purposes, and in which data cannot be stored without undergoing a screening procedure to establish suitability for storage therein. 2. Block locations reserved for special purposes, such as in main storage or on disk files. Data may be read from, but nothing may be written into, these locations.

protection, file — A device or method which prevents accidental erasure of operative data on magnetic tape reels.

protection key — Refers to a specific indicator associated with a task which appears in the program status word whenever the task in in control, and which must match the storage keys of all storage blocks which it is to use.

protocol — A protocol is essentially a set of conventions between communicating processes on the format and content of messages to be exchanged. To make implementation and usage more convenient, in sophisticated networks higher level protocols may use lower level protocols in a layered fashion.

protocol, data base — Under the data base access protocol imposed by most information storage and retrieval applications, only host commands and specified data fields will pass between the host and the controller according to standard procedures.

protocol types — It is desired to establish communication, between processes in hosts possessing different speeds, word lengths, architecture, operating systems, access controls, etc. To deal with these factors requires the development of a higher level of protocol for a very large number of pairs of processes. The development of such protocols is still in a stage of relative infancy, although quite a few have been implemented.

prototype printed circuit board — Refers to a double-sided, plated through board for designing custom interfaces to some systems. It includes a 5 volt regulator and associated filters and is used for developing Custom Interfaces.

prototyping — Prototyping represents the initial design development stage wherein, at first, it is certain that errors will be discovered which require design changes. This region is characterized by the presence of only one or two prototype units on which relatively few operating hours can be achieved, a requirement for quick design changes due to high error discovery rates and low availability of engineering time, and relative insensitivity to cost due to the swamping effects of low volume, high engineering costs, and high costs for project delays. It is in this period that design aids, emulation techniques, and supportive design techniques are essential to quick design. Good tools help assure a well tested product making it possible to achieve smooth further product development.

psec — Abbreviation for picosecond or one-trillionth of a second.

pseudocode — 1. Refers to an instruction that is not meant to be followed directly by a computer. Instead, it initiates the linking of a subroutine into the main program. 2. Refers to various codes which express programs in source language; i.e., by referring to storage locations and machine operations by symbolic names and addresses which are independent of their hardware-determined names and addresses. (Contrasted with machine-language code.) 3. An arbitrary code, independent of the hardware of a computer and designed for convenience in programming, that must be translated into computer code if it is to direct the computer.

pull operation — An operation in which an operand (or operands) is taken from the top of a pushdown stack in memory and placed in a general register (or registers). The operand remains in the stack unaltered; only a pointer value indicating the current top-of-stack is changed.

pulse — 1. The variation of a quantity having a normally constant value. This variation is characterized by a rise and a decay of a finite duration. 2. An abrupt change in voltage, either positive or negative, which conveys information to a circuit. 3. A change in the intensity or level of some medium, usually over a relatively short period of time, e.g., a shift in electric potential of a point for a short period of time compared to the time period, i.e., if the voltage level of a point shifts from −10 to +20 volts with respect to ground for a period of 2 microseconds, one says that the point received a 30 volt 2 microsecond pulse.

pulse-amplitude modulation (PAM) — The coding of a continuous or analog signal onto a uniformly-spaced sequence of constant-width pulses by amplitude-modulating the intensity of each pulse, i.e., similar to AM radio broadcasts except that the carrier is a pulse and not a sine wave.

punched card — Also called IBM card. A piece of cardboard on which information has been coded in the form of holes to be read by a machine. The holes can be of many shapes, and may be punched either by machine or by hand.

punched card entry, calculator — A "systems" approach on some units permit data or "routines" that can be used again and again. They can be pre-punched on standard 80 column cards. With the Punched Card Programmer users can combine punched cards with their own calculations and get the results they want... without having to reenter the data through the keyboard. Or users can run entire programs from beginning to end... all automatically!

punched card format — The standard IBM-type card is $7\text{-}3/8$ inches by $3\text{-}1/4$ inches and consists of 80 vertical columns, numbered from left to right. The rows reading from top down are numbered 12, 11, 0, 1, through 9. Usually only the 0 through 9 rows are actually printed on the cards, it being understood that the 12 row is the first row on the top of the card and the 11 row is the second row just above the 0 row. For a numeric code, a single punch for any particular column in a given row indicates the numerical value, i.e., if row 4 in column 5 is punched, it indicates the number 4 in column 5. Alphabetic characters consist of combinations of 12 and some single digit, 11 and some single digit or 0 and some single digit 2 through 9.

punched card programmer, calculator — For repetitive calculations, users can use the Punched Card Programmer to read up to 60 steps of programming automatically by following instructional codes on punched cards.

punched card verifier — A machine which ensures that data punched into punched cards is the same as the data on the original documents from which it was punched. The process of manual punching from initial documents is repeated and the machine recognizes any difference in key depressions.

punched paper tape — Refers to paper tape on which information has been (or may be) stored or recorded in the form of partially-punched (chadless) holes. Each character of information is punched in binary representation in a column across the width of the tape. There are usually 5 to 8 punch positions (channels or levels) per column. The channels or levels, run in rows parallel to the length of the tape. The punch positions are normally spaced ten to the inch.

punch position — The row position of a punched hole in a specific column of a punched card. In an 80-column punch card the rows are designated 0 to 9, X or Y; in a 90-column card the rows are designated 0, 1, 3, 5, 7, and 9.

punch, summary — A card punch operating in conjunction with another machine, commonly a tabulator, to punch into cards data which have been summarized or calculated by the other machine.

punch, X — 1. A punch in the X or 11 row of an 80-column card. 2. A punch in position 11 of a column. The X punch is often used to control or select, or to indicate a negative number as if it were a minus sign. Also called an 11-punch. Synonymous with eleven (11) punch.

punctuation — A means of making the display or printout easier to read and more meaningful. This is accomplished in several ways. On many electronic calculators, groups of three digits are separated by a space (triple spacing), thus denoting where the comma would be. Other calculators actually display or print the comma. Some calculators even have manually positionable markers on the display to separate the digits. Decimal points are standard on most electronic calculators and are part of the punctuation.

purification, data — The reduction of the number of errors as much as possible prior to using data in an automatic data processing system.

pushdown list — A list of items in which the last item entered becomes the first item of the list and the relative position of each of the other items is pushed back one.

pushdown nesting — As data is transferred into storage, each word in turn enters the top register and is then "pushed down" the column from register to register to make room for the subsequent words as they are assigned. When a word is transferred out of the storage, again only from the top register, other data in the storage moves back up the column from register to register to fill the space left empty. This is accomplished either through programs or the equipment itself.

push-down queue — A last in, first out, (LIFO) method of queuing in which the last item attached to the queue is the first to be withdrawn.

pushdown stack — Arithmetic and register operations in a microprocessor have evolved such that there is capability for both decimal and binary arithmetic. Because of the pin limitation off-chip to memory, most architectures use a push-down stack of some sort. The stack helps the programmer minimize register transfers, facilitates counting and sorting, and limits needless transfers to and from main memory.

push-down stack (p-stack) register — A register developed to receive information from the Program Counter and store the address location of the instructions which have been pushed down during an interrupt. This stack can be used for subroutining. Its size determines the level of subroutine nesting in a 16 work register. When instructions are returned they are popped back on a last-in-first-out (LIFO) basis.

push operation — An operation in which an operand (or operands) from a general register (or registers) is stored into the new top location of a push-down stack in memory.

pushup list — A list of items in which each item is entered at the end of the list and the previous items maintain their same relative position in the list.

pushup storage — A technique in which the next item of data to be retrieved is the oldest, i.e., been in the queue the longest.

pyramid reporting — This form of reporting requires a constant review of data so that only pertinent information goes up the line of command until the final decision is made on the basis of a brief but meaningful summary.

Q

QTAM — Queued Teleprocessing Access Method.

quadrant — One of four quarters of the rectangular coordinate dimensioning system.

quadratic — Indicating or relating to a function of the form $f(x) = ax^2 + bx + c$, where $a \neq 0$.

quadratic equation — A pure quadratic equation is sometimes called an incomplete quadratic equation because the 1st power of the unknown quantity is missing.

quadratic programming — A program of an objective quadratic function stated in maxims that are subject to linear constraints. This is one of the few convex programming problems, aside from linear programming, which have solution algorithms that terminate in a finite number of steps.

quadratic programming O. R. — In operations research, a particular case of nonlinear programming in which the function to be maximized or minimized is a quadratic function and the constraints are linear functions.

quality assurance — A planned, systematic pattern of actions necessary to provide suitable confidence that an item will perform satisfactorily in actual operation.

quality control calculator application — A pharmaceuticals manufacturer of proprietary and ethical ophthalmic preparations develops products that range from contact lens cleaning solutions for both conventional and the new "soft" lenses to antibiotic ointments. In the manufacture of any pharmaceutical product, quality control is one of the most important functions of the organization. Automation of quality control procedures have a high priority and thus "AutoAnalyzer" I and II systems were teamed with interface systems and programmable calculators to provide a completely-automated active ingredient assay system for their products.

quanta — The intervals of a set or group used to quantize a function. Units of time in a queue.

quantitative analysis techniques — Generally, these are basic techniques that attempt to simulate a business problem with a normative type of model, and try to use actual or simulated data to see if the model does what it is supposed to do. Types of models include: qualitative, problem-solving, stochastic, optimal value, games, etc.

quantity — A positive or negative real number in the mathematical sense. The term quantity is preferred to the term number in referring to numeric data. The term number is used in the sense of natural number and reserved for the number of digits, the number of operations. etc.

quantity, abstract — A quantity which does not involve the idea of matter, but simply that of a mental conception; it is expressed by a letter, symbol, or figures. Thus, the number three represents an abstract idea, that is, one which has no connection with material things, while three feet presents to the mind an idea of a physical unit of measure called a foot. All numbers are abstract when the unit is abstract.

quantization — 1. The process whereby the range of values of a wave is divided into a finite number of subranges, each represented by an assigned (Quantized) value. 2. The subdivision of a continuous range into a finite number of distinct elements, and a process similar to analog-to-digital conversion: the approximation of a real (or infinite-precision) value by a number of prespecified resolution. For example, the conversion of a 1- to 100-volt signal to a 12-bit number.

quantization error — A specific guage or measure of the uncertainty, particularly that of the irretrievable information loss, which occurs as a result of the quantization of a function in an interval where it is continuous.

quantum — Refers to a unit of processing time in a time-sharing system that may be allocated for operating a program during its turn in the computer. More quanta may be allocated to higher priority programs than to lower priority programs.

quantum clock — Refers to the timing of an interval or processing time as allocated for operating each program as set in priorities used in computing systems with developed time-sharing procedures.

quantum electronics — That concerned with amplification or generation of microwave power in solid crystals, governed by quantum mechanical laws.

quartz — A mother crystal of quartz, as found in

quartz crystal

nature. It has a hexagonal cross section that is pointed at one end, and a fractured base where it was broken off the rock formation in which it grew.

quartz crystal — 1. Also called a crystal. A thin slab cut from quartz and ground to the thickness at which it will vibrate at the desired frequency when supplied with energy. It is used to accurately control the frequency of an oscillator. 2. A piezoelectric crystal which regulates an oscillator frequency.

queries, time sharing — Many organizations have problems requiring retrieval from data or document libraries. Remote terminals are being used to browse through the data file searching for material fulfilling the requirements.

query — A specific request for data, instructions, characteristics of states of switches, position in a queue, etc., while the equipment is computing or processing.

query station — A specific unit of equipment which introduces requests or queries for data, states of processing, information, etc., while the equipment is computing or processing or communicating.

queue — Refers to waiting lines resulting from temporary delays in providing service.

queue, automatic — Concerned with a specific series of interconnected registers which are designed to implement either a LIFO (Last-In-First-Out) queue or a FIFO (First-In-First-Out) queue without program manipulation. For a FIFO queue, new entries to the queue are placed in the last position and automatically jump forward to the last unoccupied position, while removal of the front entry results in all entries automatically moving forward one position. Also called push-down storage and push-up storage.

queue control block — Refers to a special control block which is designed to be used in the regulation of the sequential use of some programmer-defined facility by a set of competing tasks.

queued access method — Any access method that automatically synchronizes the transfer of data between the program using the access method and input/output devices, thereby eliminating delays for input/output operations. (The primary macro-instructions used are GET and PUT).

queue direct-access — A group of queues, or, more specifically, message-segment chains of queues, residing on a direct-access storage device. The group can include destination and process queues.

queue discipline — Refers to the methods selected to determine order of service in a queue i.e., LIFO (last in, first out) or FIFO (first in, first out), etc.

queued telecommunications access method QTAM — A method used to transfer data between main storage and remote terminals. Application programs use GET and PUT macro instructions to request the transfer of data, which is performed by a message control program. The message control program synchronizes the transfer, thus eliminating delays for input/output operations. Abbreviated QTAM.

queue, FIFO — First-in-first-out queue in which the most recent arrival is placed at the end of the waiting list and the item waiting the longest receives service first. Same as push-up list.

queue, LIFO — A last-in-first-out queue in which the most recent arrival is placed at the head or top of the list and receives service first. Same as push-down list.

queue, push-down — A first-out method of queuing in which the last item attached to the queue is the first to be withdrawn.

queue, sequential — The first-in first-out method of queuing items waiting for the processor.

queues, ready (time sharing) — Whenever a user task is in a "ready" status it can be executed or resumed. Generally a separate queue of ready tasks is maintained by the executive. Whenever a processor is available, the executive activates the task at the head of the ready queue changing its status to "running." Also called work-in-progress queue.

queue, work-in-process — Items that have had some processing and are queued by and for the computer to complete the needed processing.

queuing — Pertains to a study of the patterns involved and the time required for discrete units to move through channels, e.g., the elapsed time for auto traffic at a toll booth or employees in a cafeteria line. (in queuing theory)

queuing analysis — The study of the nature and time concerning the discrete units necessary to move through channels; e.g., the time and length of queue at service centers of grocery check-out stands, harbors, airports, etc. Queuing analysis is employed to determine lengths of lines and order, time, discipline of service.

queuing, message — The holding of messages in sequence until the destination terminal can be reached.

queuing theory — Refers to a form of probability theory useful in study delays or line-ups at servicing points.

queuing-theory problems — When a flow of goods (or customers) is bottlenecked at a particular servicing point, losses accumulate in the form of lost business, idle equipment, and unused labor. Minimizing such costs involved in waiting lines, or queues, is the object of queuing theory, an OR (operations research) technique for the most efficient handling of a line at a particular point of service.

quick-access memory — A part of memory that has relatively short access time, as compared to the main memory of the CPU.

quiet error — These are errors that occur in manual-mechanical systems and are corrected by competent people close to the system before they spread throughout the process or system.

"Quiz Kid" calculator — A special grade-school level calculator developed by National Semiconductor Corp. (Novus) in the shape of a toy figure designed for self-teaching of basic arithmetic.

quoted string — In assembler programming, a character string enclosed by apostrophes that is used in a macro instruction operand to represent a value that can include blanks. The enclosed apostrophes are part of the value represented. Contrast with character expression.

quotient — The quantity resulting from the division of a dividend by a divisor. If the dividend is not an even multiple of the divisor, the quantity left over is the remainder.

R

rack — Refers generally to the metal or other type of frame or chassis on which panels of electrical, electronic or other equipment may be mounted, such as power supply units, amplifiers, etc.

radical sign — The radical sign ($\sqrt{}$) is placed before a quantity; it shows that a root of the quantity is required. The quantity or number written at the opening of the radical sign is called the index. It shows what root is sought. When no quantity or index is written at the opening of the radical sign, the square root is indicated; if 3, as $\sqrt[3]{}$, the third root; if 4, as $\sqrt[4]{}$, the fourth root, etc.

radix — Also called the base. The total number of distinct marks or symbols used in a numbering system. For example, since the decimal numbering system uses ten symbols (0, 1, 2, 3, 4, 5, 6, 7, 8, 9), the radix is 10. In the binary numbering system the radix is 2, because there are only two marks or symbols (0, 1).

radix number, mixed — A number consisting of two or more characters, representing a sum, in which the quantity represented by each character is based on a different radix. Synonymous with mixed base number.

radix point — 1. Also called base point, and binary point, decimal point, etc., depending on the numbering system. The index which separates the integral and fractional digits of the numbering system in which the quantity is represented. 2. The dot that delineates the integer digits from the fractional digits of a number. Specifically the dot that delineates the digital position involving the zero exponent of the radix from the digital position involving the minus-one exponent of the radix. The radix point is often identified by the name of the system, e.g., binary point, octal point, or decimal point. In the writing of any number in any system, if no dot is included, the radix point is assumed to follow the rightmost digit. Synonymous with point.

RALU — Refers to Register and Arithmetic Logic Unit. The part of a chip set that performs actual operations. In older machines, this would be the accumulator or arithmetic unit.

RAM (Random Access Memory) — This type memory is random because it provides access to any storage location point in the memory immediately by means of vertical and horizontal coordinates. Information may be 'written' in or 'read' out in the same very fast procedure.

RAM control memory — Many systems use RAMs in their control memories. When RAM is used in the control memory, it is often referred to as WCS (Writeable Control Store). It can be argued that fewer bits of RAM are capable of replacing a gate than are bits of ROM. Because the control store can be altered it can be loaded with information which will tailor the device to the application or environment. Many machines can be emulated by reprogramming the control store. The important point is that bits of control store take on multiple uses.

RAM operation — During a cycle, a logical "one" on a write/I-O line is interpreted by the RAM as a write enable command and data on the bus will be written in to RAM. Generally a RAM is a nondestructive read-out device and, therefore, is always programmed to read; however, it must be instructed to "write". Because the data lines are functioning as a dual bidirection data bus during a specific cycle, it is possible for RAM to read 4 bits for example, from the designated address out to the data bus and, during the same cycle time, write 4 bits from the data bus into the designated RAM address location.

RAM/PROM comparison — RAM can be used in the same way as PROM and can be written without special equipment. However, its contents are altered when power is turned off. Many users employ RAM modules for storing intermediate computational and processing results and during initial testing of programs. PROM modules are used typically for final versions of their programs. However, many Series users need only RAM modules in their systems. For example, research laboratories in which the system is used in a variety of frequently changing applications and experiments find that a system with mostly RAM memory is often the most economical choice. With a Program Loader, programs are easily loaded into the RAM in a matter of minutes. The RAM memory has a low power standby mode that permits the use of a battery supply, if the user so desires. This allows line power to be interrupted for moderate periods without alteration of the memory contents.

RAM/ROM production control systems — Random Access Memory is used as a buffer storage to store data (such as intermediate variables used or printed during the process) which can be used in a volatile environment and stored in a volatile type memory. Random Access Memory may include I/O lines which may be used to drive input/output devices such as light-emitting-diode displays. Also available is read only type memory (ROM) which must be masked programmed and cannot be changed or altered, and Electrically Alterable Read/Only Memory (EAROM) which can be written and read back electrically and is electrically non-volatile. The basic CPU plus the memories are then tied to some type of electrical interconnection (bus) system which connects the CPU to the memories and interface modules, allowing the input/output of information and/or control of peripheral equipment.

RAM subroutine calls — Random access memories have modifiable contents. For subroutine calls and interrupts the 16-level or largerstacks are used to hold the return addresses and the contents of the state register. On some systems when the microprocessor is in the non-interrupt state one block of registers and condition code are accessible and interrupt requests may be honored. When the microprocessor is honoring, an interrupt is set equal to 1. During this time, another block of register and condition code is addressed by the processor. Further interrupt requests are kept pending until the current interrupt is serviced. Since the two or more blocks of registers and condition codes are transparent to the microinstructions, common subroutines can be used by the interrupt service routines and the background program.

RAM Terminology — For flexibility most RAM

chips are organized in one-bit or 4-bit words to let designers arrange memory access in the word lengths of their choice. For a given storage capacity, designers also have a choice of static or dynamic memory types. Static memories, essentially arrays of flip-flops, do not need the refreshing that dynamic memories require, but generally consume more power. To maintain charge storage in their memory cells, dynamic RAMs must be refreshed at least once every few milliseconds. In a typical dynamic RAM with 200 ns data access time, refresh pulses must be provided every 2 ms. Although refreshing interrupts access, its effects are minimal, and occur about once every 5000 to 10,000 read-write cycles. Implemented with n-channel MOS technology, most memory chips are compatible with 3-level TTL signal requirements, and most come packaged in dual-in-line configurations with 18 to 22 pins.

random access — 1. Access to a computer storage under conditions whereby there is no rule for predetermining the position from where the next item of information is to be obtained. 2. Describes the process of obtaining information from or placing information into a storage system where the time required for such access is independent of the location of the information most recently obtained or placed in storage. 3. Describing a device in which random access can be achieved without effective penalty in time.

random access memory — A memory whose information media are organized into discrete locations, sectors, etc., each uniquely identified by an address. Data may be obtained from such a memory by specifying the data address(es) to the memory, i.e., core, drum, disk, cards.

random access memory, CCD — Charge-coupled devices have previously been used in shift-register serial-readout memories. In random-access memories, the arrangement using CCDs in a RAM provides nondestructive readout, with access and cycle times as low as those of present MOS memories. This RAM is simple in concept, construction, and operation. It utilizes the basic functions of a CCD — storing minority carriers in a potential well, and transferring these minority carriers from the well beneath one electrode to the well beneath a neighboring electrode. The CCD unit cell is better than other one-transistor cells because it is smaller (each cell has only two surface electrodes); response time is faster (no high-resistance channels are in series with the sense circuit); construction is simple; and readout is nondestructive.

random access memory, (RAM) characteristics — The RAM consists of a number of random access memory devices that are used to store the macrocode (user program) under execution. As indicated, its size also varies with user requirements as limited by the addressing capability of the microprocessor. The I/O section consists of the necessary buffering and control interfaces for connecting the system to I/O devices such as teletypes, terminals, and other types of peripheral devices. The I/O area needs very careful consideration during the process of selecting a microprocessor system. I/O inherently creates a bottleneck in small systems for applications that require heavy I/O activity. The user must analyze his intended applications carefully to assure a satisfactory ratio between processing and I/O and to avoid having to build costly external I/O interfaces.

random access, removable — Refers to storage devices like magnetic disk packs that can be physically removed (not permanently attached).

random access storage (ROS) — Refers to a storage technique in which the time required to obtain information is independent of the location of the information most recently obtained. This strict definition must be qualified by the observation that one usually means relatively random. Thus, magnetic drums are relatively non-random access when compared to magnetic cores for main memory, but relatively random access when compared to magnetic tapes for file storage.

random errors — Those errors which can be predicted statistically.

randomize — The procedure for making numbers, data, or events random, i.e., without bias as to the selection of each number or event by assigning pseudorandom codes or characters to particular locations in storage.

random number — 1. A set of digits such that each successive digit is equally likely to be any of n digits to the base n of the number. 2. A number composed of digits selected from an orderless sequence of digits.

random-number sequence — An unpredictable array of numbers produced by chance, and satisfying one or more of the tests for randomness.

random number table — A table of random numbers is a set of numbers such that each of the digits from 0 to N has the same chance of appearing in any position in the table.

random sampling — A sample group is designed most often to be a true miniature of the universe from which it is drawn; therefore, a sample must be truly representative of the universe from which it is drawn, and the universe itself must be homogeneous. A representative sample is a random sample — that is, a sample which has been selected entirely upon the basis of a chance, in accordance with the theory of probability. If chance alone governs the selection of the various items which make up a sample, that sample will be a representative sample, provided it is large enough.

random walk — A statistical term which relates to the movement of a body to its next position, in such a way that it is likely to move in any direction with equal probability by a specified fixed distance from its current position, i.e., numbers can be involved which correspond to the distances. Mathematics techniques such as Monte Carlo are used in developing random walks.

random walk method — A variation of the Monte Carlo statistical system or method in which a problem is developed for a probabilistic solution. The "walk" factor consists of a series of traverses of long line segments. The directions; and oftentimes lengths, vary at random. The probability of reaching a defined point by a walk of this type at a given time is often given by a function that is for other interests.

range — 1. A characterization of a variable or function. All the values which a function may have. 2. The difference between the upper and lower values that can be measured by an instrument.

range key, data acquisition calculator — Key displays from memory the range previously selected for a channel pair. Users Key in new numeric code and enter.

range, error — 1. Refers to the range of all possible values of the error of a particular quantity.

2. The difference between the highest and the lowest of these values.

range, number — The span or dimension or range of values which a number (variable) can assume, and usually expressed within beginning and ending limits or using N, if such limits are unknown.

range of a DO statement — All program statements included in the repetitive execution of a DO loop operation. (FORTRAN)

rapid access loop — Refers to a section of storage, particularly in drum, tape or disk storage units, which has much faster access than the remainder of the storage. Synonymous with revolver.

raster — The bright white glow which covers the CRT when no signal is received.

rated capacity — General term for the output of an equipment, which can continue indefinitely, in conformity with a criterion, e.g., heating, distortion of signals or of waveform.

ratio — The value obtained by dividing one number by another. This value indicates their relationship to each other.

rational number — 1. These numbers are of two groups; integer and repeating decimal fractions. To be rational, the decimal portion of the number must always form a pattern that repeats endlessly. Thus, a rational number is one which may be expressed as a quotient of two numbers such as ½, – ⅔, etc. while an irrational number cannot be so exactly expressed. The representation of π (pi), most logs and roots are such numbers. 2. Any number which can be expressed as an indicated quotient of p and q, where p and q are both integers.

RCTL (Resistor-Capacitor-Transistor-Logic) —Same as

read — 1. The process of introducing data into a component or part of an automatic data-processing machine. 2. To copy, usually from one form of storage to another, particularly from external or secondary storage to internal storage. 3. To sense the meaning by arrangements of hardware. 4. To accept or copy information or data from input devices or a memory register, i.e., to read out; to position or deposit information into a storage or output medium, or a register, i.e., to read in. 5. To transcribe information from an input device to to internal or auxiliary storage.

read around number — The number of times a specific spot, digit, or location in electrostatic storage may be consulted before spillover will cause a loss of information stored in surrounding spots. The surrounding information must be restored before the loss occurs.

read-back check — Refers to a specific check or accuracy of transmission in which the information that was transmitted to an output device is returned to the information source and compared with the original information, to insure accuracy of output.

reader — Refers to device capable of sensing information stored in an off-line memory media (cards, paper tape, magnetic tape) and generating equivalent information in an on-line memory device (register, memory locations).

reader instruction, calculators — A two-step instruction is usually required to activate some card readers. The first step selects the appropriate I/O circuit, and the second sets the mode of operation. The card reader directs program control in the run mode, or loads data into memory in the learn mode. In either mode the last reader instruction must be a GO command to return control to the calculator. Then the internal program takes over, or if the original card-reader address was keyboard-generated, control is resumed by the keyboard.

reader, marked sense card (calculator) — Field statisticians, researchers and engineers can collect and record data on these cards at remote locations and then process the data on the calculator. Some units read standard size tab cards marked with soft lead pencil. They enter programs and numerical data quickly, conveniently, (and economically) into users calculators. Also, programs can be written off-line without a calculator.

reader operation, card (calculator) — As the card is inserted into the right side of the machine, it is forced against one edge of the card slot by one of two tiny leaf springs. This helps align the card with the magnetic head. Pushing the card farther into the machine causes it to activate the motor start switch when the card approaches the rubber drive roller. This turns the motor on. On some units. Each of the three switches in the card reader is activated in the same way. The card displaces a nylon ball resting on the bottom of the card slot. Movement of the ball forces a tiny finger of copper to move upward. The end point of this copper switch finger makes contact with a contact pad on the underside of the keyboard printed-circuit board. The contact point of the switch moves a distance several times the thickness of the card to provide a reliable contact. Each switch is adjusted to the proper contact position during assembly.

reader, paper tape (calculator) — Often it is more convenient to record data on punched paper tape. Most modern tape readers handle eight-level ASCII code. As in the case of the card reader, the tape reader can also often be plugged directly into the I/O bus of the calculator. But first the ASCII code must be converted to the calculator code, and the tape reader must supply its own sequential control circuitry and the means for subsequent return of control to the calculator.

Like the card reader, the tape reader requires a two-step command from either the calculator keyboard or a program stored in the calculator's memory. The first step selects the I/O circuit, and the second causes the tape reader to transfer the information on the tape to the calculator for a learn or run mode. The tape inter-record separator code is often translated into a GO command for the calculator. Control is returned either to the calculator keyboard or program, whichever initiated the tape-reader operation. The calculator's ability automatically to transfer control from calculator to tape and back, permits a user to design programs with iterative loop routines for data entry.

reader peripherals, calculators — Card readers and punched-paper-tape readers are among the more popular input peripherals. Either can supply program instructions or numerical data. Two types of card readers are commonly used — a mark-sense reader and a punched-card reader. For either marked or punched cards, many readers use a 40-column format with the information in an octal code. The 80-column tab card with a Hollerith code (or other codes) is also very popular. A card reader may either transfer data into the memory of the calculator or operate the calculator directly without intervention of the memory. Many calculators have a built-in I/O connector wired to tie a card reader directly to the calculator's bus.

read in — 1. Refers to the act of placing data in storage at a specified address. 2. To sense information contained in some source and transmit this information to an internal storage.

read only memory (ROM). — A medium scale integrated circuit storage device containing instructions preprogrammed at the manufacturer. The system can obtain program instructions from the ROM but cannot alter the data in the ROM except by ultra violet erasure, in most cases.

read only memory (ROM), blastable — Blastable read only memory (ROM) provides high-speed, non-destructive memory in applications where the contents of memory do not change. Some chips operate at a cycle time of 1.5 microseconds and, like RAM, are available in units of 1K, 2K, or 4K words on a single module.

read only memory (ROM) characteristics — The ROM is used to store the microprogram or a fixed program depending upon the microprogrammability of the CPU. The microprogram provides the translation from the higher-level user commands, such as ADD, SUBTR, etc., down to a series of detailed control codes recognizable by the microprocessor for execution. The size of the ROM varies according to user requirements within the maximum allowed capacity dictated by the addressing capability of the microprocessor.

read-only memory (ROM) programmer — A microprocessor ROM programmer is a versatile option for MicroProcessor Series (MPS) users, providing a capability for writing programs into chips used on a Programmable Read-Only Memory (PROM) module. Operating as an on-line peripheral device to a microcomputer system, the unit can be a fully self-contained subsystem that will load and verify user-generated MPS routines in individual PROM chips. Source data for loading PROMs is binary code, previously generated by an assembler or the debugging programs. The code can be in the form of paper tapes or a previously programmed PROM.

read-only memory, 32 k — The 32 k ROM opens up new areas of application, impacts hard-wired software for minicomputers and it isn't too big for calculators.

read only storage (ROS) — An inexpensive means of controlling the computer by sending pulses through preselected logic strips, which in turn set up paths for the instruction execution. The patterns of these logic strips are a microprogram which analyzes a particular instruction and determines what control paths are needed for its execution.

readout — 1. The manner in which a computer displays the processed information, e.g., digital visual display, punched tape, punched cards, automatic typewriter, etc. 2. To sense information contained in some internal storage and transmit this information to a storage external to the computer. 3. To copy data from specified addresses in storage into external storage device. 4. The act of removing and recording information from a computer or an auxiliary storage. 5. The information that is removed from computer storage and recorded in a form that the operator can interpret directly.

readout, calculator — Some units have a built-in, 16-character, 5 x 7 dot matrix, 190-line/min. thermal printer and a 32-character LED display that provides upper and lower case alphanumeric readout in a full ASCII character set. Some European and Greek character sets are ROM-addressable.

readout device — Refers to a device, consisting usually of physical equipment, the records the computer output either as a curve or as a set of printed numbers or letters.

readouts, gas discharge — Gas discharge (orange) and fluorescent (greenish blue) displays are important but less common choices for calculator readouts. Like LEDs, they too can be multiplexed, but they operate from voltages significantly higher than calculator batteries can provide directly. This necessitates a dc-to-dc converter to deliver upwards of 150 volts. There is also the potential for breakage since such readouts are largely glass. And the color options will probably become less important as LEDs boasting tints other than basic red are made available in production quantities.

readouts, liquid crystal display — Relatively new is the application of liquid crystal displays in calculators. This readout holds much promise due to extremely low current consumption, but suffers from visual contrast and reliability problems. Multiplexing liquid crystal displays also appears impractical or near-impossible, making multidigit displays a packaging nightmare. Should these roadblocks be overcome, some very interesting possibilities for "lifetime" calculators with sealed-in lithium batteries become practical.

readouts, pocket calculator LEDS — Readouts for portable and pocket-sized calculator products are available in four different varieties; light-emitting diodes (LEDs), gas discharge, fluorescent, and liquid crystal. By far, red LEDs are the most widely used, usually for practical rather than esthetic reasons, Hewlett-Packard, Litronix and Texas Instruments, among others all have LED production capability in-house, which helps solve the supply and delivery problems faced by many competitors. But LEDs offer many broad-based advantages, including 6- to 10-volt operation, making them directly compatible with batteries. LEDs may also be easily multiplexed, saving some power, but even more important, drastically cutting down the number of electrical connections needed to operate the display package. Such a time-shared system for exciting the numerals means each diode segment need not be externally accessible. Savings result in fewer LED drivers, lower packaging costs, and reduced calculator assembly time.

read punch — An input-output unit of a computing system which punches computed results into cards, reads input information into the system, and segregates output cards. The read-punch unit generally consists of a card feed, a read station, a punch station.

read-write — A small electromagnetic unit used for reading, recording, or erasing polarized spots that represent information on a magnetic tape, disk, or drum.

read-write memory (RWM) — Some systems are implemented with ROM (read only memory) program memory only. In addition, often the main PROM has all the control lines available for implementing RWM (read/write memory) program memory. In small systems ROM program memory is used for systems in fixed applications. RWM memory is used where it is desired to change the system application by the operator. RWM is a considerable step in small system complexity in hardware and programs.

ready condition — Refers to a specification or circumstance of a job or task signified when all of its requirements for execution other than control of the central processor have been satisfied.

ready status word — This status word indicates that the remote computing system is waiting for a statement entry from the terminal.

real constants — A real constant is written with a decimal point, using the decimal digits 0, 1, ..., 9. A preceding + or − sign is optional. An unsigned real constant is assumed to be positive. An integer exponent preceded by an E may follow a real constant. The exponent may have a preceding + or − sign. An unsigned exponent is assumed to be positive.

real numbers — Generally relates to set theory: i.e., an element of a set of all measurement devices, and the computer results are thereby obtained during the process of the event. For instance, the data that are recieved from measurements during a run, with real-time computation of dependent variables during the run, enables the computer to make changes in its output.

real time — 1. In solving a problem, a speed sufficient to give an answer within the actual time the problem must be solved. 2. Pertaining to the actual time during which a physical process transpires. 3. Pertaining to the performance of a computation during the actual time that the related physical process transpires in order that results of the computation can be used in guiding the physical process.

real-time clock — The circuitry which maintains time for use in program execution and event iniation.

real time executive, microcomputer — An example is a priority-oriented, multi-task software operating system designed to support real time processing on a 12-bit microcomputer. In dedicated applications the system provides comprehensive facilities for task scheduling, functional task support, input-output processing, and interactive operator communications. Tasks operating under the supervision of executives provide the mechanism of response to real time events. The occurrence of an event typically results in the scheduling of a response task. This scheduling is performed with respect to a dynamic priority structure which associates each task with a distinct priority level. Tasks scheduled for execution at a given priority level are executed before lower priority tasks are executed. A given task may be interrupted when in the process of execution and temporarily suspended, while a higher priority task is executed. The suspended task then remains in that state until all higher priority processing is complete. Support functions provided by executive enable tasks to perform input-output operations, suspend execution until certain types of conditions occur, schedule other tasks for execution, and terminate processing until rescheduled. A custom version of an executive is construction through an interactive system generation procedure. This procedure is basically one of specifying system configuration parameters and loading programs. Output from the system generation is a master object tape containing a configurated executive system.

real time input/output — Refers to information which a machine accepts as the data as it is generated by a sensor, processes or operates on the data, and furnishes the results so as to affect the operations of the data generator or some other device; i.e., the data received from an industrial process under the control of a computer or the data received from a missile under the guidance control of a computer.

real time interfaces — A host of standard interfaces can involve such tasks as controlling relays, solenoids, contact closures, limit switches, counters, and universal digital controllers are available. They are designed for high noise immunity and extremely easy hookup via screw terminal connectors. If the job concerns analog data, analog input subsystems are available.

real time option boards — Various option boards contain the major interfaces and options that most users need. Some of these include: real time clock, programmers console control, input/output interface, 12-bit parallel I/O and an asynchronous serial line unit. Extended option boards include: memory extension and timeshare control, power fail with auto restart and bootstrap leaders.

real time program — Refers to programs which operate concurrently with an external process which it is monitoring or controlling, while meeting the requirements of that process with respect to time.

real time software, microprocessor — It's the software that distinguishes various real time microprocessor systems. Software ties together the processor and peripheral capabilities of the systems. Specifically, the software is organized around two major operating systems: one for program development and one for on-line real time operation. These two systems must be totally compatible, with the programs developed capable of being directly loaded for execution. In larger configurations, they operate on-line as a background task system.

real-time terminal applications — Real-time terminal applications include the following:
1. manufacturing test,
2. factory operations,
3. traffic control,
4. air- and water-pollution monitoring,
5. pipeline, oil, and gas field operation,
6. water distribution, supply, and flood control,
7. medical monitoring,
8. railroad and truck distribution, weighing, and accounting,
9. process control,
10. other instrumentation and control systems.

real-time system — A real-time system may be thought of as a communications-oriented, data-processing system capable of performing batch-processing functions while concurrently processing inquiries, messages, and data transfer, and generating responses in a time interval directly related to the operational requirements of the system. Amplified by real-time.

reasonableness checks — Refers to various program tests made on information reaching a computer system, or being transmitted from it, to ensure that the data falls within a given range. It is one form of error control.

reasonableness tests tape — Tests provide a

recall key — means of detecting a gross error in calculation or, while posting to an account, a balance that exceeds a predetermined limit. Typical examples include payroll calculations and credit limit checks in accounts receivable. In some cases, both upper and lower limits are established; each result is then machine-compared against both units to make certain that it falls between the two.

recall key — Used to recall intermediate statistical quantities stored inside the units for example, sums of squares, sums of cross products, cell contents, etc. (some units)

recall memory key — Automatically recalls an amount from independent memory for use as a factor in any operation.

receive-only service — Service in which the data-communication channel is capable of receiving signals, but is not equipped to transmit signals.

reciprocal — The number 1 (unity) divided by a quantity — e.g., the reciprocal of 2 is ½; of 4, ¼, etc.

recharger A device used to recharge the NiCd batteries found in many smaller calculators.

record — Refers to a collection of fields; the information relating to one area of activity in a data processing activity. i.e., all information on one inventory item. Sometimes called item.

record blocking — Concerns the practice of grouping records into data blocks that can be read and/or written to magnetic tape in one operation. This enables the tape to be read more efficiently and reduces time required to read or write the file.

recorder applications, calculator — Many recorder applications require a simple keyboard input to record the decimal digits. Inventory logging systems or simple point-of-sale devices are typical of such applications. They must be portable and battery operated. In the scientific area, data must be frequently collected from meter and instrument readouts for computer processing.

record format — Refers to the design of the contents and organization of a record, ordinarily a portion of a program specification.

record gap — 1. The space between records on a tape, usually produced by tape acceleration or deceleration during the writing stage of processing. 2. A gap used to indicate the end of a record.

record group — Several records, which when placed together associate or identify with a single key which is located in one of the records. Grouping is efficient in time and space-saving on magnetic tapes.

record header — A specific record containing the description of information contained in a classification or group of records, which follow this initial document. Also known as header table.

recording density — Refers to the number of bits in a single linear track measured per unit of length of the recording medium.

recording, double-frequency, cassette (DFR) — This is often used on disc memories at high data rates. When used on a cassette, however, it requires a relatively high bandwidth for a given data rate. This method is insensitive to speed variation since each bit is self-clocked, but it is only moderately free from problems created by noise and amplitude changes. DFR is, therefore, not as reliable as other methods at data rates higher than 500 bits/second, making future expansion and improvement difficult.

recording head — A magentic head that transforms electrical variations into magnetic variations for storage on magnetic media.

recording methods, cassette data — Various methods have been used by computer enthusiasts and manufacturers to record data on audio cassette recorders. These fall into five categories: (1) simple tone burst, (2) pulse-width modulation (3) frequency shift key (FSK) as used in radio-teletypewriter or phone-line communications modems. (4) double-frequency pulse recording as used in most floppy disc systems, and (5) phase encoding as used in ANSI standard magnetic tape transports of all major computer manufacturers.
Most of these methods record data serially; that is, one bit after another. Serial recording requires a conversion from parallel to serial form (and vice versa) when used with a computer. Fortunately, most computers and terminals already have a standardized serial communications channel that transmits in a form called "non-return to zero" (NRZ).

record interface, audio cassette — Refers to a popular storage device that allows virtually unlimited memory storage for data or software. Operates by modulating audio frequencies in the record mode. Demodulates recorded data in playback mode. Connects to any medium quality cassette tape recorder.

record layout — A record must be organized or arranged in sequence as to occurrence of items and the size, distribution, etc., i.e., as the two-dimensional format of a printed page.

record program keys — (1) Read/Write. Reads a program from a card into program memory. (2) Inverse Read/Write. Writes (records) a program on the magnetic card from program memory.

records appraisal — The analysis of records for the purpose of establishing retention policy. It includes a review of the operational and legal value of records by records series.

records management — A specific program designed to provide economy and efficiency in the creation, organization, maintenance, use, and disposition of records. Thus, needless records will not be created or kept and only the valuable records will be preserved.

records, overflow — Refers to those which cannot be accommodated in assigned areas of a direct access file and which must be stored in another area where they can be retrieved by means of a reference stored in place of the records in their original assigned area.

recoverable error — Refers to an error condition that allows continued execution of a program.

rectangular coordinates — A set of three lines called axes, the intersect at a common point in space in a way that each line, or axis, is perpendicular to the plane containing the other two.

rectangular coordinates key — The key converts polar magnitude and angle in X- and Y-regiaters to rectangular x and y coordinates.

rectangular probability program — Given a and b of the probability density function $f(x) = \dfrac{1}{b-a}$ and c and d as the limit of x, this program calculates rectangular distribution based on a and b and probability $P(c < x < d)$.

recursion — 1. The continued repeating of the same operation or group of operations. 2. Any procedure A, which, while being executed, either calls itself or calls a procedure, B, which in turn calls procedure A.

recursive — Pertaining to a process that is inherently repetitive. The result of each repetition

recursive function

is usually dependent upon the result of the previous repetition.

recursive function — A mathematical function which is defined in terms of itself, i.e., an operation which takes advantage of the recursive definition of the function, resulting in either repetition of the calculations using the same function, or using the same function with a slight modification.

recursive process — In data processing, a method of computing values of functions in which each stage of processing contains all subsequent stages, i.e., the first stage is not completed until all other stages have been completed.

red tape — 1. Pertaining to administrative or overhead operations or functions that are necessary in order to maintain control of a situation; e.g., for a computer program, housekeeping involves the setting up of constants and variables to be used in a program. 2. A general term that reserves, restores, and clears the memory areas.

red-tape operation — 1. A computer operation that does not directly contribute to the solution; i.e., arithmetical, logical, and transfer operations used in modifying the address section of other instructions, in the counting cycles, and in the rearrangement data. 2. Those internal operations that are necessary to process the data, but do not contribute to any final solution.

redundancy — 1. The employment of several devices, each performing the same function, in order to improve the reliability of a particular function. 2. In the transmission of information, that fraction of the gross information content of a message which can be eliminated without loss of essential information.

redundancy check — Refers to an automatic or programmed check based on the systematic insertion in a message of bits or characters that are used for error-checking purposes; they are redundant, as they can be eliminated without the loss of essential information. Parity checking is a form of redundancy checking.

redundancy check, cyclic — Refers to a cyclic parity check character for longitudinal error control calculated from a devisor polynomial. A typical one is: $X^{16} + X^{15} + X^2 + 1$.

redundancy check, longitudinal — An error control device or system based on the arrangement of data in blocks according to some preset rule, the correctness of each character within the block being determined on the basis of the specific rule or set.

redundant character — Refers to a character specifically added to a group of characters to insure conformity with certain rules which can be used to detect computer malfunction.

redundant codes — Refers to a self-checking code which is a binary coded decimal value with an added check bit. Three redundant codes are the biquinary code, the two-out-of-five code and the quibinary code.

reenterable — Refers to a special attribute of a program that describes a routine which can be shared by several tasks concurrently ("reusable reentrant"), or which can "call" itself or a program which calls it. Special provisions are required: 1) to externalize all intermediate variables used (the "prototype control section" of the calling program), and 2) to avoid destruction of the return address by circular calling sequences.

ref chan (reference channel) data acquisition calculator — This key displays the number of the channel chosen as reference in a pre-designated block of channels. It may be used as a two-digit pointer that tells the CPU the location of channels within a binary block that have been hard wired for a specific function. Example 1: the reference channel may be used to supply a common denominator in ratio or comparative measurements. Example 2: For thermocouple measurements, channel 0 is chosen as reference channel in a block of 64 channels.

reference program table — That section of storage used as an index for operations, subroutines, and variables.

referencing, input/output — References to data on tape or disk are made symbolically. Instead of describing the address of a certain disk or tape, the programmer refers to such data with a functional name. This means the programmer need not keep in mind where data will be coming from.

register — 1. A digital-computer device capable of retaining information, often that contained in a small subset (e.g., one word) of the aggregate information. 2. A temporary storage device used for one or more words to facilitate arithmetical, logical or transferral operation. Examples are the accumulator, index, instruction and other registers. The accessibility to the CPU is basic to registers. The number of registers in a calculator is one of the prime criteria for judging its worth. 3. A memory device capable of containing one or more computer bits or words. A register has zero memory latency time and negligible memory access time.

register, accumulator — Refers to that part of the arithmetic unit in which the results of an operation remains, and into which numbers are brought to an from storage.

register, address — A register is a calculator space where an address is stored.

register addressing, memory — The direct register addressing instruction: 5 STO 10, means to store 5 directly in register 10, as indicated. Indirect addressing, on the other hand, increases the versatility of all memory registers and allows users to store the address of another memory register for future use.

register arithmetic, calculator — This means the calculator has several memories into which users can store constants or other numbers used more than once in a problem and they can call any one of these back at will so that they have to do very little writing down of numbers. Users can directly add to, subtract from, divide into, or multiply the contents of a memory register. This is handy in solving three simultaneous linear equations or doing similar problems. In addition, certain pocket calculators have a memory called an operational stack. With these, entries and intermediate answers are stored automatically and then re-entered into the calculation at the appropriate time. The vertical stack arrangement is an essential part of RPN-Reverse Polish notation.

register arrangement — To be considered in conjunction with the addressing modes, is the register arrangement. Some systems have: six general-purpose registers; a hardware stack pointer; a program counter. Registers not dedicated to any specific function can be used as determined by the instruction that is decoded: they can be used for operand storage. For example, contents of two registers can be added and stored in another register; they can contain the address of an operand or serve as pointers to the address of an operand;

they can be used for the autoincrement or autodecrement features; they can be used as index registers for convenient data and program access.

register, block — An address register of available blocks of storage that are chained together for use by the line control computer, for the allocation of incoming information.

register, buffer memory — 1. A register wherein a word is stored as it comes from memory (reading) or just prior to its entering memory (writing). See register. 2. The memory buffer serves as a buffer register for all information passing between the processor and the main memory, and serves as a buffer directly between main memory and peripheral equipment during databreak information transfers. The memory buffer is also used as a distributor shift register for the analog-to-digital converter.

register expansion, calculator — One calculating system consists of a calculator and various input and output devices to communicate with the calculator. A standard system consists of the calculator with Panaplex® display, the magnetic tape cassette drive and either the column printer or the fully alphanumeric Output Writer. One calculator series is available in three different memory configurations:

312 program steps   55 total registers
824 program steps 119 total registers
1848 program steps 247 total registers

In each configuration sixteen of the storage registers are dedicated to data only. The remaining registers are part of the program storage area, and are exchangeable with program steps in the storage area. If memory requirements expand, the smaller memories can be retrofitted to the larger capacities.

register, external — These registers, which can be referenced by the program, are located in control storage as specific addresses. These are the locations (registers) which the programmer references when he desires that some sort of computational function be carried out.

register, instruction — A temporary storage device which retains the instruction code of the instruction currently being executed. Also, known as instruction counter. The arrangement of information; an item of data which is discernible as the equivalent to a command to perform a certain operation; the sequence of operations for equivalent or programming sequences.

register, memory-address (MAR) — A special location in memory is selected for data storage or retrieval and is determined by the MAR. This register can directly address all words of the standard main memory or in any preselected field of extended main memory.

register, microcomputer — Three basic internal microcomputer registers are: an Accumulator from which all data manipulations will occur, an instruction register that will contain the instruction being executed, a program counter. The low-order 6 bits of the program counter typically will hold the address of the word in memory containing the next instruction to be executed.

register operation, hand-programmable calculator — Efficient evaluation of mathematical expressions is achieved on some units by using four temporary memory registers arranged in a stack in combination with reverse Polish (Lukaiewicz) notation. The operational stack consists of X, Y, Z, and T registers. Intermediate results stored in this stack can be automatically recalled when they are required for further processing by the calculator, eliminating the need for scratch notes or manual re-entry.

Numbers enter the stack from the bottom on a first-in, last-out basis. As a number is keyed in, it goes into the X register and is displayed; when SAVE is pressed, the number is repeated in the Y register, and any number in Y moves up to Z, any number in Z moves up to T, and T is lost. When an operation is performed on data in X and Y, the answer automatically appears on the display and the entire stack drops.

register, sequence control — A hardware register which is used by the calculator to remember the location of the next instruction to be processed in the normal sequence, but subject to branching, execute instructions, and interrupts.

register, shift — The computer register capable of shifting data as directed.

registers, programmable calculator — To use the number of registers as a measure of calculator capability, the engineer must first understand their purpose and the sizes they come in. In general, a register is a memory circuit that is big enough to store a 12-digit or longer floating-point number, its sign and a two-digit exponent with its sign. This is equivalent to four, 16-bit words. Therefore a common calculator with 100 registers has the equivalent of about 400, 16-bit words of memory. In some calculators all registers can be used interchangeably for either program or data storage. Other calculators have registers set aside for data only, while different registers hold program information only. When used for program storage, a register holds from eight to 16 steps in keyboard machines, and about eight characters of program in an algebraic machine. In judging calculator capability the number of registers alone is insufficient information. The size and allowed flexibility in using the registers must also be considered. To use total program steps as an effective measure of calculator capability, a user must know how much calculating is done with each step. In most keyboard machines, arithmetic operations use one or at most two steps. Storage and recall operations and indirect arithmetic operations call for from two to six steps. Conditional transfer operations require two to five steps. And special functions, like trig or square root, usually need only one step. A comparison of step-capacity numbers only, can be quite misleading. The types of problems that the user will be solving have a great effect on the meaning of this capacity number.

register storage, plotter commands — Various register commands for plotters provide permanent graphic solutions to problems solved by various Series Programmable Calculators. One type plotter plots the point specified by the X and Y coordinates stored in two of the calculator data registers when the plot command is given. The relationship between the variables is usually programmed in the calculator which controls the plotter. The calculator can also be used in the manual mode to transfer data coordinates directly to the plotter.

Whether users are engineers, scientists, or businessmen, a plot is often the quickest and most reliable method of translating "raw data" into "useful information". With the various types of plotters, data is plotted automatically, eliminating the tedium and inaccuracies of hand-plotting. Data reduction and precise graphical solutions to specific problems are accomplished in a minimal time. Once the plotter has given the initial graphic solution, users can modify the input data, plot again, and immediately see the results of changes made. Optimum solutions in areas of critical importance can be readily obtained with the pinpoint resolution of the plotter. The various Series Programmable Calculators and various calculator Plotters can provide graphical linear (including metric) plots, log-log, semi-log, polar plots, etc.

regression — This is the rate at which an output changes in relation to the changes in inputs; more specifically, it represents the slope of a line which graphs the comparable values of inputs (independent variables) and the output (dependent variables).

regression and design analysis programs — Some examples are:
- Simple Regression
- Multiple Regression
- Polynomial Regression
- Stepwise Regression
- One-way analysis of variance
- Factorial Design

regression, multiple — A special type of mathematical regression analysis.

regressions, statistics package — Concerns overlays individualized to polynomial regression and multiple linear regression problems. Almost totally interactive variable selection procedures permit plotting any variable against any other; calculating and plotting residuals; calculating Durbin-Watson statistics; and descriptive statistics that calculate variable means, standard variances, and correlation matrices.

rejection — Refers to a logical operation applied to two operands which will provide a result depending on the bit pattern of the operands; e.g., operating on the following 6-bit operands p = 110110, q = 011010, then r = 000001.

relation — Refers to assembler programming, the comparison of two expressions to see if the value of one is equal to, less than, or greater than the value of the other.

relational operator — In assembler programming, an operator that can be used in an arithmetic or character relation to indicate the comparison to be performed between the terms in the relation.

relational symbols —

Symbol	Sample Relation	Explanation
=	A = B	A is equal to B
<	A < B	A is less than B
< =	A <= B	A is less than or equal to B
>	A > B	A is greater than B
> =	A >= B	A is greater than or equal to B
< >	A < > B	A is not equal to B

relative address — 1. An address of a machine instruction that is referenced to an origin; e.g. R + 15 is a specific address relative to R, where R is the origin; the other R + . . . machine addresses do not need to be named. 2. A label used to identify a word in a routine or subroutine with respect to its relative position in that routine or subroutine. A relative address is translated into an absolute address by addition of some specific address for the subroutine within the main routine.

relative addressing, microprocessor — Relative addressing shortens the address part of the instruction by permitting references within some narrow range relative to a CPU register. In many systems that register is the program location counter. The address field of the instruction is added to the program location counter's value (in some cases with sign-extension) to arrive at a datum address. In larger computers, the base-displacement form of addressing is used; this relative form uses a special (base) register plus the displacement carried as an abbreviated address in the instruction to compute a storage address.

relative coding — Refers to coding in which all addresses refer to an arbitrarily selected position, or in which all addresses are represented symbolically (in a computable form).

relative data — In a program for a CRT display device, values that specify a new position for an electron beam in terms of the number of raster units in the x and y directions away from the current beam position. Contrast with absolute data.

relative frequency — Refers to a measure or calculation of the ratio of numbers of observations in a class (subset) to the total number of observations or elements constituting a population, i.e., universal subset.

relative line number — A number assigned by the user to a communications line at system generation.

relative magnitude — Refers to the magnitude relationship or comparison of one quantity to another, most often related to base magnitude and expressed as a difference from or a percentage of the base or reference.

relative order — In a program for a CRT display device, a display order that specifies that the data bytes following the order are raster unit displacements in the x and y directions from the current beam position. Contrast with absolute order.

relative origin — A symbolic origin that is assigned to a machine location by the loader.

relative redundancy (of a source) — The ratio of the redundancy of the source to the logarithm of the number of symbols available at the source.

relay — An electromechanical device in which contacts are opened and/or closed by variations in the conditions of one electric circuit and thereby affect the operation of other devices in the same or other electric circuits.

release — 1. For a computer program or system, refers to a given embodiment of operational characteristics differing significantly from predecessor or successor releases by virtue of modification for efficiency, expanded capability or to remove errors, i.e., release 22 of an operating system would be followed by release 24. (Related to "level," "version," and "modification.") 2. To let go or relinquish either by a program or manually, a storage reservation, protection or location.

reliability — The probability that a device will perform adequately for the length of time intended and under the operating environment encountered.

reliability, circuit — The percentage of time the circuit meets arbitrary standards set by the user.

reliability control — The scientific coordination and direction of technical reliability activities from a system viewpoint.

reliability, failure — The ability of an item to operate as specified for an indicated time period, often expressed as mean time between failures (MTBF) or mean time to failure (MTTF).

reliability test — Tests and analyses carried out in addition to other type tests and designed to evaluate the level of reliability in a product, etc. as well as the dependability, or stability, of this level relative to time and use under various environmental conditions.

relocatable expression — In assembler programming, an assembly-time expression whose value is affected by program relocation. A relocatable... expression can represent a relocatable address.

relocatable program — Refers to a program that is written so it may be located and executed from many areas in memory.

relocatable program loader — A program that assigns absolute origins to relocatable subroutines, object programs, and data; assigns absolute locations to each of the instructions or data, and modifies the reference to these instructions or data.

relocatable routine — Refers to a specific routine designed and stored such a way that it may be located anywhere in memory; all references to address in such routines are relative and generally must be resolved by linage-editing.

relocatable subroutine — A subroutine that can be located physically and independently in the memory–its object-time location is determined by the processor.

relocation — The modification of address constants to compensate for a change in origin of a module, program, or control section.

relocation, base address — Refers to the specific ability to augment memory references by the contents of a specific base register.

relocation dictionary (RLD) — The part of a program that contains information necessary to change addresses when it is relocated.

relocation, dynamic — The allocation of memory space in a multiprogrammed computer in order to most efficiently utilize the total memory capacity. This is accomplished automatically by the computer by its changing the area of storage occupied by given program or portion of a program. (Clarified by mapping, memory.)

remote access storage and retrieval — Refers to various remote-access storage-and-retrieval systems that involve applications such as reservation systems, insurance companies, credit checking, and similar real time operations. From the standpoint of numbers of systems in use today, remote batch probably dominates computer use of data communications.

remote batch — A method of entering jobs into the computer from a remote terminal.

remote batch, off-line — Refers to various off-line remote batches or procedures that can involve the preparation of punched cards or magnetic tapes from source documents, then the transmission of data to produce duplicate punched cards or magnetic tapes at the computer site. In an on-line system, data is fed directly into the host computer through some form of communications adapter. There are several limitations to the hard-wired communication adapters associated with most large processors, and the trend is to replace them with communications preprocessors, sometimes called "smart front ends."

remote-batch processing (Remote Job Entry)-RJE — Refers to computer programs or data being entered into a remote terminal for transmission to the central processor. Jobs can be "batched" before transmission. Results of the processing may be transmitted back to the originating point.

remote batch terminal, calculator — If large amounts of data must be transferred, then transmission error detection and recovery becomes essential. Also, to minimize communications costs, high data-transfer rates are desirable. These requirements are satisfied by a remote batch terminal configuration. Some advanced units can emulate an IBM 2780 remote batch terminal once a ROM programed for BSC protocol has been plugged in. This adds such functions as a CRC-16 checksum algorithm for error control, code conversion, insertion of synchronization and other control characters, and automatic responses for positive or negative acknowledgments. A BASIC program can incorporate the other functions characteristic of a 2780 terminal, including allocation of a 400-character buffer, record delimiters, and the option to suppress spaces.

remote calculator enhancements — With sufficient enhancement, an advanced calculator can be interfaced to instrumentation and to a graphic plotter. This means it can gather data directly from a process or experiment and present it in useful form at a remote or local site. This makes such a calculator particularly attractive as a terminal in scientific and statistical applications.

remote calculator operation example —
Mode 1. Remote calls are initiated by telephoning the calculator. The ringing circuit activates the unit which answers back a "Data terminal ready," signal. The system scans the data, sends a "Request to send", receives a "Clear to send" signal, transmits data, then terminates the call. The calculator remains dormant until the next call.
Mode 2. If operating on a leased transmission line, the calculator may initiate a scan and output data at any time without this normal handshaking process.
Mode 3. Users manually initiate a call on a dial-up line. Initiate a scan on the calculator to output the data over the line. The call must be manually terminated at the end of the data transmission.

remote communications, microprocessor — Remote communications systems disseminate information to destinations outside the system. These destinations can be interfaced to a larger host computer. The communications link and message frequency determine the resources that should be dedicated. The communications function can be carried out either with a dedicated processor in the system or combined with the concentration or processing activities. Remote I/O considerations are 1) Parallel or serial interface, 2) Single or multiple ports, 3) Synchronous or asynchronous, 4) Baud rate, 5) Communication link, 6) Information block size, 7) Simplex, half-duplex or duplex, 8) Dedicated or common bus. The remote I/O interface can be treated like any other I/O interface, in terms of activity-rate calculations.

remote console — Refers to various terminal

units in a remote computing system. Some of the distant consoles are available with each equipped with facilities to transmit and receive data to and from the central processor. Connection to the processor is normally made through a remote computing system exchange.

remote control — Any system of control performed from a distance. The control signal may be conveyed by intervening wires, sound (ultrasonics), light, or radio.

remote control central calculator — One calculator can remotely control another by loading programs in it and activating its peripherals. If a calculator is connected to a disk containing several programs, a user at another site can call up or access programs from the disk, on some systems. Communication between calculators is often combined with communication between calculator and computer.

remote control connector option — A special ROM can be used with the RS-232-C interface to allow remote control of a calculator scanning function. It can also be used with other output devices and greatly increases the flexibility of the instrument. Various functions are provided for the convenience of the user. One important advantage is that the calculator cannot be interrupted while being keyboard programmed. A remote scan request will be ignored unless the calculator is in the Auto Mode. (some systems)

remote data entry — Data collection and dissemination is simple for "dumb" or "smart" terminals. A central station such as a computer, mag-tape unit or master "intelligent" terminal can poll many terminals to pick up prepared data and return hard copy to printing terminals; most often these remote terminals operate unattended, at 1200-baud. They are used in many operations such as order entry, accounting and inventory services, branch-office reports, project accounting, general ledger preparation, and inquiry/response work.

remote debugging — Refers to using remote terminals in a mode suitable for testing of programs, most frequently found in systems designed for scientific or engineering computation.

remote inquiry — Refers to inquiry stations which when operated on-line permit humans to interrogate the computer files and receive immediate answers to inquiries. In industry they can be located at dozens of remote areas.

remote inquiry (real time) — On-line inquiry stations permit users to interrogate the computer files and receive immediate answers to their inquiries. In industry, the stations can be located at dozens of remote locations such as office, factory, warehouse, and remote branch locations. Such a system permits all levels of industrial management to obtain immediate answers to questions about inventories, work-in-process, sales and other facts.

remote job entry, RJE — RJE allows various systems to share the resources of a batch oriented computer at a speed of up to 4800 Baud. This enables such tasks as data transmission, report generation, file updating, and the compilation and running of computer programs in COBOL, FORTRAN, or RPG. The processor gives the user access to centrally located data files and access to the power necessary to process those files. Emulators compatible with HASP workstations and various terminals are available.

remote job entry (RJE) processing — Refers to processing of stacked jobs over communication lines via terminals typically equipped with line printers. Small computers also can operate as RJE stations if equipped with communications adapters.

remote keystrokes, calculator terminal — Use of the calculator's remote key allows the user a variety of commands. Specifics on some units are: .. erase screen .. accept X coordinate data .. accept Y coordinate data .. plot X-Y coordinates .. enable graphics .. disable graphics .. make hard copies (with optional hard copy unit) .. start alpha and print .. stop alpha and print .. continue alpha only .. Alpha can quickly be entered into the calculator from the terminal's typewriter keyboard. Conversely, the calculator's multi-faceted math keyboard makes a numeric conversation uncomplicated.

remote message, input/output (I/O) — This is an I/O control for obtaining messages from, and sending messages to, remote terminals. For remote message control, the I/O control handles the following functions: receipt of messages from remote terminals, sending of messages to remote terminals, automatic dial-up, and code conversion. The user supplies the system with line-control specifications and installation-oriented routines to analyze message headers. Messages received can be stored in processing queues or output-terminal queues. Macrostatements enable the installation program to obtain messages for processing and to send messages. A log of all message traffic may be stored in a secondary storage device.

remote real time terminal — Various types include: a hard-wired controller and buffer or microcomputer controlled I/O equipment, real time clock, sensor, instrument and control interfaces (i.e., discrete I/O lines), A/D converters, D/A converters, and analog multiplexers, and communications modems.

remote station — Usually input/output devices which are not at the immediate site of the computer and which permit additional input queries for data or information.

remote testing — Refers to a method designed for organizing the flow of work being processed. Programs and associated test data are independently submitted to computer operators to determine the speed of the flow of work through a computer per se or a computer system. Many tests also evaluate the discipline of the procedure and the debugging of programs, as well as diagnostic aids and the impact on memory units and storage facilities. The operator develops a detailed record of all actions taken during each test run.

re-order (to) — A procedure for placing items in a particular organizational or methodical manner or arrangement to thus facilitate the use of identifying keys which follow a prescribed pattern or set of rules, such as by alphabets, value, time sequence, etc.

repeatability — 1. Related to the close agreement among consecutive measurements of the output and measured signal values. 2. Related to the ability to achieve identical results from various runs of a computer program. 3. A quantitative measure of the agreement among repeated operations.

repeat addition and subtraction — Ability of the machine to repeat adding or subtracting a number by mere depression of the plus or minus key without re-entry.

repeat add key — On some units this adds the input number to the accumulator. The total contents of the accumulator are displayed while the individual entries are printed (aligned to the decimal switch) and truncated. "Repeat add" feature also refers to a key that will also execute a previously conditioned multiplication or division. It also executes the percent add-on sequence.

repeat counter — The repeat counter is used to control repeated operations, such as block transfer and repeated search commands. To execute a repeated instruction "k" times, the repeat counter must be loaded with "k" prior to the execution of the instruction. A repeated sequence may be suspended to process an interrupt, with circuitry providing for the completion of the repeated sequence after the interrupt has been processed.

repeat operations — Allows the addition and subtraction of a series of identical numbers by depressing the add or subtract function key repeatedly.

repertoire, instruction — 1. Refers to the set of instructions which a computing or data processing system is capable of performing. 2. The set of instructions which an automatic coding system assembles.

report generation — Refers to production of complete output reports from only a specification of the desired content and arrangement and from specifications regarding the input file.

report generator — 1. A special computer routine designed to prepare an object routine that, when later run on the computer, produces the desired report. 2. A problem oriented language capable of automatically generating the machine instructions required to transform an input file into a desired report. See generator. 3. A technique for producing complete data processing reports giving only a description of the desired content and format of the output reports, and certain information concerning the input file.

report program generator language (RPG) — A popular, problem-oriented language for commercial programming, especially in smaller installations. Like COBOL, RPG has powerful and relatively simple input/output file manipulation (including table look-up), but is relatively limited in algorithmic capabilities.

report program generator (RPG) — The report program generator provides a programming method for producing a wide variety of reports. These may range from a listing of a card deck or tape reel to a precisely arranged, calculated, and edited tabulation of data from several input sources.

representative calculating operation — A method of evaluating the speed of a calculator or computer. One method is to use one-tenth of the time required to perform nine complete additions and one complete multiplication. A complete addition or a complete multiplication time includes the time required to procure two operands from high-speed storage.

reprogrammable read only memory (ROM), bit erasable — An example: The Intel 2708/2704 are high speed 8192/4096-bit erasable and electrically programmable ROMs. The 2708/2704 are packaged in a 24 pin dual-in-line package with transparent lid. The transparent lid allows the user to expose the chip to ultraviolet light to erase the bit pattern. A new pattern can then be written into the device. A mask programmable ROM, the Intel 2308, is available for volume production runs of systems initially using the 2708/2704.

request for repetition, automatic (ARQ) — Refers to a system employing an error-detecting code and so arranged that a signal detected as being in error automatically initiates a request for retransmission.

request to send — One of the basic data set interchange leads defined in EIA Standard RS-232-B.

request to send circuit — The request-to-send circuit is used to condition the local modem for transmitting data and in half-duplex operation to control the direction of tansmission. The clear-to-send circuit indicates whether or not the modem is ready to transmit data. The interval between the request on and the response varies with the type of modem and is used to transmit preparatory signals to establish the communication path, including preparation of the distant modem to receive data.

rerun point — In a calculator program, one of a set of preselected points located in a calculator program such that if an error is detected between two such points, the problem may be rerun by returning to the last such point instead of returning to the start of the program.

rerun program — A particular routine which is designed to be used after a calculator failure, malfunction or program or operator error which reconstitutes the routine being executed from the most recent or closest rerun point.

rescue dump — A rescue dump (R dump) is the recording on magnetic tape of the entire memory, which includes the status of the system at the time the dump is made. R dumps are made so that in the event of power failure, etc., a run can be resumed from the last rescue point (R point) rather than rerunning the entire program.

rescue points — For many applications it is very desirable, indeed essential, to create rescue points (R points) from which it is known that the program can be resumed in a proper manner. If a processing mishap does occur after creating a rescue point, the operator can restart his run at any rescue point by use of the restart routine. For long runs, the liberal use of rescue points will mean that the run is, in essence, segmented. A mishap will affect only one segment and all the valid processing that preceded the establishing of the latest point is saved and need not be reprocessed.

research lab, programmable calculator uses — A research lab would conceivably consist of a programmable calculator with a large memory, matrix ROM, page printer, high-speed tape reader, and plotter. At this level, a Fourier Analysis or a two-way analysis of variance could prove invaluable.

reset — 1. To restore a storage device to a prescribed state. 2. To place a binary cell in the initial, or zero, state. (Also see Clear.) 3. To return a register or storage location to zero or to a specified initial condition.

reset flag keys, calculator — Reset Flag keys lower or clear specified flag. If Flag. Tests to see if specified flag is set. If it is, then transfer occurs to the location or label. If flag is reset, no transfer occurs. For example, 2nd if flg 3011 means if flag is set, transfer to program location 011. Or, 2nd if flg 3 A means if flag 3 is set, transfer to that segment of the program labeled A. Test Flag.

Tests to see if specified flag is set. If it is not, then transfer occurs to the location or label. If it is, no transfer. For example, INV 2nd if flg 3 A means transfer to A if flag 3 is reset. (some units)

reset key, error — Refers to a push button that when pushed acknowledges an error and resets the error detection mechanism indicated by the check light. This is required to restart a program after an error has been discovered in batch mode.

reset pulse — 1. A drive pulse which tends to reset a magnetic cell. 2. A pulse used to set a flip-flop or magnetic core to its original state.

reset switch — The reset switch, when toggled, generates a master reset condition. The processor is halted, all internal registers are set to zero, the interrupt facility is disabled, the input/output interface is initialized, and the program counter is set to a specific range. The reset switch also functions as an indicator test in that all indicators are illuminated when the reset switch is toggled.

resident — Pertaining to a program that is permanently located in storage. For example, the nucleus in main storage or a system library on direct access storage.

resident compiler — Although many microprocessors require a cross-compiler — one that runs only on a larger machine — resident compilers that use the microcomputer itself to produce their programs are technically feasible with the advanced state of microcomputer development and inexpensive peripherals. Such a compiler requires several passes to reduce a source program to machine language, using the developmental system itself, and eliminating the need for large-system support.

resident program — Refers to a program that is permanently located in storage. For example, the nucleus in main storage or a system library on direct access storage.

residual-error rate — The ratio of the number of bits, unit elements, characters and blocks incorrectly received but undetected or uncorrected by the error-control equipment, to the total number of bits, unit elements, characters, blocks that are sent.

resource — Any facility of the calculator or computing system or operating system required by a job or task and including main storage, input/output devices, the central processing unit, data sets, and control and processing programs.

resource allocation — A program which integrates the allocation of resources (men, machines, materials, money, and space) with scheduling, by time period, of project activities.

resource allocation linear programming — Linear programming (LP) is a mathematical technique in which the best allocation of limited resources may be determined by manipulation of a series of linear equations. Each factor in the problem is evaluated against all other factors in relation to the long-range goals, yielding optimum paths of action for management consideration.

resource protection — The system design of automatic procedures set to ensure that resources are accessed by well-defined operations within computations authorized to use the resources.

resource-sharing — The sharing of one central processor by several users and several peripheral devices. Principally used in connection with the sharing of time and memory.

restore — 1. Refers to return of a cycle index, a variable address, or other computer word to its initial value. See also reset. 2. Periodic regeneration of charge, especially in volatile, condenser-action storage systems.

retransmission ACK/NAK — When an error detecting scheme is used, some means must be provided for retransmission of the block in error. The receiver may signal the sender with an acknowledgment (ACK) of error-free receipt or a negative acknowledgment (NAK) of error detection. To allow for last messages, the sender usually retransmits upon receipt of a NAK or when a specified time has elapsed without receipt of an ACK. This is one form of automatic repeat request (ARQ).

return address display — One very useful feature of some advanced units is that the most recent return address can be displayed, stored in a data register, or become part of a mathematical expression. Even logic within the subroutine can be used to determine where to branch to next.

"return" key — In many calculators, the "Return" key enables the user to start at the beginning of his program again. If this key is used as part of a stored program, it stops execution of the program and returns control to the keyboard for manual operation.

revenue, marginal — The rate of change of income as a function of quantity of sales.

reverse/exchange key — Interchanges the factors in multiplication and division for increased number handling flexibility without reentry.

reverse Polish notation (RPN) — A type of logic in calculators which allows the user to enter every problem from left to right exactly as it is written. There is no need to worry about operational hierarchy as the logic system handles it all automatically. This type of logic is distinguishable because the electronic calculator has no equal key. It has an enter key instead. (see RPN definitions).

reversible process — Relates to a process whereby the flux within a magnetic materials returns to its original condition when the magnetic field is removed.

rewrite — Also called regeneration. In a storage device where the information is destroyed by being read, the restoring of information into the storage.

RF — Radio frequency; the frequency of a received carrier signal.

rheostat — Refers to an electric component in which resistance introduced into a circuit is readily variable by a knob or handle, or by mechanical means, such as an electric motor.

RI — Radio influence, radio interference, reliability index.

right shift — Refers to an operation in which digits of a word are displaced to the right. This has the effect of division in arithmetical shift.

robot — Refers to a specific device equipped with sensing instruments for detecting input signals or environmental conditions but with a reacting or guidance mechanism, which can perform sensing, calculations, etc., and with stored programs for resultant actions, i.e., a machine running itself.

robot capability — Properly programmed, the robot can solve problems in the two general areas of visual inspection and identify and attitude analysis. Available routines have the capability to extract the 2-dimensional outline of the image of an object, locate corners, find holes and separate multiple objects, identify an object on the basis of its distinguishing features, specify the grip points, acquisition and orientation of a workpiece. In one set of laboratory experiments the developmental system has identified each of four different foundry castings and determined their position.

robotics — Refers to a specific area of artificial intelligence, robots have been designed by industrial firms as well as research institutes to perform relatively simple tasks such as arranging blocks, assembling simple pumps, and mounting wheels on automobiles. The use of industrial robots is an important trend since robots can increase productivity and relieve workers from dehumanizing tasks on one hand, but could cause transitional unemployment on the other. The technology of systems and cybernetics is undergoing rapid growth and will have a profound effect on society. Such developments — by their very nature — give evidence of this impact and the corresponding need for some control.

robotics capabilities — Following is a list of currently available robot traits: (1) workspace command with six infinitely controllable articulations between the robot base and a hand extremity, (2) fast 'hands on' instinctive programming, (3) local and library memory of any size desired, (4) random program selection by external stimuli, (5) positioning repeatability to 0.3 mm (6) weight handling capability to 150 kilos, (7) intermixed point to point and path following control, (8) synchronization with moving targets, (9) compatible computer interface, (10) palletizing and depalletizing capability, (11) high reliability (at least 400 hours MTBF), and (12) all the foregoing under traditional economic justification constraints.

robot mini-control and voice-response — Robots are responsive to joystick- or voice-initiated commands, and one developmental system for programmable automation research can inspect the identity, position and orientation of parts on a moving conveyor. This commercially available industrial robot can then acquire each part and transport it to its destination. Capable of stopping whenever its appendage experiences a specified force or torque, the robot could soon be able to handle a wide range of real factory tasks in material handling and assembly operations. Additionally, it will respond to "training by showing" and will perform sophisticated part inspections. It was developed at the Stanford Research Institute, Menlo Park, Ca. The system contains hardware that includes a Unimate manipulator, TV cameras, a conveyor belt and several types of artificial appendages designed and built at the Institute. In addition, the system includes two linear diode array optical sensors, that provide voice control of the other devices; and a joystick control to aid in the training of the Unimate and the appendages.

roll-back snapshot system — A system that will restart the running program after a system failure. Snapshots of data and programs are stored at periodic intervals and the system rolls back to restart at the last recorded snapshot.

roll in — To restore in main storage, data which had been previously transferred from main storage to auxiliary storage.

roll-in/roll-out — Generally refers to a return (roll-in) to a main or internal storage unit of data and programs, which had previously been transferred (roll-out) from main or internal memory units in various external or auxiliary units.

roll out — To record the contents of main storage in auxiliary storage.

roll-over indexing — Allows depression of a key before releasing the previous key.

ROM (read only memory) — 1. A blank ROM can be considered to be a mosaic of undifferentiated cells. Many types of ROMs exist. A basic type of ROM is one programmed by a mask pattern as part of the final manufacturing stage. PROMs are 'programmable' ROMs. ROMs are relatively permanent although they can be erased with the aid of an ultraviolet irradiation instrument. Others can be electrically erased and are called EPROMs. 2. Information is stored permanently or semi-permanently and is read out, but not altered in operation.

ROM add-ons, calculator — Various calculator models allow the addition of up to 8 add-on ROMs. Five may be added as external plug-in ROMs and three as internal plug-ins on some models. There is usually no difference in the operation of a ROM installed externally versus internally. It is a simple matter of available space and design. Add-on ROMs provide additional capabilities by expanding the Command Set of some models. This allows the user to tailor his model with exactly the peripheral control and language features required.

ROM applications — Singer's new sewing machine uses ROMs to provide sequence control for complex stitch operations, and Spectra Physic's optical scanner uses ROMs to sequence a sophisticated laser controller and decode the converted optical data read from grocery labels. In addition, hundreds of other products have become feasible due to extremely low cost programmable logic provided by ROMs. ROMs have been applied so broadly that knowledge of their function is a standard tool in every logic designer's repertoire ROMs can be simulated using R/W RAMs and can be used to replace PROMs at any appropriate stage of development.

ROM bootstrap — Nearly every calculator uses at least one ROM program, the most common one being a ROM bootstrap loader. The bootstrap loader is a minimum program which, if everything in memory has been wiped out, will allow the programmer to recreate his main memory load. In one system the bootstraps executed in the RWM (Read Write Memory) of the calculator operate without destroying the user information currently residing there. For example during power turn-on, if the mass memory ROM block is present, the calculator allocates 300 words of RWM for mass memory operations. The 300 words are used for bootstrap execution and special mass memory buffers that facilitate the execution of the data transfer commands. The support software is comprised of a number of binary programs stored on a magnetic tape cassette that many mass memory users will receive These programs accomplish such functions as initial system turn-on, bootstrap verification, platter duplication, repack of mass memory files, and so on.

ROM, calculator-10-bit — One ROM consists of 10,240 bits of read-only memory, organized as 1024 words of 10 bits each. Four pages of microinstructions can be stored on one chip, and up to four chips can be addressed directly by the ACT circuit. (Arithmetic, Control and Timing)

ROM, calculator utilization — Using normal programming rules many units provide that all special functions can be stored on the cassette memory. Several advanced calculators provide user read/write memory that can be expanded from 4 to 8 kilobytes; add-on ROM allows expansion in 2-kilobyte increments up to a total of 16 kilobytes on one unit. Space is provided for up to eight ROM plug-ins. Five cigarette-pack-sized packages plug into a compartment at the side of the unit and three plug-in cards fit inside the machine. Available ROMs provide complete matrix arithmetic capability including the capability to find the determinants of an entire array with a single command; string variable capability enables the calculator to use alphanumeric data contained in strings in input and output operations, perform character-by-character comparisons of strings, and use numeric portions of strings as variables in arithmetic calculations; plotter control capability allows plotters to provide permanent graphic solutions to problems; and extended I/O allows users to command such devices as voltmeters, counters, teletypewriters, and card readers connected to the calculator. Some units are designed specifically for use with pagewidth printers that are capable of printing lines of 80 alphanumeric characters generated from a 5×7 dot matrix at rates to 250 lines/min. These printers often mount directly on top of the calculator and may be added at any time or may be replaced with a typewriter with no change in software.

ROM controlled communications calculators — In one system a powerful modem autodialer interface is being used along with three plug-in data communications ROM blocks. Also an Interface Control ROM must be installed for any data communications application. To convert the calculator to a remote batch terminal, Binary Synchronous ROM is also needed. For timesharing applications, the Interactive ROM is used along with the Interface Control ROM.

ROM-controlled plotters — Maximum plotting capability is obtained with the Plotter ROM which provides complete alphanumeric plotter output, axis generation, automatic function scaling, and special symbol point plotting on some units. This allows the user to produce finished plots that are titled, scaled, and labeled as he desires. Plotting on any size paper up to 10 inches (25 cm.) on the Y axis by 15 inches (38 cm.) on the X axis is easily accomplished by setting the pen to the lower left and upper right corners of the desired paper. The required scaling is performed automatically by the plotter to compensate for different paper sizes.

ROM custom program initialization — There are many applications for calculator users in which it is desirable to store the entire program permanently to protect against loss or accidental tampering. Dedicated systems and those with complex or lengthy programs are examples. The optional custom initialization ROM feature is a small component that is pre-programmed with a users specific system and channel-by-channel instructions. Various ROMs plug into a slot and pre-program a vast variety of functions.

ROM designed keyboards — For many disciplines users can literally design the keyboard of some models to execute the functions used most with the touch of a single key. Users can customize the three left-hand key banks by specifying individual keys, an entire bank, or a group of banks. Insert a plug-in block, overlay the associated templates, and they're ready to start solving problems. Users have a choice of modules. One, two, three different users can use any combination of three modules at the same time. Each gives special functions, plus more memory. Each block contains its own read-only memory (ROM).

ROM, extended I/O — The extended I/O ROM allows the user to command a wide variety of peripheral devices with the calculator. It expands the language of the calculator to include the I/O commands without sacrificing any of the special function keys or read/write memory. The two most important features in this ROM are the enter output statements and an automatic code inversion capability (H-P 9830-A Model 30).

ROM firmware, calculator example — To direct the various computational and control functions of some units, 3072 words of read-only memory (ROM) are used. Each ROM word contains ten bits and constitutes a calculator microinstruction. Microinstructions grouped together in blocks perform the various external functional tasks of the calculator. A task may require one block of words or several blocks woven together. For example, the CLx function requires only a few words, while the sin function uses the tan function, which uses the add function, and so on.

ROM functions — ROM is used to store the microprogram or a fixed program depending upon the microprogrammability of the CPU. The microprogram provides the translation from higher-level user commands, such as ADD, MPY, etc. down to a series of detailed codes recognizable by the microprocessor for execution. The size of the ROM varies according to user requirements within the maximum allowed capacity dictated by the addressing capability of the microprocessor.

ROM loader — A typical binary loader program is implemented in read only memory. It eliminates the manual bootstrap loading procedure. Typically consists of a 3" $\times$ 2.5" printed circuit card that plugs into sockets located inside the processor enclosure and comes complete with documentation.

ROM, matrix operation — The Matrix Operations ROM, on some units allows the user to add the matrix capability commonly found in BASIC to his Calculator. This specific ROM expands the language of the calculator to include all the matrix commands illustrated in the table without sacrificing any of the Special Function Keys or read/write memory.

ROM memory expandability — The memory of one type calculator is expandable in two separate ways. The user read/write memory is expandable from 3520 bytes (1760 words) to 7616 bytes (3808 words). Add-on read-only-memory (ROM) can be added in 2 K byte increments to a total of 16 K bytes. Users may choose the memory configuration that meets their needs. They can always add power with plug-in memory boards to solve future problems. In addition users can tailor the calculator systems with exactly the peripheral control and language features required for their application with simple plug-in ROM's.

ROM microprogramming — By microprogramming a ROM on the microprocessor chip, a logic designer can implement in one package, together with some ancillary memory, a function that often took 50 or more TTL packages. Designs can be changed by a simple software program — and reprogrammable ROMs can be used to change systems in the field. In effect, design engineers must soon become programmers to discard many tedious but formerly essential logic optimization techniques.

ROM on-line debug monitor — The On-Line Debug Monitor resident in ROMs located on the Control Console Module in some units enables users to inspect and modify microprocessor registers, memory and peripheral device registers; load and dump memory; search memory; initialize memory; and set up to eight program breakpoints.

ROM organization — The organization of the ROM bits determines the number of address (input) and output lines that will be available in a given ROM. Address input pins are the means by which a specific word in the memory is accessed or selected. If a particular ROM is organized with 32 words of eight bits per word, each word can be addressed with five input address lines ($2^5 = 32$). The address 00000 would be for word one, 00001 for word two, etc. The number of output pins for a small memory is determined by the number of bits used per word in the memory's organization. In one example, the ROM would have eight output pins.

ROM, plotter control — The plotter controller ROM provides the calculator with the additional commands that are necessary for the control of a plotter. It expands the language of the calculator to include many plotter commands without sacrificing any of the special function keys or read/write memory (H-P 9830-A, Model 30 and others).

ROM programmer, modes — A portable, semiautomatic ROM programmer can also be used to verify the data in both field and mask programmed ROMs which are pin-for-pin compatible with the various PROMs. The programmer has five modes of operation: insert (resets system and removes power from ROM socket); pre-check (verifies no programmed bits); verify (prevents programming while checking data); program (automatically programs ROM word); and remote (disables keyboard and connects control lines to remote control plug). Accessories to the programmer include a duplicator which gives the programmer the capability to duplicate automatically any ROM which is pin-for-pin compatible with PROMs. It automatically verifies that a ROM has been correctly duplicated.

ROM (Read Only Memory), calculator interface cable — Relates to a cassette for the various Calculators: The ROM enables Calculator to generate the necessary commands to write into and read from the Mass Memory. The Cassette contains the program necessary to initialize a new memory cartridge and perform a system check out.

ROMs, externally insertable — It is apparent from initial success that the convenience and extra capabilities of insertable ROMs will be extensively used in many programmable calculators. An example is the H-P 9830-A Calculator (Model 30). It allows addition of up to 8 blocks of add-on Read-Only Memory. Five may be added as external plug-in, 3 as internal plug-ins. Many more will quite likely be offered. Add-on ROMs provide additional capabilities to the calculators, permitting extension of the BASIC language with no change or lessening of the amount of read/write memory available to the user. Some of the capabilities of these specific ROMs are described elsewhere in this book.

ROM software development — ROM software development can be achieved efficiently by first using a flow chart. As part of the final design steps, a test panel, or control units, should be built to test the program after it has been loaded into ROMs. The steps generally are to determine parameters as follows: System-timing requirements; Code structures between the system and external circuitry; Code structures to and from the microprocessor; Sources of microprocessor data during all phases of its operation; Method of executive and other program control; Method of program interface and interaction; Memory structure and operation.

ROM special function programs calculator options — The versatile microprocessor within all advanced calculators provides sufficient untapped power to perform a broad range of mathematical functions and algorithms that normally might be performed in the computer. Special programming on a custom basis taps this capability, delivering the benefit of savings of thousands of dollars over off-line methods. And the functions may be performed on real time data and read out immediately in the most useful final form. There are so many possibilities that a list only scratches the surface. Users should discuss their special applications in full with manufacturers for recommendations.

ROM special system options — A variety of useful features is available which may make data collection, processing and outputting even better suited to user requirements. These features generally require the addition of only one or two special ROMs. Users should consult factory to assure compatibility if multiple options are required.

ROMs, plug-in — Optional plug-in ROMs (read only memory) on several units add up to 2,048 more program steps of single keystroke, hardwired functions. Low-cost special purpose ROMs are now available for statistics, advanced statistics, formula programming (algebraic), extended alpha listing and surveying. Custom ROMs are also available for specialized programs. Once a program has been reproduced on a custom ROM, it cannot be listed, looked at or printed. This feature gives the user complete privacy and assurance that unauthorized personnel cannot access a listing of available programs. Yet with proper instruction, programs can be run with single keystroke operation.

ROM statistics block — Often if a major portion of work is in statistics, users add the Statistics Function Keyblock to their calculator and they have powerful statistical computations, commanded by a single keystroke. Computations such as χ^2; t; linear, multi-linear, and parabolic regressions; random number generation; accumulation of sums, sums of products, and sums of squares for up to five variables; maximum/minimum search are all solved instantly. They merely enter the data, press the appropriate key, and the answer is displayed. In addition, erroneous data can be removed by the use of the exclusive CORRECT key. There is no programming or addressing required for these functions. A separate (ROM) memory block is dedicated to various statistics functions so they do not draw upon the main calculator programming memory — leaving it fully available for further problem solving needs.

ROM, string variable — The string variable ROM provides the calculator with the ability to accept and manipulate alphabetic as well as numerical information. It expands the language of the calculator to include string variables without sacrificing any of the special function keys or read/write memory. The new commands provided by the string ROM are of three main types — input, manipulation, and output.

ROM terminal systems — On some terminal units a 32K ROM (Read Only Memory) holds the operating system, including an 8K switchable bank that enables firmware expansion and flexible data communications modes via the data communications option. For even more memory, a user can address the 300K byte tape cartridge for data or programs. This adds up to an incredibly responsive computing power; at user command, at user desks.

ROM voice synthesizer example — A synthesizer in the voice-response unit turns compressed operating codes stored in 8K ROMs into human speech. The ROMs are coded with the aid of a minicomputer; each ROM stores coding for up to 8 sec of speech, or 10 to 20 separate vocabulary words. (some units)

ROM vs RAM — Writeable Control Store (WCS or RAM) leaves the design of the system open-ended. It is possible to add features or add emulation routines after the hardware design is frozen. Even though the WCS is more expensive than ROM implemented store, the flexibility provided the designer makes this trade off worthwhile. The basic reasons are that it becomes a simple problem to correct errors in the implementation of the device, and that a large library of control programs can be loaded on demand.

root — A number which produces a given number when taken as a factor an indicated number of times, i.e., 2 is the 4th root of 16.

root segment — Refers to the master of controlling segment of an overlay structure which always resides in main memory. Usually this is the first segment within the program, and it is always the first to be loaded at program initiation time.

RO (Receive Only) — A receive only printer.

round — To adjust the least significant digits retained in truncation to partially reflect the dropped portion; e.g., when rounded to the digits, the decimal number 2.7561 becomes 2.76.

round down (TRUNCATE, CUTOFF) — The ability to ignore and drop any digits beyond a certain decimal position.

round equals key — On some units this key will execute a previously conditioned operation and will print and display the answer aligned and rounded as required. In the case of addition or subtraction, the accumulator will be printed and displayed and cleared.

rounding — Often less important or less significant digits are dropped for development of increased accuracy by adding the more significant digits that are retained. The rounding rule of adding 5 in the left-most position to be dropped would then round 2.3456 to 2.346 for rounding to three decimals.

rounding error — The error that results when the less significant digits of a number are dropped and the most significant digits are then adjusted.

rounding switch — On some units this provides for selection of round-up, 5/4 round-off, and truncate for answers. Rounding will occur and the state of the rounding switch will be printed for all answers unless underflow or overflow occur.

round up — Similar to round off except that in examining the extra position, if that digit is a one or greater, it increases the previous digit by one.

routine — 1. A set of computer instructions arranged in a correct sequence and used to direct a computer in performing one or more desired operations. 2. A series of computer instructions which performs a specific, limited task.

routine, automatic — A routine that is executed independently of manual operations, but only if certain conditions occur within a program or record, or during some other process.

routine, auxiliary — A routine designed to assist in the operation of the computer and in debugging other routines.

routine channel, status (BSY) — BSY (busy) is called by drivers to determine the status of a channel. A driver cannot use a channel until the channel is free. When BSY is called, it retains control unit the channel is free. The status of each channel available to the system is contained in the channel status table (CST). This table contains one entry for each channel. Each time a driver is called, it waits for the necessary channel to be free. When an input/output operation is initiated, the driver sets the channel status at busy. Upon completion of the interrupt, the channel status is set at not busy.

routine, closed — Refers to a routine which is not inserted as a block of instructions within a main routine but is entered by basic linkage from the main routine.

routine, direct-insert — 1. A separately coded sequence of instructions that is inserted in another instruction.

routine, diagnostic — A routine used to locate a malfunction in a computer, or to aid in locating the mistakes in a computer program. Thus, in general any routine specifically designed to aid in debugging or troubleshooting. (Synonymous with malfunction routine, and related to debugging.)

routine, minimum-latency — Refers to programming in such a way that minimum waiting time is required to obtain information out of storage. (Contrasted with random-access programming.)

routine, sequence-checking — A routine that checks every instruction executed, printing certain data; e.g., to print-out the coded instruction with addresses, and the contents of each of several registers, or it may be designed to print-out only selected data, such as transfer instructions and the quantity actually transferred. The automonitor routine on some computers is an example of a sequence-checking routine.

routine, simulator — An interpretive routine designed so that programs written for one calculator can be run on a different calculator.

routine, tracing — A diagnostic routine used to provide a time history of one or more machine registers and controls during the execution of the object routine. A complete tracing routine would reveal the status of all registers and locations affected by each instruction each time the instruction is executed. Since such a trace is prohibitive in machine time, traces which provide information only following the execution of certain types of instructions are more frequently used. Furthermore, a tracing routine may be under control of the processor, or may be called in by means of a trapping feature. Related to trap.

routine, utility — A standard routine used to assist in the operation of the calculator, i.e., a conversion routine, a sorting routine, a printout routine, or a tracing routine. Synonymous with utility program.

RPN (Reverse Polish Notation) advantages — Compared to alternative logic systems, Hewlett-Packard and other adherents believe that only RPN — in combination with a 4-register operational memory stack — gives users these advantages.

1. Users can always enter their data the same way, i.e., from left to right — the same way they read an equation. Yet, there is no need for a parenthesis key; nor for a complicated "operational hierarchy."
2. Users can always proceed through their problem the same way. Once they've entered a number, they ask: "Can I perform an operation?" If yes, they do it. If no, they press ENTER↑ and key in the next number.
3. They always see all intermediate answers — as they are calculated — so that they can check the progress of their calculation as they go. As important, users can review all numbers stored in the calculator at any time by pressing a few keys. There is no "hidden" data.
4. Users don't have to think their problem all the way through beforehand unless the problem is so complex that it may require simultaneous storage of three or more intermediate answers.
5. Users can easily recover from errors since all operations are performed sequentially, immediately after pressing the appropriate key.
6. Users don't have to write down and re-enter intermediate answers, a real time-saver when working with numbers of eight or nine digits each.
7. Users can communicate with the calculator confidently, consistently because they can always proceed the same way.

RPN method — The RPN method does take some getting used to. But, once users learn it, they can use the RPN method to solve almost any mathematical expression — confidently, consistently. Proponents suggest these four easy-to-follow steps:
1. Starting at the left side of the problem, key in the first or next number.
2. Determine if any operations can be performed. If so, do all operations possible.
3. If not, press ENTER↑ to save the number for future use.
4. Repeat steps 1 through 3 until the calculation is completed.

RPN (reverse Polish notation) "computer logic" and 4 level stack — A user's problem is solved the way it is written, left to right sequence, eliminating restructuring, unnecessary keystrokes, and the handicap of having to write down intermediate solutions. And all information is at user disposal — they roll the stack (R↓) to any intermediate information desired and arrive at a solution fast, simply, and accurately. Many users address themselves to the controversy between algebraic entry and RPN. One question some ask is why proponents of algebraic entry always use an example of sum of products and never an example of product of sums — an example:

$$(2 + 3) \times (4 + 5) =$$

RPN	Algebraic
2	2
Enter	+
3	3
+	=
4	MS
Enter	5
5	+
+	4
×	=
TOTAL 9 Keystrokes	×
	MR
	=
	TOTAL 12 Keystrokes (some units add two more keystrokes)

RS-232-C interface calculator — Users can take advantage of more calculator programming and processing ability. Provides a two-way bit serial communication path for a host of RS-232-C devices. Also works with 20 mA current loop devices. One unit uses ASCII code so the calculator can converse with teleprinter terminals, CRT terminals, paper tape/punch readers and digital tape casettes. This interface is compatible with Decwriter LA30, GTE Typewriter Terminal model 5741, NCR typewriter terminal model 260-6 ASR, Teletype model ASR33, Texas Instruments models 733KSR and 733ASR, Tektronix Computer Display Terminals 4010, 4012, 4013, 4014, 4015, 4023.

RTE, real time executive — This software system provides multiprogramming, foreground-background system, with priority scheduling, interrupt handling, and program load-and-go capabilities.

run — 1. One routine or several routines automatically linked so that they form an operating unit, during which manual interruptions are not normally required to be made by the calculator operator. 2. One performance of a routine on a calculator involving loading, reading, processing and writing. 3. The execution of one or more programs that are linked to form one operating program.

run book — Refers to material needed to code document a calculator application, including problem statement, flow charts, coding, and operating instructions.

run calculate and learn modes — With some calculator systems, the run mode allows users to quickly solve complex problems with programs from prerecorded magnetic cards. The calculate mode lets them use hand-held units as powerful calculators to solve problems manually. And with the learn mode, users of these units teach the calculator unique calculating methods. In one specific line all modes can use nine levels of parentheses, 20 independent memory registers and 224 program locations. When users combine this capability with prerecorded programs, or programs they originate they have a valuable computational resource.

run indicator — The run indicator is illuminated whenever the processor is in the RUN mode.

run mode — Some units process lengthy, complex calculations automatically without it being necessary for users to know about computers or computer language for its programming power to work immediately. Users may simply select one of the many different prerecorded programs from a Basic Library or use one that he or she has written. The straightforward operation is to load the prerecorded magnetic card that lets the unit read the card's contents into program memory inserting the card above the user-defined keys. The user then enters known quantities directly into the program or into one or more of many addressable memory registers or both. Execution is completely automatic. A program runs until it encounters a halt. Users can repeat a program as often as needed, change values of their known quantities and solve for different unknowns. The stored program is unaffected.

run phase — An occasion on which the target program (after compiling) is run and often called the run phase, the target phase, or the object phase.

R/W memory-ROM calculators (BASIC) — A typical BASIC language advanced programmable Calculator has the power and memory of a minicomputer without the limitations and expense usually encountered. The units use a hardwired BASIC language compiler (the equivalent of 7,500 words) which allows the user to communicate with and program the read/write (R/W) memory without disturbing or diminishing the R/W memory itself. Also, the units employ plug-in, read-only memories (ROM's) which perform additional user (or peripheral) functions with the main R/W memory — again, without reducing memory size or disturbing the user.

The R/W user memory is always reserved and ready for programs and data. There is no loading of compilers or use of valuable memory for functions other than programs or data. A maximum of 8,000 16-bit words of user R/W memory is available in some units (in increments of 2,000 and 4,000 words). Additionally, a total of 8 plug-in ROM's provides up to 8,000 words of read-only memory over and above the R/W and compiler memories.

R/W RAM volatility — Despite all the positive aspects of semiconductor memory, it, like all other technologies, does have negative influences on system design. The first such influence one encounters is the volatility of the data in R/W semiconductor RAMs. While the problem can be overcome with a battery backup power subsystem, the cost, complexity and inconvenience of such a subsystem may prohibit its application to the problem. Making this battery backup system reliable and cost effective presents a sizable design challenge to the system designer.

S

sample — Relating to data processing, sampling is usually used in process control, weather forecasting, timesharing of equipment, on-line processing for missile guidance, etc. to obtain data on the status of various events and conditions, and also in the many mathematical, statistical, testing and automated laboratory programs.

sample analysis, statistics — One-sample analysis, refers to modular subroutines that include sort routine, histograms, censored and trimmed data t-tests, confidence intervals, and much more; many include plotting capability.

sample and hold — A circuit used to increase the interval during which a sampled signal is available, by maintaining an output equal to the input for a specified period.

sample and hold, data acquisition system — This expands the usefulness of the system by being able to measure a changing input voltage with little degradation in resolution or accuracy. Repetitive or transient waveforms can be digitized, and pulse height and step inputs can be measured.

sample, bias — Whenever a sample is selected by a method that in the long run would yield samples whose obtained measures differ systematically from the corresponding true measures, the sample drawn is the biased sample.

sample, controller — That particular controller which uses intermittently observed values of a signal such as the set point signal, the actuating error signal, or the signal representing the controlled variable to affect control action.

sample, intelligence — A sample of intelligence is a part of a signal used as evidence of the quality of the whole.

sample, statistical — A statistical sample usually relates to a small portion of the entire universe which is drawn in such a way that every value in the universe has a equal chance of being included. A sample must be representative of the universe, and the principle of the random sample is that representativeness will result from the operation of chance in the selection of the values.

sampling — 1. Obtaining the values of a function for regularly or irregularly spaced discrete values of the independent variable 2. In statistics, obtaining a sample from a population.

sampling, analog — The process by which the computer selects individual hybrid input signals from the process, converts them to the equivalent binary form, and stores the data in memory.

sampling, discrete — Discrete sampling is a sampling process in which the individual samples are sufficiently long in duration that the accuracy of information transmitted via the channel per unit time is not decreased by the sampling process.

sampling distribution — The sampling distribution is a theoretical frequency distribution of the sample means. It is called a theoretical distribution because, while it can be proved that it exists, only one value in it is known, having actually drawn only one sample. The other values are means of samples which might have been drawn. The sampling distribution can be described as the normal curve. The arithmetic mean of the sampling distribution is equal to the true mean of the universe, which is what one is trying to estimate. The standard error of the arithmetic mean is the standard deviation of the means of many distributions.

sampling, random — A sample is designed most often to be a true miniature of the universe from

sampling, scientific — which it is drawn; therefore, a sample must be truly representative of the universe from which it is drawn, and the universe itself must be homogeneous.

sampling, scientific — Scientific sampling concerns a designed selection (sample) which is a miniature of the entire universe, i.e., statistical population, so that from this sample and using established and proven mathematically precise statistical techniques one may infer characteristics and draw conclusions concerning the universe, i.e., the ultimate interest; the desired information of specific characteristics.

satellite communication — Principle of reflection or regeneration of telegraphic or telephonic signals from earth satellites, using highly directive antennae for transmission and reception, orientated by computer calculation of orbit.

satellite processor — A small processor used to support a large processor to increase its productivity. The smaller processor is used for card to tape conversion, off-line printing, and communication interface.

satisfy — An equation is said to be satisfied when the right- and left-hand members of the equation are equal after substitution of equivalent quantities for the unknown terms in the equation.

saturation testing — The testing of a program by pushing through a great many messages in an attempt to find errors that happen infrequently.

scalar — A device that produces an output equal to the input multiplied by a constant; such as a linear amplifier, a set of pulleys or speed gears. Related to scale factor.

scalar product — That of two vector quantities when the result is a scalar quantity, e.g., work = force × displacement. Known as the inner product and denoted algebraically by a dot between the vector (or by a round bracket enclosing them). Its magnitude is given by the product of their amplitudes, and the cosine of the angle between them, i.e., $A.B = AB \cos \Theta$.

scalar quantity — Any quantity which has magnitude only — e.g., time, temperature, quantity of electricity.

scale — 1. The theoretical basis of a numerical system. 2. A series of markings used for measurement or computation. 3. A defined set of values, in terms of which different quantities of the same nature can be measured. 4. In a computer, to change the units of a variable so that the problem is within its capacity. 5. To alter the units in which all variables are expressed, to bring all magnitudes within bounds dictated by need, register size, or other arbitrary limits. 6. A range of values frequently dictated by the computer word-length or routine at hand.

scale accuracy — This is expressed as a percent of scale length. Typical expression: The accuracy is plus/minus ½% of scale length.

scale factor — 1. A multiplier used by the programmer converting quantities occurring in a problem into a desired range. 2. A method of modifying the location of a decimal or binary point.

scale factors — 1. In analog computing, a proportionality factor which relates the magnitude of a variable to its representation within a computer. 2. In digital computing, the arbitrary factor which may be associated with numbers in a computer to adjust the position of the radix point so that the significant digits occupy specified columns. 3. The factor by which the number of scale divisions indicated or recorded by an instrument must be multiplied to compute the value of the measured. 4. A value used to convert a quantity from one notation to another.

scale span — The algebraic difference between the values of the actuating electrical quantity corresponding to the two ends of the scale of an instrument.

scaling — 1. The process of changing a quantity from one notation to another. 2. To place the actual decimal point of a quantity, by shifting if necessary, in the relationship to the machine decimal point, so that: (1) the quantity remains within the capacity of the machine, (2) various quantities are in the correct relationship to each other for arithmetic operations, (3) the results are computed with the actual decimal point of the quantity in the desired location.

scan — Collection of data from multiple sensors, usually through a multiplexer.

scan INTVL (interval), data acquisition calculator — Key displays the time interval setting between data scans in days, hours, minutes, and seconds. To change setting, key in numeric and enter.

scan keyboard data entry — On some systems a special ROM adds RAM memory locations for additional data which may be manually entered from the keyboard. Up to seven digits may be entered per channel location. Will be printed at the end of scan following an I/O code of 8. Users allow two open channels betweeen the scanned data and the keyboard entry data. Each group of 8 keyboard entry data channels deducts 8 channels from the maximum system size.

scanner — Refers to an instrument which automatically samples or interrogates the state of various processes, files, conditions, or physical state and initiates action in accordance with the information obtained.

scanner-calculator data acquisition system — On some systems the Digital Multimeter measures the input that has been switched in by the scanner. Therefore, the system functional capability, reading rate and specifications are essentially the same as those of the DVM. The scanner can also provide process control through contact closures on the relay actuator assembly. Scanner channel selection and multimeter programming are completely controlled by the advanced calculator. All data logging and analysis are also done by this powerful calculator.

scanning errors — Many scanning errors can be avoided by an error-scanning format that uses five rows of bar codes, and several columns of correction codes. This makes defacement or incorrect reading virtually impossible and the control codes also help regenerate partially obliterated data.

scan rate — A frequency at which data is compared or read to various predetermined sense of criteria, for the purpose of seeking certain data.

scatter format — A load module attribute that permits dynamic loading of control sections into nonadjoining areas of main storage.

scatter read — The ability of a computer to distribute data into several memory areas as it is being entered into the system from magnetic tape.

scatter-read/gather-write — Gather-write is the ability to place the information from several non-adjacent locations in main storage (for example, several logical records) into a single physical rec-

scheduler, master

ord such as a tape block. Scatter-read is the ability to place the information from a physical record into several nonadjacent locations in main memory.

scheduler, master — The scheduler permits the function of a control program what allows an operator to initiate special actions or to cause requested information to be delivered which can override the normal control functions of the system.

scheduler, program — The scheduler is called at regular intervals to decide which program in memory is to be run. A running program is temporarily terminated each time its alloted time has run out, or when it requires input/output operations with a device that is busy. A program may be terminated temporarily by user intervention to the scheduler, or it may suspend its own operation. Temporary termination does not remove the program from memory. A program may be dumped and permanently discontinued by calling the scheduler and allocator.

schematic — Refers to drawings that use conventional symbols which show the connection of components in a circuit.

schematic diagram, electrical — Refers to specific representation in graphics of an electrical circuit in which symbols are used for each circuit element, i.e., resistors, capacitors, inductors, transistors, diodes, transformers, switches etc., and wires are represented by lines. The schematic permits tracing of current paths for power and signals. Such diagrams most often are furnished by manufacturers of equipment for assistance in repairs or diagnosis.

Schottky — Refers to a bipolar technology that is faster than standard TTL but often uses more power. Today, low-power Schottky circuits are used in many computers and are becoming the standard for fast processors of various types.

Schottky bipolar microcomputer set — Various families of Schottky bipolar LSI circuits are microprogrammed in the sense that their control logic is organized around a separate read-only memory called the microprogram memory. Control signals for the various processing elements are generated by the microinstructions contained in the microprogram memory. In the implementation of a typical central processor, the microprogram interprets a higher level of instructions called macroinstructions, similar to those found in a small computer. For device controllers, the microprograms directly implement the required control functions.

scientific application — Various uses of the computer which are classified as nonbusiness and related to various scientific or research problem solving questions or programs. Such programs are relatively characterized by a low volume of input and distinctly lack volumes of processing and, again, a low volume of output.

scientific calculator, desk-top — A typical electronic programmable calculator is a MOS/LSI based desk-top unit that combines algebraic and hard-wired keyboard functions with powerful programming commands. High-speed printed output is often provided along with complete input/output peripheral capability which makes possible the use of a wide range of peripheral devices. Keyboard operation is often simple and straightforward, following algebraic rules of equation-solving, including two-level or higher nesting of arithmetic operations. Single keystroke generation of 27 or more mathematical functions is often provided. Optional user-definable keys allow users to build in a choice of several additional functions. Program and data storage memories are generally expandable at the user's option. A complete repertoire of computer-like programming instructions is provided: unconditional and conditional branching, jumping, looping, subroutines. Data may be stored and recalled under program control, and 6-level (or more) nesting of subroutines is possible. Simplified checking and debugging procedures speed up program verification. No special programming language is needed to write programs, on many such systems.

scientific calculators (low end) — Slide-rule calculators with trig and logarithmic functions, multiple memories, nesting capability plus a variety of conversions and constants are available today as low-end calculators. It is possible to build single integrated circuits that are "full-blown" scientific calculators with all the appropriate features, fast computational times and ten digit accuracy that are comparable in size and cost to the minimum function chips of a year or two ago.

scientific language — One designed for writing mathematical or scientific programs.

scientific notation — The number is entered or a result is displayed in terms of a power of 10. For example, the number 1234 is entered as $1.234 \times 10^{+3}$ and the number 0.001234 would appear as 1.234×10^{-3}.

scientific notation (E Format) (BASIC) — When a real number gets too big or too small to manage conveniently with standard notation, the BASIC interpreter converts the number to scientific notation. Numbers written in scientific notation have a fractional part called the mantissa and a power of ten part called the exponent. For example, the number $3.28E + 6$ is a number written in scientific notation; 3.28 is the mantissa and $E + 6$ is the exponent. The number $3.28E + 6$ is the same number as 3.28×10^6 which is the same number as 3280000.00.

scientific pocket calculators — A scientific calculator performs all arithmetic, log and trig calculations, including rectangular/polar conversions and common antilog evaluations. And it lets users do their trig functions in either radians or degrees. Users just flip a switch. They also generally offer full display formatting, so users can choose between fixed decimal and scientific notation.

scientific professional calculators — A professional scientific calculator should provide the standard log and trig functions, so users don't have to refer to tables or interpolate from those tables. These "full scientific" calculators also provide exponential, square root and reciprocal functions. For handling more advanced types of scientific, engineering, mathematical or statistical problems, an "advanced scientific" calculator is necessary with the built-in functions found in the full scientific machines, plus a variety of others, depending upon which model is selected. These may include: mean, standard deviation, linear regression (trend line), and U.S./metric conversions. Advanced models also offer more memory power, more sophisticated trig functions, such as rectangular coordinate/polar coordinate conversion, selectable modes (degrees, radians and, possibly grads), conversion between decimal angle and angle in degrees/minutes/seconds... and others. This added capability facilitates the handling of complex problems and can drastically reduce the time and effort necessary to solve them. For example, polar/rectangular coordinate conversions lets users add or subtract vector components in seconds, simply by pressing a few keys. The most proficient type of professional scientific pocket calculators is the programmable. When solving complex, repetitive or iterative problems, programming can be invaluable. Users enter a problem-solving sequence of keystrokes just once.... then, with just one keystroke initiate the entire sequence — as often as desired. Whatever scientific calculator is chosen, the more functions and features it has, the more capability it has to solve more types of problems — problems that are most complex — faster and easier, reducing work, and the chance for error.

scientific programmable calculator, hand-held — Low cost units permit a user to solve repetitive problems automatically. Users enter the keystrokes necessary to solve the problem only once. Thereafter, they enter the variables and press one key for an almost instant answer. These practical units require no software; no "computer" language, and no prior programming experience necessary. Various "advanced" programmables offer even more.

Their editing capability is such that users can add, change or skip steps at will. These units also offer branching and conditional test capability. Plus, typically 8 addressable memories; 72 programmed functions and operations. They operate with fixed decimal, scientific and engineering notation. The latter freezes scientific notation into multiples of $10^{\pm 3}$ for quick and easy conversions to milli-, micro-, nano-, whole numbers and fractions.

scientific sampling — Scientific sampling concerns a designed selection sample which is a miniature of the entire universe, i.e., statistical population, so that from this sample and using established and proven mathematically precise statistical techniques one may infer characteristics and draw conclusions concerning the universe, i.e., the ultimate interest; the desired information sought.

SC1 — Subcommittee 1; a subcommittee of ISO Technical Committee/97, responsible for the development of an international vocabulary for data processing.

scissoring — Removing vectors which attempt to move the graphic point off the graphic surface.

scrambled — The encoded or private form of a signal which is unintelligible except when decoded or descrambled.

scratch pad — A useful and informal term referring to or designating a unique internal storage area, supposedly reserved for intermediate results, various notations, or working area; quickly erasable storage.

scratchpad memory locations — The scratchpad memory contains individually addressable scratchpad storage locations each of which can store the address of a main-memory location. Scratchpad locations may be used for temporary storage or for indirect addressing of main memory. Only one character is necessary in an instruction address to reference a scratchpad location. This address is interpreted as a reference to the main-memory location whose address is stored in the referenced scratchpad location. Memory space is conserved by this method of addressing, since only one character is used in the address portion of the instruction. Operating time is also reduced, due to the extremely fast access time of the scratch pad memory (some systems).

SDA — Source data automation.

SDLC — Synchronous data link control; on IBM's series of compatible general-purpose terminals.

SDR — Statistical data recorder.

search — To examine a series of items for any that have a desired property or properties.

search, area — An area search relates to information retrieval by examining a collection of data or documents, but specifically those within a particular subset according to some criteria determination, i.e., belonging to some class, category, geographical area, location, etc.

search, binary — A search in which the series of items is divided into two parts, one of which is rejected, and the process repeated on the unrejected part until the item with the desired property is found. This process usually depends upon the presence of a known sequence in the series. Synonymous with dichotomizing search.

search cycle — The part of a search that is repeated for each item, which normally consists of locating the item and carrying out a comparison.

search, dichotomizing — A search in which the series of items is divided into two parts, one of which is rejected, and the process is repeated on the unrejected part until the item with the desired property is found. This process usually depends upon the presence of a known sequence in the series of items.

search, disjunctive — A search defined in terms of a logical sum, i.e., disjunctive form, in contrast to a conjunctive form or logical product.

search, key — Information that is to be compared with specific parts of data items, labels, or identifiers for identification when conducting a search.

search, records — Extended investigation of requested information resulting from a request for extraction of data or the need to check additional locations for a given record.

secondary constants — Those for a transmission line, which are derived from the primary constants. They are the characteristic impedance (impedance level) as of an infinite line, and the propagation constant (attenuation and phase delay constant).

secondary memory — A particular storage which is usually of large capacity, but also with longer access time, and which most often permits the transferring of blocks of data between it and the main storage.

secondary storage — Storage facilities forming not an integral part of the computer but indirectly linked to and controlled by calculator or the computer, e.g., magnetic drum, magnetic tapes, etc.

second function, calculator — The Second Function on most systems provides a second use for nearly every key, increasing the power of the calculator without increasing its size.

second level addressing — In addressing, a computer instruction which indicates a location where the address of the referenced operand is to be found. In some computers, the machine address indicated can itself be indirect. Such multiple levels of addressing are terminated either by prior control or by a termination symbol.

second source products — The procedure of designing a microprocessor that is oversold the market when production needs it, is not considered to be good form in electrical engineering. Products that are second-sourced (produced by another manufacturer) or otherwise entrenched are likely to be relied upon. Second sources for many products appear because of the complexity of LSI. Second sources are being developed with the cooperation of the prime source. The second source generally is no longer simply "steaming" open a competitor's package to see how to duplicate it.

section debugging, microprogram — One of the best ways to check out a microprogram is to debug it in sections. This can be done by first setting up system conditions which will force a section of code to be executed and secondly inserting Halt instructions at critical test points in the microcode. Suppose the designer sets up system conditions which should force the system to JUMP to EXIT 4. For some reason, the system never gets there but wanders off to some other point in the program. Inserting Halt instructions (Jump to self if no Halt instruction exists) for JUMPs to exits 1, 2, and 3 will cause the system to halt at one of these points and the designer can determine where the program bug is. The designer will probably find a simple coding error has caused the problem. This condition is usually hard to find by simply reading over the code.

Probably the most important rule for the microprogrammer during debug is to break his program up into a number of small segments and debug each of these. After the programmer is satisfied that each segment works, he can begin to check out the remainder of the microcode which ties the pieces together. At this point in time, additional bugs will probably be discovered in the previously checked out sections of the code.

seek — Computer process for locating specific data in a random access store. Each memory location inspected is a seek and the number of seeks governs the total search time.

seek area — Relates to disk units with multiple read-write heads. All of the data tracks under the read-write heads can be accessed without mechanical movement of the heads. If each disk surface has one read-write head, the tracks under them can be thought of as a cylinder consisting of one track from each disk.

seek time — Refers to the time that is needed to position the access mechanism of a direct access storage device at a specified position.

segment — 1. In a routine, the part short enough to be sorted entirely in the internal storage of a calculator, yet containing all the coding necessary to call in and jump automatically to other segments. 2. To divide a program into an integral number of parts, each of which performs a part of the total program and is short enough to be completely stored in internal memory. 3. A set of data that can be placed anywhere in a memory and can be addressed relative to a common origin. The origin and number of locations of a segment are called its base address and its length.

segmentation and control, automatic — Automatic segmentation and control permits the calculator to efficiently handle programs that exceed the main-memory capacity of a particular system configuration. Without reprogramming, the calculator automatically adjusts its operational procedures to allow the processing of any program on any system configuration. Segments of all programs concurrently being executed are "fitted" into available memory space for execution. Thus, the user is not forced to install a system of maximum memory capacity to accommodate one long program; he need not purchase more equipment than he normally needs for efficient operation.

segmentation overlays — A segment of a program is defined as that portion of memory which is committed by a single reference to the loader. Usually a segment overlays some other segment and may have within itself other portions which in turn overlay one another, i.e., subsegments. That part of a segment which is actually brought into memory when the loader is referenced is called the fixed part of a segment. Segments are built up from separate relocatable elements, common blocks, or other segments.

segmented program — One written in separate segments or parts. Only one, or some, of the segments may fit into memory at any one time, and the main portion of the program, remaining in memory, will call for other segments from backing storage when needed, each new segment being utilized to overlay the preceding segments.

segment, root — The master controlling segment of an overlay structure which always resides in main memory. Usually this is the first segment within the program, and it is always the first to be loaded at program initiation time; often identical to the mainline segment or program.

select — 1. To take the alternative A if the report on a condition is of one state, and alternative B if the report on the condition is of another state. 2. To choose a needed subroutine from a file of subroutines.

selecting — A data-processing function of pulling from a mass of data certain items that require special attention. Typical selections are: items containing specific digits, items for a specific date, items higher than a specific number, items below a specific number, items below two specific numbers, etc.

selection check — A check, usually an automatic check, to verify that the correct register or device is selected in the performance of an instruction.

selective calling — The ability of the transmitting station to specify which of several stations on the same line is to receive a message.

selective dump — Usually a library subroutine that is called to be used when other calculator programs are running and a dump is desired.

selective trace — A tracing routine that uses only specified criteria. Typical criteria are: instruction type (arithmetic jump), instruction location (specific region), and data location (specific region).

selector channel — Selector channels are used where high-speed devices are to be attached to a system. A single channel can operate only one I/O device at a time. Up to six selector channels can be attached to models of many calculator systems. Two or more channels connected to any system provide the ability to read, write, and compute from multiple input/output devices. See multiplexor channel.

select plus routine — A routine that determines if a device is ready to be used and, if it is, prepares a select instruction, channel command, and device order to accomplish an input/output activity or

self-adapting error recovery procedure. When this routine is entered from the channel scheduler, the sign of the accumulator is plus.

self-adapting — This pertains to the ability of a computer system to change its performance characteristics in response to its environment.

self-checking code — A code in which errors produce forbidden combinations. A single-error detecting code produces a forbidden combination if a digit gains or loses a single bit. A double-error detecting code produces a forbidden combination if a digit gains or loses either one or two bits and so forth. (Related to self-checking number and error-detecting code.)

self-checking number — A number with a suffix figure related to the figure(s) of the number, used to check the number after it has been transferred from one medium or device to another. (Related to check bit, modulo-N check, and error-detecting code.)

self-complementing code — A machine language in which the code of the complement of a digit is the complement of the code of the digit.

self-demarking code — 1. A code in which the symbols are so arranged and selected that the generation of false combinations by interaction of segments from two successive codes is prevented. 2. Same as error-detecting code.

self-learning — A special capability of a device or machine such that it can improve its capability in decision-making as programmed with instructions and based on information received, new instructions received, results of calculations, or environmental change, i.e., error histories and historical performance can and does relate to improving techniques.

self-operated controller — That specific control device in which all the energy necessary to operate the signal controlling element is derived from the control system through the sensing element.

self-organizing — Having the capability of classification or internal rearrangement, depending on the environment, in accordance with given instructions or a set of rules.

self organizing machine (SOM) — Refers to a class of machines which may be characterized loosely as containing a variable network in which the elements are organized by the machine itself, without external intervention, to meet criteria of successful operation.

self-organizing system — A system that is capable of internal reconfiguration in response to externally occurring events.

self-powered — Equipment containing its own power supply. It may be either a combination of wet and dry cells, or dry cells in conjunction with a spring-driven motor.

self-programming, hand-held units — Many hand-held units have a self-programming capability, using the calculate mode. After a user completes his program, he can store it and record it permanently by running a magnetic card through the reader. It's then in the memory and on the card. After the card is labeled it is available for repetitive problem solving. Users can insert the card and operate their units in the run mode. This saves time and effort, and greatly reduces the chance of error since there are far fewer steps to perform thereafter.

self-relocating program — Refers to a specific program that can be loaded into any area of main storage, and that contains an initialization routine to adjust its address constants so that it can be executed at that location.

self-repairing — An unusual characteristic or capability of some machines to detect, locate, repair, remove, or change (sidetrack), various types of malfunctions (or parts) during its operations and without human intervention other than supplementing such repairs as making components or parts available for automatic insertion, connections, etc.

self-resetting loop — One which contains instructions restoring all locations affecting the operation of the loop to their initial condition as at entry of the loop.

semantic error — 1. One which results in ambiguous or erroneous meaning of a computer program. Most programs have to be debugged to eliminate these errors before use. 2. Refers to an error's meaning or intent of the programmer and are definitely his responsibility. Often they are provided with an extensive set of debugging aids for manipulating and referencing a program when in search of errors in the logic and analysis.

semantics — Refers to the relationships between symbols and their intended meanings independent of their interpretation devices.

semantics, formal — A language for computer-oriented languages which acts as a compiler-compiler and contains formal semantics.

semantics, language theory — The meaning of a sentence as contrasted to syntax, which is the structure of a sentence.

semicompiled — Refers to a specific program which has been converted from source language into object code by a compiler, but which has not yet had included those subroutines explicitly or implicity called by the source program.

semiconducting material — A solid or liquid having a resistivity midway between that of an insulator and a metal.

semi-conductive — Refers to an electric device which is composed of high conductive metals and low conductive insulators designed to change the nature or strength of electrical flows in various circuits.

semiconductor — 1. A material with an electrical conductivity between that of a metal and an insulator. Its electrical conductivity, which is generally very sensitive to the presence of impurities and some structural faults, will increase as the temperature does. This is in contrast with a metal, in which conductivity decreases as its temperature rises. 2. A material whose resistivity is between that of conductors and insulators, and whose resistivity can sometimes be changed by light, an electric field or a magnetic field.

semiconductor device — A device in which the characteristic that distinguishes electronic conduction takes place within a semiconducting material.

semiconductor integrated circuits — Complex circuits fabricated by suitable and selective modification of areas on and in wafers of semiconductor material to produce patterns of interconnected passive and active elements. The circuit may be assembled from several chips and use thin-film elements or discrete components.

semiconductor memory — 1. A memory whose storage medium is a semiconductor circuit. 2. Generally semiconductor memory components are constructed using one of three basic technologies: (1) bipolar; (2) N-channel MOS; or (3) P-channel MOS. Early designs favored P-channel MOS since those technologies had already been developed for other componentry by the time it was realized that semiconductors could offer an economically feasible alternative to cores. There are many significant variations within each of the three technologies. To most experts it appears that over the long term, N-channel will be the dominant process used for semiconductor memory and processing components.

semiconductor, n-type — Relates to a semiconducting crystal material that has been doped with minute amounts of an impurity which will produce donor-type centers of electrons in the crystal lattice structure. Because electrons are negative particles, the material is called n-type, and conduction is primarily by electrons as the majority carrier of electric current.

semiconductors, bipolar — The bipolar processes of today are more mature than MOS and many variations have been tried and abandoned. The basic processes have become known by the logic circuit type built with the process, i.e., TTL — (Transistor-Transistor Logic) and ECL (Emitter Coupled Logic). Actually, all common bipolar technologies are remarkably similar, the usual difference being the number and sequences of diffusion operations required to manufacture the part.

send-only service — Service in which the data-communication channel is capable of transmitting signals, but is not equipped to receive signals.

send-receive, automatic (ASR) — A combination operator intervention or other requests for immediate transmission capability from either keyboard or paper tape. Most often used in a half-duplex circuit.

send-receive keyboard (KSR) — A combination transmitter and receiver with transmission capability from keyboard only.

send, request to — One of the basic data set interchange leads defined in EIA Standard RS-232-B.

sense — 1. Refers to the activity to examine, particularly relative to a criterion. 2. To determine the present arrangement of some element of hardware, especially a manually-set switch. 3. To read holes punched in paper.

sensing calculator — It is often necessary for a system to respond quickly to alarm conditions, operator intervention or other requests for immediate service. This service request is made via a program interrupt generated by either an event sense or a process interrupt card.

sensitivity — 1. The minimum input signal required in a radio receiver or similar device, to produce a specified output signal having a specified signal-to-noise ratio. This signal input may be expressed as power or voltage at a stipulated input network impedance. 2. Ratio of the response of a measuring device, to the magnitude of the measured quantity. It may be expressed directly in divisions per volt, milliradians per microampere, etc., or indirectly by stating a property from which sensitivity can be computed (e.g., ohms per volt for a stated deflection). 3. The degree of response of an instrument or control unit to a change in the incoming signal.

sensitivity analysis — Often refers to a test or trial of a range or number of input values to determine the response, interdependence, or friction of the output values. Sensitivity analysis is often called parametric programming because, in such investigations, one or more parameters are permitted to vary in order to determine whether or not a solution should be modified.

sensitivity ratio — 1. The degree of response of an instrument or control unit to change in the incoming signal. 2. A measured ratio of a change in output to the change in input which causes it, after steady-state has been reached, usually expressed as a numerical ratio with the units of measurement of the two quantities stated.

sensor — Refers to a transducer or other device whose input is a quantitative measure of some external physical phenomenon and whose output can be read by a computer or calculator.

sensor-based — Refers to the use of sensing devices, such as transducers or sensors, to monitor a physical process.

sensor-based system — Refers to a type of organization of components, including a calculator whose primary source of input is data from sensors and whose output can be used to control the related physical process.

sentinel — A symbol marking the beginning or end of some piece of information in digital-computer programming.

separator, file — A specific device designed for the purpose of identifying logical boundaries between items or files. Abbreviated FS.

separator, group — A specific device designed to identify logic boundaries between groups or sets of information. Abbreviated GS.

separator, record — A specific character designed for the purpose of demarcation of the logical boundary between records.

sequence — 1. To put a set of symbols into an arbitrarily defined order, i.e., to select A if A is greater than or equal to B, or select B if A is less than B. 2. An arbitrarily defined order of a set of symbols, i.e., an orderly progression of items of information or of operations in accordance with some rule.

sequence checking — Refers to a routine which checks every instruction executed and prints out certain data, e.g., to print out the coded instructions with addresses and the contents of each of several registers, or it may be designed to print out only selected data, such as transfer instructions and the quantity actually transferred.

sequence, control — The normal order of selection of instructions for execution. In some calculators one of the addresses in each instruction specifies the control sequence. In most other calculators, the sequence is consecutive except where a transfer occurs.

sequence memory, calculator — Some low-priced calculators contain a programmable sequence memory. For example, one model remembers a sequence of function-key operations up to a total of 10. This includes any sequence of plus-equals (+ =); minus-equals (− =); multiply (×); divide (÷); percent (%); add to memory (M +); subtract from memory (M −); and recall memory (RM). Clear memory (CM) cannot be used in a program, but this function is programmed by depressing recall-memory twice. Thus, the user can store a program and repeat it without having to remember the particular key operations initially required.

sequence memory, calculator operation — To insert a program in the 'sequence memory' calculator, the display and memory are first cleared. To instruct the machine to store the program, a "learn" (L) key is pressed. The sequence of data and function keys is then pressed in the proper order until the program sequence is finished, at which point, a "stop" or S key is pushed. To execute a program, the numerical data are entered and an "execute" key (E) is operated in the proper sequence. Thus one of the memories in this unit is designed to store the 10 program steps. The handheld units are battery-operated and automatically turn themselves off after 12 minutes without an entry.

sequence register — 1. Refers to a counter which is pulsed or reset following the execution of an instruction to form the new memory address which locates the next instruction. 2. A calculator register that controls the sequence of instructions.

sequence symbol — In assembler programming, a symbol used as a branching label for conditional assembly instructions. It consists of a period, followed by one to seven alphameric characters, the first of which must be alphabetic.

sequencing, automatic — The ability of equipment to put information in order or in a connected series without human intervention.

sequential-access storage — A storage technique in which the stored items of information become available only in a one after the other sequence, whether or not all the information or only some of it is desired, e.g., magnetic-tape storage. (Related to serial storage, and contrasted with random-access storage.)

sequential control — Digital-computer operation in which the instructions are set up in sequence and fed to the computer consecutively during the solution of a problem.

sequential control, PLA — A PLA can be used effectively in sequencing applications to implement flow charts of state diagrams, condition driven look up tables or arbitrary state sequencers. The input set could come from external control points ("qualifying inputs") or the PLA outputs coupled through feedback latches ("current state inputs").

sequential logic element — A device having at least one output channel and one or more input channels, all characterized by discrete states, such that the state of each output channel is determined by the previous states of the input channels.

sequential operation — The performance of actions one after the other in time. The actions referred to are of a large scale as opposed to the smaller scale operations referred to by the term serial operation. For an example of sequential operation consider A*(B*C). The two multiplications indicated follow each other sequentially. However, the processing of the individual digits in each multiplication may be either parallel or serial.

sequential processing — The processing of data that have been operated on previously to their entry into the calculator system which placed them in a definite and prescribed order.

serial — 1. Pertaining to time-sequential transmission of storage of, or logical operations on, the parts of a word in a computer — the same facilities being used for successive parts. 2. The handling of one after the other in a single facility, such as a transfer or store in a digit-by-digit time sequence, or to process a sequence of instructions one at a time, i.e., sequentially. The time sequence transmission of, storage of, or logical operations on the parts of a word, with the same facilities for successive parts.

serial adder — Refers to a logical unit which adds two binary words, one binary bit pair at a time. The least significant addition is performed first and progressively more significant additions, including carries, are performed until the sum of the two numbers is formed. Saves hardware at the expense of operating time.

serial and parallel I/O modules — Serial and parallel I/O modules are generally available for interfacing various processor buses with external devices. These modules simplify connection to peripherals when and if required, and also facilitate assembly of prototype systems without penalizing later development of customized interfaces.

serial communications — These serial input/output lines are often fully decoded on the CPU chip and provide a means of direct interface to a teletype, tape cassette or any other serial device. They also provide for direct control of user system functions or peripherals.

serial I/O (data communications) — Serial I/O for data communications provides an interface that includes a programmable synchronous and asynchronous communications-interface device, variable baud-rate generator, and jumper-selectable RS-232-C and teletypewriter drivers and receivers.

serial I/O organization — A serial I/O interface is a valuable addition to some advanced calculator systems for two reasons: First, the interface permits man-machine communications devices to be used with the system during development, production trouble-shooting, and field maintenance. By attaching a cathode-ray-tube display or teletypewriter to the serial I/O, the user design engineer or field engineer can gain access to the entire system for functional testing. He may use this interface to load diagnostic programs and then command and interrogate any part of the system. Second, the calculator may have to communicate with terminals or remote equipment via serial data-transmission links. In applications such as distributed processing, an interface to a standard serial data-communications channel is usually essential. Such channels are most commonly used to link a host processor to remote satellite processors.

serial memory system — Refers to systems designed to meet the high reliability and low cost requirements of large volume storage and CRT refresh applications. Some units feature the use of a single voltage power supply and MOS n-channel silicon gate technology. These systems are available as self-contained 20,000 words by 10 bits memory units, or are expandable to virtually any size in either word or bit length by the use of additional memory cards. They are designed for replacement of small fixed head disks and for CRT refresh applications.

serial number — Numerals usually attached to a device, machine, item or a sequence for spatial position of an item relative to other items, i.e., numbers representing a label or identifier.

serial numbering — The serial numbering of orders, invoices, checks, etc., provides control while the data is in transit. Each item or document in the series or group is assigned a successive number; and indication of the beginning and ending of numbers accompanies the group.

serial-parallel — 1. Having the property of being partially serial and partially parallel. 2. A combination of serial and parallel, i.e., serial by character, parallel by bits comprising the character. 3. Descriptive of a device which converts a serial input into a parallel output.

serial storage — Refers to the common types of storage in which time is one of the coordinates used to locate any given bit, character, or (especially) word. Storage in which words, within given groups of several words, appear one after the other in time sequence, and in which access time therefore includes a variable latency or waiting time of zero to many word-times, then said to be serial by word. Storage in which the individual bits comprising a word appear in time sequence is serial by bit. Storage for coded-decimal or other non-binary numbers in which the characters appear in time sequence is serial by character, i.e., magnetic drums are usually serial by word but may be serial by bit, or parallel by bit, or serial by character and parallel by bit, etc.

series — 1. The connecting of components end to end in a circuit, to provide a single path for the current. 2. An indicated sum of a set of terms in a mathematical expression (e.g., in an alternating or arithmetic series). 3. Said of electric components when a common current flows through them. 4. Lines in a spectrum described by a formula related to the possible energy levels of the electrons in outer shells of atoms.

series, discrete — A discrete action in use in which the differences between successive observations are always finite in character, that is, there are no values falling between the observed values. For example, shoes are made in sizes 5, 5½, 6, 6½, etc. Since no shoes are made in intermediate sizes — e.g., between 5 and 5½ — the differences between sizes are always finite.

series, divergent — A divergent series is an infinite series in which the sum of the terms is greater than any definite quantity, if enough terms are taken.

series interface board — A typical board is designed for use in assembling custom interfaces to use with various series memory systems. The interface board can be used with IC sockets, with up to 18 pins, and can be wirewrapped for quick interface connections. The I/O board plugs directly into the series connector slots. Several slots are available to accommodate up to 40 pin sockets.

series types — A succession of quantities, each derived from the preceding amount or amounts according some fixed law. The first and last terms of a series are called the extremes, and the intervening terms the means. In a series a, a + d, a + ad, a + 3d, the quantities a and a + 3d are extremes and the others are means. An ascending series is one in which the quantities increase regularly from the first term; e.g., 2, 4, 8, 16 and a, a + d, +2d, etc. are ascending. A descending series is one in which the quantities decrease regularly from the first term; e.g., 24, 12, 6, 3, and a, a − d, a − 2d, a − 3d are descending.

service bureau — Refers to computer service installations where users can rent or lease processing time on a central processor and peripheral equipment. Either can supply the programs and the center will load both program and data to be processed, process the data and transmit or deliver the results to the user in any of several forms: cards, punched tape, magnetic tape, etc. Service bureaus also provide such services as keypunching the data and preparing it for processing.

service life — The length of time a primary cell or battery needs to reach a specified final electrical condition on a service test that duplicates normal usage.

service organizations — Refers to various companies which offer and contract maintenance and operation of computers not owned or leased by them for charges and fees commensurate with the size and complexity of the system.

service program — Any of the class of standard routines that assist in the use of a calculating system and in the successful execution of problem programs, without contributing directly to control of the system or production of results.

service routine — Refers to a routine designed to assist in the actual operation of the calculator and a broad class of routines which are standardized at a particular installation for the purpose of assisting in maintenance and operation of the computer as well as the preparation of programs as opposed to routines for the actual solution of production problems. This class includes monitoring or supervisory routines, assemblers, compilers, diagnostics for calculator malfunctions, simulation of peripheral equipment, general diagnostics and input data. The distinguishing quality of service routines is that they are generally standardized so as to meet the servicing needs at a particular installation, independent of any specific production type routine requiring such services.

servo — General term for systems in which the response is determined by a drive which is actuated by the difference (error) between a set target and the actual response. A servo system aids or replaces human action, by force, time of operation or location. Error usually requires valve or transistor amplification.

servomechanism — 1. Closed-cycle system in which a small input power controls a much larger output power in a strictly proportionate manner, e.g., movement of a gun turret may be accurately controlled by movement of a small knob or wheel. 2. Any closed-loop, feedback type of control system. A servomechanism consists of the following elements (which may be distinct or combined-function elements of hardware). A. An input signal or command line, to indicate the desired state. B. An output sensor, capable of monitoring the actual output state. C. A comparator which determined the deviation from the desired state, based on the above two signals. D. An effector, which has the power to modify the output state or condition. It is not necessary for an explicit input signal to be provided, but an implicit signal must exist in those cases where an explicit signal is missing (for instance, as in the fixed-setting thermostats, or automatic level-seeking devices). The important feature of a servomechanism is its four-part closed-loop organization as outlined above. Its actual physical implementation or field of application is immaterial.

servo-system — An automatic control system for

maintaining a condition at or near a predetermined value by activation of an element such as a control rod. It compares the required condition (desired value) with the actual condition and adjusts the control element in accordance with the difference (and sometimes the rate of change of the difference).

settable timer — These units provide a convenient method of generating accurate long delays where the inputs are programmed in terms of seconds, minutes and hours. An example of this is the 24-hour timer which uses the carryout gates to generate a one second clock from a 60 hertz line source. The diodes on the time base input rectify the input signal and alternately clamp and release the internal pull up resistor. A typical input network depends on the amplitude of 60 Hertz signal available. The internal oscillators are disabled with a 1K resistor to ground.

set and subset — Whenever one can classify or describe something by a characteristic or property, he may determine that the thing belongs to the set of all things having that characteristic or property. Each thing in the set or elements in the set are subsets if identifiable by some characteristic common to each of the elements of the subject. The set that includes all of the elements having a given characteristic is called the universal set of things having the given property. A set having no elements is called the empty or null set.

set, function — A special purpose operation referring to a set of calculations within an expression, as in the sine function, square root function, etc.

set point — In a feedback control loop, the point which determines the desired value of the quantity being controlled.

set theory — Refers to a study, in the mathematical sense of the rules, for characterizing groups, sets, and elements; i.e., the theory of delimiting or combining groups.

set-up services — The action or services performed on a message before it meets the application program. Services include error checking analyzing the action code, etc.

several-for-one — A phrase often associated with a macro instruction, where one source language instruction is converted to several machine language instructions.

sexadecimal digit — A digit that is a member of the set of sixteen digits: 0 thru 9 and then A, B, C, D, E or F used in a numerical notation system using a radix of 16. All same as hexadecimal.

shannon — A specific unit of measurement of the quantity of information which is equal to that contained in a message represented by one or the other of two equally probable exclusive or exhaustive states.

shared storage — The ability to share main storage between two CPU's. This means that either machine can insert information into storage and either machine can access the data and use it.

shared files — A direct-access device that permits two systems to be linked together. Either system has access to the file.

SHARE organization — The SHARE organization coordinates the effective use of IBM data-processing systems through exchange of programming and application information, thereby seeking to reduce redundant programming effort. Programs written by SHARE members provide meaningful solutions to many data processing problems encountered in using IBM System 360 and 370 and other data processing systems and future versions of these systems and the future large systems.

sharing — 1. Refers to the interleaved time use on a device — hence, a method of operation in which a calculator facility is shared by several users concurrently. 2. The apportionment of intervals of time availability of various items of equipment to complete the performance of several tasks by interlacing (contrasted with multiprogramming). 3. The use of a device for two or more purposes during the same overall time interval, accomplished by interspersing the calculator actions in time.

shift — 1. Displacement of an ordered set of computer characters one or more places to the left or right. If the characters are the digits of a numerical expression, a shift is equivalent to multiplying by a power of the base. 2. To move information serially right or left in a register(s) of a calculator. Information shifted out of a register may be lost, or it may be re-entered at the other end of the register.

shift, arithmetic — To multiply or divide a quantity by a power of the number base; e.g., if binary 1101, which represents decimal 13, is arithmetically shifted twice to the left, the result is 110100, which represents 52, which is also obtained by multiplying (13 by 2) twice; on the other hand, if the decimal 13 were to be shifted to the left twice, the result would be the same as multiplying by 10 twice, or 1300. (Related to shift and cyclic shift.)

shift, circular — A shift in which the digits dropped-off at one end of a word are returned at the other in a circular fashion; e.g., if a register holds eight digits, 23456789, the result of a cyclic shift two columns to the left would be to change the contents of the register to 45678923. (Synonymous with end-around shift, logical shift, nonarithmetic shift, ring shift, and cyclic shift.)

shift, floating point — A shift in 4-bit increments, performed on a short-format or long-format floating-point number.

shift-in character (SI) — 1. A code extension character, used to terminate a sequence that has been introduced by the shift-out character, that makes effective the graphic characters of the standard character set. 2. A code extension character that can be used by itself to cause a return to the character set in effect prior to the departure caused by a shift-out character, usually to return to the standard character set.

shifting register — Refers to a particular register which is designed to adapt to perform shifts, i.e., a delay line register whose circulation time may be increased or decreased so as to shift the content.

shift instruction, accumulator — A computer instruction which causes the contents of an accumulator register to shift to the left or right.

shift out — 1. In a computer, to move information within a register toward one end so that as the information leaves this one end, 0's are entered into the other end.

shift phase — The time difference between the input and output signal or between any two synchronized signals of a control unit, system, or circuit.

shift register — 1. A register which provides

short circuit

short or long-term storage for either serial or parallel operation. 2. A register in which the stored data can be moved to the right or left.

short circuit — 1. Also called a short. 2. An abnormal connection of relatively low resistance between two points of a circuit. The result is a flow of excess (often damaging) current between these points. 3. Reduction of p.d. between terminals to zero by connection of a conductor of zero impedance, in which no power is dissipated. If the short-circuit is not perfect, arcing and damage may result if the circuit is not opened quickly elsewhere.

short word — A fixed word of lesser length that is capable of handling words of two different lengths. In many calculators this is referred to as a half-word because the length is exactly the half-length of a full word.

shunt — A precision low-value resistor placed across the terminals of an ammeter to increase its range. 2. Any part connected, or the act of connecting any part, in parallel with some other part. 3. In an electric circuit, a branch the winding of which is in parallel with the external or line circuit. 4. Addition of a component to divert current in a known way; e.g., from a galvanometer, to reduce temporarily its effective sensitivity. 5. Diversion of some flux from the gap in a magnetic circuit by a magnetic slide or screw in a moving-coil indicating instrument.

sidebands — 1. The frequency bands on both sides of the carrier frequency. The frequencies of the wave produced by modulation fall within these bands. During amplitude modulation with a sinewave carrier, the upper sideband includes the sum (carrier plus modulating) frequencies, and the lower sideband includes the difference (carrier minus modulating) frequencies.

sideway sum — Relates to a specific sum which is developed by adding digits without regard to position, i.e., sideways sums are brought forward by attaching various weights to the different digit positions and most often forms check digits through odd or even parity techniques.

sight check — 1. The determination by visual means whether or not a particular punch is present in all cards of a deck; to check keypunching by reading the tabulation printout of card data. 2. To verify the sorting or punching of punched cards by looking through the pattern of punched holes.

sigma (Σ, accumulate) — A key or switch that will automatically total the results of a series of calculations. This key or switch identifies an automatic register.

sign — 1. A symbol which distinguishes negative from positive quantities. 2. A symbol which indicates whether a quantity is greater or less than zero. 3. A binary indicator of the position of the magnitude of a number relative to zero.

signal — 1. A visable, audible, or other conveyor of information. 2. The intelligence, message, or effect to be conveyed over a communication system. 3. A signal wave. 4. The physical embodiment of a message.

signal conditioning — 1. Any manipulation of transducer or transmitter outputs to make them suitable for input to the computer peripheral equipment. 2. Operations such as linearizing and square-root extraction performed within the computer. 3. To process the form or mode of a signal so as to make it intelligible to, or compatible with, a given device, including such manipulation as pulse shaping, pulse clipping, digitizing and linearizing.

signal control — Various control signals are provided to control, and to ensure to orderly flow of information words between the central computer and the peripheral subsystems. These signals do not transmit data, but are used to command and identify the transfer of information words at the proper times and in the proper sequence. These control signals travel over the control lines of the input/output channel.

signal sensing — A specific signal which is often translated at the start of a message for the purpose of initiating circuit operation at the receiving end of a circuit.

signal flags, calculator — Flags are signals. Some units have five. Each is set or reset manually from the keyboard, or as part of a stored program. The flag's condition can be tested by the if flg transfer instruction.

sign bit — A single bit, used to designate the algebraic sign of the information contained in the remainder of the word.

significance — In positional representation, the factor, dependent on the digit place, by which a digit is multiplied to obtain its additive contribution in the representation of a number. Synonymous with weight.

significance, bit — Refers to the bit presence or absence in a specific location of an instruction word which distinguishes the instruction to be of certain type, for example, zero vs. one-address instruction.

significant digit — A digit that contributes to the precision of a numeral. The number of significant digits is counted beginning with the digit contributing the most value, called the most significant digit, and ending with the one contributing the least value, called the least significant digit.

significant figures (overflow sign) — This is the result displayed after automatic machine runoff. For example, when an eight-digit calculator computes 45689×98754, it will display 45115603, although the actual result is 4511560305. The last two digits, 0 and 5, are not displayed, since the machine is limited to eight digits; only the most significant ones are displayed. The symbol to the left of the result indicates that the number is larger than the display can handle (i.e., overflow sign).

significant interval — A time interval during which a given significant condition according to the code and the signal to be transmitted is, or should be transmitted.

sign off — The closing instruction to the computer system which terminates communication with the system. On a remote terminal, the user generally signs off by typing the command OFF or SIGN OFF.

sign on — The instruction which commences communication with the computer system. On a remote terminal, the user can generally receive access to the system by typing in his identification number and an appropriate password.

silicon — A metallic element when mixed with iron or steel during smelting to provide desirable magnetic properties for transformer-core materials. In its pure state, it is used as a semiconductor.

silicon on sapphire (SOS) — SOS is a technology in which a thin silicon layer is grown on a sapphire substrate, then selectively removed, leaving small silicon "islands" that are made into MOS transistors. Many fabricating techniques can be used with SOS. Because the sapphire substrate is a true insulator, not a semiconductor, this technique drastically reduces all parasite capacitance and leakage current. Because MOS performance is so sensitive to parasitic capacitance, SOS promises dramatic performance advantages over other MOS processes. It also should be possible to place transistors much closer together, with very high packing density. But SOS has not yet received good sponsorship by memory manufacturers or customers, so its technology is moving relatively slowly. Sapphire substrates are still very costly, though inherently they could be very inexpensive. SOS is a potent technology that should play an important role in high-performance memories.

simplex/duplex modems — Modems may be designed to operate in three modes: 1. Simplex, where data is transmitted (and hopefully received) in only one direction, 2. Half-duplex, where data can be transmitted in only one direction at a time, but that direction can be reversed, and 3. Full-duplex, where data may be transmitted in both directions simultaneously.

simulate — 1. Refers to the activity of representing certain features of the behavior of a physical or abstract system by the behavior of another system, e.g., to represent a physical phenomenon by means of operations performed by a computer or to represent the operations of a computer by those of another computer. 2. To imitate one system with another, primarily by software, so that the imitating system accepts the same data, executes the same computer modification, examination and modification of internal working registers, examination and modification of all the I/O points and ability to single step, run and breakpoint the program and verification of paper-tapes or other media.

simulation — 1. A type of problem in which a physical model and the conditions to which the model may be subjected are all represented by mathematical formulas. 2. The representation of physical systems and phenomena by computers, models or other equipment, e.g., an imitative type of data processing in which an automatic computer is used as a model of some entity, i.e., a chemical process. Information enters the computer to represent the factors entering the real process, the computer produces information that represents the results of the process, and the process itself. 3. In computer programming, the technique of setting up a routine for one computer to make it operate as nearly as possible like some other computer.

simulation (advantages) — Simulation is often relegated to undeserved second choice because the sheer complexity of some problems makes mathematical formulation prohibitive (if not impossible). Even when a problem can be solved by mathematical analysis, it may be more economical to solve it by simulation. Whereas analysis sets out to provide a general solution to all problems of the type being considered, simulation manipulates only the data relevant to the problem in question and thus simulation often offers a much simpler and cheaper solution.

simulation, design and monitoring — The building of a model of a system in the form of a computer program by the use of special languages. The models of a system can be adjusted easily and the system that is being designed can be tested to show the effect of any change.

simulation — man-machine — Simulation techniques clearly include models of systems in which human beings participate (operational or behavioral models). However, the possibility also exists of incorporating people within the model. In other words, the model is no longer completely computer-based but requires the active participation of a man.

simulation, microprogramming — This procedure has emulation as its chief function since a microprogram can imitate the basic instruction set of the machine being emulated. Word lengths, arithmetic, and logic details, as well as other functions of another machine, are simulated. Each fundamental instruction or operation of the imitated machine is made up of a sequence of microcoded steps allowing registers to be loaded, data to be moved, etc. Quite often the microcoded sequences which make up each basic machine operation are hardwired into a control store. Such control stores, in many new machines, are either being made from Read-Only Memory (ROM), which may be easily removed for substitution, or from semiconductor Re-loadable Control Store (RCS). Microprogramming offers user programmers opportunities to tailor their own machines to their own jobs; i.e., powerful instructions can be developed which would require only a single line of program code to complete a number of complex but repetitive jobs called for by specific installation requirements.

simulation monitoring and design — The building of a model of a system in the form of a computer program by the use of special languages. The models of a system can be adjusted easily and the system that is being designed can be tested to show the effect of any change.

simulation, physical — The use of a model of a physical system in which computing elements are used to represent some, but not all, of the subsystems.

simulation, static vs. dynamic — In a dynamic system the activity is time-dependent. This activity may be further classified as stable or unstable (under given conditions). One may choose to study steady-state or transient behavior of a dynamic system.

simulation, supervisory programs — When the supervisory program is not available, the use of a replacement program that imitates the supervisory program.

simulator — Refers to highly specific programs that emulate, imitate or substitute the logical operation of various microprocessors. These programs are designed to execute object programs generated by a cross-assembler on a machine other than the one being worked on. Simulators are very useful for checking and debugging programs prior to committing them to ROM firmware.

simulator, ROM — The ability to set, lock and monitor the ROM address register provides a convenient means for identifying the location of errors and documenting individual program changes. The simulator enables the user to insert the hundreds of little changes he will make during the

simultaneity

debugging of his program. Some of these changes will be made to correct actual errors in the microde. However, the majority will be inserted in an effort to locate and diagnose mistakes. Once the designer has the proper instrumentation at his disposal, system checkout can proceed quickly.

simultaneity — Refers to the facility of a calculator to allow input/output, on its peripherals to continue in parallel with operations in the central processor.

simultaneous calculating, live keyboards — Some types of desk-top programmable calculators permit calculations to be made at the same time that the calculator is running control programs. One type unit has a tape drive (for minicartridges), 32-character LED display, and 190-line/min. thermal printer.

simultaneous equations — Sets of equations composed of two or more, with or without a common solution, with the conditions implied by each of the equations which are imposed on all variables simultaneously.

simultaneous input/output — Generally refers to the calculators which can handle other operations concurrently with input and output operations, most often using buffers which hold input output data and information as it arrives and on a temporary basis, while other operations are executed by the CPU. Thus, the calculator need not wait for data from the very slow I/O units and may instead take it from the faster part of the buffer in massive quantities instead of as it arrives from slower units or terminals.

simultaneous processing — The performance of two or more data processing tasks at the same instant of time. Contrast with concurrent processing.

sine wave — 1. A perfectly formed electromagnetic wave with no harmonics. 2. A periodic, mathematical plotted function (quantity) which varies according to y = Rsinwt, which is an amplitude-angular-displacement plot of the projection, on a diameter, of a point moving on the circumference of a circle of radius R.

single-board subsystems — A typical complete general-purpose computer subsystem that fits on a single printed-circuit board of LSI technology consists of a central-processing unit, read/write and read-only memories, and parallel and serial input/output-interface components. They satisfy most processing and control applications needed by original-equipment manufacturers. A single-board computer greatly extends the range of computer applications by providing a single solution to three problems that have often precluded the use of conventional computers: cost; small size and lower power and design specialization.

single bus operation — No two computer I/O architectures are identical but one major difference is the use of a single bus for all data transfers or separate buses for CPU-memory and CPU-I/O transfers. These two have many pros and cons. The single bus theory of operation is that all data transfers take place on this one bus; any device capable of transmitting data on the bus can become Bus Master; any device capable of receiving data can become Bus Slave. Any bus master can transmit data to any bus slave without CPU intervention. For example: A disk (bus master) can transmit data directly to another disk or to magnetic tape (bus slave). (more commonly a disk

skip test

will transmit data directly to a CRT terminal on a refresh cycle). An Analog-to-Digital Converter (bus master) can transmit data directly to a memory module (bus slave). In each of the above cases, the CPU is not involved in the data transfer.

single step — Pertaining to a method of operating a calculator in which each step is performed in response to a single manual operation.

single step debug — One innovative feature of some units is the behavior of the SST (Single Step) key in run mode. This key was designed to help the user debug programs. It allows the user to execute his program one key phrase at a time. When the SST key is held down, the display shows the line number and the key phrase that is to be executed next. Releasing the SST key executes just that key phrase, and the numerical results appear in the display. This feature makes debugging programs quite easy because the user can tiptoe through his programs, seeing both the key phrases and their results, one phrase at a time. The display when the SST key is held down includes the step number, so checking program flow and branching is easy.

single step key — Single Step permits single stepping through a program in the learn mode. It is also used in the calculate mode to execute a program one step at a time.

single-step key, small systems — Displays step number and keycode of current program memory step when pressed; executes instruction, displays result, and moves to next step when released.

single-step operation — A method of operating an automatic calculator manually, in which a single instruction or part of an instruction is performed in response to a single operation of a manual control. This method is generally used for detecting mistakes.

single variable functions — Square. Squares number displayed. Square root. Calculates square root of number displayed. Reciprocal. Calculates reciprocal of number displayed. x Factorial. Calculates factorial of integer displayed. Two Variable Functions raise y to the x power, calculate the xth root of y, etc.

SI (superimpose) — The process which moves data from one location to another, superimposing bits or characters on the contents of specified locations.

skewed distribution — A frequency distribution of any natural phenomenon in which zero or infinity is one of its limits.

skip — Refers to an instruction to proceed to the next instruction, a blank instruction. Same as instruction, skip and instruction, no-op.

skip bus — Refers to a specific central processor bus, shared by I/O interfaces and utilized in order to test devices associated with each interface and conditional branching of the program as a result of the testing.

skip code — A functional code which instructs the machine to skip certain predetermined fields in memory.

skip instruction — An instruction having no effect other than directing the processor to proceed to another instruction designated in the storage portion.

skip test — A specific type of microinstruction designed and utilized for conditional operations based on the state of readiness of various devices or the conditions of a register.

slave station — That station which receives data from a master communications station which it either monitors or with which it complies, or in some cases, repeats to other stations, but whose output is not part of the original output.

slave system — A particular system which is connected to another system and in which the commanding or master system discharges commands and orders which are thus imitated by the slave system.

slice architecture — In a "slice" architecture, a section of the register file and ALU in a computer is placed in one package. In some systems the registers are all four bits wide; others accommodate two bits. Each end of each register is accessible through the ALU at chip's edge; two or more of these "slices" can be cascaded together to form larger word sizes. Whether instruction lengths are identical to data word size or not depends upon how the control portion of the processor is organized. In some systems another chip in the set provides 8 microprogrammed control sections.

slice, bipolar — Bipolar/LSI microprocessor slices offer several advantages over standard MOS. The bipolar speeds of "bit slice" processors, or microcontrollers, assure a precise emulation of conventional systems, which employ standard-bipolar circuits. By using microprogramming techniques, designers can replace scores of SSI and MSI packages at reduced power. And in applications such as minicomputers, processor slices provide the hardware flexibility to reduce equipment size without changes in existing software (see bit-slice).

slice-oriented circuit sets — The category of microprocessors consists of the 2-bit and 4-bit slice-oriented circuit sets, commonly built with bipolar technology, and intended for systems byond the range of the self-contained MPU circuits. Such circuits feature expansion to 16-bit (or longer) word lengths, and microprogramming, to permit tailoring the circuits to system instruction requirements. However, limitations inherent in existing circuits make it difficult to design more than a very simple system. These constraints usually consist of one or more of the following: a minimal ALU function set, restrictive data routing and inadequate I/O data ports. If additional MSI circuits are added to make these LSI circuits meet system objectives, the advantages of LSI are largely lost.

slide-rule calculator capabilities — These are intended to do (aside from addition and subtraction), the things users can do with a good log-log-duplex-decitrig slide rule: display common and natural logarithms of any number, square a number or extract its square root with a single key stroke, display the sine, cosine, tangent, or the inverse trignometric functions of any angle, instantly find the reciprocal of a number, display pi with the stroke of a special key, raise a number to any power or extract any root of a number.

slide rule calculator, hand-held — A standard unit performs all classical slide rule functions — simple arithmetic, reciprocals, factorials, expotentiation, roots, trigonometric and logarithmic functions, all in free floating decimal point or in scientific notation. Rechargeable batteries, AC Adapter/Charger and case are usually included.

slope — 1. An oblique direction. 2. The rate of change of y with respect to x. 3. The slope of a curve $y = f(x)$ is given at any point x, by the value of dy/dx evaluated at that point and a tangent to the curve at this point with the horizontal axis.

"smart" interactive terminals — Refers to new "smart terminals" to identify an interactive terminal in which part of the processing is accomplished by a microcomputer or microprocessor contained in the terminal itself. This type of terminal is sometimes referred to in the literature as an "intelligent terminal." To be considered a smart terminal the computing capability of the microcomputer in the terminal must be available to the user in a way that permits him to program it to perform part of his unique application.

"smart" terminal example — In its most rudimentary form, a smart terminal contains a CRT, a keyboard, a serial communication I/O device and a microcomputer. The microcomputer controls text editing, formatting and the protocol of communication with the host computer system. Such terminals can incorporate peripheral memory devices like tape cassettes, can be programmed independently of their roles in the larger computer system and can therefore serve several useful functions, both on- or off-line. For example, the microcomputer can serve as a communications controller and handle tasks like line switching.

"smart" terminal capabilities — Besides editing, smart terminals often offer selectable baud rates by allowing transmission from below 110 baud up to 19.2 k baud. Many terminals have buffer memory, so that blocks of data may be transmitted synchronously as well as asynchronously. Once memory is added, many terminals also offer a feature known as "scrolling." Scroll memory is available to store the information that appears on the screen. The scrolling control can move the entire display either up or down one line at a time, saving the line that disappears at the top or bottom in the scroll memory. Then, if users scroll in the opposite direction, the lines will reappear on the screen.

"smart" terminal characteristics — Microprocessor-controlled interactive smart terminals have the following characteristics:
1. self-contained storage.
2. user interaction — with the terminal or the central computer,
3. stored program,
4. part of processing accomplished in the terminal,
5. on-line via communications line with large central computer and data base,
6. human-oriented input — keyboard, light pen, etc.,
7. human-oriented output — serial printer, CRT, etc.

SME — Society of Manufacturing Engineers.

smoothing, exponential — Refers to a specific statistical technique for minimizing "noisy" fluctuations usually, in a time vs. amplitude data series; as, for example, in a scintillation or heart rate-meter:

$$X_c = X_t \cdot \frac{1}{e} + X_{t-1} \cdot \frac{1}{2e} + X_{t-2} \cdot \frac{1}{3e} \ldots;$$

snapshot program — When a trace program is an interpretive program, it is called an interpretive trace program, and when a trace program gives output only on selected instructions or for a selected set or single condition it is called a snapshot program.

snapshot system, roll-back — A system that

will restart the running program after a system failure. Snapshots of data and programs are stored at periodic intervals and the system rolls back to restart at the last recorded snapshot.

SNA — systems network architecture — Refers to IBM's standardized relationship between its virtual telecommunication access method (VTAM) and the network control program (NCP/VS).

SNR — Signal-to-noise ratio.

S/O — 1. Send only. 2. Shift-out character.

S/OFF — Sign-off.

software — 1. The term software was invented to contrast with the "iron" or hardware of a computer system. Software items are programs, languages, and procedures of a computer system. Software libraries for microprocessors are being built and assembled in heavy competition among suppliers, both manufacturers and distributors. 2. The internal programs or routines prepared professionally to simplify programming and computer operations. Uses permit the programmer to use his own language (English) or mathematics (algebra) in communicating with the calculator. 3. Various programming aids that are frequently supplied by the manufacturers to facilitate the purchaser's efficient operation of the equipment. Such software items include various assemblers, generators, subroutine libraries, compilers, operating systems, and industry-application programs.

software, common — Programs or routines which usually have common and multiple applications for many systems, i.e., report generators, sort routines, conversion programs which can be used for several routines in language common to many computers.

software cross-products (microprocessor) — These include assemblers, simulators, and various compilers. They develop versions of programs which are used for assembly, simulation or compilation of programs. A cross assembler, for example, is functionally identical to other resident assemblers. Compilers are machine-oriented systems programming languages designed specifically to generate various internal code. Assemblers often have full macro capability and allow for conditional assembly (meaning that at the time of assembly, one of several sections of code may be chosen).

software, data acquisition system — A typical set offers:
* completely interfaced and tested system routines
* prerecorded instrument control routines for fast, easy programming
* simple programming instructions and example programs to aid in user test routines
* prerecorded test programs for DVM and scanner

software development, microcomputer — Small memory and a lack of peripheral equipment often hinder applications software development for microprocessor-based microcomputers. Users can overcome the problem with hardware simulators, or they can use software tools, such as cross assemblers and editors on large machines. If a minicomputer is available, users can build hybrid simulators to give the microcomputer an artificial memory. It will not only simulate the memory functions but will also leave the hardware functions intact. The microcomputer has controlled access to the mini's memory and the user can view the result. The mini's high-speed peripherals and most microcomputer activity center on the memory. A good deal of the step-by-step diagnostic and debugging capability inherent in hardware or software simulators is retained.

software development, microprocessor — Software development for microcomputers is done several ways: a designer programmer may spend lots of time using paper tape to assemble with the microcomputer itself. In addition to the assembler, loaders for the assembled programs and diagnostics to check out the hardware are available to him. Though not always offered, a monitor or executive rather than a fullblown operating system is sufficient for microcomputers since the machines are often used in dedicated applications, not for general-purpose programming.

software development process — The steps of the basic software development cycle are as follows:
1. Problem statement
2. Design of Abstract algorithms and data structures
3. Construction of flowchart and data layouts
4. Coding of the program in the chosen language
5. Source code preparation in machine readable form often using a source code editor
6. Translation to object code or machine code (using assemblers, compilers, linkage editors)
7. Transmission of machine code to target environment (using loaders)
8. Run-time check-out of executing code (using debuggers)
9. Documentation

This series of identifiable steps serves only to illustrate roughly the various activities that are traversed from the problem statement to the tested, properly-running, well-documented program.

The problem statement can take a number of forms, each of which expresses the software development task to be performed; this problem statement serves as a goal for the creative energies of the software designer. Initial decisions are made. Abstract data structures are envisioned. Abstract algorithms are invented, discovered, deduced or induced. What once was a problem statement becomes a deterministic algorithm. This solution can be represented in a flowchart, or other representation of the algorithm, the program can be coded in whatever language chosen. This code is "disk checked" and prepared in machine-readable form so that it is acceptable to the language translator. The assembler or compiler translates this source code into object code or machine code. From there, the machine code is loaded into the target environment to be subsequently tested, debugged and documented.

software development, prototyping advantages — Depending upon the prototyping system model and configuration, some or all of the common software tools are available. The advantages of prototyping system approach can be:
1. lower out-of-pocket expense for development facilities over the term of the development, also upper limit on costs
2. convenience of local facilities
3. manufacturer support of systems software

However, the prototyping system may have the following disadvantages:
1. may require time-consuming paper tape handling
2. may not have full hardware breakpoint and trace debugging facilities

3. may not be a capable enough computer to support all the software tools, or may compromise the features of those tools
4. may not support desired peripherals
5. may only support the prototyping of one variety of microprocessor
6. may not support the debugging of the microprocessor on the user's board in his prototype.

software documents — Relating to all the documents and notations associated with the calculator i.e., manuals, circuit diagrams, etc., or programs and routines associated with the calculator; i.e., compilers, special languages, library routines.

software faults — In contrast to transmission errors and hardware faults, which are assumed to be correctable after enough retries are made, faults in the software can represent uncorrectable errors. A very important function of the communication subsystem as a whole is to detect faults of this sort, using built-in redundancies and fault-recovery mechanisms. Faults can be detected both by the communication subsystem, by maintaining dynamic consistence checks on linked lists, queue directories, and such, and by the operating system itself, by monitoring storage-protect violations, addressing and data exceptions and the like.

software functions time sharing — Software functions required in a time-shared system include: (1) allocation of hardware resources, (2) scheduling of user tasks, (3) interrupt and fault processing, (4) terminal input/output coordination, (5) centralized input/output supervision, (6) accounting, (7) interpretation and execution of system commands, (8) management of subcomponents of system, (9) management of user files, (10) miscellaneous utility functions. These functions are referred to as executive, supervisory, or monitor functions. In some time-shared systems, certain of these functions may be omitted or may be present only in a very limited way.

software library, microcomputer — A typical library of software programs available for some systems includes the following:
- Machine Language Symbolic Assembler
- Utility Programs
- Teltype Operating System
- Tape Editor Program
- Diagnostics for CPU, memory, and system peripherals
- I/O Drivers (callable subroutines) for system peripherals
- Alterable Control Operating System (ACOS)
- Micro Language Assembler
- Micro Simulator
- Cross Micro Assembler (FORTRAN)
- Cross Micro Simulator (FORTRAN)
- Integrated circuit memory MAP generators which supply control memory bit patterns for implementing fixed circuit ROM.

software, microcomputer (typical system) — Standard software for many micros includes an assembler, loader, debugging utility, source edit utility, and diagnostic programs. The assembler translates symbolic assembly language programs into executable machine programs. The loader loads object tapes produced by the assembler or debugging utility. The debugging utility aids program checkout and features multiple breakpoints, instruction trace, and several other standard functions. The source edit utility is used to generate assembly language source tapes or modify existing source tapes. The diagnostics are used to verify processor operation. The cross-assembler enables programs written for the micro to be assembled on IBM 360/370 and other series computers.

software, microprocessor — In microprocessor applications the designer-programmer tries to implement a design (previously done by logic designers on paper) through on-line programming of the microprocessor. Instead of using gate logic such as AND, OR, NAND, and NOR, the designer-programmer uses the mask, compare, and jump instructions. Most microprocessor applications involve a mixture of control operations and application computations which are interleaved in the program mainstream. Assembly language is predominant. Because of modularity and the obvious repetitious nature of so many operations, subroutines are used extensively, and subroutine nesting is facilitated by the stack register organizations in all these units.

software package — Refers to various computer programs or sets of programs used in a particular applications such as a payroll/personnel package, scientific subroutines package, etc.

software package, utility — Refers to a comprehensive library of utility software available for most series of microcomputers. The library generally includes:
- Loading and debugging program
- Text editor
- Resident assembler
- Floating point package
- Cross assembler
- PROM programming software
- Tape conversion program
- Multiply/divide package

software procedure, microprocessor —
- System definition.
- Equating definition to programs.
- Program design.
- Charting of functional flow and detailed flow.
- Instruction writing, or coding.
- Debugging.
- Editing.
- Final program layout, or ROM stacking.

software, programmable calculator — The competence of any programmable calculator depends on software-the programs that it uses. Many calculators with abundant programs are available and can save time. It is much easier to turn on a calculator and start operating than to run on a large computing unit and spend a day programming. There are times when a user might not want to do the programming and there are times when a user may want to do the programming. In this case, it's nice to have a machine which programs easily and quickly and does not demand a special language like FORTRAN or COBOL.

software storage selection, calculator — On many units users can select the programs they need from the many extensive series of software products. They can store often-used programs on handy magnetic cards or cassettes for easy instant entry into their specific model calculator.

software support, microcomputer — Manufacturers are offering sophisticated program preparation tools, extensive resident software, and fully compatible cross software packages for popular minicomputers. Included also are powerful, easy-to-use on-line debug programs to aid in checkout, text editors, assemblers, relocating linking loaders, memory dump programs, monitors and utility routines plus macro processors and language generation packages. They also offer expanding libraries of application subroutines and pertinent documentation.

Program design tends to be more detailed than that for a conventional computer. The basic assumption here is that the microprocessor functions in a stand-alone application and that, as a result, ROMs will be used to store the entire program. This restriction limits the total program unless bank-switching techniques are used. These increase the apparent size of the memory beyond the maximum rating for a microprocessor.

software test set — A comprehensive software set — including a cross-assembler, simulator, and test program generator — supports development of custom programs. Also available is a hardware simulator to verify device design in actual operating conditions prior to release of the ROM pattern to manufacturing.

software tools (microprocessor) — Several types of software tools have been, or are becoming, common in microprocessor software development, such as:
1. Source editors
2. Translators (Assemblers, and more recently, compilers)
3. Loaders and linkage editors
4. Debuggers
5. Simulators

They assist the programmer in various activities in the software development cycle. The end results of the programming effort is a series of bits, machine code that the microcomputer understands, placed at various locations in the computer's memory space. The translation by the programmer of concepts into bits is a complicated job. When such a clerical and complicated burden is placed upon human beings, our inherent fallibility couples with the incredible number of possibilities for errors, to produce what are euphemistically called "bugs."

solar cell — Photoelectric cell using silicon, which collects photons from the sun's radiation and converts the radiant energy into electrical power with reasonable efficiency. Used in spacecrafts and for remote locations lacking power supplies; i.e., for telephone amplifiers in the desert.

solder — A lead and tin alloy that melts at a fairly low temperature. It is used for making electrical connections.

solid — A state of matter in which the motion of the molecules is restricted. They tend to remain in one position, giving rise to a crystal structure. Unlike a liquid or gas, a solid has a definite shape and volume.

solid circuit — 1. A semiconductor network fabricated in one piece of material by alloying, diffusing, doping, etching cutting, and the use of necessary jumper wires. 2. Modification of properties of a material; i.e., silicon, so that components can be realized in one mass (i.e., resistors, transistors, diodes). 3. Subminiature realization of a circuit in three dimensions; e.g., as built up as parts of a semiconductor crystal or by etching or deposition on a substrate.

solid-logic technology (SLT) — 1. Refers to microelectronic circuits that are the products of solid-logic technology and are used as the basic components of the modern computing systems. Called logic circuits because they carry and control the electrical impulses that represent information within a computer, these tiny devices operate at speeds ranging from 300 down to six billionths of a second. Transistors and diodes mounted on the circuits are as small as 28 thousandths of an inch square and are protected by a film of glass 60 millionths of an inch thick. 2. Basic components of solid logic systems. These are so-called because they carry and control the electrical impulses that represent the information within a computer. These extremely small devices operate at speeds between 6 and 300×10-12 sec.

solid state — 1. Refers to various electronic components of solid materials as opposed to vacuum and gas tubes. 2. Pertains to various types of electronic components that convey or control electrons within solid materials. Transistors, germanium diodes, and magnetic cores are solid state components; vacuum and gas tubes and electromechanical relays are not.

solid state design — Refers to solid state components and circuitry of systems that offer numerous advantages including standardized production of components and the reduction of maintenance procedures. In addition to ease of maintenance, solid state circuits also impart a high degree of operating reliability to the calculator and reduce the power, cooling, and space requirements of the system at the same time.

solid-state device — 1. Any element that can control current without moving parts, heated filaments, or vacuum gaps. All semiconductors are solid-state devices, although not all solid-state devices (e.g., transformers) are semiconductors. 2. Relates to the electronic components used to convey or control electrons within solid materials, e.g., transistors, germanium diodes, and magnetic cores. Thus, vacuum and gas tubes are not included.

solid-state memory — Some series of micro- and minicomputer families are completely designed for solid-state memory. Semiconductor technology has now matured beyond the capabilities of traditional core memory, and many have integrated this new technology into computer systems of all sizes providing the system's used with large amounts of high reliable, economic mainframe memory. Metal-Oxide Semiconductor (MOS) memory. provides several advantages to the user that are not available to core memory users. While costs to produce core memory have stabilized, rapid advances in the semiconductor industry have continued to provide performance enhancements, increased density and price roll-offs. The consequence of these technological advances for the user is an end product which will remain highly competitive in price and performance over a long product life cycle.

solid-state physics — Branch of physics which covers all properties of solid materials, including electrical conduction in crystals of semiconductors and metals, superconductivity and photoconductivity.

sort — 1. To segregate items into groups according to specified criteria. Sorting involves ordering, but need not involve sequencing, for the groups may be arranged in an arbitrary order. 2. To arrange a set of items according to keys which are used as a basis for determining the sequence of the items, e.g., to arrange the records of a personnel file into alphabetical sequence by using the employee names as sort keys.

sort, block — A sort of one or more of the most significant characters of a key to serve as a means of making workable sized groups from a large volume of records to be sorted.

sort, external — The seond phase of a multipass sort program, wherein strings of data are continually merged until one string of sequenced data is formed.

sorting, criteria — 1. A character group usually forming a field, utilized in the identification or location of an item. A marked lever manually operated for copying a character; e.g., typewriter paper-tape perforater, card punch manual keyboard, digitizer or manual word generator. 2. That part of a word, record, file, etc., by which it is identified or controlled. 3. The field by which a file of records is sorted into order; e.g., the key for a file of employee records by a number, department, or letter.

sorting, digital — To sort first the keys on the least significant digit, and then to resort on next higher-order digit until the items are sorted on the most significant digit. A punched card technique.

sorting program — Refers to groups of routines or a specific program which is designed to construct other programs for performing particular types of operations is a generating program, and one of the many types which are generated are programs with procedures and processes for various types of sorts of cards, digits, information, etc. on various keys.

sort, internal — The sequencing of two or more records within the central computer memory; the first phase of a multipass sort program.

SOS — Silicon On Sapphire refers to the layers of material, and indirectly to the process of fabrication of devices which achieve bipolar speeds through MOS technology by insulating the circuit components from each other.

SOS advantages — Among advantages for military applications, SOS provides radiation protection for MSI and LSI devices operating at high speeds on low power. For military applications not requiring radiation protection, such as mobile communications systems, the benefits of low standby power and high noise immunity of CMOS-SOS offset the higher production cost of sapphire versus silicon.

source deck — Stack of program cards ready to insert into compilers of some computers operated by punched cards.

source document — 1. The original paper on which are recorded the details of a transaction. 2. See document, source.

source editors — Source editors are programs which facilitate the entry and modification of the source code into a computer system for later translation, on-line storage, off-line storage, or listing on a printer for later reference. Without a source editor the programmer would have to go through a tedious process of building his program on a unit record physical medium like cards, or through a virtually impossible process using a sequential medium like paper tape. Source editors are best designed when they take into consideration the characteristics of the language being entered and the type of communications terminal used.

source language — 1. The language used to specify computer processing; translated into object language by an assembler or compiler. 2. A compiler language such as FORTRAN from which machine-language instructions are developed by the use of translation routines or compilers. 3. The language in which the input to the FORTRAN processor is written, for example.

source-language debugging — Debugging information is requested by the user and displayed by the system in a form consistent with the source programming language.

source macro definition — In assembler programming, a macro definition included in a source module. A source macro definition can be entered into a program library; it then becomes a library macro definition.

source program — A computer program written in a language designed for ease of expression of a class of problems or procedures, by humans, e.g., symbolic or algebraic. A generator, assembler, translator or compiler routine is used to perform the mechanics of translating the source program into an object program in machine language. (Contrasted with object program.)

source recording — The recording of data in machine-readable documents, such as punched cards, punched paper tape, magnetic tapes, etc. Once in this form, the data may be transmitted, processed, or reused without manual processing.

source edit utility — The source utility facilitates the preparation and modification of symbolic assembly language source tapes. Edit is an interactive program which enables the user to perform the following functions often by way of the teletype: Construct a symbolic source tape: Insert, delete, replace and modify statements in an existing source program, and obtain a new source tape which incorporates the modifications; Obtain a state-numbered listing of the program being edited.

source language translation — The translation of a program to a target program, for example, to FORTRAN, ALGOL, etc., to machine language, the instructions being equivalent in the source program and to the automatic or problem-oriented language as FORTRAN, the translating process being completed by the machine under the control of a translator program or compiler.

source program — 1. A program that can be translated automatically into machine language. It thereby becomes an object program. 2. A computer program written in a language designed for ease of expression of a class of problems or procedures, by humans, e.g., symbolic or algebraic. A generator, assembler, translator or compiler routine is used to perform the mechanics of translating the source program into an object program in machine language.

SPA — Abbreviation for Systems and Procedures Association, an organization of management personnel.

space character — Relates to a special operating and graphic character designed to prevent a print. (SP)

space key, carriage — A specific push button, the depression of which advances the hard copy one or more lines in various type printers.

space suppression — The inhibition of platen

and/or paper movement for a line of printing.
special function keyblock examples — The following plug-in ROM's are available for some type calculator models. Each of these is described more fully in its individual technical data sheet. The Peripheral Control I Block provides general purpose control of most peripherals, and features an especially powerful control of the Plotter and Typewriter. A Mathematics Block provides mathematical functions such as sine, cosine, tangent, log, natural log, and their inverses. A User Definable Functions Block allows users to write their own mathematical functions, defining up to 25 of the left-hand keys, and use them by name. A Peripheral Control II Block provides general purpose control of most peripherals, with special emphasis on direct input/output capability. (some units)
special function keyblocks, simultaneous use — On some units up to three powerful plug-in read-only-memory (ROM) blocks can be used with the calculator at one time. Any plug-in ROM can be placed in any of the three or more slots provided, to assign special functions to the corresponding keyblock.
special function keys — Refers to a basic memory of 256 characters with expandability to 1024 characters that combines with a 32 character display typically for ease of operation. On some systems special function keys are offered for data retrieval and display format. ASCII coded keyboard and 110/300 baud rates and auto-transmit, tape play/record are added features on some units.
special function keys, calculator — There are ten special function keys in the upper-left keyboard area of some models. Each key can have two functions or programs assigned to it for a maximum of twenty. The special function keys can be used effectively in 3 different ways.
1. To represent text where text is used as a typing aid.
2. To represent functions. The functions can be single or multi-line functions and different parameters can be passed to the function from the mainline program or between functions.
3. To represent an entire program.
Programming and editing rules for the special function keys are the same as those for normal programming.
special function keys, redefinable — Some units contain sixteen high-rise finger-molded keys making available thirty-two subroutine identifiers for users own dedicated functions, giving single keystroke operation for user's own programs, calculations, or access to memory. Flexibility is built into these keyboards, since the special functions are not hardwired; they are quickly and easily redefined to relate the day-to-day changes in organization's operation.
special function keys (SFK) — Rockwell International (Unicom) and others have developed special function keys (hence (SFK) that reduce complex calculations to a few simple entries. From these hardwired keys, users can order groups of four or six. The result is a calculator that users virtually design themselves for their own applications. The potential applications are virtually endless. Some of the special function keys are: depreciation, mark-up, amortization, loan payment, power (for integer exponents) per cent change, mean, standard deviation, store in,

store out, etc. The result — complex problems become simple enough for even untrained operators.
specialized polynomial regression program — This program uses the method of least squares to calculate the coefficients of a polynomial equation of the form $Y = CX^A + DX^B$, which best fits a set of data points. (A and B are specified by the user.)
special programs, plug-in ROM's — Optional plug-in ROM's (Read Only Memory) add up to 2,048 more program steps of single keystroke, hard-wired functions on some systems. Low-cost special purpose ROM's are now available for statistics, advanced statistics, formula programming (algebraic), extended alpha listing and surveying. Custom ROM's are also available for many owner's specialized programs. Once a program has been reproduced on custom ROM, it cannot be listed, looked at or printed. This feature gives the user complete privacy and assurance that unauthorized personnel cannot access a listing of programs. Yet with proper instruction, user programs can be run with single keystroke operation. Also available are programmable ROMs i.e. PROMs.
special routine keys, calculators — Some types of molded, high-rise keys give users error-free instant access to up to 32 hard-wired Special Routines and up to 32 of their own programmed routines. Each register or program is clearly labeled with color-coded interchangeable routine strips, on some units.
specific address — An address that indicates the exact storage location where the referenced operand is to be found or stored in the actual machine-code address-numbering system. (Related to absolute code.)
specification — 1. For programming, a precise definition of the records and programs needed to carry out a particular processing function. 2. As an equipment concept, a technical or engineering description of the hardware.
specification file — 1. A file containing copies of all forms used in an activity, files by construction characteristic of the form (tab cards, flat forms, tags, continuous pinfeed). This file is developed specifically for procurement packages. 2. A reference data file containing specifications for data characteristics, report production, file layouts, etc., used in a given applications set.
specification, program — The precise and ordered definitions of logic, and scope of processing functions, that are performed by particular program or program segments.
specification sheet — Document used to describe physical appearance, construction, and special characeristics of an approved form. Used in process internal printing or outside procurement.
specific routine — A routine to solve a particular mathematical, logical, or data-handling problem in which each address refers to explicitly stated registers and locations.
speech synthesis — Scientists at the Naval Research Laboratory have developed a computer program that translates English text into synthetic speech. The program applies a limited set of letter-to-sound rules to individual words, and "sounds" them out the way a child does. Thus, it does not require a separate, dedicated computer system, separate storage for a large data base,

or computer time to break up and attempt to understand sentences. In an average sample of English text, the system pronounces correctly about 95% of the words, and most errors are obvious enough to be detected by the human operator. In some current systems, a commercial speech synthesizer is used.

speed, effective — Speed (less than rated) which can be sustained over a significant period of time and which reflects slowing effects of control codes, timing codes, error detection, retransmission, tabbing, hand keying, etc.

spooling — Refers to a procedure of temporarily storing data on disk or tape files until another aspect of processing is ready for the data (such as printing it).

SPX circuit — Abbreviation for Simplex Circuit.

square root function ($\sqrt{X}$) — Automatically calculates the quantity that, when multiplied by itself, will give the entered quantity. This capability (as with "square" and "reciprocals") is of great value where large and/or complicated numbers are involved.

square root key — Automatically computes the square root of any positive entry or result.

SST key — When one unit is in the "WRITE PROGRAM" mode, this "SINGLE STEP" key lets them step through each program instruction in the program memory, as the display shows a number for each step. This number represents the location (row and column) of the key corresponding to that particular instruction. For example, "34" refers to the key in row 3, column 4 — "RCL." (Exception: digit keys are represented by the numbers 00 to 09.) If the "SST" key is used with this unit the "RUN" mode users can execute a program one step at a time.

stack advantages — A pushdown stack is essentially a Last-in-First-Out (LIFO) buffer. As data are added, the stack moves down, with the last item added taking the top position. Stack height varies with the number of stored items, increasing or decreasing with the entering or retrieving of data. The words "push" (move down) and "pop" (retrieve the most recently stored item) are used to describe its operation. In actual practice, a hardware-implemented pushdown stack is a collection of registers with a counter which serves as a "pointer" to indicate the most recently loaded register. Registers are unloaded in the reverse of the sequence in which they were loaded. The principal benefit of the pushdown stack is an aid to compiling. By reducing the use of registers necessary for temporary storage, stack architecture can greatly decrease the number of steps required in a program, thereby reducing costs.

stack architecture — Many microcomputers have a stack architecture wherein any portion of the external memory can be used as a last-in-first-out stack to store/retrieve the contents of the accumulator, the flags, or any of the data registers. Many units contain a 16-bit stack pointer to control the addressing of this external stack. One of the major advantages of the stack is that multiple level interrupts can easily be handled since complete system status can easily be saved when an interrupt occurs and then be restored after the interrupt. Another major advantage is that almost unlimited subroutine nesting is possible.

stack control — In communications processing queues are an essential part of managing the communications work load. The ability to process stacked service requests and status words is important in conserving processor time.

stacked-job processing — A procedure of automatic job-to-job transitions, with little or no operator intervention.

stacked microcomputers — The first of the several systems was the Hypercube, an array processor now widely imitated. The Hypercube can be configured with from 16 to 256 "processor nodes." Each node has one microcomputer dedicated to system overhead and communications tasks and a second to execute user code. And each node communicates through shared memories with eight adjacent nodes. In contrast to the superscale Illiac IV array processor, which has 64 processors, the Hypercube does not split and distribute a part of a job to each processor; instead, a program remains intact within one processor node.

stack lift enable/disable, hand-held programmables — On some specific units, when users key in a new number after a calculation, the calculated result is automatically lifted in the stack, relieving users of the need to save the result (by pressing ENTER↑)before keying in the number. The same lifting action occurs if users recall a value to X from a storage register, from the Last X register, or if users recall the permanently stored value of π. Users may have observed that certain other operations also enable the Stack Lift while CLX and ENTER↑ disable the lift (after CLX and ENTER↑ are pressed). Users will generally be quite unaware of the lift status because the operation is so natural for most calculations. However, many operations have no effect on the Stack Lift.

stack, microcomputer — Microcomputers frequently have a stack in order to minimize the shortcomings of their smaller instruction sets. The stack is used by some minicomputers for monitoring program branches. It consists of up to 16 registers which provide temporary storage for a sequence of memory addresses. Two stack operations are commonly performed; a push and a pull.

stack pointer — Stack pointers are coordinated with the storing and retrieval of information in the stack. The stack pointer is decremented by one immediately following the storage in the stack of each byte of information. Conversely, the stack pointer is incremented by one immediately before retrieving each byte of information from the stack. The stack pointer may be manipulated for transferring its contents to the index register or vice versa. The address of a location is at the top of the stack.

stack push-down — Refers to a procedure which develops a reserved area of memory into which operands are pushed and from which operands are pulled on a last-in-first-out basis.

stack register — A typical stack register receives the contents of the program counter and aids in developing a multi-level program function. A 16-bit data counter can address up to 65 kilobytes of memory in some systems. More complex systems use expanded memory that can be implemented by using memory interface circuits and a direct memory access circuit (DMA).

stack, right execution (small calculators) — The automatic stack lift and automatic stack drop lets users retain and position intermediate results without reentering the numbers. This is an advantage the stack has over other data handling methods. Almost any problem can be solved by keying in the numbers in left to right order. (some units)

stack rotating, small calculators — The R↓ (roll down) key lets users review the entire stack contents at any time. To see how this key works, load the stack with the numbers 1 through 4 by pressing:

4 ENTER↑ 3 ENTER↑ 2 ENTER↑ 1

If users then press R↓, the stack contents are rotated.

staging — The moving of data from an offline or low-priority device back to an online or higher-priority device, usually on demand of the system or on request of the user. Contrast with data migration.

stand-alone desk-top programmable calculator example — One unit offers a 32-character LED display, 16-character thermal strip printer, and a typewriter-like keyboard. It has a built-in, two-track, tape cartridge drive, three I/O slots, and four ROM slots. The unit can be used as a stand-alone calculator or as a systems controller for industrial and scientific applications. It also offers interrupt; an input speed up to 400k 16 bits/sec; an output speed up to 200k 16 bits/sec; live keyboard; direct memory access; high performance, bidirectional tape drive; and extended internal calculation range ($\pm 10^{511}$ to $\pm 10^{-511}$). The unit uses N-MOS II circuitry (LSI) and will work with many instruments and peripherals, such as line printers printer/plotters, and paper tape punches and readers. (HP 9825A)

stand-alone program — Any program that operates independently of system control, generally, it is either self-loading or loaded by another stand-alone program.

standard deviation — The most widely used measure of dispersion is σ, and it enters into many other measures of statistical development. As a result of the squaring process, greater emphasis is given to extreme deviations than is the case in the mean deviation. The normal curve has been analyzed in terms of standard deviations so that this measure of dispersion can be used to facilitate comparisons or analyses based in the normal distribution.

standard deviation key — The standard deviation (a measure of dispersion around the mean) is calculated using data in the applicable storage registers and the s (standard deviation) key. Pressing fs uses the data in registers R_3 (n), R_6 (Σx^2), and R_7 (Σx) to calculate the standard deviation according to the formula:

$$s_x = \sqrt{\frac{\sum x^2 - \frac{(\Sigma x)^2}{n}}{n - 1}}$$

as used in some units.

standard interface — Refers to that specific form of interface (matching) previously designed or agreed upon so that two or several units, systems, programs, etc. may be easily joined or associated.

standardize — To adjust the exponent and mantissa of a floating-point result so that the mantissa lies in the prescribed normal range. See floating-point representation.

standard language symbols — Special graphic shapes used to represent special meanings or functions that can occur in any computer program.

standard notation (BASIC) — Real numbers written in standard notation are written with all digits displayed. For example, the number 3280000.00 is a real number written in standard notation. Imbedded spaces and commas are not allowed in the standard notation format.

standards, systems — System standards are either of the following: (1) the minimum required electrical performance characteristics of communication circuits that are based on the measured performance of existing developed circuits under the same operating conditions for which the new circuits were designed, (2) the specified characteristics necessary in order to permit interoperation of the system. (For example, the values for center frequencies for telegraph channels, test tone, etc.)

standard working — A specified combination of a transmitting and receiving system, or subscriber's lines and feeding circuits (or equivalent systems), connected by means of a distortionless variable attenuator, and employed under specific conditions to determine, by comparison, the transmission quality of other telephone systems or parts of systems.

standby — 1. Refers to a condition of some equipment which will permit complete resumption of stable operation within a short period of time. 2. A duplicate set of equipment to be used if the primary unit becomes unusable because of malfunction.

standby application — An application in which two or more computers are tied together as part of a single overall system and which, as in the case of an inquiry application, stand ready for immediate activation and appropriate action.

standby power supply — An energy generation or storage system, that can permit equipment to operate temporarily or shut down in an orderly manner.

star program — A handwritten program independently designed by a programmer and checked so that no mistakes or bugs are contained, i.e., the star program should run correctly the first time, excepting machine malfunctions.

start bit — A bit used in asynchronous transmission to precede the first bit of a character transmitted serially, signalling the start of the character.

start (in a start-stop/system) signal — Signal servicing to prepare the receiving mechanism for the reception and registration of a character, or for the control of a function.

start key — The push button on the control panel which initiates or resumes the operations of the equipment after an automatic or programmed stop.

start of heading character — A single or set of characters communicated by a polled terminal, indicating to other stations on the line that the data to follow specify the addresses of stations on the line which are to receive the answering message.

start of message (SOM) — A character or group of characters transmitted by a polled terminal to indicate addresses of stations to receive the message.

start of text character — A specific control character in communications designed to terminate and separate a heading and mark the beginning of the actual text.

start pulse — Used in Baudot teletypewriter codes for a space pulse to be transmitted just ahead of the five bits representing each character as a start element.

start-stop — A transmission method employing coded characters made up of a start bit, several (5 to 8) information bits, and a stop bit. The receiving machine stops after each character and starts again upon receipt of the first bit from the next character (the start bit). Synonymous with asynchronous.

start-stop system — A system in which each group of code elements corresponding to an alphabetical signal is preceded by a start signal which serves to prepare the receiving mechanism for the reception and registration of a character, and is followed by a stop signal which serves to bring the receiving mechanism to rest in preparation for the reception of the next character.

start time — The time between the interpretation of instructions to read or write on tape and the transfer of information to or from the tape into storage, or from storage into tape, as the case may be.

start time read — The determination or measurement of the elapsed time at the beginning of a card-read cycle before actual card reading begins.

state — A computing term relating to the condition of all the units or elements of the system, i.e., the storage data, digits in registers, settings on switches, etc., including the question, what is their state?

state, active — The state of an interrupt level that is the result of the central processor starting to process an interrupt condition.

state, armed — The state of an interrupt level wherein it can accept and remember an interrupt input signal.

state, disarmed — The state of an interrupt level that cannot accept an interrupt input signal.

state, major — Usually refers to the control state of a computer. Major control states in some systems include fetch, defer, execute, etc.

statement — In computer programming, a meaningful expression or generalized instruction in a source language.

statement number — A number that is associated with a single macrostatement so that the reference may be made to that statement in terms of its number.

statements, control — 1. Statements which are used to direct the flow of the program, either causing specific transfers or making transfers dependent upon meeting certain specified conditions. 2. Instructions which convey control information to the processor, but do not develop machine-language instructions, i.e., symbolic statements.

statements, debugging — The debugging statements are often part of the operating statements and provide a variety of methods for manipulating the program itself in an attempt to identify program errors ("bugs"). The user may: 1. insert or delete statements; 2. execute selectivity; 3. print changes of values as the change occurs and transfer control as the transfer occurs; 4. obtain a static printout of all cross-reference relationships among names and labels, and dynamic exposure of partial or imperfect execution.

static — 1. Non-movable or non-rotating, e.g., a transformer or rectifier is a static converter. 2. Electrostatic. 3. Said of all electrical disturbances to a radio system which arise through electrostatic induction, particularly from lightning flashes.

static characteristic — Curve, or set of curves, which describes relation between specified voltages and currents of electrodes under unvarying conditions, as compared with dynamic characteristic, which implies operation under normal load conditions.

static dump — A dump that is performed at a particular point in time with respect to a machine run, frequently at the end of a run.

static errors — Specific errors independent of the time variable, as contrasted with dynamic error which depends on frequency, i.e., inadequacy of the dynamic response of a computing unit.

static 4K RAM — New designs have cut memory access time significantly. One firm has a static 4k memory that features an access time of 150 nanoseconds. The static design of the device means that it will be easier to use, mainly because no clock signals will be needed to refresh stored data. Because it is static, the memory requires less power than their dynamic equivalent.

static memory — Refers to a memory device that contains no mechanical moving parts. Also a memory device that contains fixed information.

static RAM — Data is stored in a conventional bistable flip-flop and need not be refreshed.

static storage — Storage or information that is fixed, e.g., flip-flop, electro-static, etc.

static subroutine — A subroutine which involves no parameters other than the addresses of the operands.

statistic — A statistic is usually considered to be a numerical property of a sample in contrast to a parameter, which is defined as a numerical property of a distribution, i.e., a population, or universe.

statistical analysis — One of the four main techniques of operations research. Data gathering, arranging, sorting, sequencing, and evaluating are all common statistical analyses. Statistical analysis combines mathematical techniques and computer technology to handle a wide range of business and scientific problems wherever large amounts of information or data must be evaluated and analyzed.

statistical calculator — One type programmable calculator is designed for statistical calculator applications. The desk-top unit combines algebraic and hard-wired keyboard functions with powerful programming commands. High-speed printed output is provided along with complete input-output peripheral capability which makes possible the use of a wide range of peripheral devices. Program and data storage memories are expandable; a complete repertorie of computer-like programming instructions is provided: unconditional and conditional branching, jumping, looping, subroutines. Data may be stored and recalled under program control, checking and debugging procedures speed up program verification. No special language is required to program.

statistical calculator programs, examples — Various pre-wired programs include: Mean, Variance, Standard Deviation; Histogram, Median, Moving Average, Arithmetic, Geometric and Harmonic Means; Partial Correlation; Binomial, Hypergeometric, Poisson, Multinomial distributions; CHI-square, Beta and t Tests, etc.

statistical capability examples — Summations:

statistical data recorder

The "Σ +" key automatically calculates n, Σ x, Σ x², Σ y, Σ xy for statistical and vector calculations. Data may be deleted via the "Σ −" key. Mean and standard deviations: most units also calculate the mean and standard deviation of a group of data.

statistical data recorder — Under Disc Operating System (DOS) a feature that records the cumulative error status of an I/O device on the system recorder file. Abbreviated SDR.

statistical error — Refers to that arising in measurements of average count rate for random events, as a result of statistical fluctuations in the rate.

statistical expression — To make statistical analysis easy, some technical calculators feature keys that provide a running total when adding numbers; compute the sum of the squares of all entries; calculate the arithmetic mean and standard deviation; and perform averaging and vector addition and subtraction.

statistical hypothesis — In statistical analysis, a hypothesis usually takes the form of some assumption about the frequency distribution of observations whose numerical values depend upon chance.

statistical means and moments 1, 2 — The calculator solves the arithmetic, geometric, harmonic, and generalized means, the first four moments and the kurtosis and skewness of distribution are calculated for grouped or ungrouped data.

statistical method — Statistical method is designed as a technique used to obtain, analyze and present numerical data. The elements of statistical technique include: 1. the collection and assembling of data; 2. classification and condensation of data; 3. presentation of data in a textular, tabular, and graphic form; and 4. analysis of data. When data are grouped according to magnitude, the resulting series is called a frequency distribution; when grouped as to time of occurrence, it is called a time series; when grouped by geographic location, it is called spatial distribution. In addition, there are a number of special types of distributions in which the data may be arranged by kind or by degree.

statistical mistakes — Various types of mistakes to be avoided are:
1. Concealed change in the statistical unit — For example, the value of the dollar changes over time.
2. Misuse of percentages — For example, if 12 drops to 3, this is not a 300% drop because nothing can drop more than 100%. It is a drop of 75%.
3. Spurious accuracy — When working with data which are themselves approximate figures, do not carry calculations based on those figures to an excessive number of decimal places, but confine the expression of the result to the significant figures, determined with reference to the accuracy of the original data.

Other pitfalls to watch for are: (a) deductive inconsistencies; (b) emotional or dual terminology; (c) fallacy of composition; (d) bias, slants, unsystematic errors; (e) incomplete theory; (f) "missing" variables; (g) aggregation of dissimilar units; (h) improper sample.

statistical sample — A statistical sample usually relates to a small portion of the entire universe which is drawn in such a way that every value in the universe has an equal chance of being included. A sample must be representative of the universe, and the principle of the random sample is that representativeness will result from the operation of chance in the selection of the values.

statistical universe — A statistical universe (or statistical population) is a complete group of things or phenomena which are similar in certain stated respects. For example, the heights of white native-born males between the ages of 21 and 65 constitute a universe of heights similar in that they all belong to a stated class of individuals (i.e., white, native-born males).

statistics, analytical — The design and use of analytical statistics is to enable one to draw statistical inferences about the characteristics of the entire statistical "universe" of data from a small sample.

statistics, basic calculator system — The Basic Stat System: A printing desk-top system that does the following calculations.
  Linear Curve Fit
  Parabolic Curve Fit
  Mean
  Standard Deviation
  Correlation Coefficient
  Histogram
  t for paired & unpaired data

Some Basic Stat Systems add a plotter and plotter interface making the units compatible with other equipment. Some systems can handle Linear and Parabolic Curve Fit and Histograms. They draw axes as well. Some Expanded Stat systems add calculations of power, exponential and logarithmic curve fit as well as one-way analysis of variance.

statistics, Bayesian — This branch of statistics concerns estimates of (prior) probability distributions, as subsequently revised (posterior distribution) in order to incorporate new data by means of Bayes' equation. Often used in medical diagnostic programs as an alternative to analytical, sequential, or programmed diagnostic procedures.

statistics calculator, basic — One type system includes:
- printer
- built-in stat keys to calculate:
  - mean, standard deviation of single data array.
  - means, standard deviations, correlation coefficient of 2-variable array.
  - best fit straight line of the form $y = A + Bx$.
  - best fit parabola of the form $y = A + Bx + Cx^2$.
  - ten cell histogram including frequency and relative percent frequency.
  - students t for both grouped and ungrouped data.

statistics function keyblock — If a major portion of a user's work is in statistics he can add the Statistics Function Keyblock to some calculators and have powerful statistical computations, commanded by a single keystroke. Computations such as χ^2; t; linear, multi-linear, and parabolic regressions; random number generation; accumulation of sums, sums of products, and sums of squares for up to five variables; maximum/minimum search are all solved instantly as users merely enter the data, press the appropriate key, and the answer is displayed. In addition, erroneous data can be removed by the use of the exclusive CORRECT key. There is no programming or addressing required for these functions. A separate (ROM) memory block is dedicated to special statistics functions so they do not draw upon the main calculator programming memory — leaving it fully available for further problem solving needs.

statistics programs, elementary — Examples are:
- Histogram
- Cross Tabulation
- Transformation, alters columns in matrices
- Tally
- Moment
- Correlation
- t-Test
- Chi-square Test
- Survival Rate
- Probit Analysis

status and condition flags — Internal status bits are provided in most systems to designate a particular internal interrupt condition. Typically when any of the internal status bits is a 1-bit, the internal interrupt flag in file register 0 is also a 1-bit. This flag is tested by the microprogram to detect the presence of the internal interrupt condition. The internal status bits are entered via the B-bus into the selected file register by a control command, at which time the status bits are cleared. The assignments for internal status bits can be: console interrupt, DMA termination, real time clock interrupt, console step switch, power/fail restart interrupt, others.

status maps — A status report of programs and I/O operations, usually in tabular form.

status register — In some units for interfacing this 8-bit register holds information on communication errors, interface data register status, match character conditions, and communication equipment status. This register may be read onto the DAL lines by a read operation.

status word — 1. These words either indicate something about the status of the system or indicate that the system is making response to, or diagnosis of, a statement that has been entered. The majority of status words are responses to program-debugging statements and are described under the corresponding debugging statement. 2. The status word contains control information generated by the peripheral control unit and the channel synchronizer. The status word is transmitted to the central processor over the data lines.

status word CANCL — This status word indicates that the remote computing system has deleted some information.

status word ERROR — This word indicates that the remote computing system has detected an error.

status word READY — This status word indicates that the remote computing system is waiting for a statement entry from the terminal.

STD — Standard.

steady state — A stabilized condition in which the output has lined, leveled out, or reached a constant rate of change for a constant input.

step — 1. One instruction in a computer routine. 2. To cause a computer to execute one instruction.

step-by-step system — A type of line-switching system which uses step-by-step switches.

step change — The change from one value to another in a single increment and in negligible time.

STEP and LIST keys — On some units STEP and LIST keys are used for debugging and program documentation. Editing is also available in these units. The register arithmetic keys help eliminate keystrokes in the program and are useful in statistical applications. Indirect addressing of data registers is possible in the simplest manner and shortens the number of program steps users need to do successive operations on a number of pieces of data.

step counter — Refers to a counter used in the arithmetical unit to count the steps in multiplication, division, and shift operation.

stochastic — Refers to any system operation in which an element of chance cannot be excluded.

stochastic noise — Refers to that which maintains a statistically random distribution.

stochastic problem-solving, calculator — An example of this programming is: A common problem of many disciplines is the solution of irreducible equations such as $x = 5 \ln x$. Finding the answer requires clever first guesses at the solution and, based on the results of the first guess, an even more clever second guess, etc. The iterative procedure, tedious if done manually, can often be automated with calculator procedures.

stochastic programming — A generalization of linear programming in which any of the unit costs, the coefficients in the constraint equations, and the right hand sides are random variables subject to known distributions. The aim of such programming is to choose levels for the variables which will minimize the expected (rather than the actual) cost.

stochastic simulation — Properties of the representation rather than of the system itself. The introduction of random variables as essential elements of the model provides the basis for the label "stochastic" or "probabilistic". Example: a model of an inventory system in which the timing or quantity of demands for items and/or replenishment lead times are randomly distributed is stochastic. If these and other elements are taken as determined (not necessarily constant), the model is deterministic.

stochastic variable — A particular statistical variable which has a probability with which it may assume each of many possible values in a distinct set.

stop, automatic — An automatic halting of a calculator-processing operation as the result of an error detected by built-in checking devices.

stop bit — Refers to the last element of a character designed for asynchronous serial that defines the character space immediately to the left of the most significant character in accumulator storage.

stop, form — The automatic device on a printer which stops the machine when paper has run out.

stop instruction — A machine operation or routine that requires manual action other than the use of the start key to continue processing.

stop key — A push button on the control panel which can halt the processing. This often happens only after the completion of an instruction being executed at a given moment.

stop loop — A small closed loop usually designed and used for operator convenience, i.e., to indicate an error, improper use, or special result.

storage — 1. The act of storing information (also see store). 2. Sometimes called a memory. Any device in which information can be stored. 3. A calculator section used primarily for storing information in electrostatic, ferroelectric, magnetic, acoustic, optical, chemical, electronic, electrical, mechanical, etc., form. Such a section is sometimes called a memory, or a store, in British terminology. 4. Pertaining to a device into which data

storage allocation can be entered, in which they can be held, and from which they can be retrieved at a later time.

storage allocation — Executive program control of internal (main memory) and external (e.g., disk or drum) storage devices may range from helping the programmer map the contents of memory, to complicated dynamic storage allocation in a multi-processing system.

storage area, temporary — A specific area of memory which has been set aside for data which is in process of intermediate states of computation, i.e., in the CPU, such storage is often called, "scratchpad" memory.

storage, audio-cassette interface — One big-selling module allows users to connect microcomputers to any tape recorder (medium quality cassette is adequate) for inexpensive mass storage. It works by modulating (changing) digital signals from the computer to audio signals for recording data and by demodulating the audio signal for playback. Consists of a special modem board "piggy-backed" on an SIOB board.

storage, auxiliary — A storage device in addition to the main storage of a computer, e.g., magnetic tape, disk or magnetic drum. Auxiliary storage usually holds much larger amounts of information than the main storage, and the information is accessible less rapidly.

storage capacity — Also called memory capacity. The amount of information that can be retained in a storage (memory) device. It is often expressed as the number of words (given the number of digits and the base of the standard word).

storage, cartridge — Alternative to Philips cassette designed for digital applications. Data rate and capacity are typically five times the figure for cassettes, with much greater reliability.

storage, cassette — Cassettes provide the least expensive means of storage, several million bits capacity per cassette, with 10-kilobits/data rate. Most popular are upgraded versions of Philips cassette. Quality is highly variable, depending on the manufacturer.

storage, cathode ray tube — Refers to the (usually) electrostatic storage characteristics of cathode ray tubes in which the electron beam is used to sense the data.

storage cell — Refers to an elementary unit of storage, for example, a binary cell, a decimal cell.

storage, CRT — 1. Often this relates to the electrostatic storage characteristics of cathode-ray tubes in which the electron beam is used to sense the data. 2. The storage of data on a dielectric surface, such as the screen of a cathode-ray tube, in the form of the presence or absence of spots bearing electrostatic charges; these spots can persist for a short time after the removal of the electrostatic charging force. 3. A storage device used as in the foregoing description.

storage cycle — 1. Refers to a periodic sequence of events occurring when information is transferred to or from the storage device of a calculator. 2. Storing, sensing, and regeneration form parts of the storage sequence.

storage cycle time — Refers to the time required in milliseconds, microseconds, nanoseconds, etc. for a storage cycle.

storage, dedicated — The allocated, reserved or obligated, set aside, earmarked or assigned areas of storage which are committed to some specific purpose, user, or problem, i.e., exclusively reserved space on a disc storage unit for accounting procedure, problem or data set.

storage, direct-access — A type of storage device wherein access to the next position from which information is to be obtained is in no way dependent on the position from which information was previously obtained.

storage, disk cartridge — For economical mass storage, some disk cartridge systems can provide 1.6 million words of high density memory per disk drive. Generally each controller can support four disk drives. A fully expanded system can offer over 6 million words of storage. Drives have a typical access time of 50 milliseconds (average random move) and can transfer a 12-bit word in 8.32 microseconds.

storage dumping — A procedure or process designed to transfer data from one particular storage device to another or from one particular area to another.

storage, dynamic — Refers to mobility of stored data in time and space. Acoustic delay lines, in which stored data are constantly in motion relative to storage medium and require continuous regeneration, are an example of a dynamic storage device. Magnetic-core storage, in which the stored data are fixed in time and space, is an example of a static storage device.

storage element — One unit in a memory, capable of retaining one bit of information. Also the smallest area of the surface of a charge storage tube which retains information different from that of neighboring areas.

storage exchange — 1. The interchange of the total contents of two storage devices or locations, such as two registers. 2. A switching device capable of controlling and handling the flow or exchange of data between storage units or other elements of a system.

storage fill — The storing of characters in storage areas not used for data storage or the program for a particular machine run.

storage, floppy disc — "Floppies" were originally developed for low cost, low capacity data storage, and relatively low data transfer rates. Storage capacities are around a million bits with access time of several hundred milliseconds. Early floppy discs had sliding contact between head and disc during read; versions are now available with "flying head" characteristics.

storage inquiry, direct access — A process through which information can be directly requested from temporary or permanent storage devices.

storage interference — In a system with shared storage, the referencing of the same block of storage by two or more processing units.

storage, intermediate — A kind of an electronic scratchpad. As input is turned into output, it usually goes through a series of changes. An intermediate memory storage holds each of the successive changes just as long as it is needed. It can hold data picked up or developed in one program cycle for use in succeeding program cycles. It can accumulate data from cycle to cycle.

storage key — Refers to a special set of bits designed to be associated with every word or character in some block of storage, which allows tasks having a matching set of protection key bits to use that block of storage.

storage light — The light on a control console

storage list, uncommitted

panel which indicates that a parity check error has occurred on a character as it was read into storage.

storage list, uncommitted — Blocks of storage that are chained together which are not allocated at any specific moment.

storage location, temporary — Refers to a specific area of memory which has been set aside for data which is in process of intermediate states of computation, i.e., in the CPU, such storage is often called "scratch-pad" memory.

storage, magnetic core — Often refers to main storage or a storage device in which binary data are represented by the direction of magnetization in each unit of an array of magnetic material, usually in the shape of toroidal rings, but also in other forms such as wraps on bobbins. Synonymous with core storage.

storage, main — Usually the fastest storage device of a computer and the one from which instructions are executed.

storage, mass — Mass storage devices are the means of collecting, organizing and retrieving large volumes of data. Many manufacturers offer small mass storage devices tailored to a customer's needs. One dual cassette magnetic tape drive provides a total of 180,000 characters of one-line storage at low cost. Where higher capacity and speed are required, a dual floppy disk drive might be the appropriate device. It uses diskettes for low-cost random access mass memory. Some disks are capable of storing up to 128K 12-bit words; or 256K 8-bit bytes in IBM compatible format. They consist of one or two drives, a single drive electronics module, a microprogrammed controller and a power supply, enclosed in a rack-mountable chassis.

storage medium — The material on which data is recorded and which may be paper tape, cards, magnetic tape, strips, cards, or devices such as magnetic drums, etc.

storage, nondestructive — A type of storage whose location is regenerated after it is read, since it is desired and designed into the unit that the contents are to be retained at the location after reading. Drums, double cores, punched cards, most magnetic tapes, disks, etc., are examples of nondestructive storage.

storage, nonvolatile — Storage media that retains information in the absence of power and which may be made available upon restoration of power, e.g., magnetic tapes, drums, or cores.

storage, parallel — The storage of data in which all bits, characters, or especially words are essentially equally available in space, without time being one of the factors. When words are in parallel, the storage is said to be parallel by words, when characters within words, or binary digits within words or characters, are dealt with simultaneously, not one after the other, the storage is parallel by characters, or parallel by bit respectively.

storage, permanent dynamic — Storage in which the maintenance of data does not depend on a flow of energy such as magnetic disk, drum, etc.

storage protect — This hardware function provides positive protection to the system executive routine and all other programs. It not only protects against processor execution, but also against I/O (input/output) data area destruction. Because it is a hardware function rather than software, it reduces multiprogramming complexities.

storage, push-down — A storage which works as though it comprised a number of registers arranged in a column, with only the register at the top of the column connected to the rest of the storage. Each word in turn, enters the top register and is then "pushed down" the column from register to register to make room for the next words to arrive. As the words are transferred out of the storage units (out of the top register), other data in storage moves back up the column from register to register to fill the top register.

storage, push-up — Special storage which operates so as to maintain a pushdown list so that the next item of data to be retrieved is the oldest item on the list, i.e., it is pushed up in a type of queue arrangement wherein the word at the top came from the bottom in steps and has been in the longest and will go out first.

storage register — A register, is used for storing numbers. Unlike the memory register, no addition or subtraction in this register is possible. It is a place to put a number until needed later in the calculations. For example, when utilizing a constant, that number is placed into storage and recalled at the point in calculating when it is needed.

storage register arithmetic, small calculators — In some units, arithmetic operations can be performed using the number in the displayed X-register and a number in storage registers R_0 thru R_9. In storage register arithmetic, answers are placed in the storage register.

storage registers, associative — Same as associative storage. Those registers which are not identified by their name or position but which are known and addressed by the content.

storage registers, small calculators — In addition to automatic storage of intermediate results that is provided by the four-register automatic memory stack, some units also have eight or more addressable storage registers that are unaffected by operations within the stack. These storage registers allow users to set aside numbers as constants or for use in later calculations, and they can be used either manually or as part of a program.

storage, scratchpad — High-speed memory device used to store the location of an interrupted program and to retrieve the latter after the interrupting program has been completed.

storage, sequential access — A storage technique in which the items of information stored become available only in a one-after-the-other sequence, whether or not all the information or only some of it is desired, e.g., magnetic tape storage. Related to storage, serial and contrasted with storage, random access.

storage stack — A group of storage elements connected together in some fashion, i.e., a stack of data could be operated on a first-in, first-out basis.

storage, static — Storage of information that is fixed in space and available at any time, e.g., flip-flop, electrostatic, or coincident-current magnetic-core storage.

storage types, nesting — As data is transferred into storage, each word in turn enters the top register and is then "pushed down" the column from register to register to make room for the subsequent words as they are assigned. When a word is transferred out of the storage, again only from the top register, other data in the storage moves back up the column from register to register to fill the space left empty. This is accomplished either through programs or the equipment itself.

store — 1. To transfer an element of information to a device from which the unaltered information can be obtained at a later time. 2. To retain data in a device from which it can be obtained at a later time. 3. The British term for storage. 4. To put in storage. 5. To place information in a location in storage so that it may be retrieved for later use.

store and forward — Refers to communication systems in which messages are received at intermediate routing points and recorded (stored). They are then retransmitted to a further routing point or to the ultimate recipient.

store-and-forward message switching — A facility for accepting messages as rapidly as they are received from originating terminals, storing the messages, and sending the messages to destination terminals when communication channels are available.

store-and-forward switching center — A message-switching center in which the message is accepted from the sender whenever he offers it, held in a physical store, and forwarded to the receiver whenever he is able to accept it.

stored program — A set of instructions in the computer memory specifying the operations to be performed and the location of the data on which these operations are to be performed.

stored program calculator — A machine in which the instructions which specify the operations to be performed are stored in the form of coded information in main memory, along with the data currently being operated upon, making possible simple repetition of operations and the modification by the calculator of its own instructions.

stored program numerical control — A control system possessing an internal memory structure. Once programmed, the internal memory can be altered by receiving new instructions or parameters. The physical configuration of the system is not altered or affected by virtue of reprogramming.

store memory key — Automatically stores an entry or result in an independent memory.

storing and recalling data, hand-held programmables — To store a number appearing in the display (whether the result of a calculation or keystroke entry), on some systems:
1. Press STO.
2. Press a number key 1 through 9 to specify in which of the nine registers the number is to be stored.

If the selected storage register already has a number in it, the old number will be overwritten by the new one. The value in X will remain unchanged. To recall a number previously stored in one of the nine addressable memory registers; on the same system:
1. Press RCL.
2. Press a number key (1 through 9) to specify which of the nine registers the number is to be recalled from.

Recalling a number does not remove it from the storage register. Rather, a copy of the stored number is transferred to the display — the original remains in the storage register until either: (1) a new number is stored in the same register, (2) the calculator is turned off, or (3) all nine registers are cleared by pressing.

storing and recalling numbers, non-stack — Although the stack automatically holds intermediate results in some units occasionally users will find the need to set aside some number or group of numbers to be used in calculations much later. For this purpose, some units provide users with 20 or more storage locations in addition to the stack.

straight line code — Refers to repetition of a sequence of instructions, with or without address modification, by explicitly writing the instructions for each repetition. Generally straight line coding will require less execution time and more space than equivalent loop coding. If the number of repetitions is large, this type of coding is tedious unless a generator is used. The feasibility of straight line coding is limited by the space required as well as the difficulty of coding a variable number of repetitions.

stress analysis program pack — Various programs to aid the engineer with vector statics, section properties, fatigue, interference fits, Mohr circle, flat plates, beams and columns, and pressure vessels.

STRESS (structural engineering systems solver) — A language useful for structural-analysis problems in civil engineering. For design applications, larger problems, and more sophisticated modeling and analysis, this language has been replaced with STRUDL. Implemented on several computers, primarily small.

string — 1. In a list of items, a group of items that are already in sequence according to a rule. 2. A set of records which is in ascending or descending sequence according to a key contained in the records.

string block ROM — If a String ROM block is present in a calculator, alphanumeric strings of characters can also be stored in the mass memory. The maximum string size on some units is 255 characters. Strings and numeric items of any precision can be stored in mass memory files in any order.

string expressions — Refers to either numeric expressions or string expressions. A collection of variables, constants, and functions connected by operators in such a way that the expression as a whole can be reduced to a constant.

string file — Tape, wire, or string used to arrange documents for convenient reference and use.

string function (STR) — Some versions of BASIC provide a function which permits the user to extract, examine, compare or replace a specified portion of an alphanumeric string variable. The STR function operates on alphanumeric string variables, and can be used in any BASIC statement where alphanumeric variables are permissible.

string manipulation — Refers to a procedure designed for manipulating groups of contiguous characters.

strings output, calculator ROM — Strings may be output in a manner similar to numerical output using the DISP, PRINT, and WRITE statements, on some units.

string variable, calculator ROM — String Vari-

string variables applications, calculator ROM able ROM, provides some Model Calculators with the ability to accept and manipulate alphabetic, as well as numerical information. The typical ROM expands the language of these Models to include string variables without sacrificing any of the Special Function Keys or read/write memory. The new commands provided by the Strings ROM are of three main types — input, manipulation, and output.

string variables applications, calculator ROM — The use of string variables makes a program truly conversational by allowing the user to input alpha and numeric information. In addition, programs are no longer restricted to purely numerical manipulation. As a result, string variables greatly amplify the operation of most programs. The use of names, department or other alpha codes, keywords, and titles is particularly important in such applications as payroll, inventory control, engineering design, and surveying.

string variables, calculator — On one type calculator there are 26 string variables, denoted by A$, B$, ..., Z$. The user specifies the maximum size of each string variable (up to 255 characters, each) by including it in a DIM or COM statement. For purposes of input, output, and manipulation the user may reference all or any part of a string currently assigned to a string variable. To reference a part of a string, called a substring, it is only necessary to follow the string name with two parameters which specify the first and last characters of the string that are to be used. If only one parameter is given the other is assumed to be the last character in the string. For example,

A$ = SCALE AT 6.25%
A$(3,5) = ALE   A$(7) = AT 6.25%

The parameters may be expressions.

stripe recording, magnetic — Refers to magnetic recording, as the magnetic material is deposited in stripe form on a document or card, the term magnetic stripe recording is most often used.

structural engineering program package — The package consists of 12-programs. The programs included in this package are:
  Rigid Frame Analysis (7 Story, 5 Bays)
  Frame Analysis (1 Story, 8 Bays)
  Beam Analysis — Continuous Prismatic
  Wind Analysis by Cantilever Method
  Beam Analysis — Simple
  Section Properties — Concrete
  Section Properties — Steel and Aluminum
  Steel Beam Design
  Steel Column Design
  Rectangular Concrete Beam Design
  Rectangular Concrete Columns
  Retaining Wall Design

structure — 1. The organization of data within a record or file. 2. A program-defined hierarchichal ordering of data for a record. Elements within a structure may be formatted differently from each other, whereas elements in an array must all have the same format.

structure tables — These tables allow complex decision logic to be represented in tabular form. They are easy to prepare, read, and teach to others. Structure tables solved automatically offer levels of accuracy unequalled in manual systems — first, because structure table errors are reported in the same language in which the table was written and therefore can be corrected at that level; and second, the inherent accuracy of the computer lends its full power to the solution of the structure tables.

stylus, light (pen) — When this pen-like device is pointed at information displayed on the screen, it detects light from the cathode-ray tube when a beam passes within its field of view. The pen's response is transmitted to the computer which relates the computer's action to the section of the image being displayed. In this way, the operator can delete or add text, maintain tighter control over the program, and choose alternative courses of action.

subaddress — A portion of an input/output device that is accessible through an order code. For disk storage units, the module number is the subaddress.

suboptimization — The process of fulfilling or optimizing some chosen objective that is an integral part of a broader objective. Usually the broad-level objective and lower-level objective are different.

subroutine — 1. In computer technology, the portion of a routine that causes a computer to carry out a well-defined mathematical or logical operation. 2. Usually called a closed subroutine. One to which control may be transferred from a master routine, and returned to the master routine at the conclusion of the subroutine. 3. Refers to either part of a master program or routine that may be 'jumped' or 'branched' to or to an independent program in itself but usually of smaller size or importance. 4. A subroutine is a series of computer instructions to perform a specific task for many other routines. It is distinguishable from a main routine in that it requires as one of its parameters, a location specifying where to return to the main program after its function has been accomplished.

subroutine calls — The linkage between a call to a subroutine and the actual entry to the subroutine is made in a manner similar to future patching. All calls to a particular subroutine are linked in the same way. When a call to a subroutine is indicated to the loader, the address where it was last called and the name of the subroutine are entered in a subroutine call table (SCT). A subroutine should not be loaded twice, therefore a check is made to determine if it has been previously called or loaded. If a subroutine is called which is already in the table, the first call in the new program is linked to the last call specified in the new subroutine call record. When a subroutine is loaded, its name and entry address are entered in the SCT and any previous calls are patched and directed to the subroutine entry point with use of the link-back process.

subroutine, dating — A specific subroutine which computes and stores associated dates and times and is programmed for file updating relating to work with computer runs of various types, but usually time-sensitive.

subroutine, dynamic — A subroutine which involves parameters, such as decimal point position or item size, from which a relatively coded subroutine is derived. The computer itself is expected to adjust or generate the subroutine according to the parametric values chosen.

subroutine, first-order — This subroutine is entered directly from the main routine or program and subsequently returned to it.

subroutine, generalized — Subroutines that are written for easy and ready use in various programs with only minor adjustments by the programmer.

subroutine, inserted — 1. A separately coded sequence of instructions that is inserted in another instruction sequence directly in low order of the line. 2. A directly inserted subroutine to the main line program specifically where it is required. 3. A subroutine that must be relocated and inserted into the main routine at each place it is used.

subroutine, keyboard calling — A subroutine is a type of mini-program, useful whenever a task is repeatedly used in the same program. That same subroutine could also be put to use in a variety of subprograms — but it will stand alone. In some calculators, subroutines can be called from the keyboard in addition to their normal program execution. This keyboard calling makes it easier to write conveniently used modular programs. This type of program construction permits fast changes in configuration. Consequently, debugging is also simplified. For future reference any subroutine, no matter what its function, is easily stored on a magnetic tape.

subroutines, calculator — Users label subroutines symbolically. The calculator knows where to find them. And it will get the subroutine, execute and automatically remember the return address. Return addresses can be sequentially stored and recalled to permit nesting of subroutines, or can be used to compute a new starting point.

subroutine library — Refers to a set of standard and proven subroutines which is kept on file for use at any time.

subroutine package, floating point — Typical software floating point arithmetic and conversion subroutines include: decimal to floating point conversion, floating point to decimal conversion, floating point addition, floating point subtraction, floating point multiplication, floating point division, floating move, fixed to floating conversion and floating to fixed conversion.

subroutine, relocatable — A subroutine that can be located physically and independently in the memory. Its object-time location is determined by the processor.

subroutine, second removal — A subroutine which on a specific occasion is entered from a first remove subroutine is on particular occasions called a second remove subroutine, whereas, the first remove subroutine is entered directly from a program and returns to it.

subroutines, mathematical — These subroutines provide complete sets of mathematical subroutines including sine, cosine, sq. root, exponent, log, etc.

subroutines, microprogram — The use of subroutines in computer programming is well known and well understood. Frequently many microinstructions can be saved by using subroutines and using sections of microcode as subroutines in many different programs. If this is to be done, a provision must be made for storing and restoring the current address for the ROM. Many techniques for accomplishing this are known. In many microprogrammed systems this will be accomplished by placing the output from the address register onto one of the data buses where it can be stored in a register. This temporary storage register can then become one of the address sources for setting the ROM program counter.

subroutines, nest of — The process of sublevels for subroutines, wherein one subroutine will transfer control to another subroutine and so on with ultimate control climbing back through the array of subroutines to the subroutine which first transferred control.

subroutines, scientific — Several subroutines that perform standard mathematical operations are available in calculator systems. These operations include fixed-point multiplication and division; floating-point addition, subtraction, multiplication, and division; square-root extraction; matrix and statistical functions; and calculation of logarithmic and trigonometric functions.

subroutine, static — Refers to a subroutine which involves no parameters other than the addresses of the operands.

subroutine status table — Refers to the program or routine used to maintain a list of subroutines in memory and to get subroutines from a file as needed.

subroutine, symbolic label — Symbolically labeling a subroutine allows users to call a subroutine by its name rather than by its location in memory. The calculator will remember the subroutine location. All users have to do is tell the calculator which subroutine they want. The calculator finds the subroutine, executes it and automatically returns. In order to return to the proper point in the program after branching to a subroutine, the calculator automatically remembers the return address. This return address may be sequentially stored and recalled to permit nesting of subroutines, or modified to alter the return address.

subscribed array variables — An array variable followed by one or two subscripts, as in $A(9)$, $B3(1,2)$, and $Z(N)$. The subscripts refer to a specific element within the array.

subscriber station — The service provided by the common carrier to connect a customer's location to a central office. This always includes the circuit and some circuit-termination equipment, but may also include input/output equipment. Sometimes referred to as local shop.

subscript — 1. Integer numerals or symbols attached to a quantity to indicate its location in an array such as a matrix below a set name to identify a particular element or elements of that set. 2. An indexing notation, elements of that set.

subscripted variable — A variable that is followed by one or more subscripts enclosed in parentheses; used to store and refer to a large number (array) of items by a single name and a number specifying the specific element within the array, e.g. "X"(22)" refers to the twenty-second member of the array called "X."

subsegment — 1. A segment of a program is defined as that portion of memory which is committed by a single reference to the loader. Usually a segment overlays some other segment and may have within itself other portions which in turn overlay one another, i.e., subsegments. 2. That part of a segment which is actually brought into memory when the loader is referenced is called the fixed part of a segment. Segments are built up from separate relocatable elements, common blocks, or other segments.

subsegment tables — Tables referring to the subsegments in each segment.

subset — 1. A set contained within a set. 2. A subscriber apparatus in a communications network. 3. A contraction of the words "subscriber set" which has been used for many years to refer

subset, digital

to the device which is installed on a subscriber's premises. 4. A modulation/demodulation device designed to make business-machine signals compatible with the communications facilities and vice versa. A data subset accepts digital information, converts it into a suitable form for transmission over the telephone circuits, and then reconverts the data to its original form at the receiving end. 4. Any collection of objects or items contained within a larger set. 3. Contraction of subscriber's set, which is any device (but usually a telephone) installed on a subscriber's premises.

subset, digital — A collection of data in a prescribed format described by control information to which an operating system has access and which constitutes the principal unit of data storage and retrieval within the system.

subset, proper — A set, A, can have a subset, A_1 such that A intersection A_1 is not identical with A, and is thus a proper subset.

substitutable argument — A prototype card field in a macro-definition that is variable and is to be replaced with a parameter (quantity or symbol) when the macro-operation is used. It is also called a dummy argument.

substitute character — An accuracy control character intended to replace a character that is determined to be invalid, in error, or cannot be represented on a particular device. Abbreviated SUB.

substrate — In microelectronics, the physical material on which a circuit is fabricated. Its primary function is to provide mechanical support, but it may also serve a useful thermal or electrical function.

substrate, calculator — The calculator on a substrate (COS) developed by Sharp Corp was a giant step toward complete system integration. A soda-glass substrate that replaces the conventional printed-circuit board not only holds the calculator chip, but also contains the keyboard contacts and serves as the front half of the glass package for the liquid-crystal display. Logic circuits and a few discrete components are mounted on the substrate, and a power-supply subassembly is wired to it. The COS system eliminates as many intermediary components as possible. It also minimizes the amount of labor necessary for assembly, making the process engineering- and equipment-intensive.

substring — A portion of a larger string; "BC", for example, is a substring within the string "ABCD".

subsystem — Refers to a self-contained portion of a system that performs one of the major system functions usually with only minimal interaction with other portions of the system.

subsystem failure — Failures peculiar to communication subsystems include the following: 1. Mechanical and electrical faults in terminals, transmission lines, multiplexers, and control units. 2. Failures in the central processor or in main and secondary storage used to hold buffers and message queues. 3. Failures in the communication software itself, such as program "bugs," incorrect error-recovery procedures, failure to deal with terminal-user misbehavior, or failure to deal with buffer overflow (in the statistical sense). 4. Mistakes on the part of the system operators, such as incorrect tape mounts or electrical faults in the network and its terminals can be detected as transmission errors or expected replies.

subsystems, communications — To allow its central processors to function most effectively as real time systems, computers are designed with standard communication subsystems. Some recent additions to the family of subsystems enable a central processor to exchange data simultaneously with a number of remote locations over standard common-carrier communications facilities. The subsystem consists of a multiplexer or multiplexers, each of which allows simplex communication circuits to share a computer I/O channel, and communication-line terminal units which properly terminate the communication circuits and translate the data from these circuits to a form compatible with the central processor.

subsystem, standard communication — Refers to a multiplexor that permits simplex communication circuits to share an I/O channel and line terminal units.

subtotal key — On some units this key will print the accumulator contents without alignment on truncation and without altering machine status.

subtracter — Refers to a device which is capable of forming the representation of the difference between two numbers represented by signals applied to its inputs. Types: full subtracters, parallel and serial.

subtracter-adder — A logic element designed to act as an adder or a subtracter as ordered by the control signal applied to it.

subtraction key — On some units this subtracts the input number from the accumulator. The total contents of the accumulator are displayed while the individual entrys are printed aligned to the decimal switch and truncated. "Repeat subtract" feature is included. This key will also execute a previously conditional multiplication or division. It also executes the percent discount sequence.

subtrahend — 1. The number or quantity that is is subtracted from another number, called the minuend, giving a result usually called the difference, or sometimes called the remainder. 2. The quantity that is subtracted from another quantity.

successive approximations — A method (capable of high speed) of comparing an unknown against a group of weighted references (usually binary) is the process of successive approximations in an ADC — a technique similar to the orderly weighing of an unknown quantity on a precision chemical balance, using a set of weights, such as: 1 gram, ½ gram, ¼ gram, etc.

sudden death — Colloquialism for abrupt failure of transistor. (This term originally applied to point contact types where displacement of the contact frequently caused unexplained failures. Comparable breakdown of junction types may occur, e.g., as a result of thermal runaway or reverse voltages.)

suffix — A label often used in the description of an item by a programming language in order to select that item from a table in which it occurs.

sum check — Refers to a specific check developed when groups of digits are summed, usually without regard for overflow, and that sum checked

summarizing — against a previously computed sum to verify that no digits have been changed since the last summation.

summarizing — For control of operations in which data is summarized and then recorded in summary form, a final total of a key field or fields can be accumulated from the summarized data and balanced to one accumulated from the detail data. In card-to-card and tape-to-tape runs, the stored program should develop the necessary final totals of the summary data when it is recorded on the output tape; it should also balance it at the end of the run to a control total read from a control card or the tape label.

summary card — A punched card which contains totals and descriptive data resulting from an associated group of detail cards.

summary punch — A card-punching machine which can be connected to an accounting machine to punch totals or balance cards.

summation check — A redundant calculator check in which groups of digits are summed, usually without regard to overflow. The sum is then checked against a previously computed sum to verify the accuracy of the computation.

summations key — Summation calculations use the $\Sigma+$ (Sigma plus) key to total numbers for use in other calculations. These summations are particularly useful when working with vectors and statistics.

summations, vector — Useful when working with vectors as well as statistics, this function automatically calculates and stores for recall or further use: Σn, Σx, Σx^2 and Σy. Data may be deleted via the "$\Sigma-$" key.

sum of factors key — Automatically accumulates the first entries of any series of multiplication or division problems.

sum operand — Automatically sums first factors of sequence multiplication or division problems. Used when obtaining average unit price and standard deviation.

sum + key $(\Sigma+)$ — Instant conversion from polar to rectangular coordinates... or vice-versa. And vector calculations are available when users also use the $\Sigma+$ key to simultaneously accumulate two coordinates on some units. Statistical analysis is easier... because the $\Sigma+$ key provides a running total when summing numbers, keeps track of the number of entries, and automatically computes the sum of the squares. The $\bar{x}$,s key calculates the arithmetic mean and the standard deviation.

superimpose (SI) — Moves data from one location to another, superimposing bits or characters on the contents of specified locations.

superscript — In mathematical and model-building notation, a symbol written above and to the right of the base symbol to indicate a specified function or differentiation from some other similar or same base letter or character. Also the power to which a number is to be raised is placed in the superscript location, and most often to indicate a cell of a matrix or a derivation, or a unit of a particular set, if the character indicates the universal set.

supervising system — 1. Refers to a program that controls loading and relocation of routines and in some cases makes use of instructions which are unknown to the general programmer. Effectively, an executive routine is part of the machine itself (synonymous with monitor routine, supervisory routine, and supervisory program). 2. A set of coded instructions designed to process and control other sets of coded instructions. 3. A set of coded instructions used in realizing automatic coding. 4. A master set of coded instructions.

supervisor — A routine that controls the proper sequencing and positioning of segments of calculator programs in limited storage during their execution.

supervisor call instruction — An instruction that interrupts the program being executed and passes control to the supervisor so that it can perform a specific service indicated by the instruction.

supervisor-cell interrupts — Supervisor-call interrupts are caused by the program issuing an instruction to turn over control to the supervisor (the operating system). The exact cause for the call is shown in the old PSW (program status word).

supervisor overlay — A control routine that initiates and controls fetching of overlay segments on the basis of information recorded in the overlay module by linkage editor.

supervisory console — Generally the supervisory console includes the operator's control panel, a keyboard and typewriter, and a control unit for the keyboard and typewriter. Optionally, a paper-tape reader and punch may be connected to the computer through the same control unit. Information transfer between the computer and any single device is performed and output channel assigned to the console auxiliaries. Two switches mounted on the control unit permit selection of the paper-tape reader or the keyboard, and the paper-tape punch or the type printer (some computers).

supervisory control — Characters or signals which automatically actuate equipment or indicators at a remote terminal.

supervisory control action — Refers to that specific action in which the control loops operate independently, subject to intermittent corrective action, such as set point changes from an external source.

support programs — Those programs which support or aid the supervisory programs and the application programs, and include diagnostics, tesing, data generators, etc.

suppression — An optional function in either on-line or off-line printing devices that permits them to ignore certain input characters or groups of characters. See nonprint code.

surveying program pack — Various programs grouped into these common problem areas: traversing, curves, triangles and intersections, predetermined area and earthwork.

swap — Refers to systems with time sharing, to write the main storage image of a job to auxiliary storage and read the image of another job into main storage.

swapping — Refers to a design of memory multiplexing in which jobs are kept on a backing storage and periodically transferred entirely to an internal memory to be executed for a fixed time slice.

switch — 1. A mechanical or electrical device that completes or breaks the path of the current or sends it over a different path. 2. To establish

switch, function — continued

a temporary interconnection between two or more stations over communications paths. 3. A short term for a line or message switcher.

switch, function — Refers to a specific circuit having a fixed number of inputs and outputs designed such that the output information is a function of the input information, each expressed in a certain code, signal configuration, or pattern.

switching — Making, breaking, or changing the connections in an electrical circuit.

switching algebra — Relates to Boolean algebra which is applied to switching circuits, digital systems and some communications switching.

switching center — 1. A location at which incoming data from one circuit is transferred to the proper outgoing circuit. 2. A location where an incoming message is automatically or manually directed to one or more outgoing circuits, according to the intelligence contained in the message.

switching device — Any device or mechanism, either electrical or mechanical, which can place another device or circuit in an operating or non-operating state.

switch matrix — Refers to an array of circuit elements interconnected specifically to perform a particular function as interconnected, i.e., the elements are usually transistors, diodes, and relay gates completing logic functions for encoding, transliteration of characters, decoding number system transformation, word translation, etc., and most often input is taken along one dimension while output is taken along another.

switchover, automatic — An operating system which has a stand-by machine that is capable of detecting when the on-line machine is faulty and once this determination is made, to switch to itself this operation.

switch, programmed — A particular instruction which may be in the form of a numeral and may be placed in a routine to allow the calculator to select one of a number of alternative paths in its program, i.e., switch settings on the console equipment can be inspected by operators or the computer and results in changes or branches in the main program.

switch register — Some switch registers consist of up to twelve (or more) data entry switches that are used to manually alter the contents of the accumulator, program counter, or memory data register. The switch register can also be read under program control.

switch, sense — The sense switches on the operator's console provide manual control of program branching. Testing of the sense-switch settings occurs when the sense-switch instruction is given.

switch, toggle — 1. A manually operated electric switch, with a small projecting knob or arm that may be placed in either of two positions, "on" or "off," and will remain in that position until changed. 2. An electronically operated circuit that holds either of two states until changed.

symbiont control — Symbionts, besides being routines from main programs, may be concurrently performing typical off-line operations, such as tape-to-printer, independent of the main program. Symbionts may be initialized by the operator, or by a main program. Symbiont operations may be suspended, terminated, or reinitiated at any time.

symbionts — Small routines, called symbionts, run concurrently with the series of main programs. These symbionts move information back and forth between the peripherals and magnetic drum. Main programs desiring communication with these peripherals reference input/output subroutines that transfer data images between the drum and peripherals.

symbol — 1. A simplified design representing a part in a schematic circuit diagram. 2. A letter representing a particular quantity in formulas. 3. In some systems a symbol consists of up to eight letters and digits beginning with a letter. Symbols are defined by their appearance as statement labels or equality symbols. The value of a symbol, defined as a label, is the value of the location counter at the time the label was encountered. The value of a symbol, defined by equality, is the value of the expression appearing on the right of the equal sign. 4. A conventional representation of a concept or a representation of a concept upon which agreement has been reached.

symbolic addresses, calculators — Since different calculators require different detailed treatment in programming. The fine points of calculator programming must be left to the comprehensive programming manuals that are supplied with individual calculators. But there are some general programming principles of broad application. Symbolic addressing is one of the techniques that can be employed on almost all algebraic calculators. In one example the JUMP-0-0 command returns the program to its starting point. A different starting point requires a different command. Often a more convenient approach is to assign a symbolic name to the starting point. The end of the program would then command a JUMP to that symbolic name rather than zero.

symbolic addressing — Refers to a fundamental procedure or method of addressing using an address (symbolic address) chosen for convenience in programming or of the programmer in which translation of the symbolic address into an absolute address is required before it can be used in the computer.

symbolic assemblers — Nearly all manufacturers of microprocessors (and mini- and maxi-computers as well) provide symbolic assemblers — programs that ease the programming task by eliminating the need to translate instructions manually into machine-readable form. The designer can express his program in terms of mnemonics, which are abbreviations that suggest individual instructions. Then the assembler translates each mnemonic instruction into its binary representation.

symbolic assembly-language listing — The listing contains the symbolic instructions equivalent to the binary code output of the compiler. This assembly-language output listing is useful as a debugging aid. By including certain pseudo operation codes in "in-line" assembly language, the assembly language output can be assembled by the assembler routine. (If output is obtained on either cards, paper tape, or magnetic tape.) This will allow modification of programs at the assembly language level.

symbolic assembly system — A program system developed in two parts: a symbolic-language program and a computer program (processor). The processor translates a source program de-

symbolic code

veloped in symbolic language to a machine object program.

symbolic code — Refers to a specific code designed to express programs in source language; i.e., by referring to storage locations and machine operations by symbolic names and addresses which are independent of their hardware-determined names and addresses.

symbolic conversion program — Represented by the abbreviation SCP. A one-to-one compiler for symbolic addresses and operation.

symbolic data set — In coding a program, the designation used to refer to a data set, the actual data set whose data content is to be processed during a particular execution of the program is determined later. The later assignment may be an entire data set or a specific member of a directoried data set.

symbolic editor — Permits the editing of source-language programs by adding or deleting lines of text. All modification, reading, punching, etc., is controlled by symbols typed at the keyboard. The editor reads parts or all of a symbolic tape into memory where it is available for immediate examination, correction, and relisting.

symbolic instruction — An instruction in an assembly language directly translatable into a machine code. An instruction using symbols to represent or express the operator part and the address parts.

symbolic I/O assignment — A means by which problem programs can refer to an I/O device by a symbolic name. Before a program is executed, job control can be used to assign a specific I/O device to that symbolic name.

symbolic language — 1. Refers to that of a calculator program prepared in any coding other than the specific machine language, and so requiring to be assembled or compiled before it can be carried out. 2. A programming language which expresses addresses and operation codes of instructions in symbols convenient to humans rather than in machine language.

symbolic logic — 1. Refers to the study of formal logic and mathematics by means of a special written language which seeks to avoid the ambiguity and inadequacy of ordinary language. 2. The mathematical concepts, techniques and languages as used in 1, whatever their particular application or context. Synonymous with mathematical logic and related to logic.

symbolic manipulation — Because data are not usually numerical, the formal use of a symbol manipulation has resulted in specific list-processing languages. The first real list processing language or information processing language was developed by Newell, Shaw, and Simon in 1957.

symbolic name — Refers to a label used in programs written in a source language to reference data elements, peripheral units, instructions, etc.

symbolic name assignment, calculator — To assign a symbolic name to a program point, in one specific system the user presses the key labeled SYMBOL in conjunction with any other function or number key. The "name" of that key then becomes the symbol of the program point. This level of sophistication permits the recall of programs independent of their locations in memory. A program may begin at step zero or any other step. And a program's location can be changed

symmetrical

without the need to repeat all the steps, should that location be needed for something else. Symbolic addressing is a powerful tool for developing a number of concurrent programs.

symbolic parameter — In assembler programming, a variable symbol declared in the prototype statement of a macro definition. A symbolic parameter is usually assigned a value from the corresponding operand in the macro instruction that calls the macro definition. See also keyword parameter, positional parameter.

symbolic programming — 1. A program using symbols instead of numbers for the operations and locations in a computer. Although the writing of a program is easier and faster, an assembly program must be used to decode the symbols into machine language and assign instruction locations. 2. The use of arbitrary symbols to represent addresses in order to facilitate programming.

symbolic unit — 1. A mnemonic in the symbolic units table which refers to an input/output device. A symbolic unit may be assigned to an entire input/output device or to a portion of a device. 2. In coding a program, the designation used to refer to external storage, the actual storage to be used during a particular execution of the program is determined later.

symbol, logical — A sign used as an operator to denote the particular operation to be performed on the associated variables.

symbol, mnemonic — Frequently used symbols for representation of information and so selected to assist the programmer's memory in recalling meaning, as MPY for multiply.

symbols, atomic — In list processing languages, atomic symbols are sometimes referred to as atoms. When using list processing languages they may either be numeric or nonnumeric. The external representation of a nonnumeric atomic symbol is a string of letters or digits starting with a letter such as AB5, W or epsilon.

symbols, flowchart — The symbols, such as squares and circles, convey no information and must be labeled. They localize a point of interest, but convey only the most general notion of intent. The finished model must include adequate description with each symbol to explain its operation. Liberal use of footnotes is recommended to explain the "why" of operations that are not straight-forward in meaning.

symbols, functional — A block diagram term representing the functional design, i.e., the practical specification of the working relations between all parts of a system.

symbol string — A concatenation of items or characters, i.e., a one dimensional array of such items ordered only by reference to the relations between adjacent members.

symbol table control — Symbols that have been defined and used, but are no longer required, may be deleted from the symbol table. This allows room for new symbols. Thus, a very large program can be assembled with a relatively small symbol storage area.

symbol, variable — Refers to assembler programming, a symbol used in macro and conditional assembly processing that can assume any of a given set of values.

symmetrical — Refers to circuits, networks, or transducers for which the impedance level (image impedance or iterative impedance) is the same in both directions.

sync — Short for synchronous, synchronization, synchronizing, etc.

sync character — Refers to a character transmitted to establish character synchronization in synchronous communication. When the receiving station recognizes the sync character, the receiving station is said to be synchronized with the transmitting station, and communication can begin.

synchronization — 1. The precise matching of two waves or functions. 2. A process of coordinating or bringing into step the transmitted signal and the receiver's decoder used to unscramble or decode it. Usually synchronization implies a time function rather than frequency, but it can be both.

synchronize — 1. To adjust the periodicity of an electrical system so that it bears an integral relationship to the frequency of the periodic phenomenon under investigation. 2. To lock one element of a system into step with another. The term usually refers to locking a receiver to a transmitter, but it can refer to locking the data terminal equipment bit rate to the data set transmitter.

synchronizer — A storage device used to compensate for a difference in a rate of flow information or time of occurrence of events when transmitting information from one device to another.

synchronizer, channel — The channel-synchronizer signals provide for orderly transfer of the digital information. These signals do not transmit data, but are used to command and identify the transfer of data words, function words, etc., at proper times and in proper sequence.

synchronous — 1. Refers to the same frequency and phase. 2. Having a constant time interval between successive bits, characters, or events.

synchronous communications binary (BISYNC) — IBM BISYNC (Binary Synchronous Communications) describes the set of operating procedures for synchronous transmission used in teleprocessing networks. With BISYNC, some system batch terminals automatically perform error checking on all incoming data and request retransmission of a message whenever it is not received exactly as sent. As a transmitting terminal, the system automatically retransmits messages when they are not accurately received by the remote station. Because of the reliability of data transmissions using binary synchronous methods, higher speeds of data communications are possible — up to 4800 bits-per-second. Thus, it becomes economical to collect and store large amounts of data at the processor using either cassettes or mass memory subsystem and to later transmit the data to computers or terminals, including other systems.

synchronous communications interface — A typical unit provides two-way communications with devices such as a Bell 201A/B Data Set or equivalent. It operates up to 9600 baud in half or full duplex mode with fully independent transmit and receive channels. Programmable functions include parity checking, synchronization, special character recognition and character size.

synchronous data transmission — Refers to a system in which timing is derived through synchronizing characters at the beginning of each message.

synchronous device — An electronic unit in which each event or operation starts as a result of a clock signal.

synchronous machine — A machine which has an average speed exactly proportionate to the frequency of the system to which it is connected.

synchronous operation — One in which each event or the performance of each operation starts as a result of a signal generated by a clock. Contrasted with asynchronous computer, and clarified by clock frequency.

synchronous system (communications) — A system in which the sending and receiving instruments are operating at approximately the same frequency, and the phase is maintained by means of feedback.

synergetic — Refers to a combination of every unit of a system, which when combined develop a total larger than their arithmetic sum (also called synergistic).

syntactic error — Syntactic errors are considered the responsibility of the system and are further categorized as follows: Composition — typographical errors, violations of specified form, of statements and misuse of variable names (e.g., incorrect punctuation, mixed-mode expressions, undeclared arrays, etc.). Consistency — statements that are correctly composed but conflict with other statements (e.g., conflicting declaratives, illegal statement ending a DO range, failure to follow each transfer statement with a numbered statement, etc.). Completeness — programs that are incomplete (e.g., transfers to nonexistent statement numbers, improper DO nesting, illegal transfer into the range of a DO loop, etc.).

syntax — 1. Refers to the relationship among characters or groups of characters, independent of their meanings or the manner of their interpretation and use. 2. The structure of expressions in a language. 3. The rules governing the structure of a language. 4. The relationships among symbols.

syntax checker — Refers to a program that tests source statements in a programming language for violations of the syntax of that language.

synthesis — The activity of combining of parts in order to form a whole, i.e., to arrive at a circuit or a computer or program, starting from performance requirements. This can be contrasted with analysis, which arrives at performance, given the circuit or program.

synthetic language — Refers to a pseudocode or symbolic language. A fabricated language.

synthetic relationship — A relation existing between a concept that pertains to an empirical observation. Such relationships are not involved in defining concepts or terms, but in reporting the results of observations and experiments.

system — 1. Refers to a collection of parts united by some form of regulated interaction, an organized whole. 2. A collection of service routines which sequences programs through a calculator, provides conversion, I/O and debugging subroutines and makes helpful remarks to the operator is known as an operating system. 3. As used in some computing installations, the system includes, and defines the interrelationship of, hardware, service routines, processing procedures and accounting methods.

systematic errors — Those errors which have an orderly character and can be corrected by calibration.

system calculator advantages — Advanced desk-top portable calculators can help professional problem solvers increase productivity and reduce costs by providing:
- Sophisticated computer capabilities
- Immediate access and response
- Direct control of scheduling, data and processing
- Easy installation and use
- Reliability

All at an attractive purchase price.

system check — Refers to a computer performance using external program checks, not check circuits built into the hardware.

system communications processing — The transmission of data to the central computer for processing from a remote terminal as opposed to a terminal connected directly to the central computer.

system constant — System constants are permanent locations contained in the monitor (control unit). These locations contain data used by system programs. Some constants contain data that may be used by certain programs.

system constant printout — Provides automatic printout of channel-by-channel program settings for checking and file with data. When alarms are present, this option also allows printout of all alarm set points.

system control, calculator — In instrument systems, the programmable calculator is attractive as a system controller. It can now do many jobs formerly reserved for minicomputers, including process monitoring and control, R & D lab design-verification and prototype testing, and multiparameter production testing. Its user-orientation and built-in high-level languages have served to open the number-handling and computational power of the minicomputer to a much broader spectrum of users.

system controllers, calculator data acquisition system — One advanced model calculator is the standard controller for a data acquisition system. Its easy to learn algebraic languages to make it simple to write user's own test programs, even without prior programming experience. And the calculator run procedure along with the conversational alphanumeric display and printer enable relatively unskilled operators to perform complicated production tests with ease and repeatability.

While achieving programming and operating simplicity, the various programming languages have some of the best computer language features, including branching and subroutine capability. It also adds many of its own unique features such as immediate error detection and flexible statement and program line editing. A built-in magnetic card reader facilitates recording programs and data, and permits using prerecorded programs. (some systems)

system definition, microprocessor — System definition involves the major tasks to be performed by the microprocessor — which is assumed to be the central control device of the system. Data formats should be established to maximize processor control. The over-all system timing is included in this design phase to ensure that all functions can be handled within the timing constraints. Based on the system definition, the basic program structure can now be defined. Each input channel to the microprocessor represents a major program, assuming the use of more than one input device. In addition an executive program should be written to control the over-all operation of the system. Various routines — based on the different functions or command codes supplied — further subdivide the main program.

system design — The specification of the working relations between all the parts of a system in terms of their characteristic actions.

system diagnostics — Refers to programs resembling the operational program rather than a systematic logical-pattern program which will detect overall system malfunctions rather than isolate or locate faulty components.

system engineering — A method of engineering approach whereby all the elements in the control system are considered, even the smallest value and the process itself.

system firmware — Many systems include system firmware building blocks. They can be used in various systems and often assure that only application software peculiar to the application need be written by the user. The following are some firmware/software system building blocks: multiprogramming executive, macro assembly language interpreter, input/output control system, disc file management, others.

system interface (microprocessor) — Refers to devices that interconnect all other support hardware and often a TTY (teletype unit) for program assembly, simulation, PROM programming, prototype operations, and debugging.

system interrupts — System call interrrupts are programmed requests from a processing program to the control program for some action, such as initiation of an input/output operation.

system loader — One of the supervisor routines. It is used to retrieve program phases from the main image library and load them into main storage.

system, macro — A programming system with symbolic capabilities of an assembly system and the added capability of many-for-one or macro-instruction development.

system, macroinstruction — Various macroinstructions control the translation procedure and do not necessarily develop usable machine-language programs or instructions.

system monitor — A typical system monitor, which resides in the first 1k of memory, enables the user to load and execute programs stored on paper tape or other external device. The user can also write device drivers coded to suit his own particular I/O needs. Programs loaded and executed under monitor supervision can be passed parameters to control their operation. (some units)

system monitor, firmware — The monitor is a section of the firmware that dispatches data within the terminal. The processor normally executes a basic loop, in which it scans the keyboard and the data communications interface and waits for something to happen. When a character is received from either the keyboard or the data communications interface a general character interpretation subroutine is executed to determine the action to be taken. The monitor then performs the specified functions, such as putting a character on the display, transmitting a character over the data communications interface, or moving the cursor. When this has been completed, the monitor returns to the basic scan loop to look for the next input (some systems)

system organization, programmable calculator — One popular unit contains an arithmetic and register circuit, a control and timing circuit, and three read-only-memory (ROM) circuits. In this unit, each ROM is actually a quad ROM containing the equivalent of four single ROMs. The unit also has a data-register circuit. Other circuits are a program storage circuit, a card-reader control circuit, and a card read/write circuit.

The data/register circuit is made up of ten addressable data registers of 56 bits each, enough to store 14 digits each. Data register 0 is used to implement a LSTx (last x) function and always contains the previously displayed number. Registers 1 through 9 are addressable from the keyboard. Addresses and data are transferred between the data register circuit and the arithmetic and register circuit by way of a bidirectional BCD bus. The program storage circuit stores the user's program. Each program step is stored as a six-bit word. There are 100 words of storage.

system, polymolphic — A specific or particular system which can take on various forms ideally suited to the problems at hand, usually by altering, under its own control its interconnections and the functions of its component parts, i.e., it may occur with respect to logic construction or organization and a master unit controls a variety of jobs executed simultaneously and automatically.

system protection — The communications processor supports multiple terminals assigned to different application programs operating concurrently. Many control tables (i.e., terminal tables, polling lists, terminal-queue mapping tables, etc.) and other procedures such as on-line test routines, the resident linking loader, and so on, represent shared facilities and must be protected against unauthorized access. Also, the communications processor will receive system commands from the network processor requiring changes to specific control structures (i.e., routing lists). Such commands must be verified against access rights before they are accessed. (some systems)

system reliability — Hardware safeguards have been implemented to reduce the possibility of loss of the user's data. Failures can occur in any system no matter how well designed it is. For example, if primary line power fails during a write operation, that data will be lost. Improper maintenance or lack of maintenance can cause the mass memory to malfunction and data can be lost. This emphasizes the need to provide backup for any critical data. A multiple platter system makes this backup quickly and easily accomplished. Tape cassettes are another means of backup data storage and the system software also makes this easily accomplished. (some systems)

system response, time domain — Some calculators offer fast, precise analysis with complete documentation. To analyze even a very complex system with calculators, users develop a suitable model, describe its characteristic transfer function, and draw a block diagram that includes such elements as summing junctions, scalars and integrators. They then enter the system parameters in a form of coefficient matrix, and the calculator does the rest. From this they can quickly determine how stable, oscillatory, or unstable the system will be. The state variable program not only frees users from tedious mathematical computations, it gives them a printed record showing the values of the internal states of the system or network. If the calculator is controlling a plotter, users automatically get fully labeled plots of the system's dynamic response. (some systems)

system restart — 1. A restart that allows reuse of previously-initialized input and output work queues. Synonymous with warm start. 2. A restart that allows reuse of a previously-initialized link pack area. Synonymous with quick start.

systems analysis — 1. The analysis of a business activity to determine precisely what must be accomplished and how to accomplish it. 2. The organized, step-by-step study and analysis of the detailed procedure for collection, manipulation, and evaluation of information about an organization with the goal of improving control over its total operation or segments of it. 3. The examination of an activity, procedure, method, technique, or a business to determine what must be accomplished and the best method of accomplishing the necessary operations.

systems analyst — Defines the applications problem, determines system specifications, recommends equipment changes, and designs dp procedures. Devises data verification methods. Prepares block diagrams and record layouts from which a programmer prepares flow-charts. May assist in or supervise the preparation of flow-charts.

systems and support software — The wide variety of software including assemblers, compilers, subroutine libraries, operating systems, application programs, etc.

systems approach — Looking at the over-all situation rather than the narrow implications of the task at hand; particularly, looking for interrelationships between the task at hand and other functions which relate to it.

system scan display — A special ROM permits steps through the channels at rate of one/sec, displaying channel number (last 2 numbers) and current data reading. Self-timed data scans have priority and may interrupt a "display data" scan. Does not display overrange or alarms. Channel interval is disabled. (some systems)

systems compatibility — In complex systems applications, modules are completely compatible electrically, logically, and mechanically with other systems components, that include digital computers, a complete line of input/output devices, and analog interface equipment.

systems engineering — The designed implementation of a hardware and software system which results from the analysis of a control problem.

systems handbook — Refers to a concise distillation of the major characteristics of the instruction set including operation codes, addressing modes and microprocessor status for each instruction. Also includes reference to the primary aspects of system implementation including chip interfaces and timing. This document is aimed at the experienced user who understands the basics of the family and requires a concise reference book. (some systems)

system simulation — An assemblage of interacting components and processes. The interactions

systems modeling

are largely internal to the system, although links to an external environment will be recognized.

systems modeling — The representation of real world phenomena by equations — most often handled through computer simulation. Much effort has been made recently to model complex social phenomena for studying the impact of public policies. The controversy around pioneering applications of such "system dynamics" to social modeling, which started in the early 1970s, resulted in a number of extensions and refinements of this modeling approach. Among the more constructive modifications are models that emphasize individual components in any representation of the real world, the use of observed data in the structure, and the inclusion of human reaction and social cybernetics in the model. There is increased recognition that social system models merely underline the subjective nature.

system software — System software generally includes a debugging program and basic operating system, a text editor, an assembler, a linking loader, and an I/O operating system; the debugging program and basic operating system. The debugging program and basic operating system provide the user with the capabilities of address modifications, memory dumps, absolute loading, and diagnostic running of programs with breakpoint processing. The text editor offers the user editing capability for creating and maintaining source files. Text can be added, modified through a number of useful functions, and punched out on paper tape. The assembler will have the full ranges of instructions often with the options of relocatable vs. absolute code, and MACRO capacity. A linking loader is available to load relocatable codes. An I/O operating system facilitates the details of I/O programming. (some systems)

system software components — Users must choose the operating systems needed based on specific requirements. They may need more than one operating system. Typical system software often required includes: compilers, interpreters, assemblers, editors, debug assistance software and "canned" applications programs (e.g., search and sort programs).

systems study — The detailed process by which a set of procedures is determined in order to use a calculator for definite functions or operations. Also, specifications are established to be used as a basis for the selection of equipment suitable for the specific needs.

systems support, microcomputer — In supplementing the microprocessor system itself, support should be provided by the manufacturer to simplify the application of the processor and the development and prototyping of the end product. This category includes documented manuals, applicational literature, area field specialists, prototyping systems. Also generally useful are program-development software and the ability to fashion the microprocessor into different configurations.

systems test — 1. Refers to the running of the whole system against test data. 2. A complete simulation of the actual running system for purposes of testing out the adequacy of the system. 3. A test of an entire interconnected set of components for the purpose of determining proper functioning and interconnection. 4. The running of the whole system of runs making up a data processing application against test data.

system supervisor — The system supervisor is designed to allow an installation to proceed automatically from run to run with little or no computing time loss because of setting up the "next program." It is also designed to accomplish as many of the set-up and control functions as is possible prior to reading in the actual program. It is assumed that the programs are located on tape in the exact order that they are to be run. This order can be superseded by the operator. Each program on completion should transfer control to the "finish" entry point of the control program. This program will read in the next system supervisor from the library tape. Control is then transferred to the supervisor.

system utility programs — A collection of problem state programs designed for use by a system programmer in performing such functions as changing or extending the indexing structure of the catalog.

system utilization loggers — A program or a device that collects statistical information about how the system is operating.

T

table — Refers to a collection or ordering of data (such as square root values) laid out in rows and columns for reference, or stored in a computer memory as an array. In computing, elements of such a table would be obtained by direct calculation where possible (table look at) to save storage. If this was not possible the whole array would be stored and the element required determined by a comparison search (table look up).

table lockup — Refers to a method of controlling the location to which a jump or transfer is made. It is used especially when there is a large number of alternatives, as in function evaluation in scientific computations.

table look-at — Finding elements of a table by direct calculation rather than by a comparison search.

table look-up — A procedure for obtaining the value of a function from a stored table.

table look-up instruction — Refers to a specific instruction designed to speed reference to stored data which are specifically arranged, i.e., in a table or in tabular form. This instruction will direct a computer to automatically search for a named argument in a table to locate and retrieve a desired result, i.e., an operation performed instead of a calculation, in most cases, but such tables and instructions vary considerably among different computers and programs.

table simulator — A specific computer program which has the capability of computing the values in a table rather than simply looking them up as stored.

table, symbol — A mapping for a set of symbols to another set of symbols or numbers. In programming, the assembler builds a table of labels used in an assembler language program and assigns to those labels a set of relative or absolute core locations.

table, symbol control — Symbols that have been defined and used, but are no longer required, may be deleted from the symbol table. This allows room for new symbols. Thus, a very large program can be assembled with a relatively small symbol storage area.

tabular language — A composition of decision tables that become the problem-oriented language used in computation.

tag file — A file containing only selected portions ("tags") from data file records, such as sort keys, file sequence keys, etc.

tag format — The design of a record used as a tag to locate an overflow bucket.

tag sort — A sort in which addresses of records (tags), and not the records themselves, are moved during the comparison procedure.

takedown — The actions performed at the end of an equipment operating cycle to prepare the equipment for the next setup, e.g., to remove the tapes from the tape handlers at the end of a computer run is a takedown operation.

talking calculator applications — A talking calculator offers unique advantages in many applications. As an example, it will permit the user to concentrate full visual attention on the columns of printed figures or work being calculated while listening to the audio input and output, without having to shift attention back and forth from the work to look at the visual display. This capability alone can greatly increase speed and efficiency. (see audio response calculator and voice readout applications)

talking calculator features — Some characteristics are:
- Eight Functions:
  Addition
  Subtraction
  Multiplication
  Division
  Memory
  Square Root
  Percentage
  1/x
- Accumulative Memory
- Floating Decimal Point
- Mark-up and Discount
- Five function percentage keys
- Chain calculations
- Clear, natural-sounding voice fidelity
- Three Modes of Operation

talking calculator (for the blind) — Unlike most servants, a recently introduced audible calculator is heard but not seen by its master. Intended as an aid for the blind, the device has a 24-word vocabulary and recites the results of each keystroke that inputs its six-function processor. The device also incorporates a speech key that, when pressed, generates an audible readout of the contents of the calculator's display. The unit in the calculator uses an all-digital speech-generation scheme. A custom IC implements the device's synthesis algorithm. Only at the end of the synthesis process does a D/A converter transform digital data into the voltages required to simulate speech sounds.

talking calculator mode — This mode is used until operator becomes familiar with keyboard. Each entry produces an audio output associated with that entry. It has a keyboard lockout feature which guarantees audio output before new entry. This will prevent loss or clipping words.

tally — To add or subtract a digit "1" from a quantity, usually the contents of a register.

tandem system — A special system configuration in which the data proceeds through one central processor into another processor. This is a system of multiplexors and master/slave arrangements.

tape bin — A magnetic tape storage device with movable read/record heads or fixed heads for each loop. The heads and loops can move to particular or selected locations on tape thus providing more rapid access time than on plain serial reels of tape which must be rewound.

tape cartridge system — Completely implementing American National Standards Institute recording format, one series accepts byte-oriented data, and phase encodes them at 1600 bits/in. complete with preamble, postamble, and cyclic redundancy check. The system also provides timing and control for up to four ¼" tape drives. Designed for data processing applications using 8-bit bytes, the system organizes the data to bit serial on the tape. No additional parallel-to-serial converter is needed. Because bytes are not separated by start/stop bits, all available space is used for data. A 16-char preamble precedes the data for read synchronization. Data are followed immediately by a 16-char cyclic redundancy check (CRC) and a 16-char postamble. All timing is provided by a crystal-controlled oscillator in the format unit. The CRC provides precise error checking and eliminates the need for redundancy in the data portion of the record; the formatter is organized to allow independent read and write sections and can initiate the read process in either the forward or reverse direction. Commands to the system simplify interfacing to a computer or other system. Total storage is 2.875 megabytes/cartridge. (some systems)

tape cassette, advanced calculators — One type high-speed Tape Cassette lets users easily store, update, and retrieve data and programs. A fast, bidirectional search feature lets users find any file on the tape without rewinding. The unit has a minimum capacity of 6,000 registers.

tape cassette application — The write CRC and read error detection functions are executed by the controller. Peripheral Interval Timer Module is designed for real time monitoring of disk operations. In some tape cassette applications, a single PIA handles all data, status and control signals. Two op amps are used for read circuits, and a single dual comparator amplifies and digitizes data from the tape read/write head.

tape cassette calculators — Some programmable calculators bring together in one package the versatility of a desk-top calculator, the ease of the natural algebraic language, and the convenience of the tape cassette for program and data storage. With these machines users can design a system to meet their own specific needs in the business, technical, industrial, or scientific fields. These systems allow users to write, edit, and use programs to solve their problems with unprecedented time savings and ease, vs computer systems.

tape cassette capacity — For some calculators,

a single 1½ oz. tape cassette holds over 150,000 program steps or 4,000 data values or any balanced combination of the two giving the units large storage power. Such units usually have the ability to update their own memories. Reading and using every one of the 150,000 program instructions or 9,000 pieces of data on the cassette is a strong capability.

tape cassette drive manual controls — Some drives permit manual controls for forward, rewind, record, stop and eject tape cassette. Manual (or programmable) controls for writing and reading data registers or programs onto or from tape cassettes are available as when operated with midsize desk-top calculators.

tape cassette drive system — On many programmable calculator systems these systems add more programming power and greater storage capacity. With some systems the problem solving capacity is unlimited by the number of steps that can be stored in a drive system at any one time.

tape cassette memory, calculator — Though slower than core or semiconductor memories, a tape-cassette unit can be added to some calculators for long-term storage of large amounts of data. Long, complex programs can be preserved for future use. The data are organized on the tape in blocks, so that each block is handled in its entirety. When the instructions on a block are completed, the calculator signals an ADVANCE command to the tape to load the next block into the internal memory.

In this way very long programs are broken down and handled in small units. But, there are limitations to program length. First, the number of steps in a single block can't exceed the number of steps that the working memory of the calculator can employ at one time. Second, the length of tape on a cassette is limited, though several cassettes can be used successfully. Finally, the operating time for a long program can become excessive, and errors tend to increase with length of programs on many tapes.

tape cassette memory, multiple (calculator) — Though a single tape cassette serving simply as a source of information is a powerful adjunct to a calculator, the addition of a multitape unit is an even greater asset. It vastly expands flexibility. For instance, a three-tape cassette unit can store the master program on one of the tapes, allow numerical data to be transferred from the second tape into the calculator working memory, as required for arithmetic processing, and record results on the third tape.

tape cassette unit, built-in — On some units both programs and data can be recorded onto and loaded from convenient tape cassettes, either manually or under program control. Each 300' cassette has a capacity equivalent to approximately 8000 registers. Cassettes may be protected against accidental re-recording and/or secured against unauthorized use and duplication. Some types of built-in cassette ROM provides complete cassette control without taking up any of the three ROM slots or their associated keys.

tape, certified — Refers to computer tape that is machine checked on all tracks throughout each roll and is certified by the supplier to have less than a specific total number of errors or, to have zero errors.

tape, change — A paper tape or magnetic tape carrying information that is to be used to update filed information. This field information is often on a master tape. Synonymous with transaction tape.

tape channels, paper — The presence of a hole in the tape indicates the presence of a code bit. The holes are punched in channels parallel to the edge of the tape, and paper tape of 5, 6, 7, 8 information channels is in use at present. An 8-channel tape (with an additional sprocket channel for guiding the tape or for code synchronization) will commonly be of 1-in. width with codes spaced at 10 per inch along the tape.

tape character use, calculators — "IBM compatible" ½ inch (1.27 cm) wide magnetic tape is the preferred medium. Various calculator interfaces accommodate incremental recorders that record one character at a time (nine bits for 9-track seven bits for 7-track). Each mag tape character describes a single printer character, such as a digit, letter, punctuation mark, space, or housekeeping character. Data blocks correspond to data frames of the calculator and an inter-record gap is supplied. At the beginning and end of tapes a file gap may be inserted manually. The tape recorders themselves supply parity bits, vertical, horizontal, and any cyclic character redundancy codes.

tape cluster — A set of magnetic tape decks which are built into a single cabinet. Each deck is capable of independent operation and occasionally arranged to share one or more interface channels for communication with a central processor.

tape drive — A mechanism for controlling the movement of magnetic tape, commonly used to move magnetic tape past a reading or writing head or to allow automatic rewinding.

tape drive control, programmable — Some automatic programmable tape drive controls permit more sophisticated programs to be written as overlays on pre-conditioned tapes. Large programs may be divided into a number of blocks, each holding 256 steps. A command reads the next program or overlay of any number of blocks of memory at the appropriate locations. One system permits access of over 38,000 programming steps per side of tape. One system's powerful interface assembly offers both Read Only and Read/Write ports allowing it to selectively control the connected tape drives. The tape drives may be operated manually by touching the appropriate key sequence on the calculator.

tape erasure — A process by which a signal recorded on a tape is removed and the tape made ready for re-recording. Erasure may be accomplished in the two ways; in ac erasure, the tape is demagnetized by an alternating field which is reduced in amplitude from an initially high value; in dc erasure the tape is saturated by applying a primarily undirectional field.

tape, grandfather — A magnetic tape which contains basic or initial information, which is used on a second tape, and this second tape is the one which is updated according to the latest transactions or changes. When this second tape is copied, it becomes the new grandfather tape, and a series of grandfather tapes is the historical record or statistical base for further manipulation, analysis, or an audit trial. They are also backup tapes in case of accidental erasure or loss of latest developed tapes.

tape labels — 1. A tape label appears on each

reel of magnetic tape in the form of a leader and/or a trailer record; its contents will be determined to some extent by the application and the type of data found on the tape. The leader record appears as the first and the trailer record as the last on the tape. Together they provide the means for machine-performed accounting control of tape operations. Types of information which may be included in a tape label are: a name or code for the tape which identifies the application and tape data type, reel number or sequence number if there is more than one, frequency of use, record format, date of preparation or date last used, purge date, operation in which the tape was written (generally a code), name of individual chiefly responsible, output number if there are several tapes, record count, control totals, any instructions to be typed out to the operator as well as an end-of-reel or end-of-file code. 2. Every tape in the system should be identified by a tape label. Some tape labels consist of two blocks which should be assigned upon introduction. The first is an installation tape number which should be assigned upon introducing a new reel of tape into the system. This number never changes. The second identifies the information that will follow on the tape and contains dating information that will be used by special programs to further identify the tape, and to protect the information from being destroyed prematurely.

tape leader — The tape preceding or following the body of a program.

tape, magnetic — Refers to a storage device consisting of metal or plastic tape coated with magnetic material. Binary data are stored as small, magnetized spots arranged in column form across the width of the tape. A read-write head is usually associated with each row of magnetized spots so that one column can be read or written at a time as the tape is moved relative to the head.

tape, master — Usually a magnetic tape containing the main program or the data master file, which is updated by data contained in a change tape.

tape, master-file — The word "file" is used in a general sense to mean any collection of informational items similar to one another in purpose, form, and content. Thus a magnetic tape master file is a file; the term may also be applied to a punched paper tape of input items, or if convenient, to a set of cards that is equivalent in nature to either the magnetic or paper tape. File may even be applied to an accumulation of information in the processor memory.

tape, Mylar — A specific data processing tape manufactured by E.I. Dupont Nemours Co., made of polyester film with a magnetic oxide coat.

tape operating system (TOS) — 1. Refers to a powerful and flexible operating system designed for System 360/370 and other computers having a minimum 16K of memory, at least four magnetic tapes, and no random-access storage devices. 2. Basically used for smaller systems without disk drives. Some operating systems have component modules (i.e., compilers, linkage-editor, etc.) stored on a system tape and use tape libraries for storage of user program and data files. (Contrast with Disk Operating System-DOS.)

tape pack — The form taken by the tape wound onto a reel. A good pack is one that has a uniform wind, has an acceptable E value and is free from spoking, cinching and layer-to-layer adhesion.

tape perforating — The recording of data in paper tape by means of punched holes. This is generally done by a card-to-tape converter which automatically senses the information from punched cards and perforates a 5-channel or 8-channel tape used in telegraphic transmission and other common-language applications.

tape perforator, paper — For recording data in rugged environmental conditions, many suppliers recommend paper tape recording. While slower than magnetic tape, it is not so delicate and demanding of cleanliness. Further, users can tell at a glance whether the device is working, and then can read the hole pattern as a final check. Cost is lower than magnetic tape, but must be balanced against mag tape's higher density data storage, speed, and less mechanical wear on the mechanism. A standard paper tape system is one with one-inch wide tape with 8 rows of data storage, 8 level ASCII code.

tape-processing unit — Tape processing includes the functions of recording, transcribing, transmitting, receiving and converting data recorded in perforated paper tape. Data recorded in paper tape can be processed to: produce punched cards by automatic conversion, provide input for various computers, provide automatic wire transmission of all or selected data, type subsequent related records and documents, and provide master tapes, or cards, for use in repetitive data operations.

tape, punched paper — Paper tape on which information has been (or may be) stored or recorded in the form of partially-punched (chadless) holes. Each character of information is punched in binary representation in a column across the width of the tape. There are usually 5 to 8 punch positions (channels or levels) per column. The channels or levels, run in rows parallel to the length of the tape. The punch positions are normally spaced ten to the inch.

tape punch example — A typical 75 character per second tape punch can be used when data or results must additionally be stored or analyzed in a calculator or reloaded back into the calculator using compatible type tape readers. It requires a compatible Calculator Interface, however.

tape punch subsystem, advanced calculator — A typical unit combines the Tape Punch and the Optional Interface Card. The unit punches tape at 75 characters/second.

tape recorder advantages — For recording large quantities of data, the reel-to-reel magnetic tape recorder is recommended in 7-track (BCDIC) or 9-track (EBCDIC) configurations. Choice of 7- or 9- track is dictated by the calculator input chosen for data reduction. The primary advantage of magnetic tape recording is recording speed coupled with high density storage. The disadvantages are vulnerability to dirty environmental conditions, particularly dust, which can cause errors and data loss. Temperature and humidity changes can cause tape drive problems, and finally, operators cannot verify visually whether data is being recorded.

tape recorder interface — A typical interface accommodates incremental recorders that record one character at a time (nine bits for 9-track, seven bits for 7-track). Each mag tape character describes a single printer character, such as a digit, letter, punctuation mark, space, or housekeeping character. As a result, a 16-character data line on some interfaces puts 16 characters on the mag tape. Data blocks correspond to data frames of the tape recorder and an inter-record gap is supplied. At the beginning and end of tapes a file gap may be inserted manually. The tape recorders themselves supply parity bits vertical, horizontal, and any cyclic character redundancy codes.

tapes, library — Library tapes will have tape labels, skip records and control marks. However, the programs must be stored on magnetic tape according to a particular format. Library tapes may contain two types of intermixed formats — standard-format (running programs as set up by a librarian), and debugging-format (this includes check data as well as the programs to be checked).

tape, storage — A tape or ribbon or any material impregnated or coated with magnetic material on which information may be placed in the form of magnetically polarized spots.

tape strips — A material used in random access storage devices that have removable or replaceable storage, in contrast to fixed storage. Card strips and disk packs, as well as tape strips, are used to store information, but they can be removed and replaced.

tape trailer — A special strip or tape length at the end of tape reels, usually containing a type of end-of-tape marker, i.e., a hole, long blank, special magnetic spots, etc.

tape transport — Refers to the mechanism which moves magnetic or paper tape past sensing and recording heads and usually associated with data processing equipment. Synonymous with tape transport, tape drive, and feed tape.

tape, transaction — Information on a paper tape or magnetic tape that is to be used to update filed information on a master tape.

tape warning, end of — A visible magnetic strip on magnetic tape which indicates that the few feet, often five feet, of the tape remains available.

target program — The program that is the output of an automatic coding system. Often the target program is a machine-language program ready for execution, but it may well be in an intermediate language. (Synonymous with object routine, and contrasted with source program.)

target variable — Any variable which is specified as a target to receive incoming data or the results of an operation.

tariff — The published rates and specifications for a specific unit of equipment, facility or type of service provided by a communication common carrier.

task — A unit of work for the central processing unit; sometimes the basic multiprogramming unit under the control program.

task control block — The accumulation of control data relating to a particular task.

task dispatcher — A unique control routine or function which selects from the task queue or lists the next task to be processed and gives it control of the central processor.

tasking — In order to facilitate implementation of systems involving several independent processes, the processor must be able to maintain the illusion that several routines are running simultaneously. Therefore, to relieve the programmer of the job of creating this illusion, some form of multi-tasking facility must be supplied.

The basic parts of such a facility include a real-time monitor to provide a task scheduling capability and a number of commands to allow activation, deactivation, and synchronization of tasks. Other desirable features include a timing facility and a provision for interrupt handling.

task management — Refers to a set of functions of the control program or routine which controls the use of system resources other than the input/output devices by tasks.

task queue — Refers to a queue which contains all the task control blocks which are in the system at any one time.

teaching calculator — One of the first calculators specifically made for developing individual mathematical computational skills is called Classmate 88. The machine uses an individualized instruction approach to generate unlimited drill and practice exercises for more than 70 computational skills. It is used in conjunction with Operational Achievement, a skills program developed in Monroe's education center. The combination of the computer system and the skills program provide an innovative approach to developing a capability in addition, subtraction, multiplication, division, fractions, decimals and number concepts. Classmate 88 comes with survey and diagnostic testing to determine exact competence levels for individual students. With a flick of the switch, the system generates random exercises in any of the 70 skill areas. When a skill area is selected and entered on the keyboard, the Classmate 88 prints a problem for that specific skill on a tape. The student works it manually on scratch paper, enters his solution into the machine and presses a "go" button. The machine either accepts the answer as correct and automatically prints another problem or prints the student's answer and a red error indicator. The student then may do the problem again until he gets the correct answer or he may press a key to ask the machine for the right answer. Problems and student's answers are printed on the tape, providing the teacher with a record of the student's work.

teaching machines — 1. Most such units have the following characteristics: A computer monitored or controlled with continuous and active response to each unit of information presented or queried. 2. Immediate and recorded feedback from questions of the students' responses and an acknowledgment of correct or incorrect answers to the student with other alternative or remedial information and instructions. 3. A scheduling which allows the student to work at his own pace and a modular presentation allowing teacher-programmers to present materials sufficiently varied to suit individual student capabilities. The teaching machine consists of both programs and hardware. The programs are either linear or branching types, or a mixture of both. Linear programs usually consist of one or two sentences, followed by a sentence containing blanks. Progress through the program is linear in the sense that one follows the other in sequence, although skipping some frames, usually planned. Branching programs have larger units of information, such as two or three paragraphs. The student usually answers multiple-choice questions, the main path is followed if the student answers are correct. Branches provide remedial teaching or instructions for incorrect answers. The teaching machines physically have a storage unit, a display mechanism, a response panel, and communication with a central computer. Some machines will combine with slides, film strips, and microfilm.

technique — 1. The detailed procedures essential to the expert execution of an art or science. 2. The method used to collect, process, convert, transfer, and retrieve data to prepare reports.

technique flow charts — Detailed flow charts showing data and information requirements and the specific method and calculations for processing the information.

telecommunication — A general term expressing data transmission between a computing system and remotely located devices via a unit that performs the necessary format conversion and controls the rate of transmission.

telecommunication, calculator to calculator — Calculator-to-calculator communication provides a wide range of options. Full-precision data arrays can be transferred from one machine to another at rates up to 9,600 bits/second in either asynchronous or synchronous mode. BASIC programs can be transferred from the memory of one machine to the other, and for asynchronous rates up to 1,800 bits/second, one calculator can remotely control another. Programs can be loaded, run, or stopped and peripherals can be activated. If, for example, a calculator is connected to a disc containing several programs, a user at another calculator can call up and access programs from the disc via the first calculator. For data transmission where error immunity is required, two calculators can be configured as two remote batch terminals using binary synchronous communication procedures. (some units)

telecommunications access method (TCAM) — The Telecommunications Access Method (TCAM) is a communication subsystem designed to exchange messages between the communication network and a set of message queues, according to information contained in control blocks and message headers. The program which controls these operations, called the Message Control Program (MCP), is coded for each particular installation using a set of system macros, which invoke various parts of the TCAM software.

telecommunications controller, terminal system — On some systems a Telecommunication Controller allows local or remote asynchronous communication with other terminals or remote asynchronous telecommunications with "foreign" CPU's (IBM, Univac, Honeywell, et cetera). Transmission over dial-up or leased phone lines equipped with Bell 103A3 Datasets is at 100 to 300 baud or with Bell 202C Datasets at 110, 150, 300, 600 or 1,200 baud. To the foreign CPU, the host terminal appears as a Teletype Model 33 or 35. When linked directly, within 124 feet, to other host terminals, asynchronous transmission can be up to 1200 baud (some systems).

telecommunications supervisory packet — Various access systems offer telecommunications supervisory packages, that can automatically direct the output from the host system to a particular device specified by the user, or to a file in the user's library. Moreover, automatic supervision frees the user's port for execution of other on-line programs, and allows the user to periodically check the status of a job for remote job entry systems. (RJE)

telecommunications systems, calculator-based — Programmable calculators have the capacity to handle line-oriented telecommunications between other similarly programmed calculator systems. With the addition of telecommunications options, programmable calculators can, under program control, transmit, receive, store, format and convert information. Such calculators are called "systems" and many new advanced programmable calculators have "intelligent" terminal capabilities and have indeed become computers in their own right. Utilizing the BASIC statements of PRINT, PRINT USING, and INPUT, the calculators send and receive data over telephone or dedicated lines at user-selected rates of up to 1200 bauds Data which may be read from or stored into cassette or disk, can be accepted in unformatted lines of up to 64 characters or specially formatted lines of up to 192 characters on some machines. In addition, they have facilities for initiating a break signal and for decoding a selected input character as the terminating character.

teleconferencing networks — Teleconferencing refers to the use of computer networks for personal communications among widely dispersed groups of people. Systems have been implemented to support multi-party conferences via computer. Computer networks greatly facilitate personal interactions among dispersed communities. The networks are regularly used for the distribution of documentation, requests for comments, comments, gripes, and the like, and on-line collaboration is not uncommon.

teleconferencing procedures — Most regular participants have "mailboxes" or directories at particular sites to which text files may be sent. Users regularly link to one-another for assistance or simply to chat. Users have sorted themselves out into a number of special interest groups, and a kind of distributed network organization has evolved. This sort of facilitation of personal interaction which networks can achieve is perhaps their most powerful capability. Full exploitation will come with time, as more and more users adjust their work patterns to take advantage of the capabilities.

telemetering — Also called telemetry or remote metering. Measurement which, through intermediate means, can be interpreted at a distance from the primary detector. A receiving instrument converts the transmitted electrical signals into units of data, which can then be translated by data reduction into appropriate units.

telemetry — 1. Transmission to a distance of measured magnitudes by radio or telephony, with suitably coded modulation (e.g., amplitude, frequency, phase, pulse). 2. Remote sensing of operating systems by an instrument that converts transmitted electric signals into units of data.

telemetry systems, adapter unit — A data-adapter unit provides the system with greatly expanded input/output device capability. It provides direct connection for a variety of remote and local external devices, e.g., teletypewriter terminals, telemetry terminals, test instrumentation and data-acquisition equipment. The unit attaches to a selector channel or multiplexor channel. A selector channel handles high-speed input/output devices. It is overlapped with other selector channels and a multiplexor channel, in a processor's input/output control element, to provide simultaneous operations. When a selector channel is used, only one device at a time can read data into that channel, although as many as eight input/output control units can be connected to it. A multiplexor channel can handle many low- or medium-speed devices simultaneously on a character-by-character basis, or a single device in a burst of characters. The maximum data-rate capability of the unit is generally specified by the particular transmission interface adapter used, the input/output channel capacity, and the overall systems configuration (some systems).

telephone-calculator interface, CMOS — One CMOS calculator-output interface can be connected to memory buffers, printers, microprocessors and the like. And gadgeteers who don't like dial telephones might use this special interface technique to turn a 10-digit calculator into a pushbutton converter with display and storage space equal to the calculator's registers.

telephone, touch-tone audio response unit — To reduce console cost to probably the lowest possible, experiments have been conducted using ordinary touch-tone telephone hand sets. For applications with limited input requirements, this ultra-simple terminal device may suffice making such remote systems easily accessible to many users. This type of input is usually coupled with audio-response output. Magnetic tapes have words, syllables or perhaps only phonemes prerecorded. The computer puts together an aural response by stringing together sequences of these recorded elements.

telephony — The conversion of a sound signal into corresponding variations of electric current (or potential) which is then transmitted by wire or radio to a distant point where it is reconverted into sound.

teleprinter — Term used to refer to the equipment used in a printing telegraph system. A teletypewriter.

teleprinter interface, calculator — A unit designed to enable various programmable calculator models to have the capability of direct online communication to line printers, teletypes, laboratory/medical instruments, and phones with acoustic coupler or modem attachments. With the interface, numerical data, alpha of variable length, and software program input or output are accepted. Data editing, validating, and output formatting can be readily incorporated into the software programs. Various calculators will interface to peripheral devices using 20 ma. current loop, EAI RS-232C or CCITT V. 24. The coding designated character generally accepted is ASCII at 110, 150, 300, 600, or 1200 baud, either half or full duplex, usually accepted into the ENTRY registers.

teleprinter terminal — A typical small, teleprinter-type multi-copy terminal is only 22 inches wide. Its four-row keyboard generates 63 ASCII printing graphics, plus the space character, in upper case and all control characters. It has a 72-character print line, with an 86-character line available. The unit produces an original and two copies on conventional paper. Most are available in KSR, ASR and MSR configurations; and in basic, Data-Phone®, Data Access Arrangements (DAA) and acoustic-coupled arrangements.

teleprocessing network — In an operating teleprocessing network, several inquiries simultaneously might come into the system from distant cities concerning information that is contained in the disk file. The appropriate records are then taken from the disk file and the appropriate responses would be prepared and returned to the originating cities. Although this appears to be a simple function, the network requires design balance to achieve the required variety of terminal speeds and functions. The network requires: simultaneous operation of many devices operating through a single economical channel, the time-sharing and space-sharing programs that control these devices, and disk-file capacity and speed. Furthermore, it has to do all of these things concurrently with batch-job processing. The system has the data communications facilities to handle these functions as an integral part of its processing units. Special provision is made for code conversion within the processing units (some systems).

teleprocessing system — Data processing equipment used in combination with terminal equipment and communication facilities.

teleprocessing terminal — A teleprocessing terminal is used for on-line data transmission between remote process locations and a central computer system. Connection to the computer system is made by a data adapter unit or a transmission control. This system facilitates the control of natural gas and petroleum pipe lines, utility distribution systems, and the collection of process data in petroleum refineries, chemical plants, paper mills, iron and steel works, batch processes in manufacturing, and many other applications.

Teletype — Trademark of the Teletype Corporation. Usually refers to a series of different types of teleprinter equipment such as transmitters, tape punches, reperforators, page printers, utilized for communication systems.

Teletype, ASR33 — Various Teletype models may be purchased through suppliers with microcomputers. A typical unit has a pedestal base, and includes the page copy teleprinter, keyboard assembly, paper tape perforator with chad box (ASR33). Optional equipment includes modem couplers, printer disable kits, and other items. Purchase of a complete system through a specific supplier assures complete hardware compatibility.

Teletype controller — Generally the controller contains parallel-to-serial and serial-to-parallel conversion circuitry required to interface an ASR-33 teletype to various full-duplex, asynchronous operation, and a single printed circuit card mounts inside processor enclosure.

Teletype/CRT utility package — This is a library of programs that perform the most common I/O functions for a Teletype or CRT (Cathode Ray Tube) terminal. The programs are similar to the Teletype Utility Package but also provide support for CRT terminal I/O functions and therefore occupy a slightly larger portion of memory.

Teletype diagnostic — This tests the processor mounted Teletype option in a look-back diagnostic mode. If an ASR-33 Teletype is attached and operator intervention is selected, the Teletype diagnostic can test completely the keyboard, printer, paper tape reader, paper tape punch and motor on/off functions.

Teletype exchange services (TELEX & TWX) — Teletypewriter Exchange Service provides direct-dial-point-to-point connections using teleprinter equipment, such as keyboard printers, paper tape readers, and tape punches. Facilities are also available to permit computers to interface to these services. These are Western Union services.

Teletype interface and control, calculator — This interface is designed to be compatible with a Model 33 TEG Teletype or equivalent, and allows the user's Teletype to be tied on-line to the calculating systems. Gives users a variety of input/output operations such as alphanumeric input from the Teletype, hard copy alphanumeric output to the Teletype and input/output of numeric data on punched paper tape.

Teletype interface operation, calculator — Programmable calculators when interfaced to teleprinters will typically accept numerical data directly into the ENTRY register for calculation or storage in a data register; output a number from the ENTRY register through the interface to the peripheral device; generate a Carriage Return and Line Feed on the peripheral for data formatting; accept a string of up to 72 alphanumeric characters, store them in data registers and then output to a cassette or back through the interface to the peripheral for additional use. Calculators with such interfaces have the ability to output their programs to a Teletype paper punch or read them back into program memory from a paper tape reader.

Teletype microcomputer interface — A typical general purpose microcomputer with 1.5 μsec cycle time includes: 4096 word main memory, operating console, direct memory access channel, processor input-output channel, power-fail/auto-restart circuitry, interrupt system and built-in Teletype controller for 110 baud, 11-bit operation with an ASR 33 Teletype. The system is generally complete with basic software and maintenance documentation. (Note: Requires Teletype Modification Kit to be installed in Teletype.)

Teletype modification kit — A typical kit provides 20mA Teletype signal loop current; translates TTL signal levels to Teletype-compatible signal levels; contains circuitry to permit incremental control of the paper tape reader, and is designed to install in a Teletype Corporation Model 3320-3JA teletype.

teletype network — Describes a system of points, interconnected by private telegraph channels, which provide hard copy and/or telegraphic coded (5-channel) punched paper tape, as required, at both sending and receiving points. Typically, up to 20 way-stations share send-receive time on a single circuit, and can exchange information without requiring action at a switching center. If two or more circuits are provided, a switching center is required to permit cross-circuit transmission. Such networks are available on a monthly rental plus one-time installation charge basis.

Teletype terminals — Teletype and Teletype-compatible units are keyboard displays operating in an asynchronous transmission mode with ASCII code. These devices generally replace Teletype Model 33 or 35 keyboard printers and are plug-to-plug compatible with them. Also included are the Teletype Model 40 (Bell Telephone companies that offer it as a tariffed service call it Dataspeed 40) and similar units even though they are not directly compatible with the TTY-33s and 35s, because they represent an important competitive threat to the vendors or VDTs.

teletypewriter — Generic term referring to the basic equipment made by Teletype Corporation and to teleprinter equipment.

teletypewriter KSR (Keyboard Send-Receive Unit) — Receives the line signal and prints the same as an RO, but, in addition, it has a keyboard that is used for manually sending line signals. It has no paper-tape capability but is very popular for conversational time sharing and inquiry-response applications.

teletypewriter or terminal calculator output — An extremely powerful output of some calculators is the Serial USASCII interface. It makes the system compatible with a standard Teletype ASR33 teletypewriter, and any device that is mutually compatible, such as other make teletypewriter terminals, tape perforators, and CRT terminals. Since much data communications is based on this system, these system units thus acquire the facilities of a global communications network, including computer compatibility. This versatility is achieved at surprisingly low cost, making this option a very popular one. In typical use, calculator data may be fed to the ASR33 tape punch, and stored for later transmission, may be fed simultaneously via modem to a computer, and may be printed out in hard copy.

teletypewriter service, private-line — A form of teletypewriter service differing from exchange service in that it is limited to service between certain specified stations. The service may be contracted for on a full-time or part-time basis.

Telnet protocol — The Telnet protocol is extensively supported in networks and defines a network virtual terminal permitting all terminals on the network to provide a similar interface to processes in any host. This allows the use of any terminal supported by the network with any host system on the network even if that host could not support the particular terminal through its standard terminal controller.

Telpak — A service offered by telephone companies for leasing of wide band channels between two or more points. Telpak channels can be leased in groups of 60 or 240 voice grade channels.

template, calculator terminal example — The user selects the operations to be performed by the BASIC program by pressing some special-function keys. These keys are matched to the BASIC program by a special template and may be allotted the jobs of sending a canned sign-on/sign-off, single-card command, or request for job status. In addition, Job Control Language (JCL) cards can be stored in the calculator memory to further emulate 2780 functions, in some units.

tens complement — The radix complement of a numeral whose radix is ten. The tens complement is obtained by subtracting each digit of a number from 9, and adding 1 to the least significant of the resultant number. For example, the tens complement of 2456 is 7544.

terminal, addressable-pollable — A terminal is addressable when it has its own unique identifier. All data sent to the terminal must be preceded by their addresses. Pollable means that the terminal responds to status inquiries from the computer. Each terminal in the system is queried by the computer in succession. The ability of the terminal to respond to the poll and to identify itself makes it pollable. Multidrop refers to when it is possible to have a number of modems, with associated terminals, share or drop off one telephone line.

This is distinct from multipoint, where each modem has its own data link with the central computer.

terminal badge leader — A badge reader is a self-contained, remote data entry terminal. This device offers a reliable method of identifying and controlling access to a calculator and a very fast method of entering fixed data. Typically fixed alphanumeric data entry is accomplished via a 22-column static optical badge reader with no moving contacts; variable alpha-numeric data and control entry is accomplished by means of a 16-key, 30-character keyboard. The alpha-numeric display can permit complete interaction between the computer and the operator; instructions to the operator, therefore, can be tailored to the specific application. Options are available which allow a combination of controls over the audible signal, function lights, badge ejector, and keyboard lockout. This versatility permits the user to configure the terminal to offer a specific response to a badge input. The standard terminal generally contains both E1A and 20 mA interfaces. All communication is ASC11 coded. (some units.)

terminal buffer, calculator — On some systems if the central computer has too small a buffer to receive 16,000 characters at a time, it may require the terminal to send one line at a time and wait for an X-ON or similar response to send the next line. A calculator can perform this terminal function automatically with a BASIC program that stores the keyboard input on a tape cassette. On line, another BASIC program or subroutine reads and transmits the data to the calculator, the calculator now automatically responding to each X-ON by sending the next line.

terminal, calculator communications — An optionally available adapter lets users design their unit to become a terminal to a larger processor. Some advanced units provide access to remote data bases and program libraries. Information processed or developed on these units can be sent to and retrieved from a remote system. Transmission occurs at line rates of 134.5 or 300 bits per second, through a standard EIA RS-232C interface. (some units)

terminal, calculator CRT example — The second half of one system — with its CRT, teletype style keyboard and operating modes — provides a spectrum of graphics and alphanumerics. Complete with 63 upper case and numeric characters in standard ASCII form, the keyboard also includes rocker switches for:
- Local or calculator control
- Hard copies of the display via the optional (4610) hard copy unit
- Changing the keyboard from alpha to numeric code. Depending on its position, the switch permits the calculator to interpret pressed terminal keys as letters or numbers. Execution of other calculator functions is also possible with this feature.

terminal calculator operation example — When operating as a calculator, the unit reads out keystrokes and computed results onto its display. But when the calculator is configured as a timesharing terminal, characters received from a computer are first displayed. When a carriage-return signal is received, the displayed line is output on the calculator's printer. Programs or data may also be stored on tape or disk for reuse, on some units. Generally, message lengths are limited to about 15,000 to 16,000 characters by the maximum memory size. But the user can send longer programs by dividing them into segments that will fit in the memory and then sending one segment at a time.

terminal, communications — Asynchronous interfaces have switch-selectable Baud rates for maximum flexibility. Some terminals have hard copy and display with optional hard copy that provide interactive capability. In cases where the microcomputer must communicate with other computers, many suppliers offer asynchronous and synchronous interfaces for local or remote (via modem) communications. These communications capabilities make the terminals ideal tools for remote data gathering in support of a larger central computing facility.

terminal components — Refers to those needed to perform most functions: keyboard, display, microprocessor, memory, storage, printers, modems and adapters.

terminal-control functions — The types of terminal-control functions in a controller depend on the types of terminals that it was designed to service. An example of terminal control is the sending of polling characters (transmitter-start codes) to initiate transmission from a teletypewriter or the sending of addressing characters (call-directing codes) to the same type of terminal to condition it for receiving on a multiterminal line. The sending of an acknowledgment of receipt of a good block of data (ACK) or the non-receipt of the data (NACK), may be an automatic controller function. The synchronization of the two ends of the system in synchronous transmission can be accomplished by the controller.

terminal controller features — Typical capabilities include:
- Full-duplex, asynchronous operation.
- Parity, framing, and overrun detection.
- Switch-selectable even, odd, or no parity generation and checking.
- One or two stop bits.
- Teletype or RS-232C-compatible operation.
- Switch-selectable baud rates of 110 to 9600.
- Test mode operation.
- Jumper-enabled carriage-return delay for hard-copy terminals.

terminal controller functions — Functions that are handled within a controller include: 1. I/O message buffering; 2. character code conversion; 3. editing and formatting; 4. character generation for visual display; 5. refresh storage for visual display; 6. data concentration for communication lines; 7. error checking and error control.

terminal control system, disk (TCS) — Typically this is a control program which efficiently handles multiterminal operations in conjunction with the Disc Operating System. It provides task scheduling, I/O management, file access, priority dispatching and exceptionally fast task handling.

terminal cursors — Most terminals have a cursor of some sort. On the smarter terminals, the cursor can be moved around freely, but usually the movements are more restricted. Typical cursors include a line under the character at hand, a nondestructive blinking white block and a white block on which an existing character on the screen is reversed. Typical cursor keyboard commands are up, down, left, right, home and return left to next line on new line command. With the up, down, left and right keys, there is usually a repeating feature for rapid long-distance cursor movement. When cursor control keys are not enough, other interactive control devices are sometimes available as options. These include a joystick, a light pen, a trackball and a set of thumbwheel controls. These techniques are most useful on graphic terminals.

terminal, daisy-chaining — Daisy-chaining is generally the same as multidropping, except that no modems are used; however, the terminals share the same data link. The data link comes from the computer, goes to the first terminal, comes out of the first terminal and on to the second terminal, etc. All terminals share the same data link and the same computer port.

terminal data communications capabilities — Most terminals are serial asynchronous, full or half duplex and meet EIA RS-232C specifications. Both units are Bell 103 and 202 modem compatible with switch selectable data rates of 100, 150, 300, 1200 and 2400 baud. Either unit is easily interfaced to a hard copy device.

terminal display mode — Display modes include: vector, increment, character, point, vector continue, or short vector, and specify the manner in which points are to be displayed on the screen.

terminal disk multiplexer — On one system this allows the use of four system Central Processing Units with a single disk unit, to maximize use of the disk unit.

terminal dynamic memory allocation — Some terminals dynamically pack information into memory permitting 8 to 50 lines of information to be stored in 1,024 characters of display memory. With memory expansion to 8K bytes, over 3 pages of data can be stored. Twenty-four lines may be viewed at a time by using the roll up, roll down, next page and previous page keys.

terminal editing, calculator — The editing features of some calculator terminals are those of buffered, interactive terminals and are not to be found in unbuffered units. Data and programs are directly entered into the calculator's memory. This allows the user to make corrections and insert or delete lines. In some units programs to be transmitted can be entered not only in BASIC, the calculator's native language, but in FORTRAN, COBOL, or any other high-level language. The reason is that the calculator's syntax-checking function, and hence its language, can be bypassed. Once on line, the data or program to be transmitted is read out of the calculator's memory and applied to the modem instead of the printer, as would be the case for local operation.

terminal editing capabilities — New terminals operate both character by character and one block of data at a time. Terminal functions can be initated from the keyboard or from the computer. Text can be composed and edited locally before transmission to the central processor or after transmission. Editing and CPU connect times are significantly reduced by features such as:

- character or line insertion and deletion,
- addressability and positioning control (up, down, left, right and home)
- programmable protected fields in any combination of display positions,
- off-screen storage with scrolling (scroll up, scroll down, next page, previous page),
- standard horizontal tabulations and protected field tabulations,
- transparent display control codes,
- eight special function keys for user-defined routines, such as forms entry or on-line error detection, and
- positionable memory protection. (some systems)

terminal emulation calculator — One type programable calculator can emulate a time-sharing terminal or a batch terminal communicating in IBM's binary synchronous communications protocol (BSC) — capabilities that it owes to the development of communications interfaces, low-cost auxiliary mass storage, plug-in read-only memories (ROMs), and programable special-function keys. It can also vary its capabilities as either a terminal or a calculator: the user simply plugs in a different ROM and changes the names of the programable keys by laying the template associated with the ROM over the calculator's keyboard.

terminal equipment requirements, calculator — In addition to a specific Calculator and Terminal ROM, the following equipment is necessary for the operation of a calculator unit as a terminal: A Printer, a Low-speed modem with either a telephone data set or an accoustic coupler. The modem must be Electrical Industries Association (EIA) Standard RS-232-C compatible, and a Modem Interface Card.

terminal, graphic — Among the hardware features on some graphic terminals are image transformations in two or three dimensions; zooming and windowing on selected parts of the screen; function, vector and character generators (circles, ellipses, rectangles, etc.); depth cueing (change in line intensity with depth); and perspective (nonparallel planes define the viewing space). Graphic terminals are often sold with the option of a color CRT.

terminal, hand-held — Able to interact with its central processor by means of an acoustic coupler or a hard-wire connection, one specific hand-held computer terminal is a truly portable device that measures only 2 by 4.25 by 7 inches and weighs only 1.5 pounds. The unit provides all 128 ASCII characters and can display two lines of 10 characters each. A 1,000-character input buffer may be scrolled by the user. The terminal offers switch-selectable data rates of 10, 15, 20, or 120 characters per second and includes an RS-232 interface.

terminal hardware, integrated circuit design — Advances in integrated circuit design, which include MOS and LSI technology, have made it possible to compact on a few PC boards the electronic circuitry needed to control the terminal, its peripherals and communications. The cost of the electronic components for a keyboard system has been reduced over three-fold during the past few years. This cost trend should continue as LSI and other techniques of advanced circuitry design are utilized.

terminal, human factors — Key elements of human factors include the size of the screen; the number, shape and size of the characters on the screen; the color and appearance of the screen; the arrangement of the keyboard; and the sound of the keyboard. The designs should provide comfort to humans.

terminal, interactive — Various series of on-line interactive terminals give users fast video interaction plus a variety of switch-selectable transmission rates and operating modes and compatibility with computers or timesharing networks operating in asynchronous, ASCII communications codes. Some are low-density modules for simplified mechanics and low maintenance. When hard copy is needed, an electrolytic copier, on the side of some visual display units can provide a permanent record of displayed data.

terminal interfaces — Manufacturers often list under interfaces on the terminal spec sheet such comments as: "RS-232-C," "current loop," "20-mA current loop," "60-mA current loop," or a variety of computer/communications names. Interfaces, for example the RS-232-C specifies a 25-pin connector, of which only 13 pins are assigned definite functions. The 12 others are used, in whole or in part by different terminal manufacturers for different functions. Also, RS-232-C doesn't provide timing specifications.

terminal, internal memory — The internal memory should be designed so that it can be shared for programming and/or internal storage. Most terminal systems provide for 2 or 4K of memory with options to add an additional memory in 2 or 4K segments up to 32 or 64K terminal.

terminal keyboards — Refers generally to two basic types — alphanumeric and numeric. Alphanumeric keyboards are used for word processing, text processing, data processing, and teleprocessing. Numeric only keyboards are used on touch-tone telephones, accounting machines and calculators. The touch-tone telephone has come into significant use as a calculator and data input and voice output device.

terminal, keying — Concerns a combination alphanumeric/numeric keyboard for entering, editing, calling out character strings, operating peripherals and changing the function of the terminal.

terminal language, HPL calculator — HPL, a high level, formula-oriented programming language, handles subroutine nesting and 16 flags. It allows up to 26 simple variables and 26 multidimensional array variables, limited only by the size of the calculator memory. Claimed to contain the power and efficiency of FORTRAN for handling complex formulas and equations, but as easy to learn as BASIC, HPL is suited for both controller and data processing applications. The structural unit is a line composed of one or more statements separated by semicolons. Errors are indicated by error messages and line numbers in the display and are identified by a flashing cursor. Math errors can be overridden by the programmer. Programs can be debugged by commands inserted from the keyboard. Tracing can be made on the entire program, a section, or a single line. Both fixed- and floating-point formats can be set by the user. Entire lines or individual characters can be inserted, deleted, or changed. When line insertions or deletions are made, addresses are automatically renumbered.

terminal, microprocessor-controlled — The operating characteristics of "smart" terminals are controlled through firmware. The terminal's microprocessor manages memory allocation, data communications, keyboard scanning, and display control. This microprocessor implementation and the use of Single Bus architecture yield a terminal utilizing electronics and mechanics with a wide range of capabilities and potential for future enhancements.

terminal/modem interface operations — Refers to the interfaces between the terminal and modem. They contain not only digital data signals, but signals for controlling the modem and the data link. For example, when the line is turned around in half-duplex communication, the sending modem must be switched to the receiving condition, and the receiving modem must be switched to the sending condition. A modem is switched from receive to send through the EIA interface by raising to a predetermined voltage level the control lead designated as "Request to Send." When the modem's "Clear to Send" status lead turns on, it is a signal to the calculator or terminal that the modem is ready to transmit data over the data link.

terminal, parity checking — Parity checking can be one character or by block.

terminal plug-in character sets — On some terminals in addition to the standard 64 character Roman set and optional 128 Roman set, up to 3 additional 128 character sets may be added. Adjacent characters on the display may be from any of four optional character sets. Inverse video presentation of data is offered as a standard feature with underline, blinking and half-bright options. Mathematics and line drawing character sets are also widely available.

terminal polling and auto answer — Polling is the capability of addressing a terminal for data transmission to the terminal or data collection from the terminal. When the terminal has the capability of auto answering and receiving transmitting data in either a foreground or background mode, the user can optimize the communication system and at the same time get data into the computer and back in the required time frame. For example, if invoice data is only needed on a daily basis, the data can be stored in the auxiliary storage device as it is keyed during the day and automatically transferred to the host computer at night during non-prime communication hours.

terminal pop-in expandability — Digital electronics are contained on easy to remove printed circuit cards. Additional cards can be inserted for a choice of options.

terminal pre-and-post processing — An example of pre- and post-processing with the calculator used as a batch terminal is numerical control (NC) tape preparation by a midwest manufacturer. Automatic Programing of Tools (APT) language and JCL programs are stored as card images and loaded on a tape cassette under control of a Basic program. The programs not only format the card images but also provide such editing functions as deleting or inserting cards. On some units when the tape cassette is loaded, the calculator signs onto the company's main computer, indicating its intention to send the card images. Output from the APT processor is a listing of job statistics and control information for preparation of an NC tape by the calculator. The job statistics are routed to the printer, and the control information is put on cassette tape and later used off line to generate the final tape on the calculator's peripheral paper-tape punch. (some units)

terminal ROM, calculator — On one unit, because the software that enables the calculator to act as a timesharing terminal is in a separate ROM, the calculator can run local programs at the same time as it is on line to a remote computer. This combination allows data collected locally to be partially processed before being transmitted. Similarly, data from a remote computer may be massaged by a program at the calculator for further processing before readout.

terminal ROM, example — This allows a specific model to be used in conjunction with a modem or accoustic coupler as a terminal to a remote time-share system. Basically, a Terminal ROM makes the calculator work like a teleprinter when communicating with a time-share system. The calculator may also transmit or receive BASIC language programs or free text: This includes programs written in FORTRAN, ALGOL, or other programming languages. In order to provide the necessary special characters and retain single keystroke execution, the Terminal ROM makes use of four of the Special Function Keys. One Terminal ROM uses 20 8-bit bytes (10 words) of Read/Write memory to define these keys. Two of the keys correspond to the teleprinter SHIFT and CTRL keys respectively. The SAVE function key is used to retain information transmitted from the remote time-share computer to the calculator. The TRANSMIT function is used to send program lines or instructions to the time-share system, on some systems.

terminal screen, interaction advantages —
- Allows program "prompting" for entry of commands and data
- Immediate visual verification of input
- Shows intermediate and final results
- Scrolls information up or down one line at a time
- Characters may be black on white backgrounds or white on black (some units)

terminal self-test — By depressing a single button on the keyboard of some terminals users get an immediate indication of the status of the memory, firmware and display.

terminal table — An ordered collection of information consisting of a control field for the table and blocks of information on each terminal from which a message can originate, and each terminal, group of terminals, and processing program to which a message can be sent.

terminal teleprocessing — Includes the preparation, transmission and receipt of messages typically using teleprinters.

terminal, versatile keyboard — Many detachable, expanded ASCII keyboards are easy and flexible enough to fill a variety of needs. They contain a ten-key numeric pad, cursor control, tab and page control pad, editing, control and special function keys. A simplified keyboard for some units is optional.

terminal, "very low cost" — One very low cost terminals, VLCT, is used for machine language programming. It converts a three digit octal code directly into an 8 digit binary code for transmission to the computer and then displays the binary output from the computer in a 3 digital octal format. This allows users to program in octal which is much easier than programming in binary.

terminology CRT configuration — The configuration of a CRT terminal refers to the way in which it interacts with other terminals or with a host computer. Basically, terminals can either stand alone or in clustered units. The second type connects to a controller unit, communicates with it along parallel data paths and relies on it for some of its processing capabilities.

test — The process following debugging of a calculator routine, to verify that the software and/or the hardware, is functioning properly.

test and verify programs (T & V) — Test and Verify Programs (T & V) enable the user to determine whether the hardware is functioning properly or to isolate a malfunction, if one should occur. T & V programs are provided for processor, memory, and many standard peripherals and controllers.

test, bias — Refers to a form of test, usually as part of preventive maintenance or as a fault-finding or correcting operation, to test against safety margins for faults.

test card, diagnostic — Refers to a special input/output test card used to completely test all I/O functions and strappable operation configurations. The test card simulates both normal and Direct Memory Access (DMA) I/O controllers along with special purpose test logic that allows a complete test of every I/O bus signal. In addition, the test card provides connections to the power supply to test Power Fail/Restart, to the Teletype Controller to completely simulate a Teletype, to the Automatic Loader switch to completely test the automatic loader, and to other jumper option points to allow testing of every possible configuration.

test clips — Test clips offer power- and ground-seeking circuitry to eliminate the need to make separate connections from a power source to the clip. Some have buffered, over-voltage protected inputs to prevent circuit loading or LED burnout. Some particular units, while larger in overall size are connected to the unit under test via a 2-foot cable, allowing the readout section to be positioned without reference to the product under test and are provided with 100 IC reference schematic cards that can be inserted into the readout unit to aid in interpreting the display.

test data — Refers to a set of data developed specifically to test the adequacy of a calculator run or system. The data may be actual data that have been taken from previous operations, or artificial data created for this purpose.

tester devices and adapters — Refers to various devices that test all the types of MOS/LSI devices used in some systems. A functional (hot mock-up) test is performed on each chip. The tester provides fast, thorough, automatic testing of the devices in the dynamic mode.

test flag key — The Test Flag key tests to see if a

specified flag is set. If it is not, then transfer occurs to the location or label. If it is, no transfer. For example, INV 2nd if flg 3 A means transfer to A if flag 3 is reset.

test flags keys condition — The condition of the flags can be tested automatically at any point in user programs by using these "TEST FLAG 1" and "TEST FLAG 2" keys to include an appropriate test flag instruction. The program will either advance sequentially or skip over the next steps, depending on the condition of the tested flag. These keys allow users to compare the values in the X and Y registers. If the test condition is not met, the program skips over the next two steps. If the test condition is met, the program continues with the next step. This allows the users to perform conditional branches based on the results of the test. (some units)

testing — The method for examining to determine the real character or specific aspects of an item, program, or system. Acceptance testing for equipment determines capacity, capability, and reliability. Program testing determines whether programs do what they are supposed to do when used with the test, simulated, or live data.

testing, Device Under Test (DUT) — There are many types of testing requirements of today's microprocessor devices and many philosophies of test execution and pattern or sequence generation. One method turns the general-purpose tester into the natural environment of a microcomputer system. Here, a reference microprocessor in the test socket, coupled with the natural DUT environment created by the tester, allows the reference device to execute any microprocessor program. Hence, the system user can describe his microprocessor function test in the microprocessor language. The reference microprocessor executes the user written diagnostic exercise, and the tester "learns" all pin activity and saves it as the resultant truth table for future production testing.

testing nominative — Refers to various standards of performance that are established for the testing of both quantitative and qualitative system performance.

testing RAMs and ROMs — Modern RAMs and ROMs are becoming bigger and faster. In 1976, 16K RAMs came on the market, storing information at lower cost than ever before. These devices are being produced in huge quantities — millions of devices from more than a dozen major manufacturers. They incorporate the most advanced semiconductor processing techniques, to generate maximum performance (speed of access, for example). The patterns of cells used are vast. Testing them requires that the state of having a "bit" stored or not stored in the individual cell must be explored completely, so that every cell can be tested and the device characterized. Test patterns were invented to detect RAM/ROM defects rapidly, but as designs and processes evolve at a rapid rate, many "canned" patterns fail to detect faults. Even the same device, purchased at different times from different vendors, may include defects that a "proved" pattern would not detect. The reason: many patterns used in testing neglect defects of the memory device, and "pass" it where it should have "failed."

testing, self-test method — Several basic methods may be considered for microprocessor function testing. One is the "CPU Self-Test Diagnostic" method where the device exists in its natural environment with a ROM, RAM, bus controllers and peripherals. A "diagnostic program" is loaded into the RAM, or already exists in a ROM. This program when executed by the microprocessor under test, is designed to exercise as many instructions as possible under some worst-case sequence and, hopefully, worst-case data conditions in the internal registers.

testing software — The software options which are designed to make the management and development of test data easier for the user include: source editing of source files on cards, paper tape, or disc; data logging for gathering and storing selected test items for additional processing; binning summary reporting with a capability of maintaining 16 bin counters and their associated control lines; automatic histogram plotting; machine usage reporting; propagation delay testing; standard parametric testing; standard device-oriented testing; plus other unique test programs. Typical software systems offer multi-station operation — up to two parallel stations and up to four active stations plus a test compiler station. The test pattern data base and the programs are independent of each other; and programs may be compiled on line while other stations are testing, without test interruption. The system also permits programming off the front panel, with control down to a single-bit level. (some units)

test procedures, bootstrap — Terminals increasingly are becoming applications-oriented, easier to use, and more reliable. But in addition, test diagnostics can be placed in firmware, making the units self-testing. At the start of each day or shift, the operator can get the terminal to perform a test. Some units have a diagnostics program on a floppy disc and have it brought in as part of the bootstrap. It performs a hardware checkout and a display indicates to the operator where any failing point is, enabling the user to tell the customer engineer exactly what replacement part to bring.

test programs and subroutines — Frequently used test program segments can be coded once as Macros or Subroutines and then be permanently stored on a user selected device. When generating a device test, these routines can be called by the user's test program, thus reducing test generation time. Test program size is virtually unlimited as subroutines may call subroutines in up to four levels of nesting, in some systems.

test program system — A checking system used before running any problem, in which a sample problem of the same type with a known answer is run.

test run — A diagnostic run of the program, using manufactured data. The results of this run are checked against the correct answers for this problem.

tests, conditional transfers, calculator — These statements depend on tests. If test conditions are met, then transfer or branch takes place. Otherwise the regular sequence continues, as normal. Three types of tests are conducted: The display (positive, negative, zero, flashing, not flashing). Flags (set, not set). Contents of register 00 (zero or not zero).

tests, microprocessors — Currently, the major test categories available to the engineer are: the self-diagnostic method, the comparison method, algorithmic pattern generation and stored-response testing.

text editing — Refers to specific flexible editing

facilities which have been designed into the calculator program to permit the original keyboarding of textual copy without regard for the eventual format or medium for publication. Once the copy has been placed in calculator storage, it can be edited and justified easily and quickly into any required column width and for any specified type font, merely by specifying the format required. Thus, copy for a report or journal can be keyboarded and edited, then justified and output directly onto a photocomposition device for publication of the document. If later there is a request for a reprint in either the original or in an edited form, the calculator can quickly produce output suitable for printing by any of several techniques.

text editor — A text editor provides the system user with a convenient and flexible source text generation system. Source statements are entered via any source input device/file. The entered source text may be output, statements added, deleted or modified. The text editor permits the order of statements or groups of statements to be altered at any time. The final text is output to a source device/file for use as input to an Assembler.

text editor, microprocessor — With a powerful editor, users can accomplish both line and character-oriented text preparation and editing. An advanced development aid removes the tedium from program preparation and alteration. Whether users choose to develop their software on large computers or small microcomputers, software support can save time and money.

text editor, operating system — Refers to a powerful and flexible editor that runs in an Operating System (OS) environment. Editing of programs can be done symbolically on a line, word, or character basis. Text Editor includes a subroutine feature that allows repetitive editing functions to be performed with a minimum of user effort.

theft alarm, calculator — Hand-held calculators are a prime target for thieves because they can be quickly picked up and tucked out of sight. Some users physically fasten them to desks. Another approach is an audible alarm that sounds off when the calculator is unplugged from its charger. The alarm is inserted between the charger and the calculator, and draws a nominal amount of power from the charger. As long as a trickle charging current (at least 100 μA) flows into the calculator, silicon diode D1 conducts. The forward voltage drop across it keeps germanium transistor Q1 turned on. Transistor Q2, which can be almost any pnp device, is cut off, and the Sonalert alarm is silenced.

However, if the calculator is unplugged, Q1 turns off, Q2 turns on, and the Sonalert starts to howl. Obviously, if the charger is unplugged, the alarm will not operate. So, it's important either to hide the charger or secure it in some way so that the thief will not disconnect it. To prevent the alarm from becoming obvious (when it is silenced!), it's a good idea to build the alarm and the charger into one small enclosure.

thermal page-width printer — A typical alphanumeric page printer can produce full formatted output for setting up data tables, drawing simple plots, and placing text in the format desired.

thermal printer — A typical thermal printer has full set of alphanumeric characters. Prints up to 16 characters per line at 2.8 lines a second.

thermal printer, alphanumeric capability — Full editing capability is provided on most advanced units. Users can step forward or backward, delete, insert, list the program, or display the program. The alphanumeric capability provided by the thermal printer is a powerful programming tool enabling users to include printed instructions in their programs. And they can use alpha to greatly extend the number of program labels available. Some units have up to 151 labels providing lots of flexibility for even the most complex programs.

thermal printer, calculator — For high quality, hard-copy output one type Thermal Printer provides 250 lines/minute speed equivalent to 3,600 words/minute. It produces page-width, fully-formatted, alphanumeric text, tables, or simple plots.

thermal printer calculator desk-top — A desk-top model with thermal printer is a must for calculations requiring a printed record. Most are compact and light enough to carry from office to home. Typical features include:

- 10-digit, 12-column thermal printer with electric paper feed
- Addition, subtraction, multiplication, division
- Business logic
- Floating or add mode decimal selection with override capability
- Automatic constant
- Subtotals, group totals and grand totals
- Dual clear entry/clear key
- AC operation (115 V) with 8 foot cord
- Vinyl dust cover
- Compact, about 4 to 5 pounds.

thermal printer characteristics, calculator — Some unit's use of a special typing head, made up of 35 heating elements, and heat-sensitive paper eliminates the need for ribbons, ink, and the noise of impact line printers. One unit prints 56 alphanumeric characters, each composed of a 5×7 dot matrix, at a rate of 30 characters per second. Although the 80-column unit is small (weighing only 30 pounds), it is designed for high-volume printing applications.

thermal printer, programmable calculator — On some programmable calculators the Alphanumeric 16-character Thermal Printer can provide hard copy results, easily understood error messages, special user instructions, and complete program listings at the user's command.

thermal printer, subminiature — A subminiature thermal printer device which measures 2 by 5 by 1.75 inches and weighs only 20 ounces serves as the printer drive mechanism in a small and compact input-output system. It provides a readout on a 6-foot strip of heat-sensitive paper 3.7 inches in width. Images are formed by application of heated thick-film resistors to thermal paper. There is a 5 by 7 print dot matrix with 32 characters to each row. Print speed is approximately 32 lines per minute. The paper is stored in a plastic cassette internal to the printer. The electronics consists of four hybrid thick-film integrated circuits. Each IC contains 100 active integrated chips.

thesaurus — 1. An assemblage of alphabetized items (or grouped in some other concept or meaningful collection) providing the user with very close or direct synonyms or meanings, close to the term so alphabetized and used as an aid to writers, poets, programmers. 2. In computing, a

collection of words or terms used to index, classify, or sort, and then store and retrieve information in a data store or bank, i.e., main terms serve as labels, keywords, or descriptors, and when such references are cited along with the thesaurus, a very useful index is developed.

thick film — A method of manufacturing integrated circuits by depositing thin layers of materials on an insulated substrate (often ceramic) to perform electrical functions; usually only passive elements are made this way.

thin film calculator on a substrate (COS) — To accomplish this, a thin-film process was developed for coating the electrodes of the liquid-crystal display onto the glass substrate. A method was devised for depositing the thick-film wiring that serves as keyswitch contacts and interconnection circuitry, and an effective method was found for bonding the LSI calculator chip to the glass substrate. A liquid-crystal display that operates in the dynamic-scattering mode was chosen for its low power dissipation. This display had to be designed, not only for efficient calculator operation, but also to permit integration of the display packaging into the glass substrate.

three chip MOS/LSI calculator circuit set — One specific unit is a set of three MOS/LSI integrated circuits which make up the complete electronics for a 12 digit calculator driving either a gas discharge display, a printer, or both. The standard set is designed to drive the Seiko 104 printer; but having been designed for flexibility, it can be modified by users to drive other printers as well. The unit provides the four basic mathematical functions of Add, Subtract, Multiply and Divide plus percentage calculations. A memory is included with provision for subtotals as well as totals. The Add and Subtract functions utilize arithmetic logic and the Multiply and Divide functions utilize algebraic logic. The unit also provides dozens of relatively standard keys and functions: discount, exchange, list, etc. Both the input and output contain buffering designed to effectively increase the maximum operating speed of the printer.

3 M cassette — The very compact cartridge, measuring only 2½ × 3¼-inches, or smaller than a Philips cassette, can be designed into very small devices. The DC 100A holds 100,000 bytes of information and has an average transfer rate of 2,530 bytes per second. The tape speed is 30 ips (76.2 cm/s) forward and reverse, but 60 ips (152.3 cm/s) can be specially ordered. The mechanism has a 27-msec start delay and 5-millisecond stop delay.

threshold — 1. A logic operator having the property that if P is a statement, Q is a statement, R is a statement, ... , then the threshold of P, Q, R, ... is true if at least N statements are true, false if less than N statements are true, where N is a specified nonnegative integer called the threshold condition. 2. The threshold condition as in 1.

throughput — 1. Relates to the speed with which problems, programs, or segments are performed. Throughput can vary from application as well as from one piece of equipment to another although they are the same brand, and even model. 2. The total useful information processed or communicated during a specified time period.

time and frequency reference — On some units one-shot timing pulses, programmable from $1\,\mu sec$ to 40 days, and crystal-controlled pulse trains in fixed frequencies of 1, 10, 100, 1K, 10K, and 100KHz serve as time-base references for control, measurement, and data acquisition equipment.

time classification — Includes serviceable time, with subheadings of effective and ineffective time, and out of service time, with subheadings of scheduled engineering time, divided between preventive maintenance time and fault time (or down time). Additions included in total time are also such classifications as debatable time, external delays and unused time.

time, data acquisition calculator — Key displays real or elapsed time in days, hours, minutes, and seconds. Must be actuated before setting time with numeric and ENTER keys.

time interval measurement — Elapsed time between two events can be measured in the range of 10 μsec to 1 hour by counting a known frequency over the unknown interval. The program divides the accumulated count by the known frequency to determine the interval.

timer card — Various types can be programmed to generate crystal controlled, one-shot timing pulses. Time increment is variable from 1 μsec to 40 days.

timer/counter/stopwatch/elapsed timers on a chip — Typical units are complete one-chip timers which also feature low power operation. Typical power supply requirements are a three-NiCad-battery stack. External components required to complete the function are a quartz crystal, trimming capacitor, and LED display.

- Versatility of applications: precision timer, 4 stopwatch modes, 24-hour clock
- Simple to use:
  1. Function
  2. Start/Stop
  3. Reset
  4. Display
  5. Rapid Minute Advance
  6. Rapid Hour Advance
- Total integration: includes oscillator, divider, decoder driver on chip. (some units)

timer, interval — With the interval timer, the control program provides the facility to keep track of the time of day, and to interrupt periodically as required. More than one interval can be controlled at once. For example, a five-second interval between successive polling of a teleprocessing line can be specified, and at the same time a two-minute limit on the duration of a new program undergoing test can be in effect. (example)

timer, interval clock — A clock in a device which cycles the value of storage or causes a group of instructions to be periodically initiated.

timer, sequence — A succession of time-delay circuits arranged so that completion of the delay in one circuit initiates a delay in the following circuit.

timer splits — On some models, users can store intermediate time readings in registers R_0 thru R_9. These "splits" are stored by pressing any of the digit keys (0 thru 9) while the timer is running. The time reading at that instant is stored in the corresponding register. In TIMER mode, these splits can be recalled merely by pressing the same digit key with the timer stopped. In RUN mode, these times are recalled conventionally by

timer series

pressing first RCL and then the corresponding digit key. (HP-55 example)

time series — Refers to the discrete or continuous sequence of quantitative data assigned to specific moments in time, usually studied with respect to their distribution in time.

time series analysis programs — Examples are:
- Moving Average
- Seasonal Analysis
- Cyclical Analysis
- Autocovariance and Autocorrelation
- Triple Exponential Smoothing
- Crosscovariance and Crosscorrelation

time share — The use of a device for two or more purposes during the same overall time interval, accomplished by interspersing the computing component actions in time.

time-share calculator advantages —
(1) Savings in Connect Time
The calculator need not be connected to the time-share computer while programs are keyed in. Programs or data lines can be entered into the calculator memory, edited, and then the time-share connection made. The lines can be transmitted all at once to the time-share computer with considerable savings in connect time.
(2) Savings in Storage Charges
Any 'free text' lines received from a time-share system can be stored in the calculator memory as long as each line has a reference number. From the calculator memory, 'free text' lines can be stored on cassette files or on paper tape. Since most time-share services provide overnight storage to their customers at additional cost, these charges can be eliminated by using cassette or paper tape storage, as well as increasing the security of the data.
(3) 'Free text' lines can be printed without line numbers for text editing applications.
(4) The Special Function Keys can be used as typing aids for quicker and more accurate data entry.
(5) Typing and program errors are easily corrected with the calculator editing keys.
(6) The user can store and run BASIC programs in the calculator and perform calculations while in terminal mode.

time-share calculator system requirements — To use various desk-top calculators as terminals the computer time-share service must offer the following options:
- No echo-back, or suppressible echo-back.
- Low-speed operation e.g. the calculator and the Terminal ROM must be capable of transmitting up to 300 baud.
- Transmission in ASCII code.

Also the various calculators must have been designed as a general purpose stand-alone calculators. This provides a number of 'bonus' features when the units are used in terminal mode.

time shared, BASIC — Time shared BASIC is a conversational language designed to provide easy access to computers for the maxium number of people. It is especially useful in management and education where ease of access is important and is an enhancement of the original BASIC.

time-shared computer utility — Generally refers to the special computational ability of time-shared computer systems. Programs as well as data may be made available to the user. The user also may have his own programs immediately available to the central processor, may have them on call at the computer utility, or he may load them by transmitting them to the computer prior to using them. Certain data and program are shared by all users of the service; other data and programs because of proprietary nature, have restricted access. Computer utilities are generally accessed by means of data communication subsystems.

time-sharing — 1. A computing technique by which more than one terminal device can use the input, processing and output facilities of a central computer simultaneously. 2. A specific method of operation in which a computer facility is shared by several users for different purposes at (apparently) the same time. Although the computer actually services each user in sequence, the high speed of the computer makes it appear that the users are all handled simultaneously.

time sharing accounting — The executive must provide for the recognition and log-in of users. It must keep detailed records as required by the administrators of the system on the amount of central processor time, the amount of storage, and the usage of peripherals to be charged to each other. Other statistics as required may be maintained on idle time, error conditions, and the like.

time sharing BASIC, calculator — A BASIC program can be written for the calculator to take program lines input from the keyboard and store them as data on tape cassette. Then the tape is read and the program sent to the computer by another BASIC program (or a subroutine), with the calculator listening for the prompts. Because the controlling software that enables the calculator to act as a timesharing terminal is in ROM, the calculator can run local BASIC programs while on-line with a computer. Since the modem interface can be treated like any other peripheral, a local program in the calculator can interact with a user program at a timesharing system. This opens a new range of applications in which locally collected data is sent to a program at the computer. Data from the computer may also be sent to a BASIC program at the calculator. The latter capability has been used to plot data points received from a computer on a calculator plotter. Timesharing users often want to plot information received from the timeshared computer. This is not always possible because the computer system may not have the proper plotter software driver. The calculator with its plotter peripheral, can be used to receive and plot data from a computer whether or not the computer has a plotter driver.

time sharing, conversational compilers — General purpose systems usually provide languages and procedures by means of which a user may construct a program, modify it, test it, and, in some cases, add it to the file of system subcomponents. Most of the program preparation languages developed for time-sharing systems are dialects of existing languages. Processors for the languages vary from those borrowed with only slight modification from batch mode processing to conversational mode compilers designed especially for on-line use.

time sharing, dynamic data base — The data base for the problem area is very dynamic and changes are frequent. Reference to the data base is equally frequent and requires that the data base be constantly updated.

time sharing, error diagnostics — It is highly desirable in a remote system that a user's actions be closely monitored by the system, with errors in procedure or entry called to the user's attention as soon after commission as possible. The error message sent to an offending user should be provided whenever possible.

time sharing, fault processing — The executive program of a time-shared system must be in control or able to regain control at all times. User actions or executing user programs may generate unpredictable interrupt and fault conditions. The executive must process all such conditions if it is to maintain control of the system. Clock interrupts must be set up before control is given temporarily to a user program. Interrupts on completion of input/output transmission affect the ready status of deferred tasks. Interrupts from user consoles indicate user actions and requests for attention.

time sharing FORTRAN — The General Electric Missiles and Space Division at Valley Forge, Pennsylvania has implemented a time-sharing version of FORTRAN, which is available through the commercial GE Time-Sharing service. This is an extension of FORTRAN II with certain features of FORTRAN IV. Other modifications to allow operation in a time-sharing environment have also been made.

time sharing, HELP program — HELP is a question-answering program that accepts queries in natural language and responds with appropriate answers from one of several data bases associated with the system components of some Time-Sharing Systems. When a user does not know how to employ a particular service or if he runs into difficulties while using a service program, he merely types the word HELP to invoke the question-answering program. HELP places very few constraints on the user. (1) No rigid structure is imposed. (2) Unrestricted grammer and phrasing are accepted. (3) Character and the line delete (similar to strike-overs) facilitate input. (4) Reasonable misspelling is understood.

time sharing, interpretation of system commands — A user communicates with the time-sharing executive via system commands. These commands request the executive to perform one of the system functions, to call a system subcomponent, or to execute a user program. The executive accepts the system command, interprets it, and sets up a task on the user's list to be executed in accordance with the scheduling rules.

time-sharing keyboard calculator — One unit has a keyboard that has 12 special function keys that can handle 24 different operations both for program writing and in peripheral and instrument control. The keys can serve as immediate-execute keys, as call keys for subroutines and as typing aids. With the time-sharing or "live keyboard" feature, the user can perform simple calculations, examine and change program variables and list programs while the calculator is performing other peripheral or control operations. The interrupt capability apportions these operations on a priority schedule determined by the operator. The unit comes with 8-k bytes of internal read-write memory, which is expandable in 8-k increments to a total of 32-k bytes. The four optional ROM slots in the front of the machine accept ROMs that can do the following: an extended I/O which is required for interrupts and time-share features; a general I/O; a plotter; string arrays; and advanced programming. A tape cartridge can hold 250,000 bytes on two tracks (125 k/track) and has a 2750 byte/s transfer rate. The fast I/O speed, together with the simultaneous interfacing capabilities dupes for 16-bit parallel instruments and for instruments that use the IEEE Standard 488 bus, make this programmable calculator suitable as the controller of an instrumentation system. However, the calculator can also serve as a powerful computing tool.

time-sharing keyboards, controllers (calculators) — Computer-like features, long desired on desk-top calculators, are finally available with the introduction in 1975 and 1976 of several advanced programmable calculators. These machines have on-line time-sharing of their keyboards and controllers so that several computing jobs can be done simultaneously. Data for these units can be entered while the machine is calculating another program, controlling a peripheral or printing out a program. Features of one of these calculators include program interrupt, direct memory access with input speeds of up to 400 k, 16-bit words/s and output speeds of up to 200 k, 16-bit words/s, mini-cartridge tape drive for bulk memory storage, multidimensional array handling, automatic memory record and load, extended internal calculation range of $\pm 10^{115}$ to $\pm 10^{-115}$ and provisions for optional plug-in program ROMs.

The Hewlett-Packard 9825A uses the HPL formula-oriented, high-level programming language. HPL handles subroutine nesting and flags, and allows 26 simple variables and 26 multidimensional-array variables that are limited only by the size of the calculator memory. Editing of lines and characters is accomplished using a 32-character, upper and lower-case alphanumeric display together with a built-in, 16-character thermal printer. The display and printer provide the full ASCII character set. Error locations in a line are identified by a flashing cursor in the display. Fixed and floating-point formats are set from the typewriter-like keyboard.

time sharing, master/slave modes — Even with memory protection, it is still possible for a user program to wrest control from the system or to otherwise disrupt system operations unless the user program is forbidden the use of certain privileged operations. These operations include input/output, setting the clock, setting the memory protection bounds, and similar instructions affecting control of the computer. The usual solution is to have two modes of operation for the computer — master and slave. Privileged instructions can be executed only in the master mode. With such a hardware feature, the executive program of the system is the only program allowed to operate in master mode. User programs are forced to operate in slave mode and thus must remain under control.

time-sharing monitor system — The monitor system is a collection of programs remaining permanently in memory to provide overall coordination and control of the total operating system. It performs several functions. First, it permits several users' programs to be loaded into main memory simultaneously. The monitor makes use of the time-sharing hardware to prevent one user's program from interferring with other users' programs. Each program is run for a certain length of time; then the monitor switches control to another program in a rotating sequence.

time sharing option — An option of MVT and OS/VS2 that provides conversational time sharing from remote terminals. Abbreviated TSO.

time sharing, running mode — A user task is in the running mode when it is in control of a processor and is executing. A task leaves the running mode either voluntarily or involuntarily in accordance with the scheduling rules of the executive. Reasons for leaving the running mode may include: (1) request for input/output, (2) request for console response, (3) suspension on expiration of time quantum, (4) termination.

time sharing, security of user files — Each user is assigned a password composed of a string of randomly chosen characters. This password is known only to the user and to the system. At log-in the user must give his identification (name and/or account number) together with his password. The system verifies that the two match. The system may keep a table giving the authority level of the user and allow him access only to files appropriate to this level. Or a double lock may be provided by allowing the user who creates and establishes a file to specify two passwords for the file. One password authorizes reading of the file, the other authorizes modification of the entries of the file. A user specifying use of a file must know one or both of these passwords and input these to the system before being granted access to the protected data.

time-sharing terminal, calculator — Several types of programable calculators can emulate a timesharing terminal once the appropriate ROM is plugged in and the programmable keys are labeled with their special functions by the template. The routines called up by the keys intervene in the operating system to add the communications functions. For example, on some units to send data, the "transmit" special-function key is pressed after the information has been entered into the display buffer. The "shift" and "control" keys emulate their counterparts on a teletypewriter to generate special control characters for signing on, editing, ending an input sequence, and breaking transmission. These user-definable keys can be made to provide access to frequently called sequences like the telephone number of a central computer and a user identification number. In some units, an entire sign-on sequence programed in BASIC and stored in the memory may be accessed through a single key. Besides saving time, this capability simplifies the use of the terminal by inexperienced operators — though of course it is not practical if security is a consideration.

time-sharing terminal ROM calculator — The Interactive ROM converts the calculator into a timesharing terminal. It does this by taking control of the keyboard operating system. Normally, when a key is pressed, a character is displayed. Adding the Interactive ROM puts the modem interface into the keyboard loop. Then the calculator waits for keystrokes from either the keyboard or the timesharing modem and displays this information on the LED display. A full display buffer (80 characters) or a carriage return causes the information to be printed on the calculator printer. (some systems)

time-sharing terminal TRANSMIT function key — A special function key, labeled TRANSMIT on the template is programmed by a ROM to send characters typed into the display. Two other special function keys emulate the teleprinter SHIFT and CONTROL keys to generate control characters that may be required by a timeshared computer to sign on, for editing, to break, or to end input sequences.

Unlike standard teleprinter or CRT-based terminals that use paper tape or tape cassette to send programs, the calculator memory is used to send and receive programs. Instead of being prepared on paper tape, programs are entered directly into the calculator memory and edited line by line or character by character using the powerful editing features of some calculators. Programs do not have to be in compatible BASIC because the calculator syntax checking is bypassed by the ROM. For example, FORTRAN, COBOL, or line of text can be entered and edited. Once the program has been prepared, it may be stored on tape or disc as if it were a program for the calculator. To send the program to a computer, it is simply listed to the modem as if it were being listed on the printer. To receive programs to the calculator memory, a listing is requested from the computer. This is normally done by sending a LIST or similar command. To route the program to memory instead of the printer, the user sends LIST from the display by pressing the special function key labeled SAVE.

time sharing, time slices — Time quanta of a few hundred milliseconds are usually chosen. It has been shown in some time-shared systems that the smaller the time quantum the better average response time, if all user tasks are highly interactive. However, very small time slices badly penalize programs requiring a large amount of computation between console interactions. To work out of this dilemma, some systems have two ready queues; one with a small time interval for highly interactive programs, another with a large time interval for lone computation problems. This compromise technique reduces the amount of swapping and overhead on the longer running programs caused by frequent interruptions, but provides rapid response for highly interactive programs.

time sharing, waiting mode — Tasks in "waiting" mode are voluntarily suspended until some operation is complete. Upon completion of the awaited operation, the waiting task is returned to the ready mode (or in some systems to the running mode).

time slice — Refers to a designed interval of time during which a job can use a resource without being preempted.

time slicing — 1. Refers to a feature that can be used to prevent a task from monopolizing the central processing unit and thereby delaying the assignment of CPU time to other tasks. 2. In systems with time sharing, the allocation of time slices to terminal jobs.

time study — Refers to a determination of an optimum method of performing various operations as determined by a methods study of the work content of various operations. Work measurements essentially determine times required to carry out operations to a specific standard of performance by a qualified worker. Purposes for such studies help design: incentive schemes, control production, selling price, and delivery scheduling. Basic techniques are related to synthesizing time/motion studies and analytic estimating.

timing, calculator system — Timing comes to the controller from both the CPU and clock generator. Often a clock generator provides MOS clocks for the CPU and a TTL clock for the communications baud-rate generator, plus auxiliary timing functions. Some clocks, which are crystal-stabilized, run at 2.048 megahertz ± 0.1% and 18.432 MHz ± 0.1%, respectively. Some MOS clock periods from the basic instruction cycle time are 1.95 microseconds.

timing function — A typical timing function, ties the system function blocks together. This useful part provides the various clock phases needed, and makes it convenient to interface with a manual test/control panel.

timing generator — One type Precision Pacer-Timer operates Stand-Alone or Programmed and accepts Triggers, Outputs Signals Via BNCs or HP-IB, i.e. intervals from 1 microsecond to more than a day. The Timing Generator responds to trigger inputs with precision timed pulses (flags) to perform such system services as counting off time intervals, pacing measurements, and inserting known delays. Intervals from microseconds on up (1 μ to 999E8 μ) can be set into thumbwheels or programmed. Interconnected with a group of instruments or Interface Bus, the generator outputs pacing/timing signals on rear panel BNCs or interfaces. Either of two operating modes may be selected: pacer mode or timer mode.

timing generator, pacer mode — In pacer mode, pacing signals are output on a continuing basis at the end of each consecutive interval after an initial trigger signal is accepted to start off the sequence. Outputs are available two ways: as pulses at rear panel BNCs for such purposes as triggering a gate on a counter; and as signals on the — Interface Bus for any systems use. For example, the timing generator can be programmed to output Service Requests to which the Controller can respond by initiating measurement sequences at precisely timed intervals.

timing generator, timer mode — In timer mode, an external start pulse or Bus trigger begins an interval of preset length which is counted off and terminated with an output pulse or Bus signal. The function performed is essentially that of a delay generator. A typical use for short, preset delays in instrument groups is to establish settling intervals for devices to let any startup transients die away before measurements are recorded.

timing, processor — Microprocessor timing and clock generation methods affect the system, because instruction times are based on maximum clock frequencies and cycle times. Users may have to select a lower-frequency clock to optimize some system considerations, such as memory access time or clock generator synchronization with external timing.

timing signals — Electrical pulses sent throughout various machines at regular intervals to ensure absolute synchronization.

TLU (table look up) — To obtain a function value corresponding to an argument, stated or implied, from a table of function values stored in the calculator. Also, the operation of obtaining a value from a table.

tone-burst recording — Tone-burst or (cw) recording may be the simplest way of recording data, where data "1" is the presence of a tone and data "0" the absence of a tone. Because this system is basically an amplitude-modulation scheme, and very susceptible to noise, reliability suffers above 150 bits per second.

top-down method — A compiling technique using a template-matching method; prototypes for a statement of unknown nature are assumed one-by-one, until one prototype is found which matches.

topologies, alternative — Alternative network topologies include 1. highly centralized or star; 2. fully distributed, either partially or fully connected; 3. ring, which is a variant of a distributed configuration; or 4. various combinations of these.

topology, network — Network topology can be centralized or distributed. Centralized networks, also called star networks, are those in which all nodes connect to a single node. This is a description of topology, only, and implies nothing about location of computing power, network control, or user distribution. The alternative topology is distributed where, in the limit, each node is connected to every other node, although the terminology is commonly applied to topologies approaching this full connectivity. There exists a third alternative which more accurately describes a certain condition of a distributed network. This is the ring configuration commonly used in describing the Distributed Computer System. Observing the topology a ring can be seen connecting the nodes of the network. In the case of TYMNET a number of such rings are then themselves interconnected forming a multiring structure. This is a special case of a distributed network.

totals only — Relates to printing a report utilizing a punched card tabulator or a calculator printer in such a manner that for specified groups of cards or input records totals only are printed.

total time — 1. The basic categories of total time include: Serviceable time, with subheadings of effective and ineffective time and out of service time with subheadings of scheduled engineering time divided between preventive maintenance time and fault time (or down time). Added to be included in total time are also such classifications as: debatable time, external delays, and unused time. 2. The full time which is usually the total of 168 hours per week and 24 hours per day.

Touch-Tone data service — The basic difference between Touch-Tone (or other push-button calling methods) and rotary dialing is the fact that two frequencies (tones) are transmitted from the telephone instrument when a button is depressed, as compared to the DC pulses produced by a rotary dial telephone during dialing. Thus Touch-Tone has the inherent capability of sending digital data signals after a connection has been established to a distant device. This device can be a computer, a teletypewriter, or a key punch. The latter two devices require a converter to convert the 2-out-of-8 (two frequencies from a possible eight) Touch-Tone code to the ASCII or Hollerith code of the device. Data is transmitted by inserting plastic cards containing the fixed information (for example, customer name) into an ordinary card dialer and using the Touch-Tone buttons for the variable information. (Card dialers were originally developed for automatically dialing a telephone number.) The plastic cards contain up to 14 digits. The Bell System companies will only provide Touch-Tone service on a dial-up basis (including PBX systems), not on private lines.

touch-tone telephone audio-response unit — To reduce console cost to probably the lowest possible, experiments have been conducted using ordinary touch-tone telephone hand sets. For applications with limited input requirements, this ultra-simple terminal device may suffice making such remote systems easily accessible to many users. This type of input is usually coupled with audio-response output. Magnetic tapes have words, syllables or perhaps only phonemes prerecorded. The computer puts together an aural response by stringing together sequences of these recorded elements.

trace flow — A debugging device which prints out contents of various registers and memory location in a particular program segment specified by the user.

trace mode — The trace mode is a valuable tool in debugging programs. Users can either select it from the keyboard or program it to examine part of a program's activity, then cancel it with a normal statement following the suspected part of the program, on some systems. The trace mode is obtained with the TRACE key. In this mode, during program execution the printer lists the number of each line and any quantities it stores. This allows users to verify intermediate results and detect logic errors.

trace program — Pertains to a trace or diagnostic program used to perform a desired check on another program and may include instructions as its output, and intermediate results of those instructions can be arranged in the order in which the instructions are executed. When such a trace program is an interpretive type, it is called an interpretive trace program.

trace routine — An executive routine that develops a sequence record of the execution of programs to be checked or traced.

tracing routine — Refers to one of many diagnostic routines used to provide a time history of one or more machine registers and controls during the execution of the object routine. A complete tracing routine would reveal the status of all registers and locations affected by each instruction each time the instruction is executed. Since such a trace is prohibitive in machine time, traces which provide information only following the execution of certain types of instructions are more frequently used. Furthermore, a tracing routine may be under control of the processor, or may be called in by means of a trapping feature. Related to trap.

tracing structure, built-in — Various debugging, diagnostic, or error-tracing routines are built-in parts of programs, i.e., instructions to output partial results during any program execution cycle. Such instructions may be of a temporary nature and can be easily removed using various series of test instructions.

track — 1. A path which contains reproducible information left on a medium by recording means energized from a single channel. 2. In electronic computers, that portion of a moving-type storage medium accessible to a given reading station (e.g., film, drum, tapes, discs). (Also see Band and Channel.)

track address — Binary codes on magnetic tape or disc to locate data stored in other tracks by actual code patterns as indicated by the address, or by completing a count, or by simply noting their positions.

track density — The number of adjacent tracks per a given unit of distance measured in a direction perpendicular to the direction of individual tracks. The inverse of track pitch.

tracks, prerecorded — A preliminary tape-, disk-, or drum-recorded routine that simplifies programming. Relieves the programmer of the responsibility of furnishing timing or counting instructions and permits block and word addressability.

traffic — The signals or information which pass through a communications system.

traffic analysis — The obtaining of information from a study of communications traffic. Includes statistical study of message headings, receipts, acknowledgments, routing, and so on, plus a tabulation of volumes and types of messages with respect to time.

traffic control — A method of optimizing the flow of work through a factory communication system or operation by means of a computer.

trailer label — The end-of-tape file record that lists summary information concerning that file.

transaction processing systems — The collection of data at the source is an ideal application for the data access systems since this technique reduces data preparation errors and costs and reduces host CPU processing. The systems also operate efficiently with the new microprocessor-equipped families of interactive CRT terminals; with these in the system, non-technical persons can easily format the screen to resemble source documents, then enter data conversationally by filling-in blanks. Data entered through all of these interactive terminals can be transmitted concurrently to the central host system.

transaction tape — A paper tape or magnetic tape carrying information that is to be used to up-date filed information. This filed information is often on a master tape.

transaction terminal, fast food chain — An example are those that permit such stores with limited menus to input the customer's order either from a keyboard or from a mark sense sheet, the terminal calculates and prints out the total of the customer's bill and also stores information on the different items ordered for inventory purposes. These terminals are polled at night by a central computer to collect sales, inventory and record information.

transactor input station — In industry, transactor input stations can be linked with a computer system to provide a real-time processing of manufacturing data. Input stations, located at widely scattered points throughout the factory, can feed fixed and variable manufacturing data directly to the processor. The data can be processed immediately to provide management with up-to-the-

transceiver — minute information concerning all phases of operation within the plant. The ability to have data fed into the computer as the transaction occurs enables vital facts to be generated in time to be used most effectively by all levels of industrial management.

transceiver — 1. The combination of radio transmitting and receiving equipment in a common housing, usually for portable or mobile use and employing some common circuit components for both transmitting and receiving. 2. A terminal device that can both transmit and receive signals.

transceiver test systems — Various transceiver test systems provide fast, accurate, and consistently repeatable means of testing communications receivers, transmitters, power supplies, as well as complete two-way radio sets. These systems perform all the testing needs for AM and FM two-way radios operating from 10 MHz to 1300 MHz at one watt to 100 watts power output (special attenuators allow testing below one watt and above 100 watts). Some transceiver test systems are supplied with several sample test programs (measuring sensitivity, audio distortion, etc.) for use as a guide to assist in writing programs for specific needs.

transcendental functions — Transcendental functions are those such as sines, cosines, logarithms, etc.: and polar/rectangular coordinate conversions for handling vectors and complex arithmetic.

transcribe — 1. To copy, with or without translating, from one external storage medium of a computer to another. 2. To copy from a calculator into a storage medium or vice versa.

transcriber — 1. Equipment associated with a computing machine for the purpose of transferring input or output data from a record of information in a given language to the medium and language used by a digital computing machine, or from a computing machine to a record of information.

transducer — A device by means of which energy can be made to flow from one or more transmission systems to one or more other transmission systems. The energy may be in any form, such as electrical, mechanical, acoustical, etc. The term "transducer" is often restricted to a device in which the magnitude of an applied stimulus is converted into an electrica signal proportionate to the quantity of the stimulus. Usually, the variations of the phenomenon being measured are referenced to time.

transducer calculator-controller — An example of the power of the calculator as a controller is in performing on-line data analysis for output in engineering units, transducer linearization and compensation or to average noisy data, and to do statistical analysis on measurement data.

transducer conversions — Acquisition, storage, and manipulation of data are common to all engineering disciplines. The parameter of interest is usually not electrical, and must be converted, by a transducer, to an electrical signal. A broad spectrum of such transducers is available for converting physical parameters, such as acceleration, pressure, angular position, or velocity, to an electrical signal. If many measurements are necessary, the easiest course is first to convert them to analog voltages and then to digital form; alternatively, a nonelectrical quantity may be directly digitized.

transducer data logging — Charcteristics often pertain to:
- multiple channels
- low level dc volts, ac volts and
- resistance measurement capability
- time pacing
- hard copy output

transducer devices — Refers to specific elements or devices which have the capability of receiving information in the form of one physical quantity and converting it to information in the form of the same or other physical quantities. This particularly relates to specific cases of devices such as primary elements, signal transducers and various transmitters.

transducer output signals — Any instrumentation system requires consideration of four areas: transducers, measurements, linearization, and programming. Transducers develop usable electrical output signals in response to physical phenomena — specifically temerature and pressure, as in the gas turbine project. The turbine requires temperature measurements in the range from 50 to 800° C, most easily measured with a thermocouple (a junction between two dissimilar metals, which creates a voltage related to its temperature). In thermocouples, sensing and transduction take place in the same element, which requires no external power.

transducer sensing examples — Typical are:
- environmental monitoring
- gathering pipeline and well data
- furnace and flue temperature monitoring
- monitoring temperature of standard labs and environmental enclosures
- annealing and heat treating monitoring including temperature profiling
- physiological parameter monitoring

transfer bus, ASCII-calculator — In one major system the main communication paths are on the ASCII bus and can be used for direct memory access as well as for alpha and control. The transfer into and out of the program or memory can be at a megabaud rate — comparable to that in the minicomputer and fast enough to make external disk storage feasible. Often a single I/O port provides for a variety of peripherals to be connected.

transfer check — 1. Refers to a verification of transmitted data by temporarily storing, retransmitting, and comparing. Also a check to see if the transfer or jump instruction was properly performed. 2. A check which verifies that information is transferred correctly from one place to another. It is usually done by comparing each character with a copy of the same character transferred at a different time or by a different route.

transfer function — 1. A mathematical expression, frequently used by control engineers, that expresses the relationship between the outgoing and the incoming signals of a process or control element. The transfer function is useful in studies of control problems. 2. A mathematical expression or expressions that describe(s) the relationship between physical conditions at two different points in time or space in a given.

transfer function comparison — Related to tabular, graphical or mathematical statements

transfer function design — concerning the influence which systems or elements have on signals or actions compared at input and output terminals; i.e., the operation of the equivalent complex mathematical function.

transfer function design — This type design work includes analysis and synthesis of control systems, active filters, or analog circuits. Some engineers are still using the common block diagram approach to determine overall transfer characteristics. Others have found a better, faster way to design solutions. With a programmable calculator and transfer function analysis programs, users can quickly determine circuit component values from short-circuit transfer impedance functions. Or they can determine the values for the transfer function from an actual circuit. These short-circuit transfer functions — expressed in both the time constant form and the pole zero form — give 39 unique circuit configurations on some systems.

transfer keys, conditional — On some units: If Positive. Tests display register for positive or zero. If it is, transfer occurs to a location or label. If the test fails, transfer does not occur. If zero. Tests display register for zero. If it is, transfer occurs to a location or label. If not, no transfer. If Error. Tests for an error condition (flashing display). If it is, transfer occurs to a location or label. If not, no transfer. Decrement and Skip on Zero. Decrements the contents of memory register 00, then tests these contents for zero. If it is not zero, transfer occurs to a location or label. If it is, no transfer.

transfer keys, inverse conditional — On some units these reverse all the conditional transfers. For example, INV 2nd if pos tests the display and causes a transfer when the display is negative.

transfer rates — One important description of the data path, including terminal, adapter or "modem," and transmission line, is the maximum rate at which it can transfer information. Transmission capability is not the same as the net rate at which information is transferred, there is always an overhead. The maximum information transfer rate is expressed in bits per second (BPS). A bit is a binary digit, the smallest unit of information. The more meaningful, but less used, measure is the transfer rate of information bits (TRIB), which excludes all overhead. Another descriptor commonly used is baud, the number of state changes per second. There are multiple states, then each state can represent more than one bit; therefore, the BPS is greater than or equal to the baud. For example, a transmission line capable of supporting four states has a BPS rate twice its baud rate since each state represents two bits.

transfers, calculator — Up to 400k transfers per second direct memory access provides, on some units, minicomputer speeds which allow real-time data acquisition and data transfer with high-speed devices.

transfer vector — A transfer table used to communicate between two or more programs. The table is fixed in relationship with the program for which it is the transfer vector. The transfer vector provides communication linkage between that program and any remaining sub-programs.

transform — 1. To convert a current from one magnitude to another, or from one type to another. 2. In digital-computer programming, to change information in structure or composition without significantly altering the meaning or vlue at the same time. 3. To derive a new body of data from a given one according to specific procedures, often leaving some feature invariant. Related to translate.

transient error — Some errors arise which are not because of any inherent defect in tapes, machines, or programs, but because of the presence of some dust, which will disappear when the tape is physically moved again. Such errors are termed to be transient.

transient routines — These self-relocating routines are permanently stored on the system-residence device and loaded (by the supervisor) into the transient area when needed for execution.

transistor — A device made by attaching three or more wires to a small wafer of semiconducting material (a single crystal which has been specially treated so that its properties are different at the point where each wire is attached). The three wires are usually called the emitter, base, and collector. They perform functions somewhat similar to those of the cathode, grid, and plate of a vacuum tube, respectively.

transistor, field effect (FETs) — FETs, n or p channel types, using silicon provide high input impedance, resistive, bidirectional output impedance.

transistor-integrated circuit — Invented by Jack Kilby of Texas Instruments in 1958, the integrated circuit belongs to the family of semiconductors that includes transistors and diodes. All are similar in size and in the way they're fabricated. And as the name implies, the integrated circuit has considerably more electronics functions integrated on practically the same small area as the transistor. Basically, an IC measures and controls the flow of electrical current, and this enables integrated circuits of various types to control the performance of all kinds of electronics equipment.

transistorized — 1. Pertaining to equipment or a design in which transistors instead of vacuum tubes are used. 2. Said of equipment in which all circuits employ transistors and not thermionic valves.

transistors and diodes, silicon — Some logic circuits use silicon semiconductors exclusively rather than germanium components. Designed to preclude the reduced performance usually inherent with the higher forward voltage drop of silicon devices, these circuits offer such characteristic advantages of silicon over germanium as: operation over a much wider temperature range, surface passivation for protection against contamination thus providing longer life, and much lower reverse leakage permitting greater fan-in and increased switching efficiency.

transistor-transistor logic (TTL') — This is the most common form of IC logic. As a result, the relatively simple process used to produce TTL logic is a natural candidate for memory, especially since most memories are used with TTL logic. However, the TTL approach — even though the simplest bipolar process — is considerably more complicated and expensive than MOS. Since n-channel MOS can now be made as fast in performance as TTL bipolar, the importance of the TTL process to the memory market is limited. It will vie with CMOS for those applications represented by small memories of around 256 bits per chip, commonly intermixed with computer logic (distributed memory). The only advantage of both CMOS and TTL in these applications is their 100 percent compatibility with the logic (i.e., power supplies and signal levels). Of course, n-channel memories can also be made logic compatible at lower speed (2 to 3 MHz) operation. Slightly larger memories can bear the cost of having less than 100 percent compatibility, so the lower cost of n-channel will displace TTL and CMOS in all but the smallest memories.

transistor types — Three-electrode semiconductor devices with thin layer of n- (or p-) type semiconductor sandwiched between two regions of p-(or n-) type, thus forming two p-n junctions back-to-back. The emitter junction is given a forward bias and the collector junction a reverse bias. Current carriers entering the emitter diffuse through the base to the collector so it is of the order 0-98 ic. Due to the low forward resistance of the emitter junction and the high reverse resistance of the collector junction, considerable power gain is possible for signals in the emitter or base leads. The latter arrangement in the p-n-p transistor is due to hole conduction, that in an n-p-n transistor to electron conduction.

translating program — A particular program (often called a translater) which translates from one language into another, i.e., from one programming language into another programming language.

translation and/or rotation of coordinate axis program — Let (x, y) be coordinates in the old system and let (x_0, y_0) be the center of a new coordinate system rotated through an angle of θ. The new coordinates are (x', y') and are calculated by the following formulas:

1. $x' = (x - x_0) \cos \theta + (y - y_0) \sin \theta$
2. $y' = -(x - x_0) \sin \theta + (y - y_0) \cos \theta$

For no rotation put in $\theta - 0$.
For no translation put in $(x_0, y_0) = (0, 0)$

translator — Translators, a generic term for assemblers and compilers (also interpreters, which have not been used much with microcomputers) are programs which allow the programmer to express his program in a language closer to his native language for later translation to a language acceptable by a machine or subsequent loader. Sometimes translators only translate from a higher language (closer to English for example) to a lower language like assembly language (closer to machine language). Translator tools are designed with features to enhance program expression, to provide programmer services, and to remove as much clerical burden as possible.

translator, language — 1. A program which converts a language to equivalent statements in another computer language, usually for a different computer. 2. A routine which aids in the performance of natural language translations such as French to English. 3. Any assembler or compiling program which brings forth same or equivalent output from human-readable statements.

translator program — This program uses the source language program as input and produces from it a programming machine language. Like any other machine program this may either be run immediately or stored for later use.

transliterate — Refers to the activity to convert the characters of one alphabet to the corresponding characters of another alphabet.

transmission — 1. Conveying electrical energy from point to point along a path. 2. The sending of data to one or more locations or recipients. 3. The sending of data from one place for reception elsewhere. 4. In ASCII and communications, a series of characters including headings and texts. 5. Conveying electrical energy over a distance by wires, either to operate controls or indications (telemetering), acoustic information (telephony, broadcasting) or pictorial information (facsimile, television). Also used to denote radio, optical or acoustic wave propagation.

transmission control — 1. The system services many locations, some on common communication lines and some on separate lines. It supplies the equipment and programming required to handle the multiple inputs arriving in unscheduled fashion into the computer. 2. Control can communicate directly with various types of communication terminals. Examples of such terminals include the data-collection system, the data-communication systems, the process-communication system and telegraph terminals, including terminals using the new American Standard Code for information interchange.
Terminal attachments to the control can be made via common carrier-leased private telegraph, voice- or subvoice-grade lines. Accommodations also include attachment, via privately owned voice-grade communication lines and common carrier-switched voice and data networks. Multiple terminals can be attached to each communication line. However, the limiting number of terminals per line is determined by the addressing capability of that particular terminal. Each communication line is under the channel control.

transmission equipment — That large class of equipment considered peripheral to the computing equipment itself which communicates data rather than computing or processing.

transmission error control — In order to insure that transmission is occurring without errors being introduced into the data, it is necessary to establish a set of conventions between sender and receiver for detecting and correcting errors. The simplest form is a parity check on each transmitted character. This is often called a vertical redundancy check and is used to provide protection against single bit errors within characters. The longitudinal redundancy check (LRC) provides for a check across an entire message. This is done by computing a parity bit for each bit position of all the characters in the message. The most powerful form of check is the cyclic redundancy check where polynomial division is applied to the message string and the remainder used as the check digit(s). The same computation is performed at the receiving end, and the result compared. When a receiving station receives a message and determines that it is error free (using some combination of the above checks) it informs the sending station by transmitting an acknowledgment of the message (ACK). If a receiving station detects an error, it may transmit to the sending station a negative acknowledgment (NAK).

transmission preprocessor — A typical unit contains provisions for up to eight reception modes for use with character-oriented protocols (for instance, there are modes for transparent data reception and for normal text reception). The action taken in each mode and the transition from one mode to another are controlled by control tables located in main memory. A control table for an individual reception state consists of 256 bytes — one for each of the possible characters that can be received during the reception. Generally the hardware can perform block check calculations for Longitudinal Redundancy Checks (LRC) and Cyclic Redundancy Checks (CRC-16 and CRC/CCITT).

transmission speed — 1. The rate at which data is transferred. Usually measured in bits per second, characters per second, or words per minute. 2. The absolute time a signal requires to move between source and sink. This approaches the speed of light (about 186,000 miles per second) and is affected by distance, transmission medium, number of system components, etc. Same as Time, Propagation.

transmission, start-stop — Asynchronous transmission in which each group of code elements corresponding to a character signal is preceded by a start signal which serves to prepare the receiving mechanism for the reception and registration of a character, and is followed by a stop signal which serves to bring the receiving mechanism to rest in preparation for the reception of the next character.

transmission "tones" — Standard telephone company data sets at each end of the telephone line convert signals from the RTU and CTU into "tones" for transmission over the line. Conversely, the data set converts "tones" received from the lines into signals for the terminal units.

transmit — To reproduce information in a new location replacing whatever was previously stored and clearing or erasing the source of the information.

transparency — A data communication mode which enables the equipment to send and receive bit patterns of any form, without regard to their possible interpretation as control characters. Contrast with code sensitivity.

transponder — 1. A radio or satellite transmitter-receiver which transmits identifiable signals automatically when the proper interrogation is received. 2. A form of transmitter-receiver which transmits signals automatically when the correct interrogation is received; e.g., a radar beacon mounted on a flight vehicle (or missile), which comprises a receiver tuned to the radar frequency and a transmitter which radiates the received signal at an intensity appreciably higher than that of the reflected signal. The radiated signal may be coded for identification. (see satellite)

transport — 1. To convey as a whole from one storage device to another. 2. A device that moves tape past a head. (Synonymous with tape transport.)

trap — 1. A selective circuit that attenuates undesired signals but does not affect the desired ones. (Also see Wave Trap). 2. A crystal imperfection which can trap carriers. 3. An unprogrammed conditional jump to a known location, automatically activated by hardware, with the location from which the jump occurred. 4. Crystal lattice defect at which current carriers may be trapped in a semiconductor. These traps can increase recombination and generation or they may reduce the mobility of the charge carriers.

trapped instruction — A special instruction which is executed by a software routine in cases where the necessary hardware is absent and in cases where the CPU is not in the state required or an instruction whose execution was stopped or cancelled.

trapped-program interrupt — Normally, any condition that causes an interrupt should be identified as soon as possible. However, in some cases it may be more convenient to ignore this condition. To allow for this possibility, the interrupt traps may be armed or disarmed by program control. An interrupt trap is associated with each interrupt event; an interrupt may occur only if its corresponding trap is armed. Any trap may be individually armed or disarmed and its condition may be stored in memory or tested under program control.

trapping — 1. The holding of electrons or holes by any of several mechanisms in a crystal, thereby preventing them from moving. 2. A feature of some calculators whereby an unscheduled, i.e., nonprogrammed, jump is made to a predetermined location in response to a machine condition i.e., a tagged instruction.

trapping mode — Refers to a scheme used mainly in program-diagnostic procedures for certain calculators. If the trapping mode flip-flop is set and the program includes any one of certain instructions, the instruction is not performed but the next instruction is taken from location N. Program-counter contents are saved in order to resume the program after executing the diagnostic procedure.

traps — When users debug programs (move blocks of words from one memory location to another) they can insert traps in the object code, at which point, program execution halts and control is returned to the debug program.

trap settings — Refers to trap settings that control interrupt signals that then can interrupt a program in process. If a trap is armed, then the associated interrupt conditions will be permitted to interrupt the main program when they occur. A trap that has not been armed, or has been disarmed, prevents the occurrence of interrupt signals.

trap (T bit) — In some systems the program can only set or clear the trap bit (T) by popping a new PSW (program status word) off the stack. When set, a processor trap will occur through a specific location at completion of the current instruction execution, and a new processor status word will be loaded from another specific location. This T bit is especially useful in debugging programs as an efficient method of installing breakpoints.

tree — This term is often used for some types of decoders because their diagrammatic representation can resemble the branches and trunk of a tree.

tree structures — Refers to specific switching or data file addressing structures designed to select an element by reduction cascading or all members of a set by expansion cascades. If used in chained data structures, the addresses associated with each item have multiple pointers to other items, i.e., to the next row member and the next column member.

trend line analysis — The calculator determines least-squares fit of data points (x, y) where y is any value and x is integrally incremented beginning with 1.

triangle solution a, A, C program —

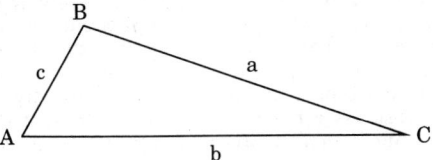

Given two angles and an opposite side this program solves the triangle for the remaining parameters by the following formulas:

$$B = 2\sin^{-1} 1 - (A + C) = \pi \text{ radians} -$$
$$(A + C) = 180° - (A + C)$$
$$= 200 \text{ grads} - (A + C)$$

$$b = \frac{a \sin B}{\sin A}$$

$$c = \frac{a \sin C}{\sin A}$$

The program works in any angular mode. However, if in degree mode all angles are assumed to be in decimal degrees.

triangle solution a, b, c program —

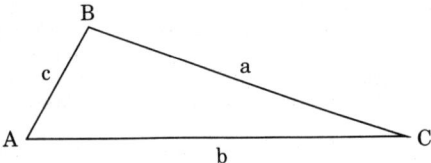

Given three sides of a triangle this program solves the triangle for the remaining parameters by the following formulas:

$$C = \cos^{-1}\left(\frac{a^2 + b^2 - c^2}{2ab}\right)$$

$$B = \sin^{-1}\left(\frac{b \sin C}{c}\right) \quad A = \sin^{-1}\left(\frac{a \sin C}{c}\right)$$

Reletter if necessary to make c the largest side. The program works in any angular mode. However, if in degree mode decimal degrees are assumed.

triangle solution a, b, C program —

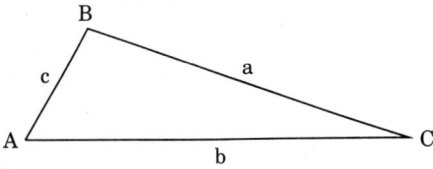

Given two sides and their included angle this program solves the triangle for the remaining parameters by the following formulas:

$$c = \sqrt{a^2 + b^2 - 2ab\cos C} \quad A = \sin^{-1}\left(\frac{a \sin C}{c}\right)$$

$$B = 2\sin^{-1} 1 - (A + C) = \pi \text{ radians} -$$
$$(A + C) = 180° - (A + C)$$
$$= 200 \text{ grads} - (A + C)$$

Reletter if necessary, to make a the smaller of a and b. This program works in any angular mode. However, if in degrees decimal degrees are assumed.

triangle solution a, B, C program —

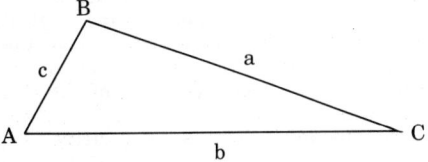

Given two angles and their included side this program solves the triangle for the remaining parameters by the following formulas:

$$A = 2\sin^{-1} 1 - (B + C) = \pi \text{ radians} -$$
$$(B + C) = 180° - (B + C)$$
$$= 200 \text{ grads} - (B + C)$$

$$b = \frac{a \sin B}{\sin A}$$

$$c = \frac{a \sin C}{\sin A}$$

The program works in any angular mode. However, if in degrees the program assumes decimal degrees.

triangle solution B, b, c program —

Given two angles and a non-included side, this program solves the triangle for the remaining parameters by the following formulas:

1. $C = \sin^{-1}\left(\frac{c \sin B}{b}\right)$

2. $A = 2\sin^{-1} 1 - (B + C) = \pi \text{ radians} -$
$(B + C) = 180° - (B + C)$
$= 200 \text{ grads} - (B + C)$

3. $a = \frac{b \sin A}{\sin B}$

If B is acute (< 90°) and b < c, a second set of solutions exists and is calculated by the following formulas:

4. $C' = 2\sin^{-1} 1 - C$

5. $A' = 2\sin^{-1} 1 - (B + C')$

6. $a' = \frac{b \sin A'}{\sin B}$

This program works in any angular mode. However, if in degrees, decimal degrees are assumed.

trig calculations — These are generally used for analyzing and making calculations from the relations of sides and angles of triangles. Some calculators give the operator the option of obtaining the answer in degrees, radians, or grads.

triggering — The starting of circuit action, which then continues for a predetermined time under its own control.

trigonometric capability — →R Rectangular/polar coordinate conversions: one can convert rectangular coordinates to polar coordinates or vice versa, enabling one to do vector arithmetic quickly, easily and accurately, on some units. For example: →HMS Angle (time) conversions: One can convert angles (times) in decimal degrees (hours) to angles (times) in degrees (hours)/minutes/seconds ... or vice versa. Many units also provides the six basic trig functions — sin x, arc sin x, cos x, arc cos x, tan x, arc tan x.

trigonometric functions (degree-radians), calculator — Typical are: Angular Mode Switch. Selects degree or radian mode for trig functions and P/R conversions. Sine. Calculates sine of the angle displayed. Cosine. Calculates cosine of the angle displayed. Tangent. Calculates tangent of the angle displayed. Inverse Sine. Calculates $\sin^{-1}$ of the number displayed. Inverse Cosine. Calculates $\cos^{-1}$ of the number displayed. Inverse Tangent. Calculates $\tan^{-1}$ of the number displayed.

triple removable flexible disk drive — This contains three disk drives, and provides storage for 786, 431 bytes of information. The removable, compact platters are interchangeable between the three disk drives of some units.

troubleshoot — 1. To search for errors in order to correct them. 2. To isolate and remove the mistakes in a program caused by the malfunction of a computer. (Related to diagnostic routine.)

troubleshooting functional modules — Troubleshooting and repair of functional modules or final assemblies can be best accomplished — with a minimum of aids — by direct component substitution. A word of warning, however, on preliminary inspection and handling of circuits: caution is needed so that solder bridges or other short circuits, or failed or improperly inserted parts, do not destroy expensive CPU or ROM chips at the moment of turn-on. It is relatively easy, while substituting components, to destroy several devices before a fault is located. And since most processor components are MOS, careful handling is required to prevent damage due to static electricity.

true credit balance — When the answer is negative, the minus sign automatically appears in the display.

truncate — To terminate a computational process in accordance with some rule, i.e., to end the evaluation of a power series at a specified term.

truncation — 1. Ending of a computational procedure in accordance with some program rule as soon as a specified accuracy has been reached. 2. Rejection of final digits in a number, thus lessening precision (but not necessarily accuracy).

truncation error — 1. The error resulting from an approximation using a finite number of terms of an infinite series. 2. The error resulting from the use of only a finite number of terms of an infinite series, or from the approximation of operations in the infinitesimal calculus by operations in the calculus of finite differences.

trunk — 1. A single message circuit between two points, both of which are switching centers and/or individual message of distribution points. 2. A communications channel between two different offices, or between groups of equipment within the same office.

trunk check — Relates to a set or group of parallel lines for transmission of data to a particular checking device or unit such as a check register, a parity checker or a comparator.

trunk, final — 1. Relating to long-distance telephone communications, that line which connects switching centers which are adjacent to each other in the line of communications such as a local center to its primary or secondary center, or a primary center to its zone center, or various zone centers to each other. A trunk is a single message circuit between two points and both of which are switching centers, or individual message distributing points. 2. A trunk-telephone line to a higher-echelon office that does not have an alternate route.

trunk hunting — A designed procedure or arrangement in which an incoming communications call is switched to the next number in sequence if the original called number is busy.

trunk, telephone — A particular telephone line between two central offices that is used to provide communications between subscribers.

truth table — 1. A mathematical table showing the Boolean-algebra relationships of variables. 2. A representation of a switching function, or truth function, in which every possible configuration of argument values 0, 1 or true-false is listed, and beside each is given the associated function value 0-1 or true-false. The number of configurations is $2^{**}n$, where n is the number of arguments, unless the function is incompletely specified, i.e., don't care conditions.

truth table, example — An example: a simple diode AND circuit, together with its logic symbol, and various possible combinations of input and output signals can be clearly summarized in a "truth table," in terms of "0" and "1". For convenience, one designates a positive voltage as "1" and a ground or negative voltage as "0". This convention is called "positive logic," and the opposite, a positive voltage meaning "0" and a ground meaning "1", is called, appropriately enough, "negative logic." Looking at a truth table, it is apparent that a "1" output can only occur when both the A and the B input are "1". This corresponds to the case where both relays must be energized, because their contacts are in series.

truth table for a NAND gate —

Inputs A B C	Output ABC
0 0 0	1
0 0 1	1
0 1 0	1
0 1 1	1
1 0 0	1
1 0 1	1
1 1 0	1
1 1 1	0

The grouping of an OR gate followed by an inverter is called a NOT OR or NOR gate. If any of the inputs has a value of 1, the output will be 0. Only if all inputs are 0 will the outputs from the NOR gate be 1. (Note that this is just the opposite of an OR gate.)

truth table for a NOR gate —

Inputs A B C	Output = A+B+C
0 0 0	1
0 0 1	0
0 1 0	0
0 1 1	0
1 0 0	0
1 0 1	0
1 1 0	0
1 1 1	0

truth table for AND gate —

Inputs I•J	Output = I•J
0 0	0
0 1	0
1 0	0
1 1	1

The output will be only if all the inputs have the value of 1.

truth table generation testing — The generation technique uses a microprocessor to develop the truth table from a user diagnostic written in the microprocessor's own machine code or assembly language. The generation program can be composed without having to know the internal architecture of the microprocessor. Only knowledge of the functions of the external device pins stated in the manufacturer's data sheet specifications are necessary.

TS dispatcher — Under TSO, a section of the time sharing interface program executed as part of the operating system dispatcher. It initiates work requested by the time sharing driver.

TSO — Time sharing option.

TSO command language — The set of commands, subcommands, and operands recognized under the time sharing option (TSO).

TTD temporary text delay — Sent by a sending station when it wishes to retain the line but is not ready to transmit. The TTD control sequence (STX ENQ) is normally sent after approximately two seconds if the sending station is not capable of transmitting within the time — thus avoiding the nominal three second time-out at the receiver.

T test — A comparison test of two units of quantitative data for the determination of their inequality, i.e., a determination of which quantity is the greater.

t test of sample means program — Computes the statistics needed to perform a one-sample or two-sample test. The computations help direct and permit the choice of t Tests to be used, especially with regard to equal or unequal population variances.

t-test, statistics package — t-test programs each have 10 or more different descriptive statistics for each sample, with histograms, tests with one tail or two tail significance levels, and 90-99% confidence intervals for means.

TTL — Refers to Transistor-Transistor Logic. The high-speed logic found in minis and mainframes. TTL is the most common bipolar technology.

TTL compatibility — Various cells can provide complete compatibility with TTL for applications where arrays are contemplated for TTL replacement or for interfacing. Specific cell connections are used for input and output compatibility. In general, the input gates must be restricted to two inputs and outputs must be buffered when interfacing with TTL when driving more than on TTL load.

TTL logic — 1. Standard TTL provides the lowest component cost of conventional logic. It is relatively fast and is unsurpassed for variety of functions. It's the standard by which all other methods are measured. It has at least four disadvantages: high power dissipation, limited noise immunity, inadequate speed for some applications and limited complexity. 2. TTL logic uses two dc flip-flops with one single-phase clock pulse to control the logic steps in a classic master-slave relationship. TTL is simple to operate, but it requires a lot of components and consequently a lot of chip area for LSI.

T^3L — A modified TTL configuration in which a third transistor is added to the TTL output of a gate (logic switch) to boost drive capabilities and increase noise immunity.

turnaround time — The particular amount of time that is required for a computation task to get from the programmer to the computer, onto the machine for a test or production run, and back to the programmer in the form of the desired results. Important problems occur when the turnaround time is excessive, especially in scientific installations.

turn-key system — A term applied to an agreement whereby a supplier will install a computer system so that he has total responsibility for building, installing, and testing the system including hardware and software.

turn-on time — The time required for an output to turn on (sink current to ground output, to go to 0-volts). It is the propagation time or time of an appropriate input signal to cause the output to go to 0 volts.

turnover — Reversing the legs of a balanced transmission circuit. This test is very important in all transmission measurements with balanced circuits, because if the same results are not obtained when any legs of the balanced system are interchanged, the presence of longitudinal currents is indicated, and no measurement can be accurate unless such currents are eliminated.

Tutor, electronic — A teaching machine which makes use of programmed instructions in the computer to help each student achieve his educational goals. Each student communicates with the computer via his own terminal. The computer will be programmed to adjust its teaching style automatically to the needs of each student, and each student will progress at this own best pace independently of others. Bright students will move from topic to topic rapidly, while slower students will be carefully tutored and given extra practice to raise them to the desired achievement levels.

tutorial lights — On some "intelligent" terminals up to 28 programmable indicator lights can be interlaced with the transaction sequence providing tutorial lead-through to an operator and/or providing a pictorial history of keyboard action while entering a transaction.

tutorial program terminal — Some firms offer hands-on introduction to terminals and extended BASIC commands. Covering operation of the keyboard, use of cartridge tapes, and the Graphics commands, the Tutor package enhances the User's Manual.

two × K contingency programs — Two-by-K Contingency Table. This program calculates CHI-Squared for a $2 \times K$ contingency table. The number of degrees of freedom, $V = K - 1$, is also calculated.

two × two contingency program — CHI-Squared Two-by-Two Contingency Table. This program calculates CHI-Squared for a Two × Two Contingency Table. CHI-Squared with Yates correction is also calculated.

two factor or randomized block analysis program — Two Way Analysis of Variance or Randomized Complete Blocks. This program will produce the Means and the Analysis of Variance for any number of entered groups with up to R replications each. The program may be used for a randomized complete block design.

two-pass assembler — An assembler which requires scanning of the source program twice.

The first pass constructs a symbol table. The second does the translation.

2^2 or 2^3 factorial analysis program — Anova for Two-Squared and Two-Cubed Factorial Experiments. Computes, by means of Yates Algorithm, the effects and the sums of squares needed for the Anova Test on two-squared and/or two-cubed factorial experiments with or without replication in each experimental cell. Two-squared or two-cubed are designed experiments with two or three factors with each factor at two levels.

two-track recording technique, self-clocking — On one unit when it records a program on one of its small magnetic cards, it places two side-by-side tracks of varying magnetic flux on the card. One track represents the logical 1's in the binary data stream coming from the program memory, and the other track represents the logical 0's. The 1 track contains a flux reversal for each 1 in the data sequence and no flux change for each 0. The 0 track contains a flux reversal for each 0 and no flux change for each 1. Various diagrams show examples. The technique is self-clocking because there is a flux transition for each bit. Thus no separate clock track is needed. The scheme also maximizes the system's tolerance to head skew and motor speed variations. The data can be recovered correctly even if a transition in one track almost overlaps a transition in the other. By contrast, other two-track schemes usually have one clock track and one data track, and may misread data when there is only minor misalignment of clock and data transitions.

two valued variable — A variable which assumes values in a set containing exactly two elements, often symbolized as 0 and 1. Synonymous with binary variable and two state variable.

two-way capacity — A CATV system with two-way capacity can conduct signals to the headend as well as away from it. Two-way or bi-directional systems now carry data; they may eventually carry full audio and video television signals either direction commercially as they already do experimentally.

TWX — Western Union teleprinter exchange service with real time direct connection between subscribers.

typewriter, calculator-control — Tables, standard forms, letters, data listings — these are just a few of the data formats users can prepare with specific type typewriters. And they can be produced with full alphanumeric capability, including upper and lower case letters, punctuation marks, and symbols. Some calculators operating through a peripheral control block, automatically controls such things as tab setting and clearing, ribbon color, and vertical and horizontal spacing. But when the calculator is not running a typewriter program, the typewriter can be operated manually.

typewriter, console monitor — The primary function of some typewriters is to monitor system and program operations. Such system conditions as ADD OVERFLOW, EXPONENT OVERFLOW, etc, and program conditions as SYNTAX ERROR, SYMBOL LENGTH, INTEGER SIZE, etc. are brought to the operator's attention via the typewriter. The typewriter also may be programmed to request information from the operator. The typewriter also may be used to enter programs and data into the central processor and to type out the results in lieu of other peripheral equipment specifically designed for these functions.

typewriter control console — The control console of the electronic data-processing system enables the operator to centrally control and monitor all processing functions. The panel is designed for efficient supervision and provides what is necessary for the operator, as the needs of the service engineers often have been placed within individual components of the system. An electric typewriter provides direct communication with the processor memory. Data can be entered into the memory through the typewriter keyboard. The processor can transmit data to the typewriter for output through the typewriter printer. Thus, through the console typewriter, the operator can interrogate the memory, input programs, and enter instructions to modify a program (some computers).

typewriter, on-line — The on-line typewriter, a standard feature of many computers, provides monitor control of operating programs. It operates on a character at a time basis under program control and communicates directly with the accumulator. Data communication is through the programmed input/output channel.

typing reperforator — A reperforator which types on chadless tape about one-half inch beyond where corresponding characters are punched. Some units type on the edge of special-width tape.

U

UART (universal asychronous transmitter) — Refers to a specific device that will interface a word parallel controller or data terminal to a bit serial communication network.

UART advantages — Because a vast majority of computers have to communicate, the PIA (Peripheral Interface Adapter) has been mated with the popular UART (Universal Asynchronous Receiver/Transmitter). In a single chip, several firms offer ACIAs (Asynchronous Communications Interface Adapter) that merge the communications-side features of a UART and one half of a PIA. This means that a single chip can incorporate all of the CPU-controlled features necessary to drive a teletypewriter or modem.

UART and ACIA differences — The characteristics of some UARTs are identical to that of an ACIA. With a UART, however, control inputs, status outputs and data buffers are accessible through unidirectional lines. Thus the I/O bus of the unit requires additional multiplexing for read or write operations. The ACIA incorporates the multiplexing circuitry, so that status, control and data registers are accessible through a single bidirectional bus.

ultraviolet erasable PROM's — ROM's are usually thought of as having permanent binary information programmed into their memories. Once information is programmed into an ordinary ROM, it cannot be altered. However, various types of PROMs are erasable. These types of PROMs permit information stored semi-permanently to be erased and new information to be reprogramed in. One type of erasable PROM can be erased by concentrated shortwave ultraviolet light. It is housed in a 16-pin dual in-line package (DIP) with a quartz top that is transparent to shortwave UV light. The 2048 bits are organized as either 256 words of four bits per word. The unwanted information is simply erased by directing UV light through the IC's quartz "window" and reprogramming as desired.

ultraviolet PROM erasure lamp — One type lamp provides complete erasures in approximately six minutes at the suggested working distance of one inch (2.5 cm). At this distance, the effective area of coverage is 2¼ × 6 inches (5.8 × 15.4 cm). When small quantities of chips are being erased, they can be placed on a simple platform to provide the proper distance from tube to chip surface.

The higher the intensity of short wave output, the shorter the exposure time required for PROM erasure. Manufacturers of programmable read only memory units are now specifying recommended unfiltered ultraviolet source for this purpose.

unconditional transfer keys, calculator — These keys include: (1) Go To. A prefix key. Moves program counter to a new program location, defined either by a 3-digit program location or a label. (2) Subroutine. A prefix key. Used with either a label or a 3-digit program location. Causes a transfer to a program segment to be used as a subroutine. (3) Indirect Go To. Transfers to the location in program memory specified by the contents of a memory register. (4) Indirect Subroutine. Transfers control to a program segment designated as a subroutine whose starting location is found in the specified memory register ... and others.

uncontrolled lines — Those lines that contain terminals that may transmit to the central processor at any time they are ready to send. The central processor must be ready at all times to accept messages from this type of terminal.

underflow — When the calculator's capacity is exceeded, some of the least significant digits are discarded and the resulting display is sometimes zero.

underflow (continue), small calculators — If a result develops that is too small in magnitude to be carried in a register ($<10^{-99}$), the register is set to zero; a running program would continue execution.

underflow indicator — 0.0000000 appears in the display and a warning light is possibly activated. In many electronic calculators that number is lost, but some provide a capability to retrieve the number.

uninterruptable power supply — On some systems, optional batteries in chassis provide an uninterruptible power supply to the program and data RAM memories to ride through a 10 minute power outage.

union — A logical operator having the property that if P is a statement and Q is a statement, then the OR of P.Q. is true if and only if at least one is true; false if all are false. P or Q is often represented by P + Q, PUQ. Related to inclusive OR and exclusive OR.

unit or event counter — A typical unit is a fully integrated unit counter suitable for driving a 7 digit, 7 segment LED display directly without external drivers. It can count to 10,000,000 for applications such as process control, traffic monitoring, etc. The unit is ideally suitable for remote battery operated systems due to the low circuit power consumption with the display switched off. Using a 3 cell NiCad stack the current consumption is typically less than $200 \mu A$ (3.6 volt nominal supply).

unit record — 1. Historically, a card containing one complete record; currently, the punched card. 2. A printed line with a maximum of 120 characters; a punched card with a maximum of 72 characters, a BCD (binary-coded decimal) tape record with a maximum of 120 characters.

unit separator — A specific character developed for the demarcation of the logical boundary between items of data that are referred to as separate and distinct units.

units key, data acquisition calculator — Key displays units code, number corresponding to MV, °C, PSI Hz, etc., for the previously selected channel pair. Users key in new numeric code and enter.

universal converter calculator — Model is pre-programmed to perform 224 conversions involving U.S., metric and imperial units of measure (feet/meters/nautical miles/etc.). It can be user-programmed for special problems. There is no limit to the number of conversion factors. Most units also do fraction calculations with impressive ease and speed.

universal digital interface systems — Typical universal digital interface systems are used where standard, off-the-shelf interface and peripheral systems fail to meet either technical or economic objectives. The universal digital interface provides a high level of programmable input and output versatility by means of various series plug-in circuit cards, each designed to perform a specific function. The primary application of some series universal digital interface, however, is sequencing and formatting binary or binary-coded-decimal information to the parallel input/output bus of advanced calculators. Because analog multiplexing and analog-to-digital conversion cards can be installed in the mainframe assembly and controlled by the calculator, the system may be used in small scale data acquisition systems.

universal interface — A typical unit provides 16 input and 16 output lines with differential transmitters and receiver for operation up to 500 feet. Can be operated in either a single or dual-channel mode.

universal vendor marking standard (UVM) — This is a standard chosen and promoted by NRMA (National Retail Merchants Association) rather than by a single equipment manufacturer. It is human readable as well as machine readable offers both internal system benefits and external customer benefits. It is a standard which can be printed by relatively inexpensive printing mechanisms of many different types. Thus, it can be implemented at less cost than systems based on print/punch, bar codes or magnetic codes. It also can be used with virtually any retail medium including credit cards, invoices and other control documents.

universal vendor marking standard (UVM) advantages — This standard seems equally attractive to general merchandise retailers and to merchandise vendors. UVM gives the merchant a powerful new tool for achieving inventory con-

unload

trol at the unit level rather than the dollar level, thereby helping to improve return on inventory investment. Its use provides a fast, easy, accurate and low-cost method of capturing the data required to keep track of unit merchandise movement from the point of sale to the point of service. It is similar to the Universal Product Code (UPC) of the supermarket industry but is read by optical character reading devices rather than bar code readers.

unload — To remove information in massive quantities as in unloading the storage contents onto a magnetic tape.

unpack — 1. To decompose packed information into a sequence of separate words or elements. 2. To recover the original data from packed data. 3. To separate combined items of information each into a separate machine word.

update — 1. To search the file (such as a particular record in a computer tape) and select one entry, then perform some operation to bring the entry up-to-date. 2. To put into a master file changes required by current information or transactions. 3. To modify an instruction so that the address numbers it contains are increased by a stated amount each time the instruction is performed.

update (verb) — To modify a master file according to current forms of information often that contained in a transaction field, according to a procedure specified as part of a data processing activity.

UPS — Uninterruptable power supply for protection and blackouts.

up time — The time during which equipment is either producing work or is available for productive work. (Contrasted with down time.)

USART, programmable — The programable USART's standard RS-232-C interface can be used to connect both synchronous and asynchronous communications devices to the calculator — (other jumper-selectable interfaces connect to standard teletypewriter lines). The USART provides full-duplex operation; that is, serial/parallel data conversions can be made simultaneously in both directions. A typical USART chip contains both receiver and transmitter buffers and control sections. In some units as a transmitter, it converts data bytes (8-bit parallel data) into serial characters 5 to 8 bits long and inserts the desired control bits or characters. As a receiver, it strips out the control characters and assembles the data into parallel bytes, which are sent to the CPU. In its synchronous mode, the device also transmits characters to keep remote units in sync when the CPU is not sending data. Often the system software specifies mode, number of sync characters, asynchronous rate (after the basic baud rate is jumper-selected, divisions of one, 16, or 64 can be programed), character length, number of stop bits, and odd/even parity. During initialization, mode-instruction words are sent by the CPU to a register on the USART chip.

USASI — United States of America Standards Institute; a former name of the American National Standard, Institute. Same as ANSI.

USASCII — An abbreviation for USA Standard Code for Information Interchange.

user area (UA) — The area on a disk where semipermanent data may be stored. This area is also used to store programs, subprograms, and subroutines. This area is contrasted with reserved areas that contain compilers, track and sector information, etc., which may not be written into.

user definable function block — On some units with the User Definable Function Block, users can customize individual keys for the operations uniquely important to users. For example, the electrical engineer will probably want voltage, impedance, capacitance, and true RMS functions; the physicist, his mass, velocity, and acceleration functions; the chemical engineer, his fluid flow and heat transfer functions. With one definable block, users can specify 5, 15, or 25 keys depending upon whether the remaining banks are being occupied by other ROM's — for these versatile systems.

user definable functions, calculator — Some specific models give users the opportunity to select from special keyboard plug-in blocks, so they can personalize their problem solving capabilities to their specific discipline. These unique features vastly extend user computing power, simplify programming, and reduce computing time. For instance, they can choose from the traditional MATHEMATICS keyboard block, the STATISTICS block, or various USER DEFINABLE FUNCTION blocks. These function blocks are completely interchangeable and require absolutely no modification to the calculator or any special tools or skills to install. To install the math functions for example, users merely insert the math memory block in the slot at the top of some calculators, place the key identification template over the left-hand block of keys, and they are ready to start solving complex mathematical problems with the touch of a single key.

user definable keys, advanced calculator — A special feature that aids the advanced calculator's role as a terminal is a set of up to 20 user-definable keys, called special function keys, that are available to store often-used sequences like telephone numbers or user sign-on codes. Only a single keystroke is needed to dial a telephone number, to send a user code, or to perform an entire sign-on sequence including dialing.

user-definable keys, preprogrammed — On some units, 13 or more keys can be preprogrammed to execute specific functions by automatically jumping to specific locations within the unit's memory.

user-definable key tag (optional on some units) — On some units (mainly desk-top) eight or more user-definable keys can be converted to user-definable operation. In the CALC (some units), each key initiates a search for a specific tag in the program memory. The keys are labeled with the customer's description for the functions, helping to eliminate operator errors.

user-definable overlays — On some units users can define eight keys with an overlay to perform special functions. They combine a series of keystrokes into a single key and label on the overlay and press their customized key and get that complex job done. It's often as simple as writing one's thoughts, only doing it on the keyboard without computer language skill. Users follow their progress on the numeric printer. They correct mistakes as they go. To keep a program for repeated use, they transfer it to a magnetic card. (some units)

user-microprogrammer processors — Current

advances in semiconductor technology have led to microprogrammed and user-microprogrammable processors having a variety of microinstruction sequencing capabilities. The primary use of microprograms is as an alternative to hardwired control sequencers in the implementation of the control function in computers with conventional instruction sets; thus, microprograms are used to implement tasks which have a relatively simple logical structure. Microprograms are being used to support special purpose architectures with instruction sets chosen to simplify programming of certain classes of algorithms; these microprograms are also being used to implement tasks which may have a relatively complex logical structure.

user profile table — In systems with time sharing, a table of user attributes kept for each active user, built from information gathered during logon.

user programmed cards — After users have completed their program they can store it and record it permanently, by running a magnetic card through the reader. Then it's in the unit and on the card. After the card is labeled it is available for repetitive problem solving. Users simply insert the card and operate the unit in the run mode. They save time and effort, and have greatly reduced the change of error since there are far fewer steps to perform.

user programs — A group of specific programs, subprograms or subroutines that have been written by the user as contrasted to manufacturer supplied programs.

users group — 1. A users group is both a means of communication among Users and a method of building a comprehensive library of programs. Specific company purchasers are often entitled to a free, one year membership in these groups. Members of the Users Group are encouraged to submit programs by entering various "Software Contests". Winners of these contests are awarded prizes. User groups often have newspapers which publish monthly and are mailed free to all members. These computer notes contain complete update on many hardware and software developments, programming tips, general calculator articles and other useful information. 2. Refers to particular organizations made up of users (as opposed to vendors) of various calculator systems to give the users an opportunity to share knowledge they have gained in using calculator computing systems, to exchange programs they have developed, and to jointly influence vendor software and hardware support and policy.

utility debug — A designed aid for the programmer in testing and debugging programs and in the performing of utility functions. Features included are:
- Display and Change Memory
- Display and Change Registers
- Punch Object Tape
- Load a Program Tape
- Execute a Program and Tape
- Breakpoint Select
- List Program
- Search Memory
- Calculate Sums and Differences

utility, financial — A general-purpose computer utility for handling massive volumes of financial transactions. In the future there is expected to be a rapid expansion of on-line, real-time banking with computer power for individual banks being supplied by large banking utilities. Retail stores are likely to be tied in, and shopping with "money cards" will become commonplace. As more and more businesses are included, the money card will largely replace both checks and currency as the normal medium of exchange.

utility functions — Auxiliary operations such as tape searching, tape-file copying, media conversion, and dynamic memory and tape dumps.

utility program — A standard routine used to assist in the operation of the calculator, e.g., a conversion routine, a sorting routine, a printout routine, or a tracing routine.

utility routines — Utility routines are likely to include: addition, subtraction and division; trigonometric functions; logorithms, exponentials and other common mathematical functions; programs to read from and write to all peripheral devices (I/O subsystem with device drivers), and programs to generate text output at a line printer, teletype or CRT terminal. The utility routines may constitute a large number of programs, but only those components actually referenced by applications programs will be loaded into memory.

utility system — A system or program that is developed to perform miscellaneous or utility functions such as card-to-tape, tape-to-printer, and other peripheral operations or suboperations.

utilization factor — A specific ratio, calculated to be a measure of the arrival rate to the service rate. In the steady state, the utilization factor represents the average fraction of time that the system is being used.

utilization loggers system — A program or a device that collects statistical information about how the system is operating.

utilization ratio — That particular measurement which is the ratio of effective time to serviceable time.

VAB (voice answer back) — Concerns various audio response units which can link a calculator system to a telephone network to provide voice responses to inquiries made from telephone-type terminals. The audio response is composed from a vocabulary prerecorded in a digital-coded voice or a disk-storage device.

validity checking — 1. Refers to a procedure for detecting invalid or distinctly unreasonable results, i.e., illogical bit combinations, high improbable numeric codes, storage addresses, etc. 2. A data screening procedure wherein data input records are checked for range, valid coding, valid representation (i.e., calendar date), etc. Related to input editing.

valid memory address — This output indicates to peripheral devices that there is a valid address on the address bus. In normal operation,

value-added carriers this signal should be utilized for enabling peripheral interfaces such as the PIA and ACIA. In many systems this signal is not three-state. One standard TTL load and 30 pF may be directly driven by this active high signal.

value-added carriers — A new class of communications common carrier now authorized to lease raw communication trunks from the transmission carriers, augment these facilities with computerized switching, and provide enhanced or "value-added" communications services. Telenet Communications Corporation, and others are now employing a fundamentally new technology, called packet switching, to provide value-added data communications services. Packet switching is a communications technology, but it has its roots in the computer field rather than in the communications field, for it was developed by computer users in order to better meet their communication requirements.

value-added network examples — Examples of existing and proposed "value-added networks" covered by this definition are TYMNET, ARPANET, and that developed by Telenet Communications Inc. Also the extensive communications networks used to distribute the services of the large commercial time-sharing companies, such as GE Information Services are included.

V-answerback — The response to a transmitter start code (TSC) of a polled station in a teletypewriter switched network if the station has no traffic to send, or the response to a call-directing code (CDC) of a station that is prepared to receive traffic.

variable — 1. Any factor or condition which can be measured, altered, or controlled (e.g., temperature, pressure, flow, liquid level, humidity, weight, chemical composition, color, etc.). 2. A quantity that can assume any of a given set of values.

variable block format — A format which allows the number of words in successive blocks to vary.

variable field — A field in which the scalar (or vector) at any point changes during the time under consideration.

variable-format messages — Messages in which line control characters are not to be deleted upon arrival nor inserted upon departure: variable-format messages are intended for terminals with similar characteristics. Contrast with fixed-format messages.

variable-length instructions — A feature which increases main memory efficiency by using only the amount necessary for the application and increases speed because the machine interprets only the fields relevant to the application. Half-word (2 byte). two-halfword (4 bytes), or three-halfword (6 bytes) instructions are used. (Some systems)

variable-length records — Records of a file in which the number of words in each record varies.

variable length records sorting — Sorting records in which the number of words, characters, bits, fields, etc. vary in length.

variable logic — That specific internal logic design which is alterable in accordance with a precompleted program which controls the various electronic interconnections of the gating elements, i.e., the instruction repertoire can be electronically changed, or the machine capability can be matched to the problem requirement. A type of variable logic.

variable name — A name selected by the programmer that represents a specific variable. Numeric variables and array variables may be named with the characters A through Z and A1 through Z9. String variables may be named with the characters A$ through Z$.

variable-point representation — A specific radix notation in which each number is represented by a single set of digits, the position of the radix point explicitly indicated by the inclusion of an appropriate character.

variable problem — 1. A multiplier used by the programmer converting quantities occurring in a problem into a desired range. 2. A method of modifying the location of a decimal or binary point.

variables, FORTRAN — Fixed point (restricted to integer values): Consisting of 1 to 6 alphanumeric characters, the first I, J, K, L, M, or N. Floating point: 1 to 6 alphanumeric characters, the first being alphabetic but not I, J, K, L, M, or N. Boolean: Floating-point names. (Some systems)

variable symbol — A symbol, corresponding to a location in memory, whose value may change as a program executes.

variable word — The specific feature in which the number of characters handled in the unit is not constant. For contrast, see fixed word.

variance — The measure of dispersion about the mean: i.e., the average of the squared deviations between observations and the mean. The square of the standard deviation.

variance analysis — Relates to the estimate of probability relatedness by comparison of between-columns variance with within-columns variance.

variance internal program — Confidence Interval on Variance. This program determines a confidence interval on the variance assuming the X's are independent, random, and from a normal distribution.

variance, standard deviation — Variance arises from a search for a number which is associated with a distribution of data to express the degree to which the numbers are spread or scattered. The variance is a widely used measure of dispersion. The standard deviation is the square root of the variance, and is expressed in the same units as the original variables.

variation — When two variables, x and y, are so related that the ratio of x to y is always constant, then x is said to vary directly as y. When two variables, x and y, are so related that y varies directly as the reciprocal of x, then y is said to vary inversely as x. Joint variation concerns two or more variables such as: z=kxy where z is stated as a joint variable of x and y, or if z = k(x/y), z thus varies directly as x and inversely as y.

vector — 1. The term for a symbol which denotes a directed quantity — i.e., one which cannot be completely described except in terms of both magnitude and direction (e.g., wind velocities, voltage and currents of electricity, and forces of all kinds). 2. A quantity having magnitude and direction, as contrasted with a scalar which has quantity only. 3. A 1-dimensional array.

vector algebra — Manipulation of symbols representing vector quantities according to laws of addition, subtraction, multiplication and division, which these quantities obey.

vector arithmetic — Many calculators are ideal for vector arithmetic problems. Once the sums of the x and y coordinates of all vectors are accumu-

vector cross product program — If $A = (a_1, a_2, a_3)$ and $B = (b_1, b_2, b_3)$ are two three dimensional vectors then the cross product of A and B is denoted by $A \times B$ and is calculated as follows:

$$A \times B = \left(\left| \begin{matrix} a_2 \, a_3 \\ b_2 \, b_3 \end{matrix} \right|, - \left| \begin{matrix} a_1 \, a_3 \\ b_1 \, b_3 \end{matrix} \right|, \left| \begin{matrix} a_1 \, a_2 \\ b_1 \, b_2 \end{matrix} \right| \right) =$$

$(a_2 \, b_3 - a_3 \, b_2, \, a_3 \, b_1 - a_1 \, b_3, \, a_1 \, b_2 - a_2 \, b_1)$

Let the solution be represented by (c_1, c_2, c_3).

vector diagram — An arrangement of vectors showing the relationships between alternating quantities having the same frequency.

vectored interrupt interface — Some bus systems provide a vectored interrupt interface for any device. Device polling is not required in processing interrupt requests. When an interrupting device receives a grant, the device passes to the processor and the interrupt vector which points to a new processor status word and the starting address of an interrupt service routine for the device.

vectored priority interrupt — An interrupt Control Unit (ICU) implements eight levels of vectored priority interrupt. The unit features automatic priority determination, programmable status and N-level interrupt expansion capability.

vectored priority interrupt — Allows virtually simultaneous processing of multiple jobs. It's easily programmed to suspend processing, gather or send data and messages to instruments and peripherals, then automatically return to the original job. (some units)

vector field — In a given region of space, the total value of some vector quantity which has a definite value at each point of the region (e.g., the distribution of magnetic intensity in a region surrounding a current-carrying conductor.)

vector function — A function which has both magnitude and direction (e.g., the magnetic intensity at a point near an electric circuit is a vector function of the current in that circuit).

vector instruction — As an example of how one powerful firmware instruction can facilitate the performance of the operating system, the Vector instruction takes an interrupt, stores the machine state, branches to the appropriate device or handle switches stacks and allocates a stack frame in just 18 microseconds. This process would take a number of sequential subroutines if it were done by the operating system. (some systems)

vector power — A vector quantity equal to the square root of the sum of the squares of the active and reactive powers. The unit is the vector-ampere.

vector summations, small calculators) — The $\Sigma+$ key can be used to sum any quantities that are in the X- and Y-registers. User can perform vector addition and subtraction using rectangular to polar coordinate conversion and the $\Sigma+$ and $\Sigma-$ keys.
Method: The true heading and ground speed are equal to the sum of the instrument vector and the wind vector. The vectors are converted to rectangular coordinates and summed using the $\Sigma+$ and $\Sigma-$ keys. Their sum is recalled by recalling the values in storage registers R_4 (Σy) and R_7 (Σx), and the new rectangular coordinates are then converted back to polar coordinates to give the vector of the actual ground speed and true heading (as used in some small systems)

vector quantity — A quantity which has both magnitude and direction such as field intensity, momentum etc. as contrasted with scaler quantities.

vector ratio — That between two alternating quantities, in which both relative amplitudes and phases are expressed as vectors.

Veitch diagram — 1. A graphical technique used for the solution of problems arising in logical circuit design. 2. A table or chart showing information contained in a truth table.

velocity — 1. A vector quantity that includes both magnitude (speed) and direction in relation to a given frame of reference. 2. Rate of motion in a given direction, employed in its higher magnitudes as a means of overcoming the force of gravity. 3. In a wave, distance travelled by a given phase of a wave divided by time taken. It is a vector quantity so that it has a magnitude and a direction expressed relative to some frame of reference.

Venn diagrams — Diagrams in which circles or elipses are used to give a graphic representation of basic logic relations . . . logic relations between classes, operations on classes, and the terms of the propositions are illustrated and defined by the inclusion, exclusion, or intersection of these figures. Shading indicates empty areas, crosses indicate areas that are not empty, and blank spaces indicate areas that may be either. Named for English logician John Venn, who devised them.

verification — The process of checking the results of one data transcription against those of another, both transcriptions usually involving manual operations. (Also see Check.)

verification mode — Refers to systems with time sharing, a mode of operation under the EDIT command in which all subcommands are acknowledged and any textual changes are displayed as they are made.

verify — 1. To check, usually with an automatic machine, one recording of data against another in order to minimize the number of human errors in the data transcription. 2. To make certain that the information being prepared for a computer is correct. 3. To determine whether a transcription of data or other operation has been accomplished accurately. 4. To check the results of keypunching.

vernier — 1. An auxiliary scale comprising subdivisions of the main measuring scale and thus permitting more accurate measurements than is possible from the main scale alone. 2. An auxiliary device used for obtaining fine adjustments.

vertical blanking — The elimination of the vertical trace on a CRT during frame flyback.

vertical display — The height, in inches, of the display area of the cathode-ray tube.

vertical feed — Indicates the attitude in which a card is placed in the hopper, enters, and traverses the card track.

vertical format — Pertaining to the vertical arrangement of data, as viewed by an observer of a document.

vertical parity — The term used to describe the method of error checking which utilizes a check or parity bit with each character.

vertical parity check — Refers to a check by summation in which the binary digits, in a character or word, are added, and the sum checked against a single, previously computed parity digit; i.e., a check tests whether the number of ones in a

vertical redundance

word is odd or even (synonymous with odd-even check, and related to redundant check and forbidden-combination check).

vertical redundance — In a parity checking system, refers to an even number of bits in odd parity system or vice versa.

vertical redundancy check — An odd parity check performed on each character of a transmitted block of ASCII-coded data as the block is received. Abbreviated VRC. See also cyclic redundancy check, longitudinal redundancy check.

vertical tabulation character — A specific control character which was developed to cause the printing or display position to be moved a measured number of lines at right angles to the line of printing.

v-f band — A voice-frequency band. A transmission facility of approximately 3000-cycle bandwidth, capable of telephone-quality communications.

V format — A data record format designed so that the logical records are of variable length and each record begins with a record length indication.

VHF (Very High Frequencies) — The range of frequencies extending from 30 to 300 MHz; also, television channels 2 through 13.

video-data terminal — In many systems video-data terminal and interrogator units include complete units which combine data entry and display. Each video data terminal operates over a single communications line and contains its own storage and character generator, capable of providing a selected character subset for display of up to 480 characters on various sized screens. (Some units)

video terminal — A computer terminal that incorporates a cathode-ray tube (CRT) for displaying information on a screen. Some terminals are designed for data entry as well as display, and feature built-in microcomputers or minicomputers both edit and format input and operate as stand-alone data processing systems.

video terminals, standard — A standard video terminal is simple to operate as well as economical and reliable for use in timesharing and inquiry systems. A typical unit is a 59-key typewriter-type keyboard with a 12-inch diagonal screen. The bright display shows 24 rows of 80 characters that have been sent or received. Transmission can be in upper-and-lower case for remote output of all 128-character ASCII characters. Capable of full- or half-duplex operation. Many units offer 11 selectable speeds ranging from 75 to 19,200 baud. (other types vary considerably)

violation of subroutines — Violation occurs when the input to the subroutine doesn't match the input as specified.

violation program, memory protect — A special program which is generated when a detection is made that a memory alteration or modification is being attempted on the contents of sections of memory which are protected by the presence of a guard bit.

virtual — Conceptual or appearing to be, rather than actually being.

virtual address — In a computer, an immediate, or real-time, address.

virtual address area — In DOS/VS, the area of virtual storage whose addresses are greater than the highest address of the real address area.

virtual address, effective — The virtual address value after only indirect addressing and/or index-

virtual memory

ing modifications have been accomplished, but before memory mapping is performed.

virtual display, calculator — A standard feature on some units is the Panaplex® display. In RUN mode, the display offers a quick and accurate check on entered data. In LEARN mode users can almost see into the memory of the system. Displaying each program step and instruction lets users debug faster and more easily while stepping through a program. A PAUSE feature displays intermediate results in ½ second increments without printing out; saves both time and paper. Final results can be shown with a fixed or floating decimal point or in scientific notation, on these units.

virtual display console — 1. Refers to the display of a message of thousands of characters of information, or tables, charts, graphs and the lines and curves of drawings as a series of points. A "light pen" (stylus), available with the display, can detect information that has been displayed on the screen and enables the operator to change information under program control. 2. There are binary displays on many computer operator's consoles. One display bit indicates the memory word parity: other display bits may indicate: 1. The next instruction; 2. The contents of any memory location; 3. The contents of the accumulator; 4. The contents of index registers.

virtual display interface — Conveys the results of computation or measurement to the observer via either a numeric or alphanumeric visual display. Particularly significant are the high voltage requirements of the gas discharge display types like the Burroughs Panaplex and Beckman (formerly Sperry) displays. Required here are voltages far in excess of traditionally acceptable monolithic IC levels.

virtual earth — Live input terminal of a high-gain directly-coupled amplifier which remains approximately at earth potential although not connected to earth.

virtual machine techniques — There is an increasing use of virtual memory and virtual-machine techniques. Memory systems, already up to ½-million bytes, can go to 250 million words in a virtual memory, and it also has the advantage of simplified software and increased reliability. A virtual machine implies virtual memory and more. It maps memory plus instructions. So when a user executes, say, an I/O instruction, the machine traps and implements it directly.

virtual memory — Virtual memory, ideally invisible to the user, involves the transfer of information one page or more at a time between primary and secondary memory, and adds only that time required for page swapping to the normal operating time. This procedure leaves the programmer free to address total storage without concern as to whether primary or secondary storage is actually being addressed, and effectively includes the large, inexpensive capacity of secondary storage in the system. Optimally, the computer should be able to operate either with or without virtual memory without major software modification. While this concept has found wide application in larger computer systems, it has played a lesser role in minicomputer applications because its simplest implementation is in software alone, which requires a substantial portion of available primary storage capacity. Benefits of virtual memory operation are therefore enhanced when it is implemented by hardware which carries out the data swapping algorithms. Higher hardware costs are usually more than compensated for by savings in software. Because today's minicomputers are so inexpensive, a virtual memory option would not cost significantly more than an integrated minicomputer plus a secondary disc storage system.

virtual memory design — The first approach involves writing a pre-assembler or modifying the assembler. Such a system could insert at the appropriate location in text, instructions to jump to a paging routine since the next address will be outside the current page boundary. This is quite an attractive approach since in the mini which some firms use, only a relatively small number of the instructions actually address memory. Under such a system page swapping would only occur when required, and the software for the most part would run at its optimum speed.

virtual-memory environments — A virtual-memory system is organized around a relatively small amount of directly accessible main storage and a large amount of secondary storage in the form of high-speed drums and disks. Programs in these systems can be constructed so as to use a great deal of memory, without worrying over much about how this memory is going to be allocated in main storage or swapped between main and secondary storage. In typical systems the virtual memory for all programs is organized in pages of perhaps 4096 bytes, this organization being transparent to each program. Then, assisted by hardware, the supervisor organizes page transfers between main and secondary storage as required without explicit intervention on the part of the program.

virtual memory, executive system — A sophisticated storage allocator can allow the programmer to write programs as if main memory were unlimited. This is termed Virtual Memory. The executive program will keep programs on disk when out of use, loading each one into memory whenever it is called for.

virtual memory, microcomputer — The memory management function of one type operating system automatically brings memory pages to main memory from the system disc as required by the currently executing program. Because some programs are inherently relocatable and because a program's pages need not be in contiguous locations, a page can be swapped from disc into any available page in memory (the memory manager just makes the appropriate map register entry). In this system a process can execute with only two pages in main memory: the code page containing the current instruction and the data page referenced by that instruction.

In one system history bits are associated with each map entry to record access and overlays occurring with a particular page. The memory manager also maintains a list of maps (each process has a separate map) active in a processor module. When memory space is needed for an overlay, the memory manager selects the map that is at the head of the map lists then selects the least accessed page in that map for overlaying. The memory manager ensures that processes are selected on an equal basis for potential overlays by putting the last map selected for overlay at the tail of the map list.

virtual memory pointer — Refers to an aid for storage efficiency. Some computers are designed so that parts of programs and data may be scattered through main memory and auxiliary storage. Various pointers or lists of pointers automatically keep track of the location of these program portions. The user of computers so designed may be unaware of this scattering procedure and most often operates computing procedures as though he were using normal memory.

virtual memory technique (VMT) — In some systems, to execute a single instruction, all that is required is that the instruction and the data on which it operates be located in the main memory. As far as the execution of the instruction is concerned the remainder of the program could reside on secondary storage such as a disk or drum. It is the task of a virtual memory system to insure that prior to executing an instruction, the instruction and its operand(s) be in main memory. If either is not in memory, then it must be located on the secondary storage, the actual site of virtual memory, and brought into memory. If this retrieval were done on a single instruction basis, the system overhead and execution degradation would be significant.

virtual memory, user-coded — Virtual memory can be provided by a user-determined form of code segmentation. This approach permits a program to be larger than the main memory and avoids the thrashing between disk and memory that often results when segmentation is totally machine determined. Some systems automatically eliminate swap out of segments that are in frequent use. A hardware-implemented variable stack design can sharply reduce the amount of memory required to execute programs. Minor data area can be wasted by unused subroutines. A data stack can also provide variable-size arrays, re-entrant code, recursive programming, and an efficient method of parameter passing to subroutines.

visual display modes — Some calculators offer several display modes. In RUN mode, a visual display can offer a quick and accurate check on entered data. In LEARN mode, a user can see into the memory of the system. Displaying each program step by step lets the user debug faster and more easily while stepping through a program. A PAUSE feature can display intermediate results, usually in ½ second increments without printing out; saving both time and paper. Final results can be shown with a fixed or floating decimal point or in scientific notation.

visual display terminals (VDTs) — VDT's include all devices which permit input to a computer (by a user, not a computer operator) through a keyboard and/or some other manual input method (light pen, cursor controls, function buttons), and whose primary output method is visual (i.e., volatile or soft copy) display of alphanumeric and/or graphical information. Excluded are devices with only a few characters' worth of display capacity — say, under 100 — since that normally implies that they have a special purpose. Many terminal devices — POS, banking, credit verification, industrial data collection terminals, etc. — now employ visual display devices using various technologies.

visual display terminal (VDT) capabilities — Terminals as data entry units for data entry are keyboard display work stations oriented toward the pure data entry function (including initial keyboarding, verification, editing, correction, reformatting, and supervisory functions) on a stand-alone basis or supported by a shared processor. The devices are normally user-programmable through parameter designations or specialized data entry-oriented languages. This category does not include general-purpose display terminals used for online applications.

visual-error representation — When a transmission has not been properly received after three successive tries, the third transmission will be printed. The line will be transmitted again and may be printed for comparison with the third transmission (some systems)

visual inquiry station — Refers to an input/output unit which permits the interrogation of an automatic data processing system by the immediate processing of data from a human or terminal (automatic) source together with the display of the results of the processing ..., on a cathode ray tube (CRT) in many cases.

visual scanner — 1. A device that scans optically and usually generates an analog or digital signal. 2. A device that optically scans printed or written data and generates their representation.

visual terminal types — There are several alternative technologies to CRT terminals, including plasma panel displays, magneto-optic displays, and injection electroluminescence light-emitting diode (LED) displays. In displays having very small number of characters plasma panel and LED techniques are being used. From a longer range standpoint the LED technology is perhaps the most promising because of its compatibility with other semiconductor LSI technologies.

voice channel — Refers to a circuit of sufficient bandwidth to permit a data transfer rate of up to 2400 bits per second. Primarily the term distinguishes this service from teleprinter grade utilizing a set or sets of data. Thus, a set of data may furnish data required for plotting more than one graph.

voice, digit-coded — A coded voice response that is output from an ARU (audio response unit).

voice entry data terminal — One specific unit replaces or complements intelligent CRT stations by enabling the user to enter data by voice. The output of each of these modified terminals is in the same format and code as that of a standard keyboard terminal. Voice input is especially valuable to personnel whose hands and eyes are already occupied in their normal work. The data are displayed for verification by the operator before entry.

voice frequency — Any frequency within that part of the audio-frequency range essential for the transmission of highly intelligible speech. Voice frequencies used for telephone transmission of speech usually lie within the range of 200 to 3,400 Hz, although the extreme ends of this range may not be transmitted at an optimum level.

voice-frequency (VF), telephone frequency — Any frequency within that part of the audio-frequency range essential for the transmission of speech of commercial quality, i.e., 300-3400 C/S.

voice grade channel — A channel suitable for transmission of speech, digital or analog data, or facsimile, generally with a frequency range of about 300 to 3000 cycles per second.

voice-operated device — Refers to a device used on a telephone circuit to permit the presence of telephone currents to effect a desired control. Such a device is used on most echo suppressors.

voice output operation — In one system each word is stored in a separate memory module, and modules may be reprogrammed or additional modules added as need determines. Maximum word duration is 0.66 seconds; maximum message duration per unit is 10.56 seconds. Message, in this case, refers to a sentence in which no words are repeated. For those who wonder about what anyone could do with a one-word system, two examples are "Fire!" and, in an aircraft ground-avoidance system, "Pull up!"

voice output systems — A lot of computers are starting to talk back. Voice units sell for under $800 in basic configurations and, because they use digitized human speech, they sound like a person speaking. A single unit can have a vocabulary of from one to 16 words. Units can be clustered to enlarge the vocabulary, but many systems are particularly designed for applications requiring limited-vocabulary, low cost voice response. However, 16 words really isn't that limited, since it permits use of 10 numbers plus six additional words. Users specify their desired vocabulary by submitting a tape recording. The words are digitized, resulting in reproduction so natural that speaker identification is possible. The output voice may be male or female and in any language.

voice readout calculator applications — Voice readout for ... telephone line identification ... aircraft fault warning ... paging equipment subscriber code identification. touch tone pad input verification ... credit authorization at point of sale (without embarrassing red light visual display) ... inventory control numeric verification ... purchase order numeric entry verification ... hospital patient monitoring alarm with room location & cause identification ... hotel wake-up time announcements ... process control warning & status reports ... fire alarm with location identification ... (see talking calculator and audio response calculator defintions)

voice readout systems, solid state — A unit called EVA — Expandable Voice Annunciator — is a new concept in electronically-synthesized voice recording and transmitting. It is a technique for digitizing and storing spoken words in Read-Only Memories (ROM). The result of whole-word storage is that the synthesized voice is so natural sounding, it is difficult to distinguish it from the original. With each word stored in its own individual ROM, it is a simple matter to access each ROM and call up the words in the sequence required for the desired message. EVA is the expandable voice annuciator. It is capable of being expanded modularly from 10 to 30 words. The first 10 words are the numeric words zero to nine with addtional words added as specified. EVA accepts either binary address or 10 mutually exclusive switch closures for the first 10 words. Other words require binary address only. EVA is being used as a calculator peripheral.

voice response calculator — A new concept in electronically-synthesized voice has achieved a technique for digitizing and storing whole-words in Metal Oxide Semiconductor (MOS) Read-Only Memories (ROM). By analyzing plotted audio wave forms, engineers have been able to develop a proprietary method for converting the analog audio signal of a word into a digital signal requiring minimal storage space. The result of whole-word storage is that the synthesized voice is natural sounding and difficult to distinguish it from the original. All of the voice inflections and natural qualities are there, so that user's can actually recognize the person whose voice was used, even though the voice is reproduced electronically. With each word stored in its own individual memory, it is a simple matter to access each ROM and call up the words in the sequence required for the desired message. Simple logic decoding can be used to accomplish this sequencing without complicated programming. The system is called EVA, for Expandable Voice Annunciator.

voice response calculator application — Voice response traditionally has been used to provide information to people using telephones as computer terminals, but there are many other reasons why calculators should speak. Many suppliers list such applications as automatic wake-up systems for motels, monitoring vital signs in hospital patients, and aircraft warning systems. In each example, instead of answering inquiries, the computer speaks when certain conditions are met or tolerances exceeded. Developments by these companies make such applications as now economically feasible for the first time. Many new model voice generators similar to the voice annunciator have been introduced. Audio tapes of the human voice are digitized and the codes compressed by a computer. The codes then are stored in read-only memories (ROMs) and used to drive the synthesizer, resulting in speech so natural that it is often possible to identify the original speaker's voice. Vocabularies may include continuous phrases as well as separate words in either a male or female voice.

Codes are transmitted from memory to the synthesizer in bursts, which means that one memory can drive multiple synthesizers concurrently, each speaking a different message.

Some models accept ASCII codes at various standard baud rates via either a parallel or a serial interface. Evaluation units with a preprogrammed 48-word vocabulary are available.

voice response calculator operation — EVA is the expandable voice annunciator. It is capable of being expanded modularly from 10 to 30 words. In the standard model, the first 10 words are the numeric words zero to nine with additional words added as specified. EVA accepts either binary address or 10 mutually exclusive switch closures for the first 10 words. Additional words, after the first 10, require binary address only. Both the sync and complete pulse are each one micro-second wide, however, each may be preselected for a longer duration pulse to meet specific requirements.

voice-response ROMs — Some applications as on-line order entry echo back information to a salesperson for verification. But many simpler applications, such as patient-monitoring in intensive-care units and talking calculators for the blind, require units smaller and cheaper than most currently available. To meet this need, one firm developed a voice-response unit whose synthesizer circuitry models the human vocal tract and operates from compressed digital word sets stored in 8K ROMs. Each ROM stores coding for up to 8 sec of continuous speech or 10 to 20 separate vocabulary words; a word requires 300 to 1000 bits. The entire unit, including synthesizer, power supply, vocabulary ROMs and interface logic to accept ASCII word selection codes, measures $2'' \times 6'' \times 10''$.

void — In character recognition, the undesired absence of ink within the outline of a character as might occur in magnetic ink characters or optical characters and is most often due to defects in the inks, paper, or printing process.

volatile — A characteristic of becoming lost or erased when power is removed, i.e., the loss of data where it is not returned or recovered when power is restored. Some such units, as tape units, are in a volatile condition if such a power loss occurs.

volatile display — The nonpermanent image appearing on the screen of a visual display terminal.

volatile dynamic storage — Refers to a specific storage unit which depends only on the external supply of power for maintenance of stored information.

volatile storage — Refers to a storage medium in which information cannot be retained without continuous power dissipation. Contrasted with storage, nonvolatile.

volt — MKSA unit of p.d. or e.m.f., such that the p.d. across a conductor is 1 volt when 1 amp in it dissipates 1 W of power. This is 1 J/s, or 10^7 erg/s, a mechanical unit.

voltage comparator — Suitable for use in a variety of applications in logic, control and instrumentation equipment, voltage comparators are available from most large semiconductor manufacturers as well as a number of the smaller specialty firms. In its basic form, the voltage comparator is essentially a modified differential amplifier with two stable output states, responding when an applied input voltage crosses a pre-established threshold level.

voltage drop — 1. Diminution of potential along a conductor, or over an apparatus, through which a current is passing. 2. Possible diminution of voltage between two terminals when current is taken from them.

voltage jump — Abrupt discontinuity in voltage drop across discharge tube, normally associated with a marked change in the geometry of the discharge.

voltage level — P-p value at any point in a network expressed relative to a specified reference level. When this is 1 volt the symbol dBv is used.

voltage monitor — Typical card converts dc input voltage (± 10 V) to equivalent 12-bit 2's complement digital word for calculator read-in.

voltage monitor card — A typical card monitors bipolar dc voltages in the range of $+10.235$ to -10.240 V, and returns a 12-bit two's complement digital word to the controller to indicate the magnitude and sign of the measured voltage. Up to 150 conversions per second can be performed as commanded by the program or an external gate input.

voltage regulator — A device that maintains or varies the terminal voltage of a generator or other machine at a predetermined value.

voltage standard — An accurately known voltage source (e.g., a standard cell) used for comparison with or calibration of other voltages.

voltmeter — An instrument for measuring potential difference. Its scale is usually graduated in volts. If graduated in millivolts or kilovolts, the instrument is usually designated as a millivoltmeter or a kilovoltmeter.

volume statistics — The groups of various pertinent facts in relation to the nature and level of operations of an area under consideration expressed in numbers (e.g., number of sellers, number of different items, orders, purchases, etc.), plus, or including, subclassifications of these data to obtain a clear understanding of the pattern of the operations.

volume, system residence — The volume i.e., disk pack etc. that contains the operating system (software).

volume test — The processing of a volume of actual data to check for program malfunctions.

VS — Virtual storage.

VTAM (vortex telecommunications method) — A special data communications software package that organizes and simplifies data-communications programming to serve remote workstations for a host computer.

(VTOC) volume table of contents — Concerns a specific index record near the beginning of each volume, which records the name, location, and extent of every file or data set residing on that particular volume. Usually not found on magnetic tapes, but often required on all disk packs and drums.

WACK, wait before transmit positive acknowledgment — WACK allows a receiving station to indicate a "temporarily-not-ready-to-receive" condition. It can be sent as a response to a text or heading block selection-sequence (multipoint) line bid (point-to-point with contention), or an ID (identification) line-bid sequence (switched network). WACK is a positive acknowledgment to the received data block or to selection. The ability to receive WACK is mandatory for all BSC stations, but the capability of sending WACK is optional (BSC).

wait — The condition a real-time program meets when it requires information from a file-storage unit and is forced to "wait" until the required-file record is accessed and brought into the main memory. File-oriented systems have this characteristic that leads to multiprogrammed approaches by interleaving and overlapping "wait" times for one program to achieve process time for another program.

waiting lines (queuing theory) — When a flow of goods (or customers) is bottlenecked at a particular servicing point, losses accumulate in the form of lost business, idle equipment, and unused labor. Minimizing such costs involved in waiting lines, or queues, is the object of queuing theory, an O/R (operations research) technique for the most efficient handling of a waiting line at a particular service point.

waiting list — Refers to a procedure for organizing and controlling the data of unprocessed operational programs. These lines are ordinarily maintained by the control program. Synonymous with queue.

waiting state — Refers to the state of an interrupt level that is armed and has received an interrupt signal, but is not yet allowed to become active.

WAIT, macroinstruction — In multithread processing, the presentation of a request on one message that causes a delay so that no processing can go on. A WAIT macro is given which shifts control to a supervisory program so that work may continue on other messages. Work on the delayed message will continue only when the cause of the delay is removed.

wait state — 1. The condition of a task that is dependent on one or more events in order to enter the ready condition. 2. The condition of a central processing unit when all operations are suspended.

watch/calculator, quartz — One type is a combination Pulsar quartz timepiece (hours, minutes, seconds, month, and date) and microminiature IC calculator. The calculator is capable of providing answers totaling up to 12 figures, displaying the first six significant digits. It has a complete calculator keyboard that enables the wearer to add, subtract, divide, or multiply. It also has a built-in memory, floating decimal point, and percentage key. The unit can be switched from calculator to timepiece at the touch of single key. The miniature calculator is operated by touching the keys with the retractable plastic tip of a 12-kt gold-filled pocket pen packaged with the unit. The unit is powered by four energy cells, which the company estimates will provide power for as many as 25 calculations and 25 time checks a day for one year.

WATS service, wide-area telephone — This is similar to WADS (wide area data service). A service which provides a special line allowing the customer to call a certain zone(s) or band(s), on a direct-distance dialing basis, for a flat monthly charge. The continental United States is divided into six bands for the purpose of rates.

watt — Abbreviated W. A unit of the electric power required to do work at the rate of 1 joule per second. It is the power expended when 1 ampere of direct current flows through a resistance of 1 ohm.

watt-hour — MKSA unit of electrical energy, being the work done by 1 W acting for 1 hour, and thus equal to 3600 J or $3 \cdot 6 \times 10^{10}$ erg.

wave — 1. A physical activity that rises and falls, or advances and retreats, periodically as it travels through a medium. 2. A propagated disturbance, usually periodic, such as a radio wave, a sound wave, or a carrier wave used for transmitting data signals. 3. A single cycle of a periodic propagated disturbance.

waveguide — Hollow metal conductor within which very high frequency energy can be transmitted efficiently in one of a number of modes of electromagnetic oscillation. Dielectric guides, consisting of rods or slabs of dielectric, operate similarly, but normally have higher losses.

wavelength — 1. Distance between two similar and successive points on an alternating wave, e.g., between successive maxima or minima; equal to the velocity of propagation divided by the frequency of the alternations when travelling along wires. 2. Distance, measured radially from the source, between two successive points in free space at which an EM or acoustic wave has the same phase; for an EM wave, it is equal in meters, to 300,000 ÷ frequency (kHz). 3. That associated with electrons in motion when considered as a wave train. It is $\lambda = h/p$, h being Planck's constant and p the momentum of the election. Similar for neutrons and other particles. 4. In a periodic wave, the instance between points of corresponding phase of two consecutive cycles.

Weibull probability program — Refers to a Weibull Distribution Parameter. For a set of data, this program calculates the Weibull Parameters B and Theta for the Weibull probability density function and the cumulative distribution function.

weighted average — An average performed on data in which some of the values are more heavily valued than others.

weighted value — The numerical value assigned to any single bit as a function of its position in the code word.

Westar transponders — 1. Each WU satellite has 12 transponders. Each transponder is designed to receive and retransmit the equivalent of one color TV signal with accompanying audio, 1,200 one-way voice circuits, or data traffic at the rate of 50 million bits per second. Each voice circuit has 4 KHz of bandwidth. 2. Expected minimum life for each satellite — seven years. 3. The Westar system is controlled from Earth Station No. 1 at Glenwood, N.J. (outside New York City) by Western Union Telegraph Co.

wheel printer — A printer where each print position is on a wheel on the face of which is engraved a type font.

who-are-you (WRU) — A transmission control character used for switching on an answerback unit in the station with which the connection has been set up, or for initiating a response including station identification and, in some applications, the type of equipment in service and the status of the station.

wideband data sets — Wideband data sets are now developed which permit data rates of 72,000 bits per second (72 Kb/sec) and 90 Kb/sec (with error control) over channels now capable of operating at 50 Kb/sec. A new switched 50 kilobit-per-second service has recently been submitted to regulatory agencies. This service enables communication at these data rates between a number of points without the need for full-period circuit.

wing panel — A panel which is added on sides of existing panels and which often contains intervention or other type switches, or warning lights.

wire — A solid or stranded group of solid cylindrical conductors having a low resistance to current flow, together with any associated insulation.

"wired city" — The concept of television and other communications, data, educational material, instructional television and information retrieval service that wired services can provide to cities and neighborhoods. Broadcast services must, of necessity, be limited by scarce spectrum space; wired services have theoretically unlimited channel capacity.

wired-in — Refers to components connected in circuits, particularly subminiature valves and semiconductor devices, which are too small to be plugged safely into a holder.

wired OR — Externally connecting separate circuits or functions so that the combination of their outputs results in an "AND" function. The point at which the separate circuits are wired together will be a "1" if all circuits feeding into this point are "1".

wire storage — A wire made of or coated with a magnetic material and used for magnetic recording.

wire wrap — Wire wrap was developed in the 1950's by Bell Labs as an alternative to soldering. Wire-wrapping consists basically of winding a number of turns of wire around a metal post with at least two sharp edges. In practice, the metal post has evolved into a standard 0.025 inch square pin. With the correct wire and tension during wrapping, a clean metal-to-metal contact results. The corrosion resistance, mechanical stability and conductivity are good enough for the technique to be used in military equipment. Wire-wrap is widely used in industry for proto-type work and, using semiautomatic and automatic machines, for short run production. Wide usage has brought with it a broad range of hardware such as tools, DIP sockets, edge connectors, and even whole logic boards.

wire-wrap advantages — Wire-wrapping offers the advantage of ease of design, freedom of layout, easy maintainability and parts replacement, ease of design change, good performance and good density. But unless users can justify wire-wrapped interconnection for applications on the basis of economics, there is no point in using it. Wire-wrapping would not enjoy its current popularity if it did not offer economic advantages over other techniques. But it is also far easier to lay out a wire-wrapped system than a printed circuit board, and there is also an increase in flexibility of component location. Design changes can be implemented by documentation changes. This is considerably easier than modifying printed circuit artwork and modifying an etched board when a design change is necessary. Replacing a component is also generally easier in a wire-wrapped system because of the plug-in feature inherent in wire-wrapping hardware. PCB components can be made pluggable, of course, by the addition of sockets, but sockets on a printed circuit board represent additional space, assembly labor and parts cost.

word — A set of characters that occupies one storage location and is treated by the computer circuits as a unit and transported as such. Ordinarily a word is treated by the control unit as an instruction.

word arrangement, communications — The standard communication subsystem accommodates four types of computer input/output words. They are the function word, input-data word, output-data word, and output-data request word.

word, call — That set of characters designed to identify, label, or place a subroutine or data into the subroutine itself or into a program of which a subroutine is a part. The call word acts as the identifier.

word, computer — A group of characters (bits) which is treated as a unit and which is stored in one computer storage location; each word being addressable, such words being instruction words with address and operation parts or a data word with alphanumeric characters of fixed or real

word (communications)

numbers. Parts of computer words are syllables, bytes, etc.

word (communications) — 1. In computing, an ordered set of characters that is the normal unit in which information may be stored, transmitted, or operated upon within a computer. 2. In telegraphy, six characters (five characters plus one space).

word, control — A word in the memory, usually the first or last of a record, or first or last word of a block, that carries indicative information for the following words, records, or blocks.

word count — Refers to record count. The first word of a record in a backing store file which indicates the length of the record to the housekeeping software and enables the software to unpack logical records from physical blocks or buckets.

word counter — Block transfer devices that function as bus masters during data transfers usually require two registers to hold the parameters of the transfer. One parameter is the transfer word count. In some systems this register (WC) is loaded by the computer with the 2's complement of the number of words to be transferred to or from memory. This number is clocked into the WORD COUNT register.

word-count register — A separate, word-count register keeps track of the progress of I/O transfers. Typically the register is loaded at the beginning of the operation with the number of data words to be transferred and decremented after each transfer. On reaching zero, the word-count register signals the completion of the transfer operation by generating an interrupt signal.

word-count register, controller — One specific 16-bit register is loaded with the complement of the number of words to be transferred, and then incremented to zero by the user's interface. The zero count is detected and the resulting signal is accessible at a wire-wrap post.

word, ERROR status — This status word indicates that the remote computing system has detected an error.

word generator, serial device tests — A word generator is useful for testing serial devices, such as shift registers, disc memories and terminals. Many serial devices actually need three inputs: data, qualifier, and clock. The generator supplies a clock signal and serial patterns up to 256 bits in length. The STROBE channel may be used as a qualifier; programming it to generate a string of 1's in the NRZ format effectively creates a wide gating pulse. It may also be used to supply word framing pulses. With the help of a generator, many of these tests can be performed economically on a wide variety of devices at incoming inspection stations or for component evaluation.

word index — The contents of a storage position or register that may be used to automatically modify the effective address of any given instruction.

word length — Longer word lengths increase efficiency and accuracy, but add complexity and cost. Most common is 16-bit, but 8, 12, 18, and 24 bits are widely used, and 32 bits is used occasionally. Word length limits the number of memory locations which can be directly accessed using single-word addresses. For greater precision and memory access, multiple-word operands and instructions are convenient features, although they increase execution times and architectural complexity. Word lengths and formats should be com-

word processing terminal

patible with peripherals to avoid complex and expensive interfacing requirements.

word-length, double — Many arithmetic instructions produce two-word results. With fixed-point multiplication, a double-length product is stored in two A registers of control storage for integer and fractional operations. Integer and fractional division is performed upon a double-length dividend with the remainder and the quotient retained in the A registers.

word-length, fixed — Having the property that a machine word always contains the same number of characters or digits.

word-length, I/O compatibility — Efficient handling of 8-bit words is important in communications processing, where 8-bit ASCII characters are typical; 8- or 16-bit machines featuring good byte-handling capabilities are required in such applications. Incompatible I/O word lengths increase difficulties encountered in interfacing with communication lines and peripherals.

word-length, variable — Having the property that a machine word may have a variable number of characters. It may be applied either to a single entry whose information content may be changed from time to time, or to a group of functionally similar entries whose corresponding components are of different lengths.

word location, effective — The storage location pointed to by the effective virtual address of a word-addressing instruction.

word, machine — A unit of information of a standard number of characters which a machine regularly handles in each transfer, i.e., a machine may regularly handle numbers or instruction in units of 36 binary digits, this is then the machine word.

word, machine-length — The selection of one of the word lengths of the equipment as a datum and thus to classify different operations as partial or multiples of these lengths for working.

word-mark — Refers to an indicator to signal the beginning or end of a word, usually in a variable word-length machine.

word, parameter — A word in a subroutine which contains one or more parameters which specify the action of the subroutine or words which contain the address of such parameters.

word, partial — A programming device which permits the selection of a portion of a machine word for processing.

word pattern — The smallest meaningful language unit recognized by a machine. It is usually composed of a group of syllables and/or words.

word period — The size or magnitude of the time interval between the occurrence of signals representing digits occupying corresponding positions in consecutive words.

word processing centers (WP) — Word processing (WP) will continue to intertwine with other office systems — namely, computers, records keeping, micrographics, photocomposition, reprographics and the like. WP will depend more than ever on the computer industry for technological developments. In turn, the computer industry will begin to depend on WP for advances in the human relations that offices are so used to. In other words, WP will be the computer market's human-relations mouthpiece. WP experts have been able to convince the technologically untouched office that it's O.K. to use automated equipment.

word processing terminal — Relates to the

word, short

preparation and dissemination of letters, memoranda, reports and articles using automated office typewriters and word processing systems.

word, short — A fixed word of lesser length that is capable of handling words of two different lengths. In many computers this is referred to as a half-word because the length is exactly the half-length of a full word.

word, shortest — A word of the shortest length a computer can use, and which is most often half of the word length of the full length word.

words, mask — The mask word modifies both the identifier word and the input word which is called up for a search comparison in a logical AND operation.

word, trap — The main storage location used to store the instruction counter and trap identification data.

work area — Refers to a portion of storage in which a data item may be processed or temporarily stored. The term often refers to a place in storage used to retain intermediate results of calculation, especially those results which will not appear directly as output from the program.

work-distribution chart — 1. A listing or inventory of the duties, responsibilities, and sequence of the personnel in the job or task force under study. 2. The establishment of each duty relationship performed by the individual in relation to the specific task or function, which includes brief volumes-of-occurrence indicators, and the estimated and projected times to perform each item of work.

working, multiple length — Refers to the use of two or more machine words to represent a number and to thus increase precision, i.e., the use of double-length procedures, double precision, etc.

working registers — The major significance of working registers lies in access time and the bit efficiency of instruction words. It takes far fewer bits to specify one of several previously defined working registers than a memory location. Whether these registers are in an external memory or in the CPU is irrelevant, so long as they can be referenced efficiently. But a faster execution time can be obtained with registers that are separate from memory. They can be accessed for read and write operations without users incurring excessive memory-cycle delays.

working routine — That routine which produces the results of the problem or program as it was designed, as contrasted with the routines which are designed for support, housekeeping, or to compile, assemble, translate, etc.

working space — A portion of the internal storage reserved for the data upon which operations are being performed. (Synonymous with temporary storage, and contrasted with program storage.)

work-in-process queue — Items that have had some processing and are queued by and for the computer to complete the needed processing.

work process schedule — Under general direction, schedules operating time of the over-all electronic data processing activity in order to ensure that the data-processing equipment is effectively and efficiently utilized.

work-output queue — Refers to various data which are output and often not immediately printed or punched into final form and are stored on some type of auxiliary storage device and thus become part of a queue which is operated or programmed with control information for disposition of this information. The computer system often is printerbound or can operate only as fast as the printer can perform.

WOROM — Write only ready only memory.

worst case — Refers to the circumstance or case in which the maximum stress is placed on a system, such as inputs or greater than expected volume.

worst-case circuit analysis — A type of circuit analysis used to determine the worst possible effect on the output parameters due to changes in the values of circuit elements. The circuit elements are set to the values within their anticipated ranges that produce the maximum detrimental changes in the output.

WPM — The abbreviation for words per minute. A common measure of speed in telegraph systems.

wraparound — Refers to: 1. The continuation of an operation from the maximum addressable location in storage to the first addressable location. 2. The continuation of register addresses from the highest register address to the lowest. 3. On a CRT display device, the continuation of an operation, i.e., a read or cursor movement, from the last character position in the display buffer to the first position in the display buffer.

wrap-around storage — Concerns an arrangement of core storage in which the lowest numbered storage location is the successor of the highest numbered one.

wristwatch calculator — In one unit the calculator has four functions, and is complete with a memory, floating decimal point and an overflow indicator. It can handle 12-figure calculations, but displays only the first six figures. In addition to the digit keys the calculator has a percent key, an add-to-memory key, a recall-memory key, and a subtract-from-memory key. Clear-entry and clear-calculator keys are also provided. The device has two main chips — a calculator and a watch chip — as well as a number of drive and interface chips to enable the two primary chips to talk to each other. For timekeeping, a command button is depressed to display hours and minutes, or seconds, or month and date, in that sequence. The wearer can change from timekeeping to the calculator function by pushing the "0" key.

wrist-watch size calculators — One miniature calculator has a 17-key unit. Its tiny keys and readout use a layer of conductive rubber. The trend toward micominiaturization in electronics has been pushed even further by the watch industry. One pioneering company responded by introducing a keyboard measuring only $3/4 \times 1$ inch with 17 keys of $5/32$-inch centers. The key array includes a moving decimal point, constant, clear, multiply, divide, add-equal, and subtract-equal keys that are as easy to read as a watch face. The full calculator would probably have either a four-digit liquid-crystal display or a six-digit light-emitting-diode (LED) readout.

wrist-watch size calculator keyboard — This pencil tip or stylus keyboard makes use of new materials technology in conductive elastomers, paints, and inks, and its capability in full-size keyboards. The miniature keyboard uses the same materials as the large subassemblies, but they are put together differently. The keyboard consists of a tiny printed-circuit board, screened with a silver paint that provides a permanently conductive contact surface. Over this is laid a 0.005-inch-thick Mylar spacer with holes directly under the keys. A layer of conductive rubber, and a Mylar legend sheet has the keys on it. When the Mylar is deflected, an electrical impulse that is set up in the conductive rubber travels through the holes in the Mylar spacer to the printed-circuit board. The keyboard was developed as a result of inquiries from watch companies, and samples were supplied to at least 10 of them in mid-1974. In volume the manufacturer says the keyboards could sell for less than $2 each. Slightly larger readout areas could accommodate several 'answer' lines, using an attached magnifier for improved clarity.

writable control store — Dynamically alterable, 256 24-bit word storage (typical) for microprograms. Enables access to additional high speed registers and read/write capabilities from memory.

write — In a computer: 1. To copy, usually from internal to external storage. 2. To transfer elements of information to an output medium. 3. To record information in a register, location, or other storage device or medium. 4. To establish a charge pattern corresponding to the input (charge-storage tubes). (Also see Read.) 5. To make a permanent or transient recording of data in a storage device or on a data medium. In the English language, the phrases "to read to" and "to write from" are often distinguished from the phrases "to write to" and "to write from" only by the viewpoint of the description. For example, the transfer of a block of data from internal storage to external storage may be called "writing to the external storage" or "reading from the internal storage," or both. 6. To record data in a storage device or a data medium. The recording need not be permanent, such as the writing on a cathode ray tube display device.

writeable control storage (WCS), RAM — One of the most significant trends in computer system architecture today is the replacement of ROM in the control store with random access storage (RAM). Writeable control storage is the name given to read/write memories used in the control portion of a system. The trend is significant because it enables the system designer to change the external characteristics of the system. The process of using control storage in a host machine to give that machine the external characteristics of another device is called emulation.

writeable control store — Writeable Control Store provides more memory for user written control instructions. In some systems with 256 24-bit words, a WCS module has enough storage capacity for many new instructions and high speed routines. Some WCS have a read access time of 140 nanoseconds, the same as the many main Control Stores. It can be dynamically altered for more extensive needs.

writeable control store, handshaking — A typical writeable-control store (WSC) consists of 512-words by 24-bits of high-speed, bipolar read/write memory. A serial "handshaking" interface for the WCS provides a universal I/O scheme that doesn't depend on the host system. Hence microprograms can be modified more quickly than when PROMS are used.

writeable control store, microcode — In some systems in addition to the regular instruction set, a special segment of RAM, containing 256 56-bit words, is set aside in models for user-programmed microcode. Called a writeable control store, it lets the sophisticated user microcode his own specialized instruction set. This is suited particularly for applications such as communications and signal processing that require efficient execution of a few rather well-defined algorithms. User microprogramming often allows these algorithms to be implemented at speeds approaching those of dedicated hardware designs with the additional benefits of greater flexibility and reduced implementation cost. Like the regular microcode, each 200-nanosecond CPU cycle executes a 56-bit microinstruction in which up to three data paths may be controlled simultaneously. (some systems)

write key — A code in the program status doubleword that is used in conjunction with a memory lock to determine whether or not a program may write into a specific page of actual addresses.

write key field — The portion of the program status doubleword that contains the write key.

write-only — The operation of transferring information from logic units or files.

write-process-read — The process of reading in one block of data, while simultaneously processing the preceding block and writing out the results of the previously processed block. Some special processors can perform concurrently on any two or three of these operations, others are limited to read/write.

write pulse — That drive pulse (or the sum of several simultaneous drive pulses) which under suitable conditions can write into a magnetic cell or set a cell, i.e., ususally to a one condition.

writing head — Refers to that magnetic head which is designed and used to write as contrasted with the read head, with which it is often combined.

writing machine — Typewriters capable of writing a document automatically from tapes or cards. They can also produce a selectively punched tape containing part of all information written on the document. Typical of many word processing devices.

writing rate — The maximum speed at which the spot on a cathode ray tube can move and still produce a satisfactory image.

writing speed — Speed of deflection of trace on phosphor, or rate of registering signals on charge storage device.

WRU — An abbreviation for Who Are You? An ASCII character used in TWX as a request for an automatic station identification sequence.

WS — An abbreviation for working storage, that specific area on a disk used to hold dynamic or working data. This area is contrasted to reserved area containing permanent information such as compilers, track and sector information, etc., and user for semipermanent storage.

x-axis — 1. The reference axis in a quartz crystal. 2. The horizontal axis in a system of rectangular coordinates.

xerographic printer — Refers to a page printer in which the character pattern is set for a full page before printing, using the principle of xerography.

xerography — 1. Non-chemical photographic process in which light discharges a charged dielectric surface. This is dusted with a dielectric powder, which adheres to the charged areas, rendering the image visable. Permanent images can be obtained by transferring particles to suitable backing surface (e.g., paper or plastic) and fixing, usually by heat. 2. A dry copying process involving the photoelectric discharge of an electrostatically charged plate. The copy is made by tumbling a resinous powder over the plate, the remaining electrostatic charge discharged and the resin transferred to paper or an offset printing master.

XMT — Transmit.

X punch — 1. A punch in the X or 11 row of an 80-column card. 2. A punch in position 11 of a column. The X punch is often used to control or select, or to indicate a negative number as if it were a minus sign. Also called an 11-punch.

X register data transfer card — On some units the data transfer card has a number of applications, the most common being remote display of six of the first seven digits of the X register of the calculator, presetting of external up/down counter systems and provision of setpoints for external high/low comparators. Upon command from the calculator, the six of the first seven digits in the X register will be transferred into storage in the card and a signal will be output from the card indicating the existence of valid data. (some systems)

X, Y coordinates CRT — A point plotting CRT used for graphic forms.

XY digitizer — This provides the capability to digitize single points or curves at a resolution of ±.005 inches over the entire digitizing surface.

X-Y plotter, advanced calculator — One type X-Y Plotter has a peripheral control function block that automatically scales user data, generates words as well as numbers, and sets up both axes, complete with labels and tick marks — all in designated units.

X-Y plotter, calculator — Histograms; pie charts; linear, log-log, and polar plots; circuit diagrams — these are just some of the things the various type X-Y Plotters can do. With a Peripheral Control Function Block, the plotter can automatically scale the data, generate words as well as numbers, and set up both axes complete with labels and tic marks — all in specific designated units.

X-Y (plotting board) recorder — A recorder that makes a record of any one voltage with respect to another.

xy recorder — A recorder that traces, on a chart, the relationship between two variables, neither of which is time. Sometimes the chart moves and one of the variables is controlled so that the relationship does increase in proportion to time.

X-Y recorder, (plotting board) — A recorder that makes a record of any one voltage with respect to another.

y-axis — 1. A line perpendicular to two parallel faces of a quart crystal. 2. The vertical axis in a system of rectangular coordinates.

Z

zatocoding system — A system of coordinate indexing.

zener — A semiconductor diode which, under reverse bias, is capable of conducting heavy currents.

zero — 1. Nothing; positive-binary zero is usually indicated by the absence of digits or pulses in a word; negative-binary zero in a computer operating on one's complements by a pulse in every pulse position in a word; in a coded-decimal machine, decimal zero and binary zero may not have the same representation. In most computers, there exists distinct and valid representation both for plus and for minus zero. 2. The combition of coded bits that the computer recognizes as zero. In most computers distinct and valid bit instructions are used for positive and negative zero.

zero-access storage — The storage for which the latency (waiting time) is small. Though once widely used, this term is becoming less acceptable, since it constitutes a misnomer.

zero-address instruction — An instruction specifying an operation in which the locations of the operands are defined by the computer code, so that no address need be given explicitly.

zero balance — The outcome of a method of balancing if details and totals are both correct.

zero balancing (accounting) — Zero balancing is an effective method of verification when both detail items (e.g., accounts payable distribution cards or records) and their summary (e.g., an accounts payable disbursement card or record) are processed together. Each detail item is accumulated minus, and the summary plus. The result is a zero balance if both are correct.

zero-based conformity — Refers to a specific value of nonconformity which is determined after various translations and/or rotations of the actual curves are made to thereby make it coincide with zero on the specified curve which minimizes the maximum deviation.

zero bit — The two high-order bits of the program counter are labeled the Z (Zero) and L (Link) bits. Typically the Z-bit will be set to 1 whenever an operation results in the accumulator bits all being clean (accumulator contains zero value); the Z bit will be zero otherwise.

zero compression — A technique of data processing used to eliminate the storing of non-significant leading zeros.

zero error — 1. Residual time delay which has to be compensated in determining readings of range. 2. Error or any instrument when indicating zero, either by pointer, angle, or display.

zero fill — Refers to a procedure to fill in characters with the representation of zeros but which does not change meaning or content.

zeroize — The procedure to fill storage space or to replace representations with zeros, i.e., the storage location may be cleared to zero, although doing so may not necessarily be the same as the meaning of zeroize. For example, if an "excess" code is used such as excess-3.

zero level — Any voltage, current or power reference when other levels are expressed in dB relative to this.

zero-level address — An instruction address in which the address part of the instruction is the operand. Same as immediate address.

zero offset — The manual insertion of dimensional data into the control unit, or feedback unit, which will add to, or subtract from, the machine position, thus altering the programmed cutter path.

zero page addressing — In some systems the zero page instructions allow for shorter code and execution times by only fetching the second byte of the instruction and assuming a zero high address byte. Careful use of the zero page can result in significant increase in code efficiency.

zero potential — Theoretically, that of a point at infinite distance, used for defining capacitance. Practically, the earth is taken as being of invariant potential. That of any large mass of metal; e.g., equipment chassis.

zero proof — A procedure or process of checking computations by adding positive and negative values so that if all computations are accurate the total of such proof would be zero, i.e., wage deduction plus net pay less gross pay would be equal to zero.

zero suppression — The elimination, in computing and data processing, of non-significant zeros to the left of the integral part of a quantity, especially before the start of printing.

zero transmission-level reference point — An arbitrary chosen point in a circuit to which all relative transmission levels are referred. The transmission level at the transmitting switchboard is frequently taken as the zero transmission-level reference point.

zone — Refers to: 1. A portion of internal storage allocated for a particular function or purpose. 2. The three top positions of 12, 11 and 0 on certain punch cards. In these positions, a second punch can be inserted so that with punches in the remaining positions 1 to 9, alphbetic charcters may be represented.

zone bits — The bits other than the four used to represent the digits in a dense binary code.

zoned format — A binary-coded decimal format in which one decimal digit consists of zone bits and numeric bits and occupies an entire byte of storage.

zone digit — Refers to the numerical key to a section of a code. Zone digits may be used independently of other punchings for control significance, etc.

zone leveling — An analogous process to zone refining, carried out during processing of semiconductors in order to distribute impurities evenly through sample.

zone, minus — That set of characters in a particular code which is associated with the adjacent bit which represents a minus sign.

zone, neutral — A range of values in the parameters of a control system in which no control action occurs.

zone, plus — Bit positions in a computer code which represent the algebraic plus sign.

zone punch — An additional punch, or punches, in a card column for purposes of expanding the number of characters that may be represented.

EPILOGUE

Conclusion: The New Directions and Future of Programmable Calculators — It appears very clear that the battles against the IBM 5100 and other major computer manufacturers' small computer systems has been joined by the makers of advanced computing calculators. The advantages seem to be on the side of the inherent characteristics of the latter: lower prices; easy direct operation by managers, department heads, clerks; immediate turn-on and versatile utility with wide ranges of low-cost peripherals; abundant and simplified-use personal software either 'free' or at 'pocket-money' costs; portability, compactness, fast and sure maintenance, and a host of others. The Wang 2200 systems, especially the PCS; the Tektronix 4051; the Hewlett-Packard 9825 and the Compucorp 400 systems are excellent competitors not only against IBM but also against Digital Equipment's PDP-8 and the bookkeeping machines made by NCR, Nixdorf and Olivetti, among others. The Wang 2200WS (work station) competes very favorably in the distributed processing market (by processing up to four jobs simultaneously) against IBM's S/32 and in the intelligent terminal market against Sycor and Datapoint and also in the minicomputer market against Data General and other makers. These major calculator systems include processors with cassette, floppy-disk, hard-disk, and tape storage and offer BASIC and other high-level languages.

At the low end of the calculator spectrum, manufacturers that supply chips to the industry as well as vendors that make their own chips are placing major emphasis on packing more power into single and multi-chip devices while holding current very low cost-per-function prices. In that respect the downward price in small but high-power hand-held and compact desk-top calculators will continue. Rockwell reported, for example, work underway on a combination programmable/printer/display chip set that pressages their (and several of their customer firm's) entry into the programmables fields. It also claims that its three-chip format including memory, CPU and ALU (Arithmetic-Logic Unit) provides extensive programming capability. The new extended 'chip power' means the calculator manufacturer no longer has to use expensive time to design, mount, and interconnect as many devices as formerly — for the main power versatility or that of peripheral capabilities. National Semiconductor Co. competes (along with many others) in this area by offering two new chips with either RPN or algebraic math, selectable by grounding the appropriate pin.

Nonvolatile Memories and One-Chip Programmables — Nonvolatile semiconductor memory is also due from National and several other manufacturers. Nonvolatile memory is the inexpensive way of storing programs in hand-held calculators for days, months, or years after the battery power supply has been switched off. It began appearing in late 1976 in a wide range of hand-held scientific calculators priced at $90 to $200. New advances in 'clocked static complementary-MOS random-access memory' having standby modes that require only a few microamperes of current, and p-channel metal-nitride-oxide-semiconductor (MNOS) memories offer retention of information for years. Thus, the production and marketing of lines of 'nonvolatile semiconductor-memory chips' will be followed by Texas Instruments, Rockwell International, Electronic Arrays, American Microsystems, Inc., Hewlett-Packard Co. and others in the next rounds of introductions of sophisticated calculators and chips. This follows the demands of the markets — calculators that draw less power and provide permanent storage plus those with more powerful memories that increase the range and number of special functions. The trends are to use C-MOS with trickle current and the inherently nonvolatile MNOS chips as noted above. The MOSTEK Corp. began the movement with its nonvolatile memory 'Checkmaster' calculator, achieved by using metal-gate-MOS with long, thin depletion loads to reduce the chip's power drain. The technique works only with machines that do not require much memory. Several chip makers are said to have series or families that have stand-by modes in the 75- to 100 microwatt range. This drain, according to some experts, is well within the natural self-discharge rate of nickel-cadmium batteries — about 2% to 3% a week. Some calculator makers are boasting of 1-kilobit chips with superspeed access times of about 500 nanoseconds, read-cycle times of 2 microseconds and write time of 1.5 to 2 microseconds. One Japanese maker has developed a 256-bit MNOS RAM that can retain data without power for at least one year, has a read-access time of 500 nanoseconds, a write-cycle time of less than 1 microsecond, a power consumption of 600 milliwatts, and a 1024-bit version of it as well.*

Besides the high interest in nonvolatile memories and one-chip programmables, the market seems to be quite receptive to hand-held and very small desk-top printer calculators. Texas Instruments' model 5050 sells for about $100 and its two programmable hand units, the SR-52 and SR-56, have printer options. Sharp has several 'printers' — the model EL-8151, model EL-1051 (vertical tape), both at about $130. Hewlett-Packard's HP-91 sells for $500 as a desk-top and performs all math, log and trig calculations as well as statistical calculations like factorials, accumulations, two-variable mean and standard deviations, linear estimates and regressions, with a very large 10-digit plus two exponent LED display. Casio has its hand-held printing calculator the model C-100P, which sells for under $80, a vertical tape unit with the four basic functions, an electronic memory and square root capability. Cannon has a broad line of printing calculators and has been offering a hand-held, thermal printing strip-tape calculator with per cent since 1972, the 'Pocketronic', under $150.

__portable collector of solar energy__ — A hand-held solar-energy collector and converter to power portable radios and calculators was scheduled to be marketed for about $30 by late summer 1976. The unit, built by M7 International of Arlington Heights, Va., uses a non-imaging solar-radiation collector, called a compound parabolic concentrator, developed by University of Chicago physicist Roland Winston. Use of the collector, which delivers 0.25 watt, reportedly reduces by 70% the number of silicon cells needed.

epilogue

Microprocessor-Controlled Desk-Top Programmable Calculators Vying for Leading Role in Controller Applications — Sophisticated calculators as programmable controllers in science labs and industrial control applications are edging minicomputers out as low-cost, easy-to-use digital handlers. The HP model 9815A desk-top calculator employs a Motorola 6800 microprocessor, has an alphanumeric keyboard and matrix printer, a 16-character Burroughs Panaplex numeric-only display and uses a mag tape mini-cartridge developed jointly with 3M Company. It features auto-diagnostics and automatic boot-strapping. Code is stored in seven, 16K-byte NMOS ROMs, and the unit interfaces to a plotter, a companion printer, etc. The step-up model, the 9825A, however is using a custom-designed hybrid microprocessor that provides very high speed computing with powerful interrupt capability and a versatile interfaces for wide-ranging control. With a 'live keyboard', two levels of 14 interrupts, DMA (Direct Memory Access), automatic memory record and extended (10^{511} to 10^{-511}) internal calculation range, transfer speeds up to 4500 readings/sec, full alphanumeric capability, a 16-character strip printer, a special formula-oriented language (HPL), it excels in controller applications as well as data processing. With less capability but perhaps even more dollar-for-dollar value, the TI SR-60 desk-top card-reading, matrix-printing, 96-key layout programmable at less than $1700 will lead many thousands of amateur and novice users into data processing automation and instrumentation control.

The Sharp PC-2600 desk-top programmable with a floppy disc that provides over 246,000 steps of programming can be custom-tailored to a wide variety of special needs. It also is controlled by a microcomputer with 98 memory registers, many peripherals. Microprocessor-based calculators have no applications limits and great user acceptance. They will become the real 'consumer computers' satisfying practically everyone.

Appendix A
Desk-Top Programable Calculator Comparison Chart

DESK-TOP PROGRAMABLE CALCULATORS***

model number	base price	language used	number of storage registers	storage register capacity (min/max)	program memory type	program memory number of steps	no. of programs available	type of display	peripheral add-ons (options)
Canon U.S.A. Inc.									
SX 320	$3,395	Canon machine language	50 min.	9.9999 × 10⁺⁹⁹ / 9.9999 × 10⁻⁹⁹	Cartridge	1,000 min.	Available Upon Request	Tape & LED	Typewriter step ROM
SX 310	$2,895		50 min.		Mag. Card	500 min.		Tape & LED	Typewriter step ROM
SX 100	$2,695		50 min.		Mag. Card	500 min.		Tape & LED	None
1614 P	$1,495		14	16	Punch Card	240		"Nixie"	Printer
1670 II	$ 995								
1210	$ 476		4	16	Punch Card	130		"Nixie"	Printer
Casio Inc.									
162 F	$295	Keyboard instruction	7	16 Digit	Hard Wire	N/A	20+	"Digitron"	None
FX-3	$345	Keyboard instruction	N/A	12 Digit	Hard Wire	N/A	20+	"Digitron"	None
Compucorp									
402 and 450	N/A	Keyboard		13 Digit	MOS	8K Bytes		CRT	Printer Disk Cassette Plotter

(Compucorp 325, 326, 327 same data as Monroe)

model number	base price	language used	number of storage registers	storage register capacity (min/max)	program memory type	program memory number of steps	no. of programs available	type of display	peripheral add-ons (options)
Hewlett-Packard Co., Calculator Prod. Div.									
9810A	$2,075	RPN	51-111	51-111	MOS	500-2,036	30* Packs	LED	Graphic plotter
9815A	$2,900	RPN	10-250	10-250	MOS	472-2,008	8* Packs	Gas Discharge	Thermal printers
9820A	$4,175	Algebraic	173-1,453	173-1,453	MOS	1,384, 11,624	18* program packs	LED	Line printer Card readers
9821A	$5,225	Algebraic	167-1,447	167-1,447	MOS	1,336 thru 11,576	10* program packs	LED	Paper tape readers
9830A	$6,800	Basic			MOS	3,520 thru 15,808 Bytes	70* Packs	LED	Paper tape punches External cassette memory Disc memory digitizer CRT display I/O expander Impact printer/plotter
9825A	$5900	HPL	10-511 to	10-511	MOS	8K to 32K Bytes	Full Range	LED	

*Packs consist of multiple programs.

model number	base price	language used	number of storage registers	storage register capacity (min/max)	program memory type	program memory number of steps	no. of programs available	type of display	peripheral add-ons (options)
Monroe Div., Litton									
1830	$2,975	Algebraic	74	1,000	RAM	512	25,000+	Print	I/O printer
1860	$3,240		74	8,000	RAM	512	25,000+	Print	Interface Read write cassette
1880	$3,240	Algebraic	74	8,000	RAM	512	25,000+	Print	Interface Read write cassette
324	$495		10	0.5K	RAM	160	500	Display	None
325	$1,795		12	0.2K	RAM	416	500	Display & Print	Interface
326-392	$795		12	0.2K	RAM	160	500	Display	Read write cassette
344	$595		10	0.2K	RAM	160	500	Display	None
354	$1,094.50		10	0.2K	RAM	160	50	Display	None

** Burroughs Corp. information not available
*** Basic Data from Industrial Research—Jan. 1976 p. 68

appendix a

Olivetti Corp. of America									
P 101	$1,695	key board/ full in- struction*	10	11 Digits	Share	120 inst.	Comprehensive library for all products	Impact Printer	None
P 602	$3,150	11	18	150 Digits	Share	384 inst.		Impact Printer	Typewriter, extended memory paper tape punch, paper tape read, plotter, single or dual drive cassette
P 652 2K	$3,500	11	120	12	Share	600 inst		Impact Printer	as above, plus disc
P 652 4K	$4,500	11	240	12	Share	1,200 inst.		Impact Printer	as above, plus disc

* In contrast to keystroke.

Rockwell International Co.									
930	N/A	Keyboard	9 basic; expandable to 99	14 digits	Mag. card	192 expandable to 960	N/A	LED	N/A
940	N/A								
960	N/A								
Sharp Electronics									
PC-1001	$495	Machine	8	$\pm 10^{99}$	MOS	64	$\approx 100+$	"Itron"	None
PC-1002	$645	Machine	8	$\pm 10^{99}$	MOS PROM	64 256	$\approx 100+$	"Itron"	None
CS 364P	$1,495	Machine	12	16 Digits	MOS	288 Steps STD. 1,152 optional	$\approx 100+$	"Nixie" & Printer	Teletype
CS-365P	$1,695	Machine	24 48 optional	16 Digits	MOS	28 Steps STD. 1,152 optional	$\approx 100+$	"Nixie" & Printer	Teletype
PC 2610	$3,200	Machine	96	16 Digits	MOS	2,048	N/A	"Pan-Plex Alpha/ Numeric Printer	Typewriter Floppy Disc
Tektronix Inc.									
31	$2,850	Algebraic	74-1,010	8 Bytes	RAM	512 to 8,192	10 Libraries	Numeric	Disc & plotter
E31	$2,495	Algebraic	74-1,010	8 Bytes	RAM	Same	9 Libraries	Numeric	None
31-53	$3,995	Algebraic	74-1,010	8 Bytes	RAM	Same	19 Programs		Disc & plotter instrumentation
4051	$6,995	Basic	Variable	8 Bytes	RAM	30,000 Max. or 1,000 Statements	7 Libraries	11 in. Graphic Storage CRT	Hard copy Joy stick plotter printer
Texas Instruments Inc.									
SR-60	$1,695	Algebraic (AOS)	100	10^{-99} to 10^{99}	Mag Card	480 to 1920 with Option	110+ Programs	LED	N/A
Victor Comptometer Corp									
4800-485	$2,195	40 Keyboard instructions	102	14 Digits plus sign and decimal	Semi-conductor MOS 1k RAM	1,000	5,001 Expanding	Numeric printer	None
4800	$1,995	40 Keyboard instructions	102	14 Digits plus sign and decimal	MOS 1k RAM	1,000	5,001 Expanding	Numeric printer	None
4700-485	$1,795	40 Keyboard instructions	54	14 Digits plus sign and decimal	MOS 1k RAM	512	5,001 Expanding	Numeric printer	None
4700	$1,595	40 Keyboard instructions	54	14 Digits plus sign and decimal	MOS 1k RAM	512	5,001 Expanding	Numeric printer	None
4900	N/A January Introduction	125+ Keyboard instructions	200	14 Digits plus sign and decimal	MOS 2k RAM	1,792	5,001 Expanding	Alpha/ Numeric printer	None

All models have mag card read/record

appendix a

Wang Laboratories									
600-2	$2,600	Machine	39	0-39	MOS	312	*	Numeric	5 Options
600-6	$2,700	Machine	103	0-103	MOS	824	*	Numeric	5 ROMS
600-14	$2,800	Machine	231	0-231	MOS	1,848	*	Numeric	14 Peripherals
700B	$5,000	Machine	120	0-120	Core	960	*	Numeric	18 Peripherals
700C	$5,200	Machine	120	0-120	Core	960	*	Numeric	
720B	$6,800	Machine	248	0-248	Core	1,984	*	Numeric	
720C	$7,000	Machine	248	0-248	Core	1,984	*	Numeric	
450	$900	Machine	64	0-40	MOS	320	General Library	Numeric	Punched & marked sense card reader
452	$1,200	Machine	64	0-40	MOS	320	General Library	Numeric	
462	$1,200	Machine	64	0-40	MOS	320	General Library	Numeric	Additional 256 program steps or 32 registers
22005	$5,400	BASIC	400	0-4,000	MOS	4,096	*	A/N	10 Options 32 Peripherals

*Extensive library of programs covering many fields of interest

APPENDIX B,
MANUFACTURER'S ADDRESS LIST

Addo (See Facit-Addo)

Addmaster Corp.—Marchant Div.
416 Junipero Serra Dr.
San Gabriel, CA 91776

Adler
1600 Route 22
Union, New Jersey 07083

APF Electronics, Inc.
444 Madison Ave.
New York, N.Y. 10022

Berkey Photo Inc.
Keystone Place
Paramus, New Jersey 07652

Brother International
680 Fifth Ave.
New Yori, N.Y. 10022

Burroughs Corporation
6071 2nd Ave.
Detroit, Michigan 48232

Canon USA
10 Nevada Drive
Lake Success, New York 11040

Casio Inc.
Suite 40011
One World Trade Center
New York, N.Y. 10048

Commodore Business Machines
901 California Ave.
Palo Alto, CA 84304

Compucorp
12312 West Olympic Blvd.
Los Angeles CA 90064

Craig Corporation
921 Artesia Blvd.
Compton, CA 90220

Facit-Addo, Inc.
501 Winsor Drive
Secaucus, New Jersey 07094

Friden, Div. of Singer Corp.
2350 Washington Ave.
San Leandro, CA 94577

Hewlett-Packard Co.
815 14th Street SW
Loveland, Colorado 85037

(Also)
Hewlett-Packard Company
19310 Pruneridge Ave.
Cupertino, CA 95014

Hermes Division
Paillard Inc.
1900 Lower Road
Linden, New Jersey 07036

C. Itoh Electronics, Inc.
200 Park Ave.
New York, N.Y. 10017

Keith Ian Co., Inc.
265 Highway 36
W. Long Branch, N.J. 07764

Litronix, Inc.
19000 Homestead Road,
Cupertioo, CA 95014

Lloyds Electronics
5 Kohner Place
East Patterson N.J. 07407

Master Specialties Co.
1640 Monrovia Ave.
Costa Mesa, CA 96227

Melcor Electronics Corp.
1750 New Highway
Farmingdale, N.Y. 11735

Monroe, Div. of Litton Industries
550 Central Ave.
Orange, New Jersey 07051

National Semiconductor Co.
Consumer Products Div.
1177 Kern Ave.
Sunnyvale, CA 94086

NCR Corporation
Main & K Streets
Dayton, Ohio 45479

Precisa Ltd.
Zurich/Switzerland

Olivetti Corp. of America
500 Park Ave.
New York, N.Y. 10016

Olympia USA, Inc.
P.O. Box 22
Somerville, New Jersey 08876

Rapid Sales Corp.
29245 Stephenson Highway
Madison Heights, MI 48071

Ricoh of America
17482 Pullman Ave.
Irvine, CA 92705

Rockwell International
Microelectronics Group
P.O. Box 3669
Anaheim, CA 98203

Royal Typewriter Co.
150 New Park Ave.
Hartford, Conn. 06106

Sanyo Electronic Trading Co.
Office Equipment Div.
51 Joseph Street
Moonachie, N.J. 07074

Seiko Time Corp.
640 Fifth Ave.
New York, N.Y. 10019

Sharp Electronics Corp.
Business Equipment Div.
10 Keystone Place
Paramus, N.J. 07652

Sinclair Radionics, Inc.
375 Park Ave.
New York, N.Y. 10022

Summit International Corp.
180 West 2950 South
Salt Lake City, UT 84115

Tektronix, Inc.
P.O. Box 500
Beaverton, Oregon 97005

Texas Instruments, Inc.
P.O. Box 5012
Calculator Products Div.
Dallas, Texas 75222

Toshiba Amcrica
Business Equipment Div.
280 Park Ave.
New York, N.Y. 10017

Unitrex of America
612 W. Walnut St.
Compton, CA 90220

Victor Comptometer Corp.
3900 No. Rockwell St.
Chicago, IL 60618

Wang Laboratories
836 North St.
Tewksbury, MA 81876

INDEX OF CALCULATOR PRODUCTS

Adler	1215P	44,48
Burroughs	C-2400	47
	C-2050	47
	2436	48
	2456	48
	C-6451	50
	C-7200	50
	C-6203	51
Canon	SX-100	71,72
	SX-310	71,72
	SX-320	71,72
Casio Minicalculator Printer		5
Biolator		5
	101-F	46
	121-F	46
	R-200	48
	R-11	48
	FX-3	51
	162-F	52
Chromerics, Inc.	Calculator-Watch	6
Commodore	4146-R	27
Compucorp	326	39,40
	325	57
	327	58
	402	76,77
	403	77
	450	78
Fondilier Corp	Calcron Calculator-Watch	6
Hanimex Pocket Calculator		5
Hewlett-Packard	HP-65	18,35,36,37,38,39
	HP-25	20,29,30
	HP-21	24,35
	HP-35	24
	HP-45	24,52
	HP-22	24,25
	HP-80	25
	HP-81	26,52
	HP-55	32,33
	HP-27	35
	HP-91	49
	HP-46	52
	HP-9805	52
	HP-9825A	54,66
	9810	64
	9815A	64,65,66
	9030	68
IBM	5100	91
Litronix	1101P	8
	2200	8,9
	2260	8
	2290	9-15
Lloyds Printer Desk-Top		44,46
Master Specialties	ARC9500	5
Melcor	SC-655	27
Monroe	Classmate-88	4
	360/65	26
	324	33
	344	34
	354	34
	326	39,40
	1450	44,57
	1930	52
	1830	72,73,74
	1880	72,73,74,75
	1860	72,73,74
Mostek	Checkmaster Calculator	5
Olivetti	Logos-68	48
	652	78,79,80

index

Olympia	402	45
	502	45
	CPD-575	46,47
	CP-162	46
	CP-181	47
Optel	Calculator-Watch	6
National Semiconductor	Novus 4510	16
	Novus 4515	16
	Novus 6030	16
	Novus 6035	17
	Nat. Semi. 4615	18
	Nat. Semi. 4640	18
	Novus 4020	32
	Novus 4025	32
	Novus 6020	32
	Novus 6025	32
Ricoh	301-P	44
	Exprint II	48
Rockwell	Calendar Calculator	5
	44RD	23
	64RD	23
	330	44,46
	310	46
	420P	48
	920	59
	930	59
	940	59
	910	60
Sharp	EL-8300	26
	EL-8200	26
	1001	56
	364P II	61
	CS-4500	72
Sinclair Scientific Programmable		15
Tektronix	E-31	86,87,88,89
	31/53	87
	4051	89,90
Telesensory "Speech Plus"	Calculator	5
Texas Instruments	TI 5050	4
	TI 1250	8
	TI2550 II	8
	SR-50A	20
	SR-51A	20
	SR-52	30,31,41,42
	SR-56	30,31
	PC-100	31,43
	TI-500	48
	SR-60	55
Time Computer Inc.	Pulsar Calculator-Watch	6
Underwood	481	48
Unitrex	80-F	8
Victor	18/1721	46
	19/4462	48
	480	70
Wang	450	57
	452	57
	462	57
	600	81,82,83
	700	83,84
	2200S	85,86